H

PAPERBACK
PORTUGUESE
DICTIONARY

English-Portuguese/Portuguese-English

This edition published in Great Britain 2001
by Chambers Harrap Publishers Ltd
7 Hopetoun Crescent, Edinburgh EH7 4AY

© Havas Éducation Référence 1999

ISBN 0 245 60699 8

HARRAP

PAPERBACK
PORTUGUESE
DICTIONARY

English-Portuguese/Portuguese-English

HARRAP

OS COMPOSTOS EM INGLÊS

Em inglês os compostos são vocábulos com um só significado, mas formados por mais de uma palavra; por exemplo **point of view**, **kiss of life**, **virtual reality** ou **West Indies**. Uma das características deste dicionário é o fato de os compostos terem uma entrada própria e seguirem rigorosamente a ordem alfabética. Assim, **blood poisoning** figura depois de **bloodhound** que por seu lado surge depois de **blood donor**.

ENGLISH COMPOUNDS

A compound is a word or expression which has a single meaning but is made up of more than one word, e.g. **point of view**, **kiss of life**, **virtual reality** and **West Indies**. It is a feature of this dictionary that English compounds appear in the A-Z list in strict alphabetical order. The compound **blood poisoning** will therefore come after **bloodhound** which itself follows **blood donor**.

MARCAS REGISTRADAS

O símbolo ® indica que a palavra em questão é uma marca registrada. Este símbolo, ou a sua eventual ausência, não afeta, no entanto, a situação legal da marca.

TRADEMARKS

Words considered to be trademarks have been designated in this dictionary by the symbol ®. However, neither the presence nor the absence of such designation should be regarded as affecting the legal status of any trademark.

AO LEITOR

E ste dicionário é ideal para atender às necessidades do estudante de inglês, seja aprendendo a língua na escola ou em casa, seja em viagens ao exterior.

É um referência prática criada para fornecer respostas claras e precisas para os inúmeros problemas encontrados no estudo da língua inglesa. Com 40 000 palavras e expressões e 55 000 traduções, incluindo abreviaturas e substantivos próprios, o dicionário permite ao usuário entender e apreciar uma grande variedade de textos.

Graças a uma cobertura detalhada do vocabulário básico da língua inglesa e a indicadores de sentido que possibilitam uma tradução acurada, escrever em inglês corretamente e com segurança deixou de ser um problema.

Não hesite em enviar-nos as suas sugestões ou dúvidas, pois elas poderão ser muito úteis e ajudar a tornar este dicionário ainda melhor.

A EDITORA

TO OUR READERS

T his dictionary is ideal for all your language needs, from language learning at school and at home to traveling abroad.

This handy reference is designed to provide fast and clear solutions to the various problems encountered when studying present-day Portuguese. With 40,000 references and 55,000 translations, including many common abbreviations and proper names, it enables the user to understand and enjoy a wide range of reading material.

Writing idiomatic Portuguese with confidence is no longer a problem thanks to the dictionary's detailed coverage of essential vocabulary and helpful sense-markers which guide the user to the most appropriate translation.

Send us your comments or queries – you will be helping to make this dictionary an even better book.

THE PUBLISHER

ABREVIATURAS		ABBREVIATIONS
abreviatura	*abrev/abbr*	abbreviation
adjetivo	*adj*	adjective
adjetivo feminino	*adj f*	feminine adjective
adjetivo masculino	*adj m*	masculine adjective
advérbio	*adv*	adverb
inglês americano	*Am*	American English
anatomia	*ANAT*	anatomy
automóvel	*AUT*	automobile, cars
auxiliar	*aux*	auxiliary
português do Brasil	*Br*	Brazilian Portuguese
inglês britânico	*Brit*	British English
comércio	*COM(M)*	commerce, business
comparativo	*comp(ar)*	comparative
informática	*COMPUT*	computers
conjunção	*conj*	conjunction
contínuo	*cont*	continuous
culinária	*CULIN*	culinary, cooking
economia	*ECON*	economics
educação, escola	*EDUC*	school, education
esporte	*ESP*	sport
interjeição	*excl*	exclamation
substantivo feminino	*f*	feminine noun
familiar	*fam*	informal
figurado	*fig*	figurative
finanças	*FIN*	finance, financial
formal	*fml*	formal
inseparável	*fus*	inseparable

– indica que o "phrasal verb" (verbo + preposição ou advérbio) não pode ser separado, colocando-se o objeto entre o verbo e a segunda partícula da locução, p. ex. com **look after** diz-se *I looked after him* mas não *I looked him after*

– shows that a phrasal verb is "fused", i.e. inseparable, e.g. **look after** where the object cannot come between the verb and the particle, e.g. *I looked after him* but not *I looked him after*

geralmente	*gen*	generally
gramática	*GRAM(M)*	grammar
familiar	*inf*	informal
informática	*INFORM*	computers
interjeição	*interj*	exclamation
invariável	*inv*	invariable
jurídico	*JUR*	juridical, legal
substantivo masculino	*m*	masculine noun
matemática	*MAT(H)*	mathematics

medicina	MED	medicine
substantivo masculino e feminino	mf	masculine and feminine noun
substantivo masculino com desinência feminina	m, f	masculine noun with a feminine inflection
termos militares	MIL	military
música	MÚS/MUS	music
substantivo	n	noun
termos náuticos	NÁUT/NAUT	nautical, maritime
numeral	num	numeral
	o.s.	oneself
pejorativo	pej	pejorative
plural	pl	plural
política	POL	politics
português de Portugal	Port	European Portuguese
particípio passado	pp	past participle
preposição	prep	preposition
pronome	pron	pronoun
passado	pt	past tense
marca registrada	®	registered trademark
religião	RELIG	religion
substantivo	s	noun
alguém	sb	somebody
educação, escola	SCH	school, education
inglês escocês	Scot	Scottish English
separável	sep	separable
– indica que o "phrasal verb" (verbo + preposição ou advérbio) pode ser separado, colocando-se o objeto entre o verbo e a segunda partícula da locução, p. ex. com **let in** diz-se *I let her in*		– shows that a phrasal verb is separable, e.g. **let in**, where the object can come between the verb and the particle, *I let her in*
singular	sg	singular
algo	sthg	something
sujeito	suj/subj	subject
superlativo	sup(erl)	superlative
termos técnicos	TEC(H)	technology
televisão	TV	television
verbo	v/vb	verb
verbo intransitivo	vi	intransitive verb
verbo impessoal	v impess / v impers	impersonal verb
verbo pronominal	vp	pronominal verb
verbo transitivo	vt	transitive verb
vulgar	vulg	vulgar
equivalente cultural	≃	cultural equivalent

TRANSCRIÇÃO FONÉTICA

PHONETIC TRANSCRIPTION

Vogais portuguesas

[a]	pá, amar
[ɛ]	sé, seta, hera
[c]	ler, mês
[i]	ir, sino, nave
[ɔ]	nota, pó
[o]	corvo, avô
[u]	azul, tribo

English vowels

[ɪ]	pit, big, rid
[e]	pet, tend
[æ]	pat, bag, mad
[ʌ]	run, cut
[ɒ]	pot, log
[ʊ]	put, full
[ə]	mother, suppose
[iː]	bean, weed
[ɑː]	barn, car, laugh
[ɔː]	born, lawn
[uː]	loop, loose
[ɜː]	burn, learn, bird

Ditongos portugueses

[aj]	faixa, mais
[ej]	leite, rei
[ɛj]	hotéis, pastéis
[ɔj]	herói, bóia
[oj]	coisa, noite
[uj]	azuis, fui
[aw]	nau, jaula
[ɛw]	céu, véu
[ew]	deus, seu
[iw]	riu, viu

English diphthongs

[ɛɪ]	bay, late, great
[aɪ]	buy, light, aisle
[ɔɪ]	boy, foil
[əʊ]	no, road, blow
[aʊ]	now, shout, town
[ɪə]	peer, fierce, idea
[ɛə]	pair, bear, share
[ʊə]	poor, sure, tour

Vogais nasais

[ã]	maçã, santo
[ẽ]	lençol, sempre
[ĩ]	fim, patim
[õ]	onde, com, honra
[ũ]	jejum, nunca

Nasal vowels

Ditongos nasais

[ãj]	cãibra, mãe
[ãw]	betão, cão
[ẽj]	bem, quem
[õj]	cordões, leões

Nasal diphthongs

Semivogais

sereia, maio	[j]
luar, quadro, poema	[w]

Semi-vowels

[j]	you, spaniel
[w]	wet, why, twin

Consoantes		Consonants
beijo, abrir	[b]	bottle, bib
casa, dique	[k]	come, kitchen
dama, prenda	[d]	dog, did
dia, bonde	[dʒ]	jet, fridge
fado, afinal	[f]	fib, physical
grande, agora	[g]	gag, great
gelo, cisne, anjo	[ʒ]	usual, measure
	[h]	how, perhaps
lata, feliz, cola	[l]	little, help
folha, ilha	[ʎ]	
mel, amigo	[m]	metal, comb
novo, mina	[n]	night, dinner
linha, sonho	[ɲ]	
anca, inglês	[ŋ]	sung, parking
pão, gripe	[p]	pop, people
cura, era	[r]	right, carry
rádio, terra	[x]	loch
cima, desse, caça	[s]	seal, peace
noz, bis, caixa, chá	[ʃ]	sheep, machine
tema, lata, porta	[t]	train, tip
tio, infantil	[tʃ]	chain, wretched
	[θ]	think, fifth
	[ð]	this, with
vela, ave	[v]	vine, livid
zelo, brisa	[z]	zip, his

[ʳ] só se pronuncia quando é seguido de uma palavra que começa por vogal.

[ʳ] is pronounced only when followed by a word beginning with a vowel.

O símbolo fonético [(x)] em português indica que o 'r' no final da palavra é quase sempre levemente pronunciado, exceto ao ser seguido por uma vogal, quando então é pronunciado [r].

The symbol [(x)] in Portuguese phonetics indicates that final 'r' is often barely sounded unless it is followed by a word beginning with a vowel, in which case it is pronounced [r].

O símbolo ['] indica a sílaba tônica, onde recai o acento principal; [ˌ] indica a sílaba subtônica, onde recai o acento secundário.

The symbol ['] indicates that the following syllable carries primary stress and [ˌ] that the following syllable carries secondary stress.

No lado português as regras de pronúncia seguidas são as do português falado no Rio de Janeiro, exceto nos verbetes seguidos pela abreviatura Port que correspondem ao português europeu e cuja pronúncia é a de Lisboa.

Portuguese phonetics reflect the language as spoken in Rio de Janeiro, except for entries marked Port, which relate specifically to European Portuguese and where the pronunciation given is that of Lisbon.

Conjugações

Chave: **A** = presente do indicativo, **B** = pretérito imperfeito do indicativo, **C** = pretérito perfeito do indicativo, **D** = pretérito mais-que-perfeito do indicativo, **E** = futuro do indicativo, **F** = condicional, **G** = presente do subjuntivo, **H** = futuro do subjuntivo, **I** = pretérito imperfeito do subjuntivo, **J** = imperativo, **K** = gerúndio, **L** = infinitivo pessoal, **M** = particípio passado.

ANDAR: **A** ando, andas, anda, andamos, andais, andam, **B** andava, andavas, andava, andávamos, andáveis, andavam, **C** andei, andaste, andou, andamos, andastes, andaram, **D** andara, andaras, andara, andáramos, andáreis, andaram, **E** andarei, andarás, andará, andaremos, andareis, andarão, **F** andaria, andarias, andaria, andaríamos, andaríeis, andariam, **G** ande, andes, ande, andemos, andeis, andem, **H** andar, andares, andar, andarmos, andardes, andarem, **I** andasse, andasses, andasse, andássemos, andásseis, andassem, **J** anda, ande, andemos, andai, andem, **K** andando, **L** andar, andares, andar, andarmos, andardes, andarem, **M** andado.

chover: **A** chove, **B** chovia, **C** choveu, **G** chova, **H** chover, **I** chovesse, **M** chovido.

COMER: **A** como, comes, come, comemos, comeis, comem, **B** comia, comias, comia, comíamos, comíeis, comiam, **C** comi, comeste, comeu, comemos, comestes, comeram, **D** comera, comeras, comera, comêramos, comêreis, comeram, **E** comerei, comerás, comerá, comeremos, comereis, comerão, **F** comeria, comerias, comeria, comeríamos, comeríeis, comeriam, **G** coma, comas, coma, comamos, comais, comam, **H** comer, comeres, comer, comermos, comerdes, comerem, **I** comesse, comesses, comesse, comêssemos, comêsseis, comessem, **J** come, coma, comamos, comei, comam, **K** comendo, **L** comer, comeres, comer, comermos, comerdes, comerem, **M** comido.

conduzir: **A** conduzo, conduzes, conduz, etc., **B** conduzia, etc., **C** conduzi, conduziste, etc., **G** conduza, etc., **I** conduzisse, etc., **J** conduz, conduza, etc., **M** conduzido.

conhecer: **A** conheço, conheces, etc., **B** conhecia, etc., **C** conheci, conheceste, etc., **D** conhecera, etc., **I** conhecesse, conhecesses, etc., **J** conhece, conheça, etc., **M** conhecido.

conseguir: **A** consigo, consegues, consegue, etc., **C** consegui, conseguiste, etc., **D** conseguira, conseguiras, etc., **E** conseguirei, conseguirás, etc., **J** consegue, consiga, consigamos, consegui, consigam.

dar: **A** dou, dás, dá, damos, dais, dão, **B** dava, etc., **C** dei, deste, deu, demos, destes, deram, **D** dera, deras, etc., **E** darei, darás, etc., **F** daria, etc., **G** dê, dês, dê, dêmos, deis, dêem, **H** der, deres, etc., **I** desse, desses, etc., **J** dá, dê, dêmos, dai, dêem, **K** dando, **L** dar, dares, dar, darmos, dardes, darem, **M** dado.

dizer: **A** digo, dizes, diz, dizemos, dizeis, dizem ; **B** dizia, dizias, etc., **C** disse, disseste, disse, dissemos, dissestes, disseram, **D** dissera, disseras, etc., **E** direi, dirás, dirá, etc., **F** diria, dirias, etc., **G** diga, digas, etc., **H** disser, disseres, disser, dissermos, disserdes, disserem, **I** dissesse, dissesses, etc., **J** diz, diga, etc., **K** dizendo, **L** dizer, dizeres, dizer, dizermos, dizerdes, dizerem, **M** dito.

dormir: A durmo, dormes, dorme, dormimos, dormis, dormem, B dormia, dormias, etc., C dormi, dormiste, etc., H dormir, dormires, etc., J dorme, durma, durmamos, dormi, durmam, M dormido.

escrever: A escrevo, escreves, etc., B escrevia, escrevias, etc., C escrevi, escreveste, escreveu, etc., D escrevera, escreveras, etc., I escrevesse, escrevesses, etc., J escreve, escreva, etc., M escrito.

ESTAR: A estou, estás, está, estamos, estais, estão, B estava, estavas, estava, estávamos, -estáveis, estavam, C estive, estiveste, esteve, estivemos, estivestes, estiveram, D estivera, estiveras, estivera, estivéramos, estivéreis, estiveram, E estarei, estarás, estará, estaremos, estareis, estarão, F estaria, estarias, estaria, estaríamos, estaríeis, estariam, G esteja, estejas, esteja, estejamos, estejais, estejam, H estiver, estiveres, estiver, estivermos, estiverdes, estiverem, I estivesse, estivesses, estivesse, estivéssemos, estivésseis, estivessem, J está, esteja, estejamos, estai, estejam, K estando, L estar, estares, estar, estarmos, estardes, estarem, M estado.

fazer: A faço, fazes, faz, etc., B fazia, fazias, etc., C fiz, fizeste, fez, fizemos, fizestes, fizeram, D fizera, fizeras, etc., E farei, farás, etc., F faria, farias, etc., G faça, faças, etc.; H fizer, fizeres, etc., I fizesse, fizesses, etc., J faz, faça, façamos, fazei, façam, M feito.

ir: A vou, vais, vai, vamos, ides, vão, B ia, ias, íamos, etc., C fui, foste, foi, fomos, fostes, foram, D fora, foras, fora, fôramos, fôreis, foram, E irei, irás, irá, iremos, ireis, irão, F iria, irias, iríamos, etc., G vá, vás, vá, vamos, vades, vão, H for, fores, for, formos, fordes, forem, I fosse, fosses, fosse, fôssemos, fôsseis, fossem, J vai, vá, vamos, ide, vão, K indo, L ir, ires, ir, irmos, irdes, irem, M ido.

ler: A leio, lês, lê, lemos, ledes, lêem, B lia, lias, etc., C li, leste, leu, etc., G leia, leias, etc., M lido.

nascer: A nasço, nasces, etc., B nascia, etc., C nasci, nasceste, nasceu, etc., D nascera, etc., G nasça, nasças, etc., H nascer, nasceres, etc., I nascesse, etc., M nascido.

negociar: A negoc(e)io, negoc(e)ias, negoc(e)ia, negociamos, negociais, negoc(e)iam, B negociava, etc., C negociei, negociaste, etc., G negoc(e)ie, negoc(e)ies, negoc(e)ie, negociemos, negocieis, negoc(e)iem, J negoc(e)ia, negoc(e)ie, negociemos, negociai, negoc(e)iem, M negociado.

oferecer: A ofereço, ofereces, etc., B oferecia, etc., C ofereci, ofereceste, ofereceu, etc., D oferecera, etc., G ofereça, ofereças, etc., I oferecesse, etc., J oferece, ofereça, ofereçamos, oferecei, ofereçam, M oferecido.

ouvir: A ouço, ouves, ouve, etc., B ouvia, etc., C ouvi, ouviste, ouviu, etc., D ouvira, etc., G ouça, ouças, etc., H ouvir, ouvires, etc., I ouvisse, ouvisses, etc., J ouve, ouça, ouçamos, ouvi, ouçam, M ouvido.

parecer: A pareço, pareces, parece, etc., B parecia, etc., C pareci, pareceste, etc., D parecera, etc., G pareça, pareças, etc., H parecer, pareceres, etc., I parecesse, parecesses, etc., M parecido.

PARTIR: A parto, partes, parte, partimos, partis, partem, **B** partia, partias, partia, partíamos, partíeis, partiam, **C** parti, partiste, partiu, partimos, partistes, partiram, **D** partira, partiras, partira, partíramos, partíreis, partiram, **G** parta, partas, parta, partamos, partais, partam, **H** partir, partires, partir, partirmos, partirdes, partirem, **I** partisse, partisses, partisse, partíssemos, partísseis, partissem, **J** parte, parta, partamos, parti, partam, **K** partindo, **L** partir, partires, partir, partirmos, partirdes, partirem, **M** partido.

passear: A passeio, passeias, passeia, passeamos, passeais, passeiam, **B** passeava, passeavas, etc., **C** passeei, passeaste, etc., **E** passearei, passearás, etc., **G** passeie, passeies, etc., **J** passeia, passeie, passeemos, passeai, passeiem, **M** passeado.

pedir: A peço, pedes, pede, etc., **C** pedi, pediste, pediu, etc., **G** peça, peças, etc., **J** pede, peça, peçamos, pedi, peçam, **M** pedido.

perder: A perco, perdes, perde, perdemos, perdeis, perdem, **C** perdi, perdeste, perdeu, etc., **F** perderia, perderias, etc., **G** perca, percas, perca, etc., **H** perder, perderes, etc., **I** perdesse, perdesses, etc., **J** perde, perca, percamos, perdei, percam, **M** perdido.

poder: A posso, podes, pode, podemos, podeis, podem, **B** podia, podias, etc., **C** pude, pudeste, pôde, pudemos, pudestes, puderam, **G** possa, possamos, etc., **H** puder, puderes, puder, etc., **I** pudesse, pudéssemos, etc.

pôr: A ponho, pões, põe, pomos, pondes, põem, **B** punha, púnhamos, etc., **C** pus, puseste, pôs, pusemos, pusestes, puseram, **D** pusera, puséramos, etc., **E** porei, porás, etc., **F** poria, porias, etc., **G** ponha, ponhas, etc., **H** puser, pusermos, etc., **I** pusesse, puséssemos, etc., **J** põe, ponha, ponhamos, ponde, ponham, **K** pondo, **L** pôr, pores, pôr, pormos, pordes, porem, **M** posto.

querer: A quero, queres, quer, queremos, quereis, querem, **C** quis, quiseste, quis, quisemos, quisestes, quiseram, **D** quisera, quiséramos, etc., **G** queira, queiramos, etc., **H** quiser, quisermos, etc., **I** quisesse, quiséssemos, etc., **J** quer, queira, queiramos, querei, queiram, **K** querendo, **L** querer, quereres, querer, querermos, quererdes, quererem, **M** querido.

rir: A rio, ris, ri, rimos, rides, riem, **B** ria, ríamos, etc., **C** ri, riste, riu, rimos, ristes, riram, **D** rira, ríramos, etc., **G** ria, rias, etc., **H** rir, rires, etc., **I** risse, ríssemos, etc., **J** ri, ria, riamos, ride, riam, **K** rindo, **M** rido.

saber: A sei, sabes, sabe, sabemos, sabeis, sabem, **B** sabia, sabíamos, etc., **C** soube, soubeste, soube, soubemos, soubestes, souberam, **D** soubera, soubéramos, etc., **G** saiba, saibas, saiba, saibamos, saibais, saibam, **H** souber, souberes, etc., **I** soubesse, soubesses, etc., **J** sabe, saiba, saibamos, sabei, saibam, **M** sabido.

sair: A saio, sais, sai, saímos, saís, saem, **B** saía, saías, etc., **C** saí, saíste, saiu, etc., **D** saíra, saíras, etc., **G** saia, saias, saia, saiamos, saiais, saiam, **H** sair, saíres, sair, etc., **I** saísse, saísses, etc., **J** sai, saia, saiamos, saí, saiam, **K** saindo, **M** saído.

SENTAR-SE: A sento-me, sentas-te, senta-se, sentamo-nos, sentais-vos, sentam-se, **B** sentava-me, sentavas-te, sentava-se, sentávamo-nos, sentáveis-vos, sentavam-se, **C** sentei-me, sentaste-te, sentou-se, sentámo-nos, sentastes-vos, sentaram-se, **D** sentara-me, sentaras-te, sentara-se, sentáramo-nos, sentáreis-vos, sentaram-se, **E** sentar-me-ei, sentar-te-ás, sentar-se-á, sentar-nos-emos, sentar-vos-eis, sentar-se-ão, **F** sentar-me-ia, sentar-te-ias, sentar-se-ia, sentar-nos-íamos, sentar-vos-íeis, sentar-se-iam, **G** me sente, te sentes, se sente, nos sentemos, vos senteis, se sentem, **H** me sentar, te sentares, se sentar, nos sentarmos, vos sentardes, se sentarem, **I** me sentasse, te sentasses, se sentasse, nos sentássemos, vos sentásseis, se sentassem, **J** senta-te, sente-se, sentemo-nos, sentai-vos, sentem-se, **K** sentando-se, **L** sentar-me, sentares-te, sentar-se, sentarmo-nos, sentardes-vos, sentarem-se, **M** sentado.

sentir: A sinto, sentes, sente, sentimos, sentis, sentem, **B** sentia, sentias, etc., **C** senti, sentiste, sentiu, etc., **D** sentira, etc., **G** sinta, sintas, etc., **I** sentisse, sentisses, etc., **H** sentir, sentires, etc., **J** sente, sinta, sintamos, senti, sintam, **M** sentido.

SER: A sou, és, é, somos, sois, são, **B** era, eras, era, éramos, éreis, eram, **C** fui, foste, foi, fomos, fostes, foram, **D** fora, foras, fora, fôramos, fôreis, foram, **F** seria, serias, seria, seríamos, seríeis, seriam, **G** seja, sejas, seja, sejamos, sejais, sejam, **H** for, fores, for, formos, fordes, forem, **I** fosse, fosses, fosse, fôssemos, fôsseis, fossem, **J** sê, seja, sejamos, sede, sejam, **K** sendo, **L** ser, seres, ser, sermos, serdes, serem, **M** sido.

TER: A tenho, tens, tem, temos, tendes, têm, **B** tinha, tinhas, tinha, tínhamos, tínheis, tinham, **C** tive, tiveste, teve, tivemos, tivestes, tiveram, **D** tivera, tiveras, tivera, tivéramos, tivéreis, tiveram, **E** terei, terás, terá, teremos, tereis, terão, **F** teria, terias, teria, teríamos, teríeis, teriam, **G** tenha, tenhas, tenha, tenhamos, tenhais, tenham, **H** tiver, tiveres, tiver, tivermos, tiverdes, tiverem, **I** tivesse, tivesses, tivesse, tivéssemos, tivésseis, tivessem, **J** tem, tenha, tenhamos, tende, tenham, **K** tendo, **L** ter, teres, ter, termos, terdes, terem, **M** tido.

trazer: A trago, trazes, traz, trazemos, trazeis, trazem, **B** trazia, trazias, etc., **C** trouxe, trouxeste, trouxe, trouxemos, trouxestes, trouxeram, **D** trouxera, trouxeras, etc., **E** trarei, trarás, trará, traremos, trareis, trarão, **F** traria, trarias, etc., **G** traga, tragas, etc., **H** trouxer, trouxeres, etc., **I** trouxesse, trouxesses, etc., **J** traz, traga, tragamos, trazei, tragam, **K** trazendo, **L** trazer, trazeres, trazer, trazermos, trazerdes, trazerem, **M** trazido.

ver: A vejo, vês, vê, vemos, vedes, vêem, **B** via, vias, etc., **C** vi, viste, viu, vimos, vistes, viram, **D** vira, viras, etc., **E** verei, verás, etc., **G** veja, vejas, veja, etc., **H** vir, vires, vir, virmos, virdes, virem, **I** visse, visses, visse, etc., **J** vê, veja, vejamos, vede, vejam, **K** vendo, **L** ver, veres, ver, vermos, verdes, verem, **M** visto.

vir: A venho, vens, vem, vimos, vindes, vêm, **B** vinha, vinhas, etc., **C** vim, vieste, veio, viemos, viestes, vieram, **D** viera, vieras, etc., **E** virei, virás, etc., **G** venha, venhas, etc., **H** vier, vieres, vier, etc., **I** viesse, viesses, etc., **J** vem, venha, venhamos, vinde, venham, **K** vindo, **L** vir, vires, vir, virmos, virdes, virem, **M** vindo.

viver: A vivo, vives, etc., **B** vivia, vivias, etc., **C** vivi, viveste, viveu, etc., **G** viva, vivas, etc., **I** vivesse, vivesses, etc., **J** vive, viva, vivamos, vivei, vivam, **M** vivido.

ENGLISH IRREGULAR VERBS

Infinitive	Past Tense	Past Participle
arise	arose	arisen
awake	awoke	awoken
be	was/were	been
bear	bore	born(e)
beat	beat	beaten
begin	began	begun
bend	bent	bent
bet	bet/betted	bet/betted
bid	bid	bid
bind	bound	bound
bite	bit	bitten
bleed	bled	bled
blow	blew	blown
break	broke	broken
breed	bred	bred
bring	brought	brought
build	built	built
burn	burnt/burned	burnt/burned
burst	burst	burst
buy	bought	bought
can	could	–
cast	cast	cast
catch	caught	caught
choose	chose	chosen
come	came	come
cost	cost	cost
creep	crept	crept
cut	cut	cut
deal	dealt	dealt
dig	dug	dug
do	did	done
draw	drew	drawn
dream	dreamed/dreamt	dreamed/dreamt
drink	drank	drunk
drive	drove	driven
eat	ate	eaten
fall	fell	fallen
feed	fed	fed
feel	felt	felt
fight	fought	fought
find	found	found
fling	flung	flung
fly	flew	flown
forget	forgot	forgotten
freeze	froze	frozen
get	got	got (Am gotten)
give	gave	given
go	went	gone
grind	ground	ground
grow	grew	grown

Infinitive	Past Tense	Past Participle
hang	hung / hanged	hung / hanged
have	had	had
hear	heard	heard
hide	hid	hidden
hit	hit	hit
hold	held	held
hurt	hurt	hurt
keep	kept	kept
kneel	knelt / kneeled	knelt / kneeled
know	knew	known
lay	laid	laid
lead	led	led
lean	leant / leaned	leant / leaned
leap	leapt / leaped	leapt / leaped
learn	learnt / learned	learnt / learned
leave	left	left
lend	lent	lent
let	let	let
lie	lay	lain
light	lit / lighted	lit / lighted
lose	lost	lost
make	made	made
may	might	–
mean	meant	meant
meet	met	met
mow	mowed	mown / mowed
pay	paid	paid
put	put	put
quit	quit / quitted	quit / quitted
read	read	read
rid	rid	rid
ride	rode	ridden
ring	rang	rung
rise	rose	risen
run	ran	run
saw	sawed	sawn
say	said	said
see	saw	seen
seek	sought	sought
sell	sold	sold
send	sent	sent
set	set	set
shake	shook	shaken
shall	should	–
shed	shed	shed
shine	shone	shone
shoot	shot	shot
show	showed	shown
shrink	shrank	shrunk

Infinitive	Past Tense	Past Participle
shut	shut	shut
sing	sang	sung
sink	sank	sunk
sit	sat	sat
sleep	slept	slept
slide	slid	slid
sling	slung	slung
smell	smelt /smelled	smelt /smelled
sow	sowed	sown /sowed
speak	spoke	spoken
speed	sped /speeded	sped /speeded
spell	spelt /spelled	spelt /spelled
spend	spent	spent
spill	spilt /spilled	spilt /spilled
spin	spun	spun
spit	spat	spat
split	split	split
spoil	spoiled /spoilt	spoiled /spoilt
spread	spread	spread
spring	sprang	sprung
stand	stood	stood
steal	stole	stolen
stick	stuck	stuck
sting	stung	stung
stink	stank	stunk
strike	struck	struck /stricken
swear	swore	sworn
sweep	swept	swept
swell	swelled	swollen /swelled
swim	swam	swum
swing	swung	swung
take	took	taken
teach	taught	taught
tear	tore	torn
tell	told	told
think	thought	thought
throw	threw	thrown
tread	trod	trodden
wake	woke /waked	woken /waked
wear	wore	worn
weave	wove /weaved	woven /weaved
weep	wept	wept
win	won	won
wind	wound	wound
wring	wrung	wrung
write	wrote	written

a [a] *artigo definido* → **o** ◆ *prep* **1.** *(introduz um complemento indireto)* to; **mostrar algo a alguém** to show sthg to sb; **diga ao Zé para vir** tell Zé to come; **pede o chapéu ao Paulo** ask Paulo for the hat. **2.** *(relativo a direção)* to; **fomos à praia** we went to the beach; **vamos ao cinema** we're going to the cinema; **cheguei a Salvador ontem** I arrived in Salvador yesterday. **3.** *(relativo a posição, lugar, distância)*: **é à esquerda/direita** it's on the left/right; **fica a 10 quilômetros** it's 10 kilometres away. **4.** *(relativo a quantidade, medida, preço)*: **aos centos/às dezenas** by the hundred/dozen; **a quanto estão as peras?** how much are the pears?; **vender algo a metro** to sell sthg by the metre. **5.** *(indica modo, maneira)*: **feito à mão** handmade; **bater à máquina** to type; **sal a gosto** salt to taste. **6.** *(relativo a velocidade)*: **dirigir a 60 km/h** to drive at 60 km/h; **ela ia a 100 por hora** she was going at 100 kilometres an hour. **7.** *(indica freqüência)*: **três vezes ao dia** three times a day; **estou lá às terças e quintas** I'm there on Tuesdays and Thursdays. **8.** *(introduz complemento de tempo)*: **as lojas abrem às 9 horas** the shops open at 9 (o'clock); **chegam daqui a 2 horas** they're arriving in 2 hours' time; **fica a dez minutos daqui** it's ten minutes from here; **à noite** at night. **9.** *(indica série)*: **de ... a** from ... to; **façam os exercícios de um a dez** do exercises one to ten.

10. *(seguido de infinitivo para exprimir momento)*: **ele começou a falar** he started speaking; **ele tropeçou ao subir no ônibus** he tripped over as he was getting on the bus.
11. *(seguido de infinitivo indicando duas ações)*: **ela sentou-se a ler** she sat down and started to read.

à [a] = **a + a**, → **a**.

aba ['aba] *f (de chapéu)* brim; *(corte de carne)* side.

abacate [abaˈkatʃi] *m* avocado.

abacaxi [abakaˈʃi] *m* pineapple.

abadia [abaˈdʒia] *f* abbey.

abafado, -da [abaˈfadu, -da] *adj (ar)* stuffy; *(tempo)* close.

abafar [abaˈfa(x)] *vt (ruído)* to muffle ◆ *vi (sufocar)* to stifle.

abaixar [abajˈʃa(x)] *vt* to lower.
❑ **abaixar-se** *vp* to stoop.

abaixo [aˈbajʃu] *adv* down; **jogar ~** *(árvore)* to cut down; **mais ~** further down; **~ de** below; **~ o governo!** down with the government!

abaixo-assinado [aˌbajʃuasiˈnadu] *(pl* **abaixo-assinados** [aˌbajʃuasiˈnaduʃ]*) m* petition.

abajur [abaˈʒu(x)] *(pl* **-res** [-riʃ]*) m* lampshade.

abalar [abaˈla(x)] *vt (estremecer)* to shake.

abalo [aˈbalu] *m*: **~ (sísmico** OU **de terra)** earth tremor.

abanar [abaˈna(x)] *vt (cabeça)* to shake; *(rabo)* to wag.

abandonado, -da [abãdoˈnadu, -da] *adj (lugar)* deserted; *(cão, carro)* abandoned.

abandonar [abãdoˈna(x)] *vt* to abandon.

abandono [abãn'donu] *m* abandonment; **ao ~** abandoned; **~ do lar** desertion.

abarcar [abax'ka(x)] *vt* to cover.

abarrotado, -da [abaxo'tadu. -da] *adj* packed.

abarrotar [abaxo'ta(x)] *vi* to be full up ♦ *vt* to pack; **a ~ de** packed with.

abastecer [abaʃte'se(x)] *vt* to supply. ❑ **abastecer-se** *vp* to stock up.

abastecimento [abaʃtesi'mẽntu] *m* supply.

abater [aba'te(x)] *vt* (*baixar*) to reduce; (*avião*) to shoot down; (*árvore*) to fell; (*animal*) to slaughter.

abatimento [abatʃi'mẽntu] *m* (*desconto*) reduction; (*fraqueza*) weakness.

abcesso [ab'sɛsu] *m* abscess.

abdicar [abdʒi'ka(x)] *vi* to abdicate.

abdómen [ab'dɔmɛn] *m* (*Port*) = **abdômen**.

abdômen [ab'domɛ] *m* (*Br*) abdomen.

abdominal [abdomi'naw] (*pl* **-ais** [-ajʃ]) *adj* abdominal. ❑ **abdominais** *mpl*: **fazer abdominais** to do sit-ups.

á-bê-cê [abe'se] *m* abc.

abecedário [abese'darju] *m* alphabet.

abeirar-se [abej'raxsi] : **abeirar-se de** *vp* + *prep* to draw near to.

abelha [a'beʎa] *f* bee.

abelhudo, -da [abe'ʎudu. -da] *adj* nosy.

aberração [abexa'sãw] (*pl* **-ões** [-õjʃ]) *f* aberration.

aberto, -ta [a'bɛxtu. -ta] *pp* → **abrir** ♦ *adj* open.

abertura [abex'tura] *f* opening; (*MÚS*) overture; **"~ fácil"** "easy to open".

abeto [a'bɛtu] *m* fir tree.

ABI *f* (*abrev de Associação Brasileira de Imprensa*) *Brazilian press association which also functions as a political pressure group.*

abismo [a'biʒmu] *m* abyss.

abóbada [a'bɔbada] *f* vault.

abóbora [a'bɔbora] *f* pumpkin.

abóbora-menina [a,bɔborame'nina] (*pl* **abóboras-meninas** [a,bɔboraʒme'ninaʃ]) *f* sweet pumpkin.

abobrinha [abo'briɲa] *f* (*Br*) courgette (*Brit*), zucchini (*Am*).

abolir [abo'li(x)] *vt* to abolish.

abominar [abomi'na(x)] *vt* to loathe.

abono [a'bonu] *m*: **~ de família** (*Port*) child benefit.

abordagem [abox'daʒẽ] (*pl* **-ns** [-ʃ]) *f* (*de tema, situação*) handling, treatment.

abordar [abox'da(x)] *vt* (*pessoa*) to approach; (*assunto*) to broach.

aborígene [abo'riʒeni] *mf* aborigine.

aborrecer [aboxe'se(x)] *vt* (*irritar*) to annoy; (*entediar*) to bore. ❑ **aborrecer-se** *vp* (*irritar-se*) to get annoyed; (*entediar-se*) to get bored.

aborrecido, -da [aboxe'sidu. -da] *adj* (*chato*) tedious; (*zangado*) annoyed.

aborrecimento [aboxesi'mẽntu] *m* (*tédio*) boredom; (*contrariedade*) annoyance.

abortar [abox'ta(x)] *vi* (*MED*) (*espontaneamente*) to have a miscarriage; (*intencionalmente*) to have an abortion.

aborto [a'boxtu] *m* (*MED*) (*espontâneo*) miscarriage; (*intencional*) abortion.

abotoar [abo'twa(x)] *vt* to button (up).

abraçar [abra'sa(x)] *vt* to hug. ❑ **abraçar-se** *vp* to hug each other.

abraço [a'brasu] *m* hug; **um ~** (*em carta, postal*) best wishes.

abrandar [abrãn'da(x)] *vt* (*dor*) to ease ♦ *vi* (*vento*) to drop; (*chuva*) to ease off.

abranger [abrã'ʒe(x)] *vt* to include.

abre-latas [abre'lataʃ] *m inv* (*Port*) tin opener (*Brit*), can opener (*Am*).

abreviação [abrevja'sãw] (*pl* **-ões** [-õjʃ]) *f* abbreviation.

abreviatura [abrevja'tura] *f* abbreviation.

abridor [abri'do(x)] (*pl* **-res** [-riʃ]) *m* (*Br*): **~ de garrafa** bottle opener; **~ de lata** tin opener (*Brit*), can opener (*Am*).

abrigar [abri'ga(x)] *vt* to shelter. ❑ **abrigar-se** *vp* to take cover.

abrigo [a'brigu] *m* shelter; **ao ~ de** under cover of.

abril [a'briw] *m* April, → **setembro**.

abrir [a'bri(x)] *vt & vi* to open; **~ o apetite** to whet one's appetite; **~ a boca** (*bocejar*) to yawn; **~ uma exceção** to make an exception; **~ mão de algo** (*fig*) to forego sthg; **~ os olhos** (*fig*) to open one's eyes. ❑ **abrir-se** *vp*: **~-se com alguém** to confide in sb.

absinto [ab'sĩntu] *m* absinthe.

absolutamente [abso,luta'mẽntʃi] *adv* absolutely.

absoluto, -ta [abso'lutu. -ta] *adj* absolute.

absolver [absow've(x)] *vt* *(perdoar)* to absolve; *(JUR)* to acquit.

absorção [absox'sãw] *f* absorption.

absorvente [absox'vẽntʃi] *adj* absorbent.

❏ **absorventes** *mpl*: **~s diários** panty liners.

absorver [absox've(x)] *vt* to absorb.

abstémio, -mia [abʃ'temju, -mja] *m, f (Port)* = **abstêmio**.

abstêmio, -mia [abʃ'temju, -mja] *m, f (Br)* teetotaller.

abstracto, -ta [abʃ'tratu, -ta] *adj (Port)* = **abstrato**.

abstrato, -ta [abʃ'tratu, -ta] *adj (Br)* abstract.

absurdo, -da [ab'suxdu, -da] *adj* absurd ♦ *m* nonsense.

abundância [abũn'dãsja] *f* abundance.

abundante [abũn'dãntʃi] *adj* abundant.

abusado, -da [abu'zadu, -da] *adj (Br: atrevido)* forward.

abusar [abu'za(x)] *vi* to overdo things; **~ de alguém** to abuse sb; **~ da bebida/do tabaco** to drink/smoke too much.

abuso [a'buzu] *m* *(de álcool, droga)* abuse; *(JUR)* indecent assault.

a.C. *(abrev de antes de Cristo)* BC.

a/c *(abrev de aos cuidados de)* c/o.

acabamento [akaba'mẽntu] *m* finish.

acabar [aka'ba(x)] *vt* to finish ♦ *vi* *(tempo, programa, filme)* to finish, to end; *(água, pão, leite)* to run out; **~ com algo** to put an end to sthg; **~ com alguém** *(matar)* to kill sb; **~ de fazer algo** to have just done sthg; **~ bem** to end well; **~ por fazer algo** to end up doing sthg.

❏ **acabar-se** *vp* to run out; **acabou-se!** that's enough!

acácia [a'kasja] *f* acacia.

academia [akade'mia] *f* academy; **~ de belas-artes** Academy of Fine Arts; **~ de ginástica** gymnasium.

açafrão [asa'frãw] *m* saffron.

acalmar [akaw'ma(x)] *vt* to calm ♦ *vi* *(vento, dor)* to abate.

❏ **acalmar-se** *vp* to calm down.

acampamento [akãmpa'mẽntu] *m* camp.

acampar [akãm'pa(x)] *vi* to camp.

acanhado, -da [aka'ɲadu, -da] *adj* shy.

acanhar-se [aka'ɲaxsi] *vp* to be shy.

ação [a'sãw] *(pl -ões* [-õjʃ]*) f (Br)* action; *(título de crédito)* share; *(de poema, peça teatral)* plot; **entrar em ~** to take action.

acarajé [akara'ʒe] *m (CULIN)* beancake fried in palm oil and served with a spicy sauce.

acariciar [akari'sja(x)] *vt* to caress.

acaso [a'kazu] *m* chance, accident; **ao ~** at random; **por ~** by chance OU accident.

acastanhado, -da [akaʃta'ɲadu, -da] *adj* brownish.

acatar [aka'ta(x)] *vt (ordem, lei)* to obey.

acção [a'sãw] *(pl -ões* [-õjʃ]*) f (Port)* = **ação**.

accionar [asju'nar] *vt (Port)* = **acionar**.

accionista [asju'niʃta] *mf (Port)* = **acionista**.

acções → acção.

aceder [ase'de(x)] *vi* to consent.

aceitar [asej'ta(x)] *vt* to accept.

aceito, -ta [a'sejtu, -ta] *pp →* **aceitar**.

acelerador [aselera'do(x)] *(pl -res* [-riʃ]*) m (AUT)* accelerator *(Brit)*, gas pedal *(Am)*.

acelerar [asele'ra(x)] *vt* to speed up ♦ *vi* to accelerate.

acenar [ase'na(x)] *vi (com braço)* to wave; *(com cabeça)* to nod.

acender [asẽn'de(x)] *vt (cigarro, vela, lareira)* to light; *(lâmpada, candeeiro)* to switch OU turn on.

aceno [a'senu] *m (with arm)* gesture; **um ~ de cabeça** a nod.

acento [a'sẽntu] *m (sinal gráfico)* accent; *(inflexão)* stress; **~ agudo/grave** acute/grave accent; **~ circunflexo** circumflex.

acepção [asep'sãw] *(pl -ões* [-õjʃ]*) f* sense.

acerca [a'sexka] : **acerca de** *prep* about, concerning.

acerola [ase'rɔla] *f* small bitter red fruit commonly used in juice and ice cream.

acertar [asex'ta(x)] *vt (relógio)* to set ♦ *vi*: **~ em** *(em alvo)* to hit; *(em resposta)* to get right; **~ com** *(com lugar, local)* to find; **acertou!** *(adivinhaste)* you got it right!

acervo [a'sexvu] *m (de museu, fundação)* collection.

aceso, -sa [a'sεzu, -za] *pp* → **acender**
♦ *adj* (*luz, lume*) on; (*discussão*) heated.

acessível [ase'sivew] (*pl* -**eis** [-ejʃ]) *adj*
accessible; (*preço*) affordable; (*pessoa*)
approachable.

acesso [a'sεsu] *m* access; (*de raiva,
histeria*) fit; **de fácil ~** easy to get to.

acessório [ase'sɔrju] *m* accessory.

acetona [ase'tona] *f* nail varnish
remover.

achado [a'ʃadu] *m* (*descoberta*) find;
(*pechincha*) bargain.

achar [a'ʃa(x)] *vt* to find; **~ que** to
think (that); **acho que não** I don't
think so; **acho que sim** I think so.

acidentado, -da [asidēn'tadu, -da]
adj (*terreno*) rough; (*viagem, férias*)
eventful ♦ *m, f* injured person.

acidental [asidēn'taw] (*pl* -**ais** [-ajʃ])
adj accidental.

acidentalmente [asidēntaw'mēntʃi]
adv accidentally.

acidente [asi'dēntʃi] *m* accident; (*de
terreno*) bump.

acidez [asi'deʒ] *f* acidity.

ácido, -da ['asidu, -da] *adj* (*sabor*)
sour ♦ *m* acid; **~ cítrico/sulfúrico** cit-
ric/sulphuric acid.

acima [a'sima] *adv* up; **mais ~** higher
up; **~ de** above; **~ de tudo** above all.

acionar [asjo'na(x)] *vt* (*Br*) to set in
motion.

acionista [asjo'niʃta] *mf* (*Br*) shareholder.

acne ['akni] *f* acne.

aço ['asu] *m* steel; **~ inoxidável** stainless steel.

acocorar-se [akoko'raxsi] *vp* to
squat (down).

ações → **ação**.

acolhimento [akoʎi'mēntu] *m* welcome.

acompanhamento [akõmpaɲa-
'mēntu] *m* (*de evolução, situação*) following; (*de prato de carne, peixe*) side dish,
side order; (*MÚS*) accompaniment.

acompanhante [akõmpa'ɲāntʃi] *mf*
companion; (*MÚS*) accompanist.

acompanhar [akõmpa'ɲa(x)] *vt* to
accompany; (*programa, situação*) to follow.

aconchegador, -ra [akõʃega'do(x),
-ra] (*mpl* -**res** [-riʃ], *fpl* -**s** [-ʃ]) *adj* cosy.

aconselhar [akõse'ʎa(x)] *vt* to advise.
⊐ **aconselhar-se** *vp* to get advice.

aconselhável [akõse'ʎavew] (*pl* -**eis**
[-ejʃ]) *adj* advisable; **pouco ~** inadvisable.

acontecer [akõnte'se(x)] *vi* to happen; (**mas**) **acontece que ...** but as it
happens ...; **aconteça o que ~** come
what may.

acontecimento [akõntesi'mēntu] *m*
event.

acordar [akox'da(x)] *vt & vi* to wake
up.

acorde [a'kɔxdʒi] *m* (*MÚS*) chord.

acordeão [akox'dʒjāw] (*pl* -**ões** [-õjʃ])
m accordion.

acordo [a'koxdu] *m* agreement; (*JUR*)
accord; **de ~!** all right!; **estar de ~ com**
to agree with; **de ~ com** in accordance
with.

acorrentar [akoxēn'ta(x)] *vt* to chain
(up).

acostamento [akoʃta'mēntu] *m* (*Br*)
hard shoulder (*Brit*), shoulder (*Am*).

acostumado, -da [akoʃtu'madu, -da]
adj: **estar ~ a algo** to be used to sthg.

acostumar-se [akoʃtu'maxsi] *vp*: **~
com algo** to get used to sthg; **~ a fazer
algo** to get used to doing sthg.

açougue [a'sogi] *m* (*Br*) butcher's
(shop).

açougueiro, -ra [aso'gejru, -ra] *m, f*
(*Br*) butcher.

A.C.P. (*abrev de Automóvel Clube de
Portugal*) = AA (*Brit*), = AAA (*Am*).

acre ['akri] *adj* (*sabor*) bitter; (*cheiro*)
acrid.

acreditar [akredʒi'ta(x)] *vi* to believe;
~ em to believe in.

acrescentar [akresēn'ta(x)] *vt* to add.

acréscimo [a'kresimu] *m* increase.

acrílica [a'krilika] *adj f* → **fibra**.

acrobata [akro'bata] *mf* acrobat.

activo, -va [a'tivu, -va] *adj* (*Port*) =
ativo.

acto ['atu] *m* (*Port*) = **ato**.

actor, -triz [a'tor, -triʃ] (*mpl* -**res**
[-reʃ], *fpl* -**zes** [-zeʃ]) *m, f* (*Port*) = **ator**.

actual [a'twal] (*pl* -**ais** [-ajʃ]) *adj* (*Port*)
= **atual**.

actuar [a'twar] *vi* (*Port*) = **atuar**.

açúcar [a'suka(x)] *m* sugar; **~ preto/
branco** brown/white sugar; **~ em
cubos** sugar cubes (*pl*); **~ mascavo** mus-
covado sugar; **~ em pó** caster sugar.

açucareiro [asuka'rejru] *m* sugar
bowl.

acumulação [akumula'sāw] (*pl* -**ões**
[-õjʃ]) *f* accumulation.

acumular [akumu'la(x)] *vt* to accumulate.

acupunctura [akupūn'tura] *f* acupuncture.

acusação [akuza'sāw] (*pl* -ões [-õjʃ]) *f* (*denúncia*) accusation; (*queixa*) complaint; (*JUR: declaração*) charge; (*JUR: acusador*) plaintiff.

acusar [aku'za(x)] *vt* to accuse; (*revelar*) to reveal.

A.D. (*abrev de Anno Domini*) AD.

adaptação [adapta'sāw] (*pl* -ões [-õjʃ]) *f* adaptation.

adaptado, -da [adap'tadu, -da] *adj* (*adequado*) appropriate.

adaptador [adapta'do(x)] (*pl* -res [-riʃ]) *m* adaptor.

adaptar [adap'ta(x)] *vt* to adapt.
❑ **adaptar-se** *vp*: **~-se a** to adapt to.

adega [a'dɛga] *f* wine cellar; **~ cooperativa** *wine cellar run by a cooperative.*

adepto, -ta [a'dɛptu, -ta] *m, f* supporter.

adequado, -da [ade'kwadu, -da] *adj* appropriate.

adereço [ade'resu] *m* (*em teatro, espetáculo*) prop.

aderente [ade'rēntʃi] *adj* (*pneu*) nonskid ◆ *mf* (*partidário*) supporter.

aderir [ade'ri(x)] *vi* to stick; **~ a algo** (*fig: a idéia, partido*) to support sthg.

adesão [ade'zāw] (*pl* -ões [-õjʃ]) *f* (*a idéia, partido*) support.

adesivo, -va [ade'zivu, -va] *adj* adhesive ◆ *m* adhesive tape.

adesões → **adesão.**

adeus [a'dewʃ] *m* goodbye ◆ *interj* goodbye!; **dizer ~** to say goodbye.

adiamento [adʒja'mēntu] *m* postponement.

adiantado, -da [adʒjān'tadu, -da] *adj* (*no tempo*) ahead of schedule; (*no espaço*) advanced ◆ *adv*: **chegar ~** to arrive early; **estar ~** (*relógio*) to be fast; **pagar ~** to pay in advance.

adiantar [adʒjān'ta(x)] *vt* (*relógio*) to put forward; (*dinheiro*) to advance; (*trabalho*) to get ahead with ◆ *v impess*: **não adianta gritar** there's no point in shouting.
❑ **adiantar-se** *vp* (*no espaço*) to get ahead.

adiante [a'dʒjāntʃi] *adv* ahead ◆ *interj* forward!; **mais ~** further on; **passar ~** to overlook; **e por aí ~** and so forth.

adiar [a'dʒja(x)] *vt* to postpone.

adição [adʒi'sāw] (*pl* -ões [-õjʃ]) *f* addition.

adicionar [adʒisjo'na(x)] *vt* (*acrescentar*) to add; (*somar*) to add up.

adições → **adição.**

adivinha [adʒi'viɲa] *f* riddle.

adivinhar [adʒivi'ɲa(x)] *vt* to guess; (*futuro*) to predict; (*decifrar*) to solve.

adjectivo [adʒɛ'tivu] *m* (*Port*) = **adjetivo.**

adjetivo [adʒɛ'tʃivu] *m* (*Br*) adjective.

adjunto, -ta [ad'ʒūntu, -ta] *m, f* assistant ◆ *adj* assistant (*antes de s*).

administração [adʒiminiʃtra'sāw] *f* administration; (*os administradores*) management; (*local*) administrative office.

administrador, -ra [adʒiminiʃtra-'do(x), -ra] (*mpl* -res [-riʃ], *fpl* -s [-ʃ]) *m, f* administrator.

administrar [adʒiminiʃ'tra(x)] *vt* to administer.

admiração [adʒimira'sāw] *f* (*espanto*) amazement; (*respeito, estima*) admiration.

admirador, -ra [adʒimira'do(x), -ra] (*mpl* -res [-riʃ], *fpl* -s [-ʃ]) *m, f* admirer.

admirar [adʒimi'ra(x)] *vt* (*contemplar*) to admire; (*espantar*) to amaze.
❑ **admirar-se** *vp* to be surprised.

admirável [adʒimi'ravew] (*pl* -eis [-ejʃ]) *adj* (*incrível*) amazing; (*digno de respeito*) admirable.

admissão [adʒimi'sāw] (*pl* -ões [-õjʃ]) *f* admission.

admitir [adʒimi'tʃi(x)] *vt* (*permitir*) to allow; (*deixar entrar*) to admit.

adoçante [ado'sāntʃi] *m* sweetener.

adoção [ado'sāw] (*pl* -ões [-õjʃ]) *f* (*Br*) adoption.

adoçar [ado'sa(x)] *vt* to sweeten.

adoecer [adoe'se(x)] *vi* to fall ill.

adolescência [adole'sēsja] *f* adolescence.

adolescente [adole'sēntʃi] *mf* adolescent.

adopção [ado'sāw] (*pl* -ões [-õjʃ]) *f* (*Port*) = **adoção.**

adorar [ado'ra(x)] *vt* to adore, to love.

adorável [ado'ravew] (*pl* -eis [-ejʃ]) *adj* adorable.

adormecer [adoxme'se(x)] *vt* to send to sleep ◆ *vi* to fall asleep.

adornar [adox'na(x)] *vt* to adorn.

adotado, -da [ado'tadu, -da] *adj* adopted.

adotar [ado'ta(x)] *vt* to adopt; *(livro)* to choose.

adquirir [adʒiki'ri(x)] *vt* to acquire.

adrenalina [adrena'lina] *f* adrenalin.

adulterar [aduwte'ra(x)] *vt* to adulterate.

adultério [aduw'tɛrju] *m* adultery.

adulto, -ta [a'duwtu, -ta] *adj & m, f* adult.

advérbio [ad'vɛxbju] *m* adverb.

adversário, -ria [adʒivɛx'sarju, -rja] *adj* opposing ♦ *m, f* opponent.

advertência [adʒivɛx'tẽsja] *f* warning.

advogado, -da [adʒivo'gadu, -da] *m, f* lawyer *(Brit)*, attorney *(Am)*.

á-é-i-ó-u [aɛ'jɔu] *m*: **aprender o ~** *(as vogais)* to learn to spell; *(o essencial de algo)* to learn the basics.

aéreo, -rea [a'ɛrju, -rja] *adj* air *(antes de s)*; *(fig: distraído)* absentminded.

aerobarco [aero'baxku] *m (Br)* hovercraft.

aerodinâmico, -ca [aerodʒi'namiku, -ka] *adj* aerodynamic.

aeródromo [aɛ'rɔdromu] *m* airfield.

aeromoça [aero'mosa] *f (Br)* air hostess.

aeromodelismo [a‚eromode'liʒmu] *m* model aeroplane making.

aeronáutica [aero'nawtʃika] *f (Br)* airforce.

aeroporto [aero'poxtu] *m* airport.

aerossol [aero'sɔw] *(pl* **-óis** [-ɔjʃ]*) m* aerosol.

afagar [afa'ga(x)] *vt* to stroke.

afastado, -da [afaʃ'tadu, -da] *adj (distante)* remote; *(retirado)* isolated.

afastar [afaʃ'ta(x)] *vt (desviar)* to move away; *(apartar)* to separate.
❏ **afastar-se** *vp (desviar-se)* to move away; *(distanciar-se)* to distance o.s.

afável [a'favɛw] *(pl* **-eis** [-ɛjʃ]*) adj* friendly.

afecto [a'fɛtu] *m (Port)* = **afeto**.

afeição [afej'sãw] *f (afecto)* affection; *(inclinação)* liking.

afetar [afe'ta(x)] *vt* to affect.

afetivo, -va [afe'tʃivu, -va] *adj (pessoa)* affectionate; *(carência, problema, vida)* emotional.

afeto [a'fɛtu] *m (Br)* affection.

afetuoso, -osa [afe'twozu, -ɔza] *adj* affectionate.

afiadeira [afja'dejra] *f (Port)* pencil sharpener.

afiado, -da [a'fjadu, -da] *adj* sharp.

afiambrado [afjãm'bradu] *m* chopped pork slices *(pl)*.

afiar [a'fja(x)] *vt* to sharpen.

aficionado, -da [afisjo'nadu, -da] *m, f* enthusiast.

afilhado, -da [afi'ʎadu, -da] *m, f* godson *(f* goddaughter*)*.

afim [a'fĩ] *(pl* **-ns** [-ʃ]*) adj* related ♦ *m (parente)* relative, relation.

afinado, -da [afi'nadu, -da] *adj (instrumento musical)* in tune; *(motor)* tuned.

afinal [afi'naw] *adv*: **~ (de contas)** after all.

afinar [afi'na(x)] *vt (instrumento, motor, travões)* to tune.

afinidade [afini'dadʒi] *f* affinity.

afins → **afim**.

afirmação [afixma'sãw] *(pl* **-ões** [-õjʃ]*) f* statement.

afirmar [afix'ma(x)] *vt* to state.

afirmativo, -va [afixma'tʃivu, -va] *adj* affirmative.

afixar [afik'sa(x)] *vt (cartaz, aviso)* to put up.

aflição [afli'sãw] *(pl* **-ões** [-õjʃ]*) f* distress.

afligir [afli'ʒi(x)] *vt* to distress.
❏ **afligir-se** *vp* to distress o.s.; **~-se com** to worry about.

aflito, -ta [a'flitu, -ta] *pp* → **afligir**.

aflorar [aflo'ra(x)] *vt (assunto, tema)* to touch on ♦ *vi* to surface.

afluência [aflu'ẽsja] *f* stream.

afluente [aflu'ẽtʃi] *m* tributary.

afobado, -da [afo'badu, -da] *adj (Br) (apressado)* rushed; *(atrapalhado)* flustered.

afogado, -da [afo'gadu, -da] *adj (pessoa)* drowned; *(motor)* flooded ♦ *m, f* drowned person.

afogador [afoga'do(x)] *(pl* **-res** [-riʃ]*) m (Br)* choke.

afogamento [afoga'mẽntu] *m* drowning.

afogar [afo'ga(x)] *vt* to drown.
❏ **afogar-se** *vp* to drown.

afónico, -ca [a'fɔniku, -ka] *adj (Port)* = **afônico**.

afônico, -ca [a'foniku, -ka] *adj (Br)*: **estar ~** to have lost one's voice.

afortunado, -da [afoxtu'nadu, -da]

adj lucky, fortunate.

afresco [aˈfreʃku] *m* (Br) fresco.

África [ˈafrika] *f*: **a ~** Africa; **a ~ do Sul** South Africa.

africano, -na [afriˈkanu, -na] *adj & m, f* African.

afro-brasileiro, -ra [ˌafrobraziˈlejru, -ra] *adj* Afro-Brazilian ◆ *m, f* Brazilian person of African extraction.

afronta [aˈfrõnta] *f* insult.

afrouxar [afroˈʃa(x)] *vt* (cinto, laço de sapato) to loosen.

afta [ˈafta] *f* mouth ulcer.

afugentar [afugẽnˈta(x)] *vt* to drive away.

afundar [afũnˈda(x)] *vt* to sink.
◻ **afundar-se** *vp* to sink.

agachar-se [agaˈʃaxsi] *vp* to squat.

agarrar [agaˈxa(x)] *vt* (apanhar, segurar) to grab; (alcançar, apanhar no ar) to catch.
◻ **agarrar-se** *vp*: **~-se a** (segurar-se a) to grab hold of; (pegar-se a) to stick to; (dedicar-se a) to get stuck into; **~-se aos livros** (fam) to study hard.

agasalhar-se [agazaˈʎaxsi] *vp* to wrap up warm.

agasalho [agaˈzaʎu] *m* (casaco) coat; (pulôver) jumper.

ágeis → **ágil**.

agência [aˈʒẽsja] *f* office; **~ bancária** branch (of a bank); **~ de câmbio** bureau de change; **~ de correio** (Br) post office; **~ funerária** funeral director's; **~ imobiliária** estate agent's (Brit), real estate office (Am); **~ de viagens** travel agent's.

agenda [aˈʒẽnda] *f* (livro) diary; (plano de reunião) agenda.

agente [aˈʒẽntʃi] *mf* (de polícia) policeman (f policewoman); (de vendas) sales representative; **"~ autorizado"** authorized agent for the sale of lottery tickets and football coupons; **~ secreto** secret agent.

ágil [ˈaʒiw] (pl **ágeis** [ˈaʒejʃ]) *adj* agile.

agilidade [aʒiliˈdadʒi] *f* agility.

ágio [ˈaʒju] *m* premium.

agir [aˈʒi(x)] *vi* to act.

agitação [aʒitaˈsãw] *f* agitation.

agitado, -da [aʒiˈtadu, -da] *adj* (pessoa) agitated; (mar) rough; (tempo) unsettled.

agitar [aʒiˈta(x)] *vt* (líquido) to shake; **"agite antes de abrir"** "shake well before opening".

◻ **agitar-se** *vp* to get agitated.

aglomeração [aglomeraˈsãw] (pl **-ões** [-õjʃ]) *f* (de pessoas) crowd; (de detritos) pile.

aglomerar [aglomeˈra(x)] *vt* to pile up.

agonia [agoˈnia] *f* (angústia) agony; (náusea) nausea; (antes da morte) death throes (pl).

agora [aˈgɔra] *adv* now; **é ~ ou nunca** it's now or never; **só ~!** at last!; **só ~ é que cheguei** I've only just arrived; **~ mesmo** right now; **~ que** now that; **essa ~!** whatever next!; **por ~** for the time being.

agosto [aˈgoʃtu] *m* (Br) August, → **setembro**.

agradar [agraˈda(x)] *vi*: **~ a alguém** to please sb.

agradável [agraˈdavɛw] (pl **-eis** [-ejʃ]) *adj* pleasant.

agradecer [agradeˈse(x)] *vt* to thank ◆ *vi*: **~ a alguém algo, ~ algo a alguém** to thank sb for sthg.

agradecido, -da [agradeˈsidu, -da] *adj* grateful; **mal ~** ungrateful; **muito ~!** many thanks!.

agradecimento [agradesiˈmẽntu] *m* thanks (pl).

agrafador [agrafaˈdor] (pl **-res** [-reʃ]) *m* (Port) stapler.

agrafo [aˈgrafu] *m* (Port) staple.

agravamento [agravaˈmẽntu] *m* worsening.

agravante [agraˈvãntʃi] *adj* aggravating ◆ *f* aggravating circumstance.

agravar [agraˈva(x)] *vt* to make worse.

agredir [agreˈdʒi(x)] *vt* to attack.

agregado [agreˈgadu] *m*: **~ familiar** household.

agressão [agreˈsãw] (pl **-ões** [-õjʃ]) *f* (ataque) attack.

agressivo, -va [agreˈsivu, -va] *adj* aggressive.

agressões → **agressão**.

agreste [aˈgrɛʃtʃi] *adj* (paisagem) wild; (tempo) stormy.

agrião [agriˈãw] (pl **-ões** [-õjʃ]) *m* watercress.

agrícola [aˈgrikola] *adj* agricultural.

agricultor, -ra [agrikuwˈto(x), -ra] (mpl **-res** [-riʃ], fpl **-s** [-ʃ]) *m, f* farmer.

agricultura [agrikuwˈtura] *f* agriculture.

agridoce [agriˈdosi] *adj* sweet-and-sour.

agriões → agrião.

agronomia [agrono'mia] f agronomy.

agrupar [agru'pa(x)] vt to group together.

água ['agwa] f water; ~ **doce/salgada** fresh/salt water; ~ **benta** holy water; ~ **corrente** running water; ~ **destilada** distilled water; ~ **mineral com gás** OU **gaseificada** fizzy OU sparkling mineral water; ~ **mineral sem gás** still mineral water; ~ **potável** drinking water; ~ **sanitária** (Br) household bleach; ~ **tônica** tonic water; **de dar ~ na boca** mouthwatering.

aguaceiro [agwa'sejru] m downpour.

água-de-colônia [ˌagwadʒiko'lɔnja] f eau de cologne.

aguado, -da [a'gwadu, -da] adj watery.

água-oxigenada [ˌagw(a)ɔksiʒe'nada] f hydrogen peroxide.

aguardar [agwar'da(x)] vt to wait for.

aguardente [agwax'dẽntʃi] f spirit (Brit), liquor (Am); ~ **de cana** rum; ~ **de pêra** pear brandy; ~ **velha** brandy.

aguarela [agwa'rɛla] f (Port) watercolour.

aguarrás [agwa'xaʃ] f turpentine.

água-viva [ˌagwa'viva] (pl **águas-vivas** [ˌagwaʒ'vivaʃ]) f jellyfish.

açucado, -da [agu'sadu, -da] adj sharp.

açuçar [agu'sa(x)] vt to sharpen.

agudo, -da [a'gudu, -da] adj (dor) sharp; (som, voz) shrill; (doença) acute.

aguentar [agwẽn'tar] vt (Port) = **agüentar**.

agüentar [agwẽn'ta(x)] vt (Br) to stand.

❑ **agüentar com** v + prep (Br) (peso) to support.

águia ['agja] f eagle.

agulha [a'guʎa] f needle.

agulheta [agu'ʎeta] f nozzle.

aí [a'i] adv there; (então) then; **por** ~ (direção) that way; (em lugar indeterminado) over there; **tem alguém por** ~ **assaltando turistas** someone is going around mugging tourists.

ai [aj] interj ouch!

AIDS [ajdʒs] f (Br) AIDS.

ainda [a'ĩnda] adv still; ~ **agora** only just; ~ **assim** even so; ~ **bem!** thank goodness!; ~ **bem que** thank goodness; ~ **não** not yet; ~ **por cima** to cap

it all; ~ **que** even though.

aipim [aj'pĩ] (pl **-ns** [-ʃ]) m cassava, manioc.

aipo ['ajpu] m celery.

ajeitar [aʒej'ta(x)] vt (cabelo) to tidy up; (gravata, saia) to straighten.

❑ **ajeitar-se** vp (acomodar-se) to make o.s. comfortable; ~-**se com algo** (saber lidar com) to get to grips with sthg.

ajoelhar-se [aʒwe'ʎaxsi] vp to kneel down.

ajuda [a'ʒuda] f help.

ajudante [aʒu'dãntʃi] mf helper.

ajudar [aʒu'da(x)] vt to help.

ajuste [a'ʒuʃtʃi] m: ~ **de contas** revenge.

Al. (abrev de alameda) Ave.

ala ['ala] f (fileira) row; (de edifício) wing.

alambique [alãm'biki] m still.

alameda [ala'meda] f avenue.

alargar [alax'ga(x)] vt (estrada) to widen; (peça de roupa) to let out; (em tempo, influência) to extend; (negócio) to expand ◆ vi (pulôver, luvas, etc) to stretch.

alarido [ala'ridu] m uproar.

alarmante [alax'mãntʃi] adj alarming.

alarme [a'laxmi] m alarm; **falso** ~, ~ **falso** false alarm.

alastrar [alaʃ'tra(x)] vt to spread.

❑ **alastrar-se** vp to spread.

alavanca [ala'vãŋka] f lever.

albergue [aw'bɛxgi] m hostel.

albufeira [awbu'fejra] f lagoon.

álbum ['awbũ] (pl **-ns** [-ʃ]) m album.

alça ['awsa] f (de vestido, combinação, arma) strap; (de bolsa, mala) handle.

alcachofra [awka'ʃofra] f artichoke.

alcançar [awkã'sa(x)] vt to reach; (apanhar) to catch up; (obter) to get; (compreender) to grasp.

alcance [aw'kãsi] m (de mão) reach; (de vista, projéctil) range; **ao** ~ **de** (de mão) within reach of; (de vista, projéctil) within range of; **fora do** ~ **de** (de mão) out of reach of; (de vista, projéctil) out of range of.

alçapão [awsa'pãw] (pl **-ões** [-õjʃ]) m trapdoor.

alcaparras [awka'paxaʃ] fpl capers.

alçapões → alçapão.

alcateia [awka'teja] f pack.

alcatifa [awka'tʃifa] f carpet.

alcatra [aw'katra] f rump.

alcatrão [awka'trãw] m tar.

álcool ['awk(w)ɔw] m (bebidas alcoólicas) alcohol; (étano) ethanol; ~ **etílico** ethyl alcohol.

alcoólatra [aw'kɔlatra] m, f alcoholic.

alcoólico, -ca [aw'kwɔliku, -ka] adj & m, f alcoholic.

Alcorão [awko'rãw] m Koran.

alcunha [aw'kuɲa] f nickname.

aldeia [aw'deja] f village.

alecrim [alɛ'krĩ] m rosemary.

alegação [alega'sãw] (pl -ões [-õjʃ]) f (acusação) allegation; (explicação) explanation; (JUR: defesa) stated defence.

alegar [alɛ'ga(x)] vt to state; (explicar) to claim.

alegoria [alego'ria] f allegory.

alegórico [alɛ'gɔriku] adj m → **carro**.

alegrar [alɛ'gra(x)] vt (pessoa) to cheer up; (ambiente, casa) to brighten up; (festa) to liven up.

❏ **alegrar-se** vp to cheer up.

alegre [a'lɛgri] adj (dia, cor) bright; (pessoa) cheerful; (fig: bêbado) merry.

alegria [alɛ'gria] f joy.

aleijado, -da [alej'ʒadu, -da] adj crippled.

aleijar [alej'ʒa(x)] vt (Br: mutilar) to cripple; (Port: machucar) to hurt.

além [a'lẽj] adv over there ♦ m: **o ~** the hereafter; **~ disso** besides; **mais ~** further on.

alemã → **alemão**.

alemães → **alemão**.

Alemanha [alɛ'maɲa] f: **a ~** Germany.

alemão, -mã [alɛ'mãw, -mã] (mpl -ães [-ãjʃ], fpl -s [-ʃ]) adj & m, f German ♦ m (língua) German.

além-mar [alẽj'ma(x)] adv & m overseas.

alentejano, -na [alẽtɛ'ʒanu, -na] adj of/relating to the Alentejo ♦ m, f native/inhabitant of the Alentejo.

alergia [alɛx'ʒia] f allergy; (fig: a trabalho, estudo) aversion.

alérgico, -ca [a'lɛxʒiku, -ka] adj allergic.

alerta [a'lɛxta] adv on the alert ♦ m alert.

alfa ['awfa] m → **comboio**.

alfabético, -ca [awfa'bɛtʃiku, -ka] adj alphabetical.

alfabeto [awfa'bɛtu] m alphabet.

alface [aw'fasi] f lettuce.

alfacinha [awfa'siɲa] mf (fam) colloquial term for a native or inhabitant of Lisbon.

alfaiate [awfa'jatʃi] m tailor.

alfândega [aw'fãdega] f customs (pl).

alfazema [awfa'zema] f lavender.

alfinete [awfi'netʃi] m pin; (jóia) brooch; **~ de gravata** tie pin; **~ de segurança** safety pin.

alforreca [awfo'xɛka] f jellyfish.

alga ['awga] f seaweed.

algarismo [awga'riʒmu] m numeral.

algazarra [awga'zaxa] f racket.

álgebra ['awʒebra] f algebra.

algemas [aw'ʒemaʃ] fpl handcuffs.

algibeira [awʒi'bejra] f pocket.

algo ['awgu] pron something.

algodão [awgo'dãw] m cotton; **~ doce** candy floss (Brit), cotton candy (Am); **~ hidrófilo** cotton wool.

alguém [aw'gẽj] pron (em afirmações) somebody, someone; (em perguntas) anybody, anyone; **ser ~** (ser importante) to be somebody.

algum, -ma [aw'gũ, -ma] (mpl -ns [-ʃ], fpl -s [-ʃ]) adj (indeterminado) some; (em interrogativas, negativas) any ♦ pron (indicando pessoa) somebody; (indicando coisa) one; (em interrogativas: pessoa) anybody; (em interrogativas: coisa) any; **~ dia** one ou some day; **alguma coisa** something, anything; **alguma vez** sometime; **não há melhora alguma** there's no improvement.

❏ **alguma** f (evento, feito) something.

❏ **alguns, algumas** pron pl some.

algures [aw'guriʃ] adv somewhere.

alheio, alheia [a'ʎeju, a'ʎeja] adj (de outrem) someone else's; (desconhecido) foreign; (distraído) distracted; **~ a** (sem consciência de) oblivious to.

alho ['aʎu] m garlic; **~ francês** (Port) leek.

alho-poró [aʎupo'rɔ] (pl alhos-porós [aʎuʃpo'rɔjʃ]) m (Br) leek.

alho-porro [aʎu'poxu] (pl alhos-porros [aʎuʃ'poxuʃ]) m wild leek.

ali [a'li] adv there; **aqui e ~** here and there; **até ~** up until then; **logo ~** just there; **por ~** (algures) around there (somewhere); **ele foi por ~** he went that way.

aliado, -da [a'ljadu, -da] *adj* allied ♦ *m*, *f* ally.

aliança [a'ljãsa] *f* alliance; *(anel)* wedding ring.

aliar [a'lja(x)] *vt* to ally.

❏ **aliar-se** *vp* to form an alliance.

aliás [a'ljaʃ] *adv (a propósito)* as a matter of fact; *(além disso)* moreover.

álibi ['alibi] *m* alibi.

alicate [ali'katʃi] *m* pliers *(pl)*.

alice [a'lisi] *f (Br)* anchovies *(pl)*.

alicerce [ali'sɛxsi] *m* foundation.

aliciante [ali'sjãntʃi] *adj* enticing ♦ *m* enticement.

aliciar [ali'sja(x)] *vt* to entice.

alienado, -da [alje'nadu, -da] *adj (pessoa)* alienated; *(bem)* transferred.

alimentação [alimẽnta'sãw] *f (alimentos)* food; *(acto)* feeding; *(dieta alimentar)* diet; *(de máquina)* supply.

alimentar [alimẽn'ta(x)] *(pl -res* [-riʃ]*) adj* food *(antes de s)* ♦ *vt (pessoa, animal)* to feed; *(máquina)* to fuel.

❏ **alimentar-se** *vp* to eat.

alimentício, -cia [alimẽn'tʃisju, -sja] *adj* nutritious.

alimento [ali'mẽntu] *m (comida)* food; *(nutrição)* nutriment.

❏ **alimentos** *mpl (Port: JUR)* alimony *(sg)*.

alinhado, -da [ali'nadu, -da] *adj (em linha)* aligned; *(pessoa)* elegant.

alinhamento [alina'mẽntu] *m (IN-FORM)* justification.

alinhar [ali'na(x)] *vt (pôr em linha)* to align; *(INFORM: texto)* to justify.

alinhavar [alina'va(x)] *vt* to tack.

alisar [ali'za(x)] *vt* to smooth.

alistar [aliʃ'ta(x)] *vt* to recruit.

❏ **alistar-se** *vp (em exército)* to enlist; *(em partido)* to join.

aliviar [ali'vja(x)] *vt (dor)* to relieve; *(peso)* to lighten.

alívio [a'livju] *m* relief; *(de peso)* lightening.

alma ['awma] *f* soul.

almoçar [awmo'sa(x)] *vi* to have lunch ♦ *vt* to have for lunch.

almoço [aw'mosu] *m* lunch.

almofada [awmo'fada] *f (de cama)* pillow; *(de sofá)* cushion; *(de carimbo)* inkpad.

almôndega [aw'mõndega] *f* meatball.

alô [a'lo] *interj (Br)* hello!

alojamento [aloʒa'mẽntu] *m (acto)* housing; *(lugar)* accommodation *(Brit)*,

accommodations *(pl) (Am)*.

alojar [alo'ʒa(x)] *vt* to put up.

❏ **alojar-se** *vp* to stay.

alpendre [aw'pẽndri] *m* porch.

alpercata [awpɛx'kata] *f* sandal.

alperce [aw'pɛxsi] *m* apricot.

Alpes ['awpiʃ] *mpl*: **os ~** the Alps.

alpinismo [awpi'niʒmu] *m* mountaineering; **fazer ~** to go climbing.

alpinista [awpi'niʃta] *mf* mountaineer.

alta ['awta] *f (de preço, valor)* rise; *(de cidade)* geographically higher and generally more wealthy part of a city; **dar ~ a** *(doente)* to discharge; **ter ~** *(de hospital)* to be discharged.

altar [aw'ta(x)] *(pl -res* [-riʃ]*) m* altar.

alteração [awtera'sãw] *(pl -ões* [-õjʃ]*) f* alteration; **sem ~** unaltered.

alterar [awte'ra(x)] *vt* to alter.

alternar [awtex'na(x)] *vt* to alternate.

alternativa [awtexna'tʃiva] *f* alternative.

altifalante [altifa'lãnte] *m (Port)* = **alto-falante**.

altitude [awtʃi'tudʒi] *f* altitude.

altivez [awtʃi'veʒ] *f (orgulho)* pride; *(arrogância)* haughtiness.

altivo, -va [aw'tʃivu, -va] *adj (orgulhoso)* proud; *(arrogante)* haughty.

alto, -ta ['awtu, -ta] *adj* high; *(pessoa, árvore, edifício)* tall; *(som, voz)* loud ♦ *interj* stop! ♦ *m (cume)* top; *(céu)* heaven ♦ *adv (falar, rir)* loud; *(relativo a posição)* high; **alta costura** haute couture; **ao ~** upright; **do ~ de** from the top of; **por ~** *(fig)* superficially; **o mais ~/a mais alta** *(pessoa)* the tallest; *(objeto)* the highest.

alto-falante ['awtofa'lãtʃi] *m (Br)* loudspeaker.

altura [aw'tura] *f (de pessoa, objecto)* height; *(de som)* level; *(altitude)* altitude; *(ocasião, época)* time; *(momento)* moment; **o muro tem um metro de ~** the wall is a metre high; **a certa** OU **dada ~** at a given moment; **nessa ~** at that time; **por ~ de** around; **estar à ~ da situação** to be equal to the task.

alucinação [alusina'sãw] *(pl -ões* [-õjʃ]*) f* hallucination.

alucinante [alusi'nãntʃi] *adj* amazing.

aludir [alu'di(x)] : **aludir a** *v + prep* to allude to.

alugar [alu'ga(x)] *vt (casa)* to rent;

(carro) to hire *(Brit)*, to rent *(Am)*.

❏ **alugar-se** *vp:* **"aluga-se" "to let"** *(Brit)*, **"for rent"** *(Am)*; **"alugam-se quartos"** "rooms to let".

aluguel [alu'gɛw] *(pl* **-éis** [-'ɛjʃ]*) m (Br) (de carro)* hire *(Brit)*, rental *(Am)*.

aluguer [alu'gɛr] *(pl* **-res** [-'reʃ]*) m (Port)* = **aluguel**.

aluir [a'lwi(x)] *vi* to collapse.

alumiar [alu'mja(x)] *vt* to light up.

alumínio [alu'minju] *m* aluminium.

aluno, -na [a'lunu, -na] *m, f (de escola)* pupil; *(de universidade)* student.

alusão [alu'zãw] *(pl* **-ões** [-'õjʃ]*) f* allusion; **fazer ~ a** to allude to.

alvejar [awve'ʒa(x)] *vt* to shoot.

alvo ['awvu] *m* target.

alvorada [awvo'rada] *f* dawn.

alvoroço [awvo'rosu] *m (gritaria)* uproar; *(excitação)* commotion.

amabilidade [amabili'dadʒi] *f* kindness.

amaciador [amasja'dor] *(pl* **-res** [-riʃ]*) m (Port) (de cabelo)* conditioner; *(para roupa)* fabric softener.

amaciante [ama'sjãntʃi] *f (Br):* **~ (de roupa)** fabric softener.

amador, -ra [ama'do(x), -ra] *(mpl* **-res** [-riʃ]*, fpl* **-s** [-ʃ]*) adj & m, f* amateur.

amadurecer [amadure'se(x)] *vi (fruta)* to ripen; *(pessoa)* to mature; *(fig: idéia)* to develop.

âmago ['amagu] *m* heart.

amainar [amaj'na(x)] *vt (vela)* to lower ✦ *vi (fig: vento, chuva)* to abate..

amaldiçoar [amawdi'swa(x)] *vt* to curse.

amálgama [a'mawgama] *f* amalgam.

amalgamar [amawga'ma(x)] *vt* to amalgamate.

amamentar [amamẽn'ta(x)] *vt* to breastfeed.

amanhã [ama'ɲã] *adv & m* tomorrow; **~ de manhã** tomorrow morning; **~ à noite/tarde** tomorrow evening/afternoon; **depois de ~** the day after tomorrow; **o ~** the future.

amanhecer [amaɲe'se(x)] *m* dawn ✦ *v impess:* **já amanheceu** dawn has broken.

amansar [amã'sa(x)] *vt* to tame.

amante [a'mãntʃi] *mf* lover; **ser ~ de** to be a lover of.

amanteigado, -da [amãntej'gadu, -da] *adj (molho)* buttery; *(queijo)* creamy.

amar [a'ma(x)] *vt* to love.

amarelado, -da [amare'ladu, -da] *adj* yellowish.

amarelinha [amare'liɲa] *f (Br: jogo)* hopscotch.

amarelo, -la [ama'rɛlu, -la] *adj & m* yellow.

amargar [amax'ga(x)] *vi* to taste bitter ✦ *vt (desilusão)* to suffer.

amargo, -ga [a'maxgu, -ga] *adj* bitter; *(fig: vida)* hard.

amarrar [ama'xa(x)] *vt (barco)* to moor; *(pessoa, animal)* to tie up.

amarrotado, -da [amaxo'tadu, -da] *adj (papel)* crumpled; *(roupa)* creased.

amarrotar [amaxo'ta(x)] *vt (papel)* to crumple (up); *(roupa)* to crease.

amassar [ama'sa(x)] *vt (cimento)* to mix; *(pão)* to knead; *(carro)* to smash up.

amável [a'mavɛw] *(pl* **-eis** [-ejʃ]*) adj* kind.

Amazonas [ama'zonaʃ] *m:* **o ~** the Amazon.

Amazônia [ama'zonja] *f:* **a ~** the Amazon region.

âmbar ['ãmbuʃ, -baʃ] *m* amber.

ambição [ãmbi'sãw] *(pl* **-ões** [-õjʃ]*) f* ambition.

ambientador [ãmbjẽnta'dor] *(pl* **-res** [-reʃ]*) m (Port):* **~ do ar** air freshener.

ambiental [ãmbjẽn'taw] *(pl* **-ais** [-ajʃ]*) adj* environmental.

ambiente [ãm'bjẽntʃi] *m (natural)* environment; *(ar)* atmosphere.

ambigüidade [ãmbigwi'dadʒi] *f* ambiguity.

ambíguo, -gua [ãm'bigwu, -gwa] *adj* ambiguous.

âmbito ['ãmbitu] *m* sphere.

ambos, -bas [ãmbuʃ, -baʃ] *adj pl* both ✦ *pron pl* both (of them).

ambrosia [ãmbro'zja] *f sweet custard pudding made with eggs and milk.*

ambulância [ãmbu'lãsja] *f* ambulance.

ambulante [ãmbu'lãntʃi] *adj* travelling.

ambulatório [ãmbula'tɔrju] *m (Br) (de hospital)* outpatients' (department); *(de escola, fábrica)* medical room.

ameaça [ame'asa] *f* threat; **sob ~** under threat.

ameaçar [amea'sa(x)] *vt* to threaten; **ameaça chover** it looks like rain.

amedrontar [amedrõn'ta(x)] *vt* to frighten.

ameixa [a'mejʃa] *f* plum.

amêndoa [a'mẽndwa] *f* almond; ~ **amarga** *almond liqueur, served chilled.*

amendoeira [amẽn'dwejra] *f* almond tree.

amendoim [amẽn'dwĩ] (*pl* **-ns** [-ʃ]) *m* peanut; ~ **torrado** roasted peanuts (*pl*).

ameno, -na [a'menu, -na] *adj* (*temperatura, clima*) mild.

América [a'mɛrika] *f*: **a ~** America; **a ~ Central** Central America; **a ~ Latina** Latin America; **a ~ do Norte** North America; **a ~ do Sul** South America.

americano, -na [ameri'kanu, -na] *adj & m, f* American.

ametista [ame't ʃiʃta] *f* amethyst.

amianto [a'mjãntu] *m* asbestos.

amido [a'midu] *m* starch; ~ **de milho** cornflour (*Brit*), cornstarch (*Am*).

amigável [ami'gavɛw] (*pl* **-eis** [-ejʃ]) *adj* friendly.

amígdalas [a'migdalaʃ] *fpl* tonsils.

amigdalite [amigda'litʃi] *f* tonsillitis.

amigo, -ga [a'migu, -ga] *m, f* friend ◆ *adj* friendly.

amistoso, -osa [amiʃ'tozu, -ɔza] *adj* friendly.

amizade [ami'zadʒi] *f* friendship.

amnésia [am'nɛzja] *f* amnesia.

amnistia [amneʃ'tia] *f* (*Port*) = **anistia**.

amolação [amola'sãw] (*pl* **-ões** [-õjʃ]) *f* (*Br*: *chateação*) nuisance.

amolar [amo'la(x)] *vt* (*afiar*) to sharpen; (*Br*: *aborrecer*) to bother.

amolecer [amole'se(x)] *vt* to soften.

amoníaco [amo'niaku] *m* ammonia.

amontoar [amõn'twa(x)] *vt* to pile up; (*dinheiro, riquezas*) to amass. ◻ **amontoar-se** *vp* to pile up.

amor [a'mo(x)] (*pl* **-res** [-riʃ]) *m* love; **fazer ~** to make love.

amora [a'mɔra] *f* (*de silva*) blackberry; (*de amoreira*) mulberry.

amordaçar [amoxda'sa(x)] *vt* to gag.

amoroso, -osa [amo'rozu, -ɔza] *adj* affectionate.

amor-perfeito [a,moxpɛx'fejtu] (*pl* **amores-perfeitos** [a,moriʃpɛx'fejtuʃ]) *m* pansy.

amor-próprio [a,mox'propriu] *m* self-esteem.

amortecedor [amoxtese'do(x)] (*pl* **-res** [-riʃ]) *m* shock absorber.

amortização [amoxtiza'sãw] (*pl* **-ões** [-õjʃ]) *f* repayment by instalments.

amortizar [amoxti'za(x)] *vt* to repay by instalments.

amostra [a'mɔʃtra] *f* sample; (*prova*) show; ~ **grátis** free sample.

amparar [ãmpa'ra(x)] *vt* to support.

amparo [ãm'paru] *m* support.

ampliação [ãmplia'sãw] (*pl* **-ões** [-õjʃ]) *f* (*de fotografia*) enlargement.

ampliar [ãmpli'a(x)] *vt* (*fotografia*) to enlarge.

amplificador [ãmplifika'do(x)] (*pl* **-res** [-riʃ]) *m* (*de som*) amplifier.

amplificar [ãmplifi'ka(x)] *vt* (*som*) to amplify.

amplitude [ãmpli'tudʒi] *f* extent.

amplo, -pla ['ãmplu, -pla] *adj* (*quarto, cama*) spacious; (*estrada*) wide; (*conhecimento*) extensive.

ampola [ãm'pola] *f* phial.

amputar [ãmpu'ta(x)] *vt* to amputate.

amuado, -da [a'mwadu, -da] *adj* sulky.

amuar [a'mwa(x)] *vi* (*criança*) to sulk.

anã → **anão**.

anacronismo [anakro'niʒmu] *m* anachronism.

anagrama [ana'grama] *m* anagram.

analfabeto, -ta [anawfa'bɛtu, -ta] *m, f & adj* illiterate.

analgésico [anaw'ʒɛziku] *m* painkiller.

analisar [anali'za(x)] *vt* to analyse.

análise [a'nalizi] *f* analysis; (*Port*: *a sangue, urina*) test; **em última ~** in the final analysis.

analista [ana'liʃta] *mf* analyst.

analogia [analo'ʒia] *f* analogy.

ananás [ana'naʃ] (*pl* **-ases** [-azeʃ]) *m* pineapple.

anão, anã [a'nãw, a'nã] (*mpl* **-ões** [-õjʃ], *fpl* **-s** [-ʃ]) *m, f* dwarf.

anarquia [anax'kia] *f* anarchy.

anatomia [anato'mia] *f* anatomy.

anca ['ãŋka] *f* hip.

anchovas [ã'ʃovaʃ] *fpl* anchovies.

ancinho [ã'siɲu] *m* rake.

âncora ['ãŋkora] *f* anchor.

andaime [ãn'dajmi] *m* scaffold.

andamento [ãnda'mẽntu] *m* (*velocidade*) speed; (*rumo*) direction; (*MÚS*) tempo; **em ~** (*em progresso*) in progress.

andar [ãn'da(x)] (*pl* **-res** [-riʃ]) *vi* to

walk ♦ *vt (distância, tempo)* to walk for ♦ *m (de edifício)* floor; *(maneira de caminhar)* walk; **ele anda um pouco deprimido ultimamente** he has been a bit depressed lately; **gosto de ~ a cavalo** I like horse-riding; **~ de avião** to fly; **~ de bicicleta** to cycle; **~ a pé** to walk; **o ~ de baixo** *(de casa)* downstairs; **o ~ de cima** *(de casa)* upstairs.

Andes [ˈãndiʃ] *mpl:* **os ~ the** Andes.

andorinha [ãndoˈriɲa] *f* swallow.

Andorra [ãˈdoxa] *s* Andorra.

anedota [aneˈdɔta] *f* joke.

anel [aˈnɛw] *(pl* **-éis** [-ˈɛjʃ]*) m* ring; *(de cabelo)* ringlet; *(de corrente)* link; **~ de noivado** engagement ring.

anemia [aneˈmia] *f* anaemia.

anestesia [anɛʃteˈzia] *f* anaesthetic; **~ geral/local** general/local anaesthetic.

anestesiar [anɛʃteˈzja(x)] *vt* to anaesthetize.

anexar [anɛkˈsa(x)] *vt* to attach; **~ algo a algo** to attach sthg to sthg.

anexo, -xa [aˈnɛksu, -ksa] *adj* attached.

anfiteatro [ãfiˈtʒatru] *m* amphitheatre; *(sala de aula)* lecture theatre.

angariar [ãŋgaˈrja(x)] *vt (dinheiro)* to raise.

angina [ãˈʒina] *f:* **~ de peito** angina (pectoris).

❏ **anginas** *fpl* tonsillitis *(sg).*

anglicano, -na [ãŋgliˈkanu, -na] *adj* Anglican.

Angola [ãŋˈgɔla] *s* Angola.

angolano, -na [ãŋgoˈlanu, -na] *adj & m, f* Angolan.

angra [ˈãŋgra] *f* inlet.

angu [ãŋˈgu] *m* a gruel made with cornflour or cassava.

ângulo [ˈãŋgulu] *m* angle.

angústia [ãŋˈguʃtʒja] *f* anguish.

animação [animaˈsãw] *f (alegria)* liveliness; *(entusiasmo)* enthusiasm; *(movimento)* bustle.

animado, -da [aniˈmadu, -da] *adj (alegre)* lively; *(entusiasmado)* enthusiastic; *(movimentado)* bustling.

animador, -ra [animaˈdo(x), -ra] *(mpl* **-res** [-riʃ]*, fpl* **-s** [-ʃ]*) adj (que alegra)* cheering; *(que encoraja)* encouraging.

animal [aniˈmaw] *(pl* **-ais** [-ajʃ]*) m* animal; **~ doméstico** pet; **~ selvagem** wild animal.

animar [aniˈma(x)] *vt (alegrar)* to cheer up.

❏ **animar-se** *vp (alegrar-se)* to cheer up.

ânimo [ˈanimu] *m* courage.

aniquilar [anikiˈla(x)] *vt* to annihilate.

anis [aˈniʃ] *(pl* **-ses** [-zɛʃ]*) m (licor)* anisette; *(planta)* aniseed.

anistia [aniʃˈtʃia] *f (Br)* amnesty.

aniversário [anivexˈsarju] *m (de pessoa)* birthday; *(de acontecimento)* anniversary; **feliz ~!** Happy Birthday!

anjo [ˈãʒu] *m* angel.

ano [ˈanu] *m* year; **quantos ~s você tem?** how old are you?; **faço ~s amanhã** it's my birthday tomorrow; **~ bissexto** leap year; **~ letivo** academic year; **Ano Novo** New Year, Hogmanay *(Scot)*; **~ após** ~ year after year.

anões → anão.

anoitecer [anojteˈse(x)] *m* dusk, nightfall ♦ *v impess* to get dark.

anomalia [anomaˈlia] *f* anomaly.

anoraque [anoˈraki] *m* anorak.

anorexia [anorɛkˈsia] *f* anorexia.

anormal [anoxˈmaw] *(pl* **-ais** [-ajʃ]*) adj* abnormal; *(idiota)* stupid; *(incomum)* unusual ♦ *m, f (idiota)* moron.

anormalidade [anoxmaliˈdadʒi] *f* abnormality.

anotação [anotaˈsãw] *(pl* **-ões** [-õjʃ]*) f* note.

anotar [anoˈta(x)] *vt* to note down.

ânsia [ˈãsja] *f* anxiety.

ansiar [ãˈsja(x)] **: ansiar por** *v + prep* to long for.

ansiedade [ãsjeˈdadʒi] *f* anxiety.

ansioso, -osa [ãˈsjozu, -ɔza] *adj* anxious.

antebraço [ãntʃiˈbrasu] *m* forearm.

antecedência [ãnteseˈdẽsja] *f:* **com ~** in advance.

antecedente [ãnteseˈdẽntʃi] *adj* preceding.

❏ **antecedentes** *mpl (médicos)* records; *(criminais)* record *(sg).*

antecipação [ãntesipaˈsãw] *(pl* **-ões** [-õjʃ]*) f* anticipation.

antecipadamente [ãntesipadaˈmẽntʃi] *adv* in advance, beforehand.

antecipar [ãntesiˈpa(x)] *vt* to anticipate.

❏ **antecipar-se** *vp* to get there first.

antemão [ãnteˈmãw] **: de antemão** *adv* beforehand.

antena [ãnˈtena] *f* aerial; **~ parabólica** satellite dish.

anteontem [ãntʃiˈõntẽ] *adv* the day before yesterday.

antepassado [ãntʃipaˈsadu] *m* ancestor.

anterior [ãnteˈrju(x)] (*pl* -res [-riʃ]) *adj* previous.

antes [ˈãntʃ] *adv* before; *(primeiramente)* first; ~ **assim** (it's) just as well; ~ **de** before; ~ **de mais** (nada) first of all; **o quanto** ~ as soon as possible.

antever [ãnteˈve(x)] *vt* to foresee.

antiaderente [ãntʃiadeˈrẽntʃi] *adj* nonstick.

antibiótico [ãntʃiˈbjɔtʃiku] *m* antibiotic.

anticaspa [ãntʃiˈkaʃpa] *adj inv* antidandruff.

anticoncepcional [ãntʃikõsepsjuˈnaw] (*pl* -ais [-ajʃ]) *adj* contraceptive.

anticonceptivo [ãntʃikõsepˈtʃivu] *m* contraceptive.

anticongelante [ãntʃikõʒeˈlãntʃi] *m* antifreeze.

anticorpo [ãntʃiˈkoxpu] *m* antibody.

antidepressivo [ãntʃidepreˈsivu] *m* antidepressant.

antídoto [ãnˈtʃidotu] *m* antidote.

antigamente [ãntʃigaˈmẽntʃi] *adv* (*antes*) formerly; *(no passado)* in the old days.

antigo, -ga [ãnˈtʃigu, -ga] *adj* *(livro, objeto)* old; *(costume, era)* ancient; *(objeto valioso)* antique.

antiguidade [ãntʃigwiˈdadʒi] *f* antiquity; *(em emprego)* seniority; **a Antiguidade** Antiquity.

⊐ **antiguidades** *fpl* antiques.

antipatia [ãntʃipaˈtʃia] *f* dislike.

antipático, -ca [ãntʃiˈpatʃiku, -ka] *adj* unfriendly.

antipatizar [ãntʃipatʃiˈza(x)] *vi:* ~ **com alguém** to dislike sb.

antiquado, -da [ãntʃiˈkwadu, -da] *adj* old-fashioned.

antiquário [ãntʃiˈkwarju] *m* antique dealer.

anti-séptico, -ca [ãntʃiˈseptʃiku, -ka] *adj* antiseptic.

antologia [ãntoloˈʒia] *f* anthology.

anual [aˈnwaw] (*pl* -ais [-ajʃ]) *adj* annual.

anuir [aˈnwi(x)] *vi* to agree.

anulação [anulaˈsãw] (*pl* -ões [-õjʃ]) *f* cancellation.

anular [anuˈla(x)] *vt* to cancel ◆ *m* ring finger.

anunciar [anũˈsja(x)] *vt* to announce; *(produto)* to advertise.

anúncio [aˈnũsju] *m* *(de produto)* advert; *(aviso)* announcement.

ânus [ˈanuʃ] *m* anus.

anzol [ãˈzɔw] (*pl* -óis [-ɔjʃ]) *m* fishhook.

ao [aw] = **a + o**, → **a**.

aonde [aˈõndʒi] *adv* where; ~ **quer que ...** wherever ....

aos [awʃ] = **a + os**, → **a**.

apagado, -da [apaˈgadu, -da] *adj* *(luz, lume)* out; *(televisão, rádio)* off; *(escrita, desenho)* faint; *(pessoa)* dull.

apagar [apaˈga(x)] *vt* *(fogo)* to put out; *(televisão, rádio, luz)* to turn OU switch off; *(escrita, desenho)* to rub out.

apaixonado, -da [apajʃoˈnadu, -da] *adj* in love; *(exaltado)* passionate; **estar** ~ **por** to be in love with.

apaixonante [apajʃoˈnãntʃi] *adj* fascinating.

apaixonar [apajʃoˈna(x)] *vt:* **o futebol apaixona as massas** football thrills the masses.

⊐ **apaixonar-se** *vp* to fall in love; ~**-se por** to fall in love with.

apalermado, -da [apalexˈmadu, -da] *adj* silly.

apalpar [apawˈpa(x)] *vt* to touch; ~ **o terreno** *(fig)* to see how the land lies.

apanhar [apaˈɲa(x)] *vt* to catch; *(levantar do chão)* to pick up; ~ **chuva** to get wet; ~ **sol** to sunbathe.

aparador [aparaˈdo(x)] (*pl* -res [-riʃ]) *m* sideboard.

apara-lápis [a.paraˈlapiʃ] *m inv* (Port) pencil sharpener.

aparar [apaˈra(x)] *vt* *(barba)* to trim; *(sebe, arbusto)* to prune; *(segurar)* to catch; *(lápis)* to sharpen.

aparecer [apareˈse(x)] *vi* *(surgir)* to appear; *(apresentar-se)* to show up; *(algo perdido)* to turn up.

aparelhagem [apareˈʎaʒẽ] (*pl* -ns [-ʃ]) *f:* ~ **(de som)** sound system, stereo.

aparelho [apaˈreʎu] *m* appliance; ~ **digestivo** digestive system; ~ **para os dentes** brace.

aparência [apaˈrẽsja] *f* appearance.

aparentar [aparẽnˈta(x)] *vt* to look like; **aparenta ter uns 40 anos** he looks about 40.

aparente [apa'rēntʃi] *adj* apparent.

Apart. *abrev* = **apartamento**.

apartado [apar'tadu] *m* (Port) P.O. Box.

apartamento [apaxta'mēntu] *m* flat *(Brit)*, apartment *(Am)*.

apatia [apa'tʃia] *f* apathy.

apavorado, -da [apavo'radu, -da] *adj* terrified.

apear-se [a'pjaxsi] *vp*: ~ **de** to get off.

apelar [ape'la(x)] *vi*: ~ **para** to appeal to.

apelido [ape'lidu] *m* (Br: *alcunha*) nickname; (Port: *nome de família*) surname.

apelo [a'pelu] *m* appeal; **fazer um** ~ **a** to appeal to.

apenas [a'penaʃ] *adv* only ◆ *conj* as soon as; **quero** ~ **um copo de água** all I want is a glass of water.

apêndice [a'pēndʒisi] *m* appendix.

apendicite [apēndʒi'sitʃi] *f* appendicitis.

aperceber-se [apexse'bexsi] *vp*: ~ **de algo** to realize; ~ **de que** (*verificar*) to realize (that).

aperfeiçoamento [apexfejswa'mēntu] *m* improvement.

aperfeiçoar [apexfej'swa(x)] *vt* to improve.

aperitivo [aperi'tʃivu] *m* (*vinho*) aperitif; (*tira-gosto*) appetizer.

apertado, -da [apex'tadu, -da] *adj* tight; (*estrada*) narrow.

apertar [apex'ta(x)] *vt* (*comprimir*) to squeeze; (*botão, interruptor*) to press; (*cinto de segurança*) to fasten; (*parafuso, porca*) to tighten; (*casaco, vestido*) to take in.

aperto [a'pextu] *m* (*de parafuso*) tightening; (*aglomeração*) crush; (*fig: dificuldade*) tight corner; ~ **de mão** handshake.

apesar [ape'za(x)] : **apesar de** *prep* despite, in spite of.

apetecer [apete'se(x)] *vi*: **apetece-me um bolo** I feel like (having) a cake; **apetece-me sair** I feel like going out.

apetite [ape'tʃitʃi] *m* appetite; **bom** ~**!** enjoy your meal!

apetitoso, -osa [apetʃi'tozu, -ɔza] *adj* appetizing.

apetrecho [ape'treʃu] *m* tool; ~**s de pesca** fishing tackle (*sg*).

apimentado, -da [apimēn'tadu, -da] *adj* (*com pimenta*) peppery; (*picante*) spicy.

apinhado, -da [api'nadu, -da] *adj*: ~ **de** packed with.

apitar [api'ta(x)] *vi* (*trem, chaleira*) to whistle; (*árbitro*) to blow the whistle.

apito [a'pitu] *m* whistle.

aplaudir [aplaw'di(x)] *vt & vi* to applaud.

aplauso [a'plawzu] *m* applause.

aplicação [aplika'sāw] (*pl* -ões [-õjʃ]) *f* (*em estudo, trabalho*) diligence; (*acessório*) appliqué; (*de dinheiro*) investment.

aplicado, -da [apli'kadu, -da] *adj* (*aluno*) diligent; (*matemática, lingüística*) applied.

aplicar [apli'ka(x)] *vt* to apply; (*curativo, injeção*) to administer.

apoderar-se [apode'raxsi] : **apoderar-se de** *vp + prep* to take control of.

apodrecer [apodre'se(x)] *vt & vi* to rot.

apoiar [apo'ja(x)] *vt* to support; ~ **algo em algo** to rest sthg on OU against sthg.

❏ **apoiar-se** *vp* to hold on; ~**-se em** OU **a** to lean on OU against.

apoio [a'poju] *m* support.

apólice [a'pɔlisi] *f*: ~ (**de seguro**) (insurance) policy.

apontador [apõnta'do(x)] (*pl* -res [-riʃ]) *m* (Br: *de lápis*) pencil sharpener.

apontamento [apõnta'mēntu] *m* note.

apontar [apõn'ta(x)] *vt* (*arma*) to aim; (*erro, falha*) to point out; (*tomar nota de*) to note down; (*razões, argumentos*) to put forward ◆ *vi*: ~ **para algo** to point to sthg.

aporrinhação [apoxiɲa'sãw] (*pl* -ões [-õjʃ]) *f* (Br: *fam: aborrecimento*) annoyance.

após [a'pɔjʃ] *prep* after ◆ *adv* afterwards.

após-barba [apɔjʒ'baxba] *adj* (Br) → **loção**.

aposentado, -da [apozēn'tadu, -da] *adj* (Br) retired ◆ *m, f* (Br) pensioner.

aposentadoria [apozēntado'ria] *f* (Br) (*fato*) retirement; (*dinheiro*) pension.

aposento [apo'zēntu] *m* room.

aposta [a'pɔʃta] *f* bet.

apostar [apoʃ'ta(x)] *vt* to bet.

apostila [apoʃˈtʃila] *f (Br)* lecture notes *(pl)*.

apóstrofo [aˈpɔʃtrofu] *m* apostrophe.

aprazível [apraˈzivew] *(pl* -**eis** [-ejʃ]) *adj* pleasant.

apreciação [apresjaˈsãw] *(pl* -**ões** [-õjʃ]) *f (avaliação)* assessment.

apreciar [apreˈsja(x)] *vt (gostar)* to like; *(avaliar)* to judge, to assess; *(paisagem, vista)* to admire.

apreender [apriẽnˈde(x)] *vt (confiscar)* to seize; *(assimilar)* to grasp.

apreensão [apriẽˈsãw] *(pl* -**ões** [-õjʃ]) *f (de bens, produtos)* seizure; *(de novos conhecimentos)* grasp; *(preocupação)* apprehension.

apreensivo, -va [apriẽˈsivu, -va] *adj* apprehensive.

aprender [aprẽnˈde(x)] *vi & vt* to learn; ~ **a fazer algo** to learn to do sthg.

aprendiz [aprẽnˈdʒiʒ] *(pl* -**zes** [-ziʃ]) *m (de ofício)* apprentice; *(principiante)* beginner.

aprendizagem [aprẽndʒiˈzaʒẽ] *f* learning.

aprendizes → aprendiz.

apresentação [aprezẽntaˈsãw] *(pl* -**ões** [-õjʃ]) *f* presentation; *(aspecto)* appearance; **a ~ do programa estará a cargo do Herman José** the programme will be presented by Herman José.

apresentador, -ra [aprezẽntaˈdo(x), -ra] *(mpl* -**res** [-riʃ], *fpl* -**s** [-ʃ]) *m, f* presenter.

apresentar [aprezẽnˈta(x)] *vt (espetáculo)* to present; *(pessoa)* to introduce; *(exibir)* to show.

❏ **apresentar-se** *vp (comparecer)* to report; **~-se a alguém** *(a desconhecido)* to introduce o.s. to sb.

apressado, -da [apreˈsadu, -da] *adj (pessoa)* rushed; *(decisão)* hasty ◆ *adv*: **sair/entrar ~** to rush in/out.

apressar-se [apreˈsaxsi] *vp* to hurry up.

aprofundar [aprofũnˈda(x)] *vt (fig: assunto)* to study in depth.

aprovação [aprovaˈsãw] *(pl* -**ões** [-õjʃ]) *f* approval; *(em exame)* pass.

aprovado, -da [aproˈvadu, -da] *adj*: **ser ~** *(EDUC)* to pass.

aprovar [aproˈva(x)] *vt* to approve; *(em exame)* to pass.

aproveitador, -ra [aprovejtaˈdo(x), -ra] *(mpl* -**res** [-riʃ], *fpl* -**s** [-ʃ]) *adj & m, f (oportunista)* opportunist.

aproveitamento [aprovejtaˈmẽntu] *m (uso)* use; *(EDUC)* progress.

❏ **aproveitamentos** *mpl* leftovers.

aproveitar [aprovejˈta(x)] *vt (a ocasião)* to take advantage of; *(férias)* to make the most of; *(utilizar)* to make use of.

❏ **aproveitar-se** *vp*: **~-se de** to take advantage of.

aproximadamente [aprosiˌmadaˈmẽntʃi] *adv* approximately.

aproximado, -da [aprosiˈmadu, -da] *adj* approximate.

aproximar [aprosiˈma(x)] *vt (objetos)* to bring closer; *(pessoas)* to bring together.

❏ **aproximar-se** *vp* to come closer; **~-se de** to approach; **aproxima-se uma pessoa/um carro** someone/a car is coming.

aptidão [aptʃiˈdãw] *(pl* -**ões** [-õjʃ]) *f* aptitude; *(vocação)* talent.

apto, -ta [ˈaptu, -ta] *adj* capable.

Apto. *abrev (Br)* = **apartamento**.

apunhalar [apuɲaˈla(x)] *vt* to stab.

apuração [apuraˈsãw] *(pl* -**ões** [-õjʃ]) *f* selection.

apurado, -da [apuˈradu, -da] *adj* selected; *(sabor)* distinctive; *(visão, olfato)* keen.

apurar [apuˈra(x)] *vt (selecionar)* to pick; *(averiguar)* to find out; *(sabor)* to bring out.

apuro [aˈpuru] *m (dificuldade)* fix; **estar em ~s** to be in a fix; **meter-se em ~s** to get into trouble.

aquarela [akwaˈrɛla] *f (Br)* watercolour.

aquário [aˈkwarju] *m* aquarium.

❏ **Aquário** *m* Aquarius.

aquático, -ca [aˈkwatʃiku, -ka] *adj* aquatic; *(ESP)* water *(antes de s)*.

aquecedor [akeseˈdo(x)] *(pl* -**res** [-riʃ]) *m* heater.

aquecer [akeˈse(x)] *vt & vi* to heat up.

❏ **aquecer-se** *vp* to warm o.s. up.

aquecimento [akesiˈmẽntu] *m* heating; **~ central** central heating.

aqueduto [akeˈdutu] *m* aqueduct.

àquela [ˈakɛla] = **a** + **aquela**, → **aquele**.

aquele, aquela [aˈkeli, aˈkɛla] *adj* that, those *(pl)* ◆ *pron* that (one); **~ ali** that one there; **~ que** *(relativo a pessoa)* the one who, those who *(pl)*; *(relativo* *a objeto)* the one which; **peça àquele homem/àquela mulher** ask that man/woman.

àquele ['akeli] = a + aquele, → aquele.

aqui [a'ki] *adv* here; **até ~** *(relativo a tempo)* up until now; **logo ~** right here; **por ~** this way; **por ~ em algum canto** somewhere around here.

aquilo [a'kilu] *pron* that; **você chama ~ de carro!** you call that a car!

àquilo ['akilu] = a + aquilo, → aquilo.

aquisição [akizi'sãw] *(pl -ões* [-õjʃ]*)* f acquisition.

ar ['a(x)] *(pl ares* [ariʃ]*)* m air; *(brisa)* breeze; **dar ~es de** to pretend to be; **dar-se ~es de importante** to put on airs (and graces); **ir ao/sair do ~** *(em rádio, TV)* to go on/off the air; **ir pelos ~es** *(explodir)* to blow up; **ter ~ de** to look OU seem like; **~ condicionado** air conditioning; **ao ~** *(lançar, atirar)* into the air; **ao ~ livre** in the open air.

árabe ['arabi] *adj & mf* Arab ♦ *m (língua)* Arabic.

aragem [a'raʒẽ] *(pl -ns* [-ʃ]*)* f breeze.

arame [a'rami] *m* wire; **~ farpado** barbed wire.

aranha [a'raɲa] *f* spider.

arara [a'rara] *f* cockatoo.

arbitragem [axbi'traʒẽ] *(pl -ns* [-ʃ]*)* f *(de jogo)* refereeing; *(de litígio)* arbitration.

arbitrar [axbi'tra(x)] *vt (jogo)* to referee.

árbitro ['axbitru] *m (de jogo)* referee.

arborizado, -da [axbori'zadu, -da] *adj* wooded.

arbusto [ax'buʃtu] *m* bush.

arca ['axka] *f* trunk.

arcaico, -ca [ax'kajku, -ka] *adj* archaic.

archote [ax'ʃotʃi] *m* torch.

arco ['axku] *m (de edifício, construção)* arch; *(curva)* arc; *(de flechas)* bow; *(brinquedo)* hoop.

arco-íris [ax'kwiriʃ] *(pl arcos-íris* [axku'ziriʃ]*)* m rainbow.

ardência [ax'dẽsja] *f (Br) (de pele)* stinging; *(de estômago)* heartburn.

ardente [ax'dẽtʃi] *adj (fig: amor, paixão)* passionate.

arder [ax'de(x)] *vi* to burn; *(pele)* to sting.

ardor [ax'do(x)] *(pl -res* [-riʃ]*)* m *(de*

pele) stinging; **com ~** ardently.

ardósia [ax'dɔzja] *f* slate.

árduo, -dua ['axdwu, -dwa] *adj* arduous.

área ['arja] *f* area; *(fig: campo de ação)* field; **~ de serviço** *(em apartamento)* utility area; **grande ~** *(em futebol)* penalty area.

areal [a'rɛaw] *(pl -ais* [-ajʃ]*)* m beach.

areia [a'reja] *f* sand; **~s movediças** quicksand *(sg)*.

arejar [are'ʒa(x)] *vt* to air ♦ *vi (fig: sair)* to get some air.

arena [a'rena] *f (de circo)* ring; *(de praça de touros)* bullring.

arenoso, -osa [are'nozu, -ɔza] *adj* sandy.

arenque [a'rẽki] *m* herring.

ares → ar.

Argentina [axʒẽtʃ'ʃina] *f:* **a ~** Argentina.

argila [ax'ʒila] *f* clay.

argola [ax'gɔla] *f (anel)* ring; *(de porta)* knocker.

❏ **argolas** *fpl (ESP)* rings; *(brincos)* hoop earrings.

argumentação [axgumẽta'sãw] *(pl -ões* [-õjʃ]*)* f argument.

argumentar [axgumẽ'ta(x)] *vt & vi* to argue.

argumento [axgu'mẽtu] *m* argument; *(de filme)* plot.

ária ['arja] *f* aria.

árido, -da ['aridu, -da] *adj* arid.

Áries ['ariʃ] *m (Br)* Aries.

arma ['axma] *f* weapon; **~ branca** knife; **~ de fogo** firearm.

armação [axma'sãw] *(pl -ões* [-õjʃ]*)* f frame; *(de animal)* horns *(pl)*; *(de barco)* rigging; *(de óculos)* frames *(pl)*.

armadilha [axma'diʎa] *f* trap.

armado, -da [ax'madu, -da] *adj* armed.

armadura [axma'dura] *f* suit of armour; *(de edifício)* framework.

armamento [axma'mẽtu] *m* armaments *(pl)*; *(de navio)* equipment.

armar [ax'ma(x)] *vt* to arm; *(tenda)* to put up.

armário [ax'marju] *m* cupboard; *(de roupa)* wardrobe.

armazém [axma'zẽ] *(pl -ns* [-ʃ]*)* m warehouse; **grande ~** *(loja)* department store.

aro ['aru] *m (de roda)* rim; *(de janela)* frame.

aroma [a'rɔma] *m* aroma; *(em iogurte, bebida)* flavour; **com ~ de morango** strawberry flavour.

arpão [ax'pãw] (*pl* **-ões** [-õjʃ]) *m* harpoon.

arqueologia [axkjolo'ʒia] *f* archeology.

arquibancada [axkibãŋ'kada] *f (Br)* grandstand.

arquipélago [axki'pɛlagu] *m* archipelago.

arquitecto, -ta [arki'tɛtu, -ta] *m, f (Port)* = **arquiteto**.

arquitectura [arkitɛ'tura] *f (Port)* = **arquitetura**.

arquiteto, -ta [axki'tɛtu, -ta] *m, f (Br)* architect.

arquitetura [axki'tɛtura] *f (Br)* architecture.

arquivo [ax'kivu] *m* archive; *(móvel)* filing cabinet; *(cartório)* registry office; *(Br: INFORM)* file.

arraial [axa'jaw] (*pl* **-ais** [-ajʃ]) *m* = fete.

arrancar [axãŋ'ka(x)] *vt (árvore, batatas)* to dig up; *(folhas, pêlos)* to pull out; *(dente)* to extract ♦ *vi (partir)* to set off; **~ algo das mãos de alguém** to snatch sthg from sb.

arranha-céus [a,xaɲa'sɛwʃ] *m inv* skyscraper.

arranhão [axa'ɲãw] (*pl* **-ões** [-õjʃ]) *m* scratch.

arranhar [axa'ɲa(x)] *vt* to scratch; *(parede, carro)* to scrape; **~ um pouco de algo** to get by in sthg.

⎿ **arranhar-se** *vp* to scratch o.s.

arranhões → arranhão.

arranjar [axã'ʒa(x)] *vt (reparar)* to fix, to repair; *(adquirir)* to get; **~ problemas** to get into trouble.

arranque [a'xãŋki] *m →* **motor.**.

arrasar [axa'za(x)] *vt* to devastate.

arrastar [axaʃ'ta(x)] *vt* to drag (along OU away).

arrecadar [axɛka'da(x)] *vt (objeto)* to store away; *(dinheiro)* to collect.

arredondado, -da [axedõn'dadu, -da] *adj (forma)* round, rounded; *(fig: valor)* rounded up.

arredondar [axedõn'da(x)] *vt (forma)* to make round; *(fig: valor)* to round up.

arredores [axe'dɔriʃ] *mpl* outskirts.

arrefecer [axɛfɛ'se(x)] *vi (tempo, ar)* to cool down; *(comida)* to get cold; *(fig: entusiasmo)* to cool.

arregaçar [axega'sa(x)] *vt (mangas, calças)* to roll up.

arreios [a'xejuʃ] *mpl (de cavalo)* harness *(sg)*.

arremedar [axeme'da(x)] *vt (imitar)* to ape.

arremessar [axeme'sa(x)] *vt (pedra, flecha)* to hurl.

arrendamento [axẽnda'mẽntu] *m (de casa)* rent.

arrendar [axẽn'da(x)] *vt (casa)* to rent; **~ uma casa a alguém** to rent (out) a house to sb.

arrendatário, -ria [axẽnda'tarju, -rja] *m, f (de casa)* tenant.

arrepender-se [axepẽn'dexsi] *vp:* **~ de (ter feito) algo** to regret (doing) sthg.

arrepiar [axe'pja(x)] *vt (pêlo, cabelo)* to make stand on end.

⎿ **arrepiar-se** *vp (de frio)* to shiver; *(de medo)* to shudder.

arrepio [axe'piu] *m (de frio)* shiver; *(de medo)* shudder.

arriscado, -da [axiʃ'kadu, -da] *adj (perigoso)* risky; *(corajoso)* daring.

arriscar [axiʃ'ka(x)] *vt (pôr em risco)* to risk.

⎿ **arriscar-se** *vp* to take a risk.

arrogância [axo'gãsja] *f (presunção)* arrogance.

arrogante [axo'gãntʃi] *adj (presumido)* arrogant.

arrombar [axõm'ba(x)] *vt (porta, janela, cofre)* to force (open).

arrotar [axo'ta(x)] *vi* to burp, to belch.

arroto [a'xotu] *m* burp, belch.

arroz [a'xoʒ] *m* rice; **~ de forno** baked dish containing rice, chicken and/or prawns, vegetables and olives.

arroz-doce [axoʒ'dosi] *m* rice pudding.

arruaça [a'xwasa] *f* street riot.

arruaceiro, -ra [axwa'sejru, -ra] *adj* riotous ♦ *m, f* rioter.

arrumado, -da [axu'madu, -da] *adj (casa, secretária, gaveta)* tidy; *(mala)* packed *(fig: resolvido)* sorted (out).

arrumar [axu'ma(x)] *vt (casa, secretária, gaveta)* to tidy up; *(mala)* to pack.

arte ['axtʃi] *f* art; **~s marciais** martial arts; **a sétima ~** cinema *(Brit)*, the movies *(pl) (Am)*.

artéria [ax'tɛrja] f artery.

arterial [axte'rjaw] (pl -ais [-ajʃ]) adj → pressão, tensão.

artesanato [axteza'natu] m craftwork, handicraft.

articulação [axtʃikula'sãw] (pl -ões [-õjʃ]) f (de ossos) joint; (de palavras) articulation.

artificial [axtʃifi'sjaw] (pl -ais [-ajʃ]) adj artificial.

artigo [ax'tʃigu] m article; (produto) item; "~s a declarar" "goods to declare"; ~s de primeira necessidade essential goods.

artista [ax'tʃiʃta] mf artist.

artístico, -ca [ax'tʃiʃtʃiku, -ka] adj artistic.

artrite [ax'tritʃi] f arthritis.

árvore ['axvori] f tree.

as [aʃ] → a.

ás ['ajʃ] (pl ases ['azeʃ]) m ace; ser um ~ to be a whizz.

às [ajʃ] = a + as, → a.

asa ['aza] f wing; (de utensílio) handle.

asa-delta [aza'dɛwta] (pl asas-delta [azaʒ'dɛwta]) f hang-glider.

ascensor [aʃsẽ'so(x)] (pl -res [-riʃ]) m (em prédio) lift (Brit), elevator (Am); (em rua, encosta) funicular.

asco ['aʃku] m disgust.

ases → ás.

asfalto [aʃ'fawtu] m asphalt.

asfixia [aʃfik'sia] f asphyxia, suffocation.

Ásia ['azja] f: a ~ Asia.

asiático, -ca [a'zjatʃiku, -ka] adj & m, f Asian.

asma ['aʒma] f asthma.

asmático, -ca [aʒ'matʃiku, -ka] adj & m, f asthmatic.

asneira [aʒ'nejra] f (tolice) nonsense; (obscenidade) swear word.

asno ['aʒnu] m donkey; (fig: estúpido) ass.

aspargo [aʃ'paxgu] m (Br) asparagus.

aspecto [aʃ'pɛktu] m appearance; (ponto de vista) aspect.

áspero, -ra ['aʃperu, -ra] adj rough; (voz) harsh.

aspirador [aʃpira'do(x)] (pl -res [-riʃ]) m vacuum cleaner, Hoover®.

aspirar [aʃpi'ra(x)] vt to vacuum, to hoover.
❏ **aspirar a** v + prep (desejar) to aspire to.

aspirina® [aʃpi'rina] f aspirin; ~ efervescente soluble aspirin.

asqueroso, -osa [aʃke'rozu, -ɔza] adj disgusting, revolting.

assado, -da [a'sadu, -da] adj & m (CULIN) roast.

assadura [asa'dura] f (de carne) roast; (em bebê) nappy rash.

assalariado, -da [asala'rjadu, -da] m, f (salaried) employee.

assaltante [asaw'tãntʃi] mf burglar.

assaltar [asaw'ta(x)] vt (pessoa) to mug; (casa) to burgle; (banco) to rob.

assalto [a'sawtu] m (a pessoa) mugging; (a casa) burglery; (a banco) robbery; (em boxe) round; ~ à mão armada armed robbery.

assar [a'sa(x)] vt to roast.

assassinar [asasi'na(x)] vt to murder.

assassínio [asa'sinju] m murder.

assassino, -na [asa'sinu, -na] m, f murderer.

assediar [ase'dʒja(x)] vt (importunar) to pester; (sexualmente) to harass.

assédio [a'sɛdʒju] m harassment; ~ sexual sexual harassment.

assegurar [asegu'ra(x)] vt to assure.
❏ **assegurar-se** vp: ~-se de que to make sure (that).

asseio [a'seju] m (limpeza) cleanliness.

assembléia [asẽm'blɛja] f assembly; (reunião) meeting; ~ geral annual general meeting; a Assembléia da República Portuguese houses of parliament.

assemelhar-se [aseme'ʎaxsi] : assemelhar-se a vp + prep to look like.

assento [a'sẽntu] m seat.

assim [a'sĩ] adv (do mesmo modo) like this; (deste modo) therefore; ~, sim! that's better!; como ~? I'm sorry?; ~ mesmo just so; ~, ~ so-so; ~ que as soon as.

assimilar [asimi'la(x)] vt to assimilate.

assinar [asi'na(x)] vt to sign; (revista) to subscribe to.

assinatura [asina'tura] f signature; (de revista) subscription; (de trem) season ticket.

assistência [asiʃ'tẽsja] f (auxílio) help; (público) audience; ~ médica medical aid.

assistir [asiʃ'tʃi(x)] vt (ajudar) to help.
❏ **assistir a** v + prep (a espetáculo) to

attend; *(a programa)* to watch; *(a acidente, acontecimento)* to witness.

assoalho [aˈsoaʎu] *m (Br: de casa)* floor.

assoar [aˈswa(x)] *vt* to blow.

❏ **assoar-se** *vp* to blow one's nose.

assobiar [asoˈbja(x)] *vi* to whistle.

assobio [asoˈbiu] *m* whistle.

associação [asosjaˈsãw] *(pl -ões* [-õjʃ]) *f* association.

assombrado, -da [asõˈbradu, -da] *adj (fig: casa, local)* haunted.

assombro [aˈsõbru] *m* amazement.

assunto [aˈsũntu] *m* subject; ~ **encerrado!** subject closed!

assustador, -ra [asuʃtaˈdo(x), -ra] *(mpl -res* [-riʃ], *fpl -s* [-ʃ]) *adj* frightening.

assustar [asuʃˈta(x)] *vt* to frighten.

❏ **assustar-se** *vp* to be frightened.

asterisco [aʃteˈriʃku] *m* asterisk.

astral [aʃˈtraw] *(pl -ais* [-ajʃ]) *m (Br: fam: humor)*: **hoje estou com baixo ~** I'm feeling out of sorts today.

astro [ˈaʃtru] *m* star.

astrologia [aʃtroloˈʒia] *f* astrology.

astronauta [aʃtroˈnawta] *mf* astronaut.

astronomia [aʃtronoˈmia] *f* astronomy.

astúcia [aʃˈtusja] *f* astuteness.

atacadista [atakaˈdiʃta] *mf* wholesaler.

atacado [ataˈkadu] *m*: **comprar por ~** to buy wholesale.

atacador [atakaˈdor] *(pl -res* [-reʃ]) *m (Port: de sapatos)* shoelace.

atacante [ataˈkãntʃi] *adj (ESP)* attacking ◆ *mf (ESP)* forward.

atacar [ataˈka(x)] *vt* to attack.

atadura [ataˈdura] *f (Br)* bandage.

atalho [aˈtaʎu] *m* short cut.

ataque [aˈtaki] *m* attack; ~ **cardíaco** heart attack.

atar [aˈta(x)] *vt (sapatos)* to lace OU do up; *(saco)* to do up; *(corda, cordão, fio)* to tie.

atarracado, -da [ataxaˈkadu, -da] *adj* stocky.

até [aˈte] *prep (limite no espaço)* as far as; *(limite no tempo)* until ◆ *adv* even; ~ **agora** so far; ~ **amanhã!** see you tomorrow!; ~ **logo!** see you later!; ~ **mais!** *(em conversa)* speak to you soon!; ~ **que enfim!** at (long) last!; ~ **porque** because.

atear [ateˈa(x)] *vt (incendiar)* to set fire to; *(avivar)* to rekindle.

atéia → **ateu**.

ateliê [ateˈlje] *m (Br)* = **atelier**.

atelier [ateˈlje] *m (Port)* studio.

atemorizar [atemoriˈza(x)] *vt* to terrify.

atenção [atẽˈsãw] *(pl -ões* [-õjʃ]) *f* attention; *(cuidado)* care; *(cortesia)* courtesy ◆ *interj* watch OU look out!; **chamar a ~ de alguém para algo** to draw sb's attention to sthg; **prestar ~** to pay attention.

atender [atẽˈde(x)] *vt (telefone)* to answer; *(em loja)* to serve; *(em hospital)* to see.

atendimento [atẽndʒiˈmẽntu] *m (de telefone)* answering; *(em loja, hospital)* service.

atentado [atẽˈtadu] *m* attempt *(on sb's life)*.

atenuante [ateˈnwãntʃi] *f* extenuating circumstance.

atenuar [ateˈnwa(x)] *vt* to soften.

aterragem [ateˈxaʒẽj] *(pl -ns* [-ʃ]) *f (Port)* = **aterrissagem**.

aterrar [ateˈxar] *vi (Port)* = **aterrissar**.

aterrissagem [atexiˈsaʒẽj] *(pl -ns* [-ʃ]) *f (Br)* landing.

aterrissar [atexiˈsa(x)] *vi (Br)* to land ◆ *vt (aterrorizar)* to terrify.

aterro [aˈtexu] *m* landfill.

aterrorizar [atexoriˈza(x)] *vt* to terrify.

atestado [ateʃˈtadu] *m* certificate; ~ **médico** doctor's certificate; ~ **de óbito** death certificate.

ateu, atéia [aˈtew, aˈteja] *m, f* atheist.

atiçar [atʃiˈsa(x)] *vt (lume)* to poke.

atingir [atʃiˈʒi(x)] *vt* to reach; *(ferir, afetar)* to hit; *(objetivo)* to achieve; *(compreender)* to grasp; *(abranger)* to cover.

atirar [atʃiˈra(x)] *vt* to throw ◆ *vi (com arma)* to shoot.

atitude [atʃiˈtudʒi] *f* attitude.

atividade [atʃiviˈdadʒi] *f* activity.

ativo, -va [aˈtʃivu, -va] *adj (Br)* active.

Atlântico [atˈlãntʃiku] *m*: **o ~** the Atlantic.

atlas [ˈatlaʃ] *m inv* atlas.

atleta [atˈleta] *mf* athlete.

atletismo [atleˈtʃiʒmu] *m* athletics *(sg)*.

atmosfera [atmoʃˈfɛra] *f* atmosphere.

ato [ˈatu] *m (Br) (acção)* action; *(de peça de teatro)* act.

atômico, -ca [aˈtomiku, -ka] *adj* atomic.

ator, atriz [aˈto(x), atriʒ] *(mpl* **-res** [-riʃ], *fpl* **-zes** [-ziʃ]) *m, f (Br)* actor *(f* actress).

atordoado, -da [atoxˈdwadu, -da] *adj* stunned.

atores → ator.

atormentado, -da [atoxmẽnˈtadu, -da] *adj* troubled.

atração [atraˈsãw] *(pl* **-ões** [-õjʃ]) *f (Br)* attraction; *(de pessoa)* attractiveness.

atracção [atraˈsãw] *(pl* **-ões** [-õjʃ]) *f (Port)* = atração.

atracções → atração.

atractivo, -va [atraˈtivu, -va] *adj (Port)* = atrativo.

atraente [atraˈẽntʃi] *adj* attractive.

atraiçoar [atrajˈswa(x)] *vt* to betray.

❏ **atraiçoar-se** *vp* to give o.s. away.

atrair [atraˈi(x)] *vt* to attract.

atrapalhar [atrapaˈʎa(x)] *vt (perturbar)* to confuse; *(dificultar)* to get in the way of.

❏ **atrapalhar-se** *vp* to get all confused.

atrás [aˈtrajʃ] *adv (detrás)* behind; *(para trás)* back there; **há dias ~** a few days ago; **~ de** *(no espaço)* behind; *(no tempo)* after; **ficar com pé ~** *(fig)* to be on one's guard.

atrasado, -da [atraˈzadu, -da] *adj (pessoa)* late; *(país, região)* backward; **chegar ~** to arrive late; **estar ~** to be late.

atrasar [atraˈza(x)] *vi (trem, ônibus)* to be delayed ♦ *vt (trabalho)* to delay; *(fig: prejudicar)* to hinder.

❏ **atrasar-se** *vp* to be late.

atraso [aˈtrazu] *m* delay; *(de país)* backwardness.

atrativo, -va [atraˈtʃivu, -va] *adj (Br)* attractive ♦ *m (Br)* attraction.

através [atraˈvɛjʃ] : **através de** *prep (pelo meio de)* through; *(por meio de)* by.

atravessar [atraveˈsa(x)] *vt (rua, rio)* to cross; *(pôr ao través)* to put across; *(fig: situação, fase)* to go through.

atrelado [atreˈladu] *m* trailer.

atrever-se [atreˈvexsi] : **atrever-se** *vp (ousar)* to dare; **~ a fazer algo** to

dare to do sthg.

atrevido, -da [atreˈvidu, -da] *adj (malcriado)* cheeky; *(audaz)* daring.

atrevimento [atreviˈmẽntu] *m (audácia)* daring; **que ~!** what a cheek!

atribuir [atriˈbwi(x)] *vt* to attribute; *(cargo)* to give.

atributo [atriˈbutu] *m* attribute.

átrio [ˈatriu] *m (de edifício)* hall.

atrito [aˈtritu] *m* friction.

❏ **atritos** *mpl* disagreements.

atriz → ator.

atropelamento [atropelaˈmẽntu] *m* road accident *(involving a pedestrian being run over)*.

atropelar [atropeˈla(x)] *vt* to run over.

atuação [atwaˈsãw] *(pl* **-ões** [-õjʃ]) *f (procedimento)* behaviour; *(em espetáculo)* acting; *(espetáculo)* performance.

atual [aˈtwaw] *(pl* **-ais** [-ajʃ]) *adj (Br) (presente)* current; *(moderno)* modern.

atualizar [atwaliˈza(x)] *vt (tornar atual)* to modernize; *(INFORM: ficheiro)* to update.

atualmente [atwawˈmẽntʃi] *adv* currently.

atuar [aˈtwa(x)] *vi (Br)* to act.

atum [aˈtũ] *m* tuna.

aturdido, -da [aturˈdʒidu, -da] *adj* stunned.

audácia [awˈdasja] *f* audacity.

audição [awdʒiˈsãw] *(pl* **-ões** [-õjʃ]) *f* hearing; *(de peça musical, concerto)* recital.

audiência [awˈdʒjẽsja] *f (JUR)* hearing.

audiovisual [awdʒjoviˈzwaw] *(pl* **-ais** [-ajʃ]) *adj* audiovisual.

auditório [awdʒiˈtɔrju] *m* auditorium; *(público ouvinte)* audience.

auge [ˈawʒi] *m* peak.

aula [ˈawla] *f* class, lesson.

aumentar [awmẽnˈta(x)] *vt & vi* to increase.

aumento [awˈmẽntu] *m* increase; *(de ordenado)* rise *(Brit)*, raise *(Am)*.

auréola [awˈrɛwla] *f* halo.

aurora [awˈrɔra] *f* dawn; **~ boreal** northern lights *(pl)*.

auscultador [awʃkuwtaˈdo(x)] *(pl* **-res** [-riʃ]) *m* receiver.

❏ **auscultadores** *mpl* headphones.

ausência [awˈzẽsja] *f* absence.

ausentar-se [awzẽnˈtaxsi] *vp*: **~ de**

(de país, sala) to leave.

ausente [aw'zẽntʃi] *adj* absent.

Austrália [awʃ'tralja] *f:* **a ~** Australia.

australiano, -na [awʃtra'ljanu, -na] *adj & m, f* Australian.

Áustria [awʃtria] *f:* **a ~** Austria.

austríaco, -ca [awʃ'triaku, -ka] *adj & m, f* Austrian.

autenticar [awtẽntʃi'ka(x)] *vt (JUR: documento, assinatura)* to authenticate.

autêntico, -ca [aw'tẽntʃiku, -ka] *adj (verdadeiro)* real; *(JUR)* authenticated.

autocarro [awto'kaxu] *m* bus; *(entre cidades)* coach; **apanhar o ~** to catch the bus.

autoclismo [awto'kliʒmu] *m (Port)* flush; **puxar o ~** to flush the toilet.

autocolante [awtoko'lãntʃi] *adj* self-adhesive ◆ *m* sticker.

autodomínio [awtodo'minju] *m* self-control.

autódromo [aw'tɔdromu] *m* race track.

auto-escola [awtɔiʃ'kɔla] *f* driving school.

auto-estima [awtɔeʃ'tʃima] *f* self-esteem.

auto-estrada [awtɔʃ'trada] *f* motorway *(Brit)*, freeway *(Am)*.

autografar [awtogra'fa(x)] *vt* to autograph.

autógrafo [aw'tɔgrafu] *m* autograph.

autolocadora [awtoloka'dora] *f (Br)* car rental.

automático, -ca [awto'matʃiku, -ka] *adj* automatic.

automatização [awtomatʃiza'sãw] *(pl* -ões [-õjʃ]) *f* automation.

automobilismo [awtomobi'liʒmu] *m* motor racing.

automobilista [awtomobi'liʃta] *mf* motorist.

automotora [awtomo'tora] *f* diesel train.

automóvel [awto'mɔvɛw] *(pl* -eis [-ejʃ]) *m* motorcar *(Brit)*, automobile *(Am)*.

autópsia [aw'tɔpsja] *f (MED)* autopsy.

autor, -ra [aw'to(x), -ra] *(mpl* -res [-riʃ], *fpl* -s [-ʃ]) *m, f* author; *(de idéia)* originator; *(de brincadeira)* instigator; *(JUR: de crime)* perpetrator.

auto-retrato [awtoxe'tratu] *m* self-portrait.

autoridade [awtori'dadʒi] *f* authority.

autorização [awtoriza'sãw] *(pl* -ões [-õjʃ]) *f* authorization.

autorizar [awtori'za(x)] *vt* to authorize.

auxiliar [awsi'lja(x)] *(pl* -res [-riʃ]) *adj* auxiliary ◆ *mf* assistant ◆ *vt* to assist.

auxílio [aw'silju] *m* help.

auxílio-desemprego [aw'silju-dʒizẽm'pregu] *(pl* **auxílios-desemprego** [aw'siljuʒdʒizẽm'pregu]) *m (Br)* unemployment benefit.

Av. *(abrev de avenida)* Ave.

avalanche [ava'lãʃi] *f* avalanche.

avaliação [avalja'sãw] *(pl* -ões [-õjʃ]) *f* assessment; *(JUR)* valuation.

avaliar [ava'lja(x)] *vt* to assess; *(gastos)* to estimate; *(valor de objeto)* to value; **a ~ por** judging by.

avançado, -da [avã'sadu, -da] *adj* advanced; *(pessoa)* progressive ◆ *m, f (ESP)* forward ◆ *m (de caravana)* awning.

avançar [avã'sa(x)] *vi* to advance.

avarento, -ta [ava'rẽntu, -ta] *adj* miserly.

avaria [ava'ria] *f* breakdown.

avariado, -da [ava'rjadu, -da] *adj* out of order; *(carro)* broken down.

ave ['avi] *f* bird.

aveia [a'veja] *f* oats *(pl).*

avelã [ave'lã] *f* hazelnut.

avenca [a'vẽŋka] *f* maidenhair fern.

avenida [ave'nida] *f* avenue.

avental [avẽn'taw] *(pl* -ais [-ajʃ]) *m* apron.

aventura [avẽn'tura] *f* adventure; *(amorosa)* affair; **partir para a ~** to set out on an adventure.

aventureiro, -ra [avẽntu'rejru, -ra] *m, f* adventurer.

averiguação [averigwa'sãw] *(pl* -ões [-õjʃ]) *f* investigation.

averiguar [averi'gwa(x)] *vt* to investigate; *(verdade)* to find out.

avesso [a'vesu] *m (de casaco, saco)* reverse; *(contrário)* opposite ◆ *adj:* **~ a** averse to; **pelo ~** inside out.

avestruz [aveʃ'truʃ] *(pl* -zes [-ziʃ]) *f* ostrich.

avião [a'vjãw] *(pl* -ões [-õjʃ]) *m* plane; **"por ~"** "by airmail".

ávido, -da ['avidu, -da] *adj:* **~ de** greedy for.

aviões → avião.

avisar [avi'za(x)] *vt* to warn; *(notificar)* to inform.

aviso [aˈvizu] *m (advertência)* warning; *(sinal, letreiro, notificação)* notice; ~ **de recepção** acknowledgement of receipt.

avistar [avifˈta(x)] *vt* to see.

avô, avó [aˈvo, aˈvɔ] *m, f* grandfather *(f* grandmother).

avós [aˈvɔʃ] *mpl* grandparents.

avulso, -sa [aˈvuwsu, -sa] *adj* separate ♦ *adv* separately.

axila [akˈsila] *f* armpit.

azar [aˈza(x)] *(pl* -**res** [-riʃ]) *m (falta de sorte)* bad luck; *(acaso)* chance; **estar com** ~ to be out of luck; **por** ~ as luck would have it.

azarado, -da [azaˈradu, -da] *m, f* unlucky person.

azares → **azar**.

azedar [azeˈda(x)] *vi* to turn sour.

azedo, -da [aˈzedu, -da] *adj* sour.

azeite [aˈzejtʃi] *m* olive oil.

azeitona [azejˈtona] *f* olive; ~**s pretas** black olives; ~**s recheadas** stuffed olives.

azevinho [azeˈviɲu] *m* holly.

azinheira [aziˈɲejra] *f* holm oak.

azul [aˈzuw] *(pl* **azuis** [aˈzujʃ]) *adj & m* blue.

azul-claro, azul-clara [a,zuwˈklaru, a,zuwˈklara] *(mpl* **azul-claros** [a,zuwˈklaruʃ], *fpl* **azul-claras** [a,zuwˈklaraʃ]) *adj* pale blue.

azulejo [azuˈlejʒu] *m* glazed tile.

azul-escuro, azul-escura [a,zuweʃˈkuru, a,zuweʃˈkura] *(mpl* **azul-escuros** [a,zuweʃˈkuruʃ], *fpl* **azul-escuras** [a,zuweʃˈkuraʃ]) *adj* dark blue.

azul-marinho [a,zuwmaˈriɲu] *adj inv* navy (blue).

azul-turquesa [a,zuwtuxˈkeza] *adj inv* turquoise.

B

baba ['baba] f dribble.

babá [ba'ba] f (Br) nanny.

babar-se [ba'baxsi] vp to dribble.

baby-sitter [bejbi'site(x)] f baby-sitter.

bacalhau [baka'ʎaw] m (peixe) cod; (em culinária) salt cod; ~ **assado (na brasa)** barbecued salt cod seasoned with olive oil and garlic, served with roast potatoes; ~ **à Brás** salt cod fried with onions and garlic then mixed with eggs, finely cut chips and olives; ~ **cru desfiado** raw pieces of salt cod seasoned with olive oil and garlic; ~ **à Gomes de Sá** pieces of salt cod, onion and potato baked with olive oil, eggs and olives.

bacia [ba'sia] f basin; (ANAT) pelvis.

baço, -ça ['basu, -sa] adj (metal, espelho) tarnished; (tinta, cor) matt ♦ m (ANAT) spleen.

bacon ['bejkõ] m bacon.

bactéria [bak'tɛrja] f bacterium.

badejo [ba'deʒu] m pollack.

badminton [bad'mĩtõ] m badminton.

bafo ['bafu] m breath.

bafômetro [ba'fometru] m (Br) Breathalyser®.

baforada [bafo'rada] f puff.

bagaço [ba'gasu] m (Port) strong spirit similar to brandy.

bagageira [baga'ʒejra] f (Port) (de carro) boot (Brit), trunk (Am); (de ônibus) luggage rack.

bagageiro [baga'ʒejru] m porter.

bagagem [ba'gaʒẽ] (pl -ns [-ʃ]) f luggage (Brit), baggage (Am); **despachar/depositar a** ~ to check in/leave one's luggage.

bagatela [baga'tɛla] f trifle.

bago ['bagu] m (de uva) grape; (de trigo) grain.

bagunça [ba'gũsa] f (Br) mess.

Bahia [ba'ia] f (Br) Bahia.

baía [ba'ia] f bay.

❑ **Baía** f (Port) = Bahia.

bailado [baj'ladu] m (ballet) ballet; (dança) dance.

bailarino, -na [bajla'rinu, -na] m, f ballet dancer.

baile ['bajli] m ball.

bainha [ba'iɲa] f (de calças, saia, etc) hem; (de espada) scabbard.

bairro ['bajxu] m neighbourhood; (divisão administrativa) district; ~ **de lata** (Port) shanty town.

baixa ['bajʃa] f (em quantidade) decrease; (de preço) reduction; (Br: médica) discharge; (em guerra) casualty.

baixar [baj'ʃa(x)] vt to lower ♦ vi (preço, valor) to come down.

❑ **baixar-se** vp to bend down.

baixo, -xa ['bajʃu, -ʃa] adj low; (pessoa) short; (qualidade) poor; (profundidade) shallow; (fig: desprezível) mean ♦ adv (falar, rir) quietly; (relativo a posição) low ♦ m (instrumento) bass; **o mais ~/a mais baixa** (pessoa) the shortest; (objeto, preço) the lowest; **para** ~ down; **por** ~ **de** under(neath); **estar em** ~ (Port: estar abatido) to be out of sorts.

bala ['bala] f bullet; (Br: doce) sweet; **à prova de** ~ bullet-proof.

balança [ba'lãsa] f scales (pl).

❑ **Balança** f (Port: signo do zodíaco) Libra.

balançar [balã'sa(x)] vt (balanço) to swing; (barco) to rock ♦ vi (balanço) to swing; (barco) to rock.

balanço [ba'lãsu] m (de criança) swing; (ação) swinging.

balão [ba'lãw] (pl -ões [-õjʃ]) m balloon; (de transporte) hot-air balloon.

balbuciar [bawbu'sja(x)] vt & vi to mumble.

barco

balbúrdia [baw'buxdʒja] *f (desordem)* shambles *(sg)*; *(barulho)* racket.

balcão [baw'kãw] *(pl -ões* [-õjʃ]) *m (de bar, loja)* counter; *(de teatro)* circle; *(de casa)* balcony; ~ **nobre/simples** *(Br: de teatro)* dress/upper circle.

balde ['bawdʒi] *m* bucket.

baldeação [hawdʒja'sãw] *(pl -ões* [-õjʃ]) *f (Br)* change; **fazer** ~ to change.

balé [ba'lɛ] *m (Br)* ballet.

baleia [ba'leja] *f* whale.

baliza [ba'liza] *f (ESP)* goal.

ballet [ba'lɛ] *m (Port)* = **balé.**

balneário [baw'njarju] *m* changing room.

balões → **balão.**

balofo, -fa [ba'lofu, -fa] *adj (pessoa)* flabby.

baloiço [ba'lojsu] *m (Port)* swing.

bálsamo ['bawsamu] *m* balsam, balm; *(fig: alívio)* comfort.

bambu [bãm'bu] *m* bamboo.

banal [ba'naw] *(pl -ais* [-ajʃ]) *adj* banal.

banana [ba'nana] *f* banana.

bananada [bana'nada] *f* dessert made with banana puree.

bananeira [bana'nejra] *f* banana tree.

banca ['bãŋka] *f (Br):* ~ **de jornais** newsstand.

bancada [bãŋ'kada] *f (de cozinha)* worktop; *(de trabalho)* bench; *(Port: de estádio)* grandstand.

bancário, -ria [bãŋ'karju, -rja] *adj* banking *(antes de s)* ♦ *m, f* bank clerk.

banco ['bãŋku] *m (de cozinha)* stool; *(de carro)* seat; *(FIN)* bank; *(de hospital)* casualty *(Brit)*, emergency room *(Am)*; ~ **de areia** sandbank; ~ **de dados** *(INFORM)* database; ~ **de jardim** (park) bench.

banda ['bãnda] *f* side; *(filarmônica)* brass band; *(de rock)* band; **de** ~ *(de lado)* sideways; **pôr de** ~ *(fig: pessoa)* to shun.

bandarilha [bãnda'riʎa] *f* barbed dart thrust into a bull's back.

bandeira [bãn'dejra] *f* flag; *(em transporte público)* destination screen; **dar** ~ *(Br: fam)* to give the game away.

bandeja [bãn'deʒa] *f* tray.

bandejão [bãnde'ʒãw] *(pl -ões* [-õjʃ]) *f (Br)* canteen meal.

bandido, -da [bãn'dʒidu, -da] *m, f* bandit.

bando ['bãndu] *m (de aves)* flock; *(de criminosos)* gang.

bandolim [bãndo'lĩ] *(pl -ns* [-ʃ]) *m* mandolin.

bangaló [bãŋga'lɔ] *m (Port)* = **bangalô.**

bangalô [bãŋga'lo] *m (Br)* bungalow.

banha ['baɲa] *f:* ~ **(de porco)** lard.

banheira [ba'ɲejra] *f* bathtub.

banheiro [ba'ɲejru] *m (Br: quarto de banho)* bathroom; *(Port: de praia, piscina)* lifeguard.

banhista [ba'ɲiʃta] *mf* bather.

banho ['baɲu] *m (em banheira)* bath; *(em piscina, mar)* swim; **tomar** ~ *(em banheira)* to have a bath; *(em chuveiro)* to have a shower; *(em piscina, mar)* to have a swim; **tomar um ~/~s de sol** to sunbathe.

banho-maria [ˌbaɲuma'ria] *m:* **cozinhar algo em** ~ to cook sthg in a bainmarie.

banir [ba'ni(x)] *vt (proibir)* to ban; *(expulsar)* to banish.

banjo ['bãʒu] *m* banjo.

banquete [bãŋ'kɛtʃi] *m* banquet.

baptismo [ba'tiʒmu] *m (Port)* = **batismo.**

baptizado [bati'zadu] *m (Port)* = **batizado.**

bar [ba(x)] *(pl -res* [-riʃ]) *m* bar.

baralhar [bara'ʎa(x)] *vt (cartas de jogar)* to shuffle; *(confundir)* to confuse. ❏ **baralhar-se** *vp* to get confused.

baralho [ba'raʎu] *m:* ~ **(de cartas)** pack (of cards) *(Brit)*, deck (of cards) *(Am)*.

barão [ba'rãw] *(pl -ões* [-õjʃ]) *m* baron.

barata [ba'rata] *f* cockroach.

barato, -ta [ba'ratu, -ta] *adj* cheap ♦ *adv* cheaply ♦ *m (Br: fam)* fun; **mais** ~ cheaper; **o mais** ~ the cheapest; **foi o maior** ~! *(Br)* it was great!

barba ['baxba] *f* beard; **fazer a** ~ to shave.

barbante [bax'bãntʃi] *m (Br)* string.

barbatana [baxba'tana] *f (de peixe)* fin; *(de nadador)* flipper.

barbeador [barbja'do(x)] *(pl -res* [-riʃ]) *m:* ~ **(elétrico)** (electric) shaver.

barbear-se [bax'bjaxsi] *vp* to shave.

barbeiro [bax'bejru] *m* barber's (shop).

barca ['baxka] *f (Br)* ferry.

barco ['baxku] *m* boat; ~ **a motor** speedboat; ~ **a remo** rowing boat; ~ **à**

vela sailing boat.

bares → bar.

barman ['baxmãn] (*pl* -s [-ʃ]) *m* barman.

barões → barão.

baronesa [baro'neza] *f* baroness.

barra ['baxa] *f* bar; (Br: foz) rivermouth; (Br: fam: situação) situation.

barraca [ba'xaka] *f* (de feira) stall; (Br: de camping) tent.

barraco [ba'xaku] *m* (Br) shack.

barragem [ba'xaʒẽ] (*pl* -ns [-ʃ]) *f* dam.

barranco [ba'xãŋku] *m* ravine.

barrar [ba'xa(x)] *vt* to bar.

barreira [ba'xejra] *f* (de rio, estrada, ESP) embankment; (ESP) hurdle; (fig: obstáculo) obstacle.

barrento, -ta [ba'xẽntu, -ta] *adj* clayey.

barrete [ba'xetʃi] *m* hat; (Port: fam: decepção) flop.

barriga [ba'xiga] *f* belly; **minha ~ está roncando** my stomach's rumbling; **~ da perna** calf; **de ~ para cima/para baixo** face up/down.

barril [ba'xiw] (*pl* -is [-iʃ]) *m* barrel.

barro ['baxu] *m* clay.

barroco, -ca [ba'xoku, -ka] *adj & m* baroque.

barulhento, -ta [baru'ʎẽntu, -ta] *adj* noisy.

barulho [ba'ruʎu] *m* (ruído) noise; (confusão) commotion; **pouco ~!** quieten down!

base ['bazi] *f* base; (de maquilhagem) foundation; (fundamento) basis.

basebol [bejze'bɔw] *m* baseball.

básico, -ca ['baziku, -ka] *adj* basic.

basílica [ba'zilika] *f* basilica.

basquete ['baʃketʃi] *m* = basquetebol.

basquetebol [baʃketʃi'bɔw] *m* basketball.

basta ['baʃta] *interj* that's enough!

bastante [baʃ'tãntʃi] *adv* (muito) a lot; (suficiente) enough ◆ *adj* (muito) a lot of; (suficiente) enough; **ele é ~ feio** he is quite ugly.

bastar [baʃ'ta(x)] *vi* to be enough.

bastidores [baʃtʃi'doreʃ] *mpl* wings.

bata ['bata] *f* (para senhora) pinafore; (para médico) (white) coat.

batalha [ba'taʎa] *f* battle; **~ naval** (jogo) battleships (sg).

batata [ba'tata] *f* potato; **~ doce** sweet potato; **~ palha** very finely cut chips; **~s assadas/cozidas** roast/boiled potatoes; **~s fritas** chips (Brit), French fries (Am); **~s fritas (de pacote)** crisps (Brit), chips (Am).

batedeira [bate'dejra] *f*: **~ (eléctrica)** mixer.

bátega ['batega] *f* downpour.

batente [ba'tẽntʃi] *m* (meia-porta) door (of double doors); (aldraba) doorknocker.

bate-papo [,batʃi'papu] (*pl* **bate-papos** [,batʃi'papuʃ]) *m* (Br) chat.

bater [ba'te(x)] *vt* to beat; (asas) to flap; (roupa) to scrub ◆ *vi* (coração) to beat; (porta, janela) to bang; **ela estava batendo queixo** her teeth were chattering because of the cold; **~ a** (porta, janela) to knock at; **~ com algo contra** OU **em algo** to crash sthg into sthg; **~ em** to hit; **~ à máquina** (Br) to type; **~ papo** (Br) to chat; **~ o pé** (teimar) to put one's foot down; **~ com o pé** to stamp one's foot; **~ com a porta** to slam the door; **bateu a bota** (fam: morrer) he popped his clogs; **ela não bate bem** she's off her head.

bateria [bate'ria] *f* (de carro, motor) battery; (MÚS) drums (pl).

baterista [bate'riʃta] *mf* drummer.

batida [ba'tʃida] *f* (Br) (de veículo) crash; (de polícia) raid; (bebida) blended drink containing "cachaça", sugar and fruit.

batido [ba'tʃidu] *m* (Port) milkshake.

batismo [ba'tʃiʒmu] *m* (Br) baptism.

batizado [batʃi'zadu] *m* (Br) christening.

batom [ba'tõ] (*pl* -ns [-ʃ]) *m* lipstick; **~ para o cieiro** (Port) chapstick.

batota [ba'tɔta] *f* (Port) cheating; **fazer ~** to cheat.

batuque [ba'tuki] *m* (Br: MÚS) Afro-Brazilian dance.

baú [ba'u] *m* trunk.

baunilha [baw'niʎa] *f* vanilla.

bazar [ba'za(x)] (*pl* -res [-riʃ]) *m* bazaar.

BB *m* (abrev de Banco do Brasil) Bank of Brazil.

BCG *m* (clínica) tuberculosis clinic; (vacina) BCG.

bêbado, -da ['bebadu, -da] *adj & m, f* drunk.

bebé [bɛ'bɛ] *m* (Port) = bebê.

bebê [be'be] *m (Br)* baby; "~ **a bordo**" "baby on board".

bebedeira [bebe'dejra] *f* drunkenness; **tomar uma** ~ to get drunk.

beber [be'be(x)] *vt & vi* to drink.

bebida [be'bida] *f* drink.

beça [ˈbɛsa] : **à beça** *adv (Br: fam)* a lot ◆ *adj (Br: fam)* loads of, a lot of; **o concerto foi bom à** ~ the concert was really good.

beco [ˈbeku] *m* alley; ~ **sem saída** dead end.

bege [ˈbɛʒi] *adj inv* beige.

begónia [beˈɡɔnja] *f (Port)* = begônia.

begônia [beˈɡonja] *f (Br)* begonia.

beija-flor [ˌbejʒaˈflo(x)] *(pl* **beija-flores** [ˌbejʒaˈfloriʃ]) *m* hummingbird.

beijar [bejˈʒa(x)] *vt* to kiss.
❑ **beijar-se** *vp* to kiss.

beijo [ˈbejʒu] *m* kiss.

beira [ˈbejra] *f (de estrada)* side; *(de rio)* bank; *(de precipício)* edge; **à** ~ **de** *(junto de)* beside; *(fig: no limiar de)* on the verge of.

beira-mar [ˌbejraˈma(x)] *f* seaside; **à** ~ by the sea.

beira-rio [ˌbejraˈxiu] *f* riverside; **à** ~ by the river.

belas-artes [ˌbɛlaˈzaxtʃiʃ] *fpl* fine arts.

beldade [bewˈdadʒi] *f* beauty.

beleza [beˈleza] *f* beauty; **que** ~! how wonderful!

belga [ˈbɛwɡa] *adj & mf* Belgian.

Bélgica [ˈbɛwʒika] *f:* **a** ~ Belgium.

beliche [beˈliʃi] *m* bunk.

beliscão [beliʃˈkãw] *(pl* **-ões** [-õjʃ]) *m* pinch.

beliscar [beliʃˈka(x)] *vt* to pinch.

beliscões → beliscão.

belo, -la [ˈbɛlu, -la] *adj* beautiful; *(homem)* handsome; *(momento)* wonderful; *(dia, sentimento, livro)* fine.

bem [bẽj] *adv* **1.** *(de forma satisfatória, correta)* well; **fala** ~ **inglês** she speaks English well; **fez** ~! you did the right thing!
2. *(exprime opinião favorável):* **estar** ~ *(de saúde)* to be well; *(de aspecto)* to look good; *(relativo a comodidade)* to be comfortable; **cheirar/saber** ~ to smell/taste good.
3. *(suficiente):* **estar** ~ to be enough.
4. *(muito)* very; **queria o bife** ~ **passado** I'd like my steak well-done; **queria uma bebida** ~ **gelada** I'd like an ice-cold drink.
5. *(bastante)* quite; **é um carro** ~ **espaçoso** it's quite a spacious car; **é um lugar** ~ **bonito** it's quite a pretty spot.
6. *(exatamente)* right; **não é** ~ **assim** it isn't quite like that; **não é** ~ **aqui é mais abaixo** it isn't here exactly, it's further down.
7. *(em locuções):* **eu** ~ **que lhe avisei** I told you so; **eu** ~ **que ajudava mas não posso** I'd be glad to help but I can't; ~ **como** as well as; ~ **feito!** it serves you right!; **está** ~! OK!, all right!; **muito** ~! very good!; **ou** ~ **que ... ou** ~ **que ...** either ...or ...; **você vai ter que ir por** ~ **ou por mal** you'll have to go whether you like it or not; **se** ~ **que** although, even though.
◆ *m* **1.** *(o que é bom)* good.
2. *(bem-estar, proveito)* good; **praticar o** ~ to do good; **é para o seu** ~ it's for your own good.
◆ *adj inv (pej):* **gente** ~ the well-heeled; **menino** ~ rich kid.
❑ **bens** *mpl (posses)* property *(sg)*; *(produtos)* goods; **bens imóveis** OU **de raiz** real estate *(sg)*; **bens de consumo** consumer goods.

bem-disposto, -osta [bẽjdʒiʃˈpoʃtu, -ɔʃta] *adj (bem humorado)* good-humoured.

bem-estar [bẽjʃˈta(x)] *m* wellbeing.

bem-vindo, -da [bẽjˈvĩndu, -da] *adj* welcome.

bendizer [bẽndʒiˈze(x)] *vt* to praise.

beneficência [benefiˈsẽsja] *f* charity.

beneficiar [benefiˈsja(x)] *vt* to benefit.

benefício [beneˈfisju] *m* benefit.

benéfico, -ca [beˈnɛfiku, -ka] *adj* beneficial.

benevolência [benevoˈlẽsja] *f* benevolence.

bengala [bẽŋˈɡala] *f* walking stick.

bengaleiro [bẽŋɡaˈlejru] *m (em casa de espetáculos)* cloakroom; *(cabide)* coat stand.

benigno, -gna [beˈnignu, -gna] *adj* benign.

bens → bem.

benzer [bẽˈze(x)] *vt* to bless.
❑ **benzer-se** *vp* to cross o.s.

berbequim [berbeˈkĩ] *(pl* **-ns** [-ʃ]) *m (Port)* drill.

berbigão [bexbiˈɡãw] *(pl* **-ões** [-õjʃ]) *m* cockle.

berço ['bexsu] *m* cot *(Brit)*, crib *(Am)*.

berlinde [ber'lindɛ] *m (Port)* marble.

beringela [beri'ʒɛla] *f (Port)* = **berinjela**.

berinjela [beri'ʒɛla] *f (Br)* aubergine *(Brit)*, eggplant *(Am)*.

berloque [bex'lɔki] *m* pendant.

bermuda [bex'muda] *f (Br)* Bermuda shorts.

besouro [be'zoru] *m* beetle.

besta ['bɛʃta] *f (cavalgadura)* mount.

besteira [beʃ'tejra] *f (Br) (fam) (asneira)* nonsense; *(insignificância)* trifle.

bestial [beʃ'tjal] *(pl* -ais [-ajʃ]*) adj (Port: fam)* brilliant.

besugo [be'zugu] *m* sea bream.

besuntar [bezũn'ta(x)] *vt* to grease.

betão [be'tãw] *m (Port)* concrete.

beterraba [bete'xaba] *f* beetroot.

betoneira [beto'nejra] *f* cement mixer.

bétula ['bɛtula] *f* birch.

bexiga [be'ʃiga] *f* bladder; **~s doidas** *(fam: varicela)* chickenpox *(sg)*.

bezerro [be'zexu] *m* calf.

BI *m (Port: abrev de Bilhete de Identidade)* ID card.

biberão [bibe'rãw] *(pl* -ões [-õjʃ]*) m (Port)* (baby's) bottle.

Bíblia ['biblia] *f* Bible.

biblioteca [biblio'tɛka] *f* library; **~ itinerante** mobile library.

bibliotecário, -ria [bibljote'karju, -rja] *m, f* librarian.

bica ['bika] *f (de água)* tap; *(Port: café)* espresso; **suar em ~(s)** to drip with sweat.

bicar [bi'ka(x)] *vt & vi* to peck.

bicha ['biʃa] *f (lombriga)* worm; *(Br: pej: homossexual)* queer; *(Port: fila)* queue.

bicho ['biʃu] *m (animal)* animal; *(inseto)* bug.

bicho-da-seda [ˌbiʃuda'seda] *(pl* **bichos-da-seda** [ˌbiʃuʃda'seda]*) m* silkworm.

bicicleta [besi'klɛta] *f* bicycle.

bico ['biku] *m (de sapato)* toe; *(de ave)* beak; *(de fogão)* burner; *(de seio)* nipple; *(Br: fam: trabalho)* odd job.

bidé [bi'dɛ] *m (Port)* = **bidê**.

bidê [bi'de] *m (Br)* bidet.

bife ['bifi] *m* steak.

bifurcação [bifuxka'sãw] *(pl* -ões [-õjʃ]*) f* fork.

bigode [bi'gɔdʒi] *m* moustache.

bijutaria [biʒuta'ria] *f (Port)* = **bijuteria**.

bijuteria [biʒute'ria] *f (Br)* costume jewellery.

bilha ['biʎa] *f (de água)* (earthenware) pot; *(de gás)* gas bottle.

bilhão [bi'ʎãw] *(pl* -ões [-õjʃ]*) num (Br: mil milhões)* thousand million *(Brit)*, billion *(Am)*; *(Port)* = **bilião**.

bilhar [bi'ʎa(x)] *(pl* -res [-riʃ]*) m (jogo)* billiards *(sg)*; *(mesa)* billiard table; **jogar ~** to play billiards.

bilhete [bi'ʎetʃi] *m* ticket; **~ de** *(Port)* single (ticket) *(Brit)*, one-way ticket *(Am)*; **~ de ida e volta** return (ticket) *(Brit)*, round-trip ticket *(Am)*; **~ de identidade** *(Port)* identity card; **~ simples** *(em metrô)* single (ticket).

bilheteira [biʎe'tejra] *f (Port)* = **bilheteria**.

bilheteria [biʎete'ria] *f (Br) (de teatro, cinema)* box office.

bilhões → **bilhão**.

bilião [bi'ljãw] *(pl* -ões [-õjʃ]*) num (Port: milhão de milhões)* billion *(Brit)*, trillion *(Am)*; *(Br)* = **bilhão**.

bilingue [bi'lĩŋgɛ] *adj (Port)* = **bilíngüe**.

bilíngüe [bi'lĩŋgwi] *adj (Br)* bilingual.

biliões → **bilião**.

bílis ['biliʃ] *f* bile.

bingo ['bĩŋgu] *m* bingo.

binóculo [bi'nɔkulu] *m* binoculars *(pl)*.

biografia [bjogra'fia] *f* biography.

biologia [bjolo'ʒia] *f* biology.

biólogo, -ga ['bjɔlogu, -ga] *m, f* biologist.

biombo ['bjõmbu] *m* screen.

biopsia [bjop'sia] *f* biopsy.

biqueira [bi'kejra] *f (de sapato)* toe.

biquíni [bi'kini] *m* bikini.

birra ['bixa] *f* tantrum; **fazer ~** to throw a tantrum.

bis [biʃ] *interj* encore!

bisavô, -vó [biza'vo, -'vɔ] *m, f* great-grandfather *(f* greatgrandmother).

bisavós [biza'vɔʃ] *mpl* great-grandparents.

biscoito [biʃ'kojtu] *m* biscuit *(Brit)*, cookie *(Am)*.

bisnaga [biʒ'naga] *f (tubo)* tube; *(Br: de pão)* French stick.

bisneto, -ta [biʒ'nɛtu, -ta] m, f great-grandson (f great-granddaughter).

bispo ['biʃpu] m bishop.

bissexto [bi'sejʃtu] adj m → ano.

bisteca [biʃ'tɛka] f (Br) steak.

bisturi [biʃtu'ri] m scalpel.

bit ['bitʃi] m bit.

bizarro, -a [bi'zaxu, -a] adj bizarre.

blasfemar [blaʃfe'ma(x)] vi to blaspheme.

blasfémia [blaʃ'fɛmja] f (Port) = **blasfêmia**.

blasfêmia [blaʃ'femja] f (Br) blasphemy.

blazer ['blejzɛ(x)] (pl -res [-riʃ]) m blazer.

bloco ['blɔku] m (de folhas) writing pad; (de apontamentos, notas) notepad; (de apartamentos, concreto) block.

bloquear [blo'kja(x)] vt to block.

blusa ['bluza] f blouse.

blusão [blu'zãw] (pl -ões [-õjʃ]) m jacket.

boa¹ → **bom**.

boa² ['boa] f boa constrictor.

boas-festas [ˌboaʒ'fɛʃtaʃ] fpl: **dar as ~ a alguém** to wish sb a Merry Christmas.

boas-vindas [ˌboaʒ'vĩdaʃ] fpl: **dar as ~ a alguém** to welcome sb.

boate ['bwatʃi] f (Br) nightclub.

boato ['bwatu] m rumour.

bobagem [bo'baʒẽ] (pl -ns [-ʃ]) f (Br) nonsense (sg).

bobina [bo'bina] f (de circuito elétrico) coil; (de fio, corda) reel.

bobo, -ba ['bobu, -ba] adj silly.

boca ['boka] f mouth; (de rua, túnel) entrance; (de fogão) ring; (Port: fam: dito provocatório) gibe.

bocado [bo'kadu] m (de pão, bolo, queijo) piece.

bocal [bo'kaw] (pl -ais [-ajʃ]) m (de castiçal) mouth; (de instrumento musical) mouthpiece.

bocejar [bose'ʒa(x)] vi to yawn.

bochecha [bu'ʃeʃa] f cheek.

bochechar [boʃe'ʃa(x)] vi to gargle.

boda ['boda] f wedding; **~s de ouro/prata** golden/silver wedding (sg).

bode ['bɔdʒi] m billy goat; **~ expiatório** scapegoat.

bofetada [bofe'tada] f slap.

boi ['boj] m ox.

bóia ['bɔja] f float; (de barco) life buoy.

boiada [bo'jada] f (Br) herd of cattle.

boiar [bo'ja(x)] vi to float.

boina ['bɔjna] f flat cap.

bola ['bɔla] f ball; (fam: cabeça) head; **dar ~ para** (Br: fam: flertar com) to flirt with; **não ser certo da ~** (Br: fam) to be away with the fairies.

bolacha [bo'laʃa] f (Port) biscuit; **~ de água e sal** water biscuit.

bolbo ['bowbu] m bulb.

boleia [bo'leja] f lift (Brit), ride (Am); **apanhar ~** to hitch a lift; **dar ~ a alguém** to give sb a lift; **pedir ~** (Port) to hitchhike.

boletim [bole'tĩ] (pl -ns [-ʃ]) m (de notícias) bulletin; (revista) newsletter; (EDUC) report; **~ meteorológico** weather forecast.

bolha ['boʎa] f (em pele) blister; (em líquido) bubble.

Bolívia [bo'livja] f: **a ~** Bolivia.

bolo ['bolu] m cake; **~ inglês** fruit cake; **dar o ~ em alguém** to stand sb up.

bolor [bo'lo(x)] m mould.

bolota [bo'lɔta] f acorn.

bolsa ['bowsa] f (mala) bag; (para dinheiro) purse; **~ de estudos** student grant; **~ de valores** stock exchange.

bolso ['bowsu] m pocket.

bom, boa ['bõ, 'boa] (mpl **bons** ['bõʃ], fpl **boas** ['boaʃ]) adj good; (bondoso) kind, nice; (são) well; (adequado) suitable; **tudo ~?** (Br: fam) how's it going?, how are you doing?

bomba ['bõmba] f (de ar, água) pump; (explosivo) bomb; **~ atômica** atomic bomb; **~ de chocolate** ≈ chocolate éclair; **~ de gasolina** petrol station (Brit), filling station (Am); **levar ~** (fam) to fail.

bombardear [bõmbax'dʒja(x)] vt to bomb.

bombazina [bõmba'zina] f (Port) corduroy.

bombeiro [bõm'bejru] m firefighter; (Br: encanador) plumber; **os ~s** (voluntários) fire brigade (Brit), fire department (Am).

bombo ['bõmbu] m bass drum.

bombom [bõm'bõ] (pl -ns [-ʃ]) m chocolate.

bondade [bõn'dadʒi] f goodness.

bonde ['bõndʒi] m (Br) tram (Brit), streetcar (Am); **ir de ~** to take the tram.

bondoso, -osa [bõn'dozu, -ɔza] *adj* kind.

boné [bɔ'nɛ] *m* cap.

boneca [bo'nɛka] *f* doll; **~ de trapos** rag doll.

boneco [bo'nɛku] *m (brinquedo)* doll; *(desenho)* matchstick figure; **~ de neve** snowman.

bonito, -ta [bo'nitu, -ta] *adj* pretty; *(homem)* good-looking; *(momento)* wonderful; *(gesto, atitude, sentimento)* kind; *(dia)* nice.

bons → bom.

bónus ['bɔnuʃ] *m inv (Port)* = **bônus**.

bônus ['bonuʃ] *m inv (Br) (de empresa)* bonus; *(de loja)* voucher.

borboleta [boxbo'leta] *f* butterfly.

borbulha [box'buʎa] *f (em pele)* pimple; *(de suco, água, champanhe)* bubble.

borbulhar [boxbu'ʎa(x)] *vi (líquido)* to bubble.

borda ['bɔxda] *f (de estrada, rio)* side; **à ~ d'água** at the water's edge.

bordado, -da [box'dadu, -da] *adj* embroidered ◆ *m* embroidery.

bordar [box'da(x)] *vt & vi* to embroider.

bordel [box'dɛw] *(pl -éis* [-ɛjʃ]*)* *m* brothel.

bordo ['boxdu] *m (de navio, passeio)* side; **a ~** on board.

borra ['boxa] *f (de café)* grounds *(pl)*; *(de vinho)* dregs *(pl)*.

borracha [bo'xaʃa] *f* rubber *(Brit)*, eraser *(Am)*; *(material)* rubber.

borracheiro [boxa'ʃejru] *m (Br) person who repairs and sells tyres at a garage*.

borrão [bo'xãw] *(pl -ões* [-õjʃ]*)* *m* blot.

borrasca [bo'xaʃka] *f* storm.

borrego [bo'xegu] *m (Port)* lamb.

borrifar [boxi'fa(x)] *vt*: **~ algo com algo** to sprinkle sthg with sthg.

borrões → borrão.

bosque ['bɔʃki] *m* wood.

bossa ['bɔsa] *f* hump; **~ nova** Brazilian musical movement from the 1960s.

bota ['bɔta] *f* boot.

botânica [bo'tanika] *f* botany, **→ botânico**.

botânico, -ca [bo'taniku, -ka] *m, f* botanist ◆ *adj m* → **jardim**.

botão [bo'tãw] *(pl -ões* [-õjʃ]*)* *m (de vestuário, aparelho)* button; *(de flor)* bud; **~ de punho** cuff link.

botar [bo'ta(x)] *vt* to put; *(vestir,*

calçar) to put on; *(suj: ave)* to lay; *(defeito)* to find; **~ algo em dia** to update sthg; **~ algo fora** to throw sthg away.

bote ['bɔtʃi] *m* boat; **~ salva-vidas** lifeboat.

botequim [botʃi'kĩ] *(pl -ns* [-ʃ]*)* *m (Br)* cafe.

botija [bo'tiʒa] *f (Port: de gás)* bottle.

botijão [botʃi'ʒãw] *(pl -ões* [-õjʃ]*)* *m (Br: de gás)* bottle.

botões → botão.

boutique [bu'tike] *f (Port)* = **butique**.

boxe ['bɔksi] *m* boxing.

braçadeira [brasa'dejra] *f (para natação)* armband; *(de cano, mangueira)* bracket; *(de cortina)* tie-back.

bracelete [brasɛ'letʃi] *m ou f* bracelet.

braço ['brasu] *m* arm; *(de viola, violino, violoncelo)* neck; *(de rio)* branch; *(de mar)* inlet; **não dar o ~ torcer** not to give in; **meter o ~ em alguém** *(Br: fam)* to hit sb; **de ~ dado** arm in arm.

bradar [bra'da(x)] *vt* to cry out ◆ *vi* to clamour.

braguilha [bra'giʎa] *f* flies *(pl)*.

branco, -ca ['brãŋku, -ka] *adj & m* white ◆ *m, f (pessoa)* white man *(f* white woman); **em ~** *(folha, cheque)* blank.

brandir [brãn'dʒi(x)] *vt* to brandish.

brando, -da ['brãndu, -da] *adj* gentle; **cozinhar em fogo ~** to simmer.

brasa ['braza] *f* ember.

brasão [bra'zãw] *(pl -ões* [-õjʃ]*)* *m* coat of arms.

Brasil [bra'ziw] *m*: **o ~** Brazil.

brasileiro, -ra [brazi'lejru, -ra] *adj & m, f* Brazilian.

Brasília [bra'zilja] *s* Brasília.

brasões → brasão.

bravio, -via [bra'viu, -via] *adj* wild.

bravo, -va ['bravu, -va] *adj (valente)* brave; *(selvagem)* wild; *(tempestuoso)* rough; *(Br: fig: furioso)* angry ◆ *interj* bravo!

brejo ['brɛʒu] *m (Br)* swamp.

breve ['brɛvi] *adj* short; **em ~** soon; **até ~!** see you soon!

brevemente [brɛvi'mẽntʃi] *adv* shortly.

briga ['briga] *f* fight.

brigada [bri'gada] *f (de trânsito)* patrol; *(de trabalhadores)* band.

brilhante [bri'ʎãntʃi] *adj (cabelo, metal)* shiny; *(olhos)* bright; *(fig: exce-*

lente) brilliant ◆ *m* diamond.
brilhar [bri'ʎa(x)] *vi* to shine.
brilho ['briʎu] *m (de cabelo, metal)* shine; *(de olhos, sol)* brightness.
brincadeira [brĩŋka'dejra] *f (jogo)* game; *(gracejo)* joke.
brincalhão, -lhona [brĩŋka'ʎãw, -'ʎona] *(mpl -ões* [-õjʃ], *fpl -s* [-ʃ]) *adj* playful ◆ *m, f* joker.
brincar [brĩŋ'ka(x)] *vi (criança)* to play; *(gracejar)* to joke.
brinco ['brĩŋku] *m* earring.
brincos-de-princesa [ˌbrĩŋkuʒ-dʒiprĩˈseza] *mpl* fuchsia *(sg)*.
brindar [brĩn'da(x)] *vi (fazer um brinde)* to drink a toast ◆ *vt (presentear);* ~ **alguém com algo** to give sthg as a present to sb; ~ **à saúde de alguém** to drink to sb.
brinde ['brĩndʒi] *m (presente)* present; **fazer um** ~ to propose a toast.
brinquedo [brĩŋ'kedu] *m* toy.
brisa ['briza] *f* breeze.
britânico, -ca [bri'taniku, -ka] *adj* British ◆ *m, f* British person; **os** ~**s** the British.
broca ['brɔka] *f* drill.
broche ['brɔʃi] *m* brooch.
brochura [bro'ʃura] *f* brochure.
brócolis ['brɔkoliʃ] *mpl (Br)* broccoli *(sg)*.
brócolos ['brɔkoluʃ] *mpl (Port)* = **brócolis**.
bronca ['brõŋka] *f (fam) (confusão)* fuss; *(Br: repreensão)* telling-off.
bronquite [brõŋ'kitʃi] *f* bronchitis.
bronze ['brõzi] *m* bronze.
bronzeado, -da [brõ'zeadu, -da] *adj* tanned ◆ *m* (sun)tan.
bronzeador [brõzea'do(x)] *(pl -res* [-riʃ]) *m* suntan cream ou lotion.
bronzear-se [brõ'zjaxsi] *vp* to get a (sun)tan.
brotar [bro'ta(x)] *vi (água)* to well up; *(flor, planta)* to sprout ◆ *vt (líquido)* to spurt.
bruços ['brusuʃ] *mpl (estilo de natação)* breaststroke *(sg)*; **de** ~ *(posição)* face down.

bruma ['bruma] *f* mist.
brusco, -ca ['bruʃku, -ka] *adj (pessoa)* brusque; *(gesto, movimento)* sudden.
brushing ['braʃĩŋ] *m* blow-dry.
brutal [bru'taw] *(pl -ais* [-ajʃ]) *adj* brutal.
bruto, -ta ['brutu, -ta] *adj* rough; *(peso)* gross; **à bruta** heavy-handedly; **em** ~ raw.
bruxa ['bruʃa] *f* witch.
bucho ['buʃu] *m (fam: ventre)* gut.
búfalo ['bufalu] *m* buffalo.
bufê [bu'fe] *m (Br) (de sala de jantar)* sideboard; *(de festas)* buffet.
bufete [bu'fetɛ] *m (Port)* = **bufê**.
bugigangas [buʒi'gãŋgaʃ] *fpl* knick-knacks.
bula ['bula] *f (de remédio)* instruction leaflet.
bule ['buli] *m (para chá)* teapot; *(para café)* coffee pot.
Bulgária [buw'garja] *f:* **a** ~ Bulgaria.
búlgaro, -ra ['buwgaru, -ra] *adj &* *m, f* Bulgarian ◆ *m (língua)* Bulgarian.
bulldozer [buw'dɔzɛ(x)] *(pl -res* [-riʃ]) *m* bulldozer.
bunda ['bũnda] *f (Br: fam)* bottom.
buraco [bu'raku] *m* hole.
burla ['burla] *f* fraud.
burlão, -lona [bur'lãw, -lona] *(mpl -ões* [-õjʃ], *fpl -s* [-ʃ]) *m, f* fraudster.
burocracia [burokra'sia] *f* bureaucracy.
burro, -a ['buxu, -a] *m, f* donkey ◆ *adj (estúpido)* stupid.
busca ['buʃka] *f* search; **em** ~ **de** in search of.
buscar [buʃ'ka(x)] *vt* to search for, to look for; **ir** ~ to pick up.
bússola ['busola] *f* compass.
bustiê [buʃ'tʃie] *m (Br)* boob tube.
busto ['buʃtu] *m* bust.
butique [bu'tʃiki] *f (Br)* boutique.
buzina [bu'zina] *f* horn.
buzinar [buzi'na(x)] *vi* to sound the horn.
búzio ['buzju] *m* conch.
B.V. *abrev* = **Bombeiros Voluntários**.

C

c/ (abrev de conta de banco) a/c.

cá ['ka] adv here; **venha ~, por favor** come here, please.

C.ª (abrev de Companhia) Co.

cabana [ka'bana] f hut.

cabeça [ka'besa] f head; (de alho) bulb; **por ~** per head; **à ~** (à frente) at the front; **de ~ para baixo** upside down; **fazer a ~ de alguém** to talk sb round; **não ter pé nem ~** to make no sense; **perder a ~** to lose one's head.

cabeçada [kabe'sada] f (pancada com a cabeça) head butt; (em futebol) header.

cabeçalho [kabe'saʎu] m masthead.

cabeceira [kabe'sejra] f head.

cabeçudo, -da [kabe'sudu, -da] adj (teimoso) stubborn.

cabedal [kabe'daw] (pl -ais [-ajʃ]) m leather.

cabeleira [kabe'lejra] f (verdadeira) head of hair; (postiça) wig.

cabeleireiro, -ra [kabelej'rejru, -ra] m, f (profissão) hairdresser ◆ m (local) hairdresser's (salon).

cabelo [ka'belu] m hair; **ir cortar o ~** to get one's hair cut.

caber [ka'be(x)] vi to fit in.

❏ **caber a** v + prep: **~ a alguém fazer algo** to be up to sb to do sthg.

cabide [ka'bidʒi] m (de chapéu) hat stand; (de roupa) (clothes) hanger.

cabine [ka'bini] f (telefônica) telephone box; (de navio, avião) cabin; (de trem) compartment.

cabisbaixo, -xa [kabiʒ'bajʃu, -ʃa] adj (fig: triste) downcast.

cabo ['kabu] m cable; (de utensílio) handle; (de terra) cape; (de exército) corporal; **até o ~** to the end; **ao ~ de** after; **de ~ a rabo** from beginning to end; **dar ~ de algo** (fam) to wreck sthg.

Cabo-Verde [ˌkabu'vexdʒi] s Cape Verde.

cabo-verdiano, -na [ˌkabuvex-'dʒjanu. -na] adj relating to Cape Verde ◆ m, f native/inhabitant of Cape Verde.

cabra ['kabra] f goat.

cabrito [ka'britu] m kid (goat); **~ assado** kid seasoned with garlic, bay leaves, "piripiri" and herbs, baked and served with potatoes.

caça ['kasa] f (ação) hunting; (animal caçado) game ◆ m (avião) fighter plane; **~ submarina** underwater fishing.

caçador, -ra [kasa'do(x), -ra] (mpl -res [-riʃ], fpl -s [-ʃ]) m, f hunter.

cação [ka'sãw] m dogfish.

caçar [ka'sa(x)] vt to hunt.

caçarola [kasa'rɔla] f (de barro) earthenware pot; (panela) saucepan.

cacau [ka'kaw] m cocoa.

cacetada [kase'tada] f blow.

cacete [ka'setʃi] m (pau) stick; **ela é chata para ~** she's a real bore!

cachaça [ka'ʃasa] f white rum.

caché [ka'ʃɛ] m (Port) = cachê.

cachê [ka'ʃe] m (Br) fee.

cachecol [kaʃe'kɔw] (pl -óis [-ɔjʃ]) m scarf.

cachimbo [ka'ʃĩmbu] m pipe.

cacho ['kaʃu] m (de uvas, flores) bunch; (de cabelo) lock.

cachorro [ka'ʃoxu] m (Port: cão pequeno) puppy; (Br: qualquer cão) dog; **~ (quente)** hot dog.

cacifo [ka'sifu] m (cofre) safe; (armário) locker.

cacto ['katu] m cactus.

cada ['kada] adj (um) each; (todos) every; **~ duas semanas** every two weeks; **~ qual** each one; **~ um/uma** each (one); **um/uma de ~ vez** one at a time; **~ vez mais** more and more; **~**

vez que every time; **aqui é ~ um por si** everyone looks out for themselves here.

cadarço [ka'daxsu] *m* (*Br*) shoelace.

cadastro [ka'daʃtru] *m* criminal record.

cadáver [ka'davɛ(x)] (*pl* -res [-riʃ]) *m* corpse.

cadê [ka'de] *adv* (*Br: fam*): ~ ...? where's ...?, where are ...? (*pl*).

cadeado [ka'dʒjadu] *m* padlock.

cadeia [ka'deja] *f* (*fila*) chain; (*prisão*) prison.

cadeira [ka'dejra] *f* (*assento*) chair; (*disciplina*) subject; ~ **de rodas** wheelchair.

cadela [ka'dɛla] *f* bitch.

cadência [ka'dẽsja] *f* rhythm.

caderno [ka'dɛrnu] *m* notebook.

caducar [kadu'ka(x)] *vi* to expire.

caduco, -ca [ka'duku, -ka] *adj* (*pessoa*) senile.

cães → **cão**.

café [ka'fɛ] *m* coffee; (*local*) cafe; ~ **com leite** white coffee; ~ **da manhã** (*Br*) breakfast; ~ **moído/solúvel** ground/instant coffee.

cafeína [kafe'ina] *f* caffeine.

cafeteira [kafe'tejra] *f* coffee pot.

cafezinho [kafe'ziɲu] *m* (*Br*) espresso.

cágado ['kagadu] *m* terrapin.

caiar [ka'ja(x)] *vt* to whitewash.

caibo ['kajbu] → **caber**.

cãibra ['kãjmbra] *f* cramp.

caipira [kaj'pira] *adj* (*Br*) provincial ♦ *mf* (*Br*) yokel.

caipirinha [kajpi'riɲa] *f* cocktail made of "cachaça", lime juice, sugar and crushed ice.

cair [ka'i(x)] *vi* to fall; (*luz*) to shine; ~ **bem/mal** (*comida*) to go down well/badly; ~ **na realidade** OU **em si** to come to one's senses; **nessa não caio eu!** I won't fall for that!

cais [kajʃ] *m inv* (*de rio, mar*) harbour; ~ **de embarque** quay.

caixa ['kajʃa] *f* box; (*seção de banco, loja*) counter; (*em supermercado*) checkout; (*banco*) savings bank; (*segurança social*) social security; (*de arma*) chamber ♦ *mf* (*profissão*) cashier; ~ **alta/baixa** upper/lower case; ~ **automático** cashpoint; ~ **de mudanças** (*Br*) gearbox; ~ **craniana**

cranium; ~ **de crédito** bank; ~ **do correio** (*em Portugal*) letterbox; (*no Brasil*) postbox; ~ **de fósforos** matchbox; ~ **de pagamento** (*em estacionamento*) cashier's desk; ~ **registadora** cash register; ~ **toráxica** thorax; ~ **de velocidades** (*Port*) gearbox.

caixão [kaj'ʃãw] (*pl* -ões [-õjʃ]) *m* coffin (*Brit*), casket (*Am*).

caixeiro [kaj'ʃejru] *m*: ~ **viajante** travelling salesman.

caixilho [kaj'ʃiʎu] *m* frame.

caixões → **caixão**.

caixote [kaj'ʃɔtʃi] *m* box; ~ **do lixo** (*Port*) bin.

caju [ka'ʒu] *m* cashew nut.

cal ['kaw] *f* lime.

calado, -da [ka'ladu, -da] *adj* quiet; **fique ~!** shut up!, be quiet!

calafrio [kala'friu] *m* shiver.

calamidade [kalami'dadʒi] *f* calamity.

calão [ka'lãw] *m* (*Port*) slang.

calar-se [ka'laxsi] *vp* to fall silent; **cale-se!** shut up!

calça ['kawsa] *f* (*Br*) trousers (*pl*).

calçada [kaw'sada] *f* pavement; (*Port: rua*) cobbled street.

calçadeira [kawsa'dejra] *f* shoehorn.

calçado, -da [kaw'sadu, -da] *adj* (*rua*) cobbled ♦ *m* footwear.

calcanhar [kawka'ɲa(x)] (*pl* -res [-riʃ]) *m* heel.

calção [kaw'sãw] (*pl* -ões [-õjʃ]) *m* (*Br*) shorts (*pl*); ~ **de banho** swimming trunks (*pl*).

calcar [kaw'ka(x)] *vt* (*pisar*) to stand on; (*comprimir*) to press down.

calçar [kaw'sa(x)] *vt* (*sapatos, meias, luvas*) to put on; (*rua, passeio*) to pave; **que número você calça?** what size (shoe) do you take?; **calço 37** I'm a (size) 37.

calcário [kaw'karju] *m* limestone.

calças ['kalsaʃ] *fpl* (*Port*) = **calça**.

calcinha [kaw'siɲa] *f* (*Br*) knickers (*pl*).

cálcio ['kawsju] *m* calcium.

calço ['kawsu] *m* wedge; ~ **de freio** brake pad.

calções [kal'sõiʃ] *mpl* (*Port*) = **calção**.

calculadora [kawkula'dora] *f* calculator; ~ **de bolso** pocket calculator.

calcular [kawku'la(x)] *vt (número, valor)* to calculate; *(conjecturar)* to reckon.

cálculo ['kawkulu] *m (aritmético, algébrico)* calculation; *(disciplina)* calculus; **pelos meus ~s estaremos lá em uma hora** I reckon we'll be there in an hour.

calda ['kawda] *f* syrup.

caldeira [kaw'dejra] *f* boiler.

caldeirada [kawdej'rada] *f (CULIN)* fish stew cooked in a tomato and herb sauce with potatoes.

caldo ['kawdu] *m (sopa)* broth; *(de carne, sopa, vegetais)* stock; *(Br: suco de fruto, planta)* juice; **~ de cana** *(Br)* thick juice made from sugarcane pulp; **~ verde** spring green soup served with "chouriço", a drop of olive oil and maize bread.

calendário [kalēn'darju] *m* calendar.

calhamaço [kaʎa'masu] *m (fam: livro)* tome.

calhar [ka'ʎa(x)] *vi (vir a propósito)*: **calhou eu estar lá** I happened to be there; **ela calhou de telefonar** she happened to ring; **~ bem/mal** to be convenient/inconvenient; **se ~** *(Port)* perhaps, maybe; **vir a ~** to come at just the right time.

calhau [ka'ʎaw] *m* stone.

calibragem [kali'braʒē] *(pl* **-ns** [-ʃ]) *f*: **~ (dos pneus)** tyre pressure.

calibre [ka'libri] *m* calibre.

cálice ['kalisi] *m (copo)* port OU liqueur glass; *(sagrado)* chalice.

calista [ka'liʃta] *mf* chiropodist *(Brit)*, podiatrist *(Am)*.

calma ['kawma] *f* calm ◆ *interj* take it easy!, calm down!; **ter ~** to keep calm.

calmante [kaw'mãntʃi] *m* tranquillizer ◆ *adj* soothing.

calmo, -ma ['kawmu, -ma] *adj* calm; *(lugar)* quiet.

calo ['kalu] *m* callus; *(de pé)* corn.

caloiro, -ra [ka'lojru, -ra] *m, f* fresher *(Brit)*, freshman *(Am)*.

calor [ka'lo(x)] *m* heat; **estar com ~** to be hot.

caloria [kalo'ria] *f* calorie.

calorífero, -ra [kalo'riferu, -ra] *adj* calorific ◆ *m* heater.

calúnia [ka'lunja] *f* slander.

calvo, -va ['kawvu, -va] *adj* bald.

cama ['kama] *f* bed; **~ de campismo** camp bed; **~ de casal** double bed; **~**

de solteiro single bed; **estar de ~** to be bedridden.

camada [ka'mada] *f* layer; *(de tinta, verniz)* coat; **a ~ do ozônio** the ozone layer.

camaleão [kama'ljãw] *(pl* **-ões** [-õjʃ]) *m* chameleon.

câmara ['kamara] *f*: **~ fotográfica** camera; **~ municipal** *(elementos)* town council; *(Port: edifício)* town hall *(Brit)*, city hall *(Am)*; **~ de vídeo** camcorder; **em ~ lenta** in slow motion.

camarada [kama'rada] *mf (de partido)* comrade; *(fam: forma de tratamento)* mate, pal ◆ *adj (preço)* good.

câmara-de-ar [kamara'dʒia(x)] *(pl* **câmaras-de-ar** [kamaraʒ'dʒia(x)]) *f* inner tube.

camarão [kama'rãw] *(pl* **-ões** [-õjʃ]) *m* shrimp.

camarata [kama'rata] *f* dormitory.

camarim [kama'rĩ] *(pl* **-ns** [-ʃ]) *m* dressing room.

camarões → camarão.

camarote [kama'rɔtʃi] *m (de navio)* cabin; *(de teatro)* box.

cambalear [kãmba'lja(x)] *vi* to stagger.

cambalhota [kãmba'ʎɔta] *f* somersault; *(trambolhão)* tumble.

câmbio ['kãmbju] *m (troca de valores)* exchange; *(preço de transação)* exchange rate; *(Br: de veículo)* gear lever.

cambraia [kãm'braja] *f* cambric.

camelo [ka'melu] *m* camel.

camelô [kame'lo] *m (Br)* street pedlar.

camião [ka'mjãw] *(pl* **-ões** [-õjʃ]) *m (Port)* = **caminhão.**

caminhada [kamiɲ'nada] *f* walk.

caminhão [kamĩ'ɲãw] *(pl* **-ões** [-õjʃ]) *m (Br)* lorry *(Brit)*, truck *(Am)*.

caminhar [kamĩ'ɲa(x)] *vi* to walk.

caminho [ka'miɲu] *m* way; *(via)* path; **estou a ~** I'm on my way; **a ~ de** on the way to; **pelo ~** on the way; **cortar ~** to take a short cut.

caminho-de-ferro [ka,miɲude'fɛxu] *(pl* **caminhos-de-ferro** [ka,miɲuʒde-'fɛxu]) *m (Port)* railway *(Brit)*, railroad *(Am)*.

caminhões → caminhão.

caminhoneiro, -ra [kamiɲo'nejru, -ra] *m, f (Br)* lorry driver *(Brit)*, truck driver *(Am)*.

caneta

caminhonete [kamjoˈnɛta] f (Br) (para passageiros) minibus; (para mercadorias) van.

camiões → camião.

camioneta [kamjuˈnɛta] f (Port) = caminhonete.

camionista [kamjuˈniʃta] mf (Port) = caminhoneiro.

camisa [kaˈmiza] f shirt.

camisa-de-forças [ka,mizadʒiˈfoxsaʃ] (pl camisas-de-forças [ka,mizadʒiˈfoxsaʃ]) f straitjacket.

camiseta [kamiˈzɛta] f (Br) T-shirt.

camisinha [kamiˈziɲa] f (Br: fam: preservativo) condom.

camisola [kamiˈzɔla] f (Port: de lã, algodão) sweater; (Br: de dormir) nightdress; ~ de gola alta (Port) polo neck (Brit), turtleneck (Am); ~ interior (Port) vest; ~ de manga curta (Port) T-shirt.

camomila [kamoˈmila] f camomile.

campainha [kãmpaˈiɲa] f bell.

campanário [kãmpaˈnarju] m belfry.

campanha [kãmˈpaɲa] f campaign; ~ eleitoral election campaign; ~ de verão/inverno summer/winter season.

campeão, -peã [kãmˈpjãw, -pjã] (mpl -ões [-õjʃ], fpl -s [-ʃ]) m, f champion.

campeonato [kãmpjoˈnatu] m championship.

campestre [kãmˈpɛʃtri] adj country (antes de s).

camping [kãmˈpĩŋ] m (Br) camping; (local) campsite.

campismo [kãmˈpiʒmu] m camping.

campista [kãmˈpiʃta] mf camper.

campo [ˈkãmpu] m country(side); (de esporte) pitch; (terreno) field; ~ de futebol football pitch; ~ de golfe golf course; ~ de jogos playing field; ~ de squash/ténis (Port) squash/tennis court; ~ de tiro firing range.

camponês, -esa [ˈkãmpoˈneʃ, -eza] (mpl -eses [-eziʃ], fpl -s [-ʃ]) m, f peasant.

camuflagem [kamuˈflaʒẽ] (pl -ns [-ʃ]) f camouflage.

camuflar [kamuˈfla(x)] vt to camouflage.

camurça [kaˈmuxsa] f suede.

cana [ˈkana] f (planta) bamboo; (material) cane; (bengala) walking stick; (Br: cana-de-açúcar) sugarcane; ir em ~ (Br: fam) to be arrested; ~ de pesca (Port) fishing rod.

Canadá [kanaˈda] m: o ~ Canada.

cana-de-açúcar [,kanadʒiaˈsuka(x)] (pl canas-de-açúcar [,kanaʒdʒiaˈsuka(x)]) f sugarcane.

canadense [kanaˈdẽsi] adj & mf (Br) Canadian.

canadiano, -na [kanaˈdjanu, -na] adj & m, f (Port) = canadense.

canal [kaˈnaw] (pl -ais [-ajʃ]) m channel; (de navegação) canal; o Canal da Mancha the (English) Channel.

canalha [kaˈnaʎa] f (Port: fam: crianças) kids (pl) ◆ mf (patife) good-for-nothing.

canalização [kanalizaˈsãw] (pl -ões [-õjʃ]) f (de água) plumbing; (de gás) piping.

canalizador, -ra [kanalizaˈdor, -ra] (mpl -res [-reʃ], fpl -s [-ʃ]) m, f (Port) plumber.

canalizar [kanaliˈza(x)] vt (água, gás) to lay pipes for; (fig: esforços, fundos) to channel.

canapé [kanaˈpɛ] m sofa.

canapê [kanaˈpe] m (Br) canapé.

canário [kaˈnarju] m canary.

canastra [kaˈnaʃtra] f large basket.

canção [kãˈsãw] (pl -ões [-õjʃ]) f song.

cancela [kãˈsɛla] f (de casa, jardim) gate; (de passagem de nível) barrier.

cancelamento [kãsɛlaˈmẽtu] m cancellation.

cancelar [kãsɛˈla(x)] vt to cancel.

câncer [ˈkãsɛ(x)] (pl -res [-riʃ]) m (Br) cancer.

⊃ Câncer m (Br) Cancer.

cancerígeno, -na [kãsɛˈriʒɛnu, -na] adj carcinogenic.

canções → canção.

cancro [ˈkãŋkru] m (Port) = câncer.

candeeiro [kãnˈdjejru] m (Br: a petróleo) oil lamp; (Port: a eletricidade) lamp.

candelabro [kãndeˈlabru] m (lustre) chandelier; (castiçal) candelabra.

candidato, -ta [kãndʒiˈdatu, -ta] m, f: ~ (a) candidate (for).

candomblé [kãndõmˈblɛ] m Afro-Brazilian religion centred around musical rituals and dance.

caneca [kaˈnɛka] f mug; (medida de cerveja) half-litre measure of beer.

canela [kaˈnɛla] f (condimento) cinnamon; (de perna) shin; esticar a ~ (fig: morrer) to kick the bucket.

caneta [kaˈnɛta] f pen; ~ de feltro

felt-tip (pen); ~ **de tinta permanente** fountain pen.

cangaceiro [kãŋga'sejru] *m (Br)* bandit.

canguru [kãŋgu'ru] *m* kangaroo.

canhão [ka'ɲãw] *(pl -ões* [-õjʃ]) *m (arma)* cannon; *(vale)* canyon.

canhoto, -ota [ka'ɲotu, -ɔta] *adj* left-handed ◆ *m, f* left-handed person.

canibal [kani'baw] *(pl -ais* [-ajʃ]) *mf* cannibal.

caniço [ka'nisu] *m* reed.

canil [ka'niw] *(pl -is* [-iʃ]) *m* kennel.

caninha [ka'niɲa] *f (Br: cachaça)* rum.

canis → **canil**.

canivete [kani'vetʃi] *m* penknife.

canja ['kãʒa] *f:* ~ **(de galinha)** chicken broth; **é ~!** it's a piece of cake!

cano ['kanu] *m* pipe; *(de arma)* barrel; ~ **de esgoto** drainpipe.

canoa [ka'noa] *f* canoe.

canoagem [ka'nwaʒẽ] *f* canoeing; **fazer ~** to go canoeing.

cansaço [kã'sasu] *m* tiredness.

cansado, -da [kã'sadu, -da] *adj:* **estar ~** to be tired.

cansar [kã'sa(x)] *vt* to tire out.

⎿ **cansar-se** *vp* to get tired.

cansativo, -va [kãsa'tʃivu, -va] *adj (fatigante)* tiring; *(maçante)* tedious.

cantar [kãn'ta(x)] *vi & vt* to sing.

cantarolar [kãntaro'la(x)] *vi & vt* to hum.

cantiga [kãn'tʃiga] *f (canção)* ballad.

cantil [kãn'tʃiw] *(pl -is* [-iʃ]) *m* flask.

cantina [kãn'tʃina] *f* canteen; *(de instituição de caridade)* soup kitchen.

cantis → **cantil**.

canto ['kãntu] *m* corner; *(forma de cantar)* singing; *(de galo)* crowing; **estou aprendendo ~** I'm having singing lessons.

cantor, -ra [kãn'to(x), -ra] *(mpl -res* [-riʃ], *fpl -s* [-ʃ]) *m, f* singer.

canudo [ka'nudu] *m* tube; *(Br: para bebida)* straw; *(fam: diploma de curso)* degree certificate.

cão ['kãw] *(pl cães* ['kãjʃ]) *m* dog; ~ **de guarda** guard dog.

caos ['kawʃ] *m* chaos.

caótico, -ca [ka'ɔtiku, -ka] *adj* chaotic.

capa ['kapa] *f (dossier, pasta)* folder;

(peça de vestuário) cape; *(de livro, caderno)* cover; ~ **impermeável** rain cape.

capacete [kapa'setʃi] *m (de moto)* crash helmet; *(de proteção)* hard hat.

capacidade [kapasi'dadʒi] *f* capacity; *(fig: talento)* ability.

capar [ka'pa(x)] *vt* to castrate; *(animal de estimação)* to neuter; *(cavalo)* to geld.

capaz [ka'paʃ] *(pl -zes* [-ziʃ]) *adj* capable; **ser ~ de fazer algo** to be able to do sthg; **é ~ de chover** it might rain.

capela [ka'pɛla] *f* chapel.

capitã → **capitão**.

capitães → **capitão**.

capital [kapi'taw] *(pl -ais* [-ajʃ]) *f & m* capital.

capitalismo [kapita'liʒmu] *m* capitalism.

capitalista [kapita'liʃta] *adj & mf* capitalist.

capitão, -tã [kapi'tãw, -tã] *(mpl -ães* [-ãjʃ], *fpl -s* [-ʃ]) *m, f* captain.

capítulo [ka'pitulu] *m* chapter.

capô [ka'po] *m (de carro)* bonnet *(Brit)*, hood *(Am)*.

capoeira [ka'pwejra] *f* coop; *(prática esportiva)* Brazilian fighting dance.

capota [ka'pɔta] *f (de carro)* bonnet *(Brit)*, hood *(Am)*.

capotar [kapo'ta(x)] *vi* to overturn.

capote [ka'pɔtʃi] *m* overcoat.

cappuccino [kapu'tʃinu] *m* cappuccino.

capricho [ka'priʃu] *m* whim.

Capricórnio [kapri'kɔrnju] *m* Capricorn.

cápsula ['kapsula] *f* capsule.

captar [kap'ta(x)] *vt (água)* to collect; *(sinal, onda)* to receive; *(atenção)* to attract.

capuz [ka'puʃ] *(pl -zes* [-ziʃ]) *m* hood.

caqui [ka'ki] *m* khaki.

cara ['kara] *f* face; *(aspecto)* appearance ◆ *m (Br: fam)* guy; **~s ou coroas?** heads or tails?; ~ **a** ~ face to face; **dar de ~ com** *(fig)* to come face to face with; **não vou com a ~ dele** I don't like the look of him; **ter ~ de poucos amigos** to look like a hard nut.

carabina [kara'bina] *f* rifle.

caracol [kara'kɔw] *(pl -óis* [-ɔjʃ]) *m*

(animal) snail; *(de cabelo)* curl.

carácter [ka'ratɛr] *(pl* **caracteres** [kara'tɛreʃ]) *m (Port)* = **caráter**.

característica [karatɛ'riʃʃika] *f* characteristic.

característico, -ca [karatɛ'riʃʃiku, -ka] *adj* characteristic.

carambola [karãm'bɔla] *f* star fruit.

caramelo [kara'mɛlu] *m* toffee.

caranguejo [karãŋ'geʒu] *m* crab.

❑ **Caranguejo** *m (Port)* Cancer.

caratê [kara'te] *m (Br)* karate.

caráter [ka'ratɛ(x)] *(pl* **-res** [-riʃ]) *m (Br)* character; *(tipo)* type.

caravana [kara'vana] *f (Port: viatura)* caravan *(Brit)*, trailer *(Am)*; *(de gente)* caravan.

carbonizado, -da [kaxboni'zadu, -da] *adj* charred.

carbono [kax'bonu] *m* carbon.

carburador [kaxbura'do(x)] *(pl* **-res** [-riʃ]) *m* carburettor.

cardápio [kax'dapju] *m (Br)* menu.

cardíaco, -ca [kax'dʒiaku, -ka] *adj* cardiac.

cardo ['kaxdu] *m* thistle.

cardume [kax'dumi] *m* shoal.

careca [ka'rɛka] *adj* bald ♦ *f* bald patch.

carecer [karɛ'se(x)] : **carecer de** *v + prep (ter falta de)* to lack; *(precisar de)* to need.

carência [ka'rẽsja] *f (falta)* lack; *(necessidade)* need.

careta [ka'rɛta] *f* grimace; **fazer ~s** to pull faces.

carga ['kaxga] *f (de barco, avião)* cargo; *(de trem, caminhão)* freight; *(de pessoa, animal)* load; *(de projétil)* charge; **~ máxima** maximum load.

cargo [ka'xgu] *m (função)* post; *(responsabilidade)* responsibility; **deixar a ~ de** to leave in charge of; **estar a ~ de** to be the responsibility of; **ter a ~** to be in charge of.

cariado, -da [ka'rjadu, -da] *adj* decayed.

caricatura [karika'tura] *f* caricature.

carícia [ka'risja] *f* caress.

caridade [kari'dadʒi] *f* charity.

cárie ['kari] *f* tooth decay.

caril [ka'riw] *m* curry powder.

carimbar [karĩm'ba(x)] *vt* to stamp.

carimbo [ka'rĩmbu] *m* stamp; *(em carta)* postmark.

carinho [ka'riɲu] *m* affection.

carinhoso, -osa [kari'ɲozu, -ɔza] *adj* affectionate.

carioca [ka'rjɔka] *mf (pessoa)* native/inhabitant of Rio de Janeiro ♦ *m (Port: café)* weak espresso; **~ de limão** *(Port)* fresh lemon infusion.

carisma [ka'riʒma] *m* charisma.

carnal [kax'naw] *(pl* **-ais** [-ajʃ]) *adj* carnal.

Carnaval [kaxna'vaw] *m* Carnival.

carne ['kaxni] *f (de comer)* meat; *(tecido muscular)* flesh; **~ de carneiro** lamb;; **~ picada** mince *(Brit)*, mincemeat *(Am)*; **~ de porco** pork; **~ de vaca** beef; **em ~ e osso** in the flesh.

carnê [kax'ne] *m (Br) (caderno)* notebook; *(de pagamentos)* payment book.

carneiro [kax'nejru] *m (animal)* sheep; *(reprodutor)* ram; *(carne)* mutton.

❑ **Carneiro** *m (Port)* Aries.

carniceiro [karni'sejru] *m (Port)* butcher.

carnudo, -da [kax'nudu, -da] *adj (lábios)* full; *(fruto)* fleshy.

caro, -ra [karu, -ra] *adj (de preço elevado)* expensive, dear; *(querido)* dear.

carochinha [karo'ʃiɲa] *f →* **história**.

caroço [ka'rosu] *m (de fruto)* stone; *(em corpo)* lump.

carona [ka'rona] *f (Br)* lift *(Brit)*, ride *(Am)*; **pegar uma ~** to hitch a lift; **dar uma ~ a alguém** to give sb a lift; **pedir ~** to hitchhike.

carpete [kax'pɛtʃi] *f* carpet.

carpinteiro [kaxpĩ'tejru] *m* carpenter.

carraça [ka'xasa] *f* tick.

carrapicho [kaxa'piʃu] *m* topknot.

carregado, -da [kaxe'gadu, -da] *adj (cor)* dark; *(tempo)* muggy; **estar ~ de** to be loaded down with.

carregador [kaxega'do(x)] *(pl* **-res** [-riʃ]) *m (em estação, hotel)* porter.

carregar [kaxe'ga(x)] *vt* to load; *(transportar)* to carry; *(pilha, bateria)* to charge ♦ *vi (pesar)* to be heavy; **~ em algo** *(exagerar)* to overdo sthg; *(Port: apertar)* to press sthg.

carreira [ka'xejra] *f (profissão)* career; *(fileira)* row; *(de transportes coletivos)* route; *(pequena corrida)* race.

carrinha [ka'xiɲa] *f (Port) (para pas-*

sageiros) minibus; *(para mercadorias)* van.

carrinho [ka'xiɲu] *m*: ~ **de bebê** pushchair *(Brit)*, stroller *(Am)*; ~ **de mão** wheelbarrow; ~ **de supermercado** trolley *(Brit)*, cart *(Am)*.

carro ['kaxu] *m* car; ~ **alegórico** carnival float; ~ **de aluguel** hire car; ~ **de corrida** racing car; ~ **de passeio** *(Br)* saloon (car) *(Brit)*, sedan *(Am)*; ~ **de praça** taxi.

carro-chefe [ˌkaxuʃˈʃefi] *(pl* **carros-chefes** [ˌkaxuʃˈʃefiʃ]) *f (Br) (coisa mais importante)* flagship; *(de desfile)* main float.

carroça [ka'xɔsa] *f* cart.

carroçaria [kaxosa'ria] *f* bodywork.

carro-leito [ˌkaxuˈlejtu] *(pl* **carros-leitos** [ˌkaxuʃˈlejtuʃ]) *f (Br)* sleeping car.

carro-restaurante [ˌkaxuxeʃtawˈrantʃi] *(pl* **carros-restaurantes** [ˌkaxuʃxeʃtawˈrantʃiʃ]) *f (Br)* dining car.

carrossel [kaxɔˈsɛw] *(pl* **-éis** [-ɛjʃ]) *m* merry-go-round *(Brit)*, carousel *(Am)*.

carruagem [ka'xwaʒẽ] *(pl* **-ns** [-ʃ]) *f (Port: vagão)* carriage *(Brit)*, car *(Am)*.

carruagem-cama [kaˌxwaʒẽˈkama] *(pl* **carruagens-cama** [kaˌxwaʒẽʃˈkama]) *f (Port)* sleeping car.

carruagem-restaurante [kaˌxwaʒẽxeʃtawˈrãntɕ] *(pl* **carruagens-restaurante** [kaˌxwaʒẽʃxeʃtawˈrãntɕ]) *f (Port)* dining car.

carta ['kaxta] *f* letter; *(mapa)* map; *(de baralho)* card; ~ **de apresentação** covering letter; ~ **(de condução)** *(Port)* driving licence *(Brit)*, driver's license *(Am)*; ~ **registrada** registered letter.

cartão [kax'tãw] *(pl* **-ões** [-õjʃ]) *m* card; *(papelão)* cardboard; ~ **bancário** bank card; ~ **de crédito** credit card; ~ **de embarque/desembarque** boarding/landing card; ~ **jovem** *young person's discount card*; ~ **multibanco** *(Port)* cashpoint card; ~ **postal** *(Br)* postcard.

cartão-de-visita [kax,tãwdʒiviˈzita] *(pl* **cartões-de-visita** [kar,tõiʒdʒiviˈzita]) *m* business card.

cartaz [kax'taʃ] *(pl* **-zes** [-ziʃ]) *m* poster.

carteira [kax'tejra] *f (de dinheiro)* wallet; *(mala de senhora)* handbag; *(de sala de aula)* desk; ~ **de identidade** *(Br)*

identity card; ~ **de motorista** *(Br)* driving licence *(Brit)*, driver's license *(Am)*.

carteiro [kax'tejru] *m* postman *(Brit)*, mailman *(Am)*.

cartões → **cartão**.

cartolina [kaxto'lina] *f* card.

cartório [kax'tɔrju] *m* registry office; ~ **notarial** notary's office.

cartucho [kax'tuʃu] *m (para mercadoria)* paper bag; *(munição)* cartridge; *(embrulho)* packet.

caruru [karu'ru] *m mashed okra or green amaranth leaves with shrimps, fish and palm oil.*

carvalho [kax'vaʎu] *m* oak.

carvão [kax'vãw] *m* coal; ~ **de lenha** charcoal.

casa ['kaza] *f* house; *(lar)* home; *(de botão)* buttonhole; **em** ~ at home; **ir para** ~ to go home; ~ **de banho** *(Port)* bathroom; ~ **de câmbio** *(Br)* bureau de change; ~ **de saúde** private hospital; **faça como se estivesse em sua** ~! make yourself at home!

casaco [ka'zaku] *m* jacket; ~ **comprido** coat; ~ **de malha** cardigan.

casado, -da [ka'zadu, -da] *adj* married.

casal [ka'zaw] *(pl* **-ais** [-ajʃ]) *m* couple.

casamento [kaza'mẽtu] *m* marriage; *(cerimônia)* wedding.

casar [ka'za(x)] *vt* to marry ♦ *vi* to get married.

❏ **casar-se** *vp* to get married.

casca ['kaʃka] *f (de ovo, noz, etc)* shell; *(de laranja, maçã, etc)* peel.

cascalho [kaʃ'kaʎu] *m* rubble.

cascata [kaʃ'kata] *f* waterfall.

cascavel [kaʃka'vɛw] *(pl* **-éis** [-ɛjʃ]) *f* rattlesnake.

casco ['kaʃku] *m (de vinho)* cask; *(de navio)* hull; *(de cavalo, boi, ovelha, etc)* hoof.

caseiro, -ra [ka'zejru, -ra] *adj* homemade; *(pessoa)* home-loving ♦ *m, f* estate worker *(provided with free accommodation for self and family).*

casino [ka'zinu] *m (Port)* = **cassino**.

caso ['kazu] *m (circunstância)* case; *(acontecimento)* affair ♦ *conj* in case; **no** ~ **de** in the event of; **"em** ~ **de emergência ..."** "in an emergency ..."; **"em** ~ **de incêndio ..."** "in case of fire ..."; **em todo o** ~ in any case;

em último ~ as a last resort; **não fazer** ~ **de algo/alguém** to ignore sthg/sb.

caspa [ˈkaʃpa] f dandruff.

casquilho [kaʃˈkiʎu] m socket.

casquinha [kaʃˈkiɲa] f (de prata, ouro) leaf; (Br: de sorvete) cone.

cassete [kaˈsɛtʃi] f cassette, tape; ~ (de vídeo) (video)tape.

cassetete [kaseˈtɛtʃi] m truncheon.

cassino [kaˈsinu] m (Br) casino.

castanha [kaʃˈtaɲa] f (fruto do castanheiro) chestnut; (fruto do cajueiro) cashew nut; ~s **assadas** roast chestnuts.

castanheiro [kaʃtaˈɲejru] m chestnut tree.

castanho, -nha [kaʃˈtaɲu, -ɲa] adj brown ◆ m (madeira) chestnut.

castelo [kaʃˈtɛlu] m castle.

castiçal [kaʃtʃiˈsaw] (pl -ais [-ajʃ]) m candlestick.

castidade [kaʃtʃiˈdadʒi] f chastity.

castigar [kaʃtʃiˈga(x)] vt to punish.

castigo [kaʃtʃigu] m punishment.

casto, -ta [ˈkaʃtu, -ta] adj chaste.

castor [kaʃˈto(x)] (pl -res [-riʃ]) m beaver.

castrar [kaʃˈtra(x)] vt to castrate.

casual [kaˈzwaw] (pl -ais [-ajʃ]) adj chance (antes de s).

casualidade [kazwaliˈdadʒi] f chance; **por** ~ by chance.

casulo [kaˈzulu] m cocoon.

catacumbas [kataˈkũbaʃ] fpl catacombs.

catálogo [kaˈtalogu] m catalogue.

catamarã [katamaˈrã] m catamaran.

catarata [kataˈrata] f waterfall; (MED) cataract; **as** ~s **do Iguaçu** the Iguaçu Falls.

catarro [kaˈtaxu] m catarrh.

catástrofe [kaˈtaʃtrofi] f catastrophe.

catatua [kataˈtua] f cockatoo.

cata-vento [kataˈvẽtu] (pl cata-ventos [kataˈvẽtuʃ]) m weather vane.

catedral [kateˈdraw] (pl -ais [-ajʃ]) f cathedral.

categoria [kategoˈria] f category; (posição) position; (qualidade) class; **de** ~ first-rate.

cativar [katʃiˈva(x)] vt to captivate.

cativeiro [katʃiˈvejru] m: **em** ~ in captivity.

católico, -ca [kaˈtɔliku, -ka] adj & m, f Catholic.

catorze [kaˈtoxzi] num fourteen, → **seis**.

caução [kawˈsãw] (pl -ões [-õjʃ]) f (JUR) bail; **pagar** ~ to pay bail.

cauda [ˈkawda] f (de animal) tail; (de manto, vestido) train.

caudal [kawˈdaw] (pl -ais [-ajʃ]) m flow.

caule [ˈkawli] m stem.

causa [ˈkawza] f (motivo) reason; (de acidente, doença) cause; (JUR: acção judicial) case; **por** ~ **de** because of.

causar [kawˈza(x)] vt to cause; ~ **danos a** to damage.

cautela [kawˈtɛla] f caution; (de loteria) part-share of a lottery ticket; **ter** ~ **com** to be careful with; **com** ~ cautiously; **à** OU **por** ~ as a safeguard.

cauteloso, -osa [kawteˈlozu, -ɔza] adj cautious.

cavala [kaˈvala] f mackerel.

cavalaria [kavalaˈria] f cavalry.

cavaleiro [kavaˈlejru] m rider; (em tourada) bullfighter on horseback; (medieval) knight.

cavalete [kavaˈletʃi] m easel.

cavalgar [kavawˈga(x)] vi to ride ◆ vt (égua, ginete) to ride; (obstáculo, barreira) to jump.

cavalheiro [kavaˈʎejru] m gentleman.

cavalinho-de-pau [kavaˌliɲudʒiˈpaw] (pl cavalinhos-de-pau [kavaˌliɲuʒdʒiˈpaw]) m hobbyhorse.

cavalo [kaˈvalu] m horse.

cavanhaque [kavaˈɲaki] m goatee (beard).

cavaquinho [kavaˈkiɲu] m small four-stringed guitar.

cavar [kaˈva(x)] vt (terra) to dig; (decote) to lower.

cave [ˈkavi] f (de vinho) wine cellar; (Port: de casa) basement.

caveira [kaˈvejra] f skull.

caverna [kaˈvɛxna] f cave.

caviar [kaˈvja(x)] m caviar.

cavidade [kaviˈdadʒi] f cavity.

caxemira [kaʃeˈmira] f cashmere.

caxumba [kaˈʃũba] f (Br) mumps (sg).

c/c (abrev de conta corrente) a/c.

CD m (abrev de compact disc) CD.

CD-i m (abrev de compact disc-

interativo) CDI.

CD-ROM [sɛdɛˈrɔmi] *m* CD-ROM.

CE *f (abrev de Comunidade Europeia)* EC.

cear [ˈsja(x)] *vi* to have dinner ◆ *vt* to have for dinner.

cebola [seˈbola] *f* onion.

cebolada [seboˈlada] *f fried onion sauce.*

cebolinha [seboˈliɲa] *f (de conserva)* pickled onions *(pl); (Br: erva comestível)* chives *(pl).*

cebolinho [seboˈliɲu] *m (Port)* chives *(pl).*

ceder [seˈdɛ(x)] *vt (lugar)* to give up; *(objeto)* to lend ◆ *vi (dar-se por vencido)* to give in; *(ponte)* to give way; *(corda, nó)* to slacken; *(chuva)* to ease up; *(vento)* to drop; **"~ a passagem"** "give way".

cedilha [seˈdiʎa] *f* cedilha. ·

cedo [ˈsedu] *adv* early; *(depressa)* soon; **muito ~** very early; **desde muito ~** *(desde criança)* from an early age; **mais ~ ou mais tarde** sooner or later.

cedro [ˈsɛdru] *m* cedar.

cegar [seˈga(x)] *vt* to blind ◆ *vi* to go blind.

cego, -ga [ˈsɛgu, -ga] *adj (pessoa)* blind; *(faca)* blunt ◆ *m, f* blind man *(f* blind woman); **às cegas** blindly.

cegonha [seˈgoɲa] *f* stork.

ceia [ˈseja] *f* supper.

cela [ˈsɛla] *f* cell.

celebração [selebraˈsãw] *(pl* -ões [-õjʃ]) *f* celebration.

celebrar [seleˈbra(x)] *vt* to celebrate; *(casamento)* to hold; *(contrato)* to sign.

célebre [ˈsɛlebri] *adj* famous.

celebridade [selebriˈdadʒi] *f* celebrity.

celeiro [seˈlejru] *m* granary.

celibatário, -ria [selibaˈtarju, -rja] *m, f* bachelor *(f* single woman).

celibato [seliˈbatu] *m* celibacy.

celofane [seloˈfani] *m* Cellophane[®].

célula [ˈsɛlula] *f* cell.

celular [seluˈla(x)] *m (Br: telefone)* mobile phone.

cem [ˈsẽ] *num* one OU a hundred; **~ mil** a hundred thousand, → **seis**.

cemitério [semiˈtɛrju] *m* cemetery.

cena [ˈsɛna] *f* scene; *(palco)* stage; **entrar em ~** *(fig)* to come on the scene; **fazer uma ~** *(fig)* to to make a scene.

cenário [seˈnarju] *m* scenery; *(de programa televisivo)* set.

cenoura [seˈnora] *f* carrot.

censo [ˈsẽsu] *f* census.

censura [sẽˈsura] *f (crítica)* criticism; *(de Estado, autoridade)* censorship.

centavo [sẽˈtavu] *m old coin equivalent to a tenth of a real.*

centeio [sẽˈteju] *m* rye.

centelha [sẽˈteʎa] *f* spark.

centena [sẽˈtena] *f* hundred; **uma ~ de pessoas** a hundred people.

centenário [sẽteˈnarju] *m* centenary.

centésimo, -ma [sẽˈtɛzimu, -ma] *num* hundredth, → **sexto**.

centígrado [sẽˈtʃigradu] *adj m* → **grau**.

centímetro [sẽˈtʃimetru] *m* centimetre.

cento [ˈsẽtu] *m* hundred; **~ e vinte** a hundred and twenty; **por ~** percent.

centopeia [sẽtoˈpeja] *f* centipede.

central [sẽˈtraw] *(pl* -ais [-ajʃ]) *adj* central ◆ *f (de instituição, organização)* head office; *(de eletricidade, energia atômica)* power station; **~ elétrica** power station; **~ nuclear** nuclear power station; **~ telefônica** telephone exchange.

centrar [sẽˈtra(x)] *vt (atenção, esforço)* to focus; *(texto, página)* to centre.

centro [ˈsẽtru] *m* centre; **~ da cidade** city centre; **~ comercial** shopping centre *(Brit)*, shopping mall *(Am)*; **~ de saúde** health clinic.

centroavante [sẽntroaˈvãntʃi] *m (Br: em futebol)* centre forward.

CEP *m (Br: abrev de Código de Endereçamento Postal)* postcode *(Brit)*, zip code *(Am).*

céptico, -ca [ˈsɛ(p)tiku, -ka] *adj (Port)* = **cético.**

cera [ˈsera] *f* wax; **~ depilatória** hair-removing OU depilatory wax.

cerâmica [seˈramika] *f (objeto)* piece of pottery; *(atividade)* ceramics *(sg).*

ceramista [seraˈmiʃta] *mf* potter.

cerca [ˈsexka] *f* fence ◆ *adv:* **~ de** about; **há ~ de uma semana** nearly a week ago.

cercar [sexˈka(x)] *vt* to surround.

cereal [seˈrjal] *(pl* -ais [-ajʃ]) *m* cereal.

cérebro [ˈsɛrebru] *m* brain.

cereja [seˈreʒa] *f* cherry.

cerimónia [seriˈmɔnja] *f (Port)* = **cerimônia**.

cerimônia [seriˈmonja] *f (Br) (religiosa)* ceremony; *(festa)* party; *(etiqueta)* formality.

cerrado, -da [seˈxadu, -da] *adj (nevoeiro)* thick.

certeza [sexˈteza] *f* certainty; **dar a ~** to confirm; **ter a ~ de que** to be sure (that); **você pode ter a ~ que vou** I'm definitely going; **com ~** *(sem dúvida)* of course; *(provavelmente)* probably; **com ~!** of course!; **de ~** definitely.

certidão [sextʃiˈdãw] *(pl* -ões [-õjʃ]*) f* certificate.

certificado [sextʃifiˈkadu] *m* certificate.

certificar-se [sextʃifiˈkaxsi] *vp* to check; **~ de algo** to check sthg.

certo, -ta [ˈsextu, -ta] *adj (exacto)* right; *(infalível)* certain ◆ *adv* correctly; **certas pessoas** certain people; **a conta não bate ~** the bill isn't quite right; **dar ~** to work out; **o ~ é ele não vir** I'm sure he won't come; **ao ~** *(exatamente)* exactly; *(provavelmente)* probably.

cerveja [sexˈveʒa] *f* beer; **~ imperial** draught beer; **~ preta** stout.

cervejaria [sexveʒaˈria] *f* bar.

cervical [sexviˈkaw] *(pl* -ais [-ajʃ]*) adj* cervical.

cessar [seˈsa(x)] *vi & vt* to cease.

cesta [ˈseʃta] *f* small basket.

cesto [ˈseʃtu] *m* basket; **~ de vime** wicker basket.

cético, -ca [ˈsɛtʃiku, -ka] *adj (Br)* sceptical ◆ *m, f (Br)* sceptic.

cetim [seˈtʃĩ] *m* satin.

céu [ˈsɛw] *m* sky; *(RELIG)* heaven; **a ~ aberto** *(fig: à vista de todos)* in broad daylight.

céu-da-boca [ˈsɛwdaˌboka] *m* roof of the mouth.

cevada [seˈvada] *f* barley; *(bebida)* barley coffee.

chá [ˈʃa] *m* tea; **~ dançante** tea dance; **~ com limão** tea with lemon; **~ de limão** lemon tea.

chacal [ʃaˈkaw] *(pl* -ais [-ajʃ]*) m* jackal.

chacota [ʃaˈkɔta] *f* mockery.

chafariz [ʃafaˈriʃ] *(pl* -zes [-ziʃ]*) m* fountain.

chafurdar [ʃafuxˈda(x)] *vi* to wallow.

chaga [ˈʃaga] *f* open wound, sore.

chalé [ʃaˈlɛ] *m* chalet.

chaleira [ʃaˈlejra] *f* kettle.

chama [ˈʃama] *f* flame.

chamada [ʃaˈmada] *f (de telefone)* call; *(de exame)* sitting; **fazer a ~** *(EDUC)* to call the register; **~ a cobrar** *(no destinatário)* reverse charge call *(Brit)*, collect call *(Am)*; **~ interurbana/local** long-distance/local call.

chamar [ʃaˈma(x)] *vt* to call ◆ *vi (telefone)* to ring.

❏ **chamar-se** *vp* to be called; **como é que você se chama?** what's your name?; **eu me chamo Carlos** my name is Carlos.

chaminé [ʃamiˈnɛ] *f* chimney; *(de lareira)* chimney-piece; *(de fábrica)* chimney stack.

champanhe [ʃãmˈpaɲi] *m* champagne.

champô [ʃãmˈpo] *(Port) m* = **xampu**.

chamuscar [ʃamuʃˈka(x)] *vt* to singe.

chance [ˈʃãsi] *f* chance.

chantagear [ʃãtaˈʒja(x)] *vt* to blackmail.

chantagem [ʃãˈtaʒẽ] *(pl* -ns [-ʃ]*) f* blackmail.

chantilly [ʃãtʃiˈli] *m* whipped cream.

chão [ˈʃãw] *m (solo)* ground; *(pavimento)* floor; **cair no ~** to fall over.

chapa [ˈʃapa] *f (Br: matrícula, placa)* numberplate *(Brit)*, license plate *(Am)*; *(Port: carroçaria)* bodywork.

chapéu [ʃaˈpɛw] *m* hat; *(de sol, chuva)* umbrella; **ser de tirar o ~** to be superb.

chapéu-de-sol [ʃaˌpɛwdʒiˈsɔw] *(pl* **chapéus-de-sol** [ʃaˌpɛwdʒiˈsɔw]*) m* parasol.

charco [ˈʃaxku] *m* puddle.

charcutaria [ʃaxkutaˈria] *f* ~ delicatessen.

charme [ˈʃaxmi] *m* charm.

charneca [ʃaxˈnɛka] *f* moor.

charrete [ʃaˈxɛtʃi] *f* chariot.

charter [ˈʃaxte(x)] *(pl* -res [-riʃ]*) m:* **(voo) ~** charter flight.

charuto [ʃaˈrutu] *m* cigar.

chassis [ʃaˈsi] *m inv* chassis.

chatear [ʃaˈtʃja(x)] *vt* to annoy.

chatice [ʃaˈtʃisi] *f (fam: tédio)* drag.

chato, -ta [ˈʃatu, -ta] *adj (fam: tedioso)*

boring; *(pé)* flat.

chauvinista [ʃoviˈniʃta] *m, f* chauvinist.

chave [ˈʃavi] *f* key.

chave-de-fendas [ʃavidʒiˈfẽndaʃ] *(pl* **chaves-de-fendas** [ʃaviʒdʒiˈfẽndaʃ]) *f* screwdriver.

chave-de-ignição [ʃavidʒigniˈsãw] *(pl* **chaves-de-ignição** [ʃaviʒdʒigniˈsãw]) *f* ignition key.

chave-inglesa [ʃaviŋˈglɛza] *(pl* **chaves-inglesas** [ʃaviʒiŋˈglɛzaʃ]) *f* monkey wrench.

chaveiro [ʃaˈvejru] *m* keyring.

chávena [ˈʃavena] *f (Port)* cup.

check-in [tʃɛˈkini] *(pl* **check-ins** [ʃɛˈkineʃ]) *m* check-in; **fazer o ~** to check in.

check-up [tʃɛˈkapi] *(pl* **check-ups** [tʃɛˈkapiʃ]) *m* check-up.

chefe [ˈʃɛfi] *mf (de trabalhadores)* boss; *(de partido)* leader; *(de empresa)* head; *(de tribo, organização)* chief.

chefe-de-estação [ʃɛfidʒiestaˈsãw] *(pl* **chefes-de-estação** [ʃɛfiʒdʒiestaˈsãw]) *m* stationmaster.

chegada [ʃeˈgada] *f* arrival; "chegadas" "arrivals"; "~s domésticas" "domestic arrivals"; "~s internacionais" "international arrivals".

chegado, -da [ʃeˈgadu, -da] *adj* close.

chegar [ʃeˈga(x)] *vi* to arrive; *(momento, altura, hora)* to come; *(ser suficiente)* to be enough; **~ bem** to arrive safely; **~ ao fim** to come to an end.

❏ **chegar-se** *vp (aproximar-se)* to come closer; *(afastar-se)* to move over; **~-se a** to come closer to.

cheia [ˈʃeja] *f* flood.

cheio, cheia [ˈʃeju, ˈʃeja] *adj* full; **~ de** full of; **estar ~** to have had enough.

cheirar [ʃejˈra(x)] *vt & vi* to smell; **~ bem/mal** to smell good/awful.

cheiro [ˈʃejru] *m* smell.

cheque [ˈʃɛki] *m* cheque; *(em xadrez)* check; **~ em branco** blank cheque; **~ sem fundos** OU **sem provisão** uncovered cheque; **~ pré-datado** pre-dated cheque; **~ de viagem** traveller's cheque; **~ visado** authorized cheque.

cheque-mate [ʃɛkiˈmatʃi] *(pl* **cheque-mates** [ʃɛkiˈmatiʃ]) *m* checkmate.

cherne [ˈʃɛxni] *m* grouper.

chiar [ˈʃja(x)] *vi* to squeak; *(porco)* to squeal; *(pneu)* to screech.

chiclete [ʃiˈklɛtʃi] *m (Br)* chewing gum.

chicória [ʃiˈkɔrja] *f* chicory.

chicote [ʃiˈkɔtʃi] *m* whip.

chifre [ˈʃifri] *m* horn.

Chile [ˈʃili] *m*: **o ~** Chile.

chimarrão [ʃimaˈxãw] *m* unsweetened *maté* tea.

chimpanzé [ʃĩmpãˈzɛ] *m* chimpanzee.

China [ˈʃina] *f*: **a ~** China.

chinelos [ʃiˈnɛluʃ] *mpl* flip-flops *(Brit)*, thongs *(Am)*; **~ (de quarto)** slippers.

chinês, -esa [ʃiˈneʃ, -eza] *(mpl* **-eses** [-eziʃ], *fpl* **-s** [-ʃ]) *adj & m, f* Chinese ◆ *m (língua)* Chinese; **isso para mim é ~** it's all double-Dutch to me!

chinó [ʃiˈnɔ] *m* toupee.

chique [ˈʃiki] *adj* chic.

chispe [ˈʃiʃpi] *m* pig's trotter.

chita [ˈʃita] *f* cotton print.

chiu [ˈʃiu] *interj* shush!

chocalhar [ʃokaˈʎa(x)] *vt (líquido)* to shake ◆ *vi (tilintar)* to jingle.

chocalho [ʃoˈkaʎu] *m* bell.

chocante [ʃoˈkãntʃi] *adj* shocking.

chocar [ʃoˈka(x)] *vi (veículos)* to crash; *(galinha)* to brood; ◆ *vt (indignar)* to shock; *(ovos)* to hatch; **~ com** *(pessoa)* to bump into; *(veículo)* to crash into.

chocho, -cha [ˈʃoʃu, -ʃa] *adj (noz)* empty; *(festa)* dull.

chocolate [ʃokoˈlatʃi] *m* chocolate; *(bebida)* chocolate drink; **~ amargo** OU **negro** plain chocolate; **~ branco** white chocolate; **~ de leite** milk chocolate; **~ em pó** cocoa.

chofer [ʃoˈfɛ(x)] *(pl* **-res** [-riʃ]) *m* driver.

chope [ˈʃopi] *m (Br)* draught beer.

choque [ˈʃɔki] *m (colisão)* crash; *(comoção)* shock.

choramingar [ʃoramĩŋˈga(x)] *vi* to snivel.

chorão, -rona [ʃoˈrãw, -ˈrona] *(mpl* **-ões** [-õjʃ], *fpl* **-s** [-ʃ]) *adj* tearful ◆ *m (árvore)* weeping willow; *(brinquedo)* baby doll that cries.

chorar [ʃoˈra(x)] *vi & vt (verter lágrimas)* to cry; **~ de rir** to cry with laughter.

chorinho [ʃoˈriɲu] *m (Br: MÚS)* type of melancholy Brazilian music.

choro [ˈʃoru] *m* crying.

chorões → **chorão**.

choupo [ˈʃopu] *m* poplar.

chouriço [ʃoˈrisu] *m (no Brasil)* black pudding; *(em Portugal)* spiced, smoked pork sausage.

chover [ʃoˈve(x)] *v impess* to rain; ~ a cântaros to pour with rain.

chuchu [ʃuˈʃu] *m* chayote; pra ~ *(Br: fam: muito)* loads.

chulé [ʃuˈlɛ] *m (fam)* foot odour.

chulo, -la [ˈʃulu, -la] *adj (Br)* vulgar ◆ *m (Port: fam)* pimp.

chumaço [ʃuˈmasu] *m* shoulder pad.

chumbar [ʃũˈba(x)] *vt (soldar)* to solder; *(atirar em)* to fire at ◆ *vi (Port: fam: reprovar)* to flunk.

chumbo [ˈʃũbu] *m* lead; *(tiro)* gunshot; a caixa está um ~ the box weighs a ton.

chupa-chupa [ʃupaˈʃupa] *(pl* chupa-chupas [ʃupaˈʃupaʃ]) *m (Port)* lollipop.

chupar [ʃuˈpa(x)] *vt* to suck.

chupeta [ʃuˈpeta] *f* dummy *(Brit)*, pacifier *(Am)*.

churrascaria [ʃuxaʃkaˈria] *f* restaurant serving barbecued meat and poultry.

churrasco [ʃuˈxaʃku] *m* barbecue.

churrasquinho [ʃuxaʃˈkiɲu] *m (Br)* kebab.

churro [ˈʃuxu] *m* fried twist of batter covered in sugar.

chutar [ʃuˈta(x)] *vt & vi* to kick.

chuteira [ʃuˈtejra] *f* football boot.

chuva [ˈʃuva] *f* rain.

chuveiro [ʃuˈvejru] *m* shower.

chuviscar [ʃuviʃˈka(x)] *vi* to drizzle.

chuvoso, -osa [ʃuˈvozu, -ɔza] *adj* rainy.

C.ᵃ *(abrev de Companhia)* Co.

ciberespaço [ˌsibereʃˈpasu] *m* cyberspace.

cibernética [sibexˈnɛtʃika] *f* cybernetics *(sg)*.

cibernético [sibexˈnɛtʃiku] *adj m* → espaço.

cicatriz [sikaˈtriʃ] *(pl -zes [-ziʃ]) f* scar.

cicatrizar [sikatriˈza(x)] *vi (ferida)* to heal (up).

cicatrizes → cicatriz.

cicerone [siseˈrɔni] *m* guide.

ciclismo [siˈkliʒmu] *m* cycling; fazer ~ to go cycling.

ciclista [siˈkliʃta] *mf* cyclist.

ciclo [ˈsiklu] *m* cycle; *(de conferências)* series.

ciclomotor [ˌsiklomoˈto(x)] *(pl -es*

[-iʃ]) *m* moped.

ciclone [siˈklɔni] *m* cyclone; *(região de baixas pressões)* depression.

cidadã → cidadão.

cidadania [sidadaˈnia] *f* citizenship.

cidadão, -dã [sidaˈdãw, -dã] *(mpl -ãos [-ãwʃ], fpl -s [-ʃ]) m, f* citizen.

cidade [siˈdadʒi] *f* city; ~ universitária campus.

cieiro [ˈsjejru] *m (Port) chapping caused by cold, windy weather.*

ciência [ˈsjẽsja] *f* science; ~s fisico-químicas physical sciences; ~s naturais natural sciences.

ciente [ˈsjẽtʃi] *adj* aware; estar ~ de to be aware of.

científico, -ca [sjẽˈtʃifiku, -ka] *adj* scientific.

cientista [sjẽˈtʃiʃta] *mf* scientist.

cifra [ˈsifra] *f* sum; *(número)* figure.

cigano, -na [siˈganu, -na] *m, f* gypsy.

cigarra [siˈgaxa] *f* cicada.

cigarreira [sigaˈxejra] *f* cigarette case.

cigarrilha [sigaˈxiʎa] *f* cigarillo.

cigarro [siˈgaxu] *m* cigarette; ~s com filtro filter-tipped cigarettes; ~s sem filtro untipped cigarettes; ~s mentolados menthol cigarettes.

cilada [siˈlada] *f* trap; caiu na ~ he fell for it.

cilindro [siˈlĩdru] *m* cylinder; *(rolo)* roller; *(de aquecimento de água)* boiler.

cílio [ˈsilju] *m* eyelash.

cima [ˈsima] *f*: de ~ from above; de ~ abaixo from top to bottom; de ~ de off; em ~ above; em ~ de on top of; para ~ up; para ~ de over; por ~ de over.

cimeira [siˈmejra] *f* summit.

cimentar [simẽˈta(x)] *vt* to cement.

cimento [siˈmẽtu] *m* cement.

cimo [ˈsimu] *m* top.

cinco [ˈsĩku] *num* five, → seis.

cineasta [siˈnjaʃta] *mf* film director.

cinema [siˈnema] *m (local)* cinema *(Brit)*, movie theater *(Am)*; *(arte)* cinema.

cinemateca [sinemaˈteka] *f (local)* filmhouse; *(coleção de filmes)* film library.

cinematográfico, -ca [sinemato ˈgrafiku, -ka] *adj* film *(antes de s)*.

cine-teatro [sineˈteatru] *m* filmhouse.

cínico, -ca ['siniku, -ka] *adj (hipócrita)* hypocritical.

cinismo [si'niʒmu] *m (hipocrisia)* hypocrisy.

cinquenta [sĩŋ'kwēnta] *num* fifty, → seis.

cinta ['sĩnta] *f (cintura)* waist; *(faixa de pano)* sash; *(roupa interior)* girdle.

cintilar [sĩntʃi'la(x)] *vi* to twinkle.

cinto ['sĩntu] *m* belt; ~ **de segurança** seatbelt.

cintura [sĩn'tura] *f* waist.

cinturão [sĩntu'rãw] (*mpl* **-ões** [-õjʃ]) *m (Br)* belt; ~ **industrial** industrial belt; ~ **verde** green belt.

cinza ['sĩza] *f* ash ◆ *adj & m (Br)* grey. ⊔ **cinzas** *fpl (restos mortais)* ashes.

cinzeiro [sĩ'zejru] *m* ashtray.

cinzel [sĩ'zɛw] (*pl* **-éis** [-ɛjʃ]) *m* chisel.

cinzento, -ta [sĩ'zēntu, -ta] *adj & m* grey.

cio ['siu] *m*: **estar no** ~ *(fêmeas)* to be on heat; *(machos)* to be in rut.

cipreste [si'prɛʃtʃi] *m* cypress.

circo ['sixku] *m* circus.

circuito [six'kwitu] *m* circuit; ~ **elétrico** electric circuit; ~ **turístico** tourist trail.

circulação [sixkula'sãw] *f* circulation; *(de veículos)* traffic.

circular [sixku'la(x)] (*pl* **-res** [-riʃ]) *vi* to circulate; *(pedestre)* to walk about; *(carro)* to drive ◆ *adj & f* circular.

círculo ['sixkulu] *m* circle; ~ **polar** polar circle.

circunferência [sixkũfe'rēsja] *f* circumference.

circunflexo [sixkũ'flɛksu] *adj m* → **acento**.

circunstância [sixkũʃ'tãsja] *f* circumstance; **nas** ~**s** under the circumstances.

círio ['sirju] *m* large candle.

cirurgia [sirux'ʒia] *f* surgery; ~ **plástica** plastic surgery.

cirurgião, -giã [sirux'ʒjãw, -ʒjã] (*mpl* **-ões** [-õjʃ], *fpl* **-s** [-ʃ]) *m, f* surgeon.

cirúrgico, -ca [si'ruxʒiku, -ka] *adj* surgical.

cirurgiões → **cirurgião**.

cisco ['siʃku] *m* speck.

cisma ['siʒma] *f* fixation.

cisne ['siʒni] *m* swan.

cisterna [siʃ'tɛxna] *f* tank.

cistite [siʃ'tʃitʃi] *f* cystitis.

citação [sita'sãw] (*pl* **-ões** [-õjʃ]) *f* quotation.

citar [si'ta(x)] *vt* to quote.

cítrico ['sitriku] *adj m* → **ácido**.

citrinos [si'trinuʃ] *mpl* citrus fruit *(sg)*.

ciúme ['sjumi] *m* jealousy; **ter** ~**s de alguém** to be jealous of sb.

ciumento, -ta [sju'mēntu, -ta] *adj* jealous.

cívico, -ca ['siviku, -ka] *adj* civic.

civil [si'viw] (*pl* **-is** [-iʃ]) *adj* civil.

civilização [siviliza'sãw] (*pl* **-ões** [-õjʃ]) *f* civilization.

civilizar [sivili'za(x)] *vt* to civilize.

civis → **civil**.

cl. *(abrev de centilitro)* cl.

clamar [kla'ma(x)] *vi* to cry out.

clamor [kla'mo(x)] (*pl* **-res** [-riʃ]) *m* outcry.

clandestino, -na [klãndeʃ'tʃinu, -na] *adj* clandestine ◆ *m, f* stowaway.

clara ['klara] *f* white.

clarabóia [klara'bɔja] *f* skylight.

clarão [kla'rãw] (*pl* **-ões** [-õjʃ]) *m* flash.

clarear [kla'rja(x)] *vi* to brighten up.

clarete [kla'retʃi] *m* rosé.

clareza [kla'reza] *f*: **falar com** ~ to speak clearly.

claridade [klari'dadʒi] *f* brightness.

clarinete [klari'netʃi] *m* clarinet.

claro, -ra ['klaru, -ra] *adj (com luz)* bright; *(cor)* light; *(preciso, sincero)* clear ◆ *adv* clearly; ~ **que sim!** of course!; **é** ~**!** of course!; **passar a noite em** ~ to have a sleepless night.

clarões → **clarão**.

classe ['klasi] *f* class; **ter** ~ to have class; **de primeira/segunda** ~ first/second class; ~ **social** social class; ~ **turística** tourist class.

clássico, -ca ['klasiku, -ka] *adj* classic; *(música)* classical.

classificação [klasifika'sãw] (*pl* **-ões** [-õjʃ]) *f* results *(pl)*.

classificados [klasefi'kaduʃ] *mpl* classified ads.

classificar [klasifi'ka(x)] *vt (EDUC: aluno)* to appraise; *(ordenar)* to classify. ⊔ **classificar-se** *vp (em competição)* to qualify.

claustro ['klawʃtru] *m* cloister.

cláusula ['klawzula] *f* clause.

clave ['klavi] *f* clef; ~ **de sol** treble clef.

clavícula [kla'vikula] *f* collarbone.
clemência [kle'mẽsja] *f* clemency.
clero ['klɛru] *m* clergy.
cliché [kli'ʃe] *m* (Port) = **clichê**.
clichê [kli'ʃe] *m* (Br) cliché.
cliente [kli'ẽntʃi] *mf* client.
clientela [kliẽn'tɛla] *f* customers (pl).
clima ['klima] *m* climate; (fig: ambiente) atmosphere.
clímax ['klimaks] *m inv* climax; **atingir o ~** to reach a climax.
clínica ['klinika] *f* clinic; **~ dentária** dental practice; **~ geral** general practice.
clínico ['kliniku] *m* clinician; **~ geral** GP.
clipe ['klipi] *m* paper clip.
cloro ['kloru] *m* chlorine.
clube ['klubi] *m* club; **~ de futebol/vídeo** football/video club.
cm. (abrev de centímetro) cm.
coador [kwa'do(x)] (pl -res [-riʃ]) *m* strainer.
coagir [kwa'ʒi(x)] *vt* to coerce.
coagular [kwagu'la(x)] *vt & vi* to clot.
coágulo ['kwagulu] *m* clot.
coalhar [kwa'ʎa(x)] *vt & vi* to curdle.
coar ['kwa(x)] *vt* to strain.
cobaia [ko'baja] *f* guinea pig.
cobarde [ko'baxdʒi] *adj & mf* = covarde.
coberta [ko'bɛxta] *f* (de cama) bedspread; (de navio) deck.
coberto, -ta [ko'bɛxtu, -ta] *adj* covered ◆ *m* shelter.
cobertor [kobex'to(x)] (pl -res [-riʃ]) *m* blanket.
cobertura [kobex'tura] *f* (tecto) roof; (Br: apartamento) penthouse; (de acontecimento, situação) coverage; **o cheque foi recusado por falta de ~** the cheque bounced due to lack of funds.
cobiça [ko'bisa] *f* (avidez) greed; (inveja) envy.
cobiçar [kobi'sa(x)] *vt* (ambicionar) to covet; (invejar) to envy.
cobra ['kɔbra] *f* snake.
cobrador, -ra [kobra'do(x), -ra] (mpl -res [-riʃ], fpl -s [-ʃ]) *m, f* (em trem, ônibus) conductor (f conductress); (de água, luz) meter reader.
cobrança [ko'brãsa] *f* (ação de cobrar) charging.
cobrar [ko'bra(x)] *vt* to charge;

(imposto, dívida) to collect.
cobre ['kɔbri] *m* copper.
cobrir [ko'bri(x)] *vt* to cover.
cocada [ko'kada] *f* dessert made with dessicated coconut and milk.
coçado, -da [ko'sadu, -da] *adj* worn.
cocaína [koka'ina] *f* cocaine.
coçar [ko'sa(x)] *vt* to scratch.
⊐ coçar-se *vp* to scratch o.s.
cóccix ['kɔksis] *m* coccyx.
cócegas ['kɔsigaʃ] *fpl:* **fazer ~** to tickle; **ter ~** to be ticklish.
coceira [ko'sejra] *f* itch.
cochichar [koʃi'ʃa(x)] *vt & vi* to whisper.
cochilo [ko'ʃilu] *m* (Br) nap; **tirar um ~** (Br) to take a nap.
coco ['koku] *m* coconut.
cócoras ['kɔkoraʃ] *fpl:* **pôr-se de ~** to squat.
côdea ['kodʒja] *f* crust.
código ['kɔdʒigu] *m* code; **~ de barras** bar code; **~ civil** civil law; **~ de trânsito** highway code; **~ postal** postcode.
codorniz [kodox'niʃ] (pl -zes [-ziʃ]) *f* quail.
coelho ['kweʎu] *m* rabbit; **~ à caçadora** rabbit cooked slowly in a white wine, onion and herb sauce which is then thickened with the rabbit's blood.
coentro ['kwẽntru] *m* coriander.
coerência [koe'rẽsja] *f* coherence.
coerente [koe'rẽntʃi] *adj* coherent.
cofre ['kɔfri] *m* safe.
cofre-forte [kɔfriʃ'fɔxti] (pl cofres-fortes [kɔfriʃ'fɔxtiʃ]) *m* safe.
cofre-noturno [kɔfrino'tuxnu] (pl cofres-noturnos [kɔfriʒno'tuxnuʃ]) *m* night safe.
cogitar [koʒi'ta(x)] *vt* to think (up) ◆ *vi* (pensar) to think.
cogumelo [kogu'mɛlu] *m* mushroom.
coice ['kojsi] *m* kick; (de arma) recoil.
coincidência [koĩsi'dẽsja] *f* coincidence; **por ~** as it happens.
coincidir [kwĩsi'di(x)] *vi* to coincide.
⊐ coincidir com *v + prep* to coincide with; (opinião) to agree with.
coisa ['kojza] *f* thing; (deseja) **mais alguma ~?** would you like anything else?; **não comprei ~ nenhuma** I didn't buy anything, I bought nothing; **alguma ~** something; **~ de** roughly; **a ~ está preta!** things are bleak!; **não ser grande ~** to be nothing special.

coitado, -da [koj'tadu, -da] *adj* poor, unfortunate ◆ *interj* poor thing!

cola ['kɔla] *f* glue.

colaborar [kolabu'ra(x)] *vi* to collaborate.

colapso [ko'lapsu] *m* collapse.

colar [ko'la(x)] (*pl* -res [-riʃ]) *vt* to glue, to stick ◆ *vi* to stick ◆ *m* necklace.

❑ **colar de** *v* + *prep* (*Br: fam*) to crib from.

colarinho [kola'riɲu] *m* collar.

colcha ['kowʃa] *f* bedspread.

colchão [kow'ʃãw] (*pl* -ões [-õjʃ]) *m* mattress; ~ **de molas/palha** spring/straw mattress.

colcheia [kow'ʃeja] *f* crotchet (*Brit*), quarter note (*Am*).

colchete [kow'ʃetʃi] *m* (*de vestuário*) hook; (*sinal de pontuação*) square bracket.

colchões → colchão.

coleção [kole'sãw] (*pl* -ões [-õjʃ]) *f* (*Br*) collection; **fazer ~ de algo** to collect sthg; ~ **de selos** stamp collection.

colecção [kule'sãw] (*pl* -ões [-õjʃ]) *f* (*Port*) = coleção.

colecionador, -ra [kolesjona'do(x), -ra] (*mpl* -res [-riʃ], *fpl* -s [-ʃ]) *m, f* collector.

coleccionar [kulesju'nar] *vt* (*Port*) = colecionar.

colecções → colecção.

colecionar [kolesjo'na(x)] *vt* (*Br*) to collect.

coleções → coleção.

colectivo, -va [kulɛ'tivu, -va] *adj* (*Port*) = coletivo.

colega [ko'lɛga] *mf* colleague; ~ **de carteira** *person you sit next to at school*; ~ **de trabalho** (work) colleague; ~ **de turma** classmate.

colégio [ko'lɛʒju] *m* school; ~ **interno** boarding school.

coleira [ko'lejra] *f* collar.

cólera ['kɔlera] *f* fury; (*MED*) cholera.

colérico, -ca [ko'lɛriku, -ka] *adj* furious.

colesterol [kolɛʃte'rɔw] *m* cholesterol.

colete [ko'letʃi] *m* waistcoat; ~ **salva-vidas** life jacket.

coletivo, -va [kolɛ'tʃivu, -va] *adj* (*Br*) (*decisão*) collective; (*reunião*) general; (*transporte*) public.

colheita [ko'ʎejta] *f* harvest.

colher¹ [ko'ʎɛ(x)] *vt* (*fruto, vegetal, flo-*

res) to pick; (*cereais*) to harvest.

colher² [ko'ʎɛ(x)] (*pl* -res [-riʃ]) *f* (*utensílio*) spoon; (*quantidade*) spoonful; ~ **de café** (*utensílio*) coffee spoon; (*quantidade*) = half teaspoon; ~ **de chá** teaspoon; ~ **de pau** wooden spoon; ~ **de sopa** (*utensílio*) soup spoon; (*quantidade*) = tablespoon.

colibri [koli'bri] *m* hummingbird.

cólica ['kɔlika] *f* colic.

colidir [koli'dʒi(x)] *vi* to collide; ~ **com** to collide with.

coligação [koliga'sãw] (*pl* -ões [-õjʃ]) *f* coalition.

colina [ko'lina] *f* hill.

colisão [koli'zãw] (*pl* -ões [-õjʃ]) *f* collision.

collants [ko'lãʃ] *mpl* tights (*Brit*), panty hose (*sg*) (*Am*).

colmeia [kow'meja] *f* beehive.

colo ['kɔlu] *m* lap; **levar uma criança no** ~ to carry a child.

colocação [koloka'sãw] (*pl* -ões [-õjʃ]) *f* placing; (*de roda, vidro*) fitting; (*emprego*) post, job.

colocar [kolo'ka(x)] *vt* to place; (*roda, vidro*) to fit; (*cortina*) to put up; (*empregar*) to employ; (*problema*) to pose.

Colômbia [ko'lõmbja] *f*: **a ~** Colombia.

cólon ['kɔlõ] *m* colon.

colónia [ku'lɔnja] *f* (*Port*) = colônia.

colônia [ko'lonja] *f* (*Br*) colony; (*perfume*) cologne; ~ **de férias** summer camp.

coloquial [kolo'kjaw] (*pl* -ais [-ajʃ]) *adj* colloquial.

colóquio [ko'lɔkju] *m* conference.

colorante [kolo'rãntʃi] *m* colouring.

colorau [kolo'raw] *m* paprika.

colorido, -da [kolo'ridu, -da] *adj* coloured; (*com muitas cores*) colourful.

colorir [kolo'ri(x)] *vt* to colour in.

coluna [ko'luna] *f* column; (*de rádio, hi-fi*) speaker; ~ **vertebral** spinal column.

com [kõ] *prep* with; (*indica causa*) because of; **só ~ muito esforço é que ele conseguiu** he only managed it through a lot of hard work; **estar ~ dor de cabeça** to have a headache; **estar ~ fome** to be hungry; **estar ~ pressa** to be in a hurry.

coma ['koma] *m ou f* (*MED*) coma.

comandante [komãn'dãntʃi] *m* (*de*

navio, polícia) commander; *(de exército)* major.

comandar [komãn'da(x)] *vt* to command, to be in charge of.

comando [ko'mãndu] *m* command; *(de máquina, sistema)* control; **estar no ~ de algo** to be in charge of sthg.

combate [kõm'batʃi] *m (luta)* fight; *(batalha)* fighting.

combater [kõmba'te(x)] *vi* to fight.

combinação [kõmbina'sãw] *(pl -ões* [-õjʃ]) *f* combination; *(acordo)* agreement; *(plano)* arrangement; *(peça de vestuário)* slip.

combinar [kõmbi'na(x)] *vt* to combine; *(planejar)* to plan ◆ *vi (cores, roupas)* to go together; **está combinado!** it's a deal!; **~ com** to go with; **~ algo com alguém** to arrange sthg with sb.

comboio [kõm'boju] *m (Port)* train; **apanhar/perder o ~** to catch/miss the train.

combustível [kõmbuʃ'tʃivew] *(pl -eis* [-ejʃ]) *m* fuel.

começar [kome'sa(x)] *vt & vi* to start, to begin; **~ a fazer algo** to start OU begin to do sthg; **~ de/por** to start from/with; **~ por fazer algo** to start by doing sthg; **para ~** to start (with).

começo [ko'mesu] *m* start, beginning.

comédia [ko'mɛdʒja] *f* comedy.

comediante [kome'dʒjãntʃi] *mf* comic actor *(f* actress).

comemorar [komemo'ra(x)] *vt* to commemorate.

comentar [komẽn'ta(x)] *vt (mencionar)* to mention; *(analisar)* to comment on; *(criticar maliciosamente)* to make comments about.

comentário [komẽn'tarju] *m* comment; *(de evento esportivo)* commentary.

comer [ko'me(x)] *(pl -res* [-riʃ]) *vt* to eat; *(em xadrez, damas)* to take ◆ *vi (alimentar-se)* to eat ◆ *m (alimento)* food; *(refeição)* meal.

comercial [komex'sjaw] *(pl -ais* [-ajʃ]) *adj* commercial.

comercialização [komexsjaliza'sãw] *f* sale.

comercializar [komexsjali'za(x)] *vt* to sell.

comerciante [komex'sjãntʃi] *mf* shopkeeper.

comércio [ko'mexsju] *m* commerce; *(lojas)* shops *(pl).*

comeres → **comer**.

comestível [komeʃ'tʃivew] *(pl -eis* [-ejʃ]) *adj* edible.

cometer [kome'te(x)] *vt (delito)* to commit; *(erro)* to make.

comichão [komi'ʃãw] *(pl -ões* [-õjʃ]) *f* itch; **fazer ~** to itch.

comício [ko'misju] *m* rally.

cómico, -ca ['kɔmiku, -ka] *adj (Port)* = **cômico.**

cômico, -ca ['komiku, -ka] *adj (Br) (actor)* comic; *(engraçado)* funny, comical.

comida [ko'mida] *f* food; *(refeição)* meal; **~ para bebê** baby food; **~ congelada** frozen food.

comigo [ko'migu] *pron* with me; **estava falando ~ mesmo** I was talking to myself.

comilão, -lona [komi'lãw, -lona] *(mpl -ões* [-õjʃ], *fpl* -s [-ʃ]) *m, f (fam)* glutton.

cominho [ko'miɲu] *m* cumin.

comissão [komi'sãw] *(pl -ões* [-õjʃ]) *f* commission.

comissário [komi'sarju] *m (de polícia)* superintendent; *(de navio)* purser; **~ de bordo** air steward.

comissões → **comissão.**

comité [komi'tɛ] *m (Port)* = **comitê.**

comitê [komi'te] *m (Br)* committee.

como ['komu] *adv* **1.** *(comparativo)* like; **não é ~ o outro** it's not like the other one; **~ quem não quer nada** casually; **~ se nada estivesse acontecendo** as if nothing was going on.
2. *(de que maneira)* how; **~?** *(o que disse)* I'm sorry?, pardon?
3. *(marca intensidade)*: **~ ele é inteligente!** he's so clever!, how clever he is!; **~ é difícil arranjar lugar para estacionar!** it's so difficult to find a parking space!; **~ você se engana!** how wrong you are!
◆ *conj* **1.** *(introduz comparação)* like; **é bonita, ~ a mãe** she's pretty, (just) like her mother.
2. *(da forma que)* as; **~ queira!** as you wish!; **seja ~ for** in any case.
3. *(por exemplo)* like, such as; **as cidades grandes ~ São Paulo** big cities like São Paulo
4. *(na qualidade de)* as; **~ mãe fiquei muito preocupada** as a mother I felt very concerned; **~ prêmio ela ganhou um carro** she won a car for a prize.
5. *(visto que)* as, since; **~ estávamos**

atrasados fomos de táxi we took a taxi as we were running late; ~ não atenderam pensamos que não estavam we thought you weren't in as there was no answer.

6. *(em locuções):* ~ deve ser *adv (corretamente)* properly.

♦ *adj (próprio)* suitable.

comoção [komo'sãw] *(pl -ões* [-õjʃ]) *f (emoção)* emotion; *(agitação)* commotion.

cómoda ['kɔmuda] *f (Port)* = cômoda.

cômoda ['komoda] *f (Br)* chest of drawers.

comodidade [komodʒi'dadʒi] *f* comfort.

comodismo [komo'dʒiʒmu] *m* complacency.

comodista [komo'dʒiʃta] *mf* complacent person.

cómodo, -da ['kɔmudu, -da] *adj (Port)* = cômodo.

cômodo, -da ['komodu, -da] *adj (Br)* comfortable.

comovedor, -ra [komove'do(x), -ra] *(mpl -res* [-riʃ], *fpl -s* [-ʃ]) *adj* moving.

comovente [komo'vẽtʃi] *adj* touching.

comover [komo've(x)] *vt* to move.

⊔ **comover-se** *vp* to be moved.

comovido, -da [komo'vidu, -da] *adj* moved.

compacto, -ta [kõm'paktu, -ta] *adj* compact; *(denso)* thick; *(sólido)* hard ♦ *m (CD)* compact disc, CD; *(Br: disco de vinil)* record.

compaixão [kõmpaj'ʃãw] *f* compassion.

companheiro, -ra [kõmpa'ɲejru, -ra] *m, f (acompanhante)* companion; *(de turma)* classmate; *(em casal)* partner.

companhia [kõmpa'ɲia] *f* company; fazer ~ a alguém to keep sb company; ~ de aviação airline; ~ de navegação shipping line; ~ de seguros insurance company; em ~ de alguém with sb.

comparação [kõmpara'sãw] *(pl -ões* [-õjʃ]) *f* comparison; não ter ~ com to bear no comparison with; em ~ com in comparison with.

comparar [kõmpa'ra(x)] *vt* to compare; ~ algo a OU com algo to compare sthg to OU with sthg.

comparecer [kõmpare'se(x)] *vi* to ap-

pear, to attend; ~ a algo to attend sthg.

compartilhar [kõmpaxtʃi'ʎa(x)] *vt* to share; ~ algo com alguém to share sthg with sb.

compartimento [kõmpaxtʃi'mẽtu] *m* compartment; *(de casa)* room.

compartir [kõmpax'tʃi(x)] *vt* to share.

compasso [kõm'pasu] *m* compasses *(pl); (MÚS)* time.

compatível [kõmpa'tʃivew] *(pl -eis* [-ejʃ]) *adj* compatible; ~ com compatible with.

compatriota [kõmpatri'ɔta] *mf* compatriot.

compensação [kõmpẽsa'sãw] *(pl -ões* [-õjʃ]) *f* compensation; *(vantagem)* advantage.

compensar [kõmpẽ'sa(x)] *vt* to compensate; *(recompensar)* to make up for; não compensa o esforço it isn't worth the effort.

competência [kõmpe'tẽsja] *f* competence; *(responsabilidade)* responsibility.

competente [kõmpe'tẽtʃi] *adj* competent.

competição [kõmpetʃi'sãw] *(pl -ões* [-õjʃ]) *f* competition.

competir [kõmpe'tʃi(x)] *vi* to compete; ~ com *(rivalizar com)* to compete with.

competitivo, -va [kõmpetʃi'tʃivu, -va] *adj* competitive.

compilar [kõmpi'la(x)] *vt* to compile.

complacente [kõmpla'sẽtʃi] *adj* indulgent.

complementar [kõmplemẽ'ta(x)] *(pl -res* [-riʃ]) *adj* complementary.

complemento [kõmple'mẽtu] *m* complement; *(em trem)* supplement.

completamente [kõmpleta'mẽtʃi] *adv* completely.

completar [kõmple'ta(x)] *vt (preencher)* to fill in; *(terminar)* to complete.

completo, -ta [kõm'pletu, -ta] *adj* completed; *(cheio)* full; *(inteiro)* complete.

complexo, -xa [kõm'plɛksu, -ksa] *adj & m* complex.

complicação [kõmplika'sãw] *(pl -ões* [-õjʃ]) *f* complication.

complicado, -da [kõmpli'kadu, -da] *adj* complicated.

complicar [kõmpli'ka(x)] *vt* to complicate.

❑ **complicar-se** *vp* to become OU get complicated.

componente [kõmpo'nẽntʃi] *mf* component.

compor [kõm'po(x)] *vt (música, poema)* to compose; *(consertar)* to repair; *(arrumar)* to tidy; *(fazer parte de)* to make up.

❑ **compor-se** *vp (arranjar-se)* to tidy o.s. up.

❑ **compor-se de** *vp + prep (ser formado por)* to be made up of.

comporta [kõm'pɔxta] *f* sluice gate.

comportamento [kõmpoxta'mẽntu] *m* behaviour.

comportar [kõmpox'ta(x)] *vt (conter em si)* to hold; *(admitir)* to permit.

❑ **comportar-se** *vp* to behave.

composição [kõmpozi'sãw] *(pl* -ões [-õjʃ]) *f* composition; *(EDUC)* essay.

compositor, -ra [kõmpozi'to(x), -ra] *(mpl* -res [-riʃ], *fpl* -s [-ʃ]) *m*, *f (MÚS)* composer.

composto, -osta [kõm'poʃtu, -ɔʃta] *m (GRAM)* compound ♦ *adj*: **ser ~ por** to be composed of.

compostura [kõmpoʃ'tura] *f* composure; *(boa educação)* manners *(pl)*.

compota [kõm'pɔta] *f* preserve.

compra ['kõmpra] *f* purchase; **ir às** OU **fazer ~s** to go shopping.

comprar [kõm'pra(x)] *vt* to buy.

compreender [kõmprjẽn'de(x)] *vt* to understand; *(incluir)* to comprise.

compreensão [kõmprjẽ'sãw] *f* understanding.

compreensivo, -va [kõmprjẽ'sivu, -va] *adj* understanding.

compressa [kõm'prɛsa] *f* compress; **~ esterilizada** sterile dressing.

comprido, -da [kõm'pridu, -da] *adj* long; **deitar-se ao ~** to lie down flat.

comprimento [kõmpri'mẽntu] *m* length; **tem 5 metros de ~** it's 5 metres long.

comprimido, -da [kõmpri'midu, -da] *adj* compressed ♦ *m* pill; **~ para dormir** sleeping pill; **~ para a dor** painkiller; **~ para o enjôo** travel sickness pill.

comprimir [kõmpri'mi(x)] *vt (apertar)* to squeeze; *(reduzir de volume)* to compress.

comprometer [kõmprome'te(x)] *vt* to compromise.

❑ **comprometer-se** *vp* to compro-

mise o.s.; **~-se a fazer algo** to commit o.s. to doing sthg.

compromisso [kõmpru'misu] *m (obrigação)* commitment; *(acordo)* agreement; **tenho um ~** I've got a prior engagement.

comprovação [kõmprova'sãw] *(pl* -ões [-õjʃ]) *f* proof.

comprovar [kõmpro'va(x)] *vt* to prove.

computador [kõmputa'do(x)] *(pl* -res [-riʃ]) *m* computer; **~ pessoal** personal computer.

comum [ko'mũ] *(pl* -ns [-ʃ]) *adj (frequente)* common; *(vulgar)* ordinary; *(partilhado)* shared.

comunhão [komu'ɲãw] *(pl* -ões [-õjʃ]) *f (RELIG)* Communion; **~ de bens** joint ownership *(in marriage)*.

comunicação [komunika'sãw] *(pl* -ões [-õjʃ]) *f* communication; *(comunicado)* announcement.

comunicado [komuni'kadu] *m* communiqué.

comunicar [komuni'ka(x)] *vt* to communicate; *(mensagem)* to pass on ♦ *vi* to communicate; **~ algo a alguém** to inform sb of sthg; **~ com** to communicate with.

comunidade [komuni'dadʒi] *f* community; **a Comunidade Européia** the European Community.

comunismo [komu'niʒmu] *m* communism.

comunista [komu'niʃta] *adj & mf* communist.

comuns → **comum**.

comutar [komu'ta(x)] *vt (pena)* to commute.

conceber [kõse'be(x)] *vt (filho)* to conceive; *(plano, sistema)* to think up.

conceder [kõse'de(x)] *vt (dar)* to give; *(prêmio, bolsa)* to award.

conceito [kõ'sejtu] *m* concept.

conceituado, -da [kõsej'twadu, -da] *adj* respected.

concelho [kõ'seʎu] *m* = municipality.

concentração [kõsẽntra'sãw] *(pl* -ões [-õjʃ]) *f* concentration; *(de pessoas)* gathering.

concentrado, -da [kõsẽn'tradu, -da] *adj (atento)* intent; *(produto, suco)* concentrated ♦ *m*: **~ de tomate** tomato purée.

concentrar [kõsẽn'tra(x)] *vt (atenção, esforços)* to concentrate; *(reunir)* to bring together.

□ **concentrar-se** *vp* to concentrate;
~-se em *(estudo, trabalho)* to concentrate on; *(lugar)* to group together in.

concepção [kõsep'sãw] *(pl* **-ões** [-õjʃ])
f concept; *(de filho)* conception.

concerto [kõ'sextu] *m* concert.

concessão [kõse'sãw] *(pl* **-ões** [-õjʃ]) *f*
(de prêmio) awarding; *(de bolsa)* granting; *(de desconto)* concession.

concessionária [kõsesjo'narja] *f (Br)*
licensed dealer; **~ automóvel** car dealer.

concessionário [kõsesju'narju] *m*
(Port) = **concessionária**.

concessões → **concessão**.

concha [ˈkõʃa] *f* shell; *(de sopa)* ladle.

conciliação [kõsilja'sãw] *(pl* **-ões**
[-õjʃ]) *f* reconciliation.

conciliar [kõsi'lja(x)] *vt* to reconcile.

concluir [kõŋklu'i(x)] *vt* to conclude;
(acabar) to finish.

conclusão [kõŋklu'zãw] *(pl* **-ões**
[-õjʃ]) *f* conclusion; **em ~** in conclusion.

concordância [kõŋkox'dãsja] *f*
agreement; **em ~ com** in accordance
with.

concordar [kõŋkox'da(x)] *vi* to agree;
~ com to agree with; **~ em fazer algo**
to agree to do sthg.

concorrência [kõŋko'xẽsja] *f* competition.

concorrente [kõŋko'xẽntʃi] *adj*
(equipe) opposing; *(produto, empresa)*
rival ◆ *mf* *(em concurso, competição)*
contestant; *(em disputa)* rival.

concorrer [kõŋko'xe(x)] *vi* to compete; **~ a algo** *(emprego, posição)* to
apply for sthg.

concretizar [kõŋkretʃi'za(x)] *vt* to
realize.

concreto, -ta [kõŋ'kretu, -ta] *adj &*
m concrete.

concurso [kõŋ'kuxsu] *m* *(de televisão)*
game show; *(de rádio)* contest; *(de
música, literatura)* competition; *(para
emprego)* open competition.

conde [ˈkõdʒi] *m* count.

condenação [kõdena'sãw] *(pl* **-ões**
[-õjʃ]) *f* condemnation; *(JUR: sentença)*
sentence.

condenar [kõde'na(x)] *vt* to condemn; *(JUR: sentenciar)* to sentence.

condensação [kõdẽsa'sãw] *f* condensation.

condensado [kõdẽ'sadu] *adj m* →
leite.

condensar [kõdẽ'sa(x)] *vt* to condense.

condescendência [kõdesẽn'dẽsja] *f*
compliance.

condescendente [kõdesẽn'dẽntʃi]
adj compliant.

condescender [kõdesẽn'de(x)] *vi* to
agree; **~ em fazer algo** to agree to do
sthg.

condessa [kõn'desa] *f* countess.

condição [kõdʒi'sãw] *(pl* **-ões** [-õjʃ])
f condition; *(classe social)* status; **estar
em boas/más condições** to be in
good/bad condition.

condicionado, -da [kõdʒisjo'nadu,
-da] *adj* restricted.

condicional [kõdʒisjo'naw] *m:* **o ~**
the conditional.

condicionar [kõdʒisjo'na(x)] *vt* to
restrict.

condições → **condição**.

condimentar [kõdʒimẽn'ta(x)] *vt* to
season.

condimento [kõdʒi'mẽntu] *m* seasoning.

condizer [kõdʒi'ze(x)] *vi* to go
together; **~ com** to go with.

condolências [kõdo'lẽsjaʃ] *fpl* condolences; **as minhas ~** my condolences.

condomínio [kõdo'minju] *m* maintenance fee.

condómino [kõn'dɔminu] *m (Port)* =
condômino.

condômino [kõn'dominu] *m (Br)* proprietor *(in a block of flats)*.

condor [kõn'do(x)] *(pl* **-res** [-riʃ]) *m*
condor.

condução [kõndu'sãw] *f (de governo)*
running; *(Br: transporte)* transport;
(Port: de veículo) driving.

conduta [kõn'duta] *f (tubo, cano)*
chute; *(comportamento)* behaviour; **~
de gás** gas piping.

condutor, -ra [kõndu'to(x), -ra] *(mpl*
-res [-riʃ], *fpl* **-s** [-ʃ]) *m, f* driver ◆ *adj*
conductive.

conduzir [kõndu'zi(x)] *vt (administrar)*
to run; *(Port: dirigir)* to drive ◆ *vi (Port:
dirigir)* to drive; **~ a** to lead to.

cone [ˈkɔni] *m* cone.

conexão [konek'sãw] *(pl* **-ões** [-õjʃ]) *f*
connection.

confecção [kõfɛk'sãw] *(pl* **-ões** [-õjʃ]) *f*

f *(de peça de vestuário)* making; *(de prato culinário)* preparation.

confeccionar [kõfeksjoˈna(x)] *vt* to make.

confecções → confecção.

confeitaria [kõfejtaˈria] *f* sweet shop *(Brit)*, candy store *(Am)*.

conferência [kõfeˈrẽsja] *f* conference.

conferir [kõfeˈri(x)] *vt* to check ♦ *vi* *(estar exato)* to be correct.

confessar [kõfeˈsa(x)] *vt* to confess.

❑ **confessar-se** *vp* to confess.

confessionário [kõfesjoˈnarju] *m* confessional.

confiança [kõfˈjãsa] *f (fé)* trust; *(segurança)* confidence; *(familiaridade)* familiarity; **ter ~ em** to trust; **ser de ~** to be reliable.

confiar [kõfˈja(x)] *vt*: **~ algo a alguém** *(segredo)* to tell sb sthg in confidence; **~ alguém a alguém** to leave sb in sb's care.

❑ **confiar em** *v + prep (pessoa)* to trust; *(futuro, resultado)* to have faith in.

confidência [kõfiˈdẽsja] *f* confidence.

confidencial [kõfidẽˈsjaw] *(pl* -ais [-ajʃ]) *adj* confidential.

confirmação [kõfixmaˈsãw] *(pl* -ões [-õjʃ]) *f* confirmation.

confirmar [kõfixˈma(x)] *vt* to confirm.

❑ **confirmar-se** *vp* to come true.

confiscar [kõfiʃˈka(x)] *vt* to confiscate.

confissão [kõfiˈsãw] *(pl* -ões [-õjʃ]) *f* confession.

conflito [kõˈflitu] *m* conflict; *(desavença)* argument.

conformar-se [kõfoxˈmaxsi] *vp* *(resignar-se)* to resign o.s.; **~ com** to resign o.s. to.

conforme [kõˈfoxmi] *conj* as ♦ *prep* *(dependendo de como)* depending on; *(de acordo com)* according to.

conformidade [kõfoxmiˈdadʒi] *f* conformity; **em ~ com** in accordance with.

confortar [kõfoxˈta(x)] *vt* to comfort.

confortável [kõfoxˈtavew] *(pl* -eis [-ejʃ]) *adj* comfortable.

conforto [kõˈfoxtu] *m* comfort.

confraternizar [kõfratexniˈza(x)] *vt* to fraternize; **~ com** to fraternize with.

confrontação [kõfrõtaˈsãw] *(pl* -ões [-õjʃ]) *f* confrontation.

confrontar [kõfrõˈta(x)] *vt* to confront; *(comparar)* to compare.

❑ **confrontar-se** *vp* to come face to face; **~-se com** *(deparar com)* to be confronted with.

confronto [kõˈfrõtu] *m* confrontation; *(comparação)* comparison.

confundir [kõfũˈdi(x)] *vt* *(pessoa)* to confuse; *(rua, significado)* to mistake; *(números)* to mix up.

❑ **confundir-se** *vp* *(enganar-se)* to make a mistake; **~-se com** *(ser muito parecido a)* to be taken for.

confusão [kõfuˈzãw] *(pl* -ões [-õjʃ]) *f* confusion; *(tumulto)* commotion; **armar ~** to cause trouble; **fazer ~** to get mixed up.

confuso, -sa [kõˈfuzu, -za] *adj* *(desordenado)* mixed up; *(obscuro)* confusing; *(confundido)* confused.

confusões → confusão.

congelado, -da [kõʒeˈladu, -da] *adj* frozen.

congelador [kõʒelaˈdor] *(pl* -res [-riʃ]) *m (Port)* freezer.

congelar [kõʒeˈla(x)] *vt & vi* to freeze.

congestão [kõʒeʃˈtãw] *(pl* -ões [-õjʃ]) *f* congestion.

congestionado, -da [kõʒeʃtʃjoˈnadu, -da] *adj* congested.

congestionamento [kõʒeʃtʃjonaˈmẽtu] *m (de trânsito)* congestion.

congestionar [kõʒeʃtʃjoˈna(x)] *vt* *(trânsito)* to block.

congestões → congestão.

congratular [kõŋgratuˈla(x)] *vt* to congratulate.

congresso [kõŋˈgresu] *m* congress.

conhaque [koˈɲaki] *m* cognac.

conhecedor, -ra [koɲeseˈdo(x), -ra] *(mpl* -res [-riʃ], *fpl* -s [-ʃ]) *m, f*: **ser ~ de** to be an authority on.

conhecer [koɲeˈse(x)] *vt* to know; *(ser apresentado a)* to meet; *(reconhecer)* to recognize.

conhecido, -da [koɲeˈsidu, -da] *adj* well-known ♦ *m, f* acquaintance.

conhecimento [koɲesiˈmẽtu] *m* knowledge; *(experiência)* experience; **dar ~ de algo a alguém** to inform sb of sthg; **tomar ~ de algo** to find out about sthg; **é do ~ de todos** it is common knowledge.

❏ **conhecimentos** *mpl* contacts; *(cultura)* knowledge *(sg)*; **(ele) é uma pessoa com ~s** he is a knowledgeable OU cultured person.

conjugado [kõʒuˈgadu] *m (Br)* studio flat.

cônjuge [ˈkõʒuʒi] *mf* spouse.

conjunção [kõʒũˈsãw] *(pl -ões* [-õjʃ]*) f (GRAM)* conjunction; *(união)* union.

conjuntiva [kõʒũˈtʃiva] *f* conjunctiva.

conjuntivite [kõʒũtʃiˈvitʃi] *f* conjunctivitis.

conjunto [kõˈʒũtu] *m* set; *(de rock)* band; *(de roupa)* outfit.

connosco [kõˈnoʃku] *pron (Port)* = **conosco**.

conosco [koˈnoʃku] *pron (Br)* with us.

conquanto [kõŋˈkwãntu] *conj* even though.

conquista [kõŋˈkiʃta] *f* conquest.

conquistar [kõŋkiʃˈta(x)] *vt* to conquer; *(posição, trabalho)* to get; *(seduzir)* to win over.

consciência [kõʃˈsjẽsja] *f* conscience; *(conhecimento)* awareness; **ter ~ de algo** to be aware of sthg; **ter a ~ pesada** to have a guilty conscience; **tomar ~ de algo** to become aware of sthg.

consciente [kõʃˈsjẽtʃi] *adj (acordado)* conscious; *(responsável)* aware ◆ *m:* **o ~** the conscious mind.

consecutivo, -va [kõseku'tʃivu, -va] *adj* consecutive.

conseguinte [kõseˈgĩtʃi] **: por conseguinte** *adv* consequently.

conseguir [kõseˈgi(x)] *vt* to get; **~ fazer algo** to manage to do sthg.

conselho [kõˈseʎu] *m* piece of advice; *(órgão coletivo)* council; **dar ~s** to give advice; **Conselho de Ministros** Cabinet.

consenso [kõˈsẽsu] *m* consensus.

consentimento [kõsẽtʃiˈmẽtu] *m* consent.

consentir [kõsẽˈtʃi(x)] *vt* to consent to.

consequência [kõseˈkwẽsja] *pron (Port)* = **conseqüência**.

conseqüência [kõseˈkwẽsja] *f (Br)* consequence; **em** OU **como ~** as a consequence.

consertar [kõsexˈta(x)] *vt* to repair, to fix.

conserto [kõˈsextu] *m* repair.

conserva [kõˈsexva] *f*: **de ~** canned, tinned.

❏ **conservas** *fpl* tinned OU canned food *(sg)*.

conservação [kõsexvaˈsãw] *f* conservation; *(de alimento)* preservation.

conservar [kõsexˈva(x)] *vt* to preserve.

conservatório [kõsexvaˈtɔrju] *m* conservatoire *(Brit)*, conservatory *(Am)*.

consideração [kõsideraˈsãw] *(pl -ões* [-õjʃ]*) f* consideration; *(crítica)* point; **ter algo em ~** to take sthg into consideration.

considerar [kõsideˈra(x)] *vt* to consider; **~ que** to consider (that).

❏ **considerar-se** *vp*: **ele considera-se o maior** he thinks he's the best.

considerável [kõsideˈravew] *(pl -eis* [-ejʃ]*) adj* considerable; *(feito, conquista)* significant.

consigo [kõˈsigu] *pron (com ele)* with him; *(com ela)* with her; *(com você)* with you; *(com eles, elas)* with them; *(relativo a coisa, animal)* with it; **ela estava a falar ~ própria** she was talking to herself.

consistência [kõsiʃˈtẽsja] *f* consistency; *(de objeto, madeira)* solidity.

consistente [kõsiʃˈtẽtʃi] *adj (coerente)* consistent; *(espesso)* thick; *(sólido)* solid.

consistir [kõsiʃˈti(x)] **: consistir em** *v + prep (ser composto por)* to consist of; *(basear-se em)* to consist in.

consoada [kõˈswada] *f* meal eaten late on Christmas Eve which traditionally consists of boiled salt cod with boiled potatoes, cabbage and boiled eggs.

consoante [kõˈswãtʃi] *f* consonant ◆ *prep (dependendo de)* depending on; *(conforme)* according to.

consolar [kõsoˈla(x)] *vt* to console.

❏ **consolar-se** *vp* to console o.s.

consomé [kõsoˈmɛ] *m (Port)* = **consomê**.

consomê [kõsoˈme] *m (Br)* consommé.

conspícuo, -cua [kõʃˈpikwu, -kwa] *adj* conspicuous.

conspiração [kõʃpiraˈsãw] *(pl -ões* [-õjʃ]*) f* conspiracy.

constante [kõʃˈtãtʃi] *adj* constant.

constar [kõʃˈta(x)] *v impess*: **consta que** ... it is said that ....

❏ **constar de** *v + prep (consistir em)* to consist of; *(figurar em)* to appear in.

constatar [kõʃta'ta(x)] *vt*: ~ **que** *(notar que)* to realize (that).

consternado, -da [kõʃter'nadu, -da] *adj* distraught.

constipação [kõʃʃipa'sãw] *(pl* -ões [-õjʃ]*) f (Br: prisão de ventre)* constipation; *(Port: resfriado)* cold.

constipado, -da [kõʃʃi'padu, -da] *adj*: **estar** ~ *(Br: ter prisão de ventre)* to be constipated; *(Port: estar resfriado)* to have a cold.

constipar-se [kõʃti'parse] *vp (Port)* to catch a cold.

constituição [kõʃtʃitwi'sãw] *(pl* -ões [-õjʃ]*) f* constitution.

constituir [kõʃtʃitwi(x)] *vt (formar)* to set up; *(representar)* to constitute.

constranger [kõʃtrã'ʒe(x)] *vt (embaraçar)* to embarrass; *(obrigar)* to force.

❏ **constranger-se** *vp (embaraçar-se)* to be embarrassed.

constrangimento [kõʃtrãʒi'mẽntu] *m (embaraço)* embarrassment; *(obrigação)* constraint.

construção [kõʃtru'sãw] *(pl* -ões [-õjʃ]*) f* construction.

construir [kõʃtru'i(x)] *vt* to build; *(frase)* to construct.

construtivo, -va [kõʃtru'tivu, -va] *adj* constructive.

construtor, -ra [kõʃtru'to(x), -ra] *(mpl* -es [-iʃ]*, fpl* -s [-ʃ]*) m, f* builder.

cônsul ['kõsuw] *(pl* -es [-iʃ]*) mf* consul.

consulado [kõsu'ladu] *m* consulate.

cônsules → **cônsul**.

consulta [kõ'suwta] *f (com médico)* appointment; *(de texto, dicionário)* consultation.

consultar [kõsuw'ta(x)] *vi (médico)* to hold a surgery ◆ *vt* to consult.

consultório [kõsuw'tɔrju] *m (de médico)* surgery.

consumidor, -ra [kõsumi'do(x), -ra] *(mpl* -res [-riʃ]*, fpl* -s [-ʃ]*) m, f* consumer.

consumir [kõsu'mi(x)] *vt & vi* to consume.

consumo [kõ'sumu] *m* consumption.

conta ['kõnta] *f (de restaurante, café, etc)* bill; *(de banco)* account; *(de colar)* bead; **a** ~**, por favor** could I have the bill, please?; **o jantar é por minha** ~ dinner's on me; **abrir uma** ~ to open an account; **dar-se** ~ **de que** to realize

(that); **fazer de** ~ **que** to pretend (that); **ter em** ~ to take into account; **tomar** ~ **de** to look after; ~ **bancária** bank account; ~ **corrente** current account; ~ **à ordem** deposit account; **vezes sem** ~ countless times.

contabilidade [kõntabeli'dadʒi] *f* accountancy; *(departamento)* accounts department.

contabilista [kõntabe'liʃta] *mf (Port)* accountant.

contacto [kõn'ta(k)tu] *m (Port)* = **contato**.

contador [kõnta'do(x)] *(pl* -res [-riʃ]*) m (Br: profissional)* accountant; *(medidor)* meter; ~ **de estórias** storyteller.

contagem [kõn'taʒẽ] *(pl* -ns [-ʃ]*) f (de gasto de água, de luz, etc)* meter-reading; *(de votos, bilhetes, etc)* counting.

contagiar [kõnta'ʒja(x)] *vt* to infect.

contágio [kõn'taʒju] *m* infection, contagion.

contagioso, -osa [kõnta'ʒjozu, -ɔza] *adj* contagious, infectious.

conta-gotas [ˌkõnta'gotaʃ] *m inv* dropper.

contaminação [kõntamina'sãw] *(pl* -ões [-õjʃ]*) f* contamination.

contaminar -[kõntami'na(x)] *vt* to contaminate.

conta-quilómetros [ˌkõntaki'lɔmetruʃ] *m inv (Port)* speedometer.

contar [kõn'ta(x)] *vt* to count; *(narrar, explicar)* to tell ◆ *vi (calcular)* to count; ~ **algo a alguém** to tell sb sthg; ~ **fazer algo** *(tencionar)* to expect to do sthg; ~ **com** to count on.

contatar [kõnta'ta(x)] *vt* to contact.

contato [kõn'tatu] *m (Br)* contact; *(de motor)* ignition; **entrar em** ~ **com** *(contatar)* to get in touch with.

contemplar [kõntẽm'pla(x)] *vt* to contemplate; ~ **alguém com algo** to give sb sthg.

contemporâneo, -nea [kõntẽmpo'ranju, -nja] *adj & m, f* contemporary.

contentamento [kõntẽnta'mẽntu] *m* contentment.

contentar [kõntẽn'ta(x)] *vt* to keep happy.

❏ **contentar a** *v + prep* to please.

❏ **contentar-se com** *vp + prep* to content o.s. with.

contente [kõn'tẽntʃi] *adj* happy.

contentor [kõntẽn'to(x)] *(pl* -es [-iʃ]*)*

m container; **~ do lixo** large bin.
conter [kõn'te(x)] *vt (ter)* to contain;
(refrear) to hold back.
❏ **conter-se** *vp* to restrain o.s.
conterrâneo, -nea [kõnteˈxanju,
-nja] *m, f* compatriot.
contestação [kõnteʃtaˈsãw] *(pl -ões*
[-õjʃ]) *f (resposta)* answer; *(polêmica)*
controversy.
contestar [kõnteʃˈta(x)] *vt (refutar)* to
dispute; *(replicar)* to answer.
conteúdo [kõnˈtjudu] *m (de recipiente)*
contents *(pl)*; *(de carta, texto)* content.
contexto [kõnˈteʃtu] *m* context.
contigo [kõnˈtigu] *pron* with you.
continente [kõntʃiˈnẽntʃi] *m* continent.
continuação [kõntʃinwaˈsãw] *(pl -ões*
[-õjʃ]) *f* continuation.
continuamente [kõnˌtʃinwaˈmẽntʃi]
adv (sem interrupção) continuously;
(repetidamente) continually.
continuar [kõntʃiˈnwa(x)] *vt* to continue ◆ *vi* to carry on; **~ a fazer algo**
to continue doing sthg; **~ com algo** to
carry on with sthg.
contínuo, -nua [kõnˈtʃinwu, -nwa]
adj (sem interrupção) continuous;
(repetido) continual ◆ *m, f* caretaker.
conto [ˈkõntu] *m (Port: mil escudos)*
thousand escudos; *(história)* story.
contornar [kõntoxˈna(x)] *vt (edifício,
muro, etc)* to go round; *(problema, situação)* to get round.
contra [ˈkõntra] *prep* against ◆ *m:*
pesar OU **ver os prós e os ~s** to weigh
up the pros and the cons.
contra-ataque [kõntraˈtaki] *m*
counterattack.
contrabaixo [kõntraˈbajʃu] *m* double bass.
contrabando [kõntraˈbãndu] *m (de
mercadorias)* smuggling; *(mercadoria)*
contraband.
contracepção [ˌkõntrasepˈsãw] *f*
contraception.
contraceptivo, -va [ˌkõntrasep-
ˈtʃivu, -va] *adj & m* contraceptive.
contradição [ˌkõntradʒiˈsãw] *(pl -ões*
[-õjʃ]) *f* contradiction.
contradizer [ˌkõntradʒiˈze(x)] *vt* to
contradict.
contrafilé [kõntrafiˈlɛ] *m (Br)* rump
steak.
contra-indicação [ˌkõntraĩndʒikaˈsãw] *(pl -ões* [-õjʃ]) *f (de medicamento)*
contraindication.
contrair [kõntraˈi(x)] *vt (doença)* to
catch, to contract; *(dívida)* to run up;
(vício, hábito) to acquire; **~ matrimônio**
to get married.
contramão [kõntraˈmãw] *f (de rua,
estrada)* the other side of the road; **ir
pela ~** to drive on the wrong side of
the road.
contrapartida [ˌkõntrapartˈʃida] *f*
compensation; **em ~** on the other
hand.
contrariar [kõntraˈrja(x)] *vt (contradizer)* to contradict; *(aborrecer)* to
annoy.
contrariedade [kõntrarjeˈdadʒi] *f*
(aborrecimento) annoyance.
contrário, -ria [kõnˈtrarju, -rja] *adj
(oposto)* opposite; *(adversário)* opposing ◆ *m:* **o ~** the opposite; **ser ~ a algo**
to be against sthg; **de ~** otherwise;
pelo ~ (quite) the contrary; **em sentido ~** in the opposite direction.
contra-senso [ˌkõntraˈsẽsu] *m (absurdo)* nonsense; *(em tradução)* mistranslation.
contrastar [kõntraʃˈta(x)] *vt & vi* to
contrast; **~ com** to contrast with.
contraste [kõnˈtraʃtʃi] *m* contrast;
em ~ com in contrast with.
contratar [kõntraˈta(x)] *vt* to hire.
contratempo [kõntraˈtẽmpu] *m* setback.
contrato [kõnˈtratu] *m* contract.
contribuinte [kõntriˈbwĩntʃi] *mf* taxpayer.
contribuir [kõntriˈbwi(x)] *vi* to contribute; **~ com algo** to contribute sthg;
~ para algo to contribute towards
sthg.
controlar [kõntroˈla(x)] *vt* to control.
❏ **controlar-se** *vp* to control o.s.
controle [kõnˈtroli] *m (Br)* control; **~
remoto** remote control.
controlo [kõnˈtrolu] *m (Port)* = **controle**.
controvérsia [kõntroˈvɛrsja] *f* controversy.
controverso, -sa [kõntroˈvɛrsu, -sa]
adj controversial.
contudo [kõnˈtudu] *conj* however.
contusão [kõntuˈzãw] *(pl -ões* [-õjʃ]) *f*
bruise.
convalescença [kõvaleʃˈsẽsa] *f* convalescence.
convenção [kõvẽˈsãw] *(pl -ões* [-õjʃ])

f convention.

convencer [kõve'se(x)] *vt* to convince; ~ **alguém a fazer algo** to persuade sb to do sthg; ~ **alguém de algo** to convince sb of sthg; ~ **alguém de que** to convince sb (that).

❏ **convencer-se** *vp* to be convinced; ~**-se de que** to become convinced (that).

convencido, -da [kõvẽ'sidu, -da] *adj* conceited.

convencional [kõvẽsjo'naw] (*pl* **-ais** [-ajʃ]) *adj* conventional.

convenções → **convenção**.

conveniente [kõve'njẽtʃi] *adj* convenient.

convento [kõ'vẽtu] *m* convent.

conversa [kõ'vexsa] *f* conversation; ~ **fiada** chitchat; **não ir na** ~ not to be taken in.

conversar [kõvex'sa(x)] *vi* to talk; ~ **com** to talk to.

conversível [kõvex'sivew] (*pl* **-eis** [-ejʃ]) *m* (*Br*: *carro*) convertible.

converter [kõvex'te(x)] *vt* (*transformar*): ~ **algo/alguém em** to convert sthg/sb into.

❏ **converter-se** *vp* to convert; ~**-se a** to convert to; ~**-se em** to turn into.

convés [kõ'vɛʃ] (*pl* **-eses** [-ɛziʃ]) *m* deck.

convidado, -da [kõvi'dadu, -da] *adj* guest (*antes de s*) ♦ *m, f* guest.

convidar [kõvi'da(x)] *vt* to invite.

convir [kõ'vi(x)] *vi* (*ser útil*) to be a good idea; (*ser adequado*) to be suitable; **é de** ~ **que** admittedly.

convite [kõ'vitʃi] *m* invitation.

convivência [kõvi'vẽsja] *f* (*vida em comum*) living together; (*familiaridade*) familiarity.

conviver [kõvi've(x)] : **conviver com** *v + prep* (*ter convivência com*) to live with; (*amigos, colegas*) to socialize with.

convívio [kõ'vivju] *m* (*convivência*) contact; (*festa*) social gathering.

convocar [kõvo'ka(x)] *vt* to summon; ~ **alguém para algo** to summon sb to sthg.

convosco [kõ'voʃku] *pron* with you.

convulsão [kõvuw'sãw] (*pl* **-ões** [-õjʃ]) *f* (*física*) convulsion; (*social*) upheaval.

cooperação [kwopera'sãw] (*pl* **-ões** [-õjʃ]) *f* cooperation.

cooperar [kwope'ra(x)] *vi* to cooperate.

cooperativa [kwopera'tiva] *f* cooperative.

coordenar [kworde'na(x)] *vt* to coordinate.

copa ['kɔpa] *f* (*divisão de casa*) pantry; (*de árvore*) top; (*de chapéu*) crown; (*Br*: *torneio esportivo*) cup.

❏ **copas** *fpl* (*naipe de cartas*) hearts.

cópia ['kɔpja] *f* copy.

copiar [ko'pja(x)] *vt* to copy ♦ *vi* (*Port*: *em exame, teste*) to cheat.

copo ['kɔpu] *m* glass; **tomar** OU **beber um** ~ to have a drink; **ser um bom** ~ (*fam*) to be able to hold one's drink.

copo-d'água [kɔpud'agwa] (*pl* **copos-d'água** [kɔpuʒd'agwa]) *m* (*Port*) reception.

coqueiro [ko'kejru] *m* coconut palm.

coquetel [koke'tɛw] (*pl* **-éis** [-ɛjʃ]) *m* cocktail.

cor[1] ['kɔ(x)] : **de cor** *adv*: **aprender/saber algo de** ~ to learn/know sthg by heart; **saber algo de** ~ **e salteado** to know sthg backwards.

cor[2] ['ko(x)] (*pl* **-res** [-riʃ]) *f* colour; **mudar de** ~ to change colour; **perder a** ~ to fade; **de** ~ (*pessoa*) coloured.

coração [kora'sãw] (*pl* **-ões** [-õjʃ]) *m* heart; **ter bom** ~ to be kind-hearted.

corado, -da [ko'radu, -da] *adj* (*pessoa*) red, flushed; (*frango, assado, etc*) brown.

coragem [ko'raʒẽ] *f* courage ♦ *interj* chin up!

corais → **coral**.

corajoso, -osa [kora'ʒozu, -ɔza] *adj* courageous.

coral [ko'raw] (*pl* **-ais** [-ajʃ]) *m* coral.

corante [ko'rãtʃi] *m* colouring; **"sem** ~**s nem conservantes"** "contains no colouring or preservatives".

corar [ko'ra(x)] *vi* to blush ♦ *vt* (*frango, assado, etc*) to brown.

Corcovado [koxko'vadu] *m*: **o** ~ the Corcovado mountain in Rio de Janeiro.

corda ['kɔrda] *f* rope; (*de instrumento musical*) string; (*de relógio, brinquedo*) clockwork; **dar** ~ **a** (*relógio, brinquedo*) to wind up; ~ **de saltar** skipping rope; ~**s vocais** vocal cords.

cordão [kor'dãw] (*pl* **-ões** [-õjʃ]) *m* (*Port*: *de sapatos*) shoelace; (*jóia*) gold chain; ~ **umbilical** umbilical cord.

cordeiro [kor'dejru] *m* lamb.

cordel [kor'dɛw] (*pl* **-éis** [-ɛiʃ]) *m* string.

cor-de-laranja [kordʒila'rãʒa] *adj inv* orange.

cor-de-rosa [ˌkordʒi'xɔza] *adj inv* pink.

cordial [kor'dʒjaw] (*pl* **-ais** [-ajʃ]) *adj* cordial.

cordilheira [kordʒi'ʎejra] *f* mountain range.

cordões → **cordão**.

cores → **cor²**.

coreto [ko'retu] *m* bandstand.

corinto [ko'rĩtu] *m* currant.

córnea ['kɔrnja] *f* cornea.

corneta [kox'neta] *f* cornet.

cornflakes® [koxni'flejkiʃ] *mpl* Cornflakes®.

coro ['koru] *m* choir; *(de música)* chorus; **em ~** in unison.

coroa [ko'roa] *f* crown; *(de enterro)* wreath.

corpo ['kɔxpu] *m* body; *(cadáver)* corpse; **~ de bombeiros** fire brigade.

corporal [koxpo'raw] (*pl* **-ais** [-ajʃ]) *adj* → **odor**.

correção [koxe'sãw] (*pl* **-ões** [-õjʃ]) *f* *(Br)* correctness; *(de exame, teste)* correction.

correcção [kuxe'sãw] (*pl* **-ões** [-õjʃ]) *f* *(Port)* = **correção**.

correções → **correção**.

corredor, -ra [koxe'do(x), -ra] (*mpl* **-res** [-riʃ], *fpl* **-s** [-ʃ]) *m, f* runner ◆ *m (de casa)* corridor.

correia [ko'xeja] *f (tira de couro)* strap; **~ da ventoinha** fan belt.

correio [ko'xeju] *m* post, mail; *(pessoa)* postman *(f* postwoman) *(Brit)*, mailman *(f* mailwoman) *(Am)*; *(local)* post office; **~ azul** *(Port)* fast mail service, ~ firstclass mail *(Brit)*; **~ eletrônico** e-mail, electronic mail; **~ expresso** express mail; **~ de voz** voice mail; **pelo ~** by post.

corrente [ko'xẽtʃi] *adj* current; *(água)* running ◆ *f* current; *(de bicicleta)* chain; **~ alternada** alternating current; **~ de ar** draught.

correr [ko'xe(x)] *vi* to run; *(tempo)* to pass; *(notícia, rumor)* to go around ◆ *vt* to run; **~ as cortinas** to draw the curtains; **~ com alguém** to get rid of sb; **~ perigo** to be in danger; **fazer algo correndo** to do sthg in a rush.

correspondência [koxeʃpõn'dẽsja] *f* correspondence.

correspondente [koxeʃpõn'dẽtʃi] *adj* corresponding ◆ *mf* correspondent.

corresponder [koxeʃpõn'de(x)] *vi* to correspond; *(retribuir)* to reciprocate; **~ a** to correspond with.

❑ **corresponder-se** *vp (escrever-se)* to write to each other; **~-se com alguém** to correspond with sb.

corretamente [koxɛta'mẽtʃi] *adv* correctly.

correto [ko'xɛtu] *adj* correct.

corretor, -ra [koxe'to(x), -ra] (*mpl* **-res** [-riʃ], *fpl* **-s** [-ʃ]) *m, f* broker ◆ *m*: *(fluido)* correction fluid; **~ de imóveis** estate agent *(Brit)*, real estate agent *(Am)*; **~ da Bolsa** stockbrocker.

corrida [ko'xida] *f (de velocidade)* race; *(tourada)* bullfight; *(de táxi)* fare; **~ de automóveis** rally; **~ de cavalos** horse race; **~ à Portuguesa** Portuguese bullfight.

corrigir [koxi'ʒi(x)] *vt* to correct.

❑ **corrigir-se** *vp* to mend one's ways.

corrimão [koxi'mãw] (*pl* **-s** [-ʃ] ou **-ões** [-õjʃ]) *m (de escada)* handrail, banister; *(de varanda)* railing.

corrimento [koxi'mẽtu] *m (de vagina)* discharge.

corrimões → **corrimão**.

corroborar [koxobo'ra(x)] *vt* to corroborate.

corromper [koxõm'pe(x)] *vt* to corrupt; *(subornar)* to bribe.

corrupção [koxup'sãw] (*pl* **-ões** [-õjʃ]) *f* corruption; **~ de menores** *(JUR)* corruption of minors.

corrupto, -ta [ko'xuptu, -ta] *adj* corrupt.

cortar [kox'ta(x)] *vt* to cut; *(carne assada)* to carve; *(gás, eletricidade)* to cut off; *(rua, estrada)* to block off ◆ *vi* to be sharp; **~ em algo** to cut back on sthg; **~ relações (com alguém)** to break up (with sb).

❑ **cortar-se** *vp* to cut o.s.

corte [kɔxtʃi] *m* cut; **~ de cabelo** haircut.

cortejo [kox'teʒu] *m* procession; **~ fúnebre** funeral procession.

cortesia [koxte'zia] *f* courtesy.

cortiça [kox'tʃisa] *f* cork.

cortiço [kox'tʃisu] *f* slum tenement.

cortina [kox'tʃina] *f* curtain.

creme

cortinados [koxtʃiˈnaduʃ] *mpl* curtains.

coruja [koˈruʒa] *f* owl.

corvina [koxˈvina] *f* black bream.

corvo [ˈkoxvu] *m* crow.

cós [ˈkɔʃ] *m inv* waistband.

coser [koˈze(x)] *vt & vi* to sew.

cosmético [koʒˈmɛtʃiku] *m* cosmetic.

cosmopolita [koʒmopoˈlita] *mf & adj* cosmopolitan.

costa [ˈkɔʃta] *f* coast; *(de montanha)* slope; **dar à ~** to wash ashore. ⊔ **costas** *fpl* back *(sg)*.

costela [koʃˈtɛla] *f* rib.

costeleta [koʃteˈleta] *f (de porco, carneiro)* chop; *(de vitela)* cutlet.

costumar [koʃtuˈma(x)] *vt*: **~ fazer algo** to usually do sthg; **ela costuma chegar na hora** she usually arrives on time ◆ *v impess*: **costuma chover muito** it tends to rain a lot.

costume [koʃˈtumi] *m (hábito)* habit; *(uso social)* custom; **como de ~** as usual; **por ~** usually.

costura [koʃˈtura] *f (atividade)* sewing; *(de operação cirúrgica)* scar.

costurar [koʃtuˈra(x)] *vt (roupa)* to sew (up); *(ferida, corte)* to stitch up.

cotação [kotaˈsãw] *(pl* **-ões** [-õjʃ]) *f (de mercadoria, título)* quoted price; **~ bancária** bank rate.

cotidiano [kotʃiˈdʒjanu] *adj (Br)* daily ◆ *m* everyday life.

cotonetes [kotoˈnɛtʃiʃ] *mpl* cotton buds.

cotovelada [kotoveˈlada] *f* poke with the elbow; **dar uma ~ em alguém** to elbow sb.

cotovelo [kotoˈvelu] *m* elbow.

cotovia [kotoˈvia] *f* lark.

coube [ˈkobi] → **caber**.

couchette [koˈʃetʃi] *f* couchette.

couraça [koˈrasa] *f (de tartaruga, cágado)* shell.

courgette [kurˈʒɛte] *f (Port)* courgette *(Brit)*, zucchini *(Am)*.

couro [ˈkoru] *m* leather; **~ cabeludo** scalp.

couve [ˈkovi] *f* cabbage; **~ lombarda** savoy cabbage; **~ à mineira** *chopped spring greens lightly fried in butter and garlic;* **~ portuguesa** kale; **~ roxa** red cabbage.

couve-de-Bruxelas [ˌkovidʒibruˈʃelaʃ] *(pl* **couves-de-Bruxelas** [ˌkoviʒdʒibruˈʃelaʃ]) *f* brussels sprout.

couve-flor [ˌkoveˈflo(x)] *(pl* **couves-flores** [ˌkoveʃˈfloreʃ]) *f* cauliflower.

couve-galega [ˌkoviɡaˈleɡa] *(pl* **couves-galegas** [ˌkoviʒɡaˈleɡaʃ]) *f* kale.

couvert [koˈve(x)] *m* cover charge.

cova [ˈkova] *f* pit; *(sepultura)* grave.

covarde [koˈvaxdʒi] *adj* cowardly ◆ *m* coward.

covardia [kovaxˈdʒia] *f* coward.

coveiro [koˈvejru] *m* gravedigger.

coxa [ˈkoʃa] *f* thigh; **~ de galinha** chicken rissole.

coxia [koˈʃia] *f* aisle.

coxo, -xa [ˈkoʃu, -ʃa] *adj* lame.

cozer [koˈze(x)] *vt* to boil; *(bolo, torta, empada)* to bake.

cozido, -da [koˈzidu, -da] *adj* boiled; *(bolo, torta, empada)* baked ◆ *m*: **~ (à portuguesa)** *a mixture of boiled meats including chicken, beef, pig's ear, "chouriço", black pudding and vegetables, served with rice.*

cozinha [koˈziɲa] *f* kitchen; *(arte)* cookery.

cozinhar [koziˈɲa(x)] *vt & vi* to cook.

cozinheiro, -ra [koziˈɲejru, -ra] *m, f* cook.

crachá [kraˈʃa] *m* badge.

crânio [ˈkranju] *m* skull.

craque [ˈkraki] *mf (fam)* expert.

cratera [kraˈtɛra] *f* crater.

cravar [kraˈva(x)] *vt*: **~ algo em algo** *(unhas)* to dig sthg into sthg; *(dentes, faca)* to sink sthg into sthg; **~ os olhos em** to stare at.

cravinho [kraˈviɲu] *m (Port)* clove.

cravo [ˈkravu] *m (flor)* carnation; *(instrumento)* harpsichord; *(Br: em rosto)* blackhead; *(Br: especiaria)* clove; *(Port: verruga)* wart.

creche [ˈkrɛʃi] *f* crèche.

credencial [kredẽsiˈaw] *(pl* **-ais** [-ajʃ]) *f (médica)* letter of referral from a GP to a specialist.

crediário [kreˈdʒjarju] *m (Br)* hire purchase *(Brit)*, installment plan *(Am)*.

crédito [ˈkrɛdʒitu] *m* credit; **comprar/vender a ~** to buy/sell on credit.

credor, -ra [kreˈdo(x), -ra] *(mpl* **-res** [-riʃ], *fpl* **-s** [-ʃ]) *m, f* creditor.

crédulo, -la [ˈkrɛdulu, -wa] *adj* gullible.

cremar [kreˈma(x)] *vt* to cremate.

crematório [kremaˈtɔrju] *m* crematorium.

creme [ˈkremi] *m* cream; *(licor)* cream

liqueur; ~ **de barba** shaving cream; ~ **hidratante** moisturizer; ~ **de leite** (Br) single cream; ~ **de limpeza** cleanser; ~ **de noite** cold cream; ~ **rinse** (Br) conditioner.

cremoso, -osa [kre'mozu, -ɔza] adj creamy.

crença ['krẽsa] f belief.

crente ['krẽntʃi] mf believer.

crepe ['krɛpi] m crepe.

crepúsculo [kre'puʃkulu] m (de manhã) daybreak; (à noite) twilight.

crer ['kre(x)] vi to believe; (supor) to suppose ◆ vt: ~ **que** (acreditar) to believe (that); (supor) to suppose (that); **ver para** ~ seeing is believing.

crescente [kre'sẽntʃi] adj growing ◆ m (fase da lua) crescent.

crescer [kre'se(x)] vi to grow; (aumentar) to rise; (sobejar) to be left (over).

crespo, -pa ['kreʃpu, -pa] adj (cabelo) very curly; (rugoso) rough.

cretino, -na [kre'tinu, -na] m, f idiot.

cria ['kria] f young.

criado, -da [kri'adu, -da] m, f servant.

criador, -ra [kria'do(x), -ra] (mpl -res [-riʃ], fpl -s [-ʃ]) m, f creator; (de animais) breeder.

criança [kri'ãsa] f child; ~ **de colo** infant; **quando** ~ as a child; **ser** ~ to be childish.

criar [kri'a(x)] vt to create; (filhos) to bring up; (animais) to raise; ~ **caso** to make trouble.

❑ **criar-se** vp (produzir-se) to form; (pessoa) to grow up.

criatividade [kriatʃivi'dadʒi] f creativity.

criativo, -va [kria'tʃivu, -va] adj creative.

criatura [kria'tura] f creature.

crime ['krimi] m crime.

criminalidade [kriminali'dadʒi] f crime.

criminoso, -osa [krimi'nozu, -ɔza] m, f criminal.

crina ['krina] f mane.

crisântemo [kri'zãntemu] m chrysanthemum.

crise ['krizi] f crisis; (em doença) attack; (de nervos, histeria) fit.

crista ['kriʃta] f (de ave) crest; (de montanha) ridge; **estar na** ~ **da onda** to be all the rage.

cristã → **cristão**.

cristal [kriʃ'taw] (pl -ais [-ajʃ]) m crystal.

cristaleira [kriʃta'lejra] f china cabinet.

cristão, -tã [kriʃ'tãw, -tã] adj & m, f Christian.

critério [kri'tɛrju] m criterion.

crítica ['kritika] f (de obra, peça, filme) review; (censura) criticism.

criticar [kritʃi'ka(x)] vt (obra) to review; (pessoa, atitude) to criticize.

crivo ['krivu] m sieve; (de regador) rose.

crocante [kro'kãntʃi] adj crunchy.

croché [krɔ'ʃɛ] m (Port) = **crochê**.

crochê [krɔ'ʃe] m (Br) crochet.

crocodilo [kroko'dilu] m crocodile.

cromo ['krɔmu] m sticker.

crónica ['krɔnika] f (Port) = **crônica**.

crônica ['kronika] f (Br) (de jornal) (newspaper) column; (conto) short story.

crónico, -ca ['krɔniku, -ka] adj (Port) = **crônico**.

crônico, -ca adj ['kroniku, -ka] (Br) (doença) chronic.

cronológico, -ca [kronoʼlɔʒiku, -ka] adj chronological.

cronometrar [kronome'tra(x)] vt to time.

cronómetro [kru'nɔmetru] m (Port) = **cronômetro**.

cronômetro [kro'nometru] m (Br) stopwatch.

croquete [krɔ'ketʃi] m croquette.

crosta ['krɔʃta] f (de ferida) scab; (da Terra) crust.

cru, crua ['kru, 'krua] adj (comida) raw; (tecido) unbleached; (realidade) harsh.

crucial [kru'sjaw] (pl -ais [-ajʃ]) adj crucial.

crucifixo [kruse'fiksu] m crucifix.

cruel [kru'ew] (pl -éis [-'ɛiʃ]) adj cruel.

cruz ['kruʃ] (pl -zes [-ziʃ]) f cross; **a Cruz Vermelha** the Red Cross.

cruzamento [kruza'mẽntu] m (em estrada) crossroads (sg); (de raças) crossbreed.

cruzar [kru'za(x)] vt to cross; (braços) to fold.

❑ **cruzar-se** vp (interceptar-se) to cross; **~-se com alguém** to bump into sb.

cruzeiro [kru'zejru] m cruise; (antiga unidade monetária) cruzeiro.

cu ['ku] m (vulg) arse (Brit), ass (Am).

Cuba libre [.kuba'libri] *f* rum and cola.

cúbico, -ca ['kubiku, -ka] *adj* cubic.

cubículo [ku'bikulu] *m* cubicle.

cubo ['kubu] *m* cube; **~ de gelo** ice cube.

cuco ['kuku] *m* cuckoo.

cueca ['kwɛka] *f* briefs *(pl)*.

cuidado, -da [kui'dadu, -da] *adj (casa, jardim, etc)* well looked after ◆ *m* care ◆ *interj* (be) careful!; **ter ~** to take care, to be careful; **aos ~s de alguém** care of sb; **com ~** carefully, with care.

cuidar [kui'da(x)] : **cuidar de** *v + prep* to take care of.

❏ **cuidar-se** *vp* to look after o.s.

cujo, -ja ['kuʒu, -ʒa] *pron (de quem)* whose; *(de que)* of which.

culinária [kuli'narja] *f* cookery.

culminar [kuwmi'na(x)] : **culminar em** *v + prep* to culminate in.

culpa ['kuwpa] *f* fault; **ter ~ de algo** to be to blame for sthg; **por ~ de** due to.

culpado, -da [kuw'padu, -da] *adj* guilty.

cultivar [kuwti'va(x)] *vt* to cultivate.

❏ **cultivar-se** *vp* to educate o.s.

culto, -ta ['kuwtu, -ta] *adj* well-educated ◆ *m* cult.

cultura [kuw'tura] *f* culture; *(agrícola)* crop; *(conhecimentos)* knowledge.

cultural [kuwtu'raw] *(pl* **-ais** [-ajʃ]) *adj* cultural.

cume ['kumi] *m* summit.

cúmplice ['kũmplisi] *mf* accomplice.

cumplicidade [kũmplisi'dadʒi] *f* complicity.

cumprimentar [kũmprimẽn'ta(x)] *vt* to greet.

cumprimento [kũmpri'mẽntu] *m* greeting.

❏ **cumprimentos** *mpl* regards; **Com os melhores ~s** Yours sincerely; **~s a ...** give my regards to ....

cumprir [kũm'pri(x)] *vt (tarefa, ordem, missão)* to carry out; *(promessa)* to keep; *(pena, sentença)* to serve; *(lei)* to obey ◆ *v impess:* **~ a alguém fazer algo** *(caber a)* to be sb's turn to do sthg; *(ser o dever de)* to be sb's responsibility to do sthg.

cúmulo ['kumulu] *m* height; **é o ~!** that's the limit!

cunha ['kuɲa] *f* wedge.

cunhado, -da [ku'ɲadu, -da] *m, f* brother-in-law *(f* sister-in-law).

cunhar [ku'ɲa(x)] *vt (moeda)* to mint.

cupão [ku'pãw] *(pl* **-ões** [-õjʃ]) *m (Port)* = **cupom**.

cupom [ku'põ] *(pl* **-ns** [-ʃ]) *m (Br)* voucher.

cúpula ['kupula] *f* dome.

cura ['kura] *f* cure; *(de queijo, presunto, etc)* curing.

curar [ku'ra(x)] *vt* to cure ◆ *vi (sarar)* to heal.

❏ **curar-se** *vp* to recover.

curativo [kura't ʃivu] *m* dressing.

curinga [ku'rĩŋga] *m (de jogo de cartas)* joker; *(Br: em futebol)* substitute.

curiosidade [kurjuzi'dadʒi] *f* curiosity.

curioso, -osa [ku'rjozu, -ɔza] *adj* curious ◆ *m, f (bisbilhoteiro)* busybody; *(espectador)* onlooker; *(amador)* amateur.

curral [ku'xaw] *(pl* **-ais** [-ajʃ]) *m* pen.

currículo [ku'xikulu] *m* curriculum vitae, CV.

curso ['kursu] *m* course; *(de universidade)* degree course; *(alunos de um curso)* year; **ter um ~ de algo** *(universitário)* to have a degree in sthg; **~ intensivo** intensive course; **~ superior** (university) degree; **em ~** *(ano, semana, etc)* current; *(em funcionamento)* in operation; *(em andamento)* in progress.

cursor [kux'so(x)] *(pl* **-res** [-riʃ]) *m (INFORM)* cursor.

curtir [kux'ti(x)] *vt (peles, couros)* to tan; *(fam: desfrutar)* to enjoy.

curto, -ta ['kuxtu, -ta] *adj* short; **a ~ prazo** in the short term.

curto-circuito [.kuxtusix'kwitu] *(pl* **curtos-circuitos** [.kuxtuʃsix'kwituʃ]) *m* short circuit.

curva ['kuxva] *f (de estrada, caminho, etc)* bend; *(de corpo)* curve.

curvar [kux'va(x)] *vt* to bend; *(cabeça)* to bow.

❏ **curvar-se** *vp (inclinar-se)* to bend over; *(fig: humilhar-se)* to lower o.s.

cuscuz [kuʃ'kuʃ] *m* couscous; *(prato árabe)* couscous served with vegetables and spicy lamb; *(prato brasileiro)* steamed seafood, eggs and peas served on couscous.

cuspir [kuʃˈpi(x)] *vi & vt* to spit.

cuspe [ˈkuʃpi] *m (Br)* spit.

cuspo [ˈkuʃpu] *m (Port)* = cuspe.

custa [ˈkuʃta] : **à custa de** *prep* at the expense of.

❏ **custas** *fpl (JUR)* costs.

custar [kuʃˈta(x)] *vt & vi (valer)* to cost; **custa muito a fazer** it's hard to do; **quanto custa?** how much is it?;

custe o que ~ at all costs, at any cost.

custo [ˈkuʃtu] *m (preço, despesa)* cost; *(fig: dificuldade)* difficulty; **~ de vida** cost of living; **a ~** with difficulty.

cutia [kuˈtʃia] *f* agouti.

cutícula [kuˈtʃikula] *f* cuticle.

c.v. *m (abrev de curriculum vitae)* C.V.

c/v *abrev* = **cave**.

D

da [da] = de + a, → de.

dá [da] → dar.

dactilografar [da(k)tilogra'far] *vt* (Port) = datilografar.

dádiva ['dadiva] *f* donation.

dado, -da ['dadu, -da] *adj* (*sociável*) sociable; (*determinado*) given ◆ *m* (de jogar) dice; (de problema, cálculo) factor; (informação) fact; ~ **que** (visto que) given that.

⊐ **dados** *mpl* (jogo) dice; (INFORM) data (sg); **jogar ~s** to play dice.

daí [da'i] *adv* = de + aí; (relativo a espaço) from there; (relativo a tempo): ~ **a um mês/um ano/dez minutos** a month/a year/ten minutes later; ~ **em** OU **por diante** from then on; **e ~?** so what?; **sai ~!** get out of there!

dali [da'li] *adv* = de + ali; (relativo a espaço) from there; (relativo a tempo): ~ **a uma semana/um mês/uma hora** a week/a month/an hour later; ~ **em** OU **por diante** from then on.

daltónico, -ca [dal'tɔniku, -ka] *adj & m, f* (Port) = daltônico.

daltônico, -ca [daw'toniku, -ka] *adj* (Br) colour-blind ◆ *m, f* (Br) colour-blind person.

dama ['dama] *f* (senhora) lady; (de jogo de damas) draught (Brit), checker (Am); (de baralho de cartas) queen; ~ **de honor** (Port) bridesmaid; ~ **de honra** (Br) bridesmaid.

⊐ **damas** *fpl* draughts (sg) (Brit), checkers (sg) (Am); **jogar ~s** to play draughts.

damasco [da'maʃku] *m* apricot.

dança ['dãsa] *f* dance; ~**s folclóricas** country dancing (sg).

dançar [dã'sa(x)] *vi* to dance; (oscilar) to sway ◆ *vt* to dance.

danceteria [dãsete'ria] *f* (Br) disco.

danificar [danifi'ka(x)] *vt* to damage.

dano ['danu] *m* damage.

dantes ['dãntiʃ] *adv* in the old days.

dão ['dãw] → dar.

Dão ['dãw] *m* Portuguese wine-producing area.

daquela [da'kɛla] = de + aquela, → de.

daquele [da'keli] = de + aquele, → de.

daqui [da'ki] *adv* = de + aqui; (deste lugar) from here; (deste momento): ~ **a um ano/mês** in a year/month; **ele saiu ~ às nove** he left here at nine; ~ **a pouco** in a little while; ~ **em** OU **por diante** from now on.

daquilo [da'kilu] = de + aquilo, → aquilo.

dar ['da(x)] *vt* 1. (entregar, presentear) to give; ~ **algo a alguém** to give sb sthg, to give sthg to sb.

2. (produzir) to produce.

3. (causar, provocar) to give; **dá-me sono/pena** it makes me sleepy/sad; **isto vai** ~ **muito que fazer** this is going to be a lot of work; **só dá problemas** it's nothing but trouble.

4. (filme, programa): **deu no noticiário hoje** it was on the news today.

5. (exprime ação) to give; ~ **um berro** to give a cry; ~ **um pontapé em alguém** to kick sb; ~ **um passeio** to go for a walk.

6. (festa, concerto) to hold; **vão** ~ **uma festa** they're going to have OU throw a party.

7. (dizer) to say; **ele me deu boa-noite** he said good night to me.

8. (ensinar) to teach; **o que é que você está dando nas suas aulas?** what are you teaching (at the moment)?; **ela dá aula numa escola** she teaches at a school; **gostaria de** ~ **aulas de Inglês** I would like to teach English.

9. (aprender, estudar) to do; **o que é que estão dando em Inglês?** what are

you doing in English (at the moment)?; **estamos dando o verbo "to be"** we're doing the verb "to be".

◆ *vi* 1. *(horas)*: **já deram cinco horas** the clock has struck five.

2. *(condizer)*: **~ com** to go with; **as cores não dão umas com as outras** the colours clash.

3. *(proporcionar)*: **~ de beber a alguém** to give sb something to drink; **~ de comer a alguém** to feed sb.

4. *(em locuções)*: **dá igual** OU **no mesmo** it doesn't matter.

❑ **dar com** *v + prep (encontrar, descobrir)* to meet; **dei com ele no cinema** I met him at the cinema.

❑ **dar em** *v + prep (resultar)*: **a discussão não vai ~ em nada** the discussion will come to nothing.

❑ **dar para** *v + prep (servir para, ser útil para)* to be good for; *(suj: varanda, janela)* to look onto; *(suj: porta)* to lead to; *(ser suficiente para)* to be enough for; *(ser possível)* to be possible; **dá para você fazer isso hoje?** could you do it today?; **dá para ir a pé?** is it within walking distance?; **não vai ~ para eu chegar a horas** I won't be able to get there on time.

❑ **dar por** *v + prep (aperceber-se de)* to notice.

❑ **dar-se** *vp*: **~-se bem/mal com alguém** to get on well/badly with sb; **não me dou bem com condimentos** spices don't agree with me; **deu-se mal com a brincadeira** his plan backfired; **~-se por vencido** to give in.

dardo ['daxdu] *m (arma)* spear; *(ESP)* javelin.

❑ **dardos** *mpl* darts *(sg)*; **jogar ~s** to play darts.

das [daʃ] = **de + as**, → **de**.

data ['data] *f* date; **~ de nascimento** date of birth.

datilografar [datʃilogra'fa(x)] *vt (Br)* to type.

datilógrafo, -fa [datʃi'lografu, -fa] *m, f (Br)* typist.

d.C. *(abrev de depois de Cristo)* AD.

de [dʒi] *prep* 1. *(indica posse)* of; **o lápis do Mário** Mário's pencil; **o carro daquele homem** that man's car; **a recepção do hotel** the hotel reception; **a casa é dela** it's her house.

2. *(indica matéria)* (made) of; **um bolo ~ chocolate** a chocolate cake; **um reló-**

gio **~ ouro** a gold watch.

3. *(indica conteúdo)* of; **um copo ~ água** a glass of water.

4. *(usado em descrições, determinações)*: **uma camisola ~ manga curta** a short-sleeved T-shirt; **uma nota ~ 50 reais** a 50-real note; **o senhor ~ preto** the man in black.

5. *(indica assunto)* about; **fale da viagem** tell me about the trip; **um livro ~ informática** a book about OU on computers; **um livro ~ geografia** a geography book.

6. *(indica origem)* from; **sou ~ Coimbra** I'm from Coimbra; **os habitantes do bairro** the locals; **um produto do Brasil** a Brazilian product.

7. *(indica tempo)*: **o jornal das nove** the nine o'clock news; **partimos às três da tarde** we left at three in the afternoon; **trabalho das nove às cinco** I work from nine to five.

8. *(indica uso)*: **a sala ~ espera** the waiting room; **uma máquina ~ calcular** a calculator; **a porta ~ entrada** the front door.

9. *(usado em denominações, nomes)* of.

10. *(indica causa, modo)*: **chorar ~ alegria** to cry with joy; **está tudo ~ pernas para o ar** everything is upside down; **morrer ~ frio** to freeze to death; **viajou ~ carro** he travelled by car.

11. *(indica autor)* by; **um filme ~ Cacá Diegues** a film by Cacá Diegues; **o último livro ~ Érico Veríssimo** Érico Veríssimo's latest book.

12. *(introduz um complemento)*: **cheio ~ gente** full of people; **desconfiar ~ alguém** to distrust sb; **difícil ~ esquecer** hard to forget; **gostar ~ algo/ alguém** to like sthg/sb.

13. *(em comparações)*: **do que** than; **mais rápido do que este** it's faster than this one.

14. *(em superlativos)* of; **o melhor ~ todos** the best of all.

15. *(dentre)* of; **uma daquelas cadeiras** one of those chairs; **um dia destes** one of these days; **um desses hotéis serve** any one of those hotels will do.

16. *(indica série)*: **~ dois em dois dias** every two days; **~ quinze em quinze minutos** every fifteen minutes; **~ três em três metros** every three metres.

debaixo [de'bajʃu] *adv* underneath; ~ **de** under.

debate [de'batʃi] *m* debate.

debater [deba'te(x)] *vt* to debate.
❑ **debater-se** *vp* to struggle.

débil ['dɛbiw] (*pl* **-beis** [-bejʃ]) *adj* weak ◆ *mf*: ~ **mental** mentally handicapped person.

debitar [debi'ta(x)] *vt* to debit.

débito ['dɛbitu] *m* debit; *(de rio)* volume.

debruçar-se [debru'saxsi] *vp* to lean over; ~ **sobre algo** *(problema, questão)* to look into sthg.

década [dɛ'kada] *f* decade; **na** ~ **de oitenta/noventa** in the 80s/90s.

decadência [deka'dẽsja] *f* decadence.

decadente [deka'dẽtʃi] *adj* decadent.

decapitar [dekapi'ta(x)] *vt* to behead.

decência [de'sẽsja] *f* decency.

decente [de'sẽtʃi] *adj* decent.

decepar [dese'pa(x)] *vt* to cut off.

decepção [dese'sãw] (*pl* **-ões** [-õjʃ]) *f* disappointment.

decidido, -da [desi'dʒidu, -da] *adj (pessoa)* determined; *(resolvido)* settled.

decidir [desi'dʒi(x)] *vt* to decide; ~ **fazer algo** to decide to do sthg.
❑ **decidir-se** *vp* to make up one's mind; ~**-se a fazer algo** to make up one's mind to do sthg.

decifrar [desi'fra(x)] *vt* to decipher.

decimal [desi'maw] (*pl* **-ais** [-ajʃ]) *adj* decimal.

décimo, -ma ['dɛsimu, -ma] *num* tenth ◆ *m (em loteria)* tenth share of a lottery ticket, → **sexto**.

decisão [desi'zãw] (*pl* **-ões** [-õjʃ]) *f (resolução)* decision.

declamar [dekla'ma(x)] *vt & vi* to recite.

declaração [deklara'sãw] (*pl* **-ões** [-õjʃ]) *f* statement; *(de amor)* declaration; ~ **amigável (de acidente automóvel)** *jointly agreed insurance statement made by drivers after an accident.*

declarar [dekla'ra(x)] *vt* to declare; "**nada a** ~" "nothing to declare".
❑ **declarar-se** *vp (confessar sentimentos)* to declare one's love; *(manifestar-se)* to express an opinion.

declínio [de'klinju] *m* decline.

declive [de'klivi] *m* slope.

decolagem [deko'laʒẽ] *f (Br) (de avião)* takeoff.

decomposição [dekõmpozi'sãw] (*pl* **-ões** [-õjʃ]) *f* decomposition.

decoração [dekora'sãw] (*pl* **-ões** [-õjʃ]) *f* decoration.

decorar [deko'ra(x)] *vt (ornamentar)* to decorate; *(memorizar)* to memorize.

decorativo, -va [dekora'tʃivu, -va] *adj* decorative.

decorrente [deko'xẽtʃi] *adj* resulting; ~ **de** resulting from.

decote [de'kɔtʃi] *m* neckline; ~ **em bico** OU **em V** V-neck; ~ **redondo** round neck.

decrescer [dekre'se(x)] *vi* to decrease.

decretar [dekre'ta(x)] *vt* to decree.

decreto [de'kretu] *m* decree.

decreto-lei [de,kretu'lej] (*pl* **decretos-lei** [de,kretuʒ'lej]) *m law issued by the Government which overrules any existing legislation*

decurso [de'kursu] *m*: **no** ~ **de** in the course of.

dedal [de'daw] (*pl* **-ais** [-ajʃ]) *m* thimble.

dedão [de'dãw] (*pl* **-ões** [-õjʃ]) *m (Br) (de mão)* thumb; *(de pé)* big toe.

dedicação [dedʒika'sãw] (*pl* **-ões** [-õjʃ]) *f* dedication.

dedicar [dedʒi'ka(x)] *vt (livro, música, obra)* to dedicate; *(tempo, atenção, energias)* to devote.
❑ **dedicar-se a** *vp + prep* to devote o.s. to; **a que se dedica?** what do you do?

dedo ['dedu] *m (de mão)* finger; *(de pé)* toe; *(medida)* inch; **levantar o** ~ to put one's hand up.

dedões → **dedão**.

dedução [dedu'sãw] (*pl* **-ões** [-õjʃ]) *f* deduction.

deduzir [dedu'zi(x)] *vt (descontar)* to deduct; *(concluir)* to deduce.

defeito [de'fejtu] *m* defect.

defeituoso, -osa [defej'twozu, -ɔza] *adj (produto)* defective.

defender [defẽ'de(x)] *vt* to defend.
❑ **defender-se** *vp* to defend o.s.; ~**-se de** to defend o.s. against.

defensor, -ra [defẽ'so(x), -ra] (*mpl* **-res** [-riʃ], *fpl* **-s** [-ʃ]) *m, f* defender.

deferimento [deferi'mẽtu] *m* approval; "**pede** ~" *expression used at the end of any formal letter of request sent to an institution or government office asking them to grant a request.*

defesa [dɛ'feza] *f* defence; *(de tese)* viva voce *(oral exam taken to support one's thesis at university).*

défice ['dɛfisi] *m* deficit.

deficiência [defi'sjēsja] *f* deficiency; *(física)* handicap.

deficiente [defi'sjēntʃi] *adj* deficient ◆ *mf* handicapped person; ~ **físico** physically handicapped person; ~ **mental** mentally handicapped person; ~ **motor** *person with a motor neurone disease.*

definição [defini'sāw] *(pl* -ões [-ōjʃ]) *f* definition.

definir [defi'ni(x)] *vt (palavra, sentido)* to define; *(estratégia, plano, regras)* to set out.

❏ **definir-se** *vp* to make one's mind up.

definitivamente [definitʃiva'mēntʃi] *adv (para sempre)* for good; *(sem dúvida)* definitely.

definitivo, -va [definitʃivu, -va] *adj (decisão, resposta)* final; *(separação, mudança)* permanent.

deformação [defoxma'sāw] *(pl* -ões [-ōjʃ]) *f (de corpo)* deformity; *(de forma, realidade)* distortion.

deformar [defox'ma(x)] *vt (corpo)* to deform; *(forma, imagem, realidade)* to distort.

defrontar [defrōn'ta(x)] *vt* to confront.

defronte [de'frōntʃi] *adv* opposite; ~ **de** opposite.

defumado, -da [defu'madu, -da] *adj* smoked.

defumar [defu'ma(x)] *vt* to smoke.

degelo [de'ʒelu] *m* thaw.

degolar [dego'la(x)] *vt* to behead.

degradante [degra'dāntʃi] *adj* degrading.

degradar [degra'da(x)] *vt* to degrade.

❏ **degradar-se** *vp (saúde, relações)* to deteriorate; *(humilhar-se)* to demean o.s.

degrau [de'graw] *m* step.

degustação [deguʃta'sāw] *f* tasting.

degustar [deguʃ'ta(x)] *vt* to taste.

dei ['dej] → **dar.**

deitar [dej'ta(x)] *vt (estender)* to lay (down); *(em cama)* to put to bed; ~ **abaixo** to knock down; ~ **fora algo** *(Port: pôr no lixo)* to throw sthg away ou out; ~ **fora** *(Port) (verter)* to spill over; *(vomitar)* to throw up.

❏ **deitar-se** *vp (na cama)* to go to bed; *(no chão)* to lie down.

deixa ['dejʃa] *f* cue.

deixar [dej'ʃa(x)] *vt* leave; *(permitir)* to allow, to let; *(vício, estudos)* to give up ◆ *vi:* ~ **de fazer algo** to stop doing sthg; **não** ~ **de fazer algo** to be sure to do sthg; **deixa que eu acabe isto** let me finish this; **você deixou a cama por fazer** you didn't make the bed; ~ **alguém fazer algo** to let sb do sthg; ~ **algo para** to leave sthg for; ~ **algo de lado** to put sthg aside; ~ **algo/alguém em paz** to leave sthg/sb alone; ~ **algo/alguém para trás** to leave sthg/sb behind; ~ **cair** to drop.

❏ **deixar-se** *vp:* ~-**se levar por** to get carried away with; **deixa de brincadeiras!** stop fooling around!; **ela não se deixou enganar** she wasn't to be fooled; ~ **de fazer algo** to stop doing sthg.

dela ['dɛla] = **de** + **ela**, → **de.**

dele ['deli] = **de** + **ele**, → **de.**

delegacia [delega'sia] *f (Br)* police station.

delegado, -da [dele'gadu, -da] *m, f (Br: de polícia)* police superintendent *(Brit),* police captain *(Am); (de turma)* form captain; *(de país, governo, instituição)* delegate.

deleitar [delej'ta(x)] *vt* to delight.

❏ **deleitar-se com** *vp + prep* to delight in.

delgado, -da [dew'gadu, -da] *adj (pessoa)* slim; *(fio, corda, pau, barra)* thin.

deliberação [delibera'sāw] *(pl* -ões [-ōjʃ]) *f* decision.

deliberar [delibe'ra(x)] *vt* to decide on ◆ *vi* to deliberate.

delicadeza [delika'deza] *f* delicacy; *(cortesia)* courtesy; *(cuidado)* care.

delícia [de'lisja] *f (sensação)* pleasure; *(manjar)* delicacy; **que** ~! how lovely!

delicioso, -osa [deli'sjozu, -ɔza] *adj* delicious.

delinear [deli'nja(x)] *vt* to outline.

delinquência [delīŋ'kwēsja] *f (Port)* = **delinqüência.**

delinqüência [delīŋ'kwēsja] *f (Br)* delinquency; ~ **juvenil** juvenile delinquency.

delinqüente [delīŋ'kwēntʃi] *mf* delinquent.

delirante [deli'rāntʃi] *adj (fig: incrível)* amazing.

delirar [deli'ra(x)] *vi* to be delirious.

delírio [de'lirju] *m (MED)* delirium; *(fig: excitação)* excitement.

delito [de'litu] *m* crime.

demais [de'majʃ] *adv (com verbos)* too much; *(com adjectivos)* too ♦ *pron*: **os/as ~ the rest**; **isto já é ~!** this really is too much!; **ser ~** *(ser o máximo)* to be brilliant.

demasia [dema'zia] : **em demasia** *adv* too much.

demasiado, -da [dema'zjadu, -da] *adj (com substantivos singulares)* too much; *(com substantivos plurais)* too many ♦ *adv (com verbos)* too much; *(com adjectivos)* too.

demência [de'mẽsja] *f* dementia.

demente [de'mẽntʃi] *adj* insane.

demissão [demi'sãw] *(pl -ões* [-õjʃ]*) f (involuntária)* dismissal; *(voluntária)* resignation; **pedir ~** to resign.

demitir [demi'tʃi(x)] *vt* to dismiss.

❏ **demitir-se** *vp* to resign.

democracia [demokra'sia] *f* democracy.

democrata [demo'krata] *mf* democrat ♦ *adj* democratic.

democrático, -ca [demo'kratʃiku, -ka] *adj* democratic.

demolição [demoli'sãw] *(pl -ões* [-õjʃ]*) f* demolition.

demolir [demo'li(x)] *vt* to demolish.

demónio [de'mɔnju] *m (Port)* = **demônio**.

demônio [de'monju] *m (Br)* devil.

demonstração [demõʃtra'sãw] *(pl -ões* [-õjʃ]*) f* demonstration; *(prova)* display.

demonstrar [demõʃ'tra(x)] *vt* to demonstrate; *(revelar)* to show.

demora [de'mɔra] *f* delay; **sem ~** without delay.

demorado, -da [demo'radu, -da] *adj (longo)* lengthy; *(lento)* slow.

demorar [demo'ra(x)] *vi* to take time ♦ *vt (tardar)* to take; *(atrasar)* to detain; **vai ~ muito?** will it take long?

❏ **demorar-se** *vp* to take too long; **demorei-me por causa do trânsito** I got held up in the traffic.

dendê [dẽn'de] *m* palm oil.

denegrir [dene'gri(x)] *vt (fig: manchar)* to blacken.

dengue [dẽn'gi] *f* dengue fever; **~ hemorrágica** chronic dengue fever.

denominação [denomina'sãw] *(pl*

-ões [-õjʃ]*) f* denomination.

denotar [deno'ta(x)] *vt* to show.

densidade [dẽsi'dadʒi] *f* density.

denso, -sa ['dẽsu, -sa] *adj* dense.

dentada [dẽn'tada] *f* bite.

dentadura [dẽnta'dura] *f (natural)* teeth *(pl)*; *(postiça)* dentures *(pl)*.

dente ['dẽntʃi] *m* tooth; *(de elefante, elefante marinho)* tusk; *(de garfo, ancinho)* prong; **~ de alho** clove of garlic; **~ do siso** wisdom tooth; **~s postiços** false teeth.

dentífrico, -ca [dẽn'tʃifriku, -ka] *adj* tooth *(antes de s)* ♦ *m* toothpaste.

dentista [dẽn'tʃiʃta] *mf* dentist.

dentre ['dẽntri] = **de + entre**, → **entre**.

dentro ['dẽntru] *adv (no interior)* in, inside; **~ de** *(relativo a espaço físico)* in, inside; *(relativo a espaço temporal)* within; **~ em pouco** OU **em breve** soon; **aqui ~** in here; **lá ~** inside; **por ~ inside**; **por ~ de** on the inside of; **estar por ~ de algo** to be in the know about sthg.

denúncia [de'nũsja] *f (revelação)* exposure; *(acusação)* accusation.

denunciar [denũ'sja(x)] *vt* to report.

deparar [depa'ra(x)] : **deparar com** *v + prep (encontrar)* to come across; *(enfrentar)* to come up against.

❏ **deparar-se** *vp (surgir)* to arise.

departamento [departa'mẽntu] *m* department.

dependência [depẽn'dẽsja] *f (de casa)* room; *(de vício, droga)* dependency; *(de chefe, pai, mãe)* dependence.

dependente [depẽn'dẽntʃi] *adj* dependent.

depender [depẽn'de(x)] *vi*: **depende ... it depends ....**

❏ **depender de** *v + prep (de droga, pai, mãe)* to be dependent on; *(de circunstâncias, tempo, dinheiro)* to depend on.

depilar [depi'la(x)] *vt* to remove hair from; *(com cera)* to wax.

depilatório, -ria [depilaˈtɔrju, -rja] *adj* hair-removing ♦ *m* depilatory.

depoimento [depoj'mẽntu] *m (em esquadra)* statement; **prestar ~** to give evidence.

depois [de'pojʃ] *adv (relativo a espaço)* after; *(relativo a tempo)* afterwards; **~ se vê!** we'll see!; **e ~?** so?; **a sobremesa fica para ~** we'll leave the dessert for later; **deixar algo para ~** to leave sthg for later; **dias/semanas/anos ~** days/weeks/years later; **~ de amanhã** the day after tomorrow; **~ de** after; **~ que** since; **logo ~** straight afterwards.

depor [dɛ'po(x)] vi *(JUR)* to give evidence ♦ vt *(governo, ministro)* to overthrow.

depositar [depozi'ta(x)] vt to pay in; **~ confiança em alguém** to place one's trust in sb.

❏ **depositar-se** vp to settle.

depósito [dɛ'pozitu] m *(em banco)* deposit; *(armazém)* warehouse; *(reservatório)* tank; *(sedimento)* sediment; **; ~ de bagagens** *(Br)* left-luggage office *(Brit)*, baggage room *(Am)*; **~ de gasolina** *(Port: de veículo)* petrol tank.

depravação [deprava'sãw] *(pl* -ões [-õjʃ]) f depravity.

depreciação [depresja'sãw] *(pl* -ões [-õjʃ]) f depreciation.

depressa [dɛ'prɛsa] adv quickly ♦ interj hurry up!; **anda ~ com isso!** hurry up with that!

depressão [depre'sãw] *(pl* -ões [-õjʃ]) f depression; **~ econômica** (economic) depression.

deprimente [depri'mẽntʃi] adj depressing.

deprimir [depri'mi(x)] vt to depress.

deputado, -da [depu'tadu, -da] m, f deputy.

deriva [dɛ'riva] f: **ir à ~** to drift; **estar à ~** to be adrift.

derivar [deri'va(x)] vi to drift.

❏ **derivar de** v + prep *(palavra, termo)* to derive from; *(produto)* to be made from; *(problema)* to stem from.

dermatologista [dɛrmatolo'ʒiʃta] mf dermatologist.

derramamento [dexama'mẽntu] m *(de líquido)* spillage; *(de lágrimas, sangue)* shedding.

derramar [dexa'ma(x)] vt *(líquido)* to spill; *(lágrimas, sangue)* to shed; *(farinha, feijão)* to drop.

derrame [dɛ'xami] m *(MED)* hemorrhage.

derrapagem [dexa'paʒẽ] *(pl* -ns [-ʃ]) f skid.

derrapar [dexa'pa(x)] vi to skid.

derreter [dexe'te(x)] vt to melt.

❏ **derreter-se** vp to melt.

derrota [dɛ'xɔta] f defeat.

derrotar [dexo'ta(x)] vt to defeat.

derrubar [dexu'ba(x)] vt *(objecto, pessoa)* to knock over; *(casa)* to knock down; *(árvore)* to cut down; *(fig: governo, sistema)* to overthrow.

desabafar [dʒizaba'fa(x)] vi to get it off one's chest.

desabamento [dʒizaba'mẽntu] m *(de terra, pedras)* landslide; *(de edifício)* collapse.

desabar [dʒiza'ba(x)] vi to collapse.

desabitado, -da [dʒizabi'tadu, -da] adj unoccupied.

desabotoar [dʒizabo'twa(x)] vt to unbutton.

desabrigado, -da [dʒizabri'gadu, -da] adj *(sem casa, lar)* homeless; *(exposto ao tempo)* exposed.

desabrochar [dʒizabro'ʃa(x)] vi to open.

desacompanhado, -da [dʒiza-kõmpa'nadu, -da] adj unaccompanied.

desaconselhar [dʒizakõse'ʎa(x)] vt: **~ algo (a alguém)** to advise (sb) against sthg.

desaconselhável [dʒizakõse'ʎavew] *(pl* -eis [-ejʃ]) adj inadvisable.

desacordado, -da [dʒizakor'dadu, -da] adj unconscious.

desacostumado, -da [dʒizakoʃtu'madu, -da] adj unaccustomed.

desacreditar [dʒizakredi'ta(x)] vt to discredit.

❏ **desacreditar-se** vp to be discredited.

desactualizado, -da [dezatwali'zadu, -da] adj *(Port)* = **desatualizado.**

desafinado, -da [dʒizafi'nadu, -da] adj *(instrumento)* out of tune; *(voz)* tuneless.

desafinar [dʒizafi'na(x)] vi to be out of tune.

desafio [dʒiza'fiu] m challenge; *(Port: de futebol, basquetebol, etc)* match.

desafortunado, -da [dʒiza-foxtu'nadu, -da] adj unlucky.

desagradar [dʒizagra'da(x)] : **desagradar a** v + prep to displease.

desaguar [dʒiza'gwa(x)] vi: **~ em** to flow into.

desajeitado, -da [dʒizaʒej'tadu, -da] adj clumsy.

desalinhado, -da [dʒizali'nadu, -da] adj untidy.

desalinho [dʒiza'liɲu] m *(em forma de vestir)* sloppiness; *(desordem)* untidiness; **em ~** in disarray.

desalojar [dʒizalo'ʒa(x)] *vt* to evict.

desamarrar [dʒizama'xa(x)] *vt* to untie.

desamparado, -da [dezãmpa'radu, -da] *adj* abandoned.

desamparar [dʒizãmpa'ra(x)] *vt* to abandon.

desanimado, -da [dʒizani'madu, -da] *adj* down.

desanimar [dʒizani'ma(x)] *vt* to discourage ♦ *vi* to lose heart.

desânimo [dʒi'zanimu] *m* dejection.

desanuviar [dʒizanu'vja(x)] *vt (fig) (cabeça)* to clear; *(espírito)* to lift ♦ *vi (céu)* to clear; *(fig: espairecer)* to unwind.

desaparafusar [dʒizaparafu'za(x)] *vt* to unscrew.

desaparecer [dʒizapare'se(x)] *vi* to disappear.

desaparecido, -da [dʒizapare'sidu, -da] *adj* missing ♦ *m, f* missing person.

desaparecimento [dʒizaparesi'mēntu] *m* disappearance.

desapertar [dʒizaper'ta(x)] *vt* to undo.

desapontado, -da [dʒizapõn'tadu, -da] *adj* disappointed.

desapontamento [dʒizapõnta'mēntu] *m* disappointment.

desapontar [dʒizapõn'ta(x)] *vt* to disappoint.

desarmamento [dʒizaxma'mēntu] *m* disarmament.

desarmar [dʒizax'ma(x)] *vt* to disarm; *(barraca, cama, estante)* to dismantle.

desarranjado, -da [dʒizaxã'ʒadu, -da] *adj* dishevelled.

desarranjar [dʒizaxã'ʒa(x)] *vt* to mess up.

desarrumado, -da [dʒizaxu'madu, -da] *adj* untidy.

desarrumar [dʒizaxu'ma(x)] *vt* to mess up.

desarticulado, -da [dʒizaxtʃiku'ladu, -da] *adj* dislocated.

desassossego [dʒizaso'segu] *m* disquiet.

desastrado, -da [dʒiza'ʃtradu, -da] *adj* clumsy.

desastre [dʒi'zaʃtri] *m (de automóvel)* accident, crash; *(desgraça)* disaster.

desatar [dʒiza'ta(x)] *vt* to untie ♦ *vi:* **~ a fazer algo** to start doing sthg; **~ a**

rir/chorar to burst out laughing/crying.

desatento, -ta [dʒiza'tēntu, -ta] *adj* distracted.

desatino [dʒiza'tinu] *m (fam: chatice)* hassle.

desatualizado, -da [dʒizatwali'zadu, -da] *adj (Br) (máquina, livro, sistema)* outdated; *(pessoa)* out of touch.

desavença [dʒiza'vēsa] *f* quarrel.

desavergonhado, -da [dʒizavexgo'ɲadu, -da] *adj* cheeky ♦ *m, f* shameless person.

desbaratar [dʒiʒbara'ta(x)] *vt* to squander.

desbastar [dʒiʒbaʃ'ta(x)] *vt (cabelo)* to thin (out).

desbotado, -da [dʒiʒbo'tadu, -da] *adj* faded.

desbotar [dʒiʒbo'ta(x)] *vt & vi* to fade.

desbravar [dʒiʒbra'va(x)] *vt* to clear.

descabido, -da [dʒiʃka'bidu, -da] *adj* inappropriate.

descafeinado, -da [dʒiʃkafej'nadu, -da] *adj* decaffeinated ♦ *m* decaffeinated coffee.

descalçar [dʒiʃkaw'sa(x)] *vt* to take off.

descalço, -ça [dʒiʃ'kawsu, -sa] *pp →* **descalçar** ♦ *adj* barefoot.

descampado, -da [dʒiʃkãm'padu, -da] *adj* exposed ♦ *m* open ground.

descansado, -da [dʒiʃkã'sadu, -da] *adj* carefree; **fique ~!** don't worry!

descansar [dʒiʃkã'sa(x)] *vi* to rest.

descanso [dʒiʃ'kãsu] *m* rest; *(Br: para prato)* place mat.

descapotável [deʃkapo'tavɛl] *(pl* **-eis** [-ejʃ]) *adj (Port: carro)* convertible.

descarado, -da [dʒiʃka'radu, -da] *adj* cheeky.

descaramento [dʒiʃkara'mēntu] *m* cheek(iness).

descarga [dʒiʃ'kaxga] *f (descarregamento)* unloading; *(de arma)* shot; *(Br: de vaso sanitário)* flush; **dar a ~** *(Br)* to flush the toilet; **~ elétrica** electrical discharge.

descarregar [dʒiʃkaxe'ga(x)] *vt (carga)* to unload; *(arma)* to fire; *(fig: raiva, frustração)* to vent.

❑ **descarregar-se** *vp (bateria, pilha)* to go flat.

descarrilamento [dʒiʃkaxila'mēntu] *m* derailment.

descarrilar [dʒiʃkaxi'la(x)] *vi* to be derailed.

descartar-se [dʒiʃkax'taxsi] : **descartar-se de** *vp* + *prep* to get rid of.

descartável [dʒiʃkax'tavew] (*pl* -**eis**) *adj* disposable.

descascar [dʒiʃkaʃ'ka(x)] *vt* (*fruta, batatas*) to peel; (*nozes*) to shell.

descendência [desẽn'dẽsja] *f* descendants (*pl*).

descendente [desẽn'dẽntʃi] *mf* descendant.

descender [desẽn'de(x)] : **descender de** *v* + *prep* to descend from.

descentralizar [dʒiʃsẽntrali'za(x)] *vt* to decentralize.

descer [de'se(x)] *vt* (*escadas, rua, montanha*) to go/come down; (*estore*) to lower ♦ *vi* (*temperatura, preço*) to go down; ~ (**de**) (*de muro, escada, mesa*) to go/come down (from); (*de cavalo*) to dismount (from); (*de carro*) to get out (of); (*de ônibus, trem*) to get off.

descida [de'sida] *f* (*de rua, estrada*) slope; (*de avião*) descent; (*de preço, valor*) fall; "**~ perigosa**" "steep descent".

descoberta [dʒiʃko'bexta] *f* (*descobrimento*) discovery; (*invento*) invention.

descobrimento [dʒiʃkobri'mẽntu] *m* discovery.

❏ **Descobrimentos** *mpl*: **os Descobrimentos** the Discoveries.

descobrir [dʒiʃko'bri(x)] *vt* to discover; (*destapar, desvendar*) to uncover.

descolagem [deʃku'laʒẽ] (*pl* -**ns** [-ʃ]) *f* (*Port*) = **decolagem**.

descolar [deʃku'lar] *vt* (*selo, fita-cola, adesivo*) to remove.

descoloração [dʒiʃkolora'sãw] (*pl* -**ões** [-õjʃ]) *f* discoloration; **fazer uma** ~ to have one's hair bleached.

descompor [dʒiʃkõm'po(x)] *vt* to reprimand.

descompostura [dʒiʃkõmpoʃ'tura] *f* reprimand; **passar uma** ~ **a alguém** to give sb a good talking to.

descomunal [dʒiʃkomu'naw] (*pl* -**ais** [-ajʃ]) *adj* huge.

desconcentrar [dʒiʃkõsẽn'tra(x)] *vt* to distract.

desconfiar [dʒiʃkõ'fja(x)] *vt*: ~ **que** to suspect (that).

❏ **desconfiar de** *v* + *prep* (*não ter confiança em*) to distrust; (*suspeitar de*) to suspect.

desconfortável [dʒiʃkõfor'tavew] (*pl* -**eis** [-ejʃ]) *adj* uncomfortable.

desconforto [dʒiʃkõ'fortu] *m* discomfort.

descongelar [dʒiʃkõʒe'la(x)] *vt* to defrost.

desconhecer [dʒiʃkoɲe'se(x)] *vt*: **desconheço a resposta** I don't know the answer; **desconheço o seu paradeiro** I don't know where he is.

desconhecido, -da [dʒiʃkoɲe'sidu, -da] *adj* unknown ♦ *m, f* stranger.

desconsolado, -da [dʒiʃkõso'ladu, -da] *adj* (*triste*) disheartened; (*insípido*) insipid.

descontar [dʒiʃkõn'ta(x)] *vt* (*deduzir*) to deduct; (*cheque*) to debit.

descontentamento [dʒiʃkõntẽnta'mẽntu] *m* discontent.

desconto [dʒiʃ'kõntu] *m* discount.

descontraído, -da [dʒiʃkõntra'idu, -da] *adj* relaxed.

descontrair [dʒiʃkõntra'i(x)] *vt* to relax.

❏ **descontrair-se** *vp* to relax.

descontrolado, -da [dʒiʃkõntro'ladu, -da] *adj* (*pessoa*) hysterical; (*máquina*) out of control.

descontrolar-se [deʃkõntru'laxsi] *vp* to lose control.

desconversar [dʒiʃkõvex'sa(x)] *vi* to change the subject.

descortinar [dʒiʃkoxtʃi'na(x)] *vt* to discover.

descoser [dʒiʃko'ze(x)] *vt* to unstitch.

❏ **descoser-se** *vp* to come apart at the seams.

descrever [dʒiʃkre've(x)] *vt* to describe.

descrição [dʒiʃkri'sãw] (*pl* -**ões** [-õjʃ]) *f* description.

descuidado, -da [dʒiʃkui'dadu, -da] *adj* untidy.

descuidar [dʒiʃkui'da(x)] *vt* to neglect.

❏ **descuidar-se** *vp* (*não ter cuidado*) to be careless.

descuido [dʒiʃ'kuidu] *m* (*imprudência*) carelessness.

desculpa [dʒiʃ'kuwpa] *f* excuse; **pedir** ~ **a alguém por algo** to apologize to sb for sthg.

desculpar [dʒiʃkuw'pa(x)] *vt* to excuse; **desculpe! machuquei-o?** I'm sorry! did I hurt you?; **desculpe, pode me dizer as horas?** excuse me, do you have the time?

❏ **desculpar-se** *vp (pedir desculpa)* to apologize; *(justificar-se)* to justify o.s.; **~-se com algo** to use sthg as an excuse.

desde ['deʒdʒi] *prep (relativamente a espaço, variedade)* from; *(relativamente a tempo)* since; **~ aí** since then; **~ que** *(relativo a tempo)* since; *(indica condição)* if.

desdém [deʒ'dẽ] *m* contempt.

desdenhar [deʒde'ɲa(x)] *vt* to scorn ♦ *vi*: **~ de** to scoff at.

desdentado, -da [dʒiʒdẽn'tadu, -da] *adj* toothless.

desdizer [dʒiʒdi'ze(x)] *vt* to contradict.

❏ **desdizer-se** *vp* to go back on one's word.

desdobrar [dʒiʒdo'bra(x)] *vt (jornal, roupa, tecido)* to unfold; *(subdividir)* to divide up.

desejar [deze'ʒa(x)] *vt* to want; **o que é que você deseja?** what would you like?; **deseja mais alguma coisa?** would you like anything else?; **desejo-lhe boa sorte!** I wish you (good) luck!

desejo [de'zeʒu] *m (vontade)* wish; *(anseio)* desire.

deselegante [dʒizele'gãntʃi] *adj* inelegant.

desembaciar [dʒizẽmba'sja(x)] *vt* to clean.

desembaraçado, -da [dʒizẽmbara'sadu, -da] *adj (desenrascado)* resourceful; *(expedito)* prompt.

desembaraçar [dʒizẽmbara'sa(x)] *vt* to untangle.

❏ **desembaraçar-se** *vp* to hurry up; **~-se de algo** to rid o.s. of sthg.

desembaraço [dʒizẽmba'rasu] *m* ease.

desembarcar [dʒizẽmbax'ka(x)] *vt (carga)* to unload ♦ *vi* to disembark.

desembarque [dʒizẽm'baxki] *m (de carga)* unloading; *(de passageiros)* disembarkation; **"desembarque"** *(Br: em aeroporto)* "arrivals".

desembocar [dʒizẽmbo'ka(x)] *vi*: **~ em** *(rio)* to flow into; *(rua, caminho)* to lead into.

desembolsar [dʒizẽmbow'sa(x)] *vt (fam: pagar)* to cough up.

desembrulhar [dʒizẽmbru'ʎa(x)] *vt*

to unwrap, to open.

desempatar [dezẽmpa'ta(x)] *vt* to decide (the winner of).

desempenhar [dʒizẽmpe'ɲa(x)] *vt* to carry out; *(papel em peça, filme)* to play.

desempenho [dʒizẽm'peɲu] *m* performance; *(de obrigação)* fulfilment.

desemperrar [dʒizẽmpe'xa(x)] *vt* to loosen.

desempregado, -da [dʒizẽmpre'gadu, -da] *m, f* unemployed person.

desemprego [dʒizẽm'pregu] *m* unemployment; **estar no ~** to be unemployed.

desencadear [dʒizẽŋka'dʒja(x)] *vt* to give rise to.

❏ **desencadear-se** *v impess (tempestade)* to break.

desencaixar [dʒizẽŋkaj'ʃa(x)] *vt* to dislodge.

❏ **desencaixar-se** *vp* to come apart.

desencaixotar [dʒizẽŋkajʃu'ta(x)] *vt* to unpack.

desencantar [dʒizẽŋkãn'ta(x)] *vt (fam: achar)* to unearth; *(desiludir)* to disillusion.

desencontrar-se [dʒizẽŋkõn'traxsi] *vp* to miss each other.

desencorajar [dʒizẽŋkora'ʒa(x)] *vt* to discourage.

desencostar [dʒizẽŋkoʃ'ta(x)] *vt* to move away.

❏ **desencostar-se** *vp*: **~-se de** to move away from.

desenferrujar [dʒizẽfexu'ʒa(x)] *vt* to remove the rust from; *(fig: língua)* to brush up; *(fig: pernas)* to stretch.

desenfreado, -da [dʒizẽfri'adu, -da] *adj* unbridled.

desenganado, -da [dʒizẽŋga'nadu, -da] *adj (doente)* incurable.

desenganar [dʒizẽŋga'na(x)] *vt (doente)* to give no hope of recovery to; *(tirar as ilusões a)* to disillusion.

desengonçado, -da [dʒizẽŋgõ'sadu, -da] *adj (pessoa)* supple; *(objeto)* loose.

desenhar [deze'ɲa(x)] *vt* to draw.

❏ **desenhar-se** *vp (aparecer)* to appear; *(esboçar-se)* to take shape.

desenho [de'zeɲu] *m* drawing; **~s animados** cartoons.

desenlace [dʒizẽ'lasi] *m (de filme, história)* ending; *(de evento)* outcome.

desenrolar [dʒizẽxo'la(x)] *vt* to unroll.

❏ **desenrolar-se** *vp (ocorrer)* to take place.

desentendido, -da [dʒizēntēn'dʒidu, -da] *adj*: **fazer-se de ~** to feign ignorance.

desenterrar [dʒizēnte'xa(x)] *vt* to dig up.

desentupir [dʒizēntu'pi(x)] *vt* to unblock.

desenvolver [dʒizēvow've(x)] *vt* to develop.

❏ **desenvolver-se** *vp* to develop.

desenvolvido, -da [dʒizēvow'vidu, -da] *adj* developed.

desenvolvimento [dʒizēvowvi'mēntu] *m* development; *(progresso)* progress; *(crescimento)* growth.

desequilibrar-se [dʒizekili'braxsi] *vp* to lose one's balance.

deserto, -ta [de'zɛxtu, -ta] *adj* deserted ◆ *m* desert.

desesperado, -da [dʒizeʃpe'radu, -da] *adj* desperate.

desesperar [dʒizeʃpe'ra(x)] *vt (levar ao desespero)* to drive to despair; *(encolerizar)* to infuriate ◆ *vi* to despair.

desfalecer [dʒiʃfale'se(x)] *vi* to faint.

desfavorável [dʒiʃfavo'ravew] *(pl* -eis [-ejʃ]) *adj* unfavourable.

desfazer [dʒiʃfa'ze(x)] *vt (costura, alinhavo, nó)* to undo; *(dúvida, engano)* to dispel; *(grupo)* to disperse; *(noivado)* to break off; *(contrato)* to dissolve; *(reduzir a polpa)* to mash (up).

❏ **desfazer-se** *vp* to disintegrate; **o vidro desfez-se em mil pedaços** the glass broke into a thousand pieces.

❏ **desfazer-se de** *vp + prep* to get rid of.

desfecho [dʒiʃ'feʃu] *m* outcome.

desfeita [dʒiʃ'fejta] *f* insult.

desfeito, -ta [dʒiʃ'fejtu, -ta] *adj (em polpa)* mashed; *(cama)* unmade; *(puzzle)* in pieces; *(fig: desfigurado)* disfigured; *(acordo, casamento)* broken.

desfiar [dʒiʃ'fja(x)] *vt (bacalhau)* to shred.

❏ **desfiar-se** *vp (tecido, camisola)* to fray.

desfigurar [dʒiʃfigu'ra(x)] *vt (feições de pessoa)* to disfigure; *(fig: verdade)* to distort.

desfiladeiro [dʒiʃfila'dejru] *m* gorge.

desfilar [dʒiʃfi'la(x)] *vi* to parade.

desfile [dʒiʃ'fili] *m* parade; **~ de moda** fashion show.

desforra [dʒiʃ'fɔxa] *f* revenge.

desfrutar [dʒiʃfru'ta(x)] : **desfrutar de** *v + prep (possuir)* to have; *(tirar proveito de)* to enjoy.

desgastante [dʒiʒgaʃ'tāntʃi] *adj* exhausting.

desgastar [dʒiʒgaʃ'ta(x)] *vt (gastar)* to wear away, to erode; *(fig: cansar)* to wear out.

❏ **desgastar-se** *vp (gastar-se)* to wear down.

desgostar [dʒiʒgoʃ'ta(x)] *vt* to upset.

❏ **desgostar a** *v + prep* to displease.

desgosto [dʒiʒ'goʃtu] *m (infelicidade)* misfortune; *(mágoa)* sorrow.

desgraça [dʒiʒ'grasa] *f* misfortune.

desgrenhado, -da [dʒiʒgre'ɲadu, -da] *adj* dishevelled.

desidratação [dezidrata'sāw] *(pl* -ões [-õjʃ]) *f* dehydration.

desidratado, -da [dʒizidra'tadu, -da] *adj* dehydrated.

desidratar [dʒizidra'ta(x)] *vt* to dehydrate.

❏ **desidratar-se** *vp* to become dehydrated.

design [de'zajni] *m* design.

designação [dezigna'sāw] *(pl* -ões [-õjʃ]) *f* designation.

designar [dezig'na(x)] *vt* to designate.

designer [de'zajne(x)] *mf* designer.

desiludir [dʒizilu'di(x)] *vt* to let down.

❏ **desiludir-se com** *vp + prep* to become disillusioned with.

desilusão [dʒizilu'zāw] *(pl* -ões [-õjʃ]) *f* disillusion.

desimpedido, -da [dʒizīmpe'dʒidu, -da] *adj (linha de telefone)* free; *(rua, trânsito)* clear.

desimpedir [dʒizīmpe'dʒi(x)] *vt* to clear.

desinchar [dʒizī'ʃa(x)] *vi* to go down.

desinfetante [dʒizīfe'tāntʃi] *adj & m* disinfectant; **~ para a boca** mouthwash.

desinfectar [dezīfe'tar] *vt (Port)* = **desinfetar**.

desinfetar [dʒizīfe'ta(x)] *vt (Br)* to disinfect.

desinibido, -da [dʒizini'bidu, -da] *adj* uninhibited.

desintegrar-se [dʒizīnte'graxsi] *vp* to disintegrate.

desinteressado, -da [dʒizīntere-

'sadu, -da] *adj* uninterested; *(altruísta)* unselfish.

desinteressar-se [dʒizĩnteˈsaxsi] : **desinteressar-se de** *vp + prep* to lose interest in.

desinteresse [dʒizĩteˈresi] *m* lack of interest; *(abnegação)* unselfishness.

desistência [deziʃˈtẽsja] *f* cancellation.

desistir [deziʃˈtʃi(x)] *vi* to give up; **~ de algo** *(de reserva, vôo)* to cancel sthg; **~ de fazer algo** *(de fumar, correr, trabalhar)* to give up doing sthg.

desleal [dʒiʒˈljaw] *(pl -ais* [-ajʃ]) *adj* disloyal.

desleixado, -da [dʒiʒlejˈʃadu, -da] *adj* slovenly.

desleixo [dʒiʒˈlejʃu] *m* carelessness.

desligado, -da [dʒiʒliˈgadu, -da] *adj (aparelho)* switched off; *(telefone)* off the hook; *(fam: aéreo)* absent-minded.

desligar [dʒiʒliˈga(x)] *vt (rádio, TV)* to switch off; *(telefone)* to put down.

deslizar [dʒiʒliˈza(x)] *vi* to slide.

deslize [dʒiʒˈlizi] *m (fig: lapso)* slip.

deslocado, -da [dʒiʒloˈkadu, -da] *adj* dislocated; *(desambientado)* out of place.

deslocar [dʒiʒloˈka(x)] *vt* to dislocate.
❏ **deslocar-se** *vp* to be put out of joint; **~-se para** to go to; **~-se com** to move with; **~-se de** to go from.

deslumbrante [dʒiʒlũmˈbrãntʃi] *adj* amazing.

deslumbrar [dʒiʒlũmˈbra(x)] *vt* to dazzle.

desmaiado, -da [dʒiʒmaˈjadu, -da] *adj (desfalecido)* unconscious; *(desbotado)* faded.

desmaiar [dʒiʒmaˈja(x)] *vi* to faint.

desmaio [dʒiʒˈmaju] *m* faint.

desmamar [dʒiʒmaˈma(x)] *vt* to wean.

desmancha-prazeres [dʒiʒˌmãʃapraˈzeriʃ] *mf inv* killjoy.

desmanchar [dʒiʒmãˈʃa(x)] *vt (desmontar)* to take apart; *(renda, costura)* to undo; *(noivado)* to break (off).
❏ **desmanchar-se** *vp* to come apart.

desmarcar [dʒiʒmaxˈka(x)] *vt (consulta, reserva)* to cancel.

desmedido, -da [dʒiʒmeˈdʒidu, -da] *adj* excessive.

desmentido [dʒiʒmẽˈtʃidu] *m* denial.

desmentir [dʒiʒmẽˈtʃi(x)] *vt (negar)* to deny; *(contradizer)* to contradict.

desmesurado, -da [dʒiʒmezuˈradu, -da] *adj* excessive.

desmontar [dʒiʒmõˈta(x)] *vt (máquina)* to dismantle; *(construção)* to take down; *(fig: intriga, combinação)* to uncover.

desmoralizar [dʒiʒmoraliˈza(x)] *vt (desanimar)* to demoralize; *(tirar o bom nome de)* to disparage.

desmoronamento [dʒiʒmoronaˈmẽntu] *m (de casa)* collapse; *(de terra)* landslide.

desmoronar [dʒiʒmoroˈna(x)] *vt* to demolish.
❏ **desmoronar-se** *vp* to collapse.

desnatado [dʒiʒnaˈtadu] *adj* **m → leite**.

desnecessário, -ria [dʒiʒneseˈsarju, -rja] *adj* unnecessary.

desnível [dʒiʒˈnivew] *(pl -eis* [-ejʃ]) *m (de terreno)* unevenness; *(de valor)* gap.

desobedecer [dʒizobedeˈse(x)] : **desobedecer a** *v + prep* to disobey.

desobediência [dʒizobeˈdʒjẽsja] *f* disobedience.

desobediente [dʒizobeˈdʒjẽntʃi] *adj* disobedient.

desobstruir [dʒizobʃtruˈi(x)] *vt* to unblock.

desocupado, -da [dʒizokuˈpadu, -da] *adj* free; *(casa, apartamento)* unoccupied.

desocupar [dʒizokuˈpa(x)] *vt* to vacate.

desodorante [dʒizodoˈrãtʃi] *adj (Br)* deodorant *(antes de s)* ◆ *m (Br)* deodorant.

desodorizante [dezoduriˈzãnte] *adj & m (Port)* = **desodorante**.

desonesto, -ta [dʒizoˈnɛʃtu, -ta] *adj* dishonest.

desordem [dʒiˈzoxdẽ] *f* disorder; **em ~** *(quarto, papéis)* untidy.

desorganizado, -da [dʒizoxganiˈzadu, -da] *adj* disorganized.

desorientação [dʒizorjẽntaˈsãw] *f* disorientation.

desorientado, -da [dʒizorjẽnˈtadu, -da] *adj* disorientated.

despachar [dʒiʃpaˈʃa(x)] *vt (bagagem, mercadorias, encomenda)* to send off.
❏ **despachar-se** *vp (apressar-se)* to hurry (up).

despedida [dʒiʃpeˈdʒida] *f* farewell.

despedir [dʒiʃpeˈdʒi(x)] *vt* to fire.
❏ **despedir-se** *vp (dizer adeus)* to say

goodbye; *(demitir-se)* to resign.

despejar [dʒiʃpeˈʒa(x)] *vt (líquido)* to empty (out); *(lixo)* to throw out; *(de casa, apartamento)* to evict.

despejo [dʒiʃˈpeʒu] *m (de casa, apartamento)* eviction.

❏ **despejos** *mpl (lixo)* rubbish *(sg) (Brit)*, garbage *(sg) (Am)*.

despensa [dʒiʃˈpẽsa] *f* larder.

despenteado, -da [dʒiʃpẽnˈtʒjadu, -da] *adj* dishevelled.

despentear [dʒiʃpẽnˈtʒja(x)] *vt* to mess up.

❏ **despentear-se** *vp* to mess up one's hair.

despercebido, -da [dʒiʃpexseˈbidu, -da] *adj* unnoticed; **fazer-se de ~** to pretend not to know; **passar ~** to go unnoticed.

desperdiçar [dʒiʃpexdʒiˈsa(x)] *vt* to waste.

desperdício [dʒiʃpexˈdʒisju] *m* waste.

❏ **desperdícios** *mpl* scraps.

despertador [dʒiʃpextaˈdo(x)] *(pl -res* [-riʃ]*)* *m* alarm clock.

despertar [dʒiʃpexˈta(x)] *vt* to wake up; *(fig: estimular)* to arouse; *(fig: dar origem a)* to give rise to ♦ *vi (acordar)* to wake up.

despesa [dʒiʃˈpeza] *f* expense.

❏ **despesas** *fpl (de empresa, organismo)* expenses.

despido, -da [dʒiʃˈpidu, -da] *adj* naked.

despir [dʒiʃˈpi(x)] *vt* to undress.

❏ **despir-se** *vp* to get undressed.

desportista [deʃpurˈtiʃta] *(Port)* = **esportista**.

desportivo, -va [deʃpurˈtivu, -va] *adj (Port)* = **esportivo**.

desporto [deʃˈportu] *m (Port)* = **esporte**.

despregar [dʒiʃpreˈga(x)] *vt* to remove.

❏ **despregar-se** *vp (soltar-se)* to come loose.

desprender [dʒiʃprẽnˈde(x)] *vt* to unfasten.

❏ **desprender-se** *vp* to come unfastened.

despreocupado, -da [dʒiʃprioku-ˈpadu, -da] *adj* carefree.

desprevenido, -da [dʒiʃpreveˈnidu, -da] *adj* unprepared.

desprezar [dʒiʃpreˈza(x)] *vt* to scorn.

desproporcionado, -da [dʒiʃpro-poxsjoˈnadu, -da] *adj* disproportionate.

desqualificar [dʒiʃkwalifiˈka(x)] *vt* to disqualify.

desquitado, -da [dʒiʃkiˈtadu, -da] *adj (Br)* separated.

dessa [ˈdɛsa] = **de + essa**, → **de**.

desse [ˈdesi] = **de + esse**, → **de**.

desta [ˈdɛʃta] = **de + esta**, → **de**.

destacar [dʒiʃtaˈka(x)] *vt (separar)* to detach; *(enfatizar)* to emphasize.

❏ **destacar-se** *vp (distinguir-se)* to stand out.

destacável [dʒiʃtaˈkavew] *(pl -eis* [-ejʃ]*)* *adj* detachable ♦ *m (de formulário)* tear-off slip; *(de revista, jornal)* supplement.

destapar [dʒiʃtaˈpa(x)] *vt* to uncover.

destaque [dʒiʃˈtaki] *m* prominence; **em ~** in focus.

deste [ˈdeʃtʃi] = **de + este**, → **de**.

destemido, -da [deʃteˈmidu, -da] *adj* fearless.

destilada [deʃtʃiˈlada] *adj f* → **água**.

destilar [deʃtʃiˈla(x)] *vt* to distil.

destinar [deʃtʃiˈna(x)] *vt*: **~ algo para** to earmark sthg for.

❏ **destinar-se a** *vp + prep (ter por fim)* to be aimed at; *(ser endereçado a)* to be addressed to.

destinatário, -ria [deʃtʃinaˈtarju, -rja] *m, f (de carta)* addressee; *(de mensagem)* recipient.

destino [deʃˈtʃinu] *m (de viagem)* destination; **o ~** *(fado)* destiny; **com ~ a Londres** *(vôo, trem)* to London.

destituir [deʃtʃiˈtwi(x)] *vt (demitir)* to dismiss.

destrancar [dʒiʃtrãnˈka(x)] *vt* to unlock.

destreza [deʃˈtreza] *f (agilidade)* deftness; *(habilidade)* dexterity.

destro, -tra [ˈdeʃtru, -tra] *adj* right-handed; *(ágil)* deft; *(hábil)* skilled.

destroços [dʒiʃˈtrɔsuʃ] *mpl* wreckage *(sg)*.

destruição [dʒiʃtruiˈsãw] *f* destruction.

destruir [dʒiʃtruˈi(x)] *vt* to destroy.

desuso [dʒiˈzuzu] *m*: **cair em ~** to fall into disuse.

desvalorização [dʒiʒvalorizaˈsãw] *(pl -ões* [-õjʃ]*)* *f* devaluation.

desvalorizar [dʒiʃvaloriˈza(x)] *vt* to devalue.

❏ **desvalorizar-se** *vp* to depreciate.

desvantagem [dʒiʒvãn'taʒẽ] *(pl -ns* [-ʃ]) *f* disadvantage.

desviar [dʒiʒ'vja(x)] *vt* to move; *(dinheiro)* to embezzle; *(trânsito)* to divert.
❏ **desviar-se** *vp* to get out of the way; **~-se de algo** to move out of the way of sthg.

desvio [dʒiʒ'viu] *m (estrada secundária)* turn-off; *(de caminho)* diversion; *(de dinheiro)* embezzlement.

detalhe [de'taʎi] *m* detail.

detectar [dete'ta(x)] *vt* to detect.

detector [dete'to(x)] *(pl -res* [-riʃ]) *m* detector; **~ de incêndios** smoke alarm; **~ de radiações** Geiger counter.

detenção [detẽ'sãw] *(pl -ões* [-õjʃ]) *f* detention; *(prisão)* arrest.

deter [de'te(x)] *vt (parar)* to stop; *(prender)* to detain.
❏ **deter-se** *vp (parar)* to stop; *(conterse)* to restrain o.s.

detergente [detex'ʒẽntʃi] *m (para louça)* washing-up liquid; *(para roupa)* detergent.

deterioração [deterjora'sãw] *f* deterioration.

deteriorar [deterjo'ra(x)] *vt (danificar)* to damage.
❏ **deteriorar-se** *vp (estragar-se)* to deteriorate.

determinação [determina'sãw] *(pl -ões* [-õjʃ]) *f (força de vontade)* determination; *(cálculo)* calculation; *(resolução)* decision; *(ordem)* order.

determinar [determi'na(x)] *vt (calcular, decidir)* to determine; *(ordenar)* to order.

detestar [detes'ta(x)] *vt* to detest.

detrás [de'trajʃ] *adv (relativo a espaço)* behind; *(relativo a tempo)* afterwards; **~ de** *(relativo a tempo)* after; **(por) ~ de** *(pela retaguarda de)* behind.

detritos [de'trituʃ] *mpl* debris *(sg).*

deturpar [detux'pa(x)] *vt* to distort.

deu ['dew] → **dar.**

deus, -sa [dewʃ, -za] *(pl -ses* [-ziʃ], *fpl* **-s** [-ʃ]) *m, f* god *(f* goddess).
❏ **Deus** *m* God.

devagar [dʒiva'ga(x)] *adv* slowly.

dever [de've(x)] *(pl -res* [-riʃ]) *m* duty
♦ *vt:* **~ algo a alguém** to owe sb sthg; **você deve lavar os dentes todos os dias** you should brush your teeth every day; **o trem deve estar atrasado** the train must be late; **~ cívico** civic duty.

❏ **deveres** *mpl (trabalho de casa)* homework *(sg).*

devidamente [de,vida'mẽntʃi] *adv* properly.

devido, -da [de'vidu, -da] *adj (correto)* proper; **~ a** due to.

devolução [devolu'sãw] *(pl -ões* [-õjʃ]) *f (de dinheiro, cheque)* refund; *(de objeto emprestado, compra)* return.

devolver [devow've(x)] *vt (dinheiro, cheque)* to refund; *(objeto emprestado, compra)* to return.

devorar [devo'ra(x)] *vt* to devour.

dez ['dɛʒ] *num* ten, → **seis.**

dezanove [deza'nɔvɛ] *num (Port)* = **dezenove.**

dezasseis [deza'sejʃ] *num (Port)* = **dezesseis.**

dezassete [deza'sɛtɛ] *num (Port)* = **dezessete.**

dezembro [de'zẽmbru] *m* December, → **setembro.**

dezena [de'zena] *f (set of)* ten.

dezenove [deze'nɔvi] *num (Br)* nineteen, → **seis.**

dezesseis [deze'sejʃ] *num (Br)* sixteen, → **seis.**

dezessete [deze'sɛtʃi] *num (Br)* seventeen, → **seis.**

dezoito [de'zɔitu] *num* eighteen, → **seis.**

DF *abrev (Br)* = **Distrito Federal.**

dia ['dʒia] *m* day; **bom ~!** good morning!; **já é de ~** it's morning already; **do ~** of the day; **qualquer ~** any day; **no ~ seguinte** the day after; **no ~ vinte** on the twentieth; **por (cada) ~** per day; **todos os ~s** every day; **um ~ destes** one of these days; **estar em ~** to be up-to-date; **pôr-se em ~** to bring o.s. up-to-date; **pôr algo em ~** to update sthg; **~ de anos** *(Port)* birthday; **o ~ a ~** daily life; **~ de folga** day off; **~ Santo** religious holiday; **~ de semana** weekday; **~ de Todos-os-Santos** All Saints' Day; **~ útil** weekday.

diabetes [dʒja'bɛtʃiʃ] *m* diabetes.

diabético, -ca [dʒja'bɛtʃiku, -ka] *adj & m, f* diabetic.

diabo ['dʒjabu] *m* devil; **porque ~ ...?** *(fam)* why the hell ...?

diafragma [dʒja'fragma] *m* diaphragm.

diagnóstico [dʒjag'nɔʃtʃiku] *m* diagnosis.

dialecto [djaˈlɛtu] *m (Port)* = dialeto.

dialeto [dʒiaˈlɛtu] *m (Br)* dialect.

dialogar [dʒialoˈga(x)] *vi* to talk.

diálogo [ˈdʒialogu] *m* dialogue.

diamante [dʒiaˈmãntʃi] *m* diamond.

diâmetro [ˈdʒiâmetru] *m* diameter.

diante [ˈdʒiãntʃi] : **diante de** *prep (relativo a tempo)* before; *(relativo a espaço)* in front of; *(perante)* in the face of.

dianteira [dʒiãnˈtejra] *f (frente)* front; *(liderança)* lead.

diapositivo [dʒiapoziˈtivu] *m* slide.

diária [ˈdʒiarja] *f (de pensão, hotel)* daily rate.

diariamente [ˌdʒiarjaˈmēntʃi] *adv* daily, every day.

diário, -ria [ˈdʒiarju, -rja] *adj* daily ◆ *m* diary.

diarreia [djaˈxaja] *f (Port)* = **diarréia**.

diarréia [dʒiaˈxeja] *f (Br)* diarrhoea.

dica [ˈdʒika] *f (fam)* hint.

dicionário [dʒisjoˈnarju] *m* dictionary; **~ de bolso** pocket dictionary.

didáctico, -ca [diˈdatiku, -ka] *adj (Port)* = **didático**.

didático, -ca [dʒiˈdatʃiku, -ka] *adj (Br)* educational.

diesel [ˈdʒizɛw] *adj inv* diesel.

dieta [ˈdʒiɛta] *f* diet.

dietético, -ca [dʒjeˈtetʃiku, -ka] *adj (produto)* dietetic.

difamar [dʒifaˈma(x)] *vt (verbalmente)* to slander; *(por escrito)* to libel.

diferença [dʒifeˈrēsa] *f* difference.

diferenciar [dʒifereˈsja(x)] *vt* to differentiate.

diferente [dʒifeˈrēntʃi] *adj* different.

difícil [diˈfisiw] *(pl* **-ceis** [-sejʃ]) *adj* difficult.

dificuldade [dʒefikuwˈdadʒi] *f* difficulty.

dificultar [dʒifikuwˈta(x)] *vt* to make difficult; *(funcionamento, progresso)* to hinder.

difundir [dʒifũnˈdi(x)] *vt (informação, notícia)* to spread; *(calor, luz)* to give off; *(programa de rádio)* to broadcast.

difusão [dʒifuˈzãw] *f (de informação, notícia)* dissemination; *(de luz, calor)* diffusion; *(por televisão, rádio)* broadcasting.

digerir [dʒiʒeˈri(x)] *vt* to digest.

digestão [dʒiʒeʃˈtãw] *f* digestion.

digestivo, -va [dʒiʒeʃˈtʃivu, -va] *adj* digestive ◆ *m* after-dinner drink.

digital [dʒiʒiˈtaw] *(pl* **-ais** [-ajʃ]) *adj* digital.

digitalizador [dʒiʒitalizaˈdo(x)] *(pl* **-res** [-riʃ]) *m* scanner.

digitar [dʒiʒiˈta(x)] *vt* to key in.

dígito [ˈdʒiʒitu] *m* digit.

dignidade [dʒigniˈdadʒi] *f* dignity.

dilatar [dʒilaˈta(x)] *vt* to expand; *(prazo)* to extend.

❏ **dilatar-se** *vp* to expand.

dilema [dʒiˈlema] *m* dilemma.

diluir [dʒiˈlwi(x)] *vt* to dilute.

dimensão [dʒimẽˈsãw] *(pl* **-ões** [-õjʃ]) *f* dimension.

diminuir [dʒimiˈnwi(x)] *vi (em preço, número, força)* to decrease; *(em volume, quantidade)* to diminish ◆ *vt (reduzir)* to reduce.

diminutivo [dʒiminuˈtʃivu] *m* diminutive.

Dinamarca [dʒinaˈmarka] *f:* **a ~** Denmark.

dinamarquês, -esa [dʒinamarˈkeʃ, -eza] *(mpl* **-eses** [-eziʃ]*, fpl* **-s** [-ʃ]) *adj & m* Danish ◆ *m, f* Dane.

dinâmico, -ca [dʒiˈnamiku, -ka] *adj* dynamic.

dinamismo [dʒinaˈmiʒmu] *m* dynamism.

dinamite [dʒinaˈmitʃi] *f* dynamite.

dínamo [ˈdʒinamu] *m* dynamo.

dinastia [dʒinaʃˈtʃia] *f* dynasty.

dinheiro [dʒiˈɲejru] *m* money; **ter ~** to have money; **~ miúdo** loose change; **~ trocado** change.

dinossauro [dʒinoˈsawru] *m* dinosaur.

dióspiro [ˈdʒjɔʃpiru] *m* sharon fruit.

diploma [dʒiˈploma] *m* diploma.

dique [ˈdʒiki] *m* dike.

direção [dʒireˈsãw] *(pl* **-ões** [-õjʃ]) *f (Br) (endereço)* address; *(de veículo)* steering; *(rumo)* direction; *(de empresa)* management.

direcção [direˈsãw] *(pl* **-ões** [-õjʃ]) *f (Port)* = **direção**.

direções → **direção**.

directo, -ta [diˈrɛtu, -ta] *adj (Port)* = **direto**.

direita [dʒiˈrejta] *f:* **a ~** *(mão)* one's right hand; *(lado)* the right hand side; *(em política)* the Right; **conduza pela ~** drive on the right; **siga pela ~** keep right; **à ~ (de)** on the right (of); **virar à ~** to turn right; **ser de ~** *(POL)* to be right-wing.

direito, -ta [dʒiˈrejtu, -ta] *adj (mão, perna, lado)* right; *(corte, linha)* straight; *(pessoa)* honest; *(justo)* fair ◆ *m (privilégio)* right; *(leis, curso)* law; *(taxa, imposto)* duty ◆ *adv (Br: correctamente)* properly; **ir ~ a** to go straight to; **ir ~ ao assunto** to get straight to the point; **pôr-se ~** to stand up straight; **sempre a ~ straight** ahead; **os ~s humanos** human rights; **não há ~!** it's not fair!

direto, -ta [dʒiˈrɛtu, -ta] *adj (Br)* direct; *(transmissão)* live.

diretor, -ra [dʒireˈto(x), -ra] *(mpl -res* [-riʃ]*, fpl -s* [-ʃ]*) m, f (de escola)* head; *(de empresa)* director.

dirigente [dʒiriˈʒẽtʃi] *mf* leader.

dirigir [dʒiriˈʒi(x)] *vt (empresa)* to run; *(filme, peça de teatro)* to direct; *(orquestra)* to conduct; *(projeto, equipe)* to head; *(Br: veículo)* to drive ◆ *vi (Br)* to drive; **~ algo a alguém** to address sthg to sb; **~ algo para algo** to point sthg towards sthg.

❏ **dirigir-se a** *vp + prep (pessoa)* to talk to; *(público, ouvintes)* to address; *(local)* to head for; **"este aviso dirige-se a todos os usuários"** "this is a public announcement".

❏ **dirigir-se para** *vp + prep* to head towards.

dirigível [dʒiriˈʒivɛw] *(pl -eis* [-ejʃ]*) m* airship.

discar [dʒiʃˈka(x)] *vt & vi* to dial.

disciplina [dʒisiˈplina] *f* discipline; *(EDUC: cadeira)* subject.

disco-jóquei [dʒiskoˈʒɔkej] *(pl disco-jóqueis* [dʒiskoˈʒɔkejʃ]*) mf* disc jockey.

disco [dʒiʃku] *m* record; *(INFORM)* disk; *(de telefone)* dial; *(em atletismo)* discus; **~ compacto** compact disc; **~ rígido** hard disk; **~ voador** flying saucer; **~s de algodão** cotton wool pads.

discordar [dʒiʃkoxˈda(x)] *vi* to disagree; **~ de alguém em algo** to disagree with sb about sthg.

discórdia [dʒiʃˈkɔrdʒa] *f* dissent; **semear a ~** to sow the seeds of dissent.

discoteca [dʒiʃkoˈtɛka] *f (para dançar)* (night)club; *(loja)* record shop *(Brit)*, record store *(Am)*; *(coleção)* record collection.

discreto, -ta [dʒiʃˈkrɛtu, -ta] *adj (pessoa)* discreet; *(roupa)* sensible.

discriminação [dʒiʃkriminaˈsãw] *f* discrimination.

discriminar [dʒiʃkrimiˈna(x)] *vt* to discriminate against.

discurso [dʒiʃˈkuxsu] *m* speech; **~ direto/indireto** direct/indirect speech.

discussão [dʒiʃkuˈsãw] *(pl -ões* [-õjʃ]*) f (debate)* discussion; *(briga)* argument.

discutir [dʒiʃkuˈti(x)] *vt (idéia, assunto)* to discuss ◆ *vi (brigar)* to argue.

disenteria [dʒizẽteˈria] *f* dysentery.

disfarçar [dʒiʃfaxˈsa(x)] *vt* to disguise ◆ *vi* to pretend.

❏ **disfarçar-se** *vp* to disguise o.s.; **~-se de** to dress up as.

disfarce [dʒiʃˈfaxsi] *m* disguise.

dislexia [dʒiʃlɛkˈsia] *f* dyslexia.

disléxico, -ca [dʒiʃˈlɛksiku, -ka] *adj & m, f* dyslexic.

disparador [dʒiʃparaˈdo(x)] *(pl -res* [-riʃ]*) m (de máquina fotográfica)* shutter release.

disparar [dʒiʃpaˈra(x)] *vt (arma, bala)* to shoot ◆ *vi (arma, máquina fotográfica)* to go off.

disparatado, -da [dʒiʃparaˈtadu, -da] *adj* foolish.

disparate [dʒiʃpaˈratʃi] *m* nonsense.

dispensar [dʒiʃpẽˈsa(x)] *vt* to do without; **~ alguém de algo** to excuse sb from sthg; **~ algo a alguém** to lend sthg to sb.

dispersar [dʒiʃpexˈsa(x)] *vt* to scatter ◆ *vi* to disperse.

❏ **dispersar-se** *vp* to disperse.

disperso, -sa [dʒiʃˈpɛrsu, -sa] *pp →* dispersar.

disponível [dʒiʃpoˈnivɛw] *(pl -eis* [-ejʃ]*) adj* available.

dispor [dʒiʃˈpo(x)] *vt (colocar)* to arrange.

❏ **dispor de** *v + prep* to have; *(de posição)* to hold.

❏ **dispor-se a** *vp + prep*: **~-se a fazer algo** to offer to do sthg.

dispositivo [dʒiʃpoziˈtivu] *m* device.

disposto, -osta [dʒiʃˈpoʃtu, -oʃta] *adj* ready; **estar ~ a fazer algo** to be prepared to do sthg; **estar bem ~** *(de bom humor)* to be in a good mood.

disputa [dʒiʃˈputa] *f (competição)* competition; *(discussão)* dispute.

disputar [dʒiʃpuˈta(x)] *vt (troféu, lugar)* to compete for.

disquete [dʒiʃˈkɛtʃi] *f* diskette.

dissimular [dʒisimuˈla(x)] *vt (fingir)* to hide; *(encobrir)* to cover up.

dissipar [dʒisi'pa(x)] *vt (cheiro, fumo)* to get rid of; *(mal-entendido, confusão)* to clear up.
❑ **dissipar-se** *vp* to disappear.

disso ['dʒisu] = **de + isso**, → **isso**.

dissolver [dʒisow've(x)] *vt* to dissolve.
❑ **dissolver-se** *vp* to dissolve.

dissuadir [dʒiswa'di(x)] *vt* to dissuade.

distância [dʒiʃ'tãsja] *f* distance; **a que ~ fica?** how far (away) is it?; **fica a um quilômetro de ~** it's one kilometre away; **à ~** from a distance.

distanciar [dʒiʃtã'sja(x)] *vt (em espaço, tempo)* to distance; *(pessoas)* to drive apart.
❑ **distanciar-se** *vp (em espaço)* to move away; *(pessoas)* to grow apart; **~-se de** *(em espaço)* to move away from; *(em idéias, atitudes, etc)* to differ from.

distante [dʒiʃ'tãntʃi] *adj* distant.

distinção [dʒiʃtʃĩ'sãw] *(pl* **-ões** [-õjʃ]) *f* distinction.

distinguir [dʒiʃtʃĩ'gi(x)] *vt (ver)* to make out; *(diferenciar)* to distinguish.
❑ **distinguir-se** *vp (diferenciar-se)* to differ; *(em exame, trabalho, estudos)* to excel o.s.

distinto, -ta [dʒiʃ'tʃĩntu, -ta] *adj (diferente)* different; *(ruído, som)* distinct; *(pessoa)* distinguished.

disto ['dʒiʃtu] = **de + isto**, → **isto**.

distorção [dʒiʃtox'sãw] *(pl* **-ões** [-õjʃ]) *f* distortion.

distração [dʒiʃtra'sãw] *(pl* **-ões** [-õjʃ]) *f (Br) (falta de atenção)* absent-mindedness; *(esquecimento, diversão)* distraction; *(descuido)* oversight.

distracção [diʃtra'sãw] *(pl* **-ões** [-õjʃ]) *f (Port)* = **distração**.

distrações → **distração**.

distraído, -da [dʒiʃtra'idu, -da] *adj* absent-minded.

distrair [dʒiʃtra'i(x)] *vt (entreter)* to amuse; *(fazer perder atenção)* to distract.
❑ **distrair-se** *vp (divertir-se)* to enjoy o.s.; *(descuidar-se)* to get distracted.

distribuição [dʒiʃtribwi'sãw] *(pl* **-ões** [-õjʃ]) *f (de correspondência postal)* delivery; *(AUT)* timing; *(de trabalho, comida)* distribution.

distribuidor, -ra [dʒiʃtribwi'do(x), -ra] *(mpl* **-res** [-riʃ], *fpl* **-s** [-ʃ]) *m, f (de produto)* distributor ♦ *m (AUT)* distributor.

distrito [dʒiʃ'tritu] *m* district; **Distrito Federal** *term for Brasília, home of Brazil's federal government.*

distúrbio [dʒiʃ'tuxbju] *m* disturbance; *(Br: MED)* disorder.

ditado [dʒi'tadu] *m (de texto, frase)* dictation; *(provérbio)* saying.

ditador, -ra [dʒita'do(x), -ra] *(mpl* **-res** [-riʃ], *fpl* **-s** [-ʃ]) *m, f* dictator.

ditadura [dʒita'dura] *f* dictatorship.

ditafone® [dʒikta'foni] *m* Dictaphone®.

ditar [dʒi'ta(x)] *vt* to dictate.

dito, -ta ['dʒitu, -ta] *pp* → **dizer**.

ditongo [dʒi'tõŋgu] *m* diphthong.

diurno, -na ['dʒjuxnu, -na] *adj* daytime.

divã [dʒi'vã] *m* divan.

divagar [dʒiva'ga(x)] *vi (afastar-se de assunto)* to digress; *(devanear)* to daydream; *(caminhar ao acaso)* to wander.

diversão [dʒivex'sãw] *(pl* **-ões** [-õjʃ]) *f (distração)* amusement.

diverso, -sa [dʒi'vexsu, -sa] *adj (variado)* diverse.
❑ **diversos, -sas** *adj pl (muitos)* various.

diversões → **diversão**.

divertido, -da [dʒivex'tʃidu, -da] *adj* amusing.

divertimento [dʒivextʃi'mẽntu] *m* amusement.

divertir [dʒivex'tʃi(x)] *vt* to amuse.
❑ **divertir-se** *vp* to enjoy o.s.

dívida ['dʒivida] *f* debt.

dividendos [dʒivi'dẽnduʃ] *mpl* dividends.

dividir [dʒivi'di(x)] *vt (repartir)* to share out; *(separar)* to separate; *(MAT)* to divide ♦ *vi (MAT)* to divide.
❑ **dividir-se** *vp (separar-se)* to split up; *(ramificar-se)* to divide.

divino, -na [dʒi'vinu, -na] *adj* divine.

divisão [dʒivi'zãw] *(pl* **-ões** [-õjʃ]) *f* division; *(de casa)* room.

divisas [dʒi'vizaʃ] *fpl (COM)* foreign currency *(sg)*.

divisões → **divisão**.

divorciado, -da [dʒivox'sjadu, -da] *adj* divorced.

divorciar-se [dʒivox'sjaxsi] *vp* to get divorced; **~-se de alguém** to divorce sb.

divórcio [dʒi'vɔxsju] *m* divorce.

divulgar [dʒivuw'ga(x)] *vt (informação,*

idéia) to disseminate; *(produto, serviço)* to market.

dizer [dʒi'ze(x)] *vt* to say; ~ **algo a alguém** to tell sb sthg; ~ **a alguém que faça algo** to tell sb to do sthg; **como se diz ...?** how do you say ...?

DJ [di'ʒej] *mf (abrev de disc-jóquei)* DJ.

do [du] = **de** + **o**, → **o**.

doação [dwa'sãw] *(pl -ões* [-õjʃ]) *f* donation.

doar ['dwa(x)] *vt* to donate.

dobra ['dɔbra] *f* fold; *(de calças)* turn-up *(Brit)*, cuff *(Am)*.

dobradiça [dobra'disa] *f* hinge.

dobrado, -da [do'bradu, -da] *adj* folded; *(Port: filme, programa de TV)* dubbed.

dobrar [do'bra(x)] *vt (jornal, lençol, roupa)* to fold; *(joelho, costas)* to bend; *(Port: filme, programa de TV)* to dub ◆ *vi (duplicar)* to double; ~ **a esquina** to turn the corner.

⊔ **dobrar-se** *vp (curvar-se)* to bend over.

dobro ['dobru] *m*: **o** ~ double.

doca ['dɔka] *f* dock.

doce ['dosi] *adj (bebida, comida)* sweet; *(pessoa)* gentle ◆ *m (sobremesa)* sweet; *(geléia, compota)* jam; ~ **de ovos** egg yolks and sugar blended and cooked, used as a filling in cakes, sweets and pastries.

dóceis → **dócil**.

docente [do'sẽtʃi] *adj* teaching ◆ *mf* teacher.

dócil ['dɔsiw] *(pl -ceis* [-sejʃ]) *adj* docile.

documentação [dokumẽta'sãw] *f (documentos)* papers *(pl)*.

documentário [dokumẽ'tarju] *m* documentary.

documento [doku'mẽtu] *m* document.

doçura [do'sura] *f (fig)* gentleness.

doença ['dwẽsa] *f* disease; ~ **venérea** venereal disease.

doente ['dwẽtʃi] *adj* ill ◆ *mf* sick person; ~ **mental** psychiatric patient.

doentio, -tia [dwẽ'tʃiu, -'tʃia] *adj (lugar, atmosfera)* unwholesome; *(pessoa)* sickly.

doer ['dwe(x)] *vi* to hurt.

doido, -da ['dojdu, -da] *adj* mad ◆ *m, f* madman *(f* madwoman); **ser ~ por** to be mad about; ~ **varrido** *(fam)* complete nutter.

dois, duas ['dojʃ, 'duaʃ] *num* two; ~ **a** ~ in twos, → **seis**.

dólar ['dɔla(x)] *(pl -res* [-riʃ]) *m* dollar.

doleiro [do'lejru] *m (Br)* black market money dealer *(usually in US dollars)*.

dolorido, -da [dolo'ridu, -da] *adj* sore.

doloroso, -osa [dolo'rozu, -ɔza] *adj* painful.

dom ['dõ] *(pl -ns* [-ʃ]) *m* gift.

domador, -ra [doma'do(x), -ra] *(mpl -res* [-riʃ], *fpl -s* [-ʃ]) *m, f* tamer.

doméstica [do'mɛʃtʃika] *f* housewife.

domesticado, -da [domeʃtʃi'kadu, -da] *adj* tame.

domesticar [domeʃtʃi'ka(x)] *vt* to tame.

doméstico, -ca [do'mɛʃtʃiku, -ka] *adj* domestic.

domicílio [domi'silju] *m* residence.

dominar [domi'na(x)] *vt* to control; *(país)* to rule; *(situação)* to be in control of; *(língua)* to be fluent in; *(incêndio)* to bring under control.

⊔ **dominar-se** *vp (conter-se)* to control o.s.

domingo [do'mĩngu] *m* Sunday, → **sexta-feira**.

domínio [do'minju] *m (controle)* control; *(autoridade)* authority; *(sector, campo)* field; *(território)* domain; *(de língua)* command.

dominó [domi'nɔ] *m (jogo)* dominoes *(sg)*; **jogar** ~ to play dominoes.

dona ['dona] *f (título)* Mrs; ~ **de casa** housewife, → **dono**.

donde ['dõde] *adv (Port)*: ~ **veio?** where did it come from?

dono, -na ['donu, -na] *m, f* owner.

dons → **dom**.

dopar [do'pa(x)] *vt* to drug.

dor ['do(x)] *(pl -res* [-riʃ]) *f (física)* pain; *(moral)* grief; ~ **de barriga** stomach-ache; ~ **de cabeça** headache; ~ **de dente** toothache; ~ **de estômago** stomachache; ~ **de garganta** sore throat; ~ **lombar** backache; ~ **de ouvido** earache; ~ **es menstruais** period pains; ~ **de cotovelo** *(fig)* jealousy.

dormente [dor'mẽtʃi] *adj* numb.

dormida [dor'mida] *f* sleep; **dar uma** ~ to have a sleep.

dormir [dor'mi(x)] *vi* to sleep ◆ *vt* to sleep (for).

dormitório [dormi'tɔrju] *m* dormitory.

dosagem [du'zaʒãj] (*pl* **-ns** [-ʃ]) *f* dosage.

dose ['dɔzi] *f (de medicamento)* dose; *(de bebida)* measure; *(em restaurante)* portion.

dossiê [do'sje] *m (Br) (de documentação, processo)* file; ~ **(escolar)** folder.

dossier [dɔ'sje] *m (Port)* = **dossiê**.

dotado, -da [do'tadu, -da] *adj (talentoso)* gifted.

dou ['do] → **dar**.

dourado, -da [do'radu, -da] *adj* golden.

doutor, -ra [do'to(x), -ra] (*mpl* **-res** [-riʃ], *fpl* **-s** [-ʃ]) *m, f (médico, pessoa doutorada)* doctor.

Doutor, -ra [do'to(x), -ra] *m, f* title attributed to anyone with a university degree.

doutrina [do'trina] *f* doctrine.

doze ['dozi] *num* twelve, → **seis**.

Dr. *(abrev de Doutor)* Dr.

Dra. *(abrev de Doutora)* Dr.

dragão [dra'gãw] (*pl* **-ões** [-õjʃ]) *m* dragon.

dragar [dra'ga(x)] *vt (rio, lago)* to dredge.

drágea ['draʒja] *f (Br)* tablet.

drageia [dra'ʒaja] *f (Port)* = **drágea**.

dragões → **dragão**.

drama ['drama] *m* drama.

dramatizar [dramatʃi'za(x)] *vt (fig)* to dramatize.

dramaturgo, -ga [drama'turgu, -ga] *m, f* playwright.

drástico, -ca ['draʃtʃiku, -ka] *adj* drastic.

drenar [dre'na(x)] *vt* to drain.

dreno ['drenu] *m (MED)* drainage tube.

driblar [dri'bla(x)] *vi & vt* to dribble.

drinque ['drĩŋki] *m (Br)* drink.

drive ['drajvi] *f (INFORM)* drive.

droga ['drɔga] *f* drug; *(coisa de má qualidade)* rubbish ♦ *interj* blast!

drogado, -da [dro'gadu, -da] *m, f* drug addict.

drogar [dro'ga(x)] *vt* to drug.

❏ **drogar-se** *vp* to take drugs.

drogaria [droga'ria] *f* chemist's *(Brit)*, drugstore *(Am)*.

dto. *abrev* = **direito**.

duas → **dois**.

dublar [du'blax] *vt (Br: filme, programa de TV)* to dub.

duche ['duʃe] *m (Port)* shower; **tomar uma** ~ to have a shower.

duende ['dwẽndʒi] *m* goblin.

dum [dũ] = **de** + **um**, → **um**.

duma ['duma] = **de** + **uma**, → **um**.

duna ['duna] *f* dune.

duns [dũʃ] = **de** + **uns**, → **um**.

dupla ['dupla] *f (par)* duo, pair; *(Br: em esporte)* doubles *(sg)*.

dúplex ['dupleks] *m inv* maisonette *(Brit)*, duplex *(Am)*.

duplicado [dupli'kadu] *m* duplicate; **em** ~ in duplicate.

duplicar [dupli'ka(x)] *vt & vi* to double.

duplo, -pla ['duplu, -pla] *adj* double ♦ *m*: **o** ~ double.

duração [dura'sãw] *f (de férias, concerto, curso)* length; *(de produto deteriorável)* shelf life.

duradouro, -ra [dura'doru, -ra] *adj* lasting.

durante [du'rãntʃi] *prep* during; ~ **3 horas** for three hours.

durar [du'ra(x)] *vi* to last.

durex® [du'rɛks] *adj (Br)* → **fita**.

dureza [du'reza] *f (de objeto, substância)* hardness; *(de caráter)* harshness.

durmo ['durmu] → **dormir**.

duro, -ra ['duru, -ra] *adj* hard; *(pão)* stale; *(carne)* tough.

dúvida ['duvida] *f* doubt; **estou em** ~ I'm not sure; **pôr em** ~ to doubt; **sem** ~! absolutely!; **tirar** ~**s** to sort queries out.

duvidoso, -osa [duvi'dozu, -ɔza] *adj* dubious.

duzentos, -tas [du'zẽntuʃ, -taʃ] *num* two hundred, → **seis**.

dúzia ['duzja] *f* dozen; **uma** ~ **de ovos** a dozen eggs; **vender à** ~ to sell by the dozen; **meia** ~ half a dozen.

E

e [i] *conj* and.

é ['ɛ] → **ser**.

E. *(abrev de Este)* E.

ébano ['ɛbanu] *m* ebony.

ébrio, ébria ['ɛbriu, 'ɛbria] *adj* inebriated.

ebulição [ibuli'sãw] *f (fervura)* boiling.

écharpe [e'ʃarpi] *f* scarf.

eclipse [e'klipsi] *m* eclipse.

eco ['ɛku] *m* echo.

ecoar [e'kwa(x)] *vi* to echo.

ecografia [ekogra'fia] *f* ultrasound.

ecologia [ekolo'ʒia] *f* ecology.

ecológico, -ca [eko'lɔʒiku, -ka] *adj* ecological.

economia [ekono'mia] *f (ciência)* economics *(sg)*; *(de país)* economy; *(poupança)* saving.

❑ **economias** *fpl* savings.

económico, -ca [iku'nɔmiku, -ka] *adj (Port)* = **econômico**.

econômico, -ca [eko'nomiku, -ka] *adj (Br) (pessoa)* frugal; *(barato)* cheap; *(carro, motor, dispositivo)* economical; *(situação, crise)* economic.

economista [ekono'miʃta] *mf* economist.

economizar [ekonomi'za(x)] *vt* to save ◆ *vi* to economize.

ecoturismo [ekotu'riʒmu] *m* ecotourism.

ecrã ['ɛkrã] *m* screen.

ECT *f (abrev de Empresa Brasileira de Correios e Telégrafos)* Brazilian postal services.

ECU ['ɛku] *m* ECU.

eczema [ek'zema] *m* eczema.

edição [edʒi'sãw] *(pl* -ões [-õjʃ]) *f (exemplares)* edition; *(publicação)* publishing.

edifício [edʒi'fisju] *m* building.

edifício-garagem [edʒifisjuga'raʒẽ] *(pl* **edifícios-garagens** [edʒifisjuʒga-** 'raʒẽ]) *m (Br)* multistorey car park *(Brit)*, multistory parking lot *(Am)*.

editar [edʒi'ta(x)] *vt (livro, revista)* to publish; *(disco)* to release; *(programa, matéria)* to edit.

editor, -ra [edʒi'to(x), -ra] *(mpl* -res [-riʃ]. *fpl* -s [-ʃ]) *m, f (que publica)* publisher; *(que edita)* editor.

editora [edʒi'tora] *f (empresa, estabelecimento)* publishing house, → **editor**.

editores → **editor**.

edredão [ɛdre'dãw] *(pl* -ões [-õjʃ]) *m (Port)* = **edredom**.

edredom [edre'dõ] *(pl* -ns [-ʃ]) *m (Br)* duvet.

educação [eduka'sãw] *f* education; *(cortesia)* manners *(pl)*.

educado, -da [edu'kadu, -da] *adj* polite.

educar [edu'ka(x)] *vt (filhos)* to bring up; *(alunos)* to educate.

efectivo, -va [efɛ'tivu, -va] *adj (Port)* = **efetivo**.

efectuar [efɛ'twar] *vt (Port)* = **efetuar**.

efeito [e'fejtu] *m* effect; **com ~** *(realmente)* really, indeed; **sem ~** invalid.

efervescente [iferveʃ'sẽtʃi] *adj* → **aspirina**.

efetivamente [efɛ.tʃiva'mẽtʃi] *adv* indeed.

efetivo, -va [efɛ'tʃivu, -va] *adj (Br) (real)* genuine; *(funcionário, empregado)* permanent.

efetuar [efe'twa(x)] *vt (Br) (realizar)* to carry out; *(compra, pagamento, viagem)* to make.

eficácia [efi'kasja] *f (de plano, solução, sistema)* effectiveness; *(de pessoa)* efficiency.

eficaz [efi'kaʃ] *(pl* -zes [-ziʃ]) *adj (plano, solução, sistema)* effective; *(pessoa)* efficient.

eficiência [efi'sjɛ̃sja] f (de plano, método, sistema) effectiveness; (de pessoa) efficiency.

eficiente [efi'sjẽntfi] adj (plano, método, sistema) effective; (pessoa) efficient.

efusivo, -va [efu'zivu, -va] adj effusive.

egoísmo [e'gwiʒmu] m selfishness.

egoísta [e'gwiʃta] adj selfish ◆ mf selfish person.

égua ['ɛgwa] f mare.

eis ['ejʃ] adv here is/are; **~ senão quando** when all of a sudden.

eixo ['ejʃu] m (de roda) axle; (de máquina) shaft; (em geometria) axis.

ejaculação [eʒakula'sãw] (pl -ões [-õjʃ]) f ejaculation.

ejacular [eʒaku'la(x)] vt & vi to ejaculate.

ela ['ɛla] pron (pessoa) she; (coisa, animal) it; (com preposição: pessoa) her; (com preposição: coisa) it; **e ~?** what about her?; **é ~** it's her; **~ mesma** OU **própria** (she) herself.
❏ **elas** pron pl they; (com preposição) them.

elaboração [elabora'sãw] f (de plano, sistema) working out, development; (de trabalho escrito) writing.

elaborar [elabo'ra(x)] vt (trabalho, texto) to work on; (plano, lista) to draw up.

elasticidade [elaʃtisi'dadʒi] f elasticity.

elástico, -ca ['elaʃtfiku, -ka] adj elastic ◆ m (material) elastic; (para segurar papel) rubber band.

ele ['eli] pron (pessoa) he; (coisa, animal) it; (com preposição: pessoa) him; (com preposição: coisa, animal) it; **e ~?** what about him?; **é ~** it's him; **~ mesmo** OU **próprio** (he) himself.
❏ **eles** pron pl they; (com preposição) them.

eléctrico, -ca [i'lɛtriku, -ka] adj (Port) = **elétrico** ◆ m (Port) tram (Brit), streetcar (Am).

electrónica [ile'trɔnika] f (Port) = **eletrônica**.

elefante [ele'fãntfi] m elephant.

elegância [ele'gãsja] f elegance; (de modos) refinement.

elegante [ele'gãntfi] adj (esbelto) slim; (bem vestido) elegant.

eleger [ele'ʒe(x)] vt (ministro, presi-

dente, deputado) to elect; (sistema, método, manual) to choose.

eleição [elej'sãw] (pl -ões [-õjʃ]) f (de ministro, presidente, deputado) election; (de sistema, método, manual) choice.
❏ **eleições** fpl elections.

eleito, -ta [e'lejtu, -ta] pp → **eleger** ◆ adj (presidente, ministro, deputado) elected.

eleitor, -ra [elej'to(x), -ra] (mpl -res [-riʃ], fpl -s [-ʃ]) m, f voter.

elementar [elemẽn'ta(x)] (pl -es [-iʃ]) adj (fundamental) basic; (primário) elementary.

elemento [ele'mẽntu] m element; (de equipa, grupo) member; (informação) factor.
❏ **elementos** mpl data (sg); **os ~s** the elements.

eletricidade [eletrisi'dadʒi] f electricity.

eletricista [eletri'siʃta] mf electrician.

elétrico, -ca [e'lɛtriku, -ka] adj (Br) electric ◆

eletrizar [eletri'za(x)] vt (fig: entusiasmar) to electrify.

eletrodoméstico [e,letrodo'mɛʃtʃiku] m electric household appliance.

eletrônica [ele'tronika] f (Br) electronics.

eletrônico, -ca [ele'troniku, -ka] adj electronic.

elevação [eleva'sãw] (pl -ões [-õjʃ]) f area of high ground.

elevado, -da [ele'vadu, -da] adj high.

elevador [eleva'do(x)] (pl -res [-riʃ]) m lift (Brit), elevator (Am).

elevar [ele'va(x)] vt to raise; (promover) to elevate.
❏ **elevar-se** vp to rise.

eliminar [elemi'na(x)] vt to eliminate.

elite [e'litfi] f elite.

elo ['ɛlu] m (de cadeia) link; **~ de ligação** (fig) link.

elogiar [elo'ʒja(x)] vt to praise.

elogio [elo'ʒiu] m praise.

eloqüência [elo'kwẽsja] f eloquence.

eloquente [ilu'kwẽnte] adj (Port) = **eloqüente**.

eloqüente [elo'kwẽntfi] adj (Br) eloquent.

em [ẽ] prep **1.** (no interior de) in; **os papéis estão naquela gaveta** the papers are in that drawer; **vivo no**

norte I live in the north.
2. *(sobre)* on; **coloca uma jarra nesta mesa** put a vase on this table.
3. *(em certo ponto de)* in; **ela está na sala** she's in the living room; **estar ~ casa/no trabalho** to be at home/at work.
4. *(relativo a cidade, país)* in; **~ Londres/Paris** in London/Paris; **~ Portugal/França** in Portugal/France; **no Brasil** in Brazil; **nos Estados Unidos** in the (United) States.
5. *(indica tempo)* in; *(dia)* on; *(época)* at; **faço isso num dia** I can do that in a day; **ela nasceu ~ 1970/num sábado** she was born in 1970/on a Saturday; **vou de férias no Verão/Natal** I'm going on holiday in the summer/at Christmas; **vou lá nas férias** I'm going there during the holidays.
6. *(indica modo)* in; **paguei ~ reais** I paid in reals; **respondi-lhe ~ português** I answered him in Portuguese; **ela gastou tudo em cigarros** she spent it all on cigarettes.
7. *(indica assunto)*: **ele é um perito ~ economia** he's an expert in economics; **nisso de computador, a Carlota é a melhor** when it comes to computers, Carlota is the best; **sou licenciada ~ Letras/Direito** I'm an arts/law graduate.
8. *(indica estado)* in; **~ boas condições** in good condition; **não descer com o trem ~ movimento** passengers should not alight until the train has stopped.
9. *(introduz complemento)*: **a palavra caiu ~ desuso** the word is no longer used; **não acredito nele** I don't believe him; **não penses nele** don't think about him.

emagrecer [emagre'se(x)] *vi* to lose weight.

emancipado, -da [emãsi'padu, -da] *adj* emancipated.

emaranhado, -da [emara'ɲadu, -da] *adj* tangled.

embaciado, -da [ẽmba'sjadu, -da] *adj* steamed up.

embaciar [ẽmba'sja(x)] *vt* to steam up.

embaixada [ẽmbajˈʃada] *f* embassy.

embaixador, -ra [ẽmbajʃaˈdo(x), -ra] *(mpl* **-res** [-riʃ], *fpl* **-s** [-ʃ]) *m, f* ambassador.

embaixatriz [ẽmbajʃaˈtriʃ] *(pl* **-zes** [-ziʃ]) *f* ambassadress.

embaixo [ẽm'bajʃu] *adv (Br) (em espaço)* downstairs; *(em lista)* at the bottom; **~ de** under(neath).

embalagem [ẽmbaˈlaʒẽ] *(pl* **-ns** [-ʃ]) *f* packaging; *(pacote)* packet.

embalar [ẽmbaˈla(x)] *vt (produto)* to package; *(bebê)* to rock.

embaraçar [ẽmbaraˈsa(x)] *vt (desconcertar)* to embarrass; *(estorvar)* to hinder.

❏ **embaraçar-se** *vp (atrapalhar-se)* to get flustered.

embaraço [ẽmbaˈrasu] *m (vergonha)* embarrassment; *(estorvo)* hindrance.

embarcação [ẽmbaxkaˈsãw] *(pl* **-ões** [-õjʃ]) *f* vessel.

embarcar [ẽmbaxˈka(x)] *vi* to board; **~ em** *(navio, avião, comboio)* to board; *(aventura, negócio)* to embark on.

embarque [ẽm'baxki] *m* boarding; **zona** OU **local de ~** boarding point.

embebedar-se [ẽmbebeˈdaxsi] *vp* to get drunk.

embeber [ẽmbeˈbe(x)] *vt* to soak; **~ algo em algo** to soak sthg in sthg.

embelezar [ẽmbeleˈza(x)] *vt* to embellish.

emblema [ẽmˈblema] *m* emblem.

embora [ẽmˈbɔra] *conj* even though ◆ *adv*: **ir(-se) ~** to leave; **vai ~!** go away!

emboscada [ẽmboʃˈkada] *f* ambush.

embraiagem [ẽmbrajˈaʒẽ] *(pl* **-ns** [-ʃ]) *f (Port)* = **embreagem**.

EMBRATUR [ẽmbraˈtu(x)] *f (abrev de Empresa Brasileira de Turismo)* Brazilian tourist board.

embreagem [ẽmbreˈaʒẽ] *(pl* **-ns** [-ʃ]) *f (Br)* clutch.

embriagar-se [ẽmbriaˈgaxsi] *vp* to get drunk.

embrulhar [ẽmbruˈʎa(x)] *vt* to wrap up; *(misturar)* to muddle up.

embrulho [ẽmˈbruʎu] *m* package.

embutido, -da [ẽmbuˈtʃidu, -da] *adj* fitted.

emendar [emẽˈda(x)] *vt* to correct.

❏ **emendar-se** *vp* to mend one's ways.

ementa [eˈmẽta] *f (Port)* menu; **~ turística** set menu.

emergência [emexˈʒẽsja] *f* emergency.

emigração [emigraˈsãw] *f* emigration.

emigrante [emiˈgrãtʃi] *mf* emigrant.

emigrar [emiˈgra(x)] *vi* to emigrate; **~**

para to emigrate to.
emissão [emi'sãw] (*pl* **-ões** [-õjʃ]) *f (de programa)* broadcast; *(de calor, gases)* emission.
emissor, -ra [emi'so(x), -ra] (*mpl* **-res** [-riʃ], *fpl* **-s** [-ʃ]) *adj* broadcasting ♦ *m (rádio)* transmitter; *(de mensagem)* sender.
emissora [emi'sora] *f (de rádio)* radio station.
emissores → emissor.
emitir [emi'tʃi(x)] *vt (calor, luz, som)* to emit; *(moeda)* to issue; *(programa)* to broadcast.
emoção [emo'sãw] (*pl* **-ões** [-õjʃ]) *f (comoção)* emotion; *(excitação)* excitement.
emoldurar [emowdu'ra(x)] *vt* to frame.
emotivo, -va [emo'tʃivu, -va] *adj* emotional.
empacotar [ẽmpako'ta(x)] *vt* to pack up.
empada [ẽm'pada] *f* pasty; **~ de galinha** chicken pasty.
empadão [ẽmpa'dãw] (*pl* **-ões** [-õjʃ]) *m* pie *(made with mashed potato)*.
empadinha [ẽmpa'dʒiɲa] *f (Br)* pasty; **~ de camarão** prawn pasty; **~ de palmito** palm-heart pasty; **~ de queijo** cheese pasty.
empadões → empadão.
empalhar [ẽmpa'ʎa(x)] *vt* to stuff.
empanturrar [ẽmpãntu'xa(x)] *vt*: **~ alguém com algo** *(fam)* to stuff sb full of sthg.
⃞ **empanturrar-se** *vp (fam)* to stuff o.s.
empatar [ẽmpa'ta(x)] *vi* to draw ♦ *vt (dinheiro)* to tie up; **~ alguém** *(estorvar a)* to get in sb's way.
empate [ẽm'patʃi] *m* draw, tie.
empenado, -da [ẽmpe'nadu, -da] *adj* warped.
empenhar [ẽmpe'ɲa(x)] *vt* to pawn.
⃞ **empenhar-se** *vp (esforçar-se)* to do one's utmost; *(endividar-se)* to get into debt; **~-se em algo** to do one's utmost to do sthg.
empestar [ẽmpeʃ'ta(x)] *vt* to stink out.
empilhar [ẽmpi'ʎa(x)] *vt* to pile up.
empinar [ẽmpi'na(x)] *vt (bicicleta, moto)* to do a wheelie on.
⃞ **empinar-se** *vp (cavalo)* to rear (up); *(bicicleta, moto)* to do a wheelie.

emplastro [ẽm'plaʃtru] *m* plaster.
empobrecer [ẽmpobre'se(x)] *vt (pessoa, país)* to impoverish; *(terreno)* to deplete ♦ *vi (pessoa, país)* to become poor; *(terreno)* to become depleted.
empolgante [ẽmpow'gãntʃi] *adj* gripping.
empreender [ẽmpriẽn'de(x)] *vt (negócio, trabalho)* to start.
empreendimento [ẽmpriẽndʒi-'mẽntu] *m (investimento)* venture; *(empenho)* investment.
empregado, -da [ẽmpre'gadu, -da] *m, f (em empresa)* employee; **~ de balcão** sales assistant; **~ de bar** barman *(f* barmaid); **~ (doméstico)** domestic servant; **~ (de mesa)** waiter *(f* waitress).
empregar [ẽmpre'ga(x)] *vt (pessoa, método, técnica)* to employ; *(dinheiro, tempo)* to spend; *(objeto, ferramenta)* to use.
⃞ **empregar-se** *vp (arranjar emprego)* to get a job; *(utilizar-se)* to be used.
emprego [ẽm'pregu] *m (trabalho, ocupação)* job; *(uso)* use; **o ~** *(em geral)* employment.
empregue [ẽm'prɛgi] *pp* → empregar.
empresa [ẽm'preza] *f* firm.
emprestado, -da [ẽmpreʃ'tadu, -da] *adj* borrowed; **pedir algo ~** to borrow sthg.
emprestar [ẽmpreʃ'ta(x)] *vt*: **~ algo a alguém** to lend sthg to sb.
empréstimo [ẽm'prɛʃtʃimu] *m* loan.
empunhar [ẽmpu'ɲa(x)] *vt* to hold.
empurrão [ẽmpu'xãw] (*pl* **-ões** [-õjʃ]) *m* shove.
empurrar [ẽmpu'xa(x)] *vt* to push; "empurre" "push".
empurrões → empurrão.
encabeçar [ẽŋkabe'sa(x)] *vt* to head.
encadernação [ẽŋkadexna'sãw] (*pl* **-ões** [-õjʃ]) *f (capa)* cover; *(ato)* binding.
encaixar [ẽŋkaj'ʃa(x)] *vt* to fit; *(fig: meter na cabeça)* to get into one's head.
⃞ **encaixar-se** *vp* to fit in.
encaixe [ẽŋ'kajʃi] *m* slot; **~ do flash** fitting *(for camera flash)*.
encaixotar [ẽŋkajʃo'ta(x)] *vt* to box.
encalhar [ẽŋka'ʎa(x)] *vt & vi* to run aground.
encaminhar [ẽŋkami'ɲa(x)] *vt (aconselhar)* to provide guidance for OU to; **~ algo/alguém para** to refer sthg/sb to.
⃞ **encaminhar-se para** *vp + prep* to head towards.

encanador, -ra [ĕŋkana'dox, -ra] *(mpl* **-res** [-riʃ], *fpl* **-s** [-ʃ]) *m, f (Br)* plumber.

encantador, -ra [ĕŋkãnta'do(x), -ra] *(mpl* **-res** [-riʃ], *fpl* **-s** [-ʃ]) *adj* delightful.

encantar [ĕŋkãn'ta(x)] *vt* to delight.

encaracolado, -da [ĕŋkarako'ladu, -da] *adj* curly.

encarar [ĕŋka'ra(x)] *vt* to face.

❏ **encarar com** *v* + *prep* to come face to face with.

encardido, -da [ĕŋkar'dʒidu, -da] *adj* grubby.

encarnado, -da [ĕŋkar'nadu, -da] *adj* scarlet, red.

encarregado, -da [ĕŋkaxe'gadu, -da] *m, f* person in charge; *(de operários)* foreman *(f* forewoman).

encarregar [ĕŋkaxe'ga(x)] *vt:* ~ **alguém de fazer algo** to put sb in charge of doing sth.

encastrado, -da [ĕŋkaʃ'tradu, -da] *adj* fitted; *(pedra em jóia)* set.

encenação [ĕsena'sãw] *(pl* **-ões** [-õjʃ]) *f (de peça teatral)* staging.

encenar [ĕse'na(x)] *vt (peça teatral)* to stage, to put on.

encerar [ĕse'ra(x)] *vt* to wax.

encerrado, -da [ĕse'xadu, -da] *adj* closed.

encerramento [ĕsexa'mĕntu] *m (de concerto, espetáculo)* end; *(de loja)* closure.

encerrar [ĕse'xa(x)] *vt* to close; *(concerto, espetáculo)* to end.

encharcar [ĕʃar'ka(x)] *vt* to soak.

❏ **encharcar-se** *vp* to get soaked.

enchente [ĕ'ʃĕntʃi] *f* flood.

enchova [ĕ'ʃova] *f (peixe)* snapper; *(Br: alice)* anchovy.

encoberto, -ta [ĕŋko'bɛxtu, -ta] *adj (céu, tempo)* overcast; *(oculto)* hidden.

encolher [ĕŋko'ʎe(x)] *vt (ombros)* to shrug; *(pernas)* to bend; *(barriga)* to pull in ♦ *vi* to shrink.

❏ **encolher-se** *vp* to huddle.

encomenda [ĕŋko'mĕnda] *f* order; **feito por** ~ made to order; ~ **postal** mail order.

encomendar [ĕŋkomĕn'da(x)] *vt* to order; ~ **algo a alguém** *(comprar)* to order sth from sb; *(obra, escultura, pintura)* to commission sth from sb.

encontrar [ĕŋkõn'tra(x)] *vt* to find; *(pessoa por acaso)* to bump into.

❏ **encontrar-se** *vp (ter encontro)* to meet; *(estar)* to be; ~**-se com alguém** to meet up with sb.

encontro [ĕŋ'kõntru] *m (profissional)* appointment; *(amoroso)* date.

encorajar [ĕŋkora'ʒa(x)] *vt* to encourage.

encorpado, -da [ĕŋkor'padu, -da] *adj (pessoa)* burly; *(vinho)* full-bodied.

encosta [ĕŋ'kɔʃta] *f* slope.

encostar [ĕŋkoʃ'ta(x)] *vt (carro)* to park; *(porta)* to leave ajar; *(cabeça)* to lay down; ~ **algo em algo** *(mesa, cadeira)* to put sth against sth; *(escada, vara)* to lean sth against sth.

❏ **encostar-se** *vp:* ~**-se a** *(parede, carro, poste)* to lean against.

encosto [ĕŋ'kɔʃtu] *m (de assento)* back.

encruzilhada [ĕŋkruzi'ʎada] *f* crossroads *(sg)*.

endereço [ĕndeˈresu] *m* address.

endireitar [ĕndirej'ta(x)] *vt* to straighten; *(objeto caído)* to put upright.

❏ **endireitar-se** *vp (pôr-se direito)* to stand up straight.

endívia [ĕn'dʒivja] *f* endive.

endoidecer [ĕndojde'se(x)] *vt* to drive mad ♦ *vi* to go mad.

endossar [ĕndo'sa(x)] *vt* to endorse.

endurecer [ĕndure'se(x)] *vt & vi* to harden.

energia [enɛx'ʒia] *f* energy; ~ **eólica/nuclear/solar** wind/nuclear/solar power.

enevoado, -da [ene'vwadu, -da] *adj* cloudy.

enfarte [ĕ'faxtʃi] *m:* ~ **(do miocárdio)** heart attack.

ênfase [ĕfazi] *f* emphasis.

enfatizar [ĕfatʃi'za(x)] *vt* to emphasize.

enfeitiçar [ĕfejtʃi'sa(x)] *vt* to bewitch.

enfermagem [ĕfex'maʒĕ] *f* nursing.

enfermaria [ĕfexma'ria] *f* ward.

enfermeiro, -ra [ĕfex'mejru, -ra] *m, f* nurse.

enferrujar [ĕfexu'ʒa(x)] *vt & vi* to rust.

enfiar [ĕ'fja(x)] *vt (calça, mangas, camisola)* to pull ou put on; ~ **algo em algo** to put sth in sth.

enfim [ĕ'fĩ] *adv (finalmente)* at last ♦ *interj* oh well!

enforcar [ẽfoxˈka(x)] *vt* to hang.
❏ **enforcar-se** *vp* to hang o.s.

enfraquecer [ẽfrakeˈse(x)] *vt & vi* to weaken.

enfrentar [ẽfrẽnˈta(x)] *vt* to confront.

enfurecer [ẽfureˈse(x)] *vt* to infuriate.
❏ **enfurecer-se** *vp* to get angry.

enganado, -da [ẽgaˈnadu, -da] *adj*: **estar ~** to be wrong; **ser ~** *(ser ludibriado)* to be deceived; *(por cônjuge)* to be cheated on.

enganar [ẽgaˈna(x)] *vt* to deceive; *(cônjuge)* to cheat on.
❏ **enganar-se** *vp* *(estar errado)* to be wrong; *(errar)* to make a mistake.

engano [ẽ'ganu] *m* mistake; **é ~** *(em conversa telefônica)* you've got the wrong number.

engarrafado, -da [ẽgaxaˈfadu, -da] *adj (líquido)* bottled; *(trânsito)* blocked.

engarrafamento [ẽgaxafaˈmẽntu] *m (de trânsito)* traffic jam; *(de líquido)* bottling.

engasgar-se [ẽgaʒˈgaxsi] *vp* to choke.

engenharia [ẽʒeɲaˈria] *f* engineering.

engenheiro, -ra [ẽʒeˈɲejru, -ra] *m, f* engineer.

engenhoso, -osa [ẽʒeˈɲozu, -ɔza] *adj* ingenious.

engessar [ẽʒeˈsa(x)] *vt* to set in a plaster cast.

englobar [ẽgloˈba(x)] *vt* to encompass.

engodo [ẽ'godu] *m* bait.

engolir [ẽgoˈli(x)] *vt* to swallow.

engomar [ẽgoˈma(x)] *vt (passar a ferro)* to iron; *(com goma)* to starch.

engordar [ẽgorˈda(x)] *vi (pessoa)* to put on weight; *(alimento)* to be fattening ◆ *vt (animal)* to fatten up.

engordurado, -da [ẽgorduˈradu, -da] *adj* greasy.

engraçado, -da [ẽgraˈsadu, -da] *adj* funny.

engravidar [ẽgraviˈda(x)] *vi* to get pregnant ◆ *vt*: **~ alguém** to get sb pregnant.

engraxar [ẽgraˈʃa(x)] *vt* to polish; *(Port: fam: professor, chefe, etc)* to butter up.

engraxate [ẽgraˈʃatʃi] *m (Br)* shoe shiner.

engrenagem [ẽgreˈnaʒẽ] *(pl* **-ns** [-ʃ]) *f* mechanism.

engrossar [ẽgroˈsa(x)] *vt & vi* to thicken.

enguia [ẽ'gia] *f* eel.

enguiçar [ẽgiˈsa(x)] *vi (motor, máquina)* to play up.

enigma [eˈnigma] *m (adivinha)* riddle; *(mistério)* enigma.

enjoado, -da [ẽˈʒwadu, -da] *adj* sick; *(em carro, barco)* travelsick.

enjoar [ẽˈʒwa(x)] *vi* to get travelsick ◆ *vt* to get sick of.

enjoo [ẽ'ʒou] *m (Port)* = **enjôo**.

enjôo [ẽ'ʒou] *m (Br) (náusea)* sickness; *(em barco, avião, ônibus)* travel sickness.

enlatado, -da [ẽlaˈtadu, -da] *adj (comida)* tinned *(Brit)*, canned *(Am)*; *(cultura, filme)* imported.
❏ **enlatados** *mpl* tinned foods *(Brit)*, canned foods *(Am)*.

enlouquecer [ẽlokeˈse(x)] *vt* to drive mad ◆ *vi* to go mad.

enorme [eˈnɔrmi] *adj* huge, enormous.

enquanto [ẽɲˈkwantu] *conj* while; **~ (que)** whereas; **por ~** for the time being.

enraivecer [ẽxajveˈse(x)] *vt* to enrage.

enraivecido, -da [ẽxajveˈsidu, -da] *adj* enraged.

enredo [ẽ'xedu] *m* plot.

enriquecer [ẽxikeˈse(x)] *vt* to make rich; *(melhorar)* to enrich ◆ *vi* to get rich.

enrolar [ẽxoˈla(x)] *vt (papel, tapete, fio)* to roll up; *(cabelo)* to curl; *(cigarro)* to roll; *(fam: enganar)* to take for a ride.

enroscar [ẽxoʃˈka(x)] *vt (tampa)* to screw on; *(parafuso)* to screw in.
❏ **enroscar-se** *vp (cobra)* to coil up; *(gato, cão)* to curl up; *(emaranhar-se)* to get tangled up.

enrugar [ẽxoˈga(x)] *vt (roupa, papel)* to crease; *(pele)* to wrinkle ◆ *vi (pele)* to wrinkle.

ensaiar [ẽsaˈja(x)] *vt (peça, dança)* to rehearse; *(sistema)* to test.

ensaio [ẽ'saju] *m (de peça, dança)* rehearsal; *(de sistema)* test; *(texto literário)* essay.

enseada [ẽ'sjada] *f* cove.

ensinamento [ẽsinaˈmẽntu] *m (lição)* teaching; *(preceito)* saying.

ensinar [ẽsiˈna(x)] *vt (em escola, universidade)* to teach; *(caminho, direção)*

to show; ~ **alguém a fazer algo** to
teach sb how to do sthg; ~ **algo a
alguém** (*língua, método*) to teach sb
sthg; (*caminho*) to show sb sthg.

ensino [ẽ'sinu] *m* (*actividade*) teaching; (*método, sistema*) education; ~
superior higher education.

ensolarado, -da [ẽsola'radu, -da] *adj*
sunny.

ensopado [ẽso'padu] *m* stew.

ensopar [ẽso'pa(x)] *vt* to soak.
❏ **ensopar-se** *vp* to get soaked.

ensurdecedor, -ra [ẽsurdese'do(x),
-ra] (*mpl* -**res** [-rif], *fpl* -**s** [-ʃ]) *adj* deaf-
ening.

ensurdecer [ẽsurde'se(x)] *vt* to deaf-
en ♦ *vi* (*ficar surdo*) to go deaf.

entalar [ẽnta'la(x)] *vt* (*dedo, pé*) to
trap; (*peça de roupa*) to tuck in.

entanto [ẽn'tãntu] : **no entanto** *conj*
however.

então [ẽn'tãw] *adv* then ♦ *interj* so!;
desde ~ since then.

enteado, -da [ẽn'tʒjadu, -da] *m, f*
stepson (*f* stepdaughter).

entender [ẽntẽn'de(x)] *vt* (*perceber*) to
understand ♦ *vi* (*compreender*) to
understand; **dar a** ~ **que** to give the
impression (that); ~ **que** to think
(that).
❏ **entender de** *v + prep* to know
about.
❏ **entender-se** *vp* to get along; **não me
entendo com isto** I can't get the hang
of this; **~-se com alguém** (*chegar a
acordo com*) to come to an agreement
with sb.

enternecedor, -ra [ẽnternese'do(x),
-ra] (*mpl* -**res** [-rif], *fpl* -**s** [-ʃ]) *adj* touching.

enternecer [ẽnterne'se(x)] *vt* to
touch.

enterrar [ẽnte'xa(x)] *vt* to bury.
❏ **enterrar-se** *vp* to sink.

enterro [ẽn'texu] *m* funeral.

entonação [ẽntona'sãw] (*pl* -**ões**
[-õjʃ]) *f* intonation.

entornar [ẽntor'na(x)] *vt* to spill.

entorse [ẽn'tɔxsi] *f* sprain.

entortar [ẽntor'ta(x)] *vt* to bend.

entrada [ẽn'trada] *f* entrance;
(*vestíbulo*) hall; (*prato*) starter; (*bilhete
para espetáculo*) ticket; (*de dicionário*)
entry; (*pagamento inicial*) down payment, deposit; **como ~, o que deseja?**
what would you like as a starter?;

"**entrada**" "way in"; "~ **livre**" "free
admission"; "~ **proibida**" "no entry".

entranhas [ẽn'traɲaʃ] *fpl* entrails.

entrar [ẽn'tra(x)] *vi* to enter, to
go/come in; (*encaixar*) to go in; ~ **com
algo** to contribute sthg; ~ **em algo**
(*penetrar, ingressar em*) to enter sthg;
(*participar em*) to take part in sthg;
entro em férias amanhã my holidays
start tomorrow; **não entremos em dis-
cussões** let's not start arguing; ~ **em
algo** (*carro*) to get in sthg; (*ônibus, trem*)
to get on sthg; (*equipe, grupo*) to join
sthg.

entre [ẽntri] *prep* between; (*no meio
de muitos*) among(st); (*cerca de*) about;
aqui ~ **nós** between you and me; ~ **si**
amongst themselves.

entreaberto, -ta [ẽntria'bextu, -ta]
adj (*janela*) half-open; (*porta*) ajar.

entreajuda [ẽntrea'ʒuda] *f* teamwork.

entrecosto [ẽntre'koʃtu] *m* spare ribs
(*pl*).

entrega [ẽn'trega] *f* (*de encomenda,
mercadoria, carta*) delivery; (*rendição*)
surrender; ~ **a domicílio** home delivery.

entregar [ẽntre'ga(x)] *vt*: ~ **algo a
alguém** (*dar*) to give sthg to sb;
(*encomenda, carta*) to deliver sthg to sb.
❏ **entregar-se** *vp* (*render-se*) to surrender; **~-se a** (*abandonar-se a*) to abandon o.s. to; (*dedicar-se a*) to dedicate
o.s. to.

entrelinha [ẽntre'liɲa] *f* line space.

entremeado, -da [ẽntri'mjadu, -da]
adj (*toucinho*) streaky.

entretanto [ẽntri'tãntu] *adv* meanwhile, in the meantime ♦ *conj* (*Br:
todavia*) however.

entreter [ẽntre'te(x)] *vt* to entertain.
❏ **entreter-se** *vp* to amuse o.s.

entrevado, -da [ẽn'trevadu, -da] *adj*
paralysed.

entrevista [ẽntre'viʃta] *f* interview.

entrevistador, -ra [ẽntre'viʃtado(x),
-ra] (*mpl* -**res** [-rif], *fpl* -**s** [-ʃ]) *m, f* interviewer.

entristecer [ẽntriʃte'se(x)] *vt* to sadden ♦ *vi* to grow sad.

entroncamento [ẽntrõŋka'mẽntu] *m*
junction.

entupido, -da [ẽntu'pidu, -da] *adj*
blocked.

entupir [ẽntu'pi(x)] *vt* to block.

❑ **entupir-se** *vp* to become blocked.

entusiasmar [ēntuʒjaʒˈma(x)] *vt* to excite.

❑ **entusiasmar-se** *vp* to get excited.

entusiasmo [ēntuˈʒjaʒmu] *m* enthusiasm.

entusiasta [ēntuˈʒjaʃta] *mf* enthusiast.

enumeração [enumeraˈsãw] (*pl* -ões [-õjʃ]) *f* enumeration.

enumerar [enumeˈra(x)] *vt* to list.

enunciado [enũˈsjadu] *m (de teste, exame)* (exam) paper.

enunciar [enũˈsja(x)] *vt* to express.

envelhecer [ēveʎeˈse(x)] *vt* to age ✦ *vi* to grow old.

envelope [ēveˈlɔpi] *m* envelope.

envenenamento [ēvenenaˈmēntu] *m* poisoning.

envenenar [ēveneˈna(x)] *vt* to poison.

❑ **envenenar-se** *vp* to poison o.s.

enveredar [ēvereˈda(x)] : **enveredar por** *v* + *prep (fig)* to take up.

envergonhado, -da [ēvergoˈɲadu, -da] *adj* shy.

envergonhar [ēvergoˈɲa(x)] *vt* to embarrass.

❑ **envergonhar-se** *vp (ter vergonha)* to be embarrassed.

envernizar [ēverniˈza(x)] *vt* to varnish.

enviar [ēˈvja(x)] *vt* to send.

envidraçado, -da [ēvidraˈsadu, -da] *adj* glazed.

envio [ēˈviu] *m* sending.

enviuvar [ēvjuˈva(x)] *vi* to be widowed.

envolver [ēvowˈve(x)] *vt (incluir)* to involve; *(embrulhar)* to wrap up; *(misturar)* to mix up.

❑ **envolver-se em** *vp* + *prep (imiscuir-se em)* to get involved in.

enxada [ēˈʃada] *f* hoe.

enxaguar [ēʃaˈgwa(x)] *vt* to rinse.

enxame [ēˈʃami] *m* swarm.

enxaqueca [ēʃaˈkɛka] *f* migraine.

enxergar [ēʃexˈga(x)] *vt (descortinar)* to see; *(avistar)* to make out.

enxerto [ēˈʃextu] *m (de planta)* cutting; *(MED: de pele)* graft.

enxofre [ēˈʃofri] *m* sulphur.

enxotar [ēʃoˈta(x)] *vt* to chase away.

enxugar [ēʃuˈga(x)] *vt & vi* to dry.

enxurrada [ēʃuˈxada] *f* torrent.

enxuto, -ta [ēˈʃutu, -ta] *adj* dry.

enzima [ēˈzima] *f* enzyme.

eólica [eˈɔlika] *adj f* → **energia**.

epicentro [epiˈsēntru] *m* epicentre.

epidemia [epideˈmia] *f* epidemic.

epilepsia [epilepˈsia] *f* epilepsy.

epílogo [eˈpilugu] *m* epilogue.

episódio [epiˈzɔdju] *m* episode.

epitáfio [epiˈtafju] *m* epitaph.

época [ˈɛpoka] *f (período)* era, period; *(estação)* season; ~ **alta/baixa** *(de turismo)* high/low season.

equação [ekwaˈsãw] (*pl* -ões [-õjʃ]) *f* equation.

Equador [ekwaˈdo(x)] *m*: **o** ~ Ecuador.

equilibrar [ekiliˈbra(x)] *vt* to balance.

❑ **equilibrar-se** *vp* to balance.

equilíbrio [ekiˈlibriu] *m* balance.

equipa [iˈkipa] *f (Port)* = **equipe**.

equipamento [eikipaˈmēntu] *m (esportivo)* kit; *(de empresa, fábrica)* equipment.

equipar [ekiˈpa(x)] *vt* to equip.

❑ **equipar-se** *vp* to kit o.s. out.

equiparar [ekipaˈra(x)] *vt* to compare.

❑ **equiparar-se** *vp* to be equal; ~-**se a** to equal.

equipe [eˈkipi] *f (Br)* team.

equitação [ekitaˈsãw] *f* (horse) riding.

equivalente [ekivaˈlēntʃi] *adj & m* equivalent.

equivocar-se [ekivoˈkaxsi] *vp* to make a mistake.

equívoco [eˈkivoku] *m* mistake.

era¹ [ˈɛra] → **ser**.

era² [ˈɛra] *f* era.

erecto, -ta [iˈrɛktu, -ta] *adj (Port)* = **ereto**.

ereto, -ta [eˈrɛtu, -ta] *adj (Br) (em pé)* upright; *(direito)* erect.

erguer [exˈge(x)] *vt (levantar)* to lift up; *(criar)* to put up.

❑ **erguer-se** *vp* to get up.

eriçado, -da [eriˈsadu, -da] *adj (cabelo, pêlo)* on end.

erigir [eriˈʒi(x)] *vt (monumento)* to erect; *(fundação)* to set up.

erosão [eroˈzãw] *f* erosion.

erótico, -ca [iˈrɔtiku, -ka] *adj* erotic.

erotismo [eroˈtiʒmu] *m* eroticism.

erradicar [exadʒiˈka(x)] *vt* to eradicate.

errado, -da [eˈxadu, -da] *adj* wrong.

errar [e'xa(x)] *vt* to get wrong ◆ *vi* *(enganar-se)* to make a mistake; *(vaguear)* to wander.

erro ['exu] *m* mistake.

errôneo, -nea [i'xonju, -nja] *adj (Port)* = errôneo.

errôneo, -nea [e'xonju, -nja] *adj (Br)* wrong.

erudição [erudʒi'sãw] *f* erudition.

erudito, -ta [eru'dʒitu, -ta] *adj* erudite.

erupção [erup'sãw] *(pl* -ões [-õjʃ]) *f* *(em pele)* rash; *(vulcânica)* eruption.

erva ['exva] *f* grass; ~ **daninha** weed.

erva-cidreira [ˌexva'sidrejra] *f* lemon verbena.

erva-doce [ˌexva'dosi] *f* aniseed.

erva-mate [ˌexva'matʃi] *f* maté, *herbal infusion drunk out of a gourd.*

ervanário [exva'narju] *m* herbalist.

ervilha [ex'viʎa] *f* pea.

ervilhas-de-cheiro [ex,viʎazdʒi-'ʃejru] *fpl* sweet peas.

és ['ɛʃ] → **ser**.

esbaforido, -da [iʒbafu'ridu, -da] *adj* breathless.

esbanjar [iʒbã'ʒa(x)] *vt (dinheiro)* to squander.

esbarrar [iʒba'xa(x)] *vi:* ~ **com** OU **contra** to bump into; ~ **em algo** *(chocar com)* to bump into sthg; *(deparar com)* to come up against sthg.

esbelto, -ta [iʒbɛwtu, -ta] *adj* slim.

esboço [iʒbosu] *m* sketch.

esbofetear [iʒbofe'tʒja(x)] *vt* to slap.

esburacar [iʒbura'ka(x)] *vt* to make holes in.

❏ **esburacar-se** *vp* to fall apart.

escabeche [iʃka'bɛʃi] *m (molho)* sauce *made from olive oil, garlic, onion and herbs, used to preserve cooked fish.*

escada [iʃ'kada] *f (de casa, edifício)* stairs *(pl)*; *(portátil)* ladder; ~ **de caracol** spiral staircase; ~ **rolante** escalator.

escadote [iʃka'dɔtʃi] *m* stepladder.

escala [iʃ'kala] *f* scale; *(de avião, navio)* stopover *(Brit)*, layover *(Am)*; **fazer** ~ *(avião)* to stop over; **em grande** ~ on a grand scale.

escalada [iʃka'lada] *f (de conflito)* escalation.

escalão [iʃka'lãw] *(pl* -ões [-õjʃ]) *m* grade.

escalar [iʃka'la(x)] *vt (montanha)* to climb.

escaldar [iʃkaw'da(x)] *vt (alimento)* to blanch ◆ *vi (estar muito quente)* to be scalding hot.

❏ **escaldar-se** *vp (queimar-se)* to scald o.s.

escalfado, -da [iʃkaw'fadu, -da] *adj (Port)* poached.

escalfar [iʃkaw'fa(x)] *vt (Port)* to poach.

escalões → **escalão**.

escalope [iʃka'lɔpi] *m* escalope.

escama [iʃ'kama] *f (de peixe)* scale.

escamar [iʃka'ma(x)] *vt (peixe)* to scale.

escandalizar [iʃkãndali'za(x)] *vt* to scandalize.

❏ **escandalizar-se** *vp* to be scandalized.

escândalo [iʃ'kãndalu] *m* scandal; **dar** ~ to cause a scene.

escangalhar [iʃkãŋga'ʎa(x)] *vt* to ruin.

❏ **escangalhar-se** *vp* to fall apart.

escaninho [iʃka'niɲu] *m* pigeonhole.

escanteio [iʃkãn'teju] *m (Br: em futebol)* corner.

escapar [iʃka'pa(x)] *vi* to escape; ~ **de** to escape from.

❏ **escapar-se** *vp (escoar-se)* to leak; *(fugir)* to escape.

escape [iʃ'kapi] *m* exhaust.

escapulir-se [iʃkapu'lixsi] *vp (Port: fugir)* to run away.

escaravelho [iʃkara'veʎu] *m* beetle.

escarlate [eʃkar'latʃi] *adj* scarlet.

escarlatina [iʃkarla'tina] *f* scarlet fever.

escárnio [iʃ'karnju] *m* mockery.

escarpado, -da [iʃkar'padu, -da] *adj* steep.

escarrar [iʃka'xa(x)] *vi* to hawk.

escassez [iʃka'seʒ] *f* scarcity.

escasso, -a [iʃ'kasu, -a] *adj* scarce.

escavação [iʃkava'sãw] *(pl* -ões [-õjʃ]) *f* dig, excavation.

escavar [iʃka'va(x)] *vt* to excavate.

esclarecer [iʃklare'se(x)] *vt* to clarify.

esclarecimento [iʃklaresi'mẽntu] *m (informação)* information; *(explicação)* explanation.

escoar [iʃ'kwa(x)] *vt* to drain away.

❏ **escoar-se** *vp* to drain away.

escocês, -esa [iʃko'seʃ, -eza] *(mpl* -eses [-eziʃ], *fpl* -s [-ʃ]) *adj* Scottish ◆ *m, f* Scot, Scotsman *(f* Scotswoman);

os escoceses the Scottish, the Scots.

Escócia [iʃ'kɔsja] *f:* **a ~** Scotland.

escola [iʃ'kɔla] *f* school; **~ politécnica** *college of higher education offering vocational degrees and training for jobs in industry*; **~ primária/secundária** primary/secondary school; **~ pública** state school; **~ de samba** *group organized to put on dance pageants during Carnival parades.*

escolar [iʃko'la(x)] (*pl* **-res** [-riʃ]) *adj* (*livro, equipamento*) school (*antes de s*).

escolha [iʃ'koʎa] *f* choice; **você tem vários livros à ~** you have several books to choose from.

escolher [iʃko'ʎe(x)] *vt & vi* to choose.

escombros [iʃ'kômbruʃ] *mpl* ruins.

esconder [iʃkõn'de(x)] *vt* to hide.

❑ **esconder-se** *vp* to hide.

esconderijo [iʃkõnde'riʒu] *m* hideaway, hiding place.

escondidas [iʃkõn'dʒidaʃ] **: às escondidas** *adv* in secret.

escondido, -da [iʃkõn'dʒidu, -da] *adj* hidden.

escorar [iʃko'ra(x)] *vt* (*edifício, muro*) to shore up; (*árvore*) to prop up.

escorpião [iʃkox'pjãw] (*pl* **-ões** [-õjʃ]) *m* scorpion.

❑ **Escorpião** *m* Scorpio.

escorrega [iʃko'xɛga] *m* slide.

escorregadio, -dia [iʃkoxega'dʒiu, -dʒia] *adj* slippery.

escorregar [iʃkoxe'ga(x)] *vi* (*involuntariamente*) to slip; (*deslizar*) to slide.

escorrer [iʃko'xe(x)] *vt* to drain ♦ *vi* (*pingar*) to drip.

escoteiro, -ra [iʃkõ'tejru, -ra] *m, f* (*Br*) (*depois dos 11 anos*) Scout (*f* Guide); (*entre os 7 e 11 anos*) Cub (*f* Brownie).

escotilha [iʃko'tiʎa] *f* hatch.

escova [iʃ'kova] *f* brush; **~ de dentes** toothbrush; **~ de unhas** nailbrush.

escovar [iʃko'va(x)] *vt* (*cabelo, dentes, roupa*) to brush; (*cão, gato*) to groom.

escravatura [iʃkrava'tura] *f* slavery.

escravo, -va [iʃ'kravu, -va] *m, f* slave.

escrever [iʃkre've(x)] *vt & vi* to write; **~ à máquina** (*Port*) to type.

❑ **escrever-se** *vp* to write to one another; **como é que se escreve ...?** how do you spell ...?

escrevinhar [iʃkrevi'ɲa(x)] *vt* to scribble.

escrita [iʃ'krita] *f* (*caligrafia*) handwriting.

escrito, -ta [iʃ'kritu, -ta] *pp* → **escrever** ♦ *adj* written; **por ~** in writing.

escritor, -ra [iʃkri'to(x), -ra] (*mpl* **-res** [-riʃ], *fpl* **-s** [-ʃ]) *m, f* writer.

escritório [iʃkri'tɔrju] *m* (*de casa*) study; (*de advogado, empresa*) office.

escritura [iʃkri'tura] *f* deed.

escrivaninha [iʃkriva'niɲa] *f* writing desk.

escrúpulo [iʃ'krupulu] *m* scruple; **não ter ~s** to have no scruples.

escudo [iʃ'kudu] *m* (*unidade monetária*) escudo; (*arma*) shield.

esculpir [iʃkuw'pi(x)] *vt* to sculpt.

escultor, -ra [iʃkuw'to(x), -ra] (*mpl* **-res** [-riʃ], *fpl* **-s** [-ʃ]) *m, f* sculptor (*f* sculptress).

escultura [iʃkuw'tura] *f* sculpture.

escuras [iʃ'kuraʃ] **: às escuras** *adv* in the dark; **ficou tudo às ~** everything went dark.

escurecer [iʃkure'se(x)] *vi* (*céu, noite*) to get dark ♦ *vt* (*tinta, água*) to darken.

escuridão [iʃkuri'dãw] *f* darkness.

escuro, -ra [iʃ'kuru, -ra] *adj* dark ♦ *m* darkness.

escutar [iʃku'ta(x)] *vt* to listen to ♦ *vi* to listen.

escuteiro, -ra [iʃku'tejru, -ra] *m, f* (*Port*) = **escoteiro**.

esfaquear [iʃfa'kja(x)] *vt* to stab.

esfarelar [iʃfare'la(x)] *vt* to crumble.

❑ **esfarelar-se** *vp* to crumble.

esfarrapado, -da [iʃfaxa'padu, -da] *adj* tattered.

esfera [iʃ'fɛra] *f* sphere.

esférico, -ca [iʃ'fɛriku, -ka] *adj* spherical ♦ *m* (*Port: bola de futebol*) football.

esferográfica [iʃfɛrɔ'grafika] *f* Biro®.

esferovite [iʃfɛrɔ'vitʃi] *m* polystyrene.

esfoladela [iʃfola'dɛla] *f* graze.

esfolar [iʃfo'la(x)] *vt* to skin.

esfomeado, -da [iʃfo'mjadu, -da] *adj* starving.

esforçado, -da [iʃfox'sadu, -da] *adj* hard-working.

esforçar-se [iʃfox'saxsi] *vp* to work hard.

esfregão [iʃfre'gãw] (*pl* **-ões** [-õjʃ]) *m* (*de louça*) scourer; (*de chão*) mop.

esfregar [iʃfre'ga(x)] *vt* (*friccionar*) to

rub; *(roupa)* to scrub; *(louça)* to scour.

esfregões → esfregão.

esfriar [iʃfri'a(x)] *vi* to cool (down); *(tempo)* to get cold.

esfuziante [iʃfu'zjãntʃi] *adj (deslumbrante)* dazzling; *(ruidoso)* buzzing.

esganar [iʒga'na(x)] *vt* to strangle.

esganiçado, -da [iʒgani'sadu, -da] *adj* shrill.

esgotado, -da [iʒgo'tadu, -da] *adj (produto)* sold out; *(cansado)* exhausted.

esgotamento [iʒgota'mẽntu] *m* exhaustion; *(mental, nervoso)* breakdown.

esgotar [iʒgo'ta(x)] *vt* to use up .

❏ **esgotar-se** *vp (produto)* to sell out; *(extenuar-se)* to exhaust o.s.

esgoto [iʒ'gotu] *m (de casa)* drain; *(de rua, cidade)* sewer.

esgrima [iʒ'grima] *f* fencing; **praticar ~** to fence.

esgueirar-se [iʒgej'raxsi] *vp* to sneak off.

esguichar [iʒgi'ʃa(x)] *vt & vi* to squirt.

esguicho [iʒ'giʃu] *m (jato de água)* squirt; *(repuxo)* sprinkler; *(de mangueira)* nozzle.

esguio, -guia [iʒ'giu, -'gia] *adj* slender.

eslavo, -va [iʒ'lavu, -va] *adj* Slavonic ◆ *m, f* Slav.

esmagador, -ra [iʒmaga'do(x), -ra] *(mpl* **-res** [-riʃ]. *fpl* **-s** [-ʃ]) *adj (vitória, maioria)* overwhelming; *(peso)* crushing.

esmagar [iʒma'ga(x)] *vt* to crush.

esmalte [iʒ'mawtʃi] *m* enamel; *(de unhas)* nail varnish.

esmeralda [iʒme'rawda] *f* emerald.

esmerar-se [iʒme'raxsi] *vp* to take great pains.

esmigalhar [iʒmiga'ʎa(x)] *vt (pão, broa, bolo)* to crumble; *(vidro, porcelana)* to shatter.

❏ **esmigalhar-se** *vp (pão, broa, bolo)* to crumble; *(vidro, porcelana)* to shatter.

esmola [iʒ'mɔla] *f*: **pedir ~** to beg.

esmurrar [iʒmu'xa(x)] *vt (dar murros em)* to punch.

espaçar [iʃpa'sa(x)] *vt* to space out.

espacial [iʃpa'sjaw] *(pl* **-ais** [-ajʃ]) *adj* space *(antes de s)*.

espaço [iʃ'pasu] *m* space; **o ~** *(outer)* space; **há ~ para muitas pessoas**

there's room for lots of people; **~ cibernético** cyberspace.

espaçoso, -osa [iʃpa'sozu, -ɔza] *adj* spacious.

espada [iʃ'pada] *f* sword.

❏ **espadas** *fpl (naipe de cartas)* spades.

espadarte [iʃpa'daxtʃi] *m* garfish.

espaguete [iʃpa'getʃi] *m (Br)* spaghetti.

espairecer [iʃpajre'se(x)] *vi* to relax.

espalhar [iʃpa'ʎa(x)] *vt (dispersar)* to scatter; *(notícia, boato)* to spread.

❏ **espalhar-se** *vp (dispersar-se)* to scatter; *(estatelar-se)* to fall over; *(notícia, boato)* to spread.

espanador [iʃpana'do(x)] *(pl* **-res** [-riʃ]) *m* feather duster.

espancar [iʃpãŋ'ka(x)] *vt* to beat (up).

Espanha [iʃ'paɲa] *f*: **a ~** = Spain.

espanhol, -la [iʃpa'ɲɔw, -la] *(mpl* **-óis** [-ɔjʃ], *fpl* **-s** [-ʃ]) *adj & m* Spanish ◆ *m, f (pessoa)* Spaniard; **os espanhóis** the Spanish.

espantalho [iʃpãn'taʎu] *m* scarecrow.

espantar [iʃpãn'ta(x)] *vt* to astonish, to astound; *(afugentar)* to scare off; **tome um café para ~ o sono** have a coffee to keep you awake.

❏ **espantar-se** *vp (admirar-se)* to be astonished; *(fugir)* to run off.

espanto [iʃ'pãntu] *m (admiração)* astonishment; *(medo)* fright.

esparadrapo [iʃpara'drapu] *m (Br)* (sticking) plaster *(Brit)*, Bandaid® *(Am)*.

espargo [eʃ'pargu] *m (Port)* asparagus.

esparguete [eʃpar'getʃ] *m (Port)* = **espaguete.**

espartilho [iʃpax'tiʎu] *m* corset.

espasmo [iʃ'paʒmu] *m* spasm.

espátula [iʃ'patula] *f* spatula.

especial [iʃpe'sjaw] *(pl* **-ais** [-ajʃ]) *adj* special; **em ~** especially; **~ para** especially for.

especialidade [iʃpesjali'dadʒi] *f* speciality.

especialista [iʃpesja'liʃta] *m, f (perito)* expert; *(médico especializado)* specialist ◆ *adj* specialist.

especiarias [iʃpesja'riaʃ] *fpl* spices.

espécie [iʃ'pɛsji] *f (tipo)* kind, sort; *(de seres vivos)* species *(sg)*; **a ~ humana** the human race; **uma ~ de** a kind ou sort of; **~ em vias de extinção** endangered species.

especificar [iʃpesifi'ka(x)] *vt* to specify.

espécime [iʃ'pɛsimi] *m* specimen.

espectáculo [cʃpɛ'takulu] *m (Port)* = espetáculo.

espectador, -ra [iʃpɛkta'do(x), -ra] *(mpl* -**res** [-riʃ], *fpl* -**s** [-ʃ]) *m, f (de programa televisivo)* viewer; *(de evento esportivo)* spectator; *(de espetáculo de circo, teatro, etc)* member of the audience.

espectro [iʃ'pɛktru] *m (fantasma)* spectre.

especulação [iʃpɛkula'sau] *(pl* -**ões** [-õiʃ]) *f* speculation.

especular [iʃpɛku'la(x)] *vi* to speculate; ~ **sobre algo** to speculate on OU about sthg.

espelho [iʃ'pɛʎu] *m* mirror; ~ **retrovisor** rear-view mirror.

espera [iʃ'pɛra] *f* wait; **estar à ~ de** to be waiting for.

esperança [iʃpe'rãsa] *f* hope.

esperar [iʃpe'ra(x)] *vt (aguardar)* to wait for; *(ter esperança em)* to expect ◆ *vi (aguardar)* to wait; ~ **que** to hope (that); **fazer alguém ~** to keep sb waiting; **ir ~ alguém** to meet sb; **como era de ~** as was to be expected.

esperma [iʃ'pɛxma] *m* sperm.

espertalhão, -lhona [iʃpɛxta'ʎãw, -ʎona] *(mpl* -**ões** [-õiʃ], *fpl* -**s** [-ʃ]) *m, f* smart aleck.

esperteza [iʃpɛx'teza] *f* cunning.

esperto, -ta [iʃ'pɛxtu, -ta] *adj (astuto)* cunning; *(activo)* lively.

espesso, -a [iʃ'pesu, -a] *adj* thick.

espessura [iʃpe'sura] *f* thickness.

espetacular [iʃpɛtaku'la(x)] *(pl* -**es** [-iʃ]) *adj* spectacular.

espetáculo [iʃpɛ'takulu] *m (Br) (de circo, teatro)* show; ~ **de luzes e som** concert and firework display, often the finale of a festival; ~ **de variedades** variety show.

espetada [cʃpɛ'tada] *f (Port)* shish kebab; ~ **mista** shish kebab with both meat and vegetable pieces.

espetar [iʃpɛ'ta(x)] *vt* to pierce. ⊔ **espetar-se** *vp* to prick o.s.

espeto [iʃ'pɛtu] *m (de ferro)* spit; *(de pau)* stake.

espevitado, -da [iʃpevi'tadu, -da] *adj* lively.

espezinhar [iʃpezi'ɲa(x)] *vt* to trample on; *(sujar)* to dirty.

espia [iʃ'pia] *f (cabo)* cable, → espião.

espião, -pia [iʃ'pjãw, -'pia] *(mpl* -**ões**

[-õiʃ], *fpl* -**s** [-ʃ]) *m, f* spy.

espiar [iʃ'pja(x)] *vt* to spy on.

espiga [iʃ'piga] *f* ear.

espinafre [iʃpi'nafri] *m* spinach.

espingarda [iʃpĩŋ'garda] *f* shotgun.

espinha [iʃ'piɲa] *f (de peixe)* bone; *(em pele)* spot; ~ **(dorsal)** backbone, spine.

espinho [iʃ'piɲu] *m (de rosa, silva)* thorn; *(de porco-espinho)* quill.

espiões → espião.

espiral [iʃpi'raw] *(pl* -**ais** [-ajʃ]) *f* spiral; **em ~** spiral.

espírito [iʃ'piritu] *m* spirit.

espiritual [iʃpiri'twaw] *(pl* -**ais** [-ajʃ]) *adj* spiritual.

espirrar [iʃpi'xa(x)] *vi (dar espirros)* to sneeze; *(esguichar)* to spit.

esplanada [iʃpla'nada] *f* esplanade.

esplêndido, -da [iʃ'plẽdidu, -da] *adj* splendid.

esplendor [iʃplẽ'do(x)] *m (luxo)* splendour; *(brilho)* brilliance.

espoleta [iʃpo'leta] *f* fuse.

esponja [iʃ'põʒa] *f* sponge; **passar uma ~ sobre o assunto** *(fig: esquecer)* to wipe the slate clean.

espontaneidade [iʃpõtanei'dadʒi] *f* spontaneity.

espontâneo, -nea [iʃpõ'tanju, -nja] *adj* spontaneous.

espora [iʃ'pɔra] *f* spur.

esporádico, -ca [iʃpo'radʒiku, -ka] *adj* sporadic.

esporte [iʃ'pɔxtʃi] *m (Br)* sport.

esportista [iʃpɔx'tʃiʃta] *mf (Br)* sportsman *(f* sportswoman).

esportivo, -va [iʃpɔx'tʃivu, -va] *adj (Br)* sports *(antes de s)*.

esposo, -sa [iʃ'pozu, -za] *m, f* husband *(f* wife).

espreguiçar-se [iʃpregi'saxsi] *vp* to stretch.

espreita [iʃ'prejta] : **à espreita** *adv* on the lookout.

espreitar [iʃprej'ta(x)] *vt* to peep at.

espremedor [iʃpreme'do(x)] *(pl* -**res** [-riʃ]) *m (juice)* squeezer.

espremer [iʃpre'me(x)] *vt* to squeeze.

espuma [iʃ'puma] *f (de mar)* surf; *(de sabão)* lather; *(de banho)* foam.

espumante [iʃpu'mãtʃi] *adj* sparkling ◆ *m* sparkling wine.

espumoso, -osa [iʃpu'mozu, -ɔza]

adj & m = **espumante.**

Esq. *(abrev de esquerdo)* L.

esquadra [iʃˈkwadra] *f* fleet; *(Port: delegacia)* police station.

esquadro [iʃˈkwadru] *m* set square.

esquecer [iʃkeˈse(x)] *vt* to forget.

❑ **esquecer-se** *vp* to forget; **~-se de algo/de fazer algo** to forget sthg/to do sthg.

esquecido, -da [iʃkeˈsidu, -da] *adj* absent-minded, forgetful ♦ *m, f* absent-minded person.

esquecimento [iʃkesiˈmẽntu] *m* forgetfulness.

esqueleto [iʃkeˈletu] *m* skeleton.

esquema [iʃˈkema] *m (diagrama)* diagram; *(sistema)* scheme.

esquentador [iʃkẽntaˈdo(x)] *(pl* -res [-riʃ]) *m (de água)* immersion heater; *(aquecedor)* heater.

esquentar [iʃkẽnˈta(x)] *vt* to heat up.

esquerda [iʃˈkexda] *f*: **a ~** *(mão)* one's left hand; *(lado)* the left-hand side; *(em política)* the Left; **dirija pela ~** drive on the left; **mantenha ~** keep left; **à ~ (de)** on the left (of); **virar à ~** to turn left; **ser de ~** *(POL)* to be left-wing.

esquerdo, -da [iʃˈkexdu, -da] *adj (mão, perna, lado)* left; *(canhoto)* left-handed.

esqui [iʃˈki] *m (utensílio)* ski; *(esporte)* skiing; **~ aquático** water-skiing.

esquiar [iʃˈkja(x)] *vi* to ski.

esquilo [iʃˈkilu] *m* squirrel.

esquina [iʃˈkina] *f* corner.

esquisito, -ta [iʃkiˈzitu, -ta] *adj (estranho)* strange, weird; *(picuinhas)* fussy.

esquivar-se [iʃkiˈvaxsi] *vp* to escape; **~ a fazer algo** to get out of doing sthg.

esquivo, -va [iʃˈkivu, -va] *adj (arisco)* shy.

esse, essa [ˈesi, ˈɛsa] *adj* that, those *(pl)* ♦ *pron* that (one), those (ones) *(pl)*; **essa é boa!** you must be joking!; **só faltava mais essa!** that's the final straw!

essência [eˈsẽsja] *f* essence.

essencial [eseˈsjaw] *(pl* -ais [-ajʃ]) *adj* essential ♦ *m*: **o ~** *(o indispensável)* the bare essentials *(pl)*; *(o importante)* the important thing.

esta → este².

está [iʃˈta] → **estar.**

estabelecer [iʃtableˈse(x)] *vt* to establish.

❑ **estabelecer-se** *vp* to establish o.s.

estabelecimento [iʃtabelesiˈmẽntu] *m (casa comercial)* business; *(instituição)* establishment; **~ de ensino** school.

estabilidade [iʃtabliˈdadʒi] *f* stability.

estabilizador [iʃtabilizaˈdo(x)] *(pl* -res [-riʃ]) *m*: **~ (de corrente)** stabilizer.

estábulo [iʃˈtabulu] *m* stable.

estaca [iʃˈtaka] *f* stake.

estação [iʃtaˈsãw] *(pl* -ões [-õjʃ]) *f (de trem, ônibus)* station; *(do ano, turismo, vendas)* season; **~ de águas** *(Br)* spa; **~ de rádio** radio station.

estacionamento [iʃtasjonaˈmẽntu] *m (acto)* parking; *(lugar)* parking space; **"~ privativo"** "private parking"; **"~ proibido"** "no parking".

estacionar [iʃtasjoˈna(x)] *vt & vi* to park.

estações → estação.

estada [iʃˈtada] *f* stay.

estadia [iʃtaˈdʒia] *f* = **estada.**

estádio [iʃˈtadʒju] *m (de futebol, atletismo)* stadium; *(fase)* phase.

estadista [iʃtaˈdʒiʃta] *mf* statesman (f stateswoman).

estado [iʃˈtadu] *m* state; **em bom/mau ~** *(objeto)* in good/bad condition; **~ civil** marital status; **~ físico** level of fitness.

❑ **Estado** *m*: **o Estado** the State; **os Estados Unidos** the United States.

estalagem [iʃtaˈlaʒẽ] *(pl* -ns [-ʃ]) *f* inn.

estalar [iʃtaˈla(x)] *vi (porcelana, vidro, osso)* to crack; *(lenha)* to crackle ♦ *vt*: **~ a língua** to click one's tongue; **~ os dedos** to snap one's fingers.

estalido [iʃtaˈlidu] *m (estalo)* crack; *(crepitação)* crackle.

estalo [iʃˈtalu] *m (ruído)* crack; **me deu um ~** *(fig)* the penny dropped.

estampado, -da [iʃtãmˈpadu, -da] *adj* printed.

estancar [iʃtãˈka(x)] *vt (líquido)* to stop; *(sangue)* to staunch ♦ *vi (sangue)* to stop.

estância [iʃˈtãsja] *f (Br: quinta)* ranch; **~ balneária** bathing resort; **~ de férias** holiday resort; **~ hidromineral** *(Br)* spa; **~ termal** spa.

estanho [iʃˈtaɲu] *m* tin.

estante [iʃˈtãntʃi] *f* bookcase.

estão [iʃˈtãw] → **estar.**

estapafúrdio, -dia [iʃtapaˈfurdʒiu, -dʒia] *adj (excêntrico)* outrageous; *(esquisito)* peculiar.

estar [iʃˈta(x)] *vi* **1.** *(com lugar)* to be; *(em casa)* to be at home, to be in; **ela estará lá à hora certa** she'll be there on time; **estarei no emprego às dez** I'll be at work at ten; **está? está lá?** *(Port: ao telefone)* hello? hello? **2.** *(exprime estado)* to be; **está quebrado** it's out of order; **~ bem/mal de saúde** to be well/unwell; **está muito calor/frio** it's very hot/cold. **3.** *(manter-se)* to be; **estive em casa toda a tarde** I was at home all afternoon; **estive esperando uma hora** I waited for an hour; **estive fora três anos** I lived abroad for three years. **4.** *(em locuções):* **está bem** OU **certo!** OK!, all right!

❏ **estar a** *v + prep (relativo a preço)* to cost, to be; *(Port: seguido de infinitivo):* **ele está a estudar** he's studying; **o camarão está a 25 reais o quilo** prawns costs OU are 25 reals a kilo.

❏ **estar de** *v + prep:* **~ de baixa/férias** to be on sick leave/holiday; **~ de saia** to be wearing a skirt; **~ de vigia** to keep watch.

❏ **estar para** *v + prep:* **~ para fazer algo** to be about to do sthg; **estou para sair** I'm about to go out, I'm just going out; **ele está para chegar** he'll be here any minute now; **não estou para brincadeiras** I'm not in the mood for silly games.

❏ **estar perante** *v + prep (frente a)* to be facing; **você está perante um gênio** you're in the presence of a genius.

❏ **estar por** *v + prep (apoiar)* to support; *(por realizar):* **a cama está por fazer** the bed hasn't been made yet; **a limpeza está por fazer** the cleaning hasn't been done yet.

❏ **estar sem** *v + prep:* **estou sem tempo** I haven't got the time; **estou sem dinheiro** I haven't got any cash; **ele está sem comer há dois dias** he hasn't eaten for two days.

estardalhaço [iʃtaxdaˈʎasu] *m* racket.

estarrecer [iʃtaxeˈse(x)] *vt* to terrify.

estatal [iʃtaˈtaw] *(pl* **-ais** [-ajʃ]) *adj* state *(antes de s).*

estático, -ca [iʃˈtatʃiku, -ka] *adj* static.

estátua [iʃˈtatwa] *f* statue.

estatura [iʃtaˈtura] *f* stature.

estatuto [iʃtaˈtutu] *m (regulamento)* statute; *(de pessoa)* status.

este¹ [ˈɛʃtʃi] *m* east; **a** OU **no ~** in the east; **a ~ de** east of.

este², esta [ˈɛʃtʃi, ˈɛʃta] *adj* this, these *(pl)* ♦ *pron* this (one), these (ones) *(pl)*; **~ mês (que vem) vou de férias** I'm going on holiday next month; **não o vi esta semana** I haven't seen him this week.

esteira [iʃˈtejra] *f (de chão)* mat; *(de praia)* beach mat.

estendal [eʃtènˈdal] *(pl* **-ais** [-ajʃ]) *m (Port)* washing line.

estender [iʃtènˈde(x)] *vt (braços, pernas)* to stretch (out); *(jornal)* to spread out; *(roupa no varal)* to hang out; *(prazo, estadia)* to extend.

❏ **estender-se** *vp (no espaço)* to stretch out; *(no tempo)* to go on.

estenografia [iʃtenograˈfia] *f* shorthand.

estepe [iʃˈtɛpi] *f* steppes *(pl).*

estéreis → estéril.

estereofónico, -ca [eʃterjoˈfoniku, -ka] *adj (Port)* = **estereofônico.**

estereofônico, -ca [iʃterjoˈfoniku, -ka] *adj (Br)* stereo(phonic).

estéril [iʃˈtɛriw] *(pl* **-reis** [-rejʃ]) *adj* infertile.

esterilizar [iʃteriliˈza(x)] *vt* to sterilize.

estética [iʃˈtɛtika] *f* aesthetics *(sg).*

estetoscópio [iʃtetoʃˈkɔpju] *m* stethoscope.

esteve [iʃˈtevi] → **estar.**

estiar [iʃtʃiˈja(x)] *vi* to stop raining.

estibordo [iʃtʃiˈbɔxdu] *m* starboard.

esticar [iʃtʃiˈka(x)] *vt* to stretch.

❏ **esticar-se** *vp* to stretch out.

estigma [iʃˈtʃigma] *m* stigma.

estilhaçar [iʃtʃiʎaˈsa(x)] *vt* to shatter.

❏ **estilhaçar-se** *vp* to shatter.

estilhaço [iʃtʃiˈʎasu] *m* splinter.

estilo [iʃˈtʃilu] *m* style.

estima [iʃˈtʃima] *f* esteem.

estimar [iʃtʃiˈma(x)] *vt* to cherish.

estimativa [iʃʃtʃimaˈtʃiva] *f* estimate.

estimulante [iʃtʃimuˈlàntʃi] *adj* stimulating ♦ *m* stimulant.

estimular [iʃtʃimuˈla(x)] *vt* to stimulate.

estipular [eʃtʃipuˈla(x)] *vt* to stipulate.

estivador, -ra [iʃtʃiva'do(x), -ra] (mpl -res [-riʃ], fpl -s [-ʃ]) m, f docker (Brit), stevedore (Am).

estive [iʃ'tivi] → estar.

estofo [iʃ'tofu] m stuffing.

estojo [iʃ'toʒu] m set; ~ **(de lápis)** pencil case; ~ **de primeiros-socorros** first-aid kit.

estômago [iʃ'tomagu] m stomach.

estontear [iʃtõn'tʃja(x)] vt to bewilder.

estore [iʃ'tɔri] m blind.

estorninho [iʃtox'niɲu] m starling.

estou [iʃ'to] → estar.

estourado, -da [iʃto'radu, -da] adj (fam: cansado) knackered.

estourar [iʃto'ra(x)] vt (balão, bola) to burst; (fam: dinheiro) to blow ◆ vi (balão, bola) to burst; (pneu) to blow out; (bomba, explosivo) to explode.

estouro [iʃ'toru] m (de balão, bola, pneu) bursting; (ruído) bang; **dar o ~** (fam: zangar-se) to blow a fuse.

estrábico, -ca [iʃ'trabiku, -ka] adj cross-eyed ◆ m, f cross-eyed person.

estrabismo [iʃtra'biʒmu] m squint.

estrada [iʃ'trada] f road; ~ **de via dupla** dual carriageway; ~ **de ferro** (Br) railway (Brit), railroad (Am); ~ **secundária** minor road.

estrado [iʃ'tradu] m platform.

estragado, -da [iʃtra'gadu, -da] adj (leite, comida) off; (pão) stale; (aparelho, máquina) out of order.

estragão [iʃtra'gãw] m tarragon.

estragar [iʃtra'ga(x)] vt (aparelho, máquina) to break; (desperdiçar) to waste.

⊃ **estragar-se** vp (comida, leite) to go off.

estrangeiro, -ra [iʃtrã'ʒejru, -ra] adj (cidade, país, língua) foreign ◆ m, f (pessoa) foreigner ◆ m: **o ~** foreign countries (pl); **ir para o ~** to go abroad; **viver no ~** to live abroad.

estrangular [iʃtrãŋgu'la(x)] vt to strangle.

estranhar [iʃtra'ɲa(x)] vt to find odd.

estranho, -nha [iʃ'traɲu, -ɲa] adj odd ◆ m, f stranger.

estratégia [iʃtra'tɛʒja] f strategy.

estrear [iʃtri'a(x)] vt (roupa, sapatos) to wear for the first time ◆ vi (peça teatral) to open; (filme) to premiere.

estreia [eʃ'traja] f (Port) = estréia.

estréia [iʃ'treja] f (Br) (de ator) debut;

(de peça teatral) opening night; (de filme) premiere.

estreitar [iʃtrej'ta(x)] vt (roupa) to take in ◆ vi (estrada, caminho) to narrow.

estreito, -ta [iʃ'trejtu, -ta] adj narrow; (roupa) tight ◆ m (canal) strait.

estrela [iʃ'trela] f star; ~ **cadente** shooting star; **ver ~s** (fig: ter dor violenta) to see stars.

estremecer [iʃtreme'se(x)] vt to shake ◆ vi (tremer) to shake; (assustar-se) to be shaken.

estria [iʃ'tria] f (em coxas, quadris, seios) stretchmark; (em superfície) groove.

estribo [iʃ'tribu] m stirrup.

estridente [iʃtri'dẽntʃi] adj strident.

estrofe [iʃ'trɔfi] f stanza.

estrondo [iʃ'trõndu] m (som) bang; (fig: pompa) ostentation.

estropiar [iʃtro'pja(x)] vt to maim.

estrume [iʃ'trumi] m manure.

estrutura [iʃtru'tura] f structure.

estuário [iʃ'twarju] m estuary.

estudante [iʃtu'dãntʃi] mf student.

estudar [iʃtu'da(x)] vt & vi to study.

estúdio [iʃ'tudʒju] m studio; (apartamento) studio flat.

estudioso, -osa [iʃtu'dʒjozu, -ɔza] adj studious.

estudo [iʃ'tudu] m study; **em ~** under consideration.

estufa [iʃ'tufa] f (de jardim) greenhouse; (de fogão) plate warmer; (tipo de fogão) heater.

estupefação [eʃtupefa'sãw] f (Br) astonishment.

estupefacção [iʃtupefa'sãw] f (Port) = estupefação.

estupefaciente [iʃtupefa'sjẽntʃi] m drug.

estupefacto, -ta [eʃtupe'fa(k)tu, -ta] adj (Port) = estupefato.

estupefato, -ta [iʃtupe'fatu, -ta] adj (Br) astounded.

estupendo, -da [iʃtu'pẽndu, -da] adj (extraordinário) remarkable; (ótimo) great.

estupidez [iʃtupi'deʃ] f stupidity.

estúpido, -da [iʃ'tupidu, -da] m, f idiot.

estupro [iʃ'tupru] m rape.

estuque [iʃ'tuki] m plaster.

esvaziar [iʒva'zja(x)] vt to empty.

esvoaçar [iʒvwa'sa(x)] *vi (ave)* to flutter.

etapa [i'tapa] *f* stage; **fazer algo por ~s** to do sthg by ou in stages.

éter ['ɛtɛ(x)] *m* ether.

eternidade [etɛxni'dadʒi] *f* eternity; **demorar/esperar uma ~** to take/wait ages.

eterno, -na [e'tɛxnu, -na] *adj* eternal.

ética ['ɛtʃika] *f* ethics *(pl)*.

ético, -ca ['ɛtʃiku, -ka] *adj* ethical.

etílico [e'tʃiliku] *adj* **m → álcool**.

etiqueta [etʃi'keta] *f (rótulo)* label, tag; *(social)* etiquette.

étnico, -ca ['ɛtniku, -ka] *adj* ethnic.

eu ['ew] *pron (sujeito)* I; **e ~?** what about me?; **sou ~** it's me; **~ mesmo** ou **próprio** (I) myself.

E.U.A. *mpl (abrev de Estados Unidos da América)* USA.

eucalipto [ewka'liptu] *m* eucalyptus.

eufemismo [ewfe'miʒmu] *m* euphemism.

euforia [ewfɔ'ria] *f* euphoria.

Eurocheque® [ewro'ʃɛki] *m* Eurocheque®.

Europa [ew'rɔpa] *f:* **a ~** Europe.

europeu, -péia [ewru'pew, -pɛja] *adj & m, f* European.

evacuação [evakwa'sãw] *(pl -ões [-õjʃ]) f* evacuation.

evacuar [eva'kwa(x)] *vt* to evacuate.

evadir-se [eva'dixsi] *vp* to escape.

Evangelho [evã'ʒɛʎu] *m*: **o ~** the Gospel.

evaporar [evapo'ra(x)] *vt* to evaporate.

❏ **evaporar-se** *vp (líquido)* to evaporate; *(fig: desaparecer)* to vanish.

evasão [eva'zãw] *(pl -ões [-õjʃ]) f (de prisão, rotina)* escape; *(evasiva)* evasion.

evasiva [eva'ziva] *f* evasion.

evasivo, -va [eva'zivu, -va] *adj* evasive.

evasões → evasão.

evento [e'vẽtu] *m* event.

eventual [evẽ'twaw] *(pl -ais [-ajʃ]) adj (possível)* possible.

evidência [evi'dẽsja] *f* evidence.

evidenciar [evidẽ'sja(x)] *vt* to show.

❏ **evidenciar-se** *vp* to draw attention to o.s.

evidente [evi'dẽtʃi] *adj* evident, obvious; **como é ~** obviously.

evitar [evi'ta(x)] *vt* to avoid; **~ que algo aconteça** to avoid sthg happening.

evocar [evo'ka(x)] *vt* to evoke.

evolução [evolu'sãw] *f* evolution.

evoluir [evo'lwi(x)] *vi* to evolve.

exacto, -ta [e'zatu, -ta] *adj (Port)* = **exato**.

exagerar [ezaʒe'ra(x)] *vt* to exaggerate.

exagero [eza'ʒeru] *m* exaggeration, overstatement; **é um ~!** it's too much!; **sem ~** seriously.

exalar [eza'la(x)] *vt* to give off.

exaltado, -da [ezaw'tadu, -da] *adj* exasperated.

exaltar [ezaw'ta(x)] *vt (elogiar)* to exalt; *(irritar)* to exasperate.

❏ **exaltar-se** *vp (irritar-se)* to lose one's temper.

exame [e'zami] *m (escolar, universitário)* exam; *(médico)* examination; **~ de aptidão física** medical.

examinar [ezami'na(x)] *vt* to examine.

exatamente [e.zata'mẽtʃi] *adv* exactly ♦ *interj* exactly!

exatidão [ezatʃi'dãw] *f (precisão)* precision; *(rigor)* accuracy; **com ~** exactly.

exato, -ta [e'zatu, -ta] *adj (Br) (preciso)* precise; *(rigoroso)* accurate; *(correto)* correct.

exaustão [ezawʃ'tãw] *f* exhaustion.

exausto, -ta [e'zawʃtu, -ta] *adj* exhausted.

exaustor [ezawʃ'to(x)] *(pl -res [-riʃ]) m* extractor fan.

exceção [e(ʃ)se'sãw] *(pl -ões [-õjʃ]) f (Br)* exception; **à** ou **com a ~ de** except for; **fora de ~** out of the ordinary; **sem ~** without exception.

excedente [ese'dẽtʃi] *m* surplus; **~s de leite/manteiga** milk/butter mountain *(sg)*.

exceder [ese'de(x)] *vt* to exceed.

❏ **exceder-se** *vp (exagerar)* to go too far; *(enfurecer-se)* to lose one's temper; **~-se em** to overdo.

excelente [ese'lẽtʃi] *adj* excellent.

excelentíssimo, -ma [eselẽ't'fisimu, -ma] *superl formal term of address used in correspondence*.

excêntrico, -ca [e'sẽtriku, -ka] *adj* eccentric.

excepção [eʃsɛ'sãw] *(pl -ões [-õjʃ]) f (Port)* = **exceção**.

excepcional [esɛsjuˈnaw] (*pl* **-ais** [-ajʃ]) *adj* exceptional.

excepções → excepção.

excepto [eˈsɛtu] *prep* (*Port*) = exceto.

excerto [eˈsɛxtu] *m* excerpt.

excessivo, -va [eseˈsivu, -va] *adj* excessive.

excesso [eˈsɛsu] *m* excess; **em ~** too much; **~ de peso** (*relativo a bagagem*) excess baggage; (*relativo a pessoa*) excess weight; **~ de velocidade** speeding.

exceto [eˈsɛtu] *prep* (*Br*) except, apart from.

excitação [esitaˈsaw] *f* (*entusiasmo*) excitement; (*irritação*) agitation.

excitado, -da [esiˈtadu, -da] *adj* (*entusiasmado*) excited; (*irritado*) agitated.

excitante [esiˈtãntʃi] *adj* exciting.

exclamação [iʃklamaˈsaw] (*pl* **-ões** [-õjʃ]) *f* exclamation.

exclamar [iʃklaˈma(x)] *vi* to exclaim.

excluir [iʃkluˈi(x)] *vt* to exclude.

exclusivo, -va [iʃkluˈzivu, -va] *adj & m* exclusive; **ter o ~ de** to corner the market in.

excursão [iʃkuxˈsaw] (*pl* **-ões** [-õjʃ]) *f* (*de ônibus*) (coach) trip.

execução [ezekuˈsaw] *f* (*de objeto*) production; (*de trabalho, plano, projeto*) execution; (*de prato culinário*) preparation; **pôr algo em ~** to put sthg into practice.

executar [ezekuˈta(x)] *vt* (*música, cena teatral*) to perform; (*desenho, pintura*) to produce; (*ordem, plano, trabalho*) to carry out; (*matar*) to execute.

executivo, -va [ezekuˈtivu, -va] *m, f* executive.

exemplar [ezẽmˈpla(x)] (*pl* **-es** [-iʃ]) *adj* exemplary ♦ *m* (*de espécie, raça*) specimen; (*de livro, revista*) copy.

exemplo [eˈzẽmplu] *m* example; **por ~** for example; **a título de ~** as an example.

exercer [ezexˈse(x)] *vt* (*profissão*) to practise; (*função*) to fulfil; (*influência*) to exercise ♦ *vi* to practise; **ela exerceu o cargo de presidente vários anos** she was the president for several years.

exercício [ezexˈsisju] *m* exercise; (*de profissão, atividade*) practice.

exercitar [ezexsiˈta(x)] *vt* to exercise.

❏ **exercitar-se** *vp* to take exercise.

exército [eˈzɛxsitu] *m* army.

exibição [ezebiˈsaw] (*pl* **-ões** [-õjʃ]) *f* show; (*de peça teatral, filme*) showing; (*Port: de quadros, esculturas*) exhibition; **em ~** (*peça teatral, filme*) showing.

exibir [eziˈbi(x)] *vt* to show; (*quadro, escultura*) to exhibit.

❏ **exibir-se** *vp* to show off.

exigência [eziˈʒẽsja] *f* demand.

exigir [eziˈʒi(x)] *vt* to demand.

existência [eziʃˈtẽsja] *f* existence.

existir [eziʃˈti(x)] *vi* to exist.

êxito [ˈezitu] *m* success; **ter ~** to be successful.

Exma. *abrev* = excelentíssima.

Exmo. *abrev* = excelentíssimo.

exorcismo [ezoxˈsiʒmu] *m* exorcism.

exorcista [ezoxˈsiʃta] *mf* exorcist.

exortação [ezoxtaˈsaw] (*pl* **-ões** [-õjʃ]) *f* exhortation.

exótico, -ca [eˈzɔtʃiku, -ka] *adj* exotic.

expansão [iʃpaˈsaw] (*pl* **-ões** [-õjʃ]) *f* (*progresso*) expansion; (*alegria*) expansiveness.

expansivo, -va [iʃpãˈsivu, -va] *adj* expansive.

expansões → expansão.

expectativa [iʃpektaˈtʃiva] *f* expectation; **ficar na ~ de** to expect.

expediente [iʃpeˈdʒjẽntʃi] *m* (*de repartição, estabelecimento comercial*) business hours (*pl*).

expedir [iʃpeˈdʒi(x)] *vt* to dispatch.

experiência [iʃpeˈrjẽsja] *f* (*ensaio*) experiment; (*conhecimento*) experience; **com ~** experienced.

experiente [iʃpeˈrjẽntʃi] *adj* experienced.

experimentar [iʃperimẽˈta(x)] *vt* (*máquina*) to test; (*carro*) to test-drive; (*peça de roupa, calçado*) to try on; (*comida, bebida*) to try; (*sensação, emoção*) to experience.

expirar [iʃpiˈra(x)] *vt* to exhale ♦ *vi* (*prazo*) to expire.

explicação [iʃplikaˈsaw] (*pl* **-ões** [-õjʃ]) *f* explanation; (*aula particular*) private lesson.

explicar [iʃpliˈka(x)] *vt* to explain.

❏ **explicar-se** *vp* to explain o.s.

explícito, -ta [iʃˈplisitu, -ta] *adj* explicit.

explodir [iʃploˈdi(x)] *vi* to explode.

exploração [iʃploraˈsaw] *f* (*investigação*) exploration; (*abuso*) exploitation.

explorar [iʃploˈra(x)] vt (investigar) to explore; (abusar de) to exploit.
explosão [iʃploˈzãw] (pl -ões [-õjʃ]) f explosion.
expor [iʃpo(x)] vt (ideia) to put forward; (situação) to explain; (exibir) to exhibit; (produtos) to display.
❑ **expor-se a** vp + prep to expose o.s. to.
exportação [iʃpoxtaˈsãw] (pl -ões [-õjʃ]) f export.
exportar [iʃpoxˈta(x)] vt to export.
exposição [iʃpoziˈsãw] (pl -ões [-õjʃ]) f (de pintura, fotografia) exhibition; (em fotografia) exposure; (de produtos) display; (narração) account; **em ~** on show.
exposto, -osta [iʃpoʃtu, -ɔʃta] adj (em exposição) on show; (produtos) on display.
expressão [iʃpreˈsãw] (pl -ões [-õjʃ]) f expression; **~ escrita** literacy; **~ oral** oral expression.
expressar [iʃpreˈsa(x)] vt to express.
❑ **expressar-se** vp to express o.s.
expressivo, -va [iʃpreˈsivu, -va] adj expressive.
expresso, -a [iʃpresu, -a] adj & m express.
expressões → expressão.
exprimir [iʃpriˈmi(x)] vt to express.
❑ **exprimir-se** vp to express o.s.
expropriar [iʃpropriˈa(x)] vt to expropriate.
expulsar [iʃpuwˈsa(x)] vt to expel.
expulso, -sa [iʃpuwsu, -sa] pp → expulsar ◆ adj expelled.
extensão [iʃtẽˈsãw] (pl -ões [-õjʃ]) f extension; (dimensão espacial) extent; (dimensão temporal) duration.
extenso, -sa [iʃtẽsu, -sa] adj long; (vasto) extensive; **escrever algo por ~** to write sthg out in full.
extensões → extensão.
extenuado, -da [iʃteˈnwadu, -da] adj worn-out.
extenuante [iʃteˈnwãntʃi] adj tiring.
exterior [iʃteˈrjo(x)] (pl -es [-iʃ]) adj outside; (calma, aparência) outward; (Br: política, comércio) foreign ◆ m (parte exterior) exterior; (aparência) outside; **o ~** (Br: o estrangeiro) foreign countries (pl); **para o/no ~** (Br) abroad.
externo, -na [iʃtɛxnu, -na] adj external; (Port: política, comércio) foreign.
extinção [iʃtĩˈsãw] f extinction.

extinguir [iʃtĩŋˈgi(x)] vt (fogo) to extinguish, to put out; (lei, norma) to abolish.
❑ **extinguir-se** vp (apagar-se) to go out; (desaparecer) to become extinct, to die out.
extinto, -ta [iʃtʃĩntu, -ta] pp → extinguir ◆ adj (espécie animal, vegetal) extinct; (fogo) extinguished; (lei, norma) defunct.
extintor [iʃtʃĩnˈto(x)] (pl -es [-iʃ]) m fire extinguisher.
extra [ˈejʃtra] adj extra ◆ m (de automóvel) spare part; (em despesa) extras (pl); (em emprego) perk.
extração [iʃtraˈsãw] (pl -ões [-õjʃ]) f (Br) extraction; (de órgão) removal; (de loteria) draw.
extracção [eʃtraˈsãw] (pl -ões [-õjʃ]) f (Port) = extração.
extrações → extração.
extracto [eʃˈtratu] m (Port) = extrato.
extraditar [iʃtradʒiˈta(x)] vt to extradite.
extrair [iʃtraˈi(x)] vt to extract; (número de loteria) to draw; **~ algo de algo** to extract sthg from sthg.
extraordinário, -ria [iʃtraordʒiˈnarju, -rja] adj extraordinary.
extrato [iʃˈtratu] m (Br) extract; (de conta bancária) statement.
extravagância [iʃtravaˈgãsja] f extravagance.
extraviado, -da [iʃtraˈvjadu, -da] adj lost.
extraviar [iʃtraˈvja(x)] vt to lose.
❑ **extraviar-se** vp to get lost.
extremidade [iʃtremiˈdadʒi] f extremity.
extremo, -ma [iʃtremu, -ma] adj (decisão, medida) drastic; (temperatura, condição) extreme ◆ m extreme; **em caso ~** if the worst comes to the worst; **ir de um ~ ao outro** (fig) to go from one extreme to the other; **chegar ao ~** to go to extremes.
extrovertido, -da [iʃtrɔvexˈtʃidu, -da] adj outgoing.
exuberante [ezubeˈrãntʃi] adj (pessoa) exuberant; (roupa) garish; (vegetação) lush.
exumar [ezuˈma(x)] vt to exhume.
ex-voto [ɛksˈvɔtu] m ex-voto.

F

fábrica ['fabrika] *f* factory.
fabricante [fabri'kãntʃi] *m* manufacturer.
fabricar [fabri'ka(x)] *vt* to make, to manufacture.
fabrico [fa'briku] *m* manufacture.
fabuloso, -osa [fabu'lozu, -ɔza] *adj* fabulous.
faca ['faka] *f* knife.
face ['fasi] *f* face; **fazer ~ a** to face up to; **em ~** opposite; **em ~ de** in view of; **~ a ~** face to face.
fáceis → **fácil**.
fachada [fa'ʃada] *f* facade.
fácil ['fasiw] (*pl* **-ceis** [-sejʃ]) *adj* easy.
facilidade [fasili'dadʒi] *f* (*destreza*) ease; (*aptidão*) aptitude; **com ~** with ease.
facilitar [fasili'ta(x)] *vt* to facilitate; **ele facilitou-nos o uso do seu equipamento** he let us use his equipment.
faço ['fasu] → **fazer**.
facto ['fa(k)tu] *m* (*Port*) = **fato**.
factor [fa(k)'tor] (*mpl* **-res** [-reʃ]) *m* (*Port*) = **fator**.
factual [fa'twal] (*pl* **-ais** [-ajʃ]) *adj* (*Port*) = **fatual**.
factura [fa'tura] *f* (*Port*) = **fatura**.
faculdade [fakuw'dadʒi] *f* faculty.
facultativo, -va [fakuwta'tʃivu, -va] *adj* optional.
fada ['fada] *f* fairy.
fadiga [fa'dʒiga] *f* fatigue.
fadista [fa'dʒiʃta] *mf* "fado" singer.
fado ['fadu] *m* (*destino*) destiny, fate; (*música*) a type of melancholy Portuguese folk song set to music.
fagulha [fa'guʎa] *f* spark.
faia ['faja] *f* beech.
faiança [fa'jãsa] *f* glazed ceramics (*pl*).
faisão [faj'zãw] (*pl* **-ões** [-õjʃ]) *m* pheasant.

faísca [fa'iʃka] *f* spark.
faisões → **faisão**.
faixa ['fajʃa] *f* (*em estrada*) lane; (*para cintura*) cummerbund; (*ligadura*) bandage; **~ (de pedestres)** (*Br*) pedestrian crossing; **~ de rodagem** lane.
fala ['fala] *f* (*dom de falar*) speech; **ser de poucas ~s** to be the silent type.
falador, -deira [fala'do(x), -dejra] (*mpl* **-res** [-riʃ], *fpl* **-s** [-ʃ]) *adj* talkative ♦ *m, f* chatterbox.
falar [fa'la(x)] *vi* to talk, to speak ♦ *vt* (*idioma*) to speak; **~ com alguém** to speak to sb; **~ de** to talk about; **para ~ a verdade** to tell the truth; **sem ~ em** not to mention; **~ claro** to speak clearly; **~ pelos cotovelos** to talk the hind legs off a donkey; **~ a sério** to be serious.
falcão [faw'kãw] (*pl* **-ões** [-õjʃ]) *m* falcon.
falecer [fale'se(x)] *vi* to pass away.
falecido, -da [fale'sidu, -da] *m, f* deceased.
falecimento [falesi'mẽntu] *m* death.
falência [fa'lẽsja] *f* bankruptcy; **ir à ~** to go bankrupt.
falha ['faʎa] *f* (*lacuna*) omission; (*em terreno, sistema*) fault.
falhar [fa'ʎa(x)] *vt* to miss ♦ *vi* (*não acertar*) to miss; (*não funcionar*) to fail; **ela falhou na primeira (tentativa)** she failed at her first attempt.
falido, -da [fa'lidu, -da] *adj* bankrupt.
falir [fa'li(x)] *vi* to go bankrupt.
falsário, -ria [faw'sarju, -rja] *m, f* forger.
falsidade [fawsi'dadʒi] *f* falseness.
falsificar [fawsifi'ka(x)] *vt* to forge.
falso, -sa [fawsu, -sa] *adj* false; (*documento, passaporte*) forged; (*dinheiro*) counterfeit; (*jóia, pele*) fake ♦ *adv:* **jurar ~** to commit perjury.

falta ['fawta] f fault; *(carência)* lack; *(em futebol)* foul; *(infração)* offence; **este aluno tem muitas ~s** this pupil has a very poor attendance record; **sinto muita ~ de um relógio** I really need a watch; **sentir ~ de** to miss; **ter ~ de algo** to be short of sthg; **à ~ de melhor** for want of anything better; **fazer algo sem ~** to do sthg without fail; **por ~ de** for lack of.

faltar [faw'ta(x)] vi *(não haver)* to be missing; *(estar ausente)* to be absent; **falta muito para as férias** the holidays are a long way off; **falta pouco para o trem chegar** the train will arrive soon; **falta sal na comida** the food needs salt; **faltam 5 km para chegarmos lá** we've got 5 km to go before we get there; **era só o que faltava!** that's all we needed!; **~ às aulas** to play truant; **~ ao trabalho** not to turn up to work.

fama ['fama] f *(reputação)* reputation; *(notoriedade)* fame; **ter ~ de ser bom/mau** *(lugar)* to have a good/bad reputation.

família [fa'milja] f family; **em ~** among friends.

familiar [fami'lja(x)] (pl **-es** [-iʃ]) adj *(ambiente, atmosfera)* informal; *(da família)* family *(antes de s)* ◆ m relative.

faminto, -ta [fa'mĩntu, -ta] adj starving.

famoso, -osa [fa'mozu, -ɔza] adj famous.

fanático, -ca [fa'natʃiku, -ka] adj fanatical ◆ m, f fanatic.

fantasia [fãnta'zia] f *(capricho)* fantasy; *(imaginação)* imagination; *(disfarce)* fancy dress.

fantasiar [fãnta'zja(x)] vi to fantasize.

❑ **fantasiar-se** vp to dress up (in fancy dress); **~-se de** to dress up as.

fantasma [fãn'taʒma] m ghost.

fantástico, -ca [fãn'taʃtʃiku, -ka] adj fantastic ◆ interj fantastic!

fantoche [fãn'tɔʃi] m puppet.

farda ['faxda] f uniform.

farei ['fa'rej] → **fazer**.

farelo [fa'rɛlu] m bran.

faringe [fa'rĩʒi] f pharynx.

farinha [fa'riɲa] f flour; **~ de centeio** rye flour; **~ integral** wholemeal flour; **~ de milho** cornflour *(Brit)*, cornstarch *(Am)*; **~ de rosca** *(Br)* breadcrumbs *(pl)*; **~ de trigo** plain flour.

farmacêutico, -ca [farma'sewtiku, -ka] adj pharmaceutical ◆ m, f pharmacist.

farmácia [fax'masja] f *(estabelecimento)* chemist's (shop) *(Brit)*, pharmacy *(Am)*; *(ciência)* pharmacy.

faro ['faru] m sense of smell.

farofa [fa'rɔfa] f cassava flour fried with onion, bacon, eggs or olives, often served with "feijoada" in Brazil.

farol [fa'rɔw] (pl **-óis** [-ɔjʃ]) m *(de veículo)* headlight; *(torre)* lighthouse; **~ alto** *(Br)* full beam *(Brit)*, high beam *(Am)*; **~ baixo** *(Br)* dipped beam *(Brit)*, low beam *(Am)*.

farpa ['faxpa] f *(de agulha)* hook; *(em tourada)* banderilla; *(em pele)* splinter.

farpado [fax'padu] adj m → **arame**.

farra ['faxa] f: **vamos cair na ~!** let's go paint the town red!

farrapo [fa'xapu] m rag.

farsa ['faxsa] f farce.

fartar-se [fax'taxsi] vp *(saciar-se)* to stuff o.s.; *(cansar-se)* to get fed up; **~-se de** *(comida)* to stuff o.s. with; *(trabalho, pessoa)* to get fed up with; **me fartei de tanto rir** I laughed my head off

farto, -ta ['faxtu, -ta] adj *(saciado)* full; **estar ~ (de)** *(cansado de)* to be fed up (with).

fartura [fax'tura] f abundance.

fascinante [fasi'nãntʃi] adj fascinating.

fascinar [fasi'na(x)] vt to fascinate.

fascismo [fa'siʒmu] m fascism.

fascista [fa'siʃta] adj & mf fascist.

fase ['fazi] f phase.

fastidioso, -osa [faʃtʃi'dʒjozu, -ɔza] adj tedious.

fatal [fa'taw] (pl **-ais** [-ajʃ]) adj fatal.

fatalidade [fatali'dadʒi] f misfortune.

fatia [fa'tʃia] f slice.

fatigante [fatʃi'gãntʃi] adj exhausting.

fato ['fatu] m fact; *(Port: terno)* suit; **ser ~ consumado** to be a fait accompli; **de ~** indeed; **pelo ~ de** because, due to the fact that; **~ de banho** *(Port)* swimsuit.

fato-macaco [,fatuma'kaku] (pl **fatos-macacos** [,fatuʒma'kakuʃ]) m *(Port)* boiler suit *(Brit)*, overall *(Am)*.

fator [fa'to(x)] (mpl **-res** [-riʃ]) m *(Br)* factor.

fatual [fa'twaw] (pl **-ais** [-ajʃ]) adj *(Br)* factual.

fatura [fa'tura] *f (Br)* invoice.

fauna ['fawna] *f* fauna.

favas ['favaʃ] *fpl* broad beans; **~ à portuguesa** *rich broad bean stew cooked with bacon, "chouriço", onion, garlic, coriander and bay leaves.*

favela [fa'vɛla] *f (Br)* shantytown, slum.

favor [fa'vo(x)] *(pl* **-res** [-riʃ]*) m* favour; **"é ~ fechar a porta"** "please close the door"; **faça ~ de entrar** do come in; **faz ~** *(para chamar a atenção)* excuse me; **fazer um ~ a alguém** to do sb a favour; **ser a ~ de** to be in favour of; **faz ~** please; **por ~** please.

favorável [favo'ravɛw] *(pl* **-eis** [-ejʃ]*) adj* favourable; **o resultado nos foi ~** the result was in our favour; **ser ~ a algo** to be in favour of sthg.

favores → favor.

favorito, -ta [favo'ritu, -ta] *adj* favourite.

fax ['faksi] *(pl* **-es** [-iʃ]*) m* fax; **~ modem** fax modem; **enviar** OU **mandar um ~** to send a fax.

faz ['faʃ]→ fazer.

fazenda [fa'zẽda] *f (Br: quinta)* ranch; *(tecido)* cloth.

fazendeiro, -ra [fazẽ'deiru, -ra] *m, f (Br)* landowner.

fazer [fa'ze(x)] *vt* **1.** *(produzir)* to make; **~ muito barulho** to make a lot of noise; **~ planos/um vestido** to make plans/a dress; **~ uma pergunta** to ask a question.
2. *(comida)* to make.
3. *(gerar)* to produce; **o chocolate faz borbulhas** chocolate gives you spots.
4. *(realizar)*: **estou fazendo um curso de computadores** I'm doing a computer course; **vamos ~ uma festa** we're having a party.
5. *(praticar)* to do; **você devia ~ mais exercício** you should exercise more; **faço jogging todas as manhãs** I go jogging every morning.
6. *(cama)* to make.
7. *(transformar)* to make; **~ alguém feliz** to make sb happy.
8. *(anos)*: **faço anos amanhã** it's my birthday tomorrow; **fazemos cinco anos de casados** we've been married (for) five years.
9. *(obrigar)* to make; **~ alguém fazer algo** to make sb do sthg; **~ alguém rir/chorar** to make sb laugh/cry.
10. *(cálculo, conta)* to do; **faz a conta para ver quanto é** work out the bill to see what it comes to.
◆ *vi* **1.** *(em teatro, cinema)*: **~ de** to play (the part of), to be.
2. *(aparentar)*: **~ como se** to act as if.
3. *(causar)*: **~ bem/mal a algo** to be good/bad for sthg; **~ bem/mal a alguém** *(suj: coisa)* to be good/bad for sb; **~ mal a alguém** *(suj: pessoa)* to hurt sb.
4. *(obrigar)*: **faça (com) que ele venha** make him come.
◆ *v impess* **1.** *(Br)*: **faz frio/calor** it's cold/hot.
2. *(tempo)*: **faz um ano que não o vejo** it's a year since I last saw him; **faz tempo que estou à espera** I've been waiting for a while; **o Sérgio partiu faz três meses** Sérgio left three months ago.
3. *(importar)*: **não faz mal se está quebrado** it doesn't matter if it's broken; **tanto faz** it doesn't matter.
❑ **fazer-se** *vp (preparar-se)* to be made; *(ser correto)*: **é assim que se faz** that's the way to do it; **~-se com** *(ser preparado com)* to be made with.
❑ **fazer-se de** *vp + prep (pretender ser)*: **ele gosta de ~-se de importante** he likes to act important; **~-se de tolo** to act stupid; **~-se de desentendido** to feign ignorance.

fé ['fɛ] *f* faith; **de boa/má ~** in good/bad faith.

febre ['febri] *f (MED)* fever; **estar com ~** to have a temperature.

febre-do-feno [febridu'fenu] *f* hay fever.

fechado, -da [fe'ʃadu, -da] *adj* shut, closed; *(torneira)* turned off; *(luz)* switched off; *(flor)* unopened; *(fig: reservado)* private; **"~ para balanço"** "closed for stocktaking"; **"~ para férias"** "closed for holidays"; **"~ para obras"** "closed for refurbishment".

fechadura [feʃa'dura] *f* lock.

fechar [fe'ʃa(x)] *vt (porta, janela)* to shut, to close; *(carro)* to lock; *(torneira)* to turn off; *(luz)* to switch off; *(negócio)* to close; *(loja, estabelecimento, fábrica)* to close down ◆ *vi (ferida)* to heal; *(estabelecimento)* to shut, to close; **~ algo à chave** to lock sthg.
❑ **fechar-se** *vp (encerrar-se)* to shut o.s

up ou away; *(calar-se)* to withdraw (into o.s.).

fecho ['feʃu] *m (de peça de vestuário)* zip *(Brit)*, zipper *(Am)*; *(de porta, janela)* lock; *(de espectáculo, acontecimento)* end; *(de colar, pulseira)* fastener; ~ éclair zip *(Brit)*, zipper *(Am)*.

fécula ['fɛkula] *f* starch; ~ de batata potato starch.

fecundar [fekũn'da(x)] *vt* to fertilize.

feder [fe'de(x)] *vi* to stink.

federação [federa'sãw] *(pl -ões [-õjʃ])* *f* federation.

fedor [fe'do(x)] *m* stench.

feijão [fej'ʒãw] *(pl -ões [-õjʃ])* *m* bean.

feijão-fradinho [fejʒãwfra'dʒinu] *(pl feijões-fradinhos [fejʒõjʒfra'dʒinuʃ])* *m* black-eyed bean *(Brit)*, black-eyed pea *(Am)*.

feijão-mulatinho [fejʒãwmula'tʃinu] *(pl feijões-mulatinhos [fejʒõjʒmula'tʃinuʃ])* *m* red bean similar to the kidney bean.

feijão-preto [fejʒãw'pretu] *(pl feijões-pretos [fejʒõjʒ'pretuʃ])* *m* black bean.

feijão-verde [fejʒãw'vexdʒi] *(pl feijões-verdes [fejʒõjʒ'vexdʒiʃ])* *m* green bean.

feijoada [fej'ʒwada] *f* bean stew; ~ brasileira black bean stew cooked with salt beef and various cuts of pork, served with "farofa", spring greens, rice and an orange; ~ à trasmontana bean stew cooked with cuts of pork and "chouriço", cabbage, carrot and herbs, served with rice.

feijões → feijão.

feio, feia ['feju, 'feja] *adj* ugly; *(atitude, situação)* nasty.

feira ['fejra] *f* market; ~ da ladra *(Port)* flea market; ~ livre *(Br)* street market; ~ do livro book fair; fazer a ~ to go to the market.

feitiçaria [fejtʃisa'ria] *f* witchcraft.

feiticeira [fejtʃi'sejra] *f* enchantress.

feiticeiro [fejtʃi'sejru] *m* wizard.

feitiço [fej'tʃisu] *m* spell.

feitio [fej'tʃiu] *m (forma)* shape; *(caráter)* temper; *(de peça de vestuário)* cut; ter bom ~ *(pessoa)* to be good-natured.

feito, -ta ['fejtu, -ta] *pp* → fazer ♦ *adj (adulto)* mature; *(realizado)* finished, done ♦ *m (façanha)* deed; ~ à mão handmade; ~ sob medida made-to-measure; ~ de made of; dito e ~ no sooner said than done.

feixe ['fejʃi] *m (de palha, lenha)* bundle; *(Br: de luz)* beam.

fel [fɛw] *m* bile.

felicidade [felisi'dadʒi] *f (contentamento)* happiness; *(boa sorte)* luck; ~s! all the best!

felicitar [felisi'ta(x)] *vt* to congratulate; ~ alguém por algo to congratulate sb on sthg.

felino, -na [fe'linu, -na] *adj* feline ♦ *m* cat.

feliz [fe'liʒ] *(pl -zes [-ziʃ])* *adj* happy; *(afortunado)* lucky; *(bem executado)* successful; Feliz Ano Novo! Happy New Year!

felizmente [feliʒ'mẽntʃi] *adv* fortunately.

felpudo, -da [few'pudu, -da] *adj* fluffy.

feltro ['fewtru] *m* felt.

fêmea ['femja] *f* female.

feminino, -na [femi'ninu, -na] *adj & m* feminine.

feminismo [feme'niʒmu] *m* feminism.

feminista [femi'niʃta] *mf* feminist.

fenda ['fẽnda] *f* crack.

fender [fẽn'de(x)] *vt* to crack.

⊔ **fender-se** *vp* to crack.

feno ['fenu] *m* hay.

fenomenal [fenome'naw] *(pl -ais [-ajʃ])* *adj* phenomenal.

fenómeno [fe'nɔmenu] *m (Port)* = fenômeno.

fenômeno [fe'nomenu] *m (Br)* phenomenon.

fera ['fɛra] *f* wild animal.

feriado [fe'rjadu] *m* public holiday; ~ nacional public holiday.

férias ['fɛrjaʃ] *fpl* holiday *(sg)*; estar de ou em ~ to be on holiday; ir de ~ to go on holiday.

ferida [fe'rida] *f (ferimento)* wound, → ferido.

ferido, -da [fe'ridu, -da] *adj (em acidente, queda)* injured; *(em combate)* wounded; *(fig: ofendido)* hurt ♦ *m, f:* houve 20 ~s 20 people were injured.

ferimento [feri'mẽntu] *m (de queda, acidente)* injury; *(de arma)* wound.

ferir [fe'ri(x)] *vt* to hurt; *(com arma)* to wound.

⊐ **ferir-se** *vp (em queda, acidente)* to hurt o.s.

fermentar [fexmẽn'ta(x)] *vi* to ferment.

fermento [fex'mẽntu] *m* yeast.

feroz [fe'rɔʃ] (*pl* **-zes** [-ziʃ]) *adj* fierce.

ferradura [fexa'dura] *f* horseshoe.

ferragens [fe'xaʒajʃ] *fpl* → **loja**.

ferramenta [fexa'mẽnta] *f (instrumento individual)* tool; *(conjunto de instrumentos)* tools *(pl)*.

ferrão [fe'xãw] (*pl* **-ões** [-õjʃ]) *m* sting.

ferreiro [fe'xejru] *m* blacksmith.

ferro ['fɛxu] *m* iron.

ferrões → **ferrão**.

ferrolho [fe'xoʎu] *m* bolt.

ferro-velho [ˌfɛxu'vɛʎu] (*pl* **ferros-velhos** [ˌfɛxuʒ'vɛʎuʃ]) *m* scrapyard.

ferrovia [fexo'via] *f (Br)* train track.

ferrugem [fe'xuʒẽ] *f (de metal)* rust; *(de chaminé)* soot.

ferry-boat [ˌfɛxi'bowt] (*pl* **ferry-boats** [ˌfɛxi'bowtʃ]) *m* ferry.

fértil ['fɛxtiw] (*pl* **-teis** [-tejʃ]) *adj* fertile.

fertilidade [fextʃili'dadʒi] *f* fertility.

fertilizante [fextʃili'zãntʃi] *m* fertilizer.

ferver [fex've(x)] *vt* to boil ◆ *vi (leite, água)* to boil; *(vinho)* to ferment; *(fig: de raiva, indignação)* to seethe.

fervor [fex'vo(x)] *m* fervour.

fervura [fex'vura] *f*: **cozer algo até levantar** ~ to bring sthg to the boil.

festa [fɛʃta] *f* party; **boas ~s!** Merry Christmas and a Happy New Year!; **~s juninas** *Brazilian religious festivals held in June in honour of the Saints*; **~s dos Santos Populares** *Portuguese religious festivals held in June in honour of St John, St Peter and St Anthony.*
⨼ **festas** *fpl (carícias)* caresses; **fazer ~s a** *(a pessoa)* to caress; *(a animal)* to stroke.

festejar [feʃte'ʒa(x)] *vt* to celebrate.

festim [feʃ'tʃĩ] (*pl* **-ns** [-ʃ]) *m* party.

festival [feʃtʃi'vaw] (*pl* **-ais** [-ajʃ]) *m (de música, cinema)* festival; *(de canção)* contest.

fétido, -da ['fɛtʃidu, -da] *adj* fetid.

feto ['fɛtu] *m (planta)* fern; *(embrião)* foetus.

fevereiro [feve'reiru] *m (Br)* February, → **setembro**.

fez [fɛʒ] → **fazer**.

fezes ['fɛziʃ] *fpl* faeces.

fiação [fja'sãw] (*pl* **-ões** [-õjʃ]) *f (fábrica)* textile mill.

fiambre ['fjãmbri] *m* ham.

fiar ['fja(x)] *vt (linho, lã)* to spin ◆ *vi (vender a crédito)* to sell on credit.
⨼ **fiar-se em** *vp + prep* to trust.

fiasco ['fjaʃku] *m* fiasco.

fibra ['fibra] *f* fibre; *(fig: coragem)* courage; **~ (acrílica)** acrylic.

ficar [fi'ka(x)] *vi* to be; *(permanecer)* to stay; *(restar)* to be· left (over); *(rico, gordo)* to get; **ele ficou todo corado** he went bright red; **essa roupa não lhe fica bem** those clothes don't suit you; **fiquei trabalhando até tarde** I worked late; **~ bem** to look good; **~ mal** not to look good; **~ com algo** to take sthg; **~ de fazer algo** to promise to do sthg; **~ em primeiro lugar** to come first; **~ por** *(custar)* to come to; **~ sem algo** to be left without sthg.

ficção [fik'sãw] *f* fiction.

ficha ['fiʃa] *f (dentária, médica)* records *(pl)*; *(EDUC: teste)* test; *(formulário)* form; *(Port: elétrica)* plug; **~ dupla/tripla** *(Port)* double/triple socket adaptor.

fichário [fi'ʃarju] *m (caixa)* index card holder; *(fichas)* index cards *(pl)*.

fictício, -cia [fik'tʃisju, -sja] *adj* fictional.

fidelidade [fideli'dadʒi] *f* fidelity; **~ (conjugal)** faithfulness (to one's partner).

fiel ['fjew] (*pl* **-éis** [-ɛiʃ]) *adj* faithful ◆ *m* believer.

fígado ['figadu] *m* liver.

figa ['figaʃ] *fpl*: **fazer ~** = to cross one's fingers.

figo ['figu] *m* fig; **~s secos** dried figs.

figueira [fi'gejra] *f* fig tree.

figura [fi'gura] *f* figure; **fazer boa/má ~** to come across well/badly.

figurante [figu'rãntʃi] *mf* extra.

figurar [figu'ra(x)] : **figurar em** *v + prep* to appear in.

figurino [figu'rinu] *m (de moda)* fashion plate.

fila ['fila] *f* queue *(Brit)*, line *(Am)*; **em ~ (indiana)** in line.

filarmónica [filar'mɔnika] *f (Port)* = **filarmônica**.

filarmônica [filax'mõnika] *f (Br)* philharmonic (orchestra).

filatelia [filate'lia] *f* stamp collecting, philately.

filé [fi'lɛ] *m (Br)* fillet.

fileira [fi'lejra] *f* row.

filete [fi'lete] *m (Port)* fillet; **~s (de pescada)** hake fillets.

filho, -lha ['fiʎu, -ʎa] *m, f* son (*f* daughter); **os nossos ~s** our children; **~ da puta** (*vulg*) bastard (*Brit*), son of a bitch (*Am*).

filhote [fiˈʎɔtʃi] *m (de cadela)* puppy; *(de raposa, urso, etc)* cub; **a mãe olhava pelos ~s** the mother looked after her young.

filial [fiˈljaw] (*pl* **-ais** [-ajʃ]) *f* branch.

filigrana [filiˈgrana] *f* filigree.

filmadora [fiwmaˈdora] *f (Br):* **~ (de vídeo)** video camera.

filmar [fiwˈma(x)] *vt* to film, to shoot.

filme ['fiwmi] *m (de cinema)* film (*Brit*), movie (*Am*); *(de máquina fotográfica)* film.

filosofia [filozoˈfia] *f* philosophy.

filósofo, -fa [fiˈlɔzofu, -fa] *m, f* philosopher.

filtrar [fiwˈtra(x)] *vt* to filter.

filtro ['fiwtru] *m* filter.

fim ['fĩ] (*pl* **-ns** [-ʃ]) *m* end; *(objetivo)* aim; **ter por ~ fazer algo** to aim to do sthg; **ter um ~ em vista** to have an end in mind; **o ~ do mundo** (*lugar distante*) the back of beyond; *(desgraça total)* the end of the world; **a ~ de** in order to; **no ~** in the end; **ao ~ e ao cabo** at the end of the day; **estar a ~ de** *(Br)* to fancy.

fim-de-semana [ˌfĩdʒiseˈmana] (*pl* **fins-de-semana** [ˌfĩʒdʒiseˈmana]) *m* weekend.

Finados [fiˈnaduʃ] *mpl:* **os ~** All Souls' Day (*sg*).

final [fiˈnaw] (*pl* **-ais** [-ajʃ]) *adj & f* (*último*) final ◆ *m* end.

finalidade [finaliˈdadʒi] *f* (*objetivo*) aim, purpose; *(de máquina)* application.

finalista [finaˈliʃta] *mf* (*em competição*) finalist; *(de curso)* finalyear student.

finanças [fiˈnãsaʃ] *fpl* finances.

fingir [fĩˈʒi(x)] *vt* to pretend.

finlandês, -esa [fĩlãnˈdeʃ, -eza] (*mpl* **-eses** [-eziʃ], *fpl* **-s** [-ʃ]) *adj & m* Finnish ◆ *m, f* Finn.

Finlândia [fĩˈlãndʒja] *f:* **a ~** Finland.

fino, -na ['finu, -na] *adj (fio, cabelo)* fine; *(roupa)* smart; *(hotel, restaurante)* exclusive; *(pessoa)* refined; *(bebida)* fortified; *(Br: fam: bom):* **ele é gente fina** he's a good sort.

fins ~ fim.

fio ['fiu] *m (de matéria têxtil)* thread; *(elétrico)* wire; *(de líquido)* trickle; **~ dental** dental floss; **~s de ovos** sweet threads of egg yolk and sugar poured over cakes, puddings and pastries; **perder o ~ à meada** to lose one's thread.

firma ['fixma] *f (Br: empresa)* firm.

firme ['fixmi] *adj* firm.

firmeza [fixˈmeza] *f (solidez)* firmness; *(estabilidade)* stability; *(fig: perseverança)* resolve.

fiscal [fiʃˈkaw] (*pl* **-ais** [-ajʃ]) *adj* fiscal ◆ *mf* (tax) inspector.

fisco ['fiʃku] *m (instituição)* = the Inland Revenue (*Brit*), ~ the Internal Revenue (*Am*).

física ['fizika] *f (ciência)* physics (*sg*), → **físico.**

físico, -ca ['fiziku, -ka] *adj* physical ◆ *m (de pessoa)* physique ◆ *m, f (profissão)* physicist.

fisionomia [fizjonoˈmia] *f* features (*pl*).

fisioterapia [ˌfizjoteraˈpia] *f* physiotherapy.

fita ['fita] *f (de tecido)* ribbon; *(fingimento)* pretence; *(filme)* film; **~ adesiva** (*Port*) adhesive tape; **~ (de cabelo)** hairband; **~ durex®** *(Br)* ~ Sellotape® *(Brit),* = Scotch tape® *(Am);* **~ isoladora** (*Port*) insulating tape; **~ (para máquina de escrever)** typewriter ribbon; **~ métrica** tape measure; **~ de vídeo** (*Br*) video cassette OU tape; **fazer ~ (fingir)** to put on an act.

fita-cola [ˌfitaˈkɔla] *f inv* (*Port*) Sellotape® *(Brit),* Scotch tape® *(Am).*

fitar [fiˈta(x)] *vt* to stare at.

fivela [fiˈvela] *f* buckle.

fixador [fiksaˈdo(x)] (*pl* **-res** [-riʃ]) *m (de cabelo)* hairspray; *(em fotografia, desenho)* fixative.

fixar [fikˈsa(x)] *vt* to fix; *(aprender de cor)* to memorize.

❏ **fixar-se** *vp (estabelecer-se)* to establish o.s.

fixo, -xa ['fiksu, -ksa] *pp* → **fixar** ◆ *adj* fixed; *(cor)* fast.

fiz ['fiʒ] → **fazer.**

flamengo [flaˈmẽngu] *adj m* → **queijo.**

flamingo [flaˈmĩngu] *m* flamingo.

flanco ['flãŋku] *m* flank.

flanela [flaˈnɛla] *f* flannel.

flash ['flaʃi] *m* flash.

flauta ['flawta] *f* flute; **~ de bisel** recorder; **~ de pã** panpipes (*pl*).

flecha ['fleʃa] *f* arrow.

fleuma ['flewma] *f* phlegm.

flexível [flekˈsivew] (*pl* **-eis** [-ejʃ]) *adj* flexible.

flippers [ˈflipərs] *mpl* pinball *(sg)*; **jogar ~** to play pinball.

floco [ˈflɔku] *m (de pêlo, lã)* fluff *(Brit)*, fuzz *(Am)*; **~ de neve** snowflake; **~s de aveia** porridge *(sg)*; **~s de milho** cornflakes.

flor [flo(x)] *(pl* **-res** [-riʃ]*) f* flower; **em ~** in bloom; **ter os nervos à ~ da pele** to be highly strung; **estar na ~ da idade** to be in one's prime.

floresta [floˈrɛʃta] *f* forest.

florido, -da [floˈridu, -da] *adj (árvore, campo, jardim)* full of flowers; *(tecido, papel)* flowery.

florista [floˈriʃta] *mf* florist ◆ *f* florist's (shop).

fluência [fluˈẽsja] *f* fluency.

fluentemente [fluẽntʃiˈmẽntʃi] *adv* fluently.

fluido, -da [fluˈidu, -da] *adj* fluid ◆ *m (líquido)* fluid; *(fam: força misteriosa)* vibes *(pl)*.

fluminense [flumiˈnẽsi] *adj* of/relating to Rio de Janeiro State.

flúor [ˈfluɔ(x)] *m* fluoride.

fluorescente [fluɾeʃˈsẽntʃi] *adj* fluorescent.

flutuante [fluˈtwãntʃi] *adj (objeto)* floating; *(preço, inflação, temperatura)* fluctuating.

flutuar [fluˈtwa(x)] *vi* to float.

fluvial [fluˈvjaw] *(pl* **-ais** [-ajʃ]*) adj* river *(antes de s)*.

fluxo [ˈfluksu] *m* flow.

fobia [foˈbia] *f* phobia.

focinho [foˈsiɲu] *m* snout.

foco [ˈfɔku] *m (de luz, lâmpada)* beam; *(de atenção)* focus; *(de doença)* centre.

fofo, -fa [ˈfofu, -fa] *adj* soft; *(bolo)* light.

fofoca [foˈfɔka] *f (Br: mexerico)* piece of gossip.

fogão [foˈgãw] *(pl* **-ões** [-õjʃ]*) m* cooker *(Brit)*, stove *(Am)*.

foge [ˈfɔʒi] → **fugir**.

fogem [ˈfɔʒẽ] → **fugir**.

fogo [ˈfogu] *(pl* **fogos** [ˈfɔguʒ]*) m* fire; **~ posto** arson.

fogo-de-artifício [ˌfogudʒiaxtʃiˈfisju] *(pl* **fogos-de-artifício** [ˌfoguʒdʒiaxtʃiˈfisju]*) m (foguetes)* fireworks *(pl)*; *(espectáculo)* firework display.

fogões → **fogão**.

fogueira [foˈgejra] *f* fire.

foguetão [fogeˈtãw] *(pl* **-ões** [-õjʃ]*) m* rocket.

foguete [foˈgetʃi] *m* rocket.

foguetões → **foguetão**.

foi [foj] → **ser, ir**.

foice [ˈfojsi] *f (pequena)* sickle; *(grande)* scythe.

folclore [fowˈklɔri] *m (música)* folk music; *(dança)* folk-dancing.

folclórico, -ca [fowˈklɔriku, -ka] *adj (música, dança)* folk *(antes de s)*; *(fig: berrante)* garish.

fôlego [ˈfolegu] *m* breath; **tomar ~** to get one's breath back.

folga [ˈfowga] *f (de trabalho)* day off; *(espaço livre)* gap; **estar de ~** to be on one's day off.

folha [ˈfoʎa] *f (de planta, árvore)* leaf; *(de jornal, livro, revista)* page; **~ de alumínio** tinfoil; **~ de cálculo** spreadsheet; **~ (de papel)** sheet of paper; **~ lisa/quadriculada** plain/squared paper; **~ pautada** lined paper.

folha-de-flandres [ˌfoʎadʒiˈflãndriʃ] *(pl* **folhas-de-flandres** [ˌfoʎaʒdʒiˈflãndriʃ]*) f* corrugated iron.

folhado, -da [foˈʎadu, -da] *adj (massa)* puff *(antes de s)*; *(bolo)* made with puff pastry ◆ *m (CULIN)* pastry.

folhagem [foˈʎaʒẽ] *f* foliage.

folhear [foˈʎja(x)] *vt* to leaf through.

folheto [foˈʎetu] *m* leaflet.

folia [foˈlia] *f* revelry.

folião, -liona [foˈljãw, -ljona] *(mpl* **-ões** [-õjʃ]*, fpl* **-s** [-ʃ]*) m, f* reveller.

fome [ˈfɔmi] *f* hunger; **estar com** OU **ter ~** to be hungry; **passar ~** to go hungry.

fone [ˈfɔni] *m (Br: de telefone)* receiver, handset.

fonética [foˈnɛtʃika] *f* phonetics *(sg)*.

fonte [ˈfõntʃi] *f (chafariz)* fountain; *(de cabeça)* temple; *(fig: de texto, trabalho, informação)* source.

fora [ˈfɔra] *adv (no exterior)* out; *(no estrangeiro)* abroad ◆ *prep* apart from ◆ *interj* get out!; **~ de série** extraordinary; **"~ de serviço"** "out of order"; **estar/ficar ~ de si** to be beside o.s.; **ficar de ~** not to join in; **~ de mão** *(dirigir)* on the wrong side of the road; **lá ~** *(no estrangeiro)* abroad; *(no exterior)* outside; **por esse país ~** throughout the country; **dar um ~ em alguém** *(Br)* to chuck sb.

foram [ˈfɔrãw] → **ser, ir**.

força [ˈfoxsa] *f (energia)* strength; *(mi-*

litar, policial) force; **~ de vontade** will power; **as ~s armadas** the armed forces; **à ~** by force; **por ~** by force; **não cheguei a horas por razões de ~ maior** I didn't arrive on time for reasons beyond my control.

forçar [foxˈsa(x)] *vt* to force.

forjar [foxˈʒa(x)] *vt* to forge.

forma[1] [ˈfɔxma] *f* shape; *(maneira)* way; **de ~ que** therefore; **de qualquer ~** anyway; **em ~ de** in the shape of; **em ~ de estrela** star-shaped; **estar em ~** to be in shape.

forma[2] [ˈfɔxma] *f (Port)* = **fôrma**.

fôrma [ˈfoxma] *f (Br) (de bolos)* cake tin; *(de sapato)* shoe tree.

formação [foxmaˈsãw] *(pl -ões* [-õjʃ]) *f* formation; *(treino)* training.

formal [foxˈmaw] *(pl -ais* [-ajʃ]) *adj* formal.

formalidade [foxmaliˈdadʒi] *f* formality.

formar [foxˈma(x)] *vt* to form; *(educar)* to train.

❑ **formar-se** *vp (terminar curso universitário)* to graduate.

formatar [foxmaˈta(x)] *vt* to format.

formidável [foxmiˈdavew] *(pl -eis* [-ejʃ]) *adj* fantastic.

formiga [foxˈmiga] *f* ant.

formoso, -osa [foxˈmozu, -ɔza] *adj* beautiful; *(homem)* handsome.

fórmula [ˈfɔxmula] *f* formula; **Fórmula 1** Formula 1.

formular [foxmuˈla(x)] *vt (palavra, frase)* to formulate; *(desejo)* to express.

formulário [foxmuˈlarju] *m* form.

fornecedor, -ra [foxneseˈdo(x), -ra] *(mpl -res* [-riʃ], *fpl -s* [-ʃ]) *m, f (de estabelecimento)* supplier; *(fam: de droga)* dealer.

fornecer [foxneˈse(x)] *vt* to supply; **~ alguém com algo** to supply sb with sthg.

❑ **fornecer-se** *vp* to stock up.

fornecimento [foxnesiˈmẽntu] *m* supply.

forno [ˈfoxnu] *m* oven.

forquilha [foxˈkiʎa] *f* fork *(Brit)*, pitchfork *(Am)*.

forrar [foˈxa(x)] *vt* to line; *(livro)* to cover.

forró [foˈxɔ] *m (Br)* party.

fortalecer [foxtaleˈse(x)] *vt* to strengthen.

fortaleza [foxtaˈleza] *f* fortress.

forte [ˈfɔxtʃi] *adj* strong; *(calor, dor)* intense; *(chuva)* heavy; *(voz, som)* loud; *(comida)* filling; *(golpe, choque)* hefty; *(bebida)* stiff ◆ *m* fort; **essa é ~!** pull the other one!

fortuna [foxˈtuna] *f* fortune.

fósforo [ˈfɔʃforu] *m (de acender)* match.

fossa [ˈfɔsa] *f* septic tank; **estar na ~** *(fig: deprimido)* to be down in the dumps.

fóssil [ˈfɔsiw] *(pl -eis* [-ejʃ]) *m* fossil.

fosso [ˈfosu] *m* moat.

foste [ˈfoʃtʃi]→ **ser, ir**.

foto [ˈfɔtu] *f* photo.

fotocópia [fotoˈkɔpja] *f* photocopy.

fotografar [fotograˈfa(x)] *vt* to photograph.

fotografia [fotograˈfia] *f (arte)* photography; *(objeto)* photograph; **~ para passaporte** passport photo.

fotógrafo, -fa [foˈtɔgrafu, -fa] *m, f* photographer.

fotómetro [foˈtɔmetru] *m* light meter.

foz [ˈfɔʃ] *f* river mouth.

fração [fraˈsãw] *(pl -ões* [-õjʃ]) *f (Br)* fraction.

fracasso [fraˈkasu] *m* failure.

fracção [fraˈsãw] *(pl -ões* [-õjʃ]) *f (Port)* = **fração**.

fraco, -ca [ˈfraku, -ka] *adj* weak; *(dor)* slight; *(chuva, vento)* light; *(voz, som)* faint; *(qualidade)* poor; **ter um ~ por alguém** *(fig: paixão)* to have a crush on sb.

frações → fração.

fractura [fraˈtura] *f (Port)* = **fratura**.

frade [ˈfradʒi] *m* friar.

frágil [ˈfraʒiw] *(pl -geis* [-ʒejʃ]) *adj* fragile.

fragmento [fragˈmẽntu] *m* fragment; *(de obra literária, manuscrito)* extract.

fragrância [fraˈgrãsja] *f* fragrance.

fralda [ˈfrawda] *f* nappy *(Brit)*, diaper *(Am)*; **~s descartáveis** disposable nappies.

framboesa [frãmˈbweza] *f* raspberry.

França [ˈfrãsa] *f*: **a ~** France.

francamente [frãŋkaˈmẽntʃi] *adv* frankly ◆ *interj* honestly!

francês, -esa [frãˈseʃ, -eza] *(mpl -eses* [-eziʃ], *fpl -s* [-ʃ]) *adj & m* French ◆ *m, f (pessoa)* Frenchman *(f* Frenchwoman); **os franceses** the French.

franco, -ca [ˈfrãŋku, -ka] *adj* frank; **para ser ~** ... to be quite honest ....

frango ['frãŋgu] *m* chicken; *(em fute-bol)* sitter; ~ **assado** roast chicken; ~ **churrasco** *barbecued chicken in a spicy sauce;* ~ **na púcara** *chicken stewed with tomatoes, onions, smoked ham, garlic, port, brandy, white wine and raisins.*

franja ['frãʒa] *f (de toalha, cortina, sofá)* fringe; *(de cabelo)* fringe *(Brit)*, bangs *(pl) (Am).*

franqueza [frãŋ'keza] *f* frankness; **com** ~ frankly.

franquia [frãŋ'kia] *f (COM)* franchise; *(selo postal)* postage; *(isenção)* exemption.

franzino, -na [frã'zinu, -na] *adj* frail.

fraqueza [fra'keza] *f* weakness; *(fome)* hunger; *(cansaço)* exhaustion.

frasco ['fraʃku] *m* jar.

frase ['frazi] *f* sentence.

fratura [fra'tura] *f (Br)* fracture.

fraude ['frawdʒi] *f* fraud.

frear [fre'a(x)] *vi (Br)* to brake.

freguês, -esa [fre'geʃ, -eza] *(mpl -eses [-eziʃ], fpl -s [-ʃ]) m, f* customer.

freio ['fraju] *m (de veículo)* brake; *(de cavalo)* bit.

freixo ['frejʃu] *m* ash.

frenético, -ca [fre'nɛtʃiku, -ka] *adj* frenetic.

frente ['frẽtʃi] *f* front; **olha-me de ~!** look me in the face!; **dar de ~ com** *(encontrar)* to bump into; **fazer ~ a** to stand up to, to confront; **ir para a ~ com** to go ahead with; ~ **fria/quente** cold/warm front; **à ~** ahead; **à ~ de** *(na dianteira de)* in front of; *(chegar, ir, partir)* ahead of; **em ~** *(defronte)* opposite; **em ~ de,** ~ **a** opposite; ~ **a** ~ face to face.

frequência [fre'kwẽsja] *f (Port)* = **freqüência.**

freqüência [fre'kwẽsja] *f (Br)* frequency; **com** ~ frequently.

freqüentar [frekwẽ'ta(x)] *vt (casa de alguém)* to visit frequently; *(curso)* to attend; *(local)* to frequent.

freqüentemente [frekwẽtʃi'mẽtʃi] *adv* frequently.

frescão [freʃ'kãw] *(pl -ões [-õjʃ]) m (Br: ônibus)* air-conditioned coach.

fresco, -ca ['freʃku, -ka] *adj* fresh; *(tempo, bebida, roupa)* cool; *(muito exigente)* fussy; *(fam:efeminado)* camp ♦ *m (Port: pintura)* fresco.

frescobol [freʃko'bɔw] *m (Br)* racquetball *(played at the beach).*

frescões → **frescão.**

frescura [freʃ'kura] *f* freshness; *(em relação a temperatura)* coolness.

fressura [fre'sura] *f* offal.

frete ['fretʃi] *m (de ônibus)* fee *(for hire of both bus and driver); (de táxi)* fare.

frevo ['frevu] *m* Brazilian carnival dance.

fricção [frik'sãw] *(pl -ões [-õjʃ]) f (esfregação)* rubbing; *(atrito)* friction.

frieira [fri'ejra] *f* chilblain.

frieza [fri'eza] *f* coldness.

frigideira [friʒi'dejra] *f* frying pan.

frigorífico [frigo'rifiku] *m* fridge.

frio, fria ['friu, 'fria] *adj & m* cold; **está** ~ it's cold; **estar com** OU **ter** ~ to be cold; **estava um** ~ **de rachar** *(fam)* it was absolutely freezing.

❑ **frios** *mpl (Br: CULIN)* cold meats.

frisar [fri'za(x)] *vt (cabelo)* to curl; *(fig: enfatizar)* to highlight.

fritar [fri'ta(x)] *vt (em pouco óleo)* to fry; *(em muito óleo)* to deep-fry.

frito, -ta ['fritu, -ta] *adj* fried; **estar** ~ *(fam)* to be done for.

fritura [fri'tura] *f (alimento frito)* fried food.

frízer ['frizex] *(pl -res [-riʃ]) m (Br) (de geladeira)* freezer; *(congelador)* deep freeze.

fronha ['froɲa] *f* pillowcase.

fronte ['frõtʃi] *f (testa)* forehead.

fronteira [frõ'tejra] *f* border; **além ~s** abroad.

frota ['frɔta] *f* fleet.

frustrado, -da [fruʃ'tradu, -da] *adj* frustrated.

frustrante [fruʃ'trãtʃi] *adj* frustrating.

fruta ['fruta] *f* fruit; ~ **em calda** fruit in syrup; ~ **da época** fruit in season.

fruta-do-conde [,frutadu'kõdʒi] *(pl frutas-do-conde* [,frutaʒdu'kõdʒi]) *f* custard apple.

frutaria [fruta'ria] *f* fruit shop.

fruto ['frutu] *m* fruit; ~**s secos** dried fruits.

tubá [fu'ba] *m* cornmeal.

fuga ['fuga] *f (de gás, água)* leak; *(evasão)* escape; **pôr-se em** ~ to run away; **em** ~ on the run.

fugir [fu'ʒi(x)] *vi* to run away; ~ **a** OU **de** to run away from.

fugitivo, -va [fuʒi'tʃivu, -va] *adj* fleeting ♦ *m, f* fugitive.

fui [ˈfuĩ] → **ser, ir**.

fulano, -na [fuˈlanu, -na] *m, f* what's-his-name (*f* what's-her-name); **era um ~ qualquer** it was just some guy.

fuligem [fuˈliʒẽ] *f* soot.

fulo, -la [ˈfulu, -la] *adj* furious; **~ da vida** fuming.

fumaça [fuˈmasa] *f* smoke.

fumador, -ra [fumaˈdor, -ra] (*mpl* **-es** [-eʃ], *fpl* **-s** [-ʃ]) *m, f* (*Port*) smoker.

fumante [fuˈmãntʃi] *mf* (*Br*) smoker.

fumar [fuˈma(x)] *vt & vi* to smoke.

fumo [ˈfumu] *m* smoke.

função [fũˈsãw] (*pl* **-ões** [-õjʃ]) *f* (*de pessoa*) role; (*de máquina*) function; **exercer a ~ de** to act as; **~ pública** civil service.

funcho [ˈfũʃu] *m* fennel.

funcionamento [fũsjonaˈmẽntu] *m* operation; **em ~** in operation; **tenho o motor em ~** I've got the engine running.

funcionar [fũsjoˈna(x)] *vi* (*máquina*) to work; (*estabelecimento*) to be open.

funcionário, -ria [fũsjoˈnarju, -rja] *m, f* employee; **~ público** civil servant.

funções → **função**.

fundação [fũndaˈsãw] (*pl* **-ões** [-õjʃ]) *f* foundation.

fundamental [fũndamẽnˈtaw] (*pl* **-ais** [-ajʃ]) *adj* fundamental.

fundamento [fũndaˈmẽntu] *m* (*motivo*) grounds (*pl*); (*justificação*) basis; **sem ~** unfounded.

fundar [fũnˈda(x)] *vt* to found; **~ algo em algo** (*basear*) to base sthg on sthg.

fundido, -da [fũnˈdʒidu, -da] *adj* (*metal*) molten; (*queijo*) melted.

fundir [fũnˈdʒi(x)] *vt* to melt.

⅃ fundir-se *vp* to melt.

fundo, -da [ˈfũndu, -da] *adj* deep ◆ *m* (*de rio, piscina, poço*) bottom; (*em economia*) fund; **ir ao ~ da questão** to get to the bottom of the matter; **sem ~** bottomless.

fúnebre [ˈfunebri] *adj* (*fig: lúgubre*) funereal.

funeral [funeˈraw] (*pl* **-ais** [-ajʃ]) *m* funeral.

fungo [ˈfũŋgu] *m* fungus.

funil [fuˈniw] (*pl* **-is** [-iʃ]) *m* funnel.

furacão [furaˈkãw] (*pl* **-ões** [-õjʃ]) *m* hurricane.

furadeira [furaˈdejra] *f* (*Br*) drill.

furado, -da [fuˈradu, -da] *adj* (*pneu*) flat; (*orelha*) pierced.

furador [furaˈdo(x)] (*pl* **-res** [-riʃ]) *m* hole punch.

furar [fuˈra(x)] *vt* (*folha*) to punch holes in; (*saco*) to make a hole in; (*pneu*) to puncture; (*orelha*) to pierce; (*fig: fila*) to jump.

furgão [fuxˈgãw] (*pl* **-ões** [-õjʃ]) *m* (*veículo*) van.

fúria [ˈfurja] *f* fury.

furnas [ˈfuxnaʃ] *fpl* hot ou thermal springs.

furo [ˈfuru] *m* (*em pneu*) puncture; (*em saco, orelha*) hole.

furtar [fuxˈta(x)] *vt* to steal.

⅃ furtar-se a *vp + prep* to avoid.

furúnculo [fuˈrũŋkulu] *m* boil.

fusão [fuˈzãw] (*pl* **-ões** [-õjʃ]) *f* fusion; (*de empresas*) merger.

fusível [fuˈzivɛw] (*pl* **-eis** [-ejʃ]) *m* fuse.

fuso [ˈfuzu] *m*: **~ horário** time zone.

fusões → **fusão**.

futebol [futʃiˈbɔw] *m* football (*Brit*), soccer (*Am*).

fútil [ˈfutʃiw] (*pl* **-teis** [-tejʃ]) *adj* (*frívolo*) frivolous; (*insignificante*) trivial; (*vão*) futile.

futilidade [futʃiliˈdadʒi] *f* (*frivolidade*) frivolity; (*coisa inútil*) triviality; (*inutilidade*) futility.

futuro, -ra [fuˈturu, -ra] *adj & m* future; **o ~** (*GRAM*) the future (tense); **de ~** in future; **no ~** in the future; **para o ~** for the future; **ter ~** to have a future.

fuzil [fuˈziw] (*pl* **-is** [-iʃ]) *m* rifle.

fuzileiro [fuziˈlejru] *m* fusilier.

fuzis → **fuzil**.

G

gabar [ga'ba(x)] *vt* to praise.

❑ **gabar-se** *vp* to boast; **~-se de algo** to boast about sthg.

gabardine [gabax'dʒini] *f* raincoat.

gabinete [gabi'netʃi] *m* (*compartimento*) booth; (*escritório*) office.

gado ['gadu] *m* cattle.

gaélico [ga'ɛliku] *m* Gaelic.

gafanhoto [gafa'ɲotu] *m* grasshopper.

gafe [gafi] *f* gaffe.

gagueira [ga'gejra] *f (Br)* stammer.

gaguejar [gage'ʒa(x)] *vi* to stutter, to stammer.

gaguez [ga'geʃ] *f (Port)* = gagueira.

gaiato, -ta [ga'jatu, -ta] *adj (Br)* funny.

gaio ['gaju] *m* jay.

gaiola [ga'jɔla] *f* cage.

gaita ['gajta] *f* pipe ◆ *interj* damn!

gaita-de-foles [gajtadʒi'fɔliʃ] (*pl* **gaitas-de-foles** [gajtaʒdʒi'fɔliʃ]) *f* bagpipes (*pl*).

gaivota [gaj'vota] *f* seagull.

gajo, -ja [ga'ʒu, -ʒa] *m, f (Port: fam)* guy (*f* girl).

gala ['gala] *f* gala.

galão [ga'lãw] (*pl* -ões [-õjʃ]) *m* (*bebida*) tall glass of milky coffee; (*medida*) gallon.

galáxia [ga'laksja] *f* galaxy.

galera [ga'lɛra] *f (Br: fam: turma)* gang.

galeria [gale'ria] *f* gallery; (*corredor, ala*) corridor; (*local para compras*) arcade; **~ de arte** art gallery.

galês, -esa [ga'leʃ, -eza] (*mpl* -eses [-eziʃ], *fpl* -s [-ʃ]) *adj & m* Welsh ◆ *m, f* Welshman (*f* Welshwoman); **os galeses** the Welsh.

galeto [ga'letu] *m (Br)* poussin (*Brit*), spring chicken (*Am*).

galgo ['gawgu] *m* greyhound.

galho ['gaʎu] *m* (*de árvore*) branch; (*de veado*) antler.

galinha [ga'liɲa] *f* hen.

galinheiro [gali'ɲejru] *m* henhouse.

galo ['galu] *m* rooster, cock; (*fam: na testa*) bump.

galochas [ga'lɔʃaʃ] *fpl* wellington boots (*Brit*), rubber boots (*Am*).

galões → galão.

galopar [galo'pa(x)] *vi* to gallop.

gama ['gama] *f* range.

gambas ['gãbaʃ] *fpl (Port)* king prawns.

gamela [ga'mɛla] *f* trough.

gamo ['gamu] *m* fallow deer.

gana ['gana] *f (fam)* (*ódio*) hatred; **ter ~s de** to feel like; **ter ~s a alguém** to hate sb.

ganância [ga'nãsja] *f* greed.

ganancioso, -osa [ganã'sjozu, -ɔza] *adj* greedy.

gancho ['gãʃu] *m* (*peça curva*) hook; (*Port: de cabelo*) hairgrip (*Brit*), bobby pin (*Am*).

ganga ['gãga] *f (Port)* denim.

gangorra [gã'goxa] *f (Br)* seesaw.

gangrena [gã'grena] *f* gangrene.

gangue ['gãgi] *f (Br: fam: turma)* gang.

ganhar [ga'ɲa(x)] *vt* to win; (*dinheiro, respeito*) to earn; (*peso*) to put on; (*velocidade*) to pick up ◆ *vi* (*vencer*) to win; **~ de alguém** to beat sb; **~ com algo** to benefit from sthg; **~ a vida** OU **o pão** to earn a living

ganho ['gaɲu] *m* gain.

ganir [ga'ni(x)] *vi* to whine.

ganso ['gãsu] *m* goose.

garagem [ga'raʒẽ] (*pl* -ns [-ʃ]) *f* garage.

garanhão [gara'ɲãw] (*pl* -ões [-õjʃ]) *m* stallion.

garantia [garãn'tʃia] *f* guarantee.

garantir [garãn'tʃi(x)] *vt* to vouch for;

~ que to guarantee (that); **eu garanto que está certo** I can assure you that it's correct.

garça ['gaxsa] f heron.

garçom [gax'sõ] (pl **-ns** [-ʃ]) m (Br) waiter.

garçon [gar'sõ] m (Port) = **garçom**.

garçonete [garso'netʃi] f (Br) waitress.

garçons → **garçom**.

gare ['gari] f platform.

garfo ['gaxfu] m (utensílio) fork; (de bicicleta) forks (pl); **ser um bom ~ to** enjoy one's food.

gargalhada [gaxga'ʎada] f shriek of laughter; **dar uma ~ to** laugh; **desatar às ~s** to burst out laughing.

gargalo [gax'galu] m neck (of a bottle).

garganta [gax'gãta] f throat.

gargarejar [gaxgare'ʒa(x)] vi to gargle.

gari [ga'ri] m (Br) road sweeper.

garoto, -ta [ga'rotu, -ta] m, f (miúdo) boy (f girl), kid; (Br: namorado) boyfriend (f girlfriend) ◆ m (Port: bebida) espresso coffee with a drop of milk.

garoupa [ga'ropa] f grouper.

garra ['gaxa] f (de animal) claw; (fig: talento, genica) flair; **ter ~ (talento)** to show great talent.

garrafa [ga'xafa] f bottle; **~ térmica** Thermos® (flask).

garrafão [gaxa'fãw] (pl **-ões** [-õjʃ]) m (utensílio) flagon; (em estrada) bottleneck.

garrote [ga'xɔtʃi] m (MED) tourniquet.

garupa [ga'rupa] f (de cavalo) hindquarters (pl).

gás ['gajʃ] (pl **gases** ['gaziʃ]) m gas; **~ butano** butane (gas); **~ lacrimogêneo** tear gas.

⊔ gases mpl (intestinais) wind (sg).

gaseificada [gazeifi'kada] adj f → **água**.

gases → **gás**.

gasóleo [ga'zɔlju] m diesel (oil).

gasolina [gazo'lina] f petrol (Brit), gas (Am); **~ sem chumbo** unleaded petrol; **~ normal/super** two-star/four-star petrol.

gasosa [ga'zɔza] f soda.

gastar [gaʃ'ta(x)] vt to use; (desperdiçar) to waste; (sola de sapato) to wear down; **~ tempo/dinheiro** (usar) to spend time/money; (desperdiçar) to waste time/money.

⊔ gastar-se vp (consumir-se) to be used; (desperdiçar-se) to be wasted; (desgastar-se) to wear down.

gasto, -ta ['gaʃtu, -ta] pp → **gastar** ◆ adj (dinheiro) spent; (água, eletricidade) used; (usado) worn ◆ m expense.

gástrico, -ca ['gaʃtriku, -ka] adj gastric.

gastrite [gaʃ'tritʃi] f gastritis.

gastrónomo, -ma [gaʃ'trɔnumu, -ma] m, f (Port) = **gastrônomo**.

gastrônomo, -ma [gaʃ'tronomu, -ma] m, f (Br) gourmet.

gatilho [ga'tʃiʎu] m trigger.

gatinhar [gatʃi'ɲa(x)] vi to crawl.

gato, -ta ['gatu, -ta] m, f cat; (Br: fam: homem, mulher bonita) dish (f babe).

gatuno, -na [ga'tunu, -na] m, f thief.

gaveta [ga'vcta] f drawer.

gaze ['gazi] f gauze.

gazela [ga'zɛla] f gazelle.

gazeta [ga'zɛta] f gazette; **fazer ~ (fam)** to play truant (Brit), to play hooky (Am).

geada ['ʒjada] f frost.

geladeira [ʒela'deira] f (Br) fridge.

gelado, -da [ʒe'ladu, -da] adj frozen ◆ m (Port) ice cream.

gelar [ʒe'la(x)] vt & vi to freeze.

gelataria [ʒelata'ria] f (Port) ice-cream parlour.

gelatina [ʒela'tʃina] f (de animal) gelatine; (de frutas) jelly (Brit), Jello® (Am).

geleia [ʒe'laja] f (Port) = **geléia**.

geléia [ʒe'lɛja] f (Br) jam (Brit), jelly (Am).

gelo ['ʒelu] m ice; **quebrar o ~ (fig)** to break the ice.

gema [ʒema] f yolk; **da ~ (genuíno)** real.

gêmeo, -mea ['ʒemju, -mja] adj & m, f (Port) = **gêmeo**.

gêmeo, -mea ['ʒemju, -mja] adj (Br) twin ◆ m, f: **os ~s** the twins; **o meu irmão ~** my twin brother.

⊔ Gêmeos m inv (Br) Gemini (sg).

gemer [ʒe'me(x)] vi to groan.

gemido [ʒe'midu] m groan.

gene ['ʒɛni] m gene.

general [ʒenc'raw] (pl **-ais** [-ajʃ]) m general.

generalizar [ʒenerali'za(x)] vt to make widespread ◆ vi to generalize.

⌐ **generalizar-se** *vp* to become widespread.

género ['ʒɛneru] *m (Port)* = **gênero**.

gênero ['ʒeneru] *m (Br) (tipo)* kind, type; *(espécie)* genus; *(GRAM)* gender; *(em literatura, pintura)* genre; **o ~ humano** the human race.

⌐ **gêneros** *mpl (Br) (mercadoria)* goods; **~s alimentícios** foodstuffs.

generosidade [ʒenerozi'dadʒi] *f* generosity.

generoso, -osa [ʒene'rozu, -ɔza] *adj* generous; *(vinho)* full-bodied.

genética [ʒe'nɛtʃika] *f* genetics *(sg)*.

gengibre [ʒẽ'ʒibri] *m* ginger.

gengiva [ʒẽ'ʒiva] *f* gum.

genial [ʒe'njaw] *(pl* **-ais** [-ajʃ]*) adj* brilliant.

génio ['ʒɛnju] *m (Port)* = **gênio**.

gênio ['ʒenju] *m (Br) (pessoa)* genius; *(irascibilidade)* temper; **ter mau ~** to have a short temper.

genital [ʒeni'taw] *(pl* **-ais** [-ajʃ]*) adj* genital.

genro ['ʒẽxu] *m* son-in-law.

gente ['ʒẽtʃi] *f (pessoas)* people *(pl)*; *(fam: família)* family; **a ~ (nós)** we; *(com preposição)* us; **toda a ~** everyone.

⌐ **gentes** *fpl*: **as ~s** the peoples.

gentil [ʒẽ'tʃiw] *(pl* **-is** [-iʃ]*) adj (amável)* kind; *(bem-educado)* polite.

genuíno, -na [ʒe'nwinu, -na] *adj* genuine.

geografia [ʒjogra'fia] *f* geography.

geologia [ʒjolo'ʒia] *f* geology.

geometria [ʒjome'tria] *f* geometry; **~ descritiva** *subject studied at secondary school by those wanting to go into architecture or engineering.*

geração [ʒera'sãw] *(pl* **-ões** [-õjʃ]*) f* generation.

gerador [ʒera'do(x)] *(pl* **-res** [-riʃ]*) m* generator.

geral [ʒe'raw] *(pl* **-ais** [-ajʃ]*) adj* general ♦ *f (em teatro)* cheapest seats at the theatre; **de um modo ~** generally speaking; **em ~** generally; **no ~** in general.

geralmente [ʒeraw'mẽtʃi] *adv* generally.

gerânio [ʒe'ranju] *m* geranium.

gerar [ʒe'ra(x)] *vt* to create.

⌐ **gerar-se** *vp* to form.

gerência [ʒe'rẽsja] *f* management.

gerente [ʒe'rẽtʃi] *mf* manager *(f* manageress).

gerir [ʒe'ri(x)] *vt* to manage.

germe ['ʒɛxmi] *m* germ.

gesso ['ʒesu] *m (MED)* plaster cast.

gesticular [ʒeʃtʃiku'la(x)] *vi* to gesticulate.

gesto ['ʒɛʃtu] *m* gesture.

gibi [ʒi'bi] *m (Br: revista)* comic.

gigante [ʒi'gãtʃi] *adj & m* giant.

gilete [ʒi'lɛte] *f (Port)* razor.

gim ['ʒĩ] *(pl* **-ns** [-ʃ]*) m* gin; **um ~ tônico** a gin and tonic.

ginásio [ʒi'nazju] *m* gym.

ginasta [ʒi'naʃta] *mf* gymnast.

ginástica [ʒi'naʃtʃika] *f* gymnastics *(sg)*; **fazer ~** to exercise.

gincana [ʒĩ'kana] *f fun obstacle race or rally held during local festivals.*

ginecologia [ʒinekolo'ʒia] *f* gynaecology.

ginecologista [ʒinekulu'ʒiʃta] *mf* gynaecologist.

ginja ['ʒĩʒa] *f* morello cherry.

gins → **gim**.

gira-discos [ʒira'diʃkuʃ] *m inv (Port)* record player.

girafa [ʒi'rafa] *f* giraffe.

girar [ʒi'ra(x)] *vi & vt* to turn.

girassol [ʒira'sɔw] *(pl* **-óis** [-ɔjʃ]*) m* sunflower.

gíria ['ʒirja] *f (calão)* slang; *(médica, académica)* jargon.

giro, -ra ['ʒiru, -ra] *adj (Port: fam: bonito)* good-looking ♦ *m (passeio)* stroll; *(de polícia)* beat; *(de vigilante)* rounds *(pl)*; **dar um ~** to go for a stroll.

giz ['ʒiʒ] *m* chalk.

glacial [gla'sjaw] *(pl* **-ais** [-ajʃ]*) adj (frio)* freezing; *(área)* glacial; *(fig: olhar, ambiente)* frosty.

gladíolo [gla'dʒiolu] *m* gladiolus.

glândula ['glãdula] *f* gland.

glaucoma [glaw'koma] *m* glaucoma.

glicerina [glise'rina] *f* glycerine.

global [glo'baw] *(pl* **-ais** [-ajʃ]*) adj* global.

globo ['globu] *m* globe; *(de lâmpada)* lampshade.

glóbulo ['glɔbulu] *m* corpuscle.

glória ['glɔrja] *f* glory.

glossário [glo'sarju] *m* glossary.

glutão, -tona [glu'tãw, -tona] *(mpl* **-ões** [-õjʃ]*, fpl* **-s** [-ʃ]*) m, f* glutton.

Goa ['goa] *s* Goa.

goela ['gwɛla] *f* gullet.

goiaba [go'jaba] *f* guava.

goiabada [goja'bada] f guava jelly.

gol ['gow] (pl **goles** ['goliʃ]) m (Br) goal.

gola ['gɔla] f collar.

gole ['gɔli] m (pequeno) sip; (grande) swig.

goleiro [go'leiru] m (Br) goalkeeper.

goles → **gol**.

golfe ['gowfi] m golf.

golfinho [gow'fiɲu] m dolphin.

golfo ['gowfu] m gulf.

golo ['golu] m (Port) = **gol**.

golpe ['gɔwpi] m cut; (pancada, choque) blow; ~ **de Estado** coup (d'état); ~ **de mestre** masterstroke.

goma ['goma] f starch.

gomo ['gomu] m segment.

gôndola ['gõndula] f gondola.

gongo ['gõŋgu] m gong.

gordo, -da ['gordu, -da] adj (pessoa, animal) fat; (leite) full-fat; (alimento) fatty; (substância) oily.

gordura [gox'dura] f (substância) fat.

gorduroso, -osa [goxdu'rozu, -ɔza] adj greasy.

gorila [go'rila] m gorilla.

gorjeta [gox'ʒeta] f tip.

gorro ['goxu] m woolly hat.

gostar [guʃ'ta(x)] : **gostar de** v + prep to like; ~ **de fazer algo** to like doing sthg.

gosto ['goʃtu] m taste; **com todo o** ~! with pleasure!; **dá** ~ **ver** it's a joy to behold; **faço** ~ **em** ... it gives me great pleasure to ...; **ter** ~ **de** (Br: saber a) to taste like; **tomar o** ~ **a algo** to take a liking to sthg; **bom/mau** ~ good/bad taste; ~ **não se discute** there's no accounting for taste.

gota ['gota] f (pingo) drop; (MED) gout; ~ **a** ~ drop by drop.

goteira [go'tejra] f (cano) gutter; (fenda) leak.

gotejar [gote'ʒa(x)] vi to drip.

governo [go'vexnu] m government; ~ **civil** = local government office.

gozar [go'za(x)] vt to enjoy ◆ vi (fam: brincar) to joke; ~ **com** (fam: troçar de) to make fun of; ~ **de** (desfrutar de) to enjoy.

gr. (abrev de grama) g.

Grã-Bretanha [grãmbre'taɲa] f: **a** ~ Great Britain.

graça ['grasa] f (gracejo) joke; (humor) humour; (elegância) grace; (atração) charm; **achar** ~ **em alguém/algo** to find sb/sthg amusing; **ter** ~ to be funny; ~**s a** thanks to; **de** ~ free (of charge);

sem ~ (desconcertado) embarrassed.

gracejar [grase'ʒa(x)] vi to joke.

gracejo [gra'seʒu] m (piada) joke; (galanteio) flirtatious remark.

gracioso, -osa [gra'sjozu, -ɔza] adj graceful.

grade ['gradʒi] f (vedação) bars (pl); (Port: de cerveja, Coca-Cola®) crate. ⅃ **grades** fpl (fam: cadeia) jail; **estar atrás das** ~**s** to be behind bars.

graduação [gradwa'sãw] (pl -**ões** [-õjʃ]) f graduation; (de bebida) alcohol content.

graduado, -da [gra'dwadu, -da] adj graduated ◆ m, f graduate.

gradual [gra'dwaw] (pl -**ais** [-ajʃ]) adj gradual.

graduar-se [gra'dwaxsi] vp to graduate.

grafia [gra'fia] f (maneira de escrever) handwriting; (ortografia) spelling.

gráfico ['grafiku] m graph.

gralha ['graʎa] f (ave) magpie; (erro tipográfico) typo.

grama¹ ['grama] m gram.

grama² ['grama] f (Br: relva) grass.

gramado [gra'madu] m (Br) (terreno) lawn; (de campo de futebol) pitch.

gramar [gra'ma(x)] vt (Port: fam: gostar de) to like; (fam: aguentar) to stand.

gramática [gra'matʃika] f grammar.

gramofone [gramo'fɔni] m gramophone.

grampeador [grãmpja'dox] (pl -**res** [-riʃ]) m (Br) stapler.

grampear [grãm'pja(x)] vt (Br) (folhas, papéis) to staple; (telefone) to tap.

grampo ['grãmpu] m (Br) (de cabelo) hairgrip (Brit), bobby pin (Am); (para grampeador) staple; (em ligação telefônica) tap.

granada [gra'nada] f grenade.

grande ['grãndʒi] adj big; (em altura) tall; (em comprimento) long; (em importância) great; (em gravidade) serious; ~ **penalidade** (em futebol) penalty.

granito [gra'nitu] m granite.

granizo [gra'nizu] m hailstones (pl), hail.

granulado, -da [granu'ladu, -da] adj granulated.

grão ['grãw] m grain; (de café) bean; (grão-de-bico) chickpeas (pl).

grão-de-bico [grãwdʒi'biku] m chickpeas (pl).

grasnar [graʒ'na(x)] vi (corvo) to caw;

(pato) to quack; *(ganso)* to honk.

gratidão [grat∫i'dãw] *f* gratitude.

gratificação [grat∫ifika'sãw] *(pl -ões* [-õj∫]) *f (gorjeta)* tip; *(remuneração)* payment.

gratificante [grat∫ifi'kãnt∫i] *adj* gratifying.

gratificar [grat∫ifi'ka(x)] *vt (dar gorjeta a)* to tip; *(recompensar)* to reward.

gratinado, -da [grat∫i'nadu, -da] *adj* au gratin.

gratinar [grat∫i'na(x)] *vi:* **pôr algo para ~** to cook sthg au gratin.

grátis ['grat∫i∫] *adv & adj inv* free.

grato, -ta ['gratu, -ta] *adj* grateful.

grau ['graw] *m* degree; **~s centigrados** degrees centigrade; **primeiro/segundo ~** *(Br)* primary/secondary school.

gravação [grava'sãw] *(pl -ões* [-õj∫]) *f* recording.

gravador [grava'do(x)] *(pl -res* [-ri∫]) *m* tape recorder.

gravar [gra'va(x)] *vt (música, conversa)* to record; *(em metal, jóia)* to engrave.

gravata [gra'vata] *f* tie.

grave ['gravi] *adj (sério)* serious; *(voz)* deep; *(tom)* low; *(GRAM: acento)* grave.

grávida ['gravida] *adj f* pregnant.

gravidade [gravi'dadʒi] *f* gravity.

gravidez [gravi'deʒ] *f* pregnancy.

gravura [gra'vura] *f (imagem)* picture.

graxa ['gra∫a] *f* shoe polish.

Grécia ['grɛsja] *f:* **a ~** Greece.

grego, -ga ['gregu, -ga] *adj & m, f* Greek ♦ *m (língua)* Greek.

grelha ['greʎa] *f* grill; **bife na ~** grilled steak.

grelhado, -da [gre'ʎadu, -da] *adj* grilled ♦ *m* grilled dish; **~ misto** mixed grill.

grelhador [greʎa'do(x)] *(pl -res* [-ri∫]) *m* barbecue; *(de fogão)* grill.

grelhar [gre'ʎa(x)] *vt* to grill.

grená [gre'na] *adj* dark red.

greta ['greta] *f* crack.

gretado, -da [gre'tadu, -da] *adj* chapped, cracked.

greve ['grɛvi] *f* strike; **fazer ~** to go on strike; **em ~** on strike; **~ de fome** hunger strike.

grilo ['grilu] *m* cricket.

grinalda [gri'nawda] *f (em funeral)* wreath; *(para cabelo)* garland.

gripe ['gripi] *f* flu; **estar com ~** to have the flu.

grisalho, -lha [gri'zaʎu, -ʎa] *adj* grey.

gritar [gri'ta(x)] *vi & vt* to shout; **~ com alguém** to shout at sb.

grito ['gritu] *m* shout; **de ~s** *(Port: fam: hilariante)* hilarious.

groselha [gro'zeʎa] *f* redcurrant.

grosseiro, -ra [gro'sejru, -ra] *adj* crude; *(tecido)* coarse.

grosso, grossa ['grosu, 'grɔsa] *adj* thick; *(Br: mal educado)* rude; *(voz)* deep; *(Port: fam: embriagado)* sloshed.

grotesco, -ca [gro'te∫ku, -ka] *adj* grotesque.

grua ['grua] *f* crane.

grunhido [gru'ɲidu] *m* grunt.

grunhir [gru'ɲi(x)] *vi* to grunt.

grupo ['grupu] *m* group; **em ~** as a group; **~ de risco** risk group; **~ sanguíneo** blood group.

gruta ['gruta] *f* cave.

guache ['gwa∫i] *m* gouache.

guaraná [gwara'na] *m fizzy drink made from guarana seeds;* **~ em pó** powdered guarana seeds.

guarda ['gwaxda] *mf (polícia)* policeman *(f* policewoman*)* ♦ *f (vigilância)* guard.

guarda-chuva [.gwaxda'∫uva] *(pl* **guarda-chuvas** [.gwarda'∫uva∫]) *m* umbrella.

guarda-costas [.gwaxda'kɔ∫ta∫] *mf inv* bodyguard.

guarda-fatos [.gwarda'fatu∫] *m inv (Port)* wardrobe.

guarda-fiscal [.gwardafi∫'kal] *(pl* **guardas-fiscais** [.gwarda∫fi∫'kaj∫]) *mf (Port)* customs and excise officer.

guarda-florestal [.gwaxdaflore∫'taw] *(pl* **guardas-florestais** [.gwaxda∫flore∫'taj∫]) *mf* forest ranger.

guarda-jóias [.gwarda'ʒɔja∫] *m inv (Port)* jewellery box.

guarda-lamas [.gwarda'lama∫] *m inv (Port)* mudguard.

guarda-louça [.gwarda'losa] *(pl* **guarda-louças** [.gwarda'losa∫]) *m* cupboard.

guardanapo [gwaxda'napu] *m* napkin; **~s de papel** paper napkins.

guarda-noturno [.gwaxdano'tuxnu] *(pl* **guardas-noturnos** [.gwaxdaʒno'tuxnu∫]) *m* night-watchman.

guardar [gwax'da(x)] *vt (vigiar)* to look after; *(arrecadar)* to put away; *(reservar)* to keep.

guarda-redes [ˌgwarda'xedeʃ] *m inv* (Port) goalkeeper.

guarda-roupa [ˌgwaxda'xopa] (*pl* **guarda-roupas** [ˌgwaxda'xopaʃ]) *m* wardrobe.

guarda-sol [gwaxda'sɔw] (*pl* **guarda-sóis** [ˌgwaxda'sɔjʃ]) *m* parasol.

guarda-vassouras [ˌgwardava'soraʃ] *m inv* (Port) skirting board (Brit), base-board (Am).

guarda-vestidos [ˌgwardaveʃ'tiduʃ] *m inv* (Port) wardrobe.

guarnecido, -da [gwaxne'sidu, -da] *adj:* ~ com garnished with.

guarnição [gwaxni'sãw] (*pl* -ões [-õjʃ]) *f* garnish.

Guatemala [gwate'mala] *f:* a ~ Guatemala.

gude [ˈgudʒi] *m* (Br) marbles (sg).

guelra [ˈgɛwxa] *f* gill.

guerra [ˈgɛxa] *f* war; **fazer ~ a** to wage war against OU on; **estar em pé de ~** to be at war.

guia [gia] *mf* (profissão) guide ◆ *m* (livro, folheto) guide; **~ intérprete** tour guide (fluent in foreign languages); **~ turístico** tourist guide.

guiador [gja'dor] (*pl* **-res** [-reʃ]) *m* (Port) = **guidom**.

guiar [ˈgja(x)] *vt* to guide; (automóvel, ônibus) to drive ◆ *vi* (dirigir) to drive.

guiché [giˈʃe] *m* (Port) = **guichê**.

guichê [giˈʃe] *m* (Br) counter.

guidom [giˈdõ] (*pl* **-ns** [-ʃ]) *m* (Br) (de automóvel) steering wheel; (de bicicleta) handlebars (pl).

guilhotina [giʎo'tʃina] *f* guillotine.

guincho [ˈgĩʃu] *m* (som) squeal; (máquina) winch.

guindaste [gĩ'daʃtʃi] *m* crane.

Guiné-Bissau [giˌnɛbi'saw] *f:* a ~ Guinea-Bissau.

guineense [giˈnjẽsi] *adj & mf* Guinean.

guisado, -da [giˈzadu, -da] *adj* stewed ◆ *m* stew.

guisar [giˈza(x)] *vt* (CULIN) to stew.

guitarra [giˈtaxa] *f* guitar.

guitarrista [gitaˈxiʃta] *mf* guitarist.

guizo [ˈgizu] *m* bell.

gula [ˈgula] *f* gluttony.

guloseima [guloˈzejma] *f* sweet (Brit), candy (Am).

guloso, -osa [guˈlozu, -ɔza] *adj* greedy ◆ *m, f* glutton; **ser ~** to have a sweet tooth.

gume [ˈgumi] *m* (cutting) edge.

guri, -ria [guˈri, -'ria] *m, f* (Br) kid.

H

h. *(abrev de hora)* h, hr.

há [a] → **haver**.

hábil ['abiw] *(pl* **-beis** [-bejʃ]*) adj (capaz)* skilful; *(astuto)* clever.

habilidade [abili'dadʒi] *f (capacidade)* ability; *(argúcia)* cleverness; *(talento)* skill.

❏ **habilidades** *fpl (malabarismos)* juggling *(sg).*

habilitação [abilita'sãw] *f* competence.

❏ **habilitações** *fpl* qualifications.

habitação [abita'sãw] *(pl* **-ões** [-õjʃ]*) f* residence.

habitante [abi'tãntʃi] *mf (de bairro)* resident; *(de país, região)* inhabitant.

habitar [abi'ta(x)] *vt* to live in ◆ *vi* to live; ~ **em** to live in.

hábito ['abitu] *m* habit; **como é ~ as** usual; **ter o ~ de fazer algo** to have a habit of doing sthg; **por ~ as** a rule.

habitual [abi'twaw] *(pl* **-ais** [-ajʃ]*) adj (rotineiro)* regular; *(freqüente)* common.

habitualmente [abitwaw'mẽntʃi] *adv* usually.

habituar [abi'twa(x)] *vt*: ~ **alguém a algo/a fazer algo** to accustom sb to sthg/to doing sthg.

❏ **habituar-se** *vp*: **~-se a** to get used to.

hálito ['alitu] *m* breath; **mau ~** bad breath.

hall [ɔw] *m (de casa)* hall; *(de teatro, hotel)* foyer; ~ **(da entrada)** (entrance) hall.

haltere [aw'tɛri] *m* dumbbell.

halterofilia [awtɛrofi'lia] *f* weightlifting.

hambúrguer [ãm'buxgɛ(x)] *(pl* **-es** [-iʃ]*) m* hamburger.

hangar [ãŋ'ga(x)] *(pl* **-res** [-riʃ]*) m* hangar.

hardware [ax'dwɛri] *m* hardware.

harmonia [axmo'nia] *f* harmony.

harmónica [ar'mɔnika] *f (Port)* = **harmônica**.

harmônica [ax'monika] *f (Br)* harmonica.

harpa ['axpa] *f* harp.

haste ['aʃtʃi] *f (de bandeira)* pole; *(de árvore)* branch.

haver [a'vɛ(x)] *v impess* **1.** *(existir, estar, ter lugar)*: **há** there is, there are *(pl);* **há um café muito bom ao fim da rua** there's a very good cafe at the end of the street; **não há nada aqui** there's nothing here; **não há correio amanhã** there's no post tomorrow.

2. *(exprime tempo)*: **estou esperando há dez minutos** I've been waiting for ten minutes; **há séculos que não vou lá** I haven't been there for ages; **há três dias que não o vejo** I haven't seen him for three days.

3. *(exprime obrigação)*: **há que esperar três dias** you'll have to wait for three days.

4. *(em locuções)*: **haja o que houver** come what may; **não há de quê!** don't mention it!

◆ *v aux (em tempos compostos)* to have; **ele havia chegado há pouco** he had just arrived; **como não havia comido estava com fome** I was hungry as I hadn't eaten; **havíamos reservado com antecedência** we'd booked in advance.

❏ **haver de** *v + prep (dever)* to have; *(exprime intenção)*: **hei-de conseguir** *(Port)* I'll make it; **hei de ir** *(Br)* I'll go.

❏ **haver-se com** *vp + prep*: **~-se com alguém** *(prestar contas a)* to answer to sb.

❏ **haveres** *mpl (pertences)* belongings; *(bens)* assets.

haxixe [a'ʃiʃi] *m* hashish.

hectare [ɛk'tari] *m* hectare.
hélice ['ɛlisi] *f* propeller.
helicóptero [eli'kɔpteru] *m* helicopter.
hélio ['ɛlju] *m* helium.
hematoma [ema'toma] *m* large bruise.
hemofílico, -ca [emo'filiku, -ka] *m, f* hemophiliac.
hemorragia [emoxa'ʒia] *f* hemorrhage; ~ **cerebral** brain hemorrhage; ~ **nasal** nosebleed.
hemorróidas [emo'xɔidaʃ] *fpl* piles, hemorrhoids.
hepatite [epa'tʃitʃi] *f* hepatitis.
hera ['ɛra] *f* ivy.
herança [e'rãsa] *f* inheritance.
herbicida [ɛxbi'sida] *m* herbicide.
herdar [ex'da(x)] *vt* to inherit.
herdeiro, -ra [ex'dejru, -ra] *m, f* heir (*f* heiress).
hermético, -ca [ex'mɛtʃiku, -ka] *adj* airtight.
hérnia ['ɛxnja] *f* hernia.
herói [e'rɔi] *m* hero.
heroína [e'rwina] *f* (*pessoa*) heroine; (*estupefaciente*) heroin.
hesitação [ezita'sãw] (*pl* **-ões** [-õjʃ]) *f* hesitation.
hesitar [ezi'ta(x)] *vi* to hesitate.
heterossexual [eterosɛk'swaw] (*pl* **-ais** [-ajʃ]) *adj & mf* heterosexual.
hibernar [ibex'na(x)] *vi* to hibernate.
híbrido, -da ['ibridu, -da] *adj* hybrid.
hidratante [idra'tãtʃi] *adj* moisturizing.
hidroavião [idroa'vjãw] (*pl* **-ões** [-õjʃ]) *m* seaplane.
hidrófilo [i'drɔfilu] *adj m* → **algodão**.
hidrogénio [idrɔ'ʒenju] *m* (*Port*) = **hidrogênio**.
hidrogênio [idro'ʒenju] *m* (*Br*) hydrogen.
hierarquia [jerar'kia] *f* hierarchy.
hífen ['ifɛn] (*pl* **-es** [-iʃ]) *m* hyphen.
hifenização [ifeniza'sãw] *f* hyphenation.
hi-fi [aj'faj] *m* hi-fi.
higiene [i'ʒjeni] *f* hygiene.
hilariante [ila'rjãtʃi] *adj* hilarious.
hino ['inu] *m* (*de país*) anthem; (*de igreja*) hymn.
hipermercado [.ipɛxmɛx'kadu] *m* hypermarket.
hipertensão [.ipɛxtẽ'sãw] *f* high blood pressure.

hípico, -ca ['ipiku, -ka] *adj* (*centro*) riding (*antes de s*); (*concurso*) show-jumping (*antes de s*).
hipismo [i'piʒmu] *m* (*equitação*) horse riding; (*competição*) show jumping.
hipnotismo [ipnɔt'siʒmu] *m* hypnotism.
hipocondríaco, -ca [.ipokõn'driaku, -ka] *m, f* hypochondriac.
hipocrisia [ipokre'zia] *f* hypocrisy.
hipócrita [i'pɔkrita] *mf* hypocrite.
hipódromo [i'pɔdrumu] *m* racecourse.
hipopótamo [ipo'pɔtamu] *m* hippopotamus.
hipoteca [ipo'tɛka] *f* mortgage.
hipótese [i'pɔtezi] *f* (*suposição*) hypothesis; (*possibilidade*) chance; **em ~ alguma** on no account; **na melhor das ~s** at best; **na pior das ~s** at worst.
histeria [iʃte'ria] *f* hysteria.
histérico, -ca [iʃ'tɛriku, -ka] *adj* hysterical.
história [iʃ'tɔrja] *f* (*de país, mundo, época*) history; (*narrativa*) story; ~ **da Arte** history of art; ~ **da carochinha** fairy tale; ~**s em quadrinhos** comic strips.
hobby ['ɔbi] (*pl* **hobbies** ['ɔbiʃ]) *m* hobby.
hoje ['oʒi] *adv* today; ~ **em dia** nowadays; **queria o jornal de** ~ I would like today's paper; **na melhor das** ~ a oito/quinze dias a week/a fortnight today; **de** ~ **em diante** from now on; **por** ~ **é só** that's all for today.
Holanda [o'lãnda] *f*: **a** ~ Holland.
holandês, -esa [olãn'deʃ, -eza] (*mpl* **-eses** [-eziʃ], *fpl* **-s** [-ʃ]) *adj* Dutch ◆ *m, f* Dutchman (*f* Dutchwoman); **os holandeses** the Dutch.
holofote [olo'fɔtʃi] *m* floodlight.
homem ['ɔmẽ] (*pl* **-ns** [-ʃ]) *m* man; **"homens"** "gentlemen."
homenagear [omena'ʒja(x)] *vt* to pay tribute to.
homenagem [ome'naʒẽ] (*pl* **-ns** [-ʃ]) *f* tribute.
homens → **homem**.
homicida [omi'sida] *mf* murderer.
homicídio [omi'sidʒju] *m* murder; ~ **involuntário** manslaughter.
homossexual [omosɛk'swaw] (*pl* **-ais** [-ajʃ]) *mf* homosexual.
honestidade [oneʃtʃi'dadʒi] *f* honesty.

honesto, -ta [o'nɛʃtu, -ta] *adj* honest.

honorário [ono'rarju] *adj* honorary.
⊔ **honorários** *mpl* fees.

honra ['õxa] *f* honour; **ter a ~ de fazer algo** to have the honour of doing sthg; **em ~ de** in honour of.

honrado, -da [õ'xadu, -da] *adj* honest.

honrar [õ'xa(x)] *vt (dívida)* to honour.
⊔ **honrar-se de** *vp + prep* to be proud of.

honroso, -osa [õ'xozu, -ɔza] *adj* honourable.

hóquei [ˈɔkej] *m (ESP)* hockey *(Brit)*, field hockey *(Am)*; **~ sobre gelo** ice hockey; **~ em patins** roller hockey.

hora [ˈɔra] *f (período de tempo)* hour; *(momento determinado)* time; **que ~s são?** what time is it?; **são cinco ~s** it's five o'clock; **a que ~s é ...?** what time is ...?; **é ~ de partir** it's time to leave; **esta na ~ do almoço** it's time for lunch; **na ~ H** in the nick of time; **~ de ponta** *(Port)* rush hour; **~s extraordinárias** overtime *(sg)*; **~s vagas** free OU spare time *(sg)*; **de ~ em ~** every hour; **na ~ on** time; **~s e ~s for hours; chegar a ~s** to arrive on time; **chegar em cima da ~** to arrive just in time; **à última ~** at the last minute.

horário [oˈrarju] *m (de trem, ônibus, escola)* timetable; *(de estabelecimento)* opening hours *(pl)*; **~ de atendimento** OU **funcionamento** opening hours *(pl)*; **~ nobre** prime time.

horizontal [orizõˈtaw] *(pl* **-ais** [-ajʃ]*) adj* horizontal.

horizonte [oriˈzõtʃi] *m* horizon.

horóscopo [oˈrɔʃkopu] *m* horoscope, stars *(pl)*.

horrendo, -da [oˈxẽdu, -da] *adj (feio)* hideous; *(chocante)* horrific.

horripilante [oxipiˈlãtʃi] *adj* horrifying.

horrível [oˈxivɛw] *(pl* **-eis** [-ejʃ]*) adj* horrible.

horror [oˈxo(x)] *(pl* **-res** [-riʃ]*) m* horror; **que ~!** how awful!; **ter ~ a algo** to have a horror of sthg; **um ~ de** *(fam)* a vast number of; **dizer ~es de alguém** to say horrible things about sb.

horta [ˈɔxta] *f* vegetable garden.

hortaliça [oxtaˈlisa] *f* greens *(pl)*.

hortelã [oxteˈlã] *f* mint.

hortelã-pimenta [oxteˌlãpiˈmẽta] *f* peppermint.

hortênsia [oxˈtẽsja] *f* hydrangea.

horticultor, -ra [oxtʃikuwˈto(x), -ra] *(mpl* **-res** [-riʃ]*, fpl* **-s** [-ʃ]*) m, f* market gardener *(Brit)*, truck farmer *(Am)*.

hortigranjeiros [oxtʃigrãˈʒeiruʃ] *mpl (Br)* vegetables.

hospedagem [oʃpeˈdaʒẽ] *f* accommodation.

hospedar [oʃpeˈda(x)] *vt* to put up.
⊔ **hospedar-se** *vp*: **~-se em** to stay at.

hóspede [ˈɔʃpedʒi] *mf* guest.

hospedeira [oʃpeˈdeira] *f (Port)*: **~ (de bordo)** air hostess.

hospício [oʃˈpisju] *m* home.

hospital [oʃpiˈtaw] *(pl* **-ais** [-ajʃ]*) m* hospital.

hospitaleiro, -ra [oʃpitaˈlejru, -ra] *adj* hospitable.

hospitalidade [oʃpitaliˈdadʒi] *f* hospitality.

hostil [oʃˈtiw] *(pl* **-is** [-iʃ]*) adj (gente, ar, comportamento)* hostile; *(vento, frio)* biting.

hotel [oˈtɛw] *(pl* **-éis** [-ɛiʃ]*) m* hotel.

houve [ˈovi] → **haver**.

hovercraft [ˌovɛxˈkraft] *m* hovercraft.

humanidade [umaniˈdadʒi] *f* humanity.
⊔ **humanidades** *fpl* humanities.

humanitário, -ria [umaniˈtarju, -rja] *adj* humanitarian.

humano, -na [uˈmanu, -na] *adj* human; *(compassivo)* humane ◆ *m* human (being).

humidade [umiˈdadʃe] *f (Port)* = **umidade.**

húmido, -da [ˈumidu, -da] *adj (Port)* = **úmido.**

humildade [umiwˈdadʒi] *f* humility.

humilde [uˈmiwdʒi] *adj (pobre)* poor; *(modesto)* humble.

humilhação [umiʎaˈsãw] *(pl* **-ões** [-õjʃ]*) f* humiliation.

humilhante [umiˈʎãtʃi] *adj* humiliating.

humilhar [umiˈʎa(x)] *vt* to humiliate.
⊔ **humilhar-se** *vp* to humble o.s.

humor [uˈmo(x)] *m* humour; **estar de bom/mau ~** to be in a good/bad mood.

humorista [umoˈriʃta] *mf* comedian *(f* comedienne*)*.

húngaro, -ra [ˈũgaru, -ra] *adj & m, f* Hungarian ◆ *m (língua)* Hungarian.

Hungria [ũˈgria] *f*: **a ~** Hungary.

hurra [ˈuxa] *interj* hurrah!

I

ia ['ia] → **ir**.

iate ['jatʃi] *m* yacht.

ibérico, -ca [i'bɛriku, -ka] *adj* Iberian.

ibero-americano, -na [i,bɛrwa-meri'kanu, -na] *adj & m, f* Latin American.

içar [i'sa(x)] *vt* to hoist.

ICM/S *m* (*Br: abrev de Imposto sobre a circulação de Mercadorias e Serviços*) = VAT (*Brit*), = sales tax (*Am*).

ícone ['ikɔni] *m* icon.

icterícia [ikte'risja] *f* jaundice.

ida ['ida] *f* (*partida*) departure; (*jornada*) outward journey.

idade [i'dadʒi] *f* age; **de ~** elderly; **de meia ~** middle-aged; **oito anos de ~** eight years of age.

ideal [i'dʒjaw] (*pl* **-ais** [-ajʃ]) *adj & m* ideal.

idealista [idʒja'liʃta] *adj* idealistic ◆ *mf* idealist.

ideia [i'daja] *f* (*Port*) = **idéia**.

idéia [i'dʒɛja] *f* (*Br*) idea; **que ~!** you must be joking!; **mudar de ~** to change one's mind; **não fazer ~** not to have a clue.

idêntico, -ca [i'dʒẽntʃiku, -ka] *adj* identical.

identidade [idʒẽntʃi'dadʒi] *f* identity.

identificação [idʒẽntʃifika'sãw] *f* identification.

identificar [idʒẽntʃifi'ka(x)] *vt* to identify.

❏ **identificar-se** *vp* to identify o.s.

ideologia [idʒjolo'ʒia] *f* ideology.

idílico, -ca [i'dʒiliku, -ka] *adj* idyllic.

idioma [i'dʒjoma] *m* language.

idiota [i'dʒjɔta] *adj* idiotic ◆ *mf* idiot.

ídolo ['idulu] *m* idol.

idóneo, -nea [i'dɔnju, -nja] *adj* (*Port*) = **idôneo**.

idôneo, -nea [i'dɔnju, -nja] *adj* (*Br*) reliable.

idoso, -osa [i'dozu, -ɔza] *adj* elderly ◆ *m, f* old man (*f* old woman); **os ~s** the elderly.

Iemanjá [jemã'ʒa] *f* goddess of the sea in Afro-Brazilian religion.

igarapé [igara'pɛ] *m* (*Br*) narrow river.

ignição [igni'sãw] *f* ignition.

ignorado, -da [igno'radu, -da] *adj* unknown.

ignorância [igno'rãsja] *f* ignorance.

ignorante [igno'rãntʃi] *mf* ignoramus.

ignorar [igno'ra(x)] *vt*: **~ algo** not to know sthg; **~ alguém** to ignore sb.

igreja [i'greʒa] *f* church.

igual [i'gwaw] (*pl* **-ais** [-ajʃ]) *adj* the same; (*parecido*) similar ◆ *m* (*pessoa*) equal; (*sinal*) equals sign; **os dois são iguais** they are (both) the same; **ser ~ a** to be the same as; **12 e 12 ~ a 24** 12 and 12 equals OU is 24; **sem ~** unrivalled.

igualar [igwa'la(x)] *vt* to make equal.

❏ **igualar-se** *vp*: **~-se a alguém** to be sb's equal; **~-se a algo** to be comparable with sthg.

igualdade [igwaw'dadʒi] *f* equality.

igualmente [igwaw'mẽntʃi] *adv* equally ◆ *interj* likewise!

ilegal [ile'gaw] (*pl* **-ais** [-ajʃ]) *adj* illegal.

ilegalidade [ilegali'dadʒi] *f* crime.

ilegítimo, -ma [ile'ʒitʃimu, -ma] *adj* (*filho*) illegitimate; (*ato*) illegal.

ilegível [ile'ʒivɛw] (*pl* **-eis** [-ejʃ]) *adj* illegible.

ileso, -sa [i'lezu, -za] *adj* unharmed.

ilha ['iʎa] *f* island.

ilícito, -ta [i'lisitu, -ta] *adj* illicit.

ilimitado, -da [ilemi'tadu, -da] *adj* unlimited.

Ilma. *abrev =* **Ilustríssima.**

Ilmo. *abrev =* **Ilustríssimo.**

ilógico, -ca [i'lɔʒiku, -ka] *adj* illogical.

iludir [ilu'di(x)] *vt* to deceive.

⊃ **iludir-se** *vp* to delude o.s.

iluminação [ilumina'sãw] *f* lighting.

iluminado, -da [ilumi'nadu, -da] *adj* illuminated, lit up.

iluminar [ilumi'na(x)] *vt* to illuminate, to light up.

ilusão [ilu'zãw] (*pl* **-ões** [-õjʃ]) *f* illusion; **não ter ilusões** to have no illusions; **perder as ilusões** to become disillusioned; ~ **ótica** optical illusion.

ilustração [iluʃtra'sãw] (*pl* **-ões** [-õjʃ]) *f* illustration.

ilustrado, -da [iluʃ'tradu, -da] *adj* illustrated.

ilustrar [iluʃ'tra(x)] *vt* (*exemplificar*) to illustrate.

ilustre [i'luʃtri] *adj* illustrious.

ilustríssimo, -ma [iluʃ'trisimu, -ma] *superl* (*em carta*) *very formal term of address used in correspondence.*

imã [i'mã] *m* (*Br*) magnet.

imaculado, -da [imaku'ladu, -da] *adj* immaculate.

imagem [i'maʒẽ] (*pl* **-ns** [-ʃ]) *f* picture; (*pessoal*) image.

imaginação [imaʒina'sãw] *f* imagination.

imaginar [imaʒi'na(x)] *vt* (*inventar*) to think up; (*supor*) to imagine.

⊃ **imaginar-se** *vp*: **ele se imagina um Adônis** he thinks he's God's gift to women.

imaginativo, -va [imaʒina'tʃivu, -va] *adj* imaginative.

íman [i'man] (*pl* **-es** [-cʃ]) *m* (*Port*) = **imã.**

imaturo, -ra [ima'turu, -ra] *adj* immature.

imbatível [ĩmba'tʃivεw] (*pl* **-eis** [-cjʃ]) *adj* unbeatable.

imbecil [ĩmbe'siw] (*pl* **-is** [-iʃ]) *adj* stupid ◆ *mf* idiot.

imediações [imedʒja'sõjʃ] *fpl* surrounding area (*sg*); **nas** ~ **de** in the vicinity of.

imediatamente [imedʒjata'mẽtʃi] *adv* immediately.

imediato, -ta [ime'dʒjatu, -ta] *adj* immediate; **de** ~ immediately.

imenso, -sa [i'mẽsu, -sa] *adj* huge ◆ *adv* a lot; **está um calor** ~ it's boiling (hot); **está um frio** ~ it's freezing (cold).

imergir [imεx'ʒi(x)] *vt* (*mergulhar*) to immerse.

imigração [imigra'sãw] *f* immigration.

imigrante [imi'grãtʃi] *mf* immigrant.

imigrar [imi'gra(x)] *vi* to immigrate.

iminente [imi'nẽtʃi] *adj* imminent.

imitação [imita'sãw] (*pl* **-ões** [-õjʃ]) *f* (*de produto*) imitation; (*de pessoa*) impersonation.

imitar [imi'ta(x)] *vt* (*produto*) to copy; (*comportamento*) to imitate; (*pessoa*) to impersonate.

imobiliária [imobi'ljarja] *f* estate agent's (*Brit*), realtor's (*Am*).

imobilizar [imobili'za(x)] *vt* to immobilize.

⊃ **imobilizar-se** *vp* to come to a standstill.

imoral [imo'raw] (*pl* **-ais** [-ajʃ]) *adj* immoral.

imóvel [i'mɔvεw] (*pl* **-eis** [-cjʃ]) *adj* motionless ◆ *m* (*prédio*) building; (*valor imóvel*) property.

impaciência [ĩmpa'sjẽsja] *f* impatience.

impaciente [ĩmpa'sjẽtʃi] *adj* impatient.

impacto [ĩm'paktu] *m* impact.

ímpar ['ĩmpa(x)] (*pl* **-res** [-riʃ]) *adj* (*número*) odd; (*objeto*) unique; (*ação*) unequalled.

imparcial [ĩmpax'sjaw] (*pl* **-ais** [-ajʃ]) *adj* impartial.

ímpares → **ímpar.**

impasse [ĩm'pasi] *m* impasse.

impecável [ĩmpe'kavεw] (*pl* **-eis** [-cjʃ]) *adj* (*trabalho, roupa, limpeza*) impeccable; (*fam: pessoa*) great.

impedido, -da [ĩmpe'dʒidu, -da] *adj* (*caminho, estrada*) blocked; (*linha*) engaged (*Brit*), busy (*Am*).

impedimento [ĩmpedʒi'mẽtu] *m* obstacle.

impedir [ĩmpe'dʒi(x)] *vt* (*trânsito, circulação*) to block; ~ **alguém de fazer algo** to prevent sb from doing sthg.

impelir [ĩmpe'li(x)] *vt* to push.

impenetrável [ĩmpene'travεw] (*pl* **-eis** [-cjʃ]) *adj* impenetrable.

impensável [ĩmpẽ'savεw] (*pl* **-eis** [-cjʃ]) *adj* unthinkable.

imperador [ĩmpera'do(x)] (*pl* **-res** [-riʃ]) *m* emperor.

imperativo, -va [ĩmpera'tʃivu, -va]

adj & m imperative.

imperatriz [ĩmpɛra'triʃ] *(pl* **-zes** [-zeʃ])* f* empress.

imperdoável [ĩmpex'dwavɛw] *(pl* **-eis** [-ejʃ])* adj* unforgivable.

imperfeição [ĩmpɛxfɛj'sãw] *(pl* **-ões** [-õjʃ])* f (defeito)* defect.

imperfeito, -ta [ĩmpɛx'fejtu, -ta] *adj* faulty ◆ *m (GRAM)* imperfect.

imperial [ĩmpɛ'rjaw] *(pl* **-ais** [-ajʃ])* f (Port: copo de cerveja) glass of draught beer.*

impermeável [ĩmpɛx'mjavɛw] *(pl* **-eis** [-ejʃ])* m* thin anorak ◆ *adj* waterproof.

impertinente [ĩmpɛxtʃi'nẽntʃi] *adj* impertinent.

imperturbável [ĩmpɛxtux'bavɛw] *(pl* **-eis** [-ejʃ])* adj* imperturbable.

impessoal [ĩmpɛ'swaw] *(pl* **-ais** [-ajʃ])* adj* impersonal.

impetuoso, -osa [ĩmpɛ'twozu, -ɔza] *adj* impetuous.

impiedade [ĩmpje'dadʒi] *f* irreverence.

implacável [ĩmpla'kavɛw] *(pl* **-eis** [-ejʃ])* adj* ruthless; *(vento, chuva, frio)* relentless.

implantação [ĩmplãnta'sãw] *f* introduction.

implementar [ĩmplɛmẽn'ta(x)] *vt* to implement.

implicar [ĩmpli'ka(x)] *vt (envolver)* to implicate; *(acarretar)* to involve.
❏ **implicar com** *v + prep* to have a go at.

implícito, -ta [ĩm'plisitu, -ta] *adj* implicit.

implorar [ĩmplo'ra(x)] *vt* to implore.

imponente [ĩmpo'nẽntʃi] *adj (grandioso)* imposing; *(altivo)* arrogant.

impopular [ĩmpopu'la(x)] *(pl* **-es** [-iʃ])* adj* unpopular.

impor [ĩm'po(x)] *vt (respeito, silêncio)* to command; *(ordem)* to impose; ~ **algo a alguém** to impose sthg on sb.
❏ **impor-se** *vp* to command respect.

importação [ĩmpoxta'sãw] *(pl* **-ões** [-õjʃ])* f* import.

importado, -da [ĩmpox'tadu, -da] *adj* imported.

importância [ĩmpox'tãsja] *f (valor)* importance; *(quantia monetária)* amount.

importante [ĩmpox'tãntʃi] *adj* important ◆ *m:* **o ~ é** ... the important thing is ....

importar [ĩmpox'ta(x)] *vt (mercadoria, produto, idéia)* to import ◆ *vi (ter importância)* to matter.
❏ **importar-se** *vp (fazer caso)* to mind; **você se importa de fechar a porta?** would you mind closing the door?

imposição [ĩmpozi'sãw] *(pl* **-ões** [-õjʃ])* f* condition.

impossibilitar [ĩmposibili'ta(x)] *vt* to prevent.

impossível [ĩmpo'sivɛw] *(pl* **-eis** [-ejʃ])* adj & m* impossible ◆ *m:* **querer o ~** to ask the impossible.

imposto [ĩm'poʃtu] *m* tax; **~ de renda** *(Br)* income tax; **~ sobre o rendimento** *(Port)* income tax; **~ sobre o valor acrescentado** *(Port)* value added tax *(Brit)*, sales tax *(Am)*.

impostor, -ra [ĩmpoʃ'to(x), -ra] *(mpl* **-res** [-riʃ]*, fpl* **-s** [-ʃ])* m, f* impostor.

impotente [ĩmpo'tẽntʃi] *adj* impotent.

impraticável [ĩmpratʃi'kavɛw] *(pl* **-eis** [-ejʃ])* adj (estrada, caminho)* impassable.

impreciso, -sa [ĩmpre'sizu, -za] *adj* vague.

impregnar [ĩmpreg'na(x)] *vt* to impregnate.
❏ **impregnar-se de** *vp + prep* to become impregnated with.

imprensa [ĩm'prẽsa] *f* press.

imprescindível [ĩmpreʃsĩn'dʒivɛw] *(pl* **-eis** [-ejʃ])* adj* indispensable.

impressão [ĩmpre'sãw] *(pl* **-ões** [-õjʃ])* f (sensação)* impression; *(de jornal, livro)* printing; **ter a ~ de que** to get the impression (that); **tenho a ~ que vai chover** I think it's going to rain; **~ digital** fingerprint; **causar boa ~** to make a good impression.

impressionante [ĩmpresju'nãntʃi] *adj (incrível)* amazing; *(comovente)* moving.

impressionar [ĩmpresju'na(x)] *vt (causar admiração a)* to amaze; *(comover)* to move.

impresso, -a [ĩm'prɛsu, -a] *adj* printed ◆ *m* form.

impressões → **impressão**.

impressora [ĩmpre'sora] *f* printer.

imprestável [ĩmpreʃ'tavɛw] *(pl* **-eis** [-ejʃ])* adj (não prestativo)* unhelpful; *(inútil)* useless.

imprevisível [ĩmprevi'zivɛw] *(pl* **-eis**

[-ejʃ]) *adj* unpredictable.

imprevisto, -ta [ĩmpreˈviʃtu, -ta] *adj* unexpected ♦ *m* unexpected event.

imprimir [ĩmpriˈmi(x)] *vt* to print.

impróprio, -pria [ĩmˈprɔpriu, -pria] *adj*: ~ **para** unsuitable for; ~ **para consumo** unfit for human consumption.

improvável [ĩmproˈvavɛw] (*pl* -eis [-ejʃ]) *adj* unlikely.

improvisar [ĩmproviˈza(x)] *vt & vi* to improvise.

improviso [ĩmproˈvizu] *m* improvisation; **de** ~ impromptu; **fazer um discurso de** ~ to make an impromptu speech.

imprudente [ĩmpruˈdẽntʃi] *adj* rash.

impulsionar [ĩmpuwsjuˈna(x)] *vt* to push forward.

impulsivo, -va [ĩmpuwˈsivu, -va] *adj* impulsive.

impulso [ĩmˈpuwsu] *m* (*incitamento*) impulse; (*de ligação telefônica*) unit.

impune [ĩmˈpuni] *adj* unpunished.

impureza [ĩmpuˈreza] *f* impurity.

impuro, -ra [ĩmˈpuru, -ra] *adj* impure.

imundície [imũnˈdʒisji] *f* (*sujeira*) dirt; (*lixo*) rubbish.

imune [iˈmuni] *adj* (*isento*): ~ **a** immune to.

inábil [iˈnabiw] (*pl* -beis [-bejʃ]) *adj* incompetent.

inabitado, -da [inabiˈtadu, -da] *adj* uninhabited.

inacabado, -da [inakaˈbadu, -da] *adj* unfinished.

inaceitável [inasejˈtavɛw] (*pl* -eis [-ejʃ]) *adj* unacceptable.

inacessível [inaseˈsivɛw] (*pl* -eis [-ejʃ]) *adj* inaccessible.

inacreditável [inakredʒiˈtavɛw] (*pl* -eis [-ejʃ]) *adj* unbelievable.

inactividade [inatviˈdadɛ] *f* (*Port*) = **inatividade.**

inadequado, -da [inadeˈkwadu, -da] *adj* inadequate.

inadiável [inaˈdʒjavɛw] (*pl* -eis [-ejʃ]) *adj* (*encontro, reunião, problema*) pressing.

inadvertido, -da [inadverˈtʃidu, -da] *adj* unnoticed.

inalador [inalaˈdo(x)] (*pl* -res [-riʃ]) *m* inhaler.

inalar [inaˈla(x)] *vt* to inhale.

inalcançável [inawkãˈsavɛw] (*pl* -eis [-ejʃ]) *adj* unattainable.

inanimado, -da [inaniˈmadu, -da] *adj* inanimate.

inaptidão [inaptʃiˈdãw] *f* unsuitability.

inapto, -pta [iˈnaptu, -pta] *adj* unsuitable.

inarticulado, -da [inaxtʃikuˈladu, -da] *adj* inarticulate.

inatingível [inatʃĩˈʒivɛw] (*pl* -eis [-ejʃ]) *adj* unattainable.

inatividade [inatʃiviˈdadʒi] *f* (*Br*) inactivity; **na** ~ (*pessoa*) out of work.

inativo, -va [inaˈtʃivu, -va] *adj* inactive; (*pessoa*) out of work.

inato, -ta [iˈnatu, -ta] *adj* innate.

inauguração [inawguraˈsãw] (*pl* -ões [-õjʃ]) *f* inauguration.

inaugurar [inawguˈra(x)] *vt* to inaugurate.

incansável [ĩkãˈsavɛw] (*pl* -eis [-ejʃ]) *adj* tireless.

incapacidade [ĩkapasiˈdadʒi] *f* inability.

incapaz [ĩkaˈpaʃ] (*pl* -zes [-ziʃ]) *adj* incapable.

incendiar [ĩsẽnˈdʒja(x)] *vt* to set fire to.

❏ **incendiar-se** *vp* to catch fire.

incêndio [ĩˈsẽndʒju] *m* fire.

incenso [ĩˈsẽsu] *m* incense.

incentivar [ĩsẽntʒiˈva(x)] *vt* to motivate.

incentivo [ĩsẽnˈtʃivu] *m* incentive.

incerteza [ĩsexˈteza] *f* doubt, uncertainty; **ficar na** ~ to be left in doubt.

incerto, -ta [ĩˈsextu, -ta] *adj* uncertain.

incesto [ĩˈsɛʃtu] *m* incest.

inchação [ĩʃaˈsãw] (*pl* -ões [-õjʃ]) *m* (*Br*) swelling.

inchaço [ĩˈʃasu] *m* swelling.

inchado, -da [ĩˈʃadu, -da] *adj* (*entumescido*) swollen; (*fig: envaidecido*) puffed up (with pride).

inchar [ĩˈʃa(x)] *vi* to swell.

incidência [ĩsiˈdẽsja] *f* incidence.

incidente [ĩsiˈdẽntʃi] *m* incident.

incineração [ĩsincraˈsãw] (*pl* -ões [-õjʃ]) *f* incineration.

incisivo, -va [ĩsiˈzivu, -va] *adj* (*fig: penetrante*) incisive ♦ *m* (*dente*) incisor.

incitar [ĩsiˈta(x)] *vt* to incite.

inclemente [ĩkleˈmẽntʃi] *adj* merciless.

inclinação [ĩklinaˈsãw] (*pl* -ões

[-õʃʃ]) f inclination.

inclinado, -da [ĩŋkli'nadu, -da] *adj* slanting.

inclinar [ĩŋkli'na(x)] *vt* to tilt.

❑ **inclinar-se** *vp* to lean.

incluir [ĩŋklu'i(x)] *vt* to include; *(inserir)* to enclose.

inclusive [ĩŋklu'zivɛ] *adv* even; **de 11 a 20, ~** from 11 to 20 inclusive.

incoerente [ĩŋkwe'rẽntʃi] *adj* incoherent.

incógnita [ĩŋ'kɔgnita] *f* enigma, mystery.

incógnito, -ta [ĩ'kɔgnitu, -ta] *adj* unknown.

incolor [ĩŋko'lo(x)] *(pl* **-res** [-riʃ]) *adj* colourless.

incomodar [ĩŋkomo'da(x)] *vt* to bother; "favor não ~" "do not disturb".

❑ **incomodar-se** *vp* to bother; **você se incomoda se eu fumar?** do you mind if I smoke?

incómodo, -da [ĩŋ'kɔmudu, -da] *adj & m (Port)* = **incômodo**.

incômodo, -da [ĩŋ'komodu, -da] *adj (Br)* uncomfortable ◆ *m (Br)* nuisance; *(menstruação)* period.

incomparável [ĩŋkõmpa'ravɛw] *(pl* **-eis** [-ejʃ]) *adj* incomparable.

incompatível [ĩŋkõmpa'tʃivɛw] *(pl* **-eis** [-ejʃ]) *adj* incompatible.

incompetente [ĩŋkõmpe'tẽntʃi] *adj & mf* incompetent.

incompleto, -ta [ĩŋkõm'plɛtu, -ta] *adj* unfinished.

incomum [ĩŋko'mũ] *(pl* **-ns** [-ʃ]) *adj* uncommon.

incomunicável [ĩŋkomuni'kavɛw] *(pl* **-eis** [-ejʃ]) *adj (isolado)* isolated; *(bens)* non-transferable.

incomuns → **incomun**.

inconcebível [ĩŋkõse'bivɛw] *(pl* **-eis** [-ejʃ]) *adj* inconceivable.

incondicional [ĩŋkõdʒisjo'naw] *(pl* **-ais** [-ajʃ]) *adj* unconditional.

inconformado, -da [ĩŋkõfox'madu, -da] *adj* unresigned.

inconfundível [ĩŋkõfũn'dʒivɛw] *(pl* **-eis** [-ejʃ]) *adj* unmistakable.

inconsciência [ĩŋkõʃ'sjẽsja] *f* thoughtlessness.

inconsciente [ĩŋkõʃ'sjẽntʃi] *adj (MED)* unconscious; *(irresponsável)* thoughtless ◆ *m* unconscious.

incontestável [ĩŋkõnteʃ'tavɛw] *(pl* **-eis** [-ejʃ]) *adj* indisputable.

inconveniência [ĩŋkõve'njẽsja] *f* inconvenience.

inconveniente [ĩŋkõve'njẽntʃi] *adj (pessoa)* tactless; *(assunto)* awkward ◆ *m (problema)* problem; *(desvantagem)* disadvantage.

incorporar [ĩŋkoxpo'ra(x)] *vt* to incorporate.

incorrecto, -ta [ĩŋku'xɛtu, -ta] *adj (Port)* = **incorreto**.

incorreto, -ta [ĩŋko'xɛtu, -ta] *adj (Br) (errado)* incorrect; *(malcriado)* rude.

incorrigível [ĩŋkoxi'ʒivɛw] *(pl* **-eis** [-ejʃ]) *adj* incorrigible.

incrédulo, -la [ĩŋ'krɛdulu, -la] *adj* incredulous.

incrível [ĩŋ'krivɛw] *(pl* **-eis** [-ejʃ]) *adj* incredible.

incubadora [ĩŋkuba'dora] *f* incubator.

inculto, -ta [ĩŋ'kuwtu, -ta] *adj (pessoa)* uneducated; *(terreno)* uncultivated.

incumbir [ĩŋkũm'bi(x)] *vt* to put in charge; **~ alguém de fazer algo** to ask sb to do sthg.

❑ **incumbir a** *v* + *prep*: **~ a alguém fazer algo** to be sb's turn to do sthg.

❑ **incumbir-se** *vp* + *prep*: **~-se de fazer algo** to take it upon o.s. to do sthg.

incurável [ĩŋku'ravɛw] *(pl* **-eis** [-ejʃ]) *adj* incurable.

indagar [ĩnda'ga(x)] *vi* to inquire.

indecente [ĩnde'sẽntʃi] *adj* indecent.

indecisão [ĩndesi'zãw] *(pl* **-ões** [-õjʃ]) *f* indecision, indecisiveness.

indeciso, -sa [ĩnde'sizu, -za] *adj (futuro, situação)* uncertain; *(pessoa)* indecisive; **estar ~** to be undecided.

indecisões → **indecisão**.

indecoroso, -osa [ĩndeku'rozo, -oza] *adj* improper.

indefeso, -sa [ĩnde'fezu, -za] *adj* defenceless.

indefinido, -da [ĩndefi'nidu, -da] *adj* indefinite.

indelicado, -da [ĩndeli'kadu, -da] *adj* offhand.

indemnizar [ĩndemni'zar] *vt (Port)* = **indenizar**.

indenização [ĩndeniza'sãw] *(pl* **-ões** [-õjʃ]) *f* compensation.

indenizar [ĩndeni'za(x)] *vt (Br)* to compensate.

independência [ĩndepẽn'dẽsja] *f*

inexequível

independence.

independente [ĩdepẽn'dẽntʃi] *adj* independent.

independentemente [ĩdepẽn‚dẽntʃi'mẽntʃi] : **independentemente de** *prep* independently of.

indescritível [ĩdeʃkri'tʃivɛw] (*pl* -eis [-ejʃ]) *adj* indescribable.

indesejável [ĩdeze'ʒavɛw] (*pl* -eis [-ejʃ]) *adj* undesirable.

indestrutível [ĩdeʃtru'tʃivɛw] (*pl* -eis [-ejʃ]) *adj* indestructible; *(fig: argumento)* watertight.

indeterminado, -da [ĩdetexmi'nadu, -da] *adj* indeterminate.

indevido, -da [ĩde'vidu, -da] *adj* inappropriate.

Índia [ˈĩdʒja] *f*: **a ~** India.

indiano, -na [ĩ'dʒjanu, -na] *adj & m, f* Indian.

indicação [ĩdʒika'sãw] (*pl* -ões [-õjʃ]) *f (de caminho, direção)* directions *(pl)*; *(sinal)* mark; *(instrução)* indication.

indicador [ĩdʒika'do(x)] (*pl* -res [-riʃ]) *m (dedo)* index finger; *(de temperatura, velocímetro)* indicator.

indicar [ĩdʒi'ka(x)] *vt* to show.

indicativo, -va [ĩdʒika'tʃivu, -va] *adj* indicative ◆ *m (de telefone)* dialling code *(Brit)*, area code *(Am)*; *(GRAM)* indicative.

índice [ˈĩdʒisi] *m (em livro)* index; *(nível)* rate; **~ de inflação** inflation rate.

indiferença [ĩdʒife'rẽsa] *f* indifference.

indiferente [ĩdʒife'rẽntʃi] *adj* indifferent; **para mim é ~** I don't care.

indígena [ĩ'dʒiʒena] *adj & mf (nativo)* native; *(índio)* Indian.

indigestão [ĩdʒiʒeʃ'tãw] *f* indigestion.

indigesto, -ta [ĩdʒi'ʒeʃtu, -ta] *adj* indigestible.

indignação [ĩdʒigna'sãw] (*pl* -ões [-õjʃ]) *f* indignation.

indigno, -gna [ĩ'dʒignu, -gna] *adj (pessoa)* unworthy; *(situação)* degrading.

índio, -dia [ˈĩdʒju, -dja] *adj & m, f* Indian.

indirecto, -ta [ĩdiˈrɛtu, -ta] *adj (Port)* = **indireto**.

indireta [ĩdʒi'rɛta] *f (fig: comentário)* dig.

indireto, -ta [ĩdʒi'rɛtu, -ta] *adj (Br)* indirect.

indisciplinado, -da [ĩdʒiʃsipli'nadu, -da] *adj* undisciplined.

indiscreto, -ta [ĩdʒiʃ'krɛtu, -ta] *adj* indiscreet.

indiscutível [ĩdʒiʃku'tʃivɛw] (*pl* -eis [-ejʃ]) *adj* indisputable.

indispensável [ĩdʒiʃpẽ'savɛw] (*pl* -eis [-ejʃ]) *adj* indispensable ◆ *m*: **o ~** the bare essentials *(pl)*.

indisposição [ĩdʒiʃpozi'sãw] (*pl* -ões [-õjʃ]) *f* stomach upset.

indisposto, -osta [ĩdʒiʃ'poʃtu, -ɔʃta] *adj* unwell.

indistinto, -ta [ĩdʒiʃ'tʃĩtu, -ta] *adj (pouco visível)* vague; *(forma, som)* faint.

individual [ĩdʒivi'dwaw] (*pl* -ais [-ajʃ]) *adj* individual; *(quarto, tarefa)* single; *(mesa)* for one.

indivíduo [ĩde'vidwu] *m* individual; *(fam: homem)* guy.

índole [ˈĩdoli] *f* nature.

indolor [ĩdo'lo(x)] (*pl* -res [-riʃ]) *adj* painless.

Indonésia [ĩdo'nɛʒja] *f*: **a ~** Indonesia.

indulgência [ĩduw'ʒẽsja] *f* leniency.

indulgente [ĩduw'ʒẽntʃi] *adj* lenient.

indumentária [ĩdumẽn'tarja] *f (traje)* costume; *(pej: farrapo)* rag.

indústria [ĩ'duʃtria] *f* industry.

induzir [ĩdu'zi(x)] *vt*: **~ alguém a fazer algo** to persuade sb to do sthg; **~ alguém em erro** to mislead sb.

inédito, -ta [i'nɛdʒitu, -ta] *adj (livro)* unpublished; *(original)* unique; *(acontecimento)* unprecedented.

ineficaz [inefi'kaʃ] (*pl* -zes [-ziʃ]) *adj* ineffective.

inegável [ine'gavɛw] (*pl* -eis [-ejʃ]) *adj* undeniable.

inércia [i'nɛxsja] *f* inertia.

inerte [i'nɛxtʃi] *adj* inert.

inesgotável [ineʒgo'tavɛw] (*pl* -eis [-ejʃ]) *adj* inexhaustible.

inesperado, -da [ineʃpe'radu, -da] *adj* unexpected.

inesquecível [ineʃke'sivɛw] (*pl* -eis [-ejʃ]) *adj* unforgettable.

inestimável [ineʃtʃi'mavɛw] (*pl* -eis [-ejʃ]) *adj* invaluable; **de valor ~** priceless.

inevitável [inevi'tavɛw] (*pl* -eis [-ejʃ]) *adj* inevitable.

inexequível [ineze'kwivɛw] (*pl* -eis [-ejʃ]) *adj* impracticable.

inexistência [inezi∫'tẽsja] *f*: ~ de lack of.

inexperiência [ine∫pe'rjẽsja] *f* inexperience.

inexperiente [ine∫pe'rjẽnt∫i] *adj* inexperienced; *(fig: inocente)* innocent.

infalível [ĩfa'livew] *(pl* -eis [-ej∫]) *adj (método, sistema, plano)* infallible; *(inevitável)* certain.

infâmia [ĩ'famja] *f* slander.

infância [ĩ'fãsja] *f* childhood.

infantário [ĩfãn'tarju] *m (Port)* nursery school.

infantil [ĩfãn'tiw] *(pl* -is [-i∫]) *adj (literatura, programa)* children's *(antes de s)*; *(pej: imaturo)* childish.

infecção [ĩfɛ'sãw] *(pl* -ões [-õj∫]) *f (MED)* infection.

infeccioso, -osa [ĩfɛ'sjozu, -ɔza] *adj* infectious.

infecções → infecção.

infectado, -da [ĩfɛ'tadu, -da] *adj* infected.

infectar [ĩfɛ'ta(x)] *vi* to get infected ♦ *vt* to infect.

infelicidade [ĩfelisi'dadʒi] *f (tristeza)* unhappiness; *(desgraça)* misfortune; **mas que ~!** what a shame!; **tive a ~ de** ... I had the misfortune of ....

infeliz [ĩfe'li∫] *(pl* -zes [-zi∫]) *adj (acontecimento, notícia)* sad; *(comentário, resposta)* inappropriate ♦ *mf* wretch; **ser ~** to be unhappy.

infelizmente [ĩfeliʒ'mẽnt∫i] *adv* unfortunately.

inferior [ĩfe'rjo(x)] *(pl* -res [-ri∫]) *adj* lower; *(em valor, qualidade)* inferior; **andar ~** downstairs.

inferno [ĩ'fɛxnu] *m*: **o Inferno** Hell; **isto é um ~!** what a nightmare!; **vá para o ~!** *(fam)* go to hell!

infertilidade [ĩfext∫ili'dadʒi] *f* infertility.

infestar [ĩfe∫'ta(x)] *vt* to infest.

infiel [ĩ'fjew] *(pl* -éis [-ɛi∫]) *adj (marido, esposa)* unfaithful; *(amigo)* disloyal.

infiltrar-se [ĩfiw'traxsi] *vp (água, chuva)* to seep in.

ínfimo, -ma [ĩ'fimu, -ma] *adj* minute; *(fig: sem importância)* pointless.

infindável [ĩfĩ'davew] *(pl* -eis [-ej∫]) *adj* endless.

infinidade [ĩfini'dadʒi] *f* infinity.

infinitivo [ĩfini't∫ivu] *m*: **o ~** *(GRAM)* the infinitive.

infinito, -ta [ĩfi'nitu, -ta] *adj & m* infinite.

inflação [ĩfla'sãw] *f* inflation.

inflamação [ĩflama'sãw] *(pl* -ões [-õj∫]) *f* inflammation.

inflamado, -da [ĩfla'madu, -da] *adj* inflamed.

inflamar [ĩfla'ma(x)] *vt (incendiar)* to set on fire, to set alight; *(fig: entusiasmar)* to inflame.

inflamável [ĩfla'mavew] *(pl* -eis [-ej∫]) *adj* inflammable *(Brit)*, flammable *(Am)*.

inflexível [ĩflɛk'sivew] *(pl* -eis [-ej∫]) *adj* inflexible; *(fig: implacável, rigoroso)* unbending.

influência [ĩflu'ẽsja] *f* influence; **ter ~** to be influential.

influente [ĩflu'ẽnt∫i] *adj* influential.

influir [ĩflu'i(x)] : **influir em** *v + prep* to influence.

informação [ĩfoxma'sãw] *(pl* -ões [-õj∫]) *f* information; *(notícia)* news *(sg)*; **ele não me deu informação nenhuma** he didn't give me any information.

❏ **informações** *fpl (serviço telefônico)* directory enquiries *(Brit)*, directory assistance *(sg) (Am)*; **"informações"** "enquiries".

informal [ĩfox'maw] *(pl* -ais [-aj∫]) *adj* informal.

informalidade [ĩfoxmali'dadʒi] *f* informality.

informar [ĩfox'ma(x)] *vt* to inform; **~ alguém de** OU **sobre algo** to inform sb of sthg.

❏ **informar-se** *vp* to find out.

informática [ĩfox'mat∫ika] *f* information technology, computing.

informativo, -va [ĩfoxma't∫ivu, -va] *adj* informative.

informatizar [ĩfuxmat∫i'za(x)] *vt* to computerize.

infortúnio [ĩfox'tunju] *m* misfortune.

infração [ĩfra'sãw] *(pl* -ões [-õj∫]) *f (Br) (de lei)* offence; *(de norma, regra)* breach.

infracção [ĩfra'sãw] *(pl* -ões [-õj∫]) *f (Port)* = infração.

infrações → infração.

infractor, -ra [ĩfra'tor, -ra] *(mpl* -res [-re∫], *fpl* -s [-∫]) *m, f (Port)* = infrator.

infrator, -ra [ĩfra'to(x), -ra] *(mpl* -res [-ri∫], *fpl* -s [-∫]) *m, f (Br)* offender.

infravermelho, -lha [ĩfravex'meʎu,

-ʎa] *adj* infrared.

infringir [ĩfrĩˈʒi(x)] *vt* to infringe.

infrutífero, -ra [ĩfruˈtʃiferu, -ra] *adj* fruitless.

infundado, -da [ĩfũnˈdadu, -da] *adj* unfounded.

ingenuidade [ĩʒenwiˈdadʒi] *f* ingenuity.

ingénuo, -nua [ĩˈʒɛnwu, -nwa] *adj & m, f (Port)* = ingênuo.

ingênuo, -nua [ĩˈʒenwu, -nwa] *adj (Br)* naive ◆ *m, f (Br)* naive person.

ingerir [ĩʒeˈri(x)] *vt* to ingest.

Inglaterra [ĩɡlaˈtɛxa] *f*: a ~ England.

inglês, -esa [ĩˈɡleʃ, -eza] *(mpl* -eses [-eziʃ], *fpl* -s [-ʃ]) *adj & m* English ◆ *m, f (pessoa)* Englishman *(f* Englishwoman); **os ingleses** the English; **para ~ ver** for show.

ingratidão [ĩɡratʃiˈdãw] *f* ingratitude.

ingrato, -ta [ĩˈɡratu, -ta] *adj (pessoa)* ungrateful; *(trabalho)* thankless.

ingrediente [ĩɡreˈdʒẽntʃi] *m* ingredient.

íngreme [ĩɡremi] *adj* steep.

ingresso [ĩˈɡresu] *m (em curso, universidade, partido)* enrolment; *(bilhete de cinema, teatro, etc)* ticket.

inhame [iˈɲami] *m* yam.

inibição [inibiˈsãw] *(pl* -ões [-õjʃ]) *f* inhibition.

inibido, -da [iniˈbidu, -da] *adj* inhibited.

inicial [iniˈsjaw] *(pl* -ais [-ajʃ]) *adj & f* initial.

iniciar [iniˈsja(x)] *vt* to start, to begin.
❑ **iniciar-se** *vp* to start.

iniciativa [inisjaˈtʃiva] *f* initiative; **ter ~** to show initiative.

início [iˈnisju] *m* start, beginning; **no ~** at first; **desde o ~** from the start.

inimigo, -ga [iniˈmiɡu, -ga] *adj* enemy *(antes de s)* ◆ *m, f* enemy.

ininterruptamente [inĩnteˌxuptaˈmẽntʃi] *adv* continuously.

injeção [ĩʒeˈsãw] *(pl* -ões [-õjʃ]) *f (Br)* injection.

injecção [ĩʒeˈsãw] *(pl* -ões [-õjʃ]) *f (Port)* = injeção.

injeções → injeção.

injectar [ĩʒeˈtar] *vt (Port)* = injetar.

injetar [ĩʒeˈta(x)] *vt (Br)* to inject.
❑ **injetar-se** *vp (Br) (fam: drogar-se)* to be on drugs.

injúria [ĩˈʒurja] *f* insult.

injuriar [ĩʒuˈrja(x)] *vt* to insult.

injustiça [ĩʒuʃˈtʃisa] *f* injustice.

injusto, -ta [ĩˈʒuʃtu, -ta] *adj* unfair.

inocência [inoˈsẽsja] *f* innocence.

inocentar [inosẽnˈta(x)] *vt*: ~ **alguém (de algo)** *(JUR)* to clear sb (of sthg).

inocente [inoˈsẽntʃi] *adj* innocent; **ser ou estar ~** to be innocent.

inoculação [inɔkulaˈsãw] *(pl* -ões [-õjʃ]) *f* inoculation.

inócuo, -cua [iˈnɔkwu, -kwa] *adj* innocuous.

inofensivo, -va [inofẽˈsivu, -va] *adj* harmless.

inoportuno, -na [inopoxˈtunu, -na] *adj (pessoa)* tactless; *(comentário, momento)* inopportune.

inovação [inovaˈsãw] *(pl* -ões [-õjʃ]) *f* innovation.

inox [iˈnoksi] *m* stainless steel.

inoxidável [inoksiˈdavɛw] *(pl* -eis [-ejʃ]) *adj (aço)* stainless; *(material)* rustproof.

inquérito [ĩˈkɛritu] *m (sondagem)* opinion poll, survey; *(de polícia, comissão)* investigation.

inquietação [ĩkjetaˈsãw] *f (agitação)* restlessness; *(preocupação)* worry.

inquietante [ĩkjeˈtãntʃi] *adj* worrying, disturbing.

inquilino, -na [ĩkiˈlinu, -na] *m, f* tenant.

insaciável [ĩsaˈsjavɛw] *(pl* -eis [-ejʃ]) *adj* insatiable.

insalubre [ĩsaˈlubri] *adj (comida, bebida)* unhealthy; *(local)* insalubrious.

insanidade [ĩsaniˈdadʒi] *f* insanity.

insatisfação [ĩsatʃiʃfaˈsãw] *(pl* -ões [-õjʃ]) *f* dissatisfaction.

insatisfatório, -ria [ĩsatʃiʃfaˈtɔrju, -rja] *adj* unsatisfactory.

insatisfeito, -ta [ĩsatʃiʃˈfejtu, -ta] *adj* dissatisfied.

inscrever [ĩʃkreˈve(x)] *vt* to enrol; ~ **alguém em algo** to enrol sb on ou for sthg.
❑ **inscrever-se** *vp*: ~-**se em algo** to enrol on ou for sthg.

inscrição [ĩʃkriˈsãw] *(pl* -ões [-õjʃ]) *f (em pedra)* inscription; *(em curso, cadeira)* enrolment.

inseticida [ĩsetʃiˈsida] *m* insecticide.

insecto [ĩˈsɛtu] *m (Port)* = inseto.

insegurança [ĩseɡuˈrãsa] *f* insecurity.

inseguro, -ra [ĩseˈɡuru, -ra] *adj (área,*

rua) unsafe; *(pessoa)* insecure.

inseminação [ĩsɛmina'sãw] *(pl* **-ões** [-õjʃ]) *f:* ~ **artificial** artificial insemination.

insensato, -ta [ĩsɛ̃'satu, -ta] *adj (decisão, comportamento)* foolish.

insensibilidade [ĩsẽsibili'dadʒi] *f* insensitivity.

insensível [ĩsɛ̃'sivɛw] *(pl* **-eis** [-ejʃ]) *adj* insensitive.

inseparável [ĩsepa'ravɛw] *(pl* **-eis** [-ejʃ]) *adj* inseparable.

inserir [ĩsɛ'ri(x)] *vt (colocar)* to insert; *(INFORM: dados)* to enter.

❏ **inserir-se em** *vp + prep (fazer parte de)* to be part of.

inseto [ĩ'sɛtu] *m (Br)* insect.

insidioso, -osa [ĩsi'dʒjozu, -ɔza] *adj* insidious.

insígnia [ĩ'signja] *f* insignia.

insignificante [ĩsignifi'kãntʃi] *adj* insignificant.

insincero, -ra [ĩsĩ'sɛru, -ra] *adj* insincere.

insinuar [ĩsi'nwa(x)] *vt* to insinuate.

insípido, -da [ĩ'sipidu, -da] *adj* insipid.

insistência [ĩsiʃ'tẽsja] *f* insistence.

insistente [ĩsiʃ'tẽntʃi] *adj* insistent.

insistir [ĩsiʃ'ti(x)] *vi* to insist; **eu estou sempre insistindo com ela para ter cuidado** I'm always telling her to be careful; ~ **em fazer algo** to insist on doing sthg.

insociável [ĩso'sjavɛw] *(pl* **-eis** [-ejʃ]) *adj* unsociable.

insolação [ĩsola'sãw] *(pl* **-ões** [-õjʃ]) *f* sunstroke.

insolente [ĩso'lẽntʃi] *adj* insolent ◆ *mf* insolent person.

insólito, -ta [ĩ'sɔlitu, -ta] *adj* unusual.

insónia [ĩ'sɔnja] *f (Port)* = **insônia**.

insônia [ĩ'sonja] *f (Br)* insomnia.

insosso, -a [ĩ'sosu, -a] *adj* bland; *(fig: pouco interessante)* insipid.

inspeção [ĩʃpɛ'sãw] *(pl* **-ões** [-õjʃ]) *f (Br)* inspection.

inspecção [ĩʃpɛ'sãw] *(pl* **-ões** [-õjʃ]) *f (Port)* = **inspeção**.

inspeccionar [ĩʃpesjo'nar] *vt (Port)* = **inspecionar**.

inspecções → **inspecção**.

inspecionar [ĩʃpesjo'na(x)] *vt (Br)* to inspect.

inspeções → **inspeção**.

inspector, -ra [ĩʃpɛ'tor, -ra] *(mpl* **-res** [-reʃ], *fpl* **-s** [-ʃ]) *m, f (Port)* = **inspetor**.

inspetor, -ra [ĩʃpe'to(x), -ra] *(mpl* **-res** [-riʃ], *fpl* **-s** [-ʃ]) *m, f (Br)* inspector.

inspiração [ĩʃpira'sãw] *(pl* **-ões** [-õjʃ]) *f* inspiration.

inspirador, -ra [ĩʃpira'do(x), -ra] *(mpl* **-res** [-riʃ], *fpl* **-s** [-ʃ]) *adj* inspiring.

inspirar [ĩʃpi'ra(x)] *vt (respirar)* to breathe in; *(fig: sugerir)* to inspire.

instabilidade [ĩʃtabili'dadʒi] *f* instability.

instalação [ĩʃtala'sãw] *(pl* **-ões** [-õjʃ]) *f* installation; ~ **elétrica** wiring.

❏ **instalações** *fpl* facilities.

instalar [ĩʃta'la(x)] *vt* to install.

❏ **instalar-se** *vp (em casa, local)* to move in; *(em cadeira)* to make o.s. comfortable.

instantâneo, -nea [ĩʃtãn'tanju, -nja] *adj* instantaneous ◆ *m* snapshot.

instante [ĩʃ'tãntʃi] *m* moment; **um ~!** just a minute!; **dentro de ~s** shortly; **de um ~ para o outro** suddenly; **nesse ~** at that moment; **num ~** in a second; **faço isso num ~** it'll only take me a minute; **por ~s** for a moment; **a qualquer ~** at any moment; **a todo o ~** all the time.

instintivo, -va [ĩʃtʃĩn'tʃivu, -va] *adj* instinctive.

instinto [ĩʃ'tʃĩntu] *m* instinct.

instituição [ĩʃtʃitwi'sãw] *(pl* **-ões** [-õjʃ]) *f* institution.

instituto [ĩʃtʃi'tutu] *m* institute; ~ **de beleza** beauty salon; ~ **de línguas** language school.

instrução [ĩʃtru'sãw] *(pl* **-ões** [-õjʃ]) *f (indicação)* instruction; *(educação)* education.

instruir [ĩʃtru'i(x)] *vt* to instruct.

instrumental [ĩʃtrumẽ'taw] *(pl* **-ais** [-ajʃ]) *adj* instrumental.

instrumento [ĩʃtru'mẽntu] *m (ferramenta)* tool; *(musical)* instrument.

instrutivo, -va [ĩʃtru'tʃivu, -va] *adj* instructive.

instrutor, -ra [ĩʃtru'to(x), -ra] *(mpl* **-res** [-riʃ], *fpl* **-s** [-ʃ]) *m, f (professor)* instructor; *(de direção)* driving instructor.

insubordinação [ĩsuboxdʒina'sãw] *(pl* **-ões** [-õjʃ]) *f (mau comportamento)* disobedience; *(rebelião)* insubordination.

insubstituível [ĩsubʃtʃi'twivɛw] *(pl*

-eis [-ejʃ]) *adj* irreplaceable.

insucesso [ĩsuˈsesu] *m* failure; **o ~ escolar** underperforming at school.

insuficiência [ĩsufiˈsjẽsja] *f (falta, carência)* lack; *(incapacidade)* failure; **~ cardíaca** heart failure.

insuficiente [ĩsufiˈsjẽtʃi] *adj* insufficient ◆ *m (EDUC: nota)* fail.

insuflável [ĩsuˈflavɛw] (*pl* **-eis** [-ejʃ]) *adj* inflatable; *(boneca)* blow-up.

insulina [ĩsuˈlina] *f* insulin.

insultar [ĩsuwˈta(x)] *vt* to insult.

insuperável [ĩsupeˈravɛw] (*pl* **-eis** [-ejʃ]) *adj* insurmountable.

insuportável [ĩsupoxˈtavɛw] (*pl* **-eis** [-ejʃ]) *adj* unbearable.

intacto, -ta [ĩˈta(k)tu, -ta] *adj (Port)* = intato.

intato, -ta [ĩˈtatu, -ta] *adj (Br)* intact.

íntegra [ˈĩtɛgra] *f*: **na ~** in full.

integral [ĩteˈgraw] (*pl* **-ais** [-ajʃ]) *adj* whole.

integrar [ĩteˈgra(x)] *vt* to include.

⊃ **integrar-se** *vp* to become integrated.

integridade [ĩtegriˈdadʒi] *f* integrity.

íntegro, -gra [ˈĩtegru, -gra] *adj* honest.

inteiramente [ĩˌtejraˈmẽtʃi] *adv* entirely.

inteirar-se [ĩtejˈraxsi] : **inteirar-se de** *vp* + *prep* to find out about.

inteiro, -ra [ĩˈtejru, -ra] *adj (todo)* whole; *(não partido)* intact.

intelectual [ĩtelɛkˈtwaw] (*pl* **-ais** [-ajʃ]) *adj & mf* intellectual.

inteligência [ĩteliˈʒẽsja] *f* intelligence.

inteligente [ĩteliˈʒẽtʃi] *adj* intelligent.

intenção [ĩtẽˈsãw] (*pl* **-ões** [-õjʃ]) *f* intention; **ter ~ de fazer algo to** intend to do sthg; **sem ~** unintentionally; **com** OU **na melhor das intenções** with the best of intentions; **ter segundas intenções** to have an ulterior motive.

intensidade [ĩtẽsiˈdadʒi] *f* intensity.

intensivo, -va [ĩtẽˈsivu, -va] *adj* intensive.

intenso, -sa [ĩˈtẽsu, -sa] *adj* intense; *(chuva)* heavy; *(trabalho)* hard; *(vento)* high.

interactivo, -va [ĩteraˈtivu, -va] *adj*

(Port) = **interativo**.

interativo, -va [ĩteraˈtʃivu, -va] *adj (Br)* interactive.

intercâmbio [ˌĩterˈkãmbju] *m* exchange.

interceder [ĩtexseˈde(x)] *vi*: **~ por alguém** to intercede on behalf of sb.

interceptar [ĩtexsepˈta(x)] *vt* to intercept.

interdição [ĩtexdʒiˈsãw] (*pl* **-ões** [-õjʃ]) *f (proibição)* ban; *(encerramento)* closure.

interditar [ĩtexdʒiˈta(x)] *vt* to *(proibir)* ban; *(encerrar)* to close; **interditaram a rua** they closed off the road.

interessado, -da [ĩtereˈsadu, -da] *adj* interested.

interessante [ĩtereˈsãtʃi] *adj* interesting.

interessar [ĩtereˈsa(x)] *vi* to be of interest; **a religião não me interessa** religion doesn't interest me; **não me interessa!** I don't care!

⊔ **interessar-se por** *vp* + *prep* to be interested in; **só agora é que ele se interessou pelo caso** he's only recently taken an interest in the affair.

interesse [ĩteˈresi] *m* interest; *(importância)* significance; *(proveito próprio)* self-interest; **no ~ de** in the interests of; **por ~** out of self-interest; **sem ~** of no interest.

interface [ĩtexˈfasi] *f* interface.

interferência [ĩtexfeˈrẽsja] *f* interference.

⊃ **interferências** *fpl (em imagem, rádio)* interference *(sg)*.

interferir [ĩtexfeˈri(x)] : **interferir em** *v* + *prep* to interfere in.

interfone [ĩtexˈfoni] *m* intercom.

interior [ĩteˈrjo(x)] (*pl* **-res** [-riʃ]) *adj (quarto, porta)* inner ◆ *m (de área, caixa)* inside; *(de casa, país)* interior.

interjeição [ĩtexʒejˈsãw] (*pl* **-ões** [-õjʃ]) *f* interjection.

interlocutor, -ra [ĩtexlokuˈto(x), -ra] (*mpl* **-res** [-riʃ], *fpl* **-s** [-ʃ]) *m, f* speaker.

interlúdio [ĩtexˈludʒju] *m* interlude.

intermediário, -ria [ĩtexmeˈdʒjarju, -rja] *m, f* intermediary.

intermédio [ĩterˈmedʒju] *m*: **por ~ de** through.

interminável [ĩtexmiˈnavɛw] (*pl* **-eis** [-ejʃ]) *adj* endless.

intermitente [ĩntexmi'tẽntʃi] *adj* intermittent.

internacional [ĩntexnasju'naw] (*pl* **-ais** [-ajʃ]) *adj* international.

internar [ĩntex'na(x)] *vt (MED)* to admit.

internato [ĩntex'natu] *m* boarding school.

Internet [ĩntex'netʃi] *f*: **a ~** the Internet.

interno, -na [ĩn'texnu, -na] *adj* internal; *(colégio)* boarding *(antes de s)*.

interpretação [ĩntexpreta'sãw] (*pl* **-ões** [-õjʃ]) *f (de texto, mensagem)* interpretation; *(de papel, canção)* performance; *(tradução)* interpreting.

interpretar [ĩntexpre'ta(x)] *vt (texto, mensagem)* to interpret; *(papel)* to play; *(música)* to perform.

intérprete [ĩn'texpretʃi] *mf* performer; *(tradutor)* interpreter.

interrogação [ĩntexoga'sãw] (*pl* **-ões** [-õjʃ]) *f (pergunta)* question; *(interrogatório)* interrogation.

interrogar [ĩntexu'ga(x)] *vt (perguntar a)* to question; *(em tribunal)* to cross-examine.

interrupção [ĩntexup'sãw] (*pl* **-ões** [-õjʃ]) *f* interruption; **sem ~** without interruption.

interruptor [ĩntexup'to(x)] (*pl* **-res** [-riʃ]) *m* switch.

interurbano, -na [ĩntexux'banu, -na] *adj (telefonema)* long-distance.

intervalo [ĩntex'valu] *m (de programa, aula)* break; *(de espetáculo)* interval.

intervenção [ĩntexvẽ'sãw] (*pl* **-ões** [-õjʃ]) *f (ação)* intervention; *(discurso)* speech; **~ cirúrgica** operation.

intervir [ĩntex'vi(x)] *vi (participar)* to participate; *(interferir)* to intervene; **~ em** *(participar em)* to participate in; *(interferir em)* to intervene in.

intestino [ĩnteʃ'tʃinu] *m* intestine; **~ delgado/grosso** small/large intestine.

intimar [ĩntʃi'ma(x)] *vt (JUR)* to summon; **~ alguém a fazer algo** to order sb to do sthg.

intimidação [ĩntʃimida'sãw] (*pl* **-ões** [-õjʃ]) *f* intimidation.

intimidade [ĩntʃimi'dadʒi] *f (proximidade)* intimacy; *(privacidade)* privacy.

intimidar [ĩntʃimi'da(x)] *vt* to intimidate.

⊔ **intimidar-se** *vp* to be intimidated.

íntimo, -ma ['ĩntʃimu, -ma] *adj (pes-soa)* close; *(sentimentos)* intimate; *(objetos)* personal ◆ *m*: **no ~** deep down; **ser ~ de alguém** to be close to sb.

intolerância [ĩntole'rãsja] *f* intolerance.

intolerante [ĩntole'rãntʃi] *adj (pessoa)* intolerant; *(lei, atitude)* rigid.

intoxicação [ĩntoksika'sãw] (*pl* **-ões** [-õjʃ]) *f* poisoning; **~ alimentar** food poisoning.

intransigente [ĩntrãzi'ʒẽntʃi] *adj* intransigent.

intransitável [ĩntrãzi'tavew] (*pl* **-eis** [-ejʃ]) *adj* impassable.

intransitivo [ĩntrãzi'tʃivu] *adj m →* verbo.

intransponível [ĩntrãʃpo'nivew] (*pl* **-eis** [-ejʃ]) *adj (rio, obstáculo)* impassable; *(problema)* insurmountable.

intratável [ĩntra'tavew] (*pl* **-eis** [-ejʃ]) *adj (pessoa)* difficult.

intravenoso, -osa [ĩntrave'nozu, -ɔza] *adj* intravenous.

intrépido, -da [ĩn'trɛpidu, -da] *adj* intrepid.

intriga [ĩn'triga] *f (de livro, história)* plot; *(bisbilhotice)* piece of gossip.

intrigante [ĩntri'gãntʃi] *adj (curioso)* intriguing; *(bisbilhoteiro)* gossipy.

introdução [ĩntrodu'sãw] (*pl* **-ões** [-õjʃ]) *f* introduction; *(inserção)* insertion.

introduzir [ĩntrodu'zi(x)] *vt (inserir)* to insert.

intrometer-se [ĩntrome'texsi] *vp* to interfere; **~ em** to meddle in.

intrometido, -da [ĩntrome'tʃidu, -da] *adj* meddling.

intromissão [ĩntromi'sãw] (*pl* **-ões** [-õjʃ]) *f* interference, meddling.

introvertido, -da [ĩntrovex'tʃidu, -da] *adj* introverted.

intruso, -sa [ĩn'truzu, -za] *m, f* intruder.

intuição [ĩntwi'sãw] (*pl* **-ões** [-õjʃ]) *f* intuition; **por ~** intuitively.

intuito [ĩn'twitu] *m* aim; **com o ~ de fazer algo** with the aim of doing sthg.

inumano, -na [inu'manu, -na] *adj* inhuman.

inúmeros, -ras [i'numeruʃ, -raʃ] *adj pl* countless.

inundação [inũnda'sãw] (*pl* **-ões** [-õjʃ]) *f* flood.

inundar [inũn'da(x)] *vt* to flood.

inútil [i'nutʃiw] (*pl* **-teis** [-tejʃ]) *adj*

(desnecessário) useless; *(vão)* pointless.

inutilmente [i,nutʃiw'mẽntʃi] *adv* in vain.

invadir [iva'di(x)] *vt* to invade.

invalidez [ivali'deʒ] *f* disability.

inválido, -da [i'validu, -da] *adj (pessoa)* disabled ◆ *m, f* disabled person.

invariável [iva'rjavɛw] *(pl* -eis [-ejʃ]) *adj* invariable.

invasão [iva'zãw] *(pl* -ões [-õjʃ]) *f* invasion.

inveja [ĩ'vɛʒa] *f* envy; **ter ~ de alguém** to envy sb.

invejar [ĩve'ʒa(x)] *vt* to envy.

invejoso, -osa [ĩve'ʒozu, -ɔza] *adj* envious.

invenção [ĩvẽ'sãw] *(pl* -ões [-õjʃ]) *f* invention.

inventar [ĩvẽ'ta(x)] *vt (criar)* to invent; *(fig: mentir)* to make up.

inventário [ĩvẽ'tarju] *m* inventory.

inventor, -ra [ĩvẽ'to(x), -ra] *(mpl* -res [-riʃ], *fpl* -s [-ʃ]) *m, f* inventor.

inverno [ĩ'vɛxnu] *m* winter; **no ~ in** the winter.

inverosímil [ĩveru'zimil] *(pl* -meis [-mejʃ]) *adj (Port)* = **inverossímil**.

inverossímil [ĩvero'simiw] *(pl* -meis [-mejʃ]) *adj (Br)* unlikely, improbable.

inversão [ĩvex'sãw] *(pl* -ões [-õjʃ]) *f* inversion; **fazer a ~ de marcha** to go into reverse.

inverso, -sa [ĩ'vɛxsu, -sa] *adj* opposite ◆ *m:* **o ~ the opposite.**

inversões → **inversão**.

inverter [ĩvex'te(x)] *vt (ordem, posição)* to invert; *(sentido, marcha)* to reverse.

invés [ĩ'vɛʃ] *m:* **ao ~ de** instead of.

investida [ĩvɛʃ'tʃida] *f (ataque)* attack; *(tentativa)* attempt.

investigação [ĩveʃtʃiga'sãw] *(pl* -ões [-õjʃ]) *f (policial)* investigation; *(científica)* research.

investigar [ĩveʃtʃi'ga(x)] *vt (acontecimento, crime)* to investigate; *(cientificamente)* to research.

investimento [ĩveʃtʃi'mẽntu] *m* investment.

investir [ĩveʃtʃi(x)] *vt* to invest ◆ *vi:* **~ (em algo)** to invest (in sthg).

inviável [ĩ'vjavɛw] *(pl* -eis [-ejʃ]) *adj* impracticable.

invisível [ĩve'zivɛw] *(pl* -eis [-ejʃ]) *adj* invisible.

invocar [ĩvo'ka(x)] *vt* to invoke.

invólucro [ĩ'vɔlukru] *m* wrapping.

involuntário, -ria [ĩvolũn'tarju, -rja] *adj* involuntary.

iodo ['jodu] *m* iodine.

ioga ['jɔga] *m ou f* yoga.

iogurte [ju'guxtʃi] *m* yoghurt.

iô-iô [jo'jo] *(pl* iô-iôs [jo'joʃ]) *m* yoyo.

ipê [i'pɛ] *m* type of Brazilian tree.

ir [i(x)] *vi* 1. *(deslocar-se)* to go; **fomos de ônibus** we went by bus; **iremos a pé** we'll go on foot, we'll walk; **vamos?** shall we go?

2. *(assistir, frequentar)* to go; **ele nunca vai às reuniões** he never goes to the meetings; **você não vai à aula?** aren't you going to your class?; **vou ao cinema muitas vezes** I go to the cinema a lot.

3. *(estender-se)* to go; **o caminho vai até ao lago** the path goes to the lake.

4. *(desenrolar-se)* to go; **isto não vai nada bem** this isn't going at all well; **como vai você?** how are you?; **como vão as coisas?** how's things?; **os negócios vão mal** business is bad.

5. *(exprime duração gradual):* **~ fazendo algo** to carry on doing sthg; **eu vou andando** I'll carry on; **va tentando!** keep trying!

6. *(seguido de infinitivo):* **vou falar com ele** I'll speak to him; **você vai gostar** you'll like it; **não vou fazer nada** I'm not going to do anything.

7. *(seguido de gerúndio):* **ia caindo** I almost fell; **ia morrendo** I nearly died.

8. *(em locuções):* **~ ter a (desembocar)** to lead to; **~ ter com (encontrar)** to meet.

❏ **ir de** *v + prep (ir disfarçado)* to go as; *(partir):* **vou de férias amanhã** I'm going on holiday tomorrow.

❏ **ir por** *v + prep (auto-estrada, escadas)* to take; **~ pela esquerda/direita** to go left/right; **~ pelo jardim** to go through the garden.

❏ **ir-se** *vp (partir)* to go; **ele já se foi** he's already left; **~-se embora** to leave.

ira ['ira] *f* rage.

irascível [iraʃ'sivɛw] *(pl* -eis [-ejʃ]) *adj* irascible.

íris ['iriʃ] *f inv* iris.

Irlanda [ix'lãnda] *f:* **a ~ Ireland, Eire; a ~ do Norte** Northern Ireland.

irlandês, -esa [ixlãn'deʃ, -eza] *(mpl* -eses [-eziʃ], *fpl* -s [-ʃ]) *adj & m* Irish ◆ *m, f (pessoa)* Irishman *(f* Irishwoman); **os irlandeses** the Irish.

irmã [ix'mã] *f (freira)* nun, → **irmão**.

irmão, -mã [ix'mãw, -mã] *m, f* brother *(f* sister).

ironia [iro'nia] *f* irony.

irra [ixa] *interj* damn!

irracional [ixasjo'naw] *(pl* -ais [-ajʃ]) *adj* irrational.

irradiação [ixadʒja'sãw] *(pl* -ões [-õjʃ]) *f* irradiation.

irradiar [ixa'dʒja(x)] *vt (luz)* to radiate.

irreal [i'xjaw] *(pl* -ais [-ajʃ]) *adj* unreal.

irreconciliável [ixekõsi'ljavɛw] *(pl* -eis [-ejʃ]) *adj* irreconcilable.

irreconhecível [ixekoɲe'sivɛw] *(pl* -eis [-ejʃ]) *adj* unrecognizable.

irrecuperável [ixekupe'ravɛw] *(pl* -eis [-ejʃ]) *adj (perdido)* irretrievable; *(estragado)* irreparable; *(doente, viciado)* incurable.

irregular [ixegu'la(x)] *(pl* -es [-iʃ]) *adj* irregular; *(superfície)* uneven.

irrelevante [ixele'vãntʃi] *adj* irrelevant.

irremediável [ixeme'dʒjavɛw] *(pl* -eis [-ejʃ]) *adj* irremediable.

irreprimível [ixepri'mivɛw] *(pl* -eis [-ejʃ]) *adj* irrepressible.

irrequieto, -ta [ixe'kjɛtu, -ta] *adj (criança)* boisterous.

irresistível [ixeziʃ'tʃivɛw] *(pl* -eis [-ejʃ]) *adj* irresistible; *(apetite, vontade)* overwhelming.

irresponsável [ixeʃpõ'savɛw] *(pl* -eis [-ejʃ]) *adj* irresponsible.

irrigação [ixiga'sãw] *(pl* -ões [-õjʃ]) *f* irrigation.

irrisório, -ria [ixi'zɔrju, -rja] *adj* derisory.

irritação [ixita'sãw] *(pl* -ões [-õjʃ]) *f* irritation; **~ de pele** OU **cutânea** (skin) rash.

irritante [ixi'tãntʃi] *adj* irritating.

irritar [ixi'ta(x)] *vt* to irritate.

❑ **irritar-se** *vp* to get irritated.

isca [iʃka] *f (para pesca)* bait.

isenção [izẽ'sãw] *(pl* -ões [-õjʃ]) *f* exemption.

isento, -ta [i'zẽntu, -ta] *adj* exempt; **~ de** exempt from.

isolado, -da [izo'ladu, -da] *adj (lugar)* remote; *(pessoa, objeto)* isolated.

isolamento [izola'mẽntu] *m (solidão)* isolation; *(de janela, cabo)* insulation.

isolar [izo'la(x)] *vt (pessoa)* to isolate; *(janela, cabo)* to insulate.

isopor® [izo'pox] *m (Br)* polystyrene.

isqueiro [iʃ'kejru] *m (de cigarro)* lighter; *(de fogão a gás)* ignition button.

isso [ˈisu] *pron* that ♦ *interj* that's it!; **como vai ~?** how's it going?; **foi por ~ que ele não veio** that's why he didn't come; **é por ~ mesmo que eu não vou!** that is exactly why I'm not going!; **~ não!** no way!; **não gosto disso** I don't like that; **não mexa nisso!** leave that alone!; **nem por ~** not really; **para ~** (in order) to do that.

istmo [ˈiʃtʃimu] *m* isthmus.

isto [ˈiʃtu] *pron* this; **disto eu não quero** I don't want any of this; **escreva nisto** write on this; **~ é** *(quer dizer)* that is (to say); **~ é que é vida!** this is the life!

Itália [iˈtalja] *f:* **a ~** Italy.

italiana [itaˈljana] *f* very strong espresso, → **italiano**.

italiano, -na [itaˈljanu, -na] *adj & m, f* Italian ♦ *m (língua)* Italian.

itálico [iˈtaliku] *m* italic type, italics *(pl)*; **em ~** in italics.

itinerário [itʃineˈrarju] *m* itinerary; **turístico** tourist route OU trail.

iúca [ˈjuka] *f* yucca.

IVA [ˈiva] *m (Port: abrev de Imposto sobre o Valor Acrescentado)* VAT *(Brit)*, sales tax *(Am)*.

J

já [ˈʒa] *adv (agora)* now; *(de seguida)* right away, at once; **até ~!** see you soon!; **é para ~!** coming up!; **~ acabei** I've already finished!; **~ que estamos aqui, podíamos ir ao cinema** since we're here, we might as well go to the cinema; **você ~ esteve em Salvador?** have you ever been to Salvador?; **você ~ foi a Salvador?** have you been to Salvador yet?; **~ não sei o que fazer** I don't know what else I can do; **desde ~** in advance; **~ era** it's past it; **~ que** since.

jabuti [ʒabuˈtʃi] *m* giant tortoise.

jabuticaba [ʒabutʃiˈkaba] *f dark red Brazilian berry with sweet white flesh.*

jacarandá [ʒakarãˈda] *m* jacaranda *(South American tree valued for its wood).*

jacaré [ʒakaˈrɛ] *m* crocodile.

jacinto [ʒaˈsĩntu] *m* hyacinth.

jacto [ˈʒatu] *m (Port)* = jato.

Jacuzzi® [ʒakuˈzi] *m* Jacuzzi®.

jade [ˈʒadʒi] *m* jade.

jaguar [ʒaˈgwa(x)] *(pl* -res [-riʃ]) *m* jaguar.

jamais [ʒaˈmajʃ] *adv* never; **o livro mais interessante que ~ li** the most interesting book I've ever read.

janeiro [ʒaˈnejru] *m* January, → setembro.

janela [ʒaˈnɛla] *f* window.

jangada [ʒãŋˈgada] *f* raft.

jantar [ʒãnˈta(x)] *(pl* -res [-riʃ]) *m* dinner ◆ *vi* to have dinner ◆ *vt* to have for dinner.

jante [ˈʒãntʃi] *f (wheel)* rim.

Japão [ʒaˈpãw] *m*: **o ~** Japan.

japonês, -esa [ʒapoˈneʃ, -eza] *(mpl* -eses [-eziʃ], *fpl* -s [-ʃ]) *adj & m, f* Japanese ◆ *m (língua)* Japanese.

jaqueta [ʒaˈketa] *f* jacket.

jararaca [ʒaraˈraka] *f extremely ven-*omous viper-like snake found in South America.

jardim [ʒaxˈdʒĩ] *(pl* -ns [-ʃ]) *m (de casa)* garden; *(público)* park; **~ botânico** botanical gardens *(pl)*; **~ de infância** kindergarten; **~ zoológico** zoo.

jardim-escola [ʒaˌdʒĩʃˈkɔla] *(pl* jardins-escolas [ʒaˌdʒĩʒˈkɔlaʃ]) *m (Port)* kindergarten.

jardineiras [ʒaxdʒiˈnejraʃ] *fpl (calças)* dungarees *(Brit)*, overalls *(Am)*.

jardineiro, -ra [ʒaxdʒiˈnejru, -ra] *m, f* gardener.

jardins → jardim.

jarra [ˈʒaxa] *f (para flores)* vase; *(para vinho)* carafe.

jarrão [ʒaˈxãw] *(pl* -ões [-õjʃ]) *m (large)* vase.

jarro [ˈʒaxu] *m (para bebida)* jug; *(flor)* arum lily.

jarrões → jarrão.

jasmim [ʒaʒˈmĩ] *(pl* -ns [-ʃ]) *m* jasmine.

jato [ˈʒatu] *m (Br)* jet.

jaula [ˈʒawla] *f* cage.

javali [ʒavaˈli] *m* wild boar.

jazer [ʒaˈze(x)] *vi* to lie.

jazigo [ʒaˈzigu] *m* tomb.

jazz [ˈdʒaz] *m* jazz.

jeans [ˈdʒiniʃ] *m inv (Br)* jeans *(pl)* ◆ *mpl (Port)* jeans.

jeito [ˈʒejtu] *m (modo)* way; *(comportamento)* manner; **não tem ~!** *(Br)* it's hopeless!; **com ~** carefully; **dar um ~ em algo** *(tornozelo, pulso)* to sprain sthg; *(reparar)* to fix sthg; **ficar sem ~** *(Br)* to feel embarrassed; **ter falta de ~ para algo** to be bad at sthg; **ter ~ para algo** to be good at sthg; **tomar ~** *(Br)* to learn one's lesson; **de ~ nenhum!** no way!

jejum [ʒeˈʒũ] *(pl* -ns [-ʃ]) *m* fast; **em ~** on an empty stomach.

jesuíta [ʒeˈzwita] *m (RELIG)* Jesuit.

jet ski [dʒɛt'ski] *m* jet-skiing.

jibóia [ʒi'bɔja] *f* boa constrictor.

jipe ['ʒipi] *m* Jeep®.

joalharia [ʒwaʎa'ria] *f (Port)* = **joalheria**.

joalheria [ʒwaʎe'ria] *f (Br) (loja)* jeweller's (shop); *(jóias)* jewellery.

joanete [ʒwa'netʃi] *m* bunion.

joaninha [ʒwa'niɲa] *f* ladybird *(Brit)*, ladybug *(Am)*.

joelheira [ʒwe'ʎeira] *f* knee pad.

joelho [ʒwɛʎu] *m* knee; **de ~s** on one's knees.

jogada [ʒo'gada] *f (lance de jogo)* go, turn; *(em xadrez)* move; *(em futebol, basquete)* shot.

jogar [ʒo'ga(x)] *vi* to play; *(em jogo de azar)* to gamble ♦ *vt* to play; *(apostar)* to bet; *(atirar)* to throw; **~ bola** to play ball; **~ às cartas** to play cards; **~ fora** *(Br)* to throw away OU out.

❏ **jogar-se a** *vp + prep (pessoa)* to lunge at; **ele jogou-se no chão** he threw himself to the floor.

jogo ['ʒogu] *(pl* **jogos** ['ʒoguʃ]) *m (de tênis, xadrez)* game; *(de futebol, rúghi)* match; *(conjunto)* set; *(jogos de azar)* gambling; **~ do bicho** *(unlicensed)* lottery in which every group of numbers is represented by an animal; **~ do galo** *(Port)* noughts and crosses *(sg)*; **~s de video** video games; **os Jogos Olímpicos** the Olympics.

jogo-da-velha [ˌʒoguda'vɛʎa] *(pl* **jogos-da-velha** [ˌʒoguʒda'vɛʎa]) *m (Br)* noughts and crosses *(sg)*.

jóia ['ʒɔja] *f (brincos, anel)* jewel; *(pagamento)* membership fee.

jóquei ['ʒɔkɛj] *m* jockey.

jornada [ʒox'nada] *f (caminhada)* journey; **~ de trabalho** working day.

jornal [ʒox'naw] *(pl* **-ais** [-ajʃ]) *m* newspaper.

jornaleiro, -ra [ʒoxna'lejru, -ra] *m, f (Br)* newsagent ♦ *m (Br)* newsagent's *(shop)*.

jornalista [ʒoxna'liʃta] *mf* journalist.

jorrar [ʒo'xa(x)] *vi* to gush.

jovem ['ʒovẽ] *(pl* **-ns** [-ʃ]) *adj* young ♦ *mf* young man *(f* young woman).

jovial [ʒo'vjaw] *(pl* **-ais** [-ajʃ]) *adj* jolly.

joystick [dʒɔj'stʃiki] *m* joystick.

juba ['ʒuba] *f* mane.

judaico, -ca [ʒu'dajku, -ka] *adj* Jewish.

judeu, -dia [ʒu'dew, -dʃia] *m, f* Jew.

judicial [ʒudʃi'sjaw] *(pl* **-ais** [-ajʃ]) *adj* legal; **o poder ~** the judiciary.

judiciária [ʒudʃi'sjarja] *f (Port) (polícia)* police; *(local)* police station.

judo ['ʒudu] *m (Port)* = **judô**.

judô [ʒu'do] *m (Br)* judo.

Jugoslávia [ʒuguʒ'lavja] *f (Port)*: **a ~** Yugoslavia.

juiz, juíza ['ʒwiʃ, 'ʒwiza] *(mpl* **-zes** [-zeʃ], *fpl* **-s** [-ʃ]) *m, f* judge; **~ de linha** *(Port: em futebol)* linesman.

juízo ['ʒwizu] *m (parecer)* opinion ♦ *interj* behave yourself!; **perder o ~** to lose one's mind; **ter ~** to be sensible.

jujuba [ʒu'ʒuba] *f (bala)* jelly bean.

julgamento [ʒuwga'mẽntu] *m (acto)* judgement; *(audiência)* trial.

julgar [ʒuw'ga(x)] *vt (JUR)* to judge; *(achar, opinar)* to think ♦ *vi (JUR)* to pass sentence.

❏ **julgar-se** *vp*: **ele julga-se o maior** he thinks he's the best.

julho ['ʒuʎu] *m* July, → **setembro**.

jumento [ʒu'mẽntu] *m* donkey.

junco [ʒ'ũŋku] *m* reed, rush.

junho ['ʒuɲu] *m* June, → **setembro**.

júnior ['ʒunjɔ(x)] *(pl* **juniores** [ʒu'njɔriʃ]) *adj* youngest ♦ *mf (ESP)* junior.

junta ['ʒũnta] *f* joint; *(POL)* junta.

juntamente [ʒũnta'mẽntʃi] : **juntamente com** *prep* together with.

juntar [ʒũn'ta(x)] *vt (reunir)* to gather together; *(dinheiro)* to save; *(adicionar)* to add; **~ o útil ao agradável** to mix business with pleasure.

❏ **juntar-se** *vp (reunir-se)* to gather round; *(encontrar-se)* to meet; *(amigarse)* to move in together.

junto, -ta ['ʒũntu, -ta] *pp* → **juntar** ♦ *adj* together ♦ *adv*: **~ de** OU **a** by; **~ com** along with.

jura ['ʒura] *f* vow.

juramento [ʒura'mẽntu] *m* oath.

jurar [ʒu'ra(x)] *vt & vi* to swear.

júri ['ʒuri] *m* jury.

jurídico, -ca [ʒu'ridʒiku, -ka] *adj* legal.

juros ['ʒuruʃ] *mpl* interest *(sg)*.

justeza [ʒuʃ'teza] *f (precisão)* precision; *(imparcialidade)* fairness.

justiça [ʒuʃˈtʃisa] f justice; *(organismo)* judiciary.

justificação [ʒuʃtʃifikaˈsãw] *(pl* **-ões** [-õjʃ])* f *(razão)* justification; *(escrita)* statement.

justificar [ʒuʃtʃifiˈka(x)] vt to justify.
□ **justificar-se** vp to justify o.s.

justificativa   [ʒuʃtʃifikaˈtiva]   f
justification.

justo, -ta [ˈʒuʃtu, -ta] adj *(exato)* precise; *(imparcial)* fair; *(cingido)* fitted.

juvenil [ʒuveˈniw] *(pl* **-is** [-iʃ])* adj *(moda, centro, literatura)* for teenagers; *(delinquente, comportamento)* juvenile.

juventude [ʒuvẽnˈtudʒi] f *(época)* youth; *(jovens)* young people *(pl)*.

K

karaokê [karaoˈke] *m* karaoke.
karaté [karaˈtɛ] *m (Port)* = **caratê**.
kart [ˈkaxtʃi] *m* go-kart.
karting [ˈkaxtʃiŋ] *m* go-karting.
ketchup [kɛˈtʃupi] *m* ketchup.
kg *(abrev de quilograma)* kg.
kit [ˈkitʃi] *m* kit.

kitchenette [kitʃiˈnɛtʃi] *f* kitchenette.
kiwi [ˈkiwi] *m* kiwi fruit.
km *(abrev de quilômetro)* km.
km/h *(abrev de quilômetro por hora)*
km/h.
KO [kɛˈɔ] *(abrev de knock-out)* KO.

L

lá [ˈla] *adv* there; **quero ~ saber!** what do I care!; **sei ~!** how should I know!; **vá ~!** go on!; **para ~ de** beyond.

lã [ˈlã] *f* wool.

-la [la] *pron* (pessoa) her; (coisa) it; (você) you.

labareda [labaˈreda] *f* flame.

lábio [ˈlabju] *m* lip.

labirinto [labiˈrĩtu] *m* labyrinth.

laboratório [laboraˈtɔrju] *m* laboratory.

laca [ˈlaka] *f* (Port) hairspray.

laço [ˈlasu] *m* bow; (de parentesco, amizade) bond.

lacónico, -ca [laˈkoniku, -ka] *adj* (Port) = **lacônico**.

lacônico, -ca [laˈkoniku, -ka] *adj* (Br) laconic.

lacrar [laˈkra(x)] *vt* to seal (with sealing wax).

lacrimogénio [lakrimoˈʒɛnju] *adj m* (Port) = **lacrimogênio**.

lacrimogêneo [lakrimoˈʒɛnju] *adj m* (Br) → **gás**.

lácteo, -tea [ˈlaktju, -tja] *adj* (produto) dairy (antes de s).

lacticínios [latiˈsinjuʃ] *mpl* (Port) = **laticínios**.

lacuna [laˈkuna] *f* (espaço vazio) gap; (esquecimento) oversight.

ladeira [laˈdejra] *f* slope.

lado [ˈladu] *m* side; (lugar) place; **gosto de me deitar de ~** I like to sleep on my side; **deixar** OU **pôr de ~** to set aside; **o ~ fraco** weak point; **o vizinho do ~** the next-door neighbour; **ao ~ de** next to, beside; **~ a ~** side by side; **de ~ a ~** from one end to the other; **de um ~ para o outro** back and forth; **por todo o ~** OU **todos os ~s** all over the place; **por um ~ ... por outro ~ ...** on the one hand ... on the other hand ....

ladrão, ladra [laˈdrãw, ˈladra] (*mpl* -ões [- õjʃ], *fpl* -s [-ʃ]) *m, f* thief.

ladrilho [laˈdriʎu] *m* floor tile.

ladrões → **ladrão**.

lagarta [laˈgaxta] *f* (bicho) caterpillar.

lagartixa [lagaxˈtʃiʃa] *f* gecko.

lagarto [laˈgaxtu] *m* lizard.

lago [ˈlagu] *m* (natural) lake; (de jardim) pond.

lagoa [laˈgoa] *f* lake.

lagosta [laˈgoʃta] *f* lobster.

lagostim [lagoʃˈtʃĩ] (*pl* -ns [-ʃ]) *m* langoustine.

lágrima [ˈlagrima] *f* tear.

laje [ˈlaʒi] *f* (de pavimento) paving stone; (de construção) slab.

lama [ˈlama] *f* mud.

lamacento, -ta [lamaˈsẽtu, -ta] *adj* muddy.

lambada [lãˈbada] *m* (dança) lambada.

lamber [lãˈbe(x)] *vt* to lick; **~ tudo** (fam) to lick the plate clean.

❏ **lamber-se** *vp* (cão) to lick o.s.; (gato) to wash o.s.

lamentar [lamẽˈta(x)] *vt* to lament.

❏ **lamentar-se** *vp* to moan.

lamentável [lamẽˈtavɛw] (*pl* -eis [-ejʃ]) *adj* regrettable.

lâmina [ˈlamina] *f* blade; **~ de barbear** razor blade.

lâmpada [ˈlãpada] *f* (light) bulb.

lampião [lãˈpjãw] (*pl* -ões [-õjʃ]) *m* lantern.

lampreia [lãˈpreja] *f* lamprey.

lança [ˈlãsa] *f* lance, spear.

lançar [lãˈsa(x)] *vt* (lança, bola, dardo) to throw; (novo filme, disco) to release; (campanha, livro, produto) to launch.

❏ **lançar-se** *vp*: **~-se a** to launch o.s. at; **~-se sobre** to throw o.s. on.

lance [ˈlãsi] *m* (em licitação) bid; (ESP: jogada) shot; (Br: fam: fato) fact; **~ de**

escada flight of stairs.

lancha ['lãʃa] f launch.

lanchar [lã'ʃa(x)] vi to have tea.

lanche ['lãʃi] m tea (light afternoon meal).

lanchonete [lãʃo'nɛtʃi] f (Br) snack bar.

lancinante [lãsi'nãntʃi] adj (dor) shooting; (grito) piercing.

lanço ['lãsu] m (Port) (em licitação) bid; ~ **de escadas** flight of stairs.

lânguido, -da ['lãŋgidu, -da] adj languid.

lantejoula [lãnte'ʒola] f sequin.

lanterna [lãn'tɛxna] f lantern; ~ **de bolso** torch (Brit), flashlight (Am).

lapela [la'pɛla] f lapel.

lápide ['lapidʒi] f (em monumento, estátua) memorial stone; (em túmulo) tombstone.

lápis ['lapiʃ] m inv pencil; ~ **de cor** coloured pencil; ~ **de cera** wax crayon; ~ **para os olhos** eyeliner.

lapiseira [lapi'zejra] f (em Portugal) ballpoint pen; (no Brasil) propelling pencil.

lapso ['lapsu] m (de tempo) period; (esquecimento) slip; **por** ~ by mistake.

laquê [la'ke] m (Br) hairspray.

lar ['la(x)] (pl **-res** [-riʃ]) m home; ~ **(de idosos)** old people's home.

laranja [la'rãʒa] f orange.

laranjada [larã'ʒada] f (Port) orangeade; (Br) orange juice.

laranjeira [larã'ʒejra] f orange tree.

lareira [la'rejra] f fireplace.

lares → **lar.**

largada [lax'gada] f start.

largar [lax'ga(x)] vt (soltar) to let go; (libertar) to set free; (deixar cair) to drop; (velas) to unfurl; (abandonar) to leave.

largo, -ga ['laxgu, -ga] adj (caminho, estrada, cama) wide; (roupa) loose ◆ m (praça) square; **tem 3 metros de** ~ it's 3 metres wide; **ao** ~ at a distance.

largura [lax'gura] f width.

laringe [la'rĩʒi] f larynx.

larva ['laxva] f larva.

-las [laʃ] pron pl (elas) them; (vocês) you.

lasanha [la'zaɲa] f lasagne.

lasca ['laʃka] f (de madeira) splinter; (de pedra) chip.

laser ['lejzɛ(x)] (pl **-res** [-riʃ]) m laser.

lástima ['laʃtʃima] f (pena) shame; (miséria) misery.

lastimável [laʃtʃi'mavɛw] (pl **-eis** [-ejʃ]) adj (acontecimento) regrettable; (erro) unfortunate; (situação, estado) deplorable.

lata ['lata] f tin; (de bebida) can; ~ **(de conserva)** tin (Brit), can (Am); ~ **de lixo** (Br) litter bin (Brit), trashcan (Am).

latão [la'tãw] (pl **-ões** [-õjʃ]) m (metal) brass; (vasilha) large can.

latejar [late'ʒa(x)] vi to throb.

latente [la'tẽntʃi] adj latent.

lateral [late'raw] (pl **-ais** [-ajʃ]) adj lateral.

laticínios [latʃi'sinjuʃ] mpl (Br) dairy products.

latido [la'tʃidu] m barking.

latifúndio [latʃi'fũndʒju] m large rural estate.

latim [la'tʃĩ] m Latin.

latino, -na [la'tʃinu, -na] adj Latin.

latino-americano, -na [la,tʃinwameri'kanu, -na] adj & m, f Latin American.

latir [la'tʃi(x)] vi to bark.

latitude [latʃi'tudʒi] f latitude.

latões → **latão.**

lava ['lava] f lava.

lavabo [la'vabu] m (pia) washbasin; (banheiro) toilet (Brit), restroom (Am).

lavagem [la'vaʒẽ] (pl **-ns** [-ʃ]) f washing; ~ **automática** automatic car wash; ~ **cerebral** brainwashing; ~ **a seco** dry-cleaning.

lavanda [la'vãnda] f lavender.

lavandaria [lavãnda'ria] f (Port) = lavanderia.

lavanderia [lavãnde'ria] f (Br) (loja, local) laundry; ~ **automática** launderette; ~ **a seco** dry cleaner's (shop).

lavar [la'va(x)] vt to wash; ~ **os dentes** to clean OU brush one's teeth; ~ **a louça** to wash the dishes; ~ **a roupa** to do the washing.

⊔ **lavar-se** vp to have a wash.

lavável [la'vavɛw] (pl **-eis** [-ejʃ]) adj washable.

lavrador, -ra [lavra'do(x), -ra] (mpl **-res** [-riʃ], fpl **-s** [-ʃ]) m, f farm labourer.

laxante [la'ʃãntʃi] adj & m laxative.

lazer [la'ze(x)] m: **horas** OU **ou momentos de** ~ spare OU free time; **centro de** ~ leisure centre.

Lda (Port: abrev de limitada) Ltd.

lê ['le] → **ler.**

leal [le'aw] (pl **-ais** [-ajʃ]) adj loyal.

leão [le'ãw] (pl **-ões** [-õjʃ]) m lion.

❑ **Leão** m Leo.

lebre ['lɛbri] f hare; **comer gato por ~** to be ripped off.

leccionar [lɛsju'nar] vt & vi (Port) = **lecionar**.

lecionar [lɛsjo'na(x)] vt & vi (Br) to teach.

lectivo, -va [lɛ'tivu, -va] adj (Port) = **letivo**.

lêem ['leẽ] → **ler**.

legal [le'gaw] (pl **-ais** [-ajʃ]) adj (segundo a Lei) legal; (Br: fam) great.

legalidade [legali'dadʒi] f legality.

legalizar [legali'za(x)] vt (actividade) to legalize; (documento, assinatura) to authenticate.

legenda [le'ʒẽda] f (em mapa) key; (em fotografia) caption; (mito) legend.

❑ **legendas** fpl (em cinema, televisão) subtitles.

legislação [leʒizla'sãw] f legislation.

legitimar [leʒiti'ma(x)] vt to legitimize; (documento, assinatura) to authenticate.

legítimo, -ma [le'ʒitʃimu, -ma] adj legitimate; (autêntico) genuine.

legível [le'ʒivɛw] (pl **-eis** [-ejʃ]) adj legible.

légua ['lɛgwa] f league; **ficar a ~s de distância** to be miles away.

legumes [le'gumeʃ] mpl vegetables.

lei ['lej] f law; **fazer tudo pela ~ do menor esforço** to do everything with the least possible effort; **segundo a ~** according to the law.

leilão [lej'lãw] (pl **-ões** [-õjʃ]) m auction.

leio ['leju] → **ler**.

leitão [lej'tãw] (pl **-ões** [-õjʃ]) m suckling pig.

leitaria [lejta'ria] f (Port) = **leiteria**.

leite ['lejtʃi] m milk; **~ gordo/meio-gordo/magro** (Port) full-fat/semi-skimmed/skimmed milk; **~ pasteurizado/ultrapasteurizado** pasteurized/UHT milk; **~ integral/desnatado** (Br) full-fat/skimmed milk; **~ achocolatado** chocolate milk; **~ de côco** coconut milk; **~ condensado** condensed milk; **~ creme** crème brûlée; **~ em pó** powdered milk.

leite-de-onça [lejtʃidʒi'õsa] m (Br) milk mixed with "cachaça".

leiteiro, -ra [lej'tejru, -ra] m, f milkman (f milkwoman).

leiteria [lejte'ria] f (Br) dairy.

leito ['lejtu] m bed.

leitões → **leitão**.

leitor, -ra [lej'to(x), -ra] (mpl **-res** [-riʃ], fpl **-s** [-ʃ]) m, f reader; (Port: professor assistente) language assistant ♦ m (de cassetes, CD) player; **~ de cassetes** cassette player; **~ de CD** CD player; **~ de vídeo** video(recorder) (Brit), VCR (Am).

leitura [lej'tura] f reading.

lema ['lema] m motto.

lembrança [lẽm'brãsa] f memory; (prenda) memento; **dê-lhe ~s** send him/her my regards.

lembrar [lẽm'bra(x)] vt (recordar) to remember; (assemelhar-se a) to look like; **~ algo a alguém** to remind sb of sthg; **~ alguém de fazer algo** to remind sb to do sthg.

❑ **lembrar-se** vp to remember; **~-se de** to remember; **~-se de fazer algo** to remember to do sthg.

leme ['lɛmi] m (posição) helm; (objeto) rudder.

lenço ['lẽsu] m handkerchief; **~ da cabeça** headscarf; **~ de papel** tissue; **~ (do pescoço)** scarf.

lençol [lẽ'sɔw] (pl **-óis** [-ɔjʃ]) m sheet; **~ de água** water table.

lenha ['lɛɲa] f firewood.

lente ['lẽtʃi] f lens; **~s de contato** contact lenses.

lentidão [lẽtʃi'dãw] f: **com ~** slowly.

lentilha [lẽ'tʃiʎa] f lentil.

lento, -ta ['lẽtu, -ta] adj slow.

leoa [le'oa] f lioness.

leões → **leão**.

leopardo [ljo'paxdu] m leopard.

lepra ['lɛpra] f leprosy.

leque ['lɛki] m fan.

ler ['le(x)] vt & vi to read.

lesão [le'zãw] (pl **-ões** [-õjʃ]) f (ferida, contusão) injury; (prejuízo) harm.

lesar [le'za(x)] vt (ferir) to injure; (prejudicar) to harm.

lésbica ['lɛʒbika] f lesbian.

lesma ['lɛʒma] f slug; (fig: pessoa lenta) slowcoach (Brit), slowpoke (Am).

lesões → **lesão**.

leste ['lɛʃtʃi] m east; **os países de ~** Eastern European countries; **a OU no ~** in the east; **a ~ de** east of; **estar a ~**

de algo *(fam)* not to have a clue about sthg.

letal [le'taw] *(pl -ais* [-ajʃ]) *adj* lethal.

letivo, -va [le'tʃivu, -va] *adj (Br) (ano)* academic, school *(antes de s)*.

letra ['letra] *f (do alfabeto)* letter; *(maneira de escrever)* handwriting; *(título de crédito)* bill; **~ maiúscula** capital letters *(pl)*; **~ de imprensa** block capitals *(pl)*; **~ de fôrma** *(Br)* block capitals *(pl)*.

❏ **letras** *fpl (área de estudo)* arts.

letreiro [le'trejru] *m* sign.

leu ['lew] → **ler**.

léu ['lɛu] *m*: **ao ~** uncovered.

leucemia [lewse'mia] *f* leukaemia.

levantamento [levãnta'mẽntu] *m* survey; **~ de peso** weightlifting.

levantar [levãn'ta(x)] *vt (erguer)* to raise, to lift; **~ dinheiro** to raise money; **~ a mesa** to clear the table; **~ vôo** to take off.

❏ **levantar-se** *vp (de cama)* to get up; *(de cadeira, chão)* to stand up.

levar [le'va(x)] *vt* to take; *(carregar)* to carry; *(induzir)* to lead; *(filme)* to show; *(fam: porrada, bofetada)* to get; **este recipiente leva cinco litros** this container holds five litres; **~ alguém a fazer algo** to make sb do sthg; **~ a cabo algo** to carry sthg out; **~ a mal algo** to take sthg the wrong way; **deixar-se ~** to get taken for a ride.

leve ['lɛvi] *adj* light.

leviandade [levjãn'dadʒi] *f* rashness.

leviano, -na [le'vjanu, -na] *adj* rash.

léxico ['lɛksiku] *m* lexicon.

lha [ʎa] = **lhe + a**, → **lhe**.

lhe [ʎi] *pron (ele)* (to) him; *(ela)* (to) her; *(você)* (to) you; **já ~ dei a chave do quarto** I've already given him/her/you the key to the room; **aquele livro ali, ela deu-lhe como presente** that book there, she gave it to him/her/you as a present.

lhes [ʎeʃ] *pron pl (eles, elas)* (to) them; *(vocês)* (to) you.

lho [ʎu] = **lhe + o, lhes + o**, → **lhe**.

li ['li] → **ler**.

libélula [li'bɛlula] *f* dragonfly.

liberação [libera'sãw] *f* liberation.

liberal [libe'raw] *(pl -ais* [-ajʃ]) *adj & mf* liberal.

liberalização [liberaliza'sãw] *f* deregulation.

liberar [libe'ra(x)] *vt (pessoa)* to free,

to liberate; *(comércio, consumo)* to deregulate.

liberdade [libex'dadʒi] *f* freedom; **pôr em ~** to set free; **tomar a ~ de fazer algo** to take the liberty of doing sthg.

libertar [libex'ta(x)] *vt* to set free.

liberto, -ta [li'bextu, -ta] *pp* → **libertar**.

libra ['libra] *f* pound.

❏ **Libra** *f (Br: signo do Zodíaco)* Libra.

lição [li'sãw] *(pl -ões* [-õjʃ]) *f* lesson; **dar uma ~ a alguém** to teach sb a lesson; **que isso lhe sirva de ~!** let that be a lesson to you!

licença [li'sẽsa] *f (autorização)* permission; *(de veículo)* registration document; *(de arma)* licence; **com ~** excuse me; **~ de maternidade** *(para mãe)* maternity leave; *(para pai)* paternity leave.

licenciado, -da [lisẽ'sjadu, -da] *m, f* graduate.

licenciatura [lisẽsja'tura] *f* degree.

liceu [li'sew] *m* = secondary school *(Brit)*, = high school *(Am)*.

lições → **lição**.

licor [li'ko(x)] *(pl -res* [-riʃ]) *m* liqueur.

lidar [li'da(x)] : **lidar com** *v + prep* to deal with.

líder ['lide(x)] *(pl -res* [-riʃ]) *mf* leader.

lido, -da ['lidu, -da] *pp* → **ler**.

liga ['liga] *f (associação)* league; *(de meias)* garter.

ligação [liga'sãw] *(pl -ões* [-õjʃ]) *f (de amor, amizade)* relationship; *(telefônica)* connection.

ligado, -da [li'gadu, -da] *adj (luz, televisão)* (switched OU turned) on.

ligadura [liga'dura] *f* bandage.

ligamento [liga'mẽntu] *m* ligament.

ligar [li'ga(x)] *vt (luz, televisão)* to switch OU turn on; *(em tomada)* to plug in ◆ *vi (telefonar)* to call; **~ para** *(telefonar para)* to call; *(dar atenção a)* to take notice of.

ligeiro, -ra [li'ʒejru, -ra] *light; (ferimento)* slight.

lilás [li'laʃ] *(pl -ases* [-aziʃ]) *m & adj* lilac.

lima ['lima] *f (Port)* file.

limão [li'mãw] *(pl -ões* [-õjʃ]) *m (Br)* lime; *(Port)* lemon.

limão-galego [li,mãwga'legu] *(pl limões-galegos* [li,mõjʒga'leguʃ]) *m (Br)* lemon.

limiar [li'mja(x)] *m* threshold; **no ~ de algo** on the threshold of sthg.

limitação [limita'sãw] (*pl* -ões [-õjʃ]) *f (de direitos, movimentos)* restriction; *(de terreno)* boundary.

❏ **limitações** *fpl (intelectuais)* limitations.

limitar [limi'ta(x)] *vt* to limit.

❏ **limitar-se** *a vp + prep* to limit o.s. to.

limite [li'mitʃi] *m* limit; *(de terreno)* boundary; **~ de velocidade** speed limit; **sem ~s** limitless; **passar dos ~s** *(fig)* to overstep the mark.

limo ['limu] *m* slime.

limoeiro [li'mwejru] *m* lemon tree.

limões → **limão**.

limonada [limo'nada] *f* lemonade.

limpador [lĩmpa'do(x)] (*pl* -res [-riʃ]) *m (Br):* **~ de pára-brisas** windscreen wiper *(Brit)*, windshield wiper *(Am)*.

limpa-pára-brisas [lĩmpapara'brizaʃ] *m inv (Port)* windscreen wiper *(Brit)*, windshield wiper *(Am)*.

limpar [lĩm'pa(x)] *vt* to clean; *(pratos)* to dry; *(boca)* to wipe; *(mãos)* to wash; *(fam: roubar)* to clean out; **~ o pó** to do the dusting.

limpa-vidros [lĩmpa'vidruʃ] *m inv (instrumento)* window wiper; *(detergente)* window-cleaning fluid.

limpeza [lĩm'peza] *f (ação)* cleaning; *(asseio)* cleanliness.

limpo, -pa ['lĩmpu, -pa] *pp* → **limpar** ♦ *adj (sem sujeira)* clean; *(céu)* clear; **estar** OU **ficar ~** *(fam)* to be broke; **tirar algo a ~** to clear sthg up.

limusine [limu'zini] *f* limousine.

lince ['lĩsi] *m* lynx.

lindo, -da ['lĩndu, -da] *adj* beautiful.

lingerie [lãʒe'xi] *f* lingerie.

lingote [lĩŋ'gɔtʃi] *m* ingot.

língua ['lĩŋgwa] *f (ANAT)* tongue; *(idioma)* language; **bater com a ~ nos dentes** *(fam: denunciar)* to grass; **dobrar a ~** to watch one's language; **morder a ~** to bite one's tongue; **ter algo na ponta da ~** to have sthg on the tip of one's tongue.

linguado [lĩŋ'gwadu] *m* sole.

linguagem [lĩŋ'gwaʒẽ] (*pl* -ns [-ʃ]) *f* language.

linguarudo, -da [lĩŋgwa'rudu, -da] *adj* gossipy.

línguas-de-gato [lĩŋgwaʒdʒi'gatu] *fpl* small, thin sweet biscuits.

lingueta [lĩŋ'gweta] *f* catch.

linguiça [lĩŋ'gwisa] *f* long, thin, spicy dry sausage made with lean pork and seasoned with paprika.

linha ['liɲa] *f* line; *(de coser)* thread; **~ jovem** teenage range; **manter a ~** to keep trim; **~ férrea** *(Port)* (train) tracks *(pl)*; **em ~** in a line.

linho ['liɲu] *m* linen.

linóleo [li'nɔlju] *m* linoleum.

liquidação [likida'sãw] (*pl* -ões [-õjʃ]) *f (de dívida)* settlement; **~ total** clearance OU closing-down sale.

liquidar [liki'da(x)] *vt (dívida)* to pay off; *(matar)* to liquidate; *(mercadorias)* to sell off.

liquidificador [likwidʒifika'do(x)] (*pl* -res [-riʃ]) *m (Br)* liquidizer, blender.

liquidificadora [likidifika'dora] *f (Port)* = **liquidificador**.

líquido, -da ['likidu, -da] *adj (substância)* liquid; *(COM)* net ♦ *m* liquid.

lírio ['lirju] *m* lily.

Lisboa [liʒ'boa] *s* Lisbon.

lisboeta [liʒ'bweta] *adj* of/relating to Lisbon ♦ *mf* native/inhabitant of Lisbon.

liso, -sa ['lizu, -za] *adj (superfície)* flat; *(cabelo)* straight; *(folha)* plain; **estar** OU **ficar ~** *(fam: sem dinheiro)* to be skint.

lista ['liʃta] *f* list; *(menu)* menu; **~ de preços** price list; **~ telefônica** telephone directory; **~ de vinhos** wine list.

listra ['liʃtra] *f* stripe.

literal [lite'raw] (*pl* -ais [-ajʃ]) *adj* literal.

literário, -ria [lite'rarju, -rja] *adj* literary.

literatura [litera'tura] *f* literature; **~ de cordel** *popular literature from the northeast of Brazil.*

litígio [li'tʃiʒju] *m* litigation.

litogravura [litɔgra'vura] *f* lithography.

litoral [lito'raw] (*pl* -ais [-ajʃ]) *adj* coastal ♦ *m:* **o ~** the coast.

litro ['litru] *m* litre.

lívido, -da ['lividu, -da] *adj* pallid.

livrar [li'vra(x)] **: livrar-se de** *vp + prep* to get rid of.

livraria [livra'ria] *f* bookshop *(Brit)*, book store *(Am)*.

livre ['livri] *adj* free; **"livre"** *(em táxi)* "for hire"; *(em W.C.)* "vacant".

livro ['livru] *m* book; **~ de bolso**

pocket-size paperback; ~ **de capa dura** hardback.

lixa ['liʃa] f sandpaper; *(para unhas)* nail file.

lixeira [li'ʃejra] f *(em prédio)* rubbish chute; *(local)* rubbish dump *(Brit)*, garbage dump *(Am)*.

lixívia [le'ʃivja] f *(Port)* bleach.

lixo ['liʃu] m rubbish *(Brit)*, garbage *(Am)*.

-lo [lu] *pron (pessoa)* him; *(coisa)* it; *(você)* you.

L.º *(abrev)* = **largo.**

lobo ['lobu] m wolf.

lóbulo ['lɔbulu] m *(de orelha)* earlobe.

local [lo'kaw] *(pl* **-ais** [-ajʃ]*)* m place ◆ *adj* local.

localidade [lokali'dadʒi] f town.

localização [lokaliza'sãw] *(pl* **-ões** [-õjʃ]*)* f location.

loção [lo'sãw] *(pl* **-ões** [-õjʃ]*)* f lotion; ~ **para após a barba** aftershave; ~ **capilar** hair lotion.

locatario, -ria [loka'tarju, -rja] m, f tenant.

loções → **loção.**

locomotiva [lokomo'tʃiva] f locomotive.

locução [loku'sãw] *(pl* **-ões** [-õjʃ]*)* f *(de filme, programa)* narration; *(GRAM)* phrase.

locutor, -ra [loku'to(x), -ra] *(mpl* **-res** [-riʃ], *fpl* **-s** [-ʃ]*)* m, f *(de rádio, televisão)* announcer.

lodo ['lodu] m mud.

lógica ['lɔʒika] f logic.

logo ['lɔgu] *adv* immediately; **mais** ~ later; ~ **de seguida** immediately; ~ **que** as soon as; ~ **agora que** now (that).

logotipo [logo'tʃipu] m logo.

loja ['lɔʒa] f shop *(Brit)*, store *(Am)*; ~ **de artigos esportivos** sports shop; ~ **de artigos fotográficos** camera shop; ~ **de brinquedos** toyshop; ~ **de bugigangas** junk shop; ~ **de ferragens** hardware shop; ~ **de lembranças** souvenir shop; ~ **de produtos dietéticos** health-food shop.

lombada [lõm'bada] f spine.

lombinho [lõm'biɲu] m tenderloin *(of pork)*.

lombo ['lõmbu] m loin; ~ **assado** roast loin of pork marinated in dry white wine and paprika, then smeared with lard or covered in bacon before cooking.

lombriga [lõm'briga] f roundworm.

lona ['lona] f canvas.

Londres ['lõndriʃ] s London.

londrino, -na ['lõn'drinu, -na] *adj* of/relating to London.

longa-metragem [,lõŋgame'traʒẽ] *(pl* **longas-metragens** [,lõŋgaʒme'traʒẽʃ]*)* f feature film.

longe ['lõʒi] *adv* far; ~ **disso!** on the contrary!; **ao** ~ in the distance; **de** ~ *(fig)* by far; **ir** ~ **demais** to go too far.

longitude [lõʒi'tudʒi] f longitude.

longo, -ga ['lõŋgu, -ga] *adj* long; **ao** ~ **de** along; **ao** ~ **dos anos** over time.

lontra ['lõntra] f otter.

-los ['luʃ] *pron pl (eles)* them; *(vocês)* you.

losango [lo'zãŋgu] m lozenge.

lotação [lota'sãw] *(pl* **-ões** [-õjʃ]*)* f *(de cinema, teatro)* capacity; **"~ esgotada"** "sold out".

lotaria [luta'ria] f *(Port)* = **loteria.**

lote ['lɔtʃi] m *(de terreno)* plot; *(de prédios)* street number.

loteria [lote'ria] f *(Br)* lottery; ~ **esportiva** = football pools *(pl)* *(Brit)*, ~ soccer sweepstakes *(pl)* *(Am)*.

loto ['lotu] m *(jogo)* lotto.

louça ['losa] f china; *(pratos, xícaras, pires, etc)* crockery.

louco, -ca ['loku, -ka] *adj* mad, crazy ◆ m, f lunatic; **estar** OU **ficar** ~ **de alegria** to be over the moon; **ser** ~ **por** to be crazy about.

loucura [lo'kura] f madness.

louro, -ra ['loru, -ra] *adj* blond ◆ m *(condimento)* bay leaf.

louva-a-deus [,lova'dewʃ] m *inv* praying mantis.

louvar [lo'va(x)] *vt* to praise.

louvável [lo'vavɛw] *(pl* **-eis** [-ejʃ]*)* adj* praiseworthy.

LP m *(abrev de long-play)* LP.

Ltda *(Br: abrev de limitada)* Ltd.

L.te *(abrev de lote)* ~ No. *(Brit)*, = # *(Am)*.

lua ['lua] f moon; **estar de** ~ to be in a mood; **viver no mundo da** ~ to have one's head in the clouds.

lua-de-mel [,luadʒi'mɛw] *(pl* **luas-de-mel** [,luaʒdʒi'mɛw]*)* f honeymoon.

luar ['lwa(x)] m moonlight.

lubrificante [lubrifi'kãntʃi] m lubricant.

lubrificar [lubrifi'ka(x)] *vt* to lubricate.

lucidez [lusi'deʃ] f clarity.

lúcido, -da ['lusidu, -da] adj lucid.

lúcio ['lusju] m pike.

lucrar [lu'kra(x)] vi to profit; ~ com to profit from.

lucrativo, -va [lukra'tʃivu, -va] adj lucrative.

lucro ['lukru] m profit.

lúdico, -ca ['ludʒiku, -ka] adj play (antes de s).

lugar [lu'ga(x)] (pl -res [-riʃ]) m place; **em primeiro** ~ (em esporte) in first place; (antes) first; **ter** ~ (ocorrer) to take place; **em** ~ **de** instead of; **dar o** ~ **a alguém** to give one's seat to sb; **tomar o** ~ **de alguém** to take sb's place.

lugar-comum [lu,gaxku'mū] (pl **lugares-comuns** [lu,gariʃku'mūʃ]) m cliché.

lugares → lugar.

lúgubre ['lugubri] adj gloomy.

lula ['lula] f squid; ~s grelhadas grilled squid served with a butter, lemon and parsley sauce.

lume ['lumi] m (fogueira) fire; (Port: chama) flame.

luminária [lumi'narja] f (Br) lamp; ~ **de mesa** table lamp; ~ **de pé** standard lamp (Brit), floor lamp (Am).

luminosidade [luminozi'dadʒi] f brightness.

luminoso, -osa [lumi'nozu, -ɔza] adj bright; (fig: idéia, solução) brilliant.

lunar [lu'na(x)] (pl -res [-riʃ]) adj lunar.

lunático, -ca [lu'natʃiku, -ka] m, f lunatic.

luneta [lu'neta] f (Br: telescópio) telescope.

lupa ['lupa] f magnifying glass.

lustre ['luʃtri] m shine; (luminária) chandelier; **dar o** ~ **em algo** to polish sthg.

lustro ['luʃtru] m shine.

luta ['luta] f fight.

lutar [lu'ta(x)] vi to fight; ~ **contra/por** to fight against/for.

luto ['lutu] m mourning; **estar de** ~ to be in mourning.

luva ['luva] f glove.

Luxemburgo [luʃēm'buxgu] m: **o** ~ Luxembourg.

luxo ['luʃu] m luxury; **de** ~ luxury (antes de s).

luxuoso, -osa [lu'ʃwozu, -ɔza] adj luxurious.

luxúria [lu'ʃurja] f lust.

luxuriante [luʃu'rjãntʃi] adj luxuriant.

luz ['luʃ] (pl -zes [-ziʃ]) f light; **dar à** ~ **(um menino)** to give birth (to a baby boy); ~ **do sol** sunlight.

luzir [lu'zi(x)] vi to glow.

lycra® ['likra] f Lycra®.

M

ma [ma] = me + a, → me.

má → mau.

maca ['maka] f stretcher.

maçã [ma'sã] f apple; ~ **assada** baked apple.

macabro, -bra [ma'kabru, -bra] adj macabre.

macacão [maka'kãw] (pl -ões [-õjʃ]) m (roupa) jumpsuit; (protetor) boiler suit (Brit), overall (Am).

macaco, -ca [ma'kaku, -ka] m, f monkey ♦ m (AUT) jack.

macacões → macacão.

maçã-de-adão [ma,sãdʒja'dãw] (pl maçãs-de-adão [ma,sãdʒja'dãw]) f Adam's apple.

maçador, -ra [masa'dor, -ra] (mpl -res [-reʃ], fpl -s [-ʃ]) adj (Port) boring.

maçaneta [masa'neta] f knob.

maçante [ma'sãntʃi] adj (Br) boring.

maçapão [masa'pãw] m marzipan.

maçarico [masariku] m blowtorch.

maçaroca [masa'rɔka] f corncob.

macarrão [maka'xãw] m (Br: massa) pasta; (Port: tipo de massa) macaroni.

Macau [ma'kaw] s Macao.

macedônia [mase'donja] f mixed vegetables (pl); ~ **(de frutas)** fruit salad.

macete [ma'setʃi] m mallet.

machado [ma'ʃadu] m axe.

machismo [ma'ʃiʒmu] m male chauvinism.

machista [ma'ʃiʃta] adj chauvinistic ♦ m male chauvinist.

macho ['maʃu] adj m (animal) male; (homem) virile ♦ m (animal) male.

machucado, -da [maʃu'kadu, -da] adj (Br: ferido) hurt.

machucar [maʃu'kax] vt (Br) to hurt. ❑ **machucar-se** vp (Br) to hurt o.s.

maciço, -ça [ma'sisu, -sa] adj solid.

macieira [ma'sjejra] f apple tree.

macio, -cia [ma'siu, -'sia] adj soft.

maço ['masu] m mallet; ~ **(de cigarros)** packet (of cigarettes); ~ **de folhas** block of paper.

macumba [ma'kũmba] f voodoo.

madeira [ma'dejra] f wood.

Madeira [ma'dejra] m (vinho) Madeira ♦ f: a ~ Madeira.

madeixa [ma'dejʃa] f (de cabelo) lock.

madrasta [ma'draʃta] f stepmother.

madrepérola [,madre'pɛrola] f mother-of-pearl.

madressilva [,madre'siwva] f honeysuckle.

madrinha [ma'driɲa] f (de baptismo) godmother.

madrugada [madru'gada] f (amanhecer) dawn; (noite) early morning; de ~ (fig: muito cedo) at the crack of dawn.

madrugar [madru'ga(x)] vi to get up very early.

maduro, -ra [ma'duru, -ra] adj mature; (fruto) ripe.

mãe ['mãj] f mother.

maestro [ma'ɛʃtru] m conductor.

magia [ma'ʒia] f magic.

mágico, -ca ['maʒiku, -ka] adj magical ♦ m, f magician.

magistrado, -da [maʒiʃ'tradu, -da] m, f magistrate.

magnético, -ca [mag'nɛtʃiku, -ka] adj magnetic.

magnífico, -ca [mag'nifiku, -ka] adj magnificent.

magnitude [magni'tudʒi] f magnitude.

magnólia [mag'nɔlja] f magnolia.

mago, -ga ['magu, -ga] m, f wizard (f witch).

mágoa ['magwa] f sorrow.

magoado, -da [ma'gwadu, -da] adj hurt.

magoar [ma'gwa(x)] vt to hurt.

❏ **magoar-se** *vp* to hurt o.s.

magro, -gra ['magru, -gra] *adj* thin.

maio ['maju] *m* May, → **setembro**.

maiô [ma'jo] *m (Br) (de ginástica)* leotard; *(de banho)* swimsuit.

maionese [majo'nɛzi] *f* mayonnaise.

maior [ma'jɔ(x)] *(pl* **-res** *[-riʃ]) adj (em tamanho)* bigger; *(em número)* higher; *(em quantidade, importância)* greater ♦ *mf:* **o/a ~** *(em tamanho)* the biggest; *(em número)* the highest; *(em quantidade, importância)* the greatest; **ser ~ de idade** to be an adult; **a ~ parte de** most of.

maioria [majo'ria] *f* majority.

maioridade [majori'dadʒi] *f* adulthood.

mais ['majʃ] *adv* **1.** *(em comparações)* more; **a Ana é ~ alta/inteligente** Ana is taller/ more intelligent; **~ do que** more than; **~ ... do que ...** more ... than ...; **é ~ alta do que eu** she's taller than me; **bebeu um copo a ~!** he's had one too many!; **deram-me dinheiro a ~** they gave me too much money. **2.** *(como superlativo):* **o/a ~ ...** the most ...; **o ~ engraçado/ inteligente** the funniest/most intelligent. **3.** *(indica adição)* any more; **não necessito de ~ trabalho** I don't need any more work; **não necessito de ~ ninguém** I don't need anyone else. **4.** *(indica intensidade):* **que dia ~ feliz!** what a great day!; **que casa ~ feia!** what a horrible house! **5.** *(indica preferência):* **vale ~ a pena ficar em casa** it would be better to stay at home; **gosto ~ de comida chinesa** I prefer Chinese food. **6.** *(em locuções):* **de ~ a ~** *(ainda por cima)* what's more; **~ ou menos** more or less; **por ~ que se esforce** however hard he tries; **sem ~ nem menos** for no apparent reason; **uma vez ~, ~ uma vez** once OU yet again.
♦ *adj inv* **1.** *(em comparações)* more; **eles têm ~ dinheiro** they have more money; **está ~ calor hoje** it's hotter today; **~ ... do que** more ... than. **2.** *(como superlativo)* the most; **a pessoa que ~ discos vendeu** the person who sold (the) most records; **os que ~ dinheiro têm** those who have (the) most money. **3.** *(indica adição)* more; **~ água, por favor** I'd like some more water,

please; **~ alguma coisa?** anything else?; **tenho ~ três dias de férias** I've got another three days' holiday left.
♦ *conj* and; **eu ~ o Luís vamos** Luís and I are going; **quero uma sopa ~ pão com manteiga** I'd like some soup and some bread and butter.
♦ *prep (indica soma)* plus; **dois ~ dois são quatro** two plus two is four.

maitre ['mɛtrɛ] *m (Br)* head waiter.

major [ma'ʒɔ(x)] *(pl* **-res** *[-riʃ]) m* major.

mal ['maw] *(pl* **-les** *[-liʃ]) m (doença)* illness; *(dano)* harm ♦ *adv (erradamente)* wrong ♦ *conj (assim que)* as soon as; **o ~ evil;** **~ cheguei, telefonei logo** I phoned the minute I arrived; **estar ~** *(de saúde)* to be ill; **cheirar ~** to smell; **não faz ~** it doesn't matter; **ouço/vejo ~** I can't hear/see very well; **passar ~** *(ter enjôo)* to feel sick.

mala ['mala] *f (de mão, roupa)* bag; *(do carro)* boot *(Brit),* trunk *(Am);* **~ frigorífica** cool box; **~ de viagem** suitcase; **fazer as ~s** to pack.

malabarismo [malaba'riʒmu] *m* juggling; **fazer ~s** to juggle.

malabarista [malaba'riʃta] *mf* juggler.

mal-acabado, -da [‚mawaka'badu, -da] *adj (Br)* badly finished.

malagueta [mala'geta] *f* chilli (pepper).

malandro, -dra [ma'lãndru, -dra] *adj (preguiçoso)* lazy; *(matreiro)* crafty ♦ *m, f (patife)* rogue.

malária [ma'larja] *f* malaria.

malcriado, -da [mawkri'adu, -da] *adj* rude.

maldade [maw'dadʒi] *f* evil.

maldição [mawdi'sãw] *(pl* **-ões** *[-õjʃ]) f* curse.

maldito, -ta [maw'dʒitu, -ta] *adj* damned.

maldizer [mawdʒi'ze(x)] *vt (amaldiçoar)* to curse; *(falar mal de)* to speak ill of.

maldoso, -osa [maw'dozu, -ɔza] *adj* evil.

mal-educado, -da [‚maledu'kadu, -da] *adj* rude.

malefício [male'fisju] *m* hazard.

mal-entendido [‚malĩntẽn'dʒidu] *(pl* **mal-entendidos** [‚malĩntẽn'diduʃ]) *m* misunderstanding.

males → **mal**.

mal-estar [maleʃˈta(x)] (*pl* **mal-estares** [maleʃˈtareʃ]) *m* (*dor física*) discomfort; (*inquietude*) uneasiness.

maleta [maˈleta] *f* travel bag.

malfeitor, -ra [mawfejˈto(x), -ra] (*mpl* **-res** [-riʃ], *fpl* **-s** [-ʃ]) *m, f* criminal.

malha [ˈmaʎa] *f* (*tecido*) wool; (*em rede*) mesh; (*Br: de ginástica*) leotard; **fazer ~** (*Port*) to knit.

malhado, -da [maˈʎadu, -da] *adj* (*animal*) mottled.

malhar [maˈʎa(x)] *vt* to thresh ◆ *vi* (*fam: fazer ginástica*) to work out.

mal-humorado, -da [malumoˈradu, -da] *adj* bad-tempered.

malícia [maˈlisja] *f* malice.

maligno, -gna [maˈlignu, -gna] *adj* malignant.

malmequer [mawmɛˈkɛ(x)] (*pl* **-es** [-iʃ]) *m* marigold.

mal-passado, -da [mawpaˈsadu, -da] *adj* (*bife*) rare.

malta [ˈmawta] *f* (*fam*) gang.

maltratar [mawtraˈta(x)] *vt* (*bater em*) to ill-treat; (*descuidar, estragar*) to damage.

maluco, -ca [maˈluku, -ka] *adj* crazy ◆ *m, f* lunatic.

malvadez [mawvaˈdeʃ] *f* wickedness.

malvado, -da [mawˈvadu, -da] *adj* wicked.

mama [ˈmama] *f* breast.

mamadeira [mamaˈdeira] *f* (*Br*) baby's bottle.

mamão [maˈmãw] (*pl* **-ões** [-õjʃ]) *m* papaya, pawpaw.

mamar [maˈma(x)] *vi* to be breastfed; **dar de ~ a** (*amamentar*) to breast-feed; (*com mamadeira*) to bottle-feed.

mamífero [maˈmiferu] *m* mammal.

mamilo [maˈmilu] *m* nipple.

maminha [maˈmiɲa] *f* (*Br*) very tender rump steak.

mamões → **mamão**.

manada [maˈnada] *f* herd.

mancar [mãŋˈka(x)] *vi* to limp.

mancha [ˈmãʃa] *f* (*em animal, pele*) mark, spot; (*nódoa*) stain.

Mancha [ˈmãʃa] *f*: **o canal da ~** the English Channel.

manchar [mãˈʃa(x)] *vt* to stain.

manchete [mãˈʃetʃi] *f* (*Br: de jornal*) headline.

manco, -ca [ˈmãŋku, -ka] *adj* lame.

mandar [mãnˈda(x)] *vi* to be in charge

◆ *vt*: **~ alguém fazer algo** to tell sb to do sthg; **~ fazer algo** to have sthg done; **~ alguém passear** (*fam*) to send sb packing; **~ vir** (*encomendar*) to send for; **~ alguém à merda** (*vulg*) to tell sb to piss off; **~ em** to be in charge of; **ele gosta de ~ nos outros** he likes to boss everyone about ou around.

mandioca [mãnˈdʒɔka] *f* cassava, manioc; (**farinha de**) **~** cassava (flour).

maneira [maˈnejra] *f* way; **de uma ~ geral** as a rule; **temos de fazer tudo à ~ dele** we have to do everything his way; **de ~ alguma** ou **nenhuma!** certainly not!; **de ~ que** so (that); **de qualquer ~** (*de todo jeito*) anyway; (*em desordem*) any old how; **desta ~** in this way; **de toda a ~** anyway; **de tal ~ ... que ... so ... that ...**; **de uma ~ ou de outra** one way or another.

❏ **maneiras** *fpl*: **ter ~s** to have good manners; **não ter ~s** to have bad manners.

manejar [maneˈʒa(x)] *vt* (*carro*) to drive; (*barco*) to sail.

manejável [maneˈʒavɛw] (*pl* **-eis** [-ejʃ]) *adj* manageable.

manequim [maneˈkĩ] (*pl* **-ns** [-ʃ]) *m* (*em vitrine*) dummy ◆ *mf* (*pessoa*) model.

maneta [maˈneta] *adj* one-handed; (*sem braço*) one-armed.

manga [ˈmãŋga] *f* (*de peça de vestuário*) sleeve; (*fruto*) mango; **em ~s de camisa** in shirtsleeves.

mangueira [mãŋˈgejra] *f* (*para regar, lavar*) hose; (*árvore*) mango tree.

manha [ˈmaɲa] *f*: **ter ~** to be sharp; **fazer ~** to put on an act.

manhã [maˈɲã] *f* morning; **de ~** in the morning; **duas da ~** two in the morning; **ontem de ~** yesterday morning.

mania [maˈnia] *f* (*obsessão*) obsession; (*hábito*) habit.

manicómio [maniˈkɔmju] *m* (*Port*) = **manicômio**.

manicômio [maniˈkomju] *m* (*Br*) asylum.

manicura [maniˈkura] *f* = **manicure**.

manicure [maniˈkuri] *f* manicure.

manifestação [manifeʃtaˈsãw] (*pl* **-ões** [-õjʃ]) *f* (*expressão*) expression; (*POL*) demonstration.

manifestar [manifeʃˈta(x)] *vt* (*afeto, fúria, etc*) to express.

❏ **manifestar-se** *vp* (*protestar*) to

demonstrate.

manipular [manipu'la(x)] *vt (máquina)* to handle; *(fig: influenciar)* to manipulate.

manivela [mani'vɛla] *f* crank.

manjericão [mãʒeri'kãw] *m* basil.

manobra [ma'nɔbra] *f (de carro)* manoeuvre; *(de trem)* shunting.

mansão [mã'sãw] *(pl -ões* [-õjʃ]) *f* mansion.

mansidão [mãsi'dãw] *f (de pessoa)* gentleness; *(de animal)* tameness.

manso, -sa ['mãsu, -sa] *adj (animal)* tame; *(mar)* calm.

mansões → **mansão**.

manta ['mãnta] *f* blanket.

manteiga [mãn'tejga] *f* butter; **~ de cacau** cocoa butter.

manteigueira [mãntej'gejra] *f* butter dish.

manter [mãn'te(x)] *vt* to keep; *(família)* to support; *(relação)* to have; **~ a palavra** to keep one's word.

❏ **manter-se** *vp* to stay, to remain; **~-se em forma** to keep fit.

manual [ma'nwaw] *(pl -ais* [-ajʃ]) *adj* manual ◆ *m* manual, guide; **~ (escolar)** textbook.

manuscrito, -ta [manuʃ'kritu, -ta] *adj* hand-written ◆ *m* manuscript.

manusear [manu'zea(x)] *vt (livro)* to handle; *(objeto, ferramenta)* to use.

manutenção [manutẽ'sãw] *f* maintenance.

mão ['mãw] *f (ANAT)* hand; *(de estrada)* side; **apertar a ~** to shake hands; **dar a ~ a alguém** to hold sb's hand; *(fig: ajudar)* to help sb out; **de ~s dadas** hand in hand; **à ~** *(lavar, escrever)* by hand; **dar uma ~ a alguém** to give OU lend sb a hand; **estar à ~** to be handy; **ter algo à ~** to have sthg to hand.

mão-de-obra [mãw'dʒiɔbra] *f* workforce.

mapa ['mapa] *m* map; **~ das estradas** road map.

mapa-múndi [ˌmapa'mũndʒi] *(pl* **mapas-múndi** [ˌmapaʒ'mũndʒi]) *m* world map.

maquete [ma'kɛtʃi] *f* model.

maquiagem [maki'aʒãj] *(pl -ns* [-ʃ]) *f* make-up.

maquiar [ma'kjax] *vt (Br)* to make up.

❏ **maquiar-se** *vp (Br)* to put one's make-up on.

maquilhar [maki'ʎa(x)] *vt (Port)* = **maquiar**.

máquina ['makina] *f* machine; **~ de barbear** shaver; **~ de costura** sewing machine; **~ de escrever** typewriter; **~ de filmar** film camera; **~ fotográfica** camera; **~ de lavar** *(para roupa)* washing machine; *(para louça)* dishwasher; **~ de secar** tumble-dryer.

maquinaria [makina'ria] *f* machinery.

mar ['ma(x)] *(pl -res* [-riʃ]) *m* sea; **~ alto, alto ~** high seas *(pl)*; **por ~** by sea.

maracujá [maraku'ʒa] *m* passion fruit.

maravilha [mara'viʎa] *f* wonder; **que ~!** how wonderful!; **correr às mil ~s** to be a great success; **dizer ~s de** to rave about; **fazer ~s** to do wonders.

maravilhoso, -osa [maravi'ʎozu, -ɔza] *adj* wonderful.

marca ['maxka] *f* mark; *(de carro, roupa)* make, brand; **~ registrada** trademark; **de ~** *(roupa)* designer *(antes de s)*.

marcação [maxka'sãw] *(pl -ões* [-õjʃ]) *f* booking; **a ~ de consultas realiza-se entre as nove e as dez** appointments must be made between nine and ten.

marcar [max'ka(x)] *vt (assinalar, indicar)* to mark; *(lugar)* to book; *(número)* to dial; *(ESP)* to score; **~ encontro com alguém** to arrange to meet sb; **~ uma consulta/hora** to make an appointment.

marcha ['maxʃa] *f (desfile)* march; *(ritmo)* pace; **~s populares** colourful processions during local festivals; **~ à ré** *(Br)* reverse.

marcha-atrás [ˌmaxʃa'trajʃ] *f inv (Port: de carro)* reverse; **fazer ~** to reverse.

marchar [max'ʃa(x)] *vi* to march.

marcial [max'sjaw] *(pl -ais* [-ajʃ]) *adj* martial.

marco ['maxku] *m (em estrada, caminho)* landmark; *(moeda)* mark; **~ do correio** *(Port)* postbox.

março ['marsu] *m* March, → **setembro**.

maré [ma're] *f* tide; **estar de boa ~** to be in good spirits.

maré-alta [marɛ'awta] *(pl* **marés-altas** [marɛ'zawtaʃ]) *f* high tide.

maré-baixa [marɛ'bajʃa] *(pl* **marés-**

baixas [marɛʒˈbajʃaʃ]) *f* low tide.

maremoto [mareˈmotu] *m* tidal wave.

mares → mar.

marfim [maxˈfĩ] *m* ivory.

margarida [maxgaˈrida] *f* daisy.

margarina [maxgaˈrina] *f* margarine.

margem [ˈmaxʒẽ] (*pl* -ns [-ʃ]) *f (de rio)* bank; *(em texto, livro, documento)* margin; **à ~ da sociedade** on the fringe of society; **pôr à ~** *(fig: ignorar)* to leave out; **pôr-se à ~** not to take part.

marginal [maxʒiˈnaw] (*pl* -ais [-ajʃ]) *adj* marginal ♦ *mf* criminal.

marido [maˈridu] *m* husband.

marimbondo [marĩmˈbõndu] *m (Br)* wasp.

marina [maˈrina] *f* marina.

marinada [mariˈnada] *f* marinade.

marinha [maˈriɲa] *f* navy.

marinheiro, -ra [mariˈɲejru, -ra] *m, f* sailor.

marionete [marjoˈnɛtʃi] *f* puppet.

mariposa [mariˈpoza] *f (ESP)* butterfly; *(inseto)* moth.

marisco [maˈriʃku] *m* shellfish.

marítimo, -ma [maˈritʃimu, -ma] *adj* sea *(antes de s)*.

marketing [ˈmarketʃĩŋ] *m* marketing.

marmelada [maxmeˈlada] *f* quince jelly.

marmeleiro [maxmeˈlejru] *m* quince tree.

marmelo [maxˈmɛlu] *m* quince.

mármore [ˈmaxmori] *m* marble.

marquise [maxˈkizi] *f* conservatory.

Marrocos [maˈxɔkuʃ] *s* Morocco.

marrom [maˈxõ] (*pl* -ns [-ʃ]) *adj (Br)* brown.

martelar [maxteˈla(x)] *vt* to hammer in.

martelo [maxˈtɛlu] *m* hammer.

mártir [ˈmaxti(x)] (*pl* -res [-riʃ]) *mf* martyr.

mas¹ [maʃ] = me + as, → me.

mas² [ma(j)ʃ] *conj* but ♦ *m*: **nem ~ nem meio ~!** no buts!

mascar [maʃˈka(x)] *vt* to chew.

máscara [ˈmaʃkara] *f* mask.

mascarar-se [maʃkaˈraxsi] *vp* to dress up.

mascavo [maʃˈkavu] *adj m* → açúcar.

mascote [maʃˈkɔtʃi] *f* mascot.

masculino, -na [maʃkuˈlinu, -na] *adj* masculine; *(sexo)* male.

masoquista [mazuˈkiʃta] *adj* masochistic ♦ *mf* masochist.

massa [ˈmasa] *f (espaguete, lasanha)* pasta; *(de pão)* dough; *(de bolo)* mix; **~ folhada** *(Port)* puff pastry; **~ folheada** *(Br)* puff pastry; **em ~** *(fig: em grande número)* en masse.

massacre [maˈsakri] *m* massacre.

massagear [masaˈʒea(x)] *vt (Br)* to massage.

massagem [maˈsaʒẽ] (*pl* -ns [-ʃ]) *f* massage.

massagista [masaˈʒiʃta] *mf* masseur *(f* masseuse*)*.

massajar [masaˈʒar] *vt (Port)* = **massagear**.

mastigar [maʃtʃiˈga(x)] *vt* to chew.

mastro [ˈmaʃtru] *m (NÁUT)* mast; *(de bandeira)* pole.

masturbar-se [maʃtuxˈbaxsi] *vp* to masturbate.

mata [ˈmata] *f (bosque)* wood; *(Br: floresta)* forest.

mata-borrão [ˌmataboˈxãw] (*pl* **mata-borrões** [ˌmataboˈxõjʃ]) *m* blotting paper.

matadouro [mataˈdoru] *m* slaughterhouse.

matar [maˈta(x)] *vt* to kill; *(fome)* to stay; *(sede)* to quench; **~ aula** *(Br)* to skip class; **~ o tempo** to pass the time. ⊔ **matar-se** *vp (suicidar-se)* to kill o.s.; **~-se de fazer algo** to kill o.s. doing sthg.

mata-ratos [ˌmataˈxatuʃ] *m inv* rat poison.

mate [ˈmatʃi] *adj (sem brilho)* matt; ♦ *m (Br: planta, infusão)* maté, *herbal infusion drunk out of a gourd*.

matemática [mateˈmatʃika] *f* mathematics *(sg)*.

matéria [maˈtɛrja] *f (substância)* matter; *(EDUC)* subject; *(material)* material **em ~ de** on the subject of.

material [mateˈrjaw] (*pl* -ais [-ajʃ]) *adj (bens)* material ♦ *m* materials *(pl)*; **~ escolar** school materials *(pl)*.

matéria-prima [maˌtɛrjaˈprima] (*pl* **matérias-primas** [maˌtɛrjaʃˈprimaʃ]) *f* raw material.

maternidade [matexniˈdadʒi] *f (hospital)* maternity hospital.

matinê [matʃiˈne] *f (Br)* matinée.

matinée [matiˈne] *f (Port)* = **matinê**.

matizado, -da [matʃiˈzadu, -da] *adj* speckled.

mato ['matu] *m (Br: bosque)* wood; *(tipo de vegetação)* bush.

matrícula [ma'trikula] *f (de carro)* numberplate *(Brit)*, license plate *(Am)*; *(em escola, universidade)* matriculation.

matrimónio [matri'mɔnju] *m (Port) (casamento)* = **matrimônio**.

matrimônio [matri'monju] *m (Br)* marriage.

matriz [ma'triʃ] *(pl -zes* [-ziʃ]*) f (de foto, tipografia)* original; *(igreja)* mother church; *(COM: sede)* head office.

maturidade [maturi'dadʒi] *f* maturity.

matuto, -ta [ma'tutu, -ta] *adj (Br: provinciano)* provincial.

mau, má ['maw, 'ma] *adj* bad; **nada ~!** not bad at all!

mausoléu [mawzo'lɛu] *m* mausoleum.

maus-tratos [mawʃ'tratuʃ] *mpl* abuse *(sg)*.

maxilar [maksi'la(x)] *(pl -res* [-riʃ]*) m* jaw.

máximo, -ma ['masimu, -ma] maximum; *(temperatura, nota)* highest ◆ *m*: **o ~** the most; **faz o ~ que você puder** do your best; **no ~** at most; **ao ~** to the full.

⌐ **máximos** *mpl (Port)* full beam headlights *(Brit)*, high beams *(Am)*.

me [mi] *pron (complemento direto)* me; *(complemento indireto)* (to) me; *(reflexo)* myself; **eu nunca ~ engano** I'm never wrong; **eu ~ machuquei** I hurt myself; **você já ~ contou essa história** you've already told me that story; **vou-~ embora** *(Port)* I'm going.

meados ['mjaduʃ] *mpl*: **em ~ de** in the middle of.

mecânica [me'kanika] *f* mechanics *(sg)*, → **mecânico**.

mecânico, -ca [me'kaniku, -ka] *adj* mechanical ◆ *m, f* mechanic.

mecanismo [meka'niʒmu] *m* mechanism.

mecha ['mɛʃa] *f (de vela)* wick; *(de cabelo)* tuft; **fazer ~ no cabelo** to have one's hair highlighted.

meço ['mɛsu] → **medir**.

medalha [me'daʎa] *f* medal.

média ['mɛdʒja] *f* average; **à ~ de** at an average of; **em ~** on average; **ter ~ de** *(EDUC)* to average.

mediano, -na [me'dʒjanu, -na] *adj (médio)* medium; *(sofrível)* average.

mediante [me'dʒjãntʃi] *prep* by means of, through; **irei ~ certas condições** I'll go on certain conditions.

medicação [medʒika'sãw] *(pl -ões* [-õjʃ]*) f* medication.

medicamento [medʒika'mẽntu] *m* medicine.

medicina [medʒi'sina] *f* medicine.

médico, -ca ['mɛdʒiku, -ka] *m, f* doctor; **~ de clínica geral** GP, general practitioner.

medida [me'dʒida] *f (grandeza, quantidade)* measurement; *(precaução, decisão)* measure; **feito sob ~** made to measure; **ficar na ~** to be a perfect fit; **em certa ~** to a certain extent; **na ~ do possível** as far as possible; **à ~ que** as; **tomar ~s** to take steps OU measures.

medieval [medʒje'vaw] *(pl -ais* [-ajʃ]*) adj* medieval.

médio, -dia ['mɛdʒju, -dʒja] *adj (tamanho)* medium; *(qualidade)* average ◆ *m (dedo)* middle finger; *(EDUC: nota)* pass.

⌐ **médios** *mpl (Port)* dipped headlights *(Brit)*, low beams *(Am)*.

mediocre [me'dʒjukri] *adj* mediocre.

medir [me'dʒi(x)] *vt* to measure; **quanto (é que) você mede?** how tall are you?; **eu meço 1,70 m** I'm 5 foot 7 inches.

meditar [medʒi'ta(x)] *vi* to meditate; **~ sobre algo** to think sthg over.

Mediterrâneo [medʒite'xanju] *m*: **o (mar) ~** the Mediterranean (Sea).

medo ['medu] *m* fear; **ter ~** to be frightened; **ter ~ de** to be afraid of; **você pode ir sem ~ porque não é perigoso** don't be afraid to go as it isn't dangerous.

medonho, -nha [me'doɲu, -ɲa] *adj (feio)* hideous.

medroso, -osa [me'drozu, -ɔza] *adj* frightened.

medula [me'dula] *f (bone)* marrow.

medusa [me'duza] *f* jellyfish.

megabyte [mega'bajtʃi] *m* megabyte.

meia ['mɛja] *f (Br: em número)* six; **~ de leite** white coffee.

meia-calça [,meja'kawsa] *(pl meias-calças* [,meaʃ'kawsaʃ]*) f* tights *(pl)* *(Brit)*, pantyhose *(Am)*.

meia-hora [,meja'ɔra] *(pl meias-horas* [,meja'zoraʃ]*) f* half an hour.

meia-idade [‚mejej'dadʒi] *f* middle age; **de ~** middle-aged.

meia-noite [‚meja'nojtʃi] *f* midnight.

meias ['mejaʃ] *fpl* socks; **~ de lycra** Lycra® tights.

meias-medidas [‚mejaʒme'dʒidaʃ] *fpl*: **não estar com ~** not to be content with half measures.

meias-palavras [‚mejaʃpa'lavraʃ] *fpl*: **não ser de ~** not to mince one's words.

meigo, -ga ['mejgu, -ga] *adj* sweet.

meio, meia ['meju, 'meja] *adj* half ♦ *m (modo, recurso)* way; *(social)* circles *(pl)*; **meia pensão** half board; **~ ambiente** environment; **~ bilhete** half-fare; **a meia voz** under one's breath; **no ~ de** *(duas coisas)* between; *(rua, mesa, multidão)* in the middle of.

meio-dia [‚meju'dʒia] *m* midday, noon.

meio-quilo [‚meju'kilu] *(pl* **meios-quilos** [‚mejuʃ'kiluʃ]) *m* half a kilo.

meio-seco [‚meju'seku] *adj m (vinho)* medium dry.

mel ['mɛw] *m* honey.

melaço [me'lasu] *m* molasses *(pl)*.

melado, -da [me'ladu, -da] *adj (Br: pegajoso)* sticky.

melancia [melã'sia] *f* watermelon.

melancolia [melãŋko'lia] *f* melancholy.

melancólico, -ca [melãŋ'kɔliku, -ka] *adj* melancholy.

melão [me'lãw] *(pl* **-ões** [-õjʃ]) *m* melon.

melga ['mɛlga] *f (Port) (insecto)* midge; *(fam: pessoa chata)* pest.

melhor [me'ʎɔ(x)] *(pl* **-res** [-riʃ]) *adj & adv* better ♦ *m*: **o/a ~** *(pessoa, coisa)* the best one; **o ~ a fazer é ...** the best thing to do is ...; **o ~ é não ir** it would be best not to go; **ou ~** or rather; **tanto ~!** all the better!; **estar ~** *(de saúde)* to feel better; **ser do ~ que há** to be the best there is; **cada vez ~** better and better.

melhorar [meʎo'ra(x)] *vt* to improve ♦ *vi* to get better, to improve.

melhores → **melhor**.

melindrar [melĩ'dra(x)] *vt* to hurt.

melindroso, -osa [melĩ'drozu, -ɔza] *adj (pessoa)* touchy; *(assunto, questão, problema)* delicate.

melodia [melo'dʒia] *f* tune.

melodrama [melo'drama] *m* melodrama.

melodramático, -ca [melodra'matʃiku, -ka] *adj* melodramatic.

melões → **melão**.

melro ['mewxu] *m* blackbird.

membro ['mẽmbru] *m (perna, braço)* limb; *(de clube, associação)* member.

memorando [memo'rãndu] *m* memorandum, memo.

memória [me'mɔrja] *f* memory; **de ~** off by heart.

memorizar [memori'za(x)] *vt* to memorize.

mencionar [mẽsjo'na(x)] *vt* to mention.

mendigar [mẽndʒi'ga(x)] *vi* to beg.

mendigo, -ga [mẽn'dʒigu, -ga] *m, f* beggar.

meningite [menĩ'ʒitʃi] *f* meningitis.

menino, -na [me'ninu, -na] *m, f* boy *(f* girl).

menopausa [meno'pawza] *f* menopause.

menor [me'nɔ(x)] *(pl* **-res** [-riʃ]) *adj (em tamanho)* smaller; *(em número)* lower; *(em importância)* minor; *(mínimo)* least ♦ *mf* minor; **não faço a ~ idéia** I haven't got a clue; **o/a ~** the least; *(em tamanho)* the smallest; **ser ~ de idade** to be underage.

menos ['menuʃ] *adv* **1.** *(em comparações)* less; **a Ana é ~ inteligente** Ana is less intelligent, Ana isn't as intelligent; **~ do que** less than; **~ ... do que** less ... than; **tenho ~ trabalho do que ele** I have less work than him; **tenho um livro a ~** I'm one book short; **deram-me 5 reais a ~** they gave me 5 reals too little. **2.** *(como superlativo)*: **o/a ~ ...** the least ...; **o ~ caro/interessante** the cheapest/least interesting. **3.** *(Port: com as horas)*: **são dez ~ um quarto** it's a quarter to ten. **4.** *(em locuções)*: **a ~ que** unless; **ao ~, pelo ~** at least; **isso é o de ~** that's the least of it; **pouco ~ de** just under.
♦ *adj inv* **1.** *(em comparações)* less, fewer *(pl)*; **como ~ carne** I eat less meat; **eles têm ~ posses** they've got fewer possessions; **está ~ frio do que ontem** it's not as cold as it was yesterday; **~ ... do que** less ... than, fewer ... than *(pl)*. **2.** *(como superlativo)* (the) least, (the)

fewest *(pl)*; **as que ~ bolos comeram** those who ate (the) fewest cakes; **os que ~ dinheiro têm** those who have (the) least money.

◆ *prep* **1.** *(exceto)* except (for); **todos gostaram ~ ele** they all liked it except (for) him; **tudo ~ isso** anything but that.

2. *(indica subtração)* minus; **três ~ dois é igual a um** three minus two equals one.

menosprezar [menuʃpreˈza(x)] *vt* to underrate.

mensageiro, -ra [mẽsaˈʒejru, -ra] *m, f* messenger.

mensagem [mẽsaˈʒẽ] *(pl* **-ns** [-ʃ]) *f* message.

mensal [mẽˈsaw] *(pl* **-ais** [-ajʃ]) *adj* monthly.

mensalmente [mẽsawˈmẽntʃi] *adv* monthly.

menstruação [mẽʃtruaˈsãw] *f* menstruation.

mentalidade [mẽntaliˈdadʒi] *f* mentality.

mente [ˈmẽntʃi] *f* mind; **ter em ~ fazer algo** to plan to do sthg.

mentir [mẽnˈti(x)] *vi* to lie.

mentira [mẽnˈtira] *f* lie ◆ *interj* rubbish!; **parece ~!** I can't believe it!

mentiroso, -osa [mẽntʃiˈrozu, -ɔza] *m, f* liar.

mentol [mẽnˈtɔw] *m* menthol.

menu [meˈnu] *m* menu.

mercado [mexˈkadu] *m* market; **~ municipal** (town) market; **~ negro** black market.

❑ **Mercado** *m*: **o Mercado Único** the Single European Market.

mercadoria [mexkadoˈria] *f* goods *(pl)*.

mercearia [mexsjaˈria] *f* grocer's (shop).

MERCOSUL [mexkoˈsuw] *m* South American economic community comprising Argentina, Brasil, Paraguay and Uruguay.

mercúrio [mexˈkurju] *m* mercury.

mercurocromo [mexkuroˈkromu] *m* Mercurochrome® *(antibacterial lotion)*.

merecer [mereˈse(x)] *vt* to deserve.

merecido, -da [mereˈsidu, -da] *adj* deserved.

merenda [meˈrẽnda] *f (lanche)* tea *(light afternoon meal)*; *(em excursão)* picnic.

merengue [meˈrẽŋgi] *m* meringue.

mergulhador, -ra [mergu ʎaˈdo(x),

-ra] *(mpl* **-res** [-riʃ], *fpl* **-s** [-ʃ]) *m, f* diver.

mergulhar [mergu ʎa(x)] *vi* to dive
◆ *vt*: **~ algo em algo** to dip sthg in sthg.

mergulho [mexˈguʎu] *m* dive; **dar um ~** to dive.

meridiano [meriˈdʒjanu] *m* meridian.

meridional [meridʒjoˈnaw] *(pl* **-ais** [-ajʃ]) *adj* southern.

mérito [ˈmɛritu] *m* merit; **por ~ próprio** on one's own merits.

mês [ˈmeʃ] *(pl* **meses** [ˈmeziʃ]) *m* month; **todo ~** every month; **(de) ~ a ~** every month; **por ~** a OU per month.

mesa [ˈmeza] *f* table; **estar na ~** to be at the table.

mesada [meˈzada] *f* monthly allowance.

mesa-de-cabeceira [ˌmezadʒikabeˈsejra] *(pl* **mesas-de-cabeceira** [ˌmezaʒdʒikabeˈsejra]) *f* bedside table.

mescla [ˈmɛʃkla] *f* mixture.

mesclar [meʃˈkla(x)] *vt* to mix.

meses → **mês**.

meseta [meˈzeta] *f* plateau.

mesmo, -ma [ˈmeʒmu, -ma] *adj* same
◆ *adv (até)* even; *(exatamente)* exactly; *(para enfatizar)* really ◆ *pron*: **o ~/a mesma** the same; **eu ~** I myself; **comprou-o para ele ~/ela mesma** he/she bought it for himself/herself; **isso ~!** that's it!; **~ assim** even so; **~ que** OU **se** even if; **nem ~** not even; **o ~ que** the same thing as; **valer o ~ que** to cost the same as; **só ~** only.

mesquinho, -nha [meʃˈkiɲu, -ɲa] *adj* mean.

mesquita [meʃˈkita] *f* mosque.

mestiço, -ça [meʃˈtʃisu, -sa] *adj* of mixed race ◆ *m, f* person of mixed race.

mestre [ˈmɛʃtri] *m* master.

mestre-de-cerimônias [ˌmɛʃtredʒiseriˈmonjaʃ] *(pl* **mestres-de-cerimônias** [ˌmɛʃtriʒdʒiseriˈmonjaʃ]) *m* master of ceremonies; *(em festa)* host.

mestre-sala [ˌmɛʃtriˈsala] *(pl* **mestres-sala** [ˌmɛʃtriʃˈsala]) *m (Br: em desfile)* principal figure on a carnival float.

meta [ˈmɛta] *f (em corrida)* finishing line; *(objetivo)* goal.

metabolismo [metaboˈliʒmu] *m* metabolism.

metade [meˈtadʒi] *f* half; **~ do preço** half-price; **fazer as coisas pela ~** to do things half-heartedly; **fazer algo na ~ do tempo** to do sthg in half the time.

metáfora [meˈtafora] *f* metaphor.

metal [me'taw] (*pl* **-ais** [-ajʃ]) *m* metal.

metálico, -ca [me'taliku, -ka] *adj (objeto)* metal; *(som)* metallic.

metalurgia [metalux'ʒia] *f* metallurgy.

meteorito [metʃu'ritu] *m* meteorite.

meteoro [me'tʃoru] *m* meteor.

meteorologia [meteorolo'ʒia] *f (ciência)* meteorology; *(em televisão)* weather report.

meter [me'te(x)] *vt* to put; ~ algo/alguém em algo to put sthg/sb in sthg; ~ medo to be frightening; ~ medo em alguém to frighten sb.

⏘ **meter-se** *vp* to get involved; ~-se em algo to get involved in sthg; ~-se na vida dos outros to poke one's nose into other people's business; ~-se onde não é chamado to stick one's oar in; ~-se com alguém to have a go at sb.

meticuloso, -osa [metʃiku'lozu, -ɔza] *adj* meticulous.

metódico, -ca [me'tɔdʒiku, -ka] *adj* methodical.

método [metodu] *m* method; com ~ methodically; sem ~ haphazardly.

metralhadora [metraʎa'dora] *f* machine gun.

métrico, -ca ['metriku, -ka] *adj* metric.

metro ['metru] *m (medida)* metre; *(fita métrica)* tape measure; *(Port: abrev de metropolitano)* = metrô.

metrô [me'tro] *m (Br) (abrev de metropolitano)* underground *(Brit)*, subway *(Am)*.

metropolitano [metropoli'tanu] *m* underground *(Brit)*, subway *(Am)*.

meu, minha ['mew, 'miɲa] *adj* my ♦ *pron:* o ~/a minha mine; um amigo ~ a friend of mine; os ~s *(a minha família)* my family.

mexer [me'ʃe(x)] *vt (corpo)* to move; *(CULIN)* to stir ♦ *vi (mover-se)* to move; ~ em algo to touch sthg.

⏘ **mexer-se** *vp (despachar-se)* to hurry up; *(mover-se)* to move; mexa-se! get a move on!

mexerica [meʃe'rika] *f (Br)* tangerine.

mexerico [meʃe'riku] *m* gossip.

México ['meʃiku] *m:* o ~ Mexico.

mexido, -da [me'ʃidu, -da] *adj* lively.

mexilhão [meʃi'ʎãw] *(pl* **-ões** [-õjʃ]) *m* mussel.

mg *(abrev de miligrama)* mg.

miar ['mja(x)] *vi* to miaow.

micróbio [mi'krɔbju] *m* germ.

microfone [mikro'fɔni] *m* microphone.

microondas [mikro'õndaʃ] *m inv* microwave.

microscópio [mikroʃ'kɔpju] *m* microscope.

migalha [mi'gaʎa] *f* crumb.

migração [migra'sãw] *(pl* **-ões** [-õjʃ]) *f* migration.

mijar [mi'ʒa(x)] *vi (vulg)* to piss.

mil ['miw] *num* a OU one thousand; três ~ three thousand; ~ novecentos e noventa e sete nineteen ninety-seven; → seis.

milagre [mi'lagri] *m* miracle.

milénio [mi'lɛnju] *m (Port)* = milênio.

milênio [mi'lenju] *m (Br)* millennium.

mil-folhas [miw'foʎaʃ] *m inv* millefeuille *(Brit)*, napoleon *(Am)*.

milha ['miʎa] *f* mile.

milhão [mi'ʎãw] *(pl* **-ões** [-õjʃ]) *num* million; um ~ de pessoas OU indivíduos a million people, → seis.

milhar [mi'ʎa(x)] *(pl* **-res** [-riʃ]) *num* thousand, → seis.

milho ['miʎu] *m* maize *(Brit)*, corn *(Am)*; ~ doce sweetcorn.

milhões → milhão.

miligrama [mili'grama] *m* milligram.

mililitro [mili'litru] *m* millilitre.

milímetro [mi'limetru] *m* millimetre.

milionário, -ria [miljo'narju, -rja] *m, f* millionaire *(f* millionairess).

militante [mili'tãntʃi] *mf* militant.

mim ['mi] *pron (com preposição: complemento indireto)* me; *(com preposição: reflexo)* myself; a ~, você não engana you don't fool me; comprei-o para ~ *(mesmo* OU **próprio)** I bought it for myself.

mimado, -da [mi'madu, -da] *adj* spoilt.

mimar [mi'ma(x)] *vt (criança)* to spoil; *(por gestos)* to mimic.

mímica ['mimika] *f* mime.

mimo ['mimu] *m* cuddle; dar ~s a alguém to spoil sb; ser um ~ to be great.

mina ['mina] *f (de carvão, ouro)* mine.

mindinho [mĩn'dʒiɲu] *m* little finger.

mineiro, -ra [mi'nejru, -ra] *m, f* miner.

mineral [mineˈraw] (*pl* **-ais** [-ajʃ]) *m* mineral.

minério [miˈnɛrju] *m* ore.

minha → **meu**.

minhoca [miˈɲɔka] *f* earthworm.

miniatura [minjaˈtura] *f* miniature; **em ~** in miniature.

mini-mercado [ˌminimexˈkadu] *m* corner shop.

mínimo, -ma [ˈminimu, -ma] *adj* minimum ♦ *m*: **o ~** the minimum; **não faço a mínima idéia!** I haven't got a clue!; **no ~** at least.

mini-saia [ˌminiˈsaja] *f* (*Port*) = **minissaia**.

minissaia [ˌminiˈsaja] *f* (*Br*) miniskirt.

ministério [miniʃˈterju] *m* ministry.

ministro, -tra [miˈniʃtru, -tra] *m, f* minister.

minoria [minoˈria] *f* minority; **estar em ~** to be in the minority.

minúscula [miˈnuʃkula] *f* small letter; **em ~s** in small letters.

minúsculo, -la [miˈnuʃkulu, -la] *adj* (*muito pequeno*) minuscule, tiny; (*letra*) small.

minuto [miˈnutu] *m* minute; **só um ~!** hang on a minute!; **contar os ~s** to count the minutes; **dentro de poucos ~s** in a few minutes; **em poucos ~s** in no time at all.

miolo [ˈmjolu] *m* (*de pão, bolo*) soft part of bread or cake.

❏ **miolos** *mpl* brains.

míope [ˈmjupi] *adj* shortsighted.

miopia [mjuˈpia] *f* shortsightedness.

miosótis [mjoˈzɔtʃiʃ] *m inv* forget-me-not.

miradouro [miraˈdoru] *m* viewpoint.

miragem [miˈraʒẽ] (*pl* **-ns** [-ʃ]) *f* mirage.

mirar [miˈra(x)] *vt* (*observar*) to look at.

❏ **mirar-se** *vp*: **~-se em algo** to look at o.s. in sthg.

miscelânea [miʃseˈlanja] *f* (*mistura*) mixture; (*fig: confusão*) jumble.

miserável [mizeˈravew] (*pl* **-eis** [-ejʃ]) *adj* (*pobre*) poverty-stricken; (*desgraçado*) unfortunate.

miséria [miˈzɛrja] *f* (*pobreza*) poverty; (*desgraça*) misery; (*sordidez*) squalor; (*pouca quantidade*) pittance.

misericórdia [mizeriˈkɔrdja] *f* mercy; **pedir ~** to ask for mercy.

missa [ˈmisa] *f* mass.

missão [miˈsãw] (*pl* **-ões** [-õjʃ]) *f* mission.

míssil [ˈmisiw] (*pl* **-eis** [-ejʃ]) *m* missile.

missionário, -ria [misjoˈnarju, -rja] *m, f* missionary.

missões → **missão**.

mistério [miʃˈterju] *m* mystery.

misterioso, -osa [miʃteˈrjozu, -ɔza] *adj* mysterious.

misto, -ta [ˈmiʃtu, -ta] *adj* mixed ♦ *m* (*CULIN*): **~ quente** toasted sandwich filled with cheese and ham.

mistura [miʃˈtura] *f* mixture.

misturar [miʃtuˈra(x)] *vt* to mix; (*fig: confundir*) to mix up.

mito [ˈmitu] *m* myth.

miúdo, -da [ˈmjudu, -da] *adj* small ♦ *m, f* kid.

❏ **miúdos** *mpl*: **~s de galinha** giblets; **trocar algo em ~s** to explain sthg.

ml (*abrev de mililitro*) ml.

mm (*abrev de milímetro*) mm.

mo [mu] = **me + o**, → **me**.

mobília [moˈbilja] *f* furniture.

mobiliário [mobiˈljarju] *m* furnishings (*pl*).

moçambicano, -na [mosãmbiˈkanu, -na] *adj* of/relating to Mozambique ♦ *m, f* native/inhabitant of Mozambique.

Moçambique [mosãmˈbiki] *s* Mozambique.

mocassim [mokaˈsĩ] (*pl* **-ns** [-ʃ]) *mpl* mocassin.

mochila [moˈʃila] *f* rucksack.

mocidade [mosiˈdadʒi] *f* youth.

moço, -ça [ˈmosu, -sa] *adj* young ♦ *m, f* boy (*f* girl); **~ de recados** errand boy.

mocotó [mokoˈtɔ] *m* (*Br*) shank.

moda [ˈmɔda] *f* fashion; **à ~ de** in the style of; **estar fora de ~** to be out of fashion; **estar na ~** to be in fashion, to be fashionable; **sair de ~** to go out of fashion.

modalidade [modaliˈdadʒi] *f* (*de esporte*) discipline; (*de pagamento*) method.

modelo [moˈdelu] *m* model; (*de roupa*) design; **servir de ~** to serve as an example; **tomar por ~** to take as an example.

modem [ˈmɔdɛm] *m* modem.

moderado, -da [modeˈradu, -da] *adj* moderate.

moderar [modeˈra(x)] *vt* (*restringir*) to moderate; (*reunião, debate*) to chair.

modernizar [modɛxniˈza(x)] *vt* to modernize.

moderno, -na [moˈdɛxnu, -na] *adj* modern.

modéstia [moˈdɛʃtja] *f* modesty; ~ à **parte** modesty aside.

modesto, -ta [moˈdɛʃtu, -ta] *adj* modest.

modificar [modʒifiˈka(x)] *vt* to modify.

❑ **modificar-se** *vp* to change.

modo [ˈmɔdu] *m* way; *(GRAM)* mood; ~ **de usar** instructions *(pl)*; **com bons** ~s politely; **com maus** ~s impolitely; **de certo** ~ in some ways; **de** ~ **nenhum!** no way!; **de** ~ **que** so (that); **de qualquer** ~ anyway; **de tal** ~ **que** so much that.

módulo [ˈmɔdulu] *m* *(EDUC)* module; *(Port: de ônibus, elétrico)* ticket.

moeda [ˈmwɛda] *f* *(de metal)* coin; *(em geral)* currency; ~ **estrangeira** foreign currency.

moer [ˈmwɛ(x)] *vt* to grind.

mofo [ˈmofu] *m* mould.

mogno [ˈmɔgnu] *m* mahogany.

moído, -da [ˈmwidu, -da] *adj* *(café, pimenta)* ground; **estar** ~ *(fam: estar cansado)* to be done in; **ter o corpo** ~ to be all aches and pains.

moinho [ˈmwiɲu] *m* mill; ~ **de café** coffee grinder; ~ **de vento** windmill.

mola [ˈmɔla] *f* *(em colchão, sofá)* spring; *(Port: de abotoar)* press stud *(Brit)*, snap fastener *(Am)*; ~ **de roupa** clothes peg *(Brit)*, clothes pin *(Am)*.

molar [moˈla(x)] *(pl* **-res** [-riʃ]) *m* molar.

moldar [mowˈda(x)] *vt* to mould.

moldura [mowˈdura] *f* frame.

mole [ˈmɔli] *adj* soft; *(pessoa)* docile.

molécula [muˈlɛkula] *f* molecule.

molestar [moleʃˈta(x)] *vt* *(maltratar)* to hurt; *(aborrecer)* to annoy.

molhar [moˈʎa(x)] *vt* to wet.

❑ **molhar-se** *vp* to get wet.

molheira [moˈʎejra] *f* gravy boat.

molho¹ [ˈmoʎu] *m* sauce; ~ **de tomate** tomato sauce; **pôr de** ~ to soak.

molho² [ˈmɔʎu] *m* *(de lenha)* stack; *(de palha, erva)* bundle; ~ **de chaves** bunch of keys.

molinete [moliˈnetʃi] *m* *(de cana de pesca)* reel.

momentaneamente [momẽntanjaˈmẽntʃi] *adv* momentarily.

momento [moˈmẽntu] *m* moment; **um** ~! just a moment!; **a qualquer** ~ any minute now; **até o** ~ (up) until now; **de/neste** ~ at the moment; **dentro de** ~s shortly; **de um** ~ **para o outro** any time now; **em dado** ~ at any given moment; **por** ~s for a second.

monarca [moˈnaxka] *mf* monarch.

monarquia [monaxˈkia] *f* monarchy.

monge [ˈmõʒi] *m* monk.

monitor, -ra [moniˈto(x), -ra] *(mpl* **-res** [-riʃ], *fpl* **-s** [-ʃ]) *m, f* *(em colônia de férias)* activities coordinator ◆ *m* *(de televisão)* (television) screen; *(de computador)* monitor, VDU.

monopólio [monoˈpɔlju] *m* monopoly.

monossílabo [monoˈsilabu] *m* monosyllable.

monotonia [monotoˈnia] *f* monotony.

monótono, -na [moˈnɔtonu, -na] *adj* *(pessoa)* tedious; *(vida, trabalho)* monotonous.

monstro [ˈmõʃtru] *m* monster.

montagem [mõnˈtaʒẽ] *(pl* **-ns** [-ʃ]) *f* *(de máquina)* assembly; *(de esquema)* drawing up; *(de fotografia)* montage; *(de filme)* editing.

montanha [mõnˈtaɲa] *f* mountain.

montanha-russa [mõnˈtaɲaˈrusa] *(pl* **montanhas-russas** [mõnˈtaɲaʃˈrusaʃ]) *f* roller coaster.

montanhismo [mõntaˈɲiʒmu] *m* mountaineering.

montanhoso, -osa [mõntaˈɲozu, -ɔza] *adj* mountainous.

montante [mõnˈtãntʃi] *m* total.

montar [mõnˈta(x)] *vt* *(barraca)* to put up; *(acampamento)* to set up; *(máquina)* to assemble; *(filme)* to edit ◆ *vi* *(fazer hipismo)* to ride; ~ **a cavalo** to ride (a horse).

monte [ˈmõntʃi] *m* *(montanha)* mountain; **comida aos** ~s loads of food; **um** ~ **de**, ~s **de** *(fam)* loads OU masses of; **a** ~ piled up.

montra [ˈmõntra] *f* *(Port)* (window) display.

monumental [monumẽnˈtaw] *(pl* **-ais** [-ajʃ]) *adj* *(enorme)* monumental; *(grandioso)* magnificent.

monumento [monuˈmẽntu] *m* monument; ~ **comemorativo** memorial.

moqueca [moˈkɛka] *f* stew made of

fish, seafood and eggs, seasoned with parsley, coriander, lemon, onion, coconut milk, palm oil and peppercorns.

morada [mu'rada] *f (Port)* address.

moradia [mora'dia] *f* house.

morador, -ra [mora'do(x), -ra] *(mpl -res* [-riʃ], *fpl -s* [-ʃ]) *m, f* resident.

moral [mo'raw] *(pl -ais* [-ajʃ]) *adj* moral ♦ *f (social)* morals *(pl); (conclusão)* moral ♦ *m (ânimo, disposição)* morale.

morango [mo'rãŋgu] *m* strawberry.

morar [mo'ra(x)] *vi* to live.

mórbido, -da ['mɔxbidu, -da] *adj* morbid.

morcego [mox'segu] *m* bat.

mordaça [mox'dasa] *f (em pessoa)* gag; *(em animal)* muzzle.

morder [mox'de(x)] *vt* to bite.

mordida [mox'dida] *f* bite.

mordomo [mox'domu] *m* butler.

moreno, -na [mo'renu, -na] *adj (tez, pele)* dark; *(de sol)* tanned.

morfina [mox'fina] *f* morphine.

moribundo, -da [mori'būndu, -da] *adj* dying.

morno, morna ['mɔxnu, 'mɔxna] *adj* lukewarm.

morrer [mo'xe(x)] *vi* to die; *(fogo, luz)* to die down; *(Br: motor)* to stall; **estou morrendo de fome** I'm starving; **~ de vontade de fazer algo** to be dying to do sthg.

morro ['moxu] *m (monte)* hill; *(Br: favela)* slum.

mortadela [moxta'dɛla] *f* Mortadella, *large pork sausage served cold in thin slices.*

mortal [mox'taw] *(pl -ais* [-ajʃ]) *adj (pessoa, animal)* mortal; *(acidente, ferida)* fatal; *(doença)* terminal ♦ *mf* mortal.

mortalha [mox'taʎa] *f (de cadáver)* shroud.

mortalidade [moxtali'dadʒi] *f* mortality; **~ infantil** infant mortality.

morte ['mɔxtʃi] *f (natural)* death; *(homicídio)* murder; **estar pensando na ~** *(Br)* to have a good wallow; **ser de ~** *(fam: cômico)* to be hysterical.

mortífero, -ra [mox'tʃiferu, -ra] *adj* lethal.

morto, morta ['mɔxtu, 'mɔxta] *pp →* **matar** ♦ *adj* dead ♦ *m, f* dead person; **estar ~** to be dead; **estar ~ para fazer algo** to be dying to do sthg; **estar ~ de**

cansaço/fome to be exhausted/starving; **ser ~** to be killed.

mos [moʃ] = **me + os**, → **me**.

mosaico [mo'zajku] *m* mosaic.

mosca ['moʃka] *f* fly; **acertar na ~** to hit the nail on the head.

moscatel [moʃka'tεw] *(pl -éis* [-εiʃ]) *m* Muscatel, *sweet white liqueur wine.*

mosquiteiro [moʃki'tejru] *m* mosquito net.

mosquito [moʃ'kitu] *m* mosquito.

mostarda [moʃ'taxda] *f* mustard.

mosteiro [moʃ'tejru] *m* monastery.

mostrador [moʃtra'do(x)] *(pl -es* [-iʃ]) *m (de relógio)* face; *(de velocímetro)* dial.

mostrar [moʃ'tra(x)] *vt* to show; **~ algo a alguém** to show sthg to sb, to show sb sthg; **~ interesse em** to show an interest in.

mostruário [moʃtru'arju] *m* showcase.

mota ['mɔta] *f (Port)* = **moto**.

mote ['mɔtʃi] *m* motto.

motel [mɔ'tεw] *(pl -éis* [-εiʃ]) *m* motel.

motim [mo'tʃi] *(pl -ns* [-ʃ]) *m* uprising.

motivar [motʃi'va(x)] *vt (causar)* to cause; *(aluno)* to motivate.

motivo [mo'tʃivu] *m* motive; **por ~ de** due to; **sem ~s** for no reason.

moto ['mɔtu] *f* motorbike.

motocicleta [ˌmotosi'klɛta] *f* moped.

motocross [moto'krɔsi] *m* motocross.

motor [mo'to(x)] *(pl -res* [-riʃ]) *m* engine, motor; **~ de arranque** starter motor.

motorista [moto'riʃta] *mf* driver.

motosserra [moto'sexa] *f* chain saw.

mourisco, -ca [mo'riʃku, -ka] *adj* Moorish.

Mouros ['moruʃ] *mpl:* **os ~** the Moors.

mousse ['muse] *f (Port)* = **musse**.

movediça [move'dʒisa] *adj f →* **areia**.

móvel ['mɔvew] *(pl -eis* [-ejʃ]) *adj* mobile ♦ *m* piece of furniture.

❏ **móveis** *mpl* furniture *(sg).*

mover [mo've(x)] *vt* to move; *(campanha)* to instigate.

❏ **mover-se** *vp* to move.

movimentado, -da [movimẽn'tadu, -da] *adj (rua, local)* busy.

movimento [movi'mẽntu] *m* movement; *(em rua, estabelecimento)* activity;

em ~ in motion.

MPB f (Br: abrev de Música Popular Brasileira) generic name for Brazilian popular music.

muco ['muku] m mucus.

mudança [mu'dãsa] f (modificação) change; (de casa) move; (de veículo) gear.

mudar [mu'da(x)] vt (alterar) to change; (de posição) to move ♦ vi (alterar-se) to change.

❏ **mudar de** v + prep to change; (de casa) to move; ~ **de idéia** to change one's mind; ~ **de roupa** to change (one's clothes).

❏ **mudar-se** vp to move (house); ~-**se para** to move to.

mudez [mu'deʒ] f muteness.

mudo, -da ['mudu, -da] adj (pessoa) dumb; (cinema) silent; **ficar** ~ (fig) to be lost for words.

muito, -ta ['mũĩtu, -ta] adj a lot of ♦ pron a lot ♦ adv (com verbo) a lot; (com adjetivo) very; **já não tenho** ~ **tempo** I don't have much time left; **há** ~ **tempo** a long time ago; **tenho** ~ **sono** I'm really tired; ~ **bem!** very good!; ~ **antes** long before; ~ **pior** much ou far worse; **quando** ~ at the most; **querer** ~ **a alguém** to care about sb a great deal; **não ganho** ~ I don't earn much.

mula ['mula] f mule.

mulato, -ta [mu'latu, -ta] adj & m, f mulatto.

muleta [mu'leta] f crutch.

mulher [mu'ʎɛ(x)] (pl -res [-riʃ]) f woman; (esposa) wife.

multa ['muwta] f fine; **levar uma** ~ to get a fine.

multar [muw'ta(x)] vt to fine.

multidão [muwti'dãw] (pl -ões [-õjʃ]) f (de pessoas) crowd; (de coisas) host.

multinacional [ˌmuwtʃinasju'naw] (pl -ais [-ajʃ]) f multinational.

multiplicar [muwtʃipli'ka(x)] vt & vi to multiply; ~ **por** to multiply by.

❏ **multiplicar-se** vp (reproduzir-se) to multiply.

múltiplo, -pla ['muwtʃiplu, -pla] adj & m multiple.

múmia ['mumja] f mummy.

mundial [mũn'dʒjaw] (pl -ais [-ajʃ]) adj world (antes de s) ♦ m (de futebol) World Cup; (de atletismo, etc) World Championships (pl).

mundo ['mũndu] m world; **o outro** ~ the hereafter; **não é nada do outro** ~ it's nothing out of the ordinary; **por nada deste** ~ for the world; **vai ser o fim do** ~ all hell will break loose; **todo (o)** ~ (Br) everyone, everybody; **viver no** ~ **da lua** to live in a world of one's own.

munição [muni'sãw] (pl -ões [-õjʃ]) f ammunition.

municipal [munisi'paw] (pl -ais [-ajʃ]) adj town (antes de s), municipal.

município [muni'sipju] m (cidade) town; (organismo) town council.

munições → munição.

munir [mu'ni(x)] vt: ~ **alguém de algo** to supply sb with sthg.

❏ **munir-se de** vp + prep to arm o.s. with.

mural [mu'raw] (pl -ais [-ajʃ]) m mural.

muralha [mu'raʎa] f wall; (fortaleza) ramparts (pl).

murchar [mux'ʃa(x)] vi to wilt.

murcho, -cha ['muxʃu, -ʃa] adj (flor, planta) wilted; (fig: sem animação) listless.

murmurar [muxmu'ra(x)] vt to murmur.

murmúrio [mux'murju] m murmur.

muro ['muru] m wall.

murro ['muxu] m punch; **dar um** ~ **em alguém** to punch sb; **dar um** ~ **em algo** to thump sthg.

murta ['muxta] f myrtle.

musa ['muza] f muse.

musculação [muʃkula'sãw] f body building.

músculo ['muʃkulu] m muscle.

musculoso, -osa [muʃku'lozu, -ɔza] adj muscular.

museu [mu'zew] m museum; ~ **de arte moderna** modern art gallery.

musgo ['muʒgu] m moss.

música ['muzika] f music; ~ **clássica/folclórica** classical/folk music; ~ **de câmara** chamber music; ~ **pop** pop music; ~ **sinfônica** orchestral music; **dançar conforme a** ~ (fig) to play along.

músico ['muziku] m musician.

musse ['musi] f (Br) mousse; ~ **de chocolate** chocolate mousse.

mútuo, -tua ['mutwu, -twa] adj mutual; **de** ~ **acordo** by mutual agreement.

N

N (*abrev de Norte*) N.

na [na] = em + a, → **em**.

-na [na] *pron (pessoa)* her; *(coisa)* it; *(você)* you.

nabo ['nabu] *m (planta)* turnip.

nação [na'sãw] *(pl -ões* [-õjʃ]) *f* nation.

nacional [nasjo'naw] *(pl -ais* [-ajʃ]) *adj* national.

nacionalidade [nasjonali'dadʒi] *f* nationality.

nacionalismo [nasjona'liʒmu] *m* nationalism.

nações → **nação**.

nada ['nada] *pron (coisa nenhuma)* nothing; *(em negativas)* anything ♦ *adv:* **não gosto ~ disto** I don't like it at all; **não dei por ~** I didn't notice a thing; **de ~!** don't mention it!; **~ de novo** nothing new; **ou tudo ou ~** all or nothing; **antes de mais ~** first of all; **é uma coisa de ~** it's nothing (at all); **não prestar** OU **servir para ~** to be no help at all, to be useless; **não serve de ~ resmungar** there's no point moaning.

nadador, -ra [nada'do(x), -ra] *(mpl -res* [-riʃ]. *fpl -s* [-ʃ]) *m, f* swimmer; **~ salvador** lifeguard.

nadar [na'da(x)] *vi* to swim; **~ em** *(fig: ter muito de)* to be swimming in.

nádegas ['nadegaʃ] *fpl* buttocks.

naipe ['najpi] *m* suit.

namorado, -da [namo'radu, -da] *m, f* boyfriend *(f* girlfriend).

não [nãw] *adv (em respostas)* no; *(em negativas)* not; **ainda ~ o vi** I still haven't seen him; **~ é aqui, pois ~?** it isn't here, is it?; **~ tem mais ingressos** there aren't any tickets left; **~ é?** isn't it?; **pelo sim, pelo ~** just in case.

não-fumador, -ra [nãwfuma'dor, -ra] *(mpl -res* [-rɛʃ], *fpl -s* [-ʃ]) *m, f (Port)* = **não-fumante**.

não-fumante [nãwfu'mãntʃi] *mf (Br)* non-smoker.

napa ['napa] *f* leatherette.

naquela [na'kɛla] = em + aquela, → **em**.

naquele [na'keli] = em + aquele, → **em**.

naquilo [na'kilu] = em + aquilo, → **em**.

narciso [nax'sizu] *m* narcissus.

narcótico [nax'kɔtʃiku] *m* narcotic.

narina [na'rina] *f* nostril.

nariz [na'riʃ] *(pl -zes* [-ziʃ]) *m* nose; **meter o ~ em tudo** to be a busybody; **torcer o ~ (para algo)** *(fig)* to turn one's nose up (at sth).

narração [naxa'sãw] *(pl -ões* [-õjʃ]) *f (ato)* narration; *(conto, história)* narrative.

narrar [na'xa(x)] *vt* to narrate.

narrativa [naxa'tʃiva] *f* narrative.

nas [naʃ] = em + as, → **em**.

-nas [naʃ] *pron pl (elas)* them; *(vocês)* you.

nascença [naʃ'sẽsa] *f* birth; **de ~** *(problema, defeito)* congenital.

nascente [naʃ'sẽntʃi] *f (de rio)* source; *(de água)* spring.

nascer [naʃ'se(x)] *vi (pessoa, animal)* to be born; *(planta)* to sprout; *(sol)* to rise ♦ *m (de sol)* sunrise; *(de lua)* moonrise; **~ para ser algo** to be born to be sthg.

nascimento [naʃsi'mẽntu] *m* birth.

nata ['nata] *f* cream.

⊐ **natas** *fpl (Port: para bater)* whipping cream *(sg).*

natação [nata'sãw] *f* swimming.

natal [na'taw] *(pl -ais* [-ajʃ]) *adj (aldeia, cidade)* home *(antes de s).*

⊐ **Natal** *m* Christmas; **Feliz Natal!** Merry Christmas!

nativo, -va [na'tʃivu, -va] *adj & m, f* native.

NATO ['natu] f NATO.

natural [natu'raw] (pl -ais [-ajʃ]) adj natural; **ao ~** (fruta) fresh; **como é ~** as is only natural; **é ~ que** it's understandable (that); **ser ~ de** to be from.

naturalidade [naturali'dadʒi] f (origem) birthplace; (simplicidade) naturalness.

naturalmente [naturaw'mẽntʃi] adv naturally ◆ interj naturally!, of course!

natureza [natu'reza] f nature; **da mesma ~** of the same kind; **~ morta** still life; **por ~** by nature.

❏ **Natureza** f: **a Natureza** Nature.

nau ['naw] f ship.

naufragar [nawfra'ga(x)] vi to be wrecked.

naufrágio [naw'fraʒju] m shipwreck.

náusea ['nawzca] f nausea; **dar ~s a alguém** to make sb feel sick.

náutico, -ca ['nawtʃiku, -ka] adj (atividade) water (antes de s); (clube) sailing (antes de s).

navalha [na'vaʎa] f penknife.

nave ['navi] f (de igreja) nave; **~ espacial** spaceship.

navegação [navega'sãw] f navigation.

navegar [nave'ga(x)] vi to sail; **~ na Internet** to surf the Net.

navio [na'viu] m ship.

NB (abrev de Note Bem) NB.

NE (abrev de Nordeste) NE.

neblina [ne'blina] f mist.

necessário, -ria [nese'sarju, -rja] adj necessary ◆ m: **o ~** the bare necessities (pl); **quando ~** when necessary; **se ~** if necessary; **é ~ passaporte** you need your passport.

necessidade [nesesi'dadʒi] f (carência) necessity, need; **de primeira ~** essential; **sem ~** needlessly; **ter ~ de fazer algo** to need to do sthg; **fazer uma ~** (fam) to relieve o.s.

necessitar [nesesi'ta(x)] vt to need.

❏ **necessitar de** v + prep to need; **~ de fazer algo** to need to do sthg.

necrotério [nekro'terju] m morgue.

néctar ['nekta(x)] (pl -res [-riʃ]) m nectar.

neerlandês, -esa [nexlãn'deʃ, -eza] (mpl -eses [-eziʃ], fpl -s [-ʃ]) adj & m Dutch ◆ m, f (pessoa) Dutchman (f Dutchwoman); **os neerlandeses** the Dutch.

nefasto, -ta [ne'faʃtu, -ta] adj (acontecimento) terrible; (atmosfera) bad.

negar [ne'ga(x)] vt to deny.

❏ **negar-se** vp: **~-se algo** to deny o.s. sthg; **~-se a fazer algo** to refuse to do sthg.

negativa [nega'tiva] f (Port) (EDUC) fail; **ter ~** to fail.

negativo, -va [nega'tʃivu, -va] adj negative; (saldo bancário) overdrawn; (temperatura) minus ◆ m (de filme, fotografia) negative.

negligência [negli'ʒẽsja] f negligence.

negligente [negli'ʒẽntʃi] adj negligent.

negociação [negosja'sãw] (pl -ões [-õjʃ]) f negotiation.

negociar [nego'sja(x)] vt (acordo, preço) to negotiate ◆ vi (COM) to do business.

negócio [ne'gɔsju] m business; (transação) deal; **fazer ~s com alguém** to do business with sb; **~ da China** easy money; **~s escusos** shady deals.

negro, -gra ['negru, -gra] adj black; (céu) dark; (raça) negro; (fig: difícil) bleak ◆ m, f black man (f black woman).

nela ['nela] = em + ela, → em.

nele ['neli] = em + ele, → em.

nem [nẽ] adv not even ◆ conj: **não gosto ~ de cerveja ~ de vinho** I don't like either beer or wine; **não gosto ~ de um ~ de outro** I don't like either of them; **~ por isso** not really; **~ que** even if; **~ sempre** not always; **~ tudo** not everything; **~ ... ~** neither ... nor; **~ um ~ outro** neither one nor the other; **~ pensar!** (fam) don't even think of it!

nenhum, -ma [ne'ɲũ, -ma] (mpl -ns [-ʃ], fpl -s [-ʃ]) adj no ◆ pron none; **não comprei livros nenhuns** I didn't buy any books; **não quero nenhuma bebida** I don't want a drink; **não tive problema ~** I didn't have any problems; **~ professor é perfeito** no teacher is perfect; **~ de** none of, not one of; **~ dos dois** neither of them.

neozelandês, -esa [neozelãn'deʃ, -eza] (mpl -eses [-eziʃ], fpl -s [-ʃ]) adj of/relating to New Zealand ◆ m, f native/inhabitant of New Zealand.

nervo ['nexvu] nerve; (em carne) sinew.

❏ **nervos** mpl (fam) nerves.

nervosismo [nɛxvo'ziʒmu] *m* nerves (*pl*).

nêspera ['neʃpɛra] *f* loquat, *plum-like yellow fruit*.

nessa ['nɛsa] = em + essa, → em.

nesse ['nɛsi] = em + esse, → em.

nesta ['nɛʃta] = em + esta, → em.

neste ['neʃtʃi] = em + este, → em.

neto, -ta ['nɛtu, -ta] *m, f* grandson (*f* granddaughter).

neurose [new'rɔzi] *f* neurosis.

neutralidade [newtrali'dadʒi] *f* neutrality.

neutralizar [newtrali'za(x)] *vt* to neutralize.

neutro, -tra ['newtru, -tra] *adj* neutral; (*GRAM*) neuter.

nevar [ne'va(x)] *v impess* to snow; **está nevando** it's snowing.

neve ['nɛvi] *f* snow.

névoa ['nɛvwa] *f* mist.

nevoeiro [ne'vwejru] *m* fog.

Nicarágua [nika'ragwa] *f*: **a ~** Nicaragua.

nicotina [niko'tʃina] *f* nicotine.

ninguém [nĩŋ'gãj] *pron* nobody, no one; (*em negativas*) anyone, anybody; **não tem ~ (em casa)** there's nobody in; **não vi ~** I didn't see anyone.

ninho ['niɲu] *m* nest; (*fig: lar*) home.

níquel ['nikɛw] (*pl* **-eis** [-ejʃ]) *m* nickel.

nissei [ni'sej] *mf* (*Br*) Brazilian of Japanese parentage.

nisso ['nisu] = em + isso, → em.

nisto ['niʃtu] = em + isto, → em.

nitidez [nitʃi'deʃ] *f* clarity.

nítido, -da ['nitʃidu, -da] *adj* clear.

nitrato [ni'tratu] *m* nitrate; **~ de prata** silver nitrate (*for the treatment of warts and corns*).

nível [nivew] (*pl* **-eis** [-ejʃ]) *m* level; (*qualidade*) quality; **ao ~ de** in terms of; **~ de vida** standard of living.

no [nu] = em + o, → em.

nó ['nɔ] *m* knot; (*em dedo*) knuckle; **dar um ~** to tie a knot; **dar o ~** (*casar-se*) to tie the knot.

nº (*abrev de número*) no.

-no [nu] *pron* (*pessoa*) him; (*coisa*) it; (*você*) you.

NO (*abrev de Noroeste*) NW.

nobre ['nɔbri] *adj* noble.

noção [no'sãw] (*pl* **-ões** [-õjʃ]) *f* notion.

nocivo, -va [no'sivu, -va] *adj* (*produto*) noxious; (*alimento*) unwholesome.

noções → noção.

nocturno, -na [no'turnu, -na] *adj* (*Port*) = noturno.

nódoa ['nɔdwa] *f* (*em roupa, toalha*) stain; (*em reputação*) blemish; **~ negra** (*Port*) bruise.

nogueira [no'gejra] *f* walnut tree.

noite ['nojtʃi] *f* night; (*fim da tarde*) evening; **boa ~!** good night!; **à ~** at night; **esta ~** (*mais tarde*) tonight; (*ao fim da tarde*) this evening; **dia e ~** night and day; **por ~** a OU per night; **da ~ para o dia** overnight.

noivado [noj'vadu] *m* engagement.

noivo, -va ['nojvu, -va] *m, f* fiancé (*f* fiancée); **estar ~ de alguém** to be engaged to sb.

❏ **noivos** *mpl* bride and groom; **eles estão ~s** they are engaged.

nojento, -ta [no'ʒẽntu, -ta] *adj* disgusting.

nojo ['noʒu] *m* disgust, revulsion; **dar ~** to be disgusting; **ter** OU **sentir ~ de** to be disgusted by.

nome ['nomi] *m* name; (*GRAM*) noun; **~ de batismo** Christian name; **~ completo** full name; **~ próprio, primeiro ~** first name; **em ~ de** on behalf of.

nomeação [nomja'sãw] (*pl* **-ões** [-õjʃ]) *f* (*para prêmio*) nomination; (*para cargo*) appointment.

nomeadamente [no,mjada'mẽntʃi] *adv* namely.

nomear [no'mja(x)] *vt* (*mencionar nome de*) to name; (*para prêmio*) to nominate; (*para cargo*) to appoint.

nonagésimo, -ma [nona'ʒɛzimu, -ma] *num* ninetieth, → **sexto**.

nono, -na ['nonu, -na] *num* ninth, → **sexto**.

nora ['nɔra] *f* (*familiar*) daughter-in-law; (*para água*) waterwheel.

nordeste [nɔx'dɛʃtʃi] *m* northeast; **no ~** in the northeast.

norma ['nɔxma] *f* (*padrão*) standard; (*regra*) rule; **por ~** as a rule.

normal [nɔx'maw] (*pl* **-ais** [-ajʃ]) *adj* normal.

normalmente [nɔxmaw'mẽntʃi] *adv* normally.

noroeste [nɔ'rwɛʃtʃi] *m* northwest; **no ~** in the northwest.

norte ['nɔxtʃi] *adj* (*vento, direção*) northerly ♦ *m* north; **a** OU **no ~** in the north; **ao ~ de** north of.

norte-americano, -na [ˌnɔxtʒiameri'kanu, -na] *adj & m, f* (North) American.

Noruega [no'rwɛga] *f:* **a** ~ Norway.

norueguês, -esa [norwe'geʃ, -eza] (*mpl* **-eses** [-eziʃ], *fpl* **-s** [-ʃ]) *adj & m, f* Norwegian ♦ *m* (*língua*) Norwegian.

nos¹ [noʃ] = **em** + **os**, → **em**.

nos² [noʃ] *pron pl* (*complemento direto*) us; (*complemento indireto*) (to) us; (*reflexo*) ourselves; (*recíproco*) each other, one another; ; **ela** ~ **falou** she told us; **nós nos machucamos** we hurt ourselves; **não** ~ **deixem!** don't leave us!; **nunca** ~ **enganamos** we're never wrong; ~ **beijamos** we kissed (each other); **odiamo-**~ we hate each other; **vamo-**~ **embora** (*Port*) we're going.

nós ['nɔʃ] *pron pl* (*sujeito*) we; (*complemento*) us; **e** ~? what about us?; **somos** ~ it's us; ~ **mesmos** OU **próprios** we ourselves.

-nos [noʃ] *pron pl* (*eles*) them; (*vocês*) you, → **nos²**.

nosso, -a ['nosu, -a] *adj our* ♦ *pron:* **o** ~/**a nossa** ours; **um amigo** ~ a friend of ours; **os** ~**s** (*a nossa família*) our family.

nostalgia [noʃtaw'ʒia] *f* nostalgia.

nostálgico, -ca [noʃtaw'ʒiku, -ka] *adj* nostalgic.

nota ['nɔta] *f* note; (*classificação*) mark; **tomar** ~ **de algo** to make a note of sthg.

notário, -ria [no'tarju, -rja] *m, f* notary (public).

notável [no'tavɛw] (*pl* **-eis** [-ejʃ]) *adj* (*ilustre*) distinguished; (*extraordinário*) outstanding.

notebook ['notʃibuki] *m* (*INFORM*) notebook.

notícia [no'tʃisja] *f* piece of news. ❑ **notícias** *fpl* (*noticiário*) news (*sg*).

noticiário [notʃi'sjarju] *m* news bulletin, newscast.

notificar [notʃifi'ka(x)] *vt* to notify.

notório, -ria [no'tɔrju, -rja] *adj* well-known.

noturno, -na [no'tuxnu, -na] *adj* (*Br*) (*atividade*) night (*antes de s*); (*aula*) evening (*antes de s*); (*pessoa, animal*) nocturnal.

nova ['nɔva] *f* piece of news; **ter boas** ~**s** to have some good news.

Nova Iorque [ˌnɔva'jɔxki] *s* New York.

novamente [ˌnɔva'mẽntʃi] *adv* again.

novato, -ta [no'vatu, -ta] *m, f* beginner.

Nova Zelândia [ˌnɔvaze'lãndja] *f:* **a** ~ New Zealand.

nove ['nɔvi] *num* nine, → **seis**.

novecentos, -tas [ˌnɔve'sẽntuʃ, -taʃ] *num* nine hundred, → **seis**.

novela [no'vɛla] *f* (*livro*) novella; (*Br:* *em televisão*) soap opera.

novelo [no'vɛlu] *m* ball.

novembro [no'vẽmbru] *m* November, → **setembro**.

noventa [no'vẽnta] *num* ninety, → **seis**.

novidade [novi'dadʒi] *f* (*notícia*) piece of news; (*em vestuário*) latest fashion; (*novo disco*) new release; **há** ~**s?** any news?; ~ **editorial** latest publication.

novilho [no'viʎu] *m* (*animal*) bullock (2–3 *years old*); (*carne*) beef.

novo, nova ['novu, 'nɔva] *adj* new; (*jovem*) young; ~ **em folha** brand new.

noz ['nɔʃ] (*pl* **-zes** [-ziʃ]) *f* walnut.

noz-moscada [ˌnɔʒmoʃ'kada] *f* nutmeg.

nu, nua ['nu, 'nua] *adj* naked; ~ **em pêlo** stark naked.

nublado, -da [nu'bladu, -da] *adj* cloudy.

nuca ['nuka] *f* nape (of the neck).

nuclear [nukle'a(x)] (*pl* **-res** [-riʃ]) *adj* nuclear.

núcleo ['nukliu] *m* nucleus.

nudez [nu'deʒ] *f* nudity.

nudista [nu'dʒiʃta] *mf* nudist.

nulo, -la ['nulu, -la] *adj* (*sem efeito, valor*) null and void; (*incapaz*) useless; (*nenhum*) nonexistent.

num [nũ] = **em** + **um**, → **em**.

numa ['numa] = **em** + **uma**, → **em**.

numeral [nume'raw] (*pl* **-ais** [-ajʃ]) *m* numeral.

numerar [nume'ra(x)] *vt* to number.

numerário [nume'rarju] *m* cash.

número ['numeru] *m* number; (*de sapatos, peça de vestuário*) size; (*de revista*) issue; ~ **de código** PIN number; ~ **de contribuinte** = National Insurance number (*Brit*), = social security number (*Am*); ~ **de passaporte** passport number; ~ **de telefone** telephone number.

numeroso, -osa [nume'rozu, -ɔza] *adj* (*família, grupo*) large; (*vantagens, ocasiões*) numerous.

numismática [numiʒ'matʃika] *f*

numismatics *(sg)*.

nunca ['nũŋka] *adv* never; **mais do que** ~ more than ever; ~ **mais** never again; ~ **se sabe** you never know; ~ **na vida** never ever.

nuns [nũʃ] = em + uns, → em.

núpcias ['nupsjaʃ] *fpl* marriage *(sg)*.

nutrição [nutri·sãw] *f* nutrition.

nutrir [nu·tri(x)] *vt (fig: acalentar)* to nurture; ~ **uma paixão por alguém** to carry a torch for sb.

nutritivo, -va [nutri·tʃivu, -va] *adj* nutritious.

nuvem ['nuvẽ] *(pl* **-ns** [-ʃ]) *f* cloud.

N.W. *(abrev de Noroeste)* NW.

o, a [u, a] (*mpl* **os** [uʃ], *fpl* **as** [aʃ]) *artigo definido* **1.** (*com substantivo genérico*) the; **a casa** the house; **o hotel** the hotel; **os alunos** the students. **2.** (*com substantivo abstrato*): **a vida** life; **o amor** love; **os nervos** nerves. **3.** (*com adjetivo substantivado*): **o melhor/pior** the best/worst; **vou fazer o possível** I'll do what I can. **4.** (*com nomes geográficos*): **a Inglaterra** England; **o Amazonas** the Amazon; **o Brasil** Brazil; **os Estados Unidos** the United States; **os Pirineus** the Pyrenees. **5.** (*indicando posse*): **quebrei o nariz** I broke my nose; **estou com os pés frios** my feet are cold. **6.** (*com nome de pessoa*): **o Hernani** Hernani; **a Helena** Helena; **o Sr. Mendes** Mr Mendes. **7.** (*por cada*) a, per; **3 reais a dúzia** 3 reals a dozen. **8.** (*com datas*) the; **o dois de Abril** the second of April, April the second. ◆ *pron* **1.** (*pessoa*) him (*f* her), them (*pl*); **eu a deixei alí** I left her there; **ela o amava muito** she loved him very much; **não os vi** I didn't see them. **2.** (*você, vocês*) you; **prazer em conhecê-los, meus senhores** pleased to meet you, gentlemen. **3.** (*coisa*) it, them (*pl*); **onde estão os papéis? não consigo achá-los** where are the papers? I can't find them. **4.** (*em locuções*): **o/a da esquerda** the one on the left; **os que desejarem vir terão de pagar** those who wish to come will have to pay; **o que (é que) ...?** what ...?; **o que (é que) está acontecendo** what's going on? ; **era o que eu pensava** it's just as I thought; **o quê?** what?

oásis [ɔ'azifiʃ] *m inv* oasis.

ob. (*abrev de observação*) = NB.

oba [ɔba] *interj* (*Br*) (*de surpresa*) wow!; (*saudação*) hi!

obedecer [obede'se(x)] *vi* to do as one is told, to obey; **~ a** to obey.

obediente [obe'dʒjẽntʃi] *adj* obedient.

obesidade [obezi'dadʒi] *f* obesity.

obeso, -sa [o'bezu, -za] *adj* obese.

óbito ['ɔbitu] *m* death.

obituário [obi'twarju] *m* obituary.

objeção [obʒe'sãw] (*pl* **-ões** [-õjʃ]) *f* (*Br*) objection.

objecção [obʒe'sãw] (*pl* **-ões** [-õjʃ]) *f* (*Port*) = objeção.

objecto [obʒɛtu] *m* (*Port*) = objeto.

objector [obʒɛ'tor] (*pl* **-res** [-reʃ]) *m* (*Port*): **~ de consciência** conscientious objector.

objetiva [obʒɛ'tʃiva] *f* (*de máquina fotográfica*) lens.

objetivo, -va [obʒɛ'tʃivu, -va] *adj & m* objective.

objeto [ob'ʒɛtu] *m* (*Br*) object.

oboé [o'bwɛ] *m* oboe.

obra [ɔbra] *f* work; (*construção*) building site; **~ de arte** work of art; **~ de caridade** (*instituição*) charity.

❏ **obras** *fpl* (*reparações*) repairs; "**em obras**" "closed for refurbishment".

obra-prima [ˌɔbra'prima] (*pl* **obras-primas** [ˌɔbraʃ'primaʃ]) *f* masterpiece.

obrigação [obriga'sãw] (*pl* **-ões** [-õjʃ]) *f* obligation; (*título de crédito*) bond.

obrigado, -da [obri'gadu, -da] *interj* thank you!; **muito ~!** thank you very much!

obrigar [obri'ga(x)] *vt*: **~ alguém a fazer algo** to force sb to do sthg.

obrigatório, -ria [obriga'tɔrju, -rja] *adj* compulsory.

obs. *abrev* = **observações**.

obsceno, -na [obʃ'senu, -na] *adj* obscene.

observação [obsɛxva'sãw] (*pl* **-ões** [-õjʃ]) *f* observation; *(de lei, regra)* observance.

❏ **observações** *fpl (em formulário)* remarks.

observador, -ra [obsɛxva'do(x), -ra] (*mpl* **-res** [-riʃ], *fpl* **-s** [-ʃ]) *m, f* observer.

observar [obsɛx'va(x)] *vt* to observe; *(dizer)* to remark.

observatório [obsɛxva'tɔrju] *m* observatory.

obsessão [obsɛ'sãw] (*pl* **-ões** [-õjʃ]) *f* obsession.

obsoleto, -ta [obso'lɛtu, -ta] *adj* obsolete.

obstáculo [obʃ'takulu] *m* obstacle.

obstetra [obʃ'tɛtra] *mf* obstetrician.

obstinado, -da [obʃtʃi'nadu, -da] *adj* obstinate.

obstrução [obʃtru'sãw] (*pl* **-ões** [-õjʃ]) *f* obstruction.

obter [ob'te(x)] *vt* to get.

obturação [obtura'sãw] (*pl* **-ões** [-õjʃ]) *f (de dente)* filling.

obturador [obtura'do(x)] (*pl* **-res** [-riʃ]) *m (de máquina fotográfica)* shutter.

óbvio, -via [ˈɔbvju, -vja] *adj* obvious; **como é ~** obviously.

ocasião [oka'zjãw] (*pl* **-ões** [-õjʃ]) *f (momento determinado)* occasion; *(oportunidade)* opportunity; **nessa ~** at the time; **por ~ de** during.

Oceania [o'sjanja] *f*: **a ~** Oceania.

oceano [o'sjanu] *m* ocean.

ocidental [osidẽn'taw] (*pl* **-ais** [-ajʃ]) *adj* western.

❏ **ocidentais** *mpl*: **os ocidentais** Westerners.

ocidente [osi'dẽntʃi] *m* west.

❏ **Ocidente** *m*: **o Ocidente** the West.

ócio [ˈɔsju] *m* leisure.

oco, oca [ˈoku, ˈoka] *adj* hollow.

ocorrência [oko'xẽsja] *f (incidente)* incident; *(freqüência)* occurrence.

ocorrer [oko'xe(x)] *vi* to happen.

octogésimo, -ma [okto'ʒɛzimu, -ma] *num* eightieth, → **sexto**.

oculista [oku'liʃta] *mf (médico)* optometrist; *(vendedor)* optician.

óculos [ˈɔkuluʃ] *mpl* glasses; **~ escuros** sunglasses.

ocultar [okuw'ta(x)] *vt* to hide.

❏ **ocultar-se** *vp* to hide.

oculto, -ta [o'kuwtu, -ta] *pp* → **ocultar**.

ocupação [okupa'sãw] (*pl* **-ões** [-õjʃ]) *f* occupation.

ocupado, -da [oku'padu, -da] *adj (casa)* occupied; *(lugar, assento)* taken; *(pessoa)* busy; **"ocupado"** "engaged".

ocupar [oku'pa(x)] *vt* to take up; *(casa)* to live in; *(tempo)* to occupy.

❏ **ocupar-se** *vp* to keep o.s. busy; **~-se a fazer algo** to spend one's time doing sthg; **~-se de** to see to.

odiar [o'dʒja(x)] *vt* to hate.

ódio [ˈɔdʒju] *m* hatred.

odor [o'do(x)] (*pl* **-res** [-riʃ]) *m* odour; **~ corporal** body odour.

oeste [ˈwɛʃtʃi] *m* west; **a OU no ~** in the west; **a ~ de** to the west of.

ofegante [ofe'gãntʃi] *adj* breathless.

ofegar [ofe'ga(x)] *vi* to pant.

ofender [ofẽn'de(x)] *vt* to offend.

❏ **ofender-se** *vp* to take offence; **~-se com algo** to take offence at sthg.

oferecer [ofere'se(x)] *vt* to offer; *(dar)* to give; **~ algo a alguém** *(presente, ajuda, lugar)* to give sb sthg; *(emprego)* to offer sb sthg.

❏ **oferecer-se** *vp*: **~-se para fazer algo** to offer to do sthg.

oferta [o'fɛxta] *f (presente)* gift; *(de emprego)* offer; *(COM)* supply.

oficial [ofi'sjaw] (*pl* **-ais** [-ajʃ]) *adj* official ◆ *mf (em marinha, exército)* officer.

oficina [ofi'sina] *f* garage.

ofício [o'fisju] *m (profissão)* trade; *(carta)* official letter.

oftalmologista [ɔftawmolo'ʒiʃta] *mf* ophthalmologist.

ofuscar [ofuʃ'ka(x)] *vt* to dazzle.

oi [ˈoj] *interj (Br)* hi!

oitavo, -va [oj'tavu, -va] *num* eighth, → **sexto**.

oitenta [oj'tẽnta] *num* eighty, → **seis**.

oito [ˈojtu] *num* eight; **nem ~ nem oitenta!** there's no need to exaggerate!, → **seis**.

oitocentos, -tas [ojto'sẽntuʃ, -taʃ] *num* eight hundred, → **seis**.

OK [ɔ'kej] *interj* OK!

olá [ɔ'la] *interj* hello!

olaria [ola'ria] *f* pottery.

oleado [o'ljadu] *m* oil cloth; *(vestimenta)* oilskins *(pl).*

óleo [ˈɔlju] *m* oil; **~ de cozinha** (cooking) oil; **~ de bronzear** suntan oil; **~ de girassol/soja** sunflower/soya oil; **~ vegetal** vegetable oil.

oleoduto [oljo'dutu] *m* pipeline *(for oil)*.

oleoso, -osa [o'ljozu, -ɔza] *adj* greasy.

olfacto [ol'fatu] *m (Port)* = **olfato**.

olfato [ow'fatu] *m (Br)* sense of smell.

olhadela [oʎa'dɛla] *f* glance; **dar uma ~ em algo** to have a quick look at sthg.

olhar [o'ʎa(x)] *(pl* **-res** [-riʃ]) *vt* to look at ♦ *vi* to look ♦ *m* look; **~ para** to look at; **~ por** to look after.

olheiras [o'ʎejraʃ] *fpl*: **ter ~** to have dark rings under one's eyes.

olho [o'ʎu] *(pl* **olhos** ['oʎuʃ]) *m* eye; **~ mágico** peephole; **a ~ nu** with the naked eye; **a ~s vistos** visibly; **aos ~s de** in the eyes of; **custar os ~s da cara** to cost an arm and a leg; **não pregar ~** not to sleep a wink; **ver com bons/maus ~s** to approve/disapprove of.

olho-de-sogra [oʎudʒi'sɔgra] *(pl* **olhos-de-sogra** [ɔʎuʃdʒi'sɔgra]) *m* cake made with dates and coconut.

olímpico, -ca [o'lĩmpiku, -ka] *adj* Olympic.

oliveira [oli'vejra] *f* olive tree.

ombro ['õmbru] *m* shoulder; **encolher os ~s** to shrug one's shoulders.

omelete [ome'letʃi] *f* omelette.

omissão [omi'sãw] *(pl* **-ões** [-õjʃ]) *f* omission.

omitir [omi'ti(x)] *vt* to omit.

omnipotente [,ɔmnipo'tẽntʃi] *adj* omnipotent.

omoplata [omo'plata] *f* shoulder-blade.

onça ['õsa] *f (animal)* jaguar; *(medida)* ounce.

onda ['õnda] *f* wave; **~ média/longa/curta** medium/long/short wave; **fazer ~** *(fam: criar problemas)* to make waves; **ir na ~** *(deixar-se enganar)* to fall for it.

onde ['õndʒi] *adv* where; **por ~ vamos?** which way are we going?

ondulado, -da [õndu'ladu, -da] *adj (cabelo)* wavy; *(superfície)* rippled.

oneroso, -osa [one'rozu, -ɔza] *adj* expensive.

ONG *f (abrev de Organização Não Governamental)* NGO.

ônibus ['onibuʃ] *m inv (Br)* bus.

ónix ['ɔniks] *m* onyx.

ontem ['õntẽ] *adv* yesterday; **~ de manhã/à tarde** yesterday morning/afternoon; **~ à noite** last night.

ONU ['ɔnu] *f (abrev de Organização das Nações Unidas)* UN.

onze ['õzi] *num* eleven, → **seis**.

opaco, -ca [o'paku, -ka] *adj* opaque.

opala [o'pala] *f* opal.

opção [op'sãw] *(pl* **-ões** [-õjʃ]) *f* option.

ópera ['ɔpera] *f* opera.

operação [opera'sãw] *(pl* **-ões** [-õjʃ]) *f* operation; *(comercial)* transaction.

operador, -ra [opera'do(x), -ra] *(mpl* **-res** [-riʃ], *fpl* **-s** [-ʃ]) *m, f*: **~ de computadores** computer operator.

operar [ope'ra(x)] *vi (MED)* to operate ♦ *vt (MED)* to operate on.

❑ **operar-se** *vp (realizar-se)* to take place.

operário, -ria [ope'rarju, -rja] *m, f* worker.

opereta [ope'reta] *f* operetta.

opinar [opi'na(x)] *vt* to think ♦ *vi* to give one's opinion.

opinião [opi'njãw] *(pl* **-ões** [-õjʃ]) *f* opinion; **na minha ~** in my opinion; **na ~ dele** in his opinion; **ser da ~ que** to be of the opinion that; **a ~ pública** public opinion.

ópio ['ɔpju] *m* opium.

oponente [opo'nẽntʃi] *mf* opponent.

opor-se [o'poxsi] *vp* to object; **~ a** to oppose.

oportunidade [opoxtuni'dadʒi] *f* opportunity.

oportuno, -na [opox'tunu, -na] *adj* opportune.

oposição [opozi'sãw] *f* opposition; *(diferença)* contrast; **a ~** *(POL)* the Opposition.

oposto, -osta [o'poʃtu, -ɔʃta] *adj* opposite ♦ *m*: **o ~** the opposite; **~ a** opposite.

opressão [opre'sãw] *(pl* **-ões** [-õjʃ]) *f* oppression.

opressivo, -va [opre'sivu, -va] *adj* oppressive.

opressões → **opressão**.

oprimir [opri'mi(x)] *vt* to oppress.

optar [op'ta(x)] *vi* to choose; **~ por algo** to opt for sthg; **~ por fazer algo** to opt to do sthg, to choose to do sthg.

optimismo [ɔtʃi'miʒmu] *m (Port)* = **otimismo**.

óptimo, -ma ['ɔtimu, -ma] *adj (Port)* = **ótimo**.

ora ['ɔra] *interj* come on! ◆ *conj* well ◆ *adv*: **por ~** for now; **~ essa!** well, well!; **~ ..., ~ ...** one minute ..., the next ....

oração [ora'sãw] *(pl -ões [-õjʃ]) f (prece)* prayer; *(frase)* clause.

orador, -ra [ora'do(x), -ra] *(mpl -res [-riʃ], fpl -s [-ʃ]) m, f* (public) speaker.

oral [o'raw] *(pl -ais [-ajʃ]) adj & f* oral.

orangotango [orãŋgo'tãŋgu] *m* orangutang.

orar [o'ra(x)] *vi (discursar)* to give a speech; *(rezar)* to pray.

órbita ['ɔxbita] *f (de olho)* socket; *(de planeta)* orbit; *(fig: de ação, influência)* sphere.

orçamento [oxsa'mẽntu] *m (de Estado, empresa)* budget; *(para trabalho, serviço)* estimate.

ordem ['ɔxdẽ] *(pl -ns [-ʃ]) f* order; **até segunda ~** until further notice; **de primeira ~** first-rate; **de tal ~ que** such that; **pôr algo em ~** to tidy sthg up; **por ~** in order; **por ~ de alguém** on the orders of sb; **sempre às ordens!** don't mention it!

ordenado [oxde'nadu] *m* wage.

ordenhar [oxde'ɲa(x)] *vt* to milk.

ordens → **ordem**.

ordinário, -ria [oxdʒi'narju, -rja] *adj (grosseiro)* crude.

orégano [o'rɛganu] *m (Br)* oregano.

orégão [o'rɛgãw] *m (Port)* = **orégano**.

orelha [o'reʎa] *f (ANAT)* ear; *(de calçado)* tongue.

orfanato [oxfa'natu] *m* orphanage.

órfão, -fã ['ɔxfãw, -fã] *m, f* orphan.

orfeão [ox'fẽãw] *(pl -ões [-õjʃ]) m* choral society.

orgânico, -ca [ox'ganiku, -ka] *adj* organic.

organismo [oxga'niʒmu] *m* body.

organização [oxganiza'sãw] *(pl -ões [-õjʃ]) f* organization.

órgão ['ɔxgãw] *m* organ; *(de empresa)* body; **~s sexuais** OU **genitais** sexual organs, genitals.

orgasmo [ox'gaʒmu] *m* orgasm.

orgia [ox'ʒia] *f* orgy.

orgulhar-se [oxgu'ʎaxsi] : **orgulhar-se de** *vp + prep* to be proud of.

orgulho [ox'guʎu] *m* pride.

orientação [orjẽnta'sãw] *(pl -ões [-õjʃ]) f* direction; **~ escolar** careers advice *(at school)*; **~ profissional** careers advice.

oriental [orjẽn'taw] *(pl -ais [-ajʃ]) adj (do este)* eastern; *(do Extremo Oriente)* oriental.

ɔ orientais *mpl*: **os orientais** the Orientals.

orientar [orjẽn'ta(x)] *vt (guiar)* to direct; *(aconselhar)* to advise.

ɔ orientar-se por *vp + prep* to follow.

oriente [o'rjẽntʃi] *m* east.

ɔ Oriente *m*: **o Oriente** the Orient.

orifício [ori'fisju] *m* orifice.

origem [o'riʒẽ] *(pl -ns [-ʃ]) f* origin.

original [oriʒi'naw] *(pl -ais [-ajʃ]) adj & m* original.

originar [oriʒi'na(x)] *vt* to cause.

ɔ originar-se *vp* to arise.

oriundo, -da [o'rjũndu, -da] *adj*: **~ de** from.

orixá [ori'ʃa] *mf (Br)* god or goddess of any of the Afro-Brazilian religions.

ornamentar [oxnamẽn'ta(x)] *vt* to decorate.

ornamento [oxna'mẽntu] *m* ornament.

ornitologia [oxnitolo'ʒia] *f* ornithology.

orquestra [ox'kɛʃtra] *f* orchestra.

orquídea [ox'kidʒia] *f* orchid.

ortografia [oxtogra'fia] *f* spelling.

ortopedia [oxtope'dʒia] *f* orthopaedics *(sg)*.

ortopédico, -ca [oxtp'pɛdʒiku, -ka] *adj* orthopaedic.

ortopedista [oxtɔpe'dʒiʃta] *mf* orthopaedic surgeon.

orvalho [ox'vaʎu] *m* dew.

os → o.

oscilação [oʃsila'sãw] *(pl -ões [-õjʃ]) f (balanço)* swinging; *(variação)* fluctuation.

oscilar [oʃsi'la(x)] *vi (balançar)* to swing; *(variar)* to fluctuate; **~ entre** to fluctuate between.

osso ['osu] *(pl ossos ['ɔsuʃ]) m* bone.

ostensivamente [oʃtẽ,siva'mẽntʃi] *adv* ostentatiously.

ostensivo, -va [oʃtẽ'sivu, -va] *adj (provocatório)* blatant; *(exibicionista)* ostentatious.

ostentar [oʃtẽn'ta(x)] *vt* to show off.

ostra ['oʃtra] *f* oyster.

OTAN [o'tã] *f (abrev de Organização do Tratado do Atlântico Norte)* = **NATO**.

otimismo [otʃiˈmiʒmu] *m (Br)* optimism.

ótimo, -ma [ˈɔtʃimu, -ma] *adj (Br)* great ◆ *interj (Br)* great!, excellent!

otorrinolaringologista [ˌoto-ˌxinolaˌrĩŋoloˈʒiʃta] *mf* ear, nose and throat specialist.

ou [o] *conj* or; ~ ... ~ either ... or.

ouço [ˈosu] → **ouvir.**

ouriço [oˈrisu] *m (de castanheiro)* shell.

ouriço-cacheiro [oˌrisukaˈʃejru] *(pl* **ouriços-cacheiros** [oˌrisuʃkaˈʃejruʃ]) *m* hedgehog.

ouriço-do-mar [oˌrisuduˈma(x)] *(pl* **ouriços-do-mar** [oˌrisuʒduˈma(x)]) *m* sea urchin.

ourives [oˈriviʃ] *mf inv* jeweller.

ourivesaria [orivezaˈria] *f* jeweller's (shop).

ouro [ˈoru] gold; ~ **de lei** *19.25-carat gold.*

◡ **ouros** *mpl (naipe de cartas)* diamonds.

Ouro Preto [ˌoruˈpretu] *s* Ouro Preto.

ousadia [ozaˈdʒia] *f* audacity.

ousar [oˈza(x)] *vt* to dare to.

outdoor [awtˈdɔr] *m (propaganda)* outdoor advertising; *(cartaz)* hoarding *(Brit)*, billboard *(Am)*.

outono [oˈtonu] *m* autumn *(Brit)*, fall *(Am)*.

outro, -tra [ˈotru, -tra] *adj* another *(sg)*, other *(pl)* ◆ *pron (outra coisa)* another *(sg)*, others *(pl)*; *(outra pessoa)* someone else; **o ~/a outra** the other (one); **os ~s** the others; ~ **copo** another glass; ~**s dois copos** another two

glasses; ~ **dia** another day; **no ~ dia** *(no dia seguinte)* the next day; *(relativo a dia passado)* the other day; **um ou ~** one or the other; **um após o ~** one after the other.

outubro [oˈtubru] *m* October, → **setembro.**

ouve [ˈovi] → **ouvir.**

ouvido [oˈvidu] *m (ANAT)* ear; *(audição)* hearing; **dar ~s a alguém** to listen to sb; **ser todo ~s** to be all ears; **ter bom ~** to have good hearing; **tocar de ~** to play by ear.

ouvinte [oˈvĩntʃi] *mf* listener.

ouvir [oˈvi(x)] *vt & vi* to hear; **você está ouvindo?** are you listening?; **estar ouvindo algo/alguém** to be listening to sthg/sb.

ovação [ovaˈsãw] *(pl* **-ões** [-õjʃ]) *f* ovation.

oval [oˈvaw] *(pl* **-ais** [-ajʃ]) *adj* oval.

ovário [oˈvarju] *m* ovary.

ovelha [oˈveʎa] *f* sheep; *(fêmea)* ewe; ~ **negra** black sheep.

OVNI [ˈɔvni] *m (abrev de Objeto Voador Não Identificado)* UFO.

ovo [ˈovu] *(pl* **ovos** [ˈɔvuʃ]) *m* egg; ~ **cozido/escalfado** boiled/poached egg; ~ **estrelado** fried egg; ~**s mexidos** scrambled eggs; ~**s de Páscoa** Easter eggs.

óvulo [ˈɔvulu] *m* ovum.

oxigénio [oksiˈʒɛnju] *m (Port)* = **oxigênio.**

oxigênio [oksiˈʒɛnju] *m (Br)* oxygen.

ozônio [oˈzonju] *m (Br)* ozone.

ozono [oˈzonu] *m (Port)* = **ozônio.**

P

p. *(abrev de página)* p.

P. *(abrev de Praça)* = Sq.

pá ['pa] *f (utensílio)* spade ◆ *m (Port: fam: forma de tratamento)* mate *(Brit)*, man *(Am)*.

pacato, -ta [pa'katu, -ta] *adj* easy-going.

paciência [pa'sjēsja] *f* patience; **perder a ~** to lose one's patience; **ter ~** to be patient.

paciente [pa'sjēntʃi] *adj & mf* patient.

pacífico, -ca [pa'sifiku, -ka] *adj* peaceful.

❑ **Pacífico** *m*: **o Pacífico** the Pacific.

pacifista [pasi'fiʃta] *mf* pacifist.

paçoca [pa'sɔka] *f (prato)* a dish made with fresh or dried meat, cooked and minced, then fried and mixed with corn-flour or cassava; *(doce)* dessert made from ground peanuts, milk, eggs and sugar.

pacote [pa'kɔtʃi] *m* packet; *(em turismo)* package; **~ de açúcar** *(pequeno)* packet of sugar.

padaria [pada'ria] *f* bakery.

padecer [pade'se(x)]: **padecer de** *v + prep* to suffer from.

padeiro, -ra [pa'dejru, -ra] *m, f* baker.

padrão [pa'drãw] *(pl -ões* [-õjʃ]) *m (de produto)* model; *(de tecido)* pattern; **~ de vida** standard of living.

padrasto [pa'draʃtu] *m* stepfather.

padre ['padri] *m* priest.

padrinho [pa'driɲu] *m* godfather.

padrões → padrão.

pães → pão.

pág. *(abrev de página)* p.

pagamento [paga'mēntu] *m* payment; **~ em dinheiro** OU **numerário** cash payment; **~ a prestações** hire purchase *(Brit)*, installment plan *(Am)*.

pagar [pa'ga(x)] *vt* to pay; *(estudos)* to pay for; *(fig: consequências)* to suffer ◆ *vi*: **~ por** *(sofrer consequências por)* to pay for; **~ algo a alguém** to pay sb sthg; **quanto você pagou pelo bilhete?** how much did you pay for the ticket? **~ à vista** to pay cash up front.

página ['paʒina] *f* page; **as Páginas Amarelas** the Yellow Pages®.

pago, -ga ['pagu, -ga] *pp →* **pagar.**

pagode [pa'gɔdʒi] *m (fam: farra)* fun.

págs. *(abrev de páginas)* pp.

pai ['paj] *m* father.

pai-de-santo [,pajdʒi'sãntu] *(pl pais-de-santo* [,pajʒdʒi'sãntu]) *m "candomblé"* or *"umbanda"* priest.

painel [paj'nɛw] *(pl -éis* [-ɛjʃ]) *m* panel; *(de veículo)* dashboard; **~ solar** solar panel.

paio ['paju] *m very lean "chouriço".*

pais ['pajʃ] *mpl (progenitores)* parents.

país [pa'iʃ] *(pl -ses* [-ziʃ]) *m* country.

paisagem [paj'zaʒãj] *(pl -ns* [-ʃ]) *f (vista)* view; *(pintura)* landscape.

País de Gales [pa,iʒdʒi'galiʃ] *m*: **o ~** Wales.

países → país.

paixão [paj'ʃãw] *(pl -ões* [-õjʃ]) *f* passion.

pajé [pa'ʒɛ] *m (Br)* witch doctor.

palacete [pala'setʃi] *m* small palace.

palácio [pa'lasju] *m* palace; **Palácio da Justiça** Law Courts *(pl)*.

paladar [pala'da(x)] *(pl -res* [-riʃ]) *m* taste.

palafita [pala'fita] *f* house on stilts.

palavra [pa'lavra] *f* word ◆ *interj* honest!; **dar a ~ a alguém** to give sb the opportunity to speak.

palavrão [pala'vrãw] *(pl -ões* [-õjʃ]) *m* swearword.

palavras-cruzadas [pa,lavraʃkru-'zadaʃ] *fpl* crossword (puzzle) *(sg)*.

palavrões → palavrão.

palco ['pawku] *m* stage.

palerma [pa'lɛxma] *mf* fool.

palestra [pa'lɛʃtra] *f* lecture.

paleta [pa'leta] *f* palette.

paletó [pale'tɔ] *m* jacket.

palha ['paʎa] *f* straw.

palhaço [pa'ʎasu] *m* clown.

palhinha [pa'ʎiɲa] *f* straw.

pálido, -da ['palidu, -da] *adj* pale.

paliteiro [pali'tejru] *m* toothpick holder.

palito [pa'litu] *m (para dentes)* toothpick; **~ de fósforo** matchstick; **ser um ~** *(fig: pessoa)* to be as thin as a rake.

palma ['pawma] *f* palm.

❑ **palmas** *fpl* clapping *(sg)*; **bater ~s** to clap; **uma salva de ~s** a round of applause.

palmeira [paw'mejra] *f* palm tree.

palmito [paw'mitu] *m* palm heart.

palmo ['pawmu] *m* (hand) span; **~ a ~** inch by inch.

PALOP *mpl (abrev de Países Africanos de Língua Oficial Portuguesa)*: **os ~** acronym for African countries where Portuguese is an official language.

palpável [paw'pavɛw] *(pl* **-eis** [-ejʃ]*) adj* tangible.

pálpebra ['pawpebra] *f* eyelid.

palpitação [pawpita'sãw] *(pl* **-ões** [-õjʃ]*) f* beating.

palpitar [pawpi'ta(x)] *vi* to beat.

palpite [paw'pitʃi] *m* tip; *(suposição)* hunch.

paludismo [palu'dʒiʒmu] *m* malaria.

pamonha [pa'moɲa] *f cake made from maize, coconut milk, butter, cinnamon, sweet herbs and sugar, and baked wrapped in banana skin.*

Panamá [pana'ma] *m*: **o ~** Panama.

pancada [pãŋ'kada] *f (com pau, mão)* blow; *(choque)* knock; *(de relógio)* stroke; **dar ~ em alguém** to beat sb up; **~ d'água** sudden downpour; **ser ~** *(fam)* to be crazy.

pâncreas ['pãŋkrjaʃ] *m inv* pancreas.

panda ['pãnda] *m* panda.

pandeiro [pãn'dejru] *m* tambourine.

pandemónio [pãnde'mɔnju] *m (Port)* = **pandemônio**.

pandemônio [pãnde'moɲu] *m (Br)* pandemonium.

pane ['pani] *f* breakdown.

panela [pa'nɛla] *f* pot; **~ de pressão** pressure cooker.

panfleto [pã'fletu] *m* pamphlet.

pânico ['paniku] *m* panic; **entrar em ~** to panic.

pano ['panu] *m (tecido)* cloth; *(em teatro)* curtain; **~ de fundo** backdrop.

panorama [pano'rama] *m* panorama.

panqueca [pãŋ'kɛka] *f* pancake.

pantanal [pãnta'naw] *(pl* **-ais** [-ajʃ]*) m* swampland.

❑ **Pantanal** *m*: **o Pantanal** the Pantanal.

pântano ['pãntanu] *m* swamp.

pantera [pãn'tɛra] *f* panther.

pantomima [pãnto'mima] *f* mime, dumb show.

pantufas [pãn'tufaʃ] *fpl* slippers.

pão ['pãw] *(pl* **pães** ['pãjʃ]*) m* bread; **~ de centeio** rye bread; **~ de fôrma** loaf; **~ francês** roll; **~ integral** wholemeal bread; **~ de leite** *small sweet bread glazed with egg yolk before baking*; **~ ralado** *(Port)* breadcrumbs *(pl)*; **~ de segunda** crusty white loaf; **o Pão de Açúcar** Sugar Loaf Mountain; **comer o ~ que o diabo amassou** *(fig)* to have a rough time of it.

pão-de-ló [ˌpãwdʒi'lɔ] *(pl* **pães-de-ló** [ˌpãjʒdʒi'lɔ]*) m* sponge cake.

papa ['papa] *f (para bebê)* baby food ♦ *m* pope; *(fig: ás)* ace.

papagaio [papa'gaju] *m (ave)* parrot; *(brinquedo)* kite.

papeira [pa'pejra] *f (Port)* mumps *(sg)*.

papel [pa'pɛw] *(pl* **-éis** [-ɛjʃ]*) m* paper; **~ A4** A4 paper; **~ de alumínio** tinfoil; **~ de carta** writing paper; **~ de embrulho** wrapping paper; **~ higiênico** toilet paper; **~ de máquina** typing paper; **~ de parede** wallpaper; **~ químico** *(Port)* carbon paper; **~ reciclado** recycled paper; **~ vegetal** *(de cozinha)* greaseproof paper; *(de desenho)* tracing paper.

papelão [pape'lãw] *m* cardboard.

papelaria [papela'ria] *f* stationer's (shop).

papel-carbono [paˌpɛwkax'bonu] *m (Br)* carbon paper.

papo ['papu] *m (de ave)* crop; *(Br: conversa)* chat; **levar** OU **bater um ~** *(Br: fam)* to (have a) chat; **~s de anjo** *small pastries made of syrup, jam, eggs and cinnamon, dusted with sugar on serving.*

papo-furado [ˌpapufu'radu] *m (Br: fam)* nonsense.

papoila [pa'pojla] f = **papoula**.

papo-seco [,papu'seku] (pl **papos-secos** [,papuʃ'sekuʃ]) m roll.

papoula [pa'pola] f poppy.

paquerar [pake'ra(x)] vt (Br: fam) to flirt with, to chat up ◆ vi (Br: fam) to flirt.

paquete [pa'ketʃi] m (navio) (steam-powered) ocean liner.

par ['pa(x)] (pl **-res** [-riʃ]) adj (número) even ◆ m pair; (casal) couple; **estar a ~ de** algo to be up to date on sthg; **~es masculinos/femininos/mistos** (Port: em tênis) men's/women's/mixed doubles; **a ~** side by side; **aos ~es** in pairs.

para ['para] prep 1. (exprime finalidade, destinação) for; **um telefonema ~ o senhor** a phone call for you; **queria algo ~ comer** I would like something to eat; **~ que serve isto?** what's this for?

2. (indica motivo, objetivo) (in order) to; **cheguei mais cedo ~ arranjar lugar** I arrived early (in order) to get a place; **era só ~ lhe agradar** I only wanted to please you.

3. (indica direção) towards; **apontou ~ cima/baixo** he pointed upwards/downwards; **olhei ~ ela** I looked at her; **seguiu ~ o aeroporto** he headed for the airport; **vá ~ casa!** go home!

4. (relativo a tempo) for; **quero isso pronto ~ amanhã** I want it done for tomorrow; **estará pronto ~ a semana/o ano** it'll be ready next week/year; **são quinze ~ as três** it's a quarter to three (Brit), it's a quarter of three (Am).

5. (em comparações): **é caro demais ~ as minhas posses** it's too expensive for my budget; **~ o que come, está magro** he's thin, considering how much he eats.

6. (relativo a opinião, sentimento): **~ mim** as far as I'm concerned.

7. (exprime a iminência): **estar ~ fazer algo** to be about to do sthg; **o ônibus está ~ sair** the bus is about to leave; **ele está ~ chegar** he'll be here any minute now.

8. (em locuções): **~ mais de** well over; **~ que** so that; **é ~ já!** coming up!

parabéns [para'bẽʃ] mpl congratulations ◆ interj (em geral) congratulations!; (por aniversário) happy birthday!; **dar os ~ a alguém** (em geral) to congratulate sb; (por aniversário) to wish sb a happy birthday; **você está de ~** you're to be congratulated.

parabólica [para'bɔlika] f satellite dish.

pára-brisas [,para'brizaʃ] m inv windscreen (Brit), windshield (Am).

pára-choques [,para'ʃɔkiʃ] m inv bumper.

parada [pa'rada] f (de jogo) bet, stake; (militar) parade; **~ (de ônibus)** (Br) (bus) stop.

paradeiro [para'dejru] m whereabouts (pl).

parado, -da [pa'radu, -da] adj (pessoa, animal) motionless; (carro) stationary; (máquina) switched off; (sem vida) dull.

paradoxo [para'dɔksu] m paradox.

parafina [para'fina] f paraffin.

parafrasear [parafra'zja(x)] vt to paraphrase.

parafuso [para'fuzu] m screw.

paragem [pa'raʒẽ] (pl **-ns** [-ʃ]) f stop, halt; **~ (de autocarro)** (Port) (bus) stop.

parágrafo [pa'ragrafu] m paragraph.

Paraguai [para'gwaj] m: **o ~** Paraguay.

paraíso [para'izu] m paradise.

pára-lamas [para'lamaʃ] m inv mudguard (Brit), fender (Am).

paralelo, -la [para'lɛlu, -la] adj & m parallel; **sem ~** unparalleled.

paralisar [parali'za(x)] vt to paralyse.

paralisia [parali'zia] f paralysis.

paralítico, -ca [para'litiku, -ka] m, f paralytic.

paranóico, -ca [para'nɔiku, -ka] m, f (fam) nutter ◆ adj paranoid.

parapeito [para'pejtu] m windowsill.

pára-quedas [,para'kedaʃ] m inv parachute.

pára-quedista [,parake'diʃta] mf parachutist.

parar [pa'ra(x)] vt & vi to stop; **"pare, escute, olhe"** "stop, look and listen"; **ir ~ em** to end up in; **~ de fazer algo** to stop doing sthg; **sem ~** non-stop.

pára-raios [,para'xajuʃ] m inv lightning conductor (Brit), lightning rod (Am).

parasita [para'zita] m parasite.

parceiro, -ra [pax'sejru, -ra] m, f partner.

parcela [pax'sɛla] f (de soma) item; (fragmento) fragment, bit.

parceria [paxse'ria] *f* partnership.

parcial [par'sjaw] (*pl* **-ais** [-ajʃ]) *adj* (*não completo*) partial; (*faccioso*) biased.

parcómetro [par'kɔmetru] *m* (*Port*) = **parquímetro**.

pardal [pax'daw] (*pl* **-ais** [-ajʃ]) *m* house sparrow.

pardo, -da ['paxdu, -da] *adj* dark grey.

parecer [pare'se(x)] *vi* to look ◆ *m* opinion ◆ *v impess*: **parece que vai chover** it looks like rain, it looks as if it's going to rain; **parece-me que sim** I think so; **ao que parece** by the look of things; **que lhe parece?** what do you think?

❑ **parecer-se** *vp* to look alike; **~-se com alguém** to look like sb.

parecido, -da [pare'sidu, -da] *adj* similar; **são muito ~s** they are very alike.

paredão [pare'dãw] (*pl* **-ões** [-õjʃ]) *m* thick wall.

parede [pa'redʒi] *f* wall; **morar ~s meias com** to live next door to.

paredões → **paredão**.

parente, -ta [pa'rẽtʃi, -ta] *m, f* relative; **~ próximo** close relative.

parêntese [pa'rẽtezi] *m* (*sinal*) bracket; (*frase*) parenthesis; **entre ~s** in brackets.

pares → **par**.

pargo ['paxgu] *m* sea bream.

parir [pa'ri(x)] *vt* to give birth to ◆ *vi* to give birth.

parlamento [paxla'mẽtu] *m* parliament.

paróquia [pa'rɔkja] *f* parish.

parque ['paxki] *m* park; **~ de campismo** (*Port*) campsite (*Brit*), campground (*Am*); **~ de diversões** amusement park; **~ de estacionamento** car park (*Brit*), parking lot (*Am*); **~ industrial** industrial estate; **~ infantil** (*Port*) playground; **~ nacional** national park; **~ natural** nature reserve.

parquímetro [pax'kimetru] *m* parking meter.

parte ['paxtʃi] *f* part; (*fração*) bit; (*JUR*) party; **dar ~ de** (*informar*) to report; **fazer ~ de** to be part of; **tomar ~ de** to take part in; **em outra ~** somewhere else; **por toda a ~** everywhere; **da ~ de** on behalf of; **de ~ a ~** mutual; **em ~** in part.

parteira [pax'tejra] *f* midwife.

participação [paxtʃisipa'sãw] (*pl* **-ões** [-õjʃ]) *f* participation; (*comunicado*) announcement; (*em negócio*) involvement; (*a polícia, autoridade*) report.

participante [paxtʃisi'pãtʃi] *mf* participant.

participar [paxtʃisi'pa(x)] *vi* to participate ◆ *vt*: **~ algo a alguém** (*informar*) to inform sb of sthg; (*comunicar*) to report sthg to sb; **~ de algo** to take part in sthg.

particípio [paxtʃi'sipju] *m* participle; **~ passado/presente** past/present participle.

particular [paxtʃiku'la(x)] (*pl* **-res** [-riʃ]) *adj* (*individual*) particular; (*privado*) private, privately owned.

partida [pax'tʃida] *f* (*saída*) departure; (*em esporte*) match; **estar de ~** to be about to leave; **à ~** at the beginning.

partidário, -ria [partʃi'darju, -rja] *m, f* supporter.

partido, -da [pax'tʃidu, -da] *adj* broken ◆ *m*: **~ (político)** (political) party.

partilhar [paxtʃi'ʎa(x)] *vt* to share.

partir [pax'tʃi(x)] *vt* to break ◆ *vi* (*ir embora*) to leave, to depart; **ele partiu para o estrangeiro** he went abroad; **~ de** (*lugar*) to leave; **a ~ de** from; **a ~ de agora** from now on.

❑ **partir-se** *vp* (*quebrar-se*) to break.

parto ['paxtu] *m* birth.

parvo, -va ['paxvu, -va] *m, f* idiot.

Páscoa ['paʃkwa] *f* Easter; **~ feliz!** Happy Easter!

pasmado, -da [paʒ'madu, -da] *adj* dumbstruck.

passa ['pasa] *f* (*fruto*) raisin.

passadeira [pasa'dejra] *f* (*Port: para peões*) pedestrian crossing.

passado, -da [pa'sadu, -da] *adj* (*no passado*) past; (*anterior*) last ◆ *m* past; **mal ~** (*CULIN: bife, carne*) rare; **bem ~** (*CULIN: bife, carne*) well-done.

passageiro, -ra [pasa'ʒejru, -ra] *m, f* passenger ◆ *adj* passing.

passagem [pa'saʒẽ] (*pl* **-ns** [-ʃ]) *f* passage; (*bilhete*) ticket; **~ de ano** New Year, Hogmanay (*Scot*); **~ de ida** (*Br*) single (ticket) (*Brit*), one-way ticket (*Am*); **~ de ida e volta** (*Br*) return (ticket) (*Brit*), round-trip ticket (*Am*); **~ de nível** level crossing; **~ subterrânea** subway (*Brit*), underpass (*Am*).

passaporte [pasa'pɔrtʃi] *m* passport.

passar [pa'sa(x)] *vt* **1.** *(deslizar, filtrar)*: ~ **algo por algo** to pass sthg through sthg; **ela passou a mão pelo cabelo** she ran her hand through her hair; **passou o creme bronzeador nos braços** he put suntan cream on his arms; ~ **por água** to rinse.
2. *(chegar, fazer chegar)* to pass; **pode me passar o sal?** would you pass me the salt?
3. *(a ferro)*: ~ **algo (a ferro)**, ~ **(a ferro) algo** to iron sthg; **você já passou a roupa (a ferro)?** have you done the ironing yet?
4. *(contagiar)* to pass on.
5. *(mudar)*: ~ **algo para** to move sthg to.
6. *(ultrapassar)* to pass.
7. *(tempo)* to spend; **passei um ano em Portugal** I spent a year in Portugal.
8. *(exame)* to pass.
9. *(fronteira)* to cross.
10. *(vídeo, disco)* to put on.
11. *(em televisão, cinema)* to show.
12. *(admitir)*: **deixar** ~ **algo** to let sthg pass.
♦ *vi* **1.** *(ir, circular)* to go; **o (ônibus) 7 não passa por aqui** the number 7 doesn't come this way.
2. *(revisor, ônibus)*: **já passou o (ônibus) 7/o revisor?** has the number 7/the ticket inspector been?
3. *(tempo)* to go by; **já passa das dez horas** it's past ten o'clock; **o tempo passa muito depressa** time flies.
4. *(terminar)* to be over; **o verão já passou** summer's over; **a dor já passou** the pain's gone.
5. *(a nível diferente)* to go up; **ele passou para o segundo ano** he went up into second year; **passa para primeira (velocidade)** go into first (gear); **quero** ~ **para um nível mais alto** I want to move up to a more advanced level.
6. *(mudar de ação, tema)*: ~ **a** to move on to.
7. *(em locuções)*: **como você tem passado?** *(de saúde)* how have you been?; ~ **bem** *(tempo, férias)* to enjoy; **passe bem!** good day to you!; ~ **mal** *(de saúde)* to feel ill; **não** ~ **de** to be no more than; ~ **(bem) sem** to be fine without; **não** ~ **sem** never to go without; **o que passou, passou** let bygones be bygones.
❏ **passar por** *v + prep (ser considerado*

como) to pass as OU for; *(fig: atravessar)* to go through; **fazer-se** ~ **por** to pass o.s. off as.
❏ **passar-se** *vp (acontecer)* to happen; **o que é que se passa?** what's going on?.
passarela [pasa'rɛla] *f (Br: de rua, estrada)* pedestrian crossing; *(para desfile de moda)* catwalk.
pássaro ['pasaru] *m* bird.
passatempo [.pasa'tẽmpu] *m* hobby, pastime.
passe ['pasi] *m (de ônibus)* (bus) pass; *(de trem)* season ticket.
passear [pa'sja(x)] *vt (cão)* to walk ♦ *vi* to go for a walk.
passeata [pa'sjata] *f (passeio)* stroll; *(Br: marcha de protesto)* demonstration.
passeio [pa'saju] *m (em rua)* pavement *(Brit)*, sidewalk *(Am)*; *(caminhada)* walk.
passional [pasjo'naw] *(pl* -**ais** [-ajʃ]*) adj* passionate.
passista [pa'siʃta] *mf (Br) skilled samba dancer, especially one who dances in Carnival parades in Brazil.*
passível [pa'sivew] *(pl* -**eis** [-ejʃ]*) adj*: ~ **de** liable to.
passivo, -va [pa'sivu, -va] *adj* passive ♦ *m (COM)* liabilities *(pl)*.
passo ['pasu] *m (movimento)* step; *(modo de andar)* walk; *(ritmo)* pace; **dar o primeiro** ~ to make the first move; **a dois** ~**s (de)** round the corner (from); **ao** ~ **que** whilst; ~ **a** ~ step by step.
pasta ['paʃta] *f* briefcase; *(de escola)* satchel; *(para papéis)* folder; *(de ministro)* portfolio; *(massa)* paste; ~ **dentífrica** OU **de dentes** toothpaste.
pastar [paʃ'ta(x)] *vi* to graze.
pastel [paʃ'tɛw] *(pl* -**éis** [-ɛiʃ]*) m* pie; *(em pintura)* pastel; *(Port: bolo)* cake; ~ **de bacalhau** small cod fishcake; ~ **de carne** = sausage roll; ~ **de galinha** chicken pasty.
pastelaria [paʃtela'ria] *f (local)* patisserie; *(comida)* pastries *(pl)*.
pasteurizado, -da [paʃtewri'zadu, -da] *adj* pasteurized.
pastilha [paʃ'tiʎa] *f (doce)* pastille; *(medicamento)* tablet, pill; ~ **(elástica)** *(Port)* (chewing) gum; ~ **para a garganta** throat lozenge; ~ **para a tosse** cough sweet.
pasto ['paʃtu] *m* pasture.
pastor, -ra [paʃ'to(x), -ra] *(mpl* -**res** [-riʃ], *fpl* -**s** [-ʃ]*) m, f* shepherd *(f* shep-

herdess) ◆ *m* minister.

pata ['pata] *f (perna de animal)* leg; *(pé de gato, cão)* paw; *(pé de cavalo, cabra)* hoof.

patamar [pata'ma(x)] *(pl -res* [-riʃ]) *m* landing.

paté [pa'te] *m (Port)* = **patê**.

patê [pa'te] *m (Br)* pâté.

patente [pa'tẽntʃi] *adj (visível)* obvious ◆ *f (de máquina, invento)* patent; *(de militar)* rank.

paternal [patex'naw] *(pl -ais* [-ajʃ]) *adj (afetuoso)* fatherly.

pateta [pa'tɛta] *mf* twit.

patético, -ca [pa'tɛtʃiku, -ka] *adj* pathetic.

patife [pa'tʃifi] *m* scoundrel.

patim [pa'tʃĩ] *(pl -ns* [-ʃ]) *m (de rodas)* roller skate; *(de gelo)* ice skate.

patinação [patʃina'sãw] *f (Br)* skating; ~ **artística** figure skating; ~ **no gelo** ice skating.

patinagem [patʃi'naʒẽ] *f (Port)* = **patinação**.

patinar [patʃi'na(x)] *vi (com patins)* to skate; *(veículo)* to spin.

patins → **patim**.

pátio ['patʃju] *m* patio.

pato ['patu] *m* duck.

patologia [patolo'ʒia] *f* pathology.

patológico, -ca [pato'lɔʒiku, -ka] *adj* pathological.

patrão, -troa [pa'trãw, -'troa] *(mpl -ões* [-õjʃ], *fpl -s* [-ʃ]) *m, f* boss.

pátria ['patria] *f* native country.

patrimônio [patri'monju] *m (Port)* = **patrimônio**.

patrimônio [patri'monju] *m (Br) (de empresa, fundação)* assets *(pl); (herança)* inheritance; ~ **nacional** national heritage.

patriota [patri'ɔta] *mf* patriot.

patroa → **patrão**.

patrocinador, -ra [patrosina'do(x), -ra] *(mpl -res* [-riʃ], *fpl -s* [-ʃ]) *m, f* sponsor.

patrocinar [patrosi'na(x)] *vt* to sponsor.

patrões → **patrão**.

patrulha [pa'truʎa] *f* patrol.

pau ['paw] *m* stick.

⌐ **paus** *mpl (naipe de cartas)* clubs.

paulista [paw'liʃta] *mf* native/inhabitant of São Paulo.

pausa ['pawza] *f (intervalo)* break;

(silêncio) pause.

pauta ['pawta] *f (de alunos)* register; *(de música)* stave.

pavão [pa'vãw] *(pl -ões* [-õjʃ]) *m* peacock.

pavê [pa've] *m liqueur-soaked sponge fingers set in layers with a sweet filling made from melted chocolate, egg yolks and butter.*

pavilhão [pavi'ʎãw] *(pl -ões* [-õjʃ]) *m* pavilion; ~ **esportivo** sports pavilion.

pavimentar [pavimẽn'ta(x)] *vt* to pave.

pavimento [pavi'mẽntu] *m (de estrada, rua)* road surface; *(andar de edifício)* floor.

pavões → **pavão**.

pavor [pa'vo(x)] *m* terror; **ter ~ de** to be terrified of.

paz ['paʃ] *(pl -zes* [-ziʃ]) *f* peace; **deixar algo/alguém em ~** to leave sthg/sb in peace; **fazer as ~es** to make (it) up; **que descanse em ~** (may he/she) rest in peace.

PC *m (abrev de Personal Computer)* PC.

Pça. *(abrev de praça)* Sq.

pé ['pɛ] *m* foot; *(de planta)* stem, stalk; *(em vinho)* dregs *(pl)*; **andar na ponta dos ~s** to walk on tiptoe; **pôr-se de ~** to stand up; **ter ~ *(em água)*** to be able to stand; **não ter ~ *(em água)*** not to be able to touch the bottom; **a ~** on foot; **ao ~ de** near; **em ou ~ ~** standing (up); **em ~ de igualdade** on an equal footing.

peão ['pjãw] *(pl -ões* [-õjʃ]) *m (Port: indivíduo a pé)* pedestrian; *(em xadrez)* pawn.

peça ['pɛsa] *f* piece; *(divisão de casa)* room; ~ **(de teatro)** play.

pecado [pe'kadu] *m* sin.

pechincha [pe'ʃĩʃa] *f* bargain.

peço ['pɛsu] → **pedir**.

peculiar [peku'lja(x)] *(pl -es* [-iʃ]) *adj* peculiar.

pedaço [pe'dasu] *m* piece; *(de tempo)* while; **andamos um bom ~** we walked a good part of the way; **estou aqui há ~** I've been here for a while; **estar caindo aos ~s** to be falling to bits.

pedágio [pe'daʒju] *m (Br)* toll.

pedal [pe'daw] *(pl -ais* [-ajʃ]) *m* pedal.

pede ['pedʒi] → **pedir**.

pé-de-cabra [,pede'kabra] *(pl pés-de-cabra* [,peʒde'kabra]) *m* crowbar.

pé-de-moleque [ˌpɛdʒimoˈlɛki] (*pl* **pés-de-moleque** [ˌpɛdʒimoˈlɛki]) *m hard peanut nougat.*

pedestal [pedeʃˈtaw] (*pl* **-ais** [-ajʃ]) *m* pedestal.

pedestre [peˈdɛʃtri] *adj (zona, faixa)* pedestrian *(antes de s)* ♦ *m (Br: indivíduo a pé)* pedestrian.

pediatra [peˈdʒjatra] *mf* paediatrician.

pediatria [pedʒjaˈtria] *f* paediatrics *(sg.)*

pedido [peˈdʒidu] *m* request; *(em restaurante)* order; **a ~ de alguém** at sb's request.

pedinte [peˈdʒĩtʃi] *mf* beggar.

pedir [peˈdʒi(x)] *vt (em restaurante, bar)* to order; *(preço)* to ask ♦ *vi (mendigar)* to beg; **~ algo a alguém** to ask sb for sthg; **~ a alguém que faça algo** to ask sb to do sthg; **~ algo emprestado a alguém** to borrow sthg from sb.

pedra [ˈpɛdra] *f* stone; *(lápide)* tombstone; *(granizo)* hailstone; *(de isqueiro)* flint; *(de dominó)* domino; **~ (preciosa)** precious stone, gem.

pedra-pomes [ˌpɛdraˈpɔmiʃ] (*pl* **pedras-pomes** [ˌpɛdraʃˈpɔmiʃ]) *f* pumice stone.

pedra-sabão [ˌpɛdrasaˈbãw] (*pl* **pedras-sabão** [ˌpɛdraʃsaˈbãw]) *f (Br)* soapstone.

pedreiro [peˈdrejru] *m* bricklayer.

pega [ˈpega] *f (ave)* magpie.

pegada [peˈgada] *f* footprint.

pegado, -da [peˈgadu, -da] *adj (colado)* stuck; *(contíguo)* adjoining.

pegajoso, -osa [pegaˈʒozu, -ɔza] *adj* sticky.

pegar [peˈga(x)] *vt* to catch; *(hábito, vício, mania)* to pick up ♦ *vi (motor)* to start; *(idéia, moda)* to catch on; *(planta)* to take; **peguei uma gripe** I got the flu; **~ em algo** to pick sthg up; **~ fogo em algo** to set fire to sthg; **~ no sono** to fall asleep.

❏ **pegar-se** *vp (agarrar-se)* to stick; *(brigar)* to come to blows.

peito [ˈpejtu] *m (seio)* breast; *(parte do tronco)* chest; *(de camisa, blusa)* front.

peitoril [pejtoˈriw] (*pl* **-is** [-iʃ]) *m* windowsill.

peixaria [pejʃaˈria] *f* fishmonger's (shop).

peixe [ˈpejʃi] *m* fish; **~ congelado** frozen fish.

❏ **Peixes** *m inv (signo do Zodíaco)* Pisces.

peixe-agulha [ˌpejʃaˈguʎa] *m* garfish.

peixe-espada [ˌpejʃeʃˈpada] *m* scabbard fish.

peixe-vermelho [ˌpejʃevexˈmeʎu] *m* carp.

pejorativo, -va [peʒoraˈtʃivu, -va] *adj* pejorative.

pela [ˈpela] = **por + a, → por.**

pelado, -da [peˈladu, -da] *adj (cabeça)* shorn; *(Br: fam: nu)* starkers; *(Port: fruta)* peeled.

pele [ˈpɛli] *f* skin; *(couro)* leather.

pelica [peˈlika] *f* kid (leather).

pelicano [peliˈkanu] *m* pelican.

película [peˈlikula] *f* film; **~ aderente** Clingfilm® (*Brit*), plastic wrap (*Am*).

pelo [ˈpelu] = **por + o, → por.**

pêlo [ˈpelu] *m (de animal)* fur; *(de pessoa)* hair.

Pelourinho [peloˈriɲu] *m:* **o ~ (de Salvador)** the *Pelourinho district in Salvador.*

peluche [peˈluʃe] *m (Port)* = **pelúcia.**

pelúcia [peˈlusja] *f* plush.

peludo, -da [peˈludu, -da] *adj* hairy.

pélvis [ˈpɛwviʃ] *m ou f inv* pelvis.

pena [ˈpena] *f (de ave)* feather; *(de escrever)* quill; *(dó)* pity; *(castigo)* sentence; **que ~!** what a shame!; **cumprir ~** to serve a prison term; **dar ~** to be a shame; **ter ~ de alguém** to feel sorry for sb; **tenho ~ de não poder ir** I'm sorry (that) I can't go; **valer a ~** to be worth one's while; **~ capital** capital punishment; **~ de morte** death penalty.

penalidade [penaliˈdadʒi] *f* penalty.

pênalti [peˈnawtʃi] *m (Br)* penalty.

penalty [peˈnalti] *m (Port)* = **pênalti.**

pendente [pẽˈdẽtʃi] *adj* pending ♦ *m* pendant.

pendurar [pẽduˈra(x)] *vt* to hang; **~ algo em algo** to hang sthg on sthg.

❏ **pendurar-se em** *vp + prep* to hang from.

penedo [peˈnedu] *m* boulder.

peneira [peˈnejra] *f* sieve.

penetrante [peneˈtrãtʃi] *adj* penetrating.

penetrar [peneˈtra(x)] : **penetrar em** *v + prep (entrar em)* to go into.

penhasco [peˈɲaʃku] *m* cliff.

penicilina [penisiˈlina] *f* penicillin.

penico [pe'niku] *m* chamber pot; *(para crianças)* potty.

península [pe'nĩsula] *f* peninsula.

pénis ['peniʃ] *m inv (Port)* = **pênis**.

pênis ['peniʃ] *m inv (Br)* penis.

penitência [peni'tẽsja] *f* penance.

penitenciária [penitẽ'sjarja] *f* prison.

penoso, -osa [pe'nozu, -ɔza] *adj* hard.

pensamento [pẽsa'mẽntu] *m (espírito)* mind; *(reflexão)* thought.

pensão [pẽ'sãw] *(pl* **-ões** [-õjʃ]*) f (hospedaria)* guesthouse; *(de invalidez, velhice)* pension; ~ **alimentícia** *(Br)* alimony, maintenance; ~ **completa** full board; ~ **residencial** – bed and breakfast.

pensar [pẽ'sa(x)] *vi (raciocinar)* to think; *(refletir)* to have a think ♦ *vt (tencionar)* to intend; ~ **em** to think about; ~ **que** to think (that); **nem** ~! no way!

pensionista [pẽsjo'niʃta] *mf (aposentado)* pensioner.

penso ['pẽsu] *m (Port)* dressing; ~ **higiénico** sanitary towel; ~ **rápido** (sticking) plaster *(Brit)*, Bandaid® *(Am)*.

pensões [pẽ'sõjʃ] → **pensão**.

pente ['pẽntʃi] *m* comb.

penteado [pẽn'tʃjadu] *m* hairstyle.

Pentecostes [pẽntʃi'kɔʃtʃiʃ] *m (católico)* Whit Sunday; *(judeu)* Pentecost.

penugem [pe'nuʒẽ] *f* down.

penúltimo, -ma [pe'nuwtʃimu, -ma] *adj* penultimate.

penumbra [pe'nũmbra] *f* semi-darkness, half-light.

penúria [pe'nurja] *f* penury.

peões → **peão**.

pepino [pe'pinu] *m* cucumber.

pequeno, -na [pe'kenu, -na] *adj* small, little; *(em comprimento)* short.

pequeno-almoço [pe,kenual'mosu] *(pl* **pequenos-almoços** [pe,kenuzal'mɔsuʃ]*) m (Port)* breakfast.

pêra ['pera] *(pl* **peras** ['peraʃ]*) f (fruto)* pear; *(barba)* goatee (beard); ~ **abacate** avocado.

perante [pe'rãntʃi] *prep* in the presence of; **estou ~ um grande problema** I've come up against a big problem.

perceber [pexse'be(x)] *vt (entender)* to understand; *(aperceber-se)* to realize.
❑ **perceber de** *v + prep* to know about.

percentagem [pexsẽn'taʒẽ] *(pl* **-ns** [-ʃ]*) f* percentage.

percevejo [pexse'veʒu] *m* bug; *(Br: tacha)* drawing pin *(Brit)*, thumbstack *(Am)*.

perco ['pexku] → **perder**.

percorrer [pexko'xe(x)] *vt (caminho, distância)* to travel; *(país)* to travel through; *(cidade, ruas)* to go round; ~ **algo com os olhos** OU **com a vista** to skim through sthg.

percurso [pex'kuxsu] *m* route.

percussão [pexku'sãw] *f* percussion.

perda ['pexda] *f* loss; *(desperdício)* waste.

perdão [pex'dãw] *m* pardon ♦ *interj* sorry!; ~**?** pardon?; **pedir ~** to ask (for) forgiveness.

perde ['pexdʒi] → **perder**.

perder [pex'de(x)] *vt* to lose; *(tempo)* to waste; *(trem, ônibus)* to miss ♦ *vi* to lose; ~ **a cabeça** to lose one's head; ~ **os sentidos** to pass out; ~ **alguém de vista** to lose sight of sb.
❑ **perder-se** *vp* to get lost.

perdição [pexdʒi'sãw] *f* downfall.

perdido, -da [pex'dʒidu, -da] *adj* lost; **"achados e ~s "** "lost property" *(Brit)*, "lost and found" *(Am)*; **ser ~ por** *(fam)* to be mad about.

perdiz [pex'dʒiʃ] *(pl* **-zes** [-ziʃ]*) f* partridge.

perdoar [pex'dwa(x)] *vt* to forgive.

perdurar [pexdu'ra(x)] *vi* to endure.

perecível [pere'sivew] *(pl* **-eis** [-ejʃ]*) adj* perishable.

peregrinação [peregrina'sãw] *(pl* **-ões** [-õjʃ]*) f* pilgrimage.

peregrino, -na [pere'grinu, -na] *m, f* pilgrim.

pereira [pe'rejra] *f* pear tree.

peremptório, -ria [perẽmp'tɔrju, -rja] *adj* peremptory.

perene [pe'reni] *adj* perennial.

perfeição [pexfej'sãw] *f* perfection.

perfeitamente [pexfejta'mẽntʃi] *adv* perfectly ♦ *interj* exactly!

perfeito, -ta [pex'fejtu, -ta] *adj* perfect.

pérfido, -da ['pexfidu, -da] *adj* malicious.

perfil [pex'fiw] *(pl* **-is** [-iʃ]*) m* profile; **de ~** in profile.

perfumaria [pexfuma'ria] *f* perfumery.

perfume [pex'fumi] *m* perfume.

perfurar [pexfu'ra(x)] *vt* to perforate, to make a hole in.

pergaminho [pexga'miɲu] *m* parchment.

pergunta [pex'gũnta] *f* question.

perguntar [pexgũn'ta(x)] *vt* to ask ♦ *vi*: ~ **por alguém** to ask after sb; ~ **sobre algo** to ask about sthg; ~ **algo a alguém** to ask sb sthg.

periferia [perife'ria] *f* outskirts *(pl)*.

perigo [pe'rigu] *m* danger; "~ **de incêndio**" "danger – fire risk"; "~ **de morte**" "danger of death"; "~ – **queda de materiais**" "danger – falling masonry".

perigoso, -osa [peri'gozu, -ɔza] *adj* dangerous.

perímetro [pe'rimetru] *m* perimeter.

periódico, -ca [pe'rjɔdiku, -ka] *adj* periodic.

período [pe'riodu] *m* period; *(de ano escolar)* term *(Brit)*, semester *(Am)*.

periquito [peri'kitu] *m* budgerigar.

perito, -ta [pe'ritu, -ta] *m, f & adj* expert; **ser ~ em algo** to be an expert in sthg.

permanecer [pexmane'se(x)] *vi* to stay, to remain.
❑ **permanecer em** *v + prep* to stay at.
❑ **permanecer por** *v + prep* to remain; **o problema permanece por resolver** the problem remains to be solved.

permanência [pexma'nẽsja] *f (estada)* stay; *(de problema, situação)* persistence.

permanente [pexma'nẽntʃi] *adj (emprego)* permanent; *(situação)* ongoing; *(dor, ruído)* continuous ♦ *f (penteado)* perm.

permissão [pexmi'sãw] *f* permission; **pedir ~ para fazer algo** to ask permission to do sthg.

permitir [pexmi'ti(x)] *vt* to allow.

perna ['pexna] *f* leg; *(de letra)* descender.

pernil [pex'niw] *(pl -is* [-iʃ]*)* *m* haunch.

pernilongo [pexni'lõŋgu] *m (Port: ave)* avocet; *(Br: mosquito)* mosquito.

pernis → **pernil**.

pérola ['perola] *f* pearl.

perpendicular [pexpẽndʒiku'la(x)] *(pl -res* [-riʃ]*)* *adj & f* perpendicular.

perpetrar [pexpe'tra(x)] *vt* to perpetrate.

perpetuar [pexpe'twa(x)] *vt* to immortalize.
❑ **perpetuar-se** *vp (eternizar-se)* to last forever; *(prolongar-se)* to last.

perplexidade [pexpleksi'dadʒi] *f* perplexity.

perplexo, -xa [pex'pleksu, -ksa] *adj* perplexed.

perseguição [pexsegi'sãw] *(pl -ões* [-õjʃ]*)* *f (de pessoa, criminoso)* pursuit; *(assédio)* persecution.

perseguir [pexse'gi(x)] *vt (seguir)* to follow; *(assediar)* to persecute.

perseverante [pexseve'rãntʃi] *adj* persevering.

perseverar [pexseve'ra(x)] *vi* to persevere.

persiana [pex'sjana] *f* blind.

persistente [pexsiʃ'tẽntʃi] *adj* persistent.

personagem [pexso'naʒẽ] *(pl -ns* [-ʃ]*)* *m ou f* character.

personalidade [pexsonali'dadʒi] *f* personality.

perspectiva [pexʃpe'tʃiva] *f* perspective.

perspicácia [pexʃpi'kasja] *f* shrewdness.

perspicaz [pexʃpi'kaʃ] *(pl -zes* [-ziʃ]*)* *adj* shrewd.

persuadir [pexswa'di(x)] *vt*: ~ **alguém de algo** to persuade sb of sthg; ~ **alguém a fazer algo** to persuade sb to do sthg.
❑ **persuadir-se** *vp* to convince o.s.

persuasão [pexswa'zãw] *f* persuasion.

persuasivo, -va [pexswa'zivu, -va] *adj* persuasive.

pertencente [pextẽ'sẽntʃi] *adj*: ~ **a** *(que pertence a)* belonging to; *(relativo a)* relating to.

pertencer [pextẽ'se(x)] *vi* to belong; ~ **a** to belong to; ~ **a alguém fazer algo** to be sb's responsibility to do sthg.

perto ['pextu] *adj* nearby ♦ *adv* near, close; ~ **de** *(relativo a tempo, quantidade)* around; *(relativo a espaço)* near; **ao ~ ou de ~** close up.

perturbar [pextux'ba(x)] *vt* to disturb.

peru [pe'ru] *m* turkey.

Peru [pe'ru] *m*: **o ~** Peru.

peruca [pe'ruka] *f* wig.

perverso, -sa [pex'vexsu, -sa] *adj (malvado)* wicked.

perverter [pexver'te(x)] *vt* to corrupt.

pervertido, -da [pexvex'tʃidu, -da] *adj* perverted.

pesadelo [peza'delu] *m* nightmare.

pesado, -da [pe'zadu, -da] *adj* heavy.

pêsames ['pezamiʃ] *mpl* condolences; **os meus ~** my condolences.

pesar [pe'za(x)] *vt* to weigh; *(fig: conseqüências)* to weigh (up) ◆ *vi (ser pesado)* to be heavy; *(influir)* to carry weight.

pesca ['peʃka] *f* fishing; **~ com linha** angling.

pescada [peʃ'kada] *f* hake.

pescadinha [peʃka'dʒiɲa] *f* whiting.

pescador, -ra [peʃka'do(x), -ra] *(mpl* **-res** [-riʃ], *fpl* **-s** [-ʃ]) *m, f* fisherman *(f* fisherwoman).

pescar [peʃ'ka(x)] *vt* to fish for ◆ *vi* to go fishing, to fish.

pescoço [peʃ'kosu] *m* neck.

peso ['pezu] *m* weight; **~ bruto/líquido** gross/net weight.

pesquisa [peʃ'kiza] *f* research.

pêssego ['pesegu] *m* peach.

pessegueiro [pese'gejru] *m* peach tree.

pessimista [pesi'miʃta] *mf* pessimist.

péssimo, -ma ['pesimu, -ma] *adj* horrendous, awful.

pessoa [pe'soa] *f* person; **quatro ~s** four people; **em ~** in person.

pessoal [pe'swaw] *(pl* **-ais** [-ajʃ]) *adj (individual)* personal; *(vida)* private ◆ *m* staff.

pestana [peʃ'tana] *f* eyelash; **queimar as ~s** *(fig: estudar muito)* to hit the books.

pestanejar [peʃtane'ʒa(x)] *vi* to blink.

peste ['peʃtʃi] *f* plague.

pesticida [peʃtʃi'sida] *m* pesticide.

pétala ['petala] *f* petal.

peteca [pe'teka] *f (Br: de badminton)* shuttlecock.

petição [petʃi'sãw] *(pl* **-ões** [-õjʃ]) *f* petition.

petinga [pe'tʃiŋga] *f* whitebait.

petiscar [petʃiʃ'ka(x)] *vt (provar)* to taste ◆ *vi (comer)* to nibble, to pick; **quem não arrisca não petisca** nothing ventured, nothing gained.

petisco [pe'tʃiʃku] *m (iguaria)* delicacy; *(tira-gosto)* snack.

petit-pois [petʃi'pwa] *mpl (Brit)* petit-pois.

petrificar [petrifi'ka(x)] *vt* to petrify.

petroleiro [petro'lejru] *m* oil tanker.

petróleo [pe'trɔlju] *m (rocha sedimentar)* petroleum; *(combustível)* oil.

petulância [petu'lãsja] *f (insolência)* impudence; *(vaidade)* arrogance.

petulante [petu'lãtʃi] *adj (insolente)* impudent; *(vaidoso)* arrogant.

pia ['pia] *f* sink; **~ batismal** font.

piada ['pjada] *f (anedota)* joke; *(dito espirituoso)* wisecrack.

pianista [pja'niʃta] *mf* pianist.

piano ['pjanu] *m* piano.

pião ['pjãw] *(pl* **-ões** [-õjʃ]) *m (brinquedo)* spinning top; *(com carro)* handbrake turn.

piar ['pja(x)] *vi* to chirp.

picada [pi'kada] *f (de ave)* peck; *(de inseto)* bite.

picadinho [pika'dʒiɲu] *m (Br)* minced meat stew.

picado, -da [pi'kadu, -da] *adj (carne)* minced *(Brit)*, ground *(Am)*; *(cebola, salsa)* chopped; *(furado)* pierced ◆ *m (ensopado)* minced meat stew.

picanha [pi'kaɲa] *f (Br)* tenderest part of rump steak, often served at the end of a "rodízio".

picante [pi'kãtʃi] *adj (apimentado)* spicy; *(fig: malicioso)* saucy.

pica-pau [,pika'paw] *(pl* **pica-paus** [,pika'pawʃ]) *m* woodpecker.

picar [pi'ka(x)] *vt (com alfinete, agulha)* to prick; *(carne)* to mince *(Brit)*, to grind *(Am)*; *(cebola, salsa)* to chop ◆ *vi (peixe)* to bite.

⌐ picar-se *vp (ferir-se)* to prick o.s.

picareta [pika'reta] *f* pick ◆ *mf (mau caráter)* crook.

picles ['pikleʃ] *mpl (Br)* pickles.

pico ['piku] *m (montanha)* peak; *(espinho)* thorn.

picolé [piko'le] *m (Br)* ice lolly *(Brit)*, Popsicle® *(Am)*.

picotado, -da [piko'tadu, -da] *adj* perforated ◆ *m* perforated edge.

piedade [pje'dadʒi] *f* pity; **ter ~ de alguém** to take pity on sb.

pifar [pi'fa(x)] *vi* to break; *(carro)* to break down; *(plano, projeto)* to fall through.

pigmento [pig'mẽtu] *m* pigment.

pijama [pi'ʒama] *m* pyjamas *(pl)*.

pikles ['pikleʃ] *mpl (Port)* = **picles**.

pilantra [pi'lãtra] *mf* crook.

pilar [pi'la(x)] *(pl* **-res** [-riʃ]) *m* pillar.

pilha ['piʎa] f battery; *(de papel, livros, etc)* pile; **uma ~ de nervos** a bundle of nerves; **~s** *(fam)* heaps of.

pilhar [pi'ʎa(x)] vt *(saquear)* to pillage; *(roubar)* to steal.

pilotar [pilo'ta(x)] vt to pilot.

piloto [pi'lotu] m *(de avião)* pilot; *(de automóvel)* driver.

pílula ['pilula] f pill; **tomar a ~** to be on the pill.

pimenta [pi'mẽnta] f pepper *(seasoning)*.

pimenta-do-reino [pi,mẽntadu-'xeinu] f (white) pepper.

pimentão [pimẽn'tãw] *(pl* -ões [-õjʃ]) m *(Br)* pepper *(vegetable)*.

pimentão-doce [pimẽntãw'dosi] m paprika.

pimento [pi'mẽntu] m *(Port)* = pimentão.

pin ['pin] m badge.

pinça ['pĩsa] f tweezers *(pl)*.

píncaro ['pĩkaru] m *(de montanha)* summit.

pincel [pĩ'sɛw] *(pl* -éis [-ɛiʃ]) m brush.

pinga ['pĩga] f *(gota)* drop; *(fam: aguardente)* booze.

pingar [pĩ'ga(x)] vi to drip.

pingente [pĩ'ʒẽntʃi] m *(de colar)* pendant; *(brinco)* pendant earring.

pingue-pongue [,pĩge'põngi] m Ping-pong®, table tennis.

pinguim [pĩŋ'gwĩ] *(pl* -ns [-ʃ]) m *(Port)* = pingüim.

pingüim [pĩŋ'gwĩ] *(pl* -ns [-ʃ]) m *(Br)* penguin.

pinhal [pi'ɲaw] *(pl* -ais [-ajʃ]) m pinewood.

pinhão [pi'ɲãw] *(pl* -ões [-õjʃ]) m pine kernel OU nut.

pinheiro [pi'ɲeiru] m pine tree.

pinho ['piɲu] m pine.

pinhões → pinhão.

pinta ['pĩta] f *(mancha)* spot; *(fam: aparência)* look; **ter ~ de** *(fam)* to look like.

pintado, -da [pĩ'tadu, -da] adj *(colorido)* coloured; **"~ de fresco"** "wet paint"; **"~ à mão"** "hand-painted".

pintar [pĩ'ta(x)] vt *(quadro, parede)* to paint; *(olhos)* to put make up on; *(cabelo)* to dye; *(desenho, boneco)* to colour in ◆ vi *(artista, pintor)* to paint; *(Br: fam: pessoa)* to turn up; *(Br: fam: problema)* to crop up; *(Br: fam: oportunidade)* to come up; **~ os lábios** to put lipstick on.

❑ **pintar-se** vp to wear make-up.

pintarroxo [pĩta'xoʃu] m linnet.

pintassilgo [pĩta'siwgu] m goldfinch.

pinto ['pĩtu] m *(pintainho)* chick.

pintor, -ra [pĩ'to(x), -ra] *(mpl* -es [-iʃ], *fpl* -s [-ʃ])* m, f painter.

pintura [pĩ'tura] f painting.

piões → pião.

piolho ['pjoʎu] m louse.

pionés [pjo'nɛʃ] *(pl* -eses [-ɛzeʃ]) m *(Port)* drawing pin *(Brit)*, thumbtack *(Am)*.

pior ['pjɔ(x)] *(pl* -res [-riʃ]) adj & adv worse ◆ m: **o/a ~** *(pessoa, coisa)* the worst one; **está cada vez ~** it's getting worse and worse; **ser do ~ que há** *(fam)* to be the pits.

piorar [pjo'ra(x)] vi to get worse ◆ vt *(situação)* to worsen.

piores → pior.

pipa ['pipa] f *(de vinho)* cask; *(Br: papagaio de papel)* kite.

pipoca [pi'pɔka] f popcorn.

pipoqueiro, -ra [pipo'keiru, -ra] m, f *(Br)* popcorn seller.

piquenique [pike'niki] m picnic.

pirâmide [pi'ramidʒi] f pyramid.

piranha [pi'raɲa] f piranha.

pirão [pi'rãw] m cassava-flour porridge, *eaten as a side dish.*

pirata [pi'rata] m pirate.

pires ['piriʃ] m inv saucer.

Pírex® ['pirɛks] m Pyrex®.

pirilampo [piri'lãmpu] m firefly.

Pirineus [piri'newʃ] mpl: **os ~** the Pyrenees.

piripiri [,piri'piri] m *(malagueta)* chilli (pepper); *(molho)* = Tabasco® sauce.

pirueta [pi'rweta] f pirouette.

pisar [pi'za(x)] vt *(com pé)* to step on; *(contundir)* to bruise.

pisca-pisca [,piʃka'piʃka] m indicator.

piscar [piʃ'ka(x)] vt *(olho)* to wink; *(olhos)* to blink ◆ vi *(luz)* to flicker.

piscina [piʃ'sina] f swimming pool; **~ ao ar livre** open-air swimming pool; **~ coberta** covered OU indoor swimming pool.

pisco ['piʃku] m robin.

piso ['pizu] m floor; **~ escorregadio/irregular** slippery/uneven surface.

pista ['piʃta] f *(indício)* clue; *(de corridas)* racetrack; *(de aviação)* runway; *(de* *dança)* dancefloor; *(de circo)* ring; ~ **de rodagem** *(Br)* carriageway.

pistácio [piʃˈtasju] *m* pistachio.

pistão [piʃˈtãw] *(pl* -ões [-õjʃ]) *m* piston.

pistola [piʃˈtɔla] *f* pistol.

pitada [piˈtada] *f* pinch.

pitanga [piˈtãŋga] *f variety of cherry.*

pitoresco, -ca [pitoˈreʃku, -ka] *adj* picturesque.

pivete [piˈvetʃi] *m (Br: criança aban-donada)* street child; *(Port: mau cheiro)* stink.

pizza [ˈpiza] *f* pizza.

pizzaria [pizaˈria] *f* pizzeria.

placa [ˈplaka] *f (de madeira, plástico)* sheet; *(de metal)* plate; *(de fogão)* hob; *(em porta)* plaque; *(em estrada)* sign; *(dentadura)* (set of) false teeth.

plágio [ˈplaʒju] *m* plagiarism.

planador [planaˈdo(x)] *(pl* -res [-riʃ]) *m* glider.

planalto [plaˈnawtu] *m* plateau.

planear [plaˈnjar] *vt (Port)* = **planejar**.

planejamento [planeʒaˈmẽtu] *m* planning; ~ **familiar** family planning.

planejar [planeˈʒa(x)] *vt (Br)* to plan; ~ **fazer algo** to plan to do sthg.

planeta [plaˈneta] *m* planet.

planetário [planeˈtarju] *m* planetarium.

planície [plaˈnisji] *f* plain.

plano, -na [ˈplanu, -na] *adj* flat ♦ *m* plan.

planta [ˈplãta] *f (vegetal)* plant; *(de pé)* sole; *(de cidade, casa)* plan.

plantão [plãˈtãw] *(pl* -ões [-õjʃ]) *m (turno)* shift; **estar de** ~ to be on duty.

plantar [plãˈta(x)] *vt* to plant.

plástica [ˈplaʃtʃika] *f* plastic surgery.

plasticina [plaʃtʃiˈsina] *f (Port)* = **plastilina**.

plástico [ˈplaʃtʃiku] *m* plastic.

plastilina [plaʃtʃiˈlina] *f (Br)* Plasticine®.

plataforma [plataˈfɔxma] *f* platform.

plátano [ˈplatanu] *m* plane (tree).

plateia [plaˈtaja] *f (Port)* = **platéia**.

platéia [plaˈteja] *f (Br) (local)* stalls *(pl)*; *(público)* audience.

platina [plaˈtʃina] *f* platinum.

platinados [platʃiˈnaduʃ] *mpl* points.

plausível [plawˈzivew] *(pl* -eis [-ejʃ]) *adj* plausible.

plebiscito [plebiʃˈsitu] *m (Br)* referendum.

plenamente [ˌplenaˈmẽtʃi] *adv* totally.

pleno, -na [ˈplenu, -na] *adj* total; ~ **de** full of; **em** ~ **dia** in broad daylight; **em** ~ **inverno** in the middle of winter.

plural [pluˈraw] *(pl* -ais [-ajʃ]) *m* plural.

plutónio [pluˈtɔnju] *m (Port)* = **plutônio**.

plutônio [pluˈtonju] *m (Br)* plutonium.

pneu [ˈpnew] *m* tyre; ~ **sobressalente** spare tyre.

pneumonia [pnewmoˈnia] *f* pneumonia.

pó [ˈpɔ] *m (poeira)* dust; *(substância pulverizada)* powder; ~ **de talco** talcum powder; **limpar o** ~ to do the dusting.

pobre [ˈpɔbri] *adj* poor ♦ *mf (pedinte)* beggar.

pobreza [poˈbreza] *f* poverty.

poça [ˈpɔsa] *f* pool.

poção [poˈsãw] *(pl* -ões [-õjʃ]) *f* potion.

pocilga [poˈsiwga] *f* pigsty.

poço [ˈposu] *m (de água, petróleo)* well; *(buraco)* pit.

poções → **poção**.

podar [poˈda(x)] *vt* to prune.

pode [ˈpɔdʒi] → **poder**.

pôde [ˈpodʒi] → **poder**.

pó-de-arroz [ˌpɔdʒjaˈxoʃ] *m* face powder.

poder [poˈde(x)] *(pl* -res [-riʃ]) *m* 1. *(político, influência)* power; **estar no** ~ to be in power; ~ **de compra** purchasing power; **não tenho** ~**es nenhuns** I'm powerless to help.
2. *(possessão)* possession; **estar em** ~ **de alguém** to be in sb's hands; **ter em seu** ~ **algo** to have sthg in one's possession.
♦ *v aux* 1. *(ser capaz de):* ~ **fazer algo** to be able to do sthg; **posso fazê-lo** I can do it; **posso ajudar?** can I help?; **você podia tê-lo feito antes** you could have done it beforehand; **não posso mais!** *(em relação a cansaço)* I've had enough!; *(em relação a comida)* I'm full up!
2. *(estar autorizado para):* ~ **fazer algo** to be allowed to do sthg; **posso fumar?** may I smoke?; **você não pode esta-**

cionar aqui you can't park here; **não pude sair ontem** I wasn't allowed (to go) out yesterday.
3. *(ser capaz moralmente)* can; **não podemos magoá-lo** we can't hurt him.
4. *(exprime possibilidade)*: **você podia ter vindo de ônibus** you could have come by bus; **cuidado que você pode se machucar!** be careful, you might hurt yourself!
5. *(exprime indignação, queixa)*: **não pode ser!** this is outrageous!; **você podia nos ter avisado!** you could have warned us!; **pudera!** no wonder!
◆ *v impess (ser possível)*: **pode não ser verdade** it might not be true; **pode acontecer a qualquer um** it could happen to anyone.
❑ **poder com** *v + prep (suportar)* to be able to stand; *(rival, adversário)* to be able to handle; *(peso)* to be able to carry; **você não pode com tanto peso** you can't carry all that; **não posso com ele** I can't stand him.

poderoso, -osa [pode'rozu, -ɔza] *adj* powerful.

podre [podri] *adj* rotten.

põe ['põi] → **pôr**.

poeira ['pwejra] *f* dust.

poema ['pwema] *m* poem.

poesia [pwi'zia] *f (gênero literário)* poetry; *(poema)* poem.

poeta ['pweta] *m* poet.

poetisa ['pwetʃiza] *f* (female) poet.

pois ['pojʃ] *conj (porque)* because; *(então)* then ◆ *interj* right!; ~ **sim!** certainly!, of course!; ~ **não? em que posso ajudá-lo?** can I help you?; ~ **bem** now then, right then.

polaco [pu'laku] *adj & m (Port)* Polish ◆ *m, f (Port)* Pole.

polegar [pole'ga(x)] (*pl* **-res** [-riʃ]) *m* thumb.

polémica [pu'lɛmika] *f (Port)* = **polêmica**.

polêmica [po'lemika] *f (Br)* controversy.

pólen ['pɔlen] *m* pollen.

polícia [po'lisja] *f* police ◆ *mf* policeman (*f* policewoman); ~ **militar** military police; ~ **rodoviária** traffic police.

policial [poli'sjaw] (*pl* **-ais** [-ajʃ]) *mf (Br)* policeman (*f* policewoman).

polido, -da [po'lidu, -da] *adj (lustroso)* polished; *(liso)* smooth.

polir [po'li(x)] *vt (dar lustre em)* to polish; *(alisar)* to smooth out; *(fig: educar)* to educate.

politécnica [pɔli'tɛknika] *adj f* → **escola**.

política [po'litʃika] *f (arte de governar)* politics *(sg)*; *(de governo, partido)* policy; ~ **externa** foreign policy; ~ **exterior** foreign policy.

político, -ca [po'litʃiku, -ka] *m, f* politician ◆ *adj* political.

pólo ['pɔlu] *m* pole; *(esporte)* polo; ~ **aquático** water polo.

polonês, -esa [polo'neʃ, -eza] (*mpl* **-eses** [-eziʃ], *fpl* **-s** [-ʃ]) *adj & m (Br)* Polish ◆ *m, f (Br)* Pole.

Polónia [pu'lɔnja] *f (Port)* = **Polônia**.

Polônia [po'lonja] *f (Br)* Poland.

polpa ['powpa] *f* pulp.

poltrona [pow'trona] *f* armchair.

poluição [polwi'sãw] *f* pollution.

poluído, -da [po'lwidu, -da] *adj* polluted.

poluir [po'lwi(x)] *vt* to pollute.

polvo ['powvu] *m* octopus.

pólvora ['pɔwvora] *f* gunpowder.

pomada [po'mada] *f* ointment; ~ **anti-séptica** antiseptic ointment.

pomar [po'ma(x)] (*pl* **-res** [-riʃ]) *m* orchard.

pombo, -ba ['põmbu, -ba] *m, f* pigeon; **pomba da paz** white dove.

pomo-de-adão [,pomodʒia'dãw] (*pl* **pomos-de-adão** [,pɔmoʒdʒia'dãw]) *m* Adam's apple.

pomposo, -osa [põm'pozu, -ɔza] *adj* pompous.

ponderação [põndera'sãw] *f* thought, consideration.

ponderado, -da [põnde'radu, -da] *adj* prudent.

ponderar [põnde'ra(x)] *vt* to consider.

pónei ['pɔnej] *m (Port)* = **pônei**.

pônei ['ponei] *m (Br)* pony.

ponho ['poɲu] → **pôr**.

ponta ['põnta] *f (de lápis)* point; *(de vara, linha, cigarro)* end; *(de superfície)* edge; *(de dedo, língua, nariz)* tip; **tenho a palavra na ~ da língua** I've got it on the tip of my tongue; **de ~ a ~** from one end to the other.

pontada [põn'tada] *f* stitch.

pontapé [põnta'pɛ] *m* kick; ~ **livre** free kick; ~ **de saída** kickoff.

pontaria [põnta'ria] *f*: **fazer ~** to take aim; **ter ~** to be a good shot.

ponte ['põntʃi] *f* bridge.

ponteiro [põn'tejru] *m (de relógio)* hand.

pontiagudo, -da [põntʃja'gudu, -da] *adj* pointed.

ponto ['põntu] *m* point; *(de costura, ferimento, tricot)* stitch; *(marca)* dot; *(sinal ortográfico)* full stop *(Brit)*, period *(Am)*; *(Br: parada)* stop *(lugar)* place; *(Port: teste, exame)* test; **às 9 em ~** at 9 on the dot; **estar a ~ de fazer algo** to be on the point of doing sthg; **até certo ~** up to a point; **dois ~s** colon; **~ cardeal** compass point; **~ de encontro** meeting point; **~ de exclamação** exclamation mark; **~ final** full stop *(Brit)*, period *(Am)*; **~ de interrogação** question mark; **~ morto** *(em veículo)* neutral; **~ de ônibus** bus stop; **~ de partida** starting point; **~ de táxi** taxi rank; **~ e vírgula** semicolon; **~ de vista** point of view.

pontuação [põntwa'sãw] *(pl* -ões [-õjʃ]) *f (em gramática)* punctuation; *(em competição)* score.

pontual [põn'twaw] *(pl* -ais [-ajʃ]) *adj* punctual.

pontuar [põn'twa(x)] *vt (texto)* to punctuate.

popa ['popa] *f* stern.

popelina [pope'lina] *f* poplin.

população [popula'sãw] *f* population.

popular [popu'la(x)] *(pl* -res [-riʃ]) *adj* popular; *(música, arte)* folk.

póquer ['pɔkɛr] *m (Port)* = **pôquer**.

pôquer ['pɔke(x)] *m (Br)* poker.

por [po(x)] *prep* **1.** *(indica causa)* because of, due to; **foi ~ sua causa** it was your fault; **~ falta de fundos** due to lack of funds; **~ hábito** through force of habit.

2. *(indica objetivo)* for; **lutar ~ algo** to fight for sthg.

3. *(indica meio, modo, agente)* by; **foi escrito pela Cristina** it was written by Cristina; **~ correio/fax** post/fax; **~ escrito** in writing; **~ avião** air mail.

4. *(relativo a tempo)* for; **partiu ~ duas semanas** he went away for two weeks.

5. *(relativo a lugar)* through; **entramos no Brasil ~ Paraguay** we crossed into Brazil via Paraguay; **está ~ aí** it's round there somewhere; **~ onde você vai?** which way are you going?; **vamos ~ aqui** we're going this way.

6. *(relativo a troca, preço)* for; **paguei apenas 20 reais ~ este casaco** I only paid 20 reals for this jacket; **troquei o carro velho ~ um novo** I exchanged my old car for a new one.

7. *(indica distribuição)* per; **25 ~ cento** 25 per cent; **são 100 reais ~ dia/mês** it's 100 reals per day/month.

8. *(em locuções)*: **~ que** why; **~ que (é que) ...?** why ...?; **~ mim tudo bem!** that's fine by me!

pôr ['po(x)] *vt* to put; *(vestir, calçar)* to put on; *(problema, dúvida, questão)* to raise; *(defeitos)* to find; *(suj: ave)* to lay; *(depositar dinheiro)* to pay in **~** *(galinhas)* to lay (eggs) ◆ *m*: **o ~ do sol** sunset; **~ algo em algo** to put sthg in/on sthg; **~ algo em funcionamento** to start sthg up; **~ algo mais baixo/alto** *(música, som)* to turn sthg down/up; **~ a mesa** OU lay the table.

⊔ **pôr-se** *vp (nervoso, contente)* to become; *(sol)* to set; **~-se a fazer algo** to begin to do sthg; **~-se de pé** to stand up.

porca ['pɔxka] *f (peça)* nut; *(animal)* sow.

porção [pox'sãw] *(pl* -ões [-õjʃ]) *f* portion, helping.

porcaria [poxka'ria] *f* rubbish; *(sujeira)* mess; *(pus)* pus; **isto é uma ~** this is rubbish; **(que) ~!** damn!

porcelana [poxse'lana] *f* porcelain.

porco ['pɔxku] *m (animal)* pig; *(carne)* pork.

porções → porção.

porco-espinho [‚pɔxkuiʃ'piɲu] *(pl* **porcos-espinhos** [‚pɔrkuziʃ'piɲuʃ]) *m* porcupine.

porém [po'rẽj] *conj* however.

pormenor [poxme'nɔ(x)] *(pl* -es [-iʃ]) *m* detail; **em ~** in detail.

pornografia [poxnogra'fia] *f* pornography.

poro ['pɔru] *m* pore.

porque ['pɔxki] *conj* because ◆ *adv (Port)* why.

porquê [pox'ke] *adv (Port)* why ◆ *m*: **o ~ de** the reason for.

porquinho-da-índia [pox‚kiɲuda'ĩndʒja] *(pl* **porquinhos-da-índia** [pox‚kiɲuʒda'ĩndʒja]) *m* guinea pig.

porra ['pɔxa] *interj (vulg)* bloody hell!

porta ['pɔxta] *f* door; **~ automática** automatic door; **~ corrediça** sliding door; **~ giratória** revolving door.

porta-aviões [ˌpɔxta'vjõiʃ] *m inv* aircraft carrier.

porta-bagagem [ˌpɔɔxtaba'gaʒẽ] (*pl* **porta-bagagens** [ˌpɔɔtaba'gaʒẽʃ]) *m* (*em carro*) boot (*Brit*), trunk (*Am*); (*em ônibus*) luggage hold; (*em trem*) luggage rack.

porta-bandeira [ˌpɔxtabãn'dejra] (*pl* **porta-bandeiras** [ˌpɔxtabãn'dejraʃ]) *mf* standard-bearer.

porta-chaves [ˌpɔxta'ʃaviʃ] *m inv* (*Port*) key ring.

portador, -ra [pɔxta'do(x), -ra] (*mpl* **-res** [-riʃ], *fpl* **-s** [-ʃ]) *'m*, *f* (*de doença, vírus*) (FIN) bearer; **ao ~** (*cheque, ação, obrigação*) to the bearer.

portagem [pur'taʒẽj] (*pl* **-ns** [-ʃ]) *f* (*Port*) toll.

porta-jóias [ˌpɔxta'ʒɔjaʃ] *m inv* jewellery box.

porta-lápis [ˌpɔxta'lapiʃ] *m inv* pencil case.

porta-luvas [ˌpɔxta'luvaʃ] *m inv* glove compartment.

porta-moedas [ˌpɔxta'mwɛdaʃ] *m inv* purse.

portanto [pɔx'tãntu] *conj* so, therefore.

portão [pɔx'tãw] (*pl* **-ões** [-õjʃ]) *m* gate.

portaria [pɔxta'ria] *f* (*de edifício*) main entrance; (*documento*) decree.

portátil [pɔx'tatʃiw] (*pl* **-eis** [-ejʃ]) *adj* (*telefone*) portable; (*computador*) laptop.

porta-voz [ˌpɔxta'vɔjʃ] (*pl* **porta-vozes** [ˌpɔxta'vɔziʃ]) *mf* spokesman (*f* spokeswoman).

porte ['pɔrtʃi] *m* (*postura*) posture; (*em caminhão*) haulage; (*em avião, navio, trem*) freight; **"~ pago"** "postage paid".

porteiro, -ra [pɔx'tejru, -ra] *m*, *f* porter.

pórtico ['pɔxtʃiku] *m* portico.

porto ['pɔxtu] *m* port.

portões → portão.

Portugal [pɔxtu'gal] *s* Portugal.

português, -esa [pɔxtu'geʃ, -eza] (*mpl* **-eses** [-eziʃ], *fpl* **-s** [-ʃ]) *adj* & *m*, *f* Portuguese ♦ *m* (*língua*) Portuguese; **à portuguesa** in the Portuguese way.

porventura [pɔxvẽn'tura] *adv* by any chance.

pôs ['pojʃ] → **pôr**.

posar [pɔ'za(x)] *vi* to pose.

posição [pɔzi'sãw] (*pl* **-ões** [-õjʃ]) *f* position; (*moral, política*) stance.

positivo, -va [pozi'tʃivu, -va] *adj* positive; (*valor, saldo*) in the black, in credit ♦ *m* (*de fotografia*) print.

posologia [pozolo'ʒia] *f* dosage.

posse ['pɔsi] *f* possession; **estar em ~ de** to be in possession of.

❏ **posses** *fpl*: **ter ~s** to be wealthy.

possessão [pose'sãw] (*pl* **-ões** [-õjʃ]) *f* (*posse*) possession, ownership; (*domínio*) control.

possessivo, -va [pose'sivu, -va] *adj* possessive.

possessões → possessão.

possibilidade [posibili'dadʒi] *f* possibility.

possibilitar [posibili'ta(x)] *vt* to make possible.

possível [po'sivew] (*pl* **-eis** [-ejʃ]) *adj* possible ♦ *m*: **fazer o ~ (para fazer algo)** to do one's best (to do sthg); **não é ~!** (*exprime incredulidade*) it's incredible!; **logo que ~** as soon as possible; **o mais cedo ~** as soon as possible; **o máximo ~** as much as possible; **se ~** if possible.

posso ['pɔsu] → **poder**.

possuir [po'swi(x)] *vt* (*carro, casa*) to own; (*desfrutar de*) to have.

postal [poʃ'taw] (*pl* **-ais** [-ajʃ]) *m* postcard; **~ ilustrado** picture postcard.

posta-restante [ˌpɔʃtaxeʃ'tãntʃi] (*pl* **postas-restantes** [ˌpɔʃtaʒxeʃ'tãntiʃ]) *f* poste restante.

poste ['pɔʃtʃi] *m* pole; **~ (de alta tensão)** pylon; **~ (de iluminação)** lamppost.

poster ['pɔʃtɛr] (*pl* **-res** [-reʃ]) *m* (*Port*) = **pôster**.

pôster ['pɔʃte(x)] (*pl* **-res** [-riʃ]) *m* (*Br*) poster.

posteridade [poʃteri'dadʒi] *f* posterity.

posterior [poʃte'rjo(x)] (*pl* **-res** [-riʃ]) *adj* (*em tempo, ordem*) subsequent; (*em espaço*) back, rear.

posteriormente [puʃterjor'mẽntʃi] *adv* subsequently.

postiço, -ça [poʃ'tʃisu, -sa] *adj* false.

postigo [poʃ'tʃigu] *m* hatch.

posto ['poʃtu] *m* (*em emprego*) position; (*de polícia, bombeiros*) station; **~ de gasolina** petrol station (*Brit*), filling station (*Am*); **~ médico** (*Port: em escola*) first-aid room; **~ de saúde** clinic; **"~ de venda autorizado"** *sign indicating* *that bus tickets can be bought.*

póstumo, -ma ['poʃtumu, -ma] *adj* posthumous.

postura [poʃ'tura] *f* posture.

potável [po'tavɛw] *adj* → **água**.

pote ['pɔtʃi] *m* jar.

potência [pu'tẽsja] *f* power.

potencial [potẽ'sjaw] (*pl* **-ais** [-ajʃ]) *adj* & *m* potential.

potente [po'tẽntʃi] *adj* powerful.

potro ['potru] *m* colt.

pouco, -ca ['poku, -ka] *adj* & *pron* (*no singular*) little, not much; (*no plural*) few, not many ◆ *adv* (*relativo a tempo*) not long; (*relativo a quantidade*) not much; (*com adjetivo*) not very ◆ *m*: **um ~ a** little, a bit; **ele come ~** he doesn't eat much; **ele é ~ inteligente/amável** he isn't very bright/friendly; **falta ~ para chegarmos lá** it won't be long before we get there; **falta ~ para o verão** it's almost summer(time); **um ~ de** a bit of; **um ~ mais de** a bit more; **custar ~** (*ser barato*) to be cheap; **ficar a ~s passos de** to be near; **daí a ~** shortly afterwards; **daqui a ~** in a little while; **há ~** a short while ago; **~ a ~** little by little; **por ~** nearly; **fazer ~ de** to make fun of.

poupa ['popa] *f* quiff.

poupança [po'pãsa] *f* saving.
❑ **poupanças** *fpl* savings.

poupar [po'pa(x)] *vt* to save ◆ *vi* to save up.

pouquinho [po'kiɲu] *m*: **só um ~** just a little; **um ~ de** a little.

pousada [po'zada] *f* building of artistic or historic interest which has been converted into a luxury hotel; **~ da juventude** (*Port*) youth hostel.

pousar [po'za(x)] *vt* to put down ◆ *vi* (*ave*) to perch; (*avião*) to land.

povo ['povu] *m* people (*pl*).

povoação [povwa'sãw] (*pl* **-ões** [-õjʃ]) *f* village.

povoar [po'vwa(x)] *vt* to populate.

p.p. (*abrev de páginas*) pp.

PR *abrev* = **Presidente da República**, → **presidente**.

praça ['prasa] *f* (*largo*) square; (*mercado*) market(place); **~ de táxis** (*Port*) taxi rank; **~ de touros** bullring.

prado ['pradu] *m* meadow.

praga ['praga] *f* plague; (*palavrão, maldição*) curse.

pragmático, -ca [prag'matʃiku, -ka]

adj pragmatic.

praia ['praja] *f* beach; **~ para nudistas** nudist beach.

prancha ['prãʃa] *f* board; **~ de saltos** diving board; **~ de surf** surfboard.

pranto ['prãntu] *m* wailing.

prata ['prata] *f* silver; **(feito) de ~** (made of) silver.

prateado, -da [pra'tʃjadu, -da] *adj* silver(y).

prateleira [prate'lejra] *f* shelf.

prática ['pratʃika] *f* (*experiência*) experience; (*de esporte*) playing; **na ~** in practice; **pôr algo em ~** to put sthg into practice; **ter ~** to have experience.

praticante [pratʃi'kãntʃi] *adj* practising ◆ *mf*: **~ de esporte** sportsman (*f* sportswoman).

praticar [pratʃi'ka(x)] *vt* to practise; (*esporte*) to play.

praticável [pratʃi'kavɛw] (*pl* **-eis** [-ejʃ]) *adj* (*ação*) feasible; (*estrada*) passable.

prático, -ca ['pratʃiku, -ka] *adj* practical.

prato ['pratu] *m* (*louça*) plate; (*refeição*) dish; **~ fundo** soup bowl; **~ da casa** speciality of the house; **~ do dia** dish of the day; **~ raso** dinner plate; **~ de sopa** (*utensílio*) soup plate; (*comida*) bowl of soup; **pôr tudo em ~s limpos** (*fam*) to make a clean breast of it.
❑ **pratos** *mpl* (MÚS) cymbals.

praxe ['praʃi] *f* (*costume*) custom; **ser de ~** to be the norm.

prazer [pra'ze(x)] (*pl* **-res** [-riʃ]) *m* pleasure; **muito ~!** pleased to meet you!; **~ em conhecê-lo!** pleased to meet you!; **o ~ é (todo) meu!** the pleasure is all mine!; **ela faz tudo a seu bel ~** she does as she pleases; **com ~** with pleasure; **por ~** for pleasure.

prazo ['prazu] *m* period; **~ de validade** expiry date; **a curto/longo/médio ~** in the short/long/medium term.

pré-aviso [prɛa'vizu] (*pl* **pré-avisos** [prɛa'vizuʃ]) *m* advance warning, prior notice.

precário, -ria [pre'karju, -rja] *adj* precarious.

precaução [prekaw'sãw] (*pl* **-ões** [-õjʃ]) *f* precaution; **por ~** as a precaution.

precaver-se [preka'vexsi] *vp* to take

precautions; ~ **contra** to take precautions against.

precavido, -da [prɛka'vidu, -da] *adj* prudent; **vim** ~ I've come prepared.

prece ['prɛsi] *f* prayer.

precedência [prese'dẽsja] *f* precedence; **ter** ~ **sobre** to take precedence over.

preceder [prese'de(x)] *vt* to precede.

precioso, -osa [pre'sjozu, -ɔza] *adj* precious.

precipício [presi'pisju] *m* precipice.

precipitação [presipita'sãw] (*pl* **-ões** [-õjʃ]) *f (pressa)* haste; *(chuva)* rainfall.

precipitar-se [presepi'taxsi] *vp (pessoa)* to act rashly; *(acontecimentos)* to gain momentum.

precisamente [pre,siza'mẽntʃi] *adv* precisely.

precisão [presi'zãw] *f* accuracy; **com** ~ accurately.

precisar [presi'za(x)] *vt (especificar)* to specify.

❑ **precisar de** *v* + *prep* to need; ~ **de fazer algo** to need to do sthg.

preciso, -sa [pre'sizu, -za] *adj* accurate, precise; **é** ~ **ter calma** keep calm; **é** ~ **passaporte** you need your passport.

preço ['presu] *m* price; ~ **de ocasião** special offer; ~ **reduzido** reduced price; ~ **de liquidação** sale price.

precoce [pre'kɔsi] *adj (criança)* precocious; *(decisão)* hasty.

preconcebido, -da [prɛkõse'bidu, -da] *adj* preconceived.

preconceito [prɛkõ'sejtu] *m* prejudice.

precursor, -ra [prekux'so(x), -ra] (*mpl* **-res** [-riʃ], *fpl* **-s** [-ʃ]) *m, f* forerunner.

predador, -ra [preda'do(x), -ra] (*mpl* **-es** [-iʃ], *fpl* **-s** [-ʃ]) *adj* predatory.

predecessor, -ra [predese'so(x), -ra] (*mpl* **-res** [-riʃ], *fpl* **-s** [-ʃ]) *m, f* predecessor.

predileção [predʒile'sãw] (*pl* **-ões** [-õjʃ]) *f (Br)* preference; **ter** ~ **por** to prefer.

predilecção [predile'sãw] (*pl* **-ões** [-õjʃ]) *f (Port)* = **predileção**.

predileções → **predileção**.

predilecto, -ta [predi'lɛtu, -ta] *adj (Port)* = **predileto**.

predileto, -ta [predʒi'lɛtu, -ta] *adj (Br)* favourite.

prédio ['prɛdʒju] *m* building; ~ **de apartamentos** block of flats *(Brit)*, apartment building *(Am)*.

predominante [predumi'nãntʃi] *adj* predominant.

predominar [predomi'na(x)] *vi* to predominate.

preencher [priẽ'ʃe(x)] *vt* to fill in.

pré-fabricado, -da [prɛfabri'kadu, -da] *adj* prefabricated.

prefácio [pre'fasju] *m* preface.

prefeito, -ta [pre'fejtu, -ta] *m, f (Br)* mayor.

prefeitura [prefej'tura] *f (Br)* town hall *(Brit)*, city hall *(Am)*.

preferência [prefe'rẽsja] *f* preference; **dar** ~ **a** to give preference to; **ter** ~ **por** to prefer, to have a preference for; **de** ~ preferably.

preferido, -da [prefe'ridu, -da] *adj* favourite.

preferir [prefe'ri(x)] *vt* to prefer; ~ **fazer algo** to prefer doing sthg; **eu preferia que viajássemos de dia** I would prefer to travel by day.

prefixo [pre'fiksu] *m* prefix.

prega ['prega] *f* pleat.

pregar¹ [pre'ga(x)] *vt (prego)* to hammer in; *(botões)* to sew on.

pregar² [pre'ga(x)] *vt (sermão)* to preach.

prego ['pregu] *m* nail; *(Br: fam: casa de penhor)* pawn shop.

preguiça [pre'gisa] *f* laziness.

pré-histórico, -ca [prɛiʃ'tɔriku, -ka] *adj* prehistoric.

prejudicar [preʒudʒi'ka(x)] *vt (pessoa)* to harm; *(carreira, relação, saúde)* to damage.

prejudicial [preʒudʒi'sjaw] (*pl* **-ais** [-ajʃ]) *adj:* ~ **para** damaging to.

prejuízo [pre'ʒwizu] *m (dano)* damage; *(em negócio)* loss; **em** ~ **de** to the detriment of; **sem** ~ **de** without detriment to.

prematuro, -ra [prema'turu, -ra] *adj* premature.

premiado, -da [pre'mjadu, -da] *adj* prizewinning.

premiar [pre'mja(x)] *vt* to award a prize to; *(recompensar)* to reward.

prémio ['prɛmju] *m (Port)* = **prêmio**.

prêmio ['premju] *m (Br) (em concurso, competição)* prize; *(recompensa)* reward; *(em seguros)* premium; **grande** ~ *(em Fórmula 1)* grand prix.

premonição [premoni'sãw] (*pl* **-ões** [-õjʃ]) *f* premonition.

pré-natal [ˌprɛna'taw] *adj* (*pl* **-ais**) (*roupa, vestuário*) maternity *(antes de s)*.

prenda ['prẽda] *f* present, gift.

prendado, -da [prẽ'dadu. -da] *adj* gifted.

prender [prẽ'de(x)] *vt* to tie up; *(pessoa)* to arrest.

❑ **prender-se** *vp* to get stuck.

prenome [pre'nome] *m* first name, Christian name.

prenunciar [prenũ'sja(x)] *vt* (*predizer*) to foretell.

preocupação [preokupa'sãw] (*pl* **-ões** [-õjʃ]) *f* worry.

preocupado, -da [prioku'padu. -da] *adj* worried.

preocupar [preoku'pa(x)] *vt* to worry.

❑ **preocupar-se** *vp* to worry; **~-se com** to worry about.

pré-pagamento [ˌprɛpaga'mẽtu] *m* prepayment.

preparação [prepara'sãw] (*pl* **-ões** [-õjʃ]) *f* preparation.

preparado, -da [prepa'radu. -da] *adj* ready ◆ *m* preparation.

preparar [prepa'ra(x)] *vt* to prepare.

❑ **preparar-se** *vp* to get ready; **~-se para algo** to get ready for sthg.

preposição [prepozi'sãw] (*pl* **-ões** [-õjʃ]) *f* preposition.

prepotente [prepo'tẽtʃi] *adj* domineering.

presença [pre'zẽsa] *f* presence; **na ~ de** in the presence of; **~ de espírito** presence of mind.

presenciar [prezẽ'sja(x)] *vt* to witness.

presente [pre'zẽtʃi] *adj & m* present; **o ~ (do indicativo)** the present tense.

preservação [prezexva'sãw] (*pl* **-ões** [-õjʃ]) *f* (*de costumes, língua*) preservation; *(de natureza)* conservation.

preservar [prezex'va(x)] *vt* to preserve.

preservativo [prezexva'tʃivu] *m* condom.

presidência [prezi'dẽsja] *f* presidency.

presidente [prezi'dẽtʃi] *mf* (*de país, organização*) president; *(de empresa, associação*) chairman *(f* chairwoman) *(Brit)*, president *(Am)*; **Presidente da Câmara** *(Port)* mayor; **Presidente da República** President of the Republic.

presidir [prezi'dʒi(x)] *vi*: **~ a algo** to chair sthg.

presilha [pre'ziʎa] *f* (belt) loop.

preso, -sa ['prezu. -za] *pp* → **prender** ◆ *adj* tied up; *(capturado*) imprisoned; *(que não se move)* stuck ◆ *m, f* (*prisioneiro*) prisoner.

pressa ['prɛsa] *f* hurry; **estar com ou ter ~** to be in a hurry ou rush; **estar sem ~** not to be in a hurry ou rush; **às ~s** quickly, hurriedly.

presságio [pre'saʒju] *m* premonition.

pressão [pre'sãw] (*pl* **-ões** [-õjʃ]) *f* pressure; **~ (arterial) alta/baixa** *(Br: MED*) high/low blood pressure; **~ atmosférica** atmospheric pressure; **~ dos pneus** tyre pressure; **estar sob ~** *(pessoa)* to be under pressure.

pressentimento [presẽtʃi'mẽtu] *m* feeling.

pressentir [presẽ'tʃi(x)] *vt*: **~ que** to have a feeling (that).

pressionar [presjo'na(x)] *vt* (*botão*) to press; *(pessoa)* to pressurize.

pressões → **pressão**.

pressupor [presu'po(x)] *vt* to presuppose.

prestação [preʃta'sãw] (*pl* **-ões** [-õjʃ]) *f* (*de serviço*) provision; *(de pagamento*) instalment; **pagar a prestações** to pay in instalments.

prestar [preʃ'ta(x)] *vt* (*ajuda*) to give; *(serviço)* to provide; *(contas)* to render; *(atenção)* to pay ◆ *vi* (*ser útil*) to be useful; **isso presta para alguma coisa?** is that any good?; **não ~** to be no good; **não ~ para nada** to be totally useless; **~ um serviço a alguém** to do sthg for sb.

❑ **prestar-se** *vp* + *prep* (*ser adequado para*) to be suitable for; *(estar disposto a)* to leave o.s. open to.

prestativo, -va [preʃta'tʃivu. -va] *adj* helpful.

prestes ['prɛʃtʃiʃ] *adj inv*: **estar ~ a fazer algo** to be just about to do sthg.

prestidigitador, -ra [preʃtʃidʒiʒita-'do(x). -ra] (*mpl* **-res** [-riʃ], *fpl* **-s** [-ʃ]) *m, f* conjurer.

prestígio [preʃ'tʃiʒju] *m* prestige.

presumir [prezu'mi(x)] *vt* to presume.

presunçoso, -osa [prezũ'sozu. -ɔza] *adj* (*pessoa*) conceited; *(discurso, artigo*) pretentious.

presunto [pre'zũtu] *m* ham.

prêt-a-porter [prɛtapɔxˈtɛ] *m inv* *(Br)* ready-to-wear clothes *(pl)*.

pretender [pretẽnˈde(x)] *vt (querer)* to want; *(afirmar)* to claim; ~ **fazer algo** to intend to do sthg.

pretensão [pretẽˈsãw] *(pl* -ões [-õjʃ]) *f (desejo)* wish, aspiration.

❑ **pretensões** *fpl (vaidade)* pretentiousness *(sg)*; **ter pretensões** to be pretentious.

pretérito [preˈteritu] *m (GRAM)* preterite, past tense; ~ **perfeito (simples)** simple past (tense); ~ **imperfeito (simples)** imperfect (tense).

pretexto [preˈtejʃtu] *m* excuse; **sob ~ algum** under no circumstances; **a ou sob o ~ de** on ou under the pretext of.

preto, -ta [ˈpretu, -ta] *adj & m, f* black; **pôr o ~ no branco** to set the record straight.

prevalecer [prevaleˈse(x)] *vi* to prevail.

prevenção [prevẽˈsãw] *(pl* -ões [-õjʃ]) *f (de doença, acidente)* prevention; *(aviso)* warning; **estar de ~** to be on guard; ~ **rodoviária** road safety and accident prevention; **por ~** as a precaution.

prevenido, -da [preveˈnidu, -da] *adj* cautious; **estar ~** to be prepared.

prevenir [preveˈni(x)] *vt (avisar)* to warn; *(evitar)* to prevent; ~ **alguém de algo** to warn sb of sthg.

preventivo, -va [prevẽˈtʃivu, -va] *adj* preventive.

prever [preˈve(x)] *vt* to foresee; *(tempo)* to forecast.

previamente [ˌprevjaˈmẽntʃi] *adv* beforehand.

prévio, -via [ˈprɛvju, -vja] *adj* prior.

previsão [previˈzãw] *(pl* -ões [-õjʃ]) *f* forecast; ~ **do tempo** weather forecast.

previsível [previˈzivew] *(pl* -eis [-ejʃ]) *adj* foreseeable.

previsões → **previsão**.

previsto, -ta [preˈviʃtu, -ta] *adj* expected; **como ~** as expected.

prezado, -da [preˈzadu, -da] *adj (querido)* dear; **Prezado ... *(fml:* em carta)** Dear ....

primária [priˈmarja] *f (EDUC)* primary school.

primário, -ria [priˈmarju, -rja] *adj (básico)* basic; *(EDUC)* primary.

primavera [primaˈvera] *f (estação)* spring; *(flor)* primrose.

primeira [priˈmejra] *f (em veículo)* first (gear), → **primeiro**.

primeiro, -ra [priˈmejru, -ra] *adj, adv & num* first ◆ *m, f*: **o ~/a primeira da turma** top of the class; **à primeira vista** at first sight; **de primeira** first-class; **em ~ lugar** firstly, first; **primeira classe** *(EDUC)* primary one *(Brit)*, first grade *(Am)*; **~s socorros** *(MED)* first aid *(sg)*; ~ **de tudo** *(antes de mais)* first of all, → **sexto**.

primeiro-ministro, primeira-ministra [priˌmejrumiˈniʃtru, priˌmejramiˈniʃtra] *(mpl* **primeiros-ministros** [priˌmejruʒmiˈniʃtruʃ], *fpl* **primeiras-ministras** [priˌmejraʒmiˈniʃtraʃ]) *m, f* prime minister.

primitivo, -va [primiˈtʃivu, -va] *adj* primitive.

primo, -ma [ˈprimu, -ma] *m, f* cousin.

primogénito, -ta [primoˈʒɛnitu, -ta] *m, f (Port)* = **primogênito**.

primogênito, -ta [primoˈʒenitu, -ta] *m, f (Br)* firstborn.

princesa [priˈseza] *f* princess.

principal [prĩsiˈpaw] *(pl* -ais [-ajʃ]) *adj* main.

principalmente [prĩsipawˈmẽntʃi] *adv* mainly, especially.

príncipe [ˈprĩsipi] *m* prince.

principiante [prĩseˈpjãntʃi] *mf* beginner.

principiar [prĩsiˈpja(x)] *vt & vi* to start, to begin.

princípio [prĩˈsipju] *m* beginning; *(moral)* principle; **partir do ~ que ...** to work on the basis that ...; **a ~** to start with; **desde o ~** from the beginning; **em ~** in principle; **por ~** on principle.

prioridade [prioriˈdadʒi] *f* priority; ~ **de passagem** *(AUT)* right of way.

prisão [priˈzãw] *(pl* -ões [-õjʃ]) *f (ato)* imprisonment; *(local)* prison; ~ **de ventre** constipation.

privação [privaˈsãw] *(pl* -ões [-õjʃ]) *f* loss.

❑ **privações** *fpl* misery *(sg)*, hardship *(sg)*.

privacidade [privasiˈdadʒi] *f* privacy.

privações → **privação**.

privada [priˈvada] *f (Br)* toilet.

privado, -da [priˈvadu, -da] *adj* private.

privar [priˈva(x)] *vt*: ~ **alguém de algo** to deprive sb of sthg.

❏ **privar-se de** *vp* + *prep* to go without.

privativo, -va [priva't∫ivu, -va] *adj* private.

privilegiado, -da [privili'ʒjadu, -da] *adj (pessoa)* privileged; *(local)* exceptional.

privilegiar [privili'ʒja(x)] *vt* to favour.

privilégio [privi'lɛʒju] *m* privilege.

proa ['proa] *f* prow.

probabilidade [probabili'dadʒi] *f* probability.

problema [pro'blema] *m* problem; **ter ~s com** to have problems with.

procedente [prose'dẽnt∫i] *adj*: **~ de** *(ônibus, trem, avião)* from.

proceder [prose'de(x)] *vi (agir)* to proceed, to act; **~ com** to proceed with.

processador [prosesa'do(x)] *(pl -es* [-i∫]) *m*: **~ de texto** word processor.

processamento [prosesa'mẽntu] *m* processing.

processar [prose'sa(x)] *vt (JUR: pessoa, empresa)* to prosecute; *(JUR: por danos pessoais, materiais)* to sue; *(INFORM: dados, texto)* to process.

processo [pro'sɛsu] *m (sistema)* process; *(JUR)* (law)suit.

procissão [prosi'sãw] *(pl -ões* [-õj∫]) *f* procession.

proclamar [prokla'ma(x)] *vt* to proclaim.

procura [pro'kura] *f (busca)* search; *(COM)* demand; **andar à ~ de** to be looking for.

procurador, -ra [prokura'do(x), -ra] *(mpl -res* [-ri∫], *fpl -s* [-∫]) *m, f* proxy; **~ da República** = Public Prosecutor.

procurar [proku'ra(x)] *vt* to look for; **~ fazer algo** to try to do sthg.

prodígio [pro'dʒiʒju] *m* prodigy.

produção [prudu'sãw] *(pl -ões* [-õj∫]) *f* production.

produtividade [produt∫ivi'dadʒi] *f* productivity.

produtivo, -va [produ't∫ivu, -va] *adj (que produz)* productive; *(lucrativo)* profitable.

produto [pro'dutu] *m* product; **~ alimentar** foodstuff; **~ de limpeza** cleaning product; **~ natural** natural product.

produtor, -ra [produ'to(x), -ra] *(mpl -res* [-ri∫], *fpl -s* [-∫]) *m, f* producer.

produzir [produ'zi(x)] *vt* to produce.

proeminente [proimi'nẽnt∫i] *adj (saliente)* protruding; *(importante)* prominent.

proeza [pro'eza] *f* deed.

profanar [profa'na(x)] *vt (igreja, cemitério)* to desecrate; *(memória)* to be disrespectful about.

profecia [profe'sia] *f* prophecy.

proferir [profe'ri(x)] *vt (discurso)* to give; *(palavra)* to utter; *(insulto)* to hurl; *(desejo)* to make; *(sentença)* to pronounce.

professor, -ra [profe'so(x), -ra] *(mpl -res* [-ri∫], *fpl -s* [-∫]) *m, f* teacher.

profeta [pro'fɛta] *m* prophet.

profetisa [profe't∫iza] *f* prophetess.

profiláctico, -ca [profi'latiku, -ka] *adj (Port)* = **profilático**.

profilático, -ca [profi'lat∫iku, -ka] *adj (Br)* prophylactic.

profissão [profi'sãw] *(pl -ões* [-õj∫]) *f* profession.

profissional [profisjo'naw] *(pl -ais* [-aj∫]) *adj & mf* professional.

profissões → **profissão**.

profundidade [profũndʒi'dadʒi] *f* depth; **tem três metros de ~** it's three metres deep.

profundo, -da [pro'fũndu, -da] *adj* deep; *(idéia, argumento, sentimento)* profound.

prognóstico [prog'nɔ∫t∫iku] *m (MED)* prognosis; *(de tempo)* forecast.

programa [pro'grama] *m* programme; *(EDUC)* syllabus, curriculum; *(INFORM)* program.

programação [programa'sãw] *(pl -ões* [-õj∫]) *f (em televisão, rádio)* programmes *(pl)*; *(INFORM)* programming.

progredir [progre'di(x)] *vi* to make progress; *(doença)* to progress; **~ em** to make progress in.

progresso [pro'gresu] *m* progress; **fazer ~s** to make progress.

proibição [proibi'sãw] *(pl -ões* [-õj∫]) *f* ban.

proibido, -da [proi'bidu, -da] *adj* prohibited; **"proibida a entrada"** "no entry"; **"~ afixar anúncios"** "stick no bills"; **"~ estacionar"** "no parking"; **"~ fumar"** "no smoking"; **"~ para menores de 18"** "adults only".

proibir [proi'bi(x)] *vt (consumo)* to forbid; *(acontecimento, publicação)* to ban; **~ alguém de fazer algo** to forbid sb to do sthg.

projeção [proʒe'sãw] (*pl* **-ões** [-õjʃ]) *f*
(*Br*) projection.
projecção [pruʒɛ'sãw] (*pl* **-ões** [-õjʃ])
f (*Port*) = projeção.
projeções → projeção.
projéctil [pruʒɛtil] (*pl* **-teis** [-tejʃ]) *m*
(*Port*) = projétil.
projecto [pruʒɛtu] *m* (*Port*) = projeto.
projector [pruʒɛ'tor] (*pl* **-res** [-reʃ]) *m*
(*Port*) = projetor.
projétil [proʒɛt'ʃiw] (*pl* **-teis** [-tejʃ]) *m*
(*Br*) projectile.
projeto [proʒɛtu] *m* (*Br*) project,
plan.
projetor [proʒe'to(x)] (*pl* **-res** [-riʃ]) *m*
(*Br*) projector; (*de luz*) spotlight.
proliferar [prolife'ra(x)] *vi* to prolifer-
ate.
prólogo ['prɔlogu] *m* prologue.
prolongado, -da [prolõŋ'gadu, -da]
adj extended.
prolongar [prolõŋ'ga(x)] *vt* (*prazo*) to
extend; (*férias, estada*) to prolong.
❏ **prolongar-se** *vp* (*demorar-se*) to last.
promessa [pro'mesa] *f* promise.
prometer [prome'te(x)] *vt* to
promise; **~ algo a alguém** to promise
sb sthg; **~ fazer algo** to promise to do
sthg; **~ que** to promise (that).
promíscuo, -cua [pro'miʃkwu, -kwa]
adj promiscuous.
promissor, -ra [promi'so(x), -ra] (*mpl*
-res [-riʃ], *fpl* **-s** [-ʃ]) *adj* promising.
promoção [promo'sãw] (*pl* **-ões**
[-õjʃ]) *f* promotion; **em ~** on special
offer.
promontório [promõn'tɔrju] *m*
headland.
promover [promo've(x)] *vt* to promote.
pronome [pro'nomi] *m* (*GRAM*) pronoun.
pronto, -ta ['prõntu, -ta] *adj* (*preparado*) ready; (*resposta*) prompt
♦ *interj* that's that!; **estar ~** to be
ready; **estar ~ para fazer algo** to be
willing to do sthg; **estar ~ para fazer
algo** to be ready to do sthg.
pronto-a-vestir [prõntwaveʃ'tʃi(x)]
m inv (*vestuário*) ready-to-wear clothes
(*pl*); (*loja*) clothes shop.
pronto-socorro [prõntuso'koxu] *m*
(*veículo*) ambulance.
pronúncia [pro'nũsja] *f* (*pronuncia-
ção*) pronunciation; (*sotaque*) accent.

pronunciar [pronũ'sja(x)] *vt* (*palavra,
frase*) to pronounce; (*discurso*) to give.
❏ **pronunciar-se** *vp* (*palavra*) to be
pronounced; (*exprimir opinião*) to
express one's opinion.
propaganda [propa'gãnda] *f* (*de produto*) advertising; (*POL*) propaganda.
propensão [propẽ'sãw] (*pl* **-ões**
[-õjʃ]) *f* propensity.
propina [pro'pina] *f* (*gorjeta*) tip.
propor [pro'po(x)] *vt* (*sugerir*) to propose; (*negócio*) to offer.
proporção [propor'sãw] (*pl* **-ões**
[-õjʃ]) *f* proportion; **em ~** in proportion.
❏ **proporções** *fpl* (*dimensões*) measurements.
proporcional [proporsjo'naw] (*pl*
-ais [-ajʃ]) *adj* proportional; **~ a** proportional to.
proporções → proporção.
propósito [pro'pɔzitu] *m* purpose; **a
~, quando e que você vai de férias?** by
the way, when are you going on holiday?; **com o ~ de** with the intention
of; **de ~** on purpose.
❏ **propósitos** *mpl* (*maneiras*) manners.
propriedade [proprje'dadʒi] *f* property; "**~ privada**" "private property".
proprietário, -ria [proprje'tarju,
-rja] *m*, *f* owner.
próprio, -pria ['prɔprju, -pria] *adj*
(*carro, casa*) own; (*adequado*) suitable;
(*característico*) particular ♦ *m*, *f*: **é o ~/a
própria** (*em conversa telefônica*) speaking; **~ para** suitable for; **~ para consumo** fit for human consumption; **eu
~** I myself; **o ~ presidente** the president himself.
prosa ['prɔza] *f* prose.
prospecto [proʃ'pɛ(k)tu] *m* leaflet.
prosperar [proʃpe'ra(x)] *vi* to prosper.
prosperidade [proʃperi'dadʒi] *f*
prosperity.
prosseguir [prose'gi(x)] *vt* (*estudos,
investigações*) to continue ♦ *vi* (*continuar*) to proceed, to carry on; **se ~
com este tipo de comportamento, será
despedido** if you continue to behave
in this way, you will be fired.
prostituta [proʃtʃi'tuta] *f* prostitute.
protagonista [protago'niʃta] *mf* protagonist.
proteção [prote'sãw] (*pl* **-ões** [-õjʃ]) *f*
(*Br*) protection.

protecção [prutɛ'sãw] (*pl* -ões [-õjʃ]) *f (Port)* = proteção.

proteções → proteção.

protector, -ra [prutɛ'tor, -ra] (*mpl* -res [-rɛʃ]. *fpl* -s [-ʃ]) *adj & m, f (Port)* = protetor.

proteger [protɛ'ʒɛ(x)] *vt* to protect.

proteína [protɛ'ina] *f* protein.

prótese ['prɔtɛzi] *f (MED)* prosthesis; ~ **dentária** dental prosthesis.

protestante [protɛʃ'tãntʃi] *adj & mf (RELIG)* Protestant.

protestar [protɛʃ'ta(x)] *vi* to protest; ~ **contra** to protest against.

protesto [pro'tɛʃtu] *m* protest.

protetor, -ra [protɛ'to(x), -ra] (*mpl* -res [-riʃ], *fpl* -s [-ʃ]) *m, f (Br)* protector ♦ *adj* protective; ~ **(solar)** sunscreen.

protocolo [proto'kɔlu] *m (em audiência)* transcription; *(regras)* protocol.

protuberância [protube'rãsja] *f* protuberance.

prova ['prɔva] *f* proof; *(ESP)* event; *(teste)* exam; **à ~ d'água** waterproof; **à ~ de fogo** fireproof; **à ~ de óleo** oil-resistant; **dar ~s de** to show; **pôr à ~** to put to the test; **prestar ~s** *(fazer exames)* to take exams.

provar [pro'va(x)] *vt (fato)* to prove; *(comida)* to try; *(roupa)* to try on.

provável [pro'vavɛw] (*pl* -eis [-ejʃ]) *adj* probable; **pouco ~** unlikely.

proveito [pro'vejtu] *m* benefit; **bom ~!** enjoy your meal!; **em ~ de** for the benefit of; **tirar ~ de algo** to benefit from sthg.

proveniente [prove'njẽntʃi] *adj:* ~ **de** (coming) from.

provérbio [pro'vɛrbju] *m* proverb.

prover-se [pro'vexsi] : **prover-se de** *vp + prep (abastecer-se de)* to provide o.s. with; *(munir-se de)* to equip o.s. with.

proveta [pro'vɛta] *f* test tube.

providência [pruvi'dẽsja] *f* measure; **tomar ~s** to take measures.

providenciar [providẽ'sja(x)] *vt* to arrange (for) ♦ *vi:* ~ **(para) que** to make sure (that).

província [pro'vĩsja] *f* province.

provisório, -ria [provi'zɔrju, -rja] *adj* temporary.

provocador, -ra [provoka'do(x), -ra] (*mpl* -res [-riʃ], *fpl* -s [-ʃ]) *adj* provocative.

provocante [provo'kãntʃi] *adj*

provocative.

provocar [provo'ka(x)] *vt (causar)* to cause; *(irritar)* to provoke.

provolone [provo'loni] *m* hard cheese made from cow's milk.

proximidade [prosimi'dadʒi] *f* proximity.

proximidades *fpl (arredores)* neighbourhood *(sg)*.

próximo, -ma ['prɔsimu, -ma] *adj (em espaço, tempo)* near; *(seguinte)* next; *(íntimo)* close ♦ *pron:* **o ~/a próxima** the next one; **quem é o ~?** who's next?; **até a próxima!** see you!; ~ **de** near (to); **nos ~s dias/meses** in the next few days/months.

prudência [pru'dẽsja] *f* care, caution.

prudente [pru'dẽntʃi] *adj* careful, cautious.

prurido [pru'ridu] *m* itch.

P.S. *(abrev de Post Scriptum)* PS.

pseudónimo [psew'dɔnimu] *m (Port)* = pseudônimo.

pseudônimo [psew'donimu] *m (Br)* pseudonym.

psicanálise [psika'nalizi] *f* psychoanalysis.

psicanalista [psikana'liʃta] *mf* psychoanalyst.

psicologia [psikolo'ʒia] *f* psychology.

psicológico, -ca [psiko'lɔʒiku, -ka] *adj* psychological.

psicólogo, -ga [psi'kɔlogu, -ga] *m, f* psychologist.

psiquiatra [psi'kjatra] *mf* psychiatrist.

puberdade [puber'dadʒi] *f* puberty.

publicação [publika'sãw] (*pl* -ões [-õjʃ]) *f* publication.

publicar [publi'ka(x)] *vt* to publish.

publicidade [publisi'dadʒi] *f (atividade, curso)* advertising; *(anúncio)* ad(vert); *(divulgação, difusão)* publicity.

público, -ca ['publiku, -ka] *adj (jardim, via)* public; *(escola)* state *(antes de s)*; *(empresa)* state-owned ♦ *m (de espetáculo)* audience; **o ~ em geral** the general public; **tornar ~ algo** to make sthg public; **em ~** in public.

pude ['pudʒi] → **poder**.

pudim [pu'dʒĩ] (*pl* -ns [-ʃ]) *m* pudding; ~ **flan** crème caramel; ~ **de leite** custard *(sg)*.

puf ['pufɛ] *interj (de enfado)* pah!; *(de cansaço)* phew!

pugilismo [puʒi'liʒmu] *m* boxing.

puído, -da ['pwidu, -da] *adj* worn.

pular [pu'la(x)] *vi* to jump ♦ *vt* to jump over.

pulga ['puwga] *f* flea; **estar com a ~ atrás da orelha** *(fig: estar suspeitoso)* to think something is up.

pulmão [puw'mãw] *(pl* **-ões** [-õjʃ]) *m* lung.

pulo ['pulu] *m* jump; **dar um ~ até** to pop over to; **dar ~s** to jump up and down; **num ~** in a flash.

pulôver [pu'lovɛ(x)] *(pl* **-res** [-riʃ]) *m* pullover.

pulsação [puwsa'sãw] *(pl* **-ões** [-õjʃ]) *f* beat.

pulseira [puw'sejra] *f* bracelet.

pulso. ['puwsu] *m* wrist; *(pulsação)* pulse; **medir** OU **tirar o ~ de alguém** to take sb's pulse.

pulverizar [puwvɛri'za(x)] *vt (com líquido)* to spray; *(reduzir a pó)* to pulverize.

punha ['puɲa] → **poder**.

punhado [pu'ɲadu] *m*: **um ~ de** a handful of.

punhal [pu'ɲaw] *(pl* **-ais** [-ajʃ]) *m* dagger.

punho ['puɲu] *m (mão fechada)* fist; *(pulso)* wrist; *(de casaco, camisa, blusa)* cuff; *(de arma, faca)* hilt.

punição [puni'sãw] *(pl* **-ões** [-õjʃ]) *f* punishment.

punir [pu'ni(x)] *vt* to punish.

pupila [pu'pila] *f* pupil.

puré [pu'rɛ] *m (Port)* = **purê**.

purê [pu're] *m (Br)* puree; **~ (de batata)** mashed potatoes *(pl)*.

pureza [pu'reza] *f* purity.

purgante [pux'gãntʃi] *m* purgative.

purificador, -ra [purifika'do(x), -ra] *(mpl* **-res** [-riʃ], *fpl* **-s** [-ʃ]) *adj* purifying ♦ *m*: **~ do ar** air freshener.

purificar [purifi'ka(x)] *vt (sangue)* to purify; *(ar)* to freshen.

puritano, -na [puri'tanu, -na] *adj* puritanical.

puro, -ra ['puru, -ra] *adj* pure; **pura lã** pure wool; **a pura verdade** the plain truth; **pura e simplesmente** simply.

puro-sangue [,puru'sãŋgi] *m inv* thoroughbred.

púrpura ['puxpura] *f* purple.

pus¹ ['puʃ] → **pôr**.

pus² ['puʃ] *m* pus.

puta ['puta] *f (vulg)* whore.

puxador [puʃa'do(x)] *(pl* **-res** [-riʃ]) *m* handle.

puxão [pu'ʃãw] *(pl* **-ões** [-õjʃ]) *m* tug.

puxar [pu'ʃa(x)] *vt (cabelo, cordel)* to pull; *(banco, cadeira)* to pull up; **"puxar", "puxe"** *(aviso em porta)* "pull"; **~ o autoclismo** *(Port)* to flush the toilet; **~ o saco de alguém** *(Br: fam)* to suck up to sb.

puxões → **puxão**.

Q

q.b. *(abrev de quanto baste)* as required.

Q.I. *m (abrev de quociente de inteligência)* IQ.

quadra ['kwadra] *f (em poesia)* quatrain; **~ de tênis/squash** *(Br)* tennis/squash court.

quadrado, -da [kwa'dradu, -da] *adj & m* square.

quadragésimo, -ma [kwadra'ʒɛzimu, -ma] *num* fortieth, → **sexto**.

quadril [kwa'driw] *(pl* **-is** [-iʃ]) *m* hip.

quadro ['kwadru] *m* picture; *(em sala de aula)* board; *(pintura)* painting.

quadro-negro [ˌkwadru'negru] *(pl* **quadros-negros** [ˌkwadruʒ'negruʃ]) *m (Br)* blackboard.

quaisquer → **qualquer**.

qual ['kwaw] *(pl* **-ais** [-ajʃ]) *adj* which ◆ *conj (fml: como)* like ◆ *interj (Br)* what! ◆ *pron (em interrogativa)* what; *(especificando)* which (one); **o/a ~** *(sujeito: pessoa)* who; *(complemento: pessoa)* whom; *(sujeito, complemento: coisa)* which; **cada ~** everyone; **~ deles …?** which one (of them) …?; **~ nada** OU **quê!** what!

qualidade [kwali'dadʒi] *f* quality; *(espécie)* type; **na ~ de** in the capacity of.

qualificação [kwalifika'sãw] *(pl* **-ões** [-õjʃ]) *f* qualification.

qualificado, -da [kwalifi'kadu, -da] *adj* qualified.

qualquer [kwaw'kɛ(x)] *(pl* **quaisquer** [kwajʃ'ke(x)]) *adj & pron* any; **está por aqui em ~ lugar** it's (around) here somewhere; **~ um deles** any of them; **~ um dos dois** either of them; **~ um** OU **pessoa** anyone, anybody; **a ~ momento** at any time.

quando ['kwãndu] *adv* when ◆ *conj* when; *(ao passo que)* while, whilst; **de ~ em ~** from time to time; **desde ~** how long; **~ mais não seja** at least; **~ muito** at (the) most; **~ quer que** whenever.

quantia [kwãn'tʃia] *f* amount, sum.

quantidade [kwãntʃi'dadʒi] *f* amount, quantity; **em ~** in large quantities.

quanto, -ta ['kwãntu, -ta] *adj* **1.** *(em interrogativas: singular)* how much; *(em interrogativas: plural)* how many; **~ tempo temos?** how much time have we got?; **~ tempo temos de esperar?** how long do we have to wait?; **quantas vezes você já esteve aqui?** how many times have you been here? **2.** *(em exclamações)* what a lot of; **~ dinheiro!** what a lot of money!; **~s erros!** what a lot of mistakes! **3.** *(em locuções)*: **uns ~s/umas quantas** some; **umas quantas pessoas** a few people.
◆ *pron* **1.** *(em interrogativas: singular)* how much; *(em interrogativas: plural)* how many; **~ você quer?** how much do you want?; **~s você quer?** how many do you want?; **~ custam?** how much do they cost? **2.** *(relativo a pessoas)*: **todos ~s** everyone who *(sg)*; **agradeceu a todos ~s o ajudaram** he thanked everyone who helped him. **3.** *(tudo o que)* everything, all; **coma ~/~s você quiser** eat as much/as many as you like; **tudo ~ disse é verdade** everything he said is true. **4.** *(compara quantidades)*: **~ mais se tem, mais se quer** the more you have, the more you want. **5.** *(em locuções)*: **não há espaço para um, ~ mais para dois** there's hardly enough room for one, let alone two; **~ a** as regards; **~ antes** as soon as possible; **~ mais não seja** at the very least; **~ mais melhor** the more the merrier;

uns ~s/umas quantas some.

quarenta [kwaˈrẽnta] *num* forty, →
seis.

quarentena [kwarẽnˈtena] *f* quarantine.

Quaresma [kwaˈrɛʒma] *f* Lent.

quarta [ˈkwarta] *f* (*em veículo*) fourth
(gear), → **quarto**.

quarta-feira [ˌkwaxtaˈfejra] (*pl*
quartas-feiras [ˌkwaxtaʃˈfejraʃ]) *f*
Wednesday, → **sexta-feira**.

quarteirão [kwaxtejˈrãw] (*pl* -ões
[- õjʃ]) *m* (*área*) block.

quartel [kwaxˈtɛw] (*pl* -éis [-ɛiʃ]) *m*
(*MIL*) barracks (*pl*).

quarteto [kwaxˈtetu] *m* quartet.

quarto, -ta [ˈkwaxtu, -ta] *num* fourth
♦ *m* (*divisão de casa*) room; (*parte*)
quarter; "**~ para alugar**" "room to
let"; **~ de banho** (*Port*) bathroom; **~
de casal** double room; **~ com duas
camas** twin room; **~ de hora** quarter
of an hour, → **sexto**.

quartzo [ˈkwaxtsu] *m* quartz.

quase [ˈkwazi] *adv* almost, nearly; **~
que caí** I almost fell over; **~ nada**
almost nothing, hardly anything; **~
nunca** hardly ever; **~ ~** very nearly; **~
sempre** nearly always.

quatro [ˈkwatru] *num* four, → **seis**.

quatrocentos, -tas [ˌkwatroˈsẽntuʃ,
-taʃ] *num* four hundred, → **seis**.

que [ki] *adj inv* **1.** (*em interrogativas*)
what, which; **~ livros você quer?**
which books do you want?; **~ dia é
hoje?** what day is it today?; **~ horas
são?** what time is it?

2. (*em exclamações*): **mas ~ belo dia!**
what a beautiful day!; **~ fome!** I'm
starving!; **~ maravilha!** how wonderful!

♦ *pron* **1.** (*em interrogativas*) what; **~ é
isso?** what's that?; **o ~ você quer?**
what do you want?; **o ~ você vai
comer?** what are you going to have (to
eat)?

2. (*uso relativo: sujeito*) who; (*coisa*)
which, that; **o homem ~ está correndo** the man who's running; **a guerra ~
começou em 1939** the war which OU
that started in 1939.

3. (*uso relativo: complemento*) whom,
that; (*coisa*) which, that; **o bolo ~ comi
era ótimo** the cake (that) I had was
great; **o homem ~ conheci** the man
(that) I met.

♦ *conj* **1.** (*com complemento direto*) that;
disse-me ~ ia de férias he told me
(that) he was going on holiday.

2. (*em comparações*): **(do) ~** than; **é
mais caro (do) ~ o outro** it's more
expensive than the other.

3. (*exprime causa*): **leva o guarda-chuva
~ está chovendo** take an umbrella as
it's raining; **vai depressa ~ você está
atrasado** you're late, so you'd better
hurry.

4. (*exprime consequência*) that; **pediu-
me tanto ~ acabei por lhe dar** he
asked me for it so persistently that I
ended up giving it to him.

5. (*exprime tempo*): **há horas ~ estou à
espera** I've been waiting for hours; **há
muito ~ lá não vou** I haven't been
there for ages.

6. (*indica desejo*) that; **espero ~ você se
divirta** I hope (that) you have a good
time; **quero ~ você o faça** I want you
to do it; **~ você seja feliz!** all the best!

7. (*em locuções*): **~ nem** like; **chorou ~
nem um bebê** he cried like a baby.

quê [ke] *interj* what! ♦ *pron* (*interrogativo*) what ♦ *m*: **um ~** (a certain)
something; **um ~ de** a touch of; **não
tem de ~!** not at all!, don't mention
it!; **sem ~ nem para ~** (*sem motivos*) for
no apparent reason.

quebra-cabeças [ˌkɛbrakaˈbesaʃ] *m
inv* (*passatempo*) puzzle; (*fig: problema*)
headache.

quebrado, -da [keˈbradu, -da] *adj*
(*partido*) broken; (*Br: enguiçado*) broken down.

quebra-mar [ˌkɛbraˈma(x)] (*pl*
quebra-mares [ˌkɛbraˈmariʃ]) *m* breakwater.

quebra-nozes [ˌkɛbraˈnɔziʃ] *m inv*
nutcracker.

quebrar [keˈbra(x)] *vt* to break; (*Br:
avariar*) to break down; "**~ em caso de
emergência**" "in case of emergency
break glass"; **~ a cara** (*Br: fig*) to come
a cropper.

❏ **quebrar-se** *vp* to break.

queda [ˈkɛda] *f* fall; **ter ~ para** (*fig:
vocação*) to have a flair for.

queijada [kejˈʒada] *f* cake made from
eggs, milk, cheese, sugar and flour.

queijo [ˈkejʒu] *m* cheese; **~ curado**
cured cheese; **~ de cabra** goat's
cheese; **~ flamengo** = Edam; **~ fresco**
fresh goat's cheese; **~ de ovelha** *hard*

cheese made from ewe's milk; ~ **prato** *soft cheese made from ewe's milk;* ~ **ralado** *grated cheese.*

queijo-de-minas [ˌkejʒudʒiˈminaʃ] *m soft, mild, white cheese.*

queimado, -da [kejˈmadu, -da] *adj* burnt; *(pelo sol)* sunburnt.

queimadura [kejmaˈdura] *f* burn; ~ **de sol** sunburn.

queimar [kejˈma(x)] *vt* to burn.

❏ **queimar-se** *vp* to burn o.s.; *(com sol)* to get sunburnt.

queima-roupa [ˌkejmaˈxopa] *f*: **à** ~ *(disparar)* point-blank; *(tiro)* at point-blank range.

queixa [ˈkejʃa] *f (lamentação)* moan; *(em polícia)* complaint; **apresentar** ~ *(em polícia)* to register a complaint; **fazer** ~ **de alguém** to complain about sb.

queixar-se [kejˈʃaxsi] *vp* to moan; ~ **a alguém (de algo)** to complain to sb (about sthg); ~ **de** to complain about.

queixo [ˈkejʃu] *m* chin; **tinha tanto frio que estava batendo** ~ he was so cold that his teeth were chattering.

queixoso, -osa [kejˈʃozu, -ɔza] *m, f (JUR)* plaintiff.

quem [ˈkẽj] *pron (interrogativo: sujeito)* who; *(interrogativo: complemento)* who, whom; *(indefinido)* whoever; ~ **diria!** who would have thought it!; ~ **é?** *(na porta)* who's there?; ~ **fala?** *(no telefone)* who's speaking?; ~ **me dera ser rico!** if only I were rich!; ~ **quer que** whoever; **seja** ~ **for** no matter who it is.

quentão [kẽˈtãw] *m alcoholic drink made with "cachaça", ginger and sugar, served hot.*

quente [ˈkẽtʃi] *adj* hot; *(roupa)* warm; *(Br: fam: informação, fonte)* reliable.

quer [kɛ(x)] *conj*: ~ ... ~ whether ... or; **quem** ~ **que seja** whoever; **onde** ~ **que seja** wherever; **o que** ~ **que seja** whatever.

querer [keˈre(x)] *vt* to want; **como quiser!** as you wish!; **por favor, queria** ... excuse me, I'd like ...; **sem** ~ *(sem intenção)* unintentionally, by accident; ~ **muito a alguém** *(amar)* to love sb; ~ **bem a alguém** to care about sb; **não** ~ **mal a alguém** to wish sb no ill; ~ **dizer** *(significar)* to mean.

❏ **querer-se** *vp*: **eles se querem muito**

they're very much in love.

querido, -da [keˈridu, -da] *adj* dear.

querosene [kerɔˈzɛni] *m* kerosene.

questão [keʃˈtãw] *(pl* **-ões** [-õjʃ]) *f* question; *(discussão)* quarrel; **há** ~ **de dez minutos** about ten minutes ago; **fazer** ~ **(de fazer algo)** to insist (on doing sthg); **pôr algo em** ~ to question sthg; **ser** ~ **de** to be a matter of; **em** ~ in question.

quiabo [ˈkjabu] *m* okra.

quibe [ˈkibi] *m Arabic dish made with mince and wholemeal flour, seasoned with mint and different spices.*

quiçá [kiˈsa] *adv* maybe.

quieto, -ta [ˈkjɛtu, -ta] *adj (parado, imóvel)* still; *(calado, calmo)* quiet.

quietude [kjeˈtudʒi] *f* tranquillity.

quilate [kiˈlatʃi] *m* carat.

quilo [ˈkilu] *m* kilo; **o** ~ **a** OU per kilo.

quilometragem [kilomeˈtraʒẽ] *(pl* **-ns** [-ʃ]) *f* ~ mileage, *distance travelled in kilometres.*

quilómetro [kiˈlometru] *m (Port)* = **quilômetro**.

quilômetro [kiˈlometru] *m (Br)* kilometre.

química [ˈkimika] *f* chemistry, → **químico**.

químico, -ca [ˈkimiku, -ka] *m, f* chemist.

quindim [kĩˈdʒĩ] *(pl* **-ns** [-ʃ]) *m dessert made with egg yolks, sugar and coconut.*

quinhão [kiˈɲãw] *(pl* **-ões** [-õjʃ]) *m* share.

quinhentos, -tas [kiˈɲẽtuʃ, -taʃ] *num* five hundred, → **seis**.

quinhões → **quinhão**.

quinquagésimo, -ma [kwĩkwaˈʒɛzimu, -ma] *num* fiftieth, → **sexto**.

quinquilharias [kĩkiʎaˈriaʃ] *fpl* junk *(sg)*.

quinta [ˈkĩta] *f* farm, → **quinto**.

quinta-feira [ˌkĩtaˈfejra] *(pl* **quintas-feiras** [ˌkĩtaʃˈfejraʃ]) *f* Thursday, → **sexta-feira**.

quintal [kĩˈtaw] *(pl* **-ais** [-ajʃ]) *m (terreno)* back garden; *(medida)* unit of weight equivalent to 60 kilos.

quinteto [kĩˈtetu] *m* quintet.

quinto, -ta [ˈkĩtu, -ta] *num* fifth, → **sexto**.

quinze [ˈkĩzi] *num* fifteen; ~ **dias** a fortnight.

quinzena [kĩˈzena] *f* fortnight.

quiosque [ˈkjɔʃki] *m* kiosk.
quis [ˈkiʃ] → querer.
quisto [ˈkiʃtu] *m* cyst.
quitanda [kiˈtãnda] *f (Br: loja)* grocer's (shop).
quites [ˈkitiʃ] *adj inv*: **estar ~ (com**

alguém) to be quits (with sb).
quociente [kwɔˈsjẽntʃi] *m* quotient.
quota [ˈkwɔta] *f (parte)* quota; *(de
clube)* membership fee.
quotidiano, -na [kutʃiˈdjanu, -na]
adj daily ◆ *m* everyday life.

R

R. *(abrev de rua)* Rd.

R$ *(abrev de real)* R$.

rã ['xã] *f* frog.

rabanada [xaba'nada] *f* French toast.

rabanete [xaba'netʃi] *m* radish.

rabicho [xa'biʃu] *m* ponytail.

rabino, -na [xa'binu. -na] *adj (criança)* naughty ◆ *m (sacerdote)* rabbi.

rabiscar [xabiʃ'ka(x)] *vi & vt* to scribble.

rabisco [xa'biʃku] *m* scrawl.

rabo ['xabu] *m (de ave, animal)* tail; *(Br: vulg: ânus)* arse; *(Port: fam: nádegas)* bum.

rabugento, -ta [xabu'ʒẽntu. -ta] *adj* grumpy.

raça ['xasa] *f* race; *(animal)* breed; **de ~** *(cão, gato)* pedigree; *(cavalo)* thoroughbred.

ração [xa'sãw] *(pl -ões* [-õjʃ]) *f (de animal)* feed; *(em prisão, tropa)* food, rations *(pl)*.

rachadura [xaʃa'dura] *f* crack.

rachar [xa'ʃa(x)] *vt (lenha)* to chop; *(conta)* to split ◆ *vi (abrir fenda)* to crack.

raciocínio [xasjo'sinju] *m* reasoning.

racional [xasjo'naw] *(pl -ais* [-ajʃ]) *adj* rational.

racismo [xa'siʒmu] *m* racism.

rações → ração.

radar [xa'da(x)] *(pl -res* [-riʃ]) *m* radar.

radiação [xadʒja'sãw] *(pl -ões* [-õjʃ]) *f* radiation.

radiador [xadʒja'do(x)] *(pl -res* [-riʃ]) *m* radiator.

radiante [xa'dʒjãntʃi] *adj* radiant.

radical [xadʒi'kaw] *(pl -ais* [-ajʃ]) *adj* radical.

rádio ['xadʒju] *m (telefonia)* radio ◆ *f (emissora)* radio station.

radioactivo, -va [xadʒjua'tivu. -va] *adj (Port)* = **radioativo**.

radioativo, -va [xadʒjoa'tʃivu. -va] *adj (Br)* radioactive.

rádio-despertador [ˌxadʒjodeʃ- pexta'do(x)] *(pl* **rádio-despertadores** [ˌxadjodeʃpexta'doriʃ]) *m* radio alarm.

radiografia [ˌxadʒjogra'fia] *f* X-ray.

radiotáxi [ˌxadʒjo'taksi] *m* minicab.

ráfia ['xafja] *f* raffia.

rafting ['xaftʃĩŋ] *m* rafting.

râguebi ['xagbi] *m (Port)* = **rúgbi**.

raia ['xaja] *f* skate.

rainha [xa'iɲa] *f* queen.

raio ['xaju] *m* ray; *(de roda)* spoke; *(relâmpago)* flash of lightning; **~s X** X-rays.

raiva ['xajva] *f (doença)* rabies *(sg)*; *(fúria)* rage; **ter ~ de alguém** to hate sb.

raivoso, -osa [xaj'vozu. -ɔza] *adj (pessoa)* furious; *(animal)* rabid.

raiz [xa'iʃ] *(pl -zes* [-ziʃ]) *f* root.

rajada [xa'ʒada] *f (de vento)* blast, gust.

ralador [xala'do(x)] *(pl -res* [-riʃ]) *m* grater.

ralar [xa'la(x)] *vt (alimentos)* to grate; *(joelho, cotovelo)* to graze.

❑ **ralar-se** *vp (fig: preocupar-se)* to worry; **não se rale com isso** don't worry about it.

ralhar [xa'ʎa(x)] *vi:* **~ com alguém** *(repreender)* to tell sb off.

rali [xa'li] *m* rally.

ralo, -la [xalu. -la] *adj (cabelo)* thin; *(café)* weak; *(sopa)* watery ◆ *m* drain.

rama ['xama] *f* foliage.

ramificar [xamifi'ka(x)] *vt (negócio)* to expand.

❑ **ramificar-se** *vp (negócio)* to branch out.

raminho [xa'miɲu] *m (de salsa, coentro, etc)* sprig.

ramo ['xamu] *m* branch; **mudar de ~** to change career.

rampa ['xãmpa] f (plataforma) ramp; (rua, ladeira) steep incline.

rancho ['xãʃu] m (de pessoas) group; (fam: refeição) meal.

ranço ['xãsu] m: **ter ~** (manteiga, azeite) to be rancid; (queijo, carne) to be off.

rancor [xãŋ'ko(x)] m resentment.

rancoroso, -osa [xãŋko'rozu, -ɔza] adj resentful.

rançoso, -osa [xã'sozu, -ɔza] adj (manteiga, azeite) rancid; (queijo, carne) off.

ranhura [xa'ɲura] f (em madeira, parede) groove; (em telefone público) slot.

rapar [xa'pa(x)] vt (raspar) to scrape; (cabelo, pernas) to shave; (barba) to shave off; (fam: roubar) to steal.

rapariga [xapa'riga] f (Port) girl.

rapaz [xa'paʒ] (pl **-zes** [-ziʃ]) m boy.

rapé [xa'pɛ] m snuff.

rapidez [xapi'deʃ] f speed.

rápido, -da ['xapidu, -da] adj fast; (breve) quick ◆ m (trem) express (train); (em rio) rapids (pl) ◆ adv quickly.

raposa [xa'poza] f fox.

rapsódia [xap'sɔdja] f rhapsody.

raptar [xap'ta(x)] vt to abduct, to kidnap.

rapto ['xaptu] m abduction, kidnapping.

raquete [xa'kɛtʃi] f racket.

raquítico, -ca [xa'kitʃiku, -ka] adj (fig: subdesenvolvido) underdeveloped.

raramente [xara'mẽtʃi] adv rarely.

rarefeito, -ta [xare'fejtu, -ta] adj rarefied.

raridade [xari'dadʒi] f rarity.

raro, -ra ['xaru, -ra] adj rare; (pouco espesso) thin; **raras vezes** rarely.

rascunhar [xaʃku'ɲa(x)] vt to draft.

rascunho [xaʃ'kuɲu] m draft.

rasgado, -da [xaʒ'gadu, -da] adj (tecido, folha) torn; (sorriso) broad.

rasgão [xaʒ'gãw] (pl **-ões** [-õjʃ]) m (em tecido, folha) tear; (em pele) cut.

rasgar [xaʒ'ga(x)] vt to tear.

⎤ **rasgar-se** vp to tear.

rasgões → **rasgão**.

raso, -sa ['xazu, -za] adj (nivelado) flat; (de pouca profundidade) shallow; (salto) low.

raspa ['xaʃpa] f (de limão, laranja) grated zest.

raspar [xaʃ'pa(x)] vt (pele de limão, laranja) to grate.

rasteira [xaʃ'tejra] f: **passar uma ~ em alguém** to trip sb up.

rasteiro, -ra [xaʃ'tejru, -ra] adj (vegetação) low-lying.

rastejante [xaʃte'ʒãntʃi] adj (planta, vegetação) trailing; (animal) crawling.

rastejar [xaʃte'ʒa(x)] vi to crawl.

rasto ['xaʃtu] m (Port) = **rastro**.

rastro ['xaʃtru] m (Br) trace.

ratazana [xata'zana] f rat.

rato ['xatu] m mouse.

ravina [xa'vina] f ravine.

razão [xa'zãw] (pl **-ões** [-õjʃ]) f reason; **dar ~ a alguém** to admit that sb is right; **ter ~** to be right; **este comportamento não tem ~ de ser** there's no reason for this kind of behaviour; **com ~** rightly so; **sem ~** for no reason.

r/c (Port: abrev de **rés-do-chão**) ground floor (Brit), first floor (Am).

ré ['xɛ] f (de navio) stern, → **réu**.

reabastecer [xjabaʃte'se(x)] vt to restock; (avião, carro) to refuel.

⎤ **reabastecer-se** vp to restock.

reação [xea'sãw] (pl **-ões** [-õjʃ]) f (Br) reaction.

reacção [xja'sãw] (pl **-ões** [-õjʃ]) f (Port) = **reação**.

reaccionário, -ria [xjasju'narju, -rja] adj (Port) = **reacionário**.

reacções → **reacção**.

reacionário, -ria [xeasjo'narju, -rja] adj (Br) reactionary.

reações → **reação**.

reagir [xea'ʒi(x)] vi: **~ (a algo)** (a provocação, idéia) to react (to sthg); (a medicamento, tratamento) to respond (to sthg).

real ['xeaw] (pl **-ais** [-ajʃ]) adj (verdadeiro) real; (relativo a rei, realeza) royal ◆ m (moeda) real, Brazilian currency.

realçar [xeaw'sa(x)] vt (cor, traço) to accentuate; (fato, idéia) to emphasize.

realejo [xea'leʒu] m barrel organ.

realeza [xea'leza] f royalty.

realidade [xeali'dadʒi] f reality; **na ~** in fact; **~ virtual** virtual reality.

realista [xea'liʃta] mf realist.

realização [xcaliza'sãw] (pl **-ões** [-õjʃ]) f (de tarefa, trabalho) carrying out; (de projeto, plano) implementation; (de sonho, desejo) fulfilment, realization; (de dinheiro) realization; (de *filme)* production.

realizador, -ra [xcaliza'do(x). -ra] *(mpl -res* [-riʃ], *fpl -s* [-ʃ]) *m, f (de filme)* director.

realizar [xcali'za(x)] *vt (tarefa, trabalho)* to carry out; *(projeto, plano)* to implement; *(sonho, desejo)* to fulfil, to realize; *(dinheiro)* to realize; *(filme)* to direct.

❏ **realizar-se** *vp (espetáculo)* to be performed; *(sonho, desejo)* to be fulfilled, to come true.

realmente [xeaw'mẽntʃi] *adv (efetivamente)* actually.

reanimar [xcani'ma(x)] *vt (MED) (depois de parada cardíaca)* to resuscitate; *(depois de desmaio)* to revive.

reatar [xea'ta(x)] *vt (conversação)* to resume; *(amizade)* to rekindle.

reaver [xea've(x)] *vt (recuperar)* to recover.

reavivar [xeavi'va(x)] *vt (memória)* to refresh; *(chama)* to rekindle.

rebaixar [xebaj'ʃa(x)] *vt (teto, preço)* to lower; *(pessoa)* to humiliate.

❏ **rebaixar-se** *vp* to lower o.s.

rebanho [xe'baɲu] *m* flock.

rebelde [xe'bɛwdʒi] *mf* rebel.

rebentar [xebẽn'ta(x)] *vi (balão, pneu)* to burst; *(bomba)* to explode; *(lâmpada)* to blow ◆ *vt (balão, pneu)* to burst; *(bomba)* to let off; **~ com algo** to destroy sthg.

rebocador [xeboka'do(x)] *(pl -res* [-riʃ]) *m (navio)* tug(boat).

rebocar [xebo'ka(x)] *vt* to tow.

rebolar [xebo'la(x)] *vi* to sway.

rebuçado [xebu'sadu] *m (Port)* sweet *(Brit)*, candy *(Am)*.

rebuliço [xebu'lisu] *m* commotion.

recado [xe'kadu] *m* message; **dar um ~ a alguém** to give sb a message; **deixar ~** to leave a message.

recaída [xeka'ida] *f* relapse; **ter uma ~** to have a relapse.

recair [xeka'i(x)] *vi:* **~ sobre** to fall upon.

recanto [xe'kãntu] *m* corner.

recapitular [xekapitu'la(x)] *vt* to sum up.

recatado, -da [xeka'tadu. -da] *adj (púdico)* modest; *(discreto)* discreet.

recauchutar [xekawʃu'ta(x)] *vt* to retread.

recear [xe'sja(x)] *vt* to fear.

receber [xese'be(x)] *vt* to receive;

(bofetada, pontapé) to get; *(dar as boas-vindas a)* to welcome; *(pessoas)* to entertain ◆ *vi (ter visitas)* to entertain.

receio [xe'saju] *m* fear.

receita [xe'sejta] *f (de médico)* prescription; *(culinária)* recipe; *(de Estado, empresa)* revenue.

receitar [xesej'ta(x)] *vt* to prescribe.

recém-casado, -da [xɛ,sẽka'zadu. -da] *m, f* newly-wed.

recém-chegado, -da [xɛ,sẽʃe'gadu. -da] *adj* recently arrived.

recém-nascido, -da [xɛ,sẽnaʃ'sidu. -da] *adj* newborn ◆ *m, f* newborn baby.

recente [xe'sẽntʃi] *adj* recent.

receoso, -osa [xe'sjozu. -ɔza] *adj* fearful; **estar ~ de** to be apprehensive about.

recepção [xesɛ'sãw] *(pl -ões* [-õjʃ]) *f* reception; *(de mensagem, carta)* receipt.

recepcionista [xesesjo'niʃta] *mf* receptionist.

recepções → **recepção**.

receptivo, -va [xesɛ'tʃivu. -va] *adj* receptive; **mostrar-se ~ a** to be receptive to.

receptor [xesɛ'to(x)] *(pl -res* [-riʃ]) *m (de mensagem)* recipient; *(televisão, rádio)* receiver.

recessão [xese'sãw] *(pl -ões* [-õjʃ]) *f* recession.

recheado, -da [xe'ʃjadu. -da] *adj (bolo, bombom)* filled; *(peru, vegetal)* stuffed.

rechear [xe'ʃja(x)] *vt (bolo)* to fill; *(peru)* to stuff.

recheio [xe'ʃeju] *m (de bolo, bombom)* filling; *(de peru, vegetal)* stuffing.

rechonchudo, -da [xeʃõ'ʃudu. -da] *adj* chubby.

recibo [xe'sibu] *m* receipt.

reciclagem [xesi'klaʒẽ] *f* recycling.

reciclar [xesi'kla(x)] *vt* to recycle.

reciclável [xesi'klavɛw] *(pl -eis* [-ejʃ]) *adj* recyclable.

recife [xe'sifi] *m* reef.

recinto [xe'sĩntu] *m (espaço delimitado)* enclosure; *(á volta de edifício)* grounds *(pl)*.

recipiente [xesi'pjẽntʃi] *m* container.

recíproco, -ca [xe'siproku. -ka] *adj* reciprocal.

recital [xesi'taw] *(pl -ais* [-ajʃ]) *m* recital.

recitar [xesi'ta(x)] *vt & vi* to recite.

reclamação [xeklama'sãw] (*pl* -ões [-õjʃ]) *f* complaint; **livro de reclamações** complaints book.

reclamar [xekla'ma(x)] *vi* to complain.

reclame [xe'klãmi] *m* advertisement.

recobrar [xeko'bra(x)] *vt* to resume.

recolher [xeko'ʎe(x)] *vt* to collect; *(passageiros)* to pick up; *(frutos, legumes)* to pick.

recolhimento [xekoʎi'mẽntu] *m (coleta)* collection; *(retiro)* retreat.

recomeçar [xekome'sa(x)] *vt* to begin again.

recomendação [xekomẽnda'sãw] (*pl* -ões [-õjʃ]) *f* recommendation.

❏ **recomendações** *fpl (cumprimentos)* (kind) regards.

recomendar [xekomẽn'da(x)] *vt* to recommend.

recomendável [xekomẽn'davɛw] (*pl* -eis [-ejʃ]) *adj* advisable; **pouco ~** *(lugar)* unsafe.

recompensa [xekõm'pẽsa] *f* reward.

recompor [xekõm'po(x)] *vt* to rearrange.

❏ **recompor-se** *vp (de susto)* to compose o.s.; *(de doença)* to recover.

reconciliação [xekõsilja'sãw] (*pl* -ões [-õjʃ]) *f* reconciliation.

reconhecer [xekoɲe'se(x)] *vt* to recognize; *(erro, culpa)* to acknowledge; *(documento, assinatura)* to witness.

reconhecimento [xekoɲesi'mẽntu] *m* recognition; *(de erro, culpa)* acknowledgement; *(de documento, assinatura)* witnessing.

reconstituir [xekõʃtʃi'twi(x)] *vt* to reconstruct.

recordação [xekorda'sãw] (*pl* -ões [-õjʃ]) *f (memória)* memory; *(presente)* keepsake, souvenir.

recordar [xekor'da(x)] *vt* to remember.

❏ **recordar-se** *vp* to remember; **~-se de** to remember.

recorrer [xeko'xe(x)] *vi (JUR)* to appeal; **~ a** to resort to.

recortar [xekor'ta(x)] *vt* to cut out.

recreio [xe'kreju] *m (tempo)* break; *(local)* playground.

recriar [xekri'a(x)] *vt* to recreate.

recriminar [xekrimi'na(x)] *vt* to reproach.

recruta [xe'kruta] *m* recruit ◆ *f* first three months of military service.

recta ['xɛta] *f (Port)* = **reta**.

rectângulo [xɛ'tãŋgulu] *m (Port)* = **retângulo**.

recto, -ta ['xɛtu, -ta] *adj (Port)* = **reto**.

recuar [xe'kwa(x)] *vt (veículo)* to back, to reverse ◆ *vi (em espaço)* to move back; *(em tempo)* to go back.

recuperação [xekupera'sãw] *f* recovery; *(de objeto, edifício antigo)* restoration.

recuperar [xekupe'ra(x)] *vt (algo perdido)* to recover; *(objeto, edifício antigo)* to restore.

❏ **recuperar-se** *vp (de choque, doença)* to recover.

recurso [xe'kuxsu] *m (JUR)* appeal; *(meio)* resort; **em último ~** as a last resort.

❏ **recursos** *mpl (bens)* resources.

recusa [xe'kuza] *f* refusal.

redactor, -ra [xeda'tor, -ra] (*mpl* -res [-reʃ], *fpl* -s [-ʃ]) *m, f (Port)* = **redator**.

redator, -ra [xeda'to(x), -ra] (*mpl* -res [-riʃ], *fpl* -s [-ʃ]) *m, f (Br) (de jornal)* editor.

rede ['xedʒi] *f (de pesca)* net; *(de vedação)* netting; *(de cabelo)* hairnet; *(para dormir)* hammock; *(de vias de comunicação)* network; *(de água, luz, gás)* mains *(pl)*.

rédea ['xedʒja] *f* rein.

redigir [xedʒi'ʒi(x)] *vt* to write.

redobrar [xedo'bra(x)] *vt* to double.

redondamente [xe,dõnda'mẽntʃi] *adv (enganar-se)* utterly.

redondo, -da [xe'dõndu, -da] *adj* round.

redor [xe'do(x)] *m*: **em** OU **ao ~ (de)** around, about.

redução [xedu'sãw] (*pl* -ões [-õjʃ]) *f* reduction.

redundância [xedũn'dãsja] *f* tautology.

reduzido, -da [xedu'zidu, -da] *adj* reduced.

reduzir [xedu'zi(x)] *vt* to reduce.

reembolsar [xjẽmbow'sa(x)] *vt* to refund.

reembolso [xjẽm'bowsu] *m* refund.

reencontro [xjẽŋ'kõntru] *m* reunion.

refazer [xefa'ze(x)] *vt* rebuild.

❏ **refazer-se** *vp* to recover.

refeição [xefej'sãw] (*pl* -ões [-õjʃ]) *f* meal; **nas refeições** at mealtimes; **~ ligeira** snack.

refeitório [xefej'tɔrju] *m* refectory, canteen.

refém [xɛ'fɛ̃] (*pl* **-ns** [-ʃ]) *mf* hostage.

referência [xefe'rẽsja] *f* reference; **fazer ~ a** to refer to.

❏ **referências** *fpl (para emprego)* references.

referendo [xefe'rẽndu] *m* referendum.

referente [xefe'rẽntʃi] *adj:* **~ a** relating to.

referir [xefe'ri(x)] *vt* to mention.

❏ **referir-se a** *vp + prep* to refer to; **no que se refere a** as regards.

refinado, -da [xefi'nadu, -da] *adj* refined.

refinaria [xefina'ria] *f* refinery.

reflectir [xefle'tir] *vt & vi (Port)* = **refletir**.

reflector [xefle'tor] (*pl* **-res** [-riʃ]) *m (Port)* = **refletor**.

refletir [xefle'tʃi(x)] *vt & vi (Br)* to reflect; **~ sobre algo** to reflect on sthg.

❏ **refletir-se em** *vp + prep (Br)* to be reflected in.

refletor [xefle'to(x)] (*pl* **-res** [-riʃ]) *m (Br)* reflector.

reflexão [xeflɛk'sãw] (*pl* **-ões** [-õjʃ]) *f* reflection.

reflexo [xe'flɛksu] *m* reflection; *(reação)* reflex (action).

reflexões → **reflexão**.

refogado, -da [xefo'gadu, -da] *adj (carne, peixe)* stewed; *(cebola)* fried ◆ *m (molho)* fried garlic and onion; *(ensopado)* stew.

refogar [xefo'ga(x)] *vt* to stew.

reforçado, -da [xefor'sadu, -da] *adj (esforço, energia)* redoubled; *(objeto, substância)* reinforced.

reforçar [xefox'sa(x)] *vt (idéia, argumento)* to back up; *(objeto, substância)* to reinforce.

reforma [xe'fɔxma] *f (de sistema)* reform; *(de casa, edifício)* refurbishment; *(de pessoa)* retirement.

reformado, -da [xefox'madu, -da] *m, f (pensionista)* pensioner.

refractário, -ria [xefra'tarju, -rja] *adj (Port)* = **refratário**.

refrão [xe'frãw] (*pl* **-ões** [-õjʃ]) *m* chorus.

refratário, -ria [xefra'tarju, -rja] *adj (Br) (ladrilho, vidro)* heat-resistant; *(utensílio)* ovenproof.

refrear [xefri'a(x)] *vt* to contain.

❏ **refrear-se** *vp* to contain o.s.

refrescante [xefreʃ'kãntʃi] *adj* refreshing.

refrescar [xefreʃ'ka(x)] *vt (suj: bebida, ar)* to refresh; *(cabeça)* to clear.

❏ **refrescar-se** *vp* to cool down.

refresco [xe'freʃku] *m* soft drink.

refrigerante [xefriʒe'rãntʃi] *m* soft drink.

refrões → **refrão**.

refugiado, -da [xefu'ʒjadu, -da] *m, f* refugee.

refugiar-se [xefu'ʒjaxsi] *vp (asilar-se)* to take refuge; *(abrigar-se)* to take shelter; *(esconder-se)* to hide.

refúgio [xe'fuʒju] *m* refuge.

refugo [xe'fugu] *m* refuse.

refutar [xefu'ta(x)] *vt* to refute.

rega ['xega] *f (de plantas)* watering; *(de terra)* irrigation.

regaço [xe'gasu] *m* lap.

regador [xega'do(x)] (*pl* **-res** [-riʃ]) *m* watering can.

regalias [xega'liaʃ] *fpl (em emprego)* perks.

regar [xe'ga(x)] *vt (plantas)* to water; *(terra)* to irrigate; *(prato, comida)* to season.

regata [xe'gata] *f* regatta.

regenerar-se [xeʒene'raxsi] *vp* to mend one's ways.

reger [xe'ʒe(x)] *vt (orquestra, banda)* to conduct.

região [xe'ʒjãw] (*pl* **-ões** [-õjʃ]) *f* region; **~ demarcada** *classification guaranteeing the source of a wine, its method of production and grape variety.*

regime [xe'ʒimi] *m (político)* regime; *(dieta)* diet.

regiões → **região**.

regional [xeʒjo'naw] (*pl* **-ais** [-ajʃ]) *adj* regional.

registado, -da [xeʒiʃ'tadu, -da] *adj (Port)* = **registrado**.

registar [xeʒiʃ'tar] *vt (Port)* = **registrar**.

registo [xe'ʒiʃtu] *m (Port)* = **registro**.

registrado, -da [xeʒiʃ'tradu, -da] *adj (Br)* registered.

registrar [xeʒiʃ'tra(x)] *vt (Br)* to register; *(acontecimento, mudança)* to record.

registro [xe'ʒiʃtru] *m (Br)* register; *(repartição)* registry office; *(de correio)* registration; **Registro Civil** registry office; **Registro Predial** registry *(for all* *matters relating to the buying and selling of property).*

regra ['xɛgra] *f* rule; **não fugir à ~** to be no exception; **(como) ~ geral** as a rule; **por ~** as a rule.

regressar [xɛgrɛ'sa(x)] *vi* to return; **~ a** to return to.

regresso [xɛ'grɛsu] *m* return; **estar de ~** to be back.

régua ['xɛgwa] *f* ruler.

regulamento [xɛgula'mẽntu] *m* regulations *(pl)*.

regular [xɛgu'la(x)] *(pl* **-res** [-riʃ]) *adj* regular; *(tamanho, qualidade)* standard; *(uniforme)* even; *(vôo)* scheduled ♦ *vt (regulamentar)* to regulate; *(mecanismo)* to adjust.

rei ['xɛj] *m* king.

reinado [xej'nadu] *m* reign.

reinar [xej'na(x)] *vi* to reign.

Reino Unido [,xejnu'nidu] *m*: **o ~** the United Kingdom.

reivindicação [xejvĩndʒika'sãw] *(pl* **-ões** [-õjʃ]) *f* claim.

reivindicar [xejvĩndi'ka(x)] *vt* to claim.

rejeição [xeʒej'sãw] *(pl* **-ões** [-õjʃ]) *f* rejection.

rejeitar [xeʒej'ta(x)] *vt* to reject.

relação [xela'sãw] *(pl* **-ões** [-õjʃ]) *f* relation; *(entre pessoas, países)* relationship; **com** OU **em ~ a** in relation to.

❏ **relações** *fpl (relacionamento)* relations; *(ato sexual)*: **ter relações com alguém** to sleep with sb; **relações públicas** public relations.

relâmpago [xe'lãmpagu] *m* flash of lightning.

relatar [xela'ta(x)] *vt (jogo de futebol)* to commentate on; *(acontecimento)* to relate.

relativo, -va [xela'tivu, -va] *adj* relative; **~ a** relating to.

relatório [xela'tɔrju] *m* report.

relaxado, -da [xela'ʃadu, -da] *adj* relaxed.

relaxante [xela'ʃãntʃi] *adj* relaxing ♦ *m (medicamento)* tranquillizer.

relaxar [xela'ʃa(x)] *vt* to relax.

❏ **relaxar-se** *vp* to relax.

relembrar [xelẽm'bra(x)] *vt* to recall.

relevo [xe'levu] *m* relief; **dar ~ a** to highlight.

religião [xeli'ʒãw] *(pl* **-ões** [-õjʃ]) *f* religion.

relíquia [xe'likja] *f* relic.

relógio [xe'lɔʒju] *m (de parede, mesa)* clock; *(de pulso)* watch; **~ de cuco** cuckoo clock; **~ de sol** sundial.

relojoaria [xeloʒwa'ria] *f* watchmaker's (shop).

relutância [xelu'tãsja] *f* reluctance.

reluzente [xelu'zẽntʃi] *adj* gleaming.

relva ['xɛlva] *f (Port)* grass.

relvado [xɛl'vadu] *m (Port) (relva)* lawn; *(campo de futebol)* football pitch.

remar [xe'ma(x)] *vi* to row.

rematar [xema'ta(x)] *vt (concluir)* to finish.

remediar [xeme'dʒja(x)] *vt* to remedy.

remédio [xe'mɛdʒju] *m* remedy; **não tem ~** *(fig)* it can't be helped.

remendar [xemẽn'da(x)] *vt* to mend.

remendo [xe'mẽndu] *m* patch.

remessa [xe'mɛsa] *f (de produtos)* shipment, consignment; *(de dinheiro)* remittance.

remetente [xeme'tẽntʃi] *mf* sender.

remeter [xeme'te(x)] *vt* to send.

remexer [xeme'ʃe(x)] *vt* to rummage through.

remo ['xɛmu] *m (longo)* oar; *(curto)* paddle.

remoção [xemo'sãw] *(pl* **-ões** [-õjʃ]) *f* removal.

remorso [xe'mɔxsu] *m* remorse.

remoto [xe'mɔtu] *adj* remote.

remover [xemo've(x)] *vt* to remove.

remuneração [xemunera'sãw] *(pl* **-ões** [-õjʃ]) *f* remuneration.

renascer [xenaʃ'se(x)] *vi* to be born again.

Renascimento [xenaʃsi'mẽntu] *m*: **o ~** the Renaissance.

renda ['xẽnda] *f (Br: rendimento)* income; *(de vestido, blusa)* lace trim; *(Port: de casa, apartamento)* rent; **imposto de ~** income tax; **~ nacional** gross national product; **famílias de baixa ~** low-income families.

renegar [xene'ga(x)] *vt* to reject.

renovação [xenova'sãw] *(pl* **-ões** [-õjʃ]) *f (de contrato, amizade)* renewal; *(de edifício)* renovation.

renovar [xeno'va(x)] *vt* to renew; *(consertar)* to renovate; *(substituir)* to replace.

rentabilidade [xẽntabili'dadʒi] *f* profitability.

rentável [xẽn'tavɛw] *(pl* **-eis** [-ejʃ]) *adj* profitable.

renúncia [xe'nũsja] f renunciation.

renunciar [xenũ'sja(x)] vt to renounce.

reparação [xcpara'sãw] (pl -ões [-õjʃ]) f (conserto) repair.

reparar [xepa'ra(x)] vt (consertar) to repair; (restaurar) to restore; ~ que to notice (that).

❏ **reparar em** v + prep (notar) to notice.

repartição [xcpaxtʃi'sãw] (pl -ões [-õjʃ]) f (partilha) division; (distribuição) distribution; (local) department; ~ **pública** government office.

repartir [xcpax'tʃi(x)] vt (partilhar) to divide; (distribuir) to distribute; ~ **algo com alguém** to share sthg with sb; ~ **algo em algo** to split sthg up into sthg.

repelente [xcpe'lẽntʃi] adj repellent ◆ m: ~ **(de insetos)** insect repellent.

repente [xe'pẽntʃi] m outburst; **de** ~ suddenly.

repentino, -na [xepẽn'tʃinu, -na] adj sudden.

repercussão [xepexku'sãw] (pl -ões [-õjʃ]) f (impacto) response; (conseqüência) repercussion.

repertório [xcpex'tɔrju] m repertoire.

repetição [xcpetʃi'sãw] (pl -ões [-õjʃ]) f repetition.

repetidamente [xepe,tʃida'mẽntʃi] adv repeatedly.

repetido, -da [xepe'tʃidu, -da] adj repeated.

repetir [xepe'tʃi(x)] vt to repeat; (prato, refeição) to have seconds of.

❏ **repetir-se** vp to happen again.

replay [xi'plej] m action replay.

replicar [xepli'ka(x)] vt: ~ **que** to reply that.

repolho [xe'poʎu] m cabbage.

repor [xc'po(x)] vt (dinheiro) to replace; ~ **algo no lugar** to put sthg back (where it belongs); ~ **a verdade** to set the record straight.

reportagem [xepox'taʒẽ] (pl -ns [-ʃ]) f (em rádio, televisão) report; (em jornal, revista) article.

repórter [xe'pɔxtɛ(x)] (pl -res [-riʃ]) mf reporter.

repousar [xcpo'za(x)] vt & vi to rest.

repreender [xepriẽn'de(x)] vt to rebuke.

represa [xe'preza] f weir.

represália [xcpre'zalja] f reprisal.

representação [xcprezẽnta'sãw] (pl -ões [-õjʃ]) f performance; (imagem) representation.

representante [xcprezẽn'tãntʃi] mf representative; ~ **oficial** authorized agent.

representar [xeprezẽn'ta(x)] vt to represent; (cena) to perform; (papel) to play; (pôr em cena) to put on; (significar) to mean ◆ vi (ator) to act.

repressão [xepre'sãw] (pl -ões [-õjʃ]) f suppression.

reprimir [xepri'mi(x)] vt to suppress.

reprise [xe'prizi] f revival.

reprodução [xeprodu'sãw] (pl -ões [-õjʃ]) f reproduction.

reproduzir [xeprodu'zi(x)] vt (evento) to reenact; (quadro, escultura) to reproduce.

❏ **reproduzir-se** vp to reproduce.

reprovar [xepro'va(x)] vt (atitude, comportamento) to disapprove of; (lei, projeto) to reject; (ano escolar, exame) to fail.

réptil ['xeptiw] (pl -teis [-tejʃ]) m reptile.

república [xe'publika] f (sistema político) republic; (de estudantes) student house, fraternity (Am); **a República Brasileira** the Brazilian Republic.

repudiar [xepu'dʒja(x)] vt to repudiate.

repugnância [xepug'nãsja] f repugnance.

repugnante [xepug'nãntʃi] adj repugnant.

repulsa [xe'puwsa] f repulsion.

repulsivo, -va [xcpuw'sivu, -va] adj repulsive.

reputação [xeputa'sãw] (pl -ões [-õjʃ]) f (fama) reputation; (importância social) standing.

requeijão [xckej'ʒãw] (pl -ões [-õjʃ]) m = cottage cheese.

requerer [xeke're(x)] vt (precisar de) to require; (por requerimento) to request.

requerimento [xckeri'mẽntu] m request form.

requintado, -da [xckĩn'tadu, -da] adj exquisite.

requinte [xe'kĩntʃi] m style.

requisito [xcki'zitu] m requirement.

❏ **requisitos** mpl (dotes) attributes.

rescindir [xeʃĩn'di(x)] vt (contrato) to break.

rés-do-chão [xɛʒduˈʃãw] *m (Port) inv* ground floor *(Brit)*, first floor *(Am)*.

resenha [xeˈzaɲa] *f (televisiva, de rádio)* listings *(pl)*.

reserva [xeˈzɛxva] *f* reservation; *(de alimentos, provisões)* reserves *(pl)*; *(de animais, plantas, vinho)* reserve; **~ de caça** game reserve; **~ natural** nature reserve.

reservado, -da [xezexˈvadu, -da] *adj* reserved; *(íntimo)* secluded.

reservar [xezexˈva(x)] *vt (quarto, lugar, bilhete)* to book; *(guardar)* to set aside.

resfriado [xeʃfriˈadu] *m (Br)* cold.

resgate [xeʒˈgatʃi] *m* ransom.

resguardar [xeʒgwaxˈda(x)] *vt* to protect.

❑ **resguardar-se** *vp*: **~-se de** to protect o.s. from.

residência [xeziˈdẽsja] *f* residence; *(acadêmica)* hall of residence.

residir [xeziˈdʒi(x)] : **residir em** *v + prep* to reside in.

resíduo [xeˈzidwu] *m* residue.

resignação [xezignaˈsãw] *f* resignation.

resignar-se [xezigˈnaxsi] *vp* to resign o.s.

resina [xeˈzina] *f* resin.

resistência [xeziʃˈtẽsja] *f (de pessoa)* stamina; *(de material, parede)* strength; *(de aquecedor elétrico)* resistor.

resistente [xeziʃˈtẽtʃi] *adj* resistant.

resistir [xeziʃˈtʒi(x)] *vi* to resist; **~ a algo** *(ataque, doença)* to resist sthg; *(suportar)* to withstand sthg.

resmungar [xeʒmũŋˈga(x)] *vt* to mutter ♦ *vi* to grumble.

resolução [xezoluˈsãw] *(pl* **-ões** [-õjʃ]) *f* resolution; *(firmeza, coragem)* resolve.

resolver [xezowˈve(x)] *vt* to solve; **~ fazer algo** to decide to do sthg.

❑ **resolver-se** *vp* to make up one's mind.

respectivo, -va [xeʃpɛˈtivu, -va] *adj* respective.

respeitar [xeʃpejˈta(x)] *vt* to respect.

❑ **respeitar a** *v + prep*: **no que respeita a** as regards.

respeitável [xeʃpejˈtavew] *(pl* **-eis** [-ejʃ]) *adj* respectable; *(fig: grande)* considerable.

respeito [xeʃˈpejtu] *m* respect; **dizer ~ a** to concern; **ter ~ por** to have respect for; **a ~ de, com ~ a** with respect to.

respiração [xeʃpiraˈsãw] *f* breathing.

respirar [xeʃpiˈra(x)] *vt & vi* to breathe.

resplandecente [xeʃplãdeˈsẽtʃi] *adj* dazzling.

responder [xeʃpõˈde(x)] *vt* to answer ♦ *vi (dar resposta)* to answer; *(replicar)* to answer back; *(ir a tribunal)* to appear (in court); *(reagir)* to respond; **~ a** *(carta, pergunta)* to answer.

❑ **responder por** *v + prep* to answer for.

responsabilidade [xeʃpõsabiliˈdadʒi] *f* responsibility.

responsabilizar [xeʃpõsabiliˈza(x)] *vt*: **~ alguém/algo por algo** to hold sb/sthg responsible for sthg.

❑ **responsabilizar-se** *vp*: **~-se por** to take responsibility for.

responsável [xeʃpõˈsavew] *(pl* **-eis** [-ejʃ]) *adj* responsible ♦ *mf* person in charge; **~ por** responsible for.

resposta [xeʃˈpɔʃta] *f* answer; *(a carta)* reply; *(reação)* response.

resquício [xeʃˈkisju] *m* vestige.

ressabiado, -da [xesaˈbjadu, -da] *adj (desconfiado)* cautious; *(ressentido)* resentful.

ressaca [xeˈsaka] *f* hangover.

ressaltar [xesawˈta(x)] *vt* to highlight ♦ *vi* to stand out.

ressentimento [xesẽtʃiˈmẽtu] *m* resentment.

ressentir-se [xesẽˈtixsi] *vp* to take offence; **~ de algo** *(sentir o efeito de)* to feel the effects of sthg.

ressurgimento [xesuxʒiˈmẽtu] *m* resurgence.

ressuscitar [xesusiˈta(x)] *vt* to resurrect ♦ *vi* to be resurrected.

restabelecer [xeʃtabeleˈse(x)] *vt* to reinstate.

❑ **restabelecer-se** *vp* to recover.

restar [xeʃˈta(x)] *vi* to be left.

restauração [xeʃtawraˈsãw] *(pl* **-ões** [-õjʃ]) *f (de edifício)* restoration; *(de forças, energia)* recovery.

restaurante [xeʃtawˈrãtʃi] *m* restaurant; **~ panorâmico** restaurant offering panoramic views over an area.

restaurar [xeʃtawˈra(x)] *vt* to restore.

restinga [xeʃˈtʃĩga] *f* sandbank.

restituir [xeʃtʃiˈtwi(x)] *vt* to return.

resto [ˈxɛʃtu] *m (sobra)* rest; *(MAT)* remainder.

❏ **restos** *mpl (sobras)* leftovers; **~s mortais** remains.

resultado [xezuw'tadu] *m* result; *(em exame, teste, competição)* results *(pl)*.

resultar [xczuw'ta(x)] *vi* to work; **~ de algo** to result from sthg; **~ em algo** to result in sthg.

resumir [xezu'mi(x)] *vt* to summarize.

❏ **resumir-se a** *vp + prep* to come down to.

resumo [xe'zumu] *m* summary; **em ~** in short.

reta ['xeta] *f (Br) (linha)* straight line; *(em estrada)* straight stretch of road.

retaguarda [,xeta'gwarda] *f* rear; **na ~** at the rear.

retalho [xe'taʎu] *m (de fazenda)* remnant; **a ~** *(Port: vender, comprar)* retail.

retaliação [xetalja'sãw] *(pl* -ões [-õjʃ]*)* f retaliation.

retaliar [xeta'lja(x)] *vt & vi* to retaliate.

retângulo [xe'tãŋgulu] *m (Br)* rectangle.

retardar [xetax'da(x)] *vt* to delay.

reter [xe'te(x)] *vt (parar)* to stop; *(impulso, lágrimas, ira)* to hold back; *(deter)* to detain; *(em memória)* to retain.

reticente [xetʃi'sẽntʃi] *adj* reticent.

retina [xe'tʃina] *f* retina.

retirada [xetʃi'rada] *f* retreat.

retirar [xetʃi'ra(x)] *vt (remover)* to remove; *(afirmação)* to withdraw.

❏ **retirar-se** *vp (recolher-se)* to retire; **~-se de algo** to withdraw from sthg; **ela retirou-se da sala** she left the room.

reto, -ta ['xɛtu, -ta] *adj & m (Br) (linha, estrada)* straight; *(justo)* upright ◆ *m (ANAT)* rectum.

retorcido, -da [xetox'sidu, -da] *adj* wrought.

retórica [xɛ'tɔrika] *f* rhetoric.

retornar [xetox'na(x)] *vi* to return; **~ a** to return to.

retraído, -da [xetra'idu, -da] *adj* retiring.

retrato [xe'tratu] *m* portrait; *(fotografia)* photograph.

retribuir [xetri'bwi(x)] *vt* to return.

retroceder [xetrose'de(x)] *vi* to go back.

retrógrado, -da [xe'trɔgradu, -da] *adj* retrograde.

retrovisor [xetrovi'zo(x)] *(pl* -es [-iʃ]*)* m rearview mirror.

réu, ré ['xɛu, 'xɛ] *m, f* accused.

reumatismo [xewma'tʃiʒmu] *m* rheumatism.

reunião [xju'njãw] *(pl* -ões [-õjʃ]*)* f meeting.

reunir [xju'ni(x)] *vt (pessoas, objetos)* to bring together; *(provas)* to gather.

❏ **reunir-se** *vp (encontrar-se)* to meet.

réveillon [xeve'jõ] *m* New Year's Eve dinner and party.

revelação [xevela'sãw] *(pl* -ões [-õjʃ]*)* f revelation; *(de fotografia)* development.

revelar [xeve'la(x)] *vt (segredo, notícia)* to reveal; *(fotografia)* to develop; *(interesse, talento)* to show.

❏ **revelar-se** *vp (manifestar-se)* to prove to be.

revendedor, -ra [xevẽnde'do(x), -ra] *(mpl* -res [-riʃ], *fpl* -s [-ʃ]*)* m, f retailer.

rever [xe've(x)] *vt (pessoa)* to see again; *(texto, trabalho)* to revise.

reverso [xe'vɛrsu] *m* back.

revés [xe'vɛʃ] *(pl* -eses [-ɛziʃ]*)* m setback; **ao ~** the wrong way round.

revestir [xeveʃ'tʃi(x)] *vt* to cover.

revezar-se [xeve'zaxsi] *vp* to take turns.

revirado, -da [xevi'radu, -da] *adj (gola, pontas)* turned-up; *(olhos)* rolling; *(casa, gaveta)* untidy.

reviravolta [xe,vira'vɔwta] *f* spin; *(fig: em situação)* U-turn.

revisão [xevi'zãw] *(pl* -ões [-õjʃ]*)* f *(de lei)* review; *(de texto, prova tipográfica)* proofreading; *(de máquina, carro)* service; *(de matéria, aula)* revision *(Brit)*, review *(Am)*.

revisor, -ra [xevi'zo(x), -ra] *(mpl* -res [-riʃ], *fpl* -s [-ʃ]*)* m, f *(em transporte público)* ticket inspector; *(de texto, provas tipográficas)* proofreader.

revista [xe'viʃta] *f (publicação)* magazine; *(peça teatral)* revue; *(inspeção)* review; **~ em quadrinhos** *(Br)* comic.

revolta [xe'vɔwta] *f (rebelião)* revolt; *(indignação)* outrage.

revoltar-se [xevow'taxsi] *vp (sublevar-se)* to revolt; *(indignar-se)* to be outraged; **~-se com algo** to be revolted by sthg.

revolução [xevolu'sãw] *(pl* -ões [-õjʃ]*)* f revolution.

revolver [xevow've(x)] *vt (papéis, lixo)*

to rummage through; *(terra)* to dig over.

revólver [xɛ'vɔwvɛ(x)] *(pl* -es [-iʃ]) *m* revolver.

rezar [xe'za(x)] *vi (orar)* to pray ◆ *vt (missa, oração)* to say.

ri ['xi] → **rir**.

riacho ['xjaʃu] *m* brook.

ribeira [xi'bejra] *f* stream.

ribeirão [xibej'rãw] *(pl* -ões [-õjʃ]) *m* stream.

ribeirinho, -nha [xibej'riɲu, -ɲa] *adj* river *(antes de s)*.

ribeirões → **ribeirão**.

rico, -ca ['xiku, -ka] *adj* rich; ~ **em** rich in.

ricota [xi'kɔta] *f* ricotta cheese.

ridicularizar [xidʒikulari'za(x)] *vt* to ridicule.

ridículo, -la [xi'dʒikulu, -la] *adj* ridiculous; *(insignificante)* laughable ◆ *m* absurdity.

rido ['xidu] → **rir**.

rifa ['xifa] *f (sorteio)* raffle; *(bilhete)* raffle ticket.

rigidez [xiʒi'deʒ] *f (de músculos, ossos)* stiffness; *(de caráter, costumes)* inflexibility.

rigor [xi'go(x)] *(pl* -res [-riʃ]) *m* rigour; *(de frio, calor, caráter)* severity.

rijo, -ja ['xiʒu, -ʒa] *adj* tough; *(pão, queijo, fruto)* hard; *(pessoa)* hardy.

rim ['xĩ] *(pl* -ns [-ʃ]) *m* kidney.
❏ **rins** *mpl (parte do corpo)* lower back *(sg)*.

rima ['xima] *f (de verso)* rhyme.
❏ **rimas** *fpl (versos)* verses.

rímel® ['ximɛw] *(pl* -eis [-ɛjʃ]) *m* mascara.

ringue ['xĩgi] *m (boxing)* ring.

rinoceronte [xinose'rõntʃi] *m* rhinoceros.

rinque ['xĩki] *m* rink.

rins → **rim**.

rio¹ ['xju] → **rir**.

rio² ['xju] *m* river; ~ **abaixo** downstream; ~ **acima** upstream.

Rio de Janeiro [xiudʒiʒa'nejru] *m:* o ~ Rio de Janeiro.

riqueza [xi'keza] *f (de país, pessoa, região)* wealth; *(de solo, cores, idéias)* richness.

rir ['xi(x)] *vi* to laugh; **desatar a** ~ to burst out laughing; **morrer de** ~ to laugh one's head off.

ris ['xiʃ] → **rir**.

risada [xi'zada] *f* laugh.

risca ['xiʃka] *f* stripe; **de** ~**s** striped.

riscar [xiʃ'ka(x)] *vt (frase)* to cross out; *(folha)* to scribble on; *(parede, carro, móvel)* to scratch.

risco ['xiʃku] *m (traço)* mark; *(linha)* line; *(em cabelo)* parting *(Brit)*, part *(Am)*; *(perigo)* risk; **correr o** ~ **de** to run the risk of; **pôr em** ~ to put at risk; ~ **ao meio/ao lado** *(relativo a cabelo)* middle/side parting.

riso ['xizu] *m* laugh; ~ **amarelo** grimace.

risoto [xi'zotu] *m* risotto.

ríspido, -da ['xiʃpidu, -da] *adj* stern.

rissol [xi'sɔl] *(pl* -óis [-ɔjʃ]) *m (Port)* = **rissole**.

rissole [xi'sɔli] *m (Br)* small semicircular fried cake with a fish or meat filling coated in breadcrumbs.

ritmo ['xitʒimu] *m (de movimento, andamento)* pace; *(em música)* rhythm; *(do coração)* beat.

ritual [xi'twaw] *(pl* -ais [-ajʃ]) *m* ritual.

riu ['xiu] → **rir**.

rival [xi'vaw] *(pl* -ais [-ajʃ]) *mf* rival.

rivalidade [xivali'dadʒi] *f* rivalry.

robalo [ro'balu] *m* sea bass.

robertos [ro'bɛrtuʃ] *mpl (Port)* puppets.

robô [rɔ'bo] *m* robot.

robusto, -ta [xo'buʃtu, -ta] *adj* robust.

roça ['xɔsa] *f (Br: zona rural)* countryside.

rocambole [xokãm'bɔli] *m (Br)* roulade.

roçar [xo'sa(x)] *vt* to brush.

rocha ['xɔʃa] *f* rock.

rochedo [xo'ʃedu] *m* crag.

rock ['xɔki] *m* rock (music).

roda ['xɔda] *f (de carro, bicicleta)* wheel; *(de saia, vestido)* flare; *(de pessoas)* circle, ring.

rodada [xo'dada] *f* round.

rodagem [xo'daʒẽ] *f* → **faixa**.

rodapé [xoda'pɛ] *f* skirting board; **nota de** ~ footnote.

rodar [xo'da(x)] *vt (fazer girar)* to turn; *(rapidamente)* to spin; *(filme)* to shoot ◆ *vi (girar)* to turn; *(rapidamente)* to spin.

rodear [xo'dea(x)] *vt* to surround.

❏ **rodear-se de** *vp + prep* to surround o.s. with.

rodela [xo'dɛla] *f* slice.

rodízio [xo'dʒizju] *m* restaurant.

rododendro [xodo'dẽndru] *m* rhododendron.

rodopiar [xodo'pja(x)] *vi* to whirl (around).

rodovia [xodo'via] *f (Br)* motorway *(Brit)*, expressway *(Am)*; **~ com pedágio** toll motorway *(Brit)*, turnpike *(Am)*.

rodoviária [xodo'vjarja] *f (local)* bus station.

roer ['xwe(x)] *vt (rato)* to gnaw (at); *(cão)* chew.

rola ['xola] *f* turtle dove.

rolar [xo'la(x)] *vi* to roll.

roleta [xo'leta] *f* roulette; **~ russa** Russian roulette.

rolha ['xoʎa] *f (de borracha, plástico)* stopper; **~ de cortiça** cork.

rolo ['xolu] *m* roller; *(fotográfico)* roll (of film); **~ de pastel** rolling pin.

romã [xo'mã] *f* pomegranate.

romance [xo'mãsi] *m* romance; *(gênero)* novel; *(sentimental)* romantic novel; **~ cor-de-rosa** = Mills and Boon; **~ policial** detective novel.

romântico, -ca [xo'mãʃiku, -ka] *adj* romantic.

romaria [xoma'ria] *f popular religious festival combining a religious ceremony and dancing, eating etc.*

romper [xõm'pe(x)] *vt (corda, cabo)* to snap; *(contrato)* to break ◆ *vi (namorados, noivos)* to split up; **~ com** to split up with.

❏ **romper-se** *vp (rasgar-se)* to tear.

ronda ['xõnda] *f (de polícia)* beat; *(de guarda-noturno)* rounds *(pl)*; **fazer a ~** to do the rounds.

rosa ['xɔza] *f* rose; **um mar de ~s** a bed of roses.

rosário [xo'zarju] *m* rosary.

rosbife [xoʒ'bifi] *m* roast beef.

rosca ['xoʃka] *f (de garrafa, tampa, parafuso)* thread; *(CULIN: pão)* ring-shaped loaf of bread; *(biscoito para bebê)* rusk.

rosé [xɔ'zɛ] *m* rosé.

roseira [xo'zejra] *f* rosebush.

rosnar [xoʒ'na(x)] *vi* to growl.

rosto ['xoʃtu] *m* face.

rota ['xɔta] *f (de navio)* course; *(de avião)* route.

rotativo, -va [xuta'tʃivu, -va] *adj* rotary.

roteiro [xo'tejru] *m* route.

rotina [xo'tʃina] *f* routine.

roto, -ta ['xotu, -ta] *pp → romper* ◆ *adj (roupa)* torn.

rótula ['xɔtula] *f* kneecap.

rotular [xotu'la(x)] *vt* to label.

rótulo ['xɔtulu] *m* label.

rotunda [xo'tũnda] *f (Port)* roundabout *(Brit)*, traffic circle *(Am)*.

roubar [xo'ba(x)] *vt & vi* to steal; **~ algo de alguém** to steal sthg from sb; **fui roubado** I've been robbed.

roubo ['xobu] *m (ato)* robbery, theft; *(coisa roubada)* stolen item; *(fig: preço exagerado)* daylight robbery.

rouco, -ca ['xoku, -ka] *adj* hoarse.

roupa ['xopa] *f (vestuário)* clothes *(pl)*; *(de cama)* bed linen.

roupão [xo'pãw] *(pl -ões* [-õjʃ]) *m* dressing gown *(Brit)*, bathrobe *(Am)*.

rouxinol [xoʃi'nɔw] *(pl -óis* [-ɔjʃ]) *m* nightingale.

roxo, -xa ['xoʃu, -ʃa] *adj* violet.

rua ['xua] *f* street ◆ *interj* get out!; **~ abaixo/acima** down/up the street.

rubéola [xu'bɛula] *f* German measles *(sg)*.

rubi [xu'bi] *m* ruby.

rubor [xu'bo(x)] *(pl -res* [-riʃ]) *m* blush.

ruborizar-se [xubori'zaxsi] *vp* to blush, to go red.

rubrica [xu'brika] *f* signature.

ruço, -ça ['xusu, -sa] *adj (grisalho)* grey.

rúcola ['xukola] *f* rocket.

rude ['xudʒi] *adj* coarse.

ruela ['xwɛla] *f* back street.

ruga ['xuga] *f (em pele)* wrinkle; *(em tecido)* crease.

rúgbi ['xugbi] *m (Br)* rugby.

rugido [xu'ʒidu] *m* roar.

rugir [xu'ʒi(x)] *vi* to roar.

ruído ['xwidu] *m* noise.

ruim ['xuĩ] *(pl -ns* [-ʃ]) *adj* bad.

ruínas ['xwinaʃ] *fpl* ruins.

ruins → ruim.

ruivo, -va ['xuivu, -va] *adj (cabelo)* red ◆ *m, f* redhead.

rum ['xũ] *m* rum.

rumar [xu'ma(x)] : **rumar a** *v + prep* to steer towards.

rumba ['xũmba] *f* rumba.

rumo ['xumu] *m* direction.

rumor [xu'mo(x)] (*pl* **-res** [-riʃ]) *m* rumour.

ruptura [xup'tura] *f (de relação, contrato)* breaking-off; *(de ligamento)* rupture.

rural [xu'raw] (*pl* **-ais** [-ajʃ]) *adj* rural.

rush ['xaʃ] *m (Br)* rush hour.

Rússia ['xusja] *f:* **a ~** Russia.

russo, -a ['xusu, -sa] *adj & m, f* Russian ◆ *m (língua)* Russian.

rústico, -ca ['xuʃtʃiku, -ka] *adj* rustic.

S

S.A. *(abrev de Sociedade Anônima)* = plc *(Brit)*, = Ltd *(Brit)*, = Inc *(Am)*.

sábado ['sabadu] *m* Saturday, → **sexta-feira**.

sabão [sa'bãw] *(pl* **-ões** [-õjʃ]) *m* soap; **~ em pó** soap powder; **levar um ~** *(fam)* to be told off; **passar um ~ em alguém** *(fam)* to tell sb off.

sabedoria [sabedo'ria] *f* wisdom.

saber [sa'be(x)] *vt* to know ◆ *vi (Port: ter sabor)* to taste ◆ *m* knowledge; **ele não sabe nada sobre computadores** he doesn't know a thing about computers; **não quero ~!** I don't want to know!; **~ fazer algo** to know how to do sthg; **sei falar inglês** I can speak English; **fazer ~ que** to make it known (that); **sem ~** unwittingly, unknowingly; **~ de** to know about; **vir** OR **ficar a ~ de algo** to find out about sthg.

sabiá [sa'bja] *f* thrush.

sabões → **sabão**.

sabonete [sabo'netʃi] *m* (bar of) soap.

saboneteira [sabone'tejra] *f* soap dish.

sabor [sa'bo(x)] *(pl* **-res** [-riʃ]) *m* *(gosto)* taste; *(aroma)* flavour.

saborear [sabo'rja(x)] *vt* (*provar*) to taste; *(comer devagar)* to savour; *(fig: sol, férias, descanso)* to enjoy.

sabores → **sabor**.

sabotagem [sabo'taʒẽ] *(pl* **-ns** [-ʃ]) *f* sabotage.

sabotar [sabo'ta(x)] *vt* to sabotage.

sabugueiro [sabu'gejru] *m* elder.

saca ['saka] *f* bag.

sacar [sa'ka(x)] *vt (Br: fam: compreender)* to understand.

sacarina [saka'rina] *f* saccharin.

saca-rolhas [‚saka'xoʎaʃ] *m inv* corkscrew.

sacarose [saka'rɔzi] *f* sucrose.

sacerdote [sasex'dɔtʃi] *m* priest.

sacho ['saʃu] *m* hoe.

saciar [sa'sja(x)] *vt (fome)* to satisfy; *(sede)* to quench.

❏ **saciar-se** *vp* to be satisfied.

saco ['saku] *m (pequeno)* bag; *(grande)* sack; **~ de água quente** hot-water bottle; **~ de dormir** sleeping bag; **~ de lixo** bin bag *(Brit)*, garbage bag *(Am)*; **~ de plástico** plastic bag; **~ de viagem** travel bag; **eu não tenho ~ de ir lá** *(fam)* I can't be bothered to go; **puxar o ~ de alguém** *(fam)* to suck up to somebody; **ser um ~** *(fam)* to be a pain.

saco-cama [‚saku'kama] *(pl* **sacos-cama** [‚sakuʃ'kama]) *m* sleeping bag.

sacola [sa'kɔla] *f* bag.

sacramento [sakra'mẽtu] *m* sacrament.

❏ **sacramentos** *mpl* last rites.

sacrificar [sakrifi'ka(x)] *vt* to sacrifice.

❏ **sacrificar-se** *vp:* **~-se por alguém** to make sacrifices for sb.

sacrilégio [sakri'lɛʒju] *m* sacrilege.

sacristia [sakriʃ'tʃia] *f* sacristy.

sacro, -cra ['sakru, -kra] *adj* sacred.

sacudir [saku'dʒi(x)] *vt* to shake.

sádico, -ca ['sadʒiku, -ka] *adj* sadistic ◆ *m, f* sadist.

sadio, -dia [sa'dʒiu, -'dia] *adj* healthy.

saem ['sajẽ] → **sair**.

safio [sa'fiu] *m (small)* conger eel.

safira [sa'fira] *f* sapphire.

Sagitário [saʒi'tarju] *m* Sagittarius.

sagrado, -da [sa'gradu, -da] *adj* holy, sacred.

saguão [sa'gwãw] *(pl* **-ões** [-õjʃ]) *m* courtyard.

saí ['saj] → **sair**.

saí [sa'i] → **sair**.

saia ['saja] *f* skirt.

saia-calça [ˌsajaˈkawsa] (*pl* **saias-calça** [ˌsajaʃˈkawsa]) *f* culottes (*pl*).

saída [saˈida] *f* exit, way out; *(de ônibus, trem)* departure; *(de problema, situação)* way out; **"~ de emergência"** "emergency exit"; **dar uma ~** to pop out; **estar de ~** to be on one's way out; **ter ~** *(produto)* to sell well.

saio [ˈsaju] → **sair**.

sair [saˈi(x)] *vi* to go/come out; *(partir)* to go, to leave; *(separar-se)* to come off; *(ser publicado)* to come out; **sai daí!** come out of there!; **~ a** *(custar)* to work out as.

❏ **sair-se** *vp*: **~-se bem/mal** to come off well/badly.

sais → **sal**.

saiu [saˈiu] → **sair**.

sal [ˈsaw] (*pl* **sais** [ˈsajʃ]) *m* salt; **sem ~** unsalted; **~ comum** OU **marinho** sea salt; **~ refinado** table salt; **sais de banho** bath salts; **sais de cheiro** smelling salts; **sais de fruta** liver salts.

sala [ˈsala] *f* room; **~ de aula** classroom; **~ de espera** waiting room; **~ (de estar)** living OU sitting room; **~ de jantar** dining room; **~ de jogos** amusement arcade.

salada [saˈlada] *f* salad; **~ de alface** green salad *(of lettuce only)*; **~ de feijão frade** black-eye bean salad with onion, parsley, garlic and egg; **~ de frutas** fruit salad; **~ mista** mixed salad; **~ russa** Russian salad; **~ de tomate** tomato salad.

saladeira [salaˈdejra] *f* salad bowl.

salamandra [salaˈmãndra] *f* salamander.

salame [saˈlami] *m* salami.

salão [saˈlãw] (*pl* **-ões** [- õjʃ]) *m* hall; *(exposição coletiva)* exhibition; **~ de beleza** beauty salon; **~ de chá** tea room; **~ de festas** reception room.

salário [saˈlarju] *m* salary; **~ mínimo** minimum wage.

salário-família [saˌlarjufaˈmilja] (*pl* **salários-família** [saˌlarjuʃfaˈmilja]) *m* (*Br*) family allowance.

saldar [sawˈda(x)] *vt* (*conta*) to settle; *(dívida)* to pay off; *(mercadorias)* to sell off at a reduced price.

saldo [ˈsawdu] *m* (*de conta bancária*) balance; **em ~** (*Port: mercadorias*) on sale.

salgadinhos [sawgaˈdʒiɲuʃ] *mpl* savoury snacks.

salgado, -da [sawˈgadu, -da] *adj* (*comida*) salty; (*bacalhau, água*) salt (*antes de s*).

salgueiro [sawˈgejru] *m* willow.

salientar [saljẽnˈta(x)] *vt* to point out.

❏ **salientar-se** *vp* (*evidenciar-se*) to excel o.s.

saliente [saˈljẽntʃi] *adj* protruding.

saliva [saˈliva] *f* saliva.

salmão [sawˈmãw] *m* salmon; **~ defumado** smoked salmon.

salmonela [sawmoˈnɛla] *f* salmonella.

salmonete [sawmoˈnetʃi] *m* red mullet.

salmoura [sawˈmora] *f* brine.

salões → **salão**.

salpicão [sawpiˈkãw] (*pl* **-ões** [-õjʃ]) *m* (*enchido*) paprika salami; (*prato*) chicken and smoked ham salad with carrot, peppers and onion.

salpicar [sawpiˈka(x)] *vt* to sprinkle; (*sujar com pingos*) to splash, to spatter.

salpicões → **salpicão**.

salsa [ˈsawsa] *f* parsley.

salsicha [sawˈsiʃa] *f* sausage.

saltar [sawˈta(x)] *vi* (*dar saltos*) to jump; (*ir pelo ar*) to fly off; **~ à vista** OU **aos olhos** to be as plain as day.

salteado, -da [sawˈteadu, -da] *adj* (*entremeado*) alternating.

salto [ˈsawtu] *m* jump; (*de calçado*) heel; **de ~ alto** high-heeled; **~ em altura** high jump; **~ baixo** OU **raso** (*de calçado*) flat OU low heel; **~ em comprimento** long jump; **~ mortal** somersault; **~ à vara** (*Port*) pole vault.

salutar [saluˈta(x)] (*pl* **-res** [-riʃ]) *adj* healthy.

salva [ˈsawva] *f* (*planta*) sage; (*bandeja*) salver; **~ de palmas** round of applause.

salvação [sawvaˈsãw] *f* salvation; (*remédio*) cure; **não haver ~** to be beyond repair.

salvaguardar [ˌsawvagwaxˈda(x)] *vt* to safeguard.

salvamento [sawvaˈmẽntu] *m* rescue.

salvar [sawˈva(x)] *vt* to save; **~ as aparências** to keep up appearances.

❏ **salvar-se** *vp* to escape.

salva-vidas [ˌsawvaˈvidaʃ] *m inv* lifeboat.

salvo, -va [ˈsawvu, -va] *pp* → **salvar** ♦ *adj* safe ♦ *prep* except; **estar a ~** to be safe; **pôr-se a ~** to escape; **~ erro**

unless I'm mistaken; **~ se** unless.

samba ['sãmba] *m* samba.

samba-canção [‚sãmbakã'sãw] *(pl* **sambas-canções** [‚sãmbaʃkã'sõiʃ]) *m* slower style of samba with romantic lyrics; *(Br: fam: cueca)* boxer shorts *(pl).*

sambar [sãm'ba(x)] *vi* to dance to samba.

sambista [sãm'biʃta] *mf (dançarino)* samba dancer.

sambódromo [sãm'bɔdromu] *m* place where samba is rehearsed and danced.

sanatório [sana'tɔrju] *m* sanatorium.

sanção [sã'sãw] *(pl* **-ões** [-õjʃ]) *f* sanction.

sandálias [sãn'daljaʃ] *fpl* sandals.

sandes ['sãndeʃ] *f inv (Port)* = **san-duíche**.

sanduíche [sãn'dwiʃi] *m (Br)* sandwich; **~ misto** ham and cheese sandwich ♦ *f (Port)* sandwich.

sanfona [sã'fona] *f (Br: acordeão)* accordion.

sangrar [sãŋ'gra(x)] *vi* to bleed.

sangria [sãŋ'gria] *f* sangria.

sangue ['sãŋgi] *m* blood; **exame de ~** blood test.

sangue-frio [‚sãŋgi'friu] *m (presença de espírito)* presence of mind.

sanguessuga [sãŋge'suga] *f* leech.

sanguíneo [sãŋ'g(w)inju] *adj m →* **vaso.**

sanidade [sani'dadʒi] *f (mental)* sanity.

sanita [sa'nita] *f (Port)* toilet bowl.

sanitários [sani'tarjuʃ] *mpl* toilets.

Santo, -ta ['sãntu, -ta] *m, f* Saint; **o ~ Padre** the Holy Father.

santuário [sãn'twarju] *m* sanctuary, shrine.

são¹ [sãw] → **ser.**

são², sã ['sãw, 'sã] *adj (saudável)* healthy; *(fruto)* unblemished; **~ e salvo** safe and sound.

São [sãw] *m* = **Santo.**

São Paulo [sãw'pawlu] *s* São Paulo.

sapataria [sapata'ria] *f* shoe shop.

sapateado [sapa'tʒjadu] *m* tap dancing.

sapateiro, -ra [sapa'tejru, -ra] *m, f* cobbler.

sapatilhas [sapa'tʃiʎaʃ] *fpl (Port: de tênis, etc)* trainers *(Brit)*, sneakers *(Am)*; *(Br: de bailarinos)* ballet shoes.

sapato [sa'patu] *m* shoe; **~s de salto**

alto high-heeled shoes.

sapé [sa'pɛ] *m (Br)* type of Brazilian grass commonly used for thatching huts.

sapo ['sapu] *m* toad.

saquinho [sa'kiɲu] *m*: **~ de chá** tea bag.

sarampo [sa'rãmpu] *m* measles *(sg).*

sarapatel [sarapa'tɛw] *(pl* **-éis** [-ɛiʃ]) *m* pork stew with liver and kidneys, toma-toes, nuts, apple and raisins.

sarar [sa'ra(x)] *vi & vt (cicatrizar)* to heal.

sarcasmo [sax'kaʒmu] *m* sarcasm.

sarda ['saxda] *f* freckle.

sardinha [sax'dʒiɲa] *f (peixe)* sardine; **~s assadas** grilled sardines.

sargento [sax'ʒẽntu] *m* sergeant.

sarjeta [sax'ʒeta] *f* gutter.

SARL *(Port: abrev de Sociedade Anónima de Responsabilidade Limitada)* **~** plc, **=** Ltd *(Brit),* **~** Inc *(Am).*

sarro ['saxu] *m (em vinho)* sediment; *(em dentes)* tartar.

satélite [sa'tɛlitʃi] *m* satellite.

sátira ['satʃira] *f* satire.

satisfação [satʃiʃfa'sãw] *(pl* **-ões** [-õjʃ]) *f* satisfaction; **não ter que dar satisfações a ninguém** not to have to answer to anyone; **pedir satisfações a alguém** to demand an explanation from sb.

satisfatório, -ria [satʃiʃfa'tɔrju, -rja] *adj* satisfactory.

satisfazer [satʃiʃfa'ze(x)] *vt (agradar a)* to satisfy; *(cumprir)* to meet ♦ *vi (ser suficiente)* to be satisfactory.

❏ **satisfazer-se** *vp*: **~-se com** to content o.s. with.

satisfeito, -ta [satʃiʃ'fejtu, -ta] *adj* satisfied; **dar-se por ~ (com)** to be sat-isfied (with).

saudação [sawda'sãw] *(pl* **-ões** [-õjʃ]) *f* greeting.

saudade [saw'dadʒi] *f* nostalgia; **ter ~s de** to miss; **ela deixou muitas ~s** everyone misses her; **matar ~s** *(de lugar)* to revisit old haunts; *(de pessoa)* to look up old friends; **sinto muitas ~s de Bahia** I miss Bahia so much.

saudar [saw'da(x)] *vt* to greet.

saudável [saw'davew] *(pl* **-eis** [-ejʃ]) *adj* healthy.

saúde [sa'udʒi] *f* health ♦ *interj* cheers!

sauna ['sawna] *f* sauna.

saveiro [sa'vejru] *m* narrow, flat-

*bottomed fishing boat with the prow high-
er than the stern.*

saxofone [saksoˈfɔni] *m* saxophone.

scanner [ˈskanɛ(x)] (*pl* **-res** [-riʃ]) *m*
scanner.

scooter [ˈskutɛ(x)] (*pl* **-res** [-riʃ]) *f*
scooter.

se [si] *pron* **1.** *(reflexo: pessoa)* himself
(*f* herself), themselves (*pl*); *(você, vocês)*
yourself, yourselves (*pl*); *(impessoal)*
oneself; **lavar~** to wash (oneself);
eles ~ perderam they got lost; **vocês ~
perderam** you got lost. **2.** *(reflexo: coisa, animal)* itself, themselves (*pl*); **o vidro partiu-~** the glass
broke. **3.** *(recíproco)* each other; **escrevem-~
regularmente** they write to each other
regularly; **não ~ cruzam** *(fam)* they
can't stand each other. **4.** *(com sujeito indeterminado):* **"aluga-~
quarto"** "room for rent"; **"vende-~"**
"for sale"; **come-~ bem aqui** the food
is very good here.
♦ *conj* **1.** *(indica condição)* if; **~ tiver
tempo, escrevo** I'll write if I have time.
2. *(indica causa)* if; **~ você está com
fome, come alguma coisa** if you're
hungry, have something to eat. **3.** *(indica comparação)* if; **~ um é feio, o
outro ainda é pior** if you think he's
ugly, you should see the other one. **4.** *(em interrogativas):* **que tal ~ fôssemos ao cinema?** how about going to
the cinema?; **e ~ ela não vier?** what if
she doesn't come? **5.** *(exprime desejo)* if; **~ pelo menos
tivesse dinheiro!** if only I had the
money! **6.** *(em interrogativa indireta)* if,
whether; **avisem-me ~ quiserem ir**
let me know if you'd like to go;
perguntei-lhe ~ gostou I asked him if
he liked it. **7.** *(em locuções):* **~ bem que** even
though, although.

sé [ˈsɛ] *f* cathedral; **~ catedral** cathedral.

sebe [ˈsebi] *f* fence; **~ viva** hedge.

sebento, -ta [seˈbẽntu, -ta] *adj*
grimy.

sebo [ˈsebu] *m* suet.

seca [ˈseka] *f* drought.

secador [sekaˈdo(x)] (*pl* **-res** [-riʃ]) *m*
hairdryer.

seção [seˈsãw] (*pl* **-ões** [-õjʃ]) *f* *(Br)*

department; **~ de achados e perdidos**
lost property office *(Brit)*, lost-and-
found office *(Am)*.

secar [seˈka(x)] *vt* to dry ♦ *vi (planta,
árvore)* to wither; *(rio, poço, lago)* to dry
up; *(roupa, cabelo)* to dry.

secção [sɛkˈsãw] (*pl* **-ões** [-õjʃ]) *f (Port)*
= **seção**.

seco, -ca [ˈseku, -ka] *pp* → **secar** ♦ *adj*
dry; *(carne, peixe, fruto)* dried; *(fig: ríspido)* curt.

secretaria [sekretaˈria] *f (de escola,
repartição pública)* secretary's office; **~
de Estado** government department.

secretária [sekreˈtarja] *f (móvel)*
desk; **~ eletrônica** *(Br)* answering
machine, → **secretário**.

secretário, -ria [sekreˈtarju, -rja] *m,
f* secretary; **Secretário de Estado**
Secretary of State.

secreto, -ta [seˈkretu, -ta] *adj* secret.

sectário, -ria [sɛkˈtarju, -rja] *adj* sec-
tarian.

sector [sɛˈtor] (*pl* **-res** [-riʃ]) *m (Port)* =
setor.

secular [sekuˈla(x)] (*pl* **-res** [-riʃ]) *adj*
ancient.

século [ˈsekulu] *m* century.

secundário, -ria [sekũnˈdarju, -rja]
adj secondary; *(estrada)* minor.

seda [ˈseda] *f* silk.

sedativo [sedaˈtivu] *m* sedative.

sede¹ [ˈsedʒi] *f (de empresa, organização)* headquarters (*pl*).

sede² [ˈsedʒi] *f* thirst; **ter ~** to be
thirsty; **ter ~ de** to thirst after; **matar
a ~** to quench one's thirst.

sedimento [sedʒiˈmẽntu] *m* sediment.

sedoso, -osa [seˈdozu, -ɔza] *adj* silky.

sedução [seduˈsãw] (*pl* **-ões** [-õjʃ]) *f*
seduction.

sedutor, -ra [seduˈto(x), -ra] (*mpl* **-res**
[-riʃ], *fpl* **-s** [-ʃ]) *adj* seductive.

seduzir [seduˈzi(x)] *vt* to seduce.

segmento [segˈmẽntu] *m* segment.

segredo [seˈgredu] *m* secret; *(reserva)*
secrecy.

segregar [segreˈga(x)] *vt (pôr de lado)*
to segregate; *(secreção)* to secrete.

❏ **segregar-se** *vp (isolar-se)* to cut o.s.
off.

seguida [seˈgida] *f*: **em ou de ~**
immediately.

seguidamente [seˌgidaˈmẽntʃi] *adv*
(sem interrupção) continuously; *(de*

seguida) straight afterwards.

seguido, -da [se'gidu, -da] *adj (contínuo)* continuous; **o manual ~ este ano é ...** the textbook we're using this year is ...; **dias/anos ~s** days/years on end; **~ de** followed by.

seguinte [se'gĩntʃi] *adj* following ♦ *mf:* **o/a ~** the next one; **o dia/mês ~** the following day/ month.

seguir [se'gi(x)] *vt* to follow; *(perseguir)* to chase; *(carreira, profissão)* to pursue ♦ *vi (continuar)* to go on, to carry on; **~ com algo** to continue with sthg; **~ para** to travel on to; **~ por** to travel on ou along; **a ~** afterwards; **a ~ a** after.

segunda [se'gũnda] *f (de veículo)* second (gear), → **segundo**.

segunda-feira [se,gũnda'fejra] *(pl* **segundas-feiras** [se,gũndaʃ'fejraʃ]*) f* Monday, → **sexta-feira**.

segundo, -da [se'gũndu, -da] *num &* *m* second ♦ *prep* according to ♦ *adv* secondly; **em segunda mão** second-hand, → **sexto**.

seguramente [se,gura'mẽntʃi] *adv* surely.

segurança [segu'rãsa] *f* security; *(sem perigo)* safety; *(confiança)* confidence; *(certeza)* certainty; **a Segurança Social** Social Security; **com ~** *(agir, afirmar)* confidently; **em ~** in safety.

segurar [segu'ra(x)] *vt (agarrar)* to hold on to.

seguro, -ra [se'guru, -ra] *adj* safe; *(firme, preso)* secure; *(mesa, cadeira)* steady; *(garantido)* guaranteed ♦ *m (de carro, casa, vida)* insurance; **estar ~** *(estar a salvo)* to be safe; *(ter certeza)* to be certain ou sure; **pôr no ~** to insure; **ser ~ de si** to be self-assured; **~ de doença** *(Port)* health insurance; **~ de responsabilidade civil** third-party insurance; **~ contra terceiros** third-party insurance; **~ contra todos os riscos** fully comprehensive insurance; **~ de viagem** travel insurance; **~ de vida** life insurance.

seguro-saúde [se,guɾusa'udʒi] *(pl* **seguros-saúde** [se,guɾuʃsa'udʒi]*) m (Br)* health insurance.

sei ['sej] → **saber**.

seio ['saju] *m* breast.

seis ['sejʃ] *adj num* six ♦ *m* six; *(dia)* sixth ♦ *mpl (temperatura)* six (degrees) ♦ *fpl:* **às ~** at six (o'clock); **(são) ~** horas (it's) six o'clock; **ele tem ~ anos** he's six years old; **eles eram ~** there were six of them; **~ de janeiro** the sixth of January; **página ~** page six; **trinta e ~** thirty-six; **o ~ de copas** the six of hearts; **estão ~ graus centígrados** it's six degrees centigrade; **de ~ em ~ semanas/horas** every six weeks/hours; **empataram ~ a ~** *(em partida)* they drew six-all; **~ a zero** *(em partida)* six-nil.

seiscentos, -tas [sejʃ'sẽntuʃ, -taʃ] *num* six hundred, → **seis**.

seita ['sejta] *f* sect.

seiva ['sejva] *f* sap.

seixo ['sejʃu] *m* pebble.

sela ['sɛla] *f* saddle.

selar [se'la(x)] *vt (cavalo, égua)* to saddle; *(carta, subscrito)* to stamp; *(documento oficial, pacto)* to seal.

seleção [sele'sãw] *f (Br) (escolha)* selection; *(equipe nacional)* team.

selecção [sɛlɛ'sãw] *f (Port)* = **seleção**.

seleccionar [sɛlɛsju'nar] *vt (Port)* = **selecionar**.

selecionar [selesjo'na(x)] *vt (Br)* to select.

selecto, -ta [sɛ'lɛtu, -ta] *adj (Port)* = **seleto**.

seleto, -ta [se'lɛtu, -ta] *adj (Br)* exclusive.

self-service [sɛwf'sɛxvisi] *(pl* **self-services** [sɛwf'sɛxviseʃ]*) m* self-service cafe or restaurant.

selim [se'lĩ] *(pl* **-ns** [-ʃ]*) m (de bicicleta)* saddle.

selo ['sɛlu] *m* stamp; **~ de garantia** *(em produto)* tamper-proof seal.

selva ['sɛwva] *f* jungle.

selvagem [sɛw'vaʒẽ] *(pl* **-ns** [-ʃ]*) adj* wild ♦ *mf (pessoa)* savage.

sem [sẽ] *prep* without; **estou ~ fazer nada há muito tempo** I haven't done anything for ages; **ele saiu ~ que eu notasse** he left without me noticing; **estar ~ água/gasolina** to be out of water/petrol; **~ mais nem menos** for no reason whatsoever; **~ data** undated.

sem-abrigo [sẽa'brigu] *mf inv* homeless person; **os ~** the homeless.

semáforos [se'mafɔɾuʃ] *mpl* traffic lights.

semana [se'mana] *f* week; **~ a ~** week by week; **por ~** ou per week; **a Semana Santa** Holy Week.

semanada [sema'nada] *f* pocket money.

semanal [sema'naw] (*pl* -ais [-ajʃ]) *adj* weekly.

semblante [sẽm'blãntʃi] *m* face.

semear [se'mja(x)] *vt (trigo, batatas, etc)* to sow; *(ódio, discórdia)* to spread.

semelhança [seme'ʎãsa] *f* resemblance; **à ~ de** like.

semelhante [seme'ʎãntʃi] *adj* similar; **~ a** like, similar to.

sémen ['sɛmen] *m (Port)* = **sêmen**.

sêmen ['semen] *m (Br)* semen.

semente [se'mẽntʃi] *f* seed.

semestral [semeʃ'traw] (*pl* -ais [-ajʃ]) *adj* half-yearly, six-monthly.

semestre [se'mɛʃtri] *m* period of six months.

seminário [semi'narju] *m (grupo de estudos)* seminar; *(para eclesiásticos)* seminary.

sêmola ['semola] *f* semolina.

semolina [semo'lina] *f* semolina.

sempre ['sẽmpri] *adv* always; **o mesmo de ~** the usual; **como ~** as usual; **para ~** forever; **~ que** whenever.

sem-vergonha [sãjvex'goɲa] *mf inv* rogue.

sena ['sena] *f in cards, the sixth of any suit.*

senado [se'nadu] *m* senate.

senão [se'nãw] *conj* otherwise.

senha ['seɲa] *f (sinal)* sign; *(palavra de acesso)* password; **~ de saída** ticket given at a venue to allow you to come and go without paying the entrance fee again.

senhor, -ra [se'ɲo(x), -ra] (*mpl* -res [-riʃ], *fpl* -s [-ʃ]) *m, f (em geral)* man *(f* woman); *(formalmente)* gentleman *(f* lady); *(antes de nome)* Mr *(f* Mrs, Ms); *(ao dirigir a palavra)* Sir *(f* Madam); **"senhoras"** "ladies"; **Caro** OU **Exmo. Senhor** *(em carta)* Dear Sir; **Cara** OU **Exma. Senhora** *(em carta)* Dear Madam; **bom dia meus senhores/minhas senhoras!** good morning (gentlemen/ladies)!

senhorio, -ria [seɲo'riu, -ria] *m, f* landlord *(f* landlady).

senil [se'niw] (*pl* -is [-iʃ]) *adj* senile.

sensação [sẽsa'sãw] (*pl* -ões [-õjʃ]) *f* sensation, feeling; *(intuição)* feeling; **causar ~** to cause a sensation.

sensacional [sẽsasjo'naw] (*pl* -ais [-ajʃ]) *adj* sensational.

sensações → sensação.

sensato, -ta [sẽ'satu, -ta] *adj* sensible.

sensível [sẽ'sivew] (*pl* -eis [-ejʃ]) *adj* sensitive.

senso ['sẽsu] *m* sense; **ter bom ~** to be sensible; **ter ~ prático** to be practical; **~ comum** common sense.

sensual [sẽ'swaw] (*pl* -ais [-ajʃ]) *adj* sensual.

sentado, -da [sẽn'tadu, -da] *adj* seated; **estar ~** to be sitting down.

sentar-se [sẽn'taxsi] *vp* to sit down.

sentença [sẽn'tesa] *f* sentence.

sentido, -da [sẽn'tʃidu, -da] *adj (melindrado)* touchy ◆ *m* sense; *(significado)* meaning; *(direção)* direction; **fazer ~** to make sense; **em certo ~** to a certain extent; **ir em ~ proibido** *(Port)* to go the wrong way up a one-way street; **(rua de) ~ único** one-way street.

sentimental [sẽntʃimẽn'taw] (*pl* -ais [-ajʃ]) *adj* sentimental.

sentimento [sẽntʃi'mẽntu] *m* feeling; **os meus ~s** my deepest sympathy.

sentinela [sẽntʃi'nela] *mf* guard; **estar de ~** to be on guard duty.

sentir [sẽn'tʃi(x)] *vt* to feel; **sinto muito!** I'm terribly sorry!; **~ falta de** to miss; **~ vontade de fazer algo** to feel like doing sthg.

◻ **sentir-se** *vp* to feel.

separação [separa'sãw] (*pl* -ões [-õjʃ]) *f* separation.

separado, -da [sepa'radu, -da] *adj (independente)* separate; *(cônjuges)* separated; **em ~** separately.

separar [sepa'ra(x)] *vt (dividir)* to separate; *(reservar)* to put aside.

◻ **separar-se** *vt* to separate.

septuagésimo, -ma [sɛptwa-'ʒɛzimu, -ma] *num* seventieth, → **sexto**.

sepultar [sepuw'ta(x)] *vt* to bury.

sepultura [sepuw'tura] *f* grave.

sequência [se'kwẽsja] *f (Port)* = **seqüência**.

seqüência [se'kwẽsja] *f (Br)* sequence.

sequer [se'kɛ(x)] *adv*: **nem ~** not even; **ele nem ~ falou comigo** he didn't even speak to me.

seqüestrador, -ra [sekweʃtra'do(x). -ra] (*mpl* -res [-riʃ], *fpl* -s [-ʃ]) *m, f* kidnapper.

sequestrar [sekeʃ'trar] *vt (Port)* = **seqüestrar**.

seqüestrar [sekweʃ'tra(x)] *vt (Br)* to kidnap, to abduct.

seqüestro [se'kwɛʃtru] *m* kidnapping, abduction.

sequóia [se'kwɔja] *f* sequoia.

ser [se(x)] *(pl -res* [-riʃ]) *m (criatura)* being; **~ humano** human being.

♦ *vi* 1. *(para descrever)* to be; **é demasiado longo** it's too long; **são bonitos** they're lovely; **sou médico** I'm a doctor.

2. *(para designar lugar, origem)* to be; **ele é do Brasil** he's from Brazil; **é em São Paulo** it's in São Paulo; **sou brasileira** I'm Brazilian.

3. *(custar)* to be; **quanto é? – são 100 reais** how much is it? – (it's) 100 reals.

4. *(com data, dia, hora)* to be; **hoje é sexta** it's Friday today; **que horas são?** what time is it?; **são seis horas** it's six o'clock.

5. *(exprime possessão)* to be; **é do Ricardo** it's Ricardo's; **este carro é seu?** is this car yours?; **os livros eram meus** the books were mine.

6. *(em locuções)*: **a não ~ que** unless; **que foi?** what's wrong?; **ou seja** in other words; **será que ele vem?** do you think he's coming?

♦ *v aux (forma a voz passiva)* to be; **foi visto na saída do cinema** he was seen on his way out of the cinema.

♦ *v impess* 1. *(exprime tempo)* to be; **é de dia/noite** it's daytime/ night; **é tarde/cedo** it's late/early.

2. *(com adjetivo)* to be; **é difícil dizer** it's difficult to say; **é fácil de ver** it's easy to see.

⌐ **ser de** *v + prep (matéria)* to be made of; *(ser adepto de)* to be a supporter of; **eles são do Flamengo** they're Flamengo supporters.

serão [se'rãw] *(pl -ões* [-õjʃ]) *m (reunião)* get-together; *(noite)* evening; **fazer ~** to stay up late.

sereia [se'reja] *f (de navio, farol)* siren; *(ser lendário)* mermaid.

serenar [sere'na(x)] *vt (acalmar)* to calm ♦ *vi (acalmar-se)* to calm down; *(tempo)* to clear up.

serenata [sere'nata] *f* serenade.

seres → ser.

seresta [se'rɛʃta] *f (Br)* = serenata.

seriado [se'rjadu] *m (Br) (TV)* series *(sg)*.

série ['sɛrji] *f* series *(sg)*; *(de bilhetes de metro)* book; **uma ~ de** a series of.

seriedade [serje'dadʒi] *f* seriousness; *(honestidade)* honesty.

seringa [se'rĩŋga] *f* syringe.

seringueira [serĩ'gejra] *f* rubber plant.

sério, -ria ['sɛrju, -rja] *adj* serious; *(honrado)* honest ♦ *adv*: **a ~?** seriously?; **levar** OU **tomar a ~** to take seriously.

sermão [sex'mãw] *(pl -ões* [-õjʃ]) *m* sermon.

serões → serão.

seronegativo, -va [seronega'tivu, -va] *adj (Port)* = **soronegativo.**

seropositivo, -va [seropuzi'tivu, -va] *adj (Port)* = **soropositivo.**

serpente [sex'pẽntʃi] *f* serpent.

serpentina [serpẽn'tʃina] *f* streamer.

serra ['sɛxa] *f (instrumento)* saw; *(em geografia)* mountain range.

serralheiro [sexa'ʎejru] *m* locksmith.

serrar [se'xa(x)] *vt* to saw.

sertanejo, -ja [sexta'neʒu, -ʒa] *adj* of/relating to the "sertão".

sertão [sex'tãw] *m remote, arid lands in the interior of northeastern Brazil.*

servente [sex'vẽntʃi] *m (de pedreiro)* (bricklayer's) mate.

serventia [sexvẽn'tʃia] *f (préstimo)* use; *(de casa, edifício, terreno)* access road OU path.

serviço [sex'visu] *m* service; *(trabalho)* work; **"fora de ~"** "out of service"; **"~ incluído"** "service included"; **~ cívico** social service.

servil [sex'viw] *(pl -is* [-iʃ]) *adj* servile.

servir [sex'vi(x)] *vt* to serve ♦ *vi (criado, empregado)* to serve; *(ser útil)* to be useful; *(roupa, calçado)* to fit; **em que posso servi-lo?** how may I help you?; **~ de algo** to serve as sthg.

⌐ **servir-se** *vp (de bebida, comida)* to help o.s.; **~-se de** *(fazer uso de)* to make use of.

servis → servil.

sessão [se'sãw] *(pl -ões* [-õjʃ]) *f (de filme)* showing; *(em televisão)* broadcast; *(de debate político, científico)* meeting; *(em tribunal)* session.

sessenta [se'sẽnta] *num* sixty, **→ seis.**

sessões → sessão.

sesta ['sɛʃta] *f* afternoon nap.

seta ['sɛta] *f* arrow.

sete ['sɛtʃi] *num* seven, → **seis**.

setecentos, -tas [sɛte'sẽntuʃ, -taʃ] *num* seven hundred, → **seis**.

setembro [se'tẽmbru] *m* September; **durante o mês de ~** during (the month of) September; **em ~** in September; **em meados de ~** in the middle of September, in mid-September; **este mês de ~** *(passado)* last September; *(futuro)* this (coming) September; **o passado/próximo mês de ~** last/next September; **no princípio/final de ~** at the beginning/end of September; **o primeiro de ~** the first of September.

setenta [se'tẽnta] *num* seventy, → **seis**.

sétimo, -ma ['sɛtʃimu, -ma] *num* seventh, → **sexto**.

setor [se'to(x)] *(pl* **-res** [-riʃ]) *m (Br) (ramo)* sector; *(seção)* section.

seu, sua ['sew, 'sua] *adj* **1.** *(dele)* his; *(dela)* her; *(de você, vocês)* your; *(deles, delas)* their; **ela trouxe o ~ carro** she brought her car; **onde estacionou a sua moto?** where did you park your motorbike?
2. *(de coisa, animal: singular)* its; *(de coisa, animal: plural)* their; **o cachorro foi para a o seu canil** the dog went into his OR its kennel.
♦ *pron:* **o ~/a sua** *(dele)* his; *(dela)* hers; *(deles, delas)* theirs; *(de coisa, animal: singular)* its; *(de coisa, animal: plural)* their; **um amigo ~** a friend of his/hers etc.; **os ~s** *(a família de cada um)* his/her etc. family.
♦ *m, f* **1.** *(pej: forma de tratamento)* you; **~ estúpido!** you idiot!; **~s irresponsáveis!** you fools!
2. *(com malícia)* you; **~ capeta!** you little rascal!; **sua danadinha!** you little so-and-so!

severidade [severi'dadʒi] *f* severity.

severo, -ra [se'vɛru, -ra] *adj (inflexível)* strict; *(grave)* severe.

sexagésimo, -ma [seksa'ʒɛzimu, -ma] *num* sixtieth, → **sexto**.

sexo ['sɛksu] *m* sex; *(órgão reprodutor)* genitals *(pl)*.

sexta-feira [sejʃta'fejra] *(pl* **sextas-feiras** [sejʃtaʃ'fejraʃ]) *f* Friday; **às sextas-feiras** on Fridays; **até ~** until Friday; **ela vem ~** she's coming on Friday; **esta ~** *(passada)* last Friday; *(próxima)* next Friday; **hoje é ~** today

is Friday; **todas as sextas-feiras** every Friday; **~ de manhã/à tarde/à noite** Friday morning/afternoon/night; **~ 12 de junho** Friday 12 June; **~ passada/próxima** last/next Friday; **~ que vem** next Friday; **Sexta-feira Santa** Good Friday.

sexto, -ta ['sejʃtu, -ta] *adj num* sixth
♦ *m (número)* sixth ♦ *m, f:* **o ~/a sexta** *(pessoa, coisa)* the sixth; **chegar em ~** to come sixth; **capítulo ~** chapter six; **em ~ lugar** in sixth place; **no ~ dia** on the sixth day; **a sexta parte** *(relativo a quantidade)* a sixth; *(de espetáculo, filme)* part six.

sexual [sek'swaw] *(pl* **-ais** [-ajʃ]) *adj* sexual.

sexualidade [sekswali'dadʒi] *f* sexuality.

sexy ['sɛksi] *adj* sexy.

shopping ['ʃɔpĩ] *m* shopping centre *(Brit)*, shopping mall *(Am)*.

short ['ʃɔxtʃi] *m (Br: calção)* shorts *(pl)*.

show ['ʃow] *m* show.

si ['si] *pron* **1.** *(complemento indireto: pessoa)* him *(f* her), them *(pl)*; *(você, vocês)* you; **ele disse que a chamada não era para ~** he said the call wasn't for him.
2. *(complemento indireto: coisa, animal)* it, them *(pl)*.
3. *(reflexo: pessoa)* himself *(f* herself), themselves *(pl)*; *(você, vocês)* yourself, yourselves *(pl)*; **comprou-o para ~ (mesmo OU próprio)** he bought it for himself; **é para ~ (mesmo OU próprio)?** is it for yourself?; **elas sabem tomar conta de ~ (mesmas OU próprias)** they know how to look after themselves; **ela é cheia de ~** *(fam)* she's full of herself.
4. *(reflexo: coisa, animal)* itself, themselves *(pl)*; **o livro, em ~, não é caro** the book itself is not expensive.
5. *(impessoal)* oneself; **é sinal de egoísmo só pensar em ~** it's a sign of selfishness to think only of oneself; **cada um por ~** each man for himself.

SIDA ['sida] *f (Port)* AIDS.

siderurgia [siderur'ʒia] *f* iron and steel industry.

sido ['sidu] → **ser**.

sidra ['sidra] *f* cider.

sífilis ['sifiliʃ] *f* syphilis.

sigilo [si'ʒilu] *m* secrecy.

sigla ['sigla] *f* acronym.
significado [signifi'kadu] *m* meaning.
significar [signifi'ka(x)] *vt* to mean.
significativo, -va [signifika'tʃivu, -va] *adj* significant.
signo ['signu] *m* sign.
sigo ['sigu] → **seguir**.
sílaba ['silaba] *f* syllable.
silenciar [silẽ'sja(x)] *vt* to silence.
silêncio [si'lẽsju] *m* silence ◆ *interj* silence!
silencioso, -osa [silẽ'sjozu, -ɔza] *adj* silent, quiet.
silhueta [si'ʎweta] *f* silhouette.
silicone [sili'kɔni] *m* silicone.
silva ['siwva] *f* bramble.
silvestre [siw'vɛʃtri] *adj* wild.
sim ['sĩ] *adv* yes; **penso que ~** I think so; **pelo ~ pelo não** just in case.
símbolo ['sĩmbolu] *m* symbol.
simetria [sime'tria] *f* symmetry.
similar [simi'la(x)] *(pl* -res [-riʃ]) *adj* similar.
simpatia [sĩmpa'tʃia] *f (carinho)* affection; *(cordialidade)* friendliness.
simpático, -ca [sĩm'patʃiku, -ka] *adj* nice; *(amigável)* friendly.
simpatizante [sĩmpatʃi'zãntʃi] *mf* sympathizer.
simpatizar [sĩmpatʃi'za(x)] : **simpatizar com** *v* + *prep* to like.
simples ['sĩmpleʃ] *adj inv* simple; *(bebida)* straight; *(bilhete de metrô)* single; **~ masculina/feminina** *(Br: em tênis)* men's/women's singles *(pl);* **queria um ~ copo de água** I just want a glass of water.
simplicidade [sĩmplisi'dadʒi] *f* simplicity.
simplificar [sĩmplifi'ka(x)] *vt* to simplify.
simular [simu'la(x)] *vt (fingir)* to feign; *(incêndio, ataque aéreo)* to simulate ◆ *vi (fingir)* to pretend.
simultaneamente [simuw,tanja-'mẽntʃi] *adv* simultaneously.
simultâneo, -nea [simuw'tanju, -nja] *adj* simultaneous; **em ~** *(programa de televisão, entrevista)* live.
sinagoga [sina'gɔga] *f* synagogue.
sinal [si'naw] *(pl* -ais [-ajʃ]) *m* sign; *(marca)* mark; *(em pele)* mole; *(de nascimento)* birthmark; *(dinheiro)* deposit; **estou aqui há uma hora e nem ~ dele** I've been here for an hour and there's been no sign of him; **dar ~ de si** to

show up; **dar sinais de cansaço** to show signs of fatigue; **em ~ de** as a mark OU sign of; **~ de alarme** alarm; **~ de interrompido** OU **de ocupado** engaged tone.
sinalização [sinaliza'sãw] *f* road signs *(pl).*
sinceridade [sĩseri'dadʒi] *f* sincerity.
sincero, -ra [sĩ'sɛru, -ra] *adj* sincere.
sindicato [sĩndʒi'katu] *m* trade union.
síndico ['sĩndʒiku] *m (Br) person chosen by other residents to organize the maintenance of an apartment block.*
síndrome ['sĩdromi] *f* syndrome.
sinfonia [sĩfo'nia] *f* symphony.
sinfônica [sĩ'fonika] *adj f* → **música**.
singelo, -la [sĩ'ʒɛlu, -la] *adj* simple.
single ['sĩgel] *m (Port)* single.
singular [sĩŋgu'la(x)] *(pl* -res [-riʃ]) *adj (único)* unique; *(extraordinário)* strange; *(GRAM)* singular ◆ *m (GRAM)* singular; **~es homens/mulheres** *(Port: em ténis)* men's/ women's singles.
sino ['sinu] *m* bell.
sinónimo [si'nɔnimu] *m (Port)* = **sinônimo.**
sinônimo [si'nonimu] *m (Br)* synonym.
sintaxe [sĩ'tasi] *f* syntax.
síntese ['sĩtezi] *f (resumo)* summary.
sintético, -ca [sĩ'tɛtʃiku, -ka] *adj (artificial)* synthetic; *(resumido)* concise.
sintoma [sĩ'toma] *m* symptom.
sintonizar [sĩntoni'za(x)] *vt (rádio)* to tune; *(estação de rádio)* to tune in to.
sinuca [si'nuka] *f (Br)* snooker.
sinuoso, -osa [si'nwozu, -ɔza] *adj (curva, caminho)* winding.
sirene [si'rɛni] *f* siren.
siri [si'ri] *m* crab.
sirvo ['sixvu] → **servir.**
sísmico [si'zmiku] *adj m* → **abalo.**
siso ['sizu] *m (common)* sense; **dente de ~** wisdom tooth.
sistema [siʃ'tema] *m* system; **~ métrico** metric system; **~ nervoso** nervous system; **Sistemas Digitais** *(disciplina)* computer studies; **por ~** systematically.
sistemático, -ca [siʃte'matʃiku, -ka] *adj* systematic.
sisudo, -da [si'zudu, -da] *adj* serious.
sítio ['sitʃju] *m (lugar)* place; *(espaço)* room, space; *(Br: chácara)* smallholding.

situação [sitwaˈsãw] (pl -ões [-õjʃ]) f (localização) position; (circunstâncias) situation; (estado, condição) condition.

situado, -da [siˈtwadu, -da] adj: **bem/mal** ~ well/badly situated; ~ **em** situated in; **está** ~ **ao norte de Brasília** it is situated to the north of Brasília.

situar [siˈtwa(x)] vt (colocar) to place; (localizar) to locate.
❏ **situar-se** vp (localizar-se) to be located.

s/l abrev = **sobreloja**.

slide [sˈlajdʒi] m slide.

slip [ˈslip] m (Port: cueca) underpants (pl).

slogan [ˈslogãn] m slogan.

smoking [ˈsmokĩŋ] m dinner jacket (Brit), tuxedo (Am).

snack-bar [snɛkˈba(x)] (pl **snack-bares** [snɛkˈbareʃ]) m snack bar.

snooker [ˈsnukɛr] m (Port) snooker.

só [ˈsɔ] adj (sem companhia) alone; (solitário) lonely ◆ adv (apenas) only; **é** ~ **pedir!** all you need to do is ask!; **um** ~ **minuto do teu tempo** just a minute of your time; **a** ~**s** alone; **não** ~ ... **como também** not only ... but also; ~ **que** only.

SO (abrev de Sudoeste) SW.

soalho [ˈswaʎu] m wooden floor.

soar [ˈswa(x)] vi & vt to sound; **soaram as 10 horas** the clock struck 10; ~ **bem** to sound right; ~ **mal** not to sound right.

sob [ˈsobi] prep under.

sobe [ˈsɔbi] → **subir**.

soberania [sobɛraˈnia] f sovereignty.

soberano, -na [sobeˈranu, -na] adj sovereign.

soberbo, -ba [suˈbexbu, -ba] adj (suntuoso) superb; (arrogante) arrogant.

sobrado [soˈbradu] m wooden floor.

sobrancelha [sobrãˈseʎa] f eyebrow.

sobrar [soˈbra(x)] vi to be left over.

sobre [ˈsobri] prep (em cima de) on (top of); (por cima de) over; (acerca de) about.

sobreaviso [sobreaˈvizu] m: **estar** OU **ficar de** ~ to be on the alert.

sobrecarga [sobreˈkaxga] f overload.

sobrecarregar [sobrekaxeˈga(x)] vt: ~ **alguém com algo** to overload sb with sthg.

sobreloja [sobreˈlɔʒa] f mezzanine.

sobremesa [sobreˈmeza] f dessert.

sobrenatural [ˌsobrenatuˈraw] (pl -ais [-ajʃ]) adj supernatural.

sobrenome [sobriˈnomi] m (Br) surname.

sobrepor [sobreˈpo(x)] vt: ~ **algo a algo** to put sthg on top of sthg.
❏ **sobrepor-se** vp (problema, trabalho) to take precedence.

sobrescrito [sobreʃˈkritu] m envelope.

sobressair [sobresaˈi(x)] vi to stand out.

sobressaltar [sobresawˈta(x)] vt to startle.
❏ **sobressaltar-se** vp to be startled.

sobressalto [sobreˈsawtu] m (susto) fright; (inquietação) anxiety.

sobretaxa [ˌsobreˈtaʃa] f surcharge.

sobretudo [sobreˈtudu] m overcoat ◆ adv especially, above all.

sobrevivência [sobreviˈvẽsja] f survival.

sobrevivente [sobreviˈvẽntʃi] mf survivor.

sobreviver [sobreviˈve(x)] vi to survive.

sobriedade [sobrieˈdadʒi] f sobriety.

sobrinho, -nha [soˈbriɲu, -ɲa] m, f nephew (f niece).

sóbrio, -bria [ˈsɔbriu, -bria] adj sober.

social [soˈsjaw] (pl -ais [-ajʃ]) adj social.

socialismo [sosjaˈliʒmu] m socialism.

socialista [sosjaˈliʃta] adj & mf socialist.

sociedade [sosjeˈdadʒi] f society; (comercial) partnership.

sócio, -cia [ˈsɔsju, -sja] m, f partner.

sociologia [sosjoloˈʒia] f sociology.

sociólogo, -ga [soˈsjɔlogu, -ga] m, f sociologist.

soco [ˈsoku] m (em pessoa) punch; (em mesa) thump.

socorrer [sokoˈxe(x)] vt to help.
❏ **socorrer-se** de vp + prep to resort to, to have recourse to.

socorro [soˈkoxu] m help ◆ interj help!; **pedir** ~ to ask for help.

soda [ˈsɔda] f (bicarbonato) bicarbonate of soda; (bebida) soda water.

sofá [soˈfa] m sofa; ~ **cama** sofa bed.

sofisticado, -da [sofiʃtʃiˈkadu, -da] adj sophisticated.

sofrer [soˈfre(x)] vt to have ◆ vi to suffer.

sofrimento [sofri'mẽntu] *m* suffering.

software [sɔf'twɛri] *m* software.

sogro, sogra ['sogru, 'sɔgra] *m, f*
father-in-law (*f* mother-in-law).

soirée [swa're] *f* soirée.

sóis → **sol**.

soja ['sɔʒa] *f* soya.

sol ['sɔw] (*pl* **sóis** ['sɔjʃ]) *m* sun.

sola ['sɔla] *f* sole.

solar [so'la(x)] (*pl* **-res** [-riʃ]) *adj* solar
♦ *m* manor(house).

soldado [sow'dadu] *m* soldier.

soleira [so'lejra] *f* threshold.

solene [so'lɛni] *adj* solemn.

soletrar [sole'tra(x)] *vt* to spell.

solicitar [solisi'ta(x)] *vt* to request.

solícito, -ta [so'lisitu, -ta] *adj* solici-
tous.

solidão [soli'dãw] *f* solitude.

solidariedade [solidarje'dadʒi] *f* solidarity.

solidário, -ria [soli'darju, -rja] *adj*
sharing; **ser ~ com** (*causa, idéia*) to
support; (*pessoa*) to stand by.

sólido, -da ['sɔlidu, -da] *adj* solid;
(*investimento, negócio*) sound.

solista [so'liʃta] *mf* soloist.

solitário, -ria [soli'tarju, -rja] *adj*
(*local*) lonely; (*pessoa*) solitary ♦ *m*
(*jóia*) solitaire.

solo ['sɔlu] *m* (*chão*) floor; (*superfície
terrestre*) ground; (*terreno arável*) land,
soil; (*MÚS*) solo.

soltar [sow'ta(x)] *vt* (*desprender*) to
release; (*desatar*) to untie; (*grito, preso*)
to let out.

❏ **soltar-se** *vp* (*desprender-se*) to come
loose; (*desatar-se*) to come undone.

solteiro, -ra [sow'tejru, -ra] *adj* single.

solto, -ta ['sowtu, -ta] *pp* → **soltar**
♦ *adj* (*livre*) loose; (*sozinho*) separate.

solução [solu'sãw] (*pl* **-ões** [-õjʃ]) *f*
solution.

soluçar [solu'sa(x)] *vi* (*ter soluços*) to
hiccup; (*chorar*) to sob.

solucionar [solusjo'na(x)] *vt* to solve.

soluço [so'lusu] *m* (*contração*) hiccup;
(*choro*) sob.

soluções → **solução**.

solúvel [so'luvew] (*pl* **-eis** [-ejʃ]) *adj*
soluble.

som ['sõ] (*pl* **-ns** [-ʃ]) *m* sound; **ao ~
de** to the sound of; **~ estereofônico**

stereo sound.

soma ['soma] *f* sum.

somar [so'ma(x)] *vt* to add up.

sombra ['sõmbra] *f* (*escuridão*) shade;
(*de corpo*) shadow; (*cosmético*) eye
shadow; **à** OU **na ~** in the shade; **sem
~ de dúvida** beyond a shadow of a
doubt.

sombrio, -bria [sõm'briu, -'bria] *adj*
(*escuro*) dark; (*melancólico*) sombre;
(*lúgubre*) gloomy.

somente [sɔ'mẽntʃi] *adv* only.

sonâmbulo, -la [so'nãmbulu, -la] *m, f*
sleepwalker.

sonda ['sõnda] *f* (*MED*) probe; **~ espacial** space probe.

sondagem [sõn'daʒẽ] (*pl* **-ns** [-ʃ]) *f*
(*opinion*) poll.

soneca [so'nɛka] *f* nap; **tirar uma ~** to
have a nap.

soneto [so'nɛtu] *m* sonnet.

sonhador, -ra [soɲa'do(x), -ra] (*mpl*
-res [-riʃ], *fpl* **-s** [-ʃ]) *m, f* dreamer.

sonhar [so'ɲa(x)] *vi* to dream; **~ acordado** to daydream; **~ com** to dream
about.

sonho ['soɲu] *m* dream; (*Br: CULIN*)
doughnut; **de ~** dream (*antes de s*).

sonífero [so'niferu] *m* sleeping pill.

sono ['sonu] *m* sleep; **estou morto de
~** I'm falling asleep; **pegar no ~** to get
to sleep; **ter ~** to be sleepy; **~ pesado**
deep sleep.

sonolento, -ta [sono'lẽntu, -ta] *adj*
sleepy.

sonoro, -ra [so'nɔru, -ra] *adj* sound
(*antes de s*).

sons → **som**.

sonso, -sa ['sõsu, -sa] *adj* two-faced.

sopa ['sopa] *f* soup; **~ de horta-
liça/legumes** cabbage/vegetable soup;
~ de marisco soup made with prawns,
onion and tomato; **ser ~** (*fam*: ser fácil)
to be a piece of cake.

soporífero [sopo'riferu] *m* sleeping
pill.

soprar [so'pra(x)] *vt* (*vela, lume*) to
blow out; (*pó*) to blow off; (*resposta*) to
whisper ♦ *vi* to blow.

sórdido, -da ['sɔrdʒidu, -da] *adj*
squalid.

soro ['soru] *m* (*MED*) serum; (*de leite*)
whey; **~ fisiológico** saline solution.

soronegativo, -va [soronega'tʃivu,
-va] *adj* (*Br*) HIV-negative.

soropositivo, -va [soropozi'tʃivu,

-va] *adj (Br)* HIV-positive.

sorridente [soxi'dẽntʃi] *adj (cara, face)* smiling; *(pessoa)* cheerful.

sorrir [so'xi(x)] *vi* to smile.

sorriso [so'xizu] *m* smile.

sorte [sɔxtʃi] *f* luck; *(destino)* fate; **boa ~!** good luck!; **tire um cartão/ número à ~** pick a card/ number; **para dar ~** for (good) luck; **estar com ~** to be in luck; **ter ~** to be lucky; **tirar a ~** to draw lots; **a ~ grande** the jackpot; **com ~** *(pessoa)* lucky; **por ~** luckily.

sortear [sox'tea(x)] *vt* to raffle.

sorteio [sox'teju] *m* raffle.

sortido, -da [sox'tʃidu, -da] *adj* assorted ◆ *m* assortment.

sortudo, -da [sox'tudu, -da] *m, f (fam)* lucky person.

sorvete [sox'vetʃi] *m (Br)* ice cream.

sorveteria [soxvete'ria] *f (Br)* ice-cream parlour.

SOS *m (abrev de Save our Souls)* SOS.

sossegado, -da [sose'gadu, -da] *adj* quiet.

sossego [so'segu] *m* peace.

sótão ['sɔtãw] *m* attic.

sotaque [so'taki] *m* accent.

sotavento [sɔta'vẽntu] *m* leeward.

soterrar [sote'xa(x)] *vt* to bury.

sou ['so] → **ser**.

soube ['sobi] → **saber**.

soufflé [su'fle] *m (Port)* = **suflê**.

soutien [su'tjã] *m (Port)* = **sutiã**.

sova ['sɔva] *f* beating.

sovaco [so'vaku] *m* armpit.

sovina [so'vina] *adj* miserly.

sozinho, -nha [sɔ'ziɲu, -ɲa] *adj* alone; **fiz tudo ~** I did it all by myself; **falar/rir ~** to talk/laugh to o.s.

spray ['sprej] *m* spray.

squash ['skwaʃ] *m* squash.

Sr. *(abrev de senhor)* Mr.

Sra. *(abrev de senhora)* Mrs, Ms.

stand [ʃ'tãnde] *(pl* **-des** [-diʃ]*) m (Port) (de automóveis)* (car) dealer; *(em feira de amostras)* stand.

stock [ʃ'tɔke] *m (Port)* stock.

stress [ʃ'trɛs] *m* stress.

sua → **seu**.

suar ['swa(x)] *vi* to sweat.

suástica ['swaʃtʃika] *f* swastika.

suave ['swavi] *adj* soft; *(brisa, curva)* gentle; *(sabor)* delicate; *(vinho)* smooth; *(cheiro)* subtle; *(dor)* slight.

suavidade [swavi'dadʒi] *f* softness; *(de brisa, curva)* gentleness; *(de sabor)* delicacy; *(de vinho)* smoothness; *(de cheiro)* subtlety.

suavizar [swavi'za(x)] *vt (cheiro, sabor)* to tone down; *(dor)* to ease ◆ *vi (chuva)* to ease; *(vento)* to drop.

subalimentação [subalimẽnta'sãw] *f* undernourishment.

subalimentado, -da [subalimẽn'tadu, -da] *adj* undernourished.

subalterno, -na [subaw'texnu, -na] *m, f & adj (subordinado)* subordinate.

subalugar [subalu'ga(x)] *vt* to sublet.

subconsciente [subkõʃ'sjẽntʃi] *m* subconscious.

subdesenvolvido, -da [subdezẽvow'vidu, -da] *adj* underdeveloped.

subdesenvolvimento [subdezẽvowvi'mẽntu] *m* underdevelopment.

súbdito, -ta ['subditu, -ta] *m, f (Port)* = **súdito**.

subentendido, -da [subẽntẽn'dʒidu, -da] *adj* implied.

subida [su'bida] *f (ladeira)* slope; *(de preços)* increase; *(de montanha, escadas)* climb.

subir [su'bi(x)] *vt (escadas, rua, encosta)* to go up; *(montanha, rochedo)* to climb; *(malas, bagagem)* to take up; *(preços, salários)* to increase; *(estore, persiana)* to raise ◆ *vi (ir para cima)* to go up; **~ a** to climb; **~ de posto** *(em emprego)* to be promoted; **~ em** *(Br: em ônibus, avião, etc)* to get on; *(Port: em Lisboa, Porto, etc)* to get on at; **~ para** *(Port)* to get on; **~ por** to go up.

súbito, -ta ['subitu, -ta] *adj* sudden; **de ~** suddenly.

subjectivo, -va [subʒɛ'tivu, -va] *adj (Port)* = **subjetivo**.

subjetivo, -va [subʒɛ'tʒivu, -va] *adj (Br)* subjective.

subjugar [subʒu'ga(x)] *vt* to overcome.

❏ **subjugar-se** *vp + prep* to give in to.

subjuntivo [subʒõn'tʃivu] *m (Br)* subjunctive.

sublime [su'blimi] *adj* sublime.

sublinhar [subli'ɲa(x)] *vt* to underline; *(com entoação)* to stress.

submarino [subma'rinu] *m* submarine.

submergir [submex'ʒi(x)] *vt (imergir)* to submerge; *(inundar)* to flood.

submeter [subme'te(x)] *vt:* ~ **algo/alguém a algo** to submit sthg/sb to sthg.

❑ **submeter-se a** *vp + prep* to submit to.

submisso, -a [sub'misu, -a] *adj* submissive.

subnutrido, -da [subnu'tridu, -da] *adj* undernourished.

subornar [subox'na(x)] *vt* to bribe.

subsídio [sub'sidju] *m* subsidy.

subsistência [subsiʃ'tẽsja] *f (sustento)* subsistence; *(permanência)* continued existence.

subsistir [subsiʃ'ti(x)] *vi (persistir)* to remain; *(sobreviver)* to subsist.

subsolo [sub'sɔlu] *m* subsoil.

substância [subʃ'tãsja] *f* substance.

substantivo [subʃtãn'tʒivu] *m* noun.

substituir [subʃtʃi'twi(x)] *vt* to substitute; ~ **a manteiga por margarina** substitute margarine for butter.

substituto, -ta [subʃtʃi'tutu, -ta] *m, f* replacement.

subterrâneo, -nea [subte'xanju, -nja] *adj* underground.

subtil [sub'til] *(pl -is* [-iʃ]*) adj (Port) =* sutil.

subtrair [subtra'i(x)] *vt* to subtract.

suburbano, -na [subux'banu, -na] *adj* suburban.

subúrbio [su'buxbju] *m* suburb.

subversivo, -va [subvex'sivu, -va] *adj* subversive.

sucata [su'kata] *f* scrap.

sucção [suk'sãw] *f* suction.

suceder [suse'de(x)] *vi* to happen.

❑ **suceder a** *v + prep (em cargo)* to succeed; *(vir depois)* to follow.

❑ **suceder-se** *vp* to happen.

sucedido, -da [suse'dʒidu, -da] *m* occurrence ◆ *adj:* **ser bem/mal** ~ to be successful/unsuccessful.

sucessão [suse'sãw] *(pl -ões* [-õjʃ]*) f* succession.

sucessivo, -va [suse'sivu, -va] *adj* successive.

sucesso [su'sɛsu] *m* success; **fazer** ~ to be successful.

sucessões → **sucessão**.

sucinto, -ta [su'sĩntu, -ta] *adj* succinct.

suco ['suku] *m (Br)* juice.

suculento, -ta [suku'lẽntu, -ta] *adj* succulent.

sucumbir [sukũm'bi(x)] *vi (desmoronar)* to crumble; *(morrer)* to die; ~ **a** to succumb to.

sucursal [sukux'saw] *(pl -ais* [-ajʃ]*) f (de banco, empresa)* branch.

sudeste [su'dɛʃtʃi] *m* southeast; **no** ~ in the southeast.

súdito, -ta ['sudʒitu, -ta] *m, f (Br)* subject.

sudoeste [su'dwɛʃtʃi] *m* southwest; **no** ~ in the southwest.

Suécia ['swɛsja] *f:* **a** ~ Sweden.

sueco, -ca ['swɛku, -ka] *adj & m* Swedish ◆ *m, f* Swede.

suéter ['swete(x)] *(pl -res* [-riʃ]*) m ou f (Br)* sweater.

suficiente [sufi'sjẽntʃi] *adj* enough ◆ *m (EDUC)* pass.

sufixo [su'fiksu] *m* suffix.

suflé [su'flɛ] *m (Port) =* **suflê**.

suflê [su'flɛ] *m (Br)* soufflé.

sufocante [sufo'kãntʃi] *adj* oppressive.

sufocar [sufo'ka(x)] *vt & vi* to suffocate.

sugar [su'ga(x)] *vt* to suck.

sugerir [suʒe'ri(x)] *vt* to suggest.

sugestão [suʒeʃ'tãw] *(pl -ões* [-õjʃ]*) f* suggestion.

sugestivo, -va [suʒeʃ'tʃivu, -va] *adj* suggestive.

sugestões → **sugestão**.

Suíça ['swisa] *f:* **a** ~ Switzerland.

suíças ['swisaʃ] *fpl* sideboards *(Brit)*, sideburns *(Am)*.

suicidar-se [swisi'daxsi] *vp* to commit suicide.

suicídio [swi'sidʒju] *m* suicide.

suíço, -ça ['swisu, -sa] *adj & m, f* Swiss.

suíte ['switʃi] *f (Br)* suite.

sujar [su'ʒa(x)] *vt* to dirty.

❑ **sujar-se** *vp* to get dirty.

sujeitar [suʒej'ta(x)] *vt:* ~ **algo/alguém a algo** to subject sthg/sb to sthg.

❑ **sujeitar-se a** *vp + prep (submeter-se a)* to conform to; **ela teve que** ~**-se a todo tipo de humilhação** she was subjected to ritual humiliation.

sujeito, -ta [su'ʒejtu, -ta] *m, f (fam: homem, mulher)* guy *(f girl)* ◆ *m (GRAM)* subject ◆ *adj:* ~ **a** subject to.

sujo, -ja [ˈsuʒu, -ʒa] *adj* dirty.

sul [ˈsuw] *m* south; **ao** ou **no ~** in the south; **ao ~ de** (to the) south of.

suma [ˈsuma] *f:* **em ~** in short.

sumário, -ria [suˈmarju, -rja] *adj (explicação)* brief; *(ordem, execução)* summary ♦ *m (resumo)* summary.

sumo [ˈsumu] *m (Port)* juice; **~ de frutas** fruit juice.

Sumol® [suˈmɔw] *(pl -óis [-ɔjʃ]) f:* **~ (de laranja)** orangeade.

sundae [ˈsãndei] *m (Br)* (ice cream) sundae.

sunga [ˈsũŋga] *f (Br)* swimming trunks *(pl).*

suor [ˈswɔ(x)] *(pl -res [-riʃ]) m* sweat; **sentir ~es frios** to break out in a cold sweat.

superar [supeˈra(x)] *vt* to overcome.

superficial [supexfiˈsjaw] *(pl -ais [-ajʃ]) adj* superficial.

superfície [supexˈfisji] *f* surface; *(área)* area; **na ~** on the surface.

supérfluo, -flua [suˈpɛxflu, -fla] *adj* superfluous.

superior [supeˈrjo(x)] *(pl -res [-riʃ]) adj* higher; *(em espaço)* top; *(em valor, quantidade)* greater ♦ *m* superior; **andar ~** top floor; **mostrar-se ~** to give o.s. airs (and graces).

superioridade [superjoriˈdadʒi] *f* superiority.

superlativo [supexlaˈtʃivu] *m* superlative.

superlotado, -da [supexloˈtadu, -da] *adj* packed.

supermercado [supexmexˈkadu] *m* supermarket.

superstição [supexʃtʃiˈsãw] *(pl -ões [-õjʃ]) f* superstition.

supersticioso, -osa [supexʃtʃiˈsjozu, -ɔza] *adj* superstitious.

superstições → superstição.

supervisão [supexviˈzãw] *f* supervision.

supervisionar [supexvizjoˈna(x)] *vt* to supervise.

suplemento [supleˈmẽntu] *m (de jornal, revista)* (colour) supplement.

suplente [suˈplẽntʃi] *adj (peça)* spare; *(pessoa)* substitute ♦ *mf (ESP)* substitute.

súplica [ˈsuplika] *f* plea.

suplicar [supliˈka(x)] *vt* to plead; **~ a alguém que faça algo** to beg sb to do sthg.

suplício [suˈplisju] *m* torture.

supor [suˈpo(x)] *vt* to presume.

❑ **supor-se** *vp:* **supõe-se que ela tenha morrido** she is presumed dead.

suportar [supoxˈta(x)] *vt (peso, carga)* to support; *(pessoa)* to stand; *(dor, desgosto)* to bear.

suporte [suˈpɔxtʃi] *m* support.

suposição [supoziˈsãw] *(pl -ões [-õjʃ]) f* supposition.

supositório [supoziˈtɔrju] *m* suppository.

suposto, -osta [suˈpoʃtu, -ɔʃta] *adj (hipotético)* supposed; *(alegado)* alleged; *(falso)* false ♦ *m* assumption.

supremo, -ma [suˈpremu, -ma] *adj* supreme.

❑ **Supremo** *m:* **o Supremo (Tribunal de Justiça)** the Supreme Court.

supressão [supreˈsãw] *(pl -ões [-õjʃ]) f (de palavra, frase)* deletion; *(de projeto, empregos)* axing.

suprimir [supriˈmi(x)] *vt (palavra, frase)* to delete; *(emprego, projeto)* to axe.

surdez [suxˈdeʒ] *f* deafness.

surdina [suxˈdʒina] *f:* **em ~** in a whisper.

surdo, -da [ˈsuxdu, -da] *adj* deaf ♦ *m, f* deaf person; **fazer-se ~** to turn a deaf ear.

surf [ˈsarfe] *m (Port)* = **surfe.**

surfe [ˈsuxfi] *m (Br)* surfing; **fazer ~** to go surfing.

surfista [suxˈfiʃta] *mf* surfer.

surgir [suxˈʒi(x)] *vi (aparecer)* to appear; *(problema, complicação)* to arise.

surpreendente [surpriẽnˈdẽntʃi] *adj* surprising.

surpreender [surpriẽnˈde(x)] *vt* to surprise.

❑ **surpreender-se** *vp* to be surprised.

surpresa [surˈpreza] *f* surprise; **fazer uma ~ a alguém** to give sb a surprise; **de ~** by surprise.

surpreso, -sa [surˈprezu, -za] *adj* surprised.

surto [ˈsurtu] *m (de doença)* outbreak.

susceptível [suʃseˈtivel] *(pl -eis [-ejʃ]) adj (Port)* = **suscetível.**

suscetível [suʃseˈtʃivew] *(pl -eis [-ejʃ]) adj (Br)* sensitive; **~ a** liable to.

suscitar [suʃsiˈta(x)] *vt* to provoke; *(interesse)* to arouse; *(dificuldades,* *problemas)* to cause.

suspeita [suʃ'pejta] *f* suspicion; **lançar ~s sobre alguém** to cast aspersions on sb, → **suspeito**.

suspeito, -ta [suʃ'pejtu, -ta] *adj* suspicious ◆ *m, f* suspect.

suspender [suʃpēn'de(x)] *vt* to suspend.

suspensão [suʃpē'sãw] (*pl* -**ões** [-õjʃ]) *f* suspension.

suspense [suʃ'pēsi] *m* suspense.

suspensões → **suspensão**.

suspensórios [suʃpē'sɔrjuʃ] *mpl* braces *(Brit)*, suspenders *(Am)*.

suspirar [suʃpi'ra(x)] *vi* to sigh; **~ por** to long for.

suspiro [suʃ'piru] *m* sigh; *(doce)* egg whites beaten with sugar used as a pie topping.

sussurrar [susu'xa(x)] *vi & vt* to whisper.

sussurro [su'suxu] *m* whisper.

sustentar [suʃtēn'ta(x)] *vt* to support; *(afirmar)* to maintain.

suster [suʃ'te(x)] *vt (segurar)* to sustain; *(respiração)* to hold.

susto ['suʃtu] *m* fright, shock; **tomar um ~** to get a fright; **pregar** OU **dar um ~ em alguém** to give sb a fright.

sutiã [su'tʃjã] *m (Br)* bra, brassiere *(Am)*.

sutil [su'tʃiw] (*pl* -**is** [-iʃ]) *adj (Br)* subtle.

SW *(abrev de Sudoeste)* SW.

T

ta [ta] = te + a, → te.

tabacaria [tabaka'ria] f tobacconist's (shop).

tabaco [ta'baku] m (cigarros) cigarettes (pl); (para cachimbo, enrolar) tobacco.

tabela [ta'bɛla] f (de horários) timetable; (de preços) price list.

taberna [ta'bɛxna] f cheap country-style pub.

tablete [ta'blɛtʃi] m ou f: ~ de chocolate bar of chocolate.

tábua [ˈtabwa] f board; ~ de passar a ferro (Port) ironing board; ~ de passar roupa (Br) ironing board.

tabuleiro [tabuˈlejru] m (para comida) tray; (de damas, xadrez) board; (de ponte) roadway.

tabuleta [tabuˈleta] f sign.

tac [ˈtaki] m (abrev de tomografia axial computorizada) CAT scan.

taça [ˈtasa] f cup; (para comida, doces) bowl; (de champanhe) glass.

tacada [taˈkada] f (em golfe) stroke; (em bilhar) shot.

tacho [ˈtaʃu] m saucepan.

taco [ˈtaku] m (de golfe) club; (de bilhar) cue; (de chão) parquet block.

táctica [ˈtatika] f (Port) = tática.

táctico, -ca [ˈtatiku, -ka] adj (Port) = tático.

tacto [ˈtatu] m (Port) = tato.

tagarela [tagaˈrɛla] adj talkative ♦ mf chatterbox.

tainha [taˈiɲa] f mullet.

tal [ˈtaw] (pl tais [ˈtajʃ]) adj such ♦ pron: o/a ~ the one; nunca ouvi falar de ~ coisa/pessoa I've never heard of such a thing/person; livros, tais como estes, são úteis books, such as these, are useful; um ~ senhor some man; na cidade ~ in such-and-such a town; que ~ um passeio? how about a walk?; que ~? how was it?; ~ e qual just like; como ~ so; para ~ for that; ~ como just as.

tala [ˈtala] f (MED) splint.

talão [taˈlãw] (pl -ões [-õjʃ]) m (de recibo, bilhete) stub; ~ de cheques (Br) cheque book.

talco [ˈtawku] m talc.

talento [taˈlẽtu] m talent.

talhar [taˈʎa(x)] vt to cut; (madeira) to carve.

❏ **talhar-se** vp (leite) to curdle.

talharim [taʎaˈrĩ] m tagliatelle.

talher [taˈʎɛ(x)] (pl -res [-riʃ]) m (set of) cutlery.

talho [ˈtaʎu] m (Port: açougue) butcher's (shop).

talo [ˈtalu] m (de flor, legume) stem.

talões → talão.

talvez [tawˈveʒ] adv perhaps, maybe; ~ sim, ~ não maybe, maybe not.

tamancos [taˈmãŋkuʃ] mpl clogs.

tamanho, -nha [taˈmaɲu, -ɲa] m (grandeza) size ♦ adj (tão grande): fiz ~ esforço I made such an effort; qual é o ~ do quarto? how big is the room?

tamanho-família [ta,maɲufaˈmilja] adj inv (Br: embalagem) family (antes de s).

tâmara [ˈtamara] f date.

tamarindo [tamaˈrĩndu] m tamarind.

também [tãˈbẽ] adv also; eu ~ me too; ele ~ não fez nada he didn't do anything either; ~ quero ir I want to go too; ela ~ vem she's coming as well; ele ~ se chama Luís he's also called Luís.

tambor [tãˈbo(x)] (pl -res [-riʃ]) m drum.

tamboril [tãboˈriw] (pl -is [-iʃ]) m (peixe) monkfish; (MÚS) small drum.

tamborim [tãboˈrĩ] (pl -ns [-ʃ])

m tambourine.

tamboris → **tamboril**.

Tâmisa [ˈtamiza] *m*: o ~ the Thames.

tampa [ˈtãmpa] *f* lid.

tampão [tãmˈpãw] (*pl* -ões [-õjʃ]) *m* tampon.

tampo [ˈtãmpu] *m* (*de mesa*) top; (*de privada*) lid.

tampões → **tampão**.

tampouco [tãmˈpoku] *adv* neither.

tanga [ˈtãŋga] *f* tanga.

tangerina [tãʒeˈrina] *f* tangerine.

tanque [ˈtãŋki] *m* tank.

tanto, -ta [ˈtãntu, -ta] *adj*
1. (*exprime grande quantidade*) so much, so many (*pl*); ~ **dinheiro** so much money; **tanta gente** so many people; **tantas flores** so many flowers; **esperei ~ tempo** I waited for so long; ~ ... **que** so much ...that.
2. (*indica quantidade indeterminada*) so much, so many (*pl*); **de ~s em ~s dias** every so many days; **são mil e ~s reais** one thousand and something reals.
3. (*em comparações*): ~ ... **como** as much ... as, as many ... as (*pl*); **bebi ~ vinho quanto você** I drank as much wine as you; **têm tanta sorte quanto você** they're as lucky as you.
♦ *adv* 1. (*exprime grande quantidade*) so much; **lhe quero ~** I love you so much; **não quero ~ assim** I don't want as much as that.
2. (*em locuções*): **de ~ falar perdi a voz** I lost my voice from talking so much; ~ **faz!** it doesn't matter!; ~ **melhor** so much the better; ~ **pior** too bad; ~ **quanto** as far as; **um ~ a** little; **é um ~ caro** it's a bit expensive; **um ~ quanto** slightly; ~ **que** (*pela simples razão que*) so much so that.
♦ *pron* 1. (*indica grande quantidade*) so much, so many (*pl*); **tenho ~!** I've got so much!; **ele não comprou ~s** he didn't buy that many.
2. (*indica igual quantidade*) as much, as many (*pl*); **havia muita gente ali, aqui não era tanta** there were a lot of people over there, but not as many over here.
3. (*indica quantidade indeterminada*) so much, so many (*pl*); **lá para as tantas ele foi embora** he left quite late; **põe uns ~s aqui uns ~s ali** put some over here and some over there; **leva ~s**

quantos você quiser take as many as you want.
4. (*em comparações*): ~ **quanto** as much as; **sabe ~ quanto eu do assunto** he knows as much as I do about the affair; **comi ~ quanto o Arnaldo** I ate as much as Arnaldo.
5. (*em locuções*): **às tantas** (*de repente*) all of a sudden; **às tantas da noite** late at night; **não é caso para ~** there's no need to make such a fuss.

tão [tãw] *adv* so; ~ ... **como** as ... as; ~ ... **que** so ... (that).

TAP [ˈtapi] *f* (*abrev de Transportes Aéreos Portugueses*) TAP (Portuguese national airline).

tapa [ˈtapa] *m* (*Br: bofetada*) slap.

tapar [taˈpa(x)] *vt* (*com cobertor, lençol*) to cover up; (*garrafa, frasco, panela*) to put the lid on; (*caixa*) to close; (*boca, ouvidos*) to cover; (*nariz*) to hold.

tapeçaria [tapesaˈria] *f* tapestry.

tapete [taˈpetʃi] *m* (*grande*) carpet; (*médio*) rug; (*pequeno*) mat; ~ **rolante** conveyor belt.

tardar [taxˈda(x)] *vi* to take a long time; **ele não tardará a chegar** he won't be long; ~ **a** OU **em fazer algo** to take a long time to do sthg; **o mais** ~ **at the latest.

tarde [ˈtaxdʒi] *f* (*até às seis*) afternoon; (*depois das seis*) evening ♦ *adv* late; **boa ~!** good afternoon/evening!; **à ~** in the afternoon/evening; **já é ~** it's too late; **mais ~** later; **nunca é ~ demais** it's never too late.

tardio, -dia [taxˈdʒiu, -ˈdia] *adj* late.

tarefa [taˈrefa] *f* task.

tarifa [taˈrifa] *f* (*preço, taxa*) charge; (*em transportes*) fare; (*lista de preços*) price list.

tartaruga [taxtaˈruga] *f* (*terrestre*) turtle; (*aquática*) tortoise.

tas [taʃ] = **te** + **as**, → **te**.

tática [ˈtatʃika] *f* (*Br*) tactic.

tático, -ca [ˈtatʃiku, -ka] *adj* (*Br*) tactical.

tato [ˈtatu] *m* (*Br*) (*sentido*) touch; (*fig: cuidado, habilidade*) tact; **ter ~** (*fig*) to be tactful.

tatuagem [taˈtwaʒẽ] (*pl* -**ns** [-ʃ]) *f* tattoo.

tauromaquia [tawromaˈkia] *f* bullfighting.

taxa [ˈtaʃa] *f* (*imposto*) tax; (*percentagem*) rate; ~ **de câmbio/juros**

exchange/interest rate.
tax-free [taks'fri] *adj inv* tax-free.
táxi ['taksi] *m* taxi.
taxímetro [tak'simetru] *m* taximeter.
tchau ['tʃaw] *interj* bye!
te [tʃi] *pron (complemento direto)* you; *(complemento indireto)* (to) you; *(reflexo)* yourself; **magoaste-~?** *(Port)* did you hurt yourself?; **vais-~ embora?** *(Port)* are you going?.
tear ['tea(x)] *(pl -res* [-riʃ]) *m* loom; **~ manual** hand loom.
teatral [tea'traw] *(pl -ais* [-ajʃ]) *adj (do teatro)* theatre *(antes de s)*; *(pessoa, comportamento)* theatrical.
teatro ['teatru] *m* theatre; **~ de fantoches** puppet show; **~ de variedades** variety *(Brit)*, vaudeville *(Am)*.
tecelagem [tese'laʒẽ] *(pl -ns* [-ʃ]) *f (local)* textile factory; *(ofício)* weaving.
tecer [te'se(x)] *vt (tapete, tecido)* to weave; *(suj: aranha)* to spin.
tecido [te'sidu] *m (pano)* fabric, cloth; *(ANAT)* tissue.
tecla ['tɛkla] *f* key.
teclado [te'kladu] *m* keyboard.
técnica ['tɛknika] *f* technique, → **técnico**.
técnico, -ca ['tɛkniku, -ka] *adj* technical ♦ *m, f (pessoa)* technician.
tecnologia [teknolo'ʒia] *f* technology; **~ da informação** information technology *(sg)*.
tecnológico, -ca [teknu'lɔʒiku, -ka] *adj* technological.
tecto ['tɛtu] *m (Port)* = **teto**.
tédio ['tɛdʒju] *m* boredom.
teia ['teja] *f* web.
teimar ['tejma(x)] *vi* to insist; **~ em** to insist on.
teimosia [tejmo'zia] *f* stubbornness.
teimoso, -osa [tej'mozu, -ɔza] *adj* stubborn.
teixo ['tejʃu] *m* yew (tree).
tel. *(abrev de telefone)* tel.
tela ['tɛla] *f* canvas; *(tecido)* fabric.
telecomandado, -da [telekomãn'dadu, -da] *adj* remote-controlled ♦ *m* remote control.
teleférico [tele'fɛriku] *m* cable car.
telefonar [telefo'na(x)] *vi* to (tele)phone; **~ para alguém** to (tele)phone sb.
telefone [tele'fɔni] *m* (tele)phone; **~ público** public payphone.

telefonema [telefo'nema] *m* (tele)phone call; **dar um ~** to make a (tele)phone call.
telefónico, -ca [tele'fɔniku, -ka] *adj (Port)* = **telefônico**.
telefônico, -ca [tele'foniku, -ka] *adj (Br)* (tele)phone *(antes de s)*.
telefonista [telefo'niʃta] *mf* switchboard operator.
telegrafar [telegra'fa(x)] *vt* to cable.
telegrama [tele'grama] *m* telegram; **~ fonado** *(Br)* Telemessage®.
telejornal [teleʒox'naw] *(pl -ais* [-ajʃ]) *m* news (on TV) *(sg)* .
telemóvel [.tele'mɔvew] *(pl -eis* [-ejʃ]) *m (Port: telefone)* mobile phone.
telenovela [teleno'vɛla] *f* soap opera.
teleobjectiva [.teleobʒe'tiva] *f (Port)* = **teleobjetiva**.
teleobjetiva [.teleobʒe'tʃiva] *f (Br)* telephoto lens.
telepatia [telepa'tʃia] *f* telepathy.
telescópio [teleʃ'kɔpju] *m* telescope.
telesqui [.teleʃ'ki] *m* ski lift.
televisão [televi'zãw] *(pl -ões* [-õjʃ]) *f* television, TV; **~ a cores** colour television; **~ preto e branco** black-and-white television; **~ por cabo/satélite** cable/satellite television.
televisor [televi'zo(x)] *(pl -res* [-riʃ]) *m* television (set).
telex [te'lɛks] *(pl -es* [-iʃ]) *m* telex.
telha ['teʎa] *f* (roof) tile.
telhado [te'ʎadu] *m* roof.
tem [tẽ] → **ter**.
têm ['tajẽ] → **ter**.
tema ['tema] *m* subject.
temer [te'me(x)] *vt* to be afraid of, to fear; **~ que** to fear (that).
temido, -da [te'midu, -da] *adj* feared.
temível [te'mivew] *(pl -eis* [-ejʃ]) *adj* frightening.
temor [te'mo(x)] *(pl -res* [-riʃ]) *m* fear.
temperado, -da [tẽmpe'radu, -da] *adj (comida)* seasoned; *(clima)* temperate.
temperamento [tẽmpera'mẽntu] *m* temperament.
temperar [tẽmpe'ra(x)] *vt* to season.
temperatura [tẽmpera'tura] *f* temperature.
tempero [tẽm'peru] *m* seasoning.
tempestade [tẽmpeʃ'tadʒi] *f* storm; **uma ~ num copo de água** a storm in a teacup.

templo ['tẽmplu] *m* temple.

tempo ['tẽmpu] *m (horas, minutos, segundos)* time; *(meteorológico)* weather; *(GRAM)* tense; **chegar a ~ de algo** to arrive in time for sthg; **chegar a ~ de fazer algo** to arrive in time to do sthg; **ganhar ~** to save time; **não ter ~ para algo** not to have time for sthg; **não ter ~ para fazer algo** not to have time to do sthg; **passar o ~ a fazer algo** to spend one's time doing sthg; **poupar ~** to save time; **recuperar o ~ perdido** to make up for lost time; **ser ~ de** to be time to; **em ~ integral** full-time; **~ livre** free time *(sg)*; **antes do ~** prematurely; **ao mesmo ~** at the same time; **dentro de pouco ~** in a little while; **no meu ~** in my day; **naquele ~** in those days; **de ~s a ~s** from time to time; **nos últimos ~s** lately; **por algum ~** for a while; **por ~ indefinido** OU **indeterminado** indefinitely.

têmpora ['tẽmpora] *f* temple.

temporada [tẽmpo'rada] *f* season; **passar uma ~ no estrangeiro/na praia** to spend some time abroad/at the beach.

temporal [tẽmpo'raw] *(pl* **-ais** [-ajʃ]*)* *m* storm.

temporário, -ria [tẽmpu'rarju, -rja] *adj* temporary.

tencionar [tẽsjo'na(x)] *vt*: **~ fazer algo** to intend to do sthg.

tenda [tẽnda] *f (para acampar)* tent; *(em mercado)* stall; *(quitanda)* greengrocer's (shop).

tendão [tẽn'dãw] *(pl* **-ões** [-õjʃ]*)* *m* tendon.

tendência [tẽn'dẽsja] *f* tendency; **ter ~ para** to tend to.

tendões → **tendão**.

tenente [te'nẽntʃi] *mf* lieutenant.

tenho [taɲu] → **ter**.

ténis ['tɛniʃ] *m inv (Port) (ESP)* tennis ◆ *mpl (Port) (sapatos)* trainers *(Brit)*, sneakers *(Am)*.

tênis ['tɛniʃ] *m inv (Br) (ESP)* tennis; *(sapatos)* trainers *(pl) (Brit)*, sneakers *(pl)(Am)*; **~ de mesa** table tennis.

tenro, -ra ['tẽxu, -xa] *adj* tender; **de tenra idade** young.

tensão [tẽ'sãw] *(pl* **-ões** [-õjʃ]*)* *f (nervosismo)* tension; *(elétrica)* voltage; **~ arterial alta/baixa** high/low blood pressure.

tenso, -sa ['tẽsu, -sa] *adj* tense.

tensões → **tensão**.

tentação [tẽnta'sãw] *(pl* **-ões** [-õjʃ]*)* *f* temptation.

tentáculo [tẽn'takulu] *m* tentacle.

tentador, -ra [tẽnta'do(x), -ra] *(mpl* **-res** [-riʃ], *fpl* **-s** [-ʃ]*)* *adj* tempting.

tentar [tẽnta(x)] *vt (seduzir)* to tempt ◆ *vi (experimentar)* to try; **~ fazer algo** to try to do sthg.

tentativa [tẽnta'tiva] *f* attempt; **à primeira ~** on one's first attempt OU go; **na ~ de fazer algo** in an attempt to do sthg.

ténue ['tɛnwe] *adj (Port)* = **tênue**.

tênue ['tɛnwi] *adj (Br)* faint; *(sabor)* mild.

teologia [tjolo'ʒia] *f* theology.

teor ['teo(x)] *m* tenor; *(de álcool, gordura)* content.

teoria [teo'ria] *f* theory; **em ~** in theory.

teoricamente [ˌtjɔrika'mẽntʃi] *adv* theoretically.

tépido, -da ['tɛpidu, -da] *adj* tepid.

ter ['te(x)] *vt* **1.** *(possuir)* to have; **a casa tem dois quartos** the house has two bedrooms; **ela tem os olhos verdes** she has green eyes; **tenho muito dinheiro** I have a lot of money; **~ saúde/juízo** to be healthy/sensible. **2.** *(indica medida, idade)* to be; **a sala tem quatro metros de largura** the room is four metres wide; **que idade você tem?** how old are you?; **tenho dez anos** I'm ten (years old). **3.** *(dor, doença)* to have (got); **~ febre** to have a temperature; **~ varicela/sarampo** to have chickenpox/measles; **tenho dor de dentes/cabeça** I've got toothache/a headache. **4.** *(sentir)*: **~ medo** to be frightened; **tenho frio/calor** I'm cold/hot; **tenho sede/fome** I'm thirsty/hungry. **5.** *(exprime sentimento)*: **~ amor/ódio a alguém** to love/hate sb; **~ carinho por alguém** to care about sb; **~ afeição por alguém** to be fond of sb. **6.** *(conter)* to hold; **esta garrafa tem um litro** this bottle holds one litre; **esta caixa tem apenas três bolos** this box only has three cakes in it. **7.** *(discussão, problema)* to have; **eles têm muitos problemas econômicos** they have a lot of money problems; **tivemos uma grande discussão** we had a big argument.

8. *(para desejar)* to have; **tenha umas boas férias!** have a good holiday!; **tenham um bom dia!** have a nice day!
9. *(ter de ir a)* to have; **não tenho aula hoje** I don't have school today; **tenho um encontro** I've got a date; **ele tinha uma reunião, mas não foi** he had a meeting, but he didn't go to it.
10. *(dar à luz)* to have; **ela teve uma menina** she had a baby girl.
◆ *v aux* **1.** *(haver)*: **eles tinham quebrado o vidro** they had broken the window; **tinha alugado a casa** she had rented the house; **tinha chovido e a estrada estava molhada** it had been raining and the road was wet.
2. *(exprime obrigação)*: **~ de fazer algo** to have to do sthg; **temos de estar lá às oito** we have to be there at eight; **tenho muito que fazer** I have a lot to do.

terapeuta [tera'pewta] *mf* therapist.
terapêutico, -ca [tera'petʃiku, -ka] *adj* therapeutic.
terapia [tera'pia] *f* therapy.
terça-feira [.texsa'fejra] *(pl* **terças-feiras** [.texsaʃ'fejraʃ]*) f* Tuesday; **Terça-feira de Carnaval** Shrove Tuesday *(Brit),* Mardi Gras *(Am),* → **sexta-feira.**
terceira [tex'sejra] *f (de veículo)* third (gear).
terceiro, -ra [tex'sejru, -ra] *num* third; **a terceira idade** old age, → **sexto.**
terço ['texsu] *m (parte)* third; *(rosário)* rosary; **rezar o ~** to say the rosary.
terebintina [terebĩn'tʃina] *f* turpentine, turps *(sg).*
termas ['texmaʃ] *fpl* hot OU thermal baths, spa *(sg).*
térmico, -ca [tex'miku, -ka] *adj* thermal; **garrafa térmica** Thermos® (flask).
terminal [texmi'naw] *(pl* **-ais** [-ajʃ]*) adj* terminal ◆ *m (INFORM)* terminal; **~ rodoviário/ferroviário** coach/rail terminus; **~ aéreo** airport terminal.
terminar [texmi'na(x)] *vt* to finish ◆ *vi* to end; **~ em algo** to end in sthg; **~ por fazer algo** to end up doing sthg.
termo ['texmu] *m* term; *(limite, fim)* end, conclusion; *(Port: recipiente)* Thermos® (flask); **pôr ~ a algo** to put an end to sthg.
termómetro [tex'mɔmetru] *m (Port)*

= termômetro.
termômetro [tex'mometru] *m (Br)* thermometer.
termostato [texmɔʃ'tatu] *m* thermostat.
terno, -na ['texnu, -na] *adj* tender.
ternura [tex'nura] *f* tenderness.
terra ['texa] *f (chão)* ground; *(substância)* earth; *(terreno)* land; *(pátria)* homeland; *(solo)* soil; *(localidade)* place; **a Terra** Earth; **~ natal** homeland, country of origin; **por ~** *(viajar)* by land; **~ a ~** down-to-earth; **cair por ~** *(fig: plano, negócio)* to fall through.
terraço [te'xasu] *m* terrace.
terramoto [texa'mɔtu] *m (Port)* = terremoto.
terremoto [texe'mɔtu] *m (Br)* earthquake.
terreiro [te'xejru] *m* square.
terreno, -na [te'xenu, -na] *adj* earthly ◆ *m* plot (of land).
térreo, -ea ['texju, -ja] *adj (andar, piso)* ground *(antes de s).*
terrestre [te'xeʃtri] *adj (de planeta)* terrestrial; *(da terra)* land *(antes de s)* ◆ *mf* earthling.
terrina [te'xina] *f* tureen.
território [texi'tɔrju] *m* territory.
terrível [te'xivew] *(pl* **-eis** [-ejʃ]*) adj* terrible.
terror [te'xo(x)] *(pl* **-res** [-riʃ]*) m* terror.
tese ['tezi] *f* thesis.
tesoura [te'zora] *f* scissors *(pl);* **~ de unha** nail scissors.
tesouro [te'zoru] *m* treasure.
testa ['tɛʃta] *f* forehead.
testamento [teʃta'mẽntu] *m* will.
testar [teʃ'ta(x)] *vt* to test, to try out.
teste ['tɛʃtʃi] *m* test; **~ de alcoolemia** *(Port)* Breathalyser® test; **~ de dosagem alcoólica** *(Br)* Breathalyser® test.
testemunha [teʃte'muɲa] *f* witness; **~ ocular** eyewitness.
testemunho [teʃte'muɲu] *m (JUR)* testimony; *(ESP)* baton *(in relay race).*
testículos [teʃ'tʃikuluʃ] *m* testicles.
tétano ['tɛtanu] *m* tetanus.
teto ['tɛtu] *m (Br)* ceiling.
tétrico, -ca ['tɛtriku, -ka] *adj* gloomy.
teu, tua ['tew, 'tua] *adj* your ◆ *pron:* **o ~/a tua** yours; **um amigo ~** a friend of

yours; **os ~s** *(a tua família)* your family.

teve ['tevi] → **ter**.

têxtil ['tejſtſiw] *(pl* **-teis** [-tejſ]) *m* textile.

texto ['tejſtu] *m (de livro)* text; *(de peça teatral)* script.

textura [tejſtura] *f* texture.

texugo [te'ſugu] *m* badger.

tez ['teſ] *f* complexion.

ti ['tſi] *pron (com preposição: complemento indireto)* you; *(com preposição: reflexo)* yourself; **compraste-o para ~ (mesmo OU próprio)?** did you buy it for yourself?

tigela [tſi'ʒɛla] *f* bowl; **de meia ~** *(fig: de pouco valor)* second-rate.

tigre ['tſigri] *m* tiger.

tijolo [tſi'ʒolu] *m* brick.

til ['tiw] *m* tilde.

tília ['tſilja] *f* lime blossom.

time ['tſimi] *m (Br)* team.

timidez [tſimi'deſ] *f* shyness.

tímido, -da ['tſimidu, -da] *adj* shy.

timoneiro [tſimo'nejru] *m (em barco)* helmsman; *(em expedição)* guide.

Timor [tſi'mo(x)] *s* Timor.

tímpano ['tſĩmpanu] *m (ANAT)* eardrum; *(MÚS)* kettledrum.

tina ['tſina] *f* tub.

tingido, -da [tſi'ʒidu, -da] *adj* dyed.

tingir [tſi'ʒi(x)] *vt* to dye.

tinha ['tſiɲa] → **ter**.

tinir [tſi'ni(x)] *vi* to ring.

tinta ['tſĩnta] *f (para escrever)* ink; *(para pintar)* paint; *(para tingir)* dye.

tinteiro [tſĩn'tejru] *m* inkwell.

tinto ['tſĩntu] *adj m* → **vinho**.

tintura [tſĩn'tura] *f:* **~ de iodo** tincture of iodine.

tinturaria [tſĩntura'ria] *f (local)* dry cleaner's (shop).

tio, tia ['tſiu, 'tſia] *m, f* uncle *(f* aunt).

típico, -ca ['tſipiku, -ka] *adj (comida, bebida, costume)* traditional; **ser ~ de** to be typical of.

tipo, -pa ['tſipu, -pa] *m* type ♦ *m, f (Port: fam: pessoa)* guy *(f* girl).

tipografia [tſipogra'fia] *f (local)* printing works *(sg)*.

tíquete-refeição [tſi,ketſixefei'sãw] *(pl* **tíquetes-refeição** [tſi,ketſiʒxefei-'sãw]) *m (Br)* luncheon voucher.

tiracolo [tſira'kɔlu] *m:* **a ~** across the shoulder.

tiragem [tſi'raʒẽ] *(pl* **-ns** [-ʃ]) *f (de jornal, revista)* circulation; *(livro)* print run.

tira-manchas [tſira'mãʃaʃ] *m inv (Br)* stain remover.

tirania [tſira'nia] *f* tyranny.

tira-nódoas [tſira'nɔdwaʃ] *m inv (Port)* = **tira-manchas**.

tirar [tſi'ra(x)] *vt* to take; *(remover)* to take off; **~ algo de alguém** *(roubar)* to steal sthg from sb; **~ algo à sorte** to pick sthg at random; **~ a mesa** *(Br)* to clear the table.

tirinhas [tſi'riɲaʃ] *fpl* strips; **às OU em ~** in strips.

tiritar [tſiri'ta(x)] *vi* to shiver.

tiro ['tſiru] *m* shot; **~ ao alvo** target shooting.

tiroteio [tſiro'teju] *m (tiros)* shooting; *(troca de disparos)* shoot-out.

título ['tſitulu] *m* title; *(documento)* bond.

tive ['tſivi] → **ter**.

to [tu] = **te + o**, → **te**.

toalete [twa'letſi] *m (Br) (banheiro)* toilet; *(roupa)* clothes *(pl)* ♦ *f:* **fazer a ~** *(Br)* to have a wash.

toalha ['twaʎa] *f* towel; **~ de banho** bath towel; **~ de mesa** tablecloth.

tobogã [tobo'gã] *m* toboggan.

toca-discos [tɔka'dʒiʃkuʃ] *m inv (Br)* record player.

toca-fitas [tɔka'fitaʃ] *m inv (Br)* cassette player.

tocar [to'ka(x)] *vt (instrumento)* to play ♦ *vi* to touch; *(campainha, sino, telefone)* to ring; *(MÚS)* to play; **~ em** *(em pessoa, objeto)* to touch; *(em assunto)* to touch on; **~ na campainha** to ring the bell. ❑ **tocar a** *v + prep:* **toca a ele pedir uma explicação** it's up to him to ask for an explanation; **no que me toca** as far as I'm concerned.

tocha ['tɔʃa] *f* torch.

todavia [toda'via] *adv* still ♦ *conj* but, however.

todo, -da ['todu, -da] *adj* all; **toda a gente** *(Port)* everyone, everybody; **~ o dia/mês** all day/month; **~ (o) mundo** *(Br)* everyone, everybody; **todas as coisas** everything *(sg)*; **~s os dias/meses** every day/month; **~s nós** all of us; **em toda a parte** everywhere; **ao ~** altogether, in total; **de ~** completely; **no ~** all in all. ❑ **todos, -das** *pron pl (pessoas)* every-

one *(sg)*, everybody *(sg)*; *(coisas)* all;
quero ~s I want them all, I want all of
them.

Todos-os-Santos [ˌtoduzuʃˈsãntuʃ] *s*
→ **dia.**

toldo [ˈtowdu] *m* awning.

tolerância [toleˈrãsja] *f* tolerance.

tolerar [toleˈra(x)] *vt* to tolerate.

tolice [toˈlisi] *f (coisa sem valor)* trifle;
(asneira) stupid thing.

tolo, -la [ˈtolu, -la] *adj* silly.

tom [ˈtõ] *(pl* **-ns** [-ʃ]) *m* tone; *(de cor)*
shade; **em ~ de graça** in jest; **ser de
bom ~** to be the done thing.

tomada [toˈmada] *f (elétrica)* socket;
(de lugar, edifício) seizure; **~ de posse**
(de governo, presidente) investiture.

tomar [toˈma(x)] *vt* to take; *(bebida)* to
have; *(lugar, edifício)* to seize; **toma!**
here you are!; **vamos ~ um café!** let's
go for a coffee!; **~ ar** to get some air;
~ o café da manhã to have breakfast;
~ posse *(de cargo político)* to take
office.

tomara [toˈmara] *interj* if only!

tomate [toˈmatʃi] *m* tomato.

tombar [tõmˈba(x)] *vt* to knock over
◆ *vi* to fall.

tombo [ˈtõmbu] *m* tumble; **levar um
~** to fall over.

tomilho [toˈmiʎu] *m* thyme.

tonalidade [tonaliˈdadʒi] *f (de som)*
key; *(de cor)* shade.

tonel [toˈnɛw] *(pl* **-éis** [-ɛiʃ]) *m (para
vinho)* vat.

tonelada [toneˈlada] *f* tonne.

tónica [ˈtɔnika] *f (Port)* = **tônica.**

tônica [ˈtonika] *f (Br):* **pôr a ~ em** to
put emphasis on .

tónico, -ca [ˈtɔniku, -ka] *adj & m
(Port)*= **tônico.**

tônico, -ca [ˈtoniku, -ka] *adj (Br)*
tonic; *(fortificante)* invigorating ◆ *m
(Br) (medicamento)* tonic.

tons → **tom.**

tonto, -ta [ˈtõntu, -ta] *adj (com ton-
turas)* dizzy; *(tolo)* silly.

tontura [tõnˈtura] *f* dizziness.

topázio [toˈpazju] *m* topaz.

tópico [ˈtɔpiku] *m* topic.

topless [tɔpˈlɛs] *adj* topless; **fazer ~**
to go topless.

topo [ˈtopu] *m* top.

toque [ˈtɔki] *m (contato)* touch; *(som)*
chime, chiming; *(de campainha)* ring.

toranja [toˈrãʒa] *f* grapefruit.

tórax [ˈtɔraks] *m* thorax.

torcedor, -ra [toxseˈdo(x), -ra] *(mpl*
-res [-riʃ], *fpl* **-s** [-ʃ]) *m, f (Br: ESP)* supporter, fan.

torcer [toxˈse(x)] *vt* to twist; *(espremer)* to wring out; **~ o nariz para algo**
to turn one's nose up at sthg.

⅃ torcer por *v + prep (apoiar)* to support.

⅃ torcer-se *vp (de riso, dor)* to double
up.

torcicolo [toxsiˈkɔlu] *m:* **ter um ~** to
have a crick in one's neck.

torcida [toxˈsida] *f (pavio)* wick; *(Br:
de futebol)* supporters *(pl)*.

torcido, -da [toxˈsidu, -da] *adj* twisted.

tordo [ˈtoxdu] *m* thrush.

tormenta [toxˈmẽnta] *f* storm.

tormento [toxˈmẽntu] *m* torment.

tornado [toxˈnadu] *m* tornado.

tornar [toxˈna(x)] *vt* to make; **~ algo
em algo** to turn sthg into sthg.

⅃ tornar a *v + prep:* **~ a fazer algo** to
do sthg again.

⅃ tornar-se *vp* to become.

torneio [toxˈneju] *m* tournament.

torneira [toxˈnejra] *f* tap, faucet
(Am).

torno [ˈtoxnu] *m:* **em ~ de** around.

tornozelo [toxnoˈzelu] *m* ankle.

torpedo [toxˈpedu] *m* torpedo.

torrada [toˈxada] *f (a slice of)* toast.

torradeira [toxaˈdejra] *f* toaster.

torrão [toˈxãw] *(pl* **-ões** [-õjʃ]) *m (de
terra)* clod; **~ de açúcar** sugar lump.

torrar [toˈxa(x)] *vt* to toast.

torre [ˈtoxi] *f (construção)* tower; *(em
xadrez)* rook, castle.

torrente [toˈxẽntʃi] *f* torrent.

torresmos [toˈxeʒmuʃ] *mpl cubes of
pork marinated in white wine and herbs,
then fried and served with boiled potatoes.*

tórrido, -da [ˈtɔxidu, -da] *adj* torrid.

torrões → **torrão.**

torta [ˈtɔrta] *f (Port)* swiss roll.

torto, torta [ˈtoxtu, ˈtɔrta] *adj* bent;
a ~ e a direito left, right and centre.

tortura [toxˈtura] *f* torture.

tos [tuʃ] = **te + os,** → **te.**

tosse [ˈtɔsi] *f* cough; **~ convulsa**
whooping cough.

tossir [toˈsi(x)] *vi* to cough.

tosta [ˈtɔʃta] *f (Port)* toasted sandwich.

tostado, -da [toʃ'tadu, -da] *adj (pão)* toasted; *(frango)* cooked till golden brown.

tostão [toʃ'tãw] *(pl* -ões [-õjʃ]) *m* = copper *(Brit)*, = dime *(Am)*; **não valer um ~ furado** not to be worth a penny.

total [to'taw] *(pl* -ais [-ajʃ]) *adj & m* total; **no ~ in** all.

totalidade [tutali'dadʒi] *f* whole; **a ~ dos meus alunos** all (of) my students; **na ~** *(no total)* in total; *(totalmente)* completely.

totalmente [totaw'mẽntʃi] *adv* totally.

touca ['toka] *f* cap; **~ de banho** *(em piscina)* swimming cap; *(em duche)* shower cap.

toucador [toka'do(x)] *(pl* -res [-riʃ]) *m* dressing table.

toucinho [to'siɲu] *m* streaky bacon; **~ defumado** smoked streaky bacon.

toucinho-do-céu [to,siɲudu'sɛu] *(pl* **toucinhos-do-céu** [to,siɲuʒdu'sɛu]) *m* pudding made with ground almonds, egg yolks, butter and sugar and covered in caramel.

toupeira [to'pejra] *f* mole.

tourada [to'rada] *f* bullfight.

toureiro [to'rejru] *m* bullfighter.

touro ['toru] *m* bull.

⌐ **Touro** *m* Taurus.

tóxico, -ca ['tɔksiku, -ka] *adj* toxic, poisonous.

Tr. *abrev* = **travessa**.

trabalhador, -ra [trabaʎa'do(x), -ra] *(mpl* -res [-riʃ], *fpl* -s [-ʃ]) *adj* hard-working ♦ *m, f* worker.

trabalhar [traba'ʎa(x)] *vi & vt* to work.

trabalho [tra'baʎu] *m* work; **~ de casa** *(EDUC)* homework; **~ de parto** labour; **~s manuais** arts and crafts *(subject studied at middle school)*.

traça ['trasa] *f* moth.

tração [tra'sãw] *f (Br)* traction.

traçar [tra'sa(x)] *vt (linha, desenho)* to draw; *(plano)* to draw up.

tracção [tra'sãw] *f (Port)* = **tração**.

traço ['trasu] *m (risco)* line; *(vestígio)* trace; *(de rosto, personalidade)* feature.

tractor [tra'tor] *(pl* -es [-eʃ]) *m (Port)* = **trator**.

tradição [tradʒi'sãw] *(pl* -ões [-õjʃ]) *f* tradition.

tradicional [tradʒisjo'naw] *(pl* -ais [-ajʃ]) *adj* traditional.

tradições → **tradição**.

tradução [tradu'sãw] *(pl* -ões [-õjʃ]) *f* translation.

tradutor, -ra [tradu'to(x), -ra] *(mpl* -res [-riʃ], *fpl* -s [-ʃ]) *m, f* translator.

traduzir [tradu'zi(x)] *vt & vi* to translate.

tráfego ['trafegu] *m* traffic.

traficante [trafi'kãntʃi] *mf* trafficker.

traficar [trafi'ka(x)] *vt* to traffic in.

tráfico ['trafiku] *m* traffic.

tragédia [tra'ʒedʒja] *f* tragedy.

trágico, -ca ['traʒiku, -ka] *adj* tragic.

trago ['tragu] → **trazer**.

traição [traj'sãw] *(pl* -ões [-õjʃ]) *f (de amigo, companheiro)* betrayal; *(de país)* treason; **à ~** treacherously.

traidor, -ra [traj'do(x), -ra] *(mpl* -res [-riʃ], *fpl* -s [-ʃ]) *m, f* traitor.

traineira [traj'nejra] *f* trawler.

traje ['traʒi] *m* clothes *(pl)*; **~ de noite** evening gown; **~ típico** traditional costume OU dress; **~s menores** underwear *(sg)*.

trajecto [tra'ʒɛtu] *m (Port)* = **trajeto**.

trajectória [traʒɛ'tɔrja] *f (Port)* = **trajetória**.

trajeto [tra'ʒɛtu] *m (Br) (caminho)* route; *(viagem)* journey, trip.

trajetória [traʒɛ'tɔrja] *f (Br)* trajectory.

tralha ['traʎa] *f (fam)* junk, stuff.

trama ['trama] *f (de fios)* weft; *(de livro, filme)* plot.

tramar [tra'ma(x)] *vt*: **~ algo** *(fam: conspirar)* to plot sthg.

trâmite ['tramitʃi] *m* procedure; **os ~s legais** legal procedures.

trampolim [trãmpo'lĩ] *(pl* -ns [-ʃ]) *m* springboard.

tranca ['trãŋka] *f* bar.

trança ['trãsa] *f* plait *(Brit)*, braid *(Am)*.

trancar [trãŋ'ka(x)] *vt* to bar.

tranquilidade [trãŋkwili'dade] *f (Port)* = **tranqüilidade**.

tranqüilidade [trãŋkwili'dadʒi] *f (Br)* peace, tranquillity.

tranqüilizante [trãŋkwili'zãntʃi] *adj* reassuring ♦ *m* tranquillizer.

tranqüilo, -la [trãŋ'kwilu, -la] *adj* calm; *(local)* peaceful.

transação [trãza'sãw] *(pl* -ões [-õjʃ]) *f (Br)* transaction.

transacção [trãza'sãw] *(pl* -ões [-õjʃ])

f (Port) = transação.

transações → transação.

transar [trãˈza(x)] *vt (Br: fam: combinar)* to arrange ◆ *vi:* ~ **com alguém** *(Br: fam)* to have it off with sb.

transatlântico, -ca [trãzatˈlãntʃiku, -ka] *adj* transatlantic ◆ *m* (ocean) liner.

transbordar [trãʒboxˈda(x)] *vi* to overflow; **a** ~ overflowing.

transbordo [trãʒˈboxdu] *m* transfer; **fazer** ~ to transfer.

transe [ˈtrãzi] *m* trance.

transeunte [trãˈzeũntʃi] *mf* passerby.

transferência [trãʃfeˈrẽsja] *f* transfer.

transferir [trãʃfeˈri(x)] *vt* to transfer.

transformador [trãʃfoxmaˈdo(x)] *(pl -res* [-riʃ]) *m* transformer.

transformar [trãʃfoxˈma(x)] *vt* to transform.

transfusão [trãʃfuˈzãw] *(pl -ões* [-õjʃ]) *f:* ~ **dé sangue** blood transfusion.

transgredir [trãʒgreˈdi(x)] *vt (lei)* to break, to violate; *(direito)* to infringe.

transgressão [trãʒgreˈsãw] *(pl -ões* [-õjʃ]) *f (de lei)* violation; *(de direito)* infringement.

transição [trãziˈsãw] *(pl -ões* [-õjʃ]) *f* transition.

transístor [trãˈziʃto(x)] *(pl -res* [-iʃ]) *m* transistor.

transitar [trãziˈta(x)] *vi* to circulate; ~ **para** to move on to; ~ **(de ano)** to go up a year.

transitivo, -va [trãziˈtʃivu, -va] *adj (GRAM)* transitive.

trânsito [ˈtrãzitu] *m* traffic; "~ **congestionado**" "heavy traffic ahead"; "~ **proibido**" "no entry" *(for vehicular traffic)*; "~ **nos dois sentidos**" "two-way traffic".

transmissão [trãʒmiˈsãw] *(pl -ões* [-õjʃ]) *f (de rádio, televisão)* broadcast, transmission; *(de mensagem)* passing on; *(de doença, genes)* transmission.

transmitir [trãʒmiˈtʃi(x)] *vt (suj: rádio, televisão)* to broadcast; *(mensagem)* to pass on; *(doença, genes)* to transmit ◆ *vi (rádio, televisão)* to broadcast, to transmit.

transparência [trãʃpaˈrẽsja] *f* transparency.

transparente [trãʃpaˈrẽntʃi] *adj* transparent; *(água)* clear; *(roupa, tecido)* see-through.

transpiração [trãʃpiraˈsãw] *f* perspiration.

transpirar [trãʃpiˈra(x)] *vi* to perspire.

transplantar [trãʃplãnˈta(x)] *vt* to transplant.

transplante [trãʃˈplãntʃi] *m (de planta, árvore)* transplanting; *(de órgão)* transplant.

transportar [trãʃpoxˈta(x)] *vt* to carry; *(suj: veículo)* to transport.

transporte [trãʃˈpoxtʃi] *m* transport; ~ **coletivo** public transport; ~**s públicos** public transport *(sg)*.

transtornar [trãʃtoxˈna(x)] *vt (pessoa)* to upset; *(reunião, rotina)* to disrupt.

transtorno [trãʃˈtoxnu] *m* disruption; **causar** ~ to cause disruption.

trapalhão, -lhona [trapaˈʎãw, -ʎona] *(mpl -ões* [-õjʃ], *fpl -s* [-ʃ]) *m, f* bungler.

trapézio [traˈpɛzju] *m* trapeze.

trapezista [trapeˈziʃta] *mf* trapeze artist.

trapo [ˈtrapu] *m* rag.

trarei [traˈrej] → trazer.

trás [ˈtrajʃ] *interj* bang! ◆ *prep & adv:* **deixar para** ~ to leave behind; **por** ~ **de** behind; **de** ~ from behind; **para** ~ back(wards).

traseira [traˈzejra] *f (de carro)* rear *(sg)*.

traseiro, -ra [traˈzejru, -ra] *adj (parte, assento)* back *(antes de s)* ◆ *m* backside.

tratado, -da [traˈtadu, -da] *adj* treated; *(assunto)* sorted out ◆ *m (acordo)* treaty; *(ensaio)* treatise.

tratamento [trataˈmẽntu] *m* treatment; *(INFORM)* processing.

tratar [traˈta(x)] *vt* to treat; ~ **alguém bem/mal** to treat sb well/badly.

❏ **tratar de** *v + prep* to deal with.

❏ **tratar-se de** *vp + prep:* **trata-se de um erro** it's a mistake; **de quem se trata?** who is it?

trator [traˈto(x)] *(pl -res* [-riʃ]) *m (Br)* tractor.

trauma [ˈtrawma] *m* trauma.

Trav. *(abrev)* = travessa.

travão [traˈvãw] *(pl -ões* [-õjʃ]) *m (Port)* brake; ~ **de mão** handbrake.

travar [traˈva(x)] *vt (combate, luta)* to wage ◆ *vi (Port)* to brake; ~ **conhecimento com alguém** to meet sb.

trave [ˈtravi] *f* beam; *(em futebol)* crossbar.

travessa [tra'vesa] f (rua) lane; (peça de louça) platter; (para cabelo) (decorative) comb.

travessão [trave'sãw] (pl -ões [-õjʃ]) m (para cabelo) (decorative) comb; (sinal gráfico) dash.

travesseiro [trave'sejru] m pillow.

travessia [trave'sia] f crossing.

travesso, -a [tra'vesu, -a] adj naughty.

travessões → travessão.

travões → travão.

traz ['trajʃ] → trazer.

trazer [tra'ze(x)] vt to bring; (vestir) to wear; (problemas) to cause; (consequências) to have.

trégua ['trɛgwa] f (descanso) break; (em conflito) truce.

treinador, -ra [trejna'do(x), -ra] (mpl -res [-riʃ], fpl -s [-ʃ]) m, f trainer.

treinar [trej'na(x)] vt to train.
❏ **treinar-se** vp to train.

treino ['trejnu] m training.

trela ['trela] f (para cão) lead.

trem ['trẽ] (pl -ns [-ʃ]) m (Br) train; **~ de aterrissagem** (de avião) landing gear; **~ de prata** luxury train which runs between Rio de Janeiro and São Paulo; **de ~** by train; **pegar o ~** to catch the train.

tremendo, -da [tre'mẽdu, -da] adj tremendous; (horrível) terrible.

tremer [tre'me(x)] vi to tremble; **~ de frio** to shiver with cold.

tremor [tre'mo(x)] (pl -res [-riʃ]) m (de frio) shivering; (de medo) trembling; **~ de terra** earthquake.

trémulo, -la ['tremulu, -la] adj (Port) = trêmulo.

trêmulo, -la ['tremulu, -la] adj (Br) (mãos, pernas) trembling; (luz) flickering; (voz) quivering.

trenó ['trɛ'nɔ] m sledge.

trens → trem.

trepadeira [trepa'dejra] f (planta) climber; (roseira) rambler.

trepar [tre'pa(x)] vt & vi to climb; **~ em** to climb up.

três ['trejʃ] num three, → seis.

trespassar [treʃpa'sa(x)] vt (loja, estabelecimento) to transfer; (transgredir) to violate.

trevas ['trɛvaʃ] fpl darkness (sg).

trevo ['trevu] m (planta) clover; (símbolo da Irlanda) shamrock.

treze ['trezi] num thirteen, → seis.

trezentos, -tas [tre'zẽtuʃ, -taʃ]

num three hundred, → seis.

triângulo [tri'ãngulu] m triangle.

tribo ['tribu] f tribe.

tribuna [tri'buna] f (de estádio) grandstand.

tribunal [tribu'naw] (pl -ais [-ajʃ]) m court.

triciclo [tri'siklu] m tricycle.

tricô [tri'ko] m knitting.

tricotar [triko'ta(x)] vt to knit.

trigésimo, -ma [tri'ʒɛzimu, -ma] num thirtieth, → sexto.

trigo ['trigu] m wheat.

trilha ['triʎa] f path; **~ sonora** (Br) soundtrack.

trilho ['triʎu] m (carril) rail; (caminho) path.

trimestral [trimeʃ'traw] (pl -ais [-ajʃ]) adj quarterly.

trimestre [tri'mɛʃtri] m quarter.

trincar [trĩŋ'ka(x)] vt to bite.

trincheira [trĩ'ʃejra] f (escavação) trench.

trinco ['trĩŋku] m latch; **fechar a porta com ~** to leave the door on the latch.

trinta ['trĩnta] num thirty, → seis.

trio ['triu] m trio; **~ elétrico** (Br) float on which a show is held and music played during carnival.

tripa ['tripa] f (intestino) gut.
❏ **tripas** fpl (dobrada) tripe (sg).

tripé ['tripɛ] m (de máquina fotográfica, telescópio) tripod; (banco) stool.

triplicar [tripli'ka(x)] vt to triple.

tripulação [tripula'sãw] (pl -ões [-õjʃ]) f crew.

tripular [tripu'la(x)] vt to man.

triste ['triʃʧi] adj (pessoa) unhappy, sad; (local) gloomy.

tristeza [triʃ'teza] f (de pessoa) sadness; (local) gloominess; **que ~!** what a shame!

triunfar [triũ'fa(x)] vi to win.

triunfo [tri'ũfu] m triumph.

trivial [tri'vjaw] (pl -ais [-ajʃ]) adj trivial.

triz ['triʃ] m (fam: momento) second; **por um ~** by the skin of one's teeth.

troca ['trɔka] f exchange, swap; **dar algo em ~ de algo** to give sthg in exchange for sthg.

troça ['trɔsa] f: **fazer ~ de** to make fun of.

trocado, -da [tro'kadu, -da] adj mixed-up.

❏ **trocados** *mpl* loose change *(sg)*.

trocar [tro'ka(x)] *vt* to change; *(idéias)* to exchange; *(confundir)* to mix up.

❏ **trocar de** *v* + *prep* to change.

❏ **trocar-se** *vp* to get changed.

troco ['troku] *m* change; *(fig: resposta)* retort; **dar o ~** *(responder)* to reply in kind; **a ~ de** in exchange for.

troço ['trosu] *m (fam) (coisa)* thing; *(tralha)* junk; **ter um ~** *(fam: passar mal)* to be taken ill.

troféu [tro'feu] *m* trophy.

tromba ['trõmba] *f (de elefante)* trunk; *(de chuva)* downpour.

trombeta [trõm'beta] *f* trumpet.

trombone [trõm'bɔni] *m:* **~ (de varas)** trombone.

trompa ['trõmpa] *f* horn.

trompete [trõm'pɛtʃi] *m* trumpet.

tronco ['trõŋku] *m* trunk.

trono ['tronu] *m* throne.

tropa ['trɔpa] *f* army.

tropeçar [trope'sa(x)] *vi* to trip; **~ em algo** to trip over sthg.

tropical [tropi'kaw] *(pl* **-ais** [-ajʃ]*) adj* tropical.

trópico ['trɔpiku] *m* tropic.

trotar [tro'ta(x)] *vi* to trot.

trotinete [trotʃi'nɛtʃi] *f (de criança)* scooter; *(pequeno trator)* (motorized) cultivator.

trouxa ['troʃa] *f* bundle.

trouxas-de-ovos [ˌtroʃaʒ'dʒiovuʃ] *fpl* dessert consisting of small bundles of "doce de ovos".

trouxe ['trosi] → **trazer.**

trovão [tro'vãw] *(pl* **-ões** [-õjʃ]*) m* clap of thunder.

trovejar [trove'ʒa(x)] *v impess* to thunder.

trovoada [tro'vwada] *f (ruído)* thunder; *(tempestade)* thunderstorm.

trovões → **trovão.**

trucidar [trusi'da(x)] *vt* to slaughter.

trufas ['trufaʃ] *fpl* truffles.

trunfo ['trũfu] *m* trump.

truque ['truki] *m* trick.

trusses ['trusɛʃ] *mpl (Port)* (men's) briefs.

truta ['truta] *f* trout.

T-shirt [tʃi'ʃartʃi] *f* T-shirt.

tu ['tu] *pron (Port)* you; **e ~?!** what about you?; **és ~?!** is that you?!; **~ mesmo** OU **próprio** you yourself.

tua → **teu.**

tuba ['tuba] *f* tuba.

tubarão [tuba'rãw] *(pl* **-ões** [-õjʃ]*) m* shark.

tuberculose [tubɛxku'lɔzi] *f* tuberculosis.

tubo ['tubu] *m* tube; **~ de ensaio** test tube; **~ de escape** *(Port)* exhaust (pipe) *(Brit)*, tail pipe *(Am)*.

tudo ['tudu] *pron inv* everything; **por ~ e por nada** over the slightest thing; **dar ~ por ~** to give one's all.

tulipa [tu'lipa] *f (Br) (planta)* tulip; *(copo)* tall beer glass.

túlipa ['tulipa] *f (Port) (planta)* tulip; *(quebra-luz)* (tulip-shaped) lampshade.

tumba ['tũmba] *f* tomb.

tumor [tu'mo(x)] *(pl* **-res** [-riʃ]*) m* tumour; **~ maligno/benigno** malignant/benign tumour.

túmulo ['tumulu] *m* tomb.

tumulto [tu'muwtu] *m (alvoroço)* commotion, ruckus; *(revolta)* uproar.

tuna ['tuna] *f:* **~ (académica)** *group of student minstrels.*

túnel ['tunew] *(pl* **-eis** [-ejʃ]*) m* tunnel.

túnica ['tunika] *f* tunic.

turbina [tux'bina] *f* turbine.

turbulência [turbu'lẽsia] *f* turbulence.

turco, -ca ['turku, -ka] *adj* Turkish ◆ *m, f (pessoa)* Turk ◆ *m (língua)* Turkish; *(tecido)* towelling.

turfe ['tuxfi] *m (Br) (hipódromo)* racecourse; *(hipismo)* horse racing.

turismo [tu'riʒmu] *m* tourism.

turista [tu'rifta] *mf* tourist.

turístico, -ca [tu'rifʧiku, -ka] *adj* tourist *(antes de s)*.

turma ['tuxma] *f (em escola)* class; *(Br: fam: amigos)* gang.

turné [tur'ne] *f (Port)* = **turnê.**

turnê ['tuxne] *f (Br)* tour.

turno ['tuxnu] *m* shift; **por seu ~** in turn; **por ~s** in shifts.

turquesa [tux'keza] *f* turquoise.

Turquia [txr'kia] *f:* **a ~** Turkey.

tutano [tu'tanu] *m* marrow.

tutela [tu'tɛla] *f* guardianship.

tutor, -ra [tu'to(x), -ra] *(mpl* **-res** [-riʃ]*. fpl* **-s** [-ʃ]*) m, f* guardian.

tutu [tu'tu] *m:* **~ à mineira** *bean stew with cassava flour, salted pork and bacon.*

TV *f (abrev de televisão)* TV.

tweed ['twidʒi] *m* tweed.

U

UE f (abrev de União Européia) EU.

UEM f (abrev de União Econômica e Monetária) EMU.

uísque [ˈwiski] m whisky.

uivar [uiˈva(x)] vi to howl.

úlcera [ˈuwsɛra] f ulcer.

ulmeiro [uwˈmejru] m elm.

ultimamente [ˌuwtʃimaˈmẽntʃi] adv lately.

ultimato [uwtʃiˈmatu] m ultimatum.

último, -ma [ˈuwtʃimu, -ma] adj last; (mais recente, novo) latest; (mais alto) top; (mais baixo) bottom ◆ m, f: **o ~/a última** (em ordem, fila) the last one; **a última** (novidade) the latest; **por ~** lastly.

ultraleve [ˌuwtraˈlɛvi] m microlight.

ultramar [ˌuwtraˈma(x)] m overseas.

ultramarino, -na [ˌuwtramaˈrinu, -na] adj overseas.

ultrapassado, -da [ˌuwtrapaˈsadu, -da] adj outdated.

ultrapassagem [ˌuwtrapaˈsaʒẽ] (pl -ns [-ʃ]) f overtaking.

ultrapassar [ˌuwtrapaˈsa(x)] vt to overtake.

ultravioleta [ˌuwtravjoˈleta] adj ultraviolet.

um, uma [ũ, ˈuma] (mpl uns [ũʃ], fpl umas [ˈumaʃ]) artigo indefinido a, an (antes de vogal ou "h" mudo); **~ homem** a man; **uma casa** a house; **uma mulher** a woman; **uma hora** an hour; **uma maçã** an apple.
◆ adj 1. (exprime quantidade, data indefinida) one, some (pl); **comprei uns livros** I bought some books; **~ dia voltarei** I'll be back one day; **vou umas semanas de férias** I'm going on holiday for a few weeks.
2. (para indicar quantidades) one; **trinta e ~ dias** thirty-one days; **~ litro/metro/quilo** a litre/metre/kilo.
3. (aproximadamente) about, around; **esperei uns dez minutos** I waited for about ten minutes; **estavam lá umas cinquenta pessoas** there were about fifty people there.
4. (para enfatizar): **está ~ frio/calor** it's so cold/hot; **estou com uma sede** I'm so thirsty; **foi ~ daqueles dias!** it was one of those days!
◆ pron (indefinido) one, some (pl) **dê ~** give me one; **pede mais uma** ask for another one; **só não gosto dum/duma** there's only one (of them) I don't like; **~ deles** one of them; **~ a ~, ~ por ~** one by one.
◆ num one, → **seis**.

umbanda [ũmˈbãnda] f Afro-Brazilian cult religion.

umbigo [ũmˈbigu] m navel.

umbral [ũmˈbraw] (pl -ais [-ajʃ]) m doorway.

umidade [umiˈdadʒi] f (Br) humidity.

úmido, -da [ˈumidu, -da] adj (Br) (tempo) humid; (superfície, tecido) damp.

unanimidade [unanemiˈdadʒi] f: **por ~** unanimously.

UNE f (Br: abrev de União Nacional de Estudantes) Brazilian students' union, ≈ NUS (Brit).

Unesco [uˈnɛʃku] f UNESCO.

unha [ˈuɲa] f nail; **fazer as ~s** to do one's nails.

união [uˈnjãw] (pl -ões [-õjʃ]) f union; (entre amigos, colegas) unity; **a União Européia** the European Union.

unicamente [ˌunikaˈmẽntʃi] adv only.

único, -ca [ˈuniku, -ka] adj (preço) fixed; (um só) only; (incomparável) unique ◆ m, f: **o ~/a única** the only one; **tamanho ~** one size.

unidade [uniˈdadʒi] f unit; (conformidade, uniformidade) unity; (união) union.

unido, -da [uˈnidu, -da] *adj* united; **eles são muito ~s** they're very close.

unificar [unifiˈka(x)] *vt* to unite.

uniforme [uniˈfɔxmi] *adj & m* uniform.

uniões → união.

unir [uˈni(x)] *vt* to join; *(pessoas, países)* to unite; *(anexar)* to attach.

❑ **unir-se** *vp* to join forces; **~-se contra** to join forces against.

unissex [uniˈsɛks] *adj inv (Br)* unisex.

unissexo [uniˈsɛksu] *adj inv (Port)* = **unissex**.

unitário, -ria [uniˈtarju, -rja] *adj* unitarian.

universal [univexˈsaw] (*pl* **-ais** [-ajʃ]) *adj* universal.

universidade [univexsiˈdadʒi] *f* university.

universo [uniˈvɛxsu] *m* universe.

uns → um.

untar [ũnˈta(x)] *vt* to grease.

urânio [uˈranju] *m* uranium.

urbano, -na [uxˈbanu, -na] *adj* urban.

urgência [uxˈʒẽsja] *f* urgency; **com ~** urgently.

❑ **Urgências** *fpl* accident and emergency *(sg)(Brit)*, emergency room *(sg)(Am)*.

urgente [uxˈʒẽntʃi] *adj* urgent.

urgentemente [uxˌʒẽntʃiˈmẽntʃi] *adv* urgently.

urina [uˈrina] *f* urine.

urinol [uriˈnɔw] (*pl* **-óis** [-ɔjʃ]) *m* urinal.

urna [ˈuxna] *f (de voto)* ballot box.

urrar [uˈxa(x)] *vi* to roar.

urso [ˈuxsu] *m* bear; **~ pardo** grizzly (bear); **~ de pelúcia** teddy bear; **~ polar** polar bear.

urticária [uxtʃiˈkarja] *f* hives *(pl)*.

urtiga [uxˈtʃiga] *f* (stinging) nettle.

Uruguai [uruˈgwaj] *m*: **o ~** Uruguay.

urze [ˈuxzi] *f* heather.

usado, -da [uˈzadu, -da] *adj* used; *(gasto)* worn.

usar [uˈza(x)] *vt (utilizar)* to use; *(vestir, calçar)* to wear.

❑ **usar de** *v + prep* to use.

❑ **usar-se** *vp* to be used; **agora usa-se muito o marrom** brown is very popular at the moment.

usina [uˈzina] *f (Br)* factory; **~ de açúcar** sugar refinery; **~ hidroelétrica** hydroelectric power station; **~ nuclear** nuclear power plant.

uso [ˈuzu] *m (utilização)* use; *(costume)* custom; **"para ~ externo"** "for external use only"; **fazer ~ de** to make use of; **para ~ próprio** for personal use.

usual [uˈzwaw] (*pl* **-ais** [-ajʃ]) *adj* common.

usufruir [uzufruˈi(x)] : **usufruir de** *v + prep (possuir)* to enjoy; *(tirar proveito de)* to make the most of.

usurpar [uzuxˈpa(x)] *vt* to usurp.

úteis → útil.

utensílio [utẽˈsilju] *m* utensil.

utente [uˈtẽnte] *mf (Port)* user.

útero [ˈutcru] *m* womb.

útil [ˈutʃiw] (*pl* **úteis** [ˈutejʃ]) *adj* useful.

utilidade [utʃiliˈdadʒi] *f (qualidade)* usefulness; *(proveito)* use; **isto não tem ~ nenhuma** this is useless.

utilização [utʃilizaˈsãw] (*pl* **-ões** [-õjʃ]) *f* use.

utilizar [utʃiliˈza(x)] *vt (empregar)* to use; *(tirar proveito de)* to make use of.

utopia [utoˈpia] *f* utopia.

U.V. *(abrev de ultra violeta)* UV.

uva [ˈuva] *f* grape.

V

V. *(abrev de vide)* v.

vá ['va] → **ir**.

vã → **vão²**.

vaca ['vaka] *f (animal)* cow; *(carne)* beef.

vacilar [vasi'la(x)] *vi (hesitar)* to waver.

vacina [va'sina] *f* vaccine.

vacinação [vasina'sãw] *f* vaccination.

vácuo ['vakwu] *m* vacuum.

vadio, -dia [va'dʒiu, -'dʒia] *adj (cão)* stray; *(pessoa)* idle.

vaga ['vaga] *f (em emprego)* vacancy; *(onda)* wave.

vagabundo, -da [vaga'bũndu, -da] *m, f* tramp.

vaga-lume [ˌvaga'lumi] *(pl* **vaga-lumes** [ˌvaga'lumeʃ]*) m* glow-worm.

vagão [va'gãw] *(pl* **-ões** [-õjʃ]*) m (de mercadorias)* wagon; *(Br: de passageiros)* carriage.

vagão-cama [vagãw'kama] *(pl* **vagões-cama** [vagõjʃ'kama]*) m (Port)* = **vagão-leito**.

vagão-leito [vagãw'lejtu] *(pl* **vagões-leito** [vagõiʒ'lejtu]*) m (Br)* sleeping car.

vagão-restaurante [vaˌgãwxeʃtaw-'rãntʃi] *(pl* **vagões-restaurante** [vaˌgõjʃxeʃtaw'rãntʃi]*) m* buffet car.

vagar [va'ga(x)] *vi (ficar livre)* to be vacant ◆ *m*: **ter ~ (para)** to have time (for).

vagaroso, -osa [vaga'rozu, -ɔza] *adj* slow.

vagem ['vaʒẽ] *(pl* **-ns** [-ʃ]*) f* pod. ⊔ **vagens** *fpl (feijão-verde)* green beans.

vagina [va'ʒina] *f* vagina.

vago, -ga ['vagu, -ga] *adj (lugar)* free; *(casa)* empty; *(indefinido)* vague.

vagões → **vagão**.

vai ['vaj] → **ir**.

vaidade [vaj'dadʒi] *f* vanity.

vaidoso, -osa [vaj'dozu, -ɔza] *adj* vain.

vais ['vajʃ] → **ir**.

vaivém [vaj'vẽ] *(pl* **-ns** [-ʃ]*) m (movimento)* to-ing and fro-ing, comings and goings *(pl)*.

vala ['vala] *f* ditch; **~ comum** *(sepultura)* common grave.

vale¹ ['vali] → **valer**.

vale² ['vali] *m (planície)* valley; **~ postal** postal order.

valente [va'lẽntʃi] *adj (corajoso)* brave; *(forte)* strong.

valer [va'le(x)] *vt (ter o valor de)* to be worth ◆ *vi (ter validade)* to count; **vale mais ...** it's better to ...; **a ~** *(de verdade)* for real; **para ~** for real. ⊔ **valer-se de** *vp + prep* to make use of.

valeta [va'leta] *f* ditch.

valete [va'letʃi] *m* jack.

valeu [va'lew] → **valer**.

valho ['vaʎu] → **valer**.

validação [valida'sãw] *f* validation.

validade [vali'dadʒi] *f* validity.

validar [vali'da(x)] *vt* to validate.

válido, -da ['validu, -da] *adj* valid; **~ até ...** *(produto)* best before ..., use by ...; *(documento)* expiry date ....

valioso, -osa [va'ljozu, -ɔza] *adj* valuable.

valor [va'lo(x)] *(pl* **-res** [-riʃ]*) m (de objeto)* value; *(em exame, teste)* point, mark; *(de pessoa)* worth; **dar ~ a** to value. ⊔ **valores** *mpl (bens, ações, etc)* securities; *(de pessoa, sociedade)* values.

valsa ['vawsa] *f* waltz.

válvula ['vawvula] *f* valve; **~ de segurança** safety valve.

vampiro [vãm'piru] *m* vampire.

vandalismo [vãnda'liʒmu] *m* vandalism.

vândalo, -la ['vãndalu, -la] *m, f* vandal.

vangloriar-se [vãŋglo'rjaxsi] *vp* to boast; ~ **de** to boast about.

vanguarda [vãŋ'gwaxda] *f* avantgarde; **esta na ~ de** to be in the forefront of.

vantagem [vãn'taʒẽ] *(pl* **-ns** [-ʃ]) *f* advantage; **tirar ~ de algo** to take advantage of sthg.

vantajoso, -osa [vãnta'ʒozu, -ɔza] *adj* advantageous.

vão¹ ['vãw] → **ir**.

vão², vã ['vãw, 'vã] *adj* useless ◆ *m*: ~ **das escadas** stairwell; ~ **da porta** doorway; **em ~** in vain.

vapor [va'po(x)] *(pl* **-res** [-riʃ]) *m (de líquido)* steam; *(gás)* vapour.

vaporizador [vaporiza'do(x)] *(pl* **-res** [-riʃ]) *m* atomizer.

vara ['vara] *f* rod; ~ **de pescar** *(Br)* fishing rod.

varal [va'raw] *(pl* **-ais** [-ajʃ]) *m (Br: de roupa)* washing line.

varanda [va'rãnda] *f* verandah.

varejeira [vare'ʒejra] *f* bluebottle.

varejo [va'reʒu] *m (Br: venda)* retail.

variação [varja'sãw] *(pl* **-ões** [-õjʃ]) *f* variation.

variado, -da [va'rjadu, -da] *adj* varied.

variar [va'rja(x)] *vt* to vary ◆ *vi* to be different; **para ~** for a change.

varicela [vari'sela] *f* chickenpox.

variedade [varje'dadʒi] *f* variety.

varinha [va'riɲa] *f*: ~ **de condão** magic wand; ~ **mágica** *(Port: eletrodoméstico)* hand blender.

varíola [va'riola] *f* smallpox.

vários, -rias ['varjuʃ, -rjaʃ] *adj pl* several.

variz [va'riʃ] *(pl* **-zes** [-ziʃ]) *f* varicose vein.

varredor, -ra [vaxe'do(x), -ra] *(mpl* **-res** [-riʃ], *fpl* **-s** [-ʃ]) *m, f (de rua)* road sweeper.

varrer [va'xe(x)] *vt* to sweep; ~ **algo da memória** to blank sthg out of one's mind.

vascular [vaʃku'la(x)] *(pl* **-es** [-iʃ]) *adj* vascular.

vasculhar [vaʃku'ʎa(x)] *vt (remexer)* to rummage through; *(investigar)* to probe into.

vaselina® [vaze'lina] *f* Vaseline®.

vasilha [va'ziʎa] *f* barrel.

vaso ['vazu] *m (para plantas)* vase; *(Br:*

jarra) large jug; *(ANAT)* vessel; ~ **sangüíneo** blood vessel; ~ **sanitário** *(Br)* toilet bowl.

vassoura [va'sora] *f* broom.

vasto, -ta ['vaʃtu, -ta] *adj* vast.

vatapá [vata'pa] *m Bahian dish made with fish or chicken and coconut milk, shrimps, bread, nuts and palm oil.*

Vaticano [vatʃi'kanu] *m*: **o ~** the Vatican.

vazio, -zia [va'ziu, -'zia] *adj* empty ◆ *m* void; ~ **de** devoid of.

Vd. *(abrev de vide)* V.

vê ['ve] → **ver**.

veado ['vjadu] *m (animal)* deer; *(carne)* venison.

vedação [veda'sãw] *(pl* **-ões** [-õjʃ]) *f* fence.

vedado, -da [ve'dadu, -da] *adj (edifício, local)* enclosed; *(recipiente)* sealed; *(interdito)* prohibited.

vedar [ve'da(x)] *vt (local, edifício)* to enclose; *(recipiente, buraco)* to seal; *(acesso, passagem)* to block.

vêem ['veẽ] → **ver**.

vegetação [veʒeta'sãw] *f* vegetation.

vegetal [veʒe'taw] *(pl* **-ais** [-ajʃ]) *m* vegetable.

vegetariano, -na [veʒeta'rjanu, -na] *adj & m, f* vegetarian.

veia ['veja] *f* vein.

veículo [ve'ikulu] *m* vehicle; "~ **longo**" "long vehicle".

veio ['veju] → **ver**.

vejo ['veʒu] → **ver**.

vela ['vela] *f (de barco)* sail; *(de iluminação)* candle; *(de motor)* spark plug.

veleiro [ve'lejru] *m* sailing ship, tall ship.

velejar [vele'ʒa(x)] *vi* to sail.

velhice [ve'ʎisi] *f* old age.

velho, -lha ['vɛʎu, -ʎa] *adj* old ◆ *m, f* old man *(f* old woman).

velocidade [velosi'dadʒi] *f* speed.

velocímetro [velo'simetru] *m* speedometer.

velocípede [velu'sipedʒi] *m*: ~ **com motor** moped.

velório [ve'lɔrju] *m* wake.

veloz [ve'lɔʃ] *(pl* **-zes** [-ziʃ]) *adj* fast.

veludo [ve'ludu] *m* velvet.

vem ['vãj] → **vir**.

vêm [vajãj] → **vir**.

vencedor, -ra [vẽse'do(x), -ra] *(mpl*

-res [-riʃ], fpl **-s** [-ʃ]) m, f winner ◆ adj winning.

vencer [vẽ'se(x)] vt (adversário) to beat; (corrida, competição) to win; (fig: obstáculo, timidez, problema) to overcome ◆ vi (em competição) to win; (prazo de pagamento) to expire; **deixar-se ~ por** (cansaço, tristeza) to give in to.

vencido, -da [vẽ'sidu, -da] adj defeated, beaten; **dar-se por ~** to accept defeat.

vencimento [vẽsi'mẽntu] m (ordenado) salary; (de prazo de pagamento) due date.

venda ['vẽnda] f (de mercadorias) sale; (mercearia) grocer's (shop); (para olhos) blindfold; **pôr à ~** to put on sale; **~ por atacado** wholesale; **~ pelo correio** mail order; **~ pelo telefone** telesales (pl); **~ a varejo** retail.

vendaval [vẽnda'vaw] (pl **-ais** [-ajʃ]) m gale.

vendedor, -ra [vẽnde'do(x), -ra] (mpl **-res** [-riʃ], fpl **-s** [-ʃ]) m, f seller; **~ de jornais** (Port) newsvendor.

vender [vẽn'de(x)] vt to sell; **~ a prestações** to sell on hire purchase (Brit), to sell by the installment plan (Am); **~ a vista** to sell for cash.

❏ **vender-se** vp: **"vende-se"** "for sale".

veneno [ve'nenu] m poison.

venenoso, -osa [vene'nozu, -ɔza] adj poisonous.

venéreo, -rea [ve'nɛrju, -rja] adj venereal.

venezianas [vene'zjanaʃ] fpl blinds.

Venezuela [vene'zwɛla] f: **a ~** Venezuela.

venho ['vaɲu] → **vir**.

vénia ['vɛnja] f (Port) = **vênia**.

vênia ['venja] f (Br) (permissão) consent; (reverência) bow.

vens ['vãjʃ] → **vir**.

ventania [vẽnta'nia] f gale.

ventilação [vẽntʃila'sãw] f ventilation.

ventilador [vẽntʃila'do(x)] (pl **-res** [-riʃ]) m (extractor) fan.

ventilar [vẽntʃi'la(x)] vt to ventilate.

vento ['vẽntu] m wind; **está muito ~** it's very windy.

ventoinha [vẽn'twiɲa] f fan.

ventre ['vẽntri] m belly.

ventrículo [vẽn'trikulu] m ventricle.

ventríloquo, -qua [vẽn'triloku, -ka] m, f ventriloquist.

ver ['ve(x)] vt to see; (televisão, filme) to watch; (perceber) to notice; (examinar) to look at ◆ vi to see ◆ m: **a meu ~** in my opinion; **deixar alguém ~ algo** to let sb see sthg; **fazer ~ a alguém que ...** to show sb that ...; **não tenho nada a ~ com isso** it's nothing to do with me.

veracidade [verasi'dadʒi] f truthfulness.

veranista [vera'niʃta] mf (summer) holidaymaker (Brit), (summer) vacationer (Am).

verão [ve'rãw] (pl **-ões** [-õjʃ]) m Summer.

verba ['vɛxba] f budget.

verbal [vex'baw] (pl **-ais** [-ajʃ]) adj verbal.

verbo ['vɛxbu] m verb; **~ intransitivo/transitivo** intransitive/transitive verb.

verdade [vex'dadʒi] f truth; **dizer a ~** to tell the truth; **a ~ é que ...** the truth is (that) ...; **na ~** actually; **de ~** real.

verdadeiro, -ra [vexda'dejru, -ra] adj (verídico) true; (genuíno) real.

verde ['vexdʒi] adj (de cor verde) green; (fruta) unripe ◆ m (cor) green.

verdura [vex'dura] f greens (pl).

vereda [ve'reda] f path.

veredicto [vere'dʒiktu] m verdict.

verga ['vexga] f (pau fino) stick; (para fazer cestos) wicker.

vergonha [vex'goɲa] f (timidez) bashfulness; (desonra) shame; **ter ~** to be shy; **ter ~ de alguém** to be ashamed of sb; **não ter ~ na cara** to be shameless.

verificação [verifika'sãw] (pl **-ões** [-õjʃ]) f checking.

verificar [verifi'ka(x)] vt to check.

❏ **verificar-se** vp (acontecer) to take place.

verme ['vexmi] m worm; (larva) maggot.

vermelho, -lha [vex'meʎu, -ʎa] adj & m red.

vermute [vex'mutʃi] m vermouth.

verniz [vex'niʃ] (pl **-zes** [-ziʃ]) m varnish.

verões → **verão**.

verosímil [veru'zimil] (pl **-meis** [-mejʃ]) adj (Port) = **verossímil**.

verossímil [vero'simiw] (pl **-meis** [-mejʃ]) adj (Br) probable.

verruga [ve'xuga] f wart; (em pé) verruca.

versão [vɛxˈsãw] (*pl* **-ões** [-õjʃ]) *f* version.

versátil [vɛxˈsatʃiw] (*pl* **-teis** [-tejʃ]) *adj* versatile.

verso [ˈvɛxsu] *m (de poema)* verse; *(de folha de papel)* other side *(of a page)*.

versões → **versão**.

vértebra [ˈvɛxtebra] *f* vertebra.

vertical [vɛxtʃiˈkaw] (*pl* **-ais** [-ajʃ]) *adj & f* vertical; **na** ~ upright, vertically.

vértice [ˈvɛxtʃisi] *m* vertex.

vertigem [vɛxˈtʃiʒẽ] (*pl* **-ns** [-ʃ]) *f*: **estou com vertigens** I feel dizzy.

vesgo, -ga [ˈveʒgu, -ga] *adj* cross-eyed.

vesícula [veˈzikula] *f*: ~ **(biliar)** gall bladder.

vespa [ˈveʃpa] *f (inseto)* wasp; *(motociclo)* scooter.

véspera [ˈveʃpera] *f* day before; **na** ~ the day before; **em** ~**s de** on the eve of.

vestiário [veʃtʃiˈarju] *m* cloakroom.

vestibular [veʃtʃibuˈlax] *m (Br)* exam taken at the end of secondary school in Brazil.

vestíbulo [veʃˈtʃibulu] *m* foyer.

vestido, -da [veʃˈtʃidu, -da] *adj*: ~ **de** dressed in ◆ *m* dress.

vestígio [veʃˈtʃiʒju] *m* trace.

vestir [veʃˈtʃi(x)] *vt* to dress.

❏ **vestir-se** *vp* to get dressed; ~**-se de** *(disfarçar-se de)* to dress up as; *(de azul, negro, etc)* to dress in, to wear.

vestuário [veʃˈtwarju] *m* clothes *(pl)*.

veterano, -na [veteˈranu, -na] *m, f* veteran.

veterinário, -ria [veteriˈnarju, -rja] *m, f* vet.

véu [ˈvɛu] *m* veil.

V. Exª *(abrev de Vossa Excelência)* very formal term of address used in correspondence.

vexame [veˈʃami] *m (escândalo)* scandal; *(humilhação)* humiliation.

vez [ˈveʃ] (*pl* **-zes** [-ziʃ]) *f* time; *(turno)* turn; **alguma** ~ **hei-de conseguir** I'll do it one day; **já lá foste alguma** ~? have you ever been there?; **perder a** ~ *(em fila)* to lose one's place; **à** ~ *(individualmente)* in turn; **de uma só** ~ in one go; **de** ~ once and for all; **de** ~ **em quando** occasionally; **mais de uma** ~ more than once; **na** OU **em** ~ **de** instead of; **outra** ~ again; **uma** ~ once; **às** ~**es** sometimes; **duas** ~**es** twice; **muitas** ~**es** often; **por** ~**es** sometimes;

poucas ~**es** rarely; **era uma** ~ ... once upon a time there was ....

vi [ˈvi] → **ver**.

via [ˈvia] *f (estrada, caminho)* route; *(meio)* way; *(documento)* copy of an official document; **por** ~ **aérea** by airmail; **por** ~ **de** by means of; **por** ~ **das dúvidas** just in case; **por** ~ **nasal** nasally; **por** ~ **oral** orally; **segunda** ~ *(de documento)* replacement; ~ **pública** public thoroughfare; ~ **rápida** *(em auto-estrada)* fast lane; *(estrada)* urban clearway *(Brit)*, expressway *(Am)*; ~ **verde** *(em portagem, ponte) lane in which one can drive through a toll without stopping, by means of an electronic device which debits the driver's account automatically*; **a Via Láctea** the Milky Way.

viaduto [viaˈdutu] *m* viaduct.

via-férrea [ˌviaˈfɛxja] (*pl* **vias-férreas** [ˌviaʃˈfɛxjaʃ]) *f (Port)* railway *(Brit)*, railroad *(Am)*.

viagem [ˈvjaʒẽ] (*pl* **-ns** [-ʃ]) *f (trajeto)* journey; *(excursão)* trip; *(de barco)* voyage; **ir de** ~ to go away; **boa** ~! have a good trip!; ~ **de negócios** business trip.

viajante [vjaˈʒãntʃi] *mf* traveller.

viajar [vjaˈʒa(x)] *vi* to travel; ~ **de** to travel by; ~ **por-***(por país, continente)* to travel through OU across; *(por terra, mar, ar)* to travel by.

viatura [vjaˈtura] *f* vehicle.

viável [ˈvjavɛw] (*pl* **-eis** [-ejʃ]) *adj (transitável)* passable; *(exequível)* feasible.

víbora [ˈvibora] *f* viper.

vibração [vibraˈsãw] (*pl* **-ões** [-õjʃ]) *f* vibration.

vibrar [viˈbra(x)] *vi* to vibrate; **ela vibrou de alegria** she was thrilled.

viciado, -da [viˈsjadu, -da] *adj*: **ser** ~ **em algo** to be addicted to sthg.

viciar [viˈsja(x)] *vt (informação)* to distort; *(documento)* to falsify; *(corromper)* to corrupt.

❏ **viciar-se** *vp*: ~**-se em** to become addicted to.

vício [ˈvisju] *m (de droga, bebida)* addiction; *(defeito)* vice; *(mau hábito)* bad habit.

vida [ˈvida] *f* life; **ganhar a** ~ to earn a living; **perder a** ~ to lose one's life; **tirar a** ~ **de alguém** to take sb's life.

videira [viˈdejra] *f* grapevine.

vídeo [ˈvidʒju] *m* video.

videocassete [ˌvidjukaˈsɛtɛ] *f (Port)* videotape.
videoclipe [ˌvidʒjoˈklipi] *m (pop)* (pop) video.
videoclube [ˌvidʒjoˈklubi] *m* video shop.
videodisco [ˌvidʒjoˈdiʃku] *m* videodisc.
videogame [ˌvidʒjoˈgejmi] *m* videogame.
videogravador [ˌvidʒjogravaˈdo(x)] (*pl* **-res** [-riʃ]) *m* videorecorder *(Brit)*, VCR *(Am)*.
vidraça [viˈdrasa] *f* windowpane.
vidrão [viˈdrãw] (*pl* **-ões** [-õjʃ]) *m (Port)* bottle bank *(Brit)*.
vidro [ˈvidru] *m* glass; *(vidraça)* pane (of glass); *(de carro)* window.
vidrões → **vidrão**.
viela [ˈvjɛla] *f* alley.
vieste [viˈɛʃtʃi] → **vir**.
viga [ˈviga] *f* beam.
vigário [viˈgarju] *m* vicar.
vigésimo, -ma [viˈʒɛzimu, -ma] *num* twentieth, → **sexto**.
vigia [viˈʒia] *f (vigilância)* watch; *(janela)* porthole ◆ *mf (guarda)* guard.
vigilância [viʒiˈlãsja] *f* vigilance.
vigor [viˈgo(x)] *m* vigour; **em ~** *(lei, norma)* in force.
vil [ˈviw] (*pl* **vis** [ˈviʃ]) *adj* despicable.
vila [ˈvila] *f (povoação)* village; *(habitação)* villa.
vilarejo [vilaˈreʒu] *m* small village.
vim [ˈvĩ] → **vir**.
vime [ˈvimi] *m* wicker.
vinagre [viˈnagri] *m* vinegar.
vinagreta [vinaˈgreta] *f* vinaigrette.
vinco [ˈvĩŋku] *m* crease.
vinda [ˈvĩnda] *f* return.
vindima [vĩnˈdʒima] *f* grape harvest.
vindo, -da [ˈvĩndu, -da] *pp* → **vir**.
vingança [vĩŋˈgãsa] *f* revenge.
vingar [vĩŋˈga(x)] *vt (desforrar-se de)* to avenge ◆ *vi (planta)* to take.
❑ **vingar-se** *vp (desforrar-se)* to take revenge; **~-se de alguém** to take revenge on sb.
vingativo, -va [vĩŋgaˈtʃivu, -va] *adj* vengeful.
vinha[1] [ˈviɲa] → **vir**.
vinha[2] [ˈviɲa] *f* vineyard.
vinha-d'alhos [ˌviɲaˈdaʎuʃ] *f meat marinade made of garlic, wine or vinegar and bayleaves.*
vinheta [viˈɲeta] *f (selo) charity sticker.*
vinho [ˈviɲu] *m* wine; **~ branco/tinto** white/red wine; **~ da casa** house wine; **~ espumante** OU **espumoso** sparkling wine; **~ de mesa** table wine; **~ moscatel** Muscatel; **~ do Porto** port; **~ rosé** rosé wine; **~ verde** *light, slightly sparkling, young wine.*
vinicultor, -ra [ˌvinikuwˈto(x), -ra] (*mpl* **-res** [-riʃ], *fpl* **-s** [-ʃ]) *m, f* wine producer.
vinil [viˈniw] *m* vinyl.
vintage [vĩnˈtagɛ] *m* vintage wine.
vinte [ˈvĩntʃi] *num* twenty, → **seis**.
viola [ˈvjɔla] *f* guitar.
violação [vjolaˈsãw] (*pl* **-ões** [-õjʃ]) *f (de direito, norma)* violation; *(estupro)* rape; *(de segredo)* disclosure.
violão [vjoˈlãw] (*pl* **-ões** [-õjʃ]) *m* guitar.
violar [vjoˈla(x)] *vt (direito, norma)* to violate; *(pessoa)* to rape; *(segredo)* to disclose, to reveal.
violência [vjoˈlẽsja] *f* violence.
violento, -ta [vjoˈlẽntu, -ta] *adj* violent.
violeta [vjoˈleta] *adj inv & f* violet.
violino [vjoˈlinu] *m* violin.
violões → **violão**.
violoncelo [vjolõˈsɛlu] *m* cello.
vir [ˈvi(x)] *vi* **1.** *(apresentar-se)* to come; **veio ver-me** he came to see me; **venho visitá-lo amanhã** I'll come and see you tomorrow.
2. *(chegar)* to arrive; **(ele) veio atrasado/adiantado** he arrived late/early; **ela veio no ônibus das onze** she came on the eleven o'clock bus.
3. *(a seguir no tempo)* to come; **a semana/o ano que vem** next week/year.
4. *(estar)* to be; **vem escrito em português** it's written in Portuguese; **vinha embalado** it came in a packet.
5. *(regressar)* to come back; **eles vêm de férias amanhã** they're coming back from holiday tomorrow; **hoje, venho mais tarde** I'll be back later today.
6. *(surgir)* to come; **o carro veio não sei de onde** the car came out of nowhere; **veio-me uma idéia** I've got an idea.
7. *(provir)*: **~ de** to come from; **venho agora mesmo de lá** I've just come from there; **~ de fazer algo** to have just been doing sthg.
8. *(em locuções)*: **~ a ser** to become;

que vem a ser isto? what's the meaning of this?; **~ abaixo** *(edifício, construção)* to collapse; **~ ao mundo** *(nascer)* to come into the world, to be born; **~ a saber (de algo)** to find out *(about sthg)*; **~ sobre** *(arremeter contra)* to lunge at; **~ a tempo de algo** to arrive in time for sthg; **~ a tempo de fazer algo** to arrive in time to do sthg.

virado, -da [vi'radu, -da] *adj (invertido)* upside down; *(tombado)* overturned; *(voltado)* turned up ♦ *m:* **~ à Paulista** *bean stew served with smoked sausage, fried eggs and pork chops;* **~ para** facing.

vira-lata [,vira'lata] *(pl* **vira-latas** [,vira'lataʃ]) *m (Br) (cão vadio)* stray dog; *(mistura de raças)* mongrel.

virar [vi'ra(x)] *vt* to turn; *(carro, camião)* to turn around; *(entornar, derrubar)* to knock over; *(Br: transformarse em)* to turn into ♦ *vi (mudar de direção)* to change direction; *(Br: mudar)* to change; **~ à direita/esquerda** to turn right/left.

❑ **virar-se** *vp (voltar-se)* to turn over; **~-se contra alguém** to turn against sb; **~-se para** to turn towards.

virgem ['virʒẽ] *(pl* **-ns** [-ʃ]) *mf* virgin ♦ *adj* virgin; *(cassete)* blank.

❑ **Virgem** *f (signo do Zodíaco)* Virgo.

vírgula ['virgula] *f* comma.

viril [vi'riw] *(pl* **-is** [-iʃ]) *adj* virile.

virilha [vi'riʎa] *f* groin.

viris → viril.

virose [vi'rɔzi] *f* viral infection.

virtual [vix'twaw] *(pl* **-ais** [-ajʃ]) *adj* virtual.

virtude [vix'tudʒi] *f* virtue; **em ~ de** due to.

vírus ['viruʃ] *m inv* virus.

vis → vil.

visão [vi'zãw] *(pl* **-ões** [-õjʃ]) *f* vision; *(capacidade de ver)* sight.

visar [vi'za(x)] *vt (com arma)* to take aim at; *(documento)* to endorse; **~ fazer algo** *(ter em vista)* to aim to do sthg.

vísceras [viʃ'seraʃ] *fpl* innards, internal organs.

viscoso, -osa [viʃ'kozu, -ɔza] *adj* viscous.

viseira [vi'zejra] *f (de boné, capacete)* peak.

visibilidade [vizibli'dadʒi] *f* visibility.

visita [vi'zita] *f* visit; *(de médico)* house call; **fazer uma ~ a alguém** to

pay sb a visit.

visitante [vizi'tãntʃi] *mf* visitor.

visitar [vizi'ta(x)] *vt* to visit.

visível [vi'zivɛw] *(pl* **-eis** [-ejʃ]) *adj* visible.

vislumbrar [viʒlũm'bra(x)] *vt* to make out.

visões → visão.

visor [vi'zo(x)] *(pl* **-res** [-riʃ]) *m (de máquina fotográfica)* viewfinder; *(de computador)* screen.

vista ['viʃta] *f (visão)* sight; *(olho)* eye; *(panorama)* view; **até à ~!** see you!; **dar nas ~s** to stand out; **ter algo em ~** to have sthg in view; **ter algo em ~** to have one's eye on sthg.

visto, -ta ['viʃtu, -ta] *pp →* **ver** ♦ *adj* well-known ♦ *m (em documento)* stamp; *(documento)* visa; **bem ~!** well spotted!; **nunca ~!** incredible!; **pelo ~** by the look of things; **~ que** since.

vistoso, -osa [viʃ'tozu, -ɔza] *adj* eye-catching.

visual [vi'zwaw] *(pl* **-ais** [-ajʃ]) *adj* visual.

vital [vi'taw] *(pl* **-ais** [-ajʃ]) *adj* vital.

vitamina [vita'mina] *f* vitamin.

vitela [vi'tɛla] *f (animal)* calf; *(carne)* veal.

vítima ['vitʃima] *f (de acusação, ataque)* victim; *(morto em guerra, acidente)* casualty.

vitória [vi'tɔrja] *f* victory.

vitória-régia [vi,tɔrja'xɛʒja] *(pl* **vitórias-régias** [vi,tɔrjaʒ'xɛʒjaʃ]) *f* water lily.

vitral [vi'traw] *(pl* **-ais** [-ajʃ]) *m* stained-glass window.

vitrina [vi'trina] *f (shop)* window.

viu ['viu] → **ver**.

viúvo, -va ['vjuvu, -va] *m, f* widower *(f* widow).

vivacidade [vivasi'dadʒi] *f* vivacity.

viveiro [vi'vejru] *m (de plantas)* nursery; *(de trutas)* farm.

vivência [vi'vẽsja] *f (experiência de vida)* experience.

vivenda [vi'vẽnda] *f* detached house.

viver [vi've(x)] *vi (ter vida)* to be alive; *(habitar)* to live ♦ *vt (momento, situação)* to experience; **~ com alguém** to live with sb; **~ de algo** to live off sthg; **~ em** to live in.

víveres ['vivɛreʃ] *mpl* supplies.

vivo, -va ['vivu, -va] *adj (com vida)* alive; *(perspicaz)* sharp; *(cor, luz)* bright; *(travesso)* cheeky; **ao ~** live.

vizinhança [viziˈnãsa] *f (vizinhos)* neighbours *(pl)*; *(arredores)* neighbourhood.

vizinho, -nha [viˈziɲu, -ɲa] *m, f* neighbour ♦ *adj (país, região)* neighbouring; *(casa)* next; **é o meu ~ do lado** he's my next-door neighbour.

voar [ˈvwa(x)] *vi* to fly.

vocabulário [vokabuˈlarju] *m* vocabulary.

vocação [vokaˈsãw] *(pl* **-ões** [-õjʃ]*) f* vocation; **ter ~ para** to have a vocation for.

vocalista [vokaˈliʃta] *mf* lead singer.

você [vɔˈse] *pron* you; **e ~?** what about you?; **é ~?!** is that you?!; **~ mesmo** OU **próprio** you yourself.

❑ **vocês** *pron pl* you; **~s mesmos** OU **próprios** you yourselves.

voga [ˈvɔga] *f*: **estar em ~** to be fashionable.

vogal [voˈgaw] *(pl* **-ais** [-ajʃ]*) f (letra)* vowel ♦ *mf (de junta, júri, assembléia)* member.

volante [voˈlãntʃi] *m (de veículo)* steering wheel.

volátil [voˈlatʃiw] *(pl* **-teis** [-tejʃ]*) adj* volatile.

vôlei [ˈvolei] *m (Br)* volleyball.

voleibol [volejˈbɔw] *m* = **vôlei**.

volta [ˈvɔwta] *f (regresso)* return; *(movimento)* turn; *(mudança)* change; *(passeio)* walk; *(em corrida)* lap; *(em competição)* round; **dá duas ~s à chave** turn the key twice; **dar uma ~** to go for a walk OU wander; **dar uma ~ de carro** to go for a drive; **dar a ~ em algo** *(tornear)* to go round sthg; **estar de ~** *(estar de regresso)* to be back; **~ e meia** *(fig)* every now and then; **em toda a ~ de** all the way round; **à ~ de** *(cerca de)* roughly, around; **por ~ de** around.

voltagem [vowˈtaʒẽ] *f* voltage.

voltar [vowˈta(x)] *vt* to turn over; *(cabeça, olhos, costas)* to turn; *(objeto de dentro para fora)* to turn inside out ♦ *vi (regressar)* to come back; *(ir de novo)* to go back; **~ a fazer algo** to do sthg again; **~ atrás** to go back; **~ para** to return to; **~ atrás na palavra** to go back on one's word; **~ a si** to come round.

❑ **voltar-se** *vp (virar-se)* to turn round;

~-se para to turn towards.

volume [voˈlumi] *m* volume; *(embrulho)* parcel.

voluntário, -ria [volũnˈtarju, -rja] *m, f* volunteer.

volúpia [voˈlupja] *f* voluptuousness.

vomitado [vomiˈtadu] *m* vomit.

vomitar [vomiˈta(x)] *vt & vi* to vomit.

vómito [ˈvɔmitu] *m (Port)* = **vômito**.

vômito [ˈvomitu] *m (Br)* vomit; **ter ânsias de ~** to feel sick.

vontade [võnˈtadʒi] *f (desejo)* wish; *(determinação)* willpower; **pôr-se à ~** to make o.s. comfortable; **ter ~ de fazer algo** to feel like doing sthg; **fazer as ~s de alguém** to pander to sb; **com ~ ou sem ela, você tem que ir** you'll have to go whether you like it or not; **contra a ~ de alguém** against sb's will; **de livre ~** of one's own free will.

voo [ˈvou] *m (Port)* = **vôo**.

vôo [ˈvou] *m (Br)* flight; **~ charter** OU **fretado** charter flight; **~ direto** direct flight; **~ doméstico** domestic flight; **~ livre** hang-gliding.

voraz [voˈraʃ] *(pl* **-zes** [-ziʃ]*) adj* voracious.

vos [vuʃ] *pron pl (complemento direto)* you; *(complemento indireto)* (to) you; *(fml: reflexo)* yourselves; *(fml: recíproco)* each other, one another; **ela chamou-~** *(Port)* she called you; **ele deu-~ isto** *(Port)* he gave this to you, he gave you this.

vós [ˈvɔʃ] *pron (sujeito, complemento direto)* you; *(complemento indireto)* (to) you; **~ mesmos** OU **próprios** you yourselves.

vosso, -a [ˈvɔsu, -a] *adj* your ♦ *pron*: **o ~/a vossa** yours; **um amigo ~** a friend of yours; **os ~s** *(a vossa família)* your family.

votação [votaˈsãw] *(pl* **-ões** [-õjʃ]*) f* vote.

votar [voˈta(x)] *vi* to vote; **~ em alguém** to vote for sb.

voto [ˈvɔtu] *m* vote.

❑ **votos** *mpl*: **fazer ~s que** to hope (that); **~s de felicidade** *(em carta)* best wishes.

vou [ˈvo] → **ir**.

voz [ˈvɔʃ] *(pl* **-zes** [-ziʃ]*) f* voice; **ter ~**

ativa em algo to have a say in sthg; **em
~ alta** aloud, out loud; **em ~ baixa**
softly.

vulcão [vuwˈkãw] (*pl* **-ões** [-õjʃ]) *m*
volcano.

vulgar [vuwˈga(x)] (*pl* **-res** [-riʃ]) *adj*
common; *(grosseiro)* vulgar.

vulgaridade [vuwgariˈdadʒi] *f (banali-
dade)* banality; *(grosseria)* vulgarity.

vulnerável [vuwncˈravɛw] (*pl* **-eis**
[-ejʃ]) *adj* vulnerable.

vulto [ˈvuwtu] *m* figure.

W

walkie-talkie [ˌwɔki'tɔki] (*pl* **walkie-talkies** [ˌwɔki'tɔkiʃ]) *m* walkie-talkie.
WC *m* (*abrev de water closet*) WC.
windsurf [wĩnd'sarf] *m* (*Port*) = windsurfe.

windsurfe [wĩnd'suxfi] *m* (*Br*) windsurfing; **fazer ~** to go windsurfing.
windsurfista [wĩndsux'fiʃta] *mf* windsurfer.

X

xadrez [ʃa'dreʃ] *m* (*jogo*) chess; (*fam: cadeia*) clink; **de ~** (*tecido, saia*) checked.
xale ['ʃali] *m* shawl.
xampu [ʃãm'pu] *m* (*Br*) shampoo.
xarope [ʃa'rɔpi] *m* syrup; **~ para a tosse** cough syrup OU mixture.
xenofobia [ʃenofo'bia] *f* xenophobia.
xenófobo, -ba [ʃe'nɔfobu, -ba] *m, f* xenophobe.
xeque-mate [ʃeke'matʃi] (*pl* **xeque-mates** [ʃeke'mateʃ]) *m* checkmate.
xerez [ʃe'reʃ] *m* sherry.

xerocar [ʃero'kax] *vt* (*Br*) to photocopy.
xerox® ['ʃerɔks] *m inv* (*Br*) (*fotocópia*) photocopy; (*máquina*) photocopier.
xícara ['ʃikara] *f* cup.
xilofone [ʃilɔ'fɔni] *m* xylophone.
xilografia [ʃilɔgra'fia] *f* wood engraving.
xingar [ʃĩŋ'gax] *vt* (*Br: insultar*) to swear at.
xinxim [ʃĩ'ʃi] (*pl* **-ns** [-ʃ]) *m* chicken or meat stew with prawns, palm oil, peanuts and ground cashew nuts.
xisto ['ʃiʃtu] *m* shale.

Z

zagueiro [za'geiru] *m* (*Br: em futebol*) defence.

Zaire ['zajri] *m*: o ~ Zaire.

zangado, -da [zãŋ'gadu, -da] *adj* angry.

zangão ['zãŋgãw] (*pl* -ões [-õjʃ]) *m* drone.

zangar [zãŋ'ga(x)] *vt* (*irritar*) to annoy. ⏺ **zangar-se** *vp* (*brigar*) to have a row; (*irritar-se*) to get angry.

zangões → **zângão**.

zaragatoa [zaraga'toa] *f* swab.

zarpar [zax'pa(x)] *vi* to set sail.

zebra ['zebra] *f* zebra.

zelador, -ra [zela'do(x), -ra] (*pl* -res [-riʃ], *fpl* -s [-ʃ]) *m, f* (*Br: de edifício*) porter.

zelar [ze'la(x)] : **zelar por** *v + prep* to look after.

zelo ['zelu] *m* care.

zeloso, -osa [ze'lozu, -ɔza] *adj* careful.

zero ['zɛru] *num* zero, nought; (*em futebol*) nil; (*em tênis*) love; **partir do** ~ to start from scratch; **ser um** ~ **à esquerda** (*fam*) to be hopeless; **abaixo de** ~ below zero, → **seis**.

ziguezague [zig'zagi] *m* zigzag; **andar aos** ~**s** to zigzag.

zinco ['zĩŋku] *m* zinc.

zíper ['zipe(x)] (*pl* -res [-riʃ]) *m* (*Br*) zip (*Brit*), zipper (*Am*).

Zodíaco [zo'dʒiaku] *m* zodiac.

zoeira ['z wejra] *f* buzzing.

zombar [zõm'ba(x)] *vi* to jeer; ~ **de** to make fun of.

zona ['zona] *f* (*de país, globo*) area; (*de corpo*) part; (MED) shingles (*sg*); ~ **comercial** shopping area; ~ **pedestre** pedestrian precinct.

zonzo, -za ['zõzu, -za] *adj* dazed.

zoo ['zu] *m* (*Port*) = **zôo**.

zôo ['zou] *m* (*Br*) zoo.

zoologia [zolo'ʒia] *f* zoology.

zoológico [zo'lɔʒiku] *adj m* → **jardim**.

zumbido [zũm'bidu] *m* buzzing.

zumbir [zũm'bi(x)] *vi* to buzz.

zunir [zu'ni(x)] *vi* (*vento*) to whistle; (*abelha*) to buzz.

zunzum [zũ'zũ] (*pl* -ns [-ʃ]) *m* (*fig: boato*) rumour.

zurrar [zu'xa(x)] *vi* to bray.

A

a [stressed eɪ, unstressed ə] indefinite article **1.** (referring to indefinite thing, person) um (uma); **a friend** um amigo (uma amiga); **a restaurant** um restaurante; **an apple** uma maçã; **she's a doctor** ela é médica.
2. (instead of the number one): **a hundred and twenty pounds** cento e vinte libras; **a month ago** há um mês; **a thousand** mil; **four and a half** quatro e meio.
3. (in prices, ratios): **three times a year** três vezes ao ano; **£2 a kilo** 2 libras o quilo.

AA n (Brit: abbr of Automobile Association) = TCB (Br), = ACP (Port).

aback [ə'bæk] adv: **to be taken ~** ficar surpreendido(-da).

abandon [ə'bændən] vt abandonar.

abattoir ['æbətwɑːʳ] n matadouro m.

abbey ['æbɪ] n abadia f.

abbreviation [ə,briːvɪ'eɪʃn] n abreviatura f.

abdicate ['æbdɪkeɪt] vi abdicar ♦ vt (responsibility) abdicar de.

abdomen ['æbdəmən] n abdômen m.

abduct [əb'dʌkt] vt seqüestrar.

aberration [,æbə'reɪʃn] n aberração f.

abeyance [ə'beɪəns] n (fml): **to fall into ~** (custom) cair em desuso; **to be in ~** (law) não estar em vigor.

abhor [əb'hɔːʳ] vt abominar.

abide [ə'baɪd] vt: **I can't ~ him** não o suporto.

⊔ abide by vt fus (rule, law) acatar.

ability [ə'bɪlətɪ] n (capability) capacidade f; (skill) habilidade f.

abject ['æbdʒekt] adj (poverty) extremo(-ma); (person, apology) humilde.

ablaze [ə'bleɪz] adj (on fire) em chamas.

able ['eɪbl] adj competente; **to be ~ to do sthg** poder fazer algo.

abnormal [æb'nɔːml] adj anormal.

aboard [ə'bɔːd] adv a bordo ♦ prep (ship, plane) a bordo de; (train, bus) em.

abode [ə'bəʊd] n (fml) residência f.

abolish [ə'bɒlɪʃ] vt abolir.

abolition [,æbə'lɪʃn] n abolição f.

aborigine [,æbə'rɪdʒənɪ] n aborígene mf (da Austrália).

abort [ə'bɔːt] vt (give up) cancelar.

abortion [ə'bɔːʃn] n aborto m; **to have an ~** fazer um aborto, abortar.

abortive [ə'bɔːtɪv] adj fracassado (-da).

about [ə'baʊt] adv **1.** (approximately) cerca de; **~ 50** cerca de 50; **at ~ six o'clock** por volta das seis horas.
2. (referring to place) por aí; **to run ~** correr de um lado para o outro; **to walk ~** caminhar por aí.
3. (on the point of): **to be ~ to do sthg** estar prestes a fazer algo.
♦ prep **1.** (concerning) sobre, acerca de; **a book ~ Scotland** um livro sobre a Escócia **what's it ~?** é sobre o quê?; **what ~ a drink?** que tal uma bebida?
2. (referring to place) por; **there are lots of hotels ~ the town** existem muitos hotéis por toda a cidade.

above [ə'bʌv] prep (higher than) por cima de; (more than) mais de ♦ adv (higher) de cima; **children aged ten and ~** crianças com mais de dez anos; **~ all** acima de tudo; **~ average** acima da média.

abrasive [ə'breɪsɪv] adj (product) abrasivo(-va); (person, manner) brusco(-ca).

abreast [ə'brest] *adv* lado a lado; **to keep ~ of sthg** manter-se ao corrente de algo.

abridged [ə'brɪdʒd] *adj* resumido (-da).

abroad [ə'brɔːd] *adv* (be, live, work) no estrangeiro; (go, move) para o estrangeiro.

abrupt [ə'brʌpt] *adj* brusco(-ca).

abscess ['æbses] *n* abcesso *m*.

abscond [əb'skɒnd] *vi* fugir.

abseil ['æbseɪl] *vi*: **to ~ down sthg** descer algo por uma corda.

absence ['æbsəns] *n* ausência *f*.

absent ['æbsənt] *adj* ausente.

absentee [,æbsən'tiː] *n* absentista *mf*.

absent-minded [-'maɪndɪd] *adj* distraído(-da).

absolute ['æbsəluːt] *adj* absoluto(-ta).

absolutely [*adv* 'æbsəluːtlɪ, *excl* ,æbsə'luːtlɪ] *adv* absolutamente ♦ *excl* sem dúvida!

absorb [əb'sɔːb] *vt* absorver.

absorbed [əb'sɔːbd] *adj*: **to be ~ in sthg** estar absorvido(-da) em algo.

absorbent [əb'sɔːbənt] *adj* absorvente.

absorption [əb'sɔːpʃn] *n* absorção *f*.

abstain [əb'steɪn] *vi*: **to ~ (from)** abster-se (de).

abstention [əb'stenʃn] *n* abstenção *f*.

abstract ['æbstrækt] *adj* abstrato(-ta) ♦ *n* (summary) resumo *m*.

absurd [əb'sɜːd] *adj* absurdo(-da).

ABTA ['æbtə] *n* associação britânica de agências de viagens.

abundant [ə'bʌndənt] *adj* abundante.

abuse [*n* ə'bjuːs, *vb* ə'bjuːz] *n* (insults) insultos *mpl*; (wrong use, maltreatment) abuso *m* ♦ *vt* (insult) insultar; (use wrongly) abusar de; (maltreat) maltratar.

abusive [ə'bjuːsɪv] *adj* ofensivo(-va).

abysmal [ə'bɪzml] *adj* péssimo(-ma).

AC (abbr of alternating current) CA.

academic [,ækə'demɪk] *adj* (educational) acadêmico(-ca) ♦ *n* professor *m* universitário (professora *f* universitária).

academy [ə'kædəmɪ] *n* academia *f*.

accelerate [ək'seləreɪt] *vi* acelerar.

acceleration [ək,selə'reɪʃn] *n* aceleração *f*.

accelerator [ək'seləreɪtər] *n* acelerador *m*.

accent ['æksent] *n* (way of speaking) pronúncia *f*, sotaque *m*; (mark in writing) acento *m*.

accept [ək'sept] *vt* aceitar; (blame, responsibility) assumir.

acceptable [ək'septəbl] *adj* aceitável.

acceptance [ək'septəns] *n* aceitação *f*.

access ['ækses] *n* acesso *m*.

accessible [ək'sesəbl] *adj* acessível.

accessories [ək'sesərɪz] *npl* acessórios *mpl*.

access road *n* estrada *f* de acesso.

accident ['æksɪdənt] *n* acidente *m*; **by ~** por acaso.

accidental [,æksɪ'dentl] *adj* acidental.

accidentally [,æksɪ'dentəlɪ] *adv* (unintentionally) acidentalmente; (by chance) por acaso.

accident insurance *n* seguro *m* contra acidentes.

accident-prone *adj* propenso(-sa) a acidentes.

acclaim [ə'kleɪm] *n* reconhecimento *m*, aclamação *f* ♦ *vt* aplaudir, aclamar.

acclimatize [ə'klaɪmətaɪz] *vi* aclimatar-se.

accommodate [ə'kɒmədeɪt] *vt* alojar.

accommodating [ə'kɒmədeɪtɪŋ] *adj* prestativo(-va).

accommodation [ə,kɒmə'deɪʃn] *n* alojamento *m*.

accommodations [ə,kɒmə'deɪʃnz] *npl* (Am) = accommodation.

accompany [ə'kʌmpənɪ] *vt* acompanhar.

accomplice [ə'kʌmplɪs] *n* cúmplice *mf*.

accomplish [ə'kʌmplɪʃ] *vt* conseguir, realizar.

accomplishment [ə'kʌmplɪʃmənt] *n* (achievement, finishing) cumprimento *m*; (feat, deed) feito *m*.

❏ **accomplishments** *npl* (skills) aptidões *fpl*.

accord [ə'kɔːd] *n*: **of one's own ~** por iniciativa própria.

accordance [ə'kɔːdəns] *n*: **in ~ with** de acordo com, conforme.

according [ə'kɔːdɪŋ] : **according to** *prep* (as stated by) segundo; (depending on) conforme.

accordingly [ə'kɔːdɪŋlɪ] *adv* (appropriately) de forma adequada; (consequently) por conseguinte.

accordion [ə'kɔ:dɪən] *n* acordeão *m*.

accost [ə'kɒst] *vt* abordar.

account [ə'kaunt] *n* (*at bank, shop*) conta *f*; (*report*) relato *m*; **to take into ~** levar em consideração; **on no ~** de modo algum OR nenhum; **on ~ of** devido a.
❑ **account for** *vt fus* (*explain*) justificar; (*constitute*) representar.

accountable [ə'kauntəbl] *adj*: **~ for** responsável por.

accountancy [ə'kauntənsɪ] *n* contabilidade *f*.

accountant [ə'kauntənt] *n* contador *m* (-ra *f*) (*Br*), contabilista *mf* (*Port*).

account number *n* número *m* de conta.

accumulate [ə'kju:mjʊleɪt] *vt* acumular.

accuracy [ækjʊrəsɪ] *n* (*of description, report*) exatidão *f*; (*of work, figures*) precisão *f*.

accurate [ækjʊrət] *adj* (*description, report*) exato(-ta); (*work, figures*) preciso(-sa).

accurately [ækjʊrətlɪ] *adv* (*describe, report*) com exatidão; (*type, measure*) com precisão.

accusation [ækju'zeɪʃn] *n* acusação *f*.

accuse [ə'kju:z] *vt*: **to ~ sb of sthg** acusar alguém de algo.

accused [ə'kju:zd] *n*: **the ~** o réu (a ré).

accustomed [ə'kʌstəmd] *adj*: **to be ~ to sthg/to doing sthg** estar acostumado(-da) a algo/a fazer algo.

ace [eɪs] *n* (*card*) ás *m*.

ache [eɪk] *vi* doer ♦ *n* dor *f*; **my leg ~s** minha perna está doendo.

achieve [ə'tʃi:v] *vt* conseguir.

achievement [ə'tʃi:vmənt] *n* (*accomplishment*) feito *m*.

Achilles' tendon [ə'kɪli:z-] *n* tendão *m* de Aquiles.

acid [æsɪd] *adj* ácido(-da) ♦ *n* ácido *m*.

acid rain *n* chuva *f* ácida.

acknowledge [ək'nɒlɪdʒ] *vt* (*accept*) reconhecer; (*letter*) acusar a recepção de.

acne [æknɪ] *n* acne *f*.

acorn [eɪkɔ:n] *n* bolota *f*.

acoustic [ə'ku:stɪk] *adj* acústico(-ca).

acquaintance [ə'kweɪntəns] *n* (*person*) conhecido *m* (-da *f*).

acquire [ə'kwaɪər] *vt* adquirir.

acquisitive [ə'kwɪzɪtɪv] *adj* consumidor(-ra).

acquit [ə'kwɪt] *vt*: **to ~ sb of sthg** (*JUR*) absolver alguém de algo; **to ~ o.s. well/badly** (*perform*) sair-se bem/mal.

acquittal [ə'kwɪtl] *n* (*JUR*) absolvição *f*.

acre [eɪkər] *n* = 4046,9 m², = meio hectare *m*.

acrid [ækrɪd] *adj* (*taste, smell*) acre.

acrimonious [ækrɪ'məʊnjəs] *adj* (*words*) azedo(-da); (*quarrel, conflict*) acrimonioso(-osa).

acrobat [ækrəbæt] *n* acrobata *mf*.

across [ə'krɒs] *prep* (*to other side of*) para o outro lado de; (*from one side to the other of*) de um lado para o outro de; (*on other side of*) do outro lado de ♦ *adv* (*to other side*) para o outro lado; **to walk/drive ~ sthg** atravessar algo (a pé/de carro); **it's 10 miles ~** tem 10 milhas de largura; **~ from** em frente de.

acrylic [ə'krɪlɪk] *n* fibra *f* acrílica.

act [ækt] *vi* atuar; (*in play, film*) representar ♦ *n* ato *m*; (*POL*) lei *f*; (*performance*) atuação *f*, número *m*; **to ~ as** (*serve as*) servir de; **to ~ like** portar-se como.

acting [æktɪŋ] *adj* substituto(-ta), interino(-na) ♦ *n* (*in play, film*) desempenho *m*; **I enjoy ~** gosto de representar.

action [ækʃn] *n* ação *f*; (*MIL*) combate *m*; **to take ~** agir; **to put sthg into ~** pôr algo em ação; **out of ~** (*machine*) avariado; (*person*) fora de ação.

action replay *n* repetição *f* (em câmara lenta) da jogada.

activate [æktɪveɪt] *vt* ativar.

active [æktɪv] *adj* ativo(-va).

actively [æktɪvlɪ] *adv* (*seek, promote*) ativamente; (*encourage, discourage*) energeticamente.

activity [æk'tɪvətɪ] *n* atividade *f*.
❑ **activities** *npl* (*leisure events*) atividades *fpl* (recreativas).

activity holiday *n* férias organizadas para crianças incluindo, entre outras, atividades desportivas.

act of God *n* catástrofe *f* natural.

actor [æktər] *n* ator *m*.

actress [æktrɪs] *n* atriz *f*.

actual [æktʃʊəl] *adj* (*real*) verdadeiro(-ra), real; (*for emphasis*) próprio (-pria).

actually [æktʃʊəlɪ] *adv* na verdade.

acumen [ˈækjumen] *n*: **business ~** jeito *m* para os negócios.

acupuncture [ˈækjupʌŋktʃəʳ] *n* acupuntura *f*.

acute [əˈkjuːt] *adj* agudo(-da).

ad [æd] *n (inf)* anúncio *m*.

AD *(abbr of Anno Domini)* d.C.

adamant [ˈædəmənt] *adj*: **to be ~** ser inflexível; **she was ~ that she wouldn't come** ela estava decidida a não vir.

Adam's apple [ˈædəmz-] *n* pomo-de-adão *m*.

adapt [əˈdæpt] *vt* adaptar ♦ *vi* adaptar-se.

adaptable [əˈdæptəbl] *adj* versátil.

adapter [əˈdæptəʳ] *n (for foreign plug)* adaptador *m*; *(for several plugs)* benjamin *m (Br)*, ficha *f* tripla *(Port)*.

add [æd] *vt (put, say in addition)* acrescentar; *(numbers, prices)* somar, adicionar.

❑ **add up** *vt sep* somar, adicionar.

❑ **add up to** *vt fus (total)* ser ao todo.

adder [ˈædəʳ] *n* víbora *f*.

addict [ˈædɪkt] *n* viciado *m* (-da *f*).

addicted [əˈdɪktɪd] *adj*: **to be ~ to sthg** ser viciado(-da) em algo.

addiction [əˈdɪkʃn] *n* vício *m*, dependência *f*.

addictive [əˈdɪktɪv] *adj (drug)* que causa dependência; *(exercise, food, TV)* que vicia.

addition [əˈdɪʃn] *n* adição *f*; **in ~** além disso; **in ~ to** além de.

additional [əˈdɪʃənl] *adj* adicional.

additive [ˈædɪtɪv] *n* aditivo *m*.

address [əˈdrɛs] *n (on letter)* , endereço *m*, direcção *f (Port)* ♦ *vt (speak to)* dirigir-se a; *(letter)* dirigir, endereçar.

address book *n* caderno *m* de endereços.

addressee [ædrɛˈsiː] *n* destinatário *m* (-ria *f*).

adenoids [ˈædɪnɔɪdz] *npl* adenóides *fpl*.

adept [əˈdɛpt] *adj*: **to be ~ (at sthg/at doing sthg)** ser especialista (em algo/em fazer algo).

adequate [ˈædɪkwət] *adj (sufficient)* suficiente; *(satisfactory)* aceitável.

adhere [ədˈhɪəʳ] *vi*: **to ~ to** *(stick to)* aderir a; *(obey)* respeitar.

adhesive [ədˈhiːsɪv] *adj* adesivo(-va) ♦ *n* cola *f*.

adhesive tape *n* fita *f* adesiva.

adjacent [əˈdʒeɪsənt] *adj* adjacente.

adjective [ˈædʒɪktɪv] *n* adjetivo *m*.

adjoining [əˈdʒɔɪnɪŋ] *adj* contíguo (-gua).

adjourn [əˈdʒɜːn] *vt (decision)* adiar; *(meeting)* interromper; *(session)* suspender ♦ *vi* suspender a sessão.

adjudicate [əˈdʒuːdɪkeɪt] *vt* julgar ♦ *vi* julgar, avaliar; **to ~ on sthg** emitir juízo OR sentença sobre algo.

adjust [əˈdʒʌst] *vt* ajustar ♦ *vi*: **to ~ to** adaptar-se a.

adjustable [əˈdʒʌstəbl] *adj* ajustável.

adjustment [əˈdʒʌstmənt] *n (to machine)* ajustamento *m*; *(settling in)* adaptação *f*.

ad lib [ˌædˈlɪb] *adj* improvisado(-da) ♦ *adv (freely)* livremente ♦ *n* improviso *m*.

❑ **ad-lib** *vi* improvisar.

administration [ədˌmɪnɪˈstreɪʃn] *n* administração *f*.

administrative [ədˈmɪnɪstrətɪv] *adj* administrativo(-va).

administrator [ədˈmɪnɪstreɪtəʳ] *n* administrador *m* (-ra *f*).

admirable [ˈædmərəbl] *adj* admirável.

admiral [ˈædmərəl] *n* almirante *m*.

admiration [ˌædməˈreɪʃn] *n* admiração *f*.

admire [ədˈmaɪəʳ] *vt* admirar.

admirer [ədˈmaɪərəʳ] *n* admirador *m* (-ra *f*).

admission [ədˈmɪʃn] *n* entrada *f*.

admission charge *n* entrada *f*.

admit [ədˈmɪt] *vt* admitir ♦ *vi*: **to ~ to sthg** admitir algo; **"~s one"** *(on ticket)* "válido para uma pessoa".

admittance [ədˈmɪtəns] *n* admissão *f*; **"no ~"** "entrada proibida".

admittedly [ədˈmɪtɪdlɪ] *adv* de fato.

admonish [ədˈmɒnɪʃ] *vt* repreender.

ad nauseam [ˌædˈnɔːzɪæm] *adv* até não poder mais.

ado [əˈduː] *n*: **without further** OR **more ~** sem mais cerimônias OR demora.

adolescence [ˌædəˈlɛsns] *n* adolescência *f*.

adolescent [ˌædəˈlɛsnt] *n* adolescente *mf*.

adopt [əˈdɒpt] *vt* adotar.

adopted [əˈdɒptɪd] *adj* adotivo(-va).

adoption [əˈdɒpʃn] *n* adoção *f*.

adorable [əˈdɔːrəbl] *adj* adorável.

adore [əˈdɔːʳ] *vt* adorar.

adorn [əˈdɔːn] *vt* enfeitar.

adrenalin [ə'drenəlin] *n* adrenalina *f*.

Adriatic [eidri'ætik] *n*: **the ~ Sea** o (mar) Adriático.

adrift [ə'drift] *adj (boat)* à deriva ◆ *adv*: **to go ~** *(fig: go wrong)* dar errado.

adult [ˈædʌlt] *n* adulto *m* (-ta *f*) ◆ *adj (entertainment, films)* para adultos; *(animal)* adulto(-ta).

adult education *n* ensino *m* para adultos.

adultery [ə'dʌltəri] *n* adultério *m*.

advance [əd'vɑːns] *n (money)* adiantamento *m*; *(movement)* avanço *m* ◆ *adj (warning)* prévio(-via); *(payment)* adiantado(-da) ◆ *vt (lend)* adiantar; *(bring forward)* avançar ◆ *vi (move forward)* avançar; *(improve)* progredir.

advance booking *n* reserva *f* antecipada.

advanced [əd'vɑːnst] *adj (student, level)* avançado(-da).

advantage [əd'vɑːntidʒ] *n (benefit)* vantagem *f*; **to take ~ of** *(opportunity, offer)* aproveitar; *(person)* aproveitar-se de.

advent [ˈædvənt] *n (arrival)* aparecimento *m*.

❑ **Advent** *n* (RELIG) Advento *m*.

adventure [əd'ventʃər] *n* aventura *f*.

adventurous [əd'ventʃərəs] *adj* aventureiro(-ra).

adverb [ˈædvɜːb] *n* advérbio *m*.

adverse [ˈædvɜːs] *adj* adverso(-sa).

advert [ˈædvɜːt] = **advertisement**.

advertise [ˈædvətaiz] *vt (product, event)* anunciar.

advertisement [əd'vɜːtismənt] *n* anúncio *m*.

advertising [ˈædvətaiziŋ] *n* publicidade *f*.

advice [əd'vais] *n* conselhos *mpl*; **a piece of ~** um conselho.

advisable [əd'vaizəbl] *adj* aconselhável.

advise [əd'vaiz] *vt* aconselhar; **to ~ sb to do sthg** aconselhar alguém a fazer algo; **to ~ sb against doing sthg** desaconselhar alguém a fazer algo.

adviser [əd'vaizər] *n* (Brit) conselheiro *m* (-ra *f*).

advisor [əd'vaizər] *(Am)* = **adviser**.

advisory [əd'vaizəri] *adj* consultivo (-va).

advocate [*n* 'ædvəkət, *vb* 'ædvəkeit] *n* (JUR) advogado *m* (-da *f*) ◆ *vt* advogar.

Aegean [iː'dʒiːən] *n*: **the ~ (Sea)** o mar Egeu.

aerial [ˈeəriəl] *n* antena *f*.

aerobics [eə'rəubiks] *n* aeróbica *f*.

aerodynamic [ˌeərəudai'næmik] *adj* aerodinâmico(-ca).

aeroplane [ˈeərəplein] *n* avião *m*.

aerosol [ˈeərəsɒl] *n* aerossol *m*.

aesthetic [iːs'θetik] *adj* estético(-ca).

affable [ˈæfəbl] *adj* afável.

affair [ə'feər] *n (event)* acontecimento *m*; *(love affair)* caso *m*; *(matter)* questão *f*.

affect [ə'fekt] *vt (influence)* afetar.

affection [ə'fekʃn] *n* afeto *m*.

affectionate [ə'fekʃnət] *adj* afetuoso(-osa).

affirm [ə'fɜːm] *vt (declare)* afirmar; *(confirm)* confirmar, ratificar.

afflict [ə'flikt] *vt* assolar; **to be ~ed with sthg** padecer de algo.

affluence [ˈæfluəns] *n* riqueza *f*.

affluent [ˈæfluənt] *adj* rico(-ca).

afford [ə'fɔːd] *vt*: **to be able to ~ sthg** *(holiday, new coat)* poder pagar algo; **I can't ~ it** não tenho dinheiro (que chegue); **I can't ~ the time** não tenho tempo.

affordable [ə'fɔːdəbl] *adj* acessível.

affront [ə'frʌnt] *n* afronta *f*, insulto *m* ◆ *vt* insultar.

afloat [ə'fləut] *adj* a flutuando *(Br)*, a flutuar *(Port)*.

afraid [ə'freid] *adj* assustado(-da); **to be ~ of** ter medo de; **I'm ~ so/not** receio que sim/não.

afresh [ə'freʃ] *adv* de novo.

Africa [ˈæfrikə] *n* África *f*.

African [ˈæfrikən] *adj* africano(-na) ◆ *n* africano *m* (-na *f*).

aft [ɑːft] *adv* na popa.

after [ˈɑːftər] *prep* depois de ◆ *conj* depois de que ◆ *adv* depois; **a quarter ~ ten** *(Am)* dez e um quarto; **to be ~ sb/sthg** *(in search of)* estar atrás de alguém/algo; **~ all** afinal de contas.

❑ **afters** *npl* (Brit: *inf*) sobremesa *f*.

aftercare [ˈɑːfteikeər] *n* assistência *f* médica pós-internamento.

aftereffects [ˈɑːftəriˌfekts] *npl* efeitos *mpl* secundários.

afterlife [ˈɑːftəlaif] *n*: **the ~** a outra vida, a vida no outro mundo.

aftermath [ˈɑːftəmɑːθ] *n (consequences)* consequências *fpl*; *(time)*: **in the ~ of** no período depois de.

afternoon [ɑːftə'nuːn] *n* tarde *f*; **good ~!** boa tarde!

afternoon tea *n* ≃ lanche *m*.

aftershave ['ɑːftəʃeɪv] *n* loção *f* para após a barba, after-shave *m*.

aftersun ['uːftəsʌn] *n* creme *m* hidratante (para depois do sol).

afterthought ['ɑːftəθɔːt] *n* idéia *f* OR reflexão *f* posterior.

afterwards ['uːftəwədz] *adv* depois, a seguir.

again [ə'gen] *adv* outra vez; **~ and ~** várias vezes; **never ~** nunca mais.

against [ə'genst] *prep* contra; **to lean ~ sthg** apoiar-se em algo; **~ the law** contra a lei.

age [eɪdʒ] *n* idade *f*; *(old age)* velhice *f*; **under ~** menor de idade; **I haven't seen him for ~s** *(inf)* há séculos que não o vejo.

aged [eɪdʒd] *adj*: **~ eight** com oito anos (de idade).

age group *n* grupo *m* etário.

age limit *n* limite *m* de idade.

agency ['eɪdʒənsɪ] *n* agência *f*.

agenda [ə'dʒendə] *n* agenda *f*.

agent ['eɪdʒənt] *n* agente *mf*.

aggravate ['ægrəveɪt] *vt (make worse)* agravar; *(annoy)* irritar.

aggregate ['ægrɪgət] *adj* total, global ♦ *n (total)* total *m*, conjunto *m*.

aggression [ə'greʃn] *n* agressividade *f*.

aggressive [ə'gresɪv] *adj* agressivo (-va).

aggrieved [ə'griːvd] *adj* ofendido (-da).

aghast [ə'gɑːst] *adj* horrorizado(-da); **~ at sthg** horrorizado com algo.

agile [*Brit* 'ædʒaɪl, *Am* 'ædʒəl] *adj* ágil.

agility [ə'dʒɪlɪtɪ] *n* agilidade *f*.

agitated ['ædʒɪteɪtɪd] *adj* agitado (-da).

AGM *abbr (Brit)* = **annual general meeting**.

agnostic [æg'nɒstɪk] *adj* agnóstico (-ca) ♦ *n* agnóstico *m* (-ca *f*).

ago [ə'gəʊ] *adv*: **a month ~** há um mês atrás; **how long ~?** há quanto tempo?

agog [ə'gɒg] *adj* ansioso(-osa); **to be all ~ (with)** estar todo excitado(-da) (com).

agonizing ['ægənaɪzɪŋ] *adj (delay)* angustiante; *(pain)* dilacerante.

agony ['ægənɪ] *n* agonia *f*.

agony aunt *n (Brit: inf)* conselheira *f* sentimental.

agree [ə'griː] *vi* concordar; **tomato soup doesn't ~ with me** não me dou bem com sopa de tomate; **to ~ to sthg** concordar com algo; **to ~ to do sthg** aceitar fazer algo.

❏ **agree on** *vt fus (time, price)* chegar a um acordo sobre.

agreeable [ə'grɪəbl] *adj (pleasant)* agradável; *(willing)*: **to be ~ to sthg** concordar com algo; **to be ~ to do sthg** concordar em fazer algo.

agreed [ə'griːd] *adj* combinado(-da).

agreement [ə'griːmənt] *n* acordo *m*; **in ~ with** de acordo com.

agricultural [ˌægrɪ'kʌltʃərəl] *adj* agrícola.

agriculture ['ægrɪkʌltʃər] *n* agricultura *f*.

aground [ə'graʊnd] *adv*: **to run ~** encalhar.

ahead [ə'hed] *adv (in front)* à frente; *(forwards)* em frente; **the months ~** os próximos meses; **to be ~ *(winning)*** estar à frente; **~ of *(in front of)*** à frente de; **~ of schedule** adiantado(-da); **they're four points ~** levam quatro pontos de vantagem.

aid [eɪd] *n* ajuda *f* ♦ *vt* ajudar; **in ~ of** em benefício de; **with the ~ of** com a ajuda de.

AIDS [eɪdz] *n* AIDS *f* (*Br*), SIDA *f* (*Port*).

ailment ['eɪlmənt] *n (fml)* mal *m*.

aim [eɪm] *n (purpose)* objetivo *m* ♦ *vt (gun, camera, hose)* apontar ♦ *vi*: **to ~ (at)** apontar (para); **to ~ to do sthg** ter como objetivo fazer algo.

aimless ['eɪmlɪs] *adj (person)* sem objetivos; *(task, existence)* sem sentido.

ain't [eɪnt] *(inf)* = **am not, are not, is not, has not, have not**.

air [eər] *n* ar *m* ♦ *vt (room)* arejar ♦ *adj* aéreo(-rea); **by ~** por avião.

air bag *n (AUT)* air bag *m*.

airbase ['eəbeɪs] *n* base *f* aérea.

airbed ['eəbed] *n* colchão *m* de ar.

airborne ['eəbɔːn] *adj* em vôo.

air-conditioned [-kən'dɪʃnd] *adj* climatizado(-da).

air-conditioning [-kən'dɪʃnɪŋ] *n* ar *m* condicionado.

aircraft ['eəkrɑːft] *(pl inv) n* avião *m*.

aircraft carrier [-ˌkærɪər] *n* porta-aviões *m inv*.

airfield ['eəfiːld] *n* aeródromo *m*.

airforce ['eəfɔːs] n aeronáutica f (Br), força f aérea (Port).

air freshener [-ˌfreʃnəʳ] n purificador m do ambiente OR do ar.

airgun ['eəgʌn] n pistola f de ar comprimido.

airhostess ['eəˌhəʊstɪs] n aeromoça f (Br), hospedeira f (Port).

airing cupboard ['eərɪŋ-] n armário onde se encontra o cilindro de aquecimento de água, usado para secar roupa.

airletter ['eəˌletəʳ] n aerograma m.

airline ['eəlaɪn] n companhia f aérea.

airliner ['eəˌlaɪnəʳ] n avião m de passageiros.

airlock ['eəlɒk] n (in tube, pipe) bolsa f de ar; (airtight chamber) câmara f OR caixa f de ar.

airmail ['eəmeɪl] n correio m aéreo; **by ~** por avião.

airplane ['eəpleɪn] n (Am) avião m.

airport ['eəpɔːt] n aeroporto m.

air raid n ataque m aéreo.

air rifle n espingarda f de ar comprimido.

airsick ['eəsɪk] adj enjoado(-da) (em avião).

airspace ['eəspeɪs] n espaço m aéreo.

air steward n comissário m de bordo.

air stewardess n aeromoça f (Br), hospedeira f (Port).

airstrip ['eəstrɪp] n pista f de aterrissagem (Br), pista f de aterragem (Port).

air terminal n terminal m aéreo.

airtight ['eətaɪt] adj hermético(-ca).

air traffic control n (people) pessoal m da torre de controle.

air traffic controller n controlador m aéreo (controladora f aérea).

airy ['eərɪ] adj arejado(-da).

aisle [aɪl] n corredor m; (in church) nave f.

aisle seat n lugar m do lado do corredor.

ajar [əˈdʒɑːʳ] adj entreaberto(-ta).

aka (abbr of also known as) também conhecido(-da) como.

alacrity [əˈlækrətɪ] n prontidão f.

alarm [əˈlɑːm] n alarme m ◆ vt alarmar.

alarm clock n despertador m.

alarmed [əˈlɑːmd] adj (person) assustado(-da); (door, car) provido(-da) de alarme.

alarming [əˈlɑːmɪŋ] adj alarmante.

alas [əˈlæs] excl ai!

Albania [ælˈbeɪnjə] n Albânia f.

Albanian [ælˈbeɪnjən] adj albanês (-esa) ◆ n (person) albanês m (-esa f); (language) albanês m.

albeit [ɔːlˈbiːɪt] conj se bem que.

Albert Hall ['ælbət-] n: **the ~** o Albert Hall.

album ['ælbəm] n álbum m.

alcohol ['ælkəhɒl] n álcool m.

alcohol-free adj sem álcool.

alcoholic [ˌælkəˈhɒlɪk] adj alcoólico (-ca) ◆ n alcoólatra mf (Br), alcoólico m (-ca f) (Port).

alcoholism ['ælkəhɒlɪzm] n alcoolismo m.

alcove ['ælkəʊv] n alcova f.

alderman ['ɔːldəmən] (pl -men [-mən]) n = vereador m (-ra f), = magistrado m (-da f) local.

ale [eɪl] n cerveja escura com alto teor alcoólico.

alert [əˈlɜːt] adj atento(-ta) ◆ vt alertar.

A level n (Brit) = vestibular m (Br), = exame m final do 12º ano (Port).

algebra ['ældʒɪbrə] n álgebra f.

Algeria [ælˈdʒɪərɪə] n Argélia f.

alias ['eɪlɪəs] adv também conhecido (-da) como.

alibi ['ælɪbaɪ] n álibi m.

alien ['eɪljən] n (foreigner) estrangeiro m (-ra f); (from outer space) extraterrestre mf.

alienate ['eɪljəneɪt] vt (friend, family) alienar, ganhar a antipatia de.

alight [əˈlaɪt] adj em chamas ◆ vi (fml: from train, bus): **to ~ (from)** apear-se (de).

align [əˈlaɪn] vt alinhar.

alike [əˈlaɪk] adj parecidos(-das) ◆ adv da mesma maneira; **to look ~** ser parecidos, parecer-se.

alimony ['ælɪmənɪ] n pensão f alimentícia (Br), alimentos mpl (Port).

alive [əˈlaɪv] adj vivo(-va).

alkali ['ælkəlaɪ] n álcali m.

all [ɔːl] adj 1. (with singular noun) todo(-da); **~ the money** o dinheiro todo; **~ the time** sempre; **we were out ~ day** estivemos fora o dia inteiro. 2. (with plural noun) todos(-das); **~ the houses** todas as casas; **~ trains stop at Tonbridge** todos os trens param em Tonbridge.

♦ *adv* **1.** *(completely)* completamente; ~ **alone** completamente só.
2. *(in scores)*: **it's two** ~ estão empatados dois a dois.
3. *(in phrases)*: ~ **but empty** quase vazio(-zia); ~ **over** *adj (finished)* terminado(-da) ♦ *prep* por todo(-da).
♦ *pron* **1.** *(everything)* todo *m* (-da *f*); **is that** ~? *(in shop)* é só isso?; **the best of** ~ o melhor de todos.
2. *(everybody)* todos, toda a gente; ~ **of us went** fomos todos.
3. *(in phrases)*: **can I help you at** ~ posso ajudar em alguma coisa?; **in** ~ *(in total)* ao todo; **in** ~ **it was a great success** resumindo, foi um grande êxito.

Allah [ˈælə] *n* Alá *m*.

all-around *(Am)* = **all-round**.

allay [əˈleɪ] *vt (fears, doubts)* dissipar; *(anger)* apaziguar.

allegation [ˌælɪˈɡeɪʃn] *n* alegação *f*.

allege [əˈledʒ] *vt* alegar.

allegedly [əˈledʒɪdlɪ] *adv* supostamente.

allergic [əˈlɜːdʒɪk] *adj*: **to be** ~ **to** ser alérgico(-ca) a.

allergy [ˈælədʒɪ] *n* alergia *f*.

alleviate [əˈliːvɪeɪt] *vt* aliviar.

alley [ˈælɪ] *n (narrow street)* ruela *f*.

alliance [əˈlaɪəns] *n (agreement)* aliança *f*.

alligator [ˈælɪɡeɪtəʳ] *n* caimão *m*.

all-in *adj (Brit: inclusive)* com tudo incluído.

all-night *adj (bar, petrol station)* aberto(-ta) toda a noite.

allocate [ˈæləkeɪt] *vt* atribuir.

allotment [əˈlɒtmənt] *n (Brit: for vegetables)* parcela de terreno municipal alugado para o cultivo de legumes e flores.

all-out *adj (effort)* máximo(-ma); *(war)* total.

allow [əˈlaʊ] *vt (permit)* permitir; *(time, money)* contar com; **to** ~ **sb to do sthg** deixar alguém fazer algo; **to be** ~**ed to do sthg** poder fazer algo.
❏ **allow for** *vt fus* contar com.

allowance [əˈlaʊəns] *n (state benefit)* subsídio *m*; *(for expenses)* ajudas *fpl* de custo; *(Am: pocket money)* mesada *f*.

alloy [ˈælɔɪ] *n* liga *f* (de metal).

all right *adv (satisfactorily)* bem; *(yes, okay)* está bem ♦ *adj*: **is it** ~ **if I smoke?** posso fumar?; **I thought the film was** ~ não achei o filme nada de especial; **is**

everything ~? está tudo bem?

all-round *adj (Brit) (versatile)* multifacetado(-da).

all-time *adj* de todos os tempos.

allusion [əˈluːʒn] *n* alusão *f*.

ally [ˈælaɪ] *n* aliado *m* (-da *f*).

almighty [ɔːlˈmaɪtɪ] *adj (inf: enormous)* tremendo(-da).

almond [ˈɑːmənd] *n* amêndoa *f*.

almost [ˈɔːlməʊst] *adv* quase.

alone [əˈləʊn] *adj & adv* sozinho (-nha); **the decision is yours** ~ a decisão é só sua; **to leave sb** ~ deixar alguém em paz; **to leave sthg** ~ parar de mexer em algo.

along [əˈlɒŋ] *prep (towards one end of)* por; *(alongside)* ao longo de ♦ *adv*: **to walk** ~ caminhar; **to bring sthg** ~ trazer algo; **all** ~ desde o princípio; ~ **with** (junto) com.

alongside [əˌlɒŋˈsaɪd] *prep* ao lado de.

aloof [əˈluːf] *adj* distante.

aloud [əˈlaʊd] *adv* em voz alta.

alphabet [ˈælfəbet] *n* alfabeto *m*.

alphabetical [ˌælfəˈbetɪkl] *adj* alfabético(-ca).

Alps [ælps] *npl*: **the** ~ os Alpes.

already [ɔːlˈredɪ] *adv* já.

alright [ˌɔːlˈraɪt] = **all right**.

Alsatian [ælˈseɪʃn] *n (dog)* pastor *m* alemão.

also [ˈɔːlsəʊ] *adv* também.

altar [ˈɔːltəʳ] *n* altar *m*.

alter [ˈɔːltəʳ] *vt* alterar.

alteration [ˌɔːltəˈreɪʃn] *n* alteração *f*.

alternate [*Brit* ɔːlˈtɜːnət, *Am* ˈɔːltɜːnət] *adj* alternado(-da).

alternating current [ˈɔːltəneɪtɪŋ-] *n* corrente *f* alterna OR alternada.

alternative [ɔːlˈtɜːnətɪv] *adj* alternativo(-va) ♦ *n* alternativa *f*.

alternatively [ɔːlˈtɜːnətɪvlɪ] *adv* em OR como alternativa.

alternative medicine *n* medicina *f* alternativa.

alternator [ˈɔːltəneɪtəʳ] *n* alternador *m*.

although [ɔːlˈðəʊ] *conj* embora, contudo.

altitude [ˈæltɪtjuːd] *n* altitude *f*.

alto [ˈæltəʊ] *(pl* -s*) n (female voice)* contralto *m*.

altogether [ˌɔːltəˈɡeðəʳ] *adv (completely)* completamente; *(in total)* ao todo, no total.

aluminium [æljʊ'mɪnɪəm] n (Brit) alumínio m.

aluminum [ə'luːmɪnəm] (Am) = aluminium.

always [ɔːlweɪz] adv sempre.

a.m. (abbr of ante meridiem): **at 2 ~ às** duas da manhã.

am [æm] → be.

amalgamate [ə'mælgəˌmeɪt] vt fundir, unir ♦ vi fundir-se, unir-se.

amass [ə'mæs] vt juntar, acumular.

amateur [æmətə'] n amador m (-ra f).

amaze [ə'meɪz] vt surpreender.

amazed [ə'meɪzd] adj espantado(-da), surpreso(-sa).

amazement [ə'meɪzmənt] n espanto m, surpresa f.

amazing [ə'meɪzɪŋ] adj espantoso (-osa), surpreendente.

Amazon ['æməzn] n (river): **the ~** o Amazonas.

ambassador [æm'bæsədə'] n embaixador m (-ra f).

amber [æmbə'] adj (traffic lights) amarelo(-la); (jewellery) âmbar.

ambiguous [æm'bɪgjʊəs] adj ambíguo(-gua).

ambition [æm'bɪʃn] n ambição f.

ambitious [æm'bɪʃəs] adj ambicioso(-osa).

ambulance ['æmbjʊləns] n ambulância f.

ambush ['æmbʊʃ] n emboscada f.

amenable [ə'miːnəbl] adj: **~ (to sthg)** favorável (a algo).

amendment [ə'mendmənt] n (to text) correção f; (to law) modificação f.

amenities [ə'miːnətɪz] npl comodidades fpl.

America [ə'merɪkə] n América f.

American [ə'merɪkən] adj americano (-na) ♦ n (person) americano m (-na f).

amiable ['eɪmɪəbl] adj amável.

amicable ['æmɪkəbl] adj amigável.

amiss [ə'mɪs] adj errado(-da) ♦ adv: **to take sthg ~** levar algo a mal.

ammonia [ə'məʊnjə] n amoníaco m.

ammunition [æmjʊ'nɪʃn] n munições fpl.

amnesia [æm'niːzɪə] n amnésia f.

amnesty ['æmnəstɪ] n anistia f.

amok [ə'mɒk] adv: **to run ~** ser tomado(-da) por uma crise de loucura furiosa.

among(st) [ə'mʌŋ(st)] prep entre.

amoral [eɪ'mɒrəl] adj (person, behaviour) amoral.

amount [ə'maʊnt] n (quantity) quantidade f; (sum) quantia f, montante m. ❑ **amount to** vt fus (total) atingir a quantia de.

amp [æmp] n ampere m; **a 13-~ plug** uma tomada de 13 amperes.

amphibious [æm'fɪbɪəs] adj anfíbio (-bia).

ample [æmpl] adj bastante.

amplifier ['æmplɪfaɪə'] n amplificador m.

amputate ['æmpjʊteɪt] vt amputar.

Amtrak ['æmtræk] n organismo regulador das ferrovias nos E.U.A.

amuck [ə'mʌk] = amok.

amuse [ə'mjuːz] vt (make laugh) divertir; (entertain) entreter.

amused [ə'mjuːzd] adj: **to be ~ at** OR **by sthg** (entertained, delighted) achar piada OR graça de algo; **to keep o.s. ~** (occupied) entreter-se.

amusement [ə'mjuːzmənt] n diversão f; divertimento m. ❑ **amusements** npl diversões fpl.

amusement arcade n sala f de jogos.

amusement park n parque m de diversões.

amusing [ə'mjuːzɪŋ] adj divertido (-da).

an [stressed æn, unstressed ən] → a.

anaemic [ə'niːmɪk] adj (Brit) (person) anêmico(-ca).

anaesthetic [ænɪs'θetɪk] n (Brit) anestesia f.

analgesic [ænæl'dʒiːsɪk] n analgésico m.

analogy [ə'nælədʒɪ] n analogia f; **by ~** por analogia.

analyse ['ænəlaɪz] vt (Brit) analisar.

analysis [ə'næləsɪs] (pl **-lyses** [-ləsiːz]) n análise f.

analyst ['ænəlɪst] n analista mf.

analytic(al) [ænə'lɪtɪk(l)] adj analítico(-ca).

analyze ['ænəlaɪz] (Am) = analyse.

anarchist ['ænəkɪst] n anarquista mf.

anarchy ['ænəkɪ] n anarquia f.

anathema [ə'næθəmə] n: **the concept is ~ to me** para mim, a idéia é inadmissível.

anatomy [ə'nætəmɪ] *n* anatomia *f*.

ANC *n* *(abbr of African National Congress)* ANC *m*.

ancestor [ænsestə'] *n* antepassado *m* (-da *f*).

anchor [æŋkə'] *n* âncora *f*.

anchovy [æntʃəvɪ] *n* anchova *f*.

ancient [eɪnʃənt] *adj* antigo(-ga).

ancillary [ænsɪlərɪ] *adj* auxiliar.

and [*strong form* ænd, *weak form* ənd, ən] *conj* e; ~ you? e você?; **a hundred ~** one cento e um; **more ~ more** cada vez mais; **to go ~ see** ir ver.

Andes [ændiːz] *npl*: **the ~** os Andes.

Andorra [æn'dɔːrə] *n* Andorra *s*.

anecdote [ænɪkdəʊt] *n* episódio *m* (cômico).

anemic [ə'niːmɪk] *(Am)* = **anaemic**.

anesthetic [ænɪs'θetɪk] *(Am)* = **anaesthetic**.

anew [ə'njuː] *adv* de novo.

angel [eɪndʒl] *n* anjo *m*.

anger [æŋɡə'] *n* raiva *f*, ira *f*.

angina [æn'dʒaɪnə] *n* angina *f* de peito.

angle [æŋɡl] *n* ângulo *m*; **at an ~** torto (torta).

angler [æŋɡlə'] *n* pescador *m* (-ra *f*) (de vara).

Anglican [æŋɡlɪkən] *adj* anglicano (-na) ♦ *n* anglicano *m* (-na *f*).

angling [æŋɡlɪŋ] *n* pesca *f* (de vara).

Angola [æŋ'ɡəʊlə] *n* Angola *s*.

Angolan [æŋ'ɡəʊlən] *adj* angolano(-na) ♦ *n* angolano *m* (-na *f*).

angry [æŋɡrɪ] *adj* *(person)* zangado (-da); *(words)* de raiva; **to get ~ (with sb)** zangar-se (com alguém).

anguish [æŋɡwɪʃ] *n* angústia *f*.

animal [ænɪml] *n* animal *m*.

animate [ænɪmət] *adj* animado(-da), vivo(-va).

animated [ænɪmeɪtɪd] *adj* animado (-da).

aniseed [ænɪsiːd] *n* erva-doce *f*, anis *m*.

ankle [æŋkl] *n* tornozelo *m*.

annex [æneks] *n* *(building)* anexo *m*.

annihilate [ə'naɪəleɪt] *vt* aniquilar.

anniversary [ænɪ'vɜːsərɪ] *n* aniversário *m*.

announce [ə'naʊns] *vt* anunciar.

announcement [ə'naʊnsmənt] *n* *(on TV, radio)* anúncio *m*; *(official)* comunicação *f*.

announcer [ə'naʊnsə'] *n* *(on TV)* apresentador *m* (-ra *f*); *(on radio)* locutor *m* (-ra *f*).

annoy [ə'nɔɪ] *vt* aborrecer, irritar.

annoyance [ə'nɔɪəns] *n* irritação *f*.

annoyed [ə'nɔɪd] *adj* aborrecido(-da), irritado(-da); **to get ~ (with)** aborrecer-se (com), irritar-se (com).

annoying [ə'nɔɪɪŋ] *adj* irritante.

annual [ænjʊəl] *adj* anual.

annual general meeting *n* assembléia *f* geral (anual).

annul [ə'nʌl] *vt* anular.

annum [ænəm] *n*: **per ~** por ano.

anomaly [ə'nɒmälɪ] *n* anomalia *f*.

anonymous [ə'nɒnɪməs] *adj* anônimo(-ma).

anorak [ænəræk] *n* anoraque *m*.

anorexia (nervosa) [ænə'reksɪə (nɜː'vəʊsə)] *n* anorexia *f* (nervosa).

another [ə'nʌðə'] *adj* outro(-tra) ♦ *pron* outro *m* (-tra *f*); **in ~ two weeks** dentro de (mais) duas semanas; **~ one** outro(-tra); **one ~** um ao outro (uma à outra); **to talk to one ~** falar um com o outro; **they love one ~** eles se amam (um ao outro); **one after ~** um após o outro.

answer [ɑːnsə'] *n* resposta *f* ♦ *vt* responder a ♦ *vi* responder; **to ~ the door** abrir a porta; **to ~ the phone** atender o telefone.

❑ **answer back** *vi* replicar.

answering machine [ɑːnsərɪŋ-] = **answerphone**.

answerphone [ɑːnsəfəʊn] *n* secretária *f* eletrônica *(Br)*, atendedor *m* de chamadas *(Port)*.

ant [ænt] *n* formiga *f*.

antagonism [æn'tæɡənɪzm] *n* antagonismo *m*.

antagonize [æn'tæɡənaɪz] *vt* antagonizar.

Antarctic [æn'tɑːktɪk] *n*: **the ~** o Antártico.

antelope [æntɪləʊp] *(pl inv* OR *-s)* *n* antílope *m*.

antenatal clinic [æntɪ'neɪtl-] *n* serviço *m* de consultas pré-natais.

antenna [æn'tenə] *n* *(Am: aerial)* antena *f*.

anthem [ænθəm] *n* hino *m*.

anthology [æn'θɒlədʒɪ] *n* antologia *f*.

antibiotics [æntɪbaɪ'ɒtɪks] *npl* antibióticos *mpl*.

antibody [æntɪ,bɒdɪ] *n* anticorpo *m*.

anticipate [æn'tɪsɪpeɪt] *vt* *(expect)* esperar; *(guess correctly)* prever.

anticipation [æn,tɪsɪ'peɪʃn] *n* antecipação *f*; **in ~ of** antecipando.

anticlimax [,æntɪ'klaɪmæks] *n* anticlímax *m inv*.

anticlockwise [,æntɪ'klɒkwaɪz] *adv* (*Brit*) no sentido contrário ao dos ponteiros do relógio.

antics [æntɪks] *npl* (*of children, animals*) brincadeiras *fpl*.

anticyclone [,æntɪ'saɪkləʊn] *n* anticiclone *m*.

antidepressant [,æntɪdə'presnt] *n* antidepressivo *m*.

antidote ['æntɪdəʊt] *n* antídoto *m*.

antifreeze ['æntɪfriːz] *n* anticongelante *m*.

antihistamine [,æntɪ'hɪstəmɪn] *n* anti-histamínico *m*.

antiperspirant [,æntɪ'pɜːspərənt] *n* desodorizante *m*.

antiquarian bookshop [,æntɪ'kweərɪən-] *n* sebo *m* (*Br*), alfarrabista *m* (*Port*).

antique [æn'tiːk] *n* antiguidade *f*.

antique shop *n* loja *f* de antiguidades.

antiseptic [,æntɪ'septɪk] *n* antiséptico *m*.

antisocial [,æntɪ'səʊʃl] *adj* anti-social.

antlers ['æntləz] *npl* chifres *mpl*.

anxiety [æŋ'zaɪətɪ] *n* ansiedade *f*.

anxious ['æŋkʃəs] *adj* ansioso(-osa).

any ['enɪ] *adj* **1.** (*in questions*) algum (-ma); **have you got ~ money?** você tem dinheiro?; **have you got ~ postcards?** você tem postais?; **have you got ~ rooms?** você tem algum quarto livre? **2.** (*in negatives*) nenhum(-ma); **I haven't got ~ money** não tenho dinheiro (nenhum); **we don't have ~ rooms** não temos quartos livres. **3.** (*no matter which*) qualquer; **take ~ books you like** leve os livros que quiser; **take ~ one you like** leve aquele que quiser.
♦ *pron* **1.** (*in questions*) algum *m* (-ma *f*); **I'm looking for a hotel – are there ~ nearby?** estou procurando um hotel – há algum aqui perto? **2.** (*in negatives*) nenhum *m* (-ma *f*); **I don't want ~ (of it)** não quero (nada); **I don't want ~ (of them)** não quero nenhum (deles). **3.** (*no matter which one*) qualquer um (qualquer uma); **you can sit at ~ of the tables** podem sentar-se em qualquer uma das mesas.

♦ *adv* **1.** (*in questions*): **~ other questions?** mais alguma pergunta?; **can you drive ~ faster?** vôce pode ir mais depressa?; **is that ~ better?** está melhor assim? **2.** (*in negatives*): **he's not ~ better** ele não está nada melhor; **we can't wait ~ longer** não podemos esperar mais; **we can't afford ~ more** não temos possibilidades para mais.

anybody ['enɪ,bɒdɪ] = anyone.

anyhow ['enɪhaʊ] *adv* (*carelessly*) de qualquer maneira; (*in any case*) em qualquer caso; (*in spite of that*) de qualquer modo.

anyone ['enɪwʌn] *pron* (*any person*) qualquer um (qualquer uma); (*in questions*) alguém; (*in negatives*) ninguém; **I don't like ~** não gosto de ninguém.

anything ['enɪθɪŋ] *pron* (*no matter what*) qualquer coisa; (*in questions*) alguma coisa; (*in negatives*) nada; **she didn't say ~** ela não disse nada.

anyway ['enɪweɪ] *adv* de qualquer forma OR modo.

anywhere ['enɪweəʳ] *adv* (*no matter where*) em/a qualquer lugar; (*in questions*) em/a algum lugar; (*in negatives*) em/a lugar nenhum; **I can't find it ~** não o encontro em lugar nenhum; **sit ~ you like** sente-se onde quiser; **we can go ~** podemos ir a qualquer lugar.

apart [ə'pɑːt] *adv* separado(-da); **to come ~** separar-se; **~ from** (*except for*) exceto, salvo; (*as well as*) para além de.

apartheid [ə'pɑːtheɪt] *n* apartheid *m*.

apartment [ə'pɑːtmənt] *n* (*Am*) apartamento *m*.

apathetic [,æpə'θetɪk] *adj* apático(-ca).

apathy ['æpəθɪ] *n* apatia *f*.

ape [eɪp] *n* macaco *m*.

aperitif [ə,perə'tiːf] *n* aperitivo *m*.

aperture ['æpə,tjʊəʳ] *n* (*of camera*) abertura *f*.

APEX ['eɪpeks] *n* (*plane ticket*) bilhete *m* APEX; (*Brit: train ticket*) *bilhete de preço reduzido não transmissível que se adquire com duas semanas de antecedência.*

apiece [ə'piːs] *adv*: **they cost £50 ~** custam 50 libras cada um.

apologetic [ə,pɒlə'dʒetɪk] *adj* cheio (cheia) de desculpas.

apologize [ə'pɒlədʒaɪz] *vi*: **to ~ (to sb for sthg)** pedir desculpa (a alguém por algo).

apology [ə'pɒlədʒɪ] *n* desculpa *f*.

apostle [ə'pɒsl] n apóstolo m.

apostrophe [ə'pɒstrəfı] n apóstrofo m.

appal [ə'pɔːl] vt (Brit) horrorizar.

appall [ə'pɔːl] (Am) = appal.

appalling [ə'pɔːlıŋ] adj horrível, terrível.

apparatus [æpə'reıtəs] n aparelho m.

apparent [ə'pærənt] adj aparente.

apparently [ə'pærəntlı] adv aparentemente.

appeal [ə'piːl] n (JUR) apelação f, recurso m; (fundraising campaign) campanha f de coleta de fundos ◆ vi (JUR) apelar, recorrer para; **to ~ to sb (for sthg)** apelar a alguém (para algo); **it doesn't ~ to me** não me atrai.

appealing [ə'piːlıŋ] adj atrativo(-va), sedutor(-ra).

appear [ə'pıər] vi aparecer; (seem) parecer; (before court) comparecer; **it ~s that** parece que.

appearance [ə'pıərəns] n (arrival) chegada f; (look) aparência f, aspecto m.

appease [ə'piːz] vt aplacar, acalmar.

appendices [ə'pendısiːz] pl → appendix.

appendicitis [ə,pendı'saıtıs] n apendicite f.

appendix [ə'pendıks] (pl -dices) n apêndice m.

appetite [æpıtaıt] n apetite m.

appetizer [æpıtaızər] n aperitivo m.

appetizing [æpıtaızıŋ] adj apetitoso(-osa).

applaud [ə'plɔːd] vt & vi aplaudir.

applause [ə'plɔːz] n palmas fpl.

apple [æpl] n maçã f.

apple charlotte [-'ʃɑːlət] n pudim de maçã e pão ralado, cozido numa forma forrada e depois coberta com fatias de pão.

apple crumble n sobremesa de maçã cozida coberta com uma mistura arenosa de farinha, manteiga e açúcar, cozida no forno.

apple juice n suco m de maçã.

apple pie n torta f de maçã.

apple sauce n purê m de maçã (servido como acompanhamento de carne de porco).

apple tart n torta f de maçã.

apple tree n macieira f.

apple turnover [-'tɜːn,əʊvər] n folheado m de maçã.

appliance [ə'plaıəns] n aparelho m;

electrical/domestic ~ eletrodoméstico m.

applicable [ə'plıkəbl] adj: **to be ~ (to)** ser aplicável (a); **if ~** se aplicável.

applicant [æplıkənt] n candidato m (-ta f).

application [æplı'keıʃn] n (for job, membership) candidatura f.

application form n formulário m de candidatura.

apply [ə'plaı] vt aplicar ◆ vi: **to ~ (to sb for sthg)** (make request) apelar (algo a alguém); **to ~ (to sb)** (be applicable) ser aplicável (a alguém).

appoint [ə'pɔınt] vt (to job, position) nomear; **to ~ sb to sthg** nomear alguém para algo; **to ~ sb as sthg** nomear alguém algo.

appointment [ə'pɔıntmənt] n (with hairdresser, businessman) hora f marcada; (with doctor) consulta f; **to have/make an ~ (with)** ter/marcar um encontro (com); **by ~** com hora marcada.

apportion [ə'pɔːʃn] vt (money) dividir; (blame) atribuir.

appraisal [ə'preızl] n análise f, avaliação f.

appreciable [ə'priːʃəbl] adj apreciável.

appreciate [ə'priːʃıeıt] vt (be grateful for) agradecer; (understand) compreender; (like, admire) apreciar.

appreciation [ə,priːʃı'eıʃn] n (gratitude) gratidão f, apreço m; (understanding) compreensão f; (liking) satisfação f.

appreciative [ə'priːʃıətıv] adj (person) agradecido(-da); (remark, gesture) de agradecimento; (audience) satisfeito(-ta).

apprehensive [æprı'hensıv] adj apreensivo(-va).

apprentice [ə'prentıs] n aprendiz m (-za f).

apprenticeship [ə'prentısʃıp] n aprendizagem f.

approach [ə'prəʊtʃ] n (road) acesso m; (to problem, situation) abordagem f ◆ vt (come nearer to) aproximar-se de; (problem, situation) abordar ◆ vi aproximar-se.

approachable [ə'prəʊtʃəbl] adj acessível.

appropriate [ə'prəʊprıət] adj apropriado(-da).

approval [ə'pru:vl] *n (favourable opinion)* aprovação *f*; *(permission)* autorização *f*.

approve [ə'pru:v] *vi*: **to ~ of sb/sthg** ver com bons olhos alguém/algo.

approximate [ə'prɒksɪmət] *adj* aproximado(-da).

approximately [ə'prɒksɪmətlɪ] *adv* aproximadamente.

Apr. *abbr* = **April**.

apricot ['eɪprɪkɒt] *n* alperce *m*, damasco *m*.

April ['eɪprəl] *n* Abril *m*, → **September**.

April Fools' Day *n* = 1° de abril *(Br)*, Dia *m* das mentiras *(Port)*.

apron ['eɪprən] *n* avental *m* (de cozinha).

apt [æpt] *adj (appropriate)* apropriado(-da); **to be ~ to do sthg** ser propenso a fazer algo.

aptitude ['æptɪtjuːd] *n* aptidão *f*; **to have an ~ for sthg** ter jeito para algo.

aquarium [ə'kweərɪəm] *(pl* **-riums** OR **-ria** [-rɪə]) *n* aquário *m*.

Aquarius [ə'kweərɪəs] *n* Aquário *m*.

aqueduct ['ækwɪdʌkt] *n* aqueduto *m*.

Arab ['ærəb] *adj* árabe ◆ *n (person)* árabe *mf*.

Arabic ['ærəbɪk] *adj* árabe ◆ *n (language)* árabe *m*.

Arabic numeral *n* número *m* arábico.

arable ['ærəbl] *adj (land)* arável; *(farm, crops)* agrícola.

arbitrary ['ɑːbɪtrərɪ] *adj* arbitrário (-ria).

arbitration [ɑːbɪ'treɪʃn] *n* arbitragem *f*; **to go to ~** recorrer a arbitragem.

arc [ɑːk] *n* arco *m*.

arcade [ɑː'keɪd] *n (for shopping)* galeria *f*; *(of video games)* sala *f* de jogos.

arch [ɑːtʃ] *n* arco *m*.

archaeologist [ɑːkɪ'ɒlədʒɪst] *n* arqueólogo *m* (-ga *f*).

archaeology [ɑːkɪ'ɒlədʒɪ] *n* arqueologia *f*.

archaic [ɑː'keɪɪk] *adj* arcaico(-ca).

archbishop [ɑːtʃ'bɪʃəp] *n* arcebispo *m*.

archeology [ɑːkɪ'ɒlədʒɪ] *etc* = **archaeology** *etc*.

archery ['ɑːtʃərɪ] *n* tiro *m* com arco e flechas.

archetypal [ɑːkɪ'taɪpl] *adj* típico (-ca).

archipelago [ɑːkɪ'peləgəʊ] *(pl* **-s** OR **-es)** *n* arquipélago *m*.

architect ['ɑːkɪtekt] *n* arquiteto *m* (-ta *f*).

architecture ['ɑːkɪtektʃəʳ] *n* arquitetura *f*.

Arctic ['ɑːktɪk] *n*: **the ~** o Ártico.

ardent ['ɑːdənt] *adj* ardente.

arduous ['ɑːdjʊəs] *adj* árduo(-dua).

are *[weak form* əʳ, *strong form* ɑːʳ] → **be**.

area ['eərɪə] *n* área *f*.

area code *n (Am)* prefixo *m* (telefônico) *(Br)*, indicativo *m* (telefónico) *(Port)*.

arena [ə'riːnə] *n (at circus)* arena *f*; *(sportsground)* estádio *m*.

aren't [ɑːnt] = **are not**.

Argentina [ɑːdʒən'tiːnə] *n* Argentina *f*.

arguably ['ɑːgjʊəblɪ] *adv* possivelmente.

argue ['ɑːgjuː] *vi*: **to ~ (with sb about sthg)** discutir (com alguém acerca de algo) ◆ *vt*: **to ~ (that)** argumentar que.

argument ['ɑːgjʊmənt] *n (quarrel)* discussão *f*; *(reason)* argumento *m*.

argumentative [ɑːgjʊ'mentətɪv] *adj (person)* propenso (-sa) a discutir.

arid ['ærɪd] *adj* árido(-da).

Aries ['eəriːz] *n* Áries *m (Br)*, Carneiro *m (Port)*.

arise [ə'raɪz] *(pt* **arose**, *pp* **arisen** [ə'rɪzn]) *vi*: **to ~ (from)** surgir (de).

aristocracy [ærɪ'stɒkrəsɪ] *n* aristocracia *f*.

aristocrat [*Brit* 'ærɪstəkræt, *Am* ə'rɪstəkræt] *n* aristocrata *mf*.

arithmetic [ə'rɪθmətɪk] *n* aritmética *f*.

arm [ɑːm] *n* braço *m*; *(of garment)* manga *f*.

armaments ['ɑːməmənts] *npl* armamento *m*.

armbands ['ɑːmbændz] *npl (for swimming)* braçadeiras *fpl*.

armchair ['ɑːmtʃeəʳ] *n* poltrona *f*.

armed [ɑːmd] *adj* armado(-da).

armed forces *npl*: **the ~** as forças armadas.

armhole ['ɑːmhəʊl] *n* manga *f*.

armor ['ɑːmər] *(Am)* = **armour**.

armour ['ɑːməʳ] *n (Brit)* armadura *f*.

armoured car ['ɑːməd-] *n (Brit)* *n* carro *m* blindado.

armpit [ˈɑːmpɪt] n axila f, sovaco m.

armrest [ˈɑːmrest] n braço m (de cadeira, sofá).

arms [ɑːmz] npl (weapons) armas fpl.

army [ˈɑːmɪ] n exército m.

A-road n (Brit) ≈ estrada f nacional.

aroma [əˈrəʊmə] n aroma m.

aromatic [ˌærəˈmætɪk] adj aromático(-ca).

arose [əˈrəʊz] pt → **arise**.

around [əˈraʊnd] adv (about, round) por aí; (present) por aí/aqui ♦ prep (surrounding) em redor de, à volta de; (to the other side of) para o outro lado de; (near) perto de; (all over) por todo (-da); (approximately) cerca de; ~ **here** (in the area) por aqui; **to turn** ~ virar-se; **to look** ~ (turn head) olhar em volta; (in shop, city) dar uma olhada.

arouse [əˈraʊz] vt (suspicion) levantar; (fear) provocar; (interest) suscitar.

arrange [əˈreɪndʒ] vt (books) arrumar; (flowers) arranjar; (meeting, event) organizar; **to** ~ **to do sthg** (with sb) combinar fazer algo (com alguém).

arrangement [əˈreɪndʒmənt] n (agreement) combinação f; (layout) disposição f; **by** ~ (tour, service) com data e hora marcada; **to make** ~**s** (to do sthg) fazer os preparativos (para fazer algo).

array [əˈreɪ] n (of objects, people) variedade f.

arrears [əˈrɪəz] npl (money owed) atrasos mpl (Br), retroactivos mpl (Port); **to be in** ~ (late) estar atrasado; **I'm paid monthly in** ~ eu sou pago sempre no fim do mês (de trabalho).

arrest [əˈrest] n detenção f, prisão f ♦ vt prender; **under** ~ sob prisão, preso.

arrival [əˈraɪvl] n chegada f; **on** ~ à chegada; **new** ~ (person) recém-chegado m (-da f).

arrive [əˈraɪv] vi chegar; **to** ~ **at** chegar a.

arrogant [ˈærəgənt] adj arrogante.

arrow [ˈærəʊ] n (for shooting) flecha f; (sign) seta f.

arsenic [ˈɑːsnɪk] n arsênico m.

arson [ˈɑːsn] n fogo m posto.

art [ɑːt] n arte f.

❑ **arts** npl (humanities) letras fpl; **the** ~**s** (fine arts) as belas-artes.

artefact [ˈɑːtɪfækt] n artefato m.

artery [ˈɑːtərɪ] n artéria f.

art gallery n (commercial) galeria f de arte; (public) museu m de arte.

arthritis [ɑːˈθraɪtɪs] n artrite f.

artichoke [ˈɑːtɪtʃəʊk] n alcachofra f.

article [ˈɑːtɪkl] n artigo m.

articulate [ɑːˈtɪkjʊlət] adj eloquente.

articulated lorry [ɑːˈtɪkjʊleɪtɪd-] n (Brit) jamanta f (Br), camião m articulado (Port).

artificial [ˌɑːtɪˈfɪʃl] adj artificial.

artillery [ɑːˈtɪlərɪ] n (guns) artilharia f.

artist [ˈɑːtɪst] n (painter) pintor m (-ra f); (performer) artista mf.

artistic [ɑːˈtɪstɪk] adj artístico(-ca).

arts centre n centro m cultural.

arty [ˈɑːtɪ] adj (pej) com pretensões artísticas.

as [unstressed əz, stressed æz] adv (in comparisons): ~ ... ~ tão ... como; **he's** ~ **tall** ~ **I am** ele é tão alto quanto eu; **twice as big** ~ duas vezes maior do que; ~ **many** ~ tantos quantos (tantas quantas); ~ **much** ~ tanto quanto.

♦ conj **1.** (referring to time) quando; ~ **the plane was coming in to land** quando o avião ia aterrissar.

2. (referring to manner) como; **do** ~ **you like** faz como você quiser; ~ **expected** ... (tal) como era de esperar ....

3. (introducing a statement) como; ~ **you know** ... como você sabe ....

4. (because) porque, como.

5. (in phrases): ~ **for** quanto a; ~ **from** a partir de; ~ **if** como se.

♦ prep (referring to function, job) como; **I work** ~ **a teacher** sou professora.

asap (abbr of as soon as possible) assim que possível.

ascent [əˈsent] n (climb) subida f.

ascertain [ˌæsəˈteɪn] vt confirmar.

ascribe [əˈskraɪb] vt: **to** ~ **sthg to** atribuir algo a.

ash [æʃ] n (from cigarette, fire) cinza f; (tree) freixo m.

ashamed [əˈʃeɪmd] adj envergonhado(-da); **to be** ~ **of** ter vergonha de; **to be** ~ **to do sthg** ter vergonha de fazer algo.

ashore [əˈʃɔːr] adv em terra; **to go** ~ desembarcar.

ashtray [ˈæʃtreɪ] n cinzeiro m.

Ash Wednesday n Quarta-feira f de Cinzas.

Asia [Brit ˈeɪʃə, Am ˈeɪʒə] n Ásia f.

Asian [Brit ˈeɪʃn, Am ˈeɪʒn] adj asiático(-ca) ♦ n asiático m (-ca f).

aside [əˈsaɪd] adv (to one side) para o

lado; **to move** ~ afastar-se.

ask [ɑːsk] vt *(person)* perguntar a; *(request)* pedir; *(invite)* convidar ♦ vi: **to ~ about sthg** *(enquire)* informar-se sobre algo; **to ~ sb about sthg** perguntar a alguém sobre algo; **to ~ sb sthg** perguntar algo a alguém; **to ~ sb to do sthg** pedir a alguém que faça algo; **to ~ sb for sthg** pedir algo a alguém; **to ~ a question** fazer uma pergunta. ❏ **ask for** vt fus *(ask to talk to)* perguntar por; *(request)* pedir.

askance [əˈskæns] adv: **to look ~ at** olhar desaprovadoramente para.

asking price [ˈɑːskɪŋ-] n preço m (pedido).

asleep [əˈsliːp] adj adormecido(-da); **to fall ~** adormecer.

asparagus [əˈspærəgəs] n aspargos *(Br)*, espargos mpl *(Port)*.

asparagus tips npl pontas fpl de aspargos.

aspect [ˈæspekt] n aspecto m.

aspiration [æspəˈreɪʃn] n aspiração f.

aspire [əˈspaɪəʳ] vi: **to ~ to** aspirar a.

aspirin [ˈæsprɪn] n aspirina f.

ass [æs] n *(animal)* asno m.

assailant [əˈseɪlənt] n agressor m (-ra f).

assassinate [əˈsæsɪneɪt] vt assasinar.

assassination [əˌsæsɪˈneɪʃn] n assassínio m, assassinato m.

assault [əˈsɔːlt] n agressão f ♦ vt agredir.

assemble [əˈsembl] vt *(bookcase, model)* montar ♦ vi reunir-se.

assembly [əˈsemblɪ] n *(at school)* reunião regular de alunos e professores.

assembly hall n *(at school)* sala f de reuniões.

assembly line n linha f de montagem.

assembly point n *(at airport, in shopping centre)* ponto m de encontro.

assent [əˈsent] n *(agreement)* aprovação f ♦ vi: **to ~ to sthg** aprovar algo.

assert [əˈsɜːt] vt *(fact, innocence)* afirmar; *(authority)* impor; **to ~ o.s.** impor-se.

assertive [əˈsɜːtɪv] adj firme.

assess [əˈses] vt avaliar.

assessment [əˈsesmənt] n avaliação f.

asset [ˈæset] n *(valuable person, thing)* elemento m valioso. ❏ **assets** npl bens mpl.

assign [əˈsaɪn] vt: **to ~ sthg to sb** *(give)* ceder algo a alguém; **to ~ sb to**

sthg *(designate)* nomear alguém para algo.

assignment [əˈsaɪnmənt] n *(task)* tarefa f; *(SCH)* trabalho m.

assimilate [əˈsɪmɪleɪt] vt *(learn)* assimilar; *(integrate)*: **to ~ sb (into sthg)** integrar alguém (em algo).

assist [əˈsɪst] vt ajudar.

assistance [əˈsɪstəns] n ajuda f; **to be of ~ (to sb)** ajudar (alguém).

assistant [əˈsɪstənt] n assistente mf, ajudante mf.

associate [n əˈsəʊʃɪət, vb əˈsəʊʃɪeɪt] n *(colleague)* colega mf; *(partner)* sócio m (-cia f) ♦ vt: **to ~ sb/sthg with** associar alguém/algo com OR a; **to be ~d with** *(attitude, person)* estar associado a.

association [əˌsəʊsɪˈeɪʃn] n associação f.

assorted [əˈsɔːtɪd] adj variado(-da).

assortment [əˈsɔːtmənt] n sortimento m *(Br)*, sortido m *(Port)*.

assume [əˈsjuːm] vt *(suppose)* supor; *(control, responsibility)* assumir.

assumption [əˈsʌmpʃn] n *(supposition)* suposição f.

assurance [əˈʃʊərəns] n *(promise)* garantia f; *(insurance)* seguro m.

assure [əˈʃʊəʳ] vt assegurar; **to ~ sb (that)** ... assegurar a alguém que ....

assured [əˈʃʊəd] adj *(confident)* seguro(-ra).

asterisk [ˈæstərɪsk] n asterisco m.

astern [əˈstɜːn] adv na popa.

asthma [ˈæsmə] n asma f.

asthmatic [æsˈmætɪk] adj asmático (-ca).

astonish [əˈstɒnɪʃ] vt surpreender.

astonished [əˈstɒnɪʃt] adj espantado(-da), surpreso(-sa).

astonishing [əˈstɒnɪʃɪŋ] adj espantoso(-osa), surpreendente.

astonishment [əˈstɒnɪʃmənt] n espanto m, surpresa f.

astound [əˈstaʊnd] vt surpreender.

astray [əˈstreɪ] adv: **to go ~** extraviar-se.

astrology [əˈstrɒlədʒɪ] n astrologia f.

astronaut [ˈæstrənɔːt] n astronauta mf.

astronomical [ˌæstrəˈnɒmɪkl] adj *(inf: very large)* astronômico(-ca).

astronomy [əˈstrɒnəmɪ] n astronomia f.

astute [əˈstjuːt] adj astuto(-ta).

asylum [əˈsaɪləm] n *(POL)* asilo m;

(mental hospital) manicômio *m*.

at [unstressed ət, stressed æt] *prep* **1.** *(indicating place, position)* em; ~ **home** em casa; ~ **the hotel** no hotel; ~ **my mother's** na casa da minha mãe; ~ **school** na escola. **2.** *(indicating direction)* para; **he threw a plate** ~ **the wall** ele atirou um prato na parede; **to look** ~ olhar para. **3.** *(indicating time):* ~ **nine o'clock** às nove horas; ~ **night** à noite; ~ **Christmas** no Natal. **4.** *(indicating rate, level, speed)* a; **it works out** ~ **£5 each** sai a 5 libras cada um; ~ **60 km/h** a 60 km/h. **5.** *(indicating activity)* a; **to be** ~ **lunch** estar almoçando; **to be good/bad** ~ **sthg** ser bom/mau em algo. **6.** *(indicating cause)* com.

ate [Brit et, Am ett] *pt* → **eat**.

atheist ['eiθiist] *n* ateu *m* (atéia *f*).

athlete ['æθli:t] *n* atleta *mf*.

athletics [æθ'letiks] *n* atletismo *m*.

Atlantic [ət'læntik] *n*: **the** ~ **(Ocean)** o (oceano) Atlântico.

atlas ['ætləs] *n* atlas *m inv*.

atmosphere ['ætməsfiə'] *n* atmosfera *f*.

atom ['ætəm] *n* átomo *m*.

atom bomb *n* bomba *f* atômica.

atomic [ə'tɒmik] *adj* atômico(-ca).

atomic bomb = atom bomb.

atomizer ['ætəmaizə'] *n* atomizador *m*, vaporizador *m*.

atone [ə'təun] *vi*: **to** ~ **for sthg** expiar algo.

A to Z *n (map)* mapa *m* da cidade.

atrocious [ə'trəuʃəs] *adj* atroz.

atrocity [ə'trɒsəti] *n* atrocidade *f*.

attach [ə'tætʃ] *vt* juntar; **to** ~ **sthg to sthg** juntar algo a algo.

attaché case [ə'tæʃei-] *n* pasta *f* (de executivo).

attachment [ə'tætʃmənt] *n (device)* acessório *m*.

attack [ə'tæk] *n* ataque *m* ♦ *vt* atacar.

attacker [ə'tækə'] *n* agressor *m* (-ra *f*).

attain [ə'tein] *vt (fml)* alcançar.

attainment [ə'teinmənt] *n (of happiness, objective)* conquista *f*; *(skill)* aquisição *f*.

attempt [ə'tempt] *n* tentativa *f* ♦ *vt* tentar; **to** ~ **to do sthg** tentar fazer algo.

attend [ə'tend] *vt (meeting, Mass)* assistir a; *(school)* frequentar. □ **attend to** *vt fus (deal with)* atender a.

attendance [ə'tendəns] *n (people at concert, match)* assistência *f*; *(at school)* frequência *f*.

attendant [ə'tendənt] *n* empregado *m* (-da *f*).

attention [ə'tenʃn] *n* atenção *f*; **to pay** ~ **(to)** prestar atenção (a).

attentive [ə'tentiv] *adj (paying attention)* atento(-ta); *(politely helpful)* atencioso(-osa).

attic ['ætik] *n* sótão *m*.

attitude ['ætitju:d] *n* atitude *f*.

attorney [ə'tə:ni] *n (Am)* advogado *m* (-da *f*).

attract [ə'trækt] *vt* atrair; *(attention)* chamar.

attraction [ə'trækʃn] *n* atração *f*; *(attractive feature)* atrativo *m*.

attractive [ə'træktiv] *adj* atraente.

attribute [ə'tribju:t] *vt*: **to** ~ **sthg to** atribuir algo a.

attrition [ə'triʃn] *n* desgaste *m*.

aubergine ['əubəʒi:n] *n (Brit)* beringela *f*.

auburn ['ɔ:bən] *adj* castanho-avermelhado(-da).

auction ['ɔ:kʃn] *n* leilão *m*.

auctioneer [ˌɔ:kʃə'niə'] *n* leiloeiro *m* (-ra *f*).

audible ['ɔ:dəbl] *adj* audível.

audience ['ɔ:diəns] *n* público *m*, audiência *f*.

audio ['ɔ:diəu] *adj* áudio *(inv)*.

audio-visual *adj* audiovisual.

audit ['ɔ:dit] *n* verificação *f* (oficial) de contas ♦ *vt* verificar.

audition [ɔ:'diʃn] *n* audição *f*.

auditor ['ɔ:ditə'] *n (of accounts)* técnico *m* (-ca *f*) de contas.

auditorium [ˌɔ:di'tɔ:riəm] *n* auditório *m*.

Aug. *abbr* = August.

augur ['ɔ:gə'] *vi*: **to** ~ **well/badly** ser bom/mau sinal.

August ['ɔ:gəst] *n* Agosto *m*, → **September**.

Auld Lang Syne [ˌɔ:ldlæŋ'sain] *n* cantiga tradicional escocesa cantada à meia-noite da véspera de Ano Novo cujo título significa "os bons tempos de outrora".

aunt [ɑ:nt] *n* tia *f*.

au pair [ˌəu'peə'] *n* au pair *mf*.

aural ['ɔ:rəl] *adj* auditivo(-va).

auspices [ˈɔːspɪsɪz] *npl*: **under the ~ of** sob os auspícios de.

auspicious [ɔːˈspɪʃəs] *adj* promissor (-ra).

austere [ɒˈstɪəʳ] *adj* austero(-ra).

austerity [ɒˈsterətɪ] *n* austeridade *f*.

Australia [ɒˈstreɪlɪə] *n* Austrália *f*.

Australian [ɒˈstreɪlɪən] *adj* australiano(-na) ♦ *n* australiano *m* (-na *f*).

Austria [ˈɒstrɪə] *n* Áustria *f*.

Austrian [ˈɒstrɪən] *adj* austríaco(-ca) ♦ *n* austríaco *m* (-ca *f*).

authentic [ɔːˈθentɪk] *adj* autêntico (-ca).

author [ˈɔːθəʳ] *n* (of book, article) autor *m* (-ra *f*); (by profession) escritor *m* (-ra *f*).

authoritarian [ɔːˌθɒrɪˈteərɪən] *adj* autoritário(-ria).

authoritative [ɔːˈθɒrɪtətɪv] *adj* (person, voice) autoritário(-ria); (report) autorizado(-da).

authority [ɔːˈθɒrɪtɪ] *n* autoridade *f*; **the authorities** as autoridades.

authorization [ˌɔːθəraɪˈzeɪʃn] *n* autorização *f*.

authorize [ˈɔːθəraɪz] *vt* autorizar; **to ~ sb to do sthg** autorizar alguém a fazer algo.

autistic [ɔːˈtɪstɪk] *adj* autista.

autobiography [ˌɔːtəbaɪˈɒɡrəfɪ] *n* autobiografia *f*.

autocratic [ˌɔːtəˈkrætɪk] *adj* autocrático(-ca).

autograph [ˈɔːtəɡrɑːf] *n* autógrafo *m*.

automatic [ˌɔːtəˈmætɪk] *adj* automático(-ca); (fine) imediato(-ta) ♦ *n* (car) carro *m* automático OR com direção assistida.

automatically [ˌɔːtəˈmætɪklɪ] *adv* automaticamente.

automobile [ˈɔːtəməbiːl] *n* (Am) automóvel *m*.

autonomy [ɔːˈtɒnəmɪ] *n* autonomia *f*.

autopsy [ˈɔːtɒpsɪ] *n* autópsia *f*.

autumn [ˈɔːtəm] *n* Outono *m*; **in (the) ~** no Outono.

auxiliary (verb) [ɔːɡˈzɪljərɪ-] *n* verbo *m* auxiliar.

avail [əˈveɪl] *n*: **to no ~** em vão.

available [əˈveɪləbl] *adj* disponível.

avalanche [ˈævəlɑːnʃ] *n* avalanche *f*.

avarice [ˈævərɪs] *n* avareza *f*.

Ave. (abbr of avenue) Av.

avenge [əˈvendʒ] *vt* vingar, vingar-se de.

avenue [ˈævənjuː] *n* avenida *f*.

average [ˈævərɪdʒ] *adj* médio(-dia) ♦ *n* média *f*; **on ~** em média.

aversion [əˈvɜːʃn] *n* aversão *f*.

avert [əˈvɜːt] *vt* (problem, accident) evitar; (eyes, glance) desviar.

aviation [ˌeɪvɪˈeɪʃn] *n* aviação *f*.

avid [ˈævɪd] *adj* ávido(-da).

avocado [ˌævəˈkɑːdəʊ] (pl **-s** OR **-es**) *n*: **~ (pear)** pêra *f* abacate.

avoid [əˈvɔɪd] *vt* evitar; **to ~ doing sthg** evitar fazer algo.

await [əˈweɪt] *vt* esperar, aguardar.

awake [əˈweɪk] (pt **awoke**, pp **awoken**) *adj* acordado(-da) ♦ *vi* acordar.

award [əˈwɔːd] *n* (prize) prêmio *m* ♦ *vt*: **to ~ sb sthg** (prize) atribuir algo a alguém; (damages, compensation) adjudicar algo a alguém.

aware [əˈweəʳ] *adj* consciente; **to be ~ of** estar consciente de.

awareness [əˈweənɪs] *n* consciência *f*.

awash [əˈwɒʃ] *adj*: **~ (with)** (fig: with letters, tourists) inundado(-da) de.

away [əˈweɪ] *adv* (go) embora; (look, turn) para outro lado; **to be ~** (not at home, in office) não estar; **it's 10 miles ~ (from here)** fica a 10 milhas (daqui); **it's two weeks ~** é daqui a duas semanas; **to go ~ on holiday** ir de férias; **to put sthg ~** guardar algo; **to take sthg ~ (from sb)** tirar algo (de alguém); **to walk/drive ~** afastar-se; **far ~** longe.

awe [ɔː] *n* respeito *m* (acompanhado de receio); **to be in ~ of sb** estar impressionado com alguém.

awesome [ˈɔːsəm] *adj* incrível.

awful [ˈɔːfəl] *adj* (very bad) horrível; (very great) imenso(-sa); **I feel ~** estou me sentindo muito mal; **how ~!** que horror!

awfully [ˈɔːflɪ] *adv* (very) muitíssimo.

awkward [ˈɔːkwəd] *adj* (position) incômodo(-da); (shape, size) pouco prático(-ca); (situation, question, task) embaraçoso(-osa); (movement) desajeitado(-da); (time) inoportuno(na).

awning [ˈɔːnɪŋ] *n* toldo *m*.

awoke [əˈwəʊk] *pt* → **awake**.

awoken [əˈwəʊkən] *pp* → **awake**.

awry [əˈraɪ] *adj* torto (torta) ♦ *adv*: **to go ~** dar errado.

axe [æks] *n* machado *m*.

axis [ˈæksɪs] (pl **axes** [ˈæksiːz]) *n* eixo *m*.

axle [ˈæksl] *n* eixo *m*.

Azores [əˈzɔːz] *npl*: **the ~** os Açores.

B

BA *abbr* = **Bachelor of Arts**.

babble ['bæbl] *vi (person)* tagarelar.

baby ['beɪbɪ] *n* bebê *m*; **to have a ~** ter um bebê; **~ sweetcorn** mini-milho *m*.

baby carriage *n (Am)* carrinho *m* de bebê.

baby food *n* comida *f* de bebê.

baby-sit *vi* tomar conta de crianças.

baby-sitter [-'sɪtəʳ] *n* baby-sitter *f*.

baby wipe *n* toalhita *f* para bebê.

bachelor ['bætʃələʳ] *n* homem *m* solteiro.

Bachelor of Arts *n* = *(titular de uma) licenciatura em letras.*

Bachelor of Science *n* = *(titular de uma) licenciatura em ciências.*

back [bæk] *adv (towards the back)* para trás ◆ *n* costas *fpl*; *(of car)* parte *f* de trás; *(of room)* fundo *m* ◆ *adj (seat, wheels)* traseiro(-ra) ◆ *vi (car, driver)* recuar ◆ *vt (support)* apoiar; **to call ~** *(telephone)* voltar a telefonar; **to give sthg ~** devolver algo; **to stand ~** afastar-se; **to write ~** responder (a carta); **at the ~ of** na traseira de; **in ~ of** *(Am)* na traseira de; **~ to front** de trás para a frente.

❑ **back up** *vt sep (support)* apoiar ◆ *vi (car, driver)* dar marcha à ré.

backache ['bækeɪk] *n* dor *f* nas costas.

backbencher [,bæk'bentʃəʳ] *n (Brit: POL)* deputado do governo ou oposição sem cargo.

backbone ['bækbəʊn] *n* coluna *f* vertebral.

backcloth ['bækklɒθ] *n (Brit)* = **backdrop**.

backdate [,bæk'deɪt] *vt*: **a pay rise ~d to June** um aumento de salário com efeito retroativo desde junho.

back door *n* porta *f* traseira.

backdrop ['bækdrɒp] *n* pano *m* de fundo.

backfire [,bæk'faɪəʳ] *vi (car)* dar estouros.

backgammon [,bæk'gæmən] *n* gamão *m*.

background ['bækgraʊnd] *n* cenário *m*; *(of person)* background *m*.

backhand ['bækhænd] *n* esquerda *f*.

backing ['bækɪŋ] *n (support)* apoio *m*; *(lining)* reforço *m*.

backlash ['bæklæʃ] *n (reaction)* contra-ataque *m*, reação *f* violenta.

backlog ['bæklɒg] *n* acumulação *f*.

back number *n* número *m* atrasado.

backpack ['bækpæk] *n* mochila *f*.

backpacker ['bækpækəʳ] *n* turista com orçamento reduzido que viaja de mochila e saco de dormir nas costas.

back pay *n* salário *m* em atraso.

back seat *n* banco *m* traseiro.

backside [,bæk'saɪd] *n (inf)* traseiro *m*.

backstage [,bæk'steɪdʒ] *adv (be, stay)* nos bastidores; *(go)* para os bastidores.

back street *n* ruela *f*.

backstroke ['bækstrəʊk] *n* costas *fpl (em natação)*.

backup ['bækʌp] *adj (plan, team)* de reserva ◆ *n (support)* apoio *m*.

backward ['bækwəd] *adj (look, movement)* para trás; *(person, country)* atrasado(-da).

backwards ['bækwədz] *adv (move, look)* para trás; *(the wrong way round)* ao contrário.

backyard [,bæk'jɑːd] *n (Brit)* quintal *m*.

bacon ['beɪkən] *n* bacon *m*, toucinho *m*; **~ and eggs** bacon frito e ovos estrelados.

bacteria [bæk'tɪərɪə] *npl* bactérias *fpl*.

bad [bæd] (compar **worse**, superl **worst**) adj mau (má); (serious) grave; (poor, weak) fraco(-ca); (rotten, off) estragado(-da); **to have a ~ back/leg** ter um problema nas costas/na perna; **don't eat that – it's ~ for you** não come isso que vai lhe fazer mal; **not ~** nada mau (má).

badge [bædʒ] n crachá m.

badger ['bædʒər] n texugo m.

badly ['bædlɪ] (compar **worse**, superl **worst**) adv (poorly) mal; (seriously) gravemente; (very much) imenso.

badly-off adj (poor) pobre, com problemas econômicos.

badly paid [-peɪd] adj mal pago(-ga).

bad-mannered [-mænəd] adj mal-educado(-da).

badminton ['bædmɪntən] n badminton m.

bad-tempered [-tempəd] adj com mau gênio.

baffle ['bæfl] vt desorientar, confundir.

bag [bæg] n (of paper, plastic) saco m, saca f; (handbag) bolsa f; (suitcase) mala f; **a ~ of crisps** um pacote de batatas fritas.

bagel ['beɪgəl] n pequeno pão em forma de anel.

baggage ['bægɪdʒ] n bagagem f.

baggage allowance n peso m limite (de bagagem).

baggage reclaim n recolhimento m de bagagem.

baggage trolley n carrinho m.

baggy ['bægɪ] adj largo(-ga).

bagpipes ['bægpaɪps] npl gaita-de-foles f.

Bahamas [bəhɑːməz] npl: **the ~ as** Baamas.

bail [beɪl] n fiança f.

bailiff ['beɪlɪf] n oficial mf de justiça.

bait [beɪt] n isca f.

bake [beɪk] vt (cake, souffle) cozer (em forno); (potatoes) assar ♦ n (CULIN) gratinado m.

baked [beɪkt] adj (cake, souffle) cozido(-da); (potatoes) assado(-da).

baked Alaska [-əlæskə] n sobremesa de bolo e sorvete coberto de merengue, que se assa no forno durante breves minutos.

baked beans npl feijão m cozido com molho de tomate.

baked potato n batata f assada com casca.

baker ['beɪkər] n padeiro m (-ra f); **~'s (shop)** padaria f.

bakery ['beɪkərɪ] n padaria f.

Bakewell tart ['beɪkwel-] n torta de massa esfarelada recheada com geléia, coberta com uma mistura de ovos, manteiga, açúcar e amêndoas raladas.

baking ['beɪkɪŋ] n (process) cozimento m.

balaclava (helmet) [bæləˈklɑːvə-] n (Brit) passa-montanhas m inv.

balance ['bæləns] n (of person) equilíbrio m; (of bank account) saldo m; (remainder) resto m ♦ vt (object) equilibrar.

balanced diet [bælənst-] n dieta f equilibrada.

balcony ['bælkənɪ] n (of house) varanda f; (of theatre) balcão m.

bald [bɔːld] adj calvo(-va), careca.

bale [beɪl] n fardo m.

Balkans ['bɔːlkənz] npl: **the ~ os** Balcãs.

Balkan States ['bɔːlkən-] = **Balkans**.

ball [bɔːl] n bola f; (of wool, string) novelo m; (dance) baile m; **on the ~** (fig) a par de tudo.

ballad ['bæləd] n balada f.

ballast ['bæləst] n lastro m.

ball bearing n rolamento m de esferas.

ball boy n apanha-bolas m inv.

ballerina [bæləˈriːnə] n bailarina f.

ballet ['bæleɪ] n bailado m, ballet m, balé m.

ballet dancer n bailarino m (-na f).

ball game n (Am: baseball match) jogo m de basebol; (inf: situation): **this is a whole new ~** isto já é outra história.

balloon [bəˈluːn] n (at party etc) balão m, bola f de soprar.

ballot ['bælət] n votação f.

ballpoint pen ['bɔːlpɔɪnt-] n esferográfica f.

ballroom ['bɔːlrʊm] n salão m de baile.

ballroom dancing n dança f de salão.

balsa(wood) ['bɔːlsə(wʊd)] n balsa f.

Baltic ['bɔːltɪk] adj báltico(-ca) ♦ n: **the ~ (Sea)** o (mar) Báltico.

Baltic Republic n: **the ~s as** Repúblicas Bálticas.

bamboo [bæmˈbuː] n bambu m.

bamboo shoots npl brotos mpl de bambu.

bamboozle [bæm'buːzl] vt (inf) enrolar, passar a perna em.

ban [bæn] n proibição f ♦ vt proibir; **to ~ sb from doing sthg** proibir alguém de fazer algo.

banana [bə'nuːnə] n banana f.

banana split n banana split m, banana cortada ao meio com sorvete, creme e calda de chocolate.

band [bænd] n (musical group) banda f; (strip of paper) tira f de papel; (rubber) elástico m.

bandage ['bændɪdʒ] n atadura f (Br), ligadura f (Port) ♦ vt ligar.

Band-Aid® ['bændeɪd] n esparadrapo m (Br), penso m rápido (Port).

B and B abbr = **bed and breakfast**.

bandit ['bændɪt] n bandido m (-da f).

bandstand ['bændstænd] n coreto m.

bandy ['bændɪ] adj com as pernas tortas.

❏ **bandy about** vt sep usar a torto e a direito.

bandy-legged [-ˌlegd] adj = **bandy**.

bang [bæŋ] n (loud noise) estrondo m ♦ vt (hit loudly) bater em; (shut loudly, injure) bater com.

banger ['bæŋər] n (Brit: inf: sausage) salsicha f; **~s and mash** salsichas com puré de batata.

bangle ['bæŋgl] n pulseira f.

bangs [bæŋz] npl (Am) franja f.

banish ['bænɪʃ] vt banir.

banister ['bænɪstər] n corrimão m.

banjo ['bændʒəʊ] n (pl -s OR -es) n banjo m.

bank [bæŋk] n (for money) banco m; (of river, lake) margem f; (slope) monte m (pequeno).

bank account n conta f bancária.

bank book n caderneta f bancária.

bank charges npl encargos mpl bancários (Br), comissões fpl bancárias (Port).

bank clerk n bancário m (-ria f) (Br), empregado m bancário (empregada f bancária) (Port).

bank draft n saque m bancário (Br), transferência f bancária (Port).

banker ['bæŋkər] n banqueiro m (-ra f).

banker's card n cartão bancário que é necessário apresentar, como garantia, sempre que se paga por cheque.

bank holiday n (Brit) feriado m.

bank manager n diretor m (-ra f) de banco.

bank note n nota f (de banco).

bankrupt ['bæŋkrʌpt] adj falido(-da).

bankruptcy ['bæŋkrəptsɪ] n falência f.

bank statement n extrato m de conta.

banner ['bænər] n cartaz m.

bannister ['bænɪstər] = **banister**.

banquet ['bæŋkwɪt] n (formal dinner) banquete m; (at Indian restaurant etc) menu m fixo (para várias pessoas).

banter ['bæntər] n piadas fpl.

bap [bæp] n (Brit) pãozinho m redondo (Br), papo-seco m (Port).

baptism ['bæptɪzm] n batismo m.

Baptist ['bæptɪst] n batista mf.

baptize [Brit bæp'taɪz, Am 'bæptaɪz] vt batizar.

bar [bɑːr] n (pub, in hotel) bar m; (counter in pub) balcão m; (of metal, soap) barra f; (of wood) tranca f; (of chocolate) barra f (Br), tablete m ou f (Port) ♦ vt (obstruct) bloquear.

barbaric [bɑː'bærɪk] adj bárbaro(-ra).

barbecue ['bɑːbɪkjuː] n (apparatus) churrasqueira f (Br), grelhador m (Port); (event) churrasco m ♦ vt assar (na churrasqueira) (Br), assar (no churrasco) (Port).

barbecue sauce n molho m para churrasco.

barbed wire [bɑːbd-] n arame m farpado.

barber ['bɑːbər] n barbeiro m; **~'s** (shop) barbearia f.

barbiturate [bɑː'bɪtjʊrət] n barbitúrio m.

bar code n código m de barras.

bare [beər] adj (feet) descalço(-ça); (head) descoberto(-ta); (arms, legs) ao léu; (room, cupboard) vazio(-zia); **the ~ minimum** o mínimo dos mínimos.

bareback ['beəbæk] adv em pêlo, sem arreios.

barefaced ['beəfeɪst] adj descarado (-da).

barefoot [ˌbeəˈfʊt] adv descalço(-ça).

barely ['beəlɪ] adv mal.

bargain ['bɑːgɪn] n (agreement) acordo m; (cheap buy) pechincha f ♦ vi (haggle) regatear.

❏ **bargain for** vt fus contar com, esperar.

bargain basement n seção f de saldos.

barge [bɑːdʒ] *n* barca *f.*
❏ **barge in** *vi*: **to ~ in on sb** interromper alguém.
baritone ['bærɪtəʊn] *n* barítono *m.*
bark [bɑːk] *n (of tree)* casca *f* ❖ *vi* latir.
barley ['bɑːlɪ] *n* cevada *f.*
barley sugar *n (Brit)* ≃ bala *f (Br)*, rebuçado *m (Port).*
barley water *n (Brit)* refrigerante feito com água e grãos de cevada, açúcar e aromas de fruta.
barmaid ['bɑːmeɪd] *n* garçonete *f (Br)*, empregada *f* de bar *(Port).*
barman ['bɑːmən] *(pl* **-men** [-mən]) *n* barman *m.*
bar meal *n* comida ligeira e rápida servida em bares.
barn [bɑːn] *n* celeiro *m.*
barometer [bə'rɒmɪtəʳ] *n* barômetro *m.*
baron ['bærən] *n* barão *m.*
baroness ['bærənɪs] *n* baronesa *f.*
baroque [bə'rɒk] *adj* barroco(-ca).
barracks ['bærəks] *npl* quartel *m.*
barrage ['bærɑːʒ] *n (of questions, criticism)* chuva *f*, avalanche *f.*
barrel ['bærəl] *n (of beer, wine, oil)* barril *m*; *(of gun)* cano *m.*
barren ['bærən] *adj (land, soil)* estéril.
barricade [bærɪ'keɪd] *n* barricada *f.*
barrier ['bærɪəʳ] *n* barreira *f.*
barring ['bɑːrɪŋ] *prep*: **~ accidents** excepto se houver acidentes.
barrister ['bærɪstəʳ] *n (Brit)* advogado *m* (-da *f*) (de tribunais superiores).
barrow ['bærəʊ] *n (market stall)* carro *m* de mão *(para venda de produtos nas feiras).*
bartender ['bɑːtendəʳ] *n (Am)* garçon *m (Br)*, empregado *m* (-da *f*) de bar *(Port).*
barter ['bɑːtəʳ] *vi* negociar.
base [beɪs] *n* base *f* ❖ *vt*: **to ~ sthg on** basear algo em; **to be ~d in** *(located)* estar sediado em.
baseball ['beɪsbɔːl] *n* basebol *m.*
baseball cap *n* boné *m* de basebol.
basement ['beɪsmənt] *n (in house)* porão *m (Br)*, cave *f (Port).*
bases ['beɪsiːz] *pl* → **basis**.
bash [bæʃ] *vt (inf)* bater com.
bashful ['bæʃful] *adj* acanhado(-da), tímido(-da).
basic ['beɪsɪk] *adj (fundamental)* bási-

co(-ca); *(accommodation, meal)* simples *(inv)* ❖ *npl*: **the ~s** os princípios básicos.
basically ['beɪsɪklɪ] *adv* no fundo.
basil ['bæzl] *n* manjericão *m.*
basin ['beɪsn] *n (washbasin)* pia *f*, lavatório *m (Port)*; *(bowl)* tigela *f*, taça *f.*
basis ['beɪsɪs] *(pl* **bases**) *n* base *f*; **on a weekly ~** semanalmente; **on the ~ of** tendo em conta.
bask [bɑːsk] *vi (sunbathe)*: **to ~ in the sun** torrar no sol, apanhar sol.
basket ['bɑːskɪt] *n* cesto *m*, cesta *f.*
basketball ['bɑːskɪtbɔːl] *n (game)* basquetebol *m.*
basmati rice [bəz'mætɪ-] *n* arroz fino e aromático usado em muitos pratos indianos.
bass¹ [beɪs] *n (singer)* baixo *m.*
bass² [bæs] *n (fish)* robalo *m.*
bass drum [beɪs-] *n* bombo *m.*
bass (guitar) [beɪs-] *n* baixo *m.*
bassoon [bə'suːn] *n* fagote *m.*
bastard ['bɑːstəd] *n (vulg)* filho-da-puta *m* (filha-da-puta *f*), cabrão *m* (-brona *f*) *(Port).*
bastion ['bæstɪən] *n (fig)* bastião *m*, baluarte *m.*
bat [bæt] *n (in cricket, baseball)* pá *f*; *(in table tennis)* raquete *f*; *(animal)* morcego *m.*
batch [bætʃ] *n* lote *m.*
bath [bɑːθ] *n* banho *m* ❖ *vt* dar banho em; **to have a ~** tomar banho.
❏ **baths** *npl (Brit: public swimming pool)* piscina *f* municipal.
bathe [beɪð] *vi (inf)* tomar banho.
bathing ['beɪðɪŋ] *n (Brit)* banho *m.*
bathing cap *n* touca *f* de banho.
bathing costume *n* traje *m* de banho *(Br)*, fato *m* de banho *(Port).*
bathrobe ['bɑːθrəʊb] *n* roupão *m.*
bathroom ['bɑːθrʊm] *n* banheiro *m (Br)*, casa *f* de banho *(Port).*
bathroom cabinet *n* armário *m* de banheiro.
bath towel *n* toalha *f* de banho.
bathtub ['bɑːθtʌb] *n* banheira *f.*
baton ['bætən] *n (of conductor)* batuta *f*; *(truncheon)* cassetete *m.*
batsman ['bætsmən] *(pl* **-men** [-mən]) *n (in cricket)* batedor *m.*
batter ['bætəʳ] *n (CULIN)* massa mole para panquecas e frituras, polme *m (Port)* ❖ *vt (wife, child)* espancar.

battered ['bætəd] *adj (CULIN)* frito em massa mole.

battery ['bætəri] *n (for radio, torch etc)* pilha *f; (for car)* bateria *f.*

battery charger [-,tʃu:dʒəʳ] *n* aparelho *m* para recarregar pilhas/baterias.

battle ['bætl] *n (in war)* batalha *f; (struggle)* luta *f.*

battlefield ['bætlfi:ld] *n* campo *m* de batalha.

battlements ['bætlmənts] *npl* ameias *fpl.*

battleship ['bætlʃip] *n* navio *m* de guerra.

bauble ['bɔːbl] *n* bugiganga *f.*

bawl [bɔːl] *vt (shout)* bradar ♦ *vi* berrar.

bay [beɪ] *n (on coast)* baía *f; (for parking)* lugar *m* para estacionamento.

bay leaf *n* folha *f* de louro.

bay window *n* janela *f* saliente.

bazaar [bəˈzuːʳ] *n* bazar *m.*

B & B *abbr* = **bed and breakfast.**

BBC *(abbr of British Broadcasting Corporation)* BBC *f*, empresa estatal britânica de radiodifusão.

BC *(abbr of before Christ)* a.C.

be [biː] *(pt was, were, pp been)* vi 1. *(exist)* ser; **there is/are** há; **are there any shops near here?** há lojas perto daqui?

2. *(describing quality, permanent condition)* ser; **he's a doctor** ele é médico; **I'm British** sou britânico; **the hotel is near the airport** o hotel é OR fica perto do aeroporto.

3. *(describing state, temporary condition)* estar; **will you ~ in the office tomorrow?** você vai estar no escritório amanhã?; **I'll ~ there at six o'clock** estarei lá às seis horas; **I'm hot/cold** estou com calor/frio, tenho calor/frio.

4. *(referring to movement)*: **has the postman been?** o correio já passou?; **have you ever been to Ireland?** você já esteve na Irlanda?; **I'll ~ there in ten minutes** estarei lá em dez minutos.

5. *(occur)* ser; **the final is in June** a final é em junho.

6. *(referring to health)* estar; **how are you?** como vai você?; **I'm fine** estou bem; **she's ill** ela está doente.

7. *(referring to age)*: **how old are you?** que idade você tem?; **I'm 14 (years old)** tenho 14 anos.

8. *(referring to cost)* ser; **how much is it?** quanto é?; **it's £10** são 10 libras.

9. *(referring to time, dates)* ser; **what time is it?** que horas são?; **it's ten o'clock** são dez horas.

10. *(referring to measurement)* ter; **I'm 60 kilos** tenho 60 quilos; **he is 6 feet tall** ele tem 2 metros de altura; **it's 10 metres wide/long** tem 10 metros de largura/comprimento.

11. *(referring to weather)* estar; **it's hot/cold** está calor/frio; **it's windy/sunny** está ventando/sol; **it's going to be nice today** vai fazer bom tempo hoje.

♦ *aux vb* 1. *(forming continuous tense)* estar; **I'm learning French** estou aprendendo francês *(Br)*, estou a aprender francês *(Port)*; **we've been visiting the museum** tivemos visitando o museu *(Br)*, andámos a visitar o museu *(Port)*.

2. *(forming passive)* ser; **she was given a rise** ela foi aumentada; **the flight was delayed** o vôo atrasou; **there are no tables to ~ had** não há mesas vagas.

3. *(with infinitive to express order)*: **you are not to leave until I say so** você só pode sair quando eu disser; **new arrivals are to wait in reception** os recém-chegados têm que esperar na recepção; **all rooms are to ~ vacated by 10 a.m.** todos os quartos têm que ser desocupados antes das 10 horas da manhã.

4. *(with infinitive to express future tense)*: **the race is to start at noon** a corrida começará ao meio-dia.

5. *(in tag questions)*: **he's very tall, isn't he?** ele é muito alto, não é?; **it's cold, isn't it?** está frio, não está?

beach [biːtʃ] *n* praia *f.*

beacon ['biːkən] *n (warning fire)* fogueira *f (de aviso); (lighthouse)* farol *m; (radio beacon)* radiofarol *m.*

bead [biːd] *n* conta *f.*

beagle ['biːgl] *n* bigle *m.*

beak [biːk] *n* bico *m.*

beaker ['biːkəʳ] *n* copo *m.*

beam [biːm] *n (of light)* raio *m; (of wood)* trave *f; (of concrete)* viga *f* ♦ *vi (smile)* sorrir alegremente.

bean [biːn] *n (haricot)* feijão *m; (pod)* feijão *m* verde; *(of coffee)* grão *m.*

beanbag ['biːnbæg] *n* espécie de pufe mole estofado com esferovite.

bean curd [-kɜːd] *n* pasta de soja em

cubos muito usada na cozinha chinesa e vegetariana.

beansprouts ['bi:nsprauts] *npl* brotos *mpl* de feijão.

bear [beəᴿ] (*pt* bore, *pp* borne) *n (animal)* urso *m* ♦ *vt* suportar, aguentar; **to ~ left/right** virar à esquerda/direita.

bearable ['beərəbl] *adj* suportável.

beard [bɪəd] *n* barba *f*.

bearer ['beərəᴿ] *n (of cheque, passport)* portador *m* (-ra *f*).

bearing ['beərɪŋ] *n (relevance)* relevância *f*; **to get one's ~s** orientar-se.

beast [bi:st] *n (animal)* animal *m*.

beastly ['bi:stlɪ] *adj* horrível.

beat [bi:t] (*pt* beat, *pp* beaten ['bi:tn]) *n (of heart, pulse)* pulsação *f*; *(MUS)* ritmo *m* ♦ *vt (defeat)* derrotar, vencer; *(hit)* bater em, agredir; *(eggs, cream)* bater.

❑ **beat down** *vi (sun)* bater; *(rain)* cair ♦ *vt sep*: **I ~ him down to £15** consegui que ele baixasse o preço para 15 libras.

❑ **beat up** *vt sep* espancar.

beating ['bi:tɪŋ] *n (hitting)* surra *f*, espancamento *m*; *(defeat)* derrota *f*.

beautiful ['bju:tɪfʊl] *adj (attractive)* lindo(-da); *(very good)* magnífico(-ca).

beautifully ['bju:təflɪ] *adv* lindamente.

beauty ['bju:tɪ] *n* beleza *f*.

beauty parlour [-'pɑ:ləᴿ] *n* instituto *m* de beleza.

beauty salon = beauty parlour.

beauty spot *n (place)* local *m* de excepcional beleza.

beaver ['bi:vəᴿ] *n* castor *m*.

became [bɪ'keɪm] *pt* → become.

because [bɪ'kɒz] *conj* porque; **~ of** por causa de.

beckon ['bekən] *vi*: **to ~ (to)** acenar (a).

become [bɪ'kʌm] (*pt* became, *pp* become) *vi* tornar-se; **what became of him?** que foi feito dele?

bed [bed] *n (for sleeping in)* cama *f*; *(of river)* leito *m*; *(of sea)* fundo *m*; *(CULIN)* base *f*, camada *f*; *(in garden)* canteiro *m*; **in ~** na cama; **to get out of ~** levantar-se (da cama); **to go to ~** ir para a cama; **to go to ~ with sb** ir para a cama com alguém; **to make the ~** fazer a cama.

bed and breakfast *n (Brit)* casa privada onde se oferece dormida e café da manhã a preços acessíveis.

bedclothes ['bedkləʊðz] *npl* roupa *f* de cama.

bedding ['bedɪŋ] *n* roupa *f* de cama.

bed linen *n* lençóis *mpl* (e fronhas).

bedraggled [bɪ'drægld] *adj* molhado e sujo (molhada e suja).

bedridden ['bed,rɪdn] *adj* acamado (-da).

bedroom ['bedrʊm] *n* quarto *m*.

bedside ['bedsaɪd] *n* cabeceira *f* (de cama).

bedside table ['bedsaɪd-] *n* mesinha *f* de cabeceira.

bedsit ['bedsɪt] *n (Brit)* quarto alugado com pia e área para cozinhar.

bedspread ['bedspred] *n* colcha *f*.

bedtime ['bedtaɪm] *n* hora *f* de dormir.

bee [bi:] *n* abelha *f*.

beech [bi:tʃ] *n* faia *f*.

beef [bi:f] *n* carne *f* de vaca; **~ Wellington** *lombo de vaca envolto em massa folhada e servido em fatias.*

beefburger ['bi:f,bɜːgəᴿ] *n* hambúrger *m*.

Beefeater ['bi:f,i:təᴿ] *n* alabardeiro *m* (da Torre de Londres).

beefsteak ['bi:f,steɪk] *n* bife *m*.

beehive ['bi:haɪv] *n* colméia *f*.

been [bi:n] *pp* → be.

beer [bɪəᴿ] *n* cerveja *f*; **to have a couple of ~s** beber OR tomar umas cervejas.

beer garden *n* bar *m* ao ar livre *(Br)*, esplanada *f (Port)*.

beer mat *n* descanso *m* para copos.

beet [bi:t] *n (sugar beet)* beterraba *m*.

beetle ['bi:tl] *n* escaravelho *m*.

beetroot ['bi:tru:t] *n* beterraba *f*.

before [bɪ'fɔ:ᴿ] *adv* antes ♦ *prep* antes de; *(fml: in front of)* em frente de ♦ *conj* antes de; **~ you leave** antes de partir; **the day ~** o dia anterior; **the week ~** last há duas semanas.

beforehand [bɪ'fɔ:hænd] *adv* de antemão.

befriend [bɪ'frend] *vt* fazer amizade com.

beg [beg] *vi* pedir ♦ *vt*: **to ~ sb to do sthg** implorar a alguém que faça algo; **to ~ for sthg** *(for money, food)* pedir algo.

began [bɪ'gæn] *pt* → begin.

beggar ['begər] n mendigo m (-ga f).
begin [bɪ'gɪn] (pt began, pp begun) vt & vi começar; **to ~ doing** OR **to do sthg** começar a fazer algo; **to ~ by doing sthg** começar por fazer algo; **to ~ with** (firstly) para começar.
beginner [bɪ'gɪnər] n principiante mf.
beginning [bɪ'gɪnɪŋ] n começo m.
begrudge [bɪ'grʌdʒ] vt: **to ~ sb sthg** (envy) envejar algo a alguém; **to ~ doing sthg** (do unwillingly) detestar fazer algo.
begun [bɪ'gʌn] pp → begin.
behalf [bɪ'hɑːf] n: **on ~ of** em nome de.
behave [bɪ'heɪv] vi comportar-se; **to ~ (o.s.)** (be good) comportar-se.
behavior [bɪ'heɪvjər] (Am) = behaviour.
behaviour [bɪ'heɪvjər] n comportamento m.
behead [bɪ'hed] vt decapitar.
behind [bɪ'haɪnd] adv (at the back) atrás ♦ prep (at the back of) atrás de ♦ n (inf) traseiro m; **to be ~ sb** (supporting) apoiar alguém; **to be ~ (schedule)** estar atrasado; **to leave sthg ~** esquecer-se de algo; **to stay ~** ficar para trás.
beige [beɪʒ] adj bege (inv).
being ['biːɪŋ] n ser m; **to come into ~** nascer.
belated [bɪ'leɪtɪd] adj tardio(-dia).
belch [beltʃ] vi arrotar.
Belgian ['beldʒən] adj belga ♦ n belga mf.
Belgian waffle n (Am) = waffle m (Br), = talassa f (Port).
Belgium ['beldʒəm] n Bélgica f.
Belgrade [,bel'greɪd] n Belgrado s.
belief [bɪ'liːf] n (faith) crença f; (opinion) opinião f.
believe [bɪ'liːv] vt (person, story) acreditar em; (think) achar ♦ vi: **to ~ in** (God, human rights) crer em; **to ~ in doing sthg** acreditar em fazer algo.
believer [bɪ'liːvər] n crente mf.
bell [bel] n (of phone, door) campainha f; (of church) sino m.
bellboy ['belbɔɪ] n bói m (Br), paquete m (em hotel, clube) (Port).
belligerent [bɪ'lɪdʒərənt] adj (aggressive) belicoso(-osa), beligerante.
bellow ['beləu] vi (person) gritar; (bull, cow) mugir.
bellows ['beləuz] n fole m.

belly ['belɪ] n (inf) barriga f.
bellyache ['belɪeɪk] n dor f de barriga.
belly button n (inf) umbigo m.
belong [bɪ'lɒŋ] vi (be in right place) pertencer; **to ~ to** pertencer a.
belongings [bɪ'lɒŋɪŋz] npl pertences mpl.
beloved [bɪ'lʌvd] adj adorado(-da).
below [bɪ'ləu] adv em baixo; (downstairs) de baixo ♦ prep abaixo de; **children ~ the age of ten** crianças com menos de dez anos.
belt [belt] n (for clothes) cinto m; (TECH) correia f.
beltway ['beltweɪ] n (Am) circunvalação f.
bemused [bɪ'mjuːzd] adj confuso (-sa), perplexo(-xa).
bench [bentʃ] n banco m.
bend [bend] (pt & pp bent) n curva f ♦ vt dobrar ♦ vi (road, river, pipe) fazer uma curva.
❑ **bend down** vi dobrar-se.
❑ **bend over** vi inclinar-se.
beneath [bɪ'niːθ] adv debaixo ♦ prep (under) debaixo de, sob.
benefactor ['benɪfæktər] n benfeitor m (-ra f).
beneficial [,benɪ'fɪʃl] adj benéfico (-ca).
benefit ['benɪfɪt] n (advantage) benefício m; (money) subsídio m ♦ vt beneficiar ♦ vi: **to ~ (from)** beneficiar-se (de); **for the ~ of** em benefício de.
Benelux ['benɪlʌks] n Benelux m.
benevolent [bɪ'nevələnt] adj benevolente.
benign [bɪ'naɪn] adj (MED) benigno (-gna).
bent [bent] pt & pp → bend.
bequeath [bɪ'kwiːð] vt (money, property) legar, deixar em testamento.
bereaved [bɪ'riːvd] adj (family) enlutado(-da).
beret ['bereɪ] n gorro m.
berk [bɜːk] n (Brit: inf) idiota mf, anta f.
Berlin [bɜː'lɪn] n Berlim s.
Bermuda shorts [bə'mjuːdə-] npl bermudas fpl.
Bern [bɜːn] n Berna s.
berry ['berɪ] n baga f.
berserk [bə'zɜːk] adj: **to go ~** ficar fora de si.
berth [bɜːθ] n (for ship) ancoradouro

m; *(in ship)* beliche m; *(in train)* couchette f.

beside [bɪˈsaɪd] *prep (next to)* junto a; **to be ~ the point** não ter nada a ver.

besides [bɪˈsaɪdz] *adv* além disso ◆ *prep* além de.

besiege [bɪˈsiːdʒ] *vt (town, fortress)* cercar.

besotted [bɪˈsɒtɪd] *adj* completamente apaixonado(-da); **to be ~ with sb** estar apaixonado por alguém.

best [best] *adj* melhor ◆ *n*: **the ~** o/a melhor; **a pint of ~** *(beer)* = uma caneca de cerveja escura; **to make the ~ of sthg** aproveitar o mais possível algo; **to do one's ~** fazer o melhor possível; **the ~ thing to do is** ... o melhor é ...; **"~ before ..."** "consumir de preferência antes de ..."; **at ~** quanto muito; **all the ~!** felicidades!; *(in letter)* um abraço!; **I like this one ~** gosto mais deste; **she played ~** ela jogou melhor.

best man *n* padrinho m *(de casamento).*

best-seller [-ˈselər] *n (book)* best-seller m.

bet [bet] *(pt & pp* **bet)** *n* aposta f ◆ *vt (gamble)* apostar ◆ *vi*: **to ~ (on)** apostar (em); **I ~ (that) you can't do it** aposto que você não consegue.

betray [bɪˈtreɪ] *vt* trair.

betrayal [bɪˈtreɪəl] *n* traição f.

better [ˈbetər] *adj & adv* melhor; **you had ~ ...** é melhor ...; **to get ~** melhorar.

better off *adj (financially)* melhor de vida; *(in a better situation)* melhor.

betting [ˈbetɪŋ] *n* apostas fpl.

betting shop *n (Brit)* casa f de apostas.

between [bɪˈtwiːn] *prep* entre; **in ~** *prep* entre ◆ *adv (space)* no meio; **"closed ~ 1 and 2"** "fechado entre a uma e as duas"; **what happened in ~?** o que aconteceu nesse entremeio?

beverage [ˈbevərɪdʒ] *n (fml)* bebida f.

beware [bɪˈweər] *vi*: **to ~ of** ter cuidado com; **"~ of the dog"** "cuidado com o cachorro".

bewildered [bɪˈwɪldəd] *adj* perplexo(-xa).

beyond [bɪˈjɒnd] *prep (on far side of)* do outro lado de; *(further than)* para além de ◆ *adv* mais além; **~ reach** fora do alcance; **to be ~ doubt** ser sem

sombra de dúvida.

bias [ˈbaɪəs] *n (prejudice)* preconceito m; *(tendency)* tendência f.

biased [ˈbaɪəst] *adj* parcial.

bib [bɪb] *n (for baby)* babador m *(Br)*, bibe m *(Port).*

bible [ˈbaɪbl] *n* bíblia f.

bicarbonate of soda [baɪˈkuːbənət-] *n* bicarbonato m de soda.

biceps [ˈbaɪseps] *n* bíceps m *inv.*

bicker [ˈbɪkər] *vi* discutir.

bicycle [ˈbaɪsɪkl] *n* bicicleta f.

bicycle path *n* pista f para ciclistas.

bicycle pump *n* bomba f *(de bicicleta).*

bid [bɪd] *(pt & pp* **bid)** *n (at auction)* lanço m; *(attempt)* tentativa f ◆ *vt (money)* oferecer ◆ *vi*: **to ~ (for)** licitar (para).

bidet [ˈbiːdeɪ] *n* bidê m.

bifocals [ˌbaɪˈfəʊklz] *npl* óculos mpl bifocais.

big [bɪg] *adj* grande; **my ~ brother** o meu irmão mais velho; **how ~ is it?** de que tamanho é?

Big Dipper [-ˈdɪpər] *n (Brit: rollercoaster)* montanha f russa; *(Am: constellation)*: **the ~** a Ursa Maior.

bigheaded [ˌbɪgˈhedɪd] *adj (inf)* convencido(-da).

bigot [ˈbɪgət] *n* preconceituoso m *(-osa f).*

big toe *n* dedão m *(do pé).*

big top *n (tent)* tenda f de circo.

big wheel *n (Brit: at fairground)* roda f gigante.

bike [baɪk] *n (inf) (bicycle)* bicicleta f; *(motorcycle)* moto f.

biking [ˈbaɪkɪŋ] *n*: **to go ~** andar de bicicleta.

bikini [bɪˈkiːnɪ] *n* biquíni m.

bikini bottom *n* calça f de biquíni *(Br)*, cuecas fpl de bikini *(Port).*

bikini top *n* sutiã m de biquíni *(Br)*, soutien m de bikini *(Port).*

bilingual [baɪˈlɪŋgwəl] *adj* bilíngüe.

bill [bɪl] *n (for meal, electricity, hotel)* conta f; *(Am: bank note)* nota f; *(at cinema, theatre)* programa m; *(POL)* projeto m de lei; **can I have the ~ please?** a conta, por favor.

billboard [ˈbɪlbɔːd] *n* quadro m de anúncios *(Br)*, placar m *(publicitário) (Port).*

billfold [ˈbɪlfəʊld] *n (Am)* carteira f *(de bolso).*

billiards [ˈbɪljədz] n bilhar m.

billion [ˈbɪljən] n (thousand million) bilhão m (Br), mil milhões (Port); (Brit: million million) trilhão m (Br), bilhão (Port).

Bill of Rights n: the ~ os dez primeiros direitos e liberdades do cidadão americano que constam da constituição dos Estados Unidos.

bimbo [ˈbɪmbəʊ] (pl -s OR -es) n (inf: pej) pessoa jovem e bonita mas pouco inteligente.

bin [bɪn] n caixote m do lixo; (for bread, flour) caixa f; (on plane) compartimento m para a bagagem.

bind [baɪnd] (pt & pp bound) vt (tie up) atar.

binder [ˈbaɪndər] n (cover) capa f de argolas, dossier m.

binding [ˈbaɪndɪŋ] n (of book) encadernação f; (for ski) peças fpl de fixação (dos esquis).

bingo [ˈbɪŋgəʊ] n bingo m.

binoculars [bɪˈnɒkjʊləz] npl binóculo m.

biodegradable [ˌbaɪəʊdɪˈgreɪdəbl] adj biodegradável.

biography [baɪˈɒgrəfɪ] n biografia f.

biological [ˌbaɪəˈlɒdʒɪkl] adj biológico (-ca).

biology [baɪˈɒlədʒɪ] n biologia f.

birch [bɜːtʃ] n videoiro m.

bird [bɜːd] n (small) pássaro m; (large) ave f; (Brit: inf: woman) garota (Br), gaja f (Port).

birdie [ˈbɜːdɪ] n (bird) passarinho m; (in golf) birdie m.

bird-watching [-ˌwɒtʃɪŋ] n: I like ~ eu gosto de observar pássaros.

Biro® [ˈbaɪərəʊ] n esferográfica f.

birth [bɜːθ] n nascimento m; **by ~ de** nascimento; **to give ~ to** dar à luz.

birth certificate n certidão f de nascimento.

birth control n contracepção f.

birthday [ˈbɜːθdeɪ] n aniversário m; **happy ~!** feliz aniversário!

birthday card n cartão m de aniversário.

birthday party n festa f de aniversário OR de anos.

birthmark [ˈbɜːθmɑːk] n sinal m (de nascença).

birthplace [ˈbɜːθpleɪs] n local m de nascimento.

biscuit [ˈbɪskɪt] n (Brit) biscoito m

(Br), bolacha f (Port); (Am: scone) bolo ou pão de massa não levedada que se come com geléia ou algo salgado.

bisect [baɪˈsekt] vt (in geometry) bissectar; (subj: road, corridor) dividir em dois.

bishop [ˈbɪʃəp] n bispo m.

bison [ˈbaɪsn] n bisonte m.

bistro [ˈbiːstrəʊ] (pl -s) n bar-restaurante m.

bit [bɪt] pt → **bite** ♦ n (piece) pedaço m, bocado m; (of drill) broca f; (of bridle) freio m; **a ~** um pouco; **a ~ of money** um pouco de dinheiro; **to do a ~ of walking** andar um pouco; **not a ~** nem um pouco; **~ by ~** pouco a pouco.

bitch [bɪtʃ] n cadela f.

bitchy [ˈbɪtʃɪ] adj (inf) maldoso(-osa), venenoso(-osa).

bite [baɪt] (pt bit, pp bitten) n (when eating) dentada f; (from insect) picada f; (from snake) mordedura f ♦ vt morder; (subj: insect) picar; **to have a ~ to eat** mordiscar algo.

biting [ˈbaɪtɪŋ] adj (very cold) penetrante; (caustic) mordaz.

bitter [ˈbɪtər] adj amargo(-ga); (cold, wind) glacial; (argument, conflict) violento(-ta) ♦ n (Brit: beer) tipo de cerveja amarga.

bitter lemon n limonada f (amarga).

bitterness [ˈbɪtənɪs] n (of taste, food) amargor m; (of weather, wind) rigor m; (of person) rancor m, amargura f; (of argument, conflict) violência f.

bizarre [bɪˈzɑːr] adj estranho(-nha).

black [blæk] adj preto(-ta); (coffee, tea) sem leite, preto(-ta); (humour) negro (-gra) ♦ n (colour) preto m, negro m; (person) negro m (-gra f).
❑ **black out** vi desmaiar, perder os sentidos.

black and white adj a preto e branco.

blackberry [ˈblækbrɪ] n amora f silvestre.

blackbird [ˈblækbɜːd] n melro m.

blackboard [ˈblækbɔːd] n quadro m (negro).

black cherry n cereja f preta.

blackcurrant [ˌblækˈkʌrənt] n groselha f preta.

blacken [ˈblækn] vt (make dark) enfuscar ♦ vi (sky) escurecer.

black eye *n* olho *m* roxo.
Black Forest gâteau *n* bolo de chocolate em camadas com creme e cerejas em compota de cerejas.
blackhead ['blækhed] *n* cravo *m* (Br), ponto *m* negro (Port).
black ice *n* gelo *m* (transparente no solo).
blackmail ['blækmeɪl] *n* chantagem *f* ♦ *vt* chantagear.
blackout ['blækaut] *n* (power cut) corte *m* de energia.
black pepper *n* pimenta *f* preta.
black pudding *n* (Brit) = chouriço *m* (Br), morcela *f* (Port).
Black Sea *n*: the ~ o Mar Negro.
black sheep *n* (fig) ovelha *f* negra.
blacksmith ['blæksmɪθ] *n* ferreiro *m*.
bladder ['blædə'] *n* bexiga *f*.
blade [bleɪd] *n* (of knife, saw) lâmina *f*; (of propeller, oar) pá *f*; (of grass) pedaço *m*.
blame [bleɪm] *n* culpa *f* ♦ *vt* culpar; **to ~ sb for sthg** culpar alguém de algo; **to ~ sthg on sb** pôr a culpa de algo em alguém.
bland [blænd] *adj* (food) insosso(-a).
blank [blæŋk] *adj* (space, page, cassette) em branco; (expression) confuso(-sa) ♦ *n* (empty space) espaço *m* em branco.
blank cheque *n* cheque *m* em branco.
blanket ['blæŋkɪt] *n* cobertor *m*.
blasphemy ['blæsfəmɪ] *n* blasfêmia *f*.
blast [blɑːst] *n* (explosion) explosão *f*; (of air, wind) rajada *f* ♦ *excl* (inf) raios!; **at full ~** no máximo.
blasted ['blɑːstɪd] *adj* (inf: for emphasis) maldito(-ta).
blatant ['bleɪtənt] *adj* (discrimination, lie) puro(-ra); (disobedience) ostensivo(-va).
blaze [bleɪz] *n* (fire) incêndio *m* ♦ *vi* (fire) arder; (sun, light) brilhar intensamente.
blazer ['bleɪzə'] *n* blazer *m*.
bleach [bliːtʃ] *n* água *f* sanitária (Br), lixívia *f* (Port) ♦ *vt* (clothes) branquear; (hair) descolorar.
bleached [bliːtʃt] *adj* (hair) oxigenado(-da); (jeans) debotado(-da).
bleachers ['bliːtʃərz] *npl* (Am: SPORT) arquibancada *f* descoberta.
bleak [bliːk] *adj* (weather) escuro(-ra); (day, city) sombrio(-bria).

bleary-eyed [,blɪərɪ'aɪd] *adj* com os olhos inchados.
bleat [bliːt] *n* (of sheep, goat) balido *m* ♦ *vi* (sheep, goat) balir; (fig: complain) lamuriar-se.
bleed [bliːd] (pt & pp **bled** [bled]) *vi* sangrar.
blemish ['blemɪʃ] *n* (flaw) defeito *m*, falha *f*; (pimple, scar) marca *f*; (fig: on name, reputation) mancha *f*.
blend [blend] *n* (of coffee, whisky) mistura *f* ♦ *vt* misturar.
blender ['blendə'] *n* liquidificador *m*.
bless [bles] *vt* abençoar; **~ you!** (said after sneeze) saúde!
blessing ['blesɪŋ] *n* bênção *f*.
blew [bluː] *pt* → blow.
blimey ['blaɪmɪ] *excl* (Brit: inf) nossa!
blind [blaɪnd] *adj* cego(-ga) ♦ *n* (for window) persiana *f* ♦ *npl*: **the ~** os cegos.
blind alley *n* beco *m* sem saída.
blind corner *n* curva *f* sem visibilidade.
blindfold ['blaɪndfəʊld] *n* venda *f* ♦ *vt* vendar os olhos de.
blind spot *n* (AUT) ponto *m* cego.
blink [blɪŋk] *vi* piscar os olhos.
blinkers ['blɪŋkəz] *npl* (Brit) antolhos *mpl*.
bliss [blɪs] *n* felicidade *f* absoluta.
blister ['blɪstə'] *n* bolha *f* (d'água).
blizzard ['blɪzəd] *n* tempestade *f* de neve.
bloated ['bləʊtɪd] *adj* inchado(-da).
blob [blɒb] *n* gota *f*.
block [blɒk] *n* bloco *m*; (Am: in town, city) quarteirão *m* ♦ *vt* obstruir; **to have a ~ed (up) nose** estar com o nariz entupido.
❑ **block up** *vt sep* entupir.
blockage ['blɒkɪdʒ] *n* obstrução *f*.
blockbuster ['blɒkbʌstə'] *n* (inf: book) best-seller *m*; (film) sucesso *m* de bilheteira.
block capitals *npl* letra *f* maiúscula OR de imprensa.
block letters *npl* letra *f* maiúscula OR de imprensa.
block of flats *n* bloco *m* de apartamentos, prédio *m*.
bloke [bləʊk] *n* (Brit: inf) cara *m* (Br), tipo *m* (Port).
blond [blɒnd] *adj* louro(-ra) ♦ *n* louro *m*.

blonde [blɒnd] *adj* louro(-ra) ◆ *n* loura *f*.

blood [blʌd] *n* sangue *m*.

blood donor *n* doador *m* (-ra *f*) de sangue.

blood group *n* grupo *m* sangüíneo.

bloodhound ['blʌdhaʊnd] *n* sabujo *m*, cão *m* de caça.

blood poisoning *n* septicemia *f*.

blood pressure *n* pressão *f* arterial *(Br)*, tensão *f* arterial *(Port)*; **to have high/low ~** ter a pressão (arterial) alta/baixa.

bloodshed ['blʌdʃed] *n* derramamento *m* de sangue, carnificina *f*.

bloodshot ['blʌdʃɒt] *adj* injetado (-da) de sangue.

blood test *n* exame *m* de sangue.

bloodthirsty ['blʌd,θɜːstɪ] *adj* sedento(-ta) de sangue.

blood transfusion *n* transfusão *f* de sangue.

bloody ['blʌdɪ] *adj* (hands, handkerchief) ensangüentado(-da); *(Brit: vulg: damn)* maldito(-ta) ◆ *adv (Brit: vulg)*: **you ~ idiot!** seu idiota!

bloody mary [-'meərɪ] *n* vodka com suco de tomate e especiarias.

bloom [bluːm] *n* flor *f* ◆ *vi* florir; **in ~** em flor.

blossom ['blɒsəm] *n* flor *f*.

blot [blɒt] *n* borrão *m*.

blotch [blɒtʃ] *n* mancha *f*.

blotting paper ['blɒtɪŋ-] *n* papel *m* mata-borrão.

blouse [blaʊz] *n* blusa *f*.

blow [bləʊ] *(pt blew, pp blown) vt (subj: wind)* fazer voar; *(whistle, trumpet)* soprar em; *(bubbles)* fazer ◆ *vi* soprar; *(fuse)* queimar, rebentar ◆ *n (hit)* golpe *m*; **to ~ one's nose** assoar-se, assoar o nariz.

❏ **blow up** *vt sep (cause to explode)* explodir; *(inflate)* encher ◆ *vi (explode)* explodir; *(storm)* cair.

blow-dry *n* brushing *m* ◆ *vt* secar *(com secador)*.

blowlamp ['bləʊlæmp] *n (Brit)* maçarico *m*.

blown [bləʊn] *pp* → **blow**.

blowout ['bləʊaʊt] *n (of tyre)*: **they had a ~ on the motorway** o pneu furou quando estavam na auto-estrada.

blowtorch ['bləʊtɔːtʃ] = **blow lamp**.

BLT *n* sanduíche de bacon grelhado, alface e tomate.

blubber ['blʌbəʳ] *n (of whale)* gordura *f* de baleia ◆ *vi (pej: weep)* choramingar.

blue [bluː] *adj* azul; *(film)* pornográfico(-ca) ◆ *n* azul *m*.

❏ **blues** *n (MUS)* blues *m inv*.

bluebell ['bluːbel] *n* campainha-azul *f*, bom-dia *m*.

blueberry ['bluːbərɪ] *n* arando *m*, uva-do-monte *f*.

bluebottle ['bluː,bɒtl] *n* mosca *f* varejeira.

blue cheese *n* queijo *m* azul.

blue jeans *npl (Am)* jeans *m inv (Br)*, calças *fpl* de ganga *(Port)*.

blueprint ['bluːprɪnt] *n (plan, programme)* plano *m*, projecto *m*.

bluff [blʌf] *n (cliff)* penhasco *m* ◆ *vi* blefar *(Br)*, fazer bluff *(Port)*.

blunder ['blʌndəʳ] *n* asneira *f*.

blunt [blʌnt] *adj (knife)* cego(-ga); *(pencil)* por afiar; *(fig: person)* franco(-ca).

blurb [blɜːb] *n (inf)* texto publicitário que aparece normalmente na contracapa de um livro.

blurred [blɜːd] *adj* desfocado(-da).

blurt [blɜːt] : **blurt out** *vt sep* deixar escapar.

blush [blʌʃ] *vi* corar.

blusher ['blʌʃəʳ] *n* blush *m*.

blustery ['blʌstərɪ] *adj* tempestuoso (-osa).

BMX *(abbr of bicycle motorcross)* BMX *f*.

BO *abbr* = **body odour**.

boar [bɔːʳ] *n (male pig)* porco *m*; *(wild pig)* javali *m*.

board [bɔːd] *n (plank)* tábua *f*; *(for surfing, diving)* prancha *f*; *(notice board)* quadro *m*; *(for games)* tabuleiro *m*; *(blackboard)* quadro *m* (negro); *(of company)* direção *f*; *(hardboard)* madeira *f* compensada *(Br)*, contra-placado *m (Port)* ◆ *vt (plane, ship)* embarcar em; **~ and lodging** dormida e refeições; **full ~** pensão completa; **half ~** meia pensão; **on ~** *adv* a bordo ◆ *prep (plane, ship)* a bordo de; *(bus)* em.

boarder ['bɔːdəʳ] *n (lodger)* pensionista *mf*; *(at school)* aluno *m* interno (aluna *f* interna).

board game *n* jogo *m* de tabuleiro.

boarding ['bɔːdɪŋ] *n* embarque *m*.

boarding card *n* cartão *m* de embarque.

boardinghouse [ˈbɔːdɪŋhaʊs, *pl* -haʊzɪz] *n* pensão *f*.

boarding school *n* colégio *m* interno.

board of directors *n* direção *f*.

boast [bəʊst] *vi*: **to ~ (about sthg)** gabar-se (de algo).

boastful [ˈbəʊstfʊl] *adj* convencido (-da).

boat [bəʊt] *n* barco *m*; **by ~** de barco.

boater [ˈbəʊtəʳ] *n* (*hat*) chapéu *m* de palha.

boat train *n* (*Brit*) trem *m* (*Br*), comboio *m* (*Port*) (*de ligação com um barco, ferryboat*).

bob [bɒb] *n* (*hairstyle*) corte *m* direito.

bobbin [ˈbɒbɪn] *n* bobina *f*, carreto *m*.

bobby [ˈbɒbɪ] *n* (*Brit: inf: policeman*) guarda *m*, policial *m* (*Br*), polícia *m* (*Port*).

bobby pin *n* (*Am*) grampo *m* de cabelo (*em forma de U*).

bobsleigh [ˈbɒbsleɪ] *n* trenó *m*, bobsleigh *m*.

body [ˈbɒdɪ] *n* corpo *m*; (*of car*) carroçeria *f*; (*organization*) organismo *m*; (*of wine*) maturação *f*.

body building *n* musculação *f*, culturismo *m* (*Port*).

bodyguard [ˈbɒdɪgɑːd] *n* guarda-costas *mf*.

body odour *n* odor *m* corporal.

bodywork [ˈbɒdɪwɜːk] *n* carroçeria *f*.

bog [bɒg] *n* zona *f* pantanosa.

bogged down [ˌbɒgd-] *adj*: **~ in sthg** (*in mud, snow*) enterrado(-da) em algo; **don't get ~ in too many details** não entre em demasiados detalhes.

bogus [ˈbəʊgəs] *adj* falso(-sa).

boil [bɔɪl] *vt* (*water*) ferver; (*kettle*) pôr para ferver; (*food*) cozer ◆ *vi* ferver ◆ *n* (*on skin*) furúnculo *m*.

boiled egg [bɔɪld-] *n* ovo *m* cozido.

boiled potatoes [bɔɪld-] *npl* batatas *fpl* cozidas.

boiler [ˈbɔɪləʳ] *n* esquentador *m* (*da água*).

boiler suit *n* (*Brit*) macacão *m* (*Br*), fato-macaco *m* (*Port*).

boiling (hot) [ˈbɔɪlɪŋ-] *adj* (*inf*) (*person*) morto(-morta) de calor; (*weather*) abrazador(-ra); (*water*) fervendo.

boiling point [ˈbɔɪlɪŋ-] *n* ponto *m* de ebulição; **to reach ~** ferver.

boisterous [ˈbɔɪstərəs] *adj* (*child,*

behaviour) irrequieto(-ta).

bold [bəʊld] *adj* (*brave*) audaz.

bollard [ˈbɒlɑːd] *n* (*Brit: on road*) poste *m*.

bolt [bəʊlt] *n* (*on door, window*) ferrolho *m*; (*screw*) parafuso *m* (*com porca*) ◆ *vt* (*door, window*) fechar com ferrolho.

bomb [bɒm] *n* bomba *f* ◆ *vt* bombardear.

bombard [bɒmˈbɑːd] *vt* bombardear.

bomb disposal squad *n* equipe *f* (*de desmontamento*) de explosivos.

bomber [ˈbɒməʳ] *n* (*plane*) bombardeiro *m*.

bombing [ˈbɒmɪŋ] *n* bombardeio *m*.

bomb scare *n* ameaça *f* de bomba.

bomb shelter *n* abrigo *m* (*antiaéreo*).

bond [bɒnd] *n* (*tie, connection*) laço *m*.

bone [bəʊn] *n* (*of person, animal*) osso *m*; (*of fish*) espinha *f*.

boned [bəʊnd] *adj* (*chicken*) desossado(-da); (*fish*) sem espinhas.

bone-dry *adj* completamente seco (-ca).

bone-idle *adj* preguiçoso(-osa), malandro(-dra).

boneless [ˈbəʊnləs] *adj* (*chicken, pork*) desossado(-da).

bonfire [ˈbɒnˌfaɪəʳ] *n* fogueira *f*.

Bonfire Night *n* (*Brit*) 5 de novembro, *celebrado com fogueiras e fogo de artifício*.

Bonn [bɒn] *n* Bonn.

bonnet [ˈbɒnɪt] *n* (*Brit: of car*) capota *f*.

bonny [ˈbɒnɪ] *adj* (*Scot*) bonito(-ta).

bonus [ˈbəʊnəs] (*pl* **-es**) *n* bônus *m inv*.

bony [ˈbəʊnɪ] *adj* (*chicken*) cheio (cheia) de ossos; (*fish*) cheio (cheia) de espinhas.

boo [buː] *vi* vaiar.

booby trap [ˈbuːbɪ-] *n* (*bomb*) (*bomba*) armadilha *f*; (*prank*) peça *f* (*Br*), partida *f* (*Port*).

boogie [ˈbuːgɪ] *vi* (*inf*) sacudir o esqueleto.

book [bʊk] *n* livro *m*; (*for writing in*) caderno *m*; (*of stamps, matches*) carteira *f*; (*of tickets*) caderneta *f* ◆ *vt* (*reserve*) reservar.

❑ **book in** *vi* (*at hotel*) preencher o registro.

bookable [ˈbʊkəbl] *adj* (*seats, flight*) reservável.

bookcase [ˈbʊkkeɪs] *n* estante *f* (para livros).

booking [ˈbʊkɪŋ] *n (reservation)* reserva *f*.

booking office *n* bilheteira *f*.

bookkeeping [ˈbʊkˌkiːpɪŋ] *n* contabilidade *f*.

booklet [ˈbʊklɪt] *n* folheto *m*.

bookmaker's [ˈbʊkˌmeɪkəz] *n* casa *f* de apostas.

bookmark [ˈbʊkmɑːk] *n* marcador *m* de livros.

bookshelf [ˈbʊkʃelf] (*pl* -shelves [-ʃelvz]) *n (shelf)* prateleira *f* (para livros); *(bookcase)* estante *f* (para livros).

bookshop [ˈbʊkʃɒp] *n* livraria *f*.

bookstall [ˈbʊkstɔːl] *n* quiosque *m* de venda de livros.

bookstore [ˈbʊkstɔːr] = **bookshop**.

book token *n* espécie de vale para comprar livros.

boom [buːm] *n (sudden growth)* boom *m* ♦ *vi (voice, guns)* ribombar.

boost [buːst] *vt* aumentar; *(spirits, morale)* levantar.

booster [ˈbuːstər] *n (injection)* reforço *m* de vacina.

boot [buːt] *n (shoe)* bota *f*; *(Brit: of car)* porta-malas *m (Br)*, porta-bagagem *m (Port)*.

booth [buːð] *n (for telephone)* cabine *f*; *(at fairground)* barraca *f*.

booty [ˈbuːtɪ] *n* saque *m*, despojos *mpl*.

booze [buːz] *n (inf)* álcool *m* ♦ *vi (inf)* beber, encher a cara.

bop [bɒp] *n (inf: dance)*: **to have a ~** sacudir o esqueleto.

border [ˈbɔːdər] *n (of country)* fronteira *f*; *(edge)* borda *f*; **the Borders** região de Escócia que faz fronteira com a Inglaterra.

borderline [ˈbɔːdəlaɪn] *n (fig: uncertain division)* fronteira *f* ♦ *adj*: **a ~ case** um caso duvidoso, uma situação indecisa.

bore [bɔːr] *pt* → **bear** ♦ *n (inf)* seca *f* ♦ *vt (person)* entediar, aborrecer; *(hole)* fazer.

bored [bɔːd] *adj* entediado(-da).

boredom [ˈbɔːdəm] *n* tédio *m*.

boring [ˈbɔːrɪŋ] *adj* maçante *(Br)*, aborrecido(-da) *(Port)*.

born [bɔːn] *adj*: **to be ~** nascer.

borne [bɔːn] *pp* → **bear**.

borough [ˈbʌrə] *n* município *m*.

borrow [ˈbɒrəʊ] *vt*: **to ~ sthg (from sb)** pedir algo emprestado (a alguém).

Bosnia [ˈbɒznɪə] *n* Bósnia *f*.

Bosnia-Herzegovina [-ˌheətsəgəˈviːnə] *n* Bósnia-Herzegovina *f*.

Bosnian [ˈbɒznɪən] *adj* bósnio(-nia) ♦ *n* bósnio *m* (-nia *f*).

bosom [ˈbʊzəm] *n* peito *m*.

boss [bɒs] *n* chefe *mf*.

❑ **boss around** *vt sep* dar ordens a.

bossy [ˈbɒsɪ] *adj* mandão(-dona).

botanical garden [bəˈtænɪkl-] *n* jardim *m* botânico.

botch [bɒtʃ] : **botch up** *vt sep (inf: plan)* dar cabo de; **they really ~ed it up** fizeram um belo serviço!

both [bəʊθ] *adj* ambos(-bas) ♦ *pron* ambos *mpl* (-bas *fpl*) ♦ *adv*: **he speaks ~ French and German** ele fala francês e alemão; **~ of them** ambos(-bas), os dois (as duas); **~ of us** nós dois (nós duas).

bother [ˈbɒðər] *vt (worry)* preocupar; *(annoy, pester)* incomodar ♦ *vi* preocupar-se ♦ *n (trouble)* incômodo *m*, amolação *f*; **I can't be ~ed** não posso me dar ao trabalho; **it's no ~!** não incomoda nada.

bottle [ˈbɒtl] *n* garrafa *f*; *(for baby)* mamadeira *f (Br)*, biberão *m (Port)*; *(of shampoo, medicine)* frasco *m*.

bottle bank *n* ponto *m* de descarte de vidros para reciclagem *(Br)*, vidrão *m (Port)*.

bottled [ˈbɒtld] *adj* engarrafado(-da); **~ beer** cerveja *f* de garrafa; **~ water** água *f* mineral (engarrafada).

bottleneck [ˈbɒtlnek] *n (in traffic)* engarrafamento *m*.

bottle opener [-ˌəʊpnər] *n* abridor *m* de garrafas, saca-rolhas *m inv*.

bottom [ˈbɒtəm] *adj (lowest)* de baixo; *(last, worst)* último(-ma) ♦ *n* fundo *m*; *(of hill)* base *f*; *(buttocks)* traseiro *m* ♦ *adv*: **I came ~ in the exam** tirei a nota mais baixa do exame.

bough [baʊ] *n* ramo *m*.

bought [bɔːt] *pt & pp* → **buy**.

boulder [ˈbəʊldər] *n* pedregulho *m*.

bounce [baʊns] *vi (rebound)* pinchar; *(jump)* saltar; **his cheque ~d** ele passou um cheque sem fundos!

bouncer [ˈbaʊnsər] *n (inf)* segurança *m*, gorila *m*.

bouncy castle *n* castelo de ar para as crianças pularem em cima dele.

bound [baʊnd] *pt & pp* → **bind** ♦ *vi* correr aos pulos ♦ *adj*: **he's ~ to get it wrong** o mais certo é ele enganar-se; **it's ~ to rain** vai chover na certa; **it's out of ~s** é zona proibida; **to be ~ for** *(plane, train)* (ir) com destino a.

boundary ['baʊndrɪ] *n* fronteira *f*.

bouquet [buˈkeɪ] *n (of flowers)* ramo *m*; *(of wine)* aroma *m*, bouquet *m*.

bourbon ['bɜːbən] *n* bourbon *m*.

bout [baʊt] *n (of illness)* ataque *m*; *(of activity)* período *m*.

boutique [buːˈtiːk] *n* boutique *f*.

bow[1] [baʊ] *n (of head)* reverência *f*; *(of ship)* proa *f* ♦ *vi (bend head)* inclinar a cabeça.

bow[2] [bəʊ] *n (knot)* laço *m*; *(weapon, MUS)* arco *m*.

bowels ['baʊəlz] *npl (ANAT)* intestinos *mpl*.

bowl [bəʊl] *n* taça *f*, tigela *f*; *(for washing up)* bacia *f*; *(of toilet)* vaso *m (Br)*, sanita *f (Port)*.

❏ **bowls** *npl* jogo de gramado que consiste em arremessar bolas grandes o mais perto possível de uma bola pequena.

bow-legged [ˌbəʊˈlegɪd] *adj* com as pernas tortas.

bowler ['bəʊlər] *n (in cricket)* lançador *m (-ra f)*; **~ (hat)** chapéu-coco *m*.

bowling ['bəʊlɪŋ] *n*: **to go ~** ir jogar boliche *(Br)*, ir jogar bowling *(Port)*.

bowling alley *n* lugar onde se joga bowling.

bowling green *n* gramado *m (Br)*, relvado *m (Port) (para jogar "bowls")*.

bow tie [ˌbəʊ-] *n* laço *m*.

box [bɒks] *n* caixa *f*; *(on form)* quadrado *m*; *(in theatre)* camarote *m* ♦ *vi* jogar boxe; **a ~ of chocolates** uma caixa de bombons.

boxer ['bɒksər] *n* pugilista *m*, lutador *m* de boxe.

boxer shorts *npl* boxers *mpl*.

boxing ['bɒksɪŋ] *n* boxe *m*.

Boxing Day *n* o dia 26 de dezembro.

boxing gloves *npl* luvas *fpl* de boxe.

boxing ring *n* ringue *m* de boxe.

box office *n* bilheteira *f*.

boxroom ['bɒksrʊm] *n (Brit)* quarto *m* pequeno.

boy [bɔɪ] *n* rapaz *m* ♦ *excl (inf)*: **(oh) ~!** que bom!

boycott ['bɔɪkɒt] *vt* boicotar.

boyfriend ['bɔɪfrend] *n* namorado *m*.

boyish ['bɔɪɪʃ] *adj (man)* juvenil.

boy scout *n* escoteiro *m*.

BR *abbr* = **British Rail**.

bra [brɑː] *n* sutiã *m (Br)*, soutien *m (Port)*.

brace [breɪs] *n (for teeth)* aparelho *m* (para os dentes).

❏ **braces** *npl (Brit)* suspensórios *mpl*.

bracelet ['breɪslɪt] *n* pulseira *f*.

bracken ['brækn] *n* samambaia *f (Br)*, feto *m (Port)*.

bracket ['brækɪt] *n (written symbol)* parêntese *m*; *(support)* suporte *m*.

brag [bræg] *vi* gabar-se; **to ~ about sthg** gabar-se de algo.

braid [breɪd] *n (hairstyle)* trança *f*; *(on clothes)* galão *m*.

brain [breɪn] *n* cérebro *m*.

brainchild ['breɪntʃaɪld] *n* invenção *f*, idéia *f*.

brainwash ['breɪnwɒʃ] *vt* fazer uma lavagem cerebral em.

brainwave ['breɪnweɪv] *n* idéia *f* genial OR brilhante.

brainy ['breɪnɪ] *adj (inf)* esperto(-ta), **she's really ~** ela é um crânio.

braised [breɪzd] *adj* estufado(-da).

brake [breɪk] *n* freio *m (Br)*, travão *m (Port)* ♦ *vi* frear *(Br)*, travar *(Port)*.

brake block *n* calço *m* do freio.

brake fluid *n* líquido *m* para os freios.

brake light *n* luz *f* de freio.

brake pad *n* patilha *f* OR calço *m* do travão.

brake pedal *n* pedal *m* do freio.

bramble ['bræmbl] *n (bush)* silva *f*.

bran [bræn] *n* farelo *m*.

branch [brɑːntʃ] *n (of tree, subject)* ramo *m*; *(of bank)* agência *f*; *(of company)* sucursal *f*, filial *f*.

❏ **branch off** *vi* ramificar-se.

branch line *n* ramal *m*.

brand [brænd] *n* marca *f* ♦ *vt*: **to ~ sb (as)** rotular alguém (de).

brandish ['brændɪʃ] *vt (weapon)* brandir, empunhar; *(letter etc)* agitar.

brand-new *adj* novo (nova) em folha.

brandy ['brændɪ] *n* conhaque *m*.

brash [bræʃ] *adj (pej)* insolente.

brass [brɑːs] *n* latão *m*.

brass band *n* banda *f* de música.

brasserie ['bræsərɪ] *n* = snack-bar *m*.

brassiere [*Brit* 'bræsɪər, *Am* brəˈzɪr] *n* sutiã *m (Br)*, soutien *m (Port)*.

brat [bræt] *n (inf)* criança *f* mimada.

bravado [brə'vɑːdəʊ] *n* bravata *f*.

brave [breɪv] *adj* valente.

bravery ['breɪvərɪ] *n* valentia *f*.

bravo [,brɑː'vəʊ] *excl* bravo!

brawl [brɔːl] *n* rixa *f*.

brawn [brɔːn] *n (muscle)* músculos *mpl*, força *f* física; *(Brit: meat)* carne de porco, normalmente da cabeça, enlatada semelhante a paté.

bray [breɪ] *vi (donkey)* zurrar.

brazen ['breɪzn] *adj* descarado(-da).

brazier ['breɪzjər] *n* braseira *f*.

Brazil [brə'zɪl] *n* Brasil *m*.

Brazilian [brə'zɪljən] *adj* brasileiro (-ra) ♦ *n* brasileiro *m* (-ra *f*).

brazil nut *n* castanha-do-pará *f*.

breach [briːtʃ] *vt (contract)* quebrar; *(confidence)* abusar de.

bread [bred] *n* pão *m*; ~ **and butter** pão com manteiga.

bread bin *n (Brit)* caixa *f* para pão.

breadboard ['bredbɔːd] *n* tábua *f* para cortar pão.

bread box *(Am)* = **bread bin**.

breadcrumbs ['bredkrʌmz] *npl* farinha *f* de rosca *(Br)*, pão *m* ralado *(Port)*.

breaded ['bredɪd] *adj* panado(-da), à milanesa.

bread knife *n* faca *f* do pão.

bread roll *n* pãozinho *m (Br)*, carcaça *f (Port)*.

breadth [bretθ] *n* largura *f*.

break [breɪk] *(pt* **broke**, *pp* **broken**) *n (interruption)* interrupção *f*; *(in line)* corte *m*; *(rest, pause)* pausa *f*; *(SCH: playtime)* recreio *m* ♦ *vt (damage)* partir, quebrar; *(disobey)* ir contra; *(fail to fulfil)* quebrar; *(a record)* bater; *(news)* dar; *(journey)* interromper ♦ *vi (become damaged)* partir, quebrar; *(dawn)* romper; *(voice)* mudar; **without a** ~ sem parar; **a lucky** ~ um golpe de sorte; **to** ~ **one's leg** quebrar a pernã.

❏ **break down** *vi (car, machine)* enguiçar ♦ *vt sep (door, barrier)* derrubar.

❏ **break in** *vi* entrar à força.

❏ **break off** *vt (detach)* partir; *(holiday)* interromper ♦ *vi (stop suddenly)* parar.

❏ **break out** *vi (fire)* começar; *(war)* estourar; *(panic)* instaurar-se; **to** ~ **out in a rash** ganhar alergia.

❏ **break up** *vi (with spouse, partner)* separar-se; *(meeting, marriage)* terminar; *(school, pupils)* terminar as aulas.

breakage ['breɪkɪdʒ] *n* danos *mpl*.

breakdown ['breɪkdaʊn] *n (of car)* enguiço *m*, avaria *f*; *(in communications, negotiation)* ruptura *f*; *(mental)* esgotamento *m*.

breakdown truck *n* reboque *m (Br)*, pronto-socorro *m (Port)*.

breakfast ['brekfəst] *n* café *m* da manhã *(Br)*, pequeno-almoço *m (Port)*; **to have** ~ tomar o café da manhã; **to have sthg for** ~ comer algo no café da manhã.

breakfast cereal *n* cereal *m* (para o café da manhã).

breakfast television *n (Brit)* programação *f* matinal *(na televisão)*.

break-in *n* assalto *m*.

breakneck ['breɪknek] *adj*: **at** ~ **speed** a toda a velocidade, a uma velocidade vertiginosa.

breakthrough ['breɪkθruː] *n* avanço *m*.

breakup ['breɪkʌp] *n (of relationship)* dissolução *f*.

breakwater ['breɪk,wɔːtər] *n* quebramar *m*.

breast [brest] *n* peito *m*.

breastbone ['brestbəʊn] *n* esterno *m*.

breast-feed *vt* amamentar.

breaststroke ['breststrəʊk] *n* nado *m* de peito *(Br)*, bruços *mpl (Port)*.

breath [breθ] *n* hálito *m*; **out of** ~ sem fôlego; **to go for a** ~ **of fresh air** sair para respirar ar fresco; **to take a deep** ~ respirar fundo.

Breathalyser® ['breθəlaɪzər] *n (Brit)*: **I was given a** ~ **test** tive que soprar no bafômetro *m (Br)* OR balão *m (Port)*.

Breathalyzer® ['breθəlaɪzər] *(Am)* = **Breathalyser®**.

breathe [briːð] *vi* respirar.

❏ **breathe in** *vi* inspirar.

❏ **breathe out** *vi* expirar.

breather ['briːðər] *n (inf)* pausa *f* (para tomar fôlego).

breathing ['briːðɪŋ] *n* respiração *f*.

breathless ['breθlɪs] *adj* sem fôlego.

breathtaking ['breθ,teɪkɪŋ] *adj* incrível.

breed [briːd] *(pt & pp* **bred** [bred]) *n (of animal)* raça *f*; *(of plant)* espécie *f* ♦ *vt* criar ♦ *vi* reproduzir-se.

breeze [briːz] *n* brisa *f*.

breezy ['briːzɪ] *adj (weather, day)* ventoso(-osa).

brevity ['brevɪtɪ] *n* brevidade *f*.

brew [bruː] *vt (beer)* fabricar; *(tea, cof-*

fee) preparar ♦ *vi (tea, coffee)* repousar; **has the tea/coffee ~ed yet?** já está pronto o chá/café?

brewer ['bruːəʳ] *n* fabricante *m* de cerveja.

brewery ['bruəri] *n* fábrica *f* de cerveja.

bribe [braib] *n* suborno *m* ♦ *vt* subornar.

bribery ['braibəri] *n* suborno *m*.

bric-a-brac ['brikəbræk] *n* bricabraque *m*.

brick [brik] *n* tijolo *m*.

bricklayer ['brik,leiəʳ] *n* pedreiro *m*.

brickwork ['brikwɜːk] *n* alvenaria *f (de tijolo)*.

bridal ['braidl] *adj (dress)* de noiva; *(suite)* nupcial.

bride [braid] *n* noiva *f*.

bridegroom ['braidgrum] *n* noivo *m*.

bridesmaid ['braidzmeid] *n* dama de honra *(room); (food)* dama *f* de honor *(Port)*.

bridge [bridʒ] *n* ponte *f; (card game)* bridge *m*.

bridle ['braidl] *n* cabeçada *f*.

bridle path *n* pista *f* para cavaleiros.

brief [briːf] *adj* breve ♦ *vt* informar; **in ~** em resumo.

❑ **briefs** *npl (for men)* cueca *f (Br)*, cuecas *fpl (Port); (for women)* calcinha *f (Br)*, cuecas *fpl (Port)*.

briefcase ['briːfkeis] *n* pasta *f (para papéis, livros)*.

briefing ['briːfiŋ] *n* briefing *m*, instruções *fpl*.

briefly ['briːfli] *adv (for a short time)* por alguns momentos; *(in few words)* em poucas palavras.

brigade [brɪ'geid] *n* brigada *f*.

brigadier [,brigə'diəʳ] *n* brigadeiro *m*.

bright [brait] *adj (light, sun, idea)* brilhante; *(room)* claro(-ra); *(colour)* vivo (-va); *(clever)* esperto(-ta); *(lively, cheerful)* alegre; *(smile)* radiante.

brighten ['braitn] *vi (become lighter)* clarear, desanuviar; *(become more cheerful)* alegrar-se.

❑ **brighten up** *vt sep* alegrar ♦ *vi (become more cheerful)* alegrar-se; *(weather)* melhorar.

brilliance ['briljəns] *n (of idea, person)* gênio *m; (of colour, light, sunshine)* brilho *m; (inf: of performance, goal)* brilhantismo *m*.

brilliant ['briljənt] *adj (light, sunshine)* brilhante; *(colour)* vivo(-va); *(idea, person)* genial; *(inf: wonderful)* fantástico (-ca).

Brillo pad® ['brɪləʊ-] *n* ≃ esponja *f* Bombril® *(Br)*, esfregão *m*. Bravo® *(Port)*.

brim [brim] *n (of hat)* aba *f*; **it's full to the ~** está cheio até à borda.

brine [brain] *n* salmoura *f*.

bring [briŋ] *(pt & pp* **brought)** *vt* trazer.

❑ **bring along** *vt sep* trazer.

❑ **bring back** *vt sep (return)* devolver; *(shopping, gift)* trazer.

❑ **bring in** *vt sep (introduce)* introduzir; *(earn)* ganhar.

❑ **bring out** *vt sep (put on sale)* pôr a venda.

❑ **bring up** *vt sep (child)* criar; *(subject)* mencionar; *(food)* vomitar.

brink [briŋk] *n:* **on the ~ of** à beira de.

brisk [brisk] *adj (quick)* rápido(-da); *(efficient)* desembaraçado(-da); *(wind)* forte.

bristle ['brisl] *n (of brush)* cerda *f; (on chin)* pêlo *m*.

Britain ['britn] *n* Grã-Bretanha *f*.

British ['britiʃ] *adj* britânico(-ca) ♦ *npl:* **the ~** os britânicos.

British Isles *npl:* **the ~** as Ilhas Británicas.

British Rail *n* companhia ferroviária británica agora privatizada.

British Telecom [-'telikɒm] *n* companhia británica de telecomunicações.

Briton ['britn] *n* britânico *m (-ca f)*.

brittle ['britl] *adj* quebradiço(-ça).

broach [brəʊtʃ] *vt (subject)* abordar.

broad [brɔːd] *adj (wide)* largo(-ga); *(wide-ranging)* amplo(-pla); *(description, outline)* geral; *(accent)* forte.

B road *n (Brit)* estrada *f* secundária.

broad bean *n* fava *f*.

broadcast ['brɔːdkaːst] *(pt & pp* **broadcast)** *n* transmissão *f* ♦ *vt* transmitir.

broaden ['brɔːdn] *vt* alargar ♦ *vi (river, road)* alargar.

broadly ['brɔːdli] *adv* em geral; **~ speaking** em termos gerais.

broadminded [,brɔːd'maindid] *adj* aberto(-ta).

broccoli ['brɒkəli] *n* brócolis *mpl (Br)*, brócolos *mpl (Port)*.

brochure ['brəʊʃəʳ] *n* folheto *m*.

broiled [brɔɪld] adj (Am) grelhado(-da).
broke [brəʊk] pt → **break** ◆ adj (inf) teso(-sa).
broken ['brəʊkn] pp → **break** ◆ adj (window, leg, glass) partido(-da); (machine) com defeito (Br), avariado (-da) (Port); (English, Portuguese) incorreto(-ta).
brolly ['brɒlɪ] n (Brit: inf) guarda-chuva m.
bronchitis [brɒŋ'kaɪtɪs] n bronquite f.
bronze [brɒnz] n bronze m.
brooch [brəʊtʃ] n broche m.
brood [bruːd] n (of animals) ninhada f ◆ vi: to ~ (over OR about sthg) cismar (com algo).
brook [brʊk] n riacho m.
broom [bruːm] n vassoura f.
broomstick ['bruːmstɪk] n cabo m de vassoura.
broth [brɒθ] n sopa consistente de verduras, com carne ou peixe.
brothel ['brɒθl] n bordel m.
brother ['brʌðər] n irmão m.
brother-in-law n cunhado m.
brought [brɔːt] pt & pp → **bring**.
brow [braʊ] n (forehead) testa f; (eyebrow) sobrancelha f.
brown [braʊn] adj marrom (Br), castanho(-nha) (Port); (skin) moreno(-na); (tanned) bronzeado(-da) ◆ n marrom m (Br), castanho m (Port).
brown bread n pão m integral.
brownie ['braʊnɪ] n (CULIN) biscoito de chocolate e nozes.
Brownie ['braʊnɪ] n fadinha f (entre os sete e os dez anos).
brown paper n papel m pardo OR de embrulho.
brown rice n arroz m integral.
brown sauce n (Brit) molho picante escuro servido especialmente com batatas fritas.
brown sugar n açúcar m mascavo.
browse [braʊz] vi (in shop) dar uma olhada; to ~ through (book, paper) passar os olhos em.
browser ['braʊzər] n: "~s welcome" "entrada livre".
bruise [bruːz] n nódoa f negra, equimose f.
brunch [brʌntʃ] n café da manhã reforçado que se toma muito tarde e que serve de almoço.
brunette [bruː'net] n morena f.
brunt [brʌnt] n: to bear OR take the

~ of sthg agüentar o pior/a maior parte de algo.
brush [brʌʃ] n (for hair, teeth) escova f; (for painting) pincel m ◆ vt (floor) varrer; (clothes) escovar; (move with hand) sacudir; to ~ one's hair escovar o cabelo; to ~ one's teeth escovar os dentes.
brusque [bruːsk] adj brusco(-ca).
Brussels ['brʌslz] n Bruxelas s.
brussels sprouts npl couves-de-Bruxelas fpl.
brutal ['bruːtl] adj brutal.
brute [bruːt] n (bully) bruto m (-ta f).
BSc abbr = Bachelor of Science.
BSE n (abbr of bovine spongiform encephalopathy) BSE f, encefalopatia f espongiforme bovina.
BT abbr = British Telecom.
bubble ['bʌbl] n bolha f; (of soap) bola f de sabão; (in fizzy drink) borbulha f.
bubble bath n espuma f de banho.
bubble gum n chiclete m (Br), pastilha f elástica (Port).
bubbly ['bʌblɪ] n (inf) espumante m.
Bucharest [,buːkə'rest] n Bucareste s.
buck [bʌk] n (Am: inf: dollar) dólar m; (male animal) macho m.
bucket ['bʌkɪt] n balde m.
Buckingham Palace ['bʌkɪŋəm-] n Palácio m de Buckingham.
buckle ['bʌkl] n fivela f ◆ vt (fasten) apertar (com fivela) ◆ vi (warp) contrair-se.
buck's fizz [,bʌks'fɪz] n bebida preparada com champanhe e suco de laranja.
bud [bʌd] n (flower) botão m; (leaf) rebento m ◆ vi (flower) florescer; (leaf) brotar.
Budapest [,bjuːdə'pest] n Budapeste s.
Buddhism ['bʊdɪzm] n budismo m.
Buddhist ['bʊdɪst] n budista mf.
budding ['bʌdɪŋ] adj (aspiring) potencial.
buddy ['bʌdɪ] n (inf) amigo m (-ga f).
budge [bʌdʒ] vi mexer-se.
budgerigar ['bʌdʒərɪgaːr] n periquito m.
budget ['bʌdʒɪt] adj (holiday, travel) econômico(-ca) ◆ n orçamento m; the Budget (Brit) o orçamento do Estado. ❑ budget for vt fus: to ~ for sthg prever as despesas de algo.
budgie ['bʌdʒɪ] n (inf) periquito m.

buff [bʌf] n (inf) fanático m (-ca f).

buffalo ['bʌfələʊ] (pl -s OR -es) n búfalo m.

buffalo wings npl (Am) asas de frango fritas servidas com um molho picante.

buffer ['bʌfər] n (on train) párachoque m.

buffet [Brit 'bʊfeɪ, Am bəˈfeɪ] n bufê m (Br), bufete m (Port).

buffet car n vagão-restaurante m (Br), carruagem-restaurante f (Port).

bug [bʌg] n (insect) bicho m; (inf: mild illness) vírus m inv ◆ vt (inf: annoy) chatear.

buggy ['bʌgɪ] n carrinho m de bebê.

bugle ['bjuːgl] n corneta f.

build [bɪld] (pt & pp built) n constituição f física ◆ vt construir.

❏ **build up** vt sep (strength, speed) ganhar ◆ vi acumular-se.

builder ['bɪldər] n constructor m (-ra f) (civil).

building ['bɪldɪŋ] n edifício m.

building site n canteiro m de obras.

building society n (Brit) sociedade financeira de crédito imobiliário.

buildup ['bɪldʌp] n (increase) aumento m (gradual).

built [bɪlt] pt & pp → **build**.

built-in adj incorporado(-da).

built-up area n zona f urbanizada.

bulb [bʌlb] n (for lamp) lâmpada f eléctrica; (of plant) bulbo m.

Bulgaria [bʌlˈgeərɪə] n Bulgária f.

Bulgarian [bʌlˈgeərɪən] adj búlgaro (-ra) ◆ n (person) búlgaro m (-ra f); (language) búlgaro m.

bulge [bʌldʒ] vi fazer volume.

bulk [bʌlk] n: the ~ of a maior parte de; in ~ a granel, em grandes quantidades.

bulky ['bʌlkɪ] adj volumoso(-osa).

bull [bʊl] n touro m.

bulldog ['bʊldɒg] n buldogue m.

bulldozer ['bʊldəʊzər] n bulldôzer m.

bullet ['bʊlɪt] n bala f.

bulletin ['bʊlətɪn] n boletim m.

bullet-proof adj à prova de bala.

bullfight ['bʊlfaɪt] n corrida f de touros, tourada f.

bullfighter ['bʊlfaɪtər] n toureiro m (-ra f).

bullfighting ['bʊlfaɪtɪŋ] n tourada f, corridas fpl de touros.

bullion ['bʊljən] n lingotes mpl.

bullock ['bʊlək] n boi m, novilho m castrado.

bullring ['bʊlrɪŋ] n praça f de touros.

bull's-eye n centro m (do alvo).

bully ['bʊlɪ] n brigão m (-gona f) ◆ vt abusar de, intimidar.

bum [bʌm] n (inf: bottom) traseiro m; (Am: inf: tramp) vagabundo m (-da f).

bum bag n (Brit) carteira f (de cintura).

bumblebee ['bʌmblbiː] n abelhão m.

bump [bʌmp] n (on surface) elevação f; (on leg) inchaço m; (on head) galo m; (sound, minor accident) pancada f ◆ vt (head, leg) bater com.

❏ **bump into** vt fus (hit) chocar com; (meet) encontrar-se com.

bumper ['bʌmpər] n (on car) párachoques m inv; (Am: on train) párachoque m.

bumpy ['bʌmpɪ] adj acidentado(-da); the flight was ~ durante o voo sentiuse um pouco de turbulência.

bun [bʌn] n (cake) pão m doce (pequeno); (bread roll) pãozinho m (Br), carcaça f (Port); (hairstyle) coque m.

bunch [bʌntʃ] n (of people) grupo m; (of flowers) ramo m; (of grapes, bananas) cacho m; (of keys) molho m.

bundle ['bʌndl] n (of clothes) trouxa f; (of notes, papers) maço m.

bung [bʌŋ] n tampo m.

bungalow ['bʌŋgələʊ] n bangalô m.

bungle ['bʌŋgl] vt arruinar, estragar.

bunion ['bʌnjən] n joanete m.

bunk [bʌŋk] n (bed) beliche m.

bunk bed n beliche m.

bunker ['bʌŋkər] n (shelter) abrigo m; (for coal) paiol m de carvão; (in golf) bunker m.

bunny ['bʌnɪ] n coelhinho m.

bunting ['bʌntɪŋ] n (flags) galhardetes mpl.

buoy [Brit bɔɪ, Am 'buːɪ] n bóia f (de sinalização).

buoyant ['bɔɪənt] adj (that floats) flutuante.

BUPA ['buːpə] n companhia seguradora britânica de seguros médicos privados.

burden ['bɜːdn] n carga f.

bureau ['bjʊərəʊ] (pl -s OR -x) n (office, branch) escritório m, centro m; (Brit: desk) escrivaninha f; (Am: chest of drawers) cômoda f.

bureaucracy [bjʊəˈrɒkrəsɪ] n burocracia f.

bureau de change [ˌbjʊərəʊdə-ˈʃɒndʒ] n agência f de câmbio.
bureaux [ˌbjʊərəʊz] pl → bureau.
burger [ˈbɜːgəʳ] n (hamburger) hambúrguer m; (made with nuts, vegetables etc) hambúrguer (vegetariano).
burglar [ˈbɜːgləʳ] n assaltante mf.
burglar alarm n alarme m (anti-roubo).
burglarize [ˈbɜːgləraɪz] (Am) = burgle.
burglary [ˈbɜːglərɪ] n assalto m.
burgle [ˈbɜːgl] vt assaltar.
burial [ˈberɪəl] n enterro m.
burly [ˈbɜːlɪ] adj troncudo(-da), bem constituído(-da).
Burma [ˈbɜːmə] n Burma s.
burn [bɜːn] (pt & pp burnt OR burned) n queimadura f ◆ vt queimar ◆ vi (be on fire) arder.
❏ **burn down** vt sep incendiar ◆ vi arder.
burner [ˈbɜːnəʳ] n (on gas cooker) bico m, boca f; (on electric cooker) placa f.
burning (hot) [ˈbɜːnɪŋ-] adj muito quente, escaldante.
Burns' Night [bɜːnz-] n 25 de janeiro, aniversário do nascimento do poeta escocês Robert Burns.
burnt [bɜːnt] pt & pp → burn.
burp [bɜːp] vi (inf) arrotar.
burrow [ˈbʌrəʊ] n toca f.
bursar [ˈbɜːsəʳ] n tesoureiro m (-ra f).
bursary [ˈbɜːsərɪ] n (Brit: scholarship, grant) bolsa f (de estudos).
burst [bɜːst] (pt & pp burst) n (of gunfire, applause) salva f ◆ vt & vi rebentar; **he ~ into the room** ele irrompeu pelo quarto adentro; **to ~ into tears** desatar a chorar; **to ~ open** (door) abrir-se de repente.
bursting [ˈbɜːstɪŋ] adj (full) cheio(-a); **~ with sthg** (excitement, pride) vibrando com algo; **to be ~ to do sthg** (eager) estar doido(-da) para fazer algo.
bury [ˈberɪ] vt enterrar.
bus [bʌs] n ônibus m (Br), autocarro m (Port); **by ~** de ônibus.
bus conductor [-kənˈdʌktəʳ] n cobrador m (-ra f) (de ônibus).
bus driver n motorista mf (de ônibus).
bush [bʊʃ] n arbusto m.
bushy [ˈbʊʃɪ] adj (eyebrows, beard) cerrado(-da); (tail) peludo(-da).

business [ˈbɪznɪs] n (commerce, trade) negócios mpl; (shop, firm) negócio m; (things to do, affair) assunto m; **let's get down to ~** passemos ao que interessa; **mind your own ~!** meta-se na sua vida!; **"~ as usual"** "aberto como de costume".
business card n cartão-de-visita m.
business class n classe f executiva.
business hours npl (of shops) horário m de funcionamento; (of offices) horário de atendimento.
businesslike [ˈbɪznɪslaɪk] adj profissional.
businessman [ˈbɪznɪsmæn] (pl -men [-men]) n homem m de negócios.
business studies npl = práticas fpl administrativas.
business trip n viagem f de negócios.
businesswoman [ˈbɪznɪsˌwʊmən] (pl -women [-wɪmɪn]) n mulher f de negócios.
busker [ˈbʌskəʳ] n (Brit) músico m (-ca f) de rua.
bus lane n faixa f para ônibus.
bus pass n passe m de ônibus.
bus shelter n abrigo m (de parada de ônibus).
bus station n (estação) rodoviária f.
bus stop n parada f de ônibus (Br), paragem f de autocarro (Port).
bust [bʌst] n (of woman) busto m ◆ adj: **to go ~** (inf) falir.
bustle [ˈbʌsl] n alvoroço m, animação f.
bus tour n excursão f (de ônibus ou camionete).
busy [ˈbɪzɪ] adj ocupado(-da); (street, office) movimentado(-da); **to be ~ doing sthg** estar ocupado fazendo algo.
busybody [ˈbɪzɪˌbɒdɪ] n (pej) mexeriqueiro m (-ra f), abelhudo m (-da f).
busy signal n (Am) sinal m de ocupado.
but [bʌt] conj mas ◆ prep menos; **you've been nothing ~ trouble** você só tem me dado trabalho; **the last ~ one** o penúltimo (a penúltima); **~ for** se não fosse.
butcher [ˈbʊtʃəʳ] n carniceiro m (-ra f); **~'s (shop)** açougue m (Br), talho m (Port).
butler [ˈbʌtləʳ] n mordomo m.
butt [bʌt] n (of rifle) coronha f; (of

cigarette, cigar) ponta *f.*
butter [ˈbʌtəʳ] *n* manteiga *f* ◆ *vt* untar com manteiga.
butter bean *n* feijão *m* branco.
buttercup [ˈbʌtəkʌp] *n* botão-de-ouro *m*, ranúnculo *m*.
butter dish *n* manteigueira *f.*
butterfly [ˈbʌtəflaɪ] *n* borboleta *f*; *(swimming stroke)* nado *m* borboleta *(Br)*, mariposa *f (Port)*.
butterscotch [ˈbʌtəskɒtʃ] *n* espécie de caramelo duro feito com manteiga.
buttocks [ˈbʌtəks] *npl* nádegas *fpl.*
button [ˈbʌtn] *n* botão *m*; *(Am: badge)* crachá *m.*
buttonhole [ˈbʌtnhəʊl] *n (hole)* casa *f* (de botão).
button mushroom *n* cogumelo *m* pequeno.
buttress [ˈbʌtrɪs] *n* contraforte *m.*
buy [baɪ] *(pt & pp* **bought)** *vt* comprar ◆ *n*: **a good ~** uma boa compra; **to ~ sthg for sb, to ~ sb sthg** comprar algo para OR de alguém.
buyer [ˈbaɪəʳ] *n (purchaser)* comprador *m* (-ra *f*).
buzz [bʌz] *vi* zumbir ◆ *n (inf: phone call)*: **to give sb a ~** dar uma ligada para alguém.
buzzer [ˈbʌzəʳ] *n* campainha *f.*
buzzword [ˈbʌzwɜːd] *n (inf)* modismo *m.*
by [baɪ] *prep* **1.** *(expressing cause, agent)* por; **he's worried ~ her absence** está preocupado com a sua ausência; **he was hit ~ a car** ele foi atropelado por um carro; **a book ~ Irvine Welsh** um livro de Irvine Welsh; **funded ~ the government** financiado pelo governo.

2. *(expressing method, means)*: **~ car/bus/plane** de carro/ônibus/avião; **~ phone/post** pelo telefone/correio; **to pay ~ credit card/cheque** pagar com cartão de crédito/cheque; **to win ~ cheating** ganhar trapaceando.
3. *(near to, beside)* junto a; **~ the sea** à beira-mar, junto ao mar.
4. *(past)* por; **a car went ~ the house** um carro passou pela casa.
5. *(via)* por; **exit ~ the door on the left** sair pela porta do lado esquerdo.
6. *(with time)*: **be there ~ nine** esteja lá às nove horas; **~ day** de dia; **it should be ready ~ now** já deve estar pronto.
7. *(expressing quantity)* a; **sold ~ the dozen** vende-se à dúzia; **prices fell ~ 20%** os preços baixaram 20%; **we charge ~ the hour** cobramos por hora.
8. *(expressing meaning)* com; **what do you mean ~ that?** que quer dizer com isso?
9. *(in division, multiplication)* por; **two metres ~ five** dois metros por cinco.
10. *(according to)* segundo; **~ law** segundo a lei; **it's fine ~ me** por mim tudo bem.
11. *(expressing gradual process)* a; **one ~ one** um a um; **day ~ day** dia a dia.
12. *(in phrases)*: **~ mistake** por engano; **~ oneself** sozinho; **~ profession** por profissão.
◆ *adv (past)*: **to go/drive ~** passar.
bye(-bye) [baɪ(baɪ)] *excl (inf)* tchau!
bypass [ˈbaɪpɑːs] *n (road)* contorno *m (Br)*, circunvalação *f (Port).*
by-product *n (product)* subproduto *m*, derivado *m*; *(fig: consequence)* consequência *f.*
bystander [ˈbaɪˌstændəʳ] *n* espectador *m* (-ra *f*).

C

C (abbr of Celsius, centigrade) C.

cab [kæb] n (taxi) táxi m; (of lorry) cabine f.

cabaret ['kæbəreɪ] n cabaré m.

cabbage ['kæbɪdʒ] n couve f.

cabin ['kæbɪn] n (on ship) camarote m; (of plane) cabine f; (wooden house) cabana f.

cabin crew n pessoal m de bordo, tripulação f.

cabinet ['kæbɪnɪt] n (cupboard) armário m; (POL) conselho m de ministros.

cable ['keɪbl] n cabo m.

cable car n teleférico m.

cable television n televisão f a cabo.

cackle ['kækl] vi cacarejar.

cactus ['kæktəs] (pl **-tuses** OR **-ti** [-taɪ]) n cacto m.

cadet [kə'det] n (in police) cadete m.

cadge [kædʒ] vt (Brit: inf): **to ~ sthg (off** OR **from sb)** filar algo (de alguém) (Br), cravar algo (a alguém) (Port).

caesarean (section) [sɪ'zeərɪən-] n (Brit) cesariana f.

Caesar salad [ˌsiːzə-] n salada de alface com anchovas, queijo parmesão e cubos de pão torrado ou frito.

cafe ['kæfeɪ] n café m.

cafeteria [ˌkæfɪ'tɪərɪə] n cantina f.

cafetière [kæf'tjeər] n cafeteira f (de êmbolo).

caffeine ['kæfiːn] n cafeína f.

cage [keɪdʒ] n gaiola f.

cagey ['keɪdʒɪ] adj (inf) reservado (-da).

cagoule [kə'guːl] n (Brit) casaco m impermeável (fino e com capuz).

cajole [kə'dʒəʊl] vt: **to ~ sb into doing sthg** induzir alguém a fazer algo.

Cajun ['keɪdʒən] adj relativo à comunidade Cajun, de origem francesa, residente na Luisiana.

cake [keɪk] n bolo m; (of soap) barra f.

caked [keɪkt] adj: **~ with mud** coberto(-ta) de lama seca.

calcium ['kælsɪəm] n cálcio m.

calculate ['kælkjʊleɪt] vt calcular.

calculating ['kælkjʊleɪtɪŋ] adj calculista.

calculation [ˌkælkjʊ'leɪʃn] n cálculo m.

calculator ['kælkjʊleɪtər] n calculadora f.

calendar ['kælɪndər] n calendário m.

calf [kɑːf] (pl **calves**) n (of cow) bezerro m (-a f), vitelo m (-la f); (part of leg) barriga f da perna.

caliber ['kælɪbər] (Am) = **calibre**.

calibre ['kælɪbər] n calibre m.

California [ˌkælɪ'fɔːnjə] n Califórnia f.

calipers ['kælɪpərz] (Am) = **callipers**.

call [kɔːl] n (visit) visita f; (phone call, at airport) chamada f; (of bird) grito m ♦ vt chamar; (say loudly) chamar por; (telephone) ligar para; (meeting, election, strike) convocar; (flight) anunciar ♦ vi (telephone) telefonar, ligar; (visit): **he ~ed to see you** ele passou aqui para lhe ver; **could I have a ~ at eight o'clock, please?** por favor, pode chamar-me às oito?; **on ~** (nurse, doctor) de plantão; **to pay sb a ~** visitar alguém; **to be ~ed** chamar-se; **what is he ~ed?** como é que ele se chama?; **this train ~s at ...** este trem pára em ...; **who's ~ing?** é da parte de quem?

❏ **call back** vt sep voltar a telefonar a ♦ vi (phone again) voltar a telefonar; (visit again) **I'll ~ back later** passo aqui mais tarde.

❏ **call for** vt fus (come to fetch) ir buscar; (demand, require) exigir.

❏ **call on** vt fus (visit) ir visitar; **to ~ on sb to do sthg** pedir a alguém para fazer algo.

❏ **call out** vt sep (name, winner) anun-

ciar; *(doctor, fire brigade)* chamar ♦ *vi*
gritar.

❏ **call up** *vt sep* (MIL) chamar, mobilizar; *(telephone)* telefonar para, ligar
para.

call box *n* cabine *f* telefônica.

caller ['kɔːləʳ] *n (visitor)* visita *f; (on
phone)* pessoa *f* que chama.

call-in *n (Am: on radio, TV) programa
em que o público participa por telefone.*

calling ['kɔːlɪŋ] *n (profession, trade)*
profissão *f; (vocation, urge)* vocação
f.

calling card *n (Am)* cartão-de-visita
m.

callipers ['kælɪpəz] *npl (Brit)* (MATH)
compasso *m;* (MED) aparelho *m* ortopédico *(para as pernas).*

callous ['kæləs] *adj (unkind)* insensível.

callus ['kæləs] *n* calo *m.*

calm [kɑːm] *adj* calmo(-ma) ♦ *vt* acalmar.

❏ **calm down** *vt sep* acalmar ♦ *vi*
acalmar-se.

Calor gas® ['kælə-] *n* gás *m* butano.

calorie ['kælərɪ] *n* caloria *f.*

calves [kɑːvz] *pl* → **calf.**

Cambodia [kæm'bəʊdjə] *n* Camboja
m.

camcorder ['kæm,kɔːdəʳ] *n* máquina *f*
de filmar (vídeos).

came [keɪm] *pt* → **come.**

camel ['kæml] *n* camelo *m.*

camembert ['kæməmbeəʳ] *n* camembert *m.*

cameo ['kæmɪəʊ] *(pl -s) n (piece of
jewellery)* camafeu *m; (in acting)* curta
aparição *f (de um ator famoso); (in writing)* boa descrição *f.*

camera ['kæmərə] *n (for photographs)*
máquina *f* OR câmara *f* fotográfica; *(for
filming)* máquina OR câmara *f* de filmar.

cameraman ['kæmərəmæn] *(pl -men*
[-men]) *n* operador *m* de câmara, cameraman *m.*

camera shop *n* loja *f* de artigos
fotográficos.

Cameroon [,kæmə'ruːn] *n* Camarões
mpl.

camisole ['kæmɪsəʊl] *n* camisola *f*
interior.

camouflage ['kæməflɑːʒ] *n* camuflagem *f* ♦ *vt* camuflar.

camp [kæmp] *n (for holidaymakers)*
colônia *f* de férias; *(for soldiers)* acam

pamento *m; (for prisoners)* campo ♦ *vi*
acampar.

campaign [kæm'peɪn] *n* campanha *f*
♦ *vi:* **to ~ (for/against)** fazer campanha (a favor de/contra).

camp bed *n* cama *f* de campanha.

camper ['kæmpəʳ] *n (person)* campista
mf; (van) trailer *m (Br)*, caravana *f*, roulotte *f (motorizada) (Port).*

campground ['kæmpgraʊnd] *n (Am)*
camping *m*, acampamento *m (Br).*

camping ['kæmpɪŋ] *n:* **to go ~** acampar.

camping stove *n* fogareiro *m* (de
campismo).

campsite ['kæmpsaɪt] *n* camping *m.*

campus ['kæmpəs] *(pl -es) n* cidade *f*
universitária.

can[1] [kæn] *n* lata *f.*

can[2] *[weak form* kən, *strong form* kæn]
(pt & conditional **could**) *aux vb* **1.** *(be
able to)* poder; **~ you help me?** podia
ajudar-me?; **I ~ see the mountains**
posso ver as montanhas.
2. *(know how to)* saber; **~ you drive?**
você sabe conduzir?; **I ~ speak
Portuguese** eu sei falar português.
3. *(be allowed to)* poder; **you can't
smoke here** você não pode fumar
aqui.
4. *(in polite requests)* poder; **~ you tell
me the time?** podia me dizer as
horas?; **~ I speak to the manager?**
posso falar com o gerente?
5. *(expressing occasional occurrence)*
poder; **it ~ get cold at night** às vezes à
noite a temperatura baixa bastante.
6. *(expressing possibility)* poder; **they
could be lost** eles podem estar perdidos.

Canada ['kænədə] *n* Canadá *m.*

Canadian [kə'neɪdɪən] *adj & n* canadense *mf (Br)*, canadiano *m* (-na *f)
(Port).*

canal [kə'næl] *n* canal *m.*

canapé ['kænəpeɪ] *n* canapé *m.*

canary [kə'neərɪ] *n* canário *m.*

cancel ['kænsl] *vt* cancelar.

cancellation [,kænsə'leɪʃn] *n* cancelamento *m.*

cancer ['kænsəʳ] *n* câncer *m (Br)*, cancro *m (Port).*

Cancer ['kænsəʳ] *n* Câncer *m (Br)*,
Caranguejo *m (Port).*

candelabra [,kændɪ'lɑːbrə] *n* candelabro *m.*

candid ['kændɪd] *adj* cândido(-da).

candidate ['kændɪdət] *n* candidato *m* (-ta *f*).

candle ['kændl] *n* vela *f*.

candlelight ['kændllaɪt] *n* luz *f* de vela.

candlelit dinner ['kændllɪt-] *n* jantar *m* à luz de vela.

candlestick ['kændlstɪk] *n* castiçal *m*.

candor ['kændər] *(Am)* = candour.

candour ['kændər] *n (Brit)* candura *f*, candor *m*.

candy ['kændɪ] *n (Am) (confectionery)* guloseimas *fpl; (sweet)* bala *f (Br)*, rebuçado *m (Port)*.

candyfloss ['kændɪflɒs] *n (Brit)* algodão *m* doce.

cane [keɪn] *n (for walking)* bengala *f; (for punishment)* palha *f; (for furniture, baskets)* verga *f*.

canine ['keɪnaɪn] *adj* canino(-na) ♦ *n:* ~ **(tooth)** (dente) canino *m*.

canister ['kænɪstər] *n (for tea)* caixa *f* (para o chá); *(for gas)* lata *f*.

cannabis ['kænəbɪs] *n* maconha *f (Br)*, haxixe *m (Port)*.

canned [kænd] *adj (food, drink)* enlatado(-da).

cannibal ['kænɪbl] *n* canibal *mf*.

cannon ['kænən] *n* canhão *m*.

cannonball ['kænənbɔːl] *n* bala *f* de canhão.

cannot ['kænɒt] = can not.

canny ['kænɪ] *adj (shrewd)* astuto(-ta).

canoe [kə'nuː] *n* canoa *f*.

canoeing [kə'nuːɪŋ] *n* canoagem *f*.

can opener *n* abridor *m* de latas *(Br)*, abre-latas *m inv (Port)*.

canopy ['kænəpɪ] *n (over bed etc)* dossel *m*.

can't [kɑːnt] = cannot.

cantaloup(e) ['kæntəluːp] *n* meloa *f*.

cantankerous [kæn'tæŋkərəs] *adj* intratável.

canteen [kæn'tiːn] *n* cantina *f*.

canter ['kæntər] *n* meio galope *m* ♦ *vi* ir a meio galope.

canvas ['kænvəs] *n (for tent, bag)* lona *f*.

canvass ['kænvəs] *vt (voters)* pedir o voto de; *(investigate)* sondar.

canyon ['kænjən] *n* desfiladeiro *m*.

cap [kæp] *n (hat)* boné *m; (of pen, bottle)* tampa *f; (contraceptive)* diafragma *m*.

capability [keɪpə'bɪlətɪ] *n* capacidade *f*.

capable ['keɪpəbl] *adj* capaz; **to be ~ of doing sthg** ser capaz de fazer algo.

capacity [kə'pæsɪtɪ] *n* capacidade *f*.

cape [keɪp] *n (of land)* cabo *m; (cloak)* capa *f*.

capers ['keɪpəz] *npl* alcaparras *fpl*.

Cape Verde [-'vɜːd] *n:* **the ~ Islands** as Ilhas de Cabo Verde.

capital ['kæpɪtl] *n (of country)* capital *f; (money)* capital *m; (letter)* maiúscula *f*.

capitalism ['kæpɪtəlɪzm] *n* capitalismo *m*.

capitalist ['kæpɪtəlɪst] *adj* capitalista ♦ *n* capitalista *mf*.

capital punishment *n* pena *f* de morte.

Capitol Hill ['kæpɪtl-] *n* o Capitólio, sede do Congresso americano, em Washington.

capitulate [kə'pɪtjuleɪt] *vi:* **to ~ to sthg** capitular perante algo.

cappuccino [,kæpʊ'tʃiːnəʊ] *(pl -s) n* cappuccino *m*.

Capricorn ['kæprɪkɔːn] *n* Capricórnio *m*.

capsicum ['kæpsɪkəm] *n* pimentão *m (Br)*, pimento *m (Port)*.

capsize [kæp'saɪz] *vi* virar-se.

capsule ['kæpsjuːl] *n* cápsula *f*.

captain ['kæptɪn] *n* capitão *m* (-tã *f*); *(of plane, ship)* comandante *mf*.

caption ['kæpʃn] *n* legenda *f*.

captivate ['kæptɪveɪt] *vt* cativar.

captive ['kæptɪv] *n* cativo *m* (-va *f*) ♦ *adj (imprisoned)* cativo(-va); *(audience, market)* seguro(-ra).

captor ['kæptər] *n* captor *m* (-ra *f*).

capture ['kæptʃər] *vt (person, animal)* capturar; *(town, castle)* tomar.

car [kɑːr] *n (motorcar)* carro *m*, automóvel *m; (railway wagon)* vagão *m (Br)*, carruagem *f (Port)*.

carafe [kə'ræf] *n* garrafa *f (de boca larga para servir vinho ou água)*.

caramel ['kærəmel] *n (sweet)* caramelo *m; (burnt sugar)* calda *f* caramelada *(Br)*, caramelo líquido *(Port)*.

carat ['kærət] *n* quilate *m;* **24-~ gold** ouro de 24 quilates.

caravan ['kærəvæn] *n (Brit)* trailer *m (Br)*, caravana *f (Port)*.

caravanning ['kærəvænɪŋ] *n (Brit):* **to go ~** passar férias num trailer.

caravan site *n (Brit)* camping *m* para trailers *(Br)*, parque *m* de campismo para caravanas *(Port)*.

carbohydrate [ˌkɑːbəʊˈhaɪdreɪt] *n (in foods)* hidrato *m* de carbono.

carbon [ˈkɑːbən] *n* carbono *m*.

carbonated [ˈkɑːbəneɪtɪd] *adj* com gás, gaseificado(-da).

carbon copy *n* cópia *f* feita com papel químico.

carbon dioxide [-daɪˈɒksaɪd] *n* dióxido *m* de carbono.

carbon monoxide [-mɒˈnɒksaɪd] *n* monóxido *m* de carbono.

car boot sale *n (Brit)* mercado de objetos usados, cuja venda se faz diretamente do porta-malas dos carros.

carburetor [ˌkɑːbəˈretər] *(Am)* = **carburettor**.

carburettor [ˌkɑːbəˈretər] *n (Brit)* carburador *m*.

carcass [ˈkɑːkəs] *n* carcaça *f*.

car crash *n* acidente *m* de carro.

card [kɑːd] *n* cartão *m*; *(postcard)* postal *m*; *(playing card)* carta *f*; *(cardboard)* cartolina *f*, papelão *m*.

❑ **cards** *npl (game)* cartas *fpl*.

cardboard [ˈkɑːdbɔːd] *n* cartolina *f*, papelão *m*.

cardboard box *n* caixa *f* de papelão.

car deck *n* convés *m* para veículos.

cardiac arrest [ˌkɑːdɪæk-] *n* parada *f* cardíaca *(Br)*, paragem *f* cardíaca *(Port)*.

cardigan [ˈkɑːdɪgən] *n* casaco *m* de malha.

cardinal [ˈkɑːdɪnl] *adj* capital ◆ *n (RELIG)* cardeal *m*.

card index *n (Brit)* fichário *m (Br)*, ficheiro *m (Port)*.

care [keər] *n (attention)* cuidado *m*; *(treatment)* cuidados *mpl* ◆ *vi (mind)* importar-se; **to take ~ of** tomar conta de; **to take ~ not to do sthg** ter cuidado para não fazer algo; **take ~!** *(goodbye)* expressão de afeto utilizada frequentemente em despedidas; **with ~** com cuidado; **would you ~ to ...?** *(fml)* você se importaria de ...?; **to ~ about** *(think important)* preocupar-se com; *(person)* querer bem a.

career [kəˈrɪər] *n* carreira *f*.

careers adviser [kəˈrɪəz-] *n* orientador *m* (-ra *f*) profissional.

carefree [ˈkeəfriː] *adj* despreocupado(-da).

careful [ˈkeəfʊl] *adj* cuidadoso(-osa); **be ~!** cuidado!

carefully [ˈkeəflɪ] *adv* cuidadosamente.

careless [ˈkeələs] *adj* descuidado (-da).

caress [kəˈres] *n* carícia *f* ◆ *vt* acariciar.

caretaker [ˈkeəˌteɪkər] *n (Brit)* porteiro *m* (-ra *f*).

car ferry *n* barco *m (de travessia que transporta carros)*.

cargo [ˈkɑːgəʊ] *(pl -es OR -s)* *n* carga *f*, carregamento *m*.

car hire *n (Brit)* aluguel *m* de carros OR automóveis.

Caribbean [*Brit* ˌkærɪˈbiːən, *Am* kəˈrɪbɪən] *n:* **the ~** *(area)* as Caraíbas.

caring [ˈkeərɪŋ] *adj* atencioso(-osa), solícito(-ta).

carnage [ˈkɑːnɪdʒ] *n* carnificina *f*.

carnation [kɑːˈneɪʃn] *n* cravo *m*.

carnival [ˈkɑːnɪvl] *n* carnaval *m*.

carnivorous [kɑːˈnɪvərəs] *adj* carnívoro(-ra).

carol [ˈkærəl] *n:* **(Christmas) ~** cântico *m* de Natal.

carousel [ˌkærəˈsel] *n (for luggage)* esteira *f* rolante *(Br)*, tapete *m* rolante *(Port)*; *(Am: merry-go-round)* carrossel *m*.

carp [kɑːp] *n* carpa *f*.

car park *n (Brit)* estacionamento *m*.

carpenter [ˈkɑːpəntər] *n* carpinteiro *m* (-ra *f*).

carpentry [ˈkɑːpəntrɪ] *n* carpintaria *f*.

carpet [ˈkɑːpɪt] *n (fitted)* carpete *f (Br)*, alcatifa *f (Port)*; *(not fitted)* tapete *m*.

car phone *n* telefone *m* de carro.

car rental *n (Am)* aluguel *m* de carros OR automóveis.

carriage [ˈkærɪdʒ] *n (Brit: of train)* carruagem *f*; *(horse-drawn)* coche *m*.

carriageway [ˈkærɪdʒweɪ] *n (Brit)* pista *f (Br)*, carril *m (Port)*.

carrier (bag) [ˈkærɪər-] *n* saco *m (de papel ou plástico)*.

carrot [ˈkærət] *n* cenoura *f*.

carrot cake *n* bolo *m* de cenoura.

carry [ˈkærɪ] *vt (bear)* carregar, levar; *(transport)* transportar, levar; *(disease)* transmitir; *(cash, passport, map)* ter (consigo); *(support)* agüentar com ◆ *vi (voice, sound)* ouvir-se.

❑ **carry on** *vi (continue)* continuar ◆ *vt fus (continue)* continuar; *(conduct)* realizar; **to ~ on doing sthg** continuar a fazer algo.

❑ **carry out** vt sep (perform) levar a cabo; (fulfil) cumprir.

carrycot ['kærɪkɒt] n (Brit) moisés m inv (Br), alcofa m de bebé (Port).

carryout ['kærɪaʊt] n (Am & Scot) comida f para levar.

carsick ['kɑːˌsɪk] adj enjoado(-da) (em carro).

cart [kɑːt] n (for transport) carroça f; (Am: in supermarket) carro m das compras; (inf: video game cartridge) cassete f.

carton ['kɑːtn] n pacote m.

cartoon [kɑː'tuːn] n (drawing) desenho m, caricatura f; (film) desenho animado.

cartridge ['kɑːtrɪdʒ] n (for gun) cartucho m; (for pen) recarga f.

cartwheel ['kɑːtwiːl] n (movement) cambalhota f lateral.

carve [kɑːv] vt (wood, stone) esculpir; (meat) cortar.

carvery ['kɑːvərɪ] n restaurante onde se servem churrascos cortados diante dos fregueses.

carving ['kɑːvɪŋ] n (wooden) talha f; (stone) gravura f.

car wash n lavagem f automática.

case [keɪs] n (Brit: suitcase) mala f; (container) caixa f; (instance, patient) caso m; (JUR: trial) causa f; **in any ~** de qualquer modo; **in ~ of** em caso de; **(just) in ~** caso; **in that ~** nesse caso.

cash [kæʃ] n dinheiro m ♦ vt: **to ~ a cheque** descontar um cheque (Br), levantar um cheque (Port); **to pay ~** pagar em dinheiro.

cash and carry n cash-and-carry m, armazém m de venda a granel.

cash box n cofre m.

cash card n = (cartão) multibanco m.

cash desk n caixa f.

cash dispenser [-ˌdɪ'spensər] n caixa m automático, multibanco m.

cashew (nut) ['kæʃuː-] n caju m, castanha f de caju.

cashier [kæ'ʃɪər] n caixa mf.

cash machine n = cash dispenser.

cashmere [kæʃ'mɪər] n caxemira f.

cashpoint ['kæʃpɔɪnt] n (Brit) caixa m automático, multibanco m.

cash register n caixa f registadora.

casing ['keɪsɪŋ] n revestimento m.

casino [kə'siːnəʊ] (pl **-s**) n casino m.

cask [kɑːsk] n casco m, barril m.

cask-conditioned [-ˌkən'dɪʃnd] adj fermentado(-da) no barril.

casket ['kɑːskɪt] n (for jewels) guardajóias m inv.

casserole ['kæsərəʊl] n (stew) ensopado m de forno; **~ (dish)** panela f de ir ao forno.

cassette [kæ'set] n cassete f.

cassette player n toca-fitas m inv (Br), leitor m de cassetes (Port).

cassette recorder n gravador m.

cast [kɑːst] (pt & pp **cast**) n (actors) elenco m; (for broken bone) gesso m ♦ vt (shadow, light, look) lançar; **to ~ doubt on** pôr em dúvida; **to ~ one's vote** votar.

❑ **cast off** vi (boat, ship) zarpar.

castaway ['kɑːstəweɪ] n náufrago m (-ga f).

caster ['kɑːstər] n (wheel) rodízio m.

caster sugar n (Brit) açúcar m branco (muito fino).

cast iron n ferro m fundido.

castle ['kɑːsl] n (building) castelo m; (in chess) torre f.

castor oil ['kɑːstər-] n óleo m de rícino.

castrate [kæ'streɪt] vt castrar.

casual ['kæʒʊəl] adj (relaxed) despreocupado(-da); (manner, clothes) informal; **~ work** trabalho m temporário.

casually ['kæʒʊəlɪ] adv (in a relaxed manner) despreocupadamente; (address, dress) informalmente.

casualty ['kæʒjʊəltɪ] n vítima mf; **~ (ward)** pronto-socorro m (Br), urgências fpl (Port).

cat [kæt] n gato m.

catalog ['kætəlɒg] (Am) = **catalogue**.

catalogue ['kætəlɒg] n catálogo m.

catalyst ['kætəlɪst] n catalisador m.

catalytic converter [ˌkætə'lɪtɪkkən'vɜːtər] n conversor m catalítico (Br), vaso m catalítico (Port).

catapult ['kætəpʌlt] n catapulta f.

cataract ['kætərækt] n (in eye) catarata f.

catarrh [kə'tɑːr] n catarro m.

catastrophe [kə'tæstrəfɪ] n catástrofe f.

catch [kætʃ] (pt & pp **caught**) vt apanhar; (attention, imagination) despertar ♦ vi (become hooked) ficar preso ♦ n (of window, door) trinco m; (snag) truque m.

❏ **catch up** *vt sep* alcançar ◆ *vi*: **to ~ up (with)** alcançar.

catching [ˈkætʃɪŋ] *adj (inf)* contagioso(-osa).

catchment area [ˈkætʃmənt-] *n zona servida por uma escola ou hospital.*

catchphrase [ˈkætʃfreɪz] *n* slogan *m.*

catchy [ˈkætʃɪ] *adj* fácil de lembrar.

categorically [ˌkætɪˈɡɒrɪklɪ] *adv* categoricamente.

category [ˈkætəɡərɪ] *n* categoria *f.*

cater [ˈkeɪtəʳ] **: cater for** *vt fus (Brit) (needs, tastes)* satisfazer; *(anticipate)* contar com.

caterer [ˈkeɪtərəʳ] *n* fornecedor *m* (-ra *f*) *(de serviço de bufê).*

catering [ˈkeɪtərɪŋ] *n (at wedding etc)* serviço *m* de bufê; *(trade)* = hotelaria *f.*

caterpillar [ˈkætəpɪləʳ] *n* lagarta *f.*

cathedral [kəˈθiːdrəl] *n* catedral *f.*

Catholic [ˈkæθlɪk] *adj* católico(-ca) ◆ *n* católico *m* (-ca *f*).

Catseyes® [ˈkætsaɪz] *npl (Brit)* refletores *mpl (em estrada).*

cattle [ˈkætl] *npl* gado *m.*

cattle grid *n* mata-burro *m (ponte de traves espaçadas, destinada a impedir a passagem de animais).*

catwalk [ˈkætwɔːk] *n* passarela *f.*

caught [kɔːt] *pt & pp* → **catch.**

cauliflower [ˈkɒlɪˌflaʊəʳ] *n* couve-flor *f.*

cauliflower cheese *n* gratinado de couve-flor com molho branco e queijo ralado.

cause [kɔːz] *n* causa *f; (justification)* razão *f* ◆ *vt* ca'usar; **to ~ sb to do sthg** fazer (com) que alguém faça algo.

causeway [ˈkɔːzweɪ] *n* calçada *f (sobre água ou zona pantanosa).*

caustic [ˈkɔːstɪk] *adj (chemical)* corrosivo(-va), cáustico(-ca); *(comment)* mordaz.

caustic soda [ˌkɔːstɪk-] *n* soda *f* cáustica.

caution [ˈkɔːʃn] *n (care)* cautela *f; (warning)* aviso *m.*

cautious [ˈkɔːʃəs] *adj* cauteloso (-osa).

cavalry [ˈkævlrɪ] *n (on horseback)* cavalaria *f.*

cave [keɪv] *n* gruta *f.*

❏ **cave in** *vi (roof, ceiling)* desabar.

caveman [ˈkeɪvmæn] *(pl -men* [-men]) *n* homem *m* das cavernas.

caviar(e) [ˈkævɪɑːʳ] *n* caviar *m.*

cavity [ˈkævətɪ] *n (in tooth)* cavidade *f.*

CB *abrev =* **Citizens' Band.**

cc *n (abbr of cubic centimetre)* cm³.

CD *n (abbr of compact disc)* CD *m.*

CDI *n (abbr of compact disc interactive)* CDI *m.*

CD player *n* som *m* CD (Br), leitor *m* de CDs (Port).

CD-ROM [ˌsiːdiːˈrɒm] *n (abbr of compact disc read only memory)* CD-ROM *m.*

CDW *n (abbr of collision damage waiver)* = franquia *f,* = seguro *m* contra choque, colisão, capotagem, incêndio.

cease [siːs] *vt & vi (fml)* cessar.

ceasefire [ˈsiːsfaɪəʳ] *n* cessar-fogo *m.*

cedar (tree) [ˈsiːdəʳ-] *n* cedro *m.*

ceilidh [ˈkeɪlɪ] *n* festa ou baile tradicional escocês ou irlandês.

ceiling [ˈsiːlɪŋ] *n* teto *m.*

celebrate [ˈselɪbreɪt] *vt & vi (victory, birthday)* celebrar.

celebration [ˌselɪˈbreɪʃn] *n (event)* celebração *f.*

❏ **celebrations** *npl (festivities)* comemorações *fpl.*

celebrity [sɪˈlebrətɪ] *n (person)* celebridade *f.*

celeriac [sɪˈlerɪæk] *n* aipo-rábano *m.*

celery [ˈselərɪ] *n* aipo *m.*

celibate [ˈselɪbət] *adj* celibatário(-ria).

cell [sel] *n (of plant, body)* célula *f; (in prison)* cela *f.*

cellar [ˈseləʳ] *n* cave *f.*

cello [ˈtʃeləʊ] *(pl -s)* *n* violoncelo *m.*

Cellophane® [ˈseləfeɪn] *n* celofane *m.*

Celsius [ˈselsɪəs] *adj* centígrado(-da).

Celt [kelt] *n* celta *mf.*

Celtic [ˈkeltɪk] *adj* celta.

cement [sɪˈment] *n* cimento *m.*

cement mixer *n* betoneira *f.*

cemetery [ˈsemɪtrɪ] *n* cemitério *m.*

censor [ˈsensəʳ] *n* censor *m* (-ra *f*) ◆ *vt* censurar.

censorship [ˈsensəʃɪp] *n* censura *f.*

census [ˈsensəs] *n (population survey)* censo *m.*

cent [sent] *n (Am)* cêntimo *m.*

centenary [senˈtiːnərɪ] *n (Brit)* centenário *m.*

centennial [senˈtenjəl] *(Am)* = **centenary.**

center [ˈsentəʳ] *(Am)* = **centre.**

centigrade [ˈsentɪɡreɪd] *adj* centígrado(-da).

centilitre ['sentɪ,liːtəʳ] n centilitro m.

centimetre ['sentɪ,miːtəʳ] n centímetro m.

centipede ['sentɪpiːd] n centopeia f.

central ['sentrəl] adj central.

Central America n América f Central.

central heating n aquecimento m central.

central locking [-'lɒkɪŋ] n fechadura f centralizada.

central reservation n (Brit) canteiro m central (Br), faixa f separadora central (Port) (em auto-estrada).

centre ['sentəʳ] n (Brit) centro m ♦ adj (Brit) central; **the ~ of attention** o centro das atenções.

century ['sentʃʊrɪ] n século m.

ceramic [sɪ'ræmɪk] adj de louça OR barro.

❑ **ceramics** npl cerâmica f.

cereal ['sɪərɪəl] n cereal m.

ceremony ['serɪmənɪ] n cerimônia f.

certain ['sɜːtn] adj certo(-ta); **she's ~ to be late** o mais certo é ela chegar atrasada; **to be ~ of sthg** ter a certeza de algo; **to make ~ (that)** assegurar-se de que.

certainly ['sɜːtnlɪ] adv (without doubt) sem dúvida; (of course) com certeza; **~ not!** de modo nenhum!; **I ~ do** com certeza que sim.

certainty ['sɜːtntɪ] n certeza f.

certificate [sə'tɪfɪkət] n (of studies, medical) certificado m; (of birth) certidão f.

certified mail ['sɜːtɪfaɪd-] n (Am) correio m registrado.

certify ['sɜːtɪfaɪ] vt (declare true) comprovar.

cervical smear [sə'vaɪkl-] n exame m de lâmina, esfregaço m cervical.

cervix ['sɜːvɪks] (pl -ixes OR -ices [-ɪsiːz]) n (of uterus) cérvix m, colo m (do útero).

cesarean (section) [sɪ'zeərɪən-] (Am) = **caesarean (section)**.

CFC n (abbr of chlorofluorocarbon) CFC m.

chaffinch ['tʃæfɪntʃ] n tentilhão m.

chain [tʃeɪn] n (of metal) corrente f; (of shops, mountains) cadeia f ♦ vt: **to ~ sthg to sthg** prender algo a algo (com corrente).

chain saw n serra f de cadeia (Br),

motoserra f (Port).

chain-smoke vi fumar um cigarro atrás do outro OR cigarro atrás de cigarro.

chain store n loja pertencente a uma cadeia.

chair [tʃeəʳ] n cadeira f.

chair lift n teleférico m (de cadeira).

chairman ['tʃeəmən] (pl -men [-mən]) n presidente m.

chairperson ['tʃeə,pɜːsn] (pl -s) n presidente mf.

chairwoman ['tʃeə,wʊmən] (pl -women [-,wɪmɪn]) n presidente f.

chalet ['ʃæleɪ] n chalé m.

chalk [tʃɔːk] n giz m; **a piece of ~** um pedaço de giz.

chalkboard ['tʃɔːkbɔːd] n (Am) quadro m.

challenge ['tʃælɪndʒ] n desafio m ♦ vt (question) questionar; **to ~ sb (to sthg)** (to fight, competition) desafiar alguém (para algo).

challenging ['tʃælɪndʒɪŋ] adj (task, job) estimulante.

chamber ['tʃeɪmbəʳ] n (room) câmara f.

chambermaid ['tʃeɪmbəmeɪd] n camareira f (Br), empregada f de quarto (Port).

chameleon [kə'miːlɪən] n camaleão m.

champagne [,ʃæm'peɪn] n champanhe m.

champion ['tʃæmpjən] n campeão m (-peã f).

championship ['tʃæmpjənʃɪp] n campeonato m.

chance [tʃɑːns] n chance f ♦ vt: **to ~ it** (inf) arriscar; **to take a ~** arriscar-se; **by ~** por acaso; **on the off ~** por se acaso.

chancellor ['tʃɑːnsələʳ] n (of country) chanceler m; (of university) reitor m (-ra f).

Chancellor of the Exchequer [,tʃɑːnsələrəvðəɪks'tʃekəʳ] n (Brit) = ministro m (-tra f) da Fazenda (Br), = ministro m (-tra f) das Finanças (Port).

chandelier [,ʃændə'lɪəʳ] n candelabro m, lustre m.

change [tʃeɪndʒ] n (alteration) mudança f; (money received back) troco m; (coins) dinheiro m trocado ♦ vt mudar; (exchange) trocar; (clothes, bedding) mudar de, trocar de ♦ vi mudar; (change clothes) trocar-se, mudar de roupa; **a ~ of clothes** uma muda de roupa; **do you have ~ for a pound?** você pode trocar uma libra?; **for a ~** para variar; **to get ~d** trocar-se, mudar de roupa; **to ~ money** trocar dinheiro; **to ~ a nappy** mudar uma fralda; **to ~ a wheel** mudar uma roda; **to ~ trains/planes** mudar de trem/avião; **all ~!** *(on train)* mudança de trem!

changeable [ˈtʃeɪndʒəbl] *adj (weather)* variável.

change machine *n* máquina automática para trocar dinheiro.

changeover [ˈtʃeɪndʒˌəʊvəʳ] *n*: **~ (to)** mudança *f* (para), passagem *f* (a).

changing room [ˈtʃeɪndʒɪŋ-] *n* vestiário *m*.

channel [ˈtʃænl] *n* canal *m*; **the (English) Channel** o Canal da Mancha.

Channel Islands *npl*: **the ~** as Ilhas do Canal da Mancha.

Channel Tunnel *n*: **the ~** o túnel do Canal da Mancha, o Eurotúnel.

chant [tʃɑːnt] *vt* entoar.

chaos [ˈkeɪɒs] *n* caos *m*.

chaotic [keɪˈɒtɪk] *adj* caótico(-ca).

chap [tʃæp] *n (Brit: inf)* sujeito *m*.

chapatti [tʃəˈpætɪ] *n* pequeno pão não fermentado de origem indiana.

chapel [ˈtʃæpl] *n* capela *f*.

chaplain [ˈtʃæplɪn] *n* capelão *m*.

chapped [tʃæpt] *adj* gretado(-da).

chapter [ˈtʃæptəʳ] *n* capítulo *m*.

character [ˈkærəktəʳ] *n* carácter *m*; *(in film, book, play)* personagem *m ou f*; *(inf: person, individual)* tipo *m*.

characteristic [ˌkærəktəˈrɪstɪk] *adj* característico(-ca) ◆ *n* característica *f*.

characterize [ˈkærəktəraɪz] *vt* caracterizar.

charade [ʃəˈrɑːd] *n* charada *f*.

❑ **charades** *n* charadas *fpl*.

charcoal [ˈtʃɑːkəʊl] *n (for barbecue)* carvão *m* (de lenha).

charge [tʃɑːdʒ] *n (price)* preço *m*, custo *m*; *(JUR)* acusação *f* ◆ *vt (money, customer)* cobrar; *(JUR)* acusar; *(battery)* carregar ◆ *vi (ask money)* cobrar; *(rush)* investir; **to be in ~ (of)** estar encarregado (de); **to take ~ (of)** encarregar-se (de); **free of ~** grátis; **there is no ~ for service** o serviço é grátis.

charge card *n* cartão de crédito que permite fazer compras num estabelecimento e pagar posteriormente.

char-grilled [ˈtʃɑːgrɪld] *adj* assado

(-da) na brasa.

chariot [ˈtʃærɪət] *n* charrete *f*.

charisma [kəˈrɪzmə] *n* carisma *m*.

charity [ˈtʃærətɪ] *n (organization)* caridade *f*; **to give to ~** contribuir para obras de caridade.

charity shop *n* loja de objetos usados cujas vendas se destinam a causas beneficentes.

charm [tʃɑːm] *n (attractiveness)* charme *m* ◆ *vt* encantar.

charming [ˈtʃɑːmɪŋ] *adj* encantador (-ra).

chart [tʃɑːt] *n (diagram)* gráfico *m*; **the ~s** as paradas de sucesso *(Br)*, os tops de vendas (de discos) *(Port)*.

charter [ˈtʃɑːtəʳ] *n (document)* carta *f* ◆ *vt (plane, boat)* fretar.

chartered accountant [ˌtʃɑːtəd-] *n* perito-contador *m*, perita-contadora *f (Br)*, técnico *m* (-ca *f*) de contas *(Port)*.

charter flight *n* vôo *m* charter.

chase [tʃeɪs] *n* perseguição *f* ◆ *vt* perseguir.

chasm [ˈkæzm] *n (deep crack)* fenda *f* profunda, abismo *m*.

chassis [ˈʃæsɪ] *(pl inv* [-sɪz]*)* *n (of vehicle)* chassis *m inv*.

chat [tʃæt] *n* conversa *f* ◆ *vi* conversar; **to have a ~ (with)** conversar (com).

❑ **chat up** *vt sep (Brit: inf)* paquerar *(Br)*, engatar *(Port)*.

chat show *n (Brit)* programa *m* de variedades, talk-show *m*.

chatter [ˈtʃætəʳ] *n (of person)* tagarelice *f* ◆ *vi (person)* tagarelar; **her teeth were ~ing** ela estava tiritando.

chatterbox [ˈtʃætəbɒks] *n (inf)* tagarela *mf*.

chatty [ˈtʃætɪ] *adj (letter)* informal; *(person)* tagarela.

chauffeur [ˈʃəʊfəʳ] *n* motorista *mf*.

chauvinist [ˈʃəʊvɪnɪst] *n (sexist)* sexista *mf*; *(nationalist)* chauvinista *mf*; **male ~** machista *m*.

cheap [tʃiːp] *adj* barato(-ta).

cheap day return *n (Brit)* bilhete de ida e volta mais barato, comprado no próprio dia e que só pode ser usado depois das 9.30.

cheaply [ˈtʃiːplɪ] *adv* barato.

cheat [tʃiːt] *n (person)* trapaceiro *m* (-ra *f*) *(Br)*, batoteiro *m* (-ra *f*) *(Port)*; *(thing)* trapaça *f (Br)*, batota *f (Port)*

♦ *vi* trapacear *(Br)*, fazer batota *(Port)*
♦ *vt*: **to ~ sb (out of sthg)** roubar algo de alguém.

check [tʃek] *n (inspection)* inspecção *f*; *(Am: bill)* conta *f*; *(Am: tick)* sinal *m* de visto; *(Am)* = **cheque** ♦ *vt* verificar ♦ *vi* informar-se; **~ for any mistakes** verifique se há erros.

❏ **check in** *vt sep (luggage)* fazer o check-in de ♦ *vi (at hotel)* registrar-se; *(at airport)* fazer o check-in.

❏ **check off** *vt sep* verificar *(em lista)*.

❏ **check out** *vi* deixar o hotel.

❏ **check up** *vi*: **to ~ up (on)** informar-se (sobre).

checked [tʃekt] *adj* quadriculado, de xadrez.

checkers [ˈtʃekəz] *n (Am)* damas *fpl*.

check-in desk *n* (balcão para o) check-in *m*.

checkmate [ˈtʃekmeɪt] *n* xeque-mate *m*.

checkout [ˈtʃekaʊt] *n* caixa *f*.

checkpoint [ˈtʃekpɔɪnt] *n* controle *m*.

checkroom [ˈtʃekrʊm] *n (Am)* vestiário *m (Br)*, bengaleiro *m (Port)*.

checkup [ˈtʃekʌp] *n* exame *m* médico geral, check-up *m*.

cheddar (cheese) *n* (queijo) chedar *m*, *queijo de vaca duro mas macio, amarelo ou alaranjado*.

cheek [tʃiːk] *n (of face)* bochecha *f*; **what a ~!** que descaramento!

cheekbone [ˈtʃiːkbəʊn] *n* malar *m*, maçã *f* do rosto.

cheeky [ˈtʃiːkɪ] *adj* descarado(-da), atrevido(-da).

cheer [tʃɪər] *n* aclamação *f* ♦ *vi* aclamar.

cheerful [ˈtʃɪəfʊl] *adj* alegre.

cheerio [ˌtʃɪərɪˈəʊ] *excl (Brit: inf)* tchau!

cheers [tʃɪəz] *excl (when drinking)* saúde!; *(Brit: inf: thank you)* obrigado!

cheese [tʃiːz] *n* queijo *m*.

cheeseboard [ˈtʃiːzbɔːd] *n* tábua *f* de queijos, *queijos diversos e biscoitos servidos no final de uma refeição*.

cheeseburger [ˈtʃiːzbɜːɡər] *n* hambúrguer *m* de queijo, cheeseburger *m*.

cheesecake [ˈtʃiːzkeɪk] *n* torta de queijo, *creme e açúcar com uma base de biscoitos triturados e guarnecida com fruta em pedaços*.

cheetah [ˈtʃiːtə] *n* chita *m*, leopardo *m*.

chef [ʃef] *n* chefe *m* (de cozinha).

chef's special *n* especialidade *f* da casa.

chemical [ˈkemɪkl] *adj* químico(-ca) ♦ *n* substância *f* química.

chemist [ˈkemɪst] *n (Brit: pharmacist)* farmacêutico *m* (-ca *f*); *(scientist)* químico *m* (-ca *f*); **~'s** *(Brit: shop)* farmácia *f*.

chemistry [ˈkemɪstrɪ] *n* química *f*.

cheque [tʃek] *n (Brit)* cheque *m*; **to pay by ~** pagar com cheque.

chequebook [ˈtʃekbʊk] *n* talão *m* de cheques *(Br)*, livro *m* de cheques *(Port)*.

cheque card *n* cartão *f* bancário *(que serve de garantia para cheques)*.

cherish [ˈtʃerɪʃ] *vt (hope, memory)* acalentar; *(privilege, right)* valorizar; *(person, thing)* estimar.

cherry [ˈtʃerɪ] *n* cereja *f*.

chess [tʃes] *n* xadrez *m*.

chessboard [ˈtʃesbɔːd] *n* tabuleiro *m* de xadrez.

chessman [ˈtʃesmæn] *(pl* **-men** [-men]*) n* pedra *f* OR peça *f* (de xadrez).

chest [tʃest] *n (of body)* peito *m*; *(box)* arca *f*.

chestnut [ˈtʃesnʌt] *n* castanha *f* ♦ *adj (colour)* marrom *(Br)*, castanho(-nha) *(Port)*.

chest of drawers *n* cómoda *f*.

chew [tʃuː] *vt* mastigar ♦ *n (sweet)* goma *f*.

chewing gum [ˈtʃuːɪŋ-] *n* chiclete *m (Br)*, pastilha *f* elástica *(Port)*.

chic [ʃiːk] *adj* chique.

chicken [ˈtʃɪkɪn] *n* galinha *f*, frango *m*.

chicken breast *n* peito *m* de galinha.

chicken Kiev [-ˈkiːev] *n* empanado de frango com recheio de manteiga, alho e ervas aromáticas.

chickenpox [ˈtʃɪkɪnpɒks] *n* catapora *f (Br)*, varicela *f (Port)*.

chickpea [ˈtʃɪkpiː] *n* grão-de-bico *m*.

chicory [ˈtʃɪkərɪ] *n* chicória *f*.

chief [tʃiːf] *adj (highest-ranking)* chefe; *(main)* principal ♦ *n* chefe *m* (-fa *f*).

chiefly [ˈtʃiːflɪ] *adv (mainly)* principalmente; *(especially)* sobretudo.

chilblain [ˈtʃɪlbleɪn] *n* frieira *f*.

child [tʃaɪld] *(pl* **children***) n (young boy, girl)* criança *f*; *(son, daughter)* filho *m* (-lha *f*).

child abuse *n* maus-tratos *mpl* infantis.

child benefit *n* (Brit) = salário-família *m* (Br), = abono *m* de família (Port).

childbirth ['tʃaɪldbɜːθ] *n* parto *m*.

childhood ['tʃaɪldhʊd] *n* infância *f*.

childish ['tʃaɪldɪʃ] *adj* (pej) infantil.

childlike ['tʃaɪldlaɪk] *adj* infantil.

childminder ['tʃaɪld,maɪndər] *n* (Brit) pessoa que toma conta de crianças em sua própria casa, ama *f* (Port).

children ['tʃɪldrən] *pl* → child.

children's home *n* lar *m* para crianças.

childrenswear ['tʃɪldrənzweər] *n* roupa *f* para crianças.

child seat *n* banco *m* para crianças.

Chile ['tʃɪli] *n* Chile *m*.

chill [tʃɪl] *n* (illness) resfriado *m* ♦ *vt* gelar; **there's a ~ in the air** o tempo está frio.

chilled [tʃɪld] *adj* fresco(-ca); **"serve ~"** "sirva fresco".

chilli ['tʃɪli] (pl -ies) *n* (vegetable) pimenta *f* OR pimentão *m* picante (Br), piripiri *m* (Port); (dish) = **chilli con carne**.

chilli con carne ['tʃɪlɪkɒn'kɑːni] *n* ensopado de carne de vaca picada com feijão e pimentão picante.

chilling ['tʃɪlɪŋ] *adj* (frightening) de fazer gelar o sangue nas veias.

chilly ['tʃɪli] *adj* frio (fria).

chime [tʃaɪm] *n* (of bell, clock) toque *m* ♦ *vi* (bell, clock) tocar.

chimney ['tʃɪmnɪ] *n* chaminé *f*.

chimneypot ['tʃɪmnɪpɒt] *n* chaminé *f*.

chimneysweep ['tʃɪmnɪswiːp] *n* limpa-chaminés *m inv*.

chimpanzee [tʃɪmpən'ziː] *n* chimpanzé *m*.

chin [tʃɪn] *n* queixo *m*.

china ['tʃaɪnə] *n* (material) porcelana *f*.

China ['tʃaɪnə] *n* China *f*.

Chinese [tʃaɪ'niːz] *adj* chinês(-esa) ♦ *n* (language) chinês *m* ♦ *npl*: **the ~** os chineses; **a ~ restaurant** um restaurante chinês.

Chinese leaves *npl* (Brit) couve *f* chinesa.

chip [tʃɪp] *n* (small piece, mark) lasca *f*; (counter) ficha *f*; (COMPUT) chip *m* ♦ *vt* lascar.

❑ **chips** *npl* (Brit: French fries) batatas

fpl fritas (em palitos); (Am: crisps) batatas fritas (de pacote).

chip shop *n* (Brit) loja onde se vende batatas fritas e filés de peixe para levar.

chiropodist [kɪ'rɒpədɪst] *n* pedicuro *m* (-ra *f*).

chirp [tʃɜːp] *vi* (bird) chilrear.

chisel ['tʃɪzl] *n* formão *m*.

chitchat ['tʃɪttʃæt] *n* (inf) conversa *f* fiada.

chives [tʃaɪvz] *npl* cebolinha *f* (Br), cebolinho *m* (Port).

chlorine ['klɔːriːn] *n* cloro *m*.

choc-ice ['tʃɒkaɪs] *n* (Brit) tipo de sorvete em forma de bloco, coberto com chocolate.

chocolate ['tʃɒkələt] *n* (food, drink) chocolate *m*; (sweet) bombom *m* ♦ *adj* de chocolate.

chocolate biscuit *n* biscoito *m* de chocolate.

choice [tʃɔɪs] *n* escolha *f* ♦ *adj* de primeira qualidade; **with the dressing of your ~** com o tempero a gosto.

choir ['kwaɪər] *n* coro *m*.

choirboy ['kwaɪəbɔɪ] *n* menino *m* de coro.

choke [tʃəʊk] *vt* sufocar ♦ *vi* (on fishbone etc) engasgar-se; (to death) sufocar ♦ *n* (AUT): **to pull out the ~** fechar o afogador.

cholera ['kɒlərə] *n* cólera *f*.

choose [tʃuːz] (pt chose, pp chosen) *vt & vi* escolher; **to ~ to do sthg** decidir fazer algo.

choos(e)y ['tʃuːzɪ] *adj* exigente.

chop [tʃɒp] *n* (of meat) costeleta *f* ♦ *vt* cortar.

❑ **chop down** *vt sep* abater.

❑ **chop up** *vt sep* picar.

chopper ['tʃɒpər] *n* (inf: helicopter) helicóptero *m*.

chopping board ['tʃɒpɪŋ-] *n* tábua *f* de cozinha.

choppy ['tʃɒpɪ] *adj* encrespado(-da).

chopsticks ['tʃɒpstɪks] *npl* pauzinhos *mpl* chineses.

chop suey [tʃɒp'suːɪ] *n* chop suey *m*, prato chinês de brotos de soja, legumes, arroz e carne de porco ou galinha com molho de soja.

chord [kɔːd] *n* acorde *m*.

chore [tʃɔːr] *n* tarefa *f*.

chorus ['kɔːrəs] *n* (part of song) refrão *m*; (group of singers, dancers) coro *m*.

chose [tʃəʊz] *pt* → **choose**.

chosen [ˈtʃəʊzn] *pp* → **choose**.

choux pastry [ʃuː-] *n* massa *f* fina.

chowder [ˈtʃaʊdəʳ] *n* sopa espessa de peixe ou marisco.

chow mein [ˌtʃaʊˈmeɪn] *n* chau-min *m*, massa de talharim frita com vegetais, carne ou marisco.

Christ [kraɪst] *n* Cristo *m*.

christen [ˈkrɪsn] *vt* (*baby*) batizar.

christening [ˈkrɪsnɪŋ] *n* batizado *m*.

Christian [ˈkrɪstʃən] *adj* cristão(-tã) ◆ *n* cristão *m* (-tã *f*).

Christianity [ˌkrɪstɪˈænətɪ] *n* cristianismo *m*.

Christian name *n* nome *m* (de batismo).

Christmas [ˈkrɪsməs] *n* Natal *m*; **Happy ~!** Feliz Natal!, Boas Festas!

Christmas card *n* cartão *m* de Natal.

Christmas carol [-ˈkærəl] *n* cântico *m* de Natal.

Christmas Day *n* dia *m* de Natal.

Christmas Eve *n* véspera *f* de Natal, noite *f* de Natal.

Christmas pudding *n* sobremesa natalícia feita com frutas cristalizadas, nozes e sebo, servida quente depois de flambada com conhaque.

Christmas tree *n* árvore *f* de Natal.

chrome [krəʊm] *n* cromo *m* (*Br*), crómio *m* (*Port*).

chronic [ˈkrɒnɪk] *adj* (*long-lasting*) crônico(-ca); (*habitual*) inveterado(-da).

chronological [ˌkrɒnəˈlɒdʒɪkl] *adj* cronológico(-ca).

chrysanthemum [krɪˈsænθəməm] *n* crisântemo *m*.

chubby [ˈtʃʌbɪ] *adj* rechonchudo (-da).

chuck [tʃʌk] *vt* (*inf*) (*throw*) atirar; (*boyfriend, girlfriend*) deixar.

❏ **chuck away** *vt sep* jogar fora.

chuckle [ˈtʃʌkl] *vi* rir (baixinho).

chum [tʃʌm] *n* (*inf*) amigão *m* (-gona *f*).

chunk [tʃʌŋk] *n* pedaço *m* (grande).

church [tʃɜːtʃ] *n* igreja *f*; **to go to ~** freqüentar a igreja.

churchyard [ˈtʃɜːtʃjɑːd] *n* cemitério *m*.

churn [tʃɜːn] *n* (*for making butter*) batedeira *f* para fazer manteiga; (*for transporting milk*) lata *f* para o leite.

chute [ʃuːt] *n* rampa *f* (*Br*), conduta *f* (*Port*).

chutney [ˈtʃʌtnɪ] *n* molho picante agridoce feito com verduras ou frutas em conserva e outros temperos.

cider [ˈsaɪdəʳ] *n* sidra *f*.

cigar [sɪˈgɑːʳ] *n* charuto *m*.

cigarette [ˌsɪgəˈret] *n* cigarro *m*.

cigarette lighter *n* isqueiro *m*.

Cinderella [ˌsɪndəˈrelə] *n* Cinderela *f*, Gata-Borralheira *f*.

cinema [ˈsɪnəmə] *n* cinema *m*.

cinnamon [ˈsɪnəmən] *n* canela *f*.

circle [ˈsɜːkl] *n* (*shape, ring*) *n* círculo *m*; (*in theatre*) balcão *m* ◆ *vt* (*draw circle around*) sublinhar em volta; (*move round*) dar voltas em torno de ◆ *vi* (*plane*) dar voltas.

circuit [ˈsɜːkɪt] *n* (*track*) circuito *m*; (*lap*) volta *f*.

circular [ˈsɜːkjʊləʳ] *adj* circular ◆ *n* circular *f*.

circulate [ˈsɜːkjʊleɪt] *vi* circular.

circulation [ˌsɜːkjʊˈleɪʃn] *n* (*of blood*) circulação *f*; (*of newspaper, magazine*) tiragem *f*.

circumcision [ˌsɜːkəmˈsɪʒn] *n* circuncisão *f*.

circumference [səˈkʌmfərəns] *n* circunferência *f*.

circumstances [ˈsɜːkəmstənsɪz] *npl* circunstâncias *fpl*; **in** OR **under the ~** dadas as circunstâncias.

circus [ˈsɜːkəs] *n* circo *m*.

CIS *n* (*abbr of Commonwealth Independent States*) CEI *f*.

cistern [ˈsɪstən] *n* (*of toilet*) cisterna *f*.

citizen [ˈsɪtɪzn] *n* (*of country*) cidadão *m* (-dã *f*); (*of town*) habitante *mf*.

Citizens' Band *n* faixa *f* do cidadão.

citrus fruit [ˈsɪtrəs-] *n* citrino *m*.

city [ˈsɪtɪ] *n* cidade *f*; **the City** a City (*centro financeiro londrino*).

city centre *n* centro *m* (da cidade).

city hall *n* (*Am*) ≃ prefeitura *f* (*Br*), câmara *f* municipal (*Port*), paços *mpl* do concelho (*Port*).

civil [ˈsɪvl] *adj* (*involving ordinary citizens*) civil; (*polite*) educado(-da), cortês.

civilian [sɪˈvɪljən] *n* civil *mf*.

civilization [ˌsɪvɪlaɪˈzeɪʃn] *n* civilização *f*.

civilized [ˈsɪvɪlaɪzd] *adj* civilizado (-da).

civil rights [ˌsɪvl-] npl direitos mpl civis.

civil servant [ˌsɪvl-] n funcionário m público (funcionária f pública).

civil service [ˌsɪvl-] n administração f pública.

civil war [ˌsɪvl-] n guerra f civil.

cl (abbr of centilitre) cl.

claim [kleɪm] n (assertion) afirmação f; (demand) reivindicação f; (for insurance) reclamação f ◆ vt (allege) afirmar; (demand) reclamar; (credit, responsibility) reivindicar ◆ vi (on insurance) reclamar uma indemnização.

claimant ['kleɪmənt] n (of benefit) reclamante mf.

claim form n impresso m de reclamação.

clam [klæm] n molusco m (Br), amêijoa f (Port).

clamber ['klæmbəʳ] vi trepar.

clamp [klæmp] n (for car) garras fpl, imobilizador m ◆ vt (car) imobilizar.

clan [klæn] n clã m.

clandestine [klæn'destɪn] adj clandestino(-na).

clap [klæp] vi aplaudir.

clapping ['klæpɪŋ] n palmas fpl.

claret ['klærət] n clarete m (Br), bordéus m (Port).

clarify ['klærɪfaɪ] vt (explain, expand on) esclarecer, clarificar.

clarinet [ˌklærə'net] n clarinete m.

clarity ['klærətɪ] n (of explanation) clareza f.

clash [klæʃ] n (noise) estrondo m; (confrontation) confrontação f ◆ vi (colours) destoar; (event, date) coincidir.

clasp [klɑːsp] n (fastener) fecho m ◆ vt agarrar (com força).

class [klɑːs] n (group of pupils, students) turma f; (teaching period) aula f; (type, social group) classe f ◆ vt: **to ~ sb/sthg (as)** classificar alguém/algo (de).

classic ['klæsɪk] adj clássico(-ca) ◆ n clássico m.

classical ['klæsɪkl] adj clássico(-ca).

classical music n música f clássica.

classification [ˌklæsɪfɪ'keɪʃn] n classificação f.

classified ads [ˌklæsɪfaɪd-] npl classificados mpl.

classify ['klæsɪfaɪ] vt classificar.

classmate ['klɑːsmeɪt] n colega mf de turma.

classroom ['klɑːsrʊm] n sala f (de aula).

classy ['klɑːsɪ] adj (inf) de classe.

clause [klɔːz] n (in legal document) cláusula f; (GRAMM) proposição f, oração f.

claustrophobic [ˌklɔːstrə'fəʊbɪk] adj (person) adj claustrofóbico(-ca).

claw [klɔː] n (of bird, cat, dog) garra f; (of crab, lobster) pinça f.

clay [kleɪ] n barro m, argila f.

clean [kliːn] adj limpo(-pa); (page) em branco; (sheets, clothes) lavado(-da) ◆ vt limpar; **to ~ one's teeth** escovar os dentes.

cleaner ['kliːnəʳ] n (person) faxineiro m (-ra f) (Br), empregado m (-da f) de limpeza (Port); (substance) produto m de limpeza.

cleaning ['kliːnɪŋ] n limpeza f.

cleanse [klenz] vt limpar.

cleanser ['klenzəʳ] n (for skin) creme m de limpeza.

clean-shaven [-'ʃeɪvn] adj sem barba nem bigode.

clear [klɪəʳ] adj claro(-ra); (unobstructed) livre; (sky) limpo(-pa) ◆ vt (area, road) desempedir; (pond) limpar; (jump over) saltar; (declare not guilty) absolver; (authorize) aprovar; (cheque) creditar ◆ vi (weather) melhorar; (fog) levantar; **the cheque will ~ in three days' time** o dinheiro estará disponível daqui a três dias; **to be ~ (about sthg)** compreender (algo); **to be ~ of sthg** (not touching) não tocar em algo; **to ~ one's throat** limpar a garganta; **to ~ one's table** tirar a mesa.

❑ **clear up** vt sep (room, toys) arrumar; (problem, confusion) clarificar ◆ vi (weather) melhorar; (tidy up) arrumar.

clearance ['klɪərəns] n autorização f; (free distance) espaço m livre.

clear-cut adj (issue, plan) bem definido(-da); (division) nítido(-da).

clearing ['klɪərɪŋ] n clareira f.

clearly ['klɪəlɪ] adv claramente; (obviously) evidentemente.

clearway ['klɪəweɪ] n (Brit) estrada onde é proibido estacionar.

cleavage ['kliːvɪdʒ] n (between breasts) colo m.

clef [klef] n clave f.

clementine ['kleməntaɪn] n clementina f.

clench [klentʃ] vt (fist, teeth) cerrar.

clergy ['klɜːdʒɪ] npl: **the ~** o clero.

clergyman [ˈklɜːdʒɪmən] (*pl* **-men** [-mən]) *n* clérigo *m*.

clerical [ˈklerɪkl] *adj* (*in office*) de escritório.

clerk [*Brit* klɑːk, *Am* klɜːrk] *n* (*in office*) empregado *m* (-da *f*) de escritório; (*Am: in shop*) empregado *m* (-da *f*).

clever [ˈklevər] *adj* (*person*) esperto (-ta); (*idea, device*) engenhoso(-osa).

click [klɪk] *n* estalido *m* ◆ *vi* (*make sound*) dar um estalido.

client [ˈklaɪənt] *n* cliente *mf*.

cliff [klɪf] *n* rochedo *m*.

climate [ˈklaɪmɪt] *n* clima *m*.

climax [ˈklaɪmæks] *n* clímax *m inv*.

climb [klaɪm] *vt* (*tree, ladder*) subir em; (*mountain*) escalar ◆ *vi* subir.

❑ **climb down** *vt fus* (*tree, ladder*) descer de; (*mountain*) descer ◆ *vi* descer.

❑ **climb up** *vt fus* (*tree, ladder*) subir em; (*mountain*) escalar.

climber [ˈklaɪmər] *n* (*person*) alpinista *mf*.

climbing [ˈklaɪmɪŋ] *n* alpinismo *m*; **to go ~** fazer alpinismo.

climbing frame *n* (*Brit*) barras de metal para as crianças treparem.

cling [klɪŋ] (*pt & pp* clung) *vi*: **to ~ to** (*hold tightly*) agarrar-se a; (*subj: clothes*) colar-se a.

clingfilm [ˈklɪŋfɪlm] *n* (*Brit*) película *f* aderente.

clinic [ˈklɪnɪk] *n* clínica *f*.

clip [klɪp] *n* clip *m* ◆ *vt* (*fasten*) segurar (com clip); (*cut*) cortar; (*ticket*) furar, validar.

clipboard [ˈklɪpbɔːd] *n* clipboard *m*, prancheta *f* com mola (*para segurar papéis*).

clippers [ˈklɪpəz] *npl* (*for hair*) máquina *f* de cortar cabelo; (*for nails*) alicate *m* de unhas (*Br*), corta-unhas *m inv* (*Port*); (*for plants, hedges*) tesoura *f* de aparar OR podar.

clipping [ˈklɪpɪŋ] *n* (*newspaper cutting*) recorte *m* de jornal.

cloak [kləʊk] *n* capa *f*.

cloakroom [ˈkləʊkrʊm] *n* (*for coats*) vestiário *m* (*Br*), bengaleiro *m* (*Port*); (*Brit: toilet*) banheiro *m* (*Br*), lavabos *mpl* (*Port*).

clock [klɒk] *n* relógio *m*; (*mileometer*) velocímetro *m* (*Br*), conta-quilómetros *m inv* (*Port*); **round the ~** noite e dia.

clockwise [ˈklɒkwaɪz] *adv* no sentido dos ponteiros do relógio.

clockwork [ˈklɒkwɜːk] *adj* de corda.

clog [klɒg] *n* tamanco *m* ◆ *vt* entupir.

close¹ [kləʊs] *adj* (*near*) junto(-ta); (*relation, friend, contact*) íntimo(-ma); (*link, resemblance*) grande; (*examination*) detalhado(-da); (*race, contest*) renhido(-da) ◆ *adv* perto; **~ by** perto; **~ to** (*near*) perto de; **~ to tears/rir**, a ponto de chorar/rir; **~ to despair** nos limites do desespero.

close² [kləʊz] *vt* fechar ◆ *vi* (*door, jar, eyes*) fechar-se; (*shop, office*) fechar; (*deadline, offer, meeting*) terminar.

❑ **close down** *vt sep & vi* fechar (definitivamente).

closed [kləʊzd] *adj* fechado(-da).

closely [ˈkləʊslɪ] *adv* (*related*) intimamente; (*follow, examine*) de perto.

closet [ˈklɒzɪt] *n* (*Am: cupboard*) armário *m*.

close-up [ˈkləʊs-] *n* primeiro plano *m*.

closing time [ˈkləʊzɪŋ-] *n* horário *m* de encerramento.

closure [ˈkləʊʒər] *n* (*of business, company*) encerramento *m*; (*of road, railway line*) bloqueio *m* (*Br*), corte *m* (*Port*).

clot [klɒt] *n* (*of blood*) coágulo *m*.

cloth [klɒθ] *n* (*fabric*) tecido *m*; (*piece of cloth*) pano *m*.

clothes [kləʊðz] *npl* roupa *f*.

clothesline [ˈkləʊðzlaɪn] *n* varal *m* (*Br*), estendal *m* (*Port*).

clothes peg *n* (*Brit*) pregador *m* de roupa (*Br*), mola *f* (*para a roupa*) (*Port*).

clothespin [ˈkləʊðzpɪn] (*Am*) = **clothes peg**.

clothes shop *n* loja *f* de vestuário.

clothing [ˈkləʊðɪŋ] *n* roupa *f*.

clotted cream [ˌklɒtɪd-] *n* creme coalhado típico da Cornualha.

cloud [klaʊd] *n* nuvem *f*.

cloudy [ˈklaʊdɪ] *adj* (*sky, day*) nublado(-da); (*liquid*) turvo(-va).

clove [kləʊv] *n* (*of garlic*) dente *m*.

❑ **cloves** *npl* (*spice*) cravo *m* (*Br*), cravinho *m* (*Port*).

clover [ˈkləʊvər] *n* trevo *m*.

clown [klaʊn] *n* palhaço *m*.

club [klʌb] *n* (*organization*) clube *m*; (*nightclub*) discoteca *f*, boate *f*; (*stick*) moca *f*.

❑ **clubs** *npl* (*in cards*) paus *mpl*.

clubbing [ˈklʌbɪŋ] *n*: **to go ~** (*inf*) ir à discoteca.

club class *n* = navigator class *f*.

club sandwich n (Am) sanduíche f (com três ou mais fatias de pão).

club soda n (Am) soda f.

cluck [klʌk] vi (hen) cacarejar.

clue [kluː] n pista f; **I haven't got a ~** não faço a mínima idéia.

clumsy ['klʌmzi] adj (person) desajeitado(-da).

clung [klʌŋ] pt & pp → cling.

cluster ['klʌstər] n cacho m ◆ vi (people) juntar-se, agrupar-se.

clutch [klʌtʃ] n embreagem f ◆ vt apertar.

clutter ['klʌtər] n desordem f ◆ vt encher.

cm (abbr of centimetre) cm.

c/o (abbr of care of) a/c.

Co. (abbr of company) C.ia.

coach [kəʊtʃ] n (bus) ônibus m (Br), autocarro m (Port); (of train) vagão m (Br), carruagem f (Port); (SPORT) treinador m (-ra f).

coach party n (Brit) grupo m de excursionistas.

coach station n rodoviária f.

coach trip n (Brit) excursão f (de ônibus).

coal [kəʊl] n carvão m.

coalition [,kəʊə'lɪʃn] n (POL) coligação f.

coal mine n mina f de carvão.

coarse [kɔːs] adj (rough) áspero(-ra); (vulgar) ordinário(-ria).

coast [kəʊst] n costa f.

coastal ['kəʊstl] adj costeiro(-ra).

coaster ['kəʊstər] n (for glass) base f para copos.

coastguard ['kəʊstgɑːd] n (person) guarda m costeiro; (organization) guarda f costeira.

coastline ['kəʊstlaɪn] n litoral m.

coat [kəʊt] n (garment) casaco m; (of animal) pêlo m ◆ vt: **to ~ sthg (with)** cobrir algo (com).

coat hanger n cabide m.

coating ['kəʊtɪŋ] n (on surface) revestimento m; (on food) camada f; **with a ~ of breadcrumbs** à milanesa.

coat of arms n brasão m.

coax [kəʊks] vt: **to ~ sb (to do** OR **into doing sthg)** convencer alguém (a fazer algo).

cobbled street ['kɒbld-] n calçada f, rua calçada com pedras arredondadas.

cobbler ['kɒblər] n sapateiro m (-ra f).

cobbles ['kɒblz] npl pedras fpl da calçada, pedras arredondadas para calçamento.

cobweb ['kɒbweb] n teia f de aranha.

Coca-Cola® [,kəʊkə'kəʊlə] n Coca-Cola® f.

cocaine [kəʊ'keɪn] n cocaína f.

cock [kɒk] n (male chicken) galo m.

cock-a-leekie [,kɒkə'liːkɪ] n caldo de galinha com alho-poró, cenoura e grãos de cevada.

cockerel ['kɒkrəl] n galo m jovem.

cockles ['kɒklz] npl berbigão m.

Cockney ['kɒknɪ] (pl -s) n (person) londrino m (-na f) (dos bairros populares do leste de Londres); (dialect, accent) dialeto ou pronúncia do leste de Londres.

cockpit ['kɒkpɪt] n cabine f.

cockroach ['kɒkrəʊtʃ] n barata f.

cocktail ['kɒkteɪl] n coquetel m.

cocktail party n coquetel m.

cock-up n (Brit: vulg) asneira f; **to make a ~ (of sthg)** fazer uma merda (de algo).

cocoa ['kəʊkəʊ] n cacau m.

coconut ['kəʊkənʌt] n coco m.

cod [kɒd] (pl inv) n bacalhau m.

code [kəʊd] n (system) código m; (dialling code) indicativo m.

cod-liver oil n óleo m de fígado de bacalhau.

coeducational [,kəʊedjuː'keɪʃənl] adj misto(-ta).

coffee ['kɒfɪ] n café m; **black ~** café; **white ~** = café m com leite (Br), = meia f de leite (Port); **ground/instant ~** café moído/instantâneo.

coffee bar n (Brit) café m.

coffee break n intervalo m para o café, hora f da bica (Port).

coffee morning n (Brit) reunião matinal, normalmente com fins beneficentes, em que se serve café.

coffeepot ['kɒfɪpɒt] n bule m para o café.

coffee shop n (cafe) café m; (in shops, airports) cafeteria f.

coffee table n mesa f pequena e baixa.

coffin ['kɒfɪn] n caixão m.

cog (wheel) [kɒg-] n roda f dentada.

coherent [kəʊ'hɪərənt] adj (logical) coerente.

coil [kɔɪl] n (of rope) rolo m; (Brit: contraceptive) DIU m ◆ vt enrolar.

coin [kɔɪn] *n* moeda *f.*

coinbox ['kɔɪnbɒks] *n (Brit)* telefone *m* público (de moedas).

coincide [,kəʊɪn'saɪd] *vi:* **to ~ (with)** coincidir (com).

coincidence [kəʊ'ɪnsɪdəns] *n* coincidência *f.*

coincidental [kəʊ,ɪnsɪ'dentl] *adj:* **any similarity is purely ~** qualquer semelhança é pura coincidência.

coke [kəʊk] *n (fuel)* coque *m; (inf: cocaine)* coca *f.*

Coke® [kəʊk] *n* Coca-Cola® *f.*

colander ['kʌləndər] *n* coador *m (Br),* escorregador *m (Port).*

cold [kəʊld] *adj* frio (fria) ◆ *n (illness)* resfriado *m (Br),* constipação *f (Port); (low temperature)* frio *m;* **to get ~** arrefecer; **to catch (a) ~** resfriar-se *(Br),* apanhar uma constipação *(Port).*

cold-blooded *adj (person)* insensível, sem dó nem piedade; *(killing)* a sangue-frio.

cold cuts *(Am)* = **cold meats**.

cold meats *npl* frios *mpl (Br),* carnes *fpl* frias *(Port).*

cold sore *n* herpes *f* labial.

coleslaw ['kəʊlslɔː] *n* salada de couve, cenoura e cebola picadas com maionese.

colic ['kɒlɪk] *n* cólica *f.*

collaborate [kə'læbəreɪt] *vi* colaborar.

collapse [kə'læps] *vi (building, tent)* cair; *(from exhaustion, illness)* ter um colapso.

collar ['kɒlər] *n (of coat, blouse)* gola *f; (of shirt)* colarinho *m; (of dog, cat)* coleira *f.*

collarbone ['kɒləbəʊn] *n* clavícula *f.*

colleague ['kɒliːg] *n* colega *mf.*

collect [kə'lekt] *vt (gather)* colher; *(as a hobby)* colecionar; *(go and get)* ir buscar; *(money)* cobrar ◆ *vi (dust, leaves)* acumular-se; *(crowd)* juntar-se ◆ *adv (Am):* **to call (sb) ~** fazer uma chamada a cobrar (para o destinatário).

collection [kə'lekʃn] *n* coleção *f; (of money)* cobrança *f; (of mail)* coleta *f (Br),* tiragem *f (Port).*

collector [kə'lektər] *n (as a hobby)* colecionador *m (-ra f).*

college ['kɒlɪdʒ] *n (school)* colégio *m; (Brit: of university)* organismo independente, formado por estudantes e professores, em que se dividem certas

universidades britânicas; *(Am: university)* universidade *f.*

collide [kə'laɪd] *vi:* **to ~ (with)** chocar (com).

collie ['kɒlɪ] *n* collie *m.*

colliery ['kɒljərɪ] *n* mina *f* de carvão.

collision [kə'lɪʒn] *n* colisão *f.*

colloquial [kə'ləʊkwɪəl] *adj* familiar, coloquial.

cologne [kə'ləʊn] *n* água-de-colônia *f.*

colon ['kəʊlən] *n (GRAMM)* dois pontos *mpl.*

colonel ['kɜːnl] *n* coronel *m.*

colonial [kə'ləʊnjəl] *adj (rule, power)* colonial.

colonize ['kɒlənaɪz] *vt (subj: people)* colonizar.

colony ['kɒlənɪ] *n* colônia *f.*

color ['kʌlər] *(Am)* = **colour**.

colossal [kə'lɒsl] *adj* colossal.

colour ['kʌlər] *n* cor *f* ◆ *adj (photograph, film)* a cores ◆ *vt (hair)* pintar; *(food)* colorir.

❑ **colour in** *vt sep* colorir.

colour-blind *adj* daltónico(-ca).

coloured ['kʌləd] *adj (having colour)* colorido(-da); *(person)* de cor; **brightly ~** de cores vivas.

colourful ['kʌləful] *adj (picture, garden, scenery)* colorido(-da); *(fig: person, place)* animado(-da).

colouring ['kʌlərɪŋ] *n (of food)* corante *m; (complexion)* tez *f.*

colouring book *n* livro *m* de colorir.

colour supplement *n* suplemento *m* a cores.

colour television *n* televisão *f* a cores.

colt [kəʊlt] *n* potro *m.*

column ['kɒləm] *n* coluna *f.*

coma ['kəʊmə] *n* coma *m* ou *f.*

comb [kəʊm] *n* pente *m* ◆ *vt:* **to ~ one's hair** pentear o cabelo.

combat ['kɒmbæt] *n* combate *m* ◆ *vt* combater.

combination [,kɒmbɪ'neɪʃn] *n* combinação *f.*

combine [kəm'baɪn] *vt:* **to ~ sthg (with)** combinar algo (com).

combine harvester ['kɒmbaɪn-'hɑːvɪstər] *n* máquina *f* de ceifar e debulhar.

come [kʌm] *(pt* came, *pp* come) *vi* 1. *(move)* vir; **we came by taxi** nós viemos de táxi; ~ **and see!** venha ver!; ~ **here!** venha cá!

2. *(arrive)* chegar; **to** ~ **home** voltar para casa; **they still haven't** ~ eles ainda não chegaram; **"coming soon"** "brevemente".

3. *(in order)* vir; **to** ~ **first/last** *(in sequence)* vir primeiro/no fim; *(in competition)* chegar primeiro/em último (lugar).

4. *(reach)*: **to** ~ **up/down to** chegar a.

5. *(become)*: **to** ~ **loose/undone** desapertar-se; **to** ~ **true** realizar-se.

6. *(be sold)* vir; **they** ~ **in packs of six** vêm em pacotes de seis.

❑ **come across** *vt fus* encontrar.

❑ **come along** *vi* *(progress)* desenvolver-se; *(arrive)* aparecer; ~ **along!** *(as encouragement)* anda!; *(hurry up)* anda logo!

❑ **come apart** *vi* desfazer-se.

❑ **come back** *vi* regressar.

❑ **come down** *vi* *(price)* baixar.

❑ **come down with** *vt fus* *(illness)* apanhar.

❑ **come from** *vt fus* vir de.

❑ **come in** *vi* *(enter)* entrar; *(arrive)* chegar; *(tide)* subir; ~ **in!** entre!

❑ **come off** *vi* *(button, top)* cair; *(succeed)* resultar.

❑ **come on** *vi* *(progress)* progredir; ~ **on!** vamos lá!

❑ **come out** *vi* sair; *(sun, moon)* aparecer.

❑ **come over** *vi* *(visit)*: **I'll** ~ **over tonight** passo por aí hoje à noite.

❑ **come round** *vi* *(regain consciousness)* voltar a si; **why don't you** ~ **round tomorrow?** por que você não passa aqui amanhã?

❑ **come to** *vt fus* *(subj: bill)* ser ao todo.

❑ **come up** *vi* *(go upstairs)* subir; *(be mentioned, happen)* surgir; *(sun, moon)* aparecer.

❑ **come up with** *vt fus* *(idea)* arranjar.

comeback ['kʌmbæk] *n* *(return)* regresso *m*; **to make a** ~ *(fashion)* voltar à moda; *(actor etc)* voltar ao palco.

comedian [kə'miːdjən] *n* cómico *m* (-ca *f*).

comedy ['kɒmədɪ] *n* *(TV programme, film, play)* comédia *f*; *(humour)* humor *m*.

comet ['kɒmɪt] *n* cometa *m*.

comfort ['kʌmfət] *n* conforto *m*; *(consolation)* consolo *m* ◆ *vt* consolar.

comfortable ['kʌmftəbl] *adj* confortável; *(fig: confident)* à vontade; *(financially)* bem de vida; **to be** ~ *(after operation)* estar bem.

comfortably ['kʌmftəblɪ] *adv* *(sit, live)* confortavelmente; *(sleep)* bem ◆ *adj* *(win)* à vontade.

comic ['kɒmɪk] *adj* cómico(-ca) ◆ *n* *(person)* cómico *m* (-ca *f*); *(magazine)* histórias *fpl* em quadrinhos *(Br)*, livro *m* de banda desenhada *(Port)*.

comical ['kɒmɪkl] *adj* cómico(-ca).

comic strip *n* história *f* em quadrinhos *(Br)*, banda *f* desenhada *(Port)*.

coming ['kʌmɪŋ] *adj* *(future)* próximo(-ma), que vem ◆ *n*: ~**s and goings** idas e vindas *fpl*.

comma ['kɒmə] *n* vírgula *f*.

command [kə'mɑːnd] *n* *(order)* ordem *f*; *(mastery)* domínio *m* ◆ *vt* *(order)* ordenar; *(be in charge of)* comandar.

commander [kə'mɑːndə'] *n* comandante *m*.

commando [kə'mɑːndəʊ] *(pl* -s OR -es*)* *n* *(unit)* unidade *f* de comandos; *(soldier)* comando *m*.

commemorate [kə'meməreɪt] *vt* comemorar.

commemoration [kə,memə'reɪʃn] *n*: **in** ~ **of** em honra de.

commence [kə'mens] *vi* *(fml)* começar.

commend [kə'mend] *vt* *(praise)*: **to** ~ **sb** *(on OR for sthg)* elogiar alguém (por algo).

comment ['kɒment] *n* comentário *m* ◆ *vi* comentar.

commentary ['kɒməntrɪ] *n* *(of event)* relato *m*; *(of football, rugby match)* comentário *m*.

commentator ['kɒmənteɪtə'] *n* *(on TV, radio)* comentarista *mf* *(Br)*, comentador *m* (-ra *f*) *(Port)*.

commerce ['kɒmɜːs] *n* comércio *m*.

commercial [kə'mɜːʃl] *adj* comercial ◆ *n* anúncio *m* *(em televisão, rádio)*.

commercial break *n* intervalo *m* *(para a publicidade)*.

commiserate [kə'mɪzəreɪt] *vi*: **to** ~ **(with sb)** compadecer-se (de alguém).

commission [kə'mɪʃn] *n* comissão *f*.

commit [kə'mɪt] *vt* *(crime, sin)* cometer; **to** ~ **o.s.** *(to sthg)* comprometer-se (a algo); **to** ~ **suicide** suicidar-se.

commitment [kə'mɪtmənt] *n* *(dedication)* empenho *m*; *(responsibility)* obrigação f, compromisso m.

committee [kəˈmɪtɪ] n comitê m, comissão f.

commodity [kəˈmɒdətɪ] n produto m.

common [ˈkɒmən] adj comum; (pej: vulgar) vulgar ♦ n (Brit: land) gramado m público (Br), relvado m público (Port); **in ~** em comum.

commonly [ˈkɒmənlɪ] adv (generally) geralmente.

Common Market n Mercado m Comum.

commonplace [ˈkɒmənpleɪs] adj comum.

common room n (for teachers) sala f dos professores; (for students) sala de convívio.

common sense n senso m comum.

Commonwealth [ˈkɒmənwelθ] n: **the ~** o Commonwealth.

commotion [kəˈməʊʃn] n comoção f, agitação f.

communal [ˈkɒmjʊnl] adj (bathroom, kitchen) comum.

communicate [kəˈmjuːnɪkeɪt] vi: **to ~ (with)** comunicar (com).

communication [kəˌmjuːnɪˈkeɪʃn] n comunicação f.

communication cord n (Brit) alarme m (em trem ou metrô).

communion [kəˈmjuːnjən] n (RELIG) comunhão f.

communism [ˈkɒmjʊnɪsm] n comunismo m.

communist [ˈkɒmjʊnɪst] n comunista mf.

community [kəˈmjuːnətɪ] n comunidade f.

community centre n centro m social.

commute [kəˈmjuːt] vi deslocar-se diariamente de casa para o local de trabalho (em outra localidade).

commuter [kəˈmjuːtər] n pessoa que se desloca diariamente de casa para o local de trabalho (em outra localidade).

compact [adj kəmˈpækt, n ˈkɒmpækt] adj compacto(-ta) ♦ n (for make-up) caixa f de pó-de-arroz; (Am: car) carro m pequeno.

compact disc [ˌkɒmpækt-] n CD m, disco m compacto.

compact disc player n leitor m de CDs.

companion [kəmˈpænjən] n compa-

nheiro m (-ra f).

company [ˈkʌmpənɪ] n companhia f; **to keep sb ~** fazer companhia a alguém.

company car n carro m da empresa.

comparable [ˈkɒmprəbl] adj comparável; **~ to** OR **with** comparável a.

comparative [kəmˈpærətɪv] adj (relative) relativo(-va); (GRAMM) comparativo(-va).

comparatively [kəmˈpærətɪvlɪ] adv comparativamente.

compare [kəmˈpeər] vt: **to ~ sthg (with)** comparar algo (com); **~d with** comparado com.

comparison [kəmˈpærɪsn] n comparação f; **in ~ with** em comparação com.

compartment [kəmˈpɑːtmənt] n compartimento m.

compass [ˈkʌmpəs] n (magnetic) bússola f; **a pair of ~es** um compasso.

compassion [kəmˈpæʃn] n compaixão f.

compassionate [kəmˈpæʃənət] adj compassivo(-va).

compatible [kəmˈpætəbl] adj compatível.

compel [kəmˈpel] vt (force) obrigar; **to ~ sb to do sthg** obrigar alguém a fazer algo.

compensate [ˈkɒmpenseɪt] vt compensar ♦ vi: **to ~ (for sthg)** compensar (algo); **to ~ sb for sthg** compensar alguém por algo.

compensation [ˌkɒmpenˈseɪʃn] n compensação f.

compete [kəmˈpiːt] vi (take part) participar; **to ~ with sb for sthg** competir com alguém por algo.

competent [ˈkɒmpɪtənt] adj competente.

competition [ˌkɒmpɪˈtɪʃn] n competição f; **the ~** (rivals) a concorrência.

competitive [kəmˈpetətɪv] adj competitivo(-va).

competitor [kəmˈpetɪtər] n (in race, contest) participante mf; (COMM, in game, show) concorrente mf.

compile [kəmˈpaɪl] vt compilar.

complacency [kəmˈpleɪsnsɪ] n complacência f, auto-satisfação f.

complain [kəmˈpleɪn] vi: **to ~ (about)** queixar-se (de).

complaint [kəmˈpleɪnt] n (statement)

queixa *f*; *(illness)* problema *m*.

complement ['kɒmplɪ,ment] *vt* complementar.

complementary [,kɒmplɪ'mentərɪ] *adj* complementar.

complete [kəm'pliːt] *adj* completo (-ta); *(finished)* concluído(-da) ◆ *vt (finish)* concluir; *(a form)* preencher; *(make whole)* completar; ~ **with** completo com.

completely [kəm'pliːtlɪ] *adv* completamente.

completion [kəm'pliːʃn] *n* conclusão *f*.

complex ['kɒmpleks] *adj* complexo (-xa) ◆ *n* complexo *m*.

complexion [kəm'plekʃn] *n (of skin)* tez *f*.

complicate ['kɒmplɪkeɪt] *vt* complicar.

complicated ['kɒmplɪkeɪtɪd] *adj* complicado(-da).

complication [,kɒmplɪ'keɪʃn] *n* complicação *f*.

compliment [*n* 'kɒmplɪmənt, *vb* 'kɒmplɪment] *n* elogio *m* ◆ *vt* elogiar.

complimentary [,kɒmplɪ'mentərɪ] *adj (seat, ticket)* gratuito(-ta); *(words, person)* lisonjeiro(-ra).

comply [kəm'plaɪ] *vi*: **to ~ with sthg** *(law, standards)* cumprir algo; *(request)* respeitar algo.

component [kəm'pəʊnənt] *n* componente *mf*.

compose [kəm'pəʊz] *vt (music)* compor; *(letter, poem)* escrever; **to be ~d of** ser composto de.

composed [kəm'pəʊzd] *adj* calmo (-ma).

composer [kəm'pəʊzə'] *n* compositor *m* (-ra *f*).

composition [,kɒmpə'zɪʃn] *n* composição *f*.

compost [*Brit* 'kɒmpɒst, *Am* 'kɒmpəʊst] *n* estrume *m*.

compound ['kɒmpaʊnd] *n (substance)* composto *m*; *(word)* palavra *f* composta.

comprehend [,kɒmprɪ'hend] *vt (understand)* compreender.

comprehension [,kɒmprɪ'henʃn] *n* compreensão *f*.

comprehensive [,kɒmprɪ'hensɪv] *adj* completo(-ta).

comprehensive (school) *n (Brit)* ≈ escola *f* secundária.

compressed air [kəm'prest-] *n* ar *m* comprimido.

comprise [kəm'praɪz] *vt* ser constituído(-da) por.

compromise ['kɒmprəmaɪz] *n* compromisso *m*.

compulsive [kəm'pʌlsɪv] *adj (behaviour, gambler, liar)* compulsivo(-va).

compulsory [kəm'pʌlsərɪ] *adj* obrigatório(-ria).

computer [kəm'pjuːtə'] *n* computador *m*.

computer game *n* jogo *m* de computador.

computerized [kəm'pjuːtəraɪzd] *adj* computadorizado(-da).

computer operator *n* operador *m* (-ra *f*) de computador.

computer programmer [-'prəʊgræmə'] *n* programador *m* (-ra *f*) de computador.

computing [kəm'pjuːtɪŋ] *n* informática *f*.

comrade ['kɒmreɪd] *n* camarada *mf*.

con [kɒn] *n (inf: trick)* truque *m*; **all mod ~s** com todas as comodidades.

concave [kɒn'keɪv] *adj* côncavo(-va).

conceal [kən'siːl] *vt* esconder.

concede [kən'siːd] *vt (admit)* admitir, reconhecer ◆ *vi* ceder.

conceited [kən'siːtɪd] *adj (pej)* convencido(-da).

conceive [kən'siːv] *vt* conceber.

concentrate ['kɒnsəntreɪt] *vi* concentrar-se ◆ *vt*: **to be ~d** *(in one place)* estar concentrado; **to ~ on sthg** concentrar-se em algo.

concentrated ['kɒnsəntreɪtɪd] *adj* concentrado(-da).

concentration [,kɒnsən'treɪʃn] *n* concentração *f*.

concentration camp *n* campo *m* de concentração.

concept ['kɒnsept] *n* conceito *m*.

concern [kən'sɜːn] *n (worry)* preocupação *f*; *(matter of interest)* assunto *m*; *(COMM)* negócio *m* ◆ *vt (be about)* ser sobre; *(worry)* preocupar; *(involve)* dizer respeito a; **to be ~ed about** estar preocupado com; **to be ~ed with** tratar de; **to ~ o.s. with sthg** preocupar-se com algo; **as far as I'm ~ed** no que me diz respeito; **it's no ~ of mine** isso não me diz respeito, não é da minha conta.

concerned [kən'sɜːnd] *adj (worried)*

preocupado(-da).

concerning [kən'sɔːnɪŋ] *prep* acerca de.

concert ['kɒnsət] *n* concerto *m*.

concert hall *n* sala *f* de concertos.

concertina [ˌkɒnsə'tiːnə] *n* concertina *f*.

concession [kən'seʃn] *n* (reduced price) desconto *m*.

concise [kən'saɪs] *adj* conciso(-sa).

conclude [kən'kluːd] *vt* concluir ◆ *vi* (fml: end) terminar.

conclusion [kən'kluːʒn] *n* (decision) conclusão *f*; (end) fim *m*.

conclusive [kən'kluːsɪv] *adj* concludente, decisivo(-va).

concoction [kən'kɒkʃn] *n* (mixture, drink) mistura *f*.

concourse ['kɒŋkɔːs] *n* (hall) saguão *m* (Br), vestíbulo *m* (Port).

concrete ['kɒŋkriːt] *adj* (building, path) de concreto; (idea, plan) concreto(-ta) ◆ *n* concreto *m* (Br), betão *m* (Port).

concussion [kən'kʌʃn] *n* traumatismo *m* craniano.

condemn [kən'dem] *vt* condenar; **to ~ sb to sthg** (JUR) condenar alguém a algo.

condensation [ˌkɒnden'seɪʃn] *n* condensação *f*.

condensed milk [kən'denst-] *n* leite *m* condensado.

condescending [ˌkɒndɪ'sendɪŋ] *adj* condescendente.

condition [kən'dɪʃn] *n* (state) estado *m*; (proviso) condição *f*; **a heart/liver ~** problemas de coração/fígado; **to be out of ~** não estar em forma; **on ~ that** com a condição de.
❑ **conditions** *npl* (circumstances) condições *fpl*.

conditional [kən'dɪʃənl] *n* (GRAMM) condicional *m*.

conditioner [kən'dɪʃnəʳ] *n* amaciador *m*.

condo ['kɒndəʊ] (Am: inf) = **condominium**.

condolences ['kɒndəʊlənsɪz] *npl* condolências *fpl*.

condom ['kɒndəm] *n* preservativo *m*.

condominium [ˌkɒndə'mɪnɪəm] *n* (Am) condomínio *m*.

condone [kən'dəʊn] *vt* defender.

conducive [kən'djuːsɪv] *adj*: **~ to** ideal para.

conduct [vb kən'dʌkt, *n* 'kɒndʌkt] *vt* (investigation, business) levar a cabo; (MUS) reger ◆ *n* (fml: behaviour) conduta *f*; **to ~ o.s.** (fml) comportar-se.

conductor [kən'dʌktəʳ] *n* (MUS) maestro *m*; (on bus) cobrador *m* (-ra *f*); (Am: on train) revisor *m* (-ra *f*).

cone [kəʊn] *n* cone *m*; (for ice cream) casquinha *f* (Br), cone (Port).

confectioner's [kən'fekʃnəz] *n* (shop) confeitaria *f*.

confectionery [kən'fekʃnərɪ] *n* confeitaria *f*.

confer [kən'fɜːʳ] *vi* consultar ◆ *vt* (fml): **to ~ sthg on sb** conferir algo com alguém.

conference ['kɒnfərəns] *n* conferência *f*.

confess [kən'fes] *vi*: **to ~ (to sthg)** confessar (algo).

confession [kən'feʃn] *n* confissão *f*.

confetti [kən'fetɪ] *n* confetti *mpl*, papelinhos *mpl* (Port).

confide [kən'faɪd] *vi*: **to ~ in sb** confiar em alguém.

confidence ['kɒnfɪdəns] *n* confiança *f*; **to have ~ in** ter confiança em.

confident ['kɒnfɪdənt] *adj* (self-assured) seguro(-ra) de si; (certain) seguro(-ra).

confidential [ˌkɒnfɪ'denʃl] *adj* confidencial.

confined [kən'faɪnd] *adj* restrito(-ta).

confinement [kən'faɪnmənt] *n* reclusão *f*.

confirm [kən'fɜːm] *vt* confirmar.

confirmation [ˌkɒnfə'meɪʃn] *n* confirmação *f*; (RELIG) crisma *m*.

confiscate ['kɒnfɪskeɪt] *vt* confiscar.

conflict [*n* 'kɒnflɪkt, *vb* kən'flɪkt] *n* conflito *m* ◆ *vi*: **to ~ (with)** estar em desacordo (com).

conform [kən'fɔːm] *vi*: **to ~ (to)** obedecer (a).

confront [kən'frʌnt] *vt* confrontar.

confrontation [ˌkɒnfrʌn'teɪʃn] *n* confrontação *f*.

confuse [kən'fjuːz] *vt* confundir; **to ~ sthg with sthg** confundir algo com algo.

confused [kən'fjuːzd] *adj* confuso(-sa).

confusing [kən'fjuːzɪŋ] *adj* confuso(-sa).

confusion [kən'fjuːʒn] *n* confusão *f*.

congested [kən'dʒestɪd] *adj* (street)

congestionado(-da).

congestion [kən'dʒestʃn] *n (traffic)* congestionamento *m*.

congratulate [kən'grætʃʊleɪt] *vt*: to ~ sb (on sthg) felicitar alguém (por algo).

congratulations [kən,grætʃʊ'leɪʃənz] *excl* parabéns!

congregate ['kɒŋgrɪgeɪt] *vi* juntar-se.

congregation [,kɒŋgrɪ'geɪʃn] *n* congregação *f*.

Congress ['kɒŋgres] *n (Am)* Congresso *m*.

congressman ['kɒŋgresmən] *(pl* -men [-mən]) *n (Am: POL)* congressista *m*.

conifer ['kɒnɪfə*r*] *n* conífera *f*.

conjugation [,kɒndʒʊ'geɪʃn] *n (GRAMM)* conjugação *f*.

conjunction [kən'dʒʌŋkʃn] *n (GRAMM)* conjunção *f*.

conjunctivitis [kən,dʒʌŋktɪ'vaɪtɪs] *n* conjuntivite *f*.

conjurer ['kʌndʒərə*r*] *n* prestidigitador *m* (-ra *f*).

conker ['kɒŋkə*r*] *n (Brit)* castanha-da-Índia *f*.

conman ['kɒnmæn] *(pl* -men [-men]) *n* vigarista *mf*, burlão *m (Port)*.

connect [kə'nekt] *vt* ligar ◆ *vi*: to ~ with *(train, plane)* fazer conexão com; to ~ sthg with sthg *(associate)* ligar algo com algo.

connected [kə'nektɪd] *adj* relacionado(-da); ~ with relacionado com.

connecting flight [kə'nektɪŋ-] *n* vôo *m* de conexão.

connection [kə'nekʃn] *n* ligação *f*; a bad ~ *(on phone)* uma ligação ruim; a loose ~ *(in machine)* um fio solto; in ~ with em relação a.

connoisseur [,kɒnə'sɜː*r*] *n* conhecedor *m* (-ra *f*).

conquer ['kɒŋkə*r*] *vt* conquistar.

conquest ['kɒŋkwest] *n* conquista *f*.

conscience ['kɒnʃəns] *n* consciência *f*.

conscientious [,kɒnʃɪ'enʃəs] *adj* consciencioso(-osa).

conscious ['kɒnʃəs] *adj (awake)* consciente; *(deliberate)* deliberado(-da); to be ~ of estar consciente de.

consciousness ['kɒnʃəsnɪs] *n* consciência *f*.

conscript ['kɒnskrɪpt] *n (MIL)* recruta *mf*.

consecutive [kən'sekjʊtɪv] *adj* consecutivo(-va).

consent [kən'sent] *n* consentimento *m*.

consequence ['kɒnsɪkwəns] *n (result)* conseqüência *f*.

consequently ['kɒnsɪkwəntlɪ] *adv* conseqüentemente.

conservation [,kɒnsə'veɪʃn] *n* conservação *f*.

conservative [kən'sɜːvətɪv] *adj* conservador(-ra).

❑ **Conservative** *adj* conservador(-ra) ◆ *n* conservador *m* (-ra *f*).

conservatory [kən'sɜːvətrɪ] *n* jardim-de-inverno *m (Br)*, marquise *f (Port)*.

conserve [*n* kən'sɜːv, *vb* kən'sɜːv] *n* compota *f* ◆ *vt* preservar.

consider [kən'sɪdə*r*] *vt* considerar; to ~ doing sthg pensar em fazer algo.

considerable [kən'sɪdrəbl] *adj* considerável.

considerably [kən'sɪdrəblɪ] *adv* consideravelmente.

considerate [kən'sɪdərət] *adj (person)* gentil; that's very ~ of you que gentileza de sua parte.

consideration [kən,sɪdə'reɪʃn] *n* consideração *f*; to take sthg into ~ ter algo em consideração.

considering [kən'sɪdərɪŋ] *prep* tendo em conta.

consist [kən'sɪst] : **consist in** *vt fus* consistir em.

❑ **consist of** *vt fus* consistir em.

consistency [kən'sɪstənsɪ] *n* consistência *f*.

consistent [kən'sɪstənt] *adj* consistente.

consolation [,kɒnsə'leɪʃn] *n* consolação *f*.

console ['kɒnsəʊl] *n* consola *f*.

consonant ['kɒnsənənt] *n* consoante *f*.

conspicuous [kən'spɪkjʊəs] *adj* que dá nas vistas.

conspiracy [kən'spɪrəsɪ] *n* conspiração *f*.

constable ['kʌnstəbl] *n (Brit)* policial *mf (Br)*, polícia *mf (Port)*.

constant ['kɒnstənt] *adj* constante.

constantly ['kɒnstəntlɪ] *adv* constantemente.

constipated ['kɒnstɪpeɪtɪd] *adj*: to be ~ ter prisão de ventre.

constipation [ˌkɒnstɪ'peɪʃn] *n* prisão
f de ventre, constipação *f (Br)*.
constituency [kən'stɪtjuənsɪ] *n* círculo *m* eleitoral.
constitute ['kɒnstɪtjuːt] *vt (represent)*
constituir.
constitution [ˌkɒnstɪ'tjuːʃn] *n*
(health) constituição *f* física.
constraint [kən'streɪnt] *n (restriction)*
restrição *f*; ~ **on sthg** restrição a algo.
construct [kən'strʌkt] *vt* construir.
construction [kən'strʌkʃn] *n* construção *f*; **under** ~ em construção.
constructive [kən'strʌktɪv] *adj* construtivo(-va).
consul ['kɒnsəl] *n* cônsul *mf*.
consulate ['kɒnsjulət] *n* consulado *m*.
consult [kən'sʌlt] *vt* consultar.
consultant [kən'sʌltənt] *n (Brit: doctor)* médico *m* (-ca *f*) especialista.
consulting room [kən'sʌltɪŋ-] *n*
consultório *m*, sala *f* de consultas.
consume [kən'sjuːm] *vt* consumir.
consumer [kən'sjuːməʳ] *n* consumidor *m* (-ra *f*).
consumption [kən'sʌmpʃn] *n (use)*
consumo *m*.
contact ['kɒntækt] *n* contato *m* ♦ *vt*
contatar; **in** ~ **with** em contato com.
contact lens *n* lente *f* de contato.
contagious [kən'teɪdʒəs] *adj* contagioso(-osa).
contain [kən'teɪn] *vt* conter.
container [kən'teɪnəʳ] *n (bowl etc)*
recipiente *m*; *(for cargo)* container *m*
(Br), contentor *m (Port)*.
contaminate [kən'tæmɪneɪt] *vt* contaminar.
contemplate ['kɒntempleɪt] *vt (consider)* contemplar.
contemporary [kən'tempərərɪ] *adj*
contemporâneo(-nea) ♦ *n* contemporâneo *m* (-nea *f*).
contempt [kən'tempt] *n (scorn)* desprezo *m*; ~ **for** desprezo por.
contend [kən'tend] **: contend with** *vt*
fus enfrentar.
contender [kən'tendəʳ] *n* candidato
m (-ta *f*).
content [*adj* kən'tent, *n* 'kɒntent] *adj*
satisfeito(-ta) ♦ *n (of vitamins, fibre)*
quantidade *f*; *(of alcohol, fat)* teor *m*.
❑ **contents** *npl (things inside)* conteúdo
m; *(at beginning of book)* índice *m*.
contented [kən'tentɪd] *adj* contente,
satisfeito(-ta).

contest [*n* 'kɒntest, *vb* kən'test] *n*
(competition) concurso *m*; *(struggle)* luta
f ♦ *vt (election, seat)* candidatar-se a;
(decision, will) contestar.
contestant [kən'testənt] *n (in quiz
show)* concorrente *mf*; *(in race)* participante *mf*.
context ['kɒntekst] *n* contexto *m*.
continent ['kɒntɪnənt] *n* continente
m; **the Continent** *(Brit)* a Europa
Continental.
continental [ˌkɒntɪ'nentl] *adj (Brit:
European)* da Europa Continental.
continental breakfast *n* típico
café da manhã composto por café, pão ou
croissants, manteiga e geléia.
continental quilt *n (Brit)* edredom
m (Br), edredão *m (Port)*.
continual [kən'tɪnjuəl] *adj* contínuo
(-nua).
continually [kən'tɪnjuəlɪ] *adv* continuamente.
continue [kən'tɪnjuː] *vt & vi* continuar; **to** ~ **doing sthg** continuar a
fazer algo; **to** ~ **with sthg** continuar
com algo.
continuous [kən'tɪnjuəs] *adj* contínuo(-nua).
continuously [kən'tɪnjuəslɪ] *adv*
continuamente.
contortion [kən'tɔːʃn] *n (position)*
contorção *f*.
contour ['kɒn,tuəʳ] *n* contorno *m*.
contraband ['kɒntrəbænd] *adj* de
contrabando ♦ *n* contrabando *m*.
contraception [ˌkɒntrə'sepʃn] *n* contracepção *f*.
contraceptive [ˌkɒntrə'septɪv] *n*
anticoncepcional *m*.
contract [*n* 'kɒntrækt, *vb* kən'trækt] *n*
contrato *m* ♦ *vt (fml: illness)* contrair.
contraction [kən'trækʃn] *n (reduction
in size, length)* contração *f*.
contradict [ˌkɒntrə'dɪkt] *vt* contradizer.
contradiction [ˌkɒntrə'dɪkʃn] *n* contradição *f*.
contraflow ['kɒntrəfləu] *n (Brit)*
estreitamento e/ou inversão do sentido
normal de uma pista devido a obras ou
acidente, garrafão *m (Port)*.
contraption [kən'træpʃn] *n* gerigonça *f*.
contrary ['kɒntrərɪ] *n*: **on the** ~ pelo
cohtrário.
contrast [*n* 'kɒntrɑːst, *vb* kən'trɑːst] *n*

contraste *m* ◆ *vt* contrastar; **in ~ to** ao contrário de.

contribute [kən'trɪbjuːt] *vt (help, money)* contribuir com ◆ *vi*: **to ~ to** contribuir para.

contribution [,kɒntrɪ'bjuːʃn] *n* contribuição *f*.

contributor [kən'trɪbjutər] *n (to magazine, newspaper)* colaborador *m* (-ra *f*).

contrive [kən'traɪv] *vt (fml: manage)*: **to ~ to do sthg** conseguir fazer algo.

contrived [kən'traɪvd] *adj (plot, ending)* inverosímil; *(reaction)* forçado (-da).

control [kən'trəul] *n* controle *m* ◆ *vt* controlar; **to be in ~** controlar a situação; **out of ~** fora de controle; **under ~** sob controle.

❑ **controls** *npl (of TV, video)* controle *m (Br)*, telecomando *m (Port)*; *(of plane)* comandos *mpl*.

controller [kən'trəulər] *n (of TV, radio)* diretor *m* (-ra *f*); **financial ~** administrador *m* (-ra *f*).

control panel *n* painel *m* de controle.

control tower *n* torre *f* de controle.

controversial [,kɒntrə'vɜːʃl] *adj* controverso(-sa).

controversy ['kɒntrəvɜːsɪ, Brit kən'trɒvəsɪ] *n* controvérsia *f*.

convalesce [,kɒnvə'les] *vi* convalescer.

convenience [kən'viːnjəns] *n* conveniência *f*; **at your ~** quando (lhe) for possível.

convenience store *n (Am)* = minimercado *m (muitas vezes aberto 24 horas por dia)*.

convenient [kən'viːnjənt] *adj* conveniente.

convent ['kɒnvənt] *n* convento *m*.

conventional [kən'venʃənl] *adj* convencional.

converge [kən'vɜːdʒ] *vi* convergir; **to ~ on** convergir em.

conversation [,kɒnvə'seɪʃn] *n* conversa *f*.

conversion [kən'vɜːʃn] *n* conversão *f*.

convert [kən'vɜːt] *vt* converter; **to ~ sthg into** converter algo em.

converted [kən'vɜːtɪd] *adj (barn, loft)* convertido(-da).

convertible [kən'vɜːtəbl] *n* conversí-

vel *m (Br)*, carro *m* descapotável *(Port)*.

convex [kɒn'veks] *adj* convexo(-xa).

convey [kən'veɪ] *vt (fml: transport)* transportar; *(idea, impression)* transmitir.

conveyer belt [kən'veɪər-] *n (in airport)* esteira *f* rolante *(Br)*, tapete *m* rolante *(Port)*; *(in factory)* correia *f* transportadora.

conveyor belt [kən'veɪər-] *(Am)* = **conveyer belt**.

convict [*n* 'kɒnvɪkt, *vb* kən'vɪkt] *n* preso *m* (-sa *f*) ◆ *vt*: **to ~ sb (of)** condenar alguém (por).

conviction [kən'vɪkʃn] *n* convicção *f*; *(JUR)* condenação *f*.

convince [kən'vɪns] *vt*: **to ~ sb (of sthg)** convencer alguém (de algo); **to ~ sb to do sthg** convencer alguém a fazer algo.

convincing [kən'vɪnsɪŋ] *adj (person, argument)* convincente; *(victory, win)* esmagador(-ra).

convoy ['kɒnvɔɪ] *n* comboio *m*.

convulsion [kən'vʌlʃn] *n (MED)* convulsão *f*.

coo [kuː] *vi (bird)* arrulhar.

cook [kʊk] *n* cozinheiro *m* (-ra *f*) ◆ *vt (meal)* preparar; *(food)* cozinhar ◆ *vi (person)* cozinhar; *(food)* cozer.

cookbook ['kʊkbʊk] = **cookery book**.

cooker ['kʊkər] *n* fogão *m*.

cookery ['kʊkərɪ] *n* culinária *f*.

cookery book *n* livro *m* de culinária OR cozinha.

cookie ['kʊkɪ] *n (Am)* biscoito *m (Br)*, bolacha *f (Port)*.

cooking ['kʊkɪŋ] *n (activity)* culinária *f*; *(food)* cozinha *f*.

cooking apple *n* maçã *f* para cozer.

cooking oil *n* óleo *m* de cozinhar.

cool [kuːl] *adj (temperature)* fresco (-ca); *(calm)* calmo(-ma); *(unfriendly)* frio (fria); *(inf: great)* genial *(Br)*, bestial *(Port)* ◆ *vt* arrefecer.

❑ **cool down** *vi (become colder)* arrefecer; *(become calmer)* acalmar-se.

cool box *n (Brit)* mala *f* frigorífica.

cooler ['kuːlər] *(Am)* = **cool box**.

coop [kuːp] *n* capoeira *f*.

❑ **coop up** *vt sep (inf)* enfiar.

cooperate [kəʊ'ɒpəreɪt] *vi* cooperar.

cooperation [kəʊ,ɒpə'reɪʃn] *n* cooperação *f*.

cooperative [kəʊ'ɒpərətɪv] *adj*

(helpful) cooperante.

coordinate [kəʊˈɔːdɪneɪt] *vt* coordenar.

coordinates [kəʊˈɔːdɪnəts] *npl (clothes)* conjuntos *mpl*.

coordination [kəʊˌɔːdɪˈneɪʃn] *n* coordenação *f*.

cop [kɒp] *n (inf: policeman)* policial *mf (Br)*, polícia *mf (Port)*.

cope [kəʊp] *vi:* **to ~ with** *(problem, situation)* lidar com; *(work)* aguentar.

Copenhagen [ˌkəʊpənˈheɪgən] *n* Copenhague *s*.

copilot [ˈkəʊˌpaɪlət] *n* co-piloto *mf*.

copper [ˈkɒpəʳ] *n* cobre *m*; *(Brit: inf: coin)* = tostão *m*, *moedas de cobre no valor de um ou dois pence.*

copy [ˈkɒpɪ] *n* cópia *f*; *(of newspaper, book)* exemplar *m* ♦ *vt* copiar.

copyright [ˈkɒpɪraɪt] *n* direitos *mpl* autorais.

coral [ˈkɒrəl] *n* coral *m*.

cord [kɔːd] *n (string)* cordão *m*; *(wire)* fio *m*.

cord(uroy) [ˈkɔːd(ərɔɪ)] *n* veludo *m* cotelê *(Br)*, bombazina *f (Port)*.

core [kɔːʳ] *n (of fruit)* caroço *m*.

coriander [ˌkɒrɪˈændəʳ] *n* coentro *m*.

cork [kɔːk] *n (in bottle)* rolha *f*.

corkscrew [ˈkɔːkskruː] *n* saca-rolhas *m inv*.

corn [kɔːn] *n (Brit: crop)* cereal *m*; *(Am: maize)* milho *m*; *(on foot)* calo *m*.

corned beef [kɔːnd-] *n* carne *f* de vaca enlatada.

corner [ˈkɔːnəʳ] *n* canto *m*; *(bend in road)* curva *f*; **it's just around the ~** fica ali mesmo ao virar a esquina.

corner shop *n (Brit)* mercearia *f*, quitanda *f (Br)*, mini-mercado *m (Port)*.

cornet [ˈkɔːnɪt] *n (Brit: ice-cream cone)* casquinha *f (Br)*, cone *m (Port)*.

cornflakes [ˈkɔːnfleɪks] *npl* Cornflakes® *mpl*, flocos *mpl* de milho.

corn-on-the-cob [-kɒb] *n* espiga de milho cozida, servida com manteiga.

Cornwall [ˈkɔːnwɔːl] *n* Cornualha *f*.

coronation [ˌkɒrəˈneɪʃn] *n* coroação *f*.

corporal [ˈkɔːpərəl] *n* cabo *m*.

corporal punishment *n* castigos *mpl* corporais.

corporation [ˌkɔːpəˈreɪʃn] *n (council)* conselho *m* municipal; *(large company)* corporação *f*, companhia *f*.

corpse [kɔːps] *n* cadáver *m*.

correct [kəˈrekt] *adj* correto(-ta) ♦ *vt* corrigir.

correction [kəˈrekʃn] *n* correção *f*.

correspond [ˌkɒrɪˈspɒnd] *vi:* **to ~ (to)** *(match)* corresponder (a); **to ~ (with)** *(exchange letters)* corresponder-se (com).

correspondence [ˌkɒrɪˈspɒndəns] *n* correspondência *f*.

correspondent [ˌkɒrɪˈspɒndənt] *n* correspondente *mf*.

corresponding [ˌkɒrɪˈspɒndɪŋ] *adj* correspondente.

corridor [ˈkɒrɪdɔːʳ] *n* corredor *m*.

corrosion [kəˈrəʊʒn] *n* corrosão *f*.

corrugated iron [ˈkɒrəgeɪtɪd-] *n* ferro *m* corrugado *(Br)*, folha-deflandres *f (Port)*.

corrupt [kəˈrʌpt] *adj* corrupto(-ta).

corruption [kəˈrʌpʃn] *n* corrupção *f*.

corset [ˈkɔːsɪt] *n* espartilho *m*.

cosmetics [kɒzˈmetɪks] *npl* cosméticos *mpl*.

cosmopolitan [kɒzməˈpɒlɪtn] *adj* cosmopolita.

cost [kɒst] *(pt & pp* **cost)** *n* custo *m* ♦ *vt* custar; **how much does it ~?** quanto custa?

co-star [ˈkəʊ-] *n* co-protagonista *mf*.

costly [ˈkɒstlɪ] *adj (expensive)* caro (-ra).

costume [ˈkɒstjuːm] *n (of actor)* roupa *f (Br)*, fato *m (Port)*; *(of country, region)* traje *m*.

cosy [ˈkəʊzɪ] *adj (Brit: room, house)* aconchegante.

cot [kɒt] *n (Brit: for baby)* berço *m*; *(Am: camp bed)* cama *f* de campismo.

cottage [ˈkɒtɪdʒ] *n* casa *f* de campo.

cottage cheese *n* = requeijão *m*.

cottage pie *n (Brit)* empadão *m (de carne de vaca picada)*.

cotton [ˈkɒtn] *adj (dress, shirt)* de algodão ♦ *n (cloth)* algodão *m*; *(thread)* linha *f* (de coser).

cotton candy *n (Am)* algodão *m* doce.

cotton wool *n* algodão *m* (hidrófilo).

couch [kaʊtʃ] *n (sofa)* sofá *m*; *(at doctor's)* cama *f*.

couchette [kuːˈʃet] *n* couchette *f*.

cough [kɒf] *n* tosse *f* ♦ *vi* tossir; **to have a ~** estar com tosse.

cough mixture *n* xarope *m* para a tosse.

cough sweet n (Brit) pastilha f para a tosse.

cough syrup = cough mixture.

could [kʊd] pt → can.

couldn't ['kʊdnt] = could not.

could've ['kʊdəv] = could have.

council ['kaʊnsl] n (Brit: of town) prefeitura f (Br), câmara f (Port); (Brit: of county) = governo m civil; (organization) conselho m.

council estate n conjunto m residencial (Br), bairro m de habitação social (Port) (pertencente ao Estado).

council house n (Brit) casa f popular (Br), habitação f social (Port), casa pertencente ao Estado alugada a baixo preço.

councillor ['kaʊnsələr] n (Brit: of town, county) ~ vereador m (-ra f).

council tax n (Brit) imposto local pago à prefeitura, relativo aos serviços de saneamento, água, transportes, etc, por esta fornecidos.

counsellor ['kaʊnsələr] n (Brit) conselheiro m (-ra f).

counselor ['kaʊnsələr] (Am) = counsellor.

count [kaʊnt] vt & vi contar ♦ n (nobleman) conde m.

❏ **count on** vt fus contar com.

countdown ['kaʊntdaʊn] n contagem f decrescente.

counter ['kaʊntər] n (in shop, bank) balcão m; (in board game) ficha f.

counteract [,kaʊntər'ækt] vt compensar, contrabalançar.

counterattack [,kaʊntərə'tæk] n contra-ataque m.

counterclockwise [,kaʊntə-'klɒkwaɪz] adv (Am) no sentido contrário ao dos ponteiros do relógio.

counterfeit ['kaʊntəfɪt] adj falso(-sa) ♦ vt falsificar, forjar.

counterfoil ['kaʊntəfɔɪl] n talão m.

counterpart ['kaʊntəpɑːt] n homólogo m (-ga f).

countess ['kaʊntɪs] n condessa f.

countless ['kaʊntlɪs] adj inúmeros (-ras).

country ['kʌntrɪ] n país m; (countryside) campo m ♦ adj do campo.

country and western n música f country.

country dancing n dança f folclórica.

country house n = casa f de campo (Br), = solar m (Port).

countryman ['kʌntrɪmən] (pl -men [-mən]) n compatriota m.

country road n estrada f rural.

countryside ['kʌntrɪsaɪd] n campo m.

county ['kaʊntɪ] n (in Britain) condado m; (in US) divisão administrativa de um estado, nos EUA.

county council n (Brit) organismo que administra um condado, ~ conselho m distrital.

coup [kuː] n: ~ (d'état) golpe m de Estado.

couple ['kʌpl] n casal m; **a ~ (of)** (two) dois (duas); (a few) dois ou três (duas ou três).

coupon ['kuːpɒn] n cupom m (Br), cupão m (Port).

courage ['kʌrɪdʒ] n coragem f.

courgette [kɔː'ʒet] n (Brit) abobrinha f (Br), courgette f (Port).

courier ['kʊrɪər] n (for holidaymakers) guia mf; (for delivering letters, packages) mensageiro m (-ra f).

course [kɔːs] n curso m; (of meal) prato m; (of treatment, injections) tratamento m; (of ship, plane) rota f; (for golf) campo m; **of ~** (certainly) com certeza, claro; (evidently) claro; **of ~ not** claro que não; **in the ~ of** no decurso de.

coursework ['kɔːswɜːk] n trabalho m realizado durante o curso.

court [kɔːt] n (JUR: building, room) tribunal m; (SPORT) quadra f (Br), campo m (Port); (of king, queen) corte f.

courteous ['kɜːtjəs] adj cortês.

courtesy ['kɜːtɪsɪ] n (polite behaviour) cortesia f; **(by) ~ of** com a autorização de.

courtesy coach ['kɜːtɪsɪ-] n ônibus m gratuito (de aeroporto, hotel, etc).

courthouse ['kɔːthaʊs, pl -haʊzɪz] n (Am) tribunal m.

court shoes npl sapatos mpl (simples) de salto alto.

courtyard ['kɔːtjɑːd] n pátio m.

cousin ['kʌzn] n primo m (-ma f).

cove [kəʊv] n enseada f.

cover ['kʌvər] n cobertura f; (lid) tampa f; (of book, magazine) capa f; (blanket) coberta f ♦ vt cobrir; (travel) percorrer; (apply to) abranger; **to take ~** abrigar-se; **to be ~ed in** estar coberto de; **to ~ sthg with sthg** cobrir algo com algo.

❏ **cover up** vt sep (put cover on) cobrir; (facts, truth) encobrir.

coverage ['kʌvərɪdʒ] *n (of news)* cobertura *f* (jornalística).
cover charge *n* couvert *m*.
covering ['kʌvərɪŋ] *n (for floor etc)* revestimento *m*; *(of dust, snow etc)* camada *f*.
covering letter *n (Brit)* carta *f* de apresentação.
cover letter *(Am)* = **covering letter**.
cover note *n (Brit)* apólice *f* de seguro provisória.
cow [kaʊ] *n (animal)* vaca *f*.
coward ['kaʊəd] *n* covarde *mf*.
cowardly ['kaʊədlɪ] *adj* covarde.
cowboy ['kaʊbɔɪ] *n* cow-boy *m*, vaqueiro *m (Br)*.
cower ['kaʊə^r] *vi* encolher-se.
crab [kræb] *n* caranguejo *m*.
crack [kræk] *n (in cup, glass, wood)* rachadura *f*; *(gap)* fenda *f* ◆ *vt (cup, glass, wood)* rachar; *(nut, egg)* partir; *(inf: joke)* contar; *(whip)* estalar ◆ *vi* rachar.
cracker ['krækə^r] *n (biscuit)* bolacha *f* de água e sal; *(for Christmas) tubo de papel com uma pequena surpresa, típico do Natal, que produz um estalo ao ser aberto*.
cradle ['kreɪdl] *n* berço *m*.
craft [krɑ:ft] *n (skill, trade)* ofício *m*; *(boat: pl inv)* embarcação *f*.
craftsman ['krɑ:ftsmən] *(pl* **-men** [-mən]) *n* artesão *m*.
craftsmanship ['krɑ:ftsmənʃɪp] *n* habilidade *f*, arte *f*.
crafty ['krɑ:ftɪ] *adj* astuto(-ta).
crag [kræg] *n* penhasco *m*, rochedo *m* escarpado.
cram [kræm] *vt*: **to ~ sthg into** enfiar algo em; **to be crammed with** estar a abarrotar de.
cramp [kræmp] *n* cãibra *f*; **stomach ~s** dores *fpl* de estômago *(fortes)*.
cranberry ['krænbərɪ] *n* arando *m*.
cranberry sauce *n molho de arandos normalmente servido com peru assado*.
crane [kreɪn] *n (machine)* guindaste *m*.
crap [kræp] *n (vulg)* merda *f* ◆ *adj (vulg)*: **the film was ~** o filme era uma porcaria.
crash [kræʃ] *n (accident)* colisão *f*; *(noise)* estrondo *m* ◆ *vt (car)* bater com ◆ *vi (car, plane, train)* colidir.
❑ **crash into** *vt fus (wall)* bater contra.
crash helmet *n* capacete *m* (de proteção).
crash landing *n* aterrissagem *f* forçada *(Br)*, aterragem *f* forçada *(Port)*.
crass [kræs] *adj* grosseiro(-ra); **a ~ mistake** um erro crasso.
crate [kreɪt] *n* grade *f (para transporte de fruta, garrafas, etc)*.
crater ['kreɪtə^r] *n* cratera *f*.
crave [kreɪv] *vt* desejar (intensamente).
crawl [krɔ:l] *vi (baby, person)* engatinhar *(Br)*, gatinhar *(Port)*; *(insect)* rastejar; *(traffic)* arrastar-se ◆ *n (swimming stroke)* crawl *m*.
crawler lane ['krɔ:lə^r-] *n (Brit)* faixa *f* para veículos lentos.
crayfish ['kreɪfɪʃ] *(pl inv) n* camarão-de-água-doce *m*.
crayon ['kreɪɒn] *n* lápis *m* de cera OR giz.
craze [kreɪz] *n* moda *f*.
crazy ['kreɪzɪ] *adj* maluco(-ca), louco (ca); **to be ~ about** ser louco por.
crazy golf *n* mini-golfe *m*.
creak [kri:k] *vi (door, floorboards)* ranger; *(hinge)* chiar.
cream [kri:m] *n (food)* creme *m (Br)*, natas *fpl (Port)*; *(for face)* creme *m*; *(for burns)* pomada *f* ◆ *adj (in colour)* creme *(inv)*.
cream cake *n (Brit)* bolo *m* recheado com creme.
cream cheese *n* queijo-creme *m*, queijo *m* para barrar.
cream cracker *n (Brit)* biscoito *m* de água e sal.
cream sherry *n* xerez *m* doce.
cream tea *n (Brit) lanche composto por chá e "scones" recheados com creme e doce*.
creamy ['kri:mɪ] *adj* cremoso(-osa).
crease [kri:s] *n* vinco *m*.
creased [kri:st] *adj* vincado(-da), engelhado(-da) *(Port)*.
create [kri:'eɪt] *vt (make)* criar; *(impression)* causar; *(interest)* provocar.
creation [kri:'eɪʃn] *n* criação *f*.
creative [kri:'eɪtɪv] *adj* criativo(-va).
creature ['kri:tʃə^r] *n* criatura *f*.
crèche [kreʃ] *n (Brit)* creche *f*.
credentials [krɪ'denʃlz] *npl (papers)* identificação *f*, documentos *mpl*; *(fig: qualifications)* capacidades *fpl*; *(references)* credenciais *fpl*.
credibility [,kredə'bɪlətɪ] *n* credibilidade *f*.

credit ['kredɪt] *n (praise)* mérito *m*; *(money)* crédito *m*; *(at school, university)* cadeira terminada com nota positiva; **to be in ~** estar com saldo positivo.
❑ **credits** *npl (of film)* créditos *mpl*.

credit card *n* cartão *m* de crédito; **to pay by ~** pagar com cartão de crédito; **"all major ~s accepted"** = "aceita-se cartão de crédito".

creed [kriːd] *n* credo *m*.

creek [kriːk] *n (inlet)* angra *f*; *(Am: river)* riacho *m*.

creep [kriːp] *(pt & pp* crept) *vi (crawl)* arrastar-se ♦ *n (inf: groveller)* puxa-saco *mf (Br)*, graxista *mf (Port)*.

creepy-crawly [kriːpɪˈkrɔːlɪ] *n (inf)* bicho *m*.

cremate [krɪˈmeɪt] *vt* cremar.

cremation [krɪˈmeɪʃn] *n* cremação *f*.

crematorium [kremaˈtɔːrɪəm] *n* crematório *m*.

crepe [kreɪp] *n (thin pancake)* crepe *m*.

crepe paper *n* papel-crepe *m*.

crept [krept] *pt & pp* → **creep**.

crescent ['kresnt] *n (shape)* meia-lua *f*; *(street)* rua *f* semi-circular.

cress [kres] *n* agrião *m (muito pequeno)*.

crest [krest] *n (of bird, hill)* crista *f*; *(on coat of arms)* brasão *m*.

crevice ['krevɪs] *n* fenda *f*.

crew [kruː] *n (of ship, plane)* tripulação *f*.

crew cut *n* corte *m* à escovinha OR à máquina zero.

crew neck *n* gola *f* redonda.

crib [krɪb] *n (Am: cot)* berço *m*.

cricket ['krɪkɪt] *n (game)* críquete *m*; *(insect)* grilo *m*.

crime [kraɪm] *n* crime *m*.

criminal ['krɪmɪnl] *adj (behaviour, offence)* criminoso(-osa); *(inf: disgraceful)* vergonhoso(-osa) ♦ *n* criminoso *m* (-osa *f)*.

crimson ['krɪmzn] *adj (in colour)* carmesim *(inv)* ♦ *n* carmesim *m*.

cringe [krɪndʒ] *vi (out of fear)* encolher-se; **to ~ (at sthg)** *(inf: with embarrassment)* não saber onde se meter (perante algo).

cripple ['krɪpl] *n* aleijado *m* (-da *f)* ♦ *vt* tornar inválido(-da).

crisis ['kraɪsɪs] *(pl* crises ['kraɪsiːz]) *n* crise *f*.

crisp [krɪsp] *adj* estaladiço(-ça).
❑ **crisps** *npl (Brit)* batatas *fpl* fritas *(de pacote)*.

crispy ['krɪspɪ] *adj* estaladiço(-ça).

crisscross ['krɪskrɒs] *adj* entrecruzado(-da).

criterion [kraɪˈtɪərɪən] *(pl* **-rions** OR **-ria** [-rɪə]) *n* critério *m*.

critic ['krɪtɪk] *n (reviewer)* crítico *m* (-ca *f)*.

critical ['krɪtɪkl] *adj* crítico(-ca); *(serious)* grave; *(disparaging)* severo(-ra).

critically ['krɪtɪklɪ] *adv (seriously)* gravemente; *(crucially)* extremamente; *(analytically)* de forma crítica; *(disparagingly)* severamente.

criticism ['krɪtɪsɪzm] *n* crítica *f*; **I hate ~** detesto críticas.

criticize ['krɪtɪsaɪz] *vt* criticar.

croak [krəʊk] *vi (animal)* grasnar.

Croat ['krəʊæt] *adj* croata ♦ *n (person)* croata *mf*; *(language)* croata *m*.

Croatia [krəʊˈeɪʃə] *n* Croácia *f*.

Croatian [krəʊˈeɪʃn] = **Croat**.

crochet ['krəʊʃeɪ] *n* crochê *m*, malha *f*.

crockery ['krɒkərɪ] *n* louça *f*.

crocodile ['krɒkədaɪl] *n* crocodilo *m*.

crocus ['krəʊkəs] *(pl* **-es**) *n* crocus *m inv*.

crook [krʊk] *n (criminal)* vigarista *mf*.

crooked ['krʊkɪd] *adj (bent, twisted)* torto (torta).

crop [krɒp] *n (kind of plant)* cultura *f*; *(harvest)* colheita *f*.
❑ **crop up** *vi* surgir.

cross [krɒs] *adj* zangado(-da) ♦ *n* cruz *f*; *(mixture)* cruzamento *m* ♦ *vt (road, river, ocean)* atravessar; *(arms, legs)* cruzar; *(Brit: cheque)* barrar ♦ *vi (intersect)* cruzar-se.
❑ **cross out** *vt sep* riscar.
❑ **cross over** *vt fus (road)* atravessar.

crossbar ['krɒsbɑːr] *n* barra *f* transversal.

cross-Channel ferry *n* barco que faz a travessia do Canal da Mancha.

cross-country (running) *n* corrida *f* pelo campo *(Br)*, corta-mato *m (Port)*.

cross-eyed [-aɪd] *adj* vesgo(-ga).

crossing ['krɒsɪŋ] *n (on road)* faixa *f* para pedestres *(Br)*, passadeira *f* (para peões) *(Port)*; *(sea journey)* travessia *f*.

crossroads ['krɒsrəʊdz] *(pl inv)* *n* cruzamento *m*.

crosswalk ['krɒswɔːk] *n (Am)* faixa *f* para pedestres *(Br)*, passadeira *f* (para peões) *(Port)*.

crossword (puzzle) ['krɒswɜːd-] *n* palavras *fpl* cruzadas.

crotch [krɒtʃ] *n* entrepernas *m*.

crouch [kraʊtʃ] vi agachar-se.

crouton ['kru:tɒn] n pedaço de pão torrado ou frito, usado como guarnição em sopas.

crow [krəʊ] n corvo m.

crowbar ['krəʊbɑːʳ] n alavanca f, pé-de-cabra m.

crowd [kraʊd] n multidão f; (at match) público m.

crowded ['kraʊdɪd] adj cheio (cheia) (de gente).

crown [kraʊn] n coroa f; (of head) alto m (da cabeça).

Crown Jewels npl jóias da coroa britânica.

crucial ['kru:ʃl] adj crucial.

crucifix ['kru:sɪfɪks] n crucifixo m.

crude [kru:d] adj grosseiro(-ra).

cruel [krʊəl] adj cruel.

cruelty ['krʊəltɪ] n crueldade f.

cruet (set) ['kru:ɪt-] n galheteiro m.

cruise [kru:z] n cruzeiro m ◆ vi (plane) voar; (ship) navegar; (car) rodar.

cruiser ['kru:zəʳ] n (pleasure boat) cruzeiro m.

crumb [krʌm] n migalha f.

crumble ['krʌmbl] n sobremesa feita com fruta cozida coberta com uma massa esfarelada de farinha, açúcar e manteiga ◆ vi (building, cliff) desmoronar-se; (cheese) esmigalhar-se.

crumpet ['krʌmpɪt] n espécie de crepe pequeno que se come quente com manteiga ou geléia.

crumple ['krʌmpl] vt (dress, suit) engelhar; (letter) amarrotar.

crunch [krʌntʃ] vt (with teeth) trincar OR mastigar (fazendo ruído).

crunchy ['krʌntʃɪ] adj crocante.

crusade [kru:'seɪd] n (war) cruzada f.

crush [krʌʃ] n (drink) sumo m (de fruta) ◆ vt esmagar; (ice) partir.

crust [krʌst] n (of bread) casca f (Br), côdea f (Port); (of pie) crosta f.

crusty ['krʌstɪ] adj estaladiço(-ça).

crutch [krʌtʃ] n (stick) muleta f; (between legs) = crotch.

cry [kraɪ] n grito m ◆ vi (weep) chorar; (shout) gritar.

❑ **cry out** vi gritar.

crystal ['krɪstl] n cristal m.

crystal clear adj (motive, meaning) claro(-ra) como a água.

cub [kʌb] n (animal) cria f.

Cub [kʌb] n escoteiro entre os 8 e os 11 anos.

cubbyhole ['kʌbɪhəʊl] n cubículo m.

cube [kju:b] n cubo m.

cubicle ['kju:bɪkl] n cubículo m.

Cub Scout = Cub.

cuckoo ['kʊku:] n cuco m.

cuckoo clock n relógio m de cuco.

cucumber ['kju:kʌmbəʳ] n pepino m.

cuddle ['kʌdl] n abraço m.

cuddly toy ['kʌdlɪ-] n boneco m de pelúcia.

cue [kju:] n (in snooker, pool) taco m.

cuff [kʌf] n (of sleeve) punho m; (Am: of trousers) dobra f.

cuff links npl botões mpl de punho.

cuisine [kwɪ'zi:n] n cozinha f.

cul-de-sac ['kʌldəsæk] n beco m sem saída.

culmination [ˌkʌlmɪ'neɪʃn] n culminação f.

culottes [kju:'lɒts] npl saia-calça f.

culprit ['kʌlprɪt] n culpado m (-da f).

cult [kʌlt] n culto m ◆ adj de culto.

cultivate ['kʌltɪveɪt] vt cultivar.

cultivated ['kʌltɪveɪtɪd] adj (person) culto(-ta).

cultural ['kʌltʃərəl] adj cultural.

culture ['kʌltʃəʳ] n cultura f.

cultured ['kʌltʃəd] adj culto(-ta).

cumbersome ['kʌmbəsəm] adj pesado(-da).

cumin ['kju:mɪn] n cominho m.

cunning ['kʌnɪŋ] adj esperto(-ta).

cup [kʌp] n xícara f (Br), chávena f (Port); (trophy, competition) taça f; (of bra) taça f (Br), copa f (Port).

cupboard ['kʌbəd] n armário m.

curate ['kjʊərət] n cura m.

curator [kjʊə'reɪtəʳ] n conservador m (-ra f) (de museu, biblioteca).

curb [kɜːb] (Am) = kerb.

curd cheese [kɜːd-] n ~ requeijão m.

curdle ['kɜːdl] vi coalhar.

cure [kjʊəʳ] n (for illness) cura f ◆ vt curar.

curfew ['kɜːfju:] n toque f de recolher.

curiosity [ˌkjʊərɪ'ɒsətɪ] n curiosidade f.

curious ['kjʊərɪəs] adj curioso(-osa).

curl [kɜːl] n (of hair) caracol m ◆ vt (hair) encaracolar.

curler ['kɜːləʳ] n rolo m.

curling tongs ['kɜːlɪŋ-] npl ferro m de frisar OR encaracolar (o cabelo).

curly ['kɜːlɪ] adj encaracolado(-da).

currant ['kʌrənt] *n* corinto *m*.

currency ['kʌrənsı] *n (money)* moeda *f*.

current ['kʌrənt] *adj* actual ◆ *n* corrente *f*.

current account *n (Brit)* conta *f* corrente *(Br)*, conta *f* à ordem *(Port)*.

current affairs *npl* temas *mpl* da atualidade.

currently ['kʌrəntlı] *adv* atualmente.

curriculum [kə'rıkjələm] *n* programa *m* (de estudos).

curriculum vitae [-'viːtaı] *n (Brit)* curriculum *m* vitae.

curried ['kʌrıd] *adj* com caril.

curry ['kʌrı] *n* caril *m*.

curse [kɜːs] *vi* praguejar.

cursor ['kɜːsəʳ] *n* cursor *m*.

curt [kɜːt] *adj* seco(-ca).

curtail [kɜː'teıl] *vt (cut short)* encurtar, abreviar.

curtain ['kɜːtn] *n* cortina *f*.

curts(e)y ['kɜːtsı] *n* vênia *f (de mulher)* ◆ *vi* fazer uma vênia.

curve [kɜːv] *n* curva *f* ◆ *vi* descrever uma curva.

curved [kɜːvd] *adj* curvo(-va).

cushion ['kuʃn] *n* almofada *f*.

custard ['kʌstəd] *n* creme à base de farinha, leite e açúcar para acompanhar doces ou fruta cozida.

custody ['kʌstədı] *n* custódia *f*; **in ~** *(JUR)* sob custódia.

custom ['kʌstəm] *n (tradition)* costume *m*; **"thank you for your ~"** "obrigada pela sua visita".

customary ['kʌstəmrı] *adj* habitual.

customer ['kʌstəməʳ] *n (of shop)* cliente *mf*.

customer services *n (department)* serviço *m* de assistência a clientes.

customize ['kʌstəmaız] *vt* personalizar.

customs ['kʌstəmz] *n* alfândega *f*; **to go through ~** passar pela alfândega.

customs duty *n* impostos *mpl* alfandegários *(Br)*, direitos *mpl* alfandegários *(Port)*.

customs officer *n* inspetor *m* (-ora *f*) alfandegário *(Br)*, empregado *m* alfandegário (empregada *f* alfandegária *(Port)*.

cut [kʌt] *(pt & pp* **cut)** *n* corte *m* ◆ *vt* cortar; *(reduce)* reduzir, cortar em ◆ *vi (knife, scissors)* cortar; **~ and blow-dry** corte e brushing; **to ~ o.s.** cortar-se; **to ~ the grass** cortar a grama *(Br)*, cortar a relva *(Port)*; **to ~ sthg open** abrir algo.

❏ **cut back** *vi*: **to ~ back on sthg** cortar em algo.

❏ **cut down** *vt sep (tree)* abater.

❏ **cut down on** *vt fus* cortar em.

❏ **cut off** *vt sep* cortar; **I've been ~ off** *(on phone)* a ligação caiu; **to be ~ off** *(isolated)* estar isolado.

❏ **cut out** *vt sep (newspaper article, photo)* recortar ◆ *vi (engine)* morrer; **to ~ out fatty foods** cortar as gorduras; **~ it out!** *(inf)* pára com isso!

❏ **cut up** *vt sep* cortar.

cute [kjuːt] *adj* bonitinho(-nha) *(Br)*, giro(-ra) *(Port)*.

cut-glass *adj* de vidro biselado.

cutlery ['kʌtlərı] *n* talheres *mpl*.

cutlet ['kʌtlıt] *n (of meat)* costeleta *f*; *(of nuts, vegetables)* costeleta vegetariana.

cut-price *adj* a preço reduzido.

cutting ['kʌtıŋ] *n (from newspaper)* recorte *m*.

CV *n (Brit: abbr of curriculum vitae)* c.v. *m*.

cwt *abbr* = **hundredweight**.

cyberspace ['saıbəspeıs] *n* ciberespaço *m*.

cycle ['saıkl] *n (bicycle)* bicicleta *f*; *(series)* ciclo *m* ◆ *vi* andar de bicicleta.

cycle hire *n* aluguel *m* de bicicletas.

cycle lane *n* faixa *f* para ciclistas.

cycle path *n* pista *f* para ciclistas.

cycling ['saıklıŋ] *n* ciclismo *m*; **to go ~** ir andar de bicicleta.

cycling shorts *npl* calções *mpl* de ciclista.

cyclist ['saıklıst] *n* ciclista *mf*.

cylinder ['sılındəʳ] *n (container)* bujão *m (Br)*, botija *f (Port)*; *(in engine)* cilindro *m*.

cymbals ['sımblz] *npl* pratos *mpl*.

cynic ['sınık] *n* pessoa que não tem fé nas pessoas nem nas suas intenções.

cynical ['sınıkl] *adj* céptico(-ca) *(em relação às pessoas e às suas intenções)*.

cynicism ['sınısızm] *n* falta de fé nas pessoas e nas suas intenções.

Cypriot ['sıprıət] *adj* cipriota ◆ *n* cipriota *mf*.

Cyprus ['saıprəs] *n* Chipre *f*.

cyst [sıst] *n* quisto *m*.

czar [zɑːʳ] *n* czar *m*.

Czech [tʃek] *adj* tcheco(-ca) ◆ *n (person)* tcheco *m* (-ca *f*); *(language)* tcheco *m*.

Czechoslovakia [ˌtʃekəslə-'vækıə] *n* Tchecoslováquia *f*.

Czech Republic *n*: **the ~** a República Tcheca.

D

dab [dæb] *vt (ointment, cream)* aplicar levemente.

dachshund ['dækshʊnd] *n* (cão) salsicha *m*.

dad [dæd] *n (inf)* papá *m*.

daddy ['dædɪ] *n (inf)* papá *m*.

daddy longlegs [-'lɒŋlegz] *(pl inv)* n pernilongo *m (Br)*, melga *f (Port)*.

daffodil ['dæfədɪl] *n* narciso *m*.

daft [dɑːft] *adj (Brit: inf)* parvo(-va).

dagger ['dægəʳ] *n* punhal *m*.

daily ['deɪlɪ] *adj* diário(-ria) ◆ *adv* diariamente ◆ *n*: **a ~ (newspaper)** um jornal diário.

dainty ['deɪntɪ] *adj* delicado(-da), fino(-na).

dairy ['deərɪ] *n (on farm)* vacaria *f*; *(shop)* leitaria *f*.

dairy product *n* lacticínio *m*, produto *m* lácteo *(Port)*.

daisy ['deɪzɪ] *n* margarida *f*.

dale [deɪl] *n* vale *m*.

dam [dæm] *n* barragem *f*.

damage ['dæmɪdʒ] *n* dano *m* ◆ *vt (house, car)* danificar; *(back, leg)* machucar; *(fig: reputation, chances)* arruinar.

damn [dæm] *excl (inf)* droga! ◆ *adj (inf)* maldito(-ta); **I don't give a ~** não estou nem aí.

damned [dæmd] *adv (inf)* muito ◆ *adj (inf)* maldito(-ta); **well, I'll be ~!** nossa!

damp [dæmp] *adj* úmido(-da) ◆ *n* umidade *f*.

dampen ['dæmpən] *vt (make wet)* umedecer.

damson ['dæmzn] *n* ameixa *f* pequena, abrunho *m (Port)*.

dance [dɑːns] *n* dança *f*; *(social event)* baile *m* ◆ *vi* dançar; **to have a ~** dançar.

dance floor *n* pista *f* de dança.

dancer ['dɑːnsəʳ] *n* bailarino *m* (-na *f*).

dancing ['dɑːnsɪŋ] *n* dança *f*; **to go ~** ir dançar.

dandelion ['dændɪlaɪən] *n* dente-de-leão *m*.

dandruff ['dændrʌf] *n* caspa *f*.

Dane [deɪn] *n* dinamarquês *m* (-esa *f*).

danger ['deɪndʒəʳ] *n* perigo *m*; **in ~** em perigo.

dangerous ['deɪndʒərəs] *adj* perigoso(-osa).

dangle ['dæŋgl] *vt & vi* balançar.

Danish ['deɪnɪʃ] *adj* dinamarquês(-esa) ◆ *n (language)* dinamarquês *m*.

Danish pastry *n* bolo de massa folhada recheado com passas, ou qualquer outra fruta.

dank [dæŋk] *adj* úmido e frio (úmida e fria).

dappled ['dæpld] *adj (animal)* malhado(-da).

dare [deəʳ] *vt*: **to ~ to do sthg** ousar fazer algo, atrever-se a fazer algo; **to ~ sb to do sthg** desafiar alguém a fazer algo; **how ~ you!** como se atreve!

daredevil ['deə,devl] *n* temerário *m* (-ria *f*).

daring ['deərɪŋ] *adj* corajoso(-osa).

dark [dɑːk] *adj* escuro(-ra); *(person, skin)* moreno(-na) ◆ *n*: **after ~** depois do anoitecer; **the ~** o escuro.

dark chocolate *n* chocolate *m* amargo OR negro.

darken ['dɑːkn] *vi* escurecer.

dark glasses *npl* óculos *mpl* escuros.

darkness ['dɑːknɪs] *n* escuridão *f*.

darkroom ['dɑːkrʊm] *n* câmara *f* escura.

darling ['dɑːlɪŋ] *n (term of affection)* querido *m* (-da *f*).

dart [dɑːt] *n* dardo *m*.

❏ **darts** *n (game)* dardos *mpl*.

dartboard ['dɑːtbɔːd] *n* alvo *m (para jogo de dardos)*.

dash [dæʃ] *n (of liquid)* gota *f; (in writing)* travessão *m* ◆ *vi* precipitar-se.

dashboard ['dæʃbɔːd] *n* painel *m (Br)*, tablier *m (Port)*.

dashing ['dæʃɪŋ] *adj* fogoso(-osa).

data ['deɪtə] *n* dados *mpl*.

database ['deɪtəbeɪs] *n* banco *m* de base *(Br)*, base *f* de dados *(Port)*.

data processing [-'prəʊsesɪŋ] *n* processamento *m* de dados.

date [deɪt] *n (day)* data *f; (meeting)* encontro *m*, compromisso *m; (Am: person)* namorado *m* (-da *f*); *(fruit)* tâmara *f* ◆ *vt (cheque, letter)* datar; *(person)* sair com ◆ *vi (become unfashionable)* cair de moda; **what's the ~?** que dia é hoje?; **to have a ~ with sb** ter um encontro OR compromisso com alguém.

dated ['deɪtɪd] *adj* antiquado(-da).

date of birth *n* data *f* de nascimento.

daughter ['dɔːtə*r*] *n* filha *f*.

daughter-in-law *n* nora *f*.

daunting ['dɔːntɪŋ] *adj* assustador(-ra).

dawdle ['dɔːdl] *vi* empatar (tempo).

dawn [dɔːn] *n* amanhecer *m*, madrugada *f*.

day [deɪ] *n* dia *m;* **what ~ is it today?** que dia é hoje?; **what a lovely ~!** que lindo dia!; **to have a ~ off** ter um dia de folga; **to have a ~ out** passar o dia fora; **by ~** de dia; **the ~ after tomorrow** depois de amanhã; **the ~ before** a véspera, o dia anterior; **the ~ before yesterday** anteontem; **the following ~** o dia seguinte; **have a nice ~!** tenha um bom dia!

daybreak ['deɪbreɪk] *n* aurora *f;* **at ~** ao romper da aurora, de madrugada.

daydream ['deɪdriːm] *vi* sonhar acordado.

daylight ['deɪlaɪt] *n* luz *f* do dia.

day return *n (Brit)* bilhete de ida e volta válido por um dia.

dayshift ['deɪʃɪft] *n* turno *m* de dia.

daytime ['deɪtaɪm] *n* dia *m*.

day-to-day *adj (everyday)* quotidiano(-na).

day trip *n* excursão *f*.

daze [deɪz] *vt* aturdir ◆ *n:* **in a ~** aturdido(-da).

dazzle ['dæzl] *vt* deslumbrar.

DC *(abbr of direct current)* CC.

deactivate [diːˈæktɪˌveɪt] *vt* desactivar.

dead [ded] *adj* morto (morta); *(not lively)* sem vida, morto (morta); *(telephone line)* cortado(-da); *(battery)* gasto(-ta) ◆ *adv (precisely)* mesmo; *(inf: very)* muito; **it's ~ ahead** é mesmo em frente; **" ~ slow"** "dirija devagar".

deaden ['dedn] *vt (noise)* diminuir; *(feeling)* abrandar.

dead end *n (street)* beco *m* sem saída.

dead heat *n* empate *m*.

deadline ['dedlaɪn] *n* prazo *m*.

deadlock ['dedlɒk] *n* impasse *m*.

deadly ['dedlɪ] *adj* mortal; *(aim, accuracy)* infalível ◆ *adv* extremamente; **it was ~ boring** foi muito chato.

deaf [def] *adj* surdo(-da) ◆ *npl:* **the ~** os surdos.

deaf-and-dumb *adj* surdo-mudo (surda-muda).

deafen ['defn] *vt* ensurdecer.

deaf-mute *adj* surdo-mudo(surda-muda) ◆ *n* surdo-mudo *m* (surda-muda *f*).

deafness ['defnɪs] *n* surdez *f*.

deal [diːl] *(pt & pp* **dealt)** *n (agreement)* acordo *m* ◆ *vt (cards)* dar; **a good/bad ~** um bom/mau negócio; **a great ~ of** muito; **it's a ~!** está combinado!

❏ **deal in** *vt fus* negociar.

❏ **deal with** *vt fus (handle)* lidar com; *(be about)* tratar de.

dealer ['diːlə*r*] *n (COMM)* comerciante *mf*, negociante *mf; (in drugs)* fornecedor *m* (-ra *f*).

dealing ['diːlɪŋ] *n* comércio *m*.

❏ **dealings** *npl (business)* negociações *fpl*.

dealt [delt] *pt & pp* → **deal**.

dean [diːn] *n (of university)* reitor *m* (-ra *f*); *(of church, cathedral)* decano *m*, deão *m*.

dear [dɪə*r*] *adj (loved)* querido(-da); *(expensive)* caro(-ra) ◆ *n:* **my ~** meu querido (minha querida); **Dear Sir** Caro senhor; **Dear Madam** Cara senhora; **Dear John** Querido John; **oh ~!** meu Deus!

death [deθ] *n* morte *f*.

death penalty *n* pena *f* de morte.

debate [dɪˈbeɪt] *n* debate *m* ◆ *vt*

(wonder) considerar.
debit ['debɪt] *n* débito *m* ◆ *vt (account)* debitar em.
debris ['deɪbriː] *n (of building)* escombros *mpl; (of aeroplane)* restos *mpl*.
debt [det] *n (money owed)* dívida *f*; **to be in ~** ter dívidas.
debut ['deɪbjuː] *n* estréia *f*.
Dec. *(abbr of December)* dez.
decade ['dekeɪd] *n* década *f*.
decadence ['dekədəns] *n* decadência *f*.
decadent ['dekədənt] *adj* decadente.
decaff ['diːkæf] *n (inf)* descafeinado *m*.
decaffeinated [dɪ'kæfɪneɪtɪd] *adj* descafeinado(-da).
decanter [dɪ'kæntər] *n* garrafa *f* para licores.
decathlon [dɪ'kæθlɒn] *n* decatlo *m*.
decay [dɪ'keɪ] *n (of building)* deterioração *f; (of wood)* apodrecimento *m; (of tooth)* cárie *f* ◆ *vi (rot)* apodrecer.
deceased [dɪ'siːst] *(pl inv) adj (fml)* falecido(-da) ◆ *n:* **the ~** o falecido (a falecida).
deceit [dɪ'siːt] *n* engano *m*.
deceitful [dɪ'siːtful] *adj* enganador(-ra).
deceive [dɪ'siːv] *vt* enganar.
decelerate [diː'seləreɪt] *vi* abrandar.
December [dɪ'sembər] *n* dezembro, → September.
decent ['diːsnt] *adj* decente; *(kind)* simpático(-ca).
deception [dɪ'sepʃn] *n* decepção *f*.
deceptive [dɪ'septɪv] *adj* enganador(-ra).
decide [dɪ'saɪd] *vt (choose)* decidir ◆ *vi* tomar uma decisão; **to ~ to do sthg** decidir fazer algo.
❐ **decide on** *vt fus* decidir-se por.
decidedly [dɪ'saɪdɪdlɪ] *adv* decididamente.
deciduous [dɪ'sɪdjʊəs] *adj* decíduo(-dua).
decimal ['desɪml] *adj* decimal.
decimal point *n* vírgula *f*.
decipher [dɪ'saɪfər] *vt* decifrar.
decision [dɪ'sɪʒn] *n* decisão *f*; **to make a ~** tomar uma decisão.
decisive [dɪ'saɪsɪv] *adj (person)* decidido(-da); *(event, factor)* decisivo(-va).
deck [dek] *n (of bus)* andar *m; (of ship)* convés *m; (of cards)* baralho *m*.

deckchair ['dekʃeər] *n* espreguiçadeira *f*.
declaration [deklə'reɪʃn] *n* declaração *f*.
declare [dɪ'kleər] *vt* declarar; **to ~ that** declarar que; **"goods to ~"** "artigos a declarar"; **"nothing to ~"** "nada a declarar".
decline [dɪ'klaɪn] *n* declínio *m* ◆ *vi (get worse)* declinar; *(refuse)* recusar.
decompose [diːkəm'pəʊz] *vi* decompor-se.
decorate ['dekəreɪt] *vt* decorar.
decoration [dekə'reɪʃn] *n (wallpaper, paint, furniture)* decoração *f; (decorative object)* adorno *m*.
decorator ['dekəreɪtər] *n* decorador *m (-ra f)*.
decoy ['diːkɔɪ] *n* chamariz *m*.
decrease [*n* 'diːkriːs, *vb* diː'kriːs] *n* diminuição *f* ◆ *vi* diminuir.
decree [dɪ'kriː] *n (order, decision)* decreto *m; (Am: judgment)* sentença *f* ◆ *vt* decretar; **to ~ that** decretar que.
decrepit [dɪ'krepɪt] *adj* decrépito(-ta).
dedicate ['dedɪkeɪt] *vt* dedicar.
dedicated ['dedɪkeɪtɪd] *adj (committed)* dedicado(-da).
dedication [dedɪ'keɪʃn] *n* dedicação *f*.
deduce [dɪ'djuːs] *vt* deduzir.
deduct [dɪ'dʌkt] *vt* deduzir.
deduction [dɪ'dʌkʃn] *n* dedução *f*.
deed [diːd] *n (action)* ação *f*, ato *m*.
deep [diːp] *adj* profundo(-da); *(colour)* intenso(-sa); *(sound, voice)* grave ◆ *adv* fundo; **the pool is two metres ~** a piscina tem dois metros de profundidade; **to take a ~ breath** respirar fundo.
deep end *n (of swimming pool)* parte *f* funda.
deep freeze *n* freezer *m (Br)*, congelador *m (Port)*.
deep-fried [-'fraɪd] *adj* frito(-ta).
deep-pan *adj* de massa grossa.
deer [dɪər] *(pl inv) n* veado *m*.
defeat [dɪ'fiːt] *n* derrota *f* ◆ *vt (team, army, government)* derrotar.
defect ['diːfekt] *n* defeito *m*.
defective [dɪ'fektɪv] *adj* defeituoso(-osa).
defence [dɪ'fens] *n (Brit)* defesa *f*.
defenceless [dɪ'fenslɪs] *adj* indefeso(-sa).
defend [dɪ'fend] *vt* defender.

defender [dɪˈfendər] *n (SPORT)* defesa *mf*.

defense [dɪˈfens] *(Am)* = **defence**.

defensive [dɪˈfensɪv] *adj* defensivo (-va).

defiant [dɪˈfaɪənt] *adj* provocador (-ra).

deficiency [dɪˈfɪʃnsɪ] *n (lack)* deficiência *f*.

deficient [dɪˈfɪʃnt] *adj (inadequate)* deficiente; ~ **in** sthg deficiente em algo.

deficit [ˈdefɪsɪt] *n* déficit *m (Br)*, défice *m (Port)*.

define [dɪˈfaɪn] *vt* definir.

definite [ˈdefɪnɪt] *adj (answer, decision)* definitivo(-va); *(person)* seguro (-ra); *(improvement)* nítido(-da).

definite article *n* artigo *m* definido.

definitely [ˈdefɪnɪtlɪ] *adv (certainly)* sem dúvida (alguma); **I'll ~ go** irei de certeza.

definition [defɪˈnɪʃn] *n (of word)* definição *f*.

deflate [dɪˈfleɪt] *vt (tyre)* esvaziar.

deflect [dɪˈflekt] *vt (ball)* desviar.

defogger [diːˈfɒgər] *n (Am)* desembaciador *m*.

deformed [dɪˈfɔːmd] *adj* deformado(-da).

defrost [diːˈfrɒst] *vt (food, fridge)* descongelar; *(Am: demist)* desembaciar.

defy [dɪˈfaɪ] *vt* desafiar; **to ~ sb to do** sthg desafiar alguém a fazer algo.

degrading [dɪˈgreɪdɪŋ] *adj* degradante.

degree [dɪˈgriː] *n (unit of measurement)* grau *m*; *(qualification)* – licenciatura *f*; **a ~ of difficulty** uma certa difficuldade; **to have a ~ in** sthg ter uma licenciatura em algo.

dehydrated [diːhaɪˈdreɪtɪd] *adj* desidratado(-da).

de-ice [diːˈaɪs] *vt* descongelar.

de-icer [diːˈaɪsər] *n* produto *m* descongelante.

deity [ˈdiːɪtɪ] *n* divindade *f*.

dejected [dɪˈdʒektɪd] *adj* abatido (-da).

delay [dɪˈleɪ] *n* atraso *m* ♦ *vt* atrasar ♦ *vi* atrasar-se; **without ~** sem demora.

delayed [dɪˈleɪd] *adj (train, flight)* atrasado(-da).

delegate [*n* ˈdelɪgət, *vb* ˈdelɪgeɪt] *n*

delegado *m (-da f)* ♦ *vt (person)* delegar.

delete [dɪˈliːt] *vt* suprimir.

deli [ˈdelɪ] *abbr (inf)* = **delicatessen**.

deliberate [dɪˈlɪbərət] *adj (intentional)* deliberado(-da).

deliberately [dɪˈlɪbərətlɪ] *adv (intentionally)* deliberadamente.

delicacy [ˈdelɪkəsɪ] *n (food)* iguaria *f*.

delicate [ˈdelɪkət] *adj* delicado(-da); *(object, china)* frágil; *(taste, smell)* suave.

delicatessen [delɪkəˈtesn] *n ≈* charcutaria *f*.

delicious [dɪˈlɪʃəs] *adj* delicioso(-osa).

delight [dɪˈlaɪt] *n (feeling)* prazer *m* ♦ *vt* encantar; **to take (a) ~ in doing** sthg ter prazer em fazer algo.

delighted [dɪˈlaɪtɪd] *adj* encantado (-da).

delightful [dɪˈlaɪtfʊl] *adj* encantador(-ra).

delirious [dɪˈlɪrɪəs] *adj* delirante.

deliver [dɪˈlɪvər] *vt (goods)* entregar; *(letters, newspaper)* distribuir; *(lecture)* dar; *(baby)* fazer o parto de; *(speech)* fazer.

delivery [dɪˈlɪvərɪ] *n (of goods)* entrega *f*; *(of letters)* distribuição *f*; *(birth)* parto *m*.

delude [dɪˈluːd] *vt* enganar.

delusion [dɪˈluːʒn] *n* ilusão *f*.

de luxe [dəˈlʌks] *adj* de luxo.

delve [delv] *vi*: **to ~ into** OR **inside** sthg *(bag, cupboard)* procurar dentro de algo.

demand [dɪˈmɑːnd] *n* exigência *f*; *(claim)* reivindicação *f*; *(COMM)* procura *f* ♦ *vt* exigir; **I ~ to speak to the manager** quero falar com o gerente; **in ~** solicitado.

demanding [dɪˈmɑːndɪŋ] *adj* exigente.

demeanor [dɪˈmiːnər] *(Am)* = **demeanour**.

demeanour [dɪˈmiːnər] *n (Brit) (fml)* comportamento *m*.

demerara sugar [deməˈreərə-] *n* açúcar *m* mascavo.

demist [diːˈmɪst] *vt (Brit)* desembaciar.

demister [diːˈmɪstər] *n (Brit)* desembaciador *m*.

demo [ˈdeməʊ] *(pl* **-s***) abbr (inf)* = **demonstration**.

democracy [dɪˈmɒkrəsɪ] *n* democracia *f*.

Democrat [ˈdeməkræt] *n (Am)* democrata *mf*.

democratic [deməˈkrætɪk] *adj* democrático(-ca).

demolish [dɪˈmɒlɪʃ] *vt (building)* demolir.

demonstrate [ˈdemənstreɪt] *vt (prove)* demonstrar; *(machine, appliance)* mostrar como funciona ◆ *vi* manifestar-se.

demonstration [demənˈstreɪʃn] *n (protest)* passeata *f (Br)*, manifestação *f*; *(of machine, emotions)* demonstração *f*.

demonstrator [ˈdemənstreɪtər] *n (protester)* manifestante *mf*; *(of machine, product)* demonstrador *m* (-ra *f*).

demoralized [dɪˈmɒrəlaɪzd] *adj* desmoralizado(-da).

den [den] *n* toca *f*.

denial [dɪˈnaɪəl] *n* desmentido *m*.

denim [ˈdenɪm] *n* brim *m (Br)*, ganga *f (Port)*.

❑ **denims** *npl* jeans *m inv (Br)*, calças *fpl* de ganga *(Port)*.

denim jacket *n* casaco *m* jeans.

Denmark [ˈdenmɑːk] *n* Dinamarca *f*.

denounce [dɪˈnaʊns] *vt* denunciar.

dense [dens] *adj* denso(-sa).

density [ˈdensətɪ] *n* densidade *f*.

dent [dent] *n* mossa *f*, amolgadura *f*.

dental [ˈdentl] *adj* dentário.

dental floss [-flɒs] *n* fio *m* dental.

dental surgeon *n* cirurgião-dentista *mf*.

dental surgery *n (place)* clínica *f* dentária.

dentist [ˈdentɪst] *n* dentista *mf*; **to go to the ~'s** ir ao dentista.

dentures [ˈdentʃəz] *npl* dentadura *f* postiça.

deny [dɪˈnaɪ] *vt* negar.

deodorant [diːˈəʊdərənt] *n* deodorante *m (Br)*, desodorizante *m (Port)*.

depart [dɪˈpɑːt] *vi* partir.

department [dɪˈpɑːtmənt] *n* departamento *m*; *(of government)* = ministério *m*; *(of shop)* seção *f*.

department store *n* loja *f* de departamentos *(Br)*, grande-armazém *m (Port)*.

departure [dɪˈpɑːtʃər] *n* partida *f*; **"~s"** *(at airport)* "partidas".

departure lounge *n* sala *f* de embarque.

depend [dɪˈpend] *vi*: **it ~s** depende.

❑ **depend on** *vt fus (be decided by)* depender de; *(rely on)* confiar em; **~ing** on dependendo de.

dependable [dɪˈpendəbl] *adj* de confiança, fiável.

dependent [dɪˈpendənt] *adj (addicted)* dependente; **~ on** dependente de.

deplorable [dɪˈplɔːrəbl] *adj* deplorável.

deploy [dɪˈplɔɪ] *vt* mobilizar.

deport [dɪˈpɔːt] *vt* deportar.

deposit [dɪˈpɒzɪt] *n* depósito *m*; *(part-payment)* entrada *f* ◆ *vt (put down)* colocar; *(money in bank)* depositar.

deposit account *n (Brit)* conta *f* a prazo.

depot [ˈdiːpəʊ] *n (Am: for buses, trains)* terminal *m*.

depress [dɪˈpres] *vt (person)* deprimir.

depressed [dɪˈprest] *adj* deprimido(-da).

depressing [dɪˈpresɪŋ] *adj* deprimente.

depression [dɪˈpreʃn] *n* depressão *f*.

deprivation [ˌdeprɪˈveɪʃn] *n* privação *f*.

deprive [dɪˈpraɪv] *vt*: **to ~ sb of sthg** privar alguém de algo.

depth [depθ] *n* profundidade *f*; **to be out of one's ~** *(when swimming)* não ter pé; *(fig: unable to cope)* não estar à altura; **~ of field** *(in photography)* profundidade de campo; **in ~** a fundo.

deputy [ˈdepjʊtɪ] *adj* adjunto(-ta).

derail [dɪˈreɪl] *vt (train)* fazer descarrilhar.

derailleur [dəˈreɪljər] *n* cremalheira *f*.

derailment [dɪˈreɪlmənt] *n* descarrilhamento *m*.

derby [*Brit* ˈdɑːbɪ, *Am* ˈdɜːbɪ] *n (sports event)* competição *f* (local); *(Am: hat)* chapéu *m* de coco.

derelict [ˈderəlɪkt] *adj* abandonado(-da).

deride [dɪˈraɪd] *vt* ridicularizar.

derisory [dəˈraɪzərɪ] *adj (amount, fine)* irrisório(-ria); *(laughter, smile)* sardônico(-ca).

derivative [dɪˈrɪvətɪv] *n* derivado *m*.

derogatory [dɪˈrɒgətrɪ] *adj* depreciativo(-va).

derv [dɜːv] *n (Brit)* gasóleo *m*.

descend [dɪˈsend] *vt & vi* descer.

descendant [dɪˈsendənt] *n* descendente *mf*.

descent [dɪˈsent] *n* descida *f*.

describe [dɪˈskraɪb] *vt* descrever.

description [dɪˈskrɪpʃn] n descrição
f.

desert [n ˈdezət, vb dɪˈzɜːt] n deserto m
♦ vt abandonar.

deserted [dɪˈzɜːtɪd] adj deserto(-ta).

deserter [dɪˈzɜːtər] n desertor m (-ra
f).

desert island [ˈdezət-] n ilha f deserta.

deserve [dɪˈzɜːv] vt merecer.

deserving [dɪˈzɜːvɪŋ] adj merecedor(-ra).

design [dɪˈzaɪn] n desenho m; (art)
design m ♦ vt desenhar; to be ~ed for
ser concebido para.

designate [ˈdezɪɡneɪt] vt (appoint)
designar.

designer [dɪˈzaɪnər] n (of clothes, sunglasses) estilista mf; (of product) designer mf ♦ adj (clothes, sunglasses) de
marca.

desirable [dɪˈzaɪərəbl] adj desejável.

desire [dɪˈzaɪər] n desejo m ♦ vt desejar; it leaves a lot to be ~d deixa
muito a desejar.

desk [desk] n (in home, office) secretária f; (in school) carteira f; (at airport,
station) balcão m; (at hotel) recepção f.

desktop publishing [ˈdesktɒp-] n
desktop m publishing, editoração f
eletrônica (Br), edição f assistida por
computador (Port).

desolate [ˈdesələt] adj (place) solitário(-ria), desértico(-ca); (person) desolado(-da).

despair [dɪˈspeər] n desespero m.

despatch [dɪˈspætʃ] = dispatch.

desperate [ˈdespərət] adj desesperado(-da); to be ~ for sthg precisar de
algo desesperadamente.

desperately [ˈdespərətlɪ] adv (want,
need, love) desesperadamente; (ill) gravemente; (poor, unhappy, shy) muito,
terrivelmente.

desperation [ˌdespəˈreɪʃn] n desespero m; in ~ desesperado.

despicable [dɪˈspɪkəbl] adj desprezível.

despise [dɪˈspaɪz] vt desprezar.

despite [dɪˈspaɪt] prep apesar de.

dessert [dɪˈzɜːt] n sobremesa f.

dessertspoon [dɪˈzɜːtspuːn] n
(spoon) colher f de sobremesa; (spoonful) = colher f de sopa.

destination [ˌdestɪˈneɪʃn] n destino
m.

destined [ˈdestɪnd] adj: to be ~ for
sthg/to do sthg (intended) estar destinado(-da) a algo/a fazer algo; ~ for
(place) com destino a.

destiny [ˈdestɪnɪ] n destino m.

destitute [ˈdestɪtjuːt] adj indigente.

destroy [dɪˈstrɔɪ] vt destruir.

destruction [dɪˈstrʌkʃn] n destruição f.

detach [dɪˈtætʃ] vt separar.

detached house [dɪˈtætʃt-] n casa f
(isolada) (Br), vivenda f (Port).

detail [ˈdiːteɪl] n pormenor m, detalhe
m; in ~ em pormenor.
❏ **details** npl (facts) informações fpl.

detailed [ˈdiːteɪld] adj pormenorizado(-da), detalhado(-da).

detain [dɪˈteɪn] vt (in hospital) manter;
(delay, in custody) deter, reter.

detect [dɪˈtekt] vt detectar.

detective [dɪˈtektɪv] n detetive m; a
~ story uma história policial.

detention [dɪˈtenʃn] n (SCH) castigo
que consiste em ficar na escola depois das
aulas terem terminado.

deter [dɪˈtɜːr] (vt dissuadir, desencorajar; to ~ sb from doing sthg
dissuadir alguém de fazer algo.

detergent [dɪˈtɜːdʒənt] n detergente
m.

deteriorate [dɪˈtɪərɪəreɪt] vi deteriorar.

determination [dɪˌtɜːmɪˈneɪʃn] n
(quality) determinação f.

determine [dɪˈtɜːmɪn] vt determinar.

determined [dɪˈtɜːmɪnd] adj decidido(-da); to be ~ to do sthg estar decidido a fazer algo.

deterrent [dɪˈterənt] n meio m de
dissuasão.

detest [dɪˈtest] vt detestar.

detonate [ˈdetəneɪt] vt fazer detonar
♦ vi detonar.

detour [ˈdiːtuər] n desvio m.

detract [dɪˈtrækt] vi: to ~ from
(quality, enjoyment) diminuir, minorar;
(achievement) menosprezar.

detrain [diːˈtreɪn] vi (fml) desembarcar (de trem).

detrimental [ˌdetrɪˈmentl] adj prejudicial.

deuce [djuːs] excl (in tennis) quarenta
igual!

devastate [ˈdevəsteɪt] vt arrasar.

devastating [ˈdevəsteɪtɪŋ] adj (news,
experience, storm) devastador(-ra);

(remark, argument) arrasador(-ra); *(person, charm, beauty)* irresistível.

develop [dɪ'veləp] *vt (idea, company, land)* desenvolver; *(film)* revelar; *(machine, method)* elaborar; *(illness, habit)* contrair; *(interest)* revelar ◆ *vi (evolve)* desenvolver-se.

developing country [dɪ'veləpɪŋ-] *n* país *m* em vias de desenvolvimento.

development [dɪ'veləpmənt] *n* desenvolvimento *m*; **a housing ~** um conjunto habitacional *(Br)*, uma urbanização *(Port)*.

deviate ['di:vɪeɪt] *vi*: **to ~ from sthg** afastar-se de algo.

device [dɪ'vaɪs] *n* aparelho *m*, dispositivo *m*.

devil ['devl] *n* diabo *m*; **what the ~ …?** *(inf)* que diabo …?

devious ['di:vjəs] *adj (person, means)* desonesto(-ta).

devise [dɪ'vaɪz] *vt* conceber.

devolution [,di:və'lu:ʃn] *n (POL)* descentralização *f*.

devote [dɪ'vəʊt] *vt*: **to ~ sthg to sthg** consagrar OR dedicar algo a algo.

devoted [dɪ'vəʊtɪd] *adj* dedicado(-da).

devotion [dɪ'vəʊʃn] *n* devoção *f*.

devour [dɪ'vaʊəʳ] *vt* devorar.

devout [dɪ'vaʊt] *adj* devoto(-ta).

dew [dju:] *n* orvalho *m*.

diabetes [,daɪə'bi:ti:z] *n* diabetes *m*.

diabetic [,daɪə'betɪk] *adj (person)* diabético(-ca); *(chocolate)* para diabéticos ◆ *n* diabético *m* (-ca *f*).

diagnosis [,daɪəg'nəʊsɪs] *(pl* **-oses** [-əʊsi:z]*) n* diagnóstico *m*.

diagonal [daɪ'ægənl] *adj* diagonal.

diagram ['daɪəgræm] *n* diagrama *m*.

dial ['daɪəl] *n (of clock, radio)* mostrador *m*; *(of telephone)* disco *m* ◆ *vt* discar *(Br)*, marcar *(Port)*.

dialect ['daɪəlekt] *n* dialeto *m*.

dialling code ['daɪəlɪŋ-] *n (Brit)* código *m* de discagem *(Br)*, indicativo *m* *(Port)*.

dialling tone ['daɪəlɪŋ-] *n (Brit)* sinal *m* de discar *(Br)*, sinal de linha *(Port)*.

dialog ['daɪəlɒg] *(Am)* = **dialogue**.

dialogue ['daɪəlɒg] *n (Brit)* diálogo *m*.

dial tone *(Am)* = **dialling tone**.

diameter [daɪ'æmɪtəʳ] *n* diâmetro *m*.

diamond ['daɪəmənd] *n (gem)* diamante *m*.

❏ **diamonds** *npl (in cards)* ouros *mpl*.

diaper ['daɪpəʳ] *n (Am)* fralda *f*.

diarrhoea [,daɪə'rɪə] *n* diarréia *f*.

diary ['daɪərɪ] *n (for appointments)* agenda *f*; *(journal)* diário *m*.

dice [daɪs] *(pl inv) n* dado *m*.

diced [daɪst] *adj (food)* cortado(-da) em cubos.

dictate [dɪk'teɪt] *vt* ditar.

dictation [dɪk'teɪʃn] *n* ditado *m*.

dictator [dɪk'teɪtəʳ] *n* ditador *m* (-ra *f*).

dictatorship [dɪk'teɪtəʃɪp] *n* ditadura *f*.

dictionary ['dɪkʃənrɪ] *n* dicionário *m*.

did [dɪd] *pt* → **do**.

didn't ['dɪdnt] = **did not**.

die [daɪ] *(pt & pp* **died**, *cont* **dying***) vi* morrer; **to be dying for sthg** *(inf)* estar doido por algo; **to be dying to do sthg** *(inf)* estar doido por fazer algo.

❏ **die away** *vi* desvanecer-se.

❏ **die out** *vi* desaparecer.

diesel ['di:zl] *n (fuel)* diesel *m (Br)*, gasóleo *m (Port)*; *(car)* carro *m* diesel *(Br)*, carro *m* a gasóleo *(Port)*.

diet ['daɪət] *n* dieta *f* ◆ *vi* fazer dieta ◆ *adj* de baixa caloria.

diet Coke® *n* Coca-Cola® *f* light.

differ ['dɪfəʳ] *vi (disagree)* discordar; **to ~ (from)** *(be dissimilar)* ser diferente (de).

difference ['dɪfrəns] *n* diferença *f*; **it makes no ~** é igual, não faz diferença; **a ~ of opinion** uma divergência.

different ['dɪfrənt] *adj* diferente; **to be ~ (from)** ser diferente (de).

differently ['dɪfrəntlɪ] *adv* de outra forma.

difficult ['dɪfɪkəlt] *adj* difícil.

difficulty ['dɪfɪkəltɪ] *n* dificuldade *f*.

dig [dɪg] *(pt & pp* **dug***) vt & vi* cavar.

❏ **dig out** *vt sep (rescue)* salvar; *(find)* desenterrar.

❏ **dig up** *vt sep (from ground)* desenterrar.

digest [dɪ'dʒest] *vt* digerir.

digestion [dɪ'dʒestʃn] *n* digestão *f*.

digestive (biscuit) [dɪ'dʒestɪv-] *n (Brit)* biscoito *m* integral.

digit ['dɪdʒɪt] *n (figure)* dígito *m*; *(finger, toe)* dedo *m*.

digital ['dɪdʒɪtl] *adj* digital.

dignified ['dɪgnɪfaɪd] *adj* digno(-gna).

dignity ['dɪgnətɪ] *n* dignidade *f*.

digress [daɪˈgres] vi afastar-se do tema; **to ~ from sthg** afastar-se de algo.

digs [dɪgz] npl (Brit: inf) quarto m alugado.

dike [daɪk] n dique m.

dilapidated [dɪˈlæpɪdeɪtɪd] adj degradado(-da).

dilemma [dɪˈlemə] n dilema m.

diligent [ˈdɪlɪdʒənt] adj diligente.

dill [dɪl] n endro m.

dilute [daɪˈluːt] vt diluir.

dim [dɪm] adj (light) fraco(-ca); (room) escuro(-ra); (memory) vago(-ga); (inf: stupid) burro(-a) ◆ vt (light) diminuir, baixar.

dime [daɪm] n (Am) moeda de dez centavos.

dimensions [dɪˈmenʃnz] npl (measurements) dimensões fpl; (extent) dimensão f.

diminish [dɪˈmɪnɪʃ] vt & vi diminuir.

diminutive [dɪˈmɪnjʊtɪv] adj (fml) minúsculo(-la) ◆ n (GRAMM) diminutivo m.

dimple [ˈdɪmpl] n covinha f (no rosto).

din [dɪn] n barulho m.

dine [daɪn] vi jantar.

❑ **dine out** vi jantar fora.

diner [ˈdaɪnəʳ] n (Am: restaurant) restaurante à beira da estrada que serve refeições a preços baixos; (person) cliente mf (em restaurante).

dinghy [ˈdɪŋgɪ] n (with sail) barco m à vela; (with oars) barco a remos.

dingy [ˈdɪndʒɪ] adj miserável.

dining car [ˈdaɪnɪŋ-] n vagão-restaurante m (Br), carruagem-restaurante f (Port).

dining hall [ˈdaɪnɪŋ-] n refeitório m, cantina f.

dining room [ˈdaɪnɪŋ-] n sala f de jantar.

dinner [ˈdɪnəʳ] n (at lunchtime) almoço m; (in evening) jantar m; **to have ~** (at lunchtime) almoçar; (in evening) jantar.

dinner jacket n smoking m.

dinner party n jantar m.

dinner set n serviço m de jantar.

dinner suit n smoking m.

dinnertime [ˈdɪnətaɪm] n (at lunchtime) hora f do almoço; (in evening) hora do jantar.

dinosaur [ˈdaɪnəsɔːʳ] n dinossauro m.

dip [dɪp] n (in road, land) depressão f; (food) molho m (que se serve com legumes crus e salgadinhos) ◆ vt (into liquid) mergulhar ◆ vi (road, land) descer; **to have a ~** (swim) dar um mergulho; **to ~ one's headlights** (Brit) desligar os faróis, baixar as luzes.

diploma [dɪˈpləʊmə] n diploma m.

diplomat [ˈdɪpləmæt] n diplomata mf.

diplomatic [ˌdɪpləˈmætɪk] adj diplomático(-ca).

dipstick [ˈdɪpstɪk] n vareta f (para medir o óleo do carro).

direct [dɪˈrekt] adj direto(-ta) ◆ adv diretamente ◆ vt dirigir; (film, TV programme) realizar; (play) encenar; **can you ~ me to the railway station?** podia me mostrar o caminho para a estação?

direct current n corrente f contínua.

direction [dɪˈrekʃn] n (of movement) direção f.

❑ **directions** npl (instructions) instruções fpl; **to ask for ~s** pedir indicações.

directly [dɪˈrektlɪ] adv (exactly) exatamente; (soon) diretamente.

director [dɪˈrektəʳ] n diretor m (-ra f); (of film, TV programme) realizador m (-ra f); (of play) encenador m (-ra f).

directory [dɪˈrektərɪ] n lista f telefônica.

directory enquiries n (Brit) informações fpl.

dirt [dɜːt] n sujeira f; (earth) terra f.

dirty [ˈdɜːtɪ] adj sujo(-ja); (joke) porco (porca).

disability [ˌdɪsəˈbɪlətɪ] n deficiência f.

disabled [dɪsˈeɪbld] adj deficiente ◆ npl: **the ~** os deficientes; **"~ toilet"** "banheiro para deficientes".

disadvantage [ˌdɪsədˈvɑːntɪdʒ] n desvantagem f, inconveniente m.

disagree [ˌdɪsəˈgriː] vi (people) não estar de acordo; **to ~ with sb (about)** não concordar com alguém (sobre); **those mussels ~d with me** os mexilhões me fizeram mal.

disagreeable [ˌdɪsəˈgriːəbl] adj desagradável.

disagreement [ˌdɪsəˈgriːmənt] n (argument) discussão f; (dissimilarity) diferença f.

disallow [ˌdɪsəˈlaʊ] vt (appeal, claim) rejeitar; (goal) anular.

disappear [ˌdɪsəˈpɪəʳ] vi desaparecer.

disappearance [ˌdɪsəˈpɪərəns] n

desaparecimento *m*.
disappoint [ˌdɪsə'pɔɪnt] *vt* desiludir.
disappointed [ˌdɪsə'pɔɪntɪd] *adj* desiludido(-da).
disappointing [ˌdɪsə'pɔɪntɪŋ] *adj* decepcionante.
disappointment [ˌdɪsə'pɔɪntmənt] *n* decepção *f*, desapontamento *m*.
disapproval [ˌdɪsə'pruːvl] *n* desaprovação *f*.
disapprove [ˌdɪsə'pruːv] *vi*: **to ~ of** não aprovar.
disarmament [dɪs'ɑːməmənt] *n* desarmamento *m*.
disarray [ˌdɪsə'reɪ] *n*: **in ~** *(clothes, room)* em desordem; *(government, party)* em polvorosa.
disaster [dɪ'zɑːstəʳ] *n* desastre *m*.
disastrous [dɪ'zɑːstrəs] *adj* desastroso(-osa).
disbelief [ˌdɪsbɪ'liːf] *n*: **in** OR **with ~** com incredulidade.
disc [dɪsk] *n (Brit)* disco *m*; *(CD)* CD *m*; **to slip a ~** deslocar uma vértebra.
discard [dɪ'skɑːd] *vt* desfazer-se de.
discern [dɪ'sɜːn] *vt* discernir, distinguir.
discerning [dɪ'sɜːnɪŋ] *adj (person, taste)* exigente; *(eye)* perspicaz.
discharge [dɪst'ʃɑːdʒ] *vt (prisoner)* libertar; *(patient)* dar alta a; *(soldier)* dispensar; *(liquid)* despejar; *(smoke, gas)* emitir.
disciple [dɪ'saɪpl] *n* discíplo *m*.
discipline ['dɪsɪplɪn] *n* disciplina *f*.
disc jockey *n* discotecário *m* (-ria *f*) *(Br)*, disc-jóquei *mf*.
disclose [dɪs'kləʊz] *vt* revelar, divulgar.
disco ['dɪskəʊ] *(pl* -s) *n (place)* discoteca *f*; *(event)* baile *m*.
discoloured [dɪs'kʌləd] *adj* descolorado(-da).
discomfort [dɪs'kʌmfət] *n* desconforto *m*.
disconcert [ˌdɪskən'sɜːt] *vt* desconcertar.
disconnect [ˌdɪskə'nekt] *vt* desligar; *(telephone, gas supply)* cortar.
discontinued [ˌdɪskən'tɪnjuːd] *adj (product)* que já não se fabrica.
discotheque ['dɪskəʊtek] *n (place)* discoteca *f*.
discount ['dɪskaʊnt] *n* desconto *m*.
discourage [dɪs'kʌrɪdʒ] *vt* desencorajar; **to ~ sb from doing sthg**

desencorajar alguém de fazer algo.
discover [dɪ'skʌvəʳ] *vt* descobrir.
discovery [dɪ'skʌvərɪ] *n* descoberta *f*.
discreet [dɪ'skriːt] *adj* discreto(-ta).
discrepancy [dɪ'skrepənsɪ] *n* discrepância *f*.
discretion [dɪ'skreʃn] *n (tact)* discrição *f*; *(judgment)* discernimento *m*; **at the ~ of** ao critério de.
discriminate [dɪ'skrɪmɪneɪt] *vi*: **to ~ against sb** discriminar contra alguém.
discriminating [dɪ'skrɪmɪneɪtɪŋ] *adj (person, audience)* entendido(-da); *(taste)* refinado(-da).
discrimination [dɪˌskrɪmɪ'neɪʃn] *n* discriminação *f*.
discus ['dɪskəs] *(pl* -es) *n* disco *m*.
discuss [dɪ'skʌs] *vt* discutir.
discussion [dɪ'skʌʃn] *n* discussão *f*.
disdain [dɪs'deɪn] *n* desdém *m*; **~ for** desdém por.
disease [dɪ'ziːz] *n* doença *f*.
disembark [ˌdɪsɪm'bɑːk] *vi* desembarcar.
disgrace [dɪs'greɪs] *n* vergonha *f*; **it's a ~!** é uma vergonha!
disgraceful [dɪs'greɪsfʊl] *adj* vergonhoso(-osa).
disguise [dɪs'gaɪz] *n* disfarce *m* ◆ *vt* disfarçar; **in ~** disfarçado.
disgust [dɪs'gʌst] *n* repugnância *f*, nojo *m* ◆ *vt* enojar, repugnar.
disgusting [dɪs'gʌstɪŋ] *adj* nojento(-ta).
dish [dɪʃ] *n* prato *m*; **to do the ~es** lavar a louça; **"~ of the day"** "prato do dia".
⅃ **dish up** *vt sep* servir.
dishcloth ['dɪʃklɒθ] *n* pano *m* de prato.
disheveled [dɪ'ʃevəld] *(Am)* = **dishevelled**.
dishevelled [dɪ'ʃevəld] *adj (Brit) (hair)* despenteado(-da); *(person)* desarrumado(-da).
dishonest [dɪs'ɒnɪst] *adj* desonesto(-ta).
dish towel *n (Am)* pano *m* de prato.
dishwasher ['dɪʃˌwɒʃəʳ] *n (machine)* máquina *f* de lavar a louça.
disillusioned [ˌdɪsɪ'luːʒnd] *adj* desiludido(-da); **~ with** desiludido com.
disinclined [ˌdɪsɪn'klaɪnd] *adj*: **to be ~ to do sthg** estar pouco disposto(-osta) a fazer algo.
disinfect [ˌdɪsɪn'fekt] *vt* desinfectar.

disinfectant [ˌdɪsɪnˈfektənt] *n* desinfectante *m*.

disintegrate [dɪsˈɪntɪɡreɪt] *vi* desintegrar-se.

disinterested [dɪsˈɪntrəstɪd] *adj (impartial)* desinteressado(-da); **to be ~ in** *(inf: uninterested)* mostrar-se desinteressado por.

disk [dɪsk] *n (Am)* = **disc;** *(COMPUT)* disco *m*; *(floppy)* disquete *f*.

disk drive *n* leitor *m* de disquetes.

diskette [dɪsˈket] *n* disquete *f*.

dislike [dɪsˈlaɪk] *n* aversão *f* ♦ *vt* não gostar de; **to take a ~ to** não simpatizar com.

dislocate [ˈdɪsləkeɪt] *vt* deslocar.

dismal [ˈdɪzml] *adj (weather, place)* deprimente; *(terrible)* péssimo(-ma).

dismantle [dɪsˈmæntl] *vt* desmontar.

dismay [dɪsˈmeɪ] *n* consternação *f*.

dismiss [dɪsˈmɪs] *vt (not consider)* rejeitar; *(from job)* despedir; *(from classroom)* dispensar.

dismissal [dɪsˈmɪsl] *n (from job)* demissão *f*, despedida *f (Br)*, despedimento *m (Port)*.

disobedience [ˌdɪsəˈbiːdjəns] *n* desobediência *f*.

disobedient [ˌdɪsəˈbiːdjənt] *adj* desobediente.

disobey [ˌdɪsəˈbeɪ] *vt* desobedecer.

disorder [dɪsˈɔːdəʳ] *n (confusion)* desordem *f*; *(violence)* distúrbios *mpl*; *(illness)* problema *m*; *(mental illness)* distúrbio *m*.

disorderly [dɪsˈɔːdəlɪ] *adj (untidy)* desordenado(-da); *(unruly)* turbulento (-ta).

disorganized [dɪsˈɔːɡənaɪzd] *adj* desorganizado(-da).

disorientated *adj (Brit)* desorientado(-da).

disoriented *(Am)* = **disorientated.**

disown [dɪsˈəʊn] *vt* repudiar.

disparaging [dɪsˈpærɪdʒɪŋ] *adj* depreciativo(-va).

dispatch [dɪsˈpætʃ] *vt* enviar.

dispense [dɪsˈpens] : **dispense with** *vt fus* prescindir de, passar sem.

dispenser [dɪsˈpensəʳ] *n (device)* máquina *f* distribuidora.

dispensing chemist [dɪsˈpensɪŋ-] *n (Brit: shop)* farmácia *f*.

disperse [dɪsˈpɜːs] *vt* dispersar ♦ *vi* dispersar-se.

display [dɪsˈpleɪ] *n (of goods)* expo-

sição *f*; *(public event)* espetáculo *m*; *(readout)* visualização *f* ♦ *vt (goods)* expor; *(feeling, quality)* demonstrar; *(information)* afixar; **on ~** exposto.

displeased [dɪsˈpliːzd] *adj* descontente.

disposable [dɪsˈpəʊzəbl] *adj* descartável.

disposal [dɪsˈpəʊzl] *n (removal)* remoção *f*; **at sb's ~** à disposição de alguém.

disposed [dɪsˈpəʊzd] *adj*: **to be ~ to do sthg** *(willing)* estar disposto(-osta) a fazer algo; **to be well ~ to sthg** *(friendly)* ser favorável a algo.

disprove [dɪsˈpruːv] *(pp -d OR disproven) vt* refutar.

dispute [dɪsˈpjuːt] *n (argument)* discussão *f*; *(industrial)* conflito *m* ♦ *vt* discutir.

disqualify [dɪsˈkwɒlɪfaɪ] *vt* desqualificar; **to be disqualified from driving** *(Brit)* ter a carteira apreendida.

disregard [ˌdɪsrɪˈɡɑːd] *vt* ignorar.

disreputable [dɪsˈrepjʊtəbl] *adj* pouco respeitável.

disrupt [dɪsˈrʌpt] *vt* perturbar, transtornar.

disruption [dɪsˈrʌpʃn] *n* transtorno *m*.

dissatisfaction [ˈdɪsˌsætɪsˈfækʃn] *n* descontentamento *m*.

dissatisfied [ˌdɪsˈsætɪsfaɪd] *adj* insatisfeito(-ta).

dissect [dɪˈsekt] *vt* dissecar.

dissent [dɪˈsent] *n (disagreement)* discordância *f* ♦ *vi*: **to ~ from sthg** não concordar com algo.

dissimilar [dɪˈsɪmɪləʳ] *adj* diferente; **~ to** diferente de.

dissolve [dɪˈzɒlv] *vt* dissolver ♦ *vi* dissolver-se.

dissuade [dɪˈsweɪd] *vt*: **to ~ sb from doing sthg** dissuadir alguém de fazer algo.

distance [ˈdɪstəns] *n* distância *f*; **from a ~** de longe; **in the ~** ao longe.

distant [ˈdɪstənt] *adj* distante.

distil [dɪsˈtɪl] *vt (Brit) (liquid)* destilar; *(fig: information)* extrair.

distill [dɪsˈtɪl] *(Am)* = **distil.**

distilled water [dɪsˈtɪld-] *n* água *f* destilada.

distillery [dɪsˈtɪlərɪ] *n* destilaria *f*.

distinct [dɪsˈtɪŋkt] *adj* distinto(-ta).

distinction [dɪsˈtɪŋkʃn] *n* distinção *f*.

distinctive [dɪ'stɪŋktɪv] *adj* caracte-rístico(-ca).

distinguish [dɪ'stɪŋgwɪʃ] *vt* distin-guir; **to ~ sthg from sthg** distinguir algo de algo.

distinguished [dɪ'stɪŋgwɪʃt] *adj* dis-tinto(-ta).

distorted [dɪ'stɔːtɪd] *adj* distorcido (-da).

distract [dɪ'strækt] *vt* distrair.

distraction [dɪ'strækʃn] *n* distração *f*.

distraught [dɪ'strɔːt] *adj* cons-ternado(-da).

distress [dɪ'stres] *n* (*pain*) sofrimento *m*, dor *f*; (*anxiety*) angústia *f*.

distressing [dɪ'stresɪŋ] *adj* angustian-te.

distribute [dɪ'strɪbjuːt] *vt* distribuir.

distribution [ˌdɪstrɪ'bjuːʃn] *n* distri-buição *f*.

distributor [dɪ'strɪbjʊtəʳ] *n* (*COMM*) distribuidor *m* (-ra *f*); (*AUT*) distribui-dor *m*.

district ['dɪstrɪkt] *n* (*region*) = distrito *m*; (*of town*) ~ bairro *m*, ~ freguesia *f* (*Port*).

district attorney *n* (*Am*) = Procurador *m* (-ra *f*) da República.

district council *n* (*Brit*) ≃ junta *f* distrital (*Br*), junta *f* de freguesia (*Port*).

distrust [dɪs'trʌst] *n* desconfiança *f* ♦ *vt* desconfiar de, não confiar em.

disturb [dɪ'stɜːb] *vt* (*interrupt*) inco-modar; (*worry*) preocupar; (*move*) mexer em; **"do not ~"** "favor não incomodar".

disturbance [dɪ'stɜːbəns] *n* (*violence*) distúrbio *m*.

ditch [dɪtʃ] *n* fosso *m*.

dither ['dɪðəʳ] *vi* hesitar.

ditto ['dɪtəʊ] *adv* idem.

divan [dɪ'væn] *n* divã *m*.

dive [daɪv] (*pt Am* -d OR dove, *pt Brit* -d) *n* (*of swimmer*) mergulho *m* ♦ *vi* mergulhar; (*bird, plane*) descer em vôo picado; (*rush*) lançar-se.

diver ['daɪvəʳ] *n* mergulhador *m* (-ra *f*).

diverge [daɪ'vɜːdʒ] *vi* divergir; **to ~ from sthg** divergir de algo.

diversion [daɪ'vɜːʃn] *n* (*of traffic*) des-vio *m*; (*amusement*) diversão *f*.

diversity [daɪ'vɜːsətɪ] *n* diversidade *f*.

divert [daɪ'vɜːt] *vt* desviar.

divide [dɪ'vaɪd] *vt* dividir.
❏ **divide up** *vt sep* dividir.

dividend ['dɪvɪdend] *n* (*profit*) divi-dendo *m*.

divine [dɪ'vaɪn] *adj* divino(-na).

diving ['daɪvɪŋ] *n* mergulho *m*; **to go ~** ir mergulhar.

divingboard ['daɪvɪŋbɔːd] *n* trampo-lim *m*, prancha *f* de saltos (*Port*).

division [dɪ'vɪʒn] *n* divisão *f*; (*COMM*) departamento *m*.

divorce [dɪ'vɔːs] *n* divórcio *m* ♦ *vt* divorciar-se de.

divorced [dɪ'vɔːst] *adj* divorciado (-da).

divorcee [dɪvɔː'siː] *n* divorciado *m* (-da *f*).

DIY *abbr* = do-it-yourself.

dizzy ['dɪzɪ] *adj* tonto(-ta).

DJ *n* (*abbr of disc jockey*) DJ.

DNA *n* (*abbr of deoxyribonucleic acid*) ADN *m*.

do [duː] (*pt* did, *pp* done, *pl* dos) *aux vb* **1.** (*in negatives*): **don't ~ that!** não faça isso!; **she didn't see it** ela não o viu.

2. (*in questions*): **~ you like it?** gosta você?; **how ~ you do it?** como é que se faz?

3. (*referring to previous verb*): **~ you smoke? – yes, I ~/no, I don't** você fuma? – sim/não; **I eat more than you ~** eu como mais do que você; **no, I didn't!** não é verdade!; **so ~ I** eu tam-bém.

4. (*in question tags*): **so, you like Scotland, ~ you?** então você gosta da Escócia?; **the train leaves at five o'clock, doesn't it?** o trem sai às cinco, não é (verdade)?

5. (*for emphasis*): **I ~ like this bedroom** eu realmente gosto deste quarto; **~ come in!** faça o favor de entrar!

♦ *vt* **1.** (*perform*) fazer; **to ~ one's homework** fazer o dever de casa; **what is she doing?** o que é que ela está fazendo?; **what can I ~ for you?** em que posso ajudá-lo?

2. (*clean, brush etc*): **to ~ one's hair** pentear-se; **to ~ one's make-up** maquilhar-se; **to ~ one's teeth** esco-var os dentes.

3. (*cause*) fazer; **to ~ damage** fazer estragos; **to ~ sb good** fazer bem a alguém.

4. (*have as job*): **what do you ~?** o que você faz?

5. (*provide, offer*) fazer; **we ~ pizzas for**

under £4 vendemos pizzas por menos de 4 libras.
6. *(study)* estudar.
7. *(subj: vehicle)* ir a; **the car was ~ing 50 mph** o carro ia a 80 km/h.
8. *(inf: visit)* visitar; **we're doing Scotland next week** para a semana vamos visitar a Escócia.
♦ *vi* **1.** *(behave, act)* fazer; **~ as I say** faça como eu lhe digo.
2. *(progress, get on)*: **he did badly/well in his exam** ele foi mal/bem no exame; **how did you ~?** como é que foi?
3. *(be sufficient)* chegar; **will £5 ~?** 5 libras chega?
4. *(in phrases)*: **how do you ~?** *(greeting)* como vai?; **how are you ~ing?** como é que vão as coisas?; **what has that got to ~ with it?** o que é que isso tem a ver?
♦ *n (party)* festa *f*; **~s and don'ts** o que fazer e não fazer.
❏ **do out of** *vt sep (inf)*: **he did us out of £10** ele nos levou 10 libras a mais.
❏ **do up** *vt sep (coat, shirt)* abotoar; *(shoes, laces)* apertar, atar; *(zip)* fechar; *(decorate)* renovar; *(wrap up)* embrulhar.
❏ **do with** *vt fus (need)*: **I could ~ with a drink** eu bem que beberia alguma coisa.
❏ **do without** *vt fus* passar sem.
Doberman ['dəʊbəmən] *n (pl -s) n*: **~ (pinscher)** doberman *m*.
docile [*Brit* 'dəʊsaɪl, *Am* 'dɒsəl] *adj* dócil.
dock [dɒk] *n (for ships)* doca *f*; *(JUR)* banco *m* dos réus ♦ *vi* atracar.
docker ['dɒkə'] *n* estivador *m (-ra f)*.
docklands ['dɒkləndz] *npl (Brit)* docas *fpl*.
dockyard ['dɒkjɑːd] *n* estaleiro *m*.
doctor ['dɒktə'] *n (of medicine)* médico *m (-ca f)*, doutor *m (-ra f)*; *(academic)* doutor *m (-ra f)*; **to go to the ~'s** ir ao médico.
doctrine ['dɒktrɪn] *n* doutrina *f*.
document ['dɒkjʊmənt] *n* documento *m*.
documentary [,dɒkjʊ'mentərɪ] *n* documentário *m*.
dodge [dɒdʒ] *vt (question, responsibility, issue)* fugir a, esquivar-se a; *(missile, car)* evitar ♦ *vi* desviar-se.
Dodgems® ['dɒdʒəmz] *npl (Brit)* carrinhos *mpl* de choque.

dodgy ['dɒdʒɪ] *adj (Brit) (inf) (plan, car)* pouco confiável; *(health)* instável.
doe [dəʊ] *n (female deer)* corça *f*; *(female rabbit)* coelha *f*.
does [*weak form* dəz, *strong form* dʌz] → **do**.
doesn't ['dʌznt] = **does not**.
dog [dɒg] *n* cachorro *m (Br)*, cão *m (Port)*.
dog food *n* comida *f* para cachorros.
doggy bag ['dɒgɪ-] *n* saco que em alguns restaurantes é fornecido aos clientes para levarem o que sobrou da refeição.
do-it-yourself *n* sistema *m* faça-você-mesmo *(Br)*, bricolage *f (Port)*.
dole [dəʊl] *n (inf)*: **to be on the ~** *(Brit)* estar desempregado.
doll [dɒl] *n* boneca *f*.
dollar ['dɒlə'] *n* dólar *m*.
dolphin ['dɒlfɪn] *n* golfinho *m*.
dome [dəʊm] *n* abóbada *f*.
domestic [də'mestɪk] *adj* doméstico(-ca); *(of country)* nacional.
domestic appliance *n* eletrodoméstico *m*.
domestic flight *n* vôo *m* doméstico.
domestic science *n* economia *f* doméstica, *disciplina opcional na escola*.
dominant ['dɒmɪnənt] *adj* dominante.
dominate ['dɒmɪneɪt] *vt* dominar.
domineering [,dɒmɪ'nɪərɪŋ] *adj* autoritário(-ria), dominador(-ra).
dominoes ['dɒmɪnəʊz] *n* dominó *m*.
donate [də'neɪt] *vt* doar.
donation [də'neɪʃn] *n* doação *f*.
done [dʌn] *pp* → **do** ♦ *adj* pronto(-ta).
donkey ['dɒŋkɪ] *n* burro *m*.
donor ['dəʊnə'] *n* doador *m (-ra f)*.
don't [dəʊnt] = **do not**.
doomed [duːmd] *adj* condenado(-da); **to be ~ to** estar condenado a.
door [dɔː'] *n* porta *f*.
doorbell ['dɔːbel] *n* campainha *f*.
doorknob ['dɔːnɒb] *n* maçaneta *f*.
doorman ['dɔːmən] *(pl -men)* *n* porteiro *m*.
doormat ['dɔːmæt] *n* tapete *m*, capacho *m*.
doormen ['dɔːmən] *pl* → **doorman**.
doorstep ['dɔːstep] *n* degrau *m*; *(Brit: piece of bread)* fatia de pão bem grossa.
doorway ['dɔːweɪ] *n* entrada *f*.

dope [dəʊp] n (inf) (any illegal drug) droga f; (marijuana) erva f, maconha f.

dormitory ['dɔːmətrɪ] n dormitório m.

Dormobile® ['dɔːməbiːl] n trailer m motorizado (Br), caravana f OR roulote f (motorizada) (Port).

dosage ['dəʊsɪdʒ] n dose f.

dose [dəʊs] n (amount) dose f; (of illness) camada f.

dot [dɒt] n ponto m; **on the ~** (fig) em ponto.

dotted line ['dɒtɪd-] n pontilhado m.

double ['dʌbl] adj duplo(-pla) ♦ n (twice the amount) o dobro; (alcohol) dose f dupla ♦ vt & vi duplicar ♦ adv: **it's ~ the size** tem o dobro do tamanho; **to bend sthg ~** dobrar algo ao meio; **a ~ whisky** um whisky duplo; **~ three, four, two** três, três, quatro, dois; **~"r"** dois erres.
❏ **doubles** n (in tennis) dupla f (Br), pares mpl (Port).

double bass [-beɪs] n contrabaixo m.

double bed n cama f de casal.

double-breasted [-'brestɪd] adj trespassado(-da).

double-check vt & vi verificar duas vezes.

double chin n papada f.

double cream n (Brit) creme m de leite (Br), natas fpl espessas (Port).

double-cross vt trair.

double-decker (bus) [-'dekər-] n ônibus m de dois andares.

double doors npl porta f dupla.

double-dutch n (Brit): **that's ~ to me** isso para mim é chinês.

double-glazing [-'gleɪzɪŋ] n vidros mpl duplos.

double room n quarto m de casal.

doubt [daʊt] n dúvida f ♦ vt duvidar de; **I ~ it** duvido; **I ~ she'll be there** duvido que ela esteja lá; **in ~** (person) em dúvida; (outcome) incerto; **no ~** sem dúvida.

doubtful ['daʊtfʊl] adj (uncertain) improvável; **it's ~ that ...** (unlikely) é pouco provável que ....

doubtless ['daʊtlɪs] adv sem dúvida.

dough [dəʊ] n massa f.

doughnut ['daʊnʌt] n (without hole) = bola f de Berlim; (with hole) Donut® m.

dove[1] [dʌv] n (bird) pomba f.

dove[2] [dəʊv] pt (Am) → dive.

Dover ['dəʊvər] n Dover.

Dover sole n linguado de ótima qualidade proveniente do Canal da Mancha.

down [daʊn] adv **1.** (towards the bottom) para baixo; **~ here/there** aqui/ali em baixo; **to fall ~** cair; **to go ~** descer.
2. (along): **I'm going ~ to the shops** vou até a loja.
3. (downstairs): **I'll come ~ later** vou descer mais tarde.
4. (southwards) para baixo; **we're going ~ to London** vamos até Londres.
5. (in writing): **to write sthg ~** anotar algo.
6. (in phrases): **to go ~ with** (illness) adoecer com.
♦ prep **1.** (towards the bottom of): **they ran ~ the hill** eles correram pelo monte abaixo.
2. (along): **I was walking ~ the street** ia andando pela rua.
♦ adj (inf: depressed) deprimido(-da).
♦ n (feathers) penugem f.
❏ **downs** npl (Brit) colinas fpl.

down-and-out n mendigo m (-ga f).

downfall ['daʊnfɔːl] n queda f, ruína f.

downhearted [ˌdaʊn'hɑːtɪd] adj desanimado(-da).

downhill [ˌdaʊn'hɪl] adv: **to go ~** (walk, run, ski) descer.

Downing Street ['daʊnɪŋ-] n Downing Street.

down payment n entrada f, sinal m.

downpour ['daʊnpɔːr] n aguaceiro m.

downright ['daʊnraɪt] adj (lie) puro(-ra); (fool) completo(-ta) ♦ adv extremamente.

downstairs [ˌdaʊn'steəz] adj do andar de baixo ♦ adv no andar de baixo; **to come** OR **go ~** descer.

downstream [ˌdaʊn'striːm] adv rio abaixo.

down-to-earth adj prático(-ca).

downtown [ˌdaʊn'taʊn] adj (hotel) central; (train, bus) do centro ♦ adv (live) no centro; (go) ao centro; **~ New York** o centro de Nova Iorque.

down under adv (Brit: inf: to or in Australia) para a/na Austrália.

downward ['daʊnwəd] adj descendente.

downwards ['daʊnwədz] adv para baixo.

dowry ['daʊərɪ] n dote m.

doz. *abbr* = **dozen**.

doze [dəʊz] *vi* dormitar, cochilar.

dozen ['dʌzn] *n* dúzia *f*; **a ~ eggs** uma dúzia de ovos.

Dr *(abbr of Doctor)* Dr. *m* (Dra. *f*).

drab [dræb] *adj* sem graça.

draft [drɑːft] *n (early version)* rascunho *m*; *(money order)* ordem *f* de pagamento; *(Am)* = **draught**.

drag [dræg] *vt (pull along)* arrastar ◆ *vi (along ground)* arrastar-se; **what a ~!** *(inf)* que chatice!
❏ **drag on** *vi* arrastar-se.

dragon ['drægən] *n* dragão *m*.

dragonfly ['drægnflaɪ] *n* libélula *f*.

drain [dreɪn] *n (pipe)* esgoto *m* ◆ *vt (tank, radiator)* esvaziar ◆ *vi (vegetables, washing-up)* escorrer.

draining board ['dreɪnɪŋ-] *n* escorredor *m* de louça.

drainpipe ['dreɪnpaɪp] *n* cano *m* de esgoto *(Br)*, caleira *f (Port)*.

dram [dræm] *n (of whisky)* trago *m*.

drama ['drɑːmə] *n (play)* peça *f* de teatro; *(art)* teatro *m*; *(excitement)* drama *m*.

dramatic [drə'mætɪk] *adj* dramático(-ca).

dramatist ['dræmətɪst] *n* dramaturgo *m* (-ga *f*).

drank [dræŋk] *pt* → **drink**.

drapes [dreɪps] *npl (Am)* cortinas *fpl*, reposteiros *mpl*.

drastic ['dræstɪk] *adj* drástico(-ca).

drastically ['dræstɪklɪ] *adv* drasticamente.

draught [drɑːft] *n (Brit) (of air)* corrente *f* de ar.

draught beer *n* chope *m (Br)*, imperial *f (Port)*, fino *m (Port)*.

draughtboard ['drɑːftbɔːd] *n (Brit)* tabuleiro *m* de (jogo de) damas.

draughts [drɑːfts] *n (Brit)* damas *fpl*.

draughty ['drɑːftɪ] *adj* cheio (cheia) de correntes de ar.

draw [drɔː] *(pt* **drew**, *pp* **drawn**) *vt (with pen, pencil)* desenhar; *(line)* traçar; *(pull)* puxar; *(attract)* atrair; *(comparison)* estabelecer; *(conclusion)* chegar a ◆ *vi (with pen, pencil)* desenhar; *(SPORT)* empatar ◆ *n (SPORT: result)* empate *m*; *(lottery)* sorteio *m*; **to ~ the curtains** *(open)* abrir as cortinas; *(close)* fechar as cortinas.
❏ **draw out** *vt sep (money)* levantar.
❏ **draw up** *vt sep (list, contract)* redigir;

(plan) elaborar ◆ *vi (car, bus)* parar.

drawback ['drɔːbæk] *n* inconveniente *m*.

drawbridge ['drɔːbrɪdʒ] *n* ponte *f* levadiça.

drawer [drɔːr] *n* gaveta *f*.

drawing ['drɔːɪŋ] *n* desenho *m*.

drawing board *n* prancheta *f* de desenho.

drawing pin *n (Brit)* percevejo *m (Br)*, pionés *m (Port)*.

drawing room *n* sala *f* de estar.

drawl [drɔːl] *n* forma lenta e pouco clara de falar, alongando as vogais.

drawn [drɔːn] *pp* → **draw**.

dread [dred] *n* pavor *m* ◆ *vt (exam)* temer; **to ~ doing sthg** temer fazer algo.

dreadful ['dredfʊl] *adj* terrível.

dreadfully ['dredfʊlɪ] *adv (badly)* extremamente mal; *(extremely)* extremamente.

dream [driːm] *n* sonho *m* ◆ *vt* sonhar ◆ *vi*: **to ~ (of)** sonhar (com); **a ~ house** uma casa de sonho.

dreary ['drɪərɪ] *adj (day, weather)* sombrio(-bria); *(job, work)* monótono(-na); *(person)* enfadonho(-nha).

dregs [dregz] *npl (of tea, coffee)* borra *f*.

drench [drentʃ] *vt* encharcar, ensopar; **to be ~ed in/with sthg** estar encharcado em algo.

dress [dres] *n (for woman, girl)* vestido *m*; *(clothes)* roupa *f*, fato *m (Port)* ◆ *vt (person, baby)* vestir; *(wound)* ligar; *(salad)* temperar ◆ *vi* vestir-se; **to be ~ed in** estar vestido de; **to get ~ed** vestir-se.
❏ **dress up** *vi (in costume)* disfarçar-se; *(in best clothes)* vestir-se elegantemente.

dress circle *n* balcão *m* nobre *(Br)*, primeiro balcão *m (Port)*.

dresser ['dresər] *n (Brit: for crockery)* aparador *m*; *(Am: chest of drawers)* cômoda *f*.

dressing ['dresɪŋ] *n (for salad)* tempero *m*; *(for wound)* curativo *m (Br)*, penso *m (Port)*.

dressing gown *n* robe *m*, roupão *m*.

dressing room *n* camarim *m*.

dressing table *n* toucador *m*.

dressmaker ['dres,meɪkər] *n* costureiro *m* (-ra *f*).

dress rehearsal *n* ensaio *m* geral.

drew [druː] *pt* → **draw**.

dribble ['drɪbl] vi (liquid) pingar; (baby) babar-se.

dried [draɪd] adj (herbs, fruit, flowers) seco(-ca); (milk, eggs) em pó.

drier ['draɪə^r] = dryer.

drift [drɪft] n (of snow) monte m ♦ vi (in wind) ser levado pelo vento; (in water) ser levado pela água, derivar.

drill [drɪl] n (electric tool) furadeira f (Br), berbequim m (Port); (manual tool, of dentist) broca f ♦ vt (hole) furar.

drink [drɪŋk] (pt **drank**, pp **drunk**) n (of water, tea etc) bebida f; (alcoholic) copo m, bebida ♦ vt & vi beber; **would you like a ~?** quer beber OR tomar algo?; **to have a ~** (alcoholic) beber OR tomar um copo.

drinkable ['drɪŋkəbl] adj (safe to drink) potável; (wine) razoável.

drink-driving n (Brit) ato de dirigir sob a influência de álcool.

drinking water ['drɪŋkɪŋ-] n água f potável.

drip [drɪp] n (drop) gota f; (MED) aparelho m de soro ♦ vi pingar.

drip-dry adj que não necessita ser passado a ferro.

dripping (wet) ['drɪpɪŋ-] adj encharcado(-da).

drive [draɪv] (pt **drove**, pp **driven**) n (journey) viagem f; (in front of house) acesso m, caminho m ♦ vt (car, bus, train) dirigir (Br), conduzir (Port); (take in car) levar (em carro) ♦ vi (drive car) dirigir (Br), conduzir (Port); (travel in car) ir de carro; **to go for a ~** ir dar um passeio de carro; **it's driven by electricity** funciona a electricidade; **to ~ sb to do sthg** levar alguém a fazer algo; **to ~ sb mad** deixar alguém louco.

drivel ['drɪvl] n disparates mpl.

driven ['drɪvn] pp → drive.

driver ['draɪvə^r] n (of car, taxi) motorista mf; (of bus) condutor m (-ra f); (of train) maquinista mf.

driver's license (Am) = driving licence.

driveshaft ['draɪvʃuːft] n eixo m motor, transmissão f.

driveway ['draɪvweɪ] n acesso m, caminho m.

driving ['draɪvɪŋ] n direção f (Br), condução f (Port).

driving instructor n instrutor m (-ra f) de auto-escola.

driving lesson n aula f de direção (Br), aula f de condução (Port).

driving licence n (Brit) carteira f de motorista (Br), carta f de condução (Port).

driving school n auto-escola f (Br), escola f de condução (Port).

driving test n exame m de direção (Br), exame m de condução (Port).

drizzle ['drɪzl] n chuvisco m.

drone [drəʊn] n (sound of insect) zumbido m; (of plane, voices) ruído m.

drop [drɒp] n gota f, pingo m; (distance down) descida f; (decrease) queda f ♦ vt (let fall by accident) deixar cair; (let fall on purpose) jogar; (reduce) baixar; (from vehicle) deixar; (omit) omitir ♦ vi (fall) cair; (decrease) baixar; **to ~ a hint that** dar a entender que; **to ~ sb a line** escrever uma palavrinha a alguém.

❑ **drop in** vi (inf): **to ~ in on sb** passar por casa de alguém.

❑ **drop off** vt sep (from vehicle) deixar ♦ vi (fall asleep) adormecer; (fall off) cair.

❑ **drop out** vi (of college) abandonar os estudos; (of race) desistir.

dropout ['drɒpaʊt] n (from society) marginal mf; (from university) pessoa f que abandona os estudos.

droppings ['drɒpɪŋz] npl excrementos mpl (de animal).

drought [draʊt] n seca f.

drove [drəʊv] pt → drive.

drown [draʊn] vi afogar-se.

drowsy ['draʊzɪ] adj sonolento(-ta).

drug [drʌg] n droga f ♦ vt drogar.

drug abuse n consumo m de drogas, toxicodependência f.

drug addict n drogado m (-da f), toxicômano m (-na f).

druggist ['drʌgɪst] n (Am) farmacêutico m (-ca f).

drugstore ['drʌgstɔː^r] n (Am) farmácia f.

drum [drʌm] n (MUS) tambor m; (container) barril m; **to play the ~s** tocar bateria.

drummer ['drʌmə^r] n baterista mf.

drumstick ['drʌmstɪk] n (of chicken) perna f.

drunk [drʌŋk] pp → drink ♦ adj bêbado(-da) ♦ n bêbado m (-da f); **to get ~** embebedar-se.

drunk-driving (Am) = drink-driving.

drunken ['drʌŋkn] adj (person) bêbado(-da); (party, talk) de bêbados.

dry [draɪ] *adj* seco(-ca) ♦ *vt (hands, washing-up)* limpar, secar; *(clothes)* secar ♦ *vi* secar; **to ~ o.s.** limpar-se; **to ~ one's hair** secar o cabelo.
❑ **dry up** *vi (become dry)* secar; *(dry the dishes)* limpar.

dry-clean *vt* limpar a seco.

dry cleaner's *n* lavanderia *f.*

dryer ['draɪəʳ] *n (for clothes)* máquina *f* de secar; *(for hair)* secador *m.*

dry-roasted peanuts [-'rəʊstɪd] *npl* amendoins *mpl* torrados.

dry ski slope *n* pista *f* de ski artificial.

DSS *n (Brit)* ministério britânico da Segurança Social.

DTP *abbr* = desktop publishing.

dual ['dju:əl] *adj* duplo(-pla).

dual carriageway *n (Brit)* via *f* dupla *(Br)*, via *f* rápida *(Port)*.

dubbed [dʌbd] *adj (film)* dublado (-da) *(Br)*, dobrado(-da) *(Port)*.

dubious ['dju:bjəs] *adj (suspect)* duvidoso(-osa).

Dublin ['dʌblɪn] *n* Dublim *s.*

duchess ['dʌtʃɪs] *n* duquesa *f.*

duck [dʌk] *n* pato *m* ♦ *vi* abaixar-se.

duckling ['dʌklɪŋ] *n (animal)* patinho *m*; *(food)* pato *m.*

dud [dʌd] *adj (coin, note)* falso(-sa); *(cheque)* sem fundos *(Br)*, careca *(Port)*; *(machine, video, idea)* inútil; *(bomb, shell, bullet)* que não rebentou.

due [dju:] *adj (owed)* devido(-da); *(to be paid)* a pagar; **the train is ~ at eight o'clock** a chegada do trem está prevista para as oito; **in ~ course** no tempo devido; **~ to** devido a.

duel ['dju:əl] *n* duelo *m.*

duet [dju:'et] *n* dueto *m.*

duffel bag ['dʌfl-] *n* saco *m* tipo marinheiro.

duffel coat ['dʌfl-] *n* casaco *m (grosso de inverno com capuz).*

dug [dʌg] *pt & pp* → **dig.**

duke [dju:k] *n* duque *m.*

dull [dʌl] *adj (boring)* chato(-ta), aborrecido(-da); *(not bright)* baço(-ça); *(weather)* cinzento (-ta); *(pain)* incômodo(-da).

duly ['dju:lɪ] *adv (properly)* devidamente; *(as expected)* como era de se esperar.

dumb [dʌm] *adj (inf: stupid)* estúpido(-da); *(unable to speak)* mudo (-da).

dumbfound [dʌm'faʊnd] *vt* deixar estupefato(-ta); **to be ~ed** ficar estupefato.

dummy ['dʌmɪ] *n (Brit: for baby)* chupeta *f*; *(for clothes)* manequim *m.*

dump [dʌmp] *n (for rubbish)* lixeira *f*; *(inf: place)* espelunca *f* ♦ *vt (drop carelessly)* deixar cair; *(get rid of)* desfazer-se de.

dumper (truck) ['dʌmpəʳ-] *n (Brit)* caminhão *m* basculante *(Br)*, camião *m* basculante *(Port)*.

dumpling ['dʌmplɪŋ] *n bolinho de massa cozido e servido com ensopados.*

dump truck *(Am)* = **dumper (truck)**.

dunce [dʌns] *n* burro *m* (-a *f*).

dune [dju:n] *n* duna *f.*

dung [dʌŋ] *n* excremento *m*, bosta *f.*

dungarees [ˌdʌŋgə'ri:z] *npl (Brit: for work)* macacão *m (Br)*, fato-macaco *m (Port)*; *(fashion item)* jardineiras *fpl*; *(Am: jeans)* jeans *m inv (Br)*, calças *fpl* de ganga *(Port)*.

dungeon ['dʌndʒən] *n* masmorra *f.*

duo ['dju:əʊ] *n* duo *m.*

duplicate ['dju:plɪkət] *n* duplicado *m.*

duration [dju'reɪʃn] *n* duração *f*; **for the ~ of** durante.

during ['djʊərɪŋ] *prep* durante.

dusk [dʌsk] *n* crepúsculo *m.*

dust [dʌst] *n (in building)* pó *m*; *(on ground)* pó, poeira *f* ♦ *vt (furniture, object)* tirar o pó de.

dustbin ['dʌstbɪn] *n (Brit)* lata *f* de lixo *(Br)*, caixote *m* do lixo *(Port)*.

dustcart ['dʌstkɑ:t] *n (Brit)* caminhão *m* do lixo *(Br)*, camião *m* do lixo *(Port)*.

duster ['dʌstəʳ] *n* pano *m* de pó.

dustman ['dʌstmən] *(pl -men* [-mən]*) n (Brit)* lixeiro *m (Br)*, gari *m (Br)*, homem *m* do lixo *(Port)*.

dustpan ['dʌstpæn] *n* pá *f* de lixo.

dusty ['dʌstɪ] *adj (road)* poeirento(-ta); *(room, air)* cheio (cheia) de pó.

Dutch [dʌtʃ] *adj* holandês(-esa) ♦ *n (language)* neerlandês *m*, holandês *m* ♦ *npl*: **the ~** os holandeses.

Dutchman ['dʌtʃmən] *(pl -men* [-mən]*) n* holandês *m.*

Dutchwoman ['dʌtʃˌwʊmən] *(pl -women* [-ˌwɪmɪn]*) n* holandesa *f.*

duty ['dju:tɪ] *n (moral obligation)* dever *m*; *(tax)* taxa *f*; **to be on ~** estar de plantão; **to be off ~** estar de folga.
❑ **duties** *npl (job)* funções *fpl.*

duty chemist's *n* farmácia *f* de plantão.

duty-free *adj* livre de impostos ◆ *n (article)* artigo *m* isento de impostos alfandegários.

duty-free shop *n* duty-free shop *m*, loja *f* franca *(Port)*.

duvet ['duːveɪ] *n* edredom *m (Br)*, edredão *m (Port)*.

duvet cover *n (Brit)* capa *f* de edredom.

dwarf [dwɔːf] *(pl* **dwarves** [dwɔːvz]*) n* anão *m* (anã *f*).

dwelling ['dwelɪŋ] *n (fml)* moradia *f*.

dye [daɪ] *n* tinta *f* (para tingir) ◆ *vt* tingir.

dying ['daɪɪŋ] *cont* → **die**.

dyke [daɪk] = **dike**.

dynamic [daɪ'næmɪk] *adj* dinâmico(-ca).

dynamite ['daɪnəmaɪt] *n* dinamite *f*.

dynamo ['daɪnəməʊ] *(pl* **-s**) *n* dínamo *m*.

dynasty [*Brit* 'dɪnəstɪ, *Am* 'daɪnəstɪ] *n* dinastia *f*.

dyslexic [dɪs'leksɪk] *adj* disléxico(-ca).

E

E *(abbr of east)* E.

E111 *n* E111 *m*, impresso necessário para obter assistência médica nos outros países da União Européia.

each [iːtʃ] *adj & pron* cada; **~ one** cada um (cada uma); **~ of them** cada um deles (cada uma delas); **~ other** um ao outro; **they fought ~ other** lutaram um contra o outro; **we know ~ other** nós nos conhecemos; **one ~** um a cada um; **one of ~** um de cada.

eager [ˈiːgəʳ] *adj (pupil)* entusiasta; *(expression)* de entusiasmo; **to be ~ to do sthg** estar ansioso por fazer algo; **~ to please** doido para agradar.

eagle [ˈiːgl] *n* águia *f*.

ear [ɪəʳ] *n* orelha *f*; *(of corn)* espiga *f*.

earache [ˈɪəreɪk] *n* dor *f* de ouvidos; **I've got ~** estou com dor de ouvidos.

eardrum [ˈɪədrʌm] *n* tímpano *m*.

earl [ɜːl] *n* conde *m*.

earlier [ˈɜːlɪəʳ] *adj* anterior ◆ *adv* antes; **~ on** antes.

earlobe [ˈɪələʊb] *n* lóbulo *m* da orelha.

early [ˈɜːlɪ] *adj (before usual or arranged time)* antecipado(-da) ◆ *adv* cedo; **I need to catch an ~ train** preciso pegar um trem que passa mais cedo; **it arrived an hour ~** chegou uma hora mais cedo; **~ last year** no início do ano passado; **in the ~ morning** de madrugada; **at the earliest** o mais cedo possível, no mínimo; **~ on** cedo; **to have an ~ night** deitar-se cedo.

earn [ɜːn] *vt* ganhar; **to ~ a living** ganhar a vida.

earnest [ˈɜːnɪst] *adj* sério(-ria); **to begin in ~** começar a sério.

earnings [ˈɜːnɪŋz] *npl* rendimentos *mpl*.

earphones [ˈɪəfəʊnz] *npl* fones *mpl* de ouvido *(Br)*, auscultadores *mpl (Port)*.

earplugs [ˈɪəplʌgz] *npl* tampões *mpl*

auriculares OR para os ouvidos.

earrings [ˈɪərɪŋz] *npl* brincos *mpl*.

earshot [ˈɪəʃɒt] *n*: **within ~** ao alcance do ouvido; **out of ~** fora do alcance do ouvido.

earth [ɜːθ] *n* terra *f*; *(Brit: electrical connection)* fio *m* terra ◆ *vt (Brit: appliance)* ligar à terra; **how on ~ ...?** como diabo ...?

earthenware [ˈɜːθnweəʳ] *adj* de barro.

earthquake [ˈɜːθkweɪk] *n* terremoto *m*.

earthworm [ˈɜːθwɜːm] *n* minhoca *f*.

earwig [ˈɪəwɪg] *n* lacrainha *f (Br)*, bicha-cadela *f (Port)*.

ease [iːz] *n* facilidade *f* ◆ *vt (pain, tension)* aliviar; *(problem)* minorar; **at ~** à vontade; **with ~** com facilidade, facilmente.

❑ **ease off** *vi* diminuir.

easel [ˈiːzl] *n* cavalete *m*.

easily [ˈiːzɪlɪ] *adv (without difficulty)* facilmente; *(by far)* de longe.

east [iːst] *n* leste *m*, este *m* ◆ *adj* leste, este ◆ *adv (be situated)* a leste; *(fly, walk)* para este, para leste; **in the ~ of England** no leste da Inglaterra; **the East** *(Asia)* o Oriente.

eastbound [ˈiːstbaʊnd] *adj* em direção a leste OR ao este.

East End *n*: **the ~** o leste de Londres.

Easter [ˈiːstəʳ] *n* Páscoa *f*.

Easter egg *n* ovo *m* de Páscoa.

easterly [ˈiːstəlɪ] *adj (wind)* de leste; **in an ~ direction** em direção ao leste OR este; **the most ~ point** o ponto mais a leste OR este.

eastern [ˈiːstən] *adj* de leste, do este.

❑ **Eastern** *adj (Asian)* oriental.

Eastern Europe *n* Europa *f* de Leste.

eastward ['iːstwəd] *adj*: **in an ~ direction** em direção ao leste OR este.
eastwards ['iːstwədz] *adv* em direção ao leste OR este, para leste OR este.
easy ['iːzɪ] *adj* fácil; **to take it ~** *(relax)* levar as coisas com calma; **take it ~!** *(be calm)* tenha calma!
easy chair *n* poltrona *f*, cadeirão *m*.
easygoing [ˌiːzɪ'gəʊɪŋ] *adj* descontraído(-da).
eat [iːt] *(pt* **ate,** *pp* **eaten** ['iːtn]) *vt & vi* comer.
❑ **eat out** *vi* comer fora.
eating apple ['iːtɪŋ-] *n* maçã *f* (para comer).
eaves ['iːvz] *npl* beirais *mpl*.
ebony ['ebənɪ] *n* ébano *m*.
EC *n (abbr of European Community)* CE *f*.
eccentric [ɪk'sentrɪk] *adj* excêntrico(-ca).
echo ['ekəʊ] *(pl* **-es)** *n* eco *m* ◆ *vi* ecoar.
eclipse [ɪ'klɪps] *n* eclipse *m*.
ecological [ˌiːkə'lɒdʒɪkl] *adj* ecológico(-ca).
ecology [ɪ'kɒlədʒɪ] *n* ecologia *f*.
economic [ˌiːkə'nɒmɪk] *adj* econômico(-ca).
❑ **economics** *n* economia *f*.
economical [ˌiːkə'nɒmɪkl] *adj* econômico(-ca).
economize [ɪ'kɒnəmaɪz] *vi* economizar.
economy [ɪ'kɒnəmɪ] *n* economia *f*.
economy class *n* classe *f* turística.
economy size *adj* de tamanho econômico.
ecotourism [ˌiːkəʊ'təʊrɪzm] *n* ecoturismo *m*.
ecstasy ['ekstəsɪ] *n (great joy)* êxtase *m; (drug)* ecstasy *f*.
ecstatic [ek'stætɪk] *adj* extasiado (-da).
ECU ['ekjuː] *n* ECU *m*.
eczema ['eksɪmə] *n* eczema *m*.
edge [edʒ] *n (border)* beira *f; (of table, coin, plate)* borda *f; (of knife)* fio *m*, gume *m*.
edible ['edɪbl] *adj* comestível.
Edinburgh ['edɪnbrə] *n* Edimburgo *s*.
Edinburgh Festival *n*: **the ~** o Festival de Edimburgo.
edit ['edɪt] *vt (text)* corrigir, revisar; *(newspaper, magazine)* dirigir; *(film, programme)* montar.
edition [ɪ'dɪʃn] *n* edição *f*.

editor ['edɪtər] *n (of text)* editor *m* (-ra *f*); *(of newspaper, magazine)* diretor *m* (-ra *f*); *(of film, TV programme)* técnico *m* (-ca *f*) de montagem.
editorial [ˌedɪ'tɔːrɪəl] *n* editorial *m*.
educate ['edʒʊkeɪt] *vt* educar.
education [ˌedʒʊ'keɪʃn] *n* educação *f*.
educational [ˌedʒʊ'keɪʃənl] *adj (establishment, policy)* educacional; *(toy, experience)* didático(-ca).
eel [iːl] *n* enguia *f*.
eerie ['ɪərɪ] *adj* sinistro(-tra), arrepiante.
effect [ɪ'fekt] *n* efeito *m*; **to put sthg into ~** pôr em prática; **to take ~** *(medicine)* fazer efeito; *(law)* entrar em vigor.
effective [ɪ'fektɪv] *adj (successful)* eficaz; *(law, system)* em vigor.
effectively [ɪ'fektɪvlɪ] *adv (successfully)* eficazmente, com eficácia; *(in fact)* com efeito.
effeminate [ɪ'femɪnət] *adj* efeminado(-da).
efficiency [ɪ'fɪʃənsɪ] *n (of person)* eficiência *f; (of factory)* economia *f*.
efficient [ɪ'fɪʃənt] *adj (person)* eficiente; *(factory)* econômico(-ca).
effluent ['efluənt] *n* águas *fpl* residuais, esgotos *mpl*.
effort ['efət] *n* esforço *m*; **to make an ~ to do sthg** fazer um esforço para fazer algo; **it's not worth the ~** não vale a pena o esforço.
effortless ['efətlɪs] *adj (easy)* fácil; *(natural)* natural.
e.g. *adv* e.g., p. ex.
egg [eg] *n* ovo *m*.
egg cup *n* oveiro *m*, *pequeno suporte para ovos quentes.*
egg mayonnaise *n recheio para sanduíches composto por ovo cozido e maionese.*
eggplant ['egplɑːnt] *n (Am)* beringela *f*.
eggshell ['egʃel] *n* casca *f* de ovo.
egg white *n* clara *f* de ovo.
egg yolk *n* gema *f* de ovo.
ego ['iːgəʊ] *(pl* **-s)** *n* ego *m*, amor *m* próprio.
egoistic [ˌiːgəʊ'ɪstɪk] *adj* egoísta.
egotistic(al) [ˌiːgə'tɪstɪk(l)] *adj* egotista.
Egypt ['iːdʒɪpt] *n* Egipto *m*.
Egyptian [ɪ'dʒɪpʃn] *adj* egípcio(-cia)

♦ *n* egípcio *m* (-cia *f*).

eiderdown ['aɪdədaʊn] *n* edredom *m* *(Br)*, edredão *m* *(Port)*.

eight [eɪt] *num* oito, → **six**.

eighteen [.eɪ'tiːn] *num* dezoito, → **six**.

eighteenth [.eɪ'tiːnθ] *num* décimo oitavo (décima oitava), → **sixth**.

eighth [eɪtθ] *num* oitavo(-va), → **sixth**.

eightieth ['eɪtɪɪθ] *num* octogésimo (-ma), → **sixth**.

eighty ['eɪtɪ] *num* oitenta, → **six**.

Eire ['eərə] *n* República *f* da Irlanda.

Eisteddfod [aɪ'stedfəd] *n* festival cultural galês.

either ['aɪðər, 'iːðər] *adj*: ~ **book will do** qualquer um dos livros serve ♦ *pron*: **I'll take** ~ **(of them)** levo qualquer um (dos dois); **I don't like** ~ **(of them)** não gosto de nenhum (deles) ♦ *adv*: **I can't** ~ também não posso; ~ ... **or you ... no** ou; **I don't speak** ~ **Portuguese or English** não falo nem português nem inglês; **on** ~ **side** dos dois lados.

eject [ɪ'dʒekt] *vt (cassette)* tirar.

elaborate [ɪ'læbrət] *adj* elaborado (-da), complicado(-da).

elapse [ɪ'læps] *vi* decorrer.

elastic [ɪ'læstɪk] *n* elástico *m*.

elasticated [ɪ'læstɪkeɪtɪd] *adj* elástico(-ca).

elastic band *n (Brit)* elástico *m*.

elbow ['elbəʊ] *n* cotovelo *m*.

elder ['eldər] *adj* mais velho(-lha).

elderly ['eldəlɪ] *adj* idoso(-osa) ♦ *npl*: **the** ~ os idosos.

eldest ['eldɪst] *adj* mais velho(-lha).

elect [ɪ'lekt] *vt* eleger; **to** ~ **to do sthg** *(fml: choose)* escolher fazer algo.

election [ɪ'lekʃn] *n* eleição *f*.

electioneering [ɪ.lekʃə'nɪərɪŋ] *n* propaganda *f* eleitoral.

electorate [ɪ'lektərət] *n*: **the** ~ o eleitorado.

electric [ɪ'lektrɪk] *adj* elétrico(-ca).

electrical [ɪ'lektrɪkl] *adj* elétrico(-ca).

electrical goods *npl* eletrodomésticos *mpl*.

electric blanket *n* cobertor *m* elétrico.

electric cooker *n* fogão *m* elétrico.

electric drill *n* furadeira *f* elétrica *(Br)*, berbequim *m* (eléctrico) *(Port)*.

electric fence *n* vedação *f* eletrificada.

electric fire *n* radiador *m* OR aquecedor *m* elétrico.

electrician [.ɪlek'trɪʃn] *n* eletricista *mf*.

electricity [.ɪlek'trɪsətɪ] *n* eletricidade *f*.

electric shock *n* choque *m* elétrico.

electrocute [ɪ'lektrəkjuːt] *vt* eletrocutar.

electronic [.ɪlek'trɒnɪk] *adj* eletrônico(-ca).

electronic mail *n* correio *m* eletrônico.

elegant ['elɪgənt] *adj* elegante.

element ['elɪmənt] *n* elemento *m*; *(of fire, kettle)* resistência *f*; **the** ~**s** *(weather)* os elementos.

elementary [.elɪ'mentərɪ] *adj* elementar.

elementary school *n (Am)* escola *f* primária.

elephant ['elɪfənt] *n* elefante *m*.

elevator ['elɪveɪtər] *n (Am)* elevador *m*.

eleven [ɪ'levn] *num* onze, → **six**.

elevenses [ɪ'levnzɪz] *n (Brit)* refeição leve por volta das onze da manhã.

eleventh [ɪ'levnθ] *num* décimo primeiro (décima primeira), → **sixth**.

eligible ['elɪdʒəbl] *adj (qualified, suitable)* apto(-ta); *(bachelor)* elegível.

eliminate [ɪ'lɪmɪneɪt] *vt* eliminar.

elitist [ɪ'liːtɪst] *adj* elitista ♦ *n* elitista *mf*.

Elizabethan [ɪ.lɪzə'biːθn] *adj* isabelino(-na) *(segunda metade do séc. XVI)*.

elk [elk] *(pl inv* OR **-s**) *n* alce *m*.

elm [elm] *n* ulmeiro *m*, olmo *m*.

eloquent ['eləkwənt] *adj* eloqüente.

else [els] *adv*: **I don't want anything** ~ não quero mais nada; **anything** ~? mais alguma coisa?; **everyone** ~ os outros todos (as outras todas); **nobody** ~ mais ninguém; **nothing** ~ mais nada; **somebody** ~ mais alguém; **something** ~ outra coisa; **somewhere** ~ outro lugar; **what** ~? que mais?; **who** ~? quem mais?; **or** ~ ou então, senão.

elsewhere [els'weər] *adv (be, search)* noutro lugar; *(with verbs of motion)* para outro lado.

elude [ɪ'luːd] *vt (police, pursuers)* eludir; *(subj: fact, idea, name)* escapar a.

elusive [ɪ'luːsɪv] *adj (success, quality)* difícil de alcançar; *(person, animal)* difícil de encontrar.

e-mail *n (abbr of electronic mail)* e-mail *m*.

emancipate [ɪ'mænsɪpeɪt] *vt*: **to ~ sb from sthg** libertar alguém de algo.

embankment [ɪm'bæŋkmənt] *n (next to river)* margem *f*; *(next to road, railway)* barreira *f*.

embark [ɪm'bɑːk] *vi (board ship)* embarcar.

embarkation card [,embɑː'keɪʃn-] *n* cartão *m* de embarque.

embarrass [ɪm'bærəs] *vt* envergonhar.

embarrassed [ɪm'bærəst] *adj* envergonhado(-da).

embarrassing [ɪm'bærəsɪŋ] *adj* embaraçoso(-osa).

embarrassment [ɪm'bærəsmənt] *n* vergonha *f*.

embassy ['embəsɪ] *n* embaixada *f*.

embers ['embəz] *npl* brasas *fpl*.

emblem ['embləm] *n* emblema *m*.

embossed [ɪm'bɒst] *adj (paper)* timbrado(-da); *(wallpaper)* em relevo; *(leather)* gravado(-da); *(design, lettering)*: **~ (on sthg)** gravado (em algo).

embrace [ɪm'breɪs] *vt* abraçar.

embroidered [ɪm'brɔɪdəd] *adj* bordado(-da).

embroidery [ɪm'brɔɪdərɪ] *n* bordado *m*.

embryo ['embrɪəʊ] *(pl -s) n* embrião *m*.

emerald ['emərəld] *n* esmeralda *f*.

emerge [ɪ'mɜːdʒ] *vi (from place)* emergir, sair; *(fact, truth)* vir à tona.

emergency [ɪ'mɜːdʒənsɪ] *n* emergência *f* ♦ *adj* de emergência; **in an ~** em caso de emergência.

emergency exit *n* saída *f* de emergência.

emergency landing *n* aterissagem *f* de emergência.

emergency services *npl* serviços *mpl* de emergência.

emery board ['emərɪ-] *n* lixa *f* (para as unhas).

emigrant ['emɪgrənt] *n* emigrante *mf*.

emigrate ['emɪgreɪt] *vi* emigrar.

eminent ['emɪnənt] *adj* eminente.

emission [ɪ'mɪʃn] *n* emissão *f*.

emit [ɪ'mɪt] *vt* emitir.

emotion [ɪ'məʊʃn] *n* emoção *f*.

emotional [ɪ'məʊʃənl] *adj (situation, scene)* comovente; *(person)* emotivo(-va).

emperor ['empərər] *n* imperador *m*.

emphasis ['emfəsɪs] *(pl -ases* [-əsiːz]) *n* ênfase *f*.

emphasize ['emfəsaɪz] *vt* enfatizar, sublinhar.

emphatically [ɪm'fætɪklɪ] *adv (say, state)* enfaticamente; *(agree)* plenamente; *(disagree)* em absoluto.

empire ['empaɪər] *n* império *m*.

employ [ɪm'plɔɪ] *vt* empregar.

employed [ɪm'plɔɪd] *adj* empregado(-da).

employee [ɪm'plɔɪiː] *n* empregado *m* (-da *f*).

employer [ɪm'plɔɪər] *n* patrão *m* (-troa *f*).

employment [ɪm'plɔɪmənt] *n* emprego *m*.

employment agency *n* agência *f* de emprego.

empress ['empris] *n* imperatriz *f*.

empty ['emptɪ] *adj (containing nothing)* vazio(-zia); *(threat, promise)* vão (vã) ♦ *vt* esvaziar.

empty-handed [-'hændɪd] *adv* de mãos vazias OR a abanar.

EMU *n* UEM *f*.

emulate ['emjʊleɪt] *vt* emular.

emulsion (paint) [ɪ'mʌlʃn-] *n* tinta *f* de emulsão.

enable [ɪ'neɪbl] *vt*: **to ~ sb to do sthg** permitir a alguém fazer algo.

enamel [ɪ'næml] *n* esmalte *m*.

enchanted [ɪn'tʃuːntɪd] *adj*: **~ by OR with sthg** encantado(-da) com algo.

enchanting [ɪn'tʃuːntɪŋ] *adj* encantador(-ra).

encircle [ɪn'sɜːkl] *vt* rodear.

enclose [ɪn'kləʊz] *vt (surround)* rodear; *(with letter)* juntar.

enclosed [ɪn'kləʊzd] *adj (space)* vedado(-da).

enclosure [ɪn'kləʊʒər] *n (place)* recinto *m*.

encore ['ɒŋkɔːr] *n* bis *m* ♦ *excl* bis!

encounter [ɪn'kaʊntər] *vt* encontrar.

encourage [ɪn'kʌrɪdʒ] *vt* encorajar; **to ~ sb to do sthg** encorajar alguém a fazer algo.

encouragement [ɪn'kʌrɪdʒmənt] *n* encorajamento *m*.

encyclopedia [ɪn,saɪklə'piːdjə] *n* enciclopédia *f*.

end [end] *n* fim *m*; *(furthest point)* extremo *m*; *(of string, finger)* ponta *f*

◆ *vt* acabar, terminar; *(war, practice)* acabar com ◆ *vi* acabar, terminar; **to come to an ~** chegar ao fim; **to put an ~ to sthg** acabar com algo; **for days on ~** durante dias e dias OR dias a fio; **in the ~** no fim; **to make ~s meet** conseguir que o dinheiro chegue ao fim do mês.

⊐ **end up** *vi* acabar; **to ~ up doing sthg** acabar por fazer algo.

endanger [ɪn'deɪndʒər] *vt* pôr em risco OR perigo.

endangered species [ɪn'deɪndʒəd-] *n* espécie *f* em vias de extinção.

endearing [ɪn'dɪərɪŋ] *adj* cativante.

ending ['endɪŋ] *n (of story, film, book)* fim *m*, final *m*; *(GRAMM)* terminação *f*.

endive ['endaɪv] *n* endívia *f*.

endless ['endlɪs] *adj* infinito(-ta), sem fim.

endorsement [ɪn'dɔːsmənt] *n (of driving licence)* multa anotada na carteira de motorista.

endurance [ɪn'djuərəns] *n* resistência *f*.

endure [ɪn'djuər] *vt* suportar.

endways ['endweɪz] *adv (Brit) (not sideways)* ao comprido; *(with ends touching)* ponta com ponta, extremidade com extremidade.

endwise ['endwaɪz] *(Am)* = **endways**.

enemy ['enɪmɪ] *n* inimigo *m* (-ga *f*).

energetic [,enə'dʒetɪk] *adj* energético(-ca), ativo(-va).

energy ['enədʒɪ] *n* energia *f*.

enforce [ɪn'fɔːs] *vt (law)* aplicar, fazer cumprir.

engaged [ɪn'geɪdʒd] *adj (to be married)* noivo(-va); *(Brit: phone)* ocupado(-da) *(Br)*, impedido(-da) *(Port)*; *(toilet)* ocupado(-da); **to get ~** ficar noivo.

engaged tone *n (Brit)* sinal *m* de ocupado *(Br)*, sinal de impedido *(Port)*.

engagement [ɪn'geɪdʒmənt] *n (to marry)* noivado *m*; *(appointment)* compromisso *m*, encontro *m*.

engagement ring *n* anel *m* de noivado.

engine ['endʒɪn] *n (of vehicle)* motor *m*; *(of train)* máquina *f*.

engine driver *n (Brit)* maquinista *mf*.

engineer [,endʒɪ'nɪər] *n (of roads, machinery)* engenheiro *m* (-ra *f*); *(to do repairs)* técnico *m* (-ca *f*).

engineering [,endʒɪ'nɪərɪŋ] *n* engenharia *f*.

engineering works *npl (on railway line)* trabalhos *mpl* na linha.

England ['ɪŋglənd] *n* Inglaterra *f*.

English ['ɪŋglɪʃ] *adj* inglês(-esa) ◆ *n (language)* inglês *m* ◆ *npl*: **the ~** os ingleses.

English breakfast *n* café da manhã tradicional composto por ovos e bacon fritos, salsichas e torradas, acompanhado de café ou chá.

English Channel *n*: **the ~** o Canal da Mancha.

Englishman ['ɪŋglɪʃmən] *(pl -men* [-mən]) *n* inglês *m*.

Englishwoman ['ɪŋglɪʃ,wumən] *(pl -women* [-,wɪmɪn]) *n* inglesa *f*.

engrave [ɪn'greɪv] *vt* gravar.

engraving [ɪn'greɪvɪŋ] *n* gravura *f*.

engrossed [ɪn'grəust] *adj*: **to be ~ in sthg** estar absorto(-ta) em algo.

enhance [ɪn'hɑːns] *vt (value)* aumentar; *(reputation, chances)* melhorar; *(beauty)* realçar.

enjoy [ɪn'dʒɔɪ] *vt* gostar de; **to ~ doing sthg** gostar de fazer algo; **to ~ o.s.** divertir-se; **~ your meal!** bom apetite!

enjoyable [ɪn'dʒɔɪəbl] *adj* agradável.

enjoyment [ɪn'dʒɔɪmənt] *n* prazer *m*.

enlarge [ɪn'lɑːdʒ] *vt (photograph, building)* ampliar; *(scope)* alargar.

⊐ **enlarge on** *vt fus* desenvolver, alargar-se sobre.

enlargement [ɪn'lɑːdʒmənt] *n (of photo)* ampliação *f*.

enlightened [ɪn'laɪtnd] *adj* esclarecido(-da).

enormity [ɪ'nɔːmətɪ] *n* enormidade *f*.

enormous [ɪ'nɔːməs] *adj* enorme.

enough [ɪ'nʌf] *adj* suficiente ◆ *pron* o suficiente ◆ *adv* suficientemente; **~ time** tempo suficiente; **is that ~?** chega?; **it's not big ~** não é suficientemente grande; **I've had ~ of your cheek!** estou farto do seu atrevimento!

enquire [ɪn'kwaɪər] *vi* informar-se.

enquiry [ɪn'kwaɪərɪ] *n (question)* pergunta *f*; *(investigation)* inquérito *m*, investigação *f*; **"Enquiries"** "Informações".

enquiry desk *n* (balcão *m* de) informações *fpl*.

enraged [ɪn'reɪdʒd] *adj* enraivecido(-da).

enrol [ɪn'rəul] *vi (Brit)* matricular-se.

enroll [ɪn'rəul] *(Am)* = **enrol**.

ensue [ɪn'sjuː] *vi (fml)* surgir, acontecer.

en suite bathroom [ɒn'swiːt] *n* banheiro *m* privativo.

ensure [ɪn'ʃʊəʳ] *vt* assegurar, garantir.

entail [ɪn'teɪl] *vt (involve)* implicar.

enter ['entəʳ] *vt* entrar em; *(college, army)* entrar para; *(competition)* inscrever-se em; *(on form)* escrever ◆ *vi* entrar; *(in competition)* inscrever-se.

enterprise ['entəpraɪz] *n (business)* empresa *f*.

enterprising ['entəpraɪzɪŋ] *adj* empreendedor(-ra).

entertain [ˌentə'teɪn] *vt (amuse)* entreter.

entertainer [ˌentə'teɪnəʳ] *n* artista *mf* (de variedades).

entertaining [ˌentə'teɪnɪŋ] *adj* divertido(-da).

entertainment [ˌentə'teɪnmənt] *n (amusement)* divertimento *m*; *(show)* espetáculo *m*.

enthusiasm [ɪn'θjuːzɪæzm] *n* entusiasmo *m*.

enthusiast [ɪn'θjuːzɪæst] *n* entusiasta *mf*.

enthusiastic [ɪnˌθjuːzɪ'æstɪk] *adj* entusiástico(-ca).

entice [ɪn'taɪs] *vt* seduzir; **to ~ sb into** sthg atrair alguém para algo.

entire [ɪn'taɪəʳ] *adj* inteiro(-ra).

entirely [ɪn'taɪəlɪ] *adv* completamente.

entirety [ɪn'taɪrətɪ] *n*: **in its ~** na totalidade.

entitle [ɪn'taɪtl] *vt*: **to ~ sb to sthg** dar a alguém o direito a algo; **to ~ sb to do sthg** dar o direito a alguém de fazer algo.

entitled [ɪn'taɪtld] *adj*: **to be ~ to sthg** ter direito a algo; **to be ~ to do sthg** ter o direito de fazer algo.

entrance ['entrəns] *n* entrada *f*.

entrance examination *n* exame *m* de admissão.

entrance fee *n* entrada *f*.

entrant ['entrənt] *n (in competition)* participante *mf*.

entrepreneur [ˌɒntrəprə'nɜːʳ] *n* empresário *m* (-ria *f*).

entry ['entrɪ] *n* entrada *f*; *(in competition)* inscrição *f*, candidatura *f*; **"no ~"** *(sign on door)* "entrada proibida"; *(road sign)* "acesso proibido".

entry form *n* impresso *m* OR folha *f* de inscrição.

entry phone *n* interfone *m*.

envelope ['envələʊp] *n* envelope *m*.

envious ['envɪəs] *adj* invejoso(-osa).

environment [ɪn'vaɪərənmənt] *n* meio *m*; **the ~** o meio ambiente.

environmental [ɪnˌvaɪərən'mentl] *adj* ambiental.

environmentally friendly [ɪnˌvaɪərən'mentəlɪ-] *adj* amigo(-ga) do ambiente.

envy ['envɪ] *vt* invejar.

epic ['epɪk] *n* epopéia *f*.

epidemic [ˌepɪ'demɪk] *n* epidemia *f*.

epileptic [ˌepɪ'leptɪk] *adj* epiléptico(-ca).

episode ['epɪsəʊd] *n* episódio *m*.

equal ['iːkwəl] *adj* igual ◆ *vt* igualar; **to be ~ to** *(number)* ser igual a.

equality [ɪ'kwɒlətɪ] *n* igualdade *f*.

equalize ['iːkwəlaɪz] *vi* igualar.

equalizer ['iːkwəlaɪzəʳ] *n* gol *m* de empate *(Br)*, golo *m* da igualdade *(Port)*.

equally ['iːkwəlɪ] *adv (bad, good, matched)* igualmente; *(pay, treat)* de forma igual, da mesma forma; *(share)* por igual; *(at the same time)* ao mesmo tempo.

equal opportunities *npl* igualdade *f* de oportunidades.

equation [ɪ'kweɪʒn] *n* equação *f*.

equator [ɪ'kweɪtəʳ] *n*: **the ~** o equador.

equilibrium [ˌiːkwɪ'lɪbrɪəm] *n* equilíbrio *m*.

equip [ɪ'kwɪp] *vt*: **to ~ sb/sthg with** equipar alguém/algo com.

equipment [ɪ'kwɪpmənt] *n* equipamento *m*.

equipped [ɪ'kwɪpt] *adj*: **to be ~ with** estar equipado(-da) com.

equivalent [ɪ'kwɪvələnt] *adj* equivalente ◆ *n* equivalente *m*.

ER *n (Am: abbr of emergency room)* Urgências *fpl*.

era ['ɪərə] *n* era *f*.

eradicate [ɪ'rædɪkeɪt] *vt* erradicar.

erase [ɪ'reɪz] *vt (letter, word)* apagar.

eraser [ɪ'reɪzəʳ] *n* borracha *f* (de apagar).

erect [ɪ'rekt] *adj* erecto(-ta) ◆ *vt (tent)* montar; *(monument)* erigir.

ERM *n* mecanismo de câmbio do SME.

ermine ['ɜːmɪn] *n* arminho *m*.

erosion [ɪ'rəʊʒn] *n (of soil, rock)* erosão *f*.

erotic [ɪ'rɒtɪk] *adj* erótico(-ca).

errand ['erənd] *n* recado *m*.

erratic [ɪ'rætɪk] *adj* irregular.

error ['erə^r] *n* erro *m*.

erupt [ı'rʌpt] *vi (volcano)* entrar em erupção; *(violence, war)* estourar.

eruption [ı'rʌpʃn] *n (of volcano)* erupção *f*; *(of war)* deflagração *f*.

escalator ['eskəleıtə^r] *n* escadas *fpl* rolantes.

escalope ['eskəlɒp] *n* escalope *m*.

escape [ı'skeıp] *n* fuga *f* ◆ *vi*: **to ~ (from)** *(from prison, danger)* fugir (de); *(leak)* escapar (de).

escapism [ı'skeıpızm] *n* evasão *f* (à realidade).

escort [*n* 'eskɔːt, *vb* ı'skɔːt] *n (guard)* escolta *f* ◆ *vt* escoltar.

Eskimo ['eskıməʊ] *(pl inv OR -s) n (person)* esquimó *mf*.

espadrilles ['espə,drılz] *npl* alpercatas *fpl*.

especially [ı'speʃəlı] *adv (in particular)* sobretudo; *(on purpose)* especialmente; *(very)* particularmente.

esplanade [,esplə'neıd] *n* passeio *m*, avenida *f* à beira-mar.

espresso [ı'spresəʊ] *(pl -s) n* café *m*.

esquire [ı'skwaıə^r] *n*: **D. Lowis, ~ Exmo Sr. D. Lowis.**

essay ['eseı] *n (at school)* redação *f*, composição *f*; *(at university)* trabalho *m* escrito.

essence ['esns] *n* essência *f*; **in ~** no fundo.

essential [ı'senʃl] *adj* essencial.
  ❑ **essentials** *npl*: **the ~s** o essencial; **the bare ~s** o mínimo indispensável.

essentially [ı'senʃəlı] *adv* essencialmente.

establish [ı'stæblıʃ] *vt* estabelecer.

establishment [ı'stæblıʃmənt] *n (business)* estabelecimento *m*.

estate [ı'steıt] *n (land in country)* propriedade *f*; *(for housing)* conjunto *m* habitacional *(Br)*, urbanização *f (Port)*; *(Brit: car)* = **estate car**.

estate agency *n (Brit)* agência *f* imobiliária.

estate agent *n (Brit)* agente *m* imobiliário (agente *f* imobiliária).

estate car *n (Brit)* perua *f (Br)*, carrinha *f (Port)*.

esteem [ı'stiːm] *vt* admirar, estimar ◆ *n* consideração *f*, estima *f*.

esthetic [iːs'θetık] *(Am)* = **aesthetic**.

estimate [*n* 'estımət, *vb* 'estımeıt] *n (guess)* estimativa *f*; *(from builder, plumber)* orçamento *m* ◆ *vt* calcular.

Estonia [e'stəʊnjə] *n* Estônia *f*.

estuary ['estjʊərı] *n* estuário *m*.

etc. *(abbr of etcetera)* etc.

eternal [ı'tɜːnl] *adj (everlasting)* eterno(-na); *(fig: perpetual, continual)* contínuo(-nua).

Ethiopia [,iːθı'əʊpjə] *n* Etiópia *f*.

ethnic minority ['eθnık-] *n* minoria *f* étnica.

etiquette ['etıket] *n* etiqueta *f*.

EU *n (abbr of European Union)* UE *f*.

euphemism ['juːfəmızm] *n* eufemismo *m*.

Eurocheque ['jʊərəʊ,tʃek] *n* Eurocheque *m*.

Europe ['jʊərəp] *n* Europa *f*.

European [,jʊərə'pıən] *adj* europeu(-péia) ◆ *n* europeu *m* (-péia *f*).

European Community *n* Comunidade *f* Européia.

European Parliament *n*: **the ~** o Parlamento Europeu.

euthanasia [,juːθə'neızjə] *n* eutanásia *f*.

evacuate [ı'vækjʊeıt] *vt* evacuar.

evade [ı'veıd] *vt (person)* evitar; *(issue, responsibility)* fugir a.

evaluate [ı'væljʊeıt] *vt* avaliar.

evaporate [ı'væpəreıt] *vi* evaporar.

evaporated milk [ı'væpəreıtıd-] *n* leite *m* evaporado.

eve [iːv] *n*: **on the ~ of** na véspera de.

even [ˈiːvn] *adj (level)* plano(-na); *(equal)* igual; *(number)* par ◆ *adv (emphasizing surprise)* mesmo; *(in comparisons)* ainda; **to break ~** funcionar sem lucros nem prejuízos; **~ so** mesmo assim; **~ though** ainda que; **not ~** nem mesmo OR sequer.

evening [ˈiːvnıŋ] *n (from 5 p.m. until 8 p.m.)* fim *m* da tarde; *(from 8 p.m. onwards)* noite *f*; *(event)* serão *m*, noite *f*; **good ~!** boa tarde!, boa noite!; **in the ~** ao fim da tarde, à noite.

evening classes *npl* aulas *fpl* à noite.

evening dress *n (formal clothes)* traje *m* de cerimônia; *(woman's garment)* vestido *m* de noite.

evening meal *n* jantar *m*, refeição *f* da noite.

event [ı'vent] *n (occurrence)* acontecimento *m*; *(SPORT)* prova *f*; **in the ~ of** *(fml)* em caso de.

eventful [ı'ventfʊl] *adj* movimentado(-da), fértil em acontecimentos.

eventual [ı'ventʃʊəl] *adj* final.

eventually [ɪ'ventʃʊəlɪ] adv finalmente.

ever ['evə'] adv (at any time) alguma
vez; (in negatives) nunca; **I don't ~ do
that** nunca faço isso; **the best I've ~
seen** o melhor que já vi; **he was ~ so
angry** ele estava mesmo zangado; **for
~** (eternally) para sempre; **we've been
waiting for ~** estamos esperando há
muito tempo; **hardly ~** quase nunca;
~ since adv desde então ♦ prep desde
♦ conj desde que.

evergreen ['evəgriːn] adj de folhas
persistentes OR perenes ♦ n árvore f de
folhas persistentes OR perenes.

every ['evrɪ] adj cada; **~ day** cada dia,
todos os dias; **~ other day** dia sim, dia
não; **one in ~ ten** um em cada dez; **we
make ~ effort ...** fazemos o possível
...; **~ so often** de vez em quando.

everybody ['evrɪˌbɒdɪ] = everyone.

everyday ['evrɪdeɪ] adj diário(-ria).

everyone ['evrɪwʌn] pron toda a
gente, todos mpl (-das fpl).

everyplace ['evrɪˌpleɪs] (Am) =
everywhere.

everything ['evrɪθɪŋ] pron tudo.

everywhere ['evrɪweə'] adv (be, search)
por todo o lado; (with verbs of motion)
para todo o lado; **~ you go it's the same**
onde quer que se vá é o mesmo.

evict [ɪ'vɪkt] vt: **to ~ sb (from)** despejar alguém (de).

evidence ['evɪdəns] n prova f.

evident ['evɪdənt] adj evidente.

evidently ['evɪdəntlɪ] adv (apparently)
aparentemente; (obviously) evidentemente.

evil ['iːvl] adj mau (má) ♦ n o mal.

evolution [ˌiːvə'luːʃn] n evolução f.

ewe [juː] n ovelha f.

ex [eks] n (inf) ex mf.

exact [ɪg'zækt] adj exato(-ta); **"~ fare
ready please"** aviso em ônibus pedindo
que se pague o dinheiro exacto do bilhete,
pois não se dá troco.

exactly [ɪg'zæktlɪ] adv exatamente
♦ excl exato!

exaggerate [ɪg'zædʒəreɪt] vt & vi
exagerar.

exaggeration [ɪgˌzædʒə'reɪʃn] n exagero m.

exam [ɪg'zæm] n exame m; **to take** OR
sit an ~ fazer um exame.

examination [ɪgˌzæmɪ'neɪʃn] n exame
m.

examine [ɪg'zæmɪn] vt examinar.

examiner [ɪg'zæmɪnə'] n examinador
m (-ra f).

example [ɪg'zɑːmpl] n exemplo m; **for
~** por exemplo.

exasperate [ɪg'zæspəreɪt] vt exaspe-
rar.

excavate ['ekskəveɪt] vt escavar.

exceed [ɪk'siːd] vt ultrapassar.

exceedingly [ɪk'siːdɪŋlɪ] adv tremen-
damente.

excel [ɪk'sel] vi: **to ~ in** OR **at sthg**
distinguir-se OR sobressair-se em algo.

excellence ['eksələns] n excelência f,
perfeição f.

excellent ['eksələnt] adj excelente.

except [ɪk'sept] prep exceto, a menos
que ♦ conj exceto; **~ for** exceto; **"~ for
access"** "exceto trânsito local"; **"~ for
loading"** "exceto cargas e descargas".

excepting [ɪk'septɪŋ] prep & conj =
except.

exception [ɪk'sepʃn] n exceção f.

exceptional [ɪk'sepʃnəl] adj excecio-
nal.

excerpt ['eksɜːpt] n trecho m, excerto
m.

excess [ɪk'ses, before nouns 'ekses] adj
excessivo(-va), em excesso ♦ n excesso m.

excess baggage n excesso m de
bagagem.

excess fare n (Brit) prolongamento
m.

excessive [ɪk'sesɪv] adj excessivo(-va).

exchange [ɪks'tʃeɪndʒ] n (of telephones)
central f telefônica; (of students) intercâmbio m ♦ vt trocar; **to ~ sthg for sthg**
trocar algo por algo; **to be on an ~**
estar participando de um intercâmbio.

exchange rate n taxa f de câmbio.

excite [ɪk'saɪt] vt (person) excitar;
(interest, suspicion) provocar.

excited [ɪk'saɪtɪd] adj entusiasmado
(-da).

excitement [ɪk'saɪtmənt] n (excited
feeling) entusiasmo m; (exciting thing)
emoção f.

exciting [ɪk'saɪtɪŋ] adj emocionante,
excitante.

exclaim [ɪk'skleɪm] vt & vi exclamar.

exclamation mark [ˌeksklə'meɪʃn-]
n (Brit) ponto m de exclamação.

exclamation point [ˌeksklə'meɪʃn-]
(Am) = exclamation mark.

exclude [ɪk'skluːd] vt excluir.

excluding [ɪk'sklu:dɪŋ] *prep* excluindo.
exclusive [ɪk'sklu:sɪv] *adj* exclusivo(-va) ◆ *n* exclusivo *m*; ~ **of VAT** IVA não incluído.
excrement ['ekskrɪmənt] *n* (*fml*) excremento *m*.
excruciating [ɪk'skru:ʃieɪtɪŋ] *adj* terrível.
excursion [ɪk'skɜ:ʃn] *n* excursão *f*.
excuse [*n* ɪk'skju:s, *vb* ɪk'skju:z] *n* desculpa *f* ◆ *vt* (*forgive*) desculpar; (*let off*) dispensar; ~ **me!** (*attracting attention*) desculpe!, faz favor!; (*trying to get past*) com licença!; (*as apology*) desculpe!, perdão!
ex-directory *adj* (*Brit*) que não figura na lista telefônica.
execute ['eksɪkju:t] *vt* executar.
execution [ˌeksɪ'kju:ʃn] *n* execução *f*.
executive [ɪg'zekjʊtɪv] *adj* (*suite, travel*) para executivos ◆ *n* (*person*) executivo *m* (-va *f*).
exempt [ɪg'zempt] *adj*: ~ **(from)** isento(-ta) (de).
exemption [ɪg'zempʃn] *n* (*from taxes*) isenção *f*; (*from exam*) dispensa *f*.
exercise ['eksəsaɪz] *n* exercício *m* ◆ *vi* exercitar-se, fazer exercício; **to do** ~**s** fazer exercícios.
exercise book *n* caderno *m* (de exercícios).
exert [ɪg'zɜ:t] *vt* exercer.
exertion [ɪg'zɜ:ʃn] *n* esforço *m*.
exhale [eks'heɪl] *vt & vi* exalar.
exhaust [ɪg'zɔ:st] *vt* esgotar ◆ *n*: ~ **(pipe)** cano *m* de descarga (*Br*), tubo *m* de escape (*Port*).
exhausted [ɪg'zɔ:stɪd] *adj* exausto (-ta).
exhausting [ɪg'zɔ:stɪŋ] *adj* exaustivo(-va).
exhibit [ɪg'zɪbɪt] *n* (*in museum, gallery*) objeto *m* exposto ◆ *vt* (*in exhibition*) exibir.
exhibition [ˌeksɪ'bɪʃn] *n* (*of art*) exposição *f*.
exhilarating [ɪg'zɪləreɪtɪŋ] *adj* excitante.
exile ['eksaɪl] *n* (*condition*) exílio *m* ◆ *vt*: **to** ~ **sb from** exilar alguém de; **in** ~ no exílio.
exist [ɪg'zɪst] *vi* existir.
existence [ɪg'zɪstəns] *n* existência *f*; **to be in** ~ existir.
existing [ɪg'zɪstɪŋ] *adj* existente.
exit ['eksɪt] *n* saída *f* ◆ *vi* sair.

exorbitant [ɪg'zɔ:bɪtənt] *adj* exorbitante.
exotic [ɪg'zɒtɪk] *adj* exótico(-ca).
expand [ɪk'spænd] *vi* (*in size*) expandir-se; (*in number*) aumentar.
expansion [ɪk'spænʃn] *n* (*in size*) expansão *f*; (*in number*) aumento *m*.
expect [ɪk'spekt] *vt* esperar; **to** ~ **to do sthg** esperar fazer algo; **to** ~ **sb to do sthg** esperar que alguém faça algo; **to be** ~**ing** (*be pregnant*) estar grávida.
expectant [ɪk'spektənt] *adj* (*crowd, person*) expectante.
expectant mother *n* futura mãe *f*.
expectation [ˌekspek'teɪʃn] *n* (*hope*) esperança *f*; **it's my** ~ **that ...** creio que ...; **against** OR **contrary to all** ~**s** contra todas as expectativas, ao contrário do que seria de esperar.
expedition [ˌekspɪ'dɪʃn] *n* expedição *f*.
expel [ɪk'spel] *vt* (*from school*) expulsar.
expenditure [ɪk'spendɪtʃəʳ] *n* (*of money*) despesa *f*; (*of energy, resource*) gasto *m*, consumo *m*.
expense [ɪk'spens] *n* gasto *m*, despesa *f*; **at the** ~ **of** à custa de.
❑ **expenses** *npl* (*of business person*) gastos *mpl*, despesas *fpl*.
expensive [ɪk'spensɪv] *adj* caro(-ra).
experience [ɪk'spɪərɪəns] *n* experiência *f* ◆ *vt* passar por.
experienced [ɪk'spɪərɪənst] *adj* com experiência, experiente.
experiment [ɪk'sperɪmənt] *n* experiência *f* ◆ *vi* experimentar.
expert ['ekspɜ:t] *adj* (*advice, treatment*) especializado(-da) ◆ *n* perito *m* (-ta *f*).
expertise [ˌekspɜ:'ti:z] *n* perícia *f*, competência *f*.
expire [ɪk'spaɪəʳ] *vi* caducar.
expiry date [ɪk'spaɪərɪ-] *n* prazo *m* de validade.
explain [ɪk'spleɪn] *vt* explicar.
explanation [ˌeksplə'neɪʃn] *n* explicação *f*.
explicit [ɪk'splɪsɪt] *adj* explícito(-ta).
explode [ɪk'spləʊd] *vi* explodir.
exploit [ɪk'splɔɪt] *vt* explorar.
exploitation [ˌeksplɔɪ'teɪʃn] *n* exploração *f*.
exploration [ˌeksplə'reɪʃn] *n* exploração *f*.
explore [ɪk'splɔ:ʳ] *vt* explorar.
explorer [ɪk'splɔ:rəʳ] *n* explorador *m* (-ra *f*).
explosion [ɪk'spləʊʒn] *n* explosão *f*.

explosive [ɪkˈspləʊsɪv] n explosivo m.

export [n ˈekspɔːt, vb ɪkˈspɔːt] n exportação f ♦ vt exportar.

expose [ɪkˈspəʊz] vt expor.

exposed [ɪkˈspəʊzd] adj (place) desprotegido(-da).

exposure [ɪkˈspəʊʒə^r] n (photograph) fotografia f; (to heat, radiation) exposição f; **to die of ~** morrer de frio OR por exposição ao frio.

exposure meter n fotômetro m.

express [ɪkˈspres] adj (letter, delivery) urgente; (train) rápido(-da) ♦ n (train) expresso m ♦ vt exprimir ♦ adv: **send it ~** envie-o pelo serviço mais rápido.

expression [ɪkˈspreʃn] n expressão f.

expressive [ɪkˈspresɪv] adj expressivo(-va).

expressly [ɪkˈspreslɪ] adv expressamente.

expressway [ɪkˈspreswei] n (Am) auto-estrada f.

exquisite [ɪkˈskwɪzɪt] adj (features, manners) delicado(-da); (painting, jewellery) magnífico(-ca); (taste) requintado(-da).

extend [ɪkˈstend] vt prolongar; (hand) estender ♦ vi (stretch) estender-se.

extension [ɪkˈstenʃn] n (of building) anexo m; (for phone) ramal m (Br), extensão f (Port); (for permit) prolongamento m, prorrogação f; (for essay) prolongamento do prazo de entrega.

extension lead n extensão f.

extensive [ɪkˈstensɪv] adj vasto(-ta).

extensively [ɪkˈstensɪvlɪ] adv extensivamente.

extent [ɪkˈstent] n (of damage) dimensão f; (of knowledge) grau m; **to a certain ~** até certo ponto; **to what ~ ...?** em que medida ...?

exterior [ɪkˈstɪərɪə^r] adj exterior ♦ n (of car, building) exterior m.

exterminate [ɪkˈstɜːmɪneɪt] vt exterminar.

external [ɪkˈstɜːnl] adj externo(-na).

extinct [ɪkˈstɪŋkt] adj extinto(-ta).

extinction [ɪkˈstɪŋkʃn] n extinção f.

extinguish [ɪkˈstɪŋgwɪʃ] vt (fire, cigarette) apagar.

extinguisher [ɪkˈstɪŋgwɪʃə^r] n extintor m.

extortionate [ɪkˈstɔːʃnət] adj exorbitante.

extra [ˈekstrə] adj extra (inv) ♦ n extra m ♦ adv (more) mais, extra; **be ~ care-**ful! tenha muito cuidado!; **an ~ special** offer uma oferta extremamente especial; **we'll have to try ~ hard** temos de nos esforçar ainda mais; **~ charge** suplemento m; **~ large** XL.
☐ **extras** npl (in price) extras mpl.

extract [n ˈekstrækt, vb ɪkˈstrækt] n (of yeast, malt etc) extrato m; (from book, opera) trecho m ♦ vt (tooth) arrancar.

extractor fan [ɪkˈstræktə-] n (Brit) exaustor m.

extradite [ˈekstrədaɪt] vt: **to ~ sb from/to** extraditar alguém de/para.

extraordinary [ɪkˈstrɔːdnrɪ] adj extraordinário(-ria).

extravagance [ɪkˈstrævəgəns] n extravagância f.

extravagant [ɪkˈstrævəgənt] adj extravagante.

extreme [ɪkˈstriːm] adj extremo(-ma) ♦ n extremo m.

extremely [ɪkˈstriːmlɪ] adv extremamente.

extremist [ɪkˈstriːmɪst] adj extremista ♦ n extremista mf.

extricate [ˈekstrɪkeɪt] vt: **to ~ sthg from** retirar algo de; **to ~ o.s. from** livrar-se de.

extrovert [ˈekstrəvɜːt] n extrovertido m (-da f).

exuberance [ɪgˈzjuːbərəns] n exuberância f.

eye [aɪ] n olho m; (of needle) buraco m ♦ vt olhar para; **to keep an ~ on** vigiar.

eyeball [ˈaɪbɔːl] n globo m ocular.

eyebath [ˈaɪbɑːθ] n copo m (para lavar os olhos).

eyebrow [ˈaɪbraʊ] n sobrancelha f.

eyebrow pencil n lápis m inv de sobrancelhas.

eye drops npl colírio m (Br), gotas fpl para os olhos (Port).

eyeglasses [ˈaɪgluːsɪz] npl (Am) óculos mpl.

eyelash [ˈaɪlæʃ] n pestana f.

eyelid [ˈaɪlɪd] n pálpebra f.

eyeliner [ˈaɪlaɪnə^r] n lápis m inv para os olhos.

eye shadow n sombra f para os olhos.

eyesight [ˈaɪsaɪt] n vista f.

eyesore [ˈaɪsɔː^r] n monstruosidade f.

eyestrain [ˈaɪstreɪn] n astenopia f, vista f cansada.

eye test n exame m de vista.

eyewitness [ˌaɪˈwɪtnɪs] n testemunha mf ocular.

F

F *(abbr of Fahrenheit)* F.
fable ['feɪbl] *n* fábula *f*.
fabric ['fæbrɪk] *n (cloth)* tecido *m*.
fabulous ['fæbjʊləs] *adj* fabuloso (-osa).
facade [fə'sɑːd] *n* fachada *f*.
face [feɪs] *n* cara *f*, face *f*, rosto *m*; *(of cliff, mountain)* lado *m*; *(of clock, watch)* mostrador *m* ◆ *vt* encarar; **the hotel ~s the harbour** o hotel dá para o porto; **to be ~d with** ver-se perante.
❏ **face up to** *vt fus* fazer face a.
facecloth ['feɪsklɒθ] *n (Brit)* toalinha *f* de rosto.
face cream *n* creme *m* facial.
face-lift *n* (operação) plástica *f*; **they've given the building a ~** eles reformaram a fachada do edifício.
face powder *n* pó-de-arroz *m*.
face value *n* valor *m* nominal; **to take sthg at ~** levar algo ao pé da letra.
facial ['feɪʃl] *n* limpeza *f* facial OR de pele.
facilitate [fə'sɪlɪteɪt] *vt (fml)* facilitar.
facilities [fə'sɪlɪtiːz] *npl* instalações *fpl*.
facing ['feɪsɪŋ] *adj* oposto(-osta).
facsimile [fæk'sɪmɪlɪ] *n* fac-símile *m*.
fact [fækt] *n* fato *m*; **in ~** na realidade.
factor ['fæktər] *n* fator *m*; **~ ten suntan lotion** bronzeador com fator de proteção dez.
factory ['fæktərɪ] *n* fábrica *f*.
factual ['fæktʃʊəl] *adj* fatual.
faculty ['fækltɪ] *n (at university)* faculdade *f*.
fad [fæd] *n (of person)* mania *f* (passageira); *(of society)* moda *f* (passageira).
fade [feɪd] *vi (light, sound)* desaparecer; *(flower)* murchar; *(jeans, wallpaper)* desbotar.
faded ['feɪdɪd] *adj (jeans)* ruço(-ça),

desbotado(-da).
fag [fæg] *n (Brit: inf: cigarette)* cigarro *m*.
Fahrenheit ['færənhaɪt] *adj* Farenheit *(inv)*.
fail [feɪl] *vt (exam)* reprovar ◆ *vi (not succeed)* fracassar; *(in exam)* não passar; *(engine)* falhar; **to ~ to do sthg** *(not do)* não fazer algo.
failing ['feɪlɪŋ] *n* defeito *m* ◆ *prep*: **~ that** senão.
failure ['feɪljər] *n* fracasso *m*; *(unsuccessful person)* fracassado *m* (-da *f*); **~ to comply with the regulations ...** o não cumprimento do regulamento ....
faint [feɪnt] *adj (sound)* fraco(-ca); *(colour)* claro(-ra); *(outline)* vago(-ga); *(dizzy)* tonto(-ta) ◆ *vi* desmaiar; **I haven't the ~est idea** não faço a menor idéia.
fair [feər] *adj (decision, trial, result)* justo(-ta); *(judge, person)* imparcial; *(quite large, good)* considerável; *(SCH)* suficiente; *(hair, person)* louro(-ra); *(skin)* claro(-ra); *(weather)* bom (boa) ◆ *n* feira *f*; **~ enough!** está bem!
fairground ['feəgraʊnd] *n* espaço onde se realiza feiras beneficentes ou culturais.
fair-haired [-'heəd] *adj* louro(-ra).
fairly ['feəlɪ] *adv (quite)* bastante.
fairness ['feənɪs] *n (of decision, trial, result)* justiça *f*; *(of judge, person)* imparcialidade *f*, equidade *f*.
fairy ['feərɪ] *n* fada *f*.
fairy tale *n* conto *m* de fadas.
faith [feɪθ] *n* fé *f*.
faithful ['feɪθfʊl] *adj* fiel.
faithfully ['feɪθfʊlɪ] *adv*: **Yours ~** Atenciosamente.
fake [feɪk] *n (false thing)* imitação *f* ◆ *vt (signature, painting)* falsificar.
falcon ['fɔːlkən] *n* falcão *m*.
Falkland Islands ['fɔːklənd-] *npl*:

the ~ as Ilhas Malvinas.

Falklands ['fɔːkləndz] = **Falkland Islands**.

fall [fɔːl] (pt **fell**, pp **fallen** ['fɔːln]) vi cair; (occur) calhar ♦ n queda f; (Am: autumn) outono m; **to ~ asleep** adormecer; **to ~ ill** adoecer; **to ~ in love** apaixonar-se.

❏ **falls** npl (waterfall) quedas fpl d'água, cataratas fpl.

❏ **fall behind** vi (with work, rent) atrasar-se.

❏ **fall down** vi (lose balance) cair.

❏ **fall off** vi cair.

❏ **fall out** vi (argue) zangar-se; **my tooth fell out** meu dente caiu.

❏ **fall over** vi cair.

❏ **fall through** vi (plan, deal) falhar.

fallible ['fæləbl] adj falível.

fallout ['fɔːlaut] n (radiation) poeira f radioativa.

false [fɔːls] adj falso(-sa).

false alarm n alarme m falso.

falsely ['fɔːlslɪ] adv (accuse, imprison) injustamente; (smile, laugh) falsamente.

false teeth npl dentes mpl postiços, dentadura f (postiça).

falsify ['fɔːlsɪfaɪ] vt falsificar.

falter ['fɔːltəʳ] vi (move unsteadily) vacilar; (become weaker) enfraquecer; (hesitate, lose confidence) hesitar.

fame [feɪm] n fama f.

familiar [fə'mɪljəʳ] adj (known) familiar; (informal) íntimo(-ma) (demais); **to be ~ with** (know) conhecer, estar familiarizado(-da) com.

familiarity [fə,mɪlɪ'ærətɪ] n familiaridade f.

familiarize [fə'mɪljəraɪz] vt: **to ~ o.s. with sthg** familiarizar-se com algo; **to ~ sb with sthg** familiarizar alguém com algo.

family ['fæmlɪ] n família f ♦ adj (pack) (com) tamanho familiar; (film, holiday) para toda a família.

family doctor n médico m (-ca f) de família.

family planning clinic [-'plænɪŋ-] n consultas fpl de planejamento familiar.

family room n (at hotel) quarto m para família; (at pub, airport) sala reservada para famílias com crianças pequenas.

famine ['fæmɪn] n fome f.

famished ['fæmɪʃt] adj (inf) esfomeado(-da).

famous ['feɪməs] adj famoso(-osa).

fan [fæn] n (held in hand) leque m; (electric) ventoinha f; (enthusiast, supporter) fã mf.

fanatic [fə'nætɪk] n fanático m (-ca f).

fan belt n correia f do ventilador (Br), correia f de ventoinha (Port).

fancy ['fænsɪ] vt (inf) (feel like) ter vontade de; (be attracted to) gostar de ♦ adj (elaborate) complicado(-da); ~ **(that)!** quem diria!; ~ **going to the cinema?** que tal ir ao cinema?

fancy dress n fantasia f (Br), disfarce m (Port).

fancy-dress party n baile m à fantasia (Br), baile m de máscaras (Port).

fanfare ['fænfeəʳ] n fanfarra f.

fang [fæŋ] n dente m.

fan heater n aquecedor m (de ventoinha), termo-ventilador m.

fanlight ['fænlaɪt] n (Brit) bandeira f (de porta).

fantasize ['fæntəsaɪz] vi fantasiar.

fantastic [fæn'tæstɪk] adj fantástico (-ca).

fantasy ['fæntəsɪ] n fantasia f.

far [fɑːʳ] (compar **further** OR **farther**, superl **furthest** OR **farthest**) adv (in distance, time) longe; (in degree) muito ♦ adj (end, side) extremo(-ma); **how ~ did you go?** até onde você foi?; **how ~ is it (to London)?** qual é a distância (até Londres)?; **as ~ as** (place) até; **as ~ as I'm concerned** no que me diz respeito; **as ~ as I know** que eu saiba; ~ **better** muito melhor; **by ~** de longe; **so ~** (until now) até agora; **to go too ~** ir longe demais.

faraway ['fɑːrəweɪ] adj distante.

farce [fɑːs] n farsa f.

fare [feəʳ] n (on bus, train etc) bilhete m; (fml: food) comida f ♦ vi sair-se.

Far East n: **the ~** o Extremo Oriente.

fare stage n (Brit) = zona f, parada de ônibus a partir da qual o preço do bilhete aumenta.

farewell [feə'wel] n despedida f ♦ excl adeus!

farm [fɑːm] n fazenda f (Br), quinta f (Port).

farmer ['fɑːməʳ] n agricultor m (-ra f), fazendeiro m (-ra f) (Br).

farmhand ['fɑːmhænd] n lavrador m

(-ra *f*), trabalhador *m* (-ra *f*) agrícola.

farmhouse ['fɑːmhaʊs, *pl* -haʊzɪz] *n* casa *f* de fazenda (*Br*), casa *f* de quinta (*Port*).

farming ['fɑːmɪŋ] *n* agricultura *f*.

farmland ['fɑːmlænd] *n* terras *fpl* de lavoura, terrenos *mpl* agrícolas.

farmyard ['fɑːmjɑːd] *n* terreno *m* da fazenda (*Br*), pátio *m* da quinta (*Port*).

farther ['fɑːðəʳ] *compar* → **far**.

farthest ['fɑːðəst] *superl* → **far**.

fascinate ['fæsɪneɪt] *vt* fascinar.

fascinating ['fæsɪneɪtɪŋ] *adj* fascinante.

fascination [,fæsɪ'neɪʃn] *n* fascínio *m*, fascinação *f*.

fascism ['fæʃɪzm] *n* fascismo *m*.

fashion ['fæʃn] *n* moda *f*; (*manner*) maneira *f*; **to be in ~** estar na moda; **to be out of ~** estar fora de moda.

fashionable ['fæʃnəbl] *adj* na moda.

fashion show *n* desfile *m* de moda.

fast [fɑːst] *adj* (*quick*) rápido(-da); (*clock, watch*) adiantado(-da) ◆ *adv* (*quickly*) depressa, rápido; (*securely*) bem seguro(-ra); **to be ~ asleep** estar dormindo profundamente; **a ~ train** um trem rápido.

fasten ['fɑːsn] *vt* (*belt, coat*) apertar; (*two things*) atar.

fastener ['fɑːsnəʳ] *n* fecho *m*.

fast food *n* comida *f* rápida.

fat [fæt] *adj* gordo(-da) ◆ *n* gordura *f*.

fatal ['feɪtl] *adj* (*accident, disease*) fatal.

fate [feɪt] *n* destino *m*; **to tempt ~** tentar o diabo.

father ['fɑːðəʳ] *n* pai *m*.

Father Christmas *n* (*Brit*) Papai *m* Noel (*Br*), Pai *m* Natal (*Port*).

father-in-law *n* sogro *m*.

fathom ['fæðəm] (*pl inv* OR **-s**) *n* braça *f* ◆ *vt*: **to ~ sthg/sb (out)** compreender algo/alguém.

fatten ['fætn] *vt* engordar.

fattening ['fætnɪŋ] *adj* que engorda.

fatty ['fætɪ] *adj* gorduroso(-osa).

faucet ['fɔːsɪt] *n* (*Am*) torneira *f*.

fault [fɔːlt] *n* (*responsibility*) culpa *f*; (*defect*) falha *f*; **it's your ~** a culpa é sua.

faultless ['fɔːltlɪs] *adj* impecável, perfeito(-ta).

faulty ['fɔːltɪ] *adj* defeituoso(-osa).

fauna ['fɔːnə] *n* fauna *f*.

favor ['feɪvəʳ] (*Am*) = **favour**.

favour ['feɪvəʳ] *n* (*Brit*) (*kind act*) favor

m ◆ *vt* (*Brit*) (*prefer*) favorecer; **to be in ~ of** ser a favor de; **to do sb a ~** fazer um favor a alguém.

favourable ['feɪvrəbl] *adj* favorável.

favourite ['feɪvrɪt] *adj* preferido(-da), favorito(-ta) ◆ *n* preferido *m* (-da *f*), favorito *m* (-ta *f*).

favouritism ['feɪvrɪtɪzm] *n* favoritismo *m*.

fawn [fɔːn] *adj* bege (*inv*).

fax [fæks] *n* fax *m* ◆ *vt* (*document*) mandar por fax; (*person*) mandar um fax para.

fax machine *n* fax *m*.

fax modem *n* fax *m* modem.

fear [fɪəʳ] *n* medo *m* ◆ *vt* (*be afraid of*) ter medo de; **for ~ of** por medo de, com receio de.

fearful ['fɪəful] *adj* (*frightened*) receoso(-osa); (*frightening*) terrível.

fearless ['fɪəlɪs] *adj* destemido(-da).

feasible ['fiːzəbl] *adj* viável.

feast [fiːst] *n* banquete *m*.

feat [fiːt] *n* feito *m*.

feather ['feðəʳ] *n* pena *f*.

feature ['fiːtʃəʳ] *n* (*characteristic*) característica *f*; (*of face*) traço *m*; (*in newspaper*) artigo *m* de fundo; (*on radio, TV*) reportagem *f* ◆ *vt* (*subj: film*) ser protagonizado por.

feature film *n* longa-metragem *f*.

Feb. (*abbr of February*) fev.

February ['februərɪ] *n* fevereiro, → September.

fed [fed] *pt & pp* → **feed**.

federal ['fedrəl] *adj* federal.

federation [,fedə'reɪʃn] *n* federação *f*.

fed up *adj* farto(-ta); **to be ~ with** estar farto de.

fee [fiː] *n* (*for admission*) preço *m*; (*of doctor, solicitor*) honorários *mpl*; (*of university*) anuidade *f* (*Br*), propina *f* (*Port*).

feeble ['fiːbl] *adj* fraco(-ca).

feed [fiːd] (*pt & pp* **fed**) *vt* (*person, animal*) alimentar; (*insert*) inserir.

feedback ['fiːdbæk] *n* (*reaction*) reações *fpl*; (*criticism*) comentários *mpl*; (*electrical noise*) feedback *m*.

feeding bottle ['fiːdɪŋ-] *n* (*Brit*) mamadeira *f* (*Br*), biberão *m* (*Port*).

feel [fiːl] (*pt & pp* **felt**) *vt* (*touch*) tocar; (*experience*) sentir; (*think*) achar ◆ *vi* (*have emotion*) sentir-se ◆ *n* (*of material*) toque *m*; **I ~ like a cup of tea** eu quero tomar uma xícara de chá; **to ~ up to doing sthg** sentir-se capaz de fazer algo; **to ~ cold/hot** sentir frio/calor; **my nose ~s cold** meu nariz está frio.

feeler ['fi:lǝr] n (of insect, snail) antena m.

feeling ['fi:lɪŋ] n (emotion) sentimento m; (sensation) sensação f; (belief) opinião f; **to hurt sb's ~s** magoar alguém.

feet [fi:t] pl → foot.

fell [fel] pt → fall ♦ vt (tree) abater.

fellow ['felǝʊ] n (man) cara m (Br), tipo m (Port) ♦ adj: **my ~ students** os meus colegas.

felt [felt] pt & pp → feel ♦ n feltro m.

felt-tip pen n caneta f pilot (Br), caneta f de feltro (Port).

female ['fi:meɪl] adj fêmea ♦ n (animal) fêmea f.

feminine ['femɪnɪn] adj feminino (-na).

feminist ['femɪnɪst] n feminista mf.

fence [fens] n cerca f, vedação f.

fencing ['fensɪŋ] n (SPORT) esgrima f.

fend [fend] vi: **to ~ for o.s.** cuidar de si (mesmo OR próprio).

fender ['fendǝr] n (for fireplace) guarda-fogo m; (Am: on car) párachoques m inv.

fennel ['fenl] n funcho m.

ferment [fǝ'ment] vi (wine, beer) fermentar.

fern [fɜ:n] n samambaia f (Br), feto m (Port).

ferocious [fǝ'rǝʊʃǝs] adj feroz.

ferret ['ferɪt] n furão m.

Ferris wheel ['ferɪs-] n roda f gigante.

ferry ['ferɪ] n ferry m, barco m de travessia.

fertile ['fɜ:taɪl] adj fértil.

fertilizer ['fɜ:tɪlaɪzǝr] n adubo m, fertilizante m.

fervent ['fɜ:vǝnt] adj ferveroso(-osa); (desire) ardente.

fester ['festǝr] vi (wound, sore) criar, supurar.

festival ['festǝvl] n (of music, arts etc) festival m; (holiday) feriado m, dia m festivo.

festive ['festɪv] adj festivo(-va).

festive season n: **the ~** as festas de fim-de-ano (Br), a quadra natalícia (Port).

festivities [fes'tɪvǝtɪz] npl festividades fpl.

feta cheese ['fetǝ-] n queijo de origem grega feito com leite de ovelha.

fetch [fetʃ] vt (go and get) ir buscar; (be sold for) atingir.

fetching ['fetʃɪŋ] adj: **you look very ~ in that dress** esse vestido lhe cai muito bem.

fete [feɪt] n festa f (ao ar livre e normalmente de beneficência).

fetus ['fi:tǝs] = foetus.

feud ['fju:d] n feudo m ♦ vi lutar.

fever ['fi:vǝr] n febre f; **to have a ~** ter febre.

feverish ['fi:vǝrɪʃ] adj febril.

few [fju:] adj pouco(-ca) ♦ pron poucos mpl (-cas fpl); **the first ~ times** as primeiras vezes; **a ~** adj alguns(algumas) ♦ pron alguns mpl (algumas fpl); **quite a ~** bastantes.

fewer ['fju:ǝ] adj & pron menos.

fewest ['fju:ǝst] adj menos.

fiancé [fɪ'ɒnseɪ] n noivo m.

fiancée [fɪ'ɒnseɪ] n noiva f.

fiasco [fɪ'æskǝʊ] (pl -s) n fiasco m.

fib [fɪb] n (inf) mentira f.

fiber ['faɪbǝr] (Am) = fibre.

fibre ['faɪbǝr] n (Brit) fibra f.

fibreglass ['faɪbǝglɑ:s] n fibra f de vidro.

fickle ['fɪkl] adj inconstante, volúvel.

fiction ['fɪkʃn] n ficção f.

fictitious [fɪk'tɪʃǝs] adj fictício(-cia).

fiddle ['fɪdl] n (violin) rabeca f ♦ vi: **to ~ with sthg** brincar com algo.

fidget ['fɪdʒɪt] vi mexer-se; **stop ~ing!** fica quieto!

field [fi:ld] n campo m.

field glasses npl binóculos mpl.

field trip n viagem f de estudos.

fierce [fɪǝs] adj (animal, person) feroz; (storm, heat) violento(-ta).

fifteen [fɪf'ti:n] num quinze, → six.

fifteenth [fɪf'ti:nθ] num décimo quinto (décima quinta), → sixth.

fifth [fɪfθ] num quinto(-ta), → sixth.

fiftieth ['fɪftɪǝθ] num qüinquagésimo(-ma), → sixth.

fifty ['fɪftɪ] num cinquenta, → six.

fifty-fifty adj cinquenta por cento, fifty-fifty (inv) ♦ adv a meias, fiftyfifty.

fig [fɪg] n figo m.

fight [faɪt] (pt & pp fought) n (physical clash) briga f, luta f; (argument) discussão f; (struggle) luta ♦ vt (physically) brigar com, lutar com; (enemy, crime, injustice) lutar contra, combater ♦ vi *(physically)* brigar, lutar; *(in war)* combater; *(quarrel)* discutir; *(struggle)* lutar; **to have a ~ with sb** brigar com alguém.

❑ **fight back** *vi* defender-se.

❑ **fight off** *vt sep (attacker)* repelir *(illness)* lutar contra.

fighter ['faɪtə'] *n (plane)* caça *m*; *(soldier)* combatente *m*; *(combative person)* lutador *m* (-ra *f*).

fighting ['faɪtɪŋ] *n* luta *f*.

figurative ['fɪɡərətɪv] *adj* figurativo(va).

figure ['fɪɡə'] *n (number, statistic)* número *m*, valor *m*; *(of person)* silhueta *f*, figura *f*; *(diagram)* figura.

❑ **figure out** *vt sep (understand)* perceber, compreender.

Fiji ['fiːdʒiː] *n* Fiji *s*.

file [faɪl] *n (document holder)* capa *f*; *(information on person,* COMPUT*)* dossiê *m (Br)*, ficheiro *m (Port)*; *(tool)* lixa *f (Br)*, lima *f (Port)* ◆ *vt (complaint)* apresentar; *(petition)* fazer; *(nails)* lixar *(Br)*, limar *(Port)*; **in single ~** em fila indiana.

filing cabinet ['faɪlɪŋ-] *n* arquivo *m*.

fill [fɪl] *vt (make full)* encher; *(space)* ocupar; *(role)* desempenhar; *(tooth)* obturar *(Br)*, chumbar *(Port)*.

❑ **fill in** *vt sep (form)* preencher.

❑ **fill out** *vt sep* = **fill in**.

❑ **fill up** *vt sep* encher; **~ her up!** *(with petrol)* ateste!

filled roll [fɪld-] *n* sanduíche *m (Br)*, sandes *f inv (Port)*.

fillet ['fɪlɪt] *n* filé *m*.

fillet steak *n* filé *m (Br)*, bife *m (Port)*.

filling ['fɪlɪŋ] *n (of cake, sandwich)* recheio *m*; *(in tooth)* obturação *f (Br)*, chumbo *m (Port)* ◆ *adj* que enche.

filling station *n* posto *m* de gasolina *(Br)*, bombas *fpl* de gasolina *(Port)*.

film [fɪlm] *n (at cinema)* filme *m*; *(for camera)* filme *m (Br)*, rolo *m (Port)* ◆ *vt* filmar.

film star *n* estrela *f* de cinema.

Filofax® ['faɪləʊfæks] *n* organizador *m*, agenda *f (de folhas soltas)*.

filter ['fɪltə'] *n* filtro *m*.

filter coffee *n* café *m (de cafeteira de filtro)*.

filth [fɪlθ] *n (dirt)* sujeira *f*, porcaria *f*.

filthy ['fɪlθɪ] *adj* nojento(-ta).

fin [fɪn] *n* barbatana *f*.

final ['faɪnl] *adj (last)* último(-ma);

(decision, offer) final ◆ *n* final *f*.

finalist ['faɪnəlɪst] *n* finalista *mf*.

finally ['faɪnəlɪ] *adv* finalmente.

finance [*n* 'faɪnæns, *vb* faɪ'næns] *n (money)* financiamento *m*; *(management of money)* finanças *fpl* ◆ *vt* financiar.

❑ **finances** *npl* finanças *fpl*.

financial [fɪ'nænʃl] *adj* financeiro (-ra).

find [faɪnd] *(pt & pp* **found**) *vt* encontrar; *(find out)* descobrir; *(think)* achar, considerar ◆ *n* descoberta *f*; **to ~ the time to do sthg** arranjar tempo para fazer algo.

❑ **find out** *vt sep (fact, truth)* descobrir ◆ *vi*: **to ~ out (about sthg)** *(learn)* ficar sabendo (de algo), descobrir (algo); *(get information)* informar-se (sobre algo).

fine [faɪn] *adj (good)* bom (boa); *(thin)* fino(-na); *(wine, food)* excelente ◆ *adv (thinly)* finamente; *(well)* bem ◆ *n* multa *f* ◆ *vt* multar; **I'm ~** estou bem; **it's ~** está bem.

fine art *n* belas-artes *fpl*.

finger ['fɪŋɡə'] *n* dedo *m*.

fingernail ['fɪŋɡəneɪl] *n* unha *f*.

fingertip ['fɪŋɡətɪp] *n* ponta *f* do dedo.

finish ['fɪnɪʃ] *n (end)* fim *m*, final *m*; *(on furniture)* acabamento *m* ◆ *vt & vi* acabar, terminar; **to ~ doing sthg** acabar de fazer algo.

❑ **finish off** *vt sep* acabar, terminar.

❑ **finish up** *vi* acabar, terminar; **to ~ up doing sthg** acabar por fazer algo.

Finland ['fɪnlənd] *n* Finlândia *f*.

Finn [fɪn] *n* finlandês *m* (-esa *f*).

Finnan haddock ['fɪnən-] *n (Scot)* hadoque *m* defumado *(prato típico escocês)*.

Finnish ['fɪnɪʃ] *adj* finlandês(-esa) ◆ *n (language)* finlandês *m*.

fir [fɜː'] *n* abeto *m*.

fire ['faɪə'] *n* fogo *m*; *(uncontrolled)* incêndio *m*, fogo; *(made for cooking, heat)* fogueira *f*; *(device)* aquecedor *m* ◆ *vt (gun)* disparar; *(from job)* despedir; **on ~** em chamas; **to catch ~** incendiar-se, pegar fogo; **to make a ~** acender uma fogueira.

fire alarm *n* alarme *m* contra incêndios.

fire brigade *n (Brit)* corpo *m* de bombeiros.

fire department *(Am)* = **fire brigade**.

fire engine *n* carro *m* de bombeiros.

fire escape *n* escadas *fpl* de incêndio.

fire exit *n* saída *f* de emergência.

fire extinguisher *n* extintor *m*.

fire hazard *n*: it's a ~ constitui um risco OR perigo de incêndio.

fireman ['faɪəmən] (*pl* -men [-mən]) *n* bombeiro *m*.

fireplace ['faɪəpleɪs] *n* lareira *f*.

fire regulations *npl* normas *fpl* de segurança em caso de incêndio.

fire station *n* posto *m* de bombeiros *(Br)*, estação *f* dos bombeiros *(Port)*.

firewood ['faɪəwʊd] *n* lenha *f*.

firework display ['faɪəwɜːk-] *n* queima *f* de fogos-de-artifício.

fireworks ['faɪəwɜːks] *npl* (*rockets*) fogos-de-artifício *mpl*.

firm [fɜːm] *adj* firme ♦ *n* empresa *f*.

first [fɜːst] *adj* primeiro(-ra) ♦ *adv* primeiro; *(for the first time)* pela primeira vez ♦ *n* (*event*) estréia *f* ♦ *pron*: the ~ o primeiro (a primeira); I'll do it ~ thing (in the morning) vou fazer isso logo de manhã; ~ (gear) primeira (mudança); for the ~ time pela primeira vez; the ~ of January o dia um de janeiro; at ~ no princípio; ~ of all antes de mais nada.

first aid *n* pronto socorro *m (Br)*, primeiros-socorros *mpl (Port)*.

first-aid kit *n* estojo *m* de pronto socorro *(Br)*, estojo *m* de primeiros-socorros *(Port)*.

first class *n* (*mail*) = correspondência *f* prioritária *(Br)*, = correio-azul *m (Port)*; *(on train, plane, ship)* primeira classe *f*.

first-class *adj (stamp)* = para correio prioritário *(Br)*, = para correio-azul *(Port)*; *(ticket, work)* de primeira classe.

first floor *n (Brit: floor above ground floor)* primeiro andar *m*; *(Am: ground floor)* andar *m* térreo *(Br)*, rés-do-chão *m (Port)*.

firstly ['fɜːstlɪ] *adv* em primeiro lugar.

First World War *n*: the ~ a Primeira Guerra Mundial.

fish [fɪʃ] (*pl inv*) *n* peixe *m* ♦ *vi* pescar.

fish and chips *n* filé de peixe com batatas fritas.

fishcake ['fɪʃkeɪk] *n* croquete *m* de peixe.

fisherman ['fɪʃəmən] (*pl* -men [-mən]) *n* pescador *m*.

fish farm *n* viveiro *m* de peixes.

fish fingers *npl (Brit)* espécie de croquete alongado de peixe congelado.

fishing ['fɪʃɪŋ] *n* pesca *f*; to go ~ ir pescar.

fishing boat *n* barco *m* de pesca.

fishing rod *n* vara *f* de pescar *(Br)*, cana *f* de pesca *(Port)*.

fishmonger's ['fɪʃˌmʌŋgəʳ] *n (shop)* peixaria *f*.

fish sticks *(Am)* = fish fingers.

fish supper *n (Scot)* filé de peixe com batatas fritas.

fist [fɪst] *n* punho *m*.

fit [fɪt] *adj (healthy)* em forma ♦ *vt (be right size for)* servir a; *(a lock, kitchen, bath)* instalar; *(insert)* encaixar ♦ *vi (clothes, shoes)* servir; *(in space)* caber ♦ *n (of clothes, shoes)* tamanho *m*; *(epileptic, of coughing, anger)* ataque *m*; to be ~ for sthg ser adequado para algo; ~ to eat comestível; it doesn't ~ *(jacket, skirt)* não serve; *(object)* não cabe; to get ~ pôr-se em forma; to keep ~ manter-se em forma, manter a forma.

❏ **fit in** *vt sep (find time to do)* arranjar tempo para ♦ *vi (belong)* encaixar.

fitness ['fɪtnɪs] *n (health)* forma *f* física.

fitted carpet [fɪtəd-] *n* carpete *m (Br)*, alcatifa *f (Port)*.

fitted kitchen [fɪtəd-] *n (Brit)* cozinha *f* com armários embutidos.

fitted sheet [fɪtəd-] *n* lençol *m* capa.

fitting room ['fɪtɪŋ-] *n* cabine *f* de provas, vestiário *m*.

five [faɪv] *num* cinco, → six.

fiver ['faɪvəʳ] *n (Brit) (inf) (£5)* cinco libras *fpl*; *(£5 note)* nota *f* de cinco libras.

fix [fɪks] *vt (attach, decide on)* fixar; *(mend)* arranjar; *(drink, food)* arranjar, preparar; *(arrange)* combinar, organizar.

❏ **fix up** *vt sep*: to ~ sb up with sthg arranjar algo para alguém.

fixed [fɪkst] *adj* fixo(-xa).

fixture ['fɪkstʃəʳ] *n (SPORT)* encontro *m*; ~s and fittings equipamento *m* doméstico *(armários de cozinha, W.C., luminárias, etc)*.

fizz [fɪz] *vi (drink)* borbulhar.

fizzy ['fɪzɪ] *adj* gasoso(-osa).

flabbergasted [ˈflæbəɡuːstɪd] adj boquiaberto(-ta).

flabby [ˈflæbɪ] adj balofo(-fa), flácido (-da).

flag [flæɡ] n bandeira f.

flagpole [ˈflæɡpəʊl] n mastro m.

flagrant [ˈfleɪɡrənt] adj flagrante.

flagstone [ˈflæɡstəʊn] n laje f.

flair [fleəʳ] n (stylishness) estilo m; (talent): **to have a ~ for sthg** ter queda para algo.

flake [fleɪk] n (of snow) floco m ♦ vi desfazer-se.

flamboyant [flæmˈbɔɪənt] adj extravagante.

flame [fleɪm] n chama f.

flamingo [fləˈmɪŋɡəʊ] n flamingo m.

flammable [ˈflæməbl] adj inflamável.

flan [flæn] n torta f (Br), tarte f (Port).

flannel [ˈflænl] n (material) flanela f; (Brit: for washing face) luva f de banho. ❑ **flannels** npl calças fpl de flanela.

flap [flæp] n (of envelope) dobra f; (of tent) porta f; (of pocket) pala f ♦ vt (wings) bater.

flapjack [ˈflæpdʒæk] n (Brit: cake) biscoito ou bolo pequeno feito de flocos de aveia, manteiga e mel ao qual se podem juntar frutos secos, chocolate, etc.

flare [fleəʳ] n (signal) sinal m luminoso.

flared [fleəd] adj (trousers) à boca de sino; (skirt) de roda, evasê.

flash [flæʃ] n (of light) raio m; (for camera) flash m ♦ vi (light) brilhar; **a ~ of lightning** um relâmpago, um clarão; **to ~ one's headlights** fazer sinais com os faróis.

flashback [ˈflæʃbæk] n flashback m.

flashbulb [ˈflæʃbʌlb] n flash m.

flashgun [ˈflæʃɡʌn] n disparador m OR botão m do flash.

flashlight [ˈflæʃlaɪt] n lanterna f.

flashy [ˈflæʃɪ] adj (inf) vistoso(-osa), espalhafatoso(-osa).

flask [flɑːsk] n (Thermos) garrafa f térmica (Br), termo m (Port); (hip flask) cantil m.

flat [flæt] adj (level) plano(-na); (battery) descarregado(-da); (drink) choco (choca), que perdeu o gás; (rate, fee) fixo(-xa) ♦ n (Brit: apartment) apartamento m ♦ adv: **to lie ~** estender-se; **a ~ (tyre)** um pneu vazio OR em baixo; **~ out** a toda a velocidade, até não poder mais.

flatly [ˈflætlɪ] adv (absolutely) categoricamente.

flatmate [ˈflætmeɪt] n (Brit) colega mf de apartamento.

flatten [ˈflætn] vt (make flat) alisar. ❑ **flatten out** vt sep alisar.

flatter [ˈflætəʳ] vt lisonjear, bajular.

flattering [ˈflætərɪŋ] adj (remark, offer) lisonjeiro(-ra); (dress, colour, neckline) favorecedor(-ra).

flattery [ˈflætərɪ] n lisonja f.

flaunt [flɔːnt] vt exibir.

flavor [ˈfleɪvər] (Am) = **flavour**.

flavour [ˈfleɪvəʳ] n (Brit) sabor m.

flavoured [ˈfleɪvəd] adj aromatizado (-da); **chocolate-~** com sabor de chocolate.

flavouring [ˈfleɪvərɪŋ] n aromatizante m.

flaw [flɔː] n (in plan) falha f; (in glass, china) defeito m.

flea [fliː] n pulga f.

flea market n mercado m das pulgas (Br), feira f da ladra (Port).

flee [fliː] (pt & pp **fled** [fled]) vt fugir de ♦ vi fugir.

fleece [fliːs] n (downy material) velo m, fibra muito macia usada para fazer e forrar casacos de inverno.

fleet [fliːt] n frota f.

Flemish [ˈflemɪʃ] adj flamengo(-ga) ♦ n (language) flamengo m.

flesh [fleʃ] n (of person, animal) carne f; (of fruit, vegetable) polpa f.

flew [fluː] pt → **fly**.

flex [fleks] n cabo m elétrico.

flexible [ˈfleksəbl] adj flexível.

flick [flɪk] vt (a switch) carregar em; (with finger) dar um piparote em. ❑ **flick through** vt fus folhear.

flick knife n (Brit) navalha f de ponta em mola.

flies [flaɪz] npl (of trousers) braguilha f, fecho m.

flight [flaɪt] n vôo m; **a ~ (of stairs)** um lance de escadas.

flight attendant n (female) aeromoça f (Br), hospedeira f de bordo (Port); (male) comissário m de bordo.

flight crew n tripulação f (Br), pessoal m de bordo (Port).

flight deck n (of aircraft) cabine f de controle.

flimsy [ˈflɪmzɪ] adj (object) frágil; (clothes) leve.

fling [flɪŋ] (pt & pp **flung**) vt atirar.

flint [flɪnt] n (of lighter) pedra f.

flip [flɪp] vt (pancake, omelette, record) virar; **to ~ a coin** tirar cara ou coroa.
❑ **flip on** vt sep (switch) ligar.
❑ **flip off** vt sep (switch) desligar.

flip-flop [flɪp-] n (Brit) sandália f japonesa (Br), chinelo m de dedo (Port).

flipper ['flɪpəʳ] n barbatana f.

flirt [flɜːt] vi: **to ~ (with sb)** flertar (com alguém).

flirtatious [flɜːˈteɪʃəs] adj namorador(-ra).

float [fləʊt] n (for swimming, fishing) bóia f; (in procession) carro m; (drink) bebida servida com uma bola de sorvete ◆ vi flutuar.

flock [flɒk] n (of birds) bando m; (of sheep) rebanho m ◆ vi (people) afluir.

flood [flʌd] n enchente f, inundação f ◆ vt inundar ◆ vi transbordar.

flooding ['flʌdɪŋ] n cheia f, inundação f.

floodlight ['flʌdlaɪt] n holofote m.

floor [flɔːʳ] n (of room) chão m; (storey) andar m; (of nightclub) pista f.

floorboard ['flɔːbɔːd] n tábua f corrida.

floor show n espetáculo m de cabaré.

flop [flɒp] n (inf) fracasso m.

floppy ['flɒpɪ] adj mole.

floppy disk ['flɒpɪ-] n disquete f.

flora ['flɔːrə] n flora f.

floral ['flɔːrəl] adj (pattern) de flores.

Florida Keys [flɒrɪdə-] npl: **the ~** ilhas situadas ao largo da Flórida.

florist's ['flɒrɪsts] n (shop) florista f.

flour ['flaʊəʳ] n farinha f.

flourish ['flʌrɪʃ] vi florescer ◆ vt agitar, brandir.

flow [fləʊ] n corrente f ◆ vi correr.

flower ['flaʊəʳ] n flor f.

flowerbed ['flaʊəbed] n canteiro m.

flowerpot ['flaʊəpɒt] n vaso m.

flowery ['flaʊərɪ] adj florido(-da).

flown [fləʊn] pp → **fly**.

fl oz abbr = **fluid ounce**.

flu [fluː] n gripe f.

fluctuate ['flʌktʃʊeɪt] vi flutuar, variar.

fluency ['fluːənsɪ] n fluência f.

fluent ['fluːənt] adj: **to be ~ in Portuguese**, **to speak ~ Portuguese** falar português fluentemente.

fluff [flʌf] n (on clothes) pêlo m.

fluffy ['flʌfɪ] adj (kitten) peludo(-da); (fur, jumper) macio(-cia); (toy) de pelúcia.

fluid ['fluːɪd] n fluido m.

fluid ounce ['fluːɪd-] n = 0,03 litros.

fluke [fluːk] n (inf) acaso m.

flume [fluːm] n escorrega m aquático, rampa f.

flung [flʌŋ] pt & pp → **fling**.

flunk [flʌŋk] vt (Am: inf: exam) reprovar em.

fluorescent [flʊəˈresənt] adj fluorescente.

flush [flʌʃ] vi (toilet) funcionar ◆ vt: **to ~ the toilet** dar descarga (Br), puxar o autoclismo (Port).

flushed [flʌʃt] adj (red-faced) corado(-da).

flustered ['flʌstəd] adj agitado(-da).

flute [fluːt] n flauta f.

fly [flaɪ] (pt **flew**, pp **flown**) n (insect) mosca f; (of trousers) braguilha f, fecho m ◆ vt (plane, helicopter) pilotar; (travel by) viajar em OR com; (transport) enviar por avião ◆ vi (bird, insect, plane) voar; (passenger) viajar de avião; (pilot a plane) pilotar; (flag) estar hasteado(-da).

fly-drive n férias cujo preço inclui a viagem de avião e o aluguel de um carro.

flying ['flaɪɪŋ] n: **I'm terrified of ~** tenho medo de andar de avião.

flying saucer n disco m voador.

flying visit n visita f muito curta, visita de médico.

flyover ['flaɪˌəʊvəʳ] n (Brit) viaduto m.

flypaper ['flaɪˌpeɪpəʳ] n papel m mata-moscas.

flysheet ['flaɪʃiːt] n cobertura exterior de barraca de acampar.

fly spray n inseticida m.

FM n FM f.

foal [fəʊl] n potro m.

foam [fəʊm] n espuma f.

focus ['fəʊkəs] n (of camera) foco m ◆ vi (with camera, binoculars) focar; **in ~** focado; **out of ~** desfocado.

fodder ['fɒdəʳ] n ração f, forragem f.

foe [fəʊ] n inimigo m (-ga f).

foetus ['fiːtəs] n feto m.

fog [fɒg] n nevoeiro m, neblina f.

fogbound ['fɒgbaʊnd] adj parado(-da) por causa do nevoeiro.

foggy ['fɒgɪ] adj (weather) de nevoeiro.

foghorn ['fɒghɔːn] *n* sirene *f* de nevoeiro.

fog lamp *n* farol *m* de neblina.

foil [fɔɪl] *n (thin metal)* papel *m* OR folha *f* de alumínio.

fold [fəʊld] *n* dobra *f* ♦ *vt (paper, material)* dobrar; *(wrap)* envolver; **to ~ one's arms** cruzar os braços.

⊔ **fold up** *vi (chair, bed)* dobrar.

folder ['fəʊldə'] *n* pasta *f*.

folding ['fəʊldɪŋ] *adj (chair, table, bicycle)* articulado(-da); *(bed)* de dobrar.

foliage ['fəʊlɪɪdʒ] *n* folhagem *f*.

folk [fəʊk] *npl (people)* gente *f* ♦ *n*: ~ **(music)** música *f* tradicional.

⊔ **folks** *npl (inf: relatives)* família *f*.

folklore ['fəʊklɔː'] *n* folclore *m*.

folk song *n* canção *f* tradicional.

follow ['fɒləʊ] *vt* seguir; *(in order, time)* seguir-se a, vir a seguir de ♦ *vi (go behind)* seguir; *(in time)* seguir-se, vir a seguir; *(understand)* entender; **proceed as ~s** ... proceda da seguinte forma ...; **the results are as ~s** ... os resultados são os seguintes ...; **~ed by** seguido de.

⊔ **follow on** *vi* vir a seguir.

follower ['fɒləʊə'] *n* seguidor *m* (-ra *f*).

following ['fɒləʊɪŋ] *adj* seguinte ♦ *prep* depois de.

follow on call *n* telefonema feito com o dinheiro que sobrou da chamada precedente.

fond [fɒnd] *adj*: **to be ~ of** gostar de.

fondle ['fɒndl] *vt* acariciar.

fondue ['fɒnduː] *n* fondue *m*.

food [fuːd] *n* comida *f*.

food mixer *n* batedeira *f*.

food poisoning [-ˌpɔɪznɪŋ] *n* intoxicação *f* alimentar.

food processor [-ˌprəʊsesə'] *n* processador *m* de comida.

foodstuffs ['fuːdstʌfs] *npl* gêneros *mpl* alimentícios.

fool [fuːl] *n (idiot)* idiota *mf*; *(pudding)* mousse *f* de fruta ♦ *vt* enganar.

foolhardy ['fuːlˌhɑːdɪ] *adj* imprudente, insensato(-ta).

foolish ['fuːlɪʃ] *adj* tolo(-la).

foolproof ['fuːlpruːf] *adj (plan, system)* infalível; *(machine)* fácil de utilizar.

foot [fʊt] *(pl* feet) *n* pé *m*; *(of animal)* pata *f*; *(of hill, cliff, stairs)* pé *m*; *(measurement)* pé *m*, = 30,48 cm; **by** OR **on ~** a pé.

footage ['fʊtɪdʒ] *n* sequências *fpl*.

football ['fʊtbɔːl] *n (Brit: soccer)* futebol *m*; *(Am: American football)* futebol americano; *(Brit: in soccer)* bola *f* (de futebol); *(Am: in American football)* bola (de futebol americano).

footballer ['fʊtbɔːlə'] *n (Brit)* futebolista *mf*.

football ground *n (Brit)* campo *m* de futebol.

football pitch *n (Brit)* campo *m* de futebol.

football player *n* jogador *m* (-ra *f*) de futebol.

footbridge ['fʊtbrɪdʒ] *n* passagem *f* aérea para pedestres.

foothills ['fʊthɪlz] *npl* contrafortes *mpl*.

foothold ['fʊthəʊld] *n* ponto *m* de apoio.

footing ['fʊtɪŋ] *n (foothold)* equilíbrio *m*; **to lose one's ~** perder o equilíbrio.

footlights ['fʊtlaɪts] *npl* (luzes *fpl* da) ribalta *f*.

footnote ['fʊtnəʊt] *n* nota *f* de rodapé.

footpath ['fʊtpɑːθ, *pl* -pɑːðz] *n* caminho *m*.

footprint ['fʊtprɪnt] *n* pegada *f*.

footstep ['fʊtstep] *n* passo *m*.

footwear ['fʊtweə'] *n* calçado *m*.

for [fɔː'] *prep* **1.** *(expressing intention, purpose, reason)* para; **this book is ~ you** este livro é para você; **what did you do that ~?** para quê você fez isso?; **what's it ~?** para quê é?; **to go ~ a walk** ir dar um passeio; **"~ sale"** "vende-se"; **a town famous ~ its wine** uma cidade famosa pelo vinho; **~ this reason** por esta razão.

2. *(during)* durante; **I'm going away ~ a while** vou estar fora durante OR por algum tempo; **I've lived here ~ ten years** vivo aqui há dez anos; **we talked ~ hours** falamos horas e horas.

3. *(by, before)* para; **I'll do it ~ tomorrow** estará pronto (para) amanhã; **be there ~ 8 p.m.** tente estar lá antes das oito da noite.

4. *(on the occasion of)* por; **I got socks ~ Christmas** ganhei meias no Natal, no Natal me deram meias; **~ the first time** pela primeira vez; **what's ~ dinner?** o que há para jantar?; **~ the**

moment no momento.
5. *(on behalf of)* por; **to do sthg ~ sb** fazer algo para alguém; **to work ~ sb** trabalhar para alguém.
6. *(with time and space)* para; **there's no room ~ it** não há espaço para isso; **to have time ~ sthg** ter tempo para algo.
7. *(expressing distance)*: **road works ~ 20 miles** obras na estrada ao longo de 32 km; **we drove ~ miles** guiamos quilômetros e quilômetros.
8. *(expressing destination)* para; **a ticket ~ Edinburgh** um bilhete para Edimburgo; **this train is ~ London only** este trem só pára em Londres.
9. *(expressing price)* por; **I bought it ~ five pounds** comprei-o por cinco libras.
10. *(expressing meaning)*: **what's the Portuguese ~ "boy"?** como é que se diz "boy" em português?
11. *(with regard to)* para; **it's warm ~ November** para novembro está quente; **it's easy ~ you** para você é fácil; **respect ~ human rights** respeito pelos direitos humanos; **I feel sorry ~ them** sinto pena deles; **it's too far ~ us to walk** é longe demais para irmos a pé; **it's time ~ dinner** está na hora do jantar.

forage ['fɒrɪdʒ] *vi*: **to ~ for sthg** procurar algo.

forbid [fə'bɪd] *(pt* **-bade,** *pp* **-bidden)** *vt* proibir; **to ~ sb to do sthg** proibir alguém de fazer algo.

forbidden [fə'bɪdn] *adj* proibido(-da).

force [fɔːs] *n* força *f* ◆ *vt* forçar; **the ~s** as forças armadas; **to ~ sb to do sthg** forçar alguém a fazer algo; **to ~ one's way through (sthg)** abrir caminho (por entre algo).

forceps ['fɔːseps] *npl* fórceps *m inv*.

ford [fɔːd] *n* vau *m*.

forearm ['fɔːrɑːm] *n* antebraço *m*.

forecast ['fɔːkɑːst] *n* previsão *f*.

forecourt ['fɔːkɔːt] *n* pátio *m*.

forefinger ['fɔːfɪŋgəʳ] *n* dedo *m* indicador.

forefront ['fɔːfrʌnt] *n*: **in OR at the ~ of sthg** na vanguarda de algo.

foregone conclusion [fɔːgɒn-] *n*: **it's a ~** é mais que certo.

foreground ['fɔːgraʊnd] *n* primeiro plano *m*.

forehand ['fɔːhænd] *n* direita *f*.

forehead ['fɔːhed] *n* testa *f*.

foreign ['fɒrən] *adj* estrangeiro(-ra); *(visit)* ao estrangeiro; *(travel)* para o estrangeiro.

foreign currency *n* moeda *f* estrangeira, divisas *fpl*.

foreigner ['fɒrənəʳ] *n* estrangeiro *m* (-ra *f*).

foreign exchange *n (system)* câmbio *m*; *(money)* divisas *fpl*.

foreign minister *n* ministro *m* (-tra *f*) das relações exteriores *(Br)*, secretário *m* (-ria *f*) de Estado dos negócios estrangeiros *(Port)*.

foreign secretary *n (Brit)* ministro *m* (-tra *f*) das relações exteriores *(Br)*, ministro *m* (-tra *f*) dos negócios estrangeiros *(Port)*.

foreman ['fɔːmən] *(pl* **-men** [-mən]*)* *n* capataz *m*.

forename ['fɔːneɪm] *n (fml)* nome *m* próprio.

forensic medicine [fə'rensɪk-] *n* medicina *f* legal.

foresee [fɔː'siː] *(pt* **-saw,** *pp* **-seen)** *vt* prever.

foreseeable [fɔː'siːəbl] *adj* previsível; **in the ~ future** num futuro próximo.

foreseen [fɔː'siːn] *pp* → **foresee.**

forest ['fɒrɪst] *n* floresta *f*.

forestry ['fɒrɪstrɪ] *n* silvicultura *f*.

foretaste ['fɔːteɪst] *n* amostra *f*.

foretell [fɔː'tel] *(pt & pp* **-told)** *vt* predizer, prever.

forever [fə'revəʳ] *adv (eternally)* para sempre; *(continually)* sempre.

foreword ['fɔːwɜːd] *n* prefácio *m*.

forfeit ['fɔːfɪt] *n* penalização *f* ◆ *vt (lose)* perder.

forgave [fə'geɪv] *pt* → **forgive.**

forge [fɔːdʒ] *vt (copy)* falsificar, forjar.

forgery ['fɔːdʒərɪ] *n* falsificação *f*.

forget [fə'get] *(pt* **-got,** *pp* **-gotten)** *vt* esquecer-se de; *(person, event)* esquecer ◆ *vi* esquecer-se; **to ~ about sthg** esquecer-se de algo; **to ~ how to do sthg** esquecer-se de como se faz algo; **to ~ to do sthg** esquecer-se de fazer algo; **~ it!** esquece!

forgetful [fə'getful] *adj* esquecido (-da).

forgive [fə'gɪv] *(pt* **-gave,** *pp* **-given)** *vt* perdoar.

forgot [fə'gɒt] *pt* → **forget.**

forgotten [fə'gɒtn] *pp* → **forget.**

fork [fɔːk] *n (for eating with)* garfo *m*;

(for gardening) forquilha *f;* *(of road, path)* bifurcação *f.*

❑ **forks** *npl (of bike, motorbike)* garfo *m.*

forklift truck ['fɔːklɪft-] *n* empilhadora *f.*

forlorn [fə'lɔːn] *adj (face, expression, cry)* infeliz; *(hope, attempt)* desesperado(-da).

form [fɔːm] *n (type, shape)* forma *f;* *(piece of paper)* impresso *m,* formulário *m; (SCH)* ano *m* ◆ *vt* formar ◆ *vi* formar-se; **to be on/off ~** estar/não estar em forma; **to ~ part of** fazer parte de.

formal ['fɔːml] *adj* formal.

formality [fɔː'mælɪtɪ] *n* formalidade *f;* **it's just a ~** é só uma formalidade.

format ['fɔːmæt] *n* formato *m.*

formation [fɔː'meɪʃn] *n* formação *f.*

former ['fɔːmər] *adj (previous)* anterior; *(first)* primeiro(-ra) ◆ *pron:* **the ~** o primeiro (a primeira).

formerly ['fɔːməlɪ] *adv* antigamente.

formidable ['fɔːmɪdəbl] *adj (frightening)* temível; *(impressive)* tremendo(-da).

formula ['fɔːmjʊlə] *(pl* **-as** OR **-ae** [iː]) *n* fórmula *f.*

fort [fɔːt] *n* forte *m.*

forthcoming [fɔːθ'kʌmɪŋ] *adj (future)* próximo(-ma), que está para vir.

forthright ['fɔːθraɪt] *adj (person)* sem rodeios, direto(-ta); *(manner, opinions)* franco(-ca).

fortieth ['fɔːtɪɪθ] *num* quadragésimo(-ma), → **sixth.**

fortnight ['fɔːtnaɪt] *n (Brit)* quinzena *f,* duas semanas *fpl.*

fortress ['fɔːtrɪs] *n* fortaleza *f.*

fortunate ['fɔːtʃnət] *adj* com sorte; **she's ~ to have such a good job** ela tem a sorte de ter um emprego tão bom.

fortunately ['fɔːtʃnətlɪ] *adv* felizmente.

fortune ['fɔːtʃuːn] *n (money)* fortuna *f; (luck)* sorte *f;* **it costs a ~** *(inf)* custa uma fortuna.

fortune teller *n* cartomante *mf.*

forty ['fɔːtɪ] *num* quarenta, → **six.**

forward ['fɔːwəd] *adv* para a frente ◆ *n* avançado *m* (-da *f)* ◆ *vt (letter)* remeter; *(goods)* expedir; **to look ~ to** estar ansioso por.

forwarding address ['fɔː- wədɪŋ-] *n* novo endereço para onde o correio deve ser remitido.

forwards ['fɔːwədz] *adv* = **forward.**

fossil ['fɒsl] *n* fóssil *m.*

foster child ['fɒstə-] *n* criança sob os cuidados temporários de uma família adotiva.

foster parents *npl* família adotiva que cuida de crianças por um tempo limitado.

fought [fɔːt] *pt & pp* → **fight.**

foul [faʊl] *adj (unpleasant)* nojento(-ta) ◆ *n* falta *f.*

found [faʊnd] *pt & pp* → **find** ◆ *vt* fundar.

foundation (cream) [faʊn'deɪʃn-] *n* base *f.*

foundations [faʊn'deɪʃnz] *npl* alicerces *mpl,* fundações *fpl.*

founder ['faʊndər] *n* fundador *m* (-ra *f).*

foundry ['faʊndrɪ] *n* fundição *f.*

fountain ['faʊntɪn] *n* repuxo *m.*

fountain pen *n* caneta-tinteiro *f (Br),* caneta *f* de tinta permanente *(Port).*

four [fɔːr] *num* quatro, → **six.**

four-poster (bed) *n* cama *f* de colunas.

foursome ['fɔːsəm] *n* grupo *m* de quatro (pessoas).

four-star (petrol) *n* gasolina *f* super.

fourteen [fɔː'tiːn] *num* quatorze *(Br),* catorze, → **six.**

fourteenth [fɔː'tiːnθ] *num* décimo quarto (décima quarta), → **sixth.**

fourth [fɔːθ] *num* quarto(-ta), → **sixth.**

four-wheel drive *n (car)* veículo *m* com tração nas quatro rodas.

fowl [faʊl] *(pl inv) n* ave *f (de capoeira).*

fox [fɒks] *n* raposa *f.*

foyer ['fɔɪeɪ] *n* vestíbulo *m,* saguão *m (Br).*

fraction ['frækʃn] *n* fração *f.*

fractionally ['frækʃnəlɪ] *adv* ligeiramente.

fracture ['fræktʃər] *n* fratura *f* ◆ *vt* fraturar.

fragile ['frædʒaɪl] *adj* frágil.

fragment ['frægmənt] *n* fragmento *m.*

fragrance ['freɪɡrəns] *n* fragrância *f.*

fragrant ['freɪɡrənt] *adj* perfumado(-da).

frail [freɪl] *adj* frágil, débil.

frame [freɪm] *n (of window, photo,*

door) moldura *f,* caixilho *m;* *(of glasses, tent, bed)* armação *f;* *(of bicycle)* quadro *m* ◆ *vt (photo, picture)* emoldurar.

frame of mind *n* estado *m* de espírito.

framework ['freɪmwɔːk] *n (physical structure)* armação *f;* *(basis)* estrutura *f.*

France [frɑːns] *n* França *f.*

frank [fræŋk] *adj* franco(-ca).

frankfurter ['fræŋkfɜːtəʳ] *n* salsicha *f* alemã.

frankly ['fræŋklɪ] *adv (to be honest)* francamente; **quite ~, I don't really care** para ser franco, pouco me importa.

frantic ['fræntɪk] *adj* frenético (-ca).

fraternize ['frætənaɪz] *vi (be on friendly terms):* **to ~ with sb** fraternizar com alguém.

fraud [frɔːd] *n (crime)* fraude *f,* burla *f.*

frayed [freɪd] *adj (clothing, fabric, rope)* gasto(-ta), puído(-da).

freak [friːk] *adj* anormal ◆ *n (inf: fanatic)* fanático *m* (-ca *f).*

freckles ['freklz] *npl* sardas *fpl.*

free [friː] *adj* livre; *(costing nothing)* grátis *(inv)* ◆ *vt (prisoner)* libertar ◆ *adv (without paying)* grátis, de graça; **for ~** grátis, de graça; **~ of charge** grátis; **to be ~ to do sthg** ser livre para fazer algo.

freedom ['friːdəm] *n* liberdade *f.*

freefone ['friːfəʊn] *n (Brit)* = linha *f* verde *(Port), sistema que permite ao utilizador telefonar sem pagar.*

free gift *n* oferta *f.*

freehand ['friːhænd] *adj* desenhado(-da) à mão (livre) ◆ *adv* à mão (livre).

free house *n (Brit) pub que não está ligado a nenhuma fábrica de cervejas.*

free kick *n* (pontapé) livre *m.*

freelance ['friːlɑːns] *adj* free-lance *(inv).*

freely ['friːlɪ] *adv (speak)* à vontade; *(move)* livremente; **~ available** fácil de obter.

Freemason ['friːmeɪsn] *n* franco-maçon *m,* membro *m* da franco-maçonaria.

free period *n (SCH)* hora *f* livre, furo *m (Port).*

freepost ['friːpəʊst] *n* porte *m* pago.

free-range *adj (chicken)* do campo; **~ eggs** *ovos de galinhas criadas livremente.*

freestyle ['friːstaɪl] *n* estilo *m* livre.

free time *n* tempo *m* livre.

freeway ['friːweɪ] *n (Am)* auto-estrada *f.*

freeze [friːz] *(pt* **froze,** *pp* **frozen)** *vt* congelar ◆ *vi* gelar ◆ *v impers:* **it's freezing!** está um gelo!

freezer ['friːzəʳ] *n (deep freeze)* frízer *m (Br),* arca *f* congeladora *(Port);* *(part of fridge)* frízer *(Br),* congelador *m (Port).*

freezing ['friːzɪŋ] *adj* gelado (-da) *(Port).*

freezing point *n:* **below ~** abaixo de zero.

freight [freɪt] *n (goods)* mercadorias *fpl.*

freight train *n* trem *m* de mercadorias.

French [frentʃ] *adj* francês(-esa) ◆ *n (language)* francês *m* ◆ *npl:* **the ~** os franceses.

French bean *n* feijão *m* verde *(redondo).*

French bread *n* ~ bisnaga *f (Br),* cacete *m (Port).*

French dressing *n (in UK)* vinagrete *m; (in US)* molho *m* americano, *molho à base de ketchup e maionese.*

French fries *npl* batatas *fpl* fritas.

Frenchman ['frentʃmən] *(pl* **-men** [-mən]) *n* francês *m.*

French stick *n (Brit)* ~ bisnaga *f (Br),* cacete *m (Port).*

French toast *n* rabanada *f.*

French windows *npl* portas *fpl* envidraçadas.

Frenchwoman ['frentʃwʊmən] *(pl* **-women** [-wɪmɪn]) *n* francesa *f.*

frenetic [frə'netɪk] *adj* frenético(-ca).

frenzy ['frenzɪ] *n* frenesi *m.*

frequency ['friːkwənsɪ] *n* freqüência *f.*

frequent ['friːkwənt] *adj* freqüente.

frequently ['friːkwəntlɪ] *adv* freqüentemente.

fresh [freʃ] *adj* fresco(-ca); *(refreshing)* refrescante; *(water)* doce; *(recent)* recente; *(new)* novo (nova); **to get some ~ air** apanhar ar fresco.

fresh cream *n* creme *m (Br),* natas *fpl* frescas *(Port).*

freshen ['freʃn] : **freshen up** *vi* refrescar-se.

fresher ['freʃəʳ] *n (Brit) (inf)* calouro *m* (-ra *f).*

freshly ['freʃlı] *adv* recentemente.

freshness ['freʃnıs] *n* frescura *f*; *(of approach, ideas)* originalidade *f*.

fresh orange (juice) *n* suco *m* de laranja *(Br)*, sumo *m* de laranja natural *(Port)*.

freshwater ['freʃ,wɔːtəʳ] *adj* de água doce.

fret [fret] *vi (worry)* preocupar-se.

Fri. *(abbr of Friday)* 6ª, sex.

friar ['fraɪəʳ] *n* frade *m*.

friction ['frıkʃn] *n* fricção *f*.

Friday ['fraɪdı] *n* sexta-feira, → **Saturday.**

fridge [frıdʒ] *n* geladeira *f (Br)*, frigorífico *m (Port)*.

fridge-freezer *n (Brit)* geladeira *f* (com frízer) *(Br)*, frigorífico *m* (com congelador) *(Port)*.

fried egg [fraɪd-] *n* ovo *m* estrelado OR frito.

fried rice [fraɪd-] *n* arroz *m* frito.

friend [frend] *n* amigo *m* (-ga *f*); **to be ~s with sb** ser amigo de alguém; **to make ~s with sb** tornar-se amigo de alguém.

friendly ['frendlı] *adj* amigável; **to be ~ with sb** ser amigo(-ga) de alguém.

friendship ['frendʃıp] *n* amizade *f*.

fries [fraɪz] = **French fries.**

fright [fraɪt] *n* susto *m*; **to give sb a ~** pregar um susto em alguém.

frighten ['fraɪtn] *vt* assustar.

frightened ['fraɪtnd] *adj* assustado (-da); **to be ~** ter medo; **to be ~ of** ter medo de; **to be ~ (that)** *(worried)* ter medo que.

frightening ['fraɪtnıŋ] *adj* assustador(-ra).

frightful ['fraɪtful] *adj (very bad, unpleasant)* horrível.

frilly ['frılı] *adj* de babados *(Br)*, de folhos *(Port)*.

fringe [frındʒ] *n* franja *f*.

frisk [frısk] *vt* revistar.

fritter ['frıtəʳ] *n comida, geralmente fruta, passada por um polme e frita.*

frivolous ['frıvələs] *adj* frívolo (-la).

fro [frəʊ] *adv* → **to.**

frock [frɒk] *n* vestido *m*.

frog [frɒg] *n* rã *f*.

frogman ['frɒgmən] *(pl* **-men** [-mən]) *n* homem-rã *m*.

from [frɒm] *prep* **1.** *(expressing origin, source)* de; **I'm ~ Liverpool** sou de Liverpool; **the train ~ Manchester** o trem de Manchester; **I bought it ~ a supermarket** comprei-o num supermercado.

2. *(expressing removal, deduction)* de; **away ~ home** longe de casa; **to take sthg (away) ~ sb** tirar algo de alguém; **10% will be deducted ~ the total** será deduzido 10% do total .

3. *(expressing distance)* de; **five miles ~ London** a oito quilômetros de Londres; **it's not far ~ here** não é longe daqui.

4. *(expressing position)* de; **~ here you can see the valley** daqui vê-se o vale.

5. *(expressing what thing is made with)* de; **it's made ~ stone** é feito de pedra.

6. *(expressing starting time)* desde; **~ the moment you arrived** desde que chegou; **~ now on** de agora em diante; **~ next year** a partir do próximo ano; **open ~ nine to five** aberto das nove às cinco.

7. *(expressing change)* de; **the price has gone up ~ £1 to £2** o preço subiu de uma libra para duas; **to translate ~ German into English** traduzir do alemão para o inglês.

8. *(expressing range)* de; **tickets are ~ £10** bilhetes a partir de dez libras; **it could take ~ two to six months** pode levar de dois a seis meses.

9. *(as a result of)* de; **I'm tired ~ walking** estou cansado de andar.

10. *(expressing protection)* de; **sheltered ~ the wind** protegido do vento.

11. *(in comparisons)*: **different ~** diferente de.

fromage frais [frɒmɑːʒˈfreɪ] *n tipo de queijo cremoso.*

front [frʌnt] *adj* da frente ◆ *n* (parte da) frente *f*; *(of book)* capa *f*; *(of weather)* frente *f*; *(by the sea)* costa *f*; **in ~** em frente; **in ~ of** em frente de.

front door *n* porta *f* da frente.

frontier [frʌnˈtɪəʳ] *n* fronteira *f*.

front page *n* primeira página *f*.

front room *n* sala *f* (de estar).

front seat *n* banco *m* da frente.

front-wheel drive *n (vehicle)* veículo *m* com tração nas rodas dianteiras.

frost [frɒst] *n* geada *f*.

frostbite ['frɒstbaɪt] *n* ferida *f* causa-da pelo frio.

frosted ['frɒstɪd] *adj (glass)* fosco (-ca).

frosty ['frɒstɪ] *adj (morning, weather)* de geada.

froth [frɒθ] *n* espuma *f.*

frown [fraun] *n* cenho *m* ◆ *vi* franzir as sobrancelhas.

froze [frəʊz] *pt* → **freeze**.

frozen [frəʊzn] *pp* → **freeze** ◆ *adj* gelado(-da); *(food)* congelado (-da).

fruit [fruːt] *n (food)* fruta *f; (variety of fruit)* fruto *m;* **a piece of ~** uma fruta; **~s of the forest** frutos silvestres.

fruit cake *n* bolo *m* inglês.

fruiterer ['fruːtərər] *n (Brit)* fruteiro *m* (-ra *f*).

fruitful ['fruːtfʊl] *adj* frutífero(-ra).

fruit juice *n* suco *m* de fruta *(Br)*, sumo *m* de frutas *(Port)*.

fruitless ['fruːtlɪs] *adj* infrutífero(-ra).

fruit machine *n (Brit)* caça-níqueis *m (Br)*, slot-machine *f (Port)*.

fruit salad *n* salada *f* de fruta.

frumpy ['frʌmpɪ] *adj (inf)* careta *(Br)*, antiquado(-da) *(Port)*.

frustrate [frʌ'streɪt] *vt (person)* frus-trar; *(plan, attempt)* gorar.

frustrated [frʌ'streɪtɪd] *adj (person)* frustrado(-da); *(plan, attempt)* gorado (-da), furado(-da).

frustrating [frʌ'streɪtɪŋ] *adj* frustran-te.

frustration [frʌ'streɪʃn] *n* frustração *f.*

fry [fraɪ] *vt* fritar.

frying pan ['fraɪɪŋ-] *n* frigideira *f.*

ft *abbr* = **foot, feet**.

fudge [fʌdʒ] *n* doce *m* de leite, *doce caramelado feito com leite, açúcar e man-teiga.*

fuel [fjʊəl] *n* combustível *m.*

fuel pump *n* bomba *f* de gasolina.

fuel tank *n* tanque *m* de gasolina.

fugitive ['fjuːdʒətɪv] *n* fugitivo *m* (-va *f*).

fulfil [fʊl'fɪl] *vt (Brit) (promise, request, duty)* cumprir; *(role)* desempenhar; *(conditions, instructions, need)* satisfazer.

fulfill [fʊl'fɪl] *(Am)* = **fulfil**.

full [fʊl] *adj (filled)* cheio (cheia); *(name)* completo(-ta); *(extent, support)* total; *(maximum)* máximo(-ma); *(busy)* ocupado(-da); *(fare)* inteiro(-ra); *(fla-*

vour) rico(-ca) ◆ *adv (directly)* em cheio; **I'm ~ (up)** estou cheio; **at ~ speed** a toda a velocidade; **~ of** cheio de; **in ~** *(pay)* na totalidade; *(write)* por extenso.

full board *n* pensão *f* completa.

full-cream milk *n* leite *m* integral *(Br)*, leite *m* gordo *(Port)*.

full-length *adj (skirt, dress)* compri-do(-da) *(até aos pés)*.

full moon *n* lua *f* cheia.

full stop *n* ponto *m* final.

full-time *adj & adv* de tempo inte-gral *(Br)*, a tempo inteiro *(Port)*.

full up *adj* cheio (cheia).

fully ['fʊlɪ] *adv (completely)* completa-mente.

fully-licensed *adj* autorizado a ven-der bebidas alcoólicas.

fumble ['fʌmbl] *vi:* **he ~d in his pock-ets for his keys** ele apalpou os bolsos à procura das chaves.

fume [fjuːm] *vi (with anger)* espumar (de raiva).

❏ **fumes** *npl (from paint, alcohol)* vapo-res *mpl; (from car)* gases *mpl; (from fire)* fumaça *f.*

fun [fʌn] *n* divertimento *m*, diversão *f;* **it's good ~** é divertido; **for ~** por pra-zer; **to have ~** divertir-se; **to make ~ of** zombar de.

function ['fʌŋkʃn] *n* função *f* ◆ *vi* funcionar.

fund [fʌnd] *n* fundo *m* ◆ *vt* financiar.

❏ **funds** *npl* fundos *mpl.*

fundamental [fʌndə'mentl] *adj* fun-damental.

funding ['fʌndɪŋ] *n* financiamento *m.*

funeral ['fjuːnərəl] *n* funeral *m.*

funeral parlour *n* (agência) fune-rária *f.*

funfair ['fʌnfeər] *n* parque *m* de diversões.

fungus ['fʌŋgəs] *(pl* **-gi** [-gaɪ]*) n* fungo *m.*

funky ['fʌŋkɪ] *adj (inf: music)* funky *(inv).*

funnel ['fʌnl] *n (for pouring)* funil *m; (on ship)* chaminé *f.*

funny ['fʌnɪ] *adj (amusing)* engra-çado(-da); *(strange)* estranho(-nha); **to feel ~** *(ill)* não se sentir bem.

fur [fɜːr] *n (on animal)* pêlo *m; (gar-ment)* pele *f.*

fur coat *n* casaco *m* de peles.

furious ['fjʊərɪəs] *adj (angry)* furio-so(-osa).

furnace ['fɜːnɪs] *n* fornalha *f.*

furnish ['fɜːnɪʃ] *vt (house, room)* mobiliar.

furnished ['fɜːnɪʃt] *adj* mobiliado (-da).

furnishings ['fɜːnɪʃɪŋz] *npl* mobiliário *m.*

furniture ['fɜːnɪtʃəʳ] *n* mobília *f*; **a piece of ~** um móvel.

furrow ['fʌrəʊ] *n* rego *m*, sulco *m.*

furry ['fɜːrɪ] *adj (animal)* peludo(-da); *(toy)* de pelúcia; *(material)* com pêlo.

further ['fɜːðəʳ] *compar* → **far** ◆ *adv* mais ◆ *adj (additional)* outro (outra); **until ~ notice** até novo aviso; **it's not much ~** já não falta muito, já não é muito longe.

further education *n (Brit)* educação *f* para adultos.

furthermore [ˌfɜːðə'mɔːʳ] *adv* além disso, além do mais.

furthest ['fɜːðɪst] *superl* → **far** ◆ *adj (most distant)* mais longe OR distante ◆ *adv (in distance)* mais longe.

fury ['fjʊərɪ] *n* fúria *f.*

fuse [fjuːz] *n (of plug)* fusível *m*; *(on bomb)* detonador *m* ◆ *vi (plug, device)* queimar.

fuse box *n* caixa *f* de fusíveis.

fuss [fʌs] *n (agitation)* agitação *f*; *(complaints)* escândalo *m.*

fussy ['fʌsɪ] *adj (person)* exigente.

futile [*Brit* 'fjuːtaɪl, *Am* 'fuːtl] *adj* inútil.

futon ['fuːtɒn] *n espécie de sofá-cama japonês.*

future ['fjuːtʃəʳ] *n* futuro *m* ◆ *adj* futuro(-ra); **in ~** no futuro, de agora em diante.

G

g *(abbr of gram)* g.

gable ['geɪbl] *n* cumeeira *f*.

gadget ['gædʒɪt] *n* engenhoca *f*.

Gaelic ['geɪlɪk] *n* gaélico *m*.

gag [gæg] *n (inf: joke)* piada *f*.

gain [geɪn] *vt* ganhar; *(subj: clock, watch)* adiantar ◆ *vi (benefit)* lucrar ◆ *n* ganho *m*; **to ~ weight** engordar.

gait [geɪt] *n* andar *m*.

gal. *abbr* = **gallon.**

gala ['gɑːlə] *n (celebration)* gala *f*.

galaxy ['gæləksɪ] *n* galáxia *f*.

gale [geɪl] *n* vento *m* forte, rajada *f* de vento.

gallant ['gælənt] *adj (courageous)* corajoso(-osa).

gallery ['gælərɪ] *n* galeria *f*.

galley ['gælɪ] *n (ship)* galera *f*; *(kitchen)* cozinha *f*.

gallon ['gælən] *n (in UK)* = 4,546 litros, galão *m*; *(in US)* = 3,785 litros, galão.

gallop ['gæləp] *vi* galopar.

gallows ['gæləʊz] *(pl inv)* *n* forca *f*.

galore [gə'lɔːr] *adv* à farta, em abundância.

gamble ['gæmbl] *n* aposta *f* ◆ *vi (bet money)* apostar, jogar.

gambler ['gæmblər] *n* jogador *m* (-ra *f*).

gambling ['gæmblɪŋ] *n* jogo *m* (de azar).

game [geɪm] *n* jogo *m*; *(of tennis, snooker, chess)* partida *f*; *(wild animals, meat)* caça *f*.
❑ **games** *n (SCH)* desporto *m* ◆ *npl (sporting event)* jogos *mpl*.

gamekeeper ['geɪm,kiːpər] *n* guarda-caça *mf*, couteiro *m* (-ra *f*).

game reserve *n* reserva *f* de caça, coutada *f*.

gammon ['gæmən] *n* presunto cozido, salgado ou fumado.

gang [gæŋ] *n (of criminals)* gangue *f* (Br), bando *m* (Port); *(of friends)* grupo *m*, turma *f*.

gangrene ['gæŋgriːn] *n* gangrena *f*.

gangster ['gæŋstər] *n* bandido *m*, gangster *m*.

gangway ['gæŋweɪ] *n (for ship)* prancha *f*; *(Brit: in bus, aeroplane, theatre)* corredor *m*.

gaol [dʒeɪl] *(Brit)* = **jail.**

gap [gæp] *n (space)* espaço *m*; *(of time)* intervalo *m*; *(difference)* diferença *f*.

gape [geɪp] *vi (person)* ficar de boca aberta.

garage ['gærɑːʒ, 'gærɪdʒ] *n (for keeping car)* garagem *f*; *(Brit: for petrol)* posto *m* de gasolina; *(for repairs)* oficina *f*; *(Brit: for selling cars)* concessionária *f*.

garbage ['gɑːbɪdʒ] *n (Am: refuse)* lixo *m*.

garbage can *n (Am)* lata *f* de lixo.

garbage truck *n (Am)* caminhão *m* do lixo.

garbled ['gɑːbld] *adj* confuso (-sa).

garden ['gɑːdn] *n* jardim *m* ◆ *vi* jardinar.
❑ **gardens** *npl (public park)* jardim *m* público, parque *m*.

garden centre *n* centro *m* de jardinagem.

gardener ['gɑːdnər] *n* jardineiro *m* (-ra *f*).

gardening ['gɑːdnɪŋ] *n* jardinagem *f*.

garden peas *npl* ervilhas *fpl*.

gargle ['gɑːgl] *vi* gargarejar.

garish ['geərɪʃ] *adj* berrante.

garlic ['gɑːlɪk] *n* alho *m*.

garlic bread *n* pão untado com manteiga de alho e aquecido no forno.

garlic butter *n* manteiga *f* de alho.

garment ['gɑːmənt] *n* peça *f* de roupa.

garnish ['gɑːnɪʃ] *n* (*for decoration*) decoração *f*; (*sauce*) molho *m* ◆ *vt* decorar.

garrison ['gærɪsn] *n* guarnição *f*.

garter ['gɑːtər] *n* liga *f*.

gas [gæs] *n* gás *m*; (*Am: petrol*) gasolina *f*.

gas cooker *n* (*Brit*) fogão *m* a gás.

gas cylinder *n* bujão *m* de gás (*Br*), botija *f* de gás (*Port*).

gas fire *n* (*Brit*) aquecedor *m* a gás.

gas gauge *n* (*Am*) indicador *m* do nível de gasolina.

gash [gæʃ] *n* corte *m* (profundo) ◆ *vi* cortar, ferir.

gasket ['gæskɪt] *n* junta *f*.

gasman ['gæsmæn] (*pl* -men) *n* funcionário *m* da companhia de gás.

gas mask *n* máscara *f* antigás.

gasmen ['gæsmen] *pl* → **gasman**.

gas meter *n* medidor *m* do gás (*Br*), contador *m* do gás (*Port*).

gasoline ['gæsəliːn] *n* (*Am*) gasolina *f*.

gasp [gɑːsp] *vi* (*in shock, surprise*) ficar sem fôlego.

gas pedal *n* (*Am*) acelerador *m*.

gas station *n* (*Am*) posto *m* de gasolina (*Br*); estação *f* de serviço (*Port*).

gas stove (*Brit*) = **gas cooker**.

gas tank *n* (*Am*) tanque *m* de gasolina.

gastronomy [gæs'trɒnəmɪ] *n* gastronomia *f*.

gasworks ['gæswɜːks] (*pl inv*) *n* usina *f* de gás (*Br*), gasômetro *m* (*Br*), fábrica *f* de gás (*Port*).

gate [geɪt] *n* (*to garden, field*) portão *m*; (*at airport*) porta *f*.

gâteau ['gætəʊ] (*pl* -x [-z]) *n* (*Brit*) bolo recheado e coberto com chantilly.

gatecrash ['geɪtkræʃ] (*inf*) *vt* (*inf*) entrar sem ser convidado(-da) em, entrar de penetra em.

gateway ['geɪtweɪ] *n* (*entrance*) entrada *f*.

gather ['gæðər] *vt* (*collect*) colher; (*speed*) ganhar; (*understand*) deduzir ◆ *vi* reunir-se.

gathering ['gæðərɪŋ] *n* reunião *f*.

gaudy ['gɔːdɪ] *adj* berrante.

gauge [geɪdʒ] *n* (*for measuring*) indicador *m*, medidor *m*; (*of railway track*) distância *f* (entre os carris) ◆ *vt* (*calculate*) calcular.

gauze [gɔːz] *n* gaze *f*.

gave [geɪv] *pt* → **give**.

gay [geɪ] *adj* (*homosexual*) homossexual, gay.

gaze [geɪz] *vi*: **to ~ at** olhar (fixamente) para.

gazelle [gə'zel] *n* gazela *f*.

gazetteer [gæzɪ'tɪər] *n* índice *m* geográfico.

GB (*abbr of Great Britain*) GB.

GCSE *n* exame realizado no final do nono ano de escolaridade.

gear [gɪər] *n* (*wheel*) roda *f* de engrenagem; (*speed*) mudança *f*, velocidade *f*; (*equipment*) equipamento *m*; (*belongings*) coisas *fpl*; **in ~** engatado.

gearbox ['gɪəbɒks] *n* caixa *f* de mudança (*Br*), caixa *f* de velocidades (*Port*).

gear lever *n* alavanca *f* de mudanças.

gear shift (*Am*) = **gear lever**.

gear stick (*Brit*) = **gear lever**.

geese [giːs] *pl* → **goose**.

gel [dʒel] *n* gel *m*.

gelatine [dʒelə'tiːn] *n* gelatina *f*.

gem [dʒem] *n* pedra *f* preciosa.

Gemini ['dʒemɪnaɪ] *n* Gêmeos *m inv*.

gender ['dʒendər] *n* gênero *m*.

gene [dʒiːn] *n* gene *m*.

general ['dʒenərəl] *adj* geral ◆ *n* general *m*; **in ~** (*as a whole*) em geral; (*usually*) geralmente.

general anaesthetic *n* anestesia *f* geral.

general election *n* eleições *fpl* legislativas.

generalization [dʒenərəlaɪ'zeɪʃn] *n* generalização *f*.

general knowledge *n* cultura *f* geral.

generally ['dʒenərəlɪ] *adv* geralmente.

general practitioner [-præk'tɪʃənər] *n* clínico *m* geral.

general public *n*: **the ~** o público em geral.

general store *n* = mercearia *f*.

generate ['dʒenəreɪt] *vt* gerar.

generation [dʒenə'reɪʃn] *n* geração *f*.

generator ['dʒenəreɪtər] *n* gerador *m*.

generosity [dʒenə'rɒsətɪ] *n* generosidade *f*.

generous ['dʒenərəs] *adj* generoso (-osa).

genetic [dʒɪˈnetɪk] *adj* genético(-ca).
❑ **genetics** *n* genética *f.*
Geneva [dʒɪˈniːvə] *n* Genebra *s.*
genial [ˈdʒiːnjəl] *adj (person)* bem-humorado(-da); *(remark, smile)* amável.
genitals [ˈdʒenɪtlz] *npl* orgãos *mpl* genitais.
genius [ˈdʒiːnjəs] *n* gênio *m.*
gentle [ˈdʒentl] *adj (careful)* cuidadoso(-osa); *(kind)* gentil; *(movement, breeze)* suave.
gentleman [ˈdʒentlmən] *(pl* -men [-mən]) *n* cavalheiro *m;* **"gentlemen"** *(men's toilets)* "homens".
gently [ˈdʒentlɪ] *adv (carefully)* suavemente.
gentry [ˈdʒentrɪ] *n* pequena nobreza *f.*
gents [dʒents] *n (Brit)* banheiro *m* dos homens.
genuine [ˈdʒenjuɪn] *adj* genuíno(-na).
geographical [dʒɪəˈgræfɪkl] *adj* geográfico(-ca).
geography [dʒɪˈɒgrəfɪ] *n* geografia *f.*
geology [dʒɪˈɒlədʒɪ] *n* geologia *f.*
geometric(al) [ˌdʒɪəˈmetrɪk(l)] *adj* geométrico(-ca).
geometry [dʒɪˈɒmɪtrɪ] *n* geometria *f.*
Georgian [ˈdʒɔːdʒən] *adj (architecture etc)* georgiano(-na) *(relativo aos reinados dos reis Jorge I–IV, 1714–1830).*
geranium [dʒɪˈreɪnjəm] *n* gerânio *m.*
gerbil [ˈdʒɜːbɪl] *n* gerbilo *m,* gerbo *m.*
geriatric [ˌdʒerɪˈætrɪk] *adj* geriátrico (-ca).
German [ˈdʒɜːmən] *adj* alemão (-mã) ◆ *n (person)* alemão *m* (-mã *f);* *(language)* alemão *m.*
German measles *n* rubéola *f.*
Germany [ˈdʒɜːmənɪ] *n* Alemanha *f.*
germinate [ˈdʒɜːmɪneɪt] *vi* germinar.
germs [dʒɜːmz] *npl* germes *mpl.*
gesticulate [dʒeˈstɪkjuleɪt] *vi* gesticular.
gesture [ˈdʒestʃəʳ] *n* gesto *m.*
get [get] *(pt & pp* got, *Am pp* gotten) *vt* 1. *(obtain)* obter; *(buy)* comprar; **she got a job** ela arranjou emprego.
2. *(receive)* receber; **I got a book for Christmas** ganhei um livro no Natal.
3. *(means of transport)* apanhar; **let's ~**

a taxi vamos apanhar um táxi.
4. *(fetch)* ir buscar; **could you ~ me the manager?** *(in shop)* podia chamar o gerente?; *(on phone)* pode me passar o gerente?
5. *(illness)* apanhar; **I've got a cold** estou resfriado.
6. *(cause to become)*: **to ~ sthg done** mandar fazer algo; **to ~ sthg ready** preparar algo; **can I ~ my car repaired here?** posso mandar consertar o meu carro aqui?
7. *(ask, tell)*: **to ~ sb to do sthg** arranjar alguém para fazer algo.
8. *(move)*: **to ~ sthg out of sthg** tirar algo de algo; **I can't ~ it through the door** não consigo passar com isso na porta.
9. *(understand)* perceber; **to ~ a joke** sacar uma piada.
10. *(time, chance)* ter; **we didn't ~ the chance to see everything** não tivemos oportunidade de ver tudo.
11. *(idea, feeling)* ter; **I ~ a lot of enjoyment from it** me divirto à beça.
12. *(phone)* atender.
13. *(in phrases)*: **you ~ a lot of rain here in winter** chove muito aqui no inverno, → **have.**
◆ *vi* 1. *(become)* ficar; **it's getting late** está a ficando tarde; **to ~ ready** preparar-se; **to ~ lost** perder-se; **~ lost!** não enche o saco!, desapareça!
2. *(into particular state, position)* meter-se; **how do you ~ to Luton from here?** como é que se vai daqui para Luton?; **to ~ into the car** entrar no carro.
3. *(arrive)* chegar; **when does the train ~ here?** quando é que o trem chega aqui?
4. *(in phrases)*: **to ~ to do sthg** ter a oportunidade de fazer algo.
◆ *aux vb* ser; **to ~ delayed** atrasar-se; **to ~ killed** ser morto.
❑ **get back** *vi (return)* voltar.
❑ **get in** *vi (arrive)* chegar; *(enter)* entrar.
❑ **get off** *vi (leave)* sair.
❑ **get on** *vi (enter train, bus)* entrar; *(in relationship)* dar-se, entender-se; *(progress)*: **how are you getting on in your new job?** como você está indo no novo emprego?
❑ **get out** *vi (of car, bus, train)* sair.
❑ **get through** *vi (on phone)* conseguir ligação.

❏ **get up** *vi* levantar-se.

getaway ['getəwei] *n* fuga *f*.

get-together *n* (*inf*) reunião *f*.

geyser [*Brit* 'giːzə^r, *Am* 'gaizər] *n* (*hot spring*) géiser *m*; (*Brit: water heater*) esquentador *m*.

Ghana ['gɑːnə] *n* Gana *m*.

ghastly ['gɑːstli] *adj* (*inf: very bad*) horrível.

gherkin ['gɜːkin] *n* pequeno pepino de conserva.

ghetto ['getəʊ] (*pl* -s OR -es) *n* gueto *m*.

ghetto blaster [getəʊ,blɑːstə^r] *n* (*inf*) rádio-gravador *m* portátil.

ghost [gəʊst] *n* fantasma *m*.

giant ['dʒaɪənt] *adj* gigante ◆ *n* in *stories*) gigante *m* (-ta *f*).

gibberish ['dʒibəriʃ] *n* disparates *mpl*.

gibe [dʒaib] *n* chacota *f*, piada *f* (insultuosa).

giblets ['dʒiblits] *npl* miúdos *mpl*.

Gibraltar [dʒi'brɔːltə^r] *n* Gibraltar *s*.

giddy ['gidi] *adj* (*dizzy*) tonto(-ta).

gift [gift] *n* (*present*) presente *m*; (*talent*) dom *m*.

gift certificate (*Am*) = **gift voucher**.

gifted ['giftid] *adj* dotado(-da).

gift shop *n* loja *f* de presentes.

gift token = **gift voucher**.

gift voucher *n* (*Brit*) vale *m* para presente.

gig [gig] *n* (*inf*) concerto *m*.

gigabyte ['gigəbait] *n* gigabyte *m*, gigaocteto *m*.

gigantic [dʒai'gæntik] *adj* gigantesco(-ca).

giggle ['gigl] *vi* dar risadinha.

gill [dʒil] *n* (*measurement*) = 0,142 litros.

gills [gilz] *npl* (*of fish*) guelras *fpl*.

gilt [gilt] *adj* dourado(-da) ◆ *n* dourado *m*.

gimmick ['gimik] *n* truque *m*, artifício *m*.

gin [dʒin] *n* gim *m*; ~ **and tonic** gim tônico.

ginger ['dʒindʒə^r] *n* gengibre *m* ◆ *adj* (*colour*) cor-de-cenoura (*inv*).

ginger ale *n* ginger-ale *m*.

ginger beer *n* bebida não alcoólica de gengibre.

gingerbread ['dʒindʒəbred] *n* biscoito ou bolacha de gengibre.

ginger-haired [-'heəd] *adj* ruivo (-va).

gipsy ['dʒipsi] *n* cigano *m* (-na *f*).

giraffe [dʒi'rɑːf] *n* girafa *f*.

girder ['gɜːdə^r] *n* viga *f*.

girdle ['gɜːdl] *n* cinta *f*.

girl [gɜːl] *n* (*child*) menina *f*; (*young woman*) moça *f* (*Br*), rapariga *f* (*Port*); (*daughter*) filha *f*.

girlfriend ['gɜːlfrend] *n* (*of boy, man*) namorada *f*; (*of girl, woman*) amiga *f*.

girl guide *n* (*Brit*) = escoteira *f*.

girl scout (*Am*) = **girl guide**.

giro ['dʒairəʊ] (*pl* -s) *n* (*system*) transferência *f* bancária.

girth [gɜːθ] *n* (*of person*) (medida da) cintura *f*.

gist [dʒist] *n* ideia *f* geral; **to get the ~ (of sthg)** compreender a idéia geral (de algo).

give [giv] (*pt* gave, *pp* given ['givn]) *vt* dar; (*speech, performance*) fazer; **to ~ sb sthg** dar algo a alguém; **to ~ sb a kiss** dar um beijo em alguém; **come on, ~ me a smile!** vamos lá, dê um sorriso!; **to ~ sthg a push** empurrar algo; **~ or take a few minutes** mais minuto menos minuto; **"~ way!"** "perda de prioridade".

❏ **give away** *vt sep* (*get rid of*) dar, desfazer-se de; (*reveal*) revelar.

❏ **give back** *vt sep* devolver.

❏ **give in** *vi* desistir.

❏ **give off** *vt fus* soltar.

❏ **give out** *vt sep* (*distribute*) distribuir.

❏ **give up** *vt sep* (*seat*) ceder ◆ *vi* (*admit defeat*) desistir; **to ~ up smoking** deixar de fumar; **to ~ up chocolate** deixar de comer chocolate.

given name *n* (*Am*) nome *m* próprio OR de batismo.

glacier ['glæsjə^r] *n* glaciar *m*, geleira *f*.

glad [glæd] *adj* contente; **I'll be ~ to help** será um prazer ajudar.

gladly ['glædli] *adv* (*willingly*) com muito prazer.

glamor ['glæmər] (*Am*) = **glamour**.

glamorous ['glæmərəs] *adj* glamoroso(-osa).

glamour ['glæmə^r] *n* (*Brit*) (*of person*) charme *m*; (*of place*) elegância *f*; (*of job*) prestígio *m*.

glance [glɑːns] *n* olhadela *f* ◆ *vi*: **to ~ (at)** dar uma olhadela (em).

gland [glænd] n glândula f.

glandular fever ['glændjʊlə-] n mononucleose f infecciosa, febre f glandular.

glare [gleə^r] vi (person) lançar olhares furiosos; (sun, light) brilhar intensamente.

glaring ['gleərɪŋ] adj (error, weakness) gritante; (lights, sun) ofuscante.

glass [glɑːs] n (material) vidro m; (container, glassful) copo m ♦ adj de vidro. ❏ **glasses** npl óculos mpl.

glassware ['glɑːsweə^r] n artigos mpl de vidro.

glaze [gleɪz] n (on pottery) vitrificado m ♦ vt (pottery) vitrificar.

glazier ['gleɪzjə^r] n vidraceiro m (-ra f).

gleam [gliːm] n (of gold, candle) brilho m; (of disapproval, pride) ponta f ♦ vi (gold, candle) luzir; (with pleasure, pride) brilhar.

gleaming ['gliːmɪŋ] adj brilhante.

glee [gliː] n contentamento m, alegria f.

glen [glen] n (Scot) vale m.

glib [glɪb] adj (answer, excuse) fácil; (person) com muita lábia.

glide [glaɪd] vi (fly) planar.

glider ['glaɪdə^r] n planador m.

gliding ['glaɪdɪŋ] n vôo m planado OR sem motor.

glimmer ['glɪmə^r] n (faint light) brilho m (fraco); (trace, sign) pontinha f.

glimpse [glɪmps] n: **I only caught a ~ of her** só a vi de relance.

glisten ['glɪsn] vi brilhar.

glitter ['glɪtə^r] vi reluzir.

gloat [gləʊt] vi: **to ~ (over sthg)** regozijar-se (com algo).

global ['gləʊbl] adj (worldwide) global, mundial.

global warming [.gləʊbl'wɔːmɪŋ] n aquecimento m da atmosfera.

globe [gləʊb] n globo m; **the ~** (Earth) o globo.

gloom [gluːm] n (darkness) penumbra f; (unhappiness) tristeza f.

gloomy ['gluːmɪ] adj (room, day) sombrio(-bria); (person) triste.

glorious ['glɔːrɪəs] adj (weather, sight) esplêndido(-da); (victory, history) glorioso(-osa).

glory ['glɔːrɪ] n glória f.

gloss [glɒs] n (shine) brilho m; **~ (paint)** tinta f brilhante.

glossary ['glɒsərɪ] n glossário m.

glossy ['glɒsɪ] adj (magazine, photo) de papel couché.

glove [glʌv] n luva f.

glove compartment n portaluvas m inv.

glow [gləʊ] n luz f, brilho m ♦ vi luzir, brilhar.

glucose ['gluːkəʊs] n glucose f.

glue [gluː] n cola f ♦ vt colar.

glum [glʌm] adj triste, sorumbático(-ca).

glutton ['glʌtn] n (greedy person) glutão m (-tona f).

gnash [næʃ] vt: **to ~ one's teeth** ranger os dentes.

gnat [næt] n mosquito m.

gnaw [nɔː] vt roer.

gnome [nəʊm] n anão m.

go [gəʊ] (pt went, pp gone, pl goes) vi **1.** (move, travel) ir; **to ~ home** ir para casa; **to ~ to Portugal** ir a Portugal; **to ~ by bus** ir de ônibus; **to ~ for a walk** ir dar um passeio; **to ~ and do sthg** ir fazer algo; **to ~ in** entrar; **to ~ out** sair.

2. (leave) ir-se; **it's time for us to ~** é hora de irmos embora; **when does the bus ~?** quando é que o ônibus sai?; **~ away!** vai embora!

3. (attend) ir; **to ~ to school** ir para a escola; **which school do you ~ to?** para que escola você vai?

4. (become) ficar; **she went pale** empalideceu; **the milk has gone sour** o leite azedou.

5. (expressing future tense): **to be going to do sthg** ir fazer algo.

6. (function) funcionar; **the car won't ~** o carro não pega.

7. (stop working) ir-se; **the fuse has gone** o fusível queimou.

8. (time) passar.

9. (progress) correr; **to ~ well** correr bem.

10. (bell, alarm) tocar.

11. (match) condizer; **to ~ with** condizer com, ficar bem com; **red wine doesn't ~ with fish** vinho tinto não combina com peixe.

12. (be sold) ser vendido; **"everything must ~"** "liquidação total".

13. (fit) caber.

14. (lead) ir; **where does this path ~?** aonde é que este caminho vai dar?

15. (belong) ir, ser.

16. *(in phrases)*: **to let ~ of sthg** *(drop)* largar algo; **there are two days to ~** faltam dois dias; **to ~** *(Am: to take away)* para levar.

◆ *n* **1.** *(turn)* vez *f*; **it's your ~** é a sua vez.

2. *(attempt)* tentativa *f*; **to have a ~ at sthg** experimentar algo; **"50p a ~"** *(for game)* "50 pence cada vez".

❏ **go ahead** *vi* *(take place)* realizar-se; **~ ahead!** vai em frente!

❏ **go back** *vi* voltar.

❏ **go down** *vi* *(decrease)* diminuir; *(sun)* pôr-se; *(tyre)* esvaziar-se.

❏ **go down with** *vt fus* *(inf: illness)* apanhar.

❏ **go in** *vi* entrar.

❏ **go off** *vi* *(alarm, bell)* tocar, soar; *(go bad)* azedar; *(light, heating)* apagar-se.

❏ **go on** *vi* *(happen)* passar; *(light, heating)* acender-se; **to ~ on doing sthg** continuar a fazer algo.

❏ **go out** *vi* *(leave house)* sair; *(light, fire, cigarette)* apagar-se; *(have relationship)*: **to ~ out with sb** sair com alguém; **to ~ out for a meal** ir comer fora.

❏ **go over** *vt fus* *(check)* rever.

❏ **go round** *vi* *(revolve)* rodar; **there isn't enough cake to ~ round** não há bolo que chegue para todos.

❏ **go through** *vt fus* *(experience)* passar por; *(spend)* gastar; *(search)* revistar.

❏ **go up** *vi* *(increase)* subir.

❏ **go without** *vt fus* passar sem.

goad [gəʊd] *vt* espicaçar, incitar.

go-ahead *n* *(permission)* luz *f* verde.

goal [gəʊl] *n* *(posts)* baliza *f*; *(point scored)* gol *m*; *(aim)* objetivo *m*.

goalkeeper ['gəʊl,kiːpər] *n* goleiro *m* (-ra *f*) *(Br)*, guarda-redes *mf inv* (Port).

goalmouth ['gəʊlmaʊθ, *pl* -,maʊðz] *n* boca *f* da baliza.

goalpost ['gəʊlpəʊst] *n* poste *m* (da baliza).

goat [gəʊt] *n* cabra *f*.

gob [gɒb] *n* *(Brit: inf: mouth)* bico *m*.

gobble ['gɒbl] *vt* engolir (sem mastigar).

❏ **gobble down** *vt sep* engolir (sem mastigar).

❏ **gobble up** = **gobble down**.

go-between *n* intermediário *m* (-ria *f*).

gobsmacked ['gɒbsmækt] *adj* *(Brit: inf)*: **I was ~** fiquei de boca aberta.

go-cart = **go-kart**.

god [gɒd] *n* deus *m*.

❏ **God** *n* Deus *m*.

godchild ['gɒdtʃaɪld] (*pl* **-children** [-,tʃɪldrən]) *n* afilhado *m* (-da *f*).

goddaughter ['gɒd,dɔːtər] *n* afilhada *f*.

goddess ['gɒdɪs] *n* deusa *f*.

godfather ['gɒd,fɑːðər] *n* padrinho *m*.

godmother ['gɒd,mʌðər] *n* madrinha *f*.

gods [gɒdz] *npl*: **the ~** *(Brit: inf: in theatre)* o galinheiro.

godsend ['gɒdsend] *n*: **to be a ~** cair do céu.

godson ['gɒdsʌn] *n* afilhado *m*.

goes [gəʊz] → **go**.

goggles ['gɒglz] *npl* óculos *mpl* (protetores).

going ['gəʊɪŋ] *adj* *(available)* disponível; **the ~ rate** a tarifa em vigor.

go-kart [-kɑːt] *n* kart *m*.

gold [gəʊld] *n* ouro *m* ◆ *adj* *(bracelet, watch)* de ouro; *(colour)* dourado(-da).

golden ['gəʊldən] *adj* *(made of gold)* de ouro; *(gold-coloured)* dourado(-da).

goldfish ['gəʊldfɪʃ] (*pl inv*) *n* peixe-dourado *m*.

gold medal *n* medalha *f* de ouro.

gold-plated [-'pleɪtɪd] *adj* banhado (-da) a ouro.

golf [gɒlf] *n* golfe *m*.

golf ball *n* bola *f* de golfe.

golf club *n* *(place)* clube *m* de golfe; *(piece of equipment)* taco *m* de golfe.

golf course *n* campo *m* de golfe.

golfer ['gɒlfər] *n* jogador *m* (-ra *f*) de golfe.

gone [gɒn] *pp* → **go** ◆ *prep* *(Brit)*: **it's ~ ten** já passa das dez.

gong [gɒŋ] *n* gongo *m*.

good [gʊd] *(compar* **better**, *superl* **best)** *adj* bom (boa); *(well-behaved)* bem comportado(-da) ◆ *n* o bem; **be ~!** porte-se bem!; **to have a ~ time** divertir-se; **to be ~ at sthg** ser bom em algo; **a ~ ten minutes** uns bons dez minutos; **in ~ time** com antecedência; **to make ~ sthg** *(damage)* pagar por algo; *(loss)* compensar algo; **for ~** para sempre; **for the ~ of** para o bem de; **to do sb ~** fazer bem a alguém; **it's no ~** *(there's no point)* não vale a pena; **~ afternoon!** boa tarde!; **~ evening!** boa noite!; **~ morning!** bom dia!; ~ **night!** boa noite!.

❏ **goods** *npl* mercadorias *fpl*.

goodbye [gʊdˈbaɪ] *excl* adeus!

Good Friday *n* Sexta-feira *f* Santa.

good-humoured *adj* bem-humorado(-da).

good-looking [-ˈlʊkɪŋ] *adj* bonito(-ta).

good-natured [-ˈneɪtʃəd] *adj* amigável.

goodness [ˈgʊdnɪs] *n (kindness)* bondade *f*; *(nutritive quality)* valor *m* nutritivo ◆ *excl*: **(my) ~!** meu Deus!; **for ~ sake!** por favor!, por amor de Deus!; **thank ~!** graças a Deus!

goods train [gʊdz-] *n* trem *m* de mercadorias.

goodwill [ˌgʊdˈwɪl] *n* boa vontade *f*.

goody [ˈgʊdɪ] *n (inf: in film, book etc)* bom *m* (boa *f*).

❏ **goodies** *npl (inf: desirable things)* coisas *fpl* boas.

goose [guːs] *(pl* geese*)* *n* ganso *m*.

gooseberry [ˈgʊzbərɪ] *n* groselha *f* branca.

goosebumps [ˈguːsbʌmps] *npl (Am)* = **gooseflesh**.

gooseflesh [ˈguːsfleʃ] *n* pele *f* de galinha, pele *f* arrepiada.

goose pimples *npl (Brit)* = **gooseflesh**.

gorge [gɔːdʒ] *n* garganta *f*, desfiladeiro *m*.

gorgeous [ˈgɔːdʒəs] *adj (day, meal, countryside)* magnífico(-ca); *(inf: good-looking)* lindo(-da).

gorilla [gəˈrɪlə] *n* gorila *mf*.

gorse [gɔːs] *n* tojo *m* (arnal).

gory [ˈgɔːrɪ] *adj (film)* com muito sangue; *(scene, death)* sangrento(-ta); *(details)* escabroso(-osa).

gosh [gɒʃ] *excl (inf)* caramba!

gospel [ˈgɒspl] *n (doctrine)* evangelho *m*.

❏ **Gospel** *n* Evangelho *m*.

gossip [ˈgɒsɪp] *n (about someone)* mexerico *m*, fofoca *f*; *(chat)* conversa *f* ◆ *vi (about someone)* fofocar; *(chat)* conversar.

gossip column *n* coluna em jornal ou revista dedicada a mexericos sobre figuras públicas.

got [gɒt] *pt & pp* → **get**.

gotten [ˈgɒtn] *pp (Am)* → **get**.

goujons [ˈguːdʒɒnz] *npl* filés *mpl* (de peixe).

goulash [ˈguːlæʃ] *n* gulache *m*, prato húngaro de carne ensopada temperada com colorau ou pimentão-doce.

gourmet [ˈgʊəmeɪ] *n* gastrônomo *m* (-ma *f*) ◆ *adj* gastronómico(-ca).

govern [ˈgʌvən] *vt* governar.

governess [ˈgʌvənɪs] *n* governanta *f*, preceptora *f*.

government [ˈgʌvnmənt] *n* governo *m*.

governor [ˈgʌvənər] *n (of state, colony)* governador *m* (-ra *f*); *(of school, bank, prison)* diretor *m* (-ra *f*).

gown [gaʊn] *n (dress)* vestido *m*.

GP *abbr* = **general practitioner**.

grab [græb] *vt (take hold of)* agarrar.

grace [greɪs] *n (elegance)* graça *f*, elegância *f*; *(prayer)* ação *f* de graças.

graceful [ˈgreɪsfʊl] *adj* gracioso (-osa).

gracious [ˈgreɪʃəs] *adj (polite)* amável ◆ *excl*: **(good) ~!** santo Deus!

grade [greɪd] *n (quality)* categoria *f*; *(in exam)* nota *f*; *(Am: year at school)* ano *m* (de escolaridade).

grade crossing *n (Am)* passagem *f* de nível.

grade school *n (Am)* escola *f* primária.

gradient [ˈgreɪdjənt] *n* inclinação *f*.

gradual [ˈgrædjʊəl] *adj* gradual.

gradually [ˈgrædjʊəlɪ] *adv* gradualmente.

graduate [*n* ˈgrædjʊət, *vb* ˈgrædjʊeɪt] *n (from university)* licenciado *m* (-da *f*); *(Am: from high school)* pessoa que concluiu o ensino secundário ◆ *vi (from university)* licenciar-se, formar-se; *(Am: from high school)* concluir o ensino secundário.

graduation [ˌgrædjʊˈeɪʃn] *n (ceremony)* entrega *f* dos diplomas.

graffiti [grəˈfiːtɪ] *n* grafite *m*.

grain [greɪn] *n (seed, of sand)* grão *m*; *(crop)* cereais *mpl*; *(of salt)* pedra *f*.

gram [græm] *n* grama *m*.

grammar [ˈgræmər] *n* gramática *f*.

grammar school *n (in UK)* escola secundária tradicional para alunos dos 11 aos 18 anos, cujo acesso é ditado por um exame.

grammatical [grəˈmætɪkl] *adj (referring to grammar)* gramatical; *(grammatically correct)* (gramaticalmente) correto(-ta).

gramme [græm] = **gram**.

gramophone ['græməfoun] n gramofone m.

gran [græn] n (Brit) (inf) avó f.

grand [grænd] adj (impressive) magnífico(-ca) ◆ n (inf) (£1,000) mil libras fpl; ($1,000) mil dólares mpl.

grandchild ['græntʃaild] (pl -children [-ˌtʃildrən]) n neto m (-ta f).

granddad ['grændæd] n (inf) avô m.

granddaughter ['grænˌdɔːtəʳ] n neta f.

grandeur ['grændʒəʳ] n grandeza f, imponência f.

grandfather ['grændˌfɑːðəʳ] n avô m.

grandma ['grænmɑː] n (inf) avó f.

grandmother ['grænˌmʌðəʳ] n avó f.

grandpa ['grænpɑː] n (inf) avô m.

grandparents ['grænˌpeərənts] npl avós mpl.

grand piano n piano m de cauda.

grand slam n (in rugby, football) pleno m.

grandson ['grænsʌn] n neto m.

grandstand ['grændstænd] n tribuna f.

granite ['grænit] n granito m.

granny ['græni] n (inf) avó f.

grant [grɑːnt] n (for study) bolsa f; (POL) subsídio m ◆ vt (fml: give) conceder; **to take sthg for ~ed** considerar algo como um dado adquirido; **to take sb for ~ed** não dar o devido valor a alguém.

granulated sugar ['grænjuleitid-] n açúcar m cristalizado.

granule ['grænjuːl] n (of salt, sugar) pedrinha f; (of coffee) grânulo m.

grape [greip] n uva f.

grapefruit ['greipfruːt] n toranja f.

grapefruit juice n suco m de toranja (Br), sumo m de toranja (Port).

graph [grɑːf] n gráfico m.

graphic ['græfik] adj (vivid) minucioso(-osa).

❑ **graphics** npl (pictures) gráficos mpl.

graph paper n papel m milimétrico.

grasp [grɑːsp] vt (grip) agarrar; (understand) perceber.

grass [grɑːs] n (plant) grama f (Br), erva f (Port); (lawn) gramado m (Br), relva f (Port); "**keep off the ~**" "não pise na grama".

grasshopper ['grɑːsˌhɒpəʳ] n gafanhoto m.

grate [greit] n grelha f.

grated ['greitid] adj ralado(-da).

grateful ['greitful] adj agradecido (-da), grato(-ta).

grater ['greitəʳ] n ralador m.

grating ['greitiŋ] adj irritante ◆ n (grille) gradeamento m.

gratitude ['grætitjuːd] n gratidão f.

gratuity [grəˈtjuːiti] n (fml) gratificação f.

grave¹ [greiv] adj (mistake, news, concern) grave ◆ n sepultura f.

grave² [grɑːv] adj (accent) grave.

gravel ['grævl] n gravilha f.

gravestone ['greivstoun] n pedra f tumular.

graveyard ['greivjɑːd] n cemitério m.

gravity ['græviti] n gravidade f.

gravy ['greivi] n molho m (de carne).

gray [grei] (Am) = **grey**.

graze [greiz] vt (injure) esfolar.

grease [griːs] n gordura f.

greaseproof paper ['griːspruːf-] n (Brit) papel m vegetal.

greasy ['griːsi] adj (clothes, food) gorduroso(-osa); (skin, hair) oleoso(-osa).

great [greit] adj grande; (very good) ótimo(-ma); **(that's) ~!** ótimo!

Great Britain n Grã-Bretanha f.

Great Dane n grande dinamarquês m (cão).

great-grandchild n bisneto m (-ta f).

great-grandfather n bisavô m.

great-grandmother n bisavó f.

greatly ['greitli] adv muito.

greatness ['greitnis] n grandeza f, importância f.

Greece [griːs] n Grécia f.

greed [griːd] n (for food) gulodice f; (for money) ganância f.

greedy ['griːdi] adj (for food) guloso(-osa); (for money) ganancioso(-osa).

Greek [griːk] adj grego(-ga) ◆ n (person) grego m (-ga f); (language) grego m.

Greek salad n salada f mista (com tomate, alface, azeitonas negras e queijo de cabra).

green [griːn] adj verde ◆ n (colour) verde m; (in village) gramado m público; (on golf course) green m.

❑ **greens** npl (vegetables) verduras fpl.

green beans npl feijão m verde.

green belt n (Brit) cinturão m verde.

green card n (Brit: for car) carteira f

verde, *seguro necessário para viajar de carro no estrangeiro;* (Am: *work permit*) autorização f de permanência e trabalho.

green channel n *passagem em porto ou aeroporto reservada a passageiros sem artigos a declarar.*

greenery ['gri:nərɪ] n verde m.

greenfly ['gri:nˡflaɪ] (pl inv OR **-flies**) n pulgão m.

greengage ['gri:ngeɪdʒ] n rainha-cláudia f.

greengrocer's ['gri:ngrəʊsəz] n (shop) *loja onde se vende fruta, legumes e hortaliça.*

greenhouse ['gri:nhaʊs, pl -haʊzɪz] n estufa f.

greenhouse effect n efeito m estufa.

Greenland ['gri:nlənd] n Gronelândia f.

green light n sinal m verde.

green pepper n pimentão m (verde).

Greens [gri:nz] npl: **the ~** os Verdes.

green salad n salada f verde.

greet [gri:t] vt (say hello to) cumprimentar.

greeting ['gri:tɪŋ] n cumprimento m.

greeting card (Am) = **greetings card**.

greetings card n (Brit) cartão m de felicitações.

grenade [grəˈneɪd] n granada f.

grew [gru:] pt → **grow**.

grey [greɪ] adj cinzento(-ta); (hair) grisalho(-lha) ♦ n cinzento m; **to go ~** ganhar cabelos brancos.

grey-haired adj grisalho(-lha).

greyhound ['greɪhaʊnd] n galgo m.

grid [grɪd] n (grating) gradeamento m; (on map etc) quadrícula f.

grief [gri:f] n desgosto m; **to come to ~** fracassar.

grievance ['gri:vns] n (complaint) (motivo m de) queixa f.

grieve [gri:v] vi estar de luto.

grill [grɪl] n grelha f; (part of restaurant) grill m ♦ vt grelhar.

grille [grɪl] n (AUT) grelha f do radiador.

grilled [grɪld] adj grelhado(-da).

grim [grɪm] adj (expression) severo(-ra); (place, reality) sombrio (-bria); (news) desagradável.

grimace ['grɪməs] n careta f.

grime [graɪm] n sujeira f.

grimy ['graɪmɪ] adj sebento(-ta).

grin [grɪn] n sorriso m (largo) ♦ vi sorrir.

grind [graɪnd] (pt & pp **ground**) vt (pepper, coffee) moer.

grinder ['graɪndəʳ] n moinho m.

grip [grɪp] n (of tyres) aderência f; (handle) punho m; (bag) bolsa f de viagem; (hold) pega f ♦ vt (hold) agarrar; **to keep a firm ~ on sthg** (rope, railings) agarrar algo com força; **get a ~ on yourself!** controle-se!

gripping ['grɪpɪŋ] adj apaixonante.

grisly ['grɪzlɪ] adj horripilante, horrendo(-da).

gristle ['grɪsl] n nervo m.

grit [grɪt] n (stones) gravilha f; (sand) saibro m; (in eye) cisco m, areia f ♦ vt (road, steps) ensaibrar.

groan [grəʊn] n gemido m ♦ vi (in pain) gemer; (complain) resmungar.

groceries ['grəʊsərɪz] npl mercearia f.

grocer's ['grəʊsəz] n (shop) mercearia f.

grocery ['grəʊsərɪ] n (shop) mercearia f.

groggy ['grɒgɪ] adj tonto(-ta), zonzo(-za).

groin [grɔɪn] n virilha f.

groom [gru:m] n (of horses) cavalariço m (Br), moço m de estrebaria (Port); (bridegroom) noivo m ♦ vt (horse, dog) escovar; (candidate) preparar.

groove [gru:v] n ranhura f.

grope [grəʊp] vi: **to ~ around for sthg** procurar algo com apalpadelas.

gross [grəʊs] adj (weight, income) bruto(-ta).

grossly ['grəʊslɪ] adv (extremely) extremamente.

grotesque [grəʊˈtesk] adj grotesco(-ca).

grotto ['grɒtəʊ] (pl -s OR -es) n gruta f.

grotty ['grɒtɪ] adj (Brit: inf) mixa (Br), rasca (Port).

ground [graʊnd] pt & pp → **grind** ♦ n chão m; (SPORT) campo m ♦ adj (coffee) moído(-da) ♦ vt: **to be ~ed** (plane) não ter autorização para decolar; (Am: electrical connection) estar ligado à terra.

❑ **grounds** npl (of building) área que circunda um prédio; (of coffee) borra f; (reason) razão f, motivo m.

ground crew n pessoal m de terra.

ground floor n andar m térreo (Br), rés-do-chão m (Port).

grounding ['graʊndɪŋ] n: ~ **in sthg** conhecimentos mpl (básicos) de algo.

groundless ['graʊndlɪs] adj infundado(-da).

groundsheet ['graʊndʃiːt] n chão m OR solo m da barraca.

groundwork ['graʊndwɜːk] n trabalho m preparatório.

group [gruːp] n grupo m.

groupie ['gruːpɪ] n (inf) groupie mf, pessoa que segue o seu grupo ou artista preferido de perto indo a todos os seus concertos.

grouse [graʊs] (pl inv) n (bird) galo silvestre m.

grove [grəʊv] n (group of trees) mata f; **lemon ~** limoal m.

grovel ['grɒvl] vi (be humble) humilhar-se.

grow [grəʊ] (pt grew, pp grown) vi crescer; (become) tornar-se ◆ vt (plant, crop) cultivar; (beard) deixar crescer. ❑ **grow up** vi crescer.

growl [graʊl] vi (dog) rosnar.

grown [grəʊn] pp → **grow**.

grown-up adj adulto(-ta) ◆ n adulto m (-ta f).

growth [grəʊθ] n (increase) crescimento m; (MED) tumor m, abcesso m.

grub [grʌb] n (inf: food) comida f.

grubby ['grʌbɪ] adj (inf) porco (porca).

grudge [grʌdʒ] n ressentimento m ◆ vt: **to ~ sb sthg** invejar algo a alguém; **he seems to have a ~ against me** ele parece ter algo contra mim.

grueling ['grʊəlɪŋ] (Am) = **gruelling**.

gruelling ['grʊəlɪŋ] adj (Brit) extenuante.

gruesome ['gruːsəm] adj horripilante.

gruff [grʌf] adj áspero(-ra).

grumble ['grʌmbl] vi (complain) resmungar.

grumpy ['grʌmpɪ] adj (inf) resmungão(-gona).

grunt [grʌnt] vi grunhir.

guarantee [ˌgærən'tiː] n garantia f ◆ vt garantir.

guaranteed delivery [ˌgærən'tiːd-] n (Brit) = correio m expresso.

guard [gɑːd] n (of prisoner etc) guarda mf; (Brit: on train) guarda m; (protective

cover) proteção f ◆ vt (watch over) guardar; **to be on one's ~** estar alerta.

guard dog n cão m de guarda.

guarded ['gɑːdɪd] adj cauteloso(-osa), prudente.

guardian ['gɑːdjən] n (of child) tutor m (-ra f); (protector) guardião m (-diã f).

guard's van n (Brit) vagão m traseiro.

guerilla = **guerrilla**.

Guernsey ['gɜːnzɪ] n (place) Guernsey s.

guerrilla [gə'rɪlə] n guerrilheiro m (-ra f).

guess [ges] n suposição f ◆ vt & vi adivinhar; **I ~ (so)** é provável, imagino que sim.

guesswork ['geswɜːk] n conjetura f.

guest [gest] n (in home) convidado m (-da f); (in hotel) hóspede mf.

guesthouse ['gesthaʊs, pl -haʊzɪz] n pensão f.

guestroom ['gestrʊm] n quarto m de hóspedes.

guffaw [gʌ'fɔː] n gargalhada f ◆ vi rir às gargalhadas.

guidance ['gaɪdəns] n orientação f.

guide [gaɪd] n (for tourists) guia mf; (guidebook) guia m ◆ vt guiar. ❑ **Guide** n (Brit) = escoteira f.

guidebook ['gaɪdbʊk] n guia m.

guide dog n cão m de guia.

guided tour ['gaɪdɪd-] n visita f com guia.

guidelines ['gaɪdlaɪnz] npl diretrizes fpl.

guild [gɪld] n (association) associação f.

guillotine ['gɪlətiːn] n guilhotina f.

guilt [gɪlt] n culpa f.

guilty ['gɪltɪ] adj culpado(-da).

Guinea-Bissau [ˌgɪnɪbɪ'saʊ] n Guiné-Bissau f.

guinea pig ['gɪnɪ-] n cobaia f.

guitar [gɪ'tɑːr] n (acoustic) viola f; (electric) guitarra f.

guitarist [gɪ'tɑːrɪst] n (of acoustic guitar) tocador m (-ra f) de viola; (of electric guitar) guitarrista mf.

gulf [gʌlf] n (of sea) golfo m.

Gulf War n: **the ~** a Guerra do Golfo.

gull [gʌl] n gaivota f.

gullet ['gʌlɪt] n goela f.

gullible ['gʌləbl] adj ingênuo(-nua).

gully ['gʌlɪ] n barranco m.

gulp [gʌlp] n (of drink) gole m.

gum [gʌm] n (chewing gum, bubble gum) chiclete m (Br), pastilha f elástica (Port); (adhesive) cola f.

❑ **gums** npl (in mouth) gengivas fpl.

gumboots ['gʌmbuːts] npl (Brit) botas fpl de borracha, galochas fpl.

gun [gʌn] n (pistol) revólver m; (rifle) espingarda f; (cannon) canhão m.

gunfire ['gʌnfaɪəʳ] n tiroteio m.

gunman ['gʌnmən] (pl -men [-mən]) n pessoa f armada.

gunpoint ['gʌnpɔɪnt] n: at ~ sob ameaça de arma.

gunpowder ['gʌn,paʊdəʳ] n pólvora f.

gunshot ['gʌnʃɒt] n tiro m.

gurgle ['gɜːgl] vi gorgolejar.

gush [gʌʃ] n jorro m ◆ vi (flow out) jorrar.

gust [gʌst] n rajada f.

gut [gʌt] n (inf: stomach) bucho m.

❑ **guts** npl (inf) (intestines) tripas fpl; (courage) coragem f, peito m.

gutter ['gʌtəʳ] n (beside road) sarjeta f; (of house) calha f (Br), caleira f (Port).

gutter press n imprensa f sensacionalista.

guy [gaɪ] n (inf: man) tipo m.

❑ **guys** npl (Am: inf: people): **you ~s** vocês.

Guy Fawkes Night [-'fɔːks-] n (Brit) 5 de novembro.

guy rope n corda f (de barraca de acampar).

guzzle ['gʌzl] vt (food) devorar; (drink) emborcar.

gym [dʒɪm] n (place) ginásio m; (school lesson) ginástica f.

gymnasium [dʒɪm'neɪzjəm] (pl -iums OR -ia [-zɪə]) n ginásio m.

gymnast ['dʒɪmnæst] n ginasta mf.

gymnastics [dʒɪm'næstɪks] n ginástica f.

gym shoes npl sapatilhas fpl de ginástica.

gymslip ['dʒɪm,slɪp] n (Brit) veste f escolar (Br), bata f da escola (Port).

gynaecologist [,gaɪnə'kɒlədʒɪst] n ginecologista mf.

gynaecology [,gaɪnə'kɒlədʒɪ] n ginecologia f.

gypsy ['dʒɪpsɪ] = gipsy.

H

H *(abbr of hospital)* H ◆ *abbr* = **hot**.

haberdashery ['hæbə,dæʃərɪ] *n* *(goods)* artigos *mpl* de armarinho *(Br)*, artigos *mpl* de retrosaria *(Port)*; *(shop)* armarinho *m (Br)*, retrosaria *f (Port)*

habit ['hæbɪt] *n* hábito *m*.

habitat ['hæbɪtæt] *n* habitat *m*.

habitual [hə'bɪtʃʊəl] *adj (customary)* habitual; *(offender, smoker, drinker)* inveterado(-da).

hack [hæk] *vt* cortar, rachar.

hacksaw ['hæksɔː] *n* serra *f* para metal.

had [hæd] *pt & pp* → **have**.

haddock ['hædək] *(pl inv)* *n* hadoque *m (Br)*, eglefim *m (Port)*.

hadn't ['hædnt] = **had not**.

haggard ['hægəd] *adj (person)* abatido(-da).

haggis ['hægɪs] *n* bucho de ovelha recheado com aveia, gordura, muídos de carneiro e especiarias, cozido e servido com batatas e nabos cozidos, prato tradicional escocês.

haggle ['hægl] *vi* regatear.

Hague [heɪg] *n*: **The ~** Haia *s*.

hail [heɪl] *n* granizo *m* ◆ *v impers*: **it's ~ing** está chovendo granizo.

hailstone ['heɪlstəʊn] *n* granizo *m*, pedra *f*.

hair [heər] *n (on human head)* cabelo *m*; *(on skin)* pêlo *m*; **to have one's ~ cut** cortar o cabelo; **to wash one's ~** lavar a cabeça.

hairband ['heəbænd] *n* fita *f* para o cabelo.

hairbrush ['heəbrʌʃ] *n* escova *f* (de cabelo).

hairclip ['heəklɪp] *n* grampo *m (Br)*, gancho *m (Port)*.

haircut ['heəkʌt] *n (style)* corte *m* (de cabelo); **to have a ~** cortar o cabelo.

hairdo ['heəduː] *(pl -s)* *n* penteado *m*.

hairdresser ['heə,dresər] *n* cabeleireiro *m* (-ra *f*); **~'s** *(salon)* cabeleireiro *m*; **to go to the ~'s** ir ao cabeleireiro.

hairdryer ['heə,draɪər] *n* secador *m* de cabelo.

hair gel *n* gel *m* (para o cabelo).

hairgrip ['heəgrɪp] *n (Brit)* grampo *m (Br)*, gancho *m (Port)*.

hairnet ['heənet] *n* rede *f* para o cabelo.

hairpin ['heəpɪn] *n* grampo *m (Br)*, gancho *m (Port)*.

hairpin bend *n* curva *f* fechada.

hair-raising [-,reɪzɪŋ] *adj* de arrepiar os cabelos, arrepiante.

hair remover [-rɪ,muːvər] *n* depilatório *m*.

hair rollers [-'rəʊləz] *npl* rolos *mpl* (para o cabelo).

hair slide *n* grampo *m (Br)*, gancho *m (Port)*.

hairspray ['heəspreɪ] *n* laquê *m (Br)*, laca *f (Port)*.

hairstyle ['heəstaɪl] *n* penteado *m*.

hairy ['heərɪ] *adj (person)* cabeludo (-da); *(chest, legs)* peludo(-da).

Haiti ['heɪtɪ] *n* Haiti *m*.

hake [heɪk] *n* pescada *f*.

half [*Brit* hɑːf, *Am* hæf] *(pl* **halves***)* *n (50%)* metade *f*; *(of match)* parte *f*; *(half pint)* fino *m (Port)*, ≈ 2,5 cl; *(child's ticket)* meia passagem *f (Br)*, meio bilhete *m (Port)* ◆ *adj* meio (meia) ◆ *adv* meio; **a day and a ~** um dia e meio; **four and a ~** quatro e meio; **an hour and a ~** uma hora e meia; **~ as big as** metade do tamanho de; **~ an hour** meia-hora; **~ a dozen** meia dúzia; **~ price** a metade do preço.

half board *n* meia pensão *f*.

half-day *n* meio-dia *m*.

half fare n meia passagem f (Br), meio bilhete m (Port).

half-hearted [-'hɑːtɪd] adj pouco entusiasta.

half hour n meia-hora f; **every ~** todas as meias-horas.

half-mast n (Brit): **at ~** a meio mastro, a meia haste.

halfpenny ['heɪpnɪ] (pl **-pennies** OR **-pence**) n meio pêni m.

half portion n meia dose f.

half-price adj a metade do preço.

half term n (Brit) semana de férias na metade do trimestre escolar.

half time n intervalo m.

halfway [hɑːf'weɪ] adv (in space) a meio caminho; (in time) a meio.

halibut ['hælɪbət] (pl inv) n palmeta f.

hall [hɔːl] n (of house) entrada f, hall m; (building, large room) salão m; (country house) ~ mansão f.

hallmark ['hɔːlmɑːk] n (on silver, gold) marca f.

hallo [hə'ləʊ] = **hello**.

hall of residence n residência f universitária.

Halloween [,hæləʊ'iːn] n noite f das bruxas.

hallucinate [hə'luːsɪneɪt] vi delirar, estar com alucinações.

hallway ['hɔːlweɪ] n corredor m.

halo ['heɪləʊ] (pl **-es** OR **-s**) n halo m, auréola f.

halt [hɔːlt] vi parar ♦ n: **to come to a ~** parar.

halve [Brit hɑːv, Am hæv] vt (reduce by half) reduzir à metade; (divide in two) dividir ao meio.

halves [Brit hɑːvz, Am hævz] pl → **half**.

ham [hæm] n presunto m.

hamburger ['hæmbɜːgər] n (beefburger) hambúrguer m; (Am: mince) carne f picada.

hamlet ['hæmlɪt] n aldeia f, lugarejo m.

hammer ['hæmər] n martelo m ♦ vt (nail) martelar.

hammock ['hæmək] n rede f.

hamper ['hæmpər] n cesta f (de piquenique).

hamster ['hæmstər] n hamster m.

hamstring ['hæmstrɪŋ] n tendão m do jarrete.

hand [hænd] n mão f; (of clock, watch, dial) ponteiro m; **to give sb a ~** dar uma mão a alguém; **to get out of ~**

fugir ao controle; **by ~** à mão; **in ~** (time) disponível; **on the one ~** por um lado; **on the other ~** por outro lado.

❑ **hand in** vt sep entregar.

❑ **hand out** vt sep distribuir.

❑ **hand over** vt sep (give) entregar.

handbag ['hændbæg] n bolsa f, carteira f.

handball ['hændbɔːl] n andebol m.

handbasin ['hændbeɪsn] n pia f.

handbook ['hændbʊk] n manual m.

handbrake ['hændbreɪk] n freio m de mão (Br), travão m de mão (Port).

hand cream n creme m para as mãos.

handcuffs ['hændkʌfs] npl algemas fpl.

handful ['hændfʊl] n (amount) mãocheia f, punhado m.

handgun ['hændgʌn] n pistola f.

handicap ['hændɪkæp] n (physical, mental) deficiência f; (disadvantage) desvantagem f.

handicapped ['hændɪkæpt] adj deficiente ♦ npl: **the ~** os deficientes.

handicraft ['hændɪkræft] n artesanato m.

handiwork ['hændɪwɜːk] n obra f.

handkerchief ['hæŋkətʃɪf] (pl **-chiefs** OR **-chieves** [-tʃiːvz]) n lenço m (de mão).

handle ['hændl] n (of door, window) puxador m; (of suitcase) alça f; (of pan, knife) cabo m ♦ vt (touch) pegar em; (deal with) lidar com; (solve) tratar de; **"~ with care"** "frágil".

handlebars ['hændlbɑːz] npl guidom m (Br), guiador m (Port).

hand luggage n bagagem f de mão.

handmade [,hænd'meɪd] adj feito(-ta) à mão.

handout ['hændaʊt] n (leaflet) prospecto m.

handrail ['hændreɪl] n corrimão m.

handset ['hændset] n fone m (Br), auscultador m (Port); **"please replace the ~"** mensagem que avisa que o telefone não está bem desligado.

handshake ['hændʃeɪk] n aperto m de mão.

handsome ['hænsəm] adj bonito(-ta).

handstand ['hændstænd] n pino m.

handwriting ['hænd,raɪtɪŋ] n letra f, caligrafia f.

handy ['hændɪ] adj (useful) prático (-ca); (good with one's hands) habilido-

so(-osa); *(near)* à mão; **to come in ~**
(inf) vir mesmo a calhar.

handyman ['hændɪmæn] *(pl* **-men**
[-mɛn]) *n* faz-tudo *m*, biscoiteiro *m*.

hang [hæŋ] *(pt & pp* **hung**) *vt (on hook,
wall etc)* pendurar; *(execute: pt & pp*
hanged*)* enforcar ◆ *vi (be suspended)*
pender ◆ *n:* **to get the ~ of sthg** pegar
o jeito de algo.
❑ **hang about** *vi (Brit: inf)* rondar.
❑ **hang around** *(inf)* = **hang about**.
❑ **hang down** *vi* estar pendurado(-da).
❑ **hang on** *vi (inf: wait)* esperar.
❑ **hang out** *vt sep (washing)* pendurar
◆ *vi (inf: spend time)* passar o tempo.
❑ **hang up** *vi (on phone)* desligar.

hangar ['hæŋər] *n* hangar *m*.

hanger ['hæŋər] *n* cabide *m*.

hang gliding *n* asa-delta *f*.

hangover ['hæŋ͵ouvər] *n* ressaca *f*.

hang-up *n (inf)* complexo *m*.

hankie ['hæŋkɪ] *n (inf)* lenço *m* (de
mão).

haphazard [͵hæp'hæzəd] *adj* ao
acaso; **her work is very ~** o trabalho
dela é muito irregular.

happen ['hæpən] *vi* acontecer; **I ~ed
to bump into him** encontrei-o por
acaso.

happily ['hæpɪlɪ] *adv (luckily)* felizmente.

happiness ['hæpɪnɪs] *n* felicidade *f*.

happy ['hæpɪ] *adj* feliz; **to be ~
about sthg** *(satisfied)* estar satisfeito
(-ta) com algo; **to be ~ to do sthg** não
se importar de fazer algo; **to be ~
with sthg** estar satisfeito com algo;
Happy Birthday! Parabéns!, Feliz Aniversário!; **Happy Christmas!** Feliz
Natal!; **Happy New Year!** Feliz Ano
Novo!

happy-go-lucky *adj* despreocu-
pado(-da).

happy hour *n (inf)* período, normalmente ao fim da tarde, em que os bares
vendem as bebidas mais barato.

harass ['hærəs] *vt* assediar, importunar.

harassment ['hærəsmənt] *n* assédio
m, importúnio *m*.

harbor ['hɑːbər] *(Am)* = **harbour**.

harbour ['hɑːbər] *n (Brit)* porto *m*.

hard [hɑːd] *adj* duro(-ra); *(difficult,
strenuous)* difícil; *(forceful)* forte; *(winter, frost)* rigoroso (-osa); *(water)* calcá-
rio(-ria), duro(-ra); *(drugs)* pesado(-da)

◆ *adv (work)* muito, arduamente; *(listen)* atentamente; *(hit, rain)* com força;
to try ~ fazer um esforço.

hardback ['hɑːdbæk] *n* livro *m* enca-
dernado.

hardboard ['hɑːdbɔːd] *n* madeira *f*
compensada *(Br)*, platex *m (Port)*.

hard-boiled egg [-bɔɪld-] *n* ovo *m*
cozido.

hard cash *n* dinheiro *m* em espécie,
dinheiro *m* vivo.

hard copy *n* cópia *f* impressa.

hard disk *n* disco *m* rígido OR duro.

harden ['hɑːdn] *vt & vi* endurecer.

hard-hearted [-'hɑːtɪd] *adj* insensível.

hardly ['hɑːdlɪ] *adv:* **~ ever** quase
nunca; **I ~ know her** mal a conheço;
there's ~ any left já não há quase
nada.

hardness ['hɑːdnɪs] *n (solidness)* dureza *f*; *(difficulty)* dificuldade *f*.

hardship ['hɑːdʃɪp] *n* dificuldades *fpl*.

hard shoulder *n (Brit)* acostamento *m (Br)*, zona *f* de paragem de
urgência.

hard up *adj (inf)* teso(-sa).

hardware ['hɑːdweər] *n (tools, equipment)* ferramenta *f*; *(COMPUT)* hardware
m.

hardware shop *n* loja *f* de ferragens.

hardware store *n* loja *f* de ferragens.

hardwearing [͵hɑːd'weərɪŋ] *adj (Brit)*
resistente.

hardworking [͵hɑːd'wɜːkɪŋ] *adj* tra-
balhador(-ra).

hardy ['hɑːdɪ] *adj (person, animal)*
robusto(-ta); *(plant)* vivaz, resistente.

hare [heər] *n* lebre *f*.

harebrained ['heə͵breɪnd] *adj (inf)*
disparatado(-da), desmiolado(-da).

haricot (bean) ['hærɪkəʊ-] *n* feijão
m branco.

harm [hɑːm] *n (injury)* mal *m*; *(damage)* dano *m* ◆ *vt (injure)* magoar; *(reputation, chances)* prejudicar; *(fabric)*
danificar.

harmful ['hɑːmful] *adj* prejudicial.

harmless ['hɑːmlɪs] *adj* inofensivo
(-va).

harmonica [hɑː'mɒnɪkə] *n* harmônica
f.

harmony ['hɑːmənɪ] *n* harmonia *f*.

harness ['hɑːnɪs] *n (for horse)* arreios

mpl; (for child) andadeira *f*.

harp [hɑːp] *n* harpa *f*.

harpoon [hɑːˈpuːn] *n* arpão *m*
◆ *vt* arpear.

harpsichord [ˈhɑːpsɪkɔːd] *n* cravo *m*.

harrowing [ˈhærəʊɪŋ] *adj* horrível, horroroso(-osa).

harsh [hɑːʃ] *adj (severe)* rigoroso(-osa); *(cruel)* severo(-ra); *(sound, voice)* áspero(-ra).

harvest [ˈhɑːvɪst] *n* colheita *f*.

has [*weak form* həz, *strong form* hæz] → **have**.

has-been *n (inf)* velha glória *f*, estrela *f* do passado.

hash [hæʃ] *n (meat)* picadinho *m* de carne; **I made a real ~ of the exam** *(inf)* fui extremamente mal no exame.

hash browns [hæʃ-] *npl (Am)* bolinhos fritos de batatas e cebolas picadas.

hasn't [ˈhæznt] = **has not**.

hassle [ˈhæsl] *n (inf)* chatice *f*.

haste [heɪst] *n* pressa *f*.

hastily [ˈheɪstɪlɪ] *adv* precipitadamente.

hasty [ˈheɪstɪ] *adj (hurried)* apressado(-da); *(rash)* precipitado(-da).

hat [hæt] *n* chapéu *m*.

hatch [hætʃ] *n (for serving food)* passapratos *m* ◆ *vi (chick)* nascer.

hatchback [ˈhætʃbæk] *n* carro *m* de três OR cinco portas.

hatchet [ˈhætʃɪt] *n* machado *m*.

hatchway [ˈhætʃweɪ] *n (on ship)* escotilha *f*.

hate [heɪt] *n* ódio *m* ◆ *vt* odiar, detestar; **to ~ doing sthg** detestar fazer algo.

hateful [ˈheɪtful] *adj* detestável, odioso(-osa).

hatred [ˈheɪtrɪd] *n* ódio *m*.

hat trick *n* hat trick *m*, três gols marcados pelo mesmo jogador no mesmo jogo.

haughty [ˈhɔːtɪ] *adj* altivo(-va).

haul [hɔːl] *vt* arrastar ◆ *n*: **a long ~** um longo percurso.

haunch [hɔːntʃ] *n (of person)* quadril *m*; *(of animal)* quarto *m* traseiro.

haunt [hɔːnt] *n* sítio *m* preferido ◆ *vt (subj: ghost)* assombrar.

haunted [ˈhɔːntɪd] *adj (house)* assombrado(-da).

have [hæv] *(pt & pp* had*) aux vb* **1.** *(to form perfect tenses)*: **I ~ finished** acabei; **~ you been there? – no, I haven't** você

já esteve lá? – não; **they hadn't seen it** não o tinham visto; **we had already left** nós já tínhamos saído.
2. *(must)*: **to ~ (got) to do sthg** ter de fazer algo; **do you ~ to pay?** é preciso pagar?
◆ *vt* **1.** *(possess)*: **to ~ (got)** ter; **do you ~ OR ~ you got a double room?** você tem um quarto de casal?; **she has (got) brown hair** ela tem o cabelo castanho.
2. *(experience)* ter; **to ~ a cold** estar resfriado; **to ~ a great time** divertir-se a valer.
3. *(replacing other verbs)* ter; **to ~ breakfast** tomar o café da manhã; **to ~ dinner** jantar; **to ~ lunch** almoçar; **to ~ a bath** tomar banho; **to ~ a drink** tomar qualquer coisa, tomar um copo; **to ~ a shower** tomar um banho; **to ~ a swim** nadar; **to ~ a walk** passear.
4. *(feel)* ter; **I ~ no doubt about it** não tenho dúvida alguma OR nenhuma sobre isso.
5. *(cause to be)*: **to ~ sthg done** mandar fazer algo; **to ~ one's hair cut** cortar o cabelo.
6. *(be treated in a certain way)*: **I've had my wallet stolen** me roubaram a carteira.

haven't [ˈhævnt] = **have not**.

haversack [ˈhævəsæk] *n* mochila *f*.

havoc [ˈhævək] *n* caos *m*.

Hawaii [həˈwaɪiː] *n* Havaí *m*.

hawk [hɔːk] *n* falcão *m*.

hawker [ˈhɔːkəʳ] *n* vendedor *m* (-ra *f*) ambulante.

hay [heɪ] *n* feno *m*.

hay fever *n* febre *f* do feno.

haystack [ˈheɪstæk] *n* meda *f* de feno.

haywire [ˈheɪwaɪəʳ] *adj (inf)*: **to go ~** degringolar *(Br)*, flipar *(Port)*.

hazard [ˈhæzəd] *n* risco *m*.

hazardous [ˈhæzədəs] *adj* arriscado(-da).

hazard warning lights *npl (Brit)* pisca-alerta *m (Br)*, luzes *fpl* (avisadoras) de perigo *(Port)*.

haze [heɪz] *n* névoa *f*.

hazel [ˈheɪzl] *adj* cor-de-mel *(inv)*.

hazelnut [ˈheɪzl,nʌt] *n* avelã *f*.

hazy [ˈheɪzɪ] *adj (misty)* nublado(-da).

he [hiː] *pron* ele; **~'s tall** ele é alto.

head [hed] *n* cabeça *f; (of queue)* princípio *m; (of page, letter)* cabeçalho *m; (of table, bed)* cabeceira *f; (of company, department)* chefe *m* (-fa *f*); *(head* *teacher)* diretor *m* (-ra *f*); *(of beer)* espuma *f* ◆ *vt (list, organization)* encabeçar ◆ *vi*: **to ~ home** dirigir-se para casa; **£10 a ~** 10 libras por cabeça; **~s or tails?** cara ou coroa?

◯ **head for** *vt fus (place)* dirigir-se a.

headache ['hedeɪk] *n (pain)* dor *f* de cabeça; **I've got a ~** estou com dor de cabeça.

headband ['hedbænd] *n* fita *f* de cabelo.

head boy *n (Brit)* representante *m* estudantil.

headdress ['heddres] *n* ornamento *m* para a cabeça.

header ['hedə'] *n (in football)* cabeçada *f*.

headfirst [,hed'fɜ:st] *adv* de cabeça.

head girl *n* .(*Brit)* representante *f* estudantil.

heading ['hedɪŋ] *n* título *m*.

headlamp ['hedlæmp] *(Brit)* = **headlight**.

headlight ['hedlaɪt] *n* farol *m* (dianteiro).

headline ['hedlaɪn] *n (in newspaper)* manchete *f (Br)*, título *m (Port)*; *(on TV, radio)* notícia *f* principal.

headlong ['hedlɒŋ] *adv (at great speed)* a toda a velocidade; *(impetuously)* sem pensar; *(dive, fall)* de cabeça.

headmaster [,hed'mɑːstə'] *n* diretor *m* (de escola).

headmistress [,hed'mɪstrɪs] *n* diretora *f* (de escola).

head of state *n* chefe *m* de estado.

head-on *adj & adv* de frente.

headphones ['hedfəʊnz] *npl* fones *mpl* de ouvido *(Br)*, auscultadores *mpl (Port)*.

headquarters [,hed'kwɔ:təz] *npl (of business)* sede *f*; *(of army)* quartel *m* general; *(of police)* central *f*.

headrest ['hedrest] *n* apoio-de-cabeça *m*.

headroom ['hedrʊm] *n (under bridge)* vão *m* livre.

headscarf ['hedskɑ:f] *(pl* **-scarves** [-skɑ:vz])* *n* lenço *m* de cabeça.

headset ['hedset] *n* fones *mpl* de ouvido *(Br)*, auscultadores *mpl* com microfone *(Port)*.

head start *n* vantagem *f*, avanço *m*.

headstrong ['hedstrɒŋ] *adj* cabeçudo(-da), teimoso(-osa).

head teacher *n* diretor *m* (-ra *f*) (da escola).

head waiter *n* maître *m (Br)*, chefe *m* de mesa *(Port)*.

heal [hi:l] *vt* curar ◆ *vi* sarar.

healing ['hi:lɪŋ] *n (of a person)* cura *f*; *(of a wound)* cicatrização *f*.

health [helθ] *n* saúde *f*; **to be in good/poor ~** estar bem/mal de saúde; **your (very) good ~!** saúde!

health centre *n* centro *m* de saúde.

health food *n* comida *f* dietética.

health food shop *n* loja *f* de produtos dietéticos.

health insurance *n* seguro *m* de saúde.

health service *n* serviço *m* de saúde.

healthy ['helθɪ] *adj* saudável.

heap [hi:p] *n* monte *m*; **~s of** *(inf)* montes de.

hear [hɪə'] *(pt & pp* **heard** [hɜ:d]) *vt & vi* ouvir; **to ~ about sthg** saber de algo; **to ~ from sb** ter notícias de alguém; **have you heard of him?** você já ouviu falar dele?

hearing ['hɪərɪŋ] *n (sense)* audição *f*; *(at court)* audiência *f*; **to be hard of ~** não ouvir bem.

hearing aid *n* aparelho *m* auditivo.

hearsay ['hɪəseɪ] *n* boato *m*.

hearse [hɜːs] *n* carro *m* fúnebre.

heart [hɑːt] *n* coração *m*; **to know sthg (off) by ~** saber algo de cor; **to lose ~** perder a coragem.

◯ **hearts** *npl (in cards)* copas *fpl*.

heart attack *n* ataque *m* cardíaco.

heartbeat ['hɑːtbiːt] *n* pulsação *f*, batida *f* cardíaca.

heartbroken ['hɑːt,brəʊkn] *adj* desolado(-da), com o coração despedaçado.

heartburn ['hɑːtbɜːn] *n* azia *f*.

heart condition *n*: **to have a ~** ter problemas cardíacos OR de coração.

heartfelt ['hɑːtfelt] *adj* sincero(-ra), do fundo do coração.

hearth [hɑːθ] *n* borda *f* da lareira.

heartless ['hɑːtlɪs] *adj (person)* sem coração; *(refusal, decision)* cruel.

heartwarming ['hɑːt,wɔːmɪŋ] *adj* comovente.

hearty ['hɑːtɪ] *adj (meal)* substancial.

heat [hiːt] *n* calor *m*; *(specific temperature)* temperatura *f*.

❏ **heat up** *vt sep* aquecer.

heated ['hi:tɪd] *adj (room, swimming pool)* aquecido(-da); *(argument, discussion)* acalorado(-da).

heater ['hi:tə'] *n* aquecedor *m*.

heath [hi:θ] *n* charneca *f*.

heathen ['hi:ðn] *adj* pagão(-gã) ◆ *n* pagão *m* (-gã *f*).

heather ['heðə'] *n* urze *f*.

heating ['hi:tɪŋ] *n* aquecimento *m*.

heatstroke ['hi:tstrəʊk] *n* insolação *f*.

heat wave *n* onda *f* de calor.

heave [hi:v] *vt (push)* empurrar com força; *(pull)* puxar com força; *(lift)* levantar com força.

Heaven ['hevn] *n* paraíso *m*, céu *m*.

heavily ['hevɪlɪ] *adv* muito.

heavy ['hevɪ] *adj* pesado(-da); *(rain, fighting, traffic)* intenso(-sa); **how ~ is it?** quanto é que (isso) pesa?; **to be a ~ smoker** fumar muito.

heavy cream *n (Am)* creme *m* de leite *(Br)*, natas *fpl* espessas *(Port)*.

heavy goods vehicle *n (Brit)* veículo *m* pesado.

heavy industry *n* indústria *f* pesada.

heavy metal *n* heavy metal *m*.

heavyweight ['hevɪweɪt] *n (SPORT)* peso *m* pesado.

Hebrew ['hi:bru:] *adj* hebraico(-ca) ◆ *n (person)* hebreu *m* (-bréia *f*); *(language)* hebraico *m*, hebraico *m*.

Hebrides ['hebrɪdi:z] *npl:* **the ~ as** Hébridas.

heckle ['hekl] *vt* interromper (continuamente).

hectic ['hektɪk] *adj* agitado(-da).

he'd [hi:d] = **he had**.

hedge [hedʒ] *n* cerca *f* viva *(Br)*, sebe *f*.

hedgehog ['hedʒhɒg] *n* ouriço-cacheiro *m*.

heel [hi:l] *n (of person)* calcanhar *m*; *(of shoe)* salto *m*.

hefty ['heftɪ] *adj (person)* robusto(-ta); *(fine)* considerável.

height [haɪt] *n* altura *f*; *(peak period)* ponto *m* alto; **what ~ is it?** quanto é que mede?

heighten ['haɪtn] *vt* aumentar, intensificar ◆ *vi* aumentar, intensificar-se.

heir [eə'] *n* herdeiro *m*.

heiress ['eərɪs] *n* herdeira *f*.

heirloom ['eəlu:m] *n* relíquia *f* familiar.

held [held] *pt & pp* → **hold**.

helicopter ['helɪkɒptə'] *n* helicóptero *m*.

Hell [hel] *n* o Inferno.

he'll [hi:l] = **he will**.

hellish ['helɪʃ] *adj (inf)* terrível; **the traffic was ~** o trânsito estava um inferno.

hello [hə'ləʊ] *excl (as greeting)* oi! *(Br)*, olá! *(Port)*; *(when answering phone)* alô! *(Br)*, estou! *(Port)*; *(when phoning)* alô? *(Br)*, está? *(Port)*; *(to attract attention)* ei!

helm [helm] *n (of ship)* leme *m*.

helmet ['helmɪt] *n* capacete *m*.

help [help] *n* ajuda *f* ◆ *vt & vi* ajudar ◆ *excl* socorro!; **I can't ~ it** não consigo evitá-lo; **to ~ sb (to) do sthg** ajudar alguém a fazer algo; **to ~ o.s. (to sthg)** servir-se (de algo); **can I ~ you?** *(in shop)* posso ajudá-lo?.

❏ **help out** *vi* ajudar.

helper ['helpə'] *n (assistant)* ajudante *mf*; *(Am: cleaner)* faxineira *f (Br)*, mulher-a-dias *f (Port)*.

helpful ['helpfʊl] *adj (person)* prestativo(-va); *(useful)* útil.

helping ['helpɪŋ] *n* porção *f*; **he had a second ~ of pudding** ele repetiu a sobremesa.

helpless ['helplɪs] *adj* indefeso(-sa).

Helsinki ['helsɪŋkɪ] *n* Helsínque *s*.

hem [hem] *n* bainha *f*.

hemisphere ['hemɪˌsfɪə'] *n* hemisfério *m*.

hemline ['hemlaɪn] *n* bainha *f*.

hemophiliac [ˌhi:mə'fɪlɪæk] *n* hemofílico *m* (-ca *f*).

hemorrhage ['hemərɪdʒ] *n* hemorragia *f*.

hemorrhoids ['hemərɔɪdz] *npl* hemorróidas *fpl*.

hen [hen] *n (chicken)* galinha *f*.

hence [hens] *adv (fml: therefore)* assim; *(from now):* **ten years ~** daqui a dez anos.

henceforth [ˌhens'fɔ:θ] *adv (fml)* de hoje em diante, doravante.

henna ['henə] *n* hena *f* ◆ *vt* pintar com hena.

henpecked ['henpekt] *adj:* **he's a ~ husband** ele é um pau-mandado da mulher.

hepatitis [ˌhepə'taɪtɪs] *n* hepatite *f*.

her [hɜ:'] *adj* o seu (a sua), dela ◆ *pron*

(direct) a; *(indirect)* lhe; *(after prep)* ela; ~ **books** os livros dela, os seus livros; **I know** ~ eu a conheço; **it's** ~ é ela; **send it to** ~ mande isso para ela; **tell** ~ diz-lhe; **he's worse than** ~ ele é pior do que ela; **Zena brought it with** ~ a Zena trouxe-o consigo OR com ela.

herb [hɜːb] *n* erva *f* aromática.

herbal tea ['hɜːbl-] *n* chá *m* de ervas.

herd [hɜːd] *n (of cattle)* manada *f*; *(of sheep)* rebanho *m*.

here [hɪəʳ] *adv* aqui; ~**'s your book** aqui está o seu livro; ~ **you are** aqui tem, aqui está.

hereabout ['hɪərəˌbaʊt] *(Am)* = **hereabouts**.

hereabouts ['hɪərəˌbaʊts] *adv (Brit)* por aqui.

hereafter [ˌhɪər'ɑːftəʳ] *adv (fml) (from now on)* de hoje em diante; *(in the future)* mais tarde.

hereby [ˌhɪə'baɪ] *adv (fml: in letters)* pela presente; **I** ~ **declare this theatre open** declaro aberto este teatro.

hereditary [hɪ'redɪtrɪ] *adj (disease)* hereditário(-ria).

heresy ['herəsɪ] *n* heresia *f*.

heritage ['herɪtɪdʒ] *n* patrimônio *m*.

heritage centre *n* museu ou centro de informação em local de interesse histórico.

hermit ['hɜːmɪt] *n* eremita *mf*.

hernia ['hɜːnjə] *n* hérnia *f*.

hero ['hɪərəʊ] *(pl -es) n* herói *m*.

heroic [hɪ'rəʊɪk] *adj* heróico(-ca).

heroin ['herəʊɪn] *n* heroína *f*.

heroine ['herəʊɪn] *n* heroína *f*.

heron ['herən] *n* garça *f*.

herring ['herɪŋ] *n* arenque *m*.

hers [hɜːz] *pron* o seu (a sua), (o/a) dela; **a friend of** ~ um amigo dela OR seu; **those shoes are** ~ estes sapatos são dela OR seus; **these are mine – where are** ~? estes são os meus – onde estão os dela?

herself [hɜː'self] *pron (reflexive)* se; *(after prep)* si própria OR mesma; **she did it** ~ foi ela mesma que o fez; **she hurt** ~ ela machucou-se.

he's [hiːz] = **he is, he has**.

hesitant ['hezɪtənt] *adj* hesitante.

hesitate ['hezɪteɪt] *vi* hesitar.

hesitation [ˌhezɪ'teɪʃn] *n* hesitação *f*.

heterosexual [ˌhetərəʊ'sekʃʊəl] *adj* heterossexual ◆ *n* heterossexual *mf*.

het up [het-] *adj (inf)* nervoso(-osa).

hexagon ['heksəgən] *n* hexágono *m*.

hey [heɪ] *excl (inf)* ei!, é pá! *(Port)*.

heyday ['heɪdeɪ] *n* época *f* áurea, auge *m*.

HGV *abbr* = **heavy goods vehicle**.

hi [haɪ] *excl (inf)* oi! *(Br)*, olá! *(Port)*.

hibernate ['haɪbəneɪt] *vi* hibernar.

hiccup ['hɪkʌp] *n*: **to have (the)** ~**s** estar com OR ter soluços.

hide [haɪd] *(pt hid* [hɪd], *pp hidden* [hɪdn]) *vt* esconder; *(truth, feelings)* esconder, ocultar ◆ *vi* esconder-se ◆ *n (of animal)* pele *f*.

hide-and-seek *n* esconde-esconde *m*, escondidas *fpl*.

hideaway ['haɪdəweɪ] *n (inf)* esconde-rijo *m*, refúgio *m*.

hideous ['hɪdɪəs] *adj* horrível.

hiding ['haɪdɪŋ] *n*: **in** ~ *(concealment)* escondido(-da); **to give sb a (good)** ~ *(inf: beating)* dar uma surra em alguém.

hiding place *n* esconderijo *m*.

hierarchy ['haɪərɑːkɪ] *n* hierarquia *f*.

hi-fi ['haɪfaɪ] *n* hi-fi *m*, aparelhagem *f* de som.

high [haɪ] *adj* alto(-ta); *(wind)* forte; *(speed, quality)* grande, alto(-ta); *(opinion)* bom (boa); *(position, rank)* elevado(-da); *(sound, voice)* agudo(-da); *(inf: from drugs)* doidão(-dona) *(Br)*, pedrado(-da) *(Port)* ◆ *n (weather front)* zona *f* de alta pressão ◆ *adv* alto; **how** ~ **is it?** quanto é que (isso) mede?; **it's 10 metres** ~ mede 10 metros de altura.

high chair *n* cadeira-de-bebê *f*.

high-class *adj* de grande categoria.

Higher ['haɪəʳ] *n (Scot)* exame efetuado na Escócia no fim do ensino secundário.

higher education *n* ensino *m* superior.

high heels *npl* saltos *mpl* altos.

high jump *n* salto *m* em altura.

Highland Games ['haɪlənd-] *npl* jogos tradicionais escoceses.

Highlands ['haɪləndz] *npl*: **the** ~ região montanhosa da Escócia.

highlight ['haɪlaɪt] *n (best part)* ponto *m* alto ◆ *vt (emphasize)* destacar.

❏ **highlights** *npl (of football match etc)* pontos *mpl* altos; *(in hair)* mechas *fpl* (Br), madeixas *fpl (Port)*.

highlighter (pen) ['haɪlaɪtəʳ] *n* marcador *m*.

highly ['haɪlɪ] *adv (extremely)* extremamente; *(very well)* muito bem; **to think**

~ **of sb** admirar muito alguém.

highness ['haɪnɪs] *n*: **His/Her/ Your (Royal)** ~ Sua Alteza *f* (Real); **Their (Royal)** ~**es** Suas Altezas (Reais).

high-pitched [-'pɪtʃt] *adj* agudo (-da).

high-rise *adj*: **a** ~ **building** um espigão *(Br)*, uma torre *(Port)*.

high school *n* escola *f* secundária.

high season *n* estação *f* alta.

high-speed train *n* (trem) rápido *m*, trem *m* de grande velocidade.

high street *n (Brit)* rua *f* principal.

high-tech [-'tek] *adj (industry)* de ponta; *(design, method, furniture)* extremamente moderno(-na).

high tide *n* maré-alta *f*.

highway ['haɪweɪ] *n (Am: between towns)* auto-estrada *f*; *(Brit: any main road)* estrada *f*.

Highway Code *n (Brit)* código *m* da estrada.

hijack ['haɪdʒæk] *vt* desviar.

hijacker ['haɪdʒækəʳ] *n* pirata *m* do ar.

hike [haɪk] *n* caminhada *f*, excursão *f* a pé ◆ *vi* caminhar.

hiker ['haɪkəʳ] *n* caminhante *mf*.

hiking ['haɪkɪŋ] *n*: **to go** ~ fazer uma caminhada.

hilarious [hɪ'leərɪəs] *adj* hilariante.

hill [hɪl] *n* colina *f*, monte *m*.

hillside ['hɪlsaɪd] *n* encosta *f*.

hillwalking ['hɪlwɔːkɪŋ] *n* caminhada *f (em montanha)*.

hilly ['hɪlɪ] *adj* montanhoso (-osa).

him [hɪm] *pron (direct)* o; *(indirect)* lhe; *(after prep)* ele; **I know** ~ eu o conheço; **it's** ~ é ele; **send it to** ~ manda isso para ele; **tell** ~ diga-lhe; **she's worse than** ~ ela é pior que ele; **Tony brought it with** ~ o Tony trouxe-o consigo OR com ele.

Himalayas [hɪmə'leɪəz] *npl*: **the** ~ os Himalaias.

himself [hɪm'self] *pron (reflexive)* se; *(after prep)* si próprio OR mesmo; **he did it** ~ foi ele mesmo que o fez; **he hurt** ~ ele machucou-se.

hinder ['hɪndəʳ] *vt* impedir, atrapalhar.

hindrance ['hɪndrəns] *n (obstacle)* obstáculo *m*, impedimento *m*; *(delay)* demora *f*, atraso *m*.

hindsight ['haɪndsaɪt] *n*: **with the**

benefit of ~ em retrospecto *(Br)*, a posteriori *(Port)*.

Hindu ['hɪnduː] *adj* hindu ◆ *n (person)* hindu *mf*.

hinge [hɪndʒ] *n* dobradiça *f*.

hint [hɪnt] *n (indirect suggestion)* alusão *f*; *(piece of advice)* dica *f*, palpite *m*; *(slight amount)* ponta *f* ◆ *vi*: **to** ~ **at sthg** fazer alusão a algo.

hip [hɪp] *n* anca *f*.

hippo [hɪpəʊ] *(pl* -s) *n (inf)* = **hippopotamus**.

hippopotamus [hɪpə'pɒtəməs] *n* hipopótamo *m*.

hippy ['hɪpɪ] *n* hippy *mf*.

hire ['haɪəʳ] *vt (car, bicycle, television)* alugar; *(person)* contratar; **"for** ~**"** *(boats)* "para alugar"; *(taxi)* "livre".

❏ **hire out** *vt sep (car, bicycle, television)* alugar.

hire car *n (Brit)* carro *m* alugado.

hire purchase *n (Brit)* crediário *m (Br)*, compra *f* a prestações.

his [hɪz] *adj* o seu (a sua), dele ◆ *pron* o seu (a sua), (o/a) dele; ~ **books** os livros dele, os seus livros; **a friend of** ~ um amigo dele OR seu; **these shoes are** ~ estes sapatos são dele OR seus; **these are mine** – **where are** ~? estes são os meus – onde estão os dele?

hiss [hɪs] *n (of snake, gas etc)* silvo *m*; *(of crowd)* assobio *m* ◆ *vi (snake, gas etc)* silvar; *(crowd)* assobiar, vaiar.

historic [hɪ'stɒrɪk] *adj* histórico(-ca).

historical [hɪ'stɒrɪkəl] *adj* histórico(-ca).

history ['hɪstərɪ] *n* história *f*; *(record)* histórico *m*.

hit [hɪt] *(pt & pp hit)* *vt (strike on purpose)* bater em; *(collide with)* bater contra OR em; *(bang)* bater com; *(a target)* acertar em ◆ *n (record, play, film)* sucesso *m*.

hit-and-run *adj*: ~ **accident** atropelamento *m* com abandono da vítima.

hitch [hɪtʃ] *n (problem)* problema *m* ◆ *vi* pegar carona *(Br)*, pedir boleia *(Port)* ◆ *vt*: **to** ~ **a lift** pegar carona *(Br)*, apanhar boleia *(Port)*.

hitchhike ['hɪtʃhaɪk] *vi* pegar carona *(Br)*, pedir boleia *(Port)*.

hitchhiker ['hɪtʃhaɪkəʳ] *n* pessoa *f* que pega carona *(Br)*, pessoa *f* que viaja à boleia *(Port)*.

hi-tech [haɪ'tek] = **high-tech**.

hive [haɪv] *n (of bees)* colmeia *f*.
HIV-positive *adj* soropositivo(-va) *(Br)*, seropositivo(-va) *(Port)*.
hoard [hɔːd] *n (of food)* armazém *m*, reserva *f*; *(of money)* tesouro *m*; *(of useless objects)* tralha *f*, monte *m* ◆ *vt (food)* açambarcar; *(money)* amealhar; *(useless objects)* acumular.
hoarding [hɔːdɪŋ] *n (Brit: for adverts)* outdoor *m (Br)*, placar *m* publicitário *(Port)*.
hoarfrost [hɔːfrɒst] *n* geada *f* (branca).
hoarse [hɔːs] *adj* rouco(-ca).
hoax [hǝʊks] *n* trote *m (Br)*, trapaça *f (Port)*.
hob [hɒb] *n* parte de cima do fogão.
hobble [hɒbl] *vi* coxear, mancar.
hobby [hɒbɪ] *n* passatempo *m*.
hobbyhorse [hɒbɪhɔːs] *n (toy)* cavalinho-de-pau *m*.
hobo [hǝʊbǝʊ] *(pl* -es OR -s*) n (Am)* vagabundo *m* (-da *f*).
hock [hɒk] *n (wine)* vinho *m* branco alemão.
hockey [hɒkɪ] *n (on grass)* hóquei *m* sobre grama; *(Am: ice hockey)* hóquei sobre gelo.
hoe [hǝʊ] *n* sacho *m*.
hog [hɒg] *n (Am: pig)* porco; *(inf: greedy person)* alarde *m*, glutão *m* ◆ *vt (inf)* monopolizar.
Hogmanay [hɒgmǝneɪ] *n (Scot)* fim *m* de ano, passagem *f* de ano.
hoist [hɔɪst] *vt (load, person)* levantar, içar; *(sail, flag)* içar.
hold [hǝʊld] *(pt & pp* held*) vt* segurar; *(organize)* dar; *(contain)* conter; *(possess)* ter, possuir ◆ *vi (remain unchanged)* manter-se; *(on telephone)* esperar ◆ *n (of ship, aircraft)* porão *m*; **to ~ sb prisoner** manter alguém prisoneiro; **~ the line, please** não desligue, por favor; **to keep a firm ~ of sthg** agarrar algo com força.
❏ **hold back** *vt sep (restrain)* conter; *(keep secret)* reter.
❏ **hold on** *vi (wait, on telephone)* esperar; **to ~ on to sthg** agarrar-se a algo.
❏ **hold out** *vt sep (extend)* estender.
❏ **hold up** *vt sep (delay)* atrasar.
holdall [hǝʊldɔːl] *n (Brit)* saco *m* de viagem.
holder [hǝʊldǝr] *n (of passport, licence)* titular *mf*; *(container)* suporte *m*.
holdup [hǝʊldʌp] *n (delay)* atraso *m*.

hole [hǝʊl] *n* buraco *m*.
holiday [hɒlɪdeɪ] *n (Brit: period of time)* férias *fpl*; *(day off)* feriado *m* ◆ *vi (Brit)* passar férias; **to be on ~** estar de férias; **to go on ~** ir de férias.
holiday camp *n (Brit)* campo *m* de férias.
holidaymaker [hɒlɪdɪˌmeɪkǝr] *n (Brit)* turista *mf*.
holiday pay *n (Brit)* férias *fpl* pagas.
holiday resort *n (Brit)* estância *f* de férias.
Holland [hɒlǝnd] *n* Holanda *f*.
hollow [hɒlǝʊ] *adj* oco (oca).
holly [hɒlɪ] *n* azevinho *m*.
Hollywood [hɒlɪwʊd] *n* Hollywood *s*.
holocaust [hɒlǝkɔːst] *n* holocausto *m*; **the Holocaust** o Holocausto.
holy [hǝʊlɪ] *adj* sagrado(-da), santo (-ta).
home [hǝʊm] *n* casa *f*; *(own country)* país *m* natal; *(for old people)* lar *m* ◆ *adv (in one's home)* em casa; *(to one's home)* para casa ◆ *adj (not foreign)* nacional; *(at one's house)* caseiro(-ra); **at ~** em casa; **make yourself at ~** faça como se estivesse em sua casa; **to go ~** ir para casa; **~ address** endereço *m*; **~ number** número *m* (de telefone) de casa.
home computer *n* computador *m* pessoal.
Home Counties *npl (Brit)*: **the ~** condados situados nos arredores de Londres.
home economics *n* economia *f* doméstica, *disciplina opcional na escola*.
home help *n (Brit)* auxiliar *m* doméstico *(auxiliar f doméstica)*.
homeland [hǝʊmlænd] *n (country of birth)* pátria *f*, terra *f* natal.
homeless [hǝʊmlɪs] *npl*: **the ~** os sem-abrigo.
homely [hǝʊmlɪ] *adj (food)* caseiro (-ra), simples *(inv)*; *(place)* acolhedor(-ra); *(person, features)* sem graça.
homemade [ˌhǝʊmˈmeɪd] *adj (food)* caseiro(-ra).
homeopathic [ˌhǝʊmɪǝʊˈpæθɪk] *adj* homeopático(-ca).
homeopathy [ˌhǝʊmɪˈɒpǝθɪ] *n* homeopatia *f*.
home page *n (COMPUT)* home page *f*.
Home Secretary *n (Brit)* = Ministro *m* (-tra *f*) do Interior *(Br)*, Ministro *m* (-tra *f*) da Administração Interna *(Port)*.

homesick ['hɔumsɪk] *adj*: **to be ~** ter saudades de casa.

hometown ['hɔumtaun] *n* terra *f* (natal).

homeward ['hɔumwəd] *adj* de regresso a casa.

homewards ['hɔumwədz] *adv*: **to head ~** dirigir-se para casa; **to travel ~** viajar de regresso a casa.

homework ['hɔumwɔːk] *n* dever *m* de casa.

homicide ['hɒmɪsaɪd] *n* homicídio *m*.

homosexual [ˌhɒməˈsekʃuəl] *adj* homossexual ◆ *n* homossexual *mf*.

honest ['ɒnɪst] *adj* honesto(-ta).

honestly ['ɒnɪstlɪ] *adv* (*truthfully*) honestamente; (*to express sincerity*) a sério ◆ *excl* francamente!

honesty ['ɒnɪstɪ] *n* honestidade *f*.

honey ['hʌnɪ] *n* mel *m*.

honeycomb ['hʌnɪkɔum] *n* (*of bees*) favo *m* de mel.

honeymoon ['hʌnɪmuːn] *n* lua-de-mel *f*.

honeysuckle ['hʌnɪˌsʌkl] *n* madressilva *f*.

Hong Kong [ˌhɒŋˈkɒŋ] *n* Hong Kong *s*.

honk [hɒŋk] *vi* (*motorist*) buzinar; (*goose*) grasnar ◆ *vt*: **she ~ed her horn** ela buzinou.

honor ['ɒnər] *(Am)* = **honour**.

honorary [*Brit* 'ɒnərərɪ, *Am* ɒnəˈreərɪ] *adj* honorário(-ria); (*degree*) honoris causa.

honour ['ɒnər] *n* (*Brit*) honra *f*.

honourable ['ɒnrəbl] *adj* honrado (-da).

hood [hud] *n* (*of jacket, coat*) capuz *m*; (*on convertible car*) capota *f*; (*Am: car bonnet*) capô *m*.

hoof [huːf] *n* casco *m*.

hook [huk] *n* (*for picture, coat*) gancho *m*; (*for fishing*) anzol *m*; **off the ~** (*telephone*) fora do gancho (*Br*), desligado (*Port*).

hooked [hukt] *adj*: **to be ~** (**on sthg**) (*inf: addicted*) estar viciado(-da) (em algo).

hooligan ['huːlɪgən] *n* desordeiro *m* (-ra *f*), vândalo *m* (-la *f*).

hoop [huːp] *n* argola *f*.

hoot [huːt] *vi* (*driver*) buzinar.

hooter ['huːtər] *n* (*horn*) buzina *f*.

Hoover® ['huːvər] *n* (*Brit*) aspirador *m*.

hop [hɒp] *vi* pular com um pé só.

hope [hɔup] *n* esperança *f* ◆ *vt* esperar; **to ~ for sthg** esperar algo; **to ~ to do sthg** esperar fazer algo; **I ~ so** espero que sim.

hopeful ['hɔupful] *adj* (*optimistic*) esperançoso(-osa).

hopefully ['hɔupfəlɪ] *adv* (*with luck*) com um pouco de sorte.

hopeless ['hɔuplɪs] *adj* (*without any hope*) desesperado(-da); **he is ~!** (*inf*) (ele) é um caso perdido!

hops [hɒps] *npl* lúpulo *m*.

horizon [həˈraɪzn] *n* horizonte *m*.

horizontal [ˌhɒrɪˈzɒntl] *adj* horizontal.

hormone ['hɔːmɔun] *n* hormônio *m* (*Br*), hormona *f* (*Port*).

horn [hɔːn] *n* (*of car*) buzina *f*; (*on animal*) corno *m*, chifre *m*.

horoscope ['hɒrəskɔup] *n* horóscopo *m*.

horrendous [hɒˈrendəs] *adj* (*horrific*) horrendo(-da); (*inf: unpleasant*) terrível.

horrible ['hɒrəbl] *adj* horrível.

horrid ['hɒrɪd] *adj* (*unkind*) antipático(-ca); (*very bad*) horroroso(-osa).

horrific [hɒˈrɪfɪk] *adj* horrendo(-da).

horrify ['hɒrɪfaɪ] *vt* horrorizar.

horror ['hɒrər] *n* horror *m*.

horror film *n* filme *m* de horror.

hors d'oeuvre [ɔːˈdɜːvr] *n* aperitivo *m*, entrada *f*.

horse [hɔːs] *n* cavalo *m*.

horseback ['hɔːsbæk] *n*: **on ~** a cavalo.

horse chestnut *n* castanheiro-da-Índia *m*.

horse-drawn carriage *n* charete *f*.

horseman ['hɔːsmən] (*pl* **-men** [-mən]) *n* cavaleiro *m*.

horsepower ['hɔːsˌpauər] *n* cavalos *mpl* (vapor).

horse racing *n* corridas *fpl* de cavalos.

horseradish (sauce) ['hɔːsˌrædɪʃ-] *n* molho picante feito de rábano silvestre, tradicionalmente usado para acompanhar rosbife.

horse riding *n* equitação *f*.

horseshoe ['hɔːsʃuː] *n* ferradura *f*.

horsewoman ['hɔːsˌwumən] (*pl* **-women** [-ˌwɪmɪn]) *n* amazona *f*.

horticulture ['hɔːtɪˌkʌltʃər] *n* horticultura *f*.

hose [həʊz] *n* mangueira *f*.

hosepipe ['həʊzpaɪp] *n* mangueira *f*.

hosiery ['həʊzɪərɪ] *n* meias *fpl* e collants.

hospitable [hɒ'spɪtəbl] *adj* hospitaleiro(-ra).

hospital ['hɒspɪtl] *n* hospital *m*; **in ~** no hospital.

hospitality [,hɒspɪ'tælətɪ] *n* hospitalidade *f*.

host [həʊst] *n* (*of party, event*) anfitrião *m*; (*of show, TV programme*) apresentador *m* (-a *f*).

hostage ['hɒstɪdʒ] *n* refém *mf*.

hostel ['hɒstl] *n* (*youth hostel*) albergue *m* da juventude (*Br*), pousada *f* de juventude (*Port*).

hostess ['həʊstes] *n* (*on aeroplane*) hospedeira *f*; (*of party, event*) anfitriã *f*.

hostile [*Brit* 'hɒstaɪl, *Am* 'hɒstl] *adj* hostil.

hostility [hɒ'stɪlətɪ] *n* hostilidade *f*.

hot [hɒt] *adj* quente; (*spicy*) picante; **to be ~** (*person*) ter calor.

hot-air balloon *n* balão *m*, aeróstato *m*.

hot chocolate *n* chocolate *m* quente.

hot-cross bun *n* pequeno pão doce com passas e especiarias que se come na Páscoa.

hot dog *n* cachorro-quente *m*.

hotel [həʊ'tel] *n* hotel *m*.

hotheaded [,hɒt'hedɪd] *adj* impulsivo(-va).

hothouse ['hɒthaʊs, *pl* -haʊzɪz] *n* (*greenhouse*) estufa *f*.

hot line *n* linha direta em funcionamento 24 horas por dia.

hotplate ['hɒtpleɪt] *n* placa *f* (elétrica).

hotpot ['hɒtpɒt] *n* ensopado de carne cozido no forno e coberto com rodelas de batata.

hot-tempered [-'tempəd] *adj* exaltado(-da), irascível.

hot-water bottle *n* saco *m* de água quente.

hound [haʊnd] *n* (*dog*) cão *m* de caça ◆ *vt* (*persecute*) perseguir; **to ~ sb out** (**of somewhere**) (*drive*) escorraçar alguém (de algum lugar).

hour ['aʊəʳ] *n* hora *f*; **I've been waiting for ~s** estou esperando há horas.

hourly ['aʊəlɪ] *adj* por hora

◆ *adv* (*pay, charge*) por hora; (*depart*) de hora em hora.

house [*n* haʊs, *pl* 'haʊzɪz, *vb* haʊz] *n* casa *f*; (*SCH*) divisão dos alunos em grupos para atividades desportivas ◆ *vt* (*person*) alojar.

housecoat ['haʊskəʊt] *n* bata *f*.

household ['haʊshəʊld] *n* família *f* (*Br*), agregado *m* familiar (*Port*).

housekeeper ['haʊs,kiːpəʳ] *n* governanta *f*.

housekeeping ['haʊs,kiːpɪŋ] *n* manutenção *f* da casa.

house music *n* house music *f*.

House of Commons *n* Câmara *f* dos Comuns.

House of Lords *n* Câmara *f* dos Lordes.

House of Representatives *n* Câmara *f* dos Representantes.

Houses of Parliament *npl* Parlamento *m* britânico.

housewife ['haʊswaɪf] (*pl* -wives) *n* dona *f* de casa, doméstica *f*.

house wine *n* vinho *m* da casa.

housewives ['haʊswaɪvz] *pl* → housewife.

housework ['haʊswɜːk] *n* afazeres *m* domésticos.

housing ['haʊzɪŋ] *n* (*houses*) alojamento *m*.

housing estate *n* (*Brit*) conjunto *m* habitacional (*Br*), urbanização *f* (*Port*).

housing project (*Am*) = housing estate.

hovel ['hɒvl] *n* barraco *m*.

hover ['hɒvəʳ] *vi* (*bird, helicopter*) pairar.

hovercraft ['hɒvəkrɑːft] *n* aerobarco *m* (*Br*), hovercraft *m*.

hoverport ['hɒvəpɔːt] *n* cais *m inv* para hovercrafts.

how [haʊ] *adv* 1. (*asking about way or manner*) como; **~ do you get there?** como é que se chega lá?; **~ does it work?** como é que funciona?; **tell me ~ to do it** me diga como fazer isso. 2. (*asking about health, quality*) como; **~ are you?** como vai?; **~ are you doing?** como é que você vai?; **~ are things?** como vão as coisas?; **~ do you do?** (*greeting*) muito prazer; (*answer*) igualmente; **~ is your room?** como é o seu quarto? 3. (*asking about degree, amount*) quanto; **~ far?** a que distância?; **~ long?**

quanto tempo?; ~ **many?** quantos?; ~ **much?** quanto?; ~ **much is it?** quanto custa?; ~ **old are you?** quantos anos você tem?

4. *(in phrases):* ~ **about a drink?** que tal uma bebida?; ~ **lovely!** que lindo!

however [hau'evə^r] *adv* contudo, todavia; ~ **hard I try** por mais que tente; ~ **many there are** por muitos que sejam.

howl [haul] *vi (dog, wind)* uivar; *(person)* gritar.

hp *n (abbr of horsepower)* cv *m*.

HP *abbr* = **hire purchase**.

HQ *n (abbr of headquarters)* QG.

hr *(abbr of hour)* h.

hub [hʌb] *n (of wheel)* cubo *m*.

hub airport *n* aeroporto *m* principal.

hubbub ['hʌbʌb] *n* burburinho *m*.

hubcap ['hʌbkæp] *n* calota *f (Br)*, tampão *m (Port)*.

huddle ['hʌdl] *vi (crouch, curl up)* encolher-se; *(crowd together)* juntar-se.

hue [hju:] *n (colour)* tom *m*, matiz *m*.

huff [hʌf] *n:* **in a** ~ zangado (-da), com raiva.

hug [hʌg] *vt* abraçar ♦ *n:* **to give sb a** ~ dar um abraço em alguém.

huge [hju:dʒ] *adj* enorme.

hull [hʌl] *n* casco *m*.

hum [hʌm] *vi (bee, machine)* zumbir; *(person)* cantarolar.

human ['hju:mən] *adj* humano (-na) ♦ *n:* ~ **(being)** ser *m* humano.

humane [hju:'meɪn] *adj* humano(-na).

humanitarian [hju:,mænɪ'teərɪən] *adj* humanitário(-ria).

humanities [hju:'mænətɪz] *npl* humanidades *fpl*.

human race *n:* **the** ~ a raça humana.

human rights *npl* direitos *mpl* humanos.

humble ['hʌmbl] *adj* humilde.

humid ['hju:mɪd] *adj* úmido (-da).

humidity [hju:'mɪdətɪ] *n* umidade *f*.

humiliate [hju:'mɪlɪeɪt] *vt* humilhar.

humiliating [hju:'mɪlɪeɪtɪŋ] *adj* humilhante.

humiliation [hju:,mɪlɪ'eɪʃn] *n* humilhação *f*.

hummus ['huməs] *n* puré de grão-de-bico, alho e pasta de gergelim.

humor ['hju:mər] *(Am)* = **humour**.

humorous ['hju:mərəs] *adj (story)* humorístico(-ca); *(person)* espirituoso (-osa).

humour ['hju:mə^r] *n (Brit)* humor *m*.

hump [hʌmp] *n (bump)* elevação *f*; *(of camel)* corcova *f (Br)*, bossa *f (Port)*.

humpbacked bridge ['hʌmpbækt-] *n* ponte *f* em lomba.

hunch [hʌntʃ] *n* pressentimento *m*.

hunchback ['hʌntʃbæk] *n* corcunda *mf*.

hundred ['hʌndrəd] *num* cem; **a** ~ cem; **a** ~ **and one** cento e um, → **six**.

hundredth ['hʌndrətθ] *num* centésimo(-ma), → **sixth**.

hundredweight ['hʌndrədweɪt] *n (in UK)* = 50,8kg; *(in US)* = 45,3kg.

hung [hʌŋ] *pt & pp* → **hang**.

Hungarian [hʌŋ'geərɪən] *adj* húngaro(-ra) ♦ *n (person)* húngaro *m* (-ra *f*); *(language)* húngaro *m*.

Hungary ['hʌŋgərɪ] *n* Hungria *f*.

hunger ['hʌŋgə^r] *n* fome *f*.

hungry ['hʌŋgrɪ] *adj* esfomeado (-da); **to be** ~ estar com OR ter fome.

hunt [hʌnt] *n (Brit: for foxes)* caça *f* à raposa ♦ *vt & vi* caçar; **to** ~ **(for sthg)** *(search)* procurar (algo).

hunter ['hʌntə^r] *n* caçador *m* (-ra *f*).

hunting ['hʌntɪŋ] *n (for wild animals)* caça *f*; *(Brit: for foxes)* caça à raposa.

hurdle ['hɜ:dl] *n (SPORT)* barreira *f*.

hurl [hɜ:l] *vt* arremessar.

hurray [hu'reɪ] *excl* hurra!

hurricane ['hʌrɪkən] *n* furacão *m*.

hurriedly ['hʌrɪdlɪ] *adv* com pressa.

hurry ['hʌrɪ] *vt (person)* apressar ♦ *vi* apressar-se ♦ *n:* **to be in a** ~ estar com pressa; **to do sthg in a** ~ fazer algo com pressa.

❏ **hurry up** *vi* despachar-se.

hurt [hɜ:t] *(pt & pp* **hurt)** *vt* magoar ♦ *vi* doer; **my arm** ~**s** meu braço está doendo; **to** ~ **o.s.** magoar-se.

husband ['hʌzbənd] *n* marido *m*.

hush [hʌʃ] *n* silêncio *m* ♦ *excl* silêncio!

husky ['hʌskɪ] *adj (voice, laugh)* rouco(-ca) ♦ *n (dog)* cão *m* esquimó.

hustle ['hʌsl] *n:* ~ **and bustle** bulício *m*.

hut [hʌt] *n* cabana *f*.

hutch [hʌtʃ] *n* coelheira *f*.

hyacinth ['haɪəsɪnθ] *n* jacinto *m*.

hydrofoil ['haɪdrəfɔɪl] *n* hidrofólio *m*.
hydrogen ['haɪdrədʒən] *n* hidrogênio
m.
hyena [haɪˈiːnə] *n* hiena *f*.
hygiene ['haɪdʒiːn] *n* higiene *f*.
hygienic [haɪˈdʒiːnɪk] *adj* higiênico
(-ca).
hymn [hɪm] *n* hino *m*.
hypermarket ['haɪpə,mɑːkɪt] *n* hipermercado *m*.
hyphen ['haɪfn] *n* hífen *m*.
hypnosis [hɪpˈnəʊsɪs] *n* hipnose *f*.
hypnotize ['hɪpnətaɪz] *vt* hipnotizar.

hypocrisy [hɪˈpɒkrəsɪ] *n* hipocrisia *f*,
cinismo *m*.
hypocrite ['hɪpəkrɪt] *n* hipócrita *mf*,
cínico *m* (-ca *f*).
hypocritical [,hɪpəˈkrɪtɪkl] *adj* hipócrita, cínico(-ca).
hypodermic needle [,haɪpə-
'dɜːmɪk-] *n* agulha *f* hipodérmica.
hypothesis [haɪˈpɒθɪsɪs] (*pl* **-theses**
[-ɔːˈsiːz]) *n* hipótese *f*.
hysteria [hɪsˈtɪərɪə] *n* histeria
f.
hysterical [hɪsˈterɪkl] *adj* histérico
(-ca); *(inf: very funny)* hilariante.

I [aɪ] *pron* eu.

ice [aɪs] *n* gelo *m*; *(ice cream)* sorvete *m* *(Br)*, gelado *m* *(Port)*.

iceberg ['aɪsbɜːg] *n* icebergue *m*.

iceberg lettuce *n* alface redonda e crespa.

icebox ['aɪsbɒks] *n* *(Am)* geladeira *f* *(Br)*, frigorífico *m* *(Port)*.

ice-cold *adj* gelado(-da).

ice cream *n* sorvete *m* *(Br)*, gelado *m* *(Port)*.

ice cube *n* cubo *m* de gelo.

ice hockey *n* hóquei *m* sobre o gelo.

Iceland ['aɪslənd] *n* Islândia *f*.

Icelandic [aɪs'lændɪk] *adj* islandês (-esa) ♦ *n* *(language)* islandês *m*.

ice lolly *n* *(Brit)* picolé *m* *(Br)*, gelado *m* *(Port)*.

ice rink *n* rinque *m* (de patinagem).

ice skates *npl* patins *mpl* de lâmina.

ice-skating *n* patinagem *f* sobre o gelo; **to go ~** ir patinar no gelo.

icicle ['aɪsɪkl] *n* sincelo *m*, pingente *m* de gelo.

icing ['aɪsɪŋ] *n* glacé *m*.

icing sugar *n* açúcar *m* em pó.

icy ['aɪsɪ] *adj* gelado(-da); *(road)* com gelo.

I'd [aɪd] = **I would, I had.**

ID *n* *(abbr of identification)* (documentos *mpl* de) identificação *f*.

ID card *n* carteira *f* de identidade *(Br)*, bilhete *m* de identidade, BI *m* *(Port)*.

IDD code *n* indicativo *m* internacional automático.

idea [aɪ'dɪə] *n* ideia *f*; **I've no ~** não faço idéia.

ideal [aɪ'dɪəl] *adj* ideal ♦ *n* ideal *m*.

ideally [aɪ'dɪəlɪ] *adv* *(located, suited)* perfeitamente; *(in an ideal situation)* idealmente.

identical [aɪ'dentɪkl] *adj* idêntico(-ca).

identification [aɪ,dentɪfɪ'keɪʃn] *n* identificação *f*.

identify [aɪ'dentɪfaɪ] *vt* identificar.

identity [aɪ'dentətɪ] *n* identidade *f*.

identity card *n* carteira *f* de identidade *(Br)*, bilhete *m* de identidade *(Port)*.

ideology [,aɪdɪ'ɒlədʒɪ] *n* ideologia *f*.

idiom ['ɪdɪəm] *n* *(phrase)* expressão *f* idiomática.

idiomatic [,ɪdɪə'mætɪk] *adj* idiomático(-ca).

idiosyncrasy [,ɪdɪə'sɪŋkrəsɪ] *n* idiossincrasia *f*.

idiot ['ɪdɪət] *n* idiota *mf*.

idiotic [,ɪdɪ'ɒtɪk] *adj* idiota.

idle ['aɪdl] *adj* *(lazy)* preguiçoso (-osa); *(not working)* ocioso(-osa) ♦ *vi* *(engine)* estar em ponto morto.

idol ['aɪdl] *n* ídolo *m*.

idolize ['aɪdəlaɪz] *vt* idolatrar.

idyllic [ɪ'dɪlɪk] *adj* idílico(-ca).

i.e. *(abbr of id est)* i.e.

if [ɪf] *conj* se; **~ I were you** no seu lugar; **~ not** *(otherwise)* senão.

igloo ['ɪgluː] *n* *(pl -s)* iglu *m*.

ignite [ɪg'naɪt] *vt* inflamar ♦ *vi* inflamar-se.

ignition [ɪg'nɪʃn] *n* *(AUT)* ignição *f*.

ignition key *n* chave *f* de ignição.

ignorance ['ɪgnərəns] *n* ignorância *f*.

ignorant ['ɪgnərənt] *adj* ignorante.

ignore [ɪg'nɔːr] *vt* ignorar.

ill [ɪl] *adj* *(in health)* doente; *(bad)* mau (má).

I'll [aɪl] = **I will, I shall.**

illegal [ɪ'liːgl] *adj* ilegal.

illegible [ɪ'ledʒəbl] *adj* ilegível.

illegitimate [,ɪlɪ'dʒɪtɪmət] *adj* ilegítimo(-ma).

ill health *n*: **to suffer from ~** não ter saúde.

illicit [ɪˈlɪsɪt] *adj* ilícito(-ta).

illiteracy [ɪˈlɪtərəsɪ] *n* analfabetismo *m*.

illiterate [ɪˈlɪtərət] *adj* analfabeto (-ta).

illness [ˈɪlnɪs] *n* doença *f*.

illogical [ɪˈlɒdʒɪkl] *adj* ilógico(-ca), pouco lógico(-ca).

ill-suited *adj*: **to be ~ to sthg** ser pouco adequado(-da) para algo.

ill-treat *vt* maltratar.

illuminate [ɪˈluːmɪneɪt] *vt* iluminar.

illusion [ɪˈluːʒn] *n (false idea)* ilusão *f*; *(visual)* ilusão ótica.

illustrate [ˈɪləstreɪt] *vt* ilustrar.

illustration [ˌɪləˈstreɪʃn] *n* ilustração *f*.

illustrious [ɪˈlʌstrɪəs] *adj* ilustre.

I'm [aɪm] **= I am**.

image [ˈɪmɪdʒ] *n* imagem *f*.

imaginary [ɪˈmædʒɪnrɪ] *adj* imaginário(-ria).

imagination [ɪˌmædʒɪˈneɪʃn] *n* imaginação *f*.

imaginative [ɪˈmædʒɪnətɪv] *adj* imaginativo(-va).

imagine [ɪˈmædʒɪn] *vt* imaginar; **to ~ (that)** *(suppose)* imaginar que.

imbecile [ˈɪmbɪsiːl] *n* imbecil *mf*.

imitate [ˈɪmɪteɪt] *vt* imitar.

imitation [ˌɪmɪˈteɪʃn] *n* imitação *f* ◆ *adj (fur)* falso(-sa); **~ leather** napa *f*.

immaculate [ɪˈmækjʊlət] *adj* imaculado(-da).

immature [ˌɪməˈtjʊəʳ] *adj* imaturo (-ra).

immediate [ɪˈmiːdjət] *adj (without delay)* imediato(-ta).

immediately [ɪˈmiːdjətlɪ] *adv (at once)* imediatamente ◆ *conj (Brit)* logo que.

immense [ɪˈmens] *adj* imenso (-sa).

immersion heater [ɪˈmɜːʃn-] *n* aquecedor *m* de imersão *(Br)*, esquentador *m* eléctrico (Port).

immigrant [ˈɪmɪɡrənt] *n* imigrante *mf*.

immigration [ˌɪmɪˈɡreɪʃn] *n* imigração *f*.

imminent [ˈɪmɪnənt] *adj* iminente.

immoral [ɪˈmɒrəl] *adj* imoral.

immortal [ɪˈmɔːtl] *adj* imortal.

immune [ɪˈmjuːn] *adj*: **to be ~ to** *(MED)* estar OR ser imune a.

immunity [ɪˈmjuːnətɪ] *n (MED)* imunidade *f*.

immunize [ˈɪmjʊnaɪz] *vt* imunizar.

impact [ˈɪmpækt] *n* impacto *m*.

impair [ɪmˈpeəʳ] *vt* enfraquecer.

impartial [ɪmˈpɑːʃl] *adj* imparcial.

impassive [ɪmˈpæsɪv] *adj* impassível.

impatience [ɪmˈpeɪʃns] *n* impaciência *f*.

impatient [ɪmˈpeɪʃnt] *adj* impaciente; **to be ~ to do sthg** estar impaciente por fazer algo.

impeccable [ɪmˈpekəbl] *adj (clothes)* impecável; *(behaviour)* excelente; **he has ~ manners** ele é extremamente bem-educado.

impede [ɪmˈpiːd] *vt (person)* impedir; *(progress, negotiations)* dificultar.

impending [ɪmˈpendɪŋ] *adj* iminente.

imperative [ɪmˈperətɪv] *n (GRAMM)* imperativo *m*.

imperfect [ɪmˈpɜːfɪkt] *n (GRAMM)* imperfeito *m*.

impersonate [ɪmˈpɜːsəneɪt] *vt (for amusement)* imitar.

impersonation [ɪmˌpɜːsəˈneɪʃn] *n (for amusement)* imitação *f*; **to do ~s of sb** imitar alguém; **he was charged with ~ of a police officer** ele foi acusado de se fazer passar por um policial.

impertinent [ɪmˈpɜːtɪnənt] *adj* impertinente.

impetuous [ɪmˈpetʃʊəs] *adj* impetuoso(-osa).

impetus [ˈɪmpɪtəs] *n (momentum)* ímpeto *m*; *(stimulus)* impulso *m*.

implement [*n* ˈɪmplɪmənt, *vb* ˈɪmplɪment] *n* ferramenta *f* ◆ *vt* implementar, pôr em prática.

implication [ˌɪmplɪˈkeɪʃn] *n (consequence)* implicação *f*.

implicit [ɪmˈplɪsɪt] *adj* implícito(-ta).

implore [ɪmˈplɔːʳ] *vt*: **to ~ sb to do sthg** implorar a alguém que faça algo.

imply [ɪmˈplaɪ] *vt*: **to ~ (that)** *(suggest)* sugerir, dar a entender que.

impolite [ˌɪmpəˈlaɪt] *adj* indelicado (-da).

import [*n* ˈɪmpɔːt, *vb* ɪmˈpɔːt] *n* importação *f* ◆ *vt* importar.

importance [ɪmˈpɔːtns] *n* importância *f*.

important [ɪmˈpɔːtnt] *adj* importante.

impose [ɪmˈpəʊz] *vt* impor ◆ *vi* impor-se; **to ~ sthg on** impor algo a.

impossible [ɪmˈpɒsəbl] *adj* impossível.

imposter [ɪmˈpəʊstər] *(Am)* = **impostor**.

impostor [ɪmˈpɒstəʳ] *n* impostor *m* (-ra *f*).

impoverished [ɪmˈpɒvərɪʃt] *adj* empobrecido(-da).

impractical [ɪmˈpræktɪkl] *adj* pouco prático(-ca).

impregnable [ɪmˈpregnəbl] *adj* inexpugnável, invencível.

impress [ɪmˈpres] *vt* impressionar.

impression [ɪmˈpreʃn] *n* impressão *f*.

impressive [ɪmˈpresɪv] *adj* impressionante.

imprison [ɪmˈprɪzn] *vt* (*put in prison*) prender.

improbable [ɪmˈprɒbəbl] *adj* improvável.

improper [ɪmˈprɒpəʳ] *adj* (*incorrect, rude*) incorreto(-ta); (*illegal*) ilegal.

improve [ɪmˈpruːv] *vt & vi* melhorar.
❏ **improve on** *vt fus* melhorar.

improvement [ɪmˈpruːvmənt] *n* (*in weather, health*) melhoria *f*; (*to home*) reforma *f*.

improvise [ˈɪmprəvaɪz] *vi* improvisar.

impudent [ˈɪmpjʊdənt] *adj* insolente.

impulse [ˈɪmpʌls] *n* impulso *m*; **on ~** sem pensar duas vezes.

impulsive [ɪmˈpʌlsɪv] *adj* impulsivo(-va).

impurity [ɪmˈpjʊərətɪ] *n* impureza *f*.

in. *abbr* = **inch**.

in [ɪn] *prep* 1. (*expressing place, position*) em; **it comes ~ a box** vem numa caixa; **~ the street** na rua; **~ hospital** no hospital; **~ Scotland** na Escócia; **~ Sheffield** em Sheffield; **~ the middle** no meio; **~ the sun/rain** no sol/na chuva; **~ here/there** aqui/ali (dentro); **~ front** à frente.

2. (*participating in*) em; **who's ~ the play?** quem está na peça?

3. (*expressing arrangement*) em; **they come ~ packs of three** vêm em embalagens de três; **~ a row** em fila; **cut it ~ half** corte-o ao meio.

4. (*during*): **~ April** em abril; **~ the afternoon** à OR de tarde; **~ the morning** de manhã; **ten o'clock ~ the morning** dez (horas) da manhã; **~ 1994** em 1994; **~ summer/winter** no verão/inverno.

5. (*within*) em; (*after*) dentro de, daqui a; **it'll be ready ~ an hour** estará pronto daqui a OR dentro de uma hora; **she did everything ~ ten minutes** ela fez tudo em dez minutos; **they're arriving ~ two weeks** chegam dentro de OR daqui a duas semanas.

6. (*expressing means*): **~ writing** por escrito; **they were talking ~ English** estavam falando (em) inglês; **write ~ ink** escreva a tinta.

7. (*wearing*) de; **dressed ~ red** vestido de vermelho; **the man ~ the blue suit** o homem com o terno azul.

8. (*expressing state*) em; **to be ~ a hurry** estar com pressa; **to be ~ pain** ter dores; **to cry out ~ pain** gritar de dor OR com dores; **~ ruins** em ruínas; **~ good health** com boa saúde.

9. (*with regard to*) de; **a rise ~ prices** uma subida dos preços; **to be 50 metres ~ length** ter 50 metros de comprimento.

10. (*with numbers*): **one ~ ten** um em cada dez.

11. (*expressing age*): **she's ~ her twenties** já entrou na casa dos vinte.

12. (*with colours*): **it comes ~ green or blue** vem em verde ou azul.

13. (*with superlatives*) de; **the best ~ the world** o melhor do mundo.

◆ *adv* 1. (*inside*) dentro; **you can go ~ now** pode entrar agora.

2. (*at home, work*): **she's not ~** (ela) não está; **to stay ~** ficar em casa.

3. (*train, bus, plane*): **the train's not ~ yet** o trem ainda não chegou.

4. (*tide*): **the tide is ~** a maré está cheia.

◆ *adj* (*inf: fashionable*) na moda, in (*inv*).

inability [ˌɪnəˈbɪlətɪ] *n*: **~ (to do sthg)** incapacidade *f* (para fazer algo).

inaccessible [ˌɪnəkˈsesəbl] *adj* inacessível.

inaccurate [ɪnˈækjʊrət] *adj* incorreto(-ta).

inadequate [ɪnˈædɪkwət] *adj* (*insufficient*) insuficiente.

inadvertently [ˌɪnədˈvɜːtəntlɪ] *adv* inadvertidamente.

inappropriate [ˌɪnəˈprəʊprɪət] *adj* impróprio(-pria).

inasmuch [ˌɪnəzˈmʌtʃ] : **inasmuch as** *conj* (*fml*) visto que.

inaudible [ɪˈnɔːdɪbl] *adj* inaudível.

inauguration [ɪ.nɔːɡjʊˈreɪʃn] *n* inauguração *f*.

incapable [ɪnˈkeɪpəbl] *adj*: **to be ~ of doing sthg** ser incapaz de fazer algo.

incense [ˈɪnsens] *n* incenso *m*.

incentive [ɪnˈsentɪv] *n* incentivo *m*.

incessant [ɪnˈsesnt] *adj* incessante.

inch [ɪntʃ] *n* = 2,5 cm, polegada *f*.

incident [ˈɪnsɪdənt] *n* incidente *m*.

incidentally [.ɪnsɪˈdentəlɪ] *adv* a propósito.

incinerate [ɪnˈsɪnəreɪt] *vt* incinerar.

incisive [ɪnˈsaɪsɪv] *adj* incisivo (-va).

incite [ɪnˈsaɪt] *vt* fomentar; **to ~ sb to do sthg** incitar alguém a fazer algo.

inclination [.ɪnklɪˈneɪʃn] *n (desire)* inclinação *f*; **to have an ~ to do sthg** ter tendência a OR para fazer algo.

incline [ˈɪnklaɪn] *n* declive *m*.

inclined [ɪnˈklaɪnd] *adj (sloping)* inclinado(-da); **to be ~ to do sthg** ter a tendência para fazer algo.

include [ɪnˈkluːd] *vt* incluir.

included [ɪnˈkluːdɪd] *adj* incluído (-da); **to be ~ in sthg** estar incluído em algo.

including [ɪnˈkluːdɪŋ] *prep* incluindo.

inclusive [ɪnˈkluːsɪv] *adj*: **from the 8th to the 16th ~** do 8º ao 16º inclusive; **~ of VAT** IVA incluído.

incoherent [.ɪnkəʊˈhɪərənt] *adj* incoerente.

income [ˈɪŋkʌm] *n* rendimento *m*.

income support *n (Brit)* subsídio *para pessoas com rendimentos muito baixos ou para desempregados sem direito a auxílio-desemprego.*

income tax *n* imposto *m* sobre a renda *(Br)*, imposto *m* sobre o rendimento, IRS *m (Port)*.

incoming [ˈɪnˌkʌmɪŋ] *adj (train, plane)* de chegada; **"~ calls only"** aviso indicando que aquele telefone apenas serve para receber chamadas.

incompatible [.ɪnkəmˈpætɪbl] *adj* incompatível.

incompetent [ɪnˈkɒmpɪtənt] *adj* incompetente.

incomplete [.ɪnkəmˈpliːt] *adj* incompleto(-ta).

incomprehensible [ɪnˌkɒmprɪˈhensəbl] *adj* incompreensível.

incongruous [ɪnˈkɒŋɡrʊəs] *adj* incongruente.

inconsiderate [.ɪnkənˈsɪdərət] *adj*

sem consideração; **how ~!** que falta de consideração!

inconsistent [.ɪnkənˈsɪstənt] *adj* inconsistente.

inconspicuous [.ɪnkənˈspɪkjʊəs] *adj* que não dá nas vistas.

incontinent [ɪnˈkɒntɪnənt] *adj* incontinente.

inconvenience [.ɪnkənˈviːnjəns] *n* inconveniência *f*, inconveniente *m* ♦ *vt* incomodar, perturbar.

inconvenient [.ɪnkənˈviːnjənt] *adj* inconveniente.

incorporate [ɪnˈkɔːpəreɪt] *vt* incorporar.

incorrect [.ɪnkəˈrekt] *adj* incorreto (-ta).

increase [*n* ˈɪnkriːs, *vb* ɪnˈkriːs] *n* aumento *m* ♦ *vt & vi* aumentar; **an ~ in sthg** um aumento em algo.

increasingly [ɪnˈkriːsɪŋlɪ] *adv* cada vez mais.

incredible [ɪnˈkredəbl] *adj* incrível.

incredibly [ɪnˈkredəblɪ] *adv* incrivelmente.

incredulous [ɪnˈkredjʊləs] *adj* incrédulo(-la).

incur [ɪnˈkɜːr] *vt (expenses)* incorrer em; *(debts)* contrair.

indebted [ɪnˈdetɪd] *adj (grateful)*: **to be ~ to sb** estar em dívida com alguém.

indecent [ɪnˈdiːsnt] *adj (obscene)* indecente.

indecisive [.ɪndɪˈsaɪsɪv] *adj* indeciso (-sa).

indeed [ɪnˈdiːd] *adv (for emphasis)* de fato, realmente; *(certainly)* certamente.

indefinite [ɪnˈdefɪnɪt] *adj (time, number)* indeterminado(-da); *(answer, opinion)* vago(-ga).

indefinitely [ɪnˈdefɪnətlɪ] *adv (closed, delayed)* por tempo indeterminado.

indent [ɪnˈdent] *vt (text)* recolher.

independence [.ɪndɪˈpendəns] *n* independência *f*.

Independence Day *n feriado nacional nos Estados Unidos no dia 4 de julho em que se celebra a independência, obtida em 1776.*

independent [.ɪndɪˈpendənt] *adj* independente.

independently [.ɪndɪˈpendəntlɪ] *adv* independentemente.

independent school *n (Brit)* colégio *m* privado.

index ['ɪndɛks] *n (of book)* índice *m*; *(in library)* catálogo *m (Br)*, ficheiro *m (Port)*.

index card *n* ficha *f (de fichário)*.

index finger *n* dedo *m* indicador.

India ['ɪndjə] *n* Índia *f*.

Indian ['ɪndjən] *adj* indiano(-na) ♦ *n* indiano *m (-na f)*; **an ~ restaurant** um restaurante indiano.

Indian Ocean *n* oceano *m* Índico.

indicate ['ɪndɪkeɪt] *vi (AUT)* ligar os indicadores OR o pisca-pisca ♦ *vt* indicar.

indication [,ɪndɪ'keɪʃn] *n (suggestion)* ideia *f*; *(sign)* indício *m*.

indicator ['ɪndɪkeɪtə'] *n (AUT)* pisca-pisca *m*.

indifference [ɪn'dɪfrəns] *n* indiferença *f*.

indifferent [ɪn'dɪfrənt] *adj* indiferente.

indigenous [ɪn'dɪdʒɪnəs] *adj* nativo (-va).

indigestion [,ɪndɪ'dʒestʃn] *n* indigestão *f*.

indignant [ɪn'dɪgnənt] *adj* indignado(-da).

indigo ['ɪndɪgəʊ] *adj* anil *(inv)*, índigo *(inv)*.

indirect [,ɪndɪ'rekt] *adj* indireto(-ta).

indiscreet [,ɪndɪ'skriːt] *adj* indiscreto(-ta).

indispensable [,ɪndɪ'spensəbl] *adj* indispensável.

individual [,ɪndɪ'vɪdʒʊəl] *adj* individual ♦ *n* indivíduo *m*.

individually [,ɪndɪ'vɪdʒʊəlɪ] *adv* individualmente.

Indonesia [,ɪndə'niːzjə] *n* Indonésia *f*.

indoor ['ɪndɔː'] *adj (swimming pool)* coberto(-ta); *(sports)* em recinto fechado.

indoors [,ɪn'dɔːz] *adv* lá dentro; **to stay ~** ficar em casa; **to go ~** ir para dentro.

indulge [ɪn'dʌldʒ] *vi*: **to ~ in sthg** permitir-se algo.

indulgent [ɪn'dʌldʒənt] *adj (liberal, kind)* indulgente, complacente.

industrial [ɪn'dʌstrɪəl] *adj (machinery, products)* industrial; *(country, town)* industrializado(-da).

industrial action *n*: **to take ~** entrar em greve.

industrial estate *n (Brit)* parque *m* industrial.

industrialist [ɪn'dʌstrɪəlɪst] *n* industrial *mf*.

industrial relations *npl* relações *fpl* entre o patronato e os trabalhadores.

industrial revolution *n* revolução *f* industrial.

industrious [ɪn'dʌstrɪəs] *adj* trabalhador(-ra).

industry ['ɪndəstrɪ] *n* indústria *f*.

inebriated [ɪ'niːbrɪeɪtɪd] *adj (fml)* ébrio (ébria).

inedible [ɪn'edɪbl] *adj (unpleasant)* intragável; *(unsafe)* não comestível.

inefficient [,ɪnɪ'fɪʃnt] *adj* ineficaz.

ineligible [ɪn'elɪdʒəbl] *adj* não elegível; **to be ~ for sthg** não ter direito a algo.

inept [ɪ'nept] *adj (comment, remark)* despropositado(-da); *(person)* incapaz; **~ at sthg** inábil em algo.

inequality [,ɪnɪ'kwɒlətɪ] *n* desigualdade *f*.

inevitable [ɪn'evɪtəbl] *adj* inevitável.

inevitably [ɪn'evɪtəblɪ] *adv* inevitavelmente.

inexpensive [,ɪnɪk'spensɪv] *adj* barato(-ta).

inexperienced [,ɪnɪk'spɪərɪənst] *adj* inexperiente.

infallible [ɪn'fælɪbl] *adj* infalível.

infamous ['ɪnfəməs] *adj* infame.

infant ['ɪnfənt] *n (baby)* bebê *m*; *(young child)* criança *f (pequena)*.

infantry ['ɪnfəntrɪ] *n* infantaria *f*.

infant school *n (Brit)* primeiros três anos da escola primária.

infatuated [ɪn'fætjʊeɪtɪd] *adj*: **to be ~ with** estar apaixonado(-da) por.

infect [ɪn'fekt] *vt (cut, wound)* infectar; **to ~ sb with sthg** contagiar alguém com algo.

infected [ɪn'fektɪd] *adj* infectado (-da).

infection [ɪn'fekʃn] *n* infecção *f*.

infectious [ɪn'fekʃəs] *adj* infeccioso (-osa).

inferior [ɪn'fɪərɪə'] *adj* inferior.

infertile [ɪn'fɜːtaɪl] *adj* estéril.

infested [ɪn'festɪd] *adj*: **to be ~ with sthg** estar infestado(-da) com algo.

infiltrate ['ɪnfɪltreɪt] *vt* infiltrar-se em.

infinite ['ɪnfɪnət] *adj* infinito(-ta).

infinitely ['ɪnfɪnətlɪ] *adv* infinitamente.

infinitive [ɪnˈfɪnɪtɪv] n infinitivo m.

infinity [ɪnˈfɪnətɪ] n infinidade f.

infirmary [ɪnˈfɜːmərɪ] n hospital m.

inflamed [ɪnˈfleɪmd] adj inflamado (-da).

inflammable [ɪnˈflæməbl] adj inflamável.

inflammation [ˌɪnfləˈmeɪʃn] n inflamação f.

inflatable [ɪnˈfleɪtəbl] adj inflável.

inflate [ɪnˈfleɪt] vt inflar, insuflar.

inflation [ɪnˈfleɪʃn] n (ECON) inflação f.

inflict [ɪnˈflɪkt] vt infligir.

in-flight adj proporcionado(-da) durante o vôo.

influence [ˈɪnfluəns] vt influenciar ◆ n: ~ (on) (effect) influência f (em); **to be a bad/good ~ (on sb)** ser uma má/boa influência (para alguém).

influential [ˌɪnfluˈenʃl] adj influente.

influenza [ˌɪnfluˈenzə] n (fml) gripe f, influenza f.

inform [ɪnˈfɔːm] vt informar.

informal [ɪnˈfɔːml] adj informal.

information [ˌɪnfəˈmeɪʃn] n informação f; **a piece of ~** uma informação.

information desk n informações fpl.

information office n centro m de informações.

information technology n (tecnologia) informática f.

informative [ɪnˈfɔːmətɪv] adj informativo(-va).

infrastructure [ˈɪnfrəˌstrʌktʃəʳ] n infra-estrutura f.

infuriating [ɪnˈfjʊərieɪtɪŋ] adj extremamente irritante.

ingenious [ɪnˈdʒiːnjəs] adj engenhoso(-osa).

ingot [ˈɪŋgət] n lingote m.

ingredient [ɪnˈgriːdjənt] n ingrediente m.

inhabit [ɪnˈhæbɪt] vt viver em.

inhabitant [ɪnˈhæbɪtənt] n habitante mf.

inhale [ɪnˈheɪl] vi inalar.

inhaler [ɪnˈheɪləʳ] n inalador m.

inherently [ɪnˈhɪərəntlɪ, ɪnˈherəntlɪ] adv inerentemente.

inherit [ɪnˈherɪt] vt herdar.

inheritance [ɪnˈherɪtəns] n herança f.

inhibition [ˌɪnhɪˈbɪʃn] n inibição f.

inhospitable [ˌɪnhɒˈspɪtəbl] adj (climate, area) inóspito(-ta); (unwelcoming) pouco hospitaleiro(-ra).

in-house adj (journal, report) interno(-na); (staff) da casa ◆ adv na fonte.

initial [ɪˈnɪʃl] adj inicial ◆ vt rubricar com as iniciais.

⊔ initials npl iniciais fpl.

initially [ɪˈnɪʃəlɪ] adv inicialmente.

initiative [ɪˈnɪʃətɪv] n iniciativa f.

injection [ɪnˈdʒekʃn] n injeção f.

injure [ˈɪndʒəʳ] vt ferir; **to ~ o.s.** ferir-se.

injured [ˈɪndʒəd] adj ferido(-da).

injury [ˈɪndʒərɪ] n ferimento m; (to tendon, muscle, internal organ) lesão f.

injury time n (período de) desconto m.

injustice [ɪnˈdʒʌstɪs] n injustiça f.

ink [ɪŋk] n tinta f.

inland [adj ˈɪnlənd, adv ɪnˈlænd] adj interior ◆ adv para o interior.

Inland Revenue n (Brit) = Receita f Federal (Br), = Direcção f Geral das Contribuições e Impostos (Port).

in-laws npl (inf) (parents-in-law) sogros mpl; (others) parentes mpl afins OR por afinidade.

inlet [ˈɪnlet] n (of lake, sea) braço m; (for fuel, water) entrada f, admissão f.

inmate [ˈɪnmeɪt] n (of prison) preso m (-sa f); (of mental hospital) doente m interno (doente f interna).

inn [ɪn] n estalagem f.

innate [ɪˈneɪt] adj inato(-ta).

inner [ˈɪnəʳ] adj interior.

inner city n centro m urbano.

inner tube n câmara-de-ar f.

innocence [ˈɪnəsəns] n inocência f.

innocent [ˈɪnəsənt] adj inocente.

innocuous [ɪˈnɒkjuəs] adj (harmless) inócuo (-cua), inofensivo(-va).

innovation [ˌɪnəˈveɪʃn] n inovação f.

innovative [ˈɪnəvətɪv] adj inovador (-ra).

inoculate [ɪˈnɒkjuleɪt] vt: **to ~ sb (against sthg)** vacinar alguém (contra algo).

inoculation [ɪˌnɒkjuˈleɪʃn] n inoculação f, vacinação f.

input [ˈɪnput] vt (COMPUT) entrar.

inquire [ɪnˈkwaɪəʳ] = enquire.

inquiry [ɪnˈkwaɪərɪ] = enquiry.

inquisitive [ɪnˈkwɪzətɪv] adj curioso (-osa), inquiridor(-ra).

insane [ɪn'seɪn] *adj* louco(-ca).

inscription [ɪn'skrɪpʃn] *n (on headstone, plaque)* inscrição *f; (in book)* dedicatória *f*.

insect ['ɪnsekt] *n* inseto *m*.

insecticide [ɪn'sektɪsaɪd] *n* inseticida *m*.

insect repellent *n* repelente *m* de insetos.

insecure [ˌɪnsɪ'kjuəʳ] *adj (person)* inseguro(-ra); *(hinge, job, wall)* pouco seguro(-ra); *(investment)* arriscado(-da).

insensitive [ɪn'sensətɪv] *adj* insensível.

insert [ɪn'sɜːt] *vt* introduzir.

inside [ɪn'saɪd] *prep* dentro de ◆ *adv (go)* para dentro; *(be, stay)* lá dentro ◆ *adj* interior, interno (-na) ◆ *n*: the ~ *(interior)* o interior; *(AUT: in UK)* a (faixa da) esquerda; *(AUT: in Europe, US)* a (faixa da) direita; ~ out *(clothes)* do lado avesso.

inside lane *n (AUT) (in UK)* faixa *f* da esquerda; *(in Europe, US)* faixa da direita.

inside leg *n* altura *f* de entrepernas.

insight ['ɪnsaɪt] *n (glimpse)* idéia *f*.

insignificant [ˌɪnsɪg'nɪfɪkənt] *adj* insignificante.

insincere [ˌɪnsɪn'sɪəʳ] *adj* falso (-sa).

insinuate [ɪn'sɪnjueɪt] *vt* insinuar.

insipid [ɪn'sɪpɪd] *adj* insípido (-da).

insist [ɪn'sɪst] *vi* insistir; to ~ on doing sthg insistir em fazer algo.

insofar [ˌɪnsəʊ'fɑːʳ] : **insofar as** *conj* na medida em que.

insole ['ɪnsəʊl] *n* palmilha *f*.

insolent ['ɪnsələnt] *adj* insolente.

insomnia [ɪn'sɒmnɪə] *n* insônia *f*.

inspect [ɪn'spekt] *vt* inspecionar, examinar.

inspection [ɪn'spekʃn] *n* inspeção *f*.

inspector [ɪn'spektəʳ] *n (on bus, train)* fiscal *m; (in police force)* inspetor *m* (-ra *f*).

inspiration [ˌɪnspə'reɪʃn] *n* inspiração *f*.

inspire [ɪn'spaɪəʳ] *vt*: to ~ sb to do sthg inspirar alguém a fazer algo; to ~ sthg in sb inspirar algo a alguém.

instal [ɪn'stɔːl] *(Am)* = **install**.

install [ɪn'stɔːl] *vt (Brit)* instalar.

installation [ˌɪnstə'leɪʃn] *n* instalação *f*.

installment [ɪn'stɔːlmənt] *(Am)* = **instalment**.

instalment [ɪn'stɔːlmənt] *n (payment)* prestação *f; (episode)* episódio *m*.

instamatic (camera) [ˌɪnstə'mætɪk-] *n* máquina *f* de tirar fotografias instantâneas.

instance ['ɪnstəns] *n (example, case)* exemplo *m*; for ~ por exemplo.

instant ['ɪnstənt] *adj* instantâneo (-nea) ◆ *n* instante *m*.

instant coffee *n* café *m* instantâneo OR solúvel.

instantly ['ɪnstəntlɪ] *adv* instantaneamente.

instead [ɪn'sted] *adv* em vez disso; ~ of em vez de.

instep ['ɪnstep] *n* peito *m* do pé.

instinct ['ɪnstɪŋkt] *n* instinto *m*.

instinctive [ɪn'stɪŋktɪv] *adj* instintivo(-va).

institute ['ɪnstɪtjuːt] *n* instituto *m*.

institution [ˌɪnstɪ'tjuːʃn] *n* instituição *f*.

instruct [ɪn'strʌkt] *vt*: to ~ sb to do sthg *(tell, order)* instruir alguém que faça algo; to ~ sb in sthg *(teach)* ensinar algo a alguém.

instructions [ɪn'strʌkʃnz] *npl* instruções *fpl*.

instructor [ɪn'strʌktəʳ] *n* instrutor *m* (-ra *f*).

instrument ['ɪnstrumənt] *n* instrumento *m*.

insubordinate [ˌɪnsə'bɔːdɪnət] *adj* indisciplinado(-da).

insufficient [ˌɪnsə'fɪʃnt] *adj* insuficiente.

insulate ['ɪnsjuleɪt] *vt* isolar.

insulating tape ['ɪnsjuleɪtɪŋ-] *n* fita *f* isolante.

insulation [ˌɪnsjə'leɪʃn] *n (material)* isolamento *m*, material *m* isolante.

insulin ['ɪnsjʊlɪn] *n* insulina *f*.

insult [*n* 'ɪnsʌlt, *vb* ɪn'sʌlt] *n* insulto *m* ◆ *vt* insultar.

insurance [ɪn'ʃʊərəns] *n* seguro *m*.

insurance certificate *n* certificado *m* do seguro.

insurance company *n* companhia *f* de seguros.

insurance policy *n* apólice *f* de seguros.

insure [ɪn'ʃʊəʳ] *vt* pôr no seguro.

insured [ɪn'ʃʊəd] *adj*: to be ~ estar segurado(-da), estar no seguro.

intact [ɪn'tækt] *adj* intato(-ta).

integral ['ɪntɪgrəl] *adj* essencial; to be ~ to sthg ser essencial para algo.

integrate [ˈɪntɪgreɪt] vi integrar-se ◆ vt (include) integrar; (combine) combinar.

integrity [ɪnˈtegrɪtɪ] n integridade f.

intellect [ˈɪntəlekt] n intelecto m.

intellectual [ˌɪntəˈlektjʊəl] adj intelectual ◆ n intelectual mf.

intelligence [ɪnˈtelɪdʒəns] n inteligência f.

intelligent [ɪnˈtelɪdʒənt] adj inteligente.

intend [ɪnˈtend] vt: to be ~ed to do sthg ser suposto fazer algo; you weren't ~ed to know não era para você saber; to ~ to do sthg ter a intenção de OR tencionar fazer algo.

intense [ɪnˈtens] adj intenso(-sa).

intensely [ɪnˈtenslɪ] adv (irritating, boring) extremamente; (suffer, dislike) intensamente.

intensify [ɪnˈtensɪfaɪ] vt intensificar ◆ vi intensificar-se.

intensity [ɪnˈtensətɪ] n intensidade f.

intensive [ɪnˈtensɪv] adj intensivo (-va).

intensive care n cuidados mpl intensivos.

intent [ɪnˈtent] adj: to be ~ on doing sthg estar decidido(-da) a fazer algo.

intention [ɪnˈtenʃn] n intenção f.

intentional [ɪnˈtenʃənl] adj intencional.

intentionally [ɪnˈtenʃənəlɪ] adv intencionalmente.

interact [ˌɪntərˈækt] vi: to ~ (with sb) (communicate, cooperate) comunicar (com alguém); to ~ (with sthg) (react) interagir (com algo).

intercept [ˌɪntəˈsept] vt interceptar.

interchange [ˈɪntətʃeɪndʒ] n (on motorway) trevo m (Br), intersecção f (Port).

interchangeable [ˌɪntəˈtʃeɪndʒəbl] adj permutável.

intercity® [ˌɪntəˈsɪtɪ] n (Brit) = expresso m (Br), - (comboio) intercidades m (Port).

intercom [ˈɪntəkɒm] n intercomunicador m.

intercourse [ˈɪntəkɔːs] n (sexual) relações fpl (sexuais).

interest [ˈɪntrəst] n interesse m; (on money) juros mpl ◆ vt interessar; to take an ~ in sthg interessar-se por algo.

interested [ˈɪntrəstɪd] adj interessado(-da); to be ~ in sthg estar interessado em algo.

interesting [ˈɪntrəstɪŋ] adj interessante.

interest rate n taxa f de juro.

interface [ˈɪntəfeɪs] n (COMPUT) interface m.

interfere [ˌɪntəˈfɪəʳ] vi (meddle) interferir; to ~ with sthg (damage) interferir em algo.

interference [ˌɪntəˈfɪərəns] n (on TV, radio) interferência f.

interim [ˈɪntərɪm] adj provisório(-ria) ◆ n: in the ~ nesse meio tempo, nesse ínterim (Br).

interior [ɪnˈtɪərɪəʳ] adj interior ◆ n interior m.

interlude [ˈɪntəluːd] n interlúdio m; (at cinema, theatre) intervalo m.

intermediary [ˌɪntəˈmiːdjərɪ] n intermediário m (-ria f).

intermediate [ˌɪntəˈmiːdjət] adj intermédio(-dia).

intermission [ˌɪntəˈmɪʃn] n intervalo m.

intermittent [ˌɪntəˈmɪtənt] adj intermitente.

internal [ɪnˈtɜːnl] adj interno (-na).

internal flight n voo m interno.

Internal Revenue n (Am): the ~ = Receita f Federal (Br), = Direcção f Geral das Contribuições e Impostos (Port).

international [ˌɪntəˈnæʃənl] adj internacional.

international flight n vôo m internacional.

Internet [ˈɪntənet] n: the ~ a Internet.

interpret [ɪnˈtɜːprɪt] vi servir de intérprete.

interpreter [ɪnˈtɜːprɪtəʳ] n intérprete mf.

interrogate [ɪnˈterəgeɪt] vt interrogar.

interrogation [ɪnˌterəˈgeɪʃn] n interrogatório m.

interrupt [ˌɪntəˈrʌpt] vt interromper.

interruption [ˌɪntəˈrʌpʃn] n (comment, question, action) interrupção f; (disturbance) interrupções fpl.

intersect [ˌɪntəˈsekt] vi cruzar-se, intersectar-se ◆ vt intersectar.

intersection [ˌɪntəˈsekʃn] n (of roads) intersecção f, cruzamento m de nível.

interval [ˈɪntəvl] n intervalo m.

intervene [ˌɪntəˈviːn] vi (person) intervir; (event) interpor-se.

interview [ˈɪntəvjuː] n entrevista f ◆ vt entrevistar.

interviewer ['ıntəvju:əʳ] *n* entrevistador *m* (-ra *f*).

intestine [ın'testın] *n* intestino *m*.

intimate ['ıntımət] *adj* íntimo (-ma).

intimidate [ın'tımıdeıt] *vt* intimidar.

into ['ıntu] *prep (inside)* dentro de; *(against)* com; *(concerning)* acerca de, sobre; **4 ~ 20 goes 5 (times)** 20 dividido por 4 dá 5; **to change ~ sthg** transformar-se em algo; **to get ~ the car** entrar no carro; **to translate ~ Portuguese** traduzir para o português; **to be ~ sthg** *(inf: like)* gostar de algo.

intolerable [ın'tɒlrəbl] *adj* intolerável.

intolerant [ın'tɒlərənt] *adj* intolerante.

intoxicated [ın'tɒksıkeıtıd] *adj*: **to be ~** *(drunk)* estar embriagado(-da).

intransitive [ın'trænzətıv] *adj* intransitivo(-va).

in-tray *n* cesta *f* de correspondência.

intricate ['ıntrıkət] *adj* intrincado (-da), complicado(-da).

intriguing [ın'tri:gıŋ] *adj* intrigante.

intrinsic [ın'trınsık] *adj* intrínseco(-ca).

introduce [,ıntrə'dju:s] *vt* apresentar; **I'd like to ~ you to Fred** gostaria de lhe apresentar ao Fred.

introduction [,ıntrə'dʌkʃn] *n (to book, programme)* introdução *f*; *(to person)* apresentação *f*.

introductory [,ıntrə'dʌktrı] *adj (course, chapter)* introdutório(-ria); *(remarks)* inicial.

introvert ['ıntrəvɜ:t] *n* introvertido *m* (-da *f*).

introverted ['ıntrə,vɜ:tıd] *adj* introvertido(-da).

intrude [ın'tru:d] *vi*: **to ~ on sb** incomodar alguém; **to ~ on sthg** intrometer-se em algo.

intruder [ın'tru:dəʳ] *n* intruso *m* (-sa *f*).

intuition [,ıntju:'ıʃn] *n* intuição *f*.

inundate ['ınʌndeıt] *vt (fml: flood)* inundar; **to be ~d with sthg** *(phone calls, offers etc)* receber uma enxurrada de algo.

invade [ın'veıd] *vt* invadir.

invalid [*adj* ın'vælıd, *n* 'ınvəlıd] *adj (ticket, cheque)* não válido(-da) ♦ *n* inválido *m* (-da *f*).

invaluable [ın'væljuəbl] *adj* inestimável, valiosíssimo(-ma).

invariably [ın'veərıəblı] *adv* invariavelmente, sempre.

invasion [ın'veıʒn] *n* invasão *f*.

invent [ın'vent] *vt* inventar.

invention [ın'venʃn] *n* invenção *f*.

inventive [ın'ventıv] *adj* inventivo (-va).

inventor [ın'ventəʳ] *n* inventor *m* (-ra *f*).

inventory ['ınventrı] *n (list)* inventário *m*; *(Am: stock)* estoque *m*.

inverted commas [ın'vɜ:tıd-] *npl* aspas *fpl*.

invest [ın'vest] *vt* investir ♦ *vi*: **to ~ in sthg** investir em algo.

investigate [ın'vestıgeıt] *vt* investigar.

investigation [ın,vestı'geıʃn] *n* investigação *f*.

investment [ın'vestmənt] *n* investimento *m*.

investor [ın'vestəʳ] *n* investidor *m* (-ra *f*).

invincible [ın'vınsıbl] *adj* invencível.

invisible [ın'vızıbl] *adj* invisível.

invitation [,ınvı'teıʃn] *n* convite *m*.

invite [ın'vaıt] *vt* convidar; **to ~ sb to do sthg** *(ask)* convidar alguém para fazer algo; **to ~ sb round** convidar alguém.

inviting [ın'vaıtıŋ] *adj* convidativo (-va).

invoice ['ınvɔıs] *n* fatura *f*.

involve [ın'vɒlv] *vt (entail)* envolver; **what does it ~?** o que é que envolve?; **to be ~d in sthg** estar envolvido em algo.

involved [ın'vɒlvd] *adj (entailed)* envolvido(-da).

involvement [ın'vɒlvmənt] *n* envolvimento *m*.

inward ['ınwəd] *adj (feelings, satisfaction)* íntimo(-ma); *(flow, movement)* em direção ao interior ♦ *adv (Am)* = **inwards**.

inwards ['ınwədz] *adv* para dentro.

IOU *n* nota *f* de dívida, vale *m*.

IQ *n* QI *m*.

IRA *n (abbrev of Irish Republican Army)* IRA *m*.

Iran [ı'rɑ:n] *n* Irã *m*.

Iranian [ı'reınjən] *adj* iraniano (-na) ♦ *n (person)* iraniano *m* (-na *f*).

Iraq [ı'rɑ:k] *n* Iraque *m*.

Iraqi [ı'rɑ:kı] *adj* iraquiano(-na) ♦ *n (person)* iraquiano *m* (-na *f*).

Ireland ['aıələnd] *n* Irlanda *f*.

iris ['aıərıs] *(pl -es) n (flower)* lírio *m*; *(of eye)* íris *f*.

Irish [ˈaɪrɪʃ] adj irlandês(-esa) ◆ n (language) irlandês m ◆ npl: **the ~** os irlandeses.

Irish coffee n Irish coffee m, mistura alcoólica de uísque com café, açúcar e creme.

Irishman [ˈaɪrɪʃmən] (pl **-men** [-mən]) n irlandês m.

Irish Sea n: **the ~** o mar da Irlanda.

Irish stew n ensopado de carneiro com batatas e cebolas.

Irishwoman [ˈaɪrɪʃˌwʊmən] (pl **-women** [-ˌwɪmɪn]) n irlandesa f.

iron [ˈaɪən] n (metal) ferro m; (for clothes) ferro (de engomar OR passar); (golf club) ferro, taco m de metal ◆ vt passar a ferro.

ironic [aɪˈrɒnɪk] adj irônico(-ca).

ironing [ˈaɪənɪŋ] n (clothes to be ironed) roupa f para passar a ferro; **to do the ~** passar (a roupa) a ferro.

ironing board [ˈaɪənɪŋ-] n tábua f de engomar OR passar (a ferro).

ironmonger's [ˈaɪənˌmʌŋgəz] n (Brit) loja f de ferragens.

irony [ˈaɪrənɪ] n ironia f.

irrational [ɪˈræʃənl] adj irracional.

irrelevant [ɪˈreləvənt] adj irrelevante.

irresistible [ˌɪrɪˈzɪstəbl] adj irresistível.

irrespective [ˌɪrɪˈspektɪv] : **irrespective of** prep independentemente de.

irresponsible [ˌɪrɪˈspɒnsəbl] adj irresponsável.

irrigate [ˈɪrɪgeɪt] vt irrigar, regar.

irrigation [ˌɪrɪˈgeɪʃn] n irrigação f.

irritable [ˈɪrɪtəbl] adj irritável.

irritate [ˈɪrɪteɪt] vt irritar.

irritating [ˈɪrɪteɪtɪŋ] adj irritante.

irritation [ˌɪrɪˈteɪʃn] n irritação f.

IRS n (Am) ~ Receita f Federal (Br), ~ Direcção f Geral das Contribuições e Impostos (Port).

is [ɪz] → **be.**

Islam [ˈɪzlɑːm] n islã m.

island [ˈaɪlənd] n (in water) ilha f; (in road) abrigo m (Br), placa f (Port) (que serve de refúgio para os pedestres no meio da rua).

islander [ˈaɪləndər] n ilhéu m (ilhoa f).

isle [aɪl] n ilha f.

Isle of Man n: **the ~** a ilha de Man.

Isle of Wight [-waɪt] n: **the ~** a ilha de Wight.

isn't [ˈɪznt] = is not.

isolated [ˈaɪsəleɪtɪd] adj isolado (-da).

Israel [ˈɪzreɪəl] n Israel s.

Israeli [ɪzˈreɪlɪ] adj israelita, israelense ◆ n israelita mf, israelense mf

issue [ˈɪʃuː] n (problem, subject) questão f; (of newspaper) edição f; (of magazine) número m ◆ vt emitir.

it [ɪt] pron 1. (referring to specific thing, subject after prep) ele m (ela f); (direct object) o m (a f); (indirect object) lhe; **a free book came with ~** veio acompanhado de um livro grátis; **give ~ to me** me dê isso; **he gave ~ a kick** ele deu-lhe um pontapé; **~'s big** é grande; **~'s here** está aqui; **she hit ~** (ela) bateu-lhe; **she lost ~** (ela) perdeu-o.
2. (referring to situation, fact): **~'s a difficult question** é uma questão difícil; **I can't remember ~** não me lembro; **tell me about ~** conta-me.
3. (used impersonally): **~'s hot** está calor; **~'s six o'clock** são seis horas; **~'s Sunday** é domingo.
4. (referring to person): **~'s me** sou eu; **who is ~?** quem é?

Italian [ɪˈtæljən] adj italiano (-na) ◆ n (person) italiano m (-na f); (language) italiano m; **an ~ restaurant** um restaurante italiano.

italic [ɪˈtælɪk] adj itálico(-ca).

Italy [ˈɪtəlɪ] n Itália f.

itch [ɪtʃ] vi (person) ter coceira (Br), ter comichão (Port); **my arm ~es** estou com coceira no braço.

itchy [ˈɪtʃɪ] adj: **it's really ~** está coçando muito.

it'd [ˈɪtəd] = it would, it had.

item [ˈaɪtəm] n (object) artigo m; (on agenda) assunto m, ponto m; **a news ~** uma notícia.

itemized bill [ˈaɪtəmaɪzd-] n fatura f discriminada.

itinerary [aɪˈtɪnərərɪ] n itinerário m.

it'll [ɪtl] = it will.

its [ɪts] adj o seu (a sua), dele (dela); **the cat hurt ~ paw** o gato machucou a pata (dele) OR a (sua) pata.

it's [ɪts] = it is, it has.

itself [ɪtˈself] pron (reflexive) se; (after prep) si mesmo m (-ma f); **the house ~ is fine** a casa em si é boa.

ITV n (abbrev of Independent Television) um dos canais privados da televisão britânica.

I've [aɪv] = I have.

ivory [ˈaɪvərɪ] n marfim m.

ivy [ˈaɪvɪ] n hera f.

J

jab [dʒæb] n (Brit: inf: injection) injeção f.

jack [dʒæk] n (for car) macaco m; (playing card) valete m.

jacket ['dʒækɪt] n (garment) casaco m, blusão m; (cover) capa f; (of potato) casca f.

jacket potato n batata f assada com casca.

jack-knife vi dar uma guinada, virar na estrada.

jackpot ['dʒækpɒt] n jackpot m.

Jacuzzi® [dʒə'ku:zɪ] n jacuzzi® m.

jade [dʒeɪd] n jade m.

jagged ['dʒægɪd] adj (metal) denteado(-da); (outline, tear) irregular.

jail [dʒeɪl] n prisão f.

jailer ['dʒeɪlər] n carcereiro m (-ra f).

jam [dʒæm] n (food) geléia f (Br), compota f, doce m (Port); (of traffic) engarrafamento m; (inf: difficult situation) apuro m ◆ vt (pack tightly) enfiar (até mais não poder) ◆ vi (get stuck) emperrar; **the roads are ~med** as estradas estão congestionadas.

Jamaica [dʒə'meɪkə] n Jamaica f.

jam-packed [-'pækt] adj (inf): ~ (with) apinhado(-da) (de).

Jan. [dʒæn] (abbr of January) jan.

janitor ['dʒænɪtər] n (Am & Scot) contínuo m (-nua f).

January ['dʒænjuərɪ] n janeiro m, → September.

Japan [dʒə'pæn] n Japão m.

Japanese [ˌdʒæpə'niːz] adj japonês (-esa) ◆ n (language) japonês m ◆ npl: **the ~** os japoneses.

jar [dʒɑːr] n frasco m.

jargon ['dʒɑːgən] n jargão m.

javelin ['dʒævlɪn] n dardo m (de lançamento).

jaw [dʒɔː] n maxilar m, mandíbula f.

jawbone ['dʒɔːbəʊn] n maxilar m,

mandíbula f; (of animal) queixada f.

jazz [dʒæz] n jazz m.

jealous ['dʒeləs] adj ciumento (-ta).

jealousy ['dʒeləsɪ] n ciúmes mpl.

jeans [dʒiːnz] npl jeans m inv (Br), calças fpl de ganga (Port).

Jeep® [dʒiːp] n jipe m.

jeer [dʒɪər] vt (boo) vaiar; (mock) zombar de ◆ vi: **to ~ at sb** (boo) vaiar alguém; (mock) zombar de alguém.

Jello® ['dʒeləʊ] n (Am) gelatina f.

jelly ['dʒelɪ] n (dessert) gelatina f; (Am: jam) geléia f.

jellyfish ['dʒelɪfɪʃ] (pl inv) n água-viva f.

jeopardize ['dʒepədaɪz] vt pôr em risco.

jerk [dʒɜːk] n (movement) solavanco m; (inf: idiot) idiota mf.

jersey ['dʒɜːzɪ] n (garment) suéter m (Br), camisola f de malha (Port).

Jersey ['dʒɜːzɪ] n Jersey m.

jest [dʒest] n brincadeira f, gracejo m; **in ~** na brincadeira, gracejando.

Jesus (Christ) [dʒiːzəs-] n Jesus m (Cristo).

jet [dʒet] n jato m; (outlet) cano m de saída.

jet engine n motor m a jato.

jetfoil ['dʒetfɔɪl] n hidrofólio m.

jet lag n jet lag m, cansaço provocado pelas diferenças de fuso horário.

jet-ski n jet-ski m, moto f de água.

jetty ['dʒetɪ] n embarcadouro m.

Jew [dʒuː] n judeu m (-dia f).

jewel ['dʒuːəl] n jóia f.

◯ **jewels** npl (jewellery) jóias fpl.

jeweler's ['dʒuːələz] (Am) = jeweller's.

jeweller's ['dʒuːələz] n (Brit) joalheria f, ourivesaria f.

jewellery ['dʒuːəlrɪ] n (Brit) jóias fpl.

jewelry ['dʒuːəlrɪ] (Am) = jewellery.

Jewish ['dʒuːɪʃ] adj judaico(-ca).

jiffy ['dʒɪfɪ] n (inf): **in a ~** num instante.

jig [dʒɪg] n jiga f.

jigsaw (puzzle) ['dʒɪgsɔː-] n puzzle m.

jilt [dʒɪlt] vt deixar, abandonar.

jingle ['dʒɪŋgl] n (of advert) jingle m publicitário.

jinx [dʒɪŋks] n mau olhado m.

job [dʒɒb] n (regular work) emprego m; (task, function) trabalho m; **to lose one's ~** perder o emprego.

job centre n (Brit) centro m de emprego.

jockey ['dʒɒkɪ] n jóquei m.

jog [dʒɒg] vt (bump) empurrar (levemente) ◆ vi fazer jogging ◆ n: **to go for a ~** fazer jogging.

jogging ['dʒɒgɪŋ] n jogging m; **to go ~** fazer jogging.

john [dʒɒn] n (Am: inf: toilet) privada f.

join [dʒɔɪn] vt (club, organization) tornar-se membro de, entrar para; (fasten together, connect) ligar, unir; (come together with) unir-se a; (participate in) juntar-se a; **will you ~ me for dinner?** você me acompanha para jantar?; **to ~ the queue** entrar na fila.

⏘ join in vt fus juntar-se a, participar em ◆ vi participar.

joiner ['dʒɔɪnər] n marceneiro m (-ra f), carpinteiro m (-ra f).

joint [dʒɔɪnt] adj conjunto(-ta) ◆ n (of body) articulação f; (Brit: of meat) corte m (de carne); (in structure) junta f.

jointly ['dʒɔɪntlɪ] adv conjuntamente.

joke [dʒəʊk] n piada f, anedota f ◆ vi gozar, brincar; **it was only a ~** foi só uma brincadeira.

joker ['dʒəʊkər] n (playing card) curingão m (Br), jóquer m (Port).

jolly ['dʒɒlɪ] adj alegre ◆ adv (Brit: inf: very) muito.

jolt [dʒəʊlt] n solavanco m.

Jordan ['dʒɔːdn] n Jordânia f.

jostle ['dʒɒsl] vt empurrar, dar empurrões a ◆ vi empurrar, dar empurrões.

jot [dʒɒt]: **jot down** vt sep anotar.

journal ['dʒɜːnl] n (professional magazine) boletim m; (diary) diário m.

journalism ['dʒɜːnəlɪzm] n jornalismo m.

journalist ['dʒɜːnəlɪst] n jornalista mf.

journey ['dʒɜːnɪ] n viagem f.

jovial ['dʒəʊvjəl] adj jovial.

joy [dʒɔɪ] n (happiness) alegria f.

joyful ['dʒɔɪful] adj alegre.

joypad ['dʒɔɪpæd] n joypad m.

joyrider ['dʒɔɪraɪdər] n pessoa que rouba um carro para passear e divertir-se e que depois o abandona.

joystick ['dʒɔɪstɪk] n (of video game) joystick m, manípulo m.

Jr. (abbr of Junior) Jr.

jubilant ['dʒuːbɪlənt] adj exultante.

judge [dʒʌdʒ] n juiz m (juíza f) ◆ vt julgar.

judg(e)ment ['dʒʌdʒmənt] n (JUR) julgamento m; (opinion) parecer m; (capacity to judge) senso m.

judiciary [dʒuːˈdɪʃərɪ] n: **the ~** o poder judicial.

judo ['dʒuːdəʊ] n judô m.

jug [dʒʌg] n jarro m, jarra f.

juggernaut ['dʒʌgənɔːt] n (Brit) jamanta f (Br), camião m, TIR m (Port).

juggle ['dʒʌgl] vi fazer malabarismos.

juggler ['dʒʌglər] n malabarista mf.

juice [dʒuːs] n (from fruit, vegetables) suco m (Br), sumo m (Port); (from meat) molho m.

juicy ['dʒuːsɪ] adj (food) suculento(-ta).

jukebox ['dʒuːkbɒks] n jukebox f, máquina f de discos.

Jul. abbr = July.

July [dʒuːˈlaɪ] n julho m, → September.

jumble ['dʒʌmbl] n (mixture) miscelânea f ◆ vt: **to ~ (up)** misturar.

jumble sale n (Brit) venda de objetos em segunda mão com fins beneficentes.

jumbo ['dʒʌmbəʊ] (pl -s) adj (inf: big) gigante.

jumbo jet n jumbo m.

jump [dʒʌmp] n salto m ◆ vi (through air) saltar; (with fright) assustar-se; (increase) dar um salto ◆ vt (Am: train, bus) viajar sem bilhete em; **to ~ the queue** (Brit) furar a fila (Br), dar o golpe (Port).

jumper ['dʒʌmpər] n (Brit: pullover) pulôver m (Br), camisola f (de malha) (Port); (Am: dress) vestido m de alças.

jump leads npl cabos mpl para bateria.

jump-start vt fazer arrancar com uma ligação directa.

jumpsuit ['dʒʌmpsuːt] n macacão f.

jumpy ['dʒʌmpɪ] *adj* nervoso(-osa).

Jun. *abbr* = June.

junction ['dʒʌŋkʃn] *n (road)* cruzamento *m*; *(railway)* entroncamento *m*.

June [dʒuːn] *n* junho *m*, → September.

jungle ['dʒʌŋgl] *n* selva *f*.

junior ['dʒuːnjəʳ] *adj (of lower rank)* subalterno(-na); *(Am: after name)* júnior *(inv)* ♦ *n (younger person)*: **she's my ~** ela é mais nova do que eu.

junior high school *n (Am)* – escola *f* secundária *(para alunos entre os 12 e os 15 anos)*.

junior school *n (Brit)* escola *f* primária.

junk [dʒʌŋk] *n (inf: unwanted things)* tralha *f*.

junk food *n (inf)* comida pronta considerada pouco nutritiva ou saudável.

junkie ['dʒʌŋkɪ] *n (inf)* drogado *m* (-da *f*).

junk mail *n* papelada *f (publicitária enviada pelo correio)*.

junk shop *n* loja *f* de objetos usados.

Jupiter ['dʒuːpɪtəʳ] *n* Júpiter *m*.

jurisdiction [,dʒuərɪs'dɪkʃn] *n* jurisdição *f*.

juror ['dʒuərəʳ] *n* jurado *m* (-da *f*).

jury ['dʒuərɪ] *n* júri *m*.

just [dʒʌst] *adv (recently)* agora (mesmo); *(in the next moment)* mesmo; *(exactly)* precisamente; *(only, slightly)* só ♦ *adj* justo(-ta); **I'm ~ coming!** já vou!; **to be ~ about to do sthg** estar prestes fazendo algo; **to have ~ done sthg** acabar de fazer algo; **~ about** *(almost)* praticamente; **~ as good** igualmente bom; **~ as good as** tão bom quanto; **~ over an hour** pouco mais de uma hora; **(only) ~** *(almost not)* quase não, por pouco não; **~ a minute!** só um minuto!

justice ['dʒʌstɪs] *n* justiça *f*.

justify ['dʒʌstɪfaɪ] *vt* justificar.

jut [dʒʌt] : **jut out** *vi* sobressair.

juvenile ['dʒuːvənaɪl] *adj (young)* juvenil; *(childish)* infantil.

K

kaleidoscope [kə'laɪdəskəʊp] *n* caleidoscópio *m*.

kangaroo [ˌkæŋgə'ruː] *n* canguru *m*.

karate [kə'rɑːtɪ] *n* karatê *m*.

kayak [ˈkaɪæk] *n* kayak *m*, caiaque *m*.

KB (*COMPUT: abbr of kilobyte(s)*) KB *m*.

kebab [kɪ'bæb] *n*: **(doner)** ~ pão árabe cortado servido com carne de carneiro, salada e molho; **(shish)** ~ espeto de carne com tomate, cebola, pimentões, etc.

keel [kiːl] *n* quilha *f*.

keen [kiːn] *adj (enthusiastic)* entusiasta; *(eyesight, hearing)* apurado(-da); **to be ~ on** interessar-se por, gostar de; **to be ~ to do sthg** ter muita vontade de fazer algo.

keep [kiːp] (*pt & pp* **kept**) *vt* manter; *(book, change, object loaned)* ficar com; *(store, not tell)* guardar; *(appointment)* não faltar a; *(delay)* atrasar; *(diary)* ter ◆ *vi (food)* conservar; *(remain)* manter-se; **to ~ a record of sthg** registrar algo; **to ~ (on) doing sthg** *(do continuously)* continuar fazendo algo; *(do repeatedly)* estar sempre fazendo algo; **to ~ sb from doing sthg** impedir alguém de fazer algo; **~ back!** para trás!; **"~ in lane!"** "mantenha-se na sua faixa"; **"~ left"** "circular pela esquerda"; **"~ off the grass!"** "não pise na grama!"; **"~ out!"** "proibida a entrada"; **"~ your distance!"** "mantenha a distância"; **to ~ clear (of)** manter-se afastado (de). ❑ **keep up** *vt sep* manter ◆ *vi (maintain pace, level etc)*: **to ~ up with sb** acompanhar alguém; **~ up the good work!** continue com o bom trabalho!

keeper [ˈkiːpər] *n (in zoo)* guarda *mf*, zelador *m* (-ra *f*).

keep-fit *n (Brit)* ginástica *f*.

keepsake [ˈkiːpseɪk] *n* lembrança *f*.

keg [keg] *n* barril *m*.

kennel [ˈkenl] *n* casa *f* de cachorro, canil *m*.

Kenya [ˈkenjə] *n* Quênia *m*.

Kenyan [ˈkenjən] *adj* queniano (-na) ◆ *n* queniano *m* (-na *f*).

kept [kept] *pt & pp* → **keep**.

kerb [kɜːb] *n (Brit)* meio-fio *m (Br)*, borda *f* do passeio *(Port)*.

kernel [ˈkɜːnl] *n (of nut)* miolo *m*.

kerosene [ˈkerəsiːn] *n (Am)* querosene *m*.

ketchup [ˈketʃəp] *n* ketchup *m*, molho *m* de tomate.

kettle [ˈketl] *n* chaleira *f*; **to put the ~ on** pôr a chaleira para ferver.

key [kiː] *n* chave *f*; *(of piano, typewriter)* tecla *f* ◆ *adj* chave *(inv)*.

keyboard [ˈkiːbɔːd] *n (of typewriter, piano)* teclado *m*; *(musical instrument)* órgão *m*.

keyhole [ˈkiːhəʊl] *n* buraco *m* da fechadura.

keypad [ˈkiːpæd] *n* teclado *m* (numérico).

key ring *n* chaveiro *m (Br)*, porta-chaves *m inv (Port)*.

kg *(abbr of kilogram)* kg.

khaki [ˈkɑːkɪ] *adj* cáqui *(inv)* ◆ *n (colour)* cáqui *m*.

kick [kɪk] *n (of foot)* pontapé *m* ◆ *vt*: **to ~ sb/sthg** dar um pontapé em alguém/algo.

kickoff [ˈkɪkɒf] *n* pontapé *m* inicial.

kid [kɪd] *n (inf) (child)* garoto *m* (-ta *f*); *(young person)* criança *f* ◆ *vi (joke)* gozar, brincar.

kidnap [ˈkɪdnæp] *vt* raptar.

kidnaper [ˈkɪdnæpər] *(Am)* = **kidnapper**.

kidnapper [ˈkɪdnæpər] *n (Brit)* raptor *m* (-ra *f*).

kidnapping [ˈkɪdnæpɪŋ] *n* rapto *m*, seqüestro *m*.

kidney [ˈkɪdnɪ] *n* rim *m*.

kidney bean *n* feijão *m* vermelho.

kill [kɪl] *vt* matar; **my feet are ~ing me!** os meus pés estão me matando!

killer ['kɪlə'] *n* assassino *m* (-na *f*).

killing ['kɪlɪŋ] *n* (*murder*) assassinato *m*.

killjoy ['kɪldʒɔɪ] *n* desmancha-prazeres *mf inv*.

kiln [kɪln] *n* forno *m*, fornalha *f*.

kilo ['kiːləʊ] (*pl* **-s**) *n* quilo *m*.

kilobyte ['kɪləbaɪt] *n* kilobyte *m*.

kilogram ['kɪləgræm] *n* quilograma *m*.

kilohertz ['kɪləhɜːts] (*pl inv*) kilohertz *m*.

kilometre ['kɪlə,miːtə'] *n* quilômetro *m*.

kilowatt ['kɪləwɒt] *n* kilowatt *m*.

kilt [kɪlt] *n* kilt *m*, saia *f* escocesa.

kind [kaɪnd] *adj* amável ♦ *n* tipo *m*; **~ of** (*Am: inf*) um pouco.

kindergarten ['kɪndə,gɑːtn] *n* jardim-de-infância *m*.

kind-hearted [-'hɑːtɪd] *adj* bondoso(-osa).

kindly ['kaɪndlɪ] *adv*: **would you ~ ...?** pode fazer o favor de ...?

kindness ['kaɪndnɪs] *n* amabilidade *f*, bondade *f*.

king [kɪŋ] *n* rei *m*.

kingdom ['kɪŋdəm] *n* reino *m*.

kingfisher ['kɪŋ,fɪʃə'] *n* martim-pescador *m*, pica-peixe *m*.

king prawn *n* camarão *m* (gigante) (*Br*), gamba *f* (*Port*).

king-size bed *n* cama *f* de casal (com 160 cm de largura).

kinky ['kɪŋkɪ] *adj* (*inf*) bizarro(-a).

kiosk ['kiːɒsk] *n* (*for newspapers etc*) banca *f* de jornal (*Br*), quiosque *m* (*Port*); (*Brit: phone box*) cabine *f*.

kip [kɪp] *n* (*Brit: inf*) soneca *f* ♦ *vi* (*Brit: inf*) dormir.

kipper ['kɪpə'] *n* arenque *m* defumado.

kiss [kɪs] *n* beijo *m* ♦ *vt* beijar.

kiss of life *n* respiração *f* boca-a-boca.

kit [kɪt] *n* (*set*) estojo *m*; (*clothes*) equipamento *m*; (*for assembly*) kit *m*, modelo *m*.

kit bag *n* saco *m* de viagem.

kitchen ['kɪtʃɪn] *n* cozinha *f*.

kitchen sink *n* pia *f* da cozinha.

kitchen unit *n* módulo *m* de cozinha.

kite [kaɪt] *n* (*toy*) pipa *f* (*Br*), papagaio *m* (de papel) (*Port*).

kitten ['kɪtn] *n* gatinho *m* (-nha *f*).

kitty ['kɪtɪ] *n* (*for regular expenses*) fundo *m* comum.

kiwi fruit ['kiːwiː-] *n* kiwi *m*.

Kleenex® ['kliːneks] *n* Kleenex® *m*, lenço *m* de papel.

km (*abbr of kilometre*) km.

km/h (*abbr of kilometres per hour*) km/h.

knack [næk] *n*: **I've got the ~ (of it)** já peguei o jeito de fazer isso.

knackered ['nækəd] *adj* (*Brit: inf*) estourado(-da).

knapsack ['næpsæk] *n* mochila *f*.

knead [niːd] *vt* amassar.

knee [niː] *n* joelho *m*.

kneecap ['niːkæp] *n* rótula *f*.

kneel [niːl] (*pt & pp* **knelt** [nelt]) *vi* (*be on one's knees*) estar ajoelhado(-da) OR de joelhos; (*go down on one's knees*) ajoelhar-se.

knew [njuː] *pt* → **know**.

knickers ['nɪkəz] *npl* (*Brit*) calcinha *f* (*Br*), cuecas *fpl* (de senhora) (*Port*).

knick-knack ['nɪknæk] *n* bugiganga *f*.

knife [naɪf] (*pl* **knives**) *n* faca *f*.

knight [naɪt] *n* (*in history*) cavaleiro *m*; (*in chess*) cavalo *m*.

knighthood ['naɪthʊd] *n* (*present day title*) título *m* de "Sir".

knit [nɪt] *vt* fazer tricô.

knitted ['nɪtɪd] *adj* tricotado(-da), de malha.

knitting ['nɪtɪŋ] *n* tricô *m* (*Br*), malha *f* (*Port*).

knitting needle *n* agulha *f* de tricô.

knitwear ['nɪtweə'] *n* roupa *f* de tricô.

knives [naɪvz] *pl* → **knife**.

knob [nɒb] *n* (*on door etc*) maçaneta *f*; (*on machine*) botão *m*.

knock [nɒk] *n* (*at door*) pancada *f*, batida *f* ♦ *vt* (*hit*) bater em; (*one's head, elbow*) bater com ♦ *vi* (*at door etc*) bater.

❑ **knock down** *vt sep* (*pedestrian*) atropelar; (*building*) demolir; (*price*) baixar.

❑ **knock out** *vt sep* (*make unconscious*) deixar inconsciente; (*of competition*) eliminar.

❑ **knock over** *vt sep* (*glass, vase*) derrubar; (*pedestrian*) atropelar.

knocker ['nɒkəʳ] *n (on door)* batente *m*, aldraba *f*.

knockout ['nɒkaʊt] *n (in boxing)* nocaute *m*.

knot [nɒt] *n* nó *m*.

know [nəʊ] (*pt* knew, *pp* known) *vt* saber; *(person, place)* conhecer; **to ~ about sthg** saber (acerca) de algo; **to ~ how to do sthg** saber como fazer algo; **to ~ of** saber de; **you'll like him once you get to ~ him** você vai gostar dele quando o conhecer melhor; **to be known as** ser conhecido como; **to let sb ~ sthg** avisar alguém de algo; **you ~** *(for emphasis)* sabe.

know-all *n (Brit)* sabichão *m* (-chona *f*).

know-how *n* know-how *m*, conhecimentos *mpl*.

knowingly ['nəʊɪŋlɪ] *adv (look, smile)* com cumplicidade; *(act)* conscientemente.

knowledge ['nɒlɪdʒ] *n* saber *m*, conhecimento *m*; **to my ~** que eu saiba.

knowledgeable ['nɒlɪdʒəbl] *adj* conhecedor(-ra).

known [nəʊn] *pp* → **know**.

knuckle ['nʌkl] *n (of hand)* nó *m* do dedo; *(of pork)* mocotó *m (Br)*, chispe *m (Port)*.

koala (bear) [kəʊˈɑːlə-] *n* (urso) coala *m*.

Koran [kɒˈrɑːn] *n*: **the ~** o Corão.

kosher ['kəʊʃəʳ] *adj (meat)* limpo(-pa) (segundo a lei judaica).

kung fu [ˌkʌŋˈfuː] *n* kung-fu *m*.

Kurd [kɜːd] *n* curdo *m* (-da *f*).

Kuwait [kʊˈweɪt] *n (country)* Kuwait *m*.

L

l *(abbr of litre)* l.

L *(abbr of learner, large)* L.

lab [læb] *n (inf)* laboratório *m*.

label ['leɪbl] *n* etiqueta *f*.

labor ['leɪbər] *(Am)* = **labour**.

laboratory [*Brit* lə'bɒrətrɪ, *Am* 'læbrə,tɔːrɪ] *n* laboratório *m*.

labour ['leɪbər] *n (Brit) (work)* trabalho *m*; **in ~** *(MED)* em trabalho de parto.

labourer ['leɪbərər] *n* trabalhador *m* (-ra *f*).

Labour Party *n (Brit)* Partido *m* Trabalhista.

labour-saving *adj* que poupa trabalho.

Labrador ['læbrədɔːr] *n (dog)* cão *m* Labrador.

labyrinth ['læbərɪnθ] *n* labirinto *m*.

lace [leɪs] *n (material)* renda *f*; *(for shoe)* cardaço *m (Br)*, atacador *m (Port)*.

lace-ups *npl* sapatos *mpl* de amarrar.

lack [læk] *n* falta *f* ◆ *vt* carecer de ◆ *vi*: **to be ~ing** faltar; **he ~s confidence** falta-lhe confiança.

lacquer ['lækər] *n* laca *f*.

lad [læd] *n (inf)* garoto *m*.

ladder ['lædər] *n (for climbing)* escada *f*; *(Brit: in tights)* defeito *m*, desfiado *m (Br)*, foguete *m (Port)*.

ladies ['leɪdɪz] *n (Brit) (toilet)* banheiro *m* de senhoras.

ladies room *(Am)* = **ladies**.

ladieswear ['leɪdɪz,weər] *n* roupa *f* de senhora.

ladle ['leɪdl] *n* concha *f*.

lady ['leɪdɪ] *n (woman)* senhora *f*; *(woman of high status)* dama *f*.

ladybird ['leɪdɪbɜːd] *n (Brit)* joaninha *f*.

ladybug ['leɪdɪbʌg] *(Am)* = **ladybird**.

lady-in-waiting [-'weɪtɪŋ] *n* dama *f* de companhia.

ladylike ['leɪdɪlaɪk] *adj* elegante, distinto(-ta).

lag [læg] *vi* diminuir; **to ~ behind** *(move more slowly)* ficar para trás.

lager ['lɑːgər] *n* cerveja *f* (loura).

lagoon [lə'guːn] *n* lagoa *f*.

laid [leɪd] *pt & pp* → **lay**.

laid-back *adj (inf)* descontraído(-da).

lain [leɪn] *pp* → **lie**.

lair [leər] *n* toca *f*, covil *m*.

lake [leɪk] *n* lago *m*.

Lake District *n*: **the ~** região *de* lagos *e* montanhas *no noroeste de* Inglaterra.

lamb [læm] *n (animal)* cordeiro *m*; *(meat)* carneiro *m*.

lamb chop *n* costeleta *f* de carneiro.

lambswool ['læmzwul] *n* lã *m* de carneiro ◆ *adj* de lã de carneiro.

lame [leɪm] *adj* coxo(-xa).

lament [lə'ment] *n* lamento *m* ◆ *vt* lamentar.

laminated ['læmɪneɪtɪd] *adj* laminado(-da).

lamp [læmp] *n* lâmpada *f (Br)*, candeeiro *m (Port)*.

lamppost ['læmppəust] *n* poste *m* de iluminação.

lampshade ['læmpʃeɪd] *n* abajur *m (Br)*, quebra-luz *m (Port)*.

lance [lɑːns] *n* lança *f*.

land [lænd] *n* terra *f* ◆ *vi (plane)* aterrar; *(passengers)* desembarcar; *(fall)* cair.

landing ['lændɪŋ] *n (of plane)* aterrissagem *f (Br)*, aterragem *f (Port)*; *(on stairs)* patamar *m*.

landing card *n* cartão *m* de desembarque.

landing gear *n* trem *m* de aterrissagem.

landing strip *n* pista *f* de aterrissagem.

landlady [ˈlændˌleɪdɪ] n (of house) senhoria f; (of pub) dona f.

landlord [ˈlændlɔːd] n (of house) senhorio m; (of pub) dono m.

landmark [ˈlændmɑːk] n (in landscape, city) ponto m de referência.

landowner [ˈlændˌəʊnəʳ] n proprietário m (-ria f) rural.

landscape [ˈlændskeɪp] n paisagem f.

landslide [ˈlændslaɪd] n (of earth, rocks) deslizamento m (Br), desabamento m (Port).

lane [leɪn] n (narrow road) ruela f; (on road, motorway) pista f (Br), faixa f (Port); **"get in ~"** sinal que indica aos motoristas que devem deslocar-se para a pista adequada.

language [ˈlæŋgwɪdʒ] n (of a people, country) língua f; (system of communication, words) linguagem f.

language laboratory n laboratório m de línguas.

languish [ˈlæŋgwɪʃ] vi definhar.

lank [læŋk] adj (hair) escorrido (-da).

lanky [ˈlæŋkɪ] adj magricela.

lantern [ˈlæntən] n lanterna f.

lap [læp] n (of person) colo m; (of race) volta f.

lapel [ləˈpel] n lapela f.

lapse [læps] n lapso m ♦ vi (membership, passport) expirar (Br), caducar (Port).

lap-top (computer) n computador m portátil.

lard [lɑːd] n banha f.

larder [ˈlɑːdəʳ] n despensa f.

large [lɑːdʒ] adj grande.

largely [ˈlɑːdʒlɪ] adv em grande parte.

large-scale adj em grande escala.

lark [lɑːk] n cotovia f.

laryngitis [ˌlærɪnˈdʒaɪtɪs] n laringite f.

lasagne [ləˈzænjə] n lasanha f.

laser [ˈleɪzəʳ] n laser m.

lash [læʃ] n (eyelash) pestana f; (blow with whip) chicotada f ♦ vt (whip) chicotear; (tie) amarrar.

lass [læs] n (inf) garota f.

lasso [læˈsuː] (pl -s) n laço m ♦ vt laçar.

last [lɑːst] adj último(-ma) ♦ adv (most recently) pela última vez; (at the end) em último lugar ♦ vi durar; (be enough) chegar ♦ pron: **the ~ to come** o último a chegar; **the ~ but one** o penúltimo;

the day before ~ anteontem; **~ year** o ano passado; **the ~ year** o último ano; **at ~** finalmente.

lasting [ˈlɑːstɪŋ] adj duradouro (-ra).

lastly [ˈlɑːstlɪ] adv por último.

last-minute adj de última hora.

last name n sobrenome m (Br), apelido m (Port).

latch [lætʃ] n trinco m; **the door is on the ~** a porta está fechada com o trinco.

late [leɪt] adj (not on time) atrasado (-da); (after usual time) tardio (-dia); (dead) falecido(-da) ♦ adv (after usual time) tarde; (not on time): **the train is two hours ~** o trem está duas horas atrasado; **I had a ~ lunch** almocei tarde; **in the ~ afternoon** no fim da tarde; **in ~ June, ~ in June** no final OR fim de junho.

latecomer [ˈleɪtˌkʌməʳ] n retardatário m (-ria f).

lately [ˈleɪtlɪ] adv ultimamente.

late-night adj (chemist, supermarket) aberto(-ta) até tarde.

later [ˈleɪtəʳ] adj (train) que saia mais tarde ♦ adv: **~ (on)** mais tarde; **at a ~ date** mais tarde, posteriormente.

latest [ˈleɪtɪst] adj: **the ~ fashion** a última moda; **the ~** (in series, in fashion) o mais recente (a mais recente); **at the ~** o mais tardar.

lathe [leɪð] n torno m.

lather [ˈlɑːðəʳ] n espuma f.

Latin [ˈlætɪn] n (language) latim m.

Latin America n América f Latina.

Latin American adj latino-americano(-na) ♦ n latino-americano m (-na f).

latitude [ˈlætɪtjuːd] n latitude f.

latter [ˈlætəʳ] n: **the ~** este último (esta última).

Latvia [ˈlætvɪə] n Letônia f.

laugh [lɑːf] n riso m ♦ vi rir; **to have a ~** (Brit: inf) divertir-se.

⊔ **laugh at** vt fus (mock) rir-se de.

laughable [ˈlɑːfəbl] adj ridículo (-la).

laughing stock [ˈlɑːfɪŋ-] n alvo m de riso OR gozação.

laughter [ˈlɑːftəʳ] n risos mpl.

launch [lɔːntʃ] vt (boat) lançar ao mar; (new product) lançar.

launderette [ˌlɔːndəˈret] n lavanderia f automática.

laundry [ˈlɔːndrɪ] n (washing) roupa f

suja; *(place)* lavanderia *f*.
lava ['lɑːvə] *n* lava *f*.
lavatory ['lævətrɪ] *n* privada *f (Br)*, casa *f* de banho *(Port)*.
lavender ['lævəndər] *n* alfazema *f*.
lavish ['lævɪʃ] *adj (meal, decoration)* suntuoso(-osa).
law [lɔː] *n (JUR: rule)* lei *f*; *(study)* direito *m*; **the ~** *(JUR: set of rules)* a lei; **to be against the ~** ser contra a lei.
law-abiding [-ə,baɪdɪŋ] *adj* respeitador(-ra) da lei.
law court *n* tribunal *m*.
lawful ['lɔːfʊl] *adj* legal.
lawn [lɔːn] *n* gramado *m (Br)*, relvado *m (Port)*.
lawnmower ['lɔːn,məʊər] *n* máquina *f* de cortar grama.
lawsuit ['lɔːsuːt] *n* processo *m*.
lawyer ['lɔːjər] *n* advogado *m* (-da *f*).
lax [læks] *adj (person, behaviour, attitude)* negligente; *(standards, morals)* baixo(-xa); *(discipline)* pouco rígido (-da).
laxative ['læksətɪv] *n* laxante *m*.
lay [leɪ] *(pt & pp laid)* *pt* → **lie** ◆ *vt (place)* colocar, pôr; *(egg)* pôr; **to ~ the table** pôr a mesa.
❏ **lay off** *vt sep (worker)* despedir.
❏ **lay on** *vt sep* fornecer.
❏ **lay out** *vt sep (display)* dispor.
layabout ['leɪəbaʊt] *n (Brit: inf)* vadio *m* (-dia *f*).
lay-by *(pl lay-bys)* *n* acostamento *m (Br)*, berma *f (Port)*.
layer ['leɪər] *n* camada *f*.
layman ['leɪmən] *(pl -men* [-mən]*)* *n* leigo *m* (-ga *f*).
layout ['leɪaʊt] *n (of building)* leiaute *m (Br)*, disposição *f (Port)*; *(of streets)* traçado *m*; **"new road ~"** sinal que indica uma mudança no traçado da estrada ou rua.
laze [leɪz] *vi*: **I spent the afternoon lazing in the sun** passei a tarde no sol sem fazer nada.
lazy ['leɪzɪ] *adj* preguiçoso(-osa).
lb *abbr* = **pound**.
LCD *abbr* = **liquid crystal display**.
lead[1] [liːd] *(pt & pp led)* *vt (take)* conduzir, levar; *(team, company)* dirigir; *(race, demonstration)* estar à frente de ◆ *vi (be winning)* estar à frente ◆ *n (for dog)* trela *f*; *(cable)* cabo *m*, fio *m*; **to ~ sb to do sthg** levar alguém a fazer algo; **to ~ the way** estar à frente; **to ~**

to *(go to)* ir dar em; *(result in)* levar a; **to be in the ~** estar à frente.
lead[2] [led] *n (metal)* chumbo *m*; *(for pencil)* grafite *m (Br)*, mina *f (Port)* ◆ *adj* de chumbo.
leaded petrol ['ledɪd-] *n* gasolina *f* (com chumbo).
leader ['liːdər] *n* líder *mf*.
leadership ['liːdəʃɪp] *n* liderança *f*.
lead-free [led-] *adj* sem chumbo.
leading ['liːdɪŋ] *adj (most important)* principal.
lead singer [liːd-] *n* vocalista *mf*.
leaf [liːf] *(pl leaves)* *n (of tree)* folha *f*.
leaflet ['liːflɪt] *n* folheto *m*.
league [liːg] *n (SPORT)* campeonato *m*; *(association)* liga *f*.
leak [liːk] *n (hole)* buraco *m*; *(of gas, petrol)* vazamento *m (Br)*, fuga *f (Port)*; *(of water)* vazamento *m (Br)*, perda *f (Port)*; *(in roof)* goteira *f* ◆ *vi (roof)* ter goteiras; *(tank)* vazar.
leakage ['liːkɪdʒ] *n (of gas, petrol, water)* vazamento *m*.
lean [liːn] *(pt & pp leant OR -ed)* *adj* magro(-gra) ◆ *vi (bend)* inclinar-se ◆ *vt*: **to ~ sthg against sthg** encostar algo em algo; **to ~ on** apoiar-se em.
❏ **lean forward** *vi* inclinar-se para a frente.
❏ **lean over** *vi* abaixar-se.
leaning ['liːnɪŋ] *n*: **~ towards sthg** *(science, arts)* inclinação *f* para algo; **a magazine with Marxist ~s** uma revista com tendências marxistas.
leant [lent] *pt & pp* → **lean**.
leap [liːp] *(pt & pp leapt OR -ed)* *vi* saltar.
leapfrog ['liːpfrɒg] *n* jogo *m* de pular corniça *(Br)*, jogo *m* do eixo *(Port)* ◆ *vt* saltar.
leapt [lept] *pt & pp* → **leap**.
leap year *n* ano *m* bissexto.
learn [lɜːn] *(pt & pp learnt OR -ed)* *vt (gain knowledge of)* aprender; *(memorize)* decorar; **to ~ (how) to do sthg** aprender a fazer algo; **to ~ about sthg** *(hear about)* ficar sabendo (de) algo; *(study)* estudar algo.
learned ['lɜːnɪd] *adj* erudito(-ta).
learner (driver) ['lɜːnər-] *n* pessoa que está aprendendo a dirigir.
learning ['lɜːnɪŋ] *n* saber *m*, erudição *f*.
learnt [lɜːnt] *pt & pp* → **learn**.

lease [li:s] *n* contrato *m* de arrendamento OR aluguel ◆ *vt* arrendar, alugar; **to ~ sthg from sb** arrendar algo de alguém; **to ~ sthg to sb** arrendar algo a alguém.

leash [li:ʃ] *n* trela *f*.

least [li:st] *adv & adj* menos ◆ *pron*: **(the) ~** o mínimo; **at ~** pelo menos; **I like her the ~** ela é de quem eu gosto menos.

leather [ˈleðəʳ] *n* couro *m*, cabedal *m* (Port), pele *f*.

❐ **leathers** *npl* (of motorcyclist) roupa *f* de couro.

leave [li:v] (*pt & pp* left) *vt* deixar; (house, country) sair de ◆ *vi* (person) ir-se embora; (train, bus) sair, partir ◆ *n* (time off work) licença *f*; **to ~ a message** deixar recado, → **left**.

❐ **leave behind** *vt sep* deixar (para trás).

❐ **leave out** *vt sep* omitir.

leaves [li:vz] *pl* → **leaf**.

Lebanon [ˈlebanən] *n* Líbano *m*.

lecherous [ˈletʃərəs] *adj* (look, expression) lascivo(-va); (person) devasso(-a).

lecture [ˈlektʃəʳ] *n* (at university) aula *f*; (at conference) conferência *f*.

lecturer [ˈlektʃərəʳ] *n* professor *m* universitário (professora *f* universitária).

lecture theatre *n* anfiteatro *m*.

led [led] *pt & pp* → **lead**[1].

ledge [ledʒ] *n* (of window) peitoril *m*.

leech [li:tʃ] *n* sanguessuga *f*.

leek [li:k] *n* alho-poró *m* (Br), alho *m* francês (Port).

leer [lɪəʳ] *n* olhar *m* lascivo ◆ *vi*: **to ~ at sb** olhar lascivamente para alguém.

leeway [ˈli:wei] *n* (room to manoeuvre) margem *f* para manobra.

left [left] *pt & pp* → **leave** ◆ *adj* (not right) esquerdo(-da) ◆ *adv* (turn) à esquerda; (keep) pela esquerda ◆ *n* esquerda *f*; **on the ~** à esquerda; **to be ~ sobrar**.

left-hand *adj* esquerdo(-da).

left-hand drive *n* veículo *m* com volante do lado esquerdo.

left-handed [-ˈhændid] *adj* (person) canhoto(-ota); (implement) para canhotos.

left-luggage locker *n* (Brit) guarda-volumes *m inv* com chave (Br), cacifo *m* (para bagagem) (Port).

left-luggage office *n* (Brit) depósito *m* de bagagens.

leftover [ˈleftəʊvəʳ] *adj* a mais.

❐ **leftovers** *npl* restos *mpl*.

left-wing *adj* de esquerda.

leg [leg] *n* perna *f*; **~ of lamb** perna de carneiro.

legacy [ˈlegəsi] *n* legado *m*, herança *f*.

legal [ˈli:gl] *adj* legal.

legal aid *n* ajuda financeira estatal para pagamento de um advogado.

legalize [ˈli:gəlaiz] *vt* legalizar.

legal system *n* sistema *m* judiciário.

legal tender *n* moeda *f* corrente.

legend [ˈledʒənd] *n* lenda *f*.

leggings [ˈlegɪŋz] *npl* calças *fpl* de malha (justas).

legible [ˈledʒɪbl] *adj* legível.

legislation [ˌledʒɪsˈleɪʃn] *n* legislação *f*.

legitimate [lɪˈdʒɪtɪmət] *adj* legítimo (-ma).

legless [ˈleglɪs] *adj* (Brit: inf: drunk): **to be ~** estar bêbado(-da) que nem um gambá.

legroom [ˈlegrʊm] *n* espaço *m* para as pernas.

leg-warmers [-ˌwɔ:məz] *npl* caneleiras *fpl*, meias *fpl* sem pé.

leisure [Brit ˈleʒəʳ, Am ˈli:ʒər] *n* lazer *m*.

leisure centre *n* centro *m* de lazer.

leisurely [Brit ˈleʒəlɪ, Am ˈli:ʒərlɪ] *adj* despreocupado(-da).

leisure pool *n* parque *m* aquático.

leisure time *n* tempo *m* livre OR de lazer.

lemon [ˈlemən] *n* limão-galego *m* (Br), limão *m* (Port).

lemonade [ˌleməˈneɪd] *n* (Brit: fizzy drink) gasosa *f*; (lemon juice) limonada *f*.

lemon curd [-kɜ:d] *n* (Brit) doce *m* de limão (feito com suco de limão, açúcar, ovos e manteiga).

lemon juice *n* suco *m* de limão.

lemon meringue pie *n* torta *f* de limão e suspiro.

lemon sole *n* linguado *m*.

lemon tea *n* chá *m* de limão, ≈ carioca *m* de limão (Port).

lend [lend] (*pt & pp* lent) *vt* emprestar; **to ~ sb sthg** emprestar algo a alguém.

length [leŋθ] *n (in distance)* comprimento *m*; *(in time)* duração *f*.

lengthen ['leŋθən] *vt* aumentar.

lengthways ['leŋθweɪz] *adv* ao comprido.

lengthy ['leŋθɪ] *adj* longo(-ga).

lenient ['li:njənt] *adj* brando (-da).

lens [lenz] *n* lente *f*.

lent [lent] *pt & pp* → **lend**.

Lent [lent] *n* Quaresma *f*.

lentils ['lentlz] *npl* lentilhas *fpl*.

Leo ['li:əʊ] *n* Leão *m*.

leopard ['lepəd] *n* leopardo *m*.

leopard-skin *adj* tipo pele de leopardo.

leotard ['li:ətɑːd] *n* malha *f* de ginástica.

leper ['lepər] *n* leproso *m* (-osa *f*).

leprosy ['leprəsɪ] *n* lepra *f*.

lesbian ['lezbɪən] *adj* lésbico(-ca) ◆ *n* lésbica *f*.

less [les] *adj, adv & pron* menos; ~ **than** 20 menos de 20; **she earns ~ than him** ela ganha menos do que ele.

lessen ['lesn] *vt & vi* diminuir.

lesser ['lesər] *adj* menor; **to a ~ extent** OR **degree** em menor grau.

lesson ['lesn] *n (class)* lição *f*.

let [let] *(pt & pp* **let)** *vt (allow)* deixar; *(rent out)* alugar, arrendar; **to ~ sb do sthg** deixar alguém fazer algo; **to ~ go of sthg** largar algo; **to ~ sb have sthg** dar algo a alguém; **to ~ sb know sthg** dizer algo a alguém; **~'s go!** vamos embora!; **"to ~"** "para alugar", "aluga-se".

❑ **let in** *vt sep* deixar entrar.

❑ **let off** *vt sep (excuse)* perdoar; **can you ~ me off at the station?** pode me deixar na estação?.

❑ **let out** *vt sep (allow to go out)* deixar sair.

letdown ['letdaʊn] *n (inf)* decepção *f*.

lethal ['li:θl] *adj* letal, mortal.

lethargic [lə'θɑːdʒɪk] *adj* letárgico (-ca).

let's [lets] = **let us**.

letter ['letər] *n (written message)* carta *f*; *(of alphabet)* letra *f*.

letterbox ['letəbɒks] *n (Brit) (in door)* caixa *f* do correio; *(in street)* caixa *f* do correio *(Br)*, marco *m* do correio *(Port)*.

lettuce ['letɪs] *n* alface *f*.

leuk(a)emia [luː'kiːmɪə] *n* leucemia *f*.

level ['levl] *adj (horizontal, flat)* plano (-na) ◆ *n* nível *m*; *(storey)* andar *m*; **to be ~ with** estar no mesmo nível que.

level crossing *n (Brit)* passagem *f* de nível.

level-headed [-'hedɪd] *adj* sensato (-ta).

lever [*Brit* 'li:vər, *Am* 'levər] *n* alavanca *f*.

levy ['levɪ] *vt* lançar; **~ (on sthg)** *(financial contribution)* contribuição *f* (para algo); *(tax)* imposto *m* (sobre algo).

lewd [ljuːd] *adj (behaviour)* lascivo (-va); *(joke, song)* obsceno(-na).

liability [laɪə'bɪlətɪ] *n (responsibility)* responsabilidade *f*.

liable ['laɪəbl] *adj*: **to be ~ to do sthg** ter tendência a fazer algo; **he's ~ to be late** é provável que ele chegue tarde; **to be ~ for sthg** ser responsável por algo.

liaise [lɪ'eɪz] *vi*: **to ~ with** contatar com.

liar ['laɪər] *n* mentiroso *m* (-osa *f*).

libel ['laɪbl] *n* calúnia *f*, difamação *f* ◆ *vt* caluniar, difamar.

liberal ['lɪbərəl] *adj (tolerant)* liberal; *(generous)* generoso(-osa).

Liberal Democrat Party *n* Partido *m* Democrata Liberal.

liberate ['lɪbəreɪt] *vt* libertar.

liberty ['lɪbətɪ] *n* liberdade *f*.

Libra ['li:brə] *n* Libra *f (Br)*, Balança *f (Port)*.

librarian [laɪ'breərɪən] *n* bibliotecário *m* (-ria *f*).

library ['laɪbrərɪ] *n* biblioteca *f*.

library book *n* livro *m* da biblioteca.

Libya ['lɪbɪə] *n* Líbia *f*.

lice [laɪs] *npl* piolhos *mpl*.

licence ['laɪsəns] *n (Brit) (official document)* licença *f* ◆ *vt (Am)* = **license**.

license ['laɪsəns] *vt (Brit)* autorizar ◆ *n (Am)* = **licence**.

licensed ['laɪsənst] *adj (restaurant, bar)* autorizado(-da) a vender bebidas alcoólicas.

license plate *n (Am)* placa *f (Br)*, matrícula *f (Port)*.

licensing hours ['laɪsənsɪŋ-] *npl (Brit)* horário de abertura dos pubs.

lick [lɪk] vt lamber.

licorice [ˈlɪkərɪs] = **liquorice**.

lid [lɪd] n (cover) tampa f.

lie [laɪ] (pt **lay**, pp **lain**, cont **lying**) n mentira f ◆ vi (tell lie: pt & pp **lied**) mentir; (be horizontal) estar deitado; (lie down) deitar-se; (be situated) ficar; **to tell ~s** mentir; **to ~ about sthg** mentir sobre algo.

❑ **lie down** vi deitar-se.

Liechtenstein [ˈlɪktənstaɪn] n Liechtenstein m.

lie-down n (Brit): **to have a ~** descansar um pouco, dormir um pouco.

lie-in n (Brit): **to have a ~** dormir até (mais) tarde.

lieutenant [Brit lefˈtenənt, Am luːˈtenənt] n tenente m.

life [laɪf] (pl **lives**) n vida f.

life assurance n seguro m de vida.

life belt n bóia f (salva-vidas).

lifeboat [ˈlaɪfbəʊt] n barco m salva-vidas.

lifeguard [ˈlaɪfɡɑːd] n salva-vidas mf (Br), nadador-salvador m (nadadora-salvadora f) (Port).

life insurance n seguro m de vida.

life jacket n colete m salva-vidas.

lifelike [ˈlaɪflaɪk] adj realista.

lifelong [ˈlaɪflɒŋ] adj vitalício(-cia); (friendship) de toda a vida.

life preserver [-prɪˈzɜːvər] n (Am) (life belt) bóia f (salva-vidas); (life jacket) colete m salva-vidas.

life raft n salva-vidas m inv.

lifesaver [ˈlaɪfˌseɪvər] n salva-vidas mf (Br), (person) nadador-salvador m (nadadora-salvadora f) (Port).

life-size adj em tamanho natural.

lifespan [ˈlaɪfspæn] n tempo m de vida.

lifestyle [ˈlaɪfstaɪl] n estilo m de vida.

lifetime [ˈlaɪftaɪm] n vida f; **the chance of a ~** uma oportunidade única.

lift [lɪft] n (Brit: elevator) elevador m ◆ vt (raise) levantar ◆ vi (fog) levantar; **to give sb a ~** dar uma carona a alguém (Br), dar uma boleia a alguém (Port).

❑ **lift up** vt sep levantar.

lift-off n decolagem f.

light [laɪt] (pt & pp **lit** OR **-ed**) adj leve; (not dark) claro(-ra) ◆ n luz f; (for cigarette) fogo m (Br), lume m (Port) ◆ vt (fire, cigarette) acender; (room, stage) iluminar; **have you got a ~?** você tem fósforo OR isqueiro?; **to set ~ to sthg**

pôr fogo em algo.

❑ **lights** (traffic lights) sinais mpl de trânsito, semáforos mpl (Port).

❑ **light up** vt sep (house, road) iluminar ◆ vi (inf: light a cigarette) acender um cigarro.

light bulb n lâmpada f.

lighten [ˈlaɪtn] vt (room, ceiling) iluminar; (hair) clarear, alourar; (workload) aliviar.

lighter [ˈlaɪtər] n isqueiro m.

light-hearted [-ˈhɑːtɪd] adj alegre.

lighthouse [ˈlaɪthaʊs, pl -haʊzɪz] n farol m.

lighting [ˈlaɪtɪŋ] n iluminação f.

light meter n fotômetro m.

lightning [ˈlaɪtnɪŋ] n relâmpagos mpl.

lightweight [ˈlaɪtweɪt] adj (clothes, object) leve.

likable [ˈlaɪkəbl] adj simpático (-ca).

like [laɪk] prep como; (typical of) típico de ◆ vt gostar de; **~ this/that** assim; **what's it ~?** como é?; **to look ~ sb/sthg** parecer-se com alguém/algo; **would you ~ some more?** quer mais?; **to ~ doing sthg** gostar de fazer algo; **I'd ~ to sit down** gostaria de me sentar; **I'd ~ a drink** gostaria de beber qualquer coisa.

likeable [ˈlaɪkəbl] = **likable**.

likelihood [ˈlaɪklɪhʊd] n probabilidade f.

likely [ˈlaɪklɪ] adj provável.

liken [ˈlaɪkn] vt: **to ~ sb/sthg to** comparar alguém/algo a.

likeness [ˈlaɪknɪs] n semelhança f.

likewise [ˈlaɪkwaɪz] adv da mesma maneira; **to do ~** fazer o mesmo.

liking [ˈlaɪkɪŋ] n gosto m; **to have a ~ for** gostar de; **to be to sb's ~** estar ao gosto de alguém.

lilac [ˈlaɪlək] adj lilás (inv).

Lilo® [ˈlaɪləʊ] (pl **-s**) n (Brit) colchão m de ar.

lily [ˈlɪlɪ] n lírio m.

lily of the valley n lírio-do-vale m, lírio-convale m.

limb [lɪm] n membro m.

lime [laɪm] n (fruit) limão m (Br), lima f (Port); **~ (juice)** suco m de limão (Br), sumo m de lima (Port).

limelight [ˈlaɪmlaɪt] n: **to be in the ~** ser o centro das atenções.

limestone [ˈlaɪmstəʊn] n calcário m.

limit [ˈlɪmɪt] n limite m ◆ vt limitar; **the city ~s** os limites da cidade.

limitation [ˌlɪmɪˈteɪʃn] n limitação f.

limited [ˈlɪmɪtɪd] adj limitado (-da).

limousine [ˈlɪməziːn] n limusine f.

limp [lɪmp] adj (lettuce) murcho (-cha); (body) flácido(-da); (fabric) mole ◆ vi mancar.

limpet [ˈlɪmpɪt] n lapa f.

line [laɪn] n linha f; (row) fila f; (Am: queue) fila; (of poem, song) verso m; (for washing) varal m (Br), estendal m (Port); (rope) corda; (of business, work) ramo m; (type of product) seleção f ◆ vt (coat, drawers) forrar; **in ~** (aligned) alinhado (-da); **it's a bad ~** a linha está péssima; **the ~ is engaged** a linha está ocupada; **to drop sb a ~** (inf) mandar uma cartinha para alguém; **to stand in ~** (Am) pôr-se na fila.

❏ **line up** vt sep (arrange) organizar ◆ vi entrar na fila.

lined [laɪnd] adj (paper) pautado (-da), de linhas.

linen [ˈlɪnɪn] n (cloth) linho m; (sheets) roupa f de cama.

liner [ˈlaɪnəʳ] n (ship) transatlântico m.

linesman [ˈlaɪnzmən] (pl -men [-mən]) n juiz m de linha.

lineup [ˈlaɪnʌp] n (of players, competitors) seleção f.

linger [ˈlɪŋgəʳ] vi (smell, taste, smoke) permanecer; (person) atrasar-se.

lingerie [ˈlænʒərɪ] n roupa f de baixo (de senhora), lingerie f.

linguist [ˈlɪŋgwɪst] n lingüista mf.

linguistics [lɪŋˈgwɪstɪks] n lingüística f.

lining [ˈlaɪnɪŋ] n (of coat, jacket) forro m; (of brake) lona f (Br), patilha f (Port).

link [lɪŋk] n (connection) relação f ◆ vt ligar; **rail ~** ligação f ferroviária; **road ~** ligação rodoviária.

lino [ˈlaɪnəʊ] n (Brit) linóleo m.

lion [ˈlaɪən] n leão m.

lioness [ˈlaɪənes] n leoa f.

lip [lɪp] n (of person) lábio m.

lip-read (pt & pp lip-read) vi ler os lábios.

lip salve [-sælv] n pomada f para lábios rachados (Br), batom m para o cieiro (Port).

lipstick [ˈlɪpstɪk] n batom m.

liqueur [lɪˈkjʊəʳ] n licor m.

liquid [ˈlɪkwɪd] n líquido m.

liquid crystal display n dispositivo m cristal líquido.

liquidize [ˈlɪkwɪdaɪz] vt (Brit) liquidificar, desfazer.

liquidizer [ˈlɪkwɪdaɪzəʳ] n (Brit) liquidificador m (Br), centrifugador m (Port).

liquor [ˈlɪkəʳ] n (Am) licor m.

liquorice [ˈlɪkərɪs] n alcaçuz m.

liquor store n (Am) loja onde se vendem bebidas alcoólicas para levar.

Lisbon [ˈlɪzbən] n Lisboa s.

lisp [lɪsp] n ceceio m.

list [lɪst] n lista f ◆ vt enumerar.

listed building [ˈlɪstɪd-] n (Brit) edifício declarado de interesse histórico e artístico.

listen [ˈlɪsn] vi: **to ~ (to)** ouvir.

listener [ˈlɪsnəʳ] n (on radio) ouvinte mf.

lit [lɪt] pt & pp → **light**.

liter [ˈliːtəʳ] (Am) = **litre**.

literacy [ˈlɪtərəsɪ] n alfabetismo m.

literal [ˈlɪtərəl] adj literal.

literally [ˈlɪtərəlɪ] adv (actually) literalmente.

literary [ˈlɪtərərɪ] adj literário (-ria).

literate [ˈlɪtərət] adj (able to read and write) alfabetizado(-da); (well-read) erudito(-ta); **computer-~** versado(-da) em computadores.

literature [ˈlɪtrətʃəʳ] n literatura f.

lithe [laɪð] adj ágil.

Lithuania [ˌlɪθjʊˈeɪnjə] n Lituânia f.

litre [ˈliːtəʳ] n (Brit) litro m.

litter [ˈlɪtəʳ] n (rubbish) lixo m.

litterbin [ˈlɪtəbɪn] n (Brit) lata f de lixo (Br), caixote m do lixo (Port).

little [ˈlɪtl] adj pequeno(-na); (distance, time) curto(-ta); (not much) pouco(-ca); (sister, brother) mais novo (nova) ◆ pron pouco m (-ca f) ◆ adv pouco; **as ~ as possible** o menos possível; **~ by ~** pouco a pouco; **a ~** pron & adv um pouco ◆ adj um pouco de.

little finger n (dedo) mindinho m.

live¹ [lɪv] vi (live); (survive) sobreviver; **to ~ with sb** viver com alguém.

❏ **live together** vi viver juntos.

live² [laɪv] adj (alive) vivo(-va); (programme, performance) ao vivo; (wire) eletrificado(-da) ◆ adv ao vivo.

livelihood [ˈlaɪvlɪhʊd] n sustento m, meio m de vida.

lively [ˈlaɪvlɪ] adj (person) alegre; (place, atmosphere) animado(-da).

liven [ˈlaɪvn] : **liven up** vt sep alegrar ◆ vi (person) alegrar-se.

liver ['lɪvə'] n fígado m.

lives [laɪvz] pl → **life**.

livestock ['laɪvstɒk] n gado m.

livid ['lɪvɪd] adj (inf: angry) lívido (-da).

living ['lɪvɪŋ] adj vivo(-va) ♦ n: **to earn a ~** ganhar a vida; **what do you do for a ~?** o que é que você faz (na vida)?

living conditions npl condições fpl de vida.

living room n sala f de estar.

living standards npl nível m de vida.

lizard ['lɪzəd] n lagarto m.

llama ['lɑːmə] n lhama f.

load [ləud] n (thing carried) carga f ♦ vt carregar; **~s of** (inf) toneladas de.

loaf [ləuf] (pl loaves) n: **a ~ (of bread)** um pão de fôrma.

loafers ['ləufəz] npl (shoes) sapatos mpl sem cadarços.

loan [ləun] n empréstimo m ♦ vt emprestar.

loathe [ləuð] vt detestar.

loathsome ['ləuðsəm] adj repugnante.

loaves [ləuvz] pl → **loaf**.

lob [lɒb] n (in tennis) balão m ♦ vt (throw) atirar ao ar, lançar.

lobby ['lɒbɪ] n (hall) entrada f, hall m.

lobe [ləub] n (of ear) lóbulo m.

lobster ['lɒbstə'] n lagosta f.

local ['ləukl] adj local ♦ n (inf) (local person) habitante mf local; (Brit: pub) = bar m da esquina; (Am: bus) ônibus m (local) (Br), autocarro m (urbano) (Port); (Am: train) trem m (Br), comboio m (Port).

local anaesthetic n anestesia f local.

local authority n (Brit) autarquia f.

local call n chamada f local.

local government n administração f local.

locally ['ləukəlɪ] adv (in region) na região; (in neighbourhood) na área.

locate [Brit ləu'keɪt, Am 'ləukeɪt] vt (find) localizar; **to be ~d** ficar OR estar situado.

location [ləu'keɪʃn] n lugar m, localização f.

loch [lɒk, lɒx] n (Scot) lago m.

lock [lɒk] n (on door, drawer) fechadura f; (for bike) cadeado m; (on canal) comporta f ♦ vt fechar com chave ♦ vi

(become stuck) ficar preso.

❏ **lock in** vt sep fechar.

❏ **lock out** vt sep: **I've ~ed myself out** deixei a chave por dentro e não posso entrar.

❏ **lock up** vt sep (imprison) prender ♦ vi fechar tudo à chave.

locker ['lɒkə'] n compartimento m com chave, cacifo m.

locker room n (Am) vestiário m.

locket ['lɒkɪt] n medalhão m.

locksmith ['lɒksmɪθ] n serralheiro m (-ra f).

locomotive [ˌləukə'məutɪv] n locomotiva f.

locum ['ləukəm] n (doctor) substituto m (-ta f).

locust ['ləukəst] n gafanhoto m (viajante).

lodge [lɒdʒ] n (for skiers) refúgio m; (for hunters) pavilhão m de caça ♦ vi alojar-se.

lodger ['lɒdʒə'] n inquilino m (-na f).

lodgings ['lɒdʒɪŋz] npl quarto m alugado (em casa de família).

loft [lɒft] n sótão m.

log [lɒg] n (piece of wood) tora f, lenha f.

logbook ['lɒgbuk] n (of ship, plane) diário m de bordo; (of car) documentação f (do carro).

logic ['lɒdʒɪk] n lógica f.

logical ['lɒdʒɪkl] adj lógico(-ca).

logo ['ləugəu] (pl -s) n logotipo m.

loin [lɔɪn] n lombo m.

loiter ['lɔɪtə'] vi vadiar.

lollipop ['lɒlɪpɒp] n pirulito m (Br), chupa-chupa m (Port).

lollipop lady n (Brit) mulher, que na hora de entrada e saída das aulas, pára o trânsito para as crianças atravessarem em segurança.

lollipop man n (Brit) homem, que na hora de entrada e saída das aulas, pára o trânsito para as crianças atravessarem em segurança.

lolly ['lɒlɪ] n (inf) (lollipop) pirulito m (Br), chupa m (Port); (Brit: ice lolly) picolé m (Br), gelado m (Port).

London ['lʌndən] n Londres s.

Londoner ['lʌndənə'] n londrino m (-na f).

lone [ləun] adj solitário(-ria).

loneliness ['ləunlɪnɪs] n solidão f.

lonely ['ləunlɪ] adj (person) só; (place) isolado(-da).

loner ['ləʊnəʳ] n solitário m (-ria f).

lonesome ['ləʊnsəm] adj (Am) (inf) (person) só; (place) solitário(-ria).

long [lɒŋ] adj comprido(-da); (in time) longo(-ga) ◆ adv muito; **it's 2 metres** ~ mede 2 metros de comprimento; **it's two hours** ~ dura 2 horas; **how** ~ **is it?** (in distance) mede quanto?; (in time) dura quanto tempo?; **to take/be** ~ demorar muito; **a** ~ **time** muito tempo; **all day** ~ durante todo o dia; **as** ~ **as** desde que; **for** ~ (durante) muito tempo; **no** ~**er** já não; **so** ~! (inf) adeus!

❏ **long for** vt fus ansiar por.

long-distance adj (phone call) inter-urbano(-na).

long drink n mistura de bebida alcoólica com suco ou refrigerante servida num copo alto e estreito.

long-haul adj de longa distância.

longing ['lɒŋɪŋ] adj ansioso(-osa) ◆ n (desire) ânsia f, desejo m; (nostalgia) saudade f; **to have a** ~ **for sthg** ansiar por algo.

longitude ['lɒndʒɪtjuːd] n longitude f.

long jump n salto m em comprimento.

long-life adj de longa duração.

longsighted [lɒŋ'saɪtɪd] adj hipermetrope; **to be** ~ ter a vista cansada.

long-standing [-'stændɪŋ] adj de longa data.

long term n: **in the** ~ a longo prazo.

❏ **long-term** adj a longo prazo.

long wave n onda f longa.

longwearing [lɒŋ'weərɪŋ] adj (Am) duradouro(-ra).

longwinded [lɒŋ'wɪndɪd] adj (person) prolixo(-xa); (speech) fastidioso(-osa).

loo [luː] (pl -s) n (Brit: inf) banheiro m (Br), casa f de banho (Port).

look [lʊk] n (glance) olhadela f, olhada f; (appearance) aparência f, look m ◆ vi (with eyes) olhar; (search) procurar; (seem) parecer; **to** ~ **onto** (building, room) ter vista para, dar para; **to have a** ~ (see) dar uma olhada; (search) procurar; (good) ~**s** beleza f; **I'm just** ~**ing** (in shop) estou só olhando; ~ **out!** cuidado!

❏ **look after** vt fus (person) tomar conta de; (matter, arrangements) ocupar-se de.

❏ **look at** vt fus (observe) olhar para; (examine) analisar.

❏ **look for** vt fus procurar.

❏ **look forward to** vt fus esperar (impacientemente).

❏ **look out for** vt fus estar atento a.

❏ **look round** vt fus (town, shop) ver, dar uma volta por ◆ vi (turn head) virar-se, olhar (para trás).

❏ **look up** vt sep (in dictionary, phone book) procurar.

lookout ['lʊkaʊt] n (search): **to be on the** ~ **for sthg** andar à procura de algo.

loom [luːm] n tear m ◆ vi (rise up) erguer-se ameaçadoramente; (date) aproximar-se; (threat) pairar no ar.

❏ **loom up** vi surgir.

loony ['luːnɪ] n (inf) doido m (-da f).

loop [luːp] n argola f.

loophole ['luːphəʊl] n lacuna f.

loose [luːs] adj solto(-ta); (tooth) mole (Br), a abanar (Port); (sweets) avulso (-sa); (clothes) largo(-ga); **to let sb/sthg** ~ soltar alguém/algo.

loose change n dinheiro m trocado, trocados mpl.

loosely ['luːslɪ] adv (hold, connect) sem apertar; (translated) livremente; (associated) mais ou menos.

loosen ['luːsn] vt desapertar.

loot [luːt] n saque m ◆ vt saquear, pilhar.

looting ['luːtɪŋ] n pilhagem f.

lop [lɒp] vt (tree) derramar.

❏ **lop off** vt sep cortar.

lop-sided [-'saɪdɪd] adj torto (torta).

lord [lɔːd] n lorde m.

lorry ['lɒrɪ] n (Brit) caminhão m (Br), camião m (Port).

lorry driver n (Brit) caminhoneiro m (-ra f) (Br), camionista mf (Port).

lose [luːz] (pt & pp lost) vt perder; (subj: watch, clock) atrasar ◆ vi perder; **to** ~ **weight** emagrecer.

loser ['luːzəʳ] n (in contest) perdedor m (-ra f), vencido m (-da f).

loss [lɒs] n (losing) perda f; (of business, company) prejuízo m.

lost [lɒst] pt & pp → **lose** ◆ adj perdido(-da); **to get** ~ (lose way) perder-se.

lost-and-found office n (Am) seção f de perdidos e achados.

lost property office n (Brit) seção f de perdidos e achados.

lot [lɒt] n (at auction) lote m; (Am: car park) estacionamento m; **you take this** ~ **and I'll take the rest** leva estes que

eu levo o resto; **a ~** *(large amount)*
muito(-ta), muitos(-tas) *(pl)*; *(to a great
extent, often)* muito; **a ~ of time** muito
tempo; **a ~ of problems** muitos problemas; **the ~** *(everything)* tudo; **~s
(of)** muito(-ta), muitos(-tas) *(pl)*.
lotion ['ləʊʃn] *n* loção *f*.
lottery ['lɒtərɪ] *n* loteria *f*.
loud [laʊd] *adj (voice, music, noise)*
alto(-ta); *(colour, clothes)* berrante.
loudhailer [,laʊd'heɪlə'] *n (Brit)* megafone *m*, alto-falante *m*.
loudly ['laʊdlɪ] *adv (shout, talk)* alto;
(dress) espalhafatosamente.
loudspeaker [,laʊd'spiːkə'] *n* alto-
falante *m*.
lounge [laʊndʒ] *n (in house)* sala *f* de
estar; *(at airport)* sala de espera.
lounge bar *n (Brit)* sala mais confortável e normalmente mais cara num bar,
hotel, etc.
lousy ['laʊzɪ] *adj (inf: poor-quality)* pés-
simo(-ma).
lout [laʊt] *n* bruto *m* (-ta *f*).
lovable ['lʌvəbl] *adj* adorável.
love [lʌv] *n* amor *m*; *(in tennis)* zero *m*
♦ *vt* amar; *(music, food, art etc)* gostar
muito de, adorar; **l'd ~ a cup of coffee**
um café vinha mesmo a calhar; **to ~
doing sthg** gostar muito de fazer algo;
to be in ~ (with) estar apaixonado
(por); **(with) ~ from** *(in letter)* = beiji-
nhos de.
love affair *n* caso *m* (amoroso).
love life *n* vida *f* amorosa.
lovely ['lʌvlɪ] *adj (very beautiful)*
lindo(-da); *(very nice)* muito agradável.
lover ['lʌvə'] *n* amante *mf*.
loving ['lʌvɪŋ] *adj* carinhoso(-osa).
low [ləʊ] *adj* baixo(-xa); *(opinion)*
fraco(-ca); *(depressed)* para baixo *(Br)*,
em baixo *(Port)* ♦ *n (area of low pressure)* depressão *f*, área *f* de baixa
pressão; **we're ~ on petrol** estamos
quase sem gasolina.
low-alcohol *adj* de baixo teor alcoólico.
low-calorie *adj* de baixas calorias.
low-cut *adj* decotado(-da).
lower ['ləʊə'] *adj* inferior ♦ *vt (move
downwards)* baixar; *(reduce)* reduzir.
lower sixth *n (Brit)* primeiro de dois
anos de preparação para os "A levels".
low-fat *adj* com baixo teor de gordura.
lowly ['ləʊlɪ] *adj* humilde.

low-lying *adj* baixo(-xa).
low tide *n* maré-baixa *f*.
loyal ['lɔɪəl] *adj* leal.
loyalty ['lɔɪəltɪ] *n* lealdade *f*.
lozenge ['lɒzɪndʒ] *n (for throat)* pastilha *f* para a garganta.
LP *n* LP *m*.
L-plate *n (Brit)* placa obrigatória num
carro dirigido por alguém que ainda não
tirou carteira.
Ltd *(abbr of limited)* Ltda *(Br)*, Lda
(Port).
lubricate ['luːbrɪkeɪt] *vt* lubrificar.
lucid ['luːsɪd] *adj (writing, account)*
claro(-ra); *(person)* lúcido(-da).
luck [lʌk] *n* sorte *f*; **bad ~!** pouca
sorte!, que azar!; **good ~!** boa sorte!;
with ~ com um pouco de sorte.
luckily ['lʌkɪlɪ] *adv* felizmente, por
sorte.
lucky ['lʌkɪ] *adj (person)* sortudo (-da),
com sorte; *(event, situation)* feliz; *(number, colour)* de sorte; **to be ~** ter sorte.
lucrative ['luːkrətɪv] *adj* lucrativo
(-va).
ludicrous ['luːdɪkrəs] *adj* ridículo(-la).
lug [lʌg] *vt (inf)* arrastar.
luggage ['lʌgɪdʒ] *n* bagagem *f*.
luggage compartment *n* compartimento *m* para a bagagem.
luggage locker *n* guarda-volumes
m inv com chave *(Br)*, cacifo *m* (para
bagagem) *(Port)*.
luggage rack *n (on train)* porta-
bagagem *m*.
lukewarm ['luːkwɔːm] *adj* morno
(morna).
lull [lʌl] *n (in conversation)* pausa *f*; *(in
storm)* calmaria *f*.
lullaby ['lʌləbaɪ] *n* canção *f* de embalar.
lumbago [lʌm'beɪgəʊ] *n* lumbago *m*.
lumber ['lʌmbər] *n (Am: timber)*
madeira *f*.
lumberjack ['lʌmbədʒæk] *n* lenhador
m (-ra *f*).
luminous ['luːmɪnəs] *adj* luminoso
(-osa).
lump [lʌmp] *n (of coal, mud, butter)*
pedaço *m*; *(of sugar)* torrão *m*; *(on body)*
caroço *m*; *(on head)* galo *m*.
lump sum *n* quantia *f* global.
lumpy ['lʌmpɪ] *adj (sauce)* encaroça-
do(-da) *(Br)*, grumoso(-osa) *(Port)*;
(mattress) cheio (cheia) de altos e baixos.

lunatic ['luːnətɪk] *n (pej)* louco *m* (-ca *f*), maluco *m* (-ca *f*).

lunch [lʌntʃ] *n* almoço *m*; **to have ~** almoçar.

luncheon ['lʌntʃən] *n (fml)* almoço *m*.

luncheon meat *n tipo de mortadela enlatada.*

luncheon voucher *n (Brit)* ticket-refeição *m*.

lunch hour *n* hora *f* de almoço.

lunchtime ['lʌntʃtaɪm] *n* hora *f* de almoço.

lung [lʌŋ] *n* pulmão *m*.

lunge [lʌndʒ] *vi:* **to ~ at** atirar-se a.

lurch [lɜːtʃ] *vi (person)* cambalear.

lure [ljʊəˈ] *vt* atrair.

lurid ['ljʊərɪd] *adj (clothes, carpet)* garrido(-da); *(story, details)* chocante.

lurk [lɜːk] *vi (person)* estar à espreita *(escondido)*.

luscious ['lʌʃəs] *adj (fruit)* apetitoso (-osa).

lush [lʌʃ] *adj* luxuriante.

lust [lʌst] *n (sexual desire)* luxúria *f.*

Luxembourg ['lʌksəmbɜːg] *n* Luxemburgo *m.*

luxurious [lʌgˈʒʊərɪəs] *adj* luxuoso (-osa).

luxury ['lʌkʃərɪ] *adj* de luxo ♦ *n* luxo *m.*

LW *(abbr of long wave)* LW.

Lycra® ['laɪkrə] *n* Lycra® *f* ♦ *adj* de Lycra®.

lying ['laɪɪŋ] *cont* → **lie.**

lynch [lɪntʃ] *vt* linchar.

lyrics ['lɪrɪks] *npl* letra *f (de música).*

M

m (abbr of metre) m ◆ abbr = **mile**.
M (Brit: abbr of motorway) AE; (abbr of medium) M.
MA abbr = **Master of Arts**.
mac [mæk] n (Brit: inf: coat) impermeável m.
macaroni [,mækə'rəʊnɪ] n macarrão m.
macaroni cheese n macarrão m com queijo.
mace [meɪs] n (spice) macis m; (ornamental rod) cetro m.
machine [mə'ʃiːn] n máquina f.
machinegun [mə'ʃiːngʌn] n metralhadora f.
machinery [mə'ʃiːnərɪ] n maquinaria f.
machine-washable adj lavável à máquina.
macho ['mætʃəʊ] adj (inf) (man) macho; (attitude, opinions) machista.
mackerel ['mækrəl] (pl inv) n cavala f.
mackintosh ['mækɪntɒʃ] n (Brit) impermeável m.
mad [mæd] adj maluco(-ca); (angry) furioso(-osa); (uncontrolled) louco(-ca); **to be ~ about** (inf: like a lot) ser doido(-da) por; **like ~** como um louco OR doido.
Madagascar [,mædə'gæskəʳ] n Madagáscar s.
Madam ['mædəm] n (form of address) senhora f.
madden ['mædn] vt enfurecer.
made [meɪd] pt & pp → **make**.
madeira [mə'dɪərə] n (wine) vinho m da Madeira.
Madeira [mə'dɪərə] n (island) Madeira f.
made-to-measure adj feito (-ta) sob medida.
made-up adj (face, lips) maquiado (-da), pintado(-da); (story, excuse) inventado(-da).

madly ['mædlɪ] adv (frantically) como um louco (uma louca); **~ in love** completamente apaixonado(-da).
madman ['mædmən] (pl **madmen** [-mən]) n louco m.
madness ['mædnɪs] n (foolishness) loucura f, maluquice f.
Madrid [mə'drɪd] n Madri s.
Mafia ['mæfɪə] n: **the ~** a Máfia.
magazine [,mægə'ziːn] n (journal) revista f.
maggot ['mægət] n larva f.
magic ['mædʒɪk] n magia f.
magical ['mædʒɪkl] adj mágico(-ca).
magician [mə'dʒɪʃn] n (conjurer) mágico m (-ca f).
magistrate ['mædʒɪstreɪt] n magistrado m (-da f).
magnet ['mægnɪt] n ímã m.
magnetic [mæg'netɪk] adj magnético(-ca).
magnificent [mæg'nɪfɪsənt] adj magnífico(-ca).
magnify ['mægnɪfaɪ] vt (image) ampliar.
magnifying glass ['mægnɪfaɪɪŋ-] n lupa f.
magpie ['mægpaɪ] n pega f.
mahogany [mə'hɒgənɪ] n mogno m.
maid [meɪd] n empregada f.
maiden name ['meɪdn-] n nome m de solteira.
mail [meɪl] n correio m ◆ vt (Am) mandar OR enviar pelo correio.
mailbox ['meɪlbɒks] n (Am) (letterbox) caixa f do correio; (postbox) caixa f do correio (Br), marco m do correio (Port).
mailman ['meɪlmən] (pl **-men** [-mən]) n (Am) carteiro m.
mail order n venda f por correspondência.
mailshot ['meɪlʃɒt] n publicidade f

enviada pelo correio.

maim [meɪm] *vt* mutilar.

main [meɪn] *adj* principal.

main course *n* prato *m* principal.

main deck *n* convés *m* principal.

mainland ['meɪnlənd] *n*: **the ~** o continente.

main line *n* ferrovia *f* principal *(Br)*, linha *f* férrea principal *(Port)*.

mainly ['meɪnlɪ] *adv* principalmente.

main road *n* rua *f* principal.

mains [meɪnz] *npl*: **the ~** a rede.

mainstream ['meɪnstriːm] *adj* predominante ♦ *n*: **the ~** a corrente atual.

main street *n (Am)* rua *f* principal.

maintain [meɪn'teɪn] *vt* manter.

maintenance ['meɪntənəns] *n (of car, machine)* manutenção *f*; *(money)* pensão *f* alimentícia *(Br)*, alimentos *mpl (Port)*.

maisonette [,meɪzə'net] *n (Brit)* dúplex *m*.

maize [meɪz] *n* milho *m*.

majestic [mə'dʒestɪk] *adj* majestoso (-osa).

majesty ['mædʒəstɪ] *n* majestade *f*.
❑ **Majesty** *n*: **His/Her/Your ~** Sua Majestade.

major ['meɪdʒəʳ] *adj (important)* importante; *(most important)* principal ♦ *n (MIL)* major *m* ♦ *vi (Am)*: **to ~ in** especializar-se em *(na universidade)*.

majority [mə'dʒɒrətɪ] *n* maioria *f*.

major road *n* estrada *f* principal.

make [meɪk] *(pt & pp* **made)** *vt* 1. *(produce, manufacture)* fazer; **to be made of** ser feito de; **to ~ lunch/supper** fazer o almoço/jantar; **made in Japan** fabricado no Japão.
2. *(perform, do)* fazer; **to ~ a mistake** cometer um erro, enganar-se; **to ~ a phone call** dar um telefonema.
3. *(cause to be)* tornar; **to ~ sthg better** melhorar algo; **to ~ sb happy** fazer alguém feliz; **to ~ sthg safer** tornar algo mais seguro.
4. *(cause to do, force)* fazer; **to ~ sb do sthg** obrigar alguém a fazer algo; **it made her laugh** isso a fez rir.
5. *(amount to, total)* ser; **that ~s £5** são 5 libras.
6. *(calculate)*: **I ~ it seven o'clock** calculo que sejam sete horas; **I ~ it £4** segundo os meus cálculos são 4 libras.

7. *(profit, loss)* ter.
8. *(inf: arrive in time for)*: **we didn't ~ the 10 o'clock train** não conseguimos apanhar o trem das 10.
9. *(friend, enemy)* fazer.
10. *(have qualities for)* dar; **this would ~ a lovely bedroom** isto dava um lindo quarto.
11. *(bed)* fazer.
12. *(in phrases)*: **to ~ do** contentar-se; **to ~ good** *(loss)* compensar; *(damage)* reparar; **to ~ it** *(arrive on time)* conseguir chegar a tempo; *(be able to go)* poder ir.
♦ *n (of product)* marca *f*.
❑ **make out** *vt sep (cheque, receipt)* passar; *(form)* preencher; *(see)* distinguir; *(hear)* perceber, entender.
❑ **make up** *vt sep (invent)* inventar; *(comprise)* constituir; *(difference, extra)* cobrir.
❑ **make up for** *vt fus* compensar.

make-believe *n* invenção *f*.

maker ['meɪkəʳ] *n (of film, programme)* criador *m* (-ra *f*); *(of product)* fabricante *mf*.

makeshift ['meɪkʃɪft] *adj* improvisado(-da).

make-up *n (cosmetics)* maquiagem *f*.

malaria [mə'leərɪə] *n* malária *f*.

Malaysia [mə'leɪzɪə] *n* Malásia *f*.

male [meɪl] *adj (person)* masculino (-na); *(animal)* macho ♦ *n (animal)* macho *m*.

malevolent [mə'levələnt] *adj* malévolo(-la).

malfunction [mæl'fʌŋkʃn] *vi (fml)* funcionar mal.

malice ['mælɪs] *n* rancor *m*.

malicious [mə'lɪʃəs] *adj* maldoso (-osa).

malignant [mə'lɪgnənt] *adj (disease, tumour)* maligno(-gna).

mall [mɔːl] *n* centro *m* comercial.

mallet ['mælɪt] *n* maço *m*.

malnutrition [,mælnjuː'trɪʃn] *n* subnutrição *f*.

malt [mɔːlt] *n* malte *m*.

Malta ['mɔːltə] *n* Malta *s*.

maltreat [,mæl'triːt] *vt* maltratar.

malt whisky *n* uísque *m* de malte.

mammal ['mæml] *n* mamífero *m*.

mammoth ['mæməθ] *adj (effort, task)* tremendo(-da); *(tower, statue)* gigantesco(-ca).

man [mæn] *n* homem *m*; *(mankind)* o Homem ◆ *vt (phones, office)*: **manned 24 hours a day** aberto 24 horas (por dia).

manage ['mænɪdʒ] *vt (company, business)* gerir; *(suitcase)* poder com; *(job)* conseguir fazer; *(food)* conseguir comer OR acabar ◆ *vi (cope)* conseguir; **can you ~ Friday?** sexta-feira está bem para você?; **to ~ to do sthg** conseguir fazer algo.

manageable ['mænɪdʒəbl] *adj (task, operation)* viável, possível; *(child)* fácil de controlar; *(rate)* controlável.

management ['mænɪdʒmənt] *n (people in charge)* direção *f*, administração *f*; *(control, running)* gestão *f*.

manager ['mænɪdʒəʳ] *n (of business, bank, shop)* gerente *mf*; *(of sports team)* = treinador *m*.

manageress [,mænɪdʒə'res] *n (of business, bank, shop)* gerente *f*.

managing director ['mænɪdʒɪŋ-] *n* diretor *m* (-ra *f*) geral.

mandarin ['mændərɪn] *n (fruit)* tangerina *f*, mandarina *f*.

mane [meɪn] *n (of lion)* juba *f*; *(of horse)* crina *f*.

maneuver [mə'nuːvər] *(Am)* = **manoeuvre**.

mangetout [,mɒnʒ'tuː] *n* ervilha *f* de quebrar, ervilha-torta *f*.

mangle ['mæŋgl] *vt (crush)* amassar; *(mutilate)* mutilar.

mango ['mæŋgəʊ] *(pl* -s OR -es) *n* manga *f*.

Manhattan [mæn'hætən] *n* Manhattan *s*.

manhole ['mænhəʊl] *n* poço *m* de inspeção.

manhood ['mænhʊd] *n (age)* idade *f* adulta.

maniac ['meɪnɪæk] *n (inf: wild person)* maníaco *m* (-ca *f*), louco *m* (-ca *f*).

manic ['mænɪk] *adj* maníaco(-ca).

manicure ['mænɪkjʊəʳ] *n* manicure *f*.

manifesto [,mænɪ'festəʊ] *(pl* -s OR -es) *n* manifesto *m*.

manifold ['mænɪfəʊld] *n (AUT)* cano *m* de distribuição.

manipulate [mə'nɪpjʊleɪt] *vt (person)* manipular; *(machine, controls)* manobrar.

mankind [mæn'kaɪnd] *n* a humanidade.

manly ['mænlɪ] *adj* viril.

man-made *adj (lake)* artificial; *(fibre, fabric)* sintético(-ca).

manner ['mænəʳ] *n (way)* maneira *f*. ❏ **manners** *npl* maneiras *fpl*.

mannerism ['mænərɪzm] *n* jeito *m*.

manoeuvre [mə'nuːvəʳ] *n (Brit)* manobra *f* ◆ *vt (Brit)* manobrar.

manor ['mænəʳ] *n* = solar *m*, casa *f* senhorial.

mansion ['mænʃn] *n* mansão *f*.

manslaughter ['mæn,slɔːtəʳ] *n* homicídio *m* involuntário.

mantelpiece ['mæntlpiːs] *n* consolo *m* de lareira *(Br)*, prateleira *f* da lareira *(Port)*.

manual ['mænjʊəl] *adj* manual ◆ *n* manual *m*.

manufacture [,mænjʊ'fæktʃəʳ] *n* fabricação *f*, fabrico *m* ◆ *vt* fabricar.

manufacturer [,mænjʊ'fæktʃərəʳ] *n* fabricante *m*.

manure [mə'njʊəʳ] *n* estrume *m*.

manuscript ['mænjʊskrɪpt] *n* manuscrito *m*.

many ['menɪ] *(compar* **more**, *superl* **most)** *adj* muitos(-tas) ◆ *pron* muitos *mpl* (-tas *fpl*); **as ~ as** tantos(-tas) como; **take as ~ as you like** leve tantos quantos quiser; **twice as ~ as** o dobro de; **how ~?** quantos(-tas)?; **so ~** tantos(-tas); **too ~ people** gente demais.

map [mæp] *n* mapa *m*.

maple ['meɪpl] *n* ácer *m*, bordo *m*.

mar [mɑːʳ] *vt* prejudicar.

Mar. *abbr* = **March**.

marathon ['mærəθɒn] *n* maratona *f*.

marble ['mɑːbl] *n (stone)* mármore *m*; *(glass ball)* bola *f* de gude *(Br)*, berlinde *m (Port)*.

march [mɑːtʃ] *n (demonstration)* passeata *f (Br)*, manifestação *f (Port)* ◆ *vi (walk quickly)* marchar.

March [mɑːtʃ] *n* março *m*, → **September**.

marcher ['mɑːtʃəʳ] *n (protester)* manifestante *mf*.

mare [meəʳ] *n* égua *f*.

margarine [,mɑːdʒə'riːn] *n* margarina *f*.

marge [mɑːdʒ] *n (inf)* margarina *f*.

margin ['mɑːdʒɪn] *n* margem *f*.

marginally ['mɑːdʒɪnəlɪ] *adv* ligeiramente.

marigold ['mærɪɡəʊld] *n* malmequer *m*.

marina [mə'riːnə] *n* marina *f*.

marinated ['mærɪneɪtɪd] *adj* marinado(-da).

marine [mə'riːn] *adj* *(underwater)* marítimo(-ma) ◆ *n (Brit: in the navy)* fuzileiro *m* (-ra *f*) naval; *(Am: in the Marine Corps)* marine *mf*.

marital status ['mærɪtl-] *n* estado *m* civil.

mark [mɑːk] *n* marca *f*; *(SCH)* nota *f* ◆ *vt* marcar; *(correct)* corrigir; **(gas)** ~ **five** número cinco do termóstato (de forno a gás).

marked [mɑːkt] *adj (noticeable)* sensível.

marker ['mɑːkəʳ] *n (sign)* marca *f*.

marker pen *n* marcador *m*.

market ['mɑːkɪt] *n* mercado *m*.

market garden *n* horta *f* para fins comerciais *(Br)*, viveiro *m* agrícola *(Port)*.

marketing ['mɑːkɪtɪŋ] *n* marketing *m*.

marketplace ['mɑːkɪtpleɪs] *n* mercado *m*.

marking ['mɑːkɪŋ] *n (of exams, homework)* correção *f*.

❑ **markings** *npl (on road)* marcas *fpl* rodoviárias.

marksman ['mɑːksmən] *(pl* -**men** [-mən]) *n* atirador perito *m*.

marmalade ['mɑːməleɪd] *n* geléia *f* de laranja *(ou outro citrino)*.

maroon [mə'ruːn] *adj* grená.

marooned [mə'ruːnd] *adj* isolado(-da), preso(-sa).

marquee [mɑː'kiː] *n* tenda *f* grande.

marriage ['mærɪdʒ] *n* casamento *m*.

married ['mærɪd] *adj* casado(-da); **to get** ~ casar-se.

marrow ['mærəʊ] *n (vegetable)* abóbora *f*.

marry ['mærɪ] *vt* casar com ◆ *vi* casar-se, casar.

Mars [mɑːz] *n* Marte *m*.

marsh [mɑːʃ] *n* pântano *m*.

martial arts [mɑː'ʃl-] *npl* artes *fpl* marciais.

martyr ['mɑːtəʳ] *n* mártir *mf*.

marvel ['mɑːvl] *n* maravilha *f*; **to** ~ **at** sthg maravilhar-se com algo.

marvellous ['mɑːvələs] *adj (Brit)* maravilhoso(-osa).

marvelous ['mɑːvələs] *(Am)* = **marvellous**.

Marxism ['mɑːksɪzm] *n* marxismo *m*.

Marxist ['mɑːksɪst] *adj* marxista ◆ *n* marxista *mf*.

marzipan ['mɑːzɪpæn] *n* maçapão *m*.

mascara [mæs'kɑːrə] *n* rímel® *m*.

masculine ['mæskjʊlɪn] *adj* masculino(-na).

mash [mæʃ] *vt* desfazer.

mashed potatoes [mæʃt-] *npl* purê *m* (de batata).

mask [mɑːsk] *n* máscara *f*.

mason ['meɪsn] *n (stonemason)* pedreiro *m*; *(Freemason)* maçon *m*.

masonry ['meɪsnrɪ] *n (stones)* alvenaria *f*.

mass [mæs] *n (large amount)* monte *m*; *(RELIG)* missa *f*; ~**es (of)** *(inf: lots)* montes (de).

massacre ['mæsəkəʳ] *n* massacre *m*.

massage [*Brit* 'mæsɑːʒ, *Am* mə'sɑːʒ] *n* massagem *f* ◆ *vt* massajar.

masseur [mæ'sɜːʳ] *n* massagista *m*.

masseuse [mæ'sɜːz] *n* massagista *f*.

massive ['mæsɪv] *adj* enorme.

mass media *npl*: **the** ~ os meios de comunicação de massa.

mast [mɑːst] *n (on boat)* mastro *m*.

master ['mɑːstəʳ] *n (at school)* professor *m*; *(of servant)* patrão *m*; *(of dog)* dono *m* ◆ *vt (skill, language)* dominar.

Master of Arts *n (titular de um)* mestrado em letras.

Master of Science *n (titular de um)* mestrado em ciências.

masterpiece ['mɑːstəpiːs] *n* obra-prima *f*.

master's degree *n* mestrado *m*.

mastery ['mɑːstərɪ] *n* domínio *m*.

mat [mæt] *n (small rug)* tapete *m*; *(on table)* descanso *m* (Br), individual *m* (Port).

match [mætʃ] *n (for lighting)* fósforo *m*; *(game)* jogo *m*, encontro *m* ◆ *vt (in colour, design)* condizer com, combinar com; *(be the same as)* corresponder a; *(be as good as)* equiparar-se a ◆ *vi (in colour, design)* condizer, combinar.

matchbox ['mætʃbɒks] *n* caixa *f* de fósforos.

matching ['mætʃɪŋ] *adj* que combina.

mate [meɪt] *n (inf: friend)* amigo *m* (-ga *f*) ◆ *vi* acasalar, acasalar-se.

material [mə'tɪərɪəl] *n* material *m*; *(cloth)* tecido *m*.

❑ **materials** *npl (equipment)* material *m*.

materialistic [mə,tɪərɪəˈlɪstɪk] *adj* materialista.

maternal [məˈtɜ:nl] *adj* maternal.

maternity dress [məˈtɜ:nətɪ-] *n* vestido *m* de gestante.

maternity leave [məˈtɜ:nətɪ-] *n* licença-maternidade *f (Br)*, licença *f* de parto *(Port)*.

maternity ward [məˈtɜ:nətɪ-] *n* enfermaria *f* para parturientes.

math [mæθ] *(Am)* = maths.

mathematical [,mæθəˈmætɪkl] *adj* matemático(-ca).

mathematics [,mæθəˈmætɪks] *n* matemática *f*.

maths [mæθs] *n (Brit)* matemática *f*.

matinée [ˈmætɪneɪ] *n* matinê *f*.

matriculation [mə,trɪkjʊˈleɪʃn] *n (at university)* matrícula *f*.

matrix [ˈmeɪtrɪks] *(pl* -trixes OR -trices [-trɪsi:z]) *n (context, framework)* contexto *m*.

matron [ˈmeɪtrən] *n (Brit) (in hospital)* enfermeira-chefe *f; (in school)* enfermeira *f*.

matt [mæt] *adj* fosco(-ca) *(Br)*, mate *(Port)*.

matted [ˈmætɪd] *adj* eriçado(-da), emaranhado(-da).

matter [ˈmætər] *n (issue, situation)* assunto *m; (physical material)* matéria *f* ♦ *vi* interessar; **it doesn't ~** não tem importância; **no ~ what happens** aconteça o que acontecer; **there's something the ~ with my car** o meu carro está com algum problema; **what's the ~?** qual é o problema?; **as a ~ of course** naturalmente; **as a ~ of fact** aliás, na verdade.

matter-of-fact *adj (person)* terra-a-terra *(inv)*, prático(-ca); *(voice)* calmo (-ma).

mattress [ˈmætrɪs] *n* colchão *m*.

mature [məˈtjʊər] *adj* maduro(-ra); *(cheese)* curado(-da).

mature student *n (Brit)* estudante universitário com mais de 25 anos.

maul [mɔ:l] *vt* ferir gravemente.

mauve [məʊv] *adj* cor-de-malva *(inv)*.

max. [mæks] *(abbr of maximum)* máx.

maximum [ˈmæksɪməm] *adj* máximo (-ma) ♦ *n* máximo *m*.

may [meɪ] *aux vb* 1. *(expressing possibility)* poder; **it ~ be done as follows** pode ser feito do seguinte modo; **it ~ rain** pode chover; **they ~ have got lost** eles talvez tenham se perdido. 2. *(expressing permission)* poder; **~ I smoke?** posso fumar?; **you ~ sit, if you wish** pode sentar-se, se quiser. 3. *(when conceding a point)*: **it ~ be a long walk, but it's worth it** pode ser longe, mas vale a pena o esforço.

May *n* maio *m*, → **September**.

maybe [ˈmeɪbi:] *adv* talvez.

May Day *n* o Primeiro de Maio.

mayhem [ˈmeɪhem] *n* caos *m inv*.

mayonnaise [,meɪəˈneɪz] *n* maionese *f*.

mayor [meər] *n* = Prefeito *m (Br)*, = Presidente *m* da Câmara *(Port)*.

mayoress [ˈmeərɪs] *n* = Prefeita *f (Br)*, = Presidente *f* da Câmara *(Port)*.

maze [meɪz] *n* labirinto *m*.

MB *(abbr of megabyte)* MB *m*.

me [mi:] *pron me; (after prep)* mim; **she knows ~** ela me conhece *(Br)*, ela conhece-me *(Port)*; **it's ~** sou eu; **send it to ~** envie ele para mim *(Br)*, envia-mo *(Port)*; **tell ~** diga-me; **he's worse than ~** ele é pior que eu; **it's for ~** é para mim; **with ~** comigo.

meadow [ˈmedəʊ] *n* prado *m*.

meager [ˈmi:gər] *(Am)* = meagre.

meagre [ˈmi:gər] *adj (Brit) (amount, pay)* miserável.

meal [mi:l] *n* refeição *f*.

mealtime [ˈmi:ltaɪm] *n* hora *f* da refeição OR de comer.

mean [mi:n] *(pt & pp* meant) *adj (miserly)* sovina; *(unkind)* mau (má) ♦ *vt* querer dizer; *(be a sign of)* ser sinal de; **I ~ it** estou falando a sério; **it ~s a lot to me** é muito importante para mim; **to ~ to do sthg** ter a intenção de fazer algo, tencionar fazer algo; **to be meant to do sthg** dever fazer algo; **it's meant to be good** dizem que é bom.

meaning [ˈmi:nɪŋ] *n* significado *m*.

meaningful [ˈmi:nɪŋfʊl] *adj (glance, look)* expressivo(-va); *(relationship, remark)* profundo(-da).

meaningless [ˈmi:nɪŋlɪs] *adj* sem sentido.

means [mi:nz] *(pl inv) n (method)* meio *m* ♦ *npl (money)* recursos *mpl*; **by all ~!** claro que sim!; **by ~ of** através de.

meant [ment] *pt & pp* → **mean**.

meantime [ˈmi:ntaɪm] : **in the meantime** *adv* entretanto.

meanwhile [ˈmi:nwaɪl] *adv* entretanto, enquanto isso.

measles [ˈmi:zlz] *n* sarampo *m*.

measly ['miːzlɪ] *adj (inf)* mísero(-ra).

measure ['mɛʒəʳ] *vt* medir ♦ *n (step, action)* medida *f; (of alcohol)* dose *f;* **the room ~s 10 m²** o quarto mede 10 m².

measurement ['mɛʒəmənt] *n* medida *f.*

❏ **measurements** *npl (of person)* medidas *fpl.*

meat [miːt] *n* carne *f;* **red ~** carnes vermelhas *(pl);* **white ~** carnes brancas *(pl).*

meatball ['miːtbɔːl] *n* almôndega *f.*

meat pie *n (Brit)* empada *f* de carne.

mechanic [mɪ'kænɪk] *n* mecânico *m* (-ca *f).*

mechanical [mɪ'kænɪkl] *adj* mecânico(-ca).

mechanism ['mɛkənɪzm] *n (of machine, device)* mecanismo *m.*

medal ['mɛdl] *n* medalha *f.*

medallion [mɪ'dæljən] *n* medalhão *m.*

meddle ['mɛdl] *vi:* **to ~ (in sthg)** meter-se (em algo).

media ['miːdjə] *n or npl:* **the ~** os meios de comunicação.

median ['miːdjən] *n (Am: of road)* faixa *f* divisora central.

mediate ['miːdɪeɪt] *vi* servir de mediador; **to ~ between** servir de mediador entre.

medical ['mɛdɪkl] *adj* médico(-ca) ♦ *n* check-up *m.*

medicated ['mɛdɪkeɪtɪd] *adj* medicinal.

medication [,mɛdɪ'keɪʃn] *n* medicamento *m.*

medicine ['mɛdsɪn] *n (substance)* medicamento *m; (science)* medicina *f.*

medicine cabinet *n* armário *m* para medicamentos.

medieval [,mɛdɪ'iːvl] *adj* medieval.

mediocre [,miːdɪ'əʊkəʳ] *adj* medíocre.

meditate ['mɛdɪteɪt] *vi* meditar; **to ~ on sthg** meditar sobre algo.

Mediterranean [,mɛdɪtə'reɪnjən] *n:* **the ~ (region)** o Mediterrâneo; **the ~ (Sea)** o (mar) Mediterrâneo.

medium ['miːdjəm] *adj* médio(-dia). *(wine)* meio-seco (meia-seca).

medium-dry *adj* meio-seco (meia-seca).

medium-sized [-saɪzd] *adj* de tamanho médio.

medium wave *n* onda *f* média.

medley ['mɛdlɪ] *n (CULIN)* seleção *f.*

meek [miːk] *adj (person, voice)* dócil;

(behaviour) submisso(-a).

meet [miːt] *(pt & pp* **met)** *vt (by arrangement)* encontrar-se com; *(members of club, committee)* reunir-se com; *(by chance)* encontrar; *(get to know)* conhecer; *(go to collect)* ir buscar; *(need, requirement)* satisfazer; *(cost, expenses)* cobrir ♦ *vi (by arrangement)* encontrar-se; *(club, committee)* reunir-se; *(by chance)* encontrar-se; *(get to know each other)* conhecer-se; *(intersect)* cruzar-se; **~ me at the bar** encontre-se comigo no bar.

❏ **meet up** *vi* encontrar-se.

❏ **meet with** *vt fus (problems, resistance)* encontrar; *(Am: by arrangement)* encontrar-se com.

meeting ['miːtɪŋ] *n (for business)* reunião *f.*

meeting point *n* ponto *m* de encontro.

megabyte ['mɛgəbaɪt] *n (COMPUT)* megabyte *m.*

megaphone ['mɛgəfəʊn] *n* megafone *m,* alto-falante *m.*

melancholy ['mɛlənkəlɪ] *adj* melancólico(-ca).

mellow ['mɛləʊ] *adj (sound, colour, wine)* suave; *(person)* descontraído(-da) ♦ *vi* tornar-se mais brando(-da).

melody ['mɛlədɪ] *n* melodia *f.*

melon ['mɛlən] *n* melão *m.*

melt [mɛlt] *vi* derreter.

member ['mɛmbəʳ] *n (of party, group)* membro *m; (of club)* sócio *m* (-cia *f).*

Member of Congress *n* congressista *mf,* membro *m* do Congresso.

Member of Parliament *n* = deputado *m* (-da *f).*

membership ['mɛmbəʃɪp] *n (of party, club)* filiação *f;* **the ~** *(of party)* os membros; *(of club)* os sócios.

membership card *n* carteira *f* de membro OR filiação.

memento [mɪ'mɛntəʊ] *(pl* **-s** OR **-es)** *n* lembrança *f.*

memo ['mɛməʊ] *(pl* **-s)** *n* memorando *m.*

memoirs ['mɛmwɑːz] *fpl* memórias *fpl.*

memorandum [,mɛmə'rændəm] *(pl* **-da** [-də]) *n* memorando *m.*

memorial [mɪ'mɔːrɪəl] *n* monumento *m* comemorativo.

memorize ['mɛməraɪz] *vt* memorizar, decorar.

memory ['mɛmərɪ] n memória f; (thing remembered) lembrança f.

men [mɛn] pl → **man.**

menace ['mɛnəs] n (threat, danger) perigo m ◆ vt (threaten) ameaçar; (frighten) aterrorizar.

menacing ['mɛnəsɪŋ] adj ameaçador(-ra).

mend [mɛnd] vt arranjar.

meningitis [ˌmɛnɪn'dʒaɪtɪs] n meningite f.

menopause ['mɛnəpɔːz] n menopausa f.

men's room n (Am) banheiro m dos homens (Br), casa f de banho dos homens (Port).

menstruate ['mɛnstrʊeɪt] vi menstruar.

menstruation [ˌmɛnstrʊ'eɪʃn] n menstruação f.

menswear ['mɛnzweər] n roupa f de homem.

mental ['mɛntl] adj mental.

mental hospital n hospital m psiquiátrico.

mentality [mɛn'tælɪtɪ] n mentalidade f.

mentally handicapped ['mɛntlɪ-] adj deficiente mental ◆ npl: **the ~** os deficientes mentais.

mentally ill ['mɛntlɪ-] adj: **to be ~** ser doente mental.

mention ['mɛnʃn] vt mencionar; **don't ~ it!** de nada!, não tem de quê!

menu ['mɛnjuː] n (of food) cardápio m (Br), ementa f (Port); (COMPUT) menu m; **children's ~** menu infantil OR para crianças.

meow [mɪ'aʊ] (Am) = **miaow.**

merchandise ['mɜːtʃəndaɪz] n mercadoria f.

merchant ['mɜːtʃənt] n comerciante mf.

merchant marine (Am) = **merchant navy.**

merchant navy n (Brit) marinha f mercante.

merciful ['mɜːsɪfʊl] adj (person) misericordioso(-osa), piedoso(-osa).

merciless ['mɜːsɪlɪs] adj (person, enemy, tyrant) impiedoso(-osa); (criticism, teasing, attack) implacável.

mercury ['mɜːkjʊrɪ] n mercúrio m.

Mercury ['mɜːkjʊrɪ] n (planet) Mercúrio m.

mercy ['mɜːsɪ] n misericórdia f.

mere [mɪər] adj mero(-ra).

merely ['mɪəlɪ] adv apenas.

merge [mɜːdʒ] vi (combine) juntar-se, unir-se; **"merge"** (Am) sinal que avisa os motoristas que vão entrar na auto-estrada que devem circular pela faixa da direita.

merger ['mɜːdʒər] n fusão f.

meringue [mə'ræŋ] n merengue m, suspiro m.

merit ['mɛrɪt] n mérito m; (in exam) = bom m.

mermaid ['mɜːmeɪd] n sereia f.

merry ['mɛrɪ] adj alegre; **Merry Christmas!** Feliz Natal!

merry-go-round n carrossel m.

mesh [mɛʃ] n malha f (de rede).

mesmerize ['mɛzməraɪz] vt: **to be ~d by** ficar fascinado(-da) com.

mess [mɛs] n confusão f; **in a ~** (untidy) em desordem, de pernas para o ar.

❏ **mess about** vi (inf) (have fun) divertir-se; (behave foolishly) armar-se em tolo; **to ~ about with sthg** (interfere) mexer em algo.

❏ **mess up** vt sep (inf: ruin, spoil) estragar.

message ['mɛsɪdʒ] n mensagem f; **are there any ~s (for me)?** há algum recado (para mim)?

messenger ['mɛsɪndʒər] n mensageiro m (-ra f).

messy ['mɛsɪ] adj (untidy) desarrumado(-da).

met [mɛt] pt & pp → **meet.**

metal ['mɛtl] adj metálico(-ca), de metal ◆ n metal m.

metallic [mɪ'tælɪk] adj (sound) metálico(-ca); (paint, finish) metalizado(-da).

metalwork ['mɛtlwɜːk] n (craft) trabalho m com metal.

meteor ['mɪːtɪər] n meteoro m.

meteorology [ˌmiːtjə'rɒlədʒɪ] n meteorologia f.

meter ['mɪːtər] n (device) contador m; (Am) = **metre.**

method ['mɛθəd] n método m.

methodical [mɪ'θɒdɪkl] adj metódico(-ca).

Methodist ['mɛθədɪst] adj metodista ◆ n metodista mf.

methylated spirits ['mɛθɪleɪtɪd] n álcool m metilado OR desnaturado.

meticulous [mɪ'tɪkjʊləs] adj meticuloso(-osa).

metre ['miːtə'] *n (Brit)* metro *m*.

metric ['metrɪk] *adj* métrico(-ca).

metronome ['metrənəʊm] *n* metrô-nomo *m*.

metropolitan [,metrə'pɒlɪtn] *adj* metropolitano(-na).

mews [mjuːz] *(pl inv) n (Brit)* rua, ou pátio, ladeada por cavalariças transfor-madas em casas ou apartamentos de luxo.

Mexican ['meksɪkn] *adj* mexicano (-na) ◆ *n* mexicano *m* (-na *f*).

Mexico ['meksɪkəʊ] *n* México *m*.

mg *(abbr of milligram)* mg.

miaow [miːaʊ] *n (Brit)* mio *m* ◆ *vi (Brit)* miar.

mice [maɪs] *pl* → mouse.

mickey ['mɪkɪ] *n:* to take the ~ out of sb *(Brit: inf)* gozar alguém.

microchip ['maɪkrəʊtʃɪp] *n* microchip *m*.

microphone ['maɪkrəfəʊn] *n* microfo-ne *m*.

microscope ['maɪkrəskəʊp] *n* micros-cópio *m*.

microwave (oven) ['maɪkrəweɪv-] *n* (forno) microondas *m inv*.

midday [,mɪd'deɪ] *n* meio-dia *m*.

middle ['mɪdl] *n* meio ◆ *adj* do meio; in the ~ of the road no meio da rua; in the ~ of April em meados de abril; to be in the ~ of doing sthg estar fazen-do algo.

middle-aged *adj* de meia idade.

Middle Ages *npl:* the ~ a Idade Média.

middle-class *adj* da classe média.

Middle East *n:* the ~ o Oriente Médio.

middle name *n* segundo nome *m*.

middle school *n (in UK)* escola para crianças dos 8 aos 12 anos.

middleweight ['mɪdlweɪt] *n* peso *m* médio.

midfield [,mɪd'fiːld] *n (in football)* meio-de-campo *m*.

midge [mɪdʒ] *n* mosquito *m*.

midget ['mɪdʒɪt] *n* anão *m* (anã *f*).

midi system ['mɪdɪ-] *n* sistema *m* (de alta fidelidade) midi.

Midlands ['mɪdləndz] *npl:* the ~ regiões do centro de Inglaterra.

midnight ['mɪdnaɪt] *n* meia-noite *f*.

midst [mɪdst] *n:* in the ~ of sthg *(in space)* no meio de algo; to be in the ~ of doing sthg estar fazendo algo.

midsummer ['mɪd'sʌmə'] *n:* in ~ em pleno verão.

midway [,mɪd'weɪ] *adv* a meio.

midweek [*adj* 'mɪdwiːk, *adv* mɪd'wiːk] *adj* do meio da semana ◆ *adv* no meio da semana.

midwife ['mɪdwaɪf] *(pl* -wives [-waɪvz]*) n* parteira *f*.

midwinter ['mɪd'wɪntə'] *n:* in ~ em pleno inverno.

might [maɪt] *aux vb* **1.** *(expressing pos-sibility)* poder; **I suppose they ~ still come** acho que eles ainda podem vir; **they ~ have been killed** eles podem ter sido assassinados; **I ~ go to Wales** tal-vez vá a Gales.
2. *(fml: expressing permission)* poder; ~ **I have a few words?** podemos conver-sar?
3. *(when conceding a point):* **it ~ be expensive, but it's good quality** pode ser caro, mas é bom.
4. *(would):* **I'd hoped you ~ come too** gostaria que também pudesse vir.
◆ *n (power)* poder *m*; *(physical strength)* força *f*.

mighty ['maɪtɪ] *adj (army, ruler)* pode-roso(-osa); *(blow)* tremendo(-da).

migraine ['miːgreɪn, 'maɪgreɪn] *n* enxa-queca *f*.

migrant ['maɪgrənt] *adj (bird, animal)* migratório(-ria).

migrate [*Brit* maɪ'greɪt, *Am* 'maɪgreɪt] *vi* migrar.

mike [maɪk] *n (inf: abbr of microphone)* microfone *m*.

mild [maɪld] *adj (discomfort, pain)* ligei-ro(-ra); *(illness)* pequeno(-na); *(weath-er)* ameno(-na); *(climate)* temperado (-da); *(kind, gentle)* meigo(-ga) ◆ *n (Brit: beer)* cerveja *f* suave.

mildew ['mɪldjuː] *n* míldio *m*.

mildly ['maɪldlɪ] *adv (talk, complain, criticize)* moderadamente; *(interesting, amusing)* mais ou menos.

mile [maɪl] *n* milha *f*; it's ~s away é longíssimo.

mileage ['maɪlɪdʒ] *n* distância *f* em milhas, ~ quilometragem *f*.

mileometer [maɪ'lɒmɪtə'] *n* contador *m* de milhas, ~ conta-quilômetros *m inv*.

milestone ['maɪlstəʊn] *n (marker stone)* marco *m*; *(fig: event)* marco his-tórico.

military ['mɪlɪtrɪ] *adj* militar.

milk [mɪlk] *n* leite *m* ♦ *vt (cow)* ordenhar, mungir.

milk chocolate *n* chocolate *m* de leite.

milkman ['mɪlkmən] (*pl* **-men** [-mən]) *n* leiteiro *m*.

milk shake *n* milk-shake *m* (*Br*), batido *m* (*Port*).

milky ['mɪlkɪ] *adj (drink)* com leite.

Milky Way *n*: the ~ a Via Láctea.

mill [mɪl] *n* moinho *m*; *(factory)* fábrica *f*.

millennium [mɪ'lenɪəm] (*pl* **-niums** OR **-nnia** [-nɪə]) *n* milênio *m*.

miller ['mɪləʳ] *n* moleiro *m* (-ra *f*).

milligram ['mɪlɪɡræm] *n* miligrama *m*.

millilitre ['mɪlɪˌliːtəʳ] *n* mililitro *m*.

millimetre ['mɪlɪˌmiːtəʳ] *n* milímetro *m*.

million ['mɪljən] *n* milhão *m*; **~s** of *(fig)* milhões de.

millionaire [ˌmɪljə'neəʳ] *n* milionário *m* (-ria *f*).

millstone ['mɪlstəʊn] *n* mó *f*.

mime [maɪm] *vi* fazer mímica.

mimic ['mɪmɪk] (*pt & pp* **-ked**, *cont* **-king**) *n* imitador *m* (-ra *f*) ♦ *vt* imitar.

min. [mɪn] *(abbr of minute)* m; *(abbr of minimum)* min.

mince [mɪns] *n* (*Brit*) carne *f* moída.

mincemeat ['mɪnsmiːt] *n (sweet filling)* mistura de frutos secos e cristalizados usada para rechear tortas e bolos; *(Am: mince)* carne *f* moída.

mince pie *n* pequena torta de Natal, recheada com uma mistura de frutos secos, frutos cristalizados, açúcar e especiarias.

mind [maɪnd] *n* mente *f*; *(memory)* memória *f* ♦ *vi (be bothered)* importar-se ♦ *vt (be careful of)* ter cuidado com; *(look after)* tomar conta de; *(be bothered by)*: do you ~ the noise? o barulho está lhe incomodando?; it slipped my ~ esqueci-me; state of ~ estado *m* de espírito; to my ~ na minha opinião; to bear sthg in ~ ter algo em conta; to change one's ~ mudar de idéia; to have sthg in ~ estar pensando em algo; to have sthg on one's ~ estar preocupado com algo; to make one's ~ up decidir-se; do you ~ if ...? importa-se se ...?; I don't ~ não me importo; I wouldn't ~ a drink gostaria de beber qualquer coisa; "~ the gap!" aviso aos passageiros para estarem atentos ao espaço entre o cais e o trem; never ~! *(don't worry)* não faz mal!, não tem importância!

minder ['maɪndəʳ] *n* (*Brit: bodyguard*) guarda-costas *mf inv*.

mindful ['maɪndfʊl] *adj*: to be ~ of sthg estar consciente de algo.

mindless ['maɪndlɪs] *adj (violence, crime)* absurdo(-da), sem sentido; *(job, work)* mecânico(-ca), maçante.

mine¹ [maɪn] *pron* o meu (a minha); a friend of ~ um amigo meu; those shoes are ~ esses sapatos são meus; ~ are here – where are yours? os meus estão aqui – onde estão os seus?

mine² [maɪn] *n (for coal etc, bomb)* mina *f*.

minefield ['maɪnfiːld] *n* campo *m* de minas.

miner ['maɪnəʳ] *n* mineiro *m* (-ra *f*).

mineral ['mɪnərəl] *n* mineral *m*.

mineral water *n* água *f* mineral.

minestrone [ˌmɪnɪ'strəʊnɪ] *n* minestrone *m*, sopa de legumes com massa.

mingle ['mɪŋɡl] *vi* misturar-se.

miniature ['mɪnətʃəʳ] *adj* em miniatura ♦ *n (bottle of alcohol)* miniatura *f*.

minibar ['mɪnɪbɑːʳ] *n* minibar *m*.

minibus ['mɪnɪbʌs] *n* microônibus *m* (*Br*), carrinha *f* (*Port*).

minicab ['mɪnɪkæb] *n* (*Brit*) rádiotaxi *m*.

minimal ['mɪnɪml] *adj* mínimo(-ma).

minimum ['mɪnɪməm] *adj* mínimo (-ma) ♦ *n* mínimo *m*.

mining ['maɪnɪŋ] *n* extração *f* de minério, exploração *f* mineira.

miniskirt ['mɪnɪskɜːt] *n* mini-saia *f*.

minister ['mɪnɪstəʳ] *n (in government)* ministro *m* (-tra *f*); *(in church)* pastor *m*, ministro *m*.

ministry ['mɪnɪstrɪ] *n (of government)* ministério *m*.

mink [mɪŋk] *n (fur)* pele *f* de marta, vison *m*.

minnow ['mɪnəʊ] (*pl inv* OR **-s**) *n* vairão *m*, pequeno peixe de água doce.

minor ['maɪnəʳ] *adj* pequeno(-na) ♦ *n (fml)* menor *mf* (de idade).

minority [maɪ'nɒrətɪ] *n* minoria *f*.

minor road *n* estrada *f* secundária.

mint [mɪnt] *n (sweet)* bala *f* de hortelã (*Br*), bombom *m* de mentol (*Port*); *(plant)* hortelã *f*.

minus ['maɪnəs] *prep (in subtraction)*

menos; **it's ~ 10°C** estão 10°C abaixo de zero.

minuscule [ˈmɪnəskjuːl] *adj* minúsculo(-la).

minute¹ [ˈmɪnɪt] *n* minuto *m*; **any ~** a qualquer momento; **just a ~!** só um minuto!

minute² [maɪˈnjuːt] *adj* diminuto(-ta).

minute steak [ˌmɪnɪt-] *n* bife *m* rápido.

miracle [ˈmɪrəkl] *n* milagre *m*.

miraculous [mɪˈrækjʊləs] *adj* milagroso(-osa).

mirage [mɪˈrɑːʒ] *n* miragem *f*.

mirror [ˈmɪrəʳ] *n* espelho *m*.

misbehave [ˌmɪsbɪˈheɪv] *vi* portar-se mal.

miscalculate [ˌmɪsˈkælkjʊleɪt] *vt* calcular mal, enganar-se em ◆ *vi* enganar-se.

miscarriage [ˌmɪsˈkærɪdʒ] *n* aborto *m* (não intencional).

miscellaneous [ˌmɪsəˈleɪnjəs] *adj* diverso(-sa).

mischief [ˈmɪstʃɪf] *n* (naughty behaviour) travessuras *fpl*; (playfulness) malícia *f*.

mischievous [ˈmɪstʃɪvəs] *adj* (naughty) travesso(-a); (playful) malicioso(-osa).

misconduct [ˌmɪsˈkɒndʌkt] *n* conduta *f* imprópria.

miscount [ˌmɪsˈkaʊnt] *vt* contar mal, enganar-se em ◆ *vi* contar mal, enganar-se.

misdemeanor [ˌmɪsdɪˈmiːnər] *(Am)* = misdemeanour.

misdemeanour [ˌmɪsdɪˈmiːnəʳ] *n* (Brit: JUR) delito *m* OR crime *m* menor.

miser [ˈmaɪzəʳ] *n* avarento *m* (-ta *f*).

miserable [ˈmɪzrəbl] *adj* miserável; (unhappy) infeliz.

miserly [ˈmaɪzəlɪ] *adj* mesquinho(-nha).

misery [ˈmɪzərɪ] *n* (unhappiness) infelicidade *f*; (poor conditions) miséria *f*.

misfire [ˌmɪsˈfaɪəʳ] *vi* (car) falhar.

misfortune [mɪsˈfɔːtʃuːn] *n* (bad luck) infelicidade *f*.

misgivings [mɪsˈgɪvɪŋz] *npl* dúvidas *fpl*, receio *m*.

mishap [ˈmɪshæp] *n* incidente *m*.

misinterpret [ˌmɪsɪnˈtɜːprɪt] *vt* interpretar mal.

misjudge [ˌmɪsˈdʒʌdʒ] *vt* (distance, amount) calcular mal; (person, character) julgar mal.

mislay [ˌmɪsˈleɪ] *(pt & pp* **-laid**) *vt*: **I've mislaid my keys** não sei onde é que pus as chaves.

mislead [ˌmɪsˈliːd] *(pt & pp* **-led**) *vt* enganar.

misleading [ˌmɪsˈliːdɪŋ] *adj* enganador(-ra).

misled [ˌmɪsˈled] *pt & pp →* **mislead**.

misplace [ˌmɪsˈpleɪs] *vt*: **I've ~d my keys** não sei onde é que pus as chaves.

misprint [ˈmɪsprɪnt] *n* erro *m* de impressão, gralha *f*.

miss [mɪs] *vt* perder; (not notice) não ver; (fail to hit) falhar; (regret absence of) ter saudades de, sentir falta de; (appointment) faltar a ◆ *vi* falhar; ⊐ **miss out** *vt sep* omitir ◆ *vi* perder; **you ~ed out on a great party** você perdeu uma grande festa.

Miss [mɪs] *n* senhorita *f* (Br), Menina *f* (Port).

missile [Brit ˈmɪsaɪl, Am ˈmɪsl] *n* míssil *m*.

missing [ˈmɪsɪŋ] *adj* (lost) perdido (-da); (after accident) desaparecido(-da); **to be ~** (not there) faltar.

missing person *n* desaparecido *m* (-da *f*).

mission [ˈmɪʃn] *n* (assignment) missão *f*.

missionary [ˈmɪʃənrɪ] *n* missionário *m* (-ria *f*).

mist [mɪst] *n* bruma *f*, neblina *f*.

mistake [mɪˈsteɪk] *(pt* **-took**, *pp* **-taken**) *n* erro *m* ◆ *vt* (misunderstand) entender mal; **by ~** por engano; **to make a ~** enganar-se; **to ~ sb/sthg for** confundir alguém/algo com.

mistaken [mɪˈsteɪkn] *adj* (belief, idea) errado(-da); (person) enganado(-da); **to be ~ about** estar enganado em relação a.

Mister [ˈmɪstəʳ] *n* Senhor *m*.

mistletoe [ˈmɪsltəʊ] *n* visco-branco *m*.

mistook [mɪˈstʊk] *pt →* **mistake**.

mistreat [ˌmɪsˈtriːt] *vt* maltratar.

mistress [ˈmɪstrɪs] *n* (lover) amante *f*; (Brit: teacher) professora *f*.

mistrust [ˌmɪsˈtrʌst] *vt* desconfiar de.

misty [ˈmɪstɪ] *adj* nebuloso(-osa), nublado(-da).

misunderstand [ˌmɪsʌndəˈstænd] *(pt & pp* **-stood**) *vt & vi* compreender mal.

misunderstanding [ˌmɪsʌndəˈstændɪŋ] *n* (misinterpretation) mal-entendido *m*, engano *m*; *(quarrel)* desentendimento *m*.

misunderstood [,mɪsʌndə'stud] *pt & pp* → misunderstand.

misuse [,mɪs'juːs] *n* uso *m* indevido.

miter ['maɪtər] *(Am)* = mitre.

mitigate ['mɪtɪgeɪt] *vt* minimizar.

mitre ['maɪtər] *n (Brit: hat)* mitra *f*.

mitten ['mɪtn] *n* luva *f (com un só dedo)*.

mix [mɪks] *vt* misturar ◆ *n (for cake, sauce)* mistura *f* ◆ *vi*: **I don't like the people you ~ with** não gosto das pessoas com quem você anda; **to ~ sthg with sthg** misturar algo com algo.
◻ **mix up** *vt sep (confuse)* confundir; *(put into disorder)* misturar.

mixed [mɪkst] *adj (school)* misto(-ta).

mixed grill *n* grelhado *m* misto.

mixed salad *n* salada *f* mista.

mixed up *adj (confused)* confuso (-sa); **to be ~ in sthg** *(involved)* estar envolvido em algo.

mixed vegetables *npl* macedônia *f* (de legumes).

mixer ['mɪksər] *n (for food)* batedeira *f*; *(drink)* bebida não alcoólica que se mistura com bebidas alcoólicas.

mixture ['mɪkstʃər] *n* mistura *f*.

mix-up *n (inf)* engano *m*.

ml *(abbr of millilitre)* ml.

mm *(abbr of millimetre)* mm.

moan [məʊn] *vi (in pain, grief)* gemer; *(inf: complain)* resmungar.

moat [məʊt] *n* fosso *m*.

mobile ['məʊbaɪl] *adj* móvel.

mobile phone *n* (telefone *m*) celular *m (Br)*, telemóvel *m (Port)*.

mock [mɒk] *adj* falso(-sa) ◆ *vt* gozar com ◆ *n (Brit: exam)* exame *m* simulado *(que serve de treino)*.

mockery ['mɒkərɪ] *n (scorn)* troça *f*.

mode [məʊd] *n* modo *m*.

model ['mɒdl] *n* modelo *m*; *(fashion model)* modelo *m/f*.

modem ['məʊdem] *n* (COMPUT) modem *m*.

moderate ['mɒdərət] *adj* moderado (-da).

moderation [,mɒdə'reɪʃn] *n* moderação *f*; **in ~** com moderação.

modern ['mɒdən] *adj* moderno(-na).

modernized ['mɒdənaɪzd] *adj* modernizado(-da).

modern languages *npl* línguas *fpl*

modernas OR vivas.

modest ['mɒdɪst] *adj* modesto(-ta).

modesty ['mɒdɪstɪ] *n* modéstia *f*.

modify ['mɒdɪfaɪ] *vt* modificar.

module ['mɒdjuːl] *n* módulo *m*.

mohair ['məʊheər] *n* mohair *m*.

moist [mɔɪst] *adj* úmido(-da).

moisten ['mɔɪsn] *vt* umedecer.

moisture ['mɔɪstʃər] *n* umidade *f*.

moisturizer ['mɔɪstʃəraɪzər] *n* creme *m* hidratante.

molar ['məʊlər] *n* molar *m*.

molasses [mə'læsɪz] *n* melaço *m*.

mold [məʊld] *(Am)* = mould.

mole [məʊl] *n (animal)* toupeira *f*; *(spot)* sinal *m*.

molecule ['mɒlɪkjuːl] *n* molécula *f*.

molest [mə'lest] *vt (child)* abusar (sexualmente) de; *(woman)* assediar.

mom [mɒm] *n (Am: inf)* mãe *f*.

moment ['məʊmənt] *n* momento *m*; **at the ~** no momento; **for the ~** por agora.

momentarily [*Brit* 'məʊmentərɪlɪ, *Am* ,məʊmen'terɪlɪ] *adv (for a short time)* momentaneamente; *(Am: immediately)* dentro em pouco, em breve.

momentary ['məʊməntrɪ] *adj* momentâneo(-nea).

momentous [mə'mentəs] *adj* muito importante.

Mon. *(abbr of Monday)* 2ª, seg.

Monaco ['mɒnəkəʊ] *n* Mônaco *m*.

monarch ['mɒnək] *n* monarca *m*.

monarchy ['mɒnəkɪ] *n*: **the ~** a monarquia.

monastery ['mɒnəstrɪ] *n* mosteiro *m*.

Monday ['mʌndɪ] *n* segunda-feira *f*, → Saturday.

money ['mʌnɪ] *n* dinheiro *m*.

money belt *n* carteira *f* de cintura, cinto *m* carteira.

moneybox ['mʌnɪbɒks] *n* cofre *m (Br)*, mealheiro *m (Port)*.

money order *n* vale *m*.

mongrel ['mʌngrəl] *n* vira-lata *m (Br)*, rafeiro *m (Port)*.

monitor ['mɒnɪtər] *n (computer screen)* monitor *m* ◆ *vt (check, observe)* controlar.

monk [mʌnk] *n* monge *m*.

monkey ['mʌnkɪ] *(pl -s)* *n* macaco *m*.

monkfish ['mʌnkfɪʃ] *n* tamboril *m*.

monopolize [mə'nɒpəlaɪz] *vt* monopolizar.

monopoly [mə'nɒpəlɪ] n (COMM) monopólio m.

monorail ['mɒnəʊreɪl] n monotrilho m (Br), monocarril m (Port).

monotonous [mə'nɒtənəs] adj monótono(-a).

monsoon [mɒn'suːn] n monção f.

monster ['mɒnstə'] n monstro m.

monstrous ['mɒnstrəs] adj monstruoso(-osa).

month [mʌnθ] n mês m; **every ~** todos os meses; **in a ~'s time** daqui a um mês.

monthly ['mʌnθlɪ] adj mensal ♦ adv mensalmente.

monument ['mɒnjʊmənt] n monumento m.

monumental [ˌmɒnjʊ'mentl] adj monumental.

moo [muː] vi mugir.

mood [muːd] n humor m; **to be in a (bad) ~** estar de mau humor; **to be in a good ~** estar de bom humor.

moody ['muːdɪ] adj (bad-tempered) mal-humorado(-da); (changeable) temperamental.

moon [muːn] n lua f.

moonlight ['muːnlaɪt] n luar m.

moonlit ['muːnlɪt] adj (night) de luar; (landscape) iluminado(-da) pela lua.

moor [mɔː'] n charneca f ♦ vt atracar.

moose [muːs] (pl inv) n alce m.

mop [mɒp] n (for floor) esfregão m (Br), esfregona f (Port) ♦ vt (floor) limpar.

⊔ **mop up** vt sep (clean up) limpar.

mope [məʊp] vi andar deprimido(-da).

moped ['məʊped] n motocicleta f.

moral ['mɒrəl] adj moral ♦ n (lesson) moral f.

morale [mə'rɑːl] n moral m.

morality [mə'rælɪtɪ] n moralidade f.

morbid ['mɔːbɪd] adj mórbido(-da).

more [mɔː'] adj 1. (a larger amount of) mais; **there are ~ tourists than usual** há mais turistas que o normal.

2. (additional) mais; **are there any ~ cakes?** tem mais bolos?; **I'd like two ~ bottles** queria mais duas garrafas; **there's no ~ wine** já não tem mais vinho.

3. (in phrases): **~ and more** cada vez mais.

♦ adv 1. (in comparatives) mais; **it's ~ difficult than before** é mais difícil do que antes; **speak ~ clearly** fala de forma mais clara; **we go there ~ often**

now agora vamos lá mais freqüentemente.

2. (to a greater degree) mais; **we ought to go to the cinema ~** devíamos ir mais vezes ao cinema.

3. (in phrases): **I don't go there any ~** eu não vou mais lá; **once ~** mais uma vez; **~ or less** mais ou menos; **we'd be ~ than happy to help** teríamos imenso prazer em ajudar.

♦ pron 1. (a larger amount) mais; **I've got ~ than you** tenho mais que você; **~ than 20 types of pizza** mais de 20 tipos de pizza.

2. (an additional amount) mais; **is there any ~?** tem mais?; **there's no ~** não tem mais.

moreover [mɔː'rəʊvə'] adv (fml) além disso, além do mais.

morgue [mɔːg] n morgue f.

morning ['mɔːnɪŋ] n manhã f; **good ~!** bom dia!; **two o'clock in the ~** duas da manhã, duas da madrugada; **in the ~** (early in the day) de manhã; (tomorrow morning) amanhã de manhã.

morning-after pill n pílula f do dia seguinte.

morning sickness n enjôo m matinal.

Moroccan [mə'rɒkən] adj marroquino(-na) ♦ n marroquino m (-na f).

Morocco [mə'rɒkəʊ] n Marrocos s.

moron ['mɔːrɒn] n (inf: idiot) estúpido m (-da f), idiota mf.

morose [mə'rəʊs] adj taciturno(-na).

Morse (code) [mɔːs-] n (código de) Morse m.

morsel ['mɔːsl] n pedaço m.

mortal ['mɔːtl] adj mortal ♦ n mortal m.

mortar ['mɔːtə'] n (cement mixture) argamassa f; (gun) morteiro m.

mortgage ['mɔːgɪdʒ] n hipoteca f.

mortified ['mɔːtɪfaɪd] adj mortificado(-da).

mosaic [mə'zeɪɪk] n mosaico m.

Moscow ['mɒskəʊ] n Moscou m (Br), Moscovo m (Port).

Moslem ['mɒzləm] = **Muslim**.

mosque [mɒsk] n mesquita f.

mosquito [mə'skiːtəʊ] (pl -es) n mosquito m.

mosquito net n mosquiteiro m.

moss [mɒs] n musgo m.

most [məʊst] adj 1. (the majority of) a maioria de; **~ people agree** a maioria

das pessoas está de acordo.
2. *(the largest amount of)* mais; **I drank (the) ~ beer** fui eu que bebi mais cerveja.
♦ *adv* **1.** *(in superlatives)* mais; **the ~ expensive hotel in town** o hotel mais caro da cidade.
2. *(to the greatest degree)* mais; **I like this one ~** gosto mais deste.
3. *(fml: very)* muito; **we would be ~ grateful** ficaríamos muito gratos.
♦ *pron* **1.** *(the majority)* a maioria; **~ of the villages** a maioria das aldeias; **~ of the time** a maior parte do tempo.
2. *(the largest amount)* mais; **she earns (the) ~** ela é a que ganha mais.
3. *(in phrases)*: **at ~** no máximo; **we want to make the ~ of our stay** queremos aproveitar a nossa estada ao máximo.

mostly ['məʊstlɪ] *adv* principalmente.
MOT *n (Brit: test)* = IPO *f (Port)*, inspeção anual obrigatória para veículos com mais de três anos.
motel [məʊ'tel] *n* motel *m*.
moth [mɒθ] *n* traça *f*.
mothball ['mɒθbɔːl] *n* bola *f* de naftalina.
mother ['mʌðəʳ] *n* mãe *f*.
mother-in-law *n* sogra *f*.
mother-of-pearl *n* madrepérola *f*.
mother tongue *n* língua *f* materna.
motif [məʊ'tiːf] *n* motivo *m*.
motion ['məʊʃn] *n (movement)* movimento *m* ♦ *vi*: **to ~ to sb** fazer sinal a alguém.
motionless ['məʊʃənlɪs] *adj* imóvel.
motion picture *n (Am)* filme *m* (cinematográfico).
motivate ['məʊtɪveɪt] *vt* motivar.
motivated ['məʊtɪveɪtɪd] *adj* motivado(-da).
motivation [,məʊtɪ'veɪʃn] *n (sense of purpose)* motivação *f*.
motive ['məʊtɪv] *n* motivo *m*.
motor ['məʊtəʳ] *n* motor *m*.
Motorail® ['məʊtəreɪl] *n* auto-expresso m, trem que transporta carros e passageiros.
motorbike ['məʊtəbaɪk] *n* moto *f*.
motorboat ['məʊtəbəʊt] *n* barco *m* a motor.
motorcar ['məʊtəkɑːʳ] *n* carro m, automóvel *m*.
motorcycle ['məʊtə,saɪkl] *n* moto *f*.

motorcyclist ['məʊtə,saɪklɪst] *n* motociclista *mf*.
motoring ['məʊtərɪŋ] *n* automobilismo *m*.
motorist ['məʊtərɪst] *n* automobilista *mf*.
motor racing *n* automobilismo *m*.
motor scooter *n* lambreta *f*.
motor vehicle *n* veículo *m* motorizado.
motorway ['məʊtəweɪ] *n (Brit)* auto-estrada *f*.
mottled ['mɒtld] *adj* sarapintado (-da).
motto ['mɒtəʊ] *(pl -s)* lema *m*.
mould [məʊld] *n (Brit) (shape)* molde m, forma f; *(substance)* bolor *m* ♦ *vt (Brit) (shape)* moldar.
moulding ['məʊldɪŋ] *n (decoration)* moldura *f*.
mouldy ['məʊldɪ] *adj* bolorento(-ta).
mound [maʊnd] *n* monte *m*.
mount [maʊnt] *n (for photo)* moldura f; *(mountain)* monte *m* ♦ *vt (horse)* montar; *(photo)* emoldurar ♦ *vi (increase)* aumentar.
mountain ['maʊntɪn] *n* montanha *f*.
mountain bike *n* bicicleta *f* de montanha.
mountaineer [,maʊntɪ'nɪəʳ] *n* alpinista *mf*.
mountaineering [,maʊntɪ'nɪərɪŋ] *n*: **to go ~** fazer alpinismo.
mountainous ['maʊntɪnəs] *adj* montanhoso(-osa).
Mount Rushmore [-'rʌʃmɔːʳ] *n* o monte Rushmore.
mourn [mɔːn] *vt (person)* chorar; *(thing)* lamentar ♦ *vi* lamentar; **to ~ for sb** chorar a morte de alguém.
mourner ['mɔːnəʳ] *n (related)* parente *mf* do morto; *(unrelated)* amigo *m* (-ga *f*) do morto.
mourning ['mɔːnɪŋ] *n*: **to be in ~** estar de luto.
mouse [maʊs] *(pl mice)* *n* rato *m*.
moussaka [muːˈsɑːkə] *n* gratinado de origem grega à base de carne moída e beringela.
mousse [muːs] *n (food)* mousse f; *(for hair)* espuma *f*.
moustache [məˈstɑːʃ] *n (Brit)* bigode *m*.
mouth [maʊθ] *n* boca f; *(of river)* foz *f*.
mouthful ['maʊθfʊl] *n (of food)* bocado m; *(of drink)* gole *m*.

mouthorgan ['mauθ,ɔ:gən] n gaita-de-boca f.

mouthpiece ['mauθpi:s] n bocal m.

mouthwash ['mauθwɒʃ] n desin-fetante m para a boca.

mouth-watering [-,wɔ:tərɪŋ] adj de dar água na boca.

movable ['mu:vəbl] adj móvel.

move [mu:v] n (change of house) mudança f; (movement) movimento m; (in games) jogada f; (turn to play) vez f; (course of action) medida f ♦ vt (object) mudar; (arm, leg, lips) mexer; (emotionally) comover ♦ vi (shift) mover-se; (get out of the way) desviar-se; **to ~ (house)** mudar de casa; **to make a ~ (leave)** ir embora.

❏ **move along** vi avançar.

❏ **move in** vi (to house) mudar-se para.

❏ **move off** vi (train, car) partir.

❏ **move on** vi (after stopping) voltar a partir.

❏ **move out** vi (from house) mudar-se de.

❏ **move over** vi chegar-se para lá/cá.

❏ **move up** vi chegar-se para lá/cá.

moveable ['mu:vəbl] = **movable**.

movement ['mu:vmənt] n movimento m.

movie ['mu:vɪ] n filme m.

movie camera n câmara f de filmar.

movie theater n (Am) cinema m.

moving ['mu:vɪŋ] adj (emotionally) comovente.

mow [məu] vt: **to ~ the lawn** cortar a grama.

mower ['məuər] n máquina f de cortar grama.

mozzarella [,mɒtsə'relə] n queijo m mozzarella.

MP abbr = **Member of Parliament**.

mph (abbr of miles per hour) milhas à OR por hora.

Mr ['mɪstər] abbr Sr.

Mrs ['mɪsɪz] abbr Sra.

Ms [mɪz] abbr título que evita que se faça uma distinção entre mulheres casadas e solteiras.

MS abbr = **multiple sclerosis**.

MSc abbr = **Master of Science**.

much [mʌtʃ] (compar **more**, superl **most**) adj muito(-ta); **I haven't got ~ money** não tenho muito dinheiro; **as ~ food as you can eat** o máximo de comida que você conseguir comer; **how ~ time is left?** quanto tempo

falta?; **they have so ~ money** eles têm tanto dinheiro; **we have too ~ food** temos comida demais.

♦ adv **1.** (to a great extent) muito; **he is ~ happier** ele está muito mais feliz; **it's ~ better** é muito melhor; **he's ~ too good** ele é bom demais; **I like it very ~** gosto muitíssimo; **it's not ~ good** (inf) não é muito bom; **thank you very ~** muito obrigado.

2. (often) muitas vezes; **we don't go there ~** não vamos lá muitas vezes.

♦ pron muito; **I haven't got ~** não tenho muito; **as ~ as you like** tanto quanto (você) queira; **how ~ is it?** quanto é?; **you've got so ~** você tem tanto; **you've got too ~** você tem demais.

muck [mʌk] n (dirt) porcaria f.

❏ **muck about** vi (Brit: inf: waste time) perder tempo.

❏ **muck up** vt sep (Brit: inf) estragar.

mucky ['mʌkɪ] adj (inf) porco (porca).

mucus ['mju:kəs] n muco m.

mud [mʌd] n lama f.

muddle ['mʌdl] n: **to be in a ~** (confused) estar confuso(-sa); (in a mess) estar em desordem.

muddy ['mʌdɪ] adj lamacento(-ta).

mudguard ['mʌdgɑ:d] n guarda-lamas m inv.

muesli ['mju:zlɪ] n muesli m.

muff [mʌf] n (for hands) regalo m; (for ears) protetor m para os ouvidos.

muffin ['mʌfɪn] n (roll) pãozinho m; (cake) bolinho redondo e chato.

muffle ['mʌfl] vt (sound) abafar.

muffler ['mʌflər] n (Am: silencer) silenciador m.

mug [mʌg] n (cup) caneca f ♦ vt assaltar.

mugging ['mʌgɪŋ] n assalto m (a pessoa).

muggy ['mʌgɪ] adj abafado(-da).

mule [mju:l] n mula f.

mulled [mʌld] adj: **~ wine** vinho aquecido com especiarias e açúcar.

multicoloured ['mʌltɪ,kʌləd] adj multicolor.

multilateral [,mʌltɪ'lætərəl] adj multilateral.

multinational [,mʌltɪ'næʃənl] n multinacional f.

multiple ['mʌltɪpl] adj múltiplo(-pla).

multiple sclerosis [-sklɪ'rəusɪs] n esclerose f múltipla.

multiplex cinema ['mʌltɪpleks-] *n* cinema *m* (com várias salas).

multiplication [ˌmʌltɪplɪ'keɪʃn] *n* multiplicação *f*.

multiply ['mʌltɪplaɪ] *vt* multiplicar ♦ *vi* multiplicar-se.

multistorey (car park) [ˌmʌltɪ-'stɔːrɪ-] *n* (parque *m* de) estacionamento *m* com vários andares.

multitude ['mʌltɪtjuːd] *n* (*crowd*) multidão *f*; **a ~ of reasons** inúmeras razões.

mum [mʌm] *n* (*Brit: inf*) mãe *f*.

mumble ['mʌmbl] *vt & vi* balbuciar.

mummy ['mʌmɪ] *n* (*Brit: inf: mother*) mamãe *f*.

mumps [mʌmps] *n* caxumba *f* (*Br*), papeira *f* (*Port*).

munch [mʌntʃ] *vt* mastigar.

mundane [mʌn'deɪn] *adj* desinteressante, trivial.

municipal [mjuː'nɪsɪpl] *adj* municipal.

mural ['mjuːərəl] *n* mural *m*.

murder ['mɜːdər] *n* assassínio *m*, assassinato *m* ♦ *vt* assassinar.

murderer ['mɜːdərər] *n* assassino *m* (-na *f*).

murky ['mɜːkɪ] *adj* (*place*) sombrio (-bria), lúgubre; (*water*) sujo(-ja), turvo(-va).

murmur ['mɜːmər] *n* murmúrio *m* ♦ *vt & vi* murmurar.

muscle ['mʌsl] *n* músculo *m*.

muscular ['mʌskjʊlər] *adj* (*strong*) musculoso(-osa); (*of muscles*) muscular.

museum [mjuː'ziːəm] *n* museu *m*.

mushroom ['mʌʃrʊm] *n* cogumelo *m*.

music ['mjuːzɪk] *n* música *f*.

musical ['mjuːzɪkl] *adj* (*connected with music*) musical; (*person*) com ouvido para a música ♦ *n* musical *m*.

musical instrument *n* instrumento *m* musical.

music centre *n* (*machine*) aparelhagem *f* de som.

musician [mjuː'zɪʃn] *n* músico *m* (-ca *f*).

Muslim ['mʊzlɪm] *adj* muçulmano (-na) ♦ *n* muçulmano *m* (-na *f*).

muslin ['mʌzlɪn] *n* musselina *f*.

mussels ['mʌslz] *npl* mexilhões *mpl*.

must [mʌst] *aux vb* (*expressing obligation*) ter de; (*expressing certainty*) dever ♦ *n* (*inf*): **it's a ~** é de não perder; **I ~ go** tenho de ir; **the room ~ be vacated by ten** o quarto tem de ser desocupado antes das dez; **you ~ have seen it** você deve ter visto; **you ~ see that film** você tem de ver aquele filme; **you ~ be joking!** você deve estar brincando!

mustache ['mʌstæʃ] (*Am*) = **moustache**.

mustard ['mʌstəd] *n* mostarda *f*.

mustn't ['mʌsənt] = **must not**.

must've ['mʌstəv] = **must have**.

mute [mjuːt] *adj* mudo(-da) ♦ *n* mudo *m* (-da *f*).

mutilate ['mjuːtɪleɪt] *vt* mutilar.

mutiny ['mjuːtɪnɪ] *n* motim *m* ♦ *vi* amotinar-se.

mutter ['mʌtər] *vt* murmurar.

mutton ['mʌtn] *n* carne *f* de carneiro

mutual ['mjuːtʃʊəl] *adj* mútuo(-tua).

mutually ['mjuːtʃʊəlɪ] *adv* mutuamente.

muzzle ['mʌzl] *n* (*for dog*) focinheira *f* (*Br*), açaime *m* (*Port*).

MW *abbr* = **medium wave**.

my [maɪ] *adj* meu (minha); **~ books** os meus livros.

myself [maɪ'self] *pron* (*reflexive*) me; (*after prep*) mim; **I did it ~** eu mesmo o fiz; **I hurt ~** machuquei-me.

mysterious [mɪ'stɪərɪəs] *adj* misterioso(-osa).

mystery ['mɪstərɪ] *n* mistério *m*.

mystical ['mɪstɪkl] *adj* místico(-ca).

mystified ['mɪstɪfaɪd] *adj* confuso (-sa), perplexo(-xa).

myth [mɪθ] *n* mito *m*.

mythical ['mɪθɪkl] *adj* mítico (-ca).

mythology [mɪ'θɒlədʒɪ] *n* mitologia *f*.

N

N (abbr of north) N.

nab [næb] vt (inf: arrest) apanhar; (inf: claim quickly) agarrar.

nag [næg] vt apoquentar.

nagging ['nægɪŋ] adj (worry, suspicion) persistente; (spouse, friend) chato(-ta).

nail [neɪl] n (of finger, toe) unha f; (metal) prego m ♦ vt (fasten) pregar.

nailbrush ['neɪlbrʌʃ] n escova f de unhas.

nail file n lixa f de unhas (Br), lima f para as unhas (Port).

nail polish n esmalte m (Br), verniz m (para as unhas) (Port).

nail scissors npl tesoura f de unhas.

nail varnish n esmalte m (Br), verniz m (para as unhas) (Port).

nail varnish remover [-rə'mu:vəʳ] n acetona f, removedor m de esmalte (Br).

naive [naɪ'iːv] adj ingênuo(-nua).

naked ['neɪkɪd] adj (person) nu (nua).

name [neɪm] n nome m; (surname) sobrenome m (Br), apelido m (Port) ♦ vt (person, place, animal) chamar; (date, price) fixar; **first ~** nome próprio OR de batismo; **last ~** sobrenome (Br), apelido (Port); **what's your ~?** como você se chama?; **my ~ is ...** o meu nome é ....

namely ['neɪmlɪ] adv isto é, a saber.

namesake ['neɪmseɪk] n homônimo m.

nan bread [næn-] n pão indiano grande e achatado com condimentos.

nanny ['nænɪ] n (childminder) babá f (Br), ama f (Port); (inf: grandmother) avó f.

nap [næp] n soneca f; **to have a ~** tirar uma soneca.

nape [neɪp] n: **~ (of the neck)** nuca f.

napkin ['næpkɪn] n guardanapo m.

nappy ['næpɪ] n fralda f.

nappy liner n pequena tira descar-

tável usada com fraldas de tecido.

narcotic [nɑː'kɒtɪk] n narcótico m.

narrative ['nærətɪv] n narrativa f.

narrator [Brit nə'reɪtəʳ, Am 'næreɪtəʳ] n narrador m (-ra f).

narrow ['nærəu] adj (road, gap) estreito(-ta) ♦ vi estreitar.

narrowly ['nærəulɪ] adv por pouco, à risca.

narrow-minded [-'maɪndɪd] adj tacanho(-nha), de idéias curtas.

nasal ['neɪzl] adj nasal.

nasty ['nɑːstɪ] adj (person) mau (má); (comment) maldoso(-osa); (accident, fall) grave; (unpleasant) desgradável.

nation ['neɪʃn] n nação f.

national ['næʃənl] adj nacional ♦ n natural mf (de um país).

national anthem n hino m nacional.

National Health Service n ≃ Instituto m Nacional de Assistência Médica e Previdência Social (Br), ≃ Caixa f (de Previdência) (Port).

National Insurance n (Brit: contributions) ≃ Previdência f Social (Br), ≃ Segurança f Social (Port).

nationalist ['næʃnəlɪst] adj nacionalista ♦ n nacionalista mf.

nationality [,næʃə'nælətɪ] n nacionalidade f.

national park n parque m nacional.

national service n (Brit: MIL) serviço m militar.

National Trust n (Brit) organização britânica encarregada da preservação de prédios históricos e locais de interesse:

nationwide ['neɪʃənwaɪd] adj de âmbito nacional.

native ['neɪtɪv] adj (country) natal; (customs, population) nativo(-va) ♦ n natural mf; **a ~ speaker of English** um anglófono.

Nativity [nɔ'tɪvɪtɪ] n: the ~ a Natividade, o Natal.

NATO ['neɪtəu] n OTAN f, NATO f.

natural ['nætʃrəl] adj (ability, charm) natural; (swimmer, actor) nato(-ta).

natural gas n gás m natural.

naturally ['nætʃrəlɪ] adv (of course) naturalmente.

natural yoghurt n iogurte m natural.

nature ['neɪtʃəʳ] n natureza f.

nature reserve n reserva f natural.

naughty ['nɔːtɪ] adj (child) travesso (-a).

nausea ['nɔːzɪə] n enjôo m, náusea f.

nauseating ['nɔːsɪeɪtɪŋ] adj (food, smell) nauseabundo(-da), enjoativo (-va).

naval ['neɪvl] adj naval.

nave [neɪv] n nave f.

navel ['neɪvl] n umbigo m.

navigate ['nævɪgeɪt] vi (in boat) navegar; (in plane) calcular a rota; (in car) fazer de navegador.

navigation [,nævɪ'geɪʃn] n (piloting, steering) navegação m.

navy ['neɪvɪ] n (ships) marinha f ♦ adj: ~ (blue) azul-marinho (inv).

Nazi ['nɑːtsɪ] (pl -s) adj nazi ♦ n nazi mf.

NB (abbr of nota bene) N.B.

near [nɪəʳ] adv perto ♦ adj próximo(-ma) ♦ prep: ~ (to) (edge, object, place) perto de; **in the ~ future** num futuro próximo, em breve.

nearby [nɪə'baɪ] adv perto ♦ adj próximo(-ma).

nearly ['nɪəlɪ] adv quase.

near side n (for right-hand drive) direita f; (for left-hand drive) esquerda f.

nearsighted [,nɪə'saɪtɪd] adj (Am) míope.

neat [niːt] adj (room) arrumado(-da); (writing, work) caprichado(-da) (Br); cuidado(-da) (Port); (whisky, vodka etc) puro(-ra).

neatly ['niːtlɪ] adv cuidadosamente.

necessarily [,nesə'serɪlɪ, Brit 'nesəsrəlɪ] adv necessariamente; **not ~** não necessariamente.

necessary ['nesəsrɪ] adj necessário(-ria); **it is ~ to do it** é necessário fazê-lo.

necessity [nɪ'sesətɪ] n necessidade f.
⌐ **necessities** npl artigos mpl de primeira necessidade.

neck [nek] n (of person, animal) pescoço m; (of jumper) gola f; (of shirt) colarinho m; (of dress) decote m.

necklace ['neklɪs] n colar m.

neckline ['neklaɪn] n decote m.

necktie ['nektaɪ] n (Am) gravata f.

nectarine ['nektərɪn] n nectarina f.

need [niːd] n necessidade f ♦ vt precisar de, necessitar de; **to ~ to do sthg** precisar fazer algo.

needle ['niːdl] n agulha f.

needless ['niːdlɪs] adj desnecessário(-ria); ~ **to say** ... não é preciso dizer que ....

needlework ['niːdlwɜːk] n (SCH) costura f.

needn't ['niːdnt] = need not.

needy ['niːdɪ] adj necessitado(-da), com necessidades.

negative ['negətɪv] adj negativo(-va) ♦ n (in photography) negativo m; (GRAMM) negativa f.

neglect [nɪ'glekt] vt não prestar atenção a.

negligee ['neglɪʒeɪ] n négligé m.

negligence ['neglɪdʒəns] n negligência f.

negligible ['neglɪdʒəbl] adj insignificante.

negotiate [nɪ'gəʊʃɪeɪt] vt (agreement, deal) negociar; (obstacle, bend) transpor ♦ vi negociar; **to ~ with sb for sthg** negociar com alguém sobre algo, negociar algo com alguém.

negotiations [nɪ,gəʊʃɪ'eɪʃnz] npl negociações fpl.

negro ['niːgrəʊ] (pl -es) n negro m (-gra f).

neigh [neɪ] vi relinchar.

neighbor ['neɪbəʳ] (Am) = neighbour.

neighbour ['neɪbəʳ] n (Brit) vizinho m (-nha f).

neighbourhood ['neɪbəhʊd] n vizinhança f.

neighbouring ['neɪbərɪŋ] adj vizinho(-nha).

neighbourly ['neɪbəlɪ] adj (deed, relations) de bom vizinho (de boa vizinha); (person) bom vizinho (boa vizinha).

neither ['naɪðəʳ, 'niːðəʳ] adj: ~ **bag is big enough** nenhuma das bolsas é suficientemente grande ♦ pron: ~ **of us** nenhum m (-ma f) de nós ♦ conj: ~ **do I** nem eu; ~ ... **nor** nem ... nem.

neon light ['ni:ɒn-] n luz f de néon.
nephew ['nefju:] n sobrinho m.
Neptune ['neptju:n] n Netuno m.
nerve [nɜ:v] n (in body) nervo m; (courage) ousadia f; **what a ~!** que descaramento!
nerve-racking [-ˌrækɪŋ] adj angustiante.
nervous ['nɜ:vəs] adj nervoso(-osa).
nervous breakdown n esgotamento m nervoso.
nest [nest] n ninho m.
net [net] n rede f ♦ adj líquido(-da).
netball ['netbɔ:l] n esporte parecido com basquetebol feminino.
Netherlands ['neðələndz] npl: **the ~** os Países Baixos.
netting ['netɪŋ] n (of metal, plastic) rede f; (fabric) tule m.
nettle ['netl] n urtiga f.
network ['netwɜ:k] n rede f.
neurotic [ˌnjʊəˈrɒtɪk] adj neurótico(-ca).
neuter ['nju:tər] adj neutro(-tra).
neutral ['nju:trəl] adj neutro(-tra) ♦ n (AUT): **in ~** em ponto morto.
neutrality [nju:ˈtrælətɪ] n neutralidade f.
never ['nevər] adv nunca; **she's ~ late** ela nunca chega tarde; **~ mind!** não faz mal!
never-ending adj interminável.
nevertheless [ˌnevəðəˈles] adv contudo, todavia.
new [nju:] adj novo (nova).
newborn ['nju:bɔ:n] adj recém-nascido(-da).
newcomer ['nju:ˌkʌmər] n: **~ (to sthg)** recém-chegado m (-da f) (a algo).
newly ['nju:lɪ] adv: **~ married** recém-casado(-da).
newlyweds ['nju:lɪwedz] npl recém-casados mpl.
new potatoes npl batatas fpl tenras.
news [nju:z] n notícias fpl; (on TV) telejornal m; **a piece of ~** uma notícia.
newsagent ['nju:zeɪdʒənt] n (shop) jornaleiro m (Br), quiosque m (Port).
newsflash ['nju:zflæʃ] n flash m informativo, notícia f de última hora.
newsletter ['nju:zˌletər] n boletim m, jornal m.
newspaper ['nju:zˌpeɪpər] n jornal m.

newsreader ['nju:zˌri:dər] n (on TV) apresentador m (-ra f) do telejornal; (on radio) locutor m (-ra f) (que lê o noticiário).
newt [nju:t] n tritão m.
New Year n Ano m Novo.
New Year's Day n dia m de Ano Novo.
New Year's Eve n véspera f de Ano Novo.
New York [-jɔ:k] n: **~ (City)** (a cidade de) Nova Iorque s; **~ (State)** (o estado de) Nova Iorque.
New Zealand [-ˈzi:lənd] n Nova Zelândia f.
New Zealander [-ˈzi:ləndər] n neozelandês m (-esa f).
next [nekst] adj próximo(-ma); (room, house) do lado ♦ adv (afterwards) depois, em seguida; (on next occasion) da próxima vez; **when does the ~ bus leave?** a que horas é o próximo ônibus?; **~ month/year** o mês/ano que vem; **~ to** (by the side of) ao lado de; **the week after ~** daqui a duas semanas.
next door adv ao lado; **the house/people ~** a casa/os vizinhos do lado.
next of kin [-kɪn] n parente m mais próximo (parente f mais próxima).
NHS n (abbr of National Health Service) ≈ INAMPS m (Br), ≈ Caixa f (Port).
nib [nɪb] n aparo m.
nibble ['nɪbl] vt mordiscar.
nice [naɪs] adj (pleasant) agradável; (pretty) bonito(-ta); (kind) amável, simpático(-ca); **to have a ~ time** divertir-se; **~ to see you!** prazer em vê-lo!
nice-looking [-ˈlʊkɪŋ] adj (person) atraente; (car, room) bonito(-ta).
nicely ['naɪslɪ] adv (dressed, made) bem; (ask) educadamente, delicadamente; (behave, manage) bem; **that will do ~** está perfeito!
nickel ['nɪkl] n (metal) níquel m; (Am: coin) moeda de cinco centavos de um dólar.
nickname ['nɪkneɪm] n apelido m (Br), alcunha f (Port).
nicotine ['nɪkəti:n] n nicotina f.
niece [ni:s] n sobrinha f.
Nigeria [naɪˈdʒɪərɪə] n Nigéria f.
Nigerian [naɪˈdʒɪərɪən] adj nigeriano(-na) ♦ n nigeriano m (-na f).
night [naɪt] n noite f; **at ~** à noite; **by**

~ de noite; **last** ~ ontem à noite.

nightcap ['naɪtkæp] *n (drink)* bebida, geralmente alcoólica, que se toma antes de ir dormir.

nightclub ['naɪtklʌb] *n* boate *f (Br)*, clube *m* nocturno *(Port)*.

nightdress ['naɪtdrɛs] *n* camisola *f (Br)*, camisa *f* de noite OR de dormir *(Port)*.

nightfall ['naɪtfɔːl] *n* anoitecer *m*, o cair da noite.

nightgown ['naɪtɡaun] *n* camisola *f (Br)*, camisa *f* de dormir *(Port)*.

nightie ['naɪtɪ] *n (inf)* camisola *f (Br)*, camisa *f* de dormir *(Port)*.

nightingale ['naɪtɪŋɡeɪl] *n* rouxinol *m*.

nightlife ['naɪtlaɪf] *n* vida *f* noturna.

nightly ['naɪtlɪ] *adv* todas as noites.

nightmare ['naɪtmeəʳ] *n* pesadelo *m*.

night safe *n* cofre *m* noturno.

night school *n* aulas *fpl* noturnas.

nightshift ['naɪtʃɪft] *n* turno *m* da noite.

nightshirt ['naɪtʃɜːt] *n* camisa *f* de noite *(para homem)*.

nighttime ['naɪttaɪm] *n* noite *f*; **at** ~ durante a noite, à noite.

nil [nɪl] *n (SPORT)* zero *m*.

Nile [naɪl] *n*: **the** ~ o Nilo.

nimble ['nɪmbl] *adj (agile)* ágil.

nine [naɪn] *num* nove, → **six**.

nineteen [,naɪn'tiːn] *num* dezenove *(Br)*, dezanove *(Port)*; ~ **ninety-seven** mil novecentos e noventa e sete, → **six**.

nineteenth [,naɪn'tiːnθ] *num* décimo nono (décima nona), → **sixth**.

ninetieth [naɪntɪəθ] *num* nonagésimo(-ma), → **sixth**.

ninety ['naɪntɪ] *num* noventa, → **six**.

ninth [naɪnθ] *num* nono(-na), → **sixth**.

nip [nɪp] *vt (pinch)* beliscar.

nipple ['nɪpl] *n (of breast)* bico *m* do peito, mamilo *m*; *(of bottle)* bico *m (Br)*, tetina *f (Port)*.

nitrogen ['naɪtrədʒən] *n* azoto *m*, nitrogênio *m*.

no [nəʊ] *adv* não ♦ *adj* nenhum(-ma), algum(-ma) ♦ *n* não *m*; **I've got** ~ **money left** não tenho mais um tostão; **it is of** ~ **interest** não tem interesse (nenhum OR algum).

nobility [nə'bɪlətɪ] *n*: **the** ~ a nobreza.

noble ['nəʊbl] *adj* nobre.

nobody ['nəʊbədɪ] *pron* ninguém.

nocturnal [nɒk'tɜːnl] *adj* noturno (-na).

nod [nɒd] *vi (in agreement)* dizer que sim com a cabeça.

noise [nɔɪz] *n* barulho *m*, ruído *m*.

noisy ['nɔɪzɪ] *adj* barulhento(-ta), ruidoso(-osa).

nominate ['nɒmɪneɪt] *vt* nomear.

nonalcoholic [,nɒnælkə'hɒlɪk] *adj* sem álcool.

nonchalant [*Brit* 'nɒnʃələnt, *Am* ,nɒnʃə'lɑːnt] *adj (person, remark)* indiferente; *(gesture)* de indiferença.

nondescript [*Brit* 'nɒndɪskrɪpt, *Am* ,nɒndɪ'skrɪpt] *adj* nada de especial.

none [nʌn] *pron* nenhum *m* (-ma *f*); **there's** ~ **left** não resta nada.

nonetheless [,nʌnðə'les] *adv* todavia, contudo.

nonexistent [,nɒnɪɡ'zɪstənt] *adj* inexistente.

nonfiction [,nɒn'fɪkʃn] *n* literatura *f* não ficcional.

non-iron *adj* que não necessita de ser passado(-da) a ferro.

nonreturnable [,nɒnrɪ'tɜːnəbl] *adj* sem retorno.

nonsense ['nɒnsəns] *n (stupid words)* disparates *mpl*; *(foolish behaviour)* disparate *m*.

nonsmoker [,nɒn'sməʊkəʳ] *n* não-fumante *mf (Br)*, não-fumador *m* (-ra *f*) *(Port)*.

nonstick [,nɒn'stɪk] *adj* antiaderente.

nonstop [,nɒn'stɒp] *adj (talking, arguing)* constante; *(flight)* direto(-ta) ♦ *adv* sem parar.

noodles ['nuːdlz] *npl* miojo *m (Br)*, macaronete *m (Port)*.

nook [nʊk] *n* recanto *m*; **every** ~ **and cranny** tudo quanto é lugar.

noon [nuːn] *n* meio-dia *m*.

no one = **nobody**.

noose [nuːs] *n (lasso)* nó *m* corrediço OR corredio.

no-place *(Am)* = **nowhere**.

nor [nɔːʳ] *conj* nem; ~ **do I** nem eu, → **neither**.

norm [nɔːm] *n* norma *f*.

normal ['nɔːml] *adj* normal.

normalcy ['nɔːməlsɪ] *(Am)* = **normality**.

normality [nɔː'mælətɪ] *(Brit)* *n* normalidade *f*.

normally ['nɔːməlɪ] *adv* normalmente.

north [nɔːθ] n norte m ◆ adj norte ◆ adv (be situated) a norte; (fly, walk) para norte; **in the ~ of England** no norte de Inglaterra.

North Africa n a África do Norte, o Norte de África.

North America n a América do Norte.

northbound ['nɔːθbaund] adj em direção ao norte.

northeast [nɔːθ'iːst] n nordeste m.

northerly ['nɔːðəlɪ] adj (wind) do norte; **in a ~ direction** em direção ao norte; **the most ~ point** o ponto mais ao norte.

northern ['nɔːðən] adj do norte.

Northern Ireland n Irlanda f do Norte.

northernmost ['nɔːðənməust] adj mais ao norte.

North Korea n Coréia f do Norte.

North Pole n Pólo m Norte.

North Sea n Mar m do Norte.

northward ['nɔːθwəd] adj: **in a ~ direction** em direção ao norte.

northwards ['nɔːθwədz] adv em direção ao norte, para norte.

northwest [nɔːθ'west] n noroeste m.

Norway ['nɔːweɪ] n Noruega f.

Norwegian [nɔː'wiːdʒən] adj norueguês(-esa) ◆ n (person) norueguês m (-esa f); (language) norueguês m.

nose [nəuz] n nariz m; (of animal) focinho m.

nosebleed ['nəuzbliːd] n: **to have a ~** perder sangue pelo nariz.

no smoking area n área f reservada a não-fumantes.

nostalgia [nɒ'stældʒə] n nostalgia f.

nostril ['nɒstrəl] n narina f.

nosy ['nəuzɪ] adj bisbilhoteiro(-ra).

not [nɒt] adv não; **~ yet** ainda não; **~ at all** (pleased, interested) absolutamente nada; (in reply to thanks) não tem de quê, de nada.

notable ['nəutəbl] adj notável; **~ for** sthg notável por algo.

notably ['nəutəblɪ] adv especialmente.

note [nəut] n nota f; (message) recado m ◆ vt (notice) notar; (write down) anotar; **to take ~s** fazer anotações.

notebook ['nəutbuk] n caderno m, bloco m de anotações.

noted ['nəutɪd] adj famoso(-osa).

notepad ['nəutpæd] n bloco m de notas.

notepaper ['nəutpeɪpə'] n papel m de carta.

noteworthy ['nəut,wɜːðɪ] adj digno (-gna) de nota.

nothing ['nʌθɪŋ] pron nada; **he did ~** ele não fez nada; **~ new/interesting** nada de novo/interessante; **for ~** (for free) de graça; (in vain) para nada.

notice ['nəutɪs] vt notar ◆ n aviso m; **to take ~ of** prestar atenção a; **to hand in one's ~** demitir-se, apresentar o seu pedido de demissão.

noticeable ['nəutɪsəbl] adj visível.

notice board n quadro m de avisos (Br), placar m (de anúncios e avisos) (Port).

notify ['nəutɪfaɪ] vt: **to ~ sb of sthg** notificar alguém de algo.

notion ['nəuʃn] n noção f.

notorious [nəu'tɔːrɪəs] adj famigerado(-da).

nougat ['nuːguː] n torrone m, nugá m.

nought [nɔːt] n zero m; **~s and crosses** (Brit) jogo-da-velha m (Br), jogo m do galo (Port).

noun [naun] n substantivo m.

nourish ['nʌrɪʃ] vt alimentar.

nourishing ['nʌrɪʃɪŋ] adj nutritivo (-va).

nourishment ['nʌrɪʃmənt] n alimento m.

Nov. (abbr of November) nov.

novel ['nɒvl] n romance m ◆ adj original.

novelist ['nɒvəlɪst] n romancista mf.

novelty ['nɒvltɪ] n novidade f; (cheap object) bugiganga f.

November [nə'vembə'] n novembro m, → **September**.

novice ['nɒvɪs] n (beginner) novato m (-ta f).

now [nau] adv agora ◆ conj: **~ (that)** agora que; **by ~** já; **from ~ on** de agora em diante; **just ~** (a moment ago) agora mesmo; (at the moment) neste momento; **right ~** (at the moment) neste momento; (immediately) já, agora mesmo.

nowadays ['nauədeɪz] adv hoje em dia.

nowhere ['nəuweə'] adv em parte alguma.

nozzle ['nɒzl] n agulheta f.

nuclear ['njuːklɪəʳ] adj nuclear.

nuclear bomb n bomba f atômica.

nuclear disarmament n desarmamento m nuclear.

nuclear power n energia f nuclear.

nuclear reactor n reator m nuclear.

nude [njuːd] adj nu (nua).

nudge [nʌdʒ] vt cutucar (Br), dar uma cotovelada a (Port).

nuisance ['njuːsns] n: it's a real ~! é uma chatice!; he's such a ~! ele é um chato!

null [nʌl] adj: ~ and void nulo(-la) e sem força legal.

numb [nʌm] adj (leg, arm) dormente; (with shock, fear) atônito(-ta).

number ['nʌmbəʳ] n número m ♦ vt (give number to) numerar.

numberplate ['nʌmbəpleɪt] n chapa f (do carro) (Br), matrícula f do carro (Port).

numeral ['njuːmərəl] n numeral m, algarismo m.

numerous ['njuːmərəs] adj inúmeros(-ras).

nun [nʌn] n freira f.

nurse [nɜːs] n enfermeiro m (-ra f) ♦ vt (look after) tomar conta de.

nursery ['nɜːsərɪ] n (in house) quarto m de criança; (for plants) viveiro m para plantas.

nursery rhyme n poema m OR canção f infantil.

nursery (school) n escola f maternal (Br), infantário m (Port).

nursery slope n (ski) pista f para principiantes.

nursing ['nɜːsɪŋ] n (profession) enfermagem f.

nursing home n (for old people) lar m para idosos (privado); (for childbirth) maternidade f (privada).

nut [nʌt] n (to eat) fruto m seco (noz, avelã, etc); (of metal) porca f (de parafuso).

nutcrackers ['nʌtˌkrækəz] npl quebra-nozes m inv.

nutmeg ['nʌtmeg] n noz-moscada f.

nutritious [njuːˈtrɪʃəs] adj nutritivo(-va).

nutshell ['nʌtʃel] n: in a ~ resumindo, em poucas palavras.

nylon ['naɪlɒn] n nylon m ♦ adj de nylon.

o' [ə] abbr = **of**.

O n (zero) zero m.

oak [əʊk] n carvalho m ◆ adj de carvalho.

OAP abbr = **old age pensioner**.

oar [ɔːʳ] n remo m.

oasis [əʊˈeɪsɪs] (pl **oases** [əʊˈeɪsiːz]) n oásis m inv.

oatcake [ˈəʊtkeɪk] n biscoito m de aveia.

oath [əʊθ] n (promise) juramento m.

oatmeal [ˈəʊtmiːl] n flocos mpl de aveia.

oats [əʊts] npl aveia f.

obedience [əˈbiːdjəns] n obediência f.

obedient [əˈbiːdjənt] adj obediente.

obese [əʊˈbiːs] adj obeso(-sa).

obey [əˈbeɪ] vt obedecer a.

obituary [əˈbɪtjʊərɪ] n obituário m.

object [n ˈɒbdʒɪkt, vb ɒbˈdʒekt] n (thing) objeto m; (purpose) objetivo m; (GRAMM) objeto, complemento m ◆ vi: **to ~ (to)** opor-se (a).

objection [əbˈdʒekʃn] n objeção f.

objective [əbˈdʒektɪv] n objetivo m.

obligation [ˌɒblɪˈɡeɪʃn] n obrigação f.

obligatory [əˈblɪɡətrɪ] adj obrigatório(-ria).

oblige [əˈblaɪdʒ] vt: **to ~ sb to do sthg** obrigar alguém a fazer algo.

obliging [əˈblaɪdʒɪŋ] adj prestativo(-va).

oblique [əˈbliːk] adj oblíquo(-qua).

obliterate [əˈblɪtəreɪt] vt (destroy) destruir.

oblivion [əˈblɪvɪən] n esquecimento m.

oblivious [əˈblɪvɪəs] adj inconsciente; **to be ~ to** OR **of sthg** não ter consciência de algo.

oblong [ˈɒblɒŋ] adj retangular ◆ n retângulo m.

obnoxious [əbˈnɒkʃəs] adj horroroso(-osa).

oboe [ˈəʊbəʊ] n oboé m.

obscene [əbˈsiːn] adj obsceno(-na).

obscure [əbˈskjʊəʳ] adj (difficult to understand) obscuro(-ra); (not well-known) desconhecido(-da).

observant [əbˈzɜːvnt] adj observador(-ra).

observation [ˌɒbzəˈveɪʃn] n observação f.

observatory [əbˈzɜːvətrɪ] n observatório m.

observe [əbˈzɜːv] vt (watch, see) observar.

obsessed [əbˈsest] adj obcecado(-da).

obsession [əbˈseʃn] n obsessão f.

obsolete [ˈɒbsəliːt] adj obsoleto(-ta).

obstacle [ˈɒbstəkl] n obstáculo m.

obstetrics [bˈstetrɪks] n obstetrícia f.

obstinate [ˈɒbstənət] adj teimoso(-osa).

obstruct [əbˈstrʌkt] vt (road, path) obstruir.

obstruction [əbˈstrʌkʃn] n (in road, path) obstrução f.

obtain [əbˈteɪn] vt obter.

obtainable [əbˈteɪnəbl] adj que se pode obter.

obtuse [əbˈtjuːs] adj (fml: person) obtuso(-sa), estúpido(-da).

obvious [ˈɒbvɪəs] adj óbvio(-via).

obviously [ˈɒbvɪəslɪ] adv evidentemente.

occasion [əˈkeɪʒn] n ocasião f.

occasional [əˈkeɪʒənl] adj ocasional, esporádico(-ca).

occasionally [əˈkeɪʒnəlɪ] adv de vez em quando.

occult [ɒˈkʌlt] adj oculto(-ta).

occupant [ˈɒkjʊpənt] n (of house) inquilino m (-na f), ocupante mf; (of car, plane) ocupante.

occupation [ˌɒkjʊˈpeɪʃn] n (job) ocupação f; (pastime) passatempo m.

occupied [ˈɒkjʊpaɪd] adj (toilet) ocupado(-da).

occupier [ˈɒkjʊpaɪəʳ] n ocupante mf.

occupy [ˈɒkjʊpaɪ] vt ocupar.

occur [əˈkɜːʳ] vi ocorrer.

occurrence [əˈkʌrəns] n ocorrência f.

ocean [ˈəʊʃn] n oceano m; the ~ (Am: sea) o oceano, o mar.

oceangoing [ˈəʊʃnˌgəʊɪŋ] adj de alto mar.

o'clock [əˈklɒk] adv: it's one ~ é uma hora; it's seven ~ são sete horas; at nine ~ às nove horas.

Oct. (abbr of October) out.

octave [ˈɒktɪv] n oitava f.

October [ɒkˈtəʊbəʳ] n outubro, → September.

octopus [ˈɒktəpəs] n polvo m.

odd [ɒd] adj (strange) estranho(-nha); (number) ímpar; (not matching) sem par; (occasional) ocasional; 60 ~ miles umas 60 milhas; some ~ bits of paper alguns pedaços de papel; ~ jobs biscates mpl.

oddly [ˈɒdlɪ] adv (behave, speak, look) de forma estranha; (disappointing, uplifting) estranhamente; ~ enough, I don't care por muito estranho que pareça, pouco me importa.

odds [ɒdz] npl (in betting) apostas fpl; (chances) probabilidades fpl; ~ and ends miudezas fpl.

odds-on adj (inf): the ~ favourite o grande favorito.

odor [ˈəʊdəʳ] (Am) = odour.

odour [ˈəʊdəʳ] n (Brit) odor m.

of [ɒv] prep 1. (belonging to) de; the colour ~ the car a cor do carro.

2. (expressing amount) de; a piece ~ cake uma fatia de bolo; a fall ~ 20% uma queda de 20%; lots ~ people muita gente.

3. (containing, made from) de; a glass ~ beer um copo de cerveja; a house ~ stone uma casa de pedra; it's made ~ wood é de madeira.

4. (regarding, relating to, indicating cause) de; fear ~ spiders medo de aranhas; he died ~ cancer ele morreu de câncer.

5. (referring to time) de; the summer ~ 1969 o verão de 1969; the 26th ~ August o 26 de agosto.

6. (with towns, countries) de; the city ~

Glasgow a cidade de Glasgow.

7. (on the part of) de; that was very kind ~ you foi muito amável da sua parte.

8. (Am: in telling the time) menos, para; it's ten ~ four são dez para as quatro.

off [ɒf] adv 1. (away): to drive/walk ~ ir-se embora; to get ~ (from bus, train, etc) descer; we're ~ to Austria next week vamos para a Áustria na próxima semana.

2. (expressing removal): to take sthg ~ tirar algo.

3. (so as to stop working): to turn sthg ~ (TV, radio, engine) desligar algo; (tap) fechar algo.

4. (expressing distance or time away): it's a long way ~ (in distance) é muito longe; (in time) ainda falta muito; it's two months ~ é daqui a dois meses.

5. (not at work) de folga; I'm taking a week ~ vou tirar uma semana de férias.

♦ prep 1. (away from): to get ~ sthg descer de algo; ~ the coast ao largo da costa; just ~ the main road perto da estrada principal.

2. (indicating removal): take the lid ~ the jar tire a tampa do frasco; we'll take £20 ~ the price descontaremos 20 libras do preço.

3. (absent from): to be ~ work não estar trabalhando.

4. (inf: from) a; I bought it ~ her eu comprei isso a ela.

5. (inf: no longer liking): I'm ~ my food não tenho apetite.

♦ adj 1. (food, drink) estragado(-da).

2. (TV, radio, light) apagado(-da), desligado(-da); (tap) fechado(-da); (engine) desligado(-da).

3. (cancelled) cancelado(-da).

4. (not available): the soup's ~ não tem mais sopa.

offal [ˈɒfl] n fressura f.

off-chance n: on the ~ you'd be there no caso de você estar lá.

off colour adj (ill) indisposto(-osta).

off duty adv: when do you get ~? a que horas acaba o serviço? ♦ adj que não está de serviço;

offence [əˈfens] n (Brit) (crime) infração f, delito m; (upset) ofensa f.

offend [əˈfend] vt (upset) ofender.

offender [əˈfendəʳ] n infrator m (-ra f), transgressor m (-ra f).

offense [ə'fɛns] *(Am)* = offence.

offensive [ə'fɛnsɪv] *adj (insulting)* ofensivo(-va).

offer ['ɒfəʳ] *n* oferta *f* ◆ *vt* oferecer; **on ~** *(available)* à venda; *(reduced)* em oferta; **to ~ to do sthg** oferecer-se para fazer algo; **to ~ sb sthg** oferecer algo a alguém.

off guard *adv*: **to be caught ~** ser apanhado desprevenido (apanhada desprevenida).

offhand [ˌɒf'hænd] *adj (person)* brusco(-ca); *(greeting)* frio (fria) ◆ *adv (at this moment)* de repente.

office ['ɒfɪs] *n (room)* escritório *m*.

office block *n* edifício *m* de escritórios.

officer ['ɒfɪsəʳ] *n (MIL)* oficial *mf*; *(policeman)* polícia *mf*.

office worker *n* empregado *m* (-da *f*) de escritório.

official [ə'fɪʃl] *adj* oficial ◆ *n* funcionário *m* (-ria *f*).

officially [ə'fɪʃəlɪ] *adv* oficialmente.

off-licence *n (Brit)* loja *f* de bebidas alcoólicas (para levar).

off-line *adj (COMPUT)* off-line, fora de linha.

off-peak *adj (train, ticket)* fora das horas de rush *(Br)*, de horário azul *(Port)*.

off-putting [-pʊtɪŋ] *adj (manner)* desconcertante.

off sales *npl (Brit)* venda *f* de bebidas alcoólicas para levar.

off-season *n* época *f* baixa.

offshore ['ɒfʃɔ:ʳ] *adj (wind)* costeiro(-ra); *(oil production)* no alto mar.

off side *n (for right-hand drive)* esquerda *f*; *(for left-hand drive)* direita *f*.

offspring ['ɒfsprɪŋ] *(pl inv)* *n (fml: of people)* filhos *mpl*; *(fml: of animals)* filhotes *mpl*.

offstage [ˌɒf'steɪdʒ] *adv (go)* para os bastidores; *(be, wait)* nos bastidores.

off-the-cuff *adj* irrefletido(-da) ◆ *adv* sem pensar.

off-the-peg *adj* pronto(-ta) para vestir.

off-white *adj* branco-sujo *(inv)*.

often ['ɒfn, 'ɒftn] *adv* muitas vezes, freqüentemente; **how ~ do the buses run?** qual é a freqüência dos ônibus?; **every so ~** de vez em quando.

oh [əʊ] *excl* oh!

oil [ɔɪl] *n* óleo *m*; *(fuel)* petróleo *m*.

oilcan ['ɔɪlkæn] *n* almotolia *f*.

oilfield ['ɔɪlfi:ld] *n* campo *m* petrolífero.

oil filter *n* filtro *m* do óleo.

oil painting *n (activity)* pintura *f* a óleo; *(picture)* quadro *m* a óleo.

oil rig *n* plataforma *f* petrolífera.

oilskins ['ɔɪlskɪnz] *npl* (capa de) oleado *m*.

oil slick *n* mancha *f* negra *(Br)*, maré *f* negra *(Port)*.

oil tanker *n (ship)* petroleiro *m*; *(lorry)* camião-cisterna *m*.

oil well *n* poço *m* de petróleo.

oily ['ɔɪlɪ] *adj (cloth, hands)* oleoso (-osa); *(food)* gordurento(-ta).

ointment ['ɔɪntmənt] *n* pomada *f*, ungüento *m*.

OK [ˌəʊ'keɪ] *adj (inf)* bom (boa) ◆ *adv (inf)* bem; **is everything ~?** está tudo bem?; **is that ~?** pode ser?, você concorda?; **the film was ~** achei o filme mais ou menos.

okay [ˌəʊ'keɪ] = OK.

old [əʊld] *adj* velho(-lha); *(former)* antigo(-ga); **how ~ are you?** quantos anos você tem?; **I'm 16 years ~** tenho 16 anos; **to get ~** envelhecer.

old age *n* velhice *f*.

old age pensioner *n* aposentado *m* (-da *f*) *(Br)*, reformado *m* (-da *f*) *(Port)*.

old-fashioned [-'fæʃnd] *adj* antiquado(-da).

old people's home *n* lar *m* para idosos.

O level *n* antigo exame oficial substituído hoje em dia pelo "GCSE".

olive ['ɒlɪv] *n* azeitona *f*.

olive green *adj* verde-azeitona *(inv)*.

olive oil *n* azeite *m*.

Olympic Games [ə'lɪmpɪk-] *npl* Jogos *mpl* Olímpicos.

omelette ['ɒmlɪt] *n* omelete *f*; **mushroom ~** omelete de cogumelos.

omen ['əʊmen] *n* presságio *m*.

ominous ['ɒmɪnəs] *adj (silence, clouds)* ameaçador(-ra); *(event, sign)* de mau agouro.

omission [ə'mɪʃn] *n* omissão *f*.

omit [ə'mɪt] *vt* omitir.

on [ɒn] *prep* **1.** *(expressing position, location)* em, sobre; **it's ~ the table** está na mesa, está sobre a mesa; **put it ~ the table** ponha-o na OR sobre a mesa; **~ my right** à minha direita; **~**

the right à direita; **a picture ~ the wall** um quadro na parede; **the exhaust ~ the car** o cano de descarga do carro; **we stayed ~ a farm** ficamos numa fazenda.
2. *(with forms of transport)*: **~ the plane** no avião; **to get ~ a bus** subir num ônibus.
3. *(expressing means, method)* em; **~ foot** a pé; **~ the radio** no rádio; **~ TV** na televisão; **paid ~ an hourly basis** pago por hora.
4. *(using)* a; **it runs ~ unleaded petrol** funciona com gasolina sem chumbo; **to be ~ drugs** drogar-se; **to be ~ medication** estar tomando medicamentos.
5. *(about)* sobre; **a book ~ Germany** um livro sobre a Alemanha.
6. *(expressing time)*: **~ arrival** ao chegar; **~ Tuesday** na terça-feira; **~ 25th August** no dia 25 de agosto.
7. *(with regard to)* em, sobre; **a tax ~ imports** um imposto sobre as importações; **the effect ~ Britain** o impacto na Grã-Bretanha.
8. *(describing activity, state)*: **~ holiday** de férias; **~ offer** *(reduced)* em promoção; **~ sale** à venda.
9. *(in phrases)*: **do you have any money ~ you?** *(inf)* você tem dinheiro?; **the drinks are ~ me** as bebidas são por minha conta.
♦ *adv* 1. *(in place, covering)*: **to put one's clothes ~** vestir-se; **to put the lid ~** tapar.
2. *(film, play, programme)*: **the news is ~** está passando o noticiário OR o telejornal; **what's ~ at the cinema?** o que é que está passando no cinema?
3. *(with transport)*: **to get ~** subir.
4. *(functioning)*: **to turn sthg ~** *(TV, radio, light)* ligar OR acender algo; *(tap)* abrir algo; *(engine)* pôr algo para trabalhar.
5. *(taking place)*: **how long is the festival ~?** quanto tempo dura o festival?; **the match is already ~** o jogo já começou.
6. *(further forward)*: **to drive ~** continuar a dirigir.
7. *(in phrases)*: **I already have something ~ tonight** já tenho planos para esta noite.
♦ *adj (TV, radio, light)* ligado(-da), aceso(-sa); *(tap)* aberto(-ta); *(engine)*

funcionando.
once [wʌns] *adv (one time)* uma vez; *(in the past)* uma vez, no passado ♦ *conj* quando, assim que; **at ~** *(immediately)* imediatamente; *(at the same time)* ao mesmo tempo; **for ~** pelo menos uma vez; **~ more** *(one more time)* mais uma vez; *(again)* outra vez.
oncoming ['ɒn,kʌmɪŋ] *adj (traffic)* em sentido contrário.
one [wʌn] *num* um (uma) ♦ *adj (only)* único(-ca) ♦ *pron (object, person)* um *m* (uma *f*); *(fml: you)* cada um; **thirty-~** trinta e um; **~ fifth** um quinto; **the green ~** o verde; **I want a blue ~** quero um azul; **that ~** aquele *m* (aquela *f*), esse *m* (essa *f*); **this ~** este *m* (esta *f*); **which ~?** qual?; **the ~ I told you about** aquele de que lhe falei; **~ of my friends** um dos meus amigos; **~ day** um dia.
one-armed bandit *n* slot-machine *f*.
one-man band *n (musician)* homem-orquestra *m*.
one-off *adj (inf)* único(-ca) ♦ *n (inf: event, person)* caso *m* único; *(product)* exemplar *m* único.
one-piece (swimsuit) *n* traje *m* de banho *(Br)*, fato *m* de banho *(Port)*.
oneself [wʌn'self] *pron (reflexive)* se; *(after prep)* si próprio OR mesmo (si própria OR mesma).
one-sided [-'saɪdɪd] *adj (unequal)* desigual; *(biased)* tendencioso(-osa), parcial.
one-way *adj (street)* de sentido único; *(ticket)* de ida.
ongoing ['ɒn,gəʊɪŋ] *adj (project, discussions)* atual, em curso; *(problem)* constante.
onion ['ʌnjən] *n* cebola *f*.
onion bhaji [-'bɑːdʒɪ] *n* bolinho de cebola picada, farinha e condimentos, frito e servido como entrada.
onion rings *npl* rodelas de cebolas, fritas em massa mole.
online ['ɒnlaɪn] *adj & adv* (COMPUT) online, em linha.
onlooker ['ɒn,lʊkər] *n* espectador *m* (-ra *f*), curioso *m* (-osa *f*).
only ['əʊnlɪ] *adj* único(-ca) ♦ *adv* só; **he's an ~ child** ele é filho único; **I ~ want one** só quero um; **we've ~ just arrived** acabamos de chegar; **there's ~ just enough** só tem a conta certa;

"members ~" "só para membros"; not ~ não só.

onset ['ɒn,set] n início m.

onshore ['ɒn ʃɔːr] adj (wind) costeiro (-ra); (oil production) em terra.

onslaught ['ɒn,slɔːt] n investida f.

onto ['ɒntu:] prep (with verbs of movement) para (cima de); to get ~ sb (telephone) contatar alguém (pelo telefone).

onward ['ɒnwəd] adv = onwards
♦ adj: the ~ journey o resto da viagem.

onwards ['ɒnwədz] adv (forwards) para a frente, para diante; from now ~ daqui em diante; from October ~ de outubro em diante.

ooze [uːz] vt (charm, confidence) respirar ♦ vi ressudar; to ~ from OR out of sthg ressudar de algo.

opal ['əupl] n opala f.

opaque [əu'peik] adj opaco(-ca).

open ['əupn] adj aberto(-ta); (honest) franco(-ca) ♦ vt abrir; (start) iniciar ♦ vi (door, window, lock) abrir-se; (shop, office, bank) abrir; (start) iniciar-se, começar; are you ~ at the weekend? está aberto ao fim de semana?; wide ~ completamente aberto; in the ~ (air) ao ar livre.
❑ open onto vt fus dar para.
❑ open up vi abrir.

open-air adj ao ar livre.

opener ['əupnər] n abridor m.

opening ['əupnɪŋ] n abertura f; (opportunity) oportunidade f.

opening hours npl horário m de funcionamento.

openly ['əupnlɪ] adv abertamente.

open-minded [-'maɪndɪd] adj aberto(-ta), sem preconceitos.

open-plan adj sem divisórias.

open sandwich n canapé m (Br), sandes f inv aberta (Port).

Open University n (Brit): the ~ a Universidade Aberta.

opera ['ɒpərə] n ópera f.

opera house n teatro m de ópera.

operate ['ɒpəreit] vt (machine) trabalhar com ♦ vi (work) funcionar; to ~ on sb operar alguém.

operating room ['ɒpəreitɪŋ-] n (Am) = operating theatre

operating theatre ['ɒpəreitɪŋ-] n (Brit) sala f de operações.

operation [,ɒpə'reɪʃn] n operação f; to be in ~ (law, system) estar em vigor;

to have an ~ ser operado.

operational [,ɒpə'reɪʃənl] adj operacional.

operator ['ɒpəreitər] n (on phone) telefonista mf.

opinion [ə'pɪnjən] n opinião f; in my ~ na minha opinião.

opinionated [ə'pɪnjəneitɪd] adj opinioso(-osa) (Br), pirrónico(-ca) (Port).

opinion poll n pesquisa f de opinião pública (Br), sondagem f de opinião (Port).

opponent [ə'pəunənt] n adversário m (-ria f).

opportunist [,ɒpə'tjuːnɪst] n oportunista mf.

opportunity [,ɒpə'tjuːnətɪ] n oportunidade f.

oppose [ə'pəuz] vt opor-se a.

opposed [ə'pəuzd] adj: to be ~ to opor-se a.

opposing [ə'pəuzɪŋ] adj oposto (-osta).

opposite ['ɒpəzɪt] adj oposto(-osta) ♦ prep em frente de, frente a ♦ n: the ~ (of) o oposto (de), o contrário (de); I live in the house ~ vivo na casa em frente.

opposition [,ɒpə'zɪʃn] n (objections) oposição f; (SPORT) adversário m; the Opposition (POL) a oposição.

oppress [ə'pres] vt oprimir.

opt [ɒpt] vt: to ~ to do sthg optar por fazer algo.

optical ['ɒptɪkl] adj ótico(-ca).

optician's [ɒp'tɪʃns] n (shop) oculista m.

optimist ['ɒptɪmɪst] n otimista mf.

optimistic [,ɒptɪ'mɪstɪk] adj otimista.

optimum ['ɒptɪməm] (pl -mums, fml -ma [-mə]) adj ideal.

option ['ɒpʃn] n opção f.

optional ['ɒpʃənl] adj facultativo (-va).

or [ɔːr] conj ou; (after negative) nem; (otherwise) senão; I can't read ~ write não sei ler nem escrever.

OR abbr = operating room.

oral ['ɔːrəl] adj oral ♦ n oral f.

orally ['ɔːrəlɪ] adv (in spoken form) oralmente; (via the mouth) por via oral.

orange ['ɒrɪndʒ] adj cor-de-laranja (inv) ♦ n (fruit) laranja f; (colour) cor-de-laranja m inv.

orange juice n suco m de laranja (Br), sumo m de laranja (Port).

orange squash n (Brit) laranjada f (sem gás).

orbit ['ɔːbɪt] n órbita f.

orbital (motorway) ['ɔːbɪtl-] n (Brit) auto-estrada f (em torno de uma grande cidade).

orchard ['ɔːtʃəd] n pomar m.

orchestra ['ɔːkɪstrə] n orquestra f.

orchestral [ɔːˈkestrəl] adj para orquestra, orquestral.

orchid ['ɔːkɪd] n orquídea f.

ordeal [ɔːˈdiːl] n experiência f traumática.

order ['ɔːdəʳ] n ordem f; (in restaurant) pedido m; (COMM) encomenda f ♦ vt (command) mandar; (food, drink) pedir; (taxi) chamar; (COMM) encomendar ♦ vi (in restaurant) pedir; **in ~ to** para; **out of ~** (not working) quebrado(-da) (Br), avariado(-da) (Port); **in working ~** a funcionar; **to ~ sb to do sthg** mandar alguém fazer algo.

order form n folha f de encomenda.

orderly ['ɔːdəlɪ] adj ordenado(-da) ♦ n (in hospital) auxiliar mf.

ordinarily ['ɔːdənrəlɪ, Am ‚ɔːrdn'erəlɪ] adv geralmente.

ordinary ['ɔːdənrɪ] adj comum.

ore [ɔːʳ] n minério m.

oregano [‚ɒrɪˈgɑːnəʊ] n orégão m.

organ ['ɔːgən] n órgão m.

organic [ɔːˈgænɪk] adj orgânico(-ca).

organization [‚ɔːgənaɪˈzeɪʃn] n organização f.

organize ['ɔːgənaɪz] vt organizar.

organizer ['ɔːgənaɪzəʳ] n (person) organizador m (-ra f); (diary) agenda f.

orgasm ['ɔːgæzm] n orgasmo m.

oriental [‚ɔːrɪˈentl] adj oriental.

orientate ['ɔːrɪenteɪt] vt: **to ~ o.s.** orientar-se.

orienteering [‚ɔːrɪenˈtɪərɪŋ] n orientação f; **to go ~** fazer orientação.

origami [‚ɒrɪˈgɑːmɪ] n arte japonesa de dobrar papel criando formas de flores, animais, etc.

origin ['ɒrɪdʒɪn] n origem f.

original [əˈrɪdʒənl] adj original.

originally [əˈrɪdʒənəlɪ] adv (formerly) inicialmente.

originate [əˈrɪdʒəneɪt] vi: **to ~ (from)** nascer (de).

Orkney Islands ['ɔːknɪ-] npl: **the ~** as ilhas Órcades.

Orkneys ['ɔːknɪz] = **Orkney Islands**.

ornament ['ɔːnəmənt] n (object) peça f de decoração.

ornamental [‚ɔːnəˈmentl] adj decorativo(-va).

ornate [ɔːˈneɪt] adj ornado(-da).

ornithology [‚ɔːnɪˈθɒlədʒɪ] n ornitologia f.

orphan ['ɔːfn] n órfão m (-fã f).

orphanage ['ɔːfənɪdʒ] n orfanato m.

orthodox ['ɔːθədɒks] adj ortodoxo(-xa).

orthopaedic [‚ɔːθəˈpiːdɪk] adj ortopédico(-ca).

oscillate ['ɒsɪleɪt] vi oscilar.

Oslo ['ɒzləʊ] n Oslo s.

ostensible ['stensəbl] n aparente.

ostentatious [‚ɒstənˈteɪʃəs] adj pretensioso(-osa).

osteopath ['ɒstɪəpæθ] n osteopata mf.

ostracize ['ɒstrəsaɪz] vt marginalizar; (from party, union) condenar ao ostracismo.

ostrich ['ɒstrɪtʃ] n avestruz f.

other ['ʌðəʳ] adj outro(-tra) ♦ adv: **~ than** exceto; **the ~ (one)** o outro (a outra); **the ~ day** no outro dia; **one after the ~** um depois do outro.

❏ **others** pron pl (additional ones) outros mpl (-tras fpl); **the ~s** (remaining ones) os outros (as outras).

otherwise ['ʌðəwaɪz] adv (or else) senão; (apart from that) de resto; (differently) de outro modo.

otter ['ɒtəʳ] n lontra f.

ouch [aʊtʃ] excl ai!, au!

ought [ɔːt] aux vb dever; **you ~ to have gone** você devia ter ido; **you ~ to see a doctor** você devia ir ao médico; **the car ~ to be ready by Friday** o carro deve estar pronto sexta-feira.

ounce [aʊns] n = 28,35 gr, onça f.

our ['aʊəʳ] adj nosso(-a); **~ books** os nossos livros.

ours ['aʊəz] pron o nosso (a nossa); **a friend of ~** um amigo nosso; **these shoes are ~** estes sapatos são (os) nossos; **~ are here – where are yours?** os nossos estão aqui – onde estão os seus?

ourselves [aʊəˈselvz] pron (reflexive) nos; (after prep) nós mpl mesmos OR próprios (nós fpl mesmas OR próprias); **we did it ~** nós mesmos OR próprios o fizemos; **we hurt ~** nós nos machucamos.

oust [aʊst] *vt (fml)*: **to ~ sb from sthg** obrigar alguém a sair de algo.

out [aʊt] *adj* **1.** *(light, cigarette)* apaga-do(-da).

2. *(wrong)*: **the bill's £10 ~** há um erro de dez libras na conta.

♦ *adv* **1.** *(outside)* fora; **to get/go ~ (of)** sair (de); **it's cold ~ today** está frio lá fora hoje; **he looked ~** ele olhou para fora.

2. *(not at home, work)* fora; **to be ~** não estar em casa; **to go ~** sair.

3. *(so as to be extinguished)*: **to turn sthg ~** apagar algo; **put your cigarette ~** apague o cigarro.

4. *(expressing removal)*: **to pour sthg ~** despejar algo, jogar algo fora; **to take money ~** *(from cashpoint)* retirar dinhei-ro; **to take sthg ~ (of)** tirar algo (de).

5. *(outwards)*: **to stick ~** sobressair.

6. *(expressing distribution)*: **to hand sthg ~** distribuir algo.

7. *(in phrases)*: **to get enjoyment ~ of sthg** divertir-se com algo; **stay ~ of the sun** não se exponha ao sol; **made ~ of wood** (feito) de madeira; **five ~ of ten women** cinco em cada dez mu-lheres; **I'm ~ of cigarettes** não tenho cigarros.

outback [ˈaʊtbæk] *n*: **the ~** o interior australiano.

outboard (motor) [ˈaʊtbɔːd-] *n* motor *m* de borda.

outbreak [ˈaʊtbreɪk] *n (of disease)* surto *m*; *(of violence)* deflagração *f*.

outburst [ˈaʊtbɜːst] *n* explosão *f*.

outcast [ˈaʊtkɑːst] *n* marginalizado *m* (-da *f*), pária *mf*.

outcome [ˈaʊtkʌm] *n* resultado *m*.

outcrop [ˈaʊtkrɒp] *n* afloramento *m*.

outcry [ˈaʊtkraɪ] *n* clamor *m* (de pro-testo), protesto *m*.

outdated [ˌaʊtˈdeɪtɪd] *adj* ultrapassa-do(-da).

outdo [aʊtˈduː] *(pt -did, pp -done)* *vt* ultrapassar, vencer.

outdoor [ˈaʊtdɔːr] *adj (swimming pool, activities)* ao ar livre.

outdoors [aʊtˈdɔːz] *adv* ao ar livre.

outer [ˈaʊtər] *adj* exterior, externo (-na).

outer space *n* espaço *m* (exterior).

outfit [ˈaʊtfɪt] *n (clothes)* roupa *f*.

outgoing [ˈaʊtgəʊɪŋ] *adj (mail, train)* de saída; *(friendly, sociable)* extroverti-do(-da), aberto(-ta).

◻ **outgoings** *npl (Brit)* gastos *mpl*.

outing [ˈaʊtɪŋ] *n* excursão *f*, saída *f*.

outlaw [ˈaʊtlɔː] *n* foragido *m* (-da *f*) ♦ *vt (make illegal)* proibir.

outlay [ˈaʊtleɪ] *n* despesa *f*, gasto *m*.

outlet [ˈaʊtlet] *n (pipe)* saída *f*; **"no ~"** *(Am)* sinal que indica que a rua não tem saída.

outline [ˈaʊtlaɪn] *n (shape)* contorno *m*; *(description)* linhas *fpl* gerais, esboço *m*.

outlive [aʊtˈlɪv] *vt (subj: person)* sobreviver a.

outlook [ˈaʊtlʊk] *n (for future)* pers-pectiva *f*; *(of weather)* previsão *f*; *(atti-tude)* atitude *f*.

outlying [ˈaʊtlaɪɪŋ] *adj (remote)* remo-to(-ta); *(on edge of town)* periférico(-ca).

outnumber [ˌaʊtˈnʌmbər] *vt* ultrapas-sar OR exceder em número.

out-of-date *adj (old-fashioned)* anti-quado(-da); *(passport, licence)* expira-do(-da) *(Br)*, caducado(-da) *(Port)*.

out of doors *adv* ao ar livre.

outpatients' (department) [ˈaʊtˌpeɪʃnts-] *n* ambulatório *m* *(Br)*, consultas *fpl* externas *(Port)*.

output [ˈaʊtpʊt] *n (of factory)* pro-dução *f*; *(COMPUT: printout)* impressão *f*.

outrage [ˈaʊtreɪdʒ] *n (cruel act)* atroci-dade *f*.

outrageous [aʊtˈreɪdʒəs] *adj (shock-ing)* escandaloso(-osa).

outright [ˈaʊtraɪt] *adv (tell, deny)* categoricamente; *(own)* completamen-te, totalmente.

outset [ˈaʊtset] *n*: **from/at the ~** desde o/no início.

outside [*adv* ˌaʊtˈsaɪd, *adj, prep & n* ˈaʊtsaɪd] *adv* lá fora ♦ *prep* fora de; *(in front of)* em frente de ♦ *adj (exterior)* exterior; *(help, advice)* independente ♦ *n*: **the ~** *(of building, car, container)* o exterior; *(AUT: in UK)* a faixa direita; *(AUT: in Europe, US)* a faixa esquerda; **~ of** *(Am)* *(on the outside of)* fora de; *(apart from)* excepto; **let's go ~** vamos lá para fora; **an ~ line** uma linha ex-terna.

outside lane *n (AUT) (in UK)* faixa *f* direita; *(in Europe, US)* faixa esquerda.

outsider [aʊtˈsaɪdər] *n (socially)* estranho *m* (-nha *f*); *(in horse race)* cavalo que não estava entre os favoritos.

outsize [ˈaʊtsaɪz] *adj (clothes)* de

tamanho extra grande.

outskirts [ˈaʊtskɜːts] *npl* arredores *mpl*.

outspoken [ˌaʊtˈspəʊkn] *adj* direto (-ta); *(critic)* assumido(-da).

outstanding [ˌaʊtˈstændɪŋ] *adj (remarkable)* notável; *(problem, debt)* pendente.

outstay [aʊtˈsteɪ] *vt*: **to ~ one's welcome** abusar da hospitalidade de alguém.

outstretched [ˌaʊtˈstretʃt] *adj* estendido(-da).

outstrip [aʊtˈstrɪp] *vt (do better than)* ganhar de, vencer.

outward [ˈaʊtwəd] *adj (journey)* de ida; *(external)* exterior.

outwardly [ˈaʊtwədlɪ] *adv* aparentemente.

outwards [ˈaʊtwədz] *adv* para fora.

outweigh [aʊtˈweɪ] *vt* pesar mais (do) que.

outwit [aʊtˈwɪt] *vt* passar a perna em.

oval [ˈəʊvl] *adj* oval.

ovary [ˈəʊvərɪ] *n* ovário *m*.

ovation [əʊˈveɪʃn] *n* ovação *f*.

oven [ˈʌvn] *n* forno *m*.

oven glove *n* luva *f* de cozinha.

ovenproof [ˈʌvnpruːf] *adj* refratário(-ria).

oven-ready *adj* pronto(-ta) para assar (no forno).

over [ˈəʊvər] *prep* **1.** *(above)* por cima de; **a bridge ~ the road** uma ponte por cima da estrada.
2. *(across)* por cima de; **with a view ~ the square** com vista sobre a praça; **to step ~ sthg** passar por cima de algo; **it's just ~ the road** é logo do outro lado da rua.
3. *(covering)* sobre; **put a plaster ~ the wound** põe um band-aid na ferida.
4. *(more than)* mais de; **it cost ~ £1,000** custou mais de 1.000 libras.
5. *(during)* em; **~ the past two years** nos últimos dois anos.
6. *(with regard to)* sobre; **an argument ~ the price** uma discussão sobre o preço.
♦ *adv* **1.** *(downwards)*: **to bend ~** abaixar-se; **to fall ~** cair; **to push sthg ~** empurrar algo.
2. *(referring to position, movement)*: **to fly ~ to Canada** ir ao Canadá de avião; **~ here** aqui; **~ there** ali.

3. *(round to other side)*: **to turn sthg ~** virar algo.
4. *(more)*: **children aged 12 and ~** crianças com 12 anos ou mais.
5. *(remaining)*: **to be (left) ~** restar.
6. *(to one's house)*: **to invite sb ~ for dinner** convidar alguém para jantar.
7. *(in phrases)*: **all ~ the world/country** por todo o mundo/país.
♦ *adj (finished)*: **to be ~** acabar, terminar; **it's (all) ~!** acabou-se!

overall [*adv* ˌəʊvərˈɔːl, *n* ˈəʊvərɔːl] *adv (in general)* no geral ♦ *n (Brit: coat)* bata *f*; *(Am: boiler suit)* macacão *m (Br)*, fato-macaco *m (Port)*; **how much does it cost ~?** quanto custa ao todo?.
❑ **overalls** *npl (Brit: boiler suit)* macacão *m (Br)*, fato-macaco *m (Port)*; *(Am: dungarees)* jardineiras *fpl*.

overawe [ˌəʊvərˈɔː] *vt* impressionar.

overbearing [ˌəʊvəˈbeərɪŋ] *adj* autoritário(-ria).

overboard [ˈəʊvəbɔːd] *adv (from ship)* ao mar.

overbooked [ˌəʊvəˈbʊkt] *adj (flight)*: **to be ~** ter mais reservas que lugares.

overcame [ˌəʊvəˈkeɪm] *pt* → **overcome**.

overcast [ˌəʊvəˈkɑːst] *adj* encoberto(-ta).

overcharge [ˌəʊvəˈtʃɑːdʒ] *vt* cobrar demasiado a.

overcoat [ˈəʊvəkəʊt] *n* sobretudo *m*.

overcome [ˌəʊvəˈkʌm] *(pt* **-came**, *pp* **-come)** *vt (defeat)* vencer.

overcooked [ˌəʊvəˈkʊkt] *adj* cozido (-da) demais OR demasiado.

overcrowded [ˌəʊvəˈkraʊdɪd] *adj* superlotado(-da); *(country)* com excesso populacional.

overcrowding [ˌəʊvəˈkraʊdɪŋ] *n* superlotação *f*; *(of country)* excesso *m* populacional.

overdo [ˌəʊvəˈduː] *(pt* **-did**, *pp* **-done)** *vt (exaggerate)* exagerar em; **to ~ it** exagerar.

overdone [ˌəʊvəˈdʌn] *pp* → **overdo**
♦ *adj (food)* cozido(-da) demais OR demasiado.

overdose [ˈəʊvədəʊs] *n* overdose *f*, dose *f* excessiva.

overdraft [ˈəʊvədrɑːft] *n* saldo *m* negativo.

overdrawn [ˌəʊvəˈdrɔːn] *adj*: **to be ~** estar com saldo negativo.

overdue [ˌəʊvəˈdjuː] *adj* atrasado(-da).

over easy adj (Am: egg) frito(-ta) dos dois lados.

overestimate [,əʊvər'estɪmeɪt] vt (quantity, bill) exagerar (no cálculo de); (enthusiasm, importance) sobrestimar.

overexposed [,əʊvərɪk'spəʊzd] adj (photograph) demasiado exposto (-osta).

overflow [vb ,əʊvə'fləʊ, n 'əʊvəfləʊ] vi transbordar ♦ n (pipe) cano m de descarga.

overgrown [,əʊvə'grəʊn] adj coberto(-ta) de ervas daninhas.

overhaul [,əʊvə'hɔːl] n (of machine, car) revisão f.

overhead [adj 'əʊvəhed, adv ,əʊvə'hed] adj aéreo(-rea) ♦ adv no alto.

overhead locker n compartimento m superior.

overhead projector n retroprojetor m.

overhear [,əʊvə'hɪər] (pt & pp -heard) vt ouvir (casualmente).

overheat [,əʊvə'hiːt] vi aquecer demais.

overjoyed [,əʊvə'dʒɔɪd] adj: to be ~ (at sthg) estar contentíssimo(-ma) (com algo).

overland [,əʊvə'lænd] adv por terra.

overlap [,əʊvə'læp] vi sobrepor-se.

overleaf [,əʊvə'liːf] adv no verso.

overload [,əʊvə'ləʊd] vt sobrecarregar.

overlook [vb ,əʊvə'lʊk, n 'əʊvəlʊk] vt (subj: building, room) dar para; (miss) não reparar em ♦ n: (scenic) ~ (Am) miradouro m.

overnight [adv ,əʊvə'naɪt, adj 'əʊvənaɪt] adv (during the night) durante a noite ♦ adj (train, journey) noturno(-na); **why don't you stay ~?** por que é que você não fica para dormir?

overnight bag n saco m de viagem.

overpass ['əʊvəpɑːs] n viaduto m.

overpower [,əʊvə'paʊər] vt (in fight) dominar; (fig: overwhelm) tomar conta de.

overpowering [,əʊvə'paʊərɪŋ] adj intenso(-sa).

overran [,əʊvə'ræn] pt → overrun.

overrated [,əʊvə'reɪtɪd] adj: **I think the film is totally ~** não acho que o filme seja tão bom como se diz.

override [,əʊvə'raɪd] (pt -rode, pp -ridden) vt (be more important than) pre-

valecer sobre; (overrule: decision) ir contra.

overrule [,əʊvə'ruːl] vt (person) desautorizar; (decision) ir contra; (objection, request) rejeitar, negar.

overrun [,əʊvə'rʌn] (pt -ran, pp -run) vi (last too long) alongar-se, ultrapassar o tempo previsto ♦ vt (occupy) invadir; **to be ~ with sthg** (fig: covered, filled) ser invadido(-da) por algo.

oversaw [,əʊvə'sɔː] pt → oversee.

overseas [adv ,əʊvə'siːz, adj 'əʊvəsiːz] adv (go) para o estrangeiro; (live) no estrangeiro ♦ adj estrangeiro(-ra); ~ **territories** territórios mpl ultramarinos.

oversee [,əʊvə'siː] (pt -saw, pp -seen) vt supervisionar.

overseer ['əʊvə,siːər] n supervisor m (-ra f).

overshadow [,əʊvə'ʃædəʊ] vt: **to be ~ed by** (eclipsed) ser ofuscado(-da) por; (spoiled) ser toldado(-da) por.

overshoot [,əʊvə'ʃuːt] (pt & pp -shot) vt passar.

oversight ['əʊvəsaɪt] n descuido m.

oversleep [,əʊvə'sliːp] (pt & pp -slept) vi dormir demais, acordar tarde (Port).

overt ['əʊvɜːt, əʊ'vɜːt] adj manifesto(-ta), notório(-ria).

overtake [,əʊvə'teɪk] (pt -took, pp -taken) vt & vi ultrapassar; **"no overtaking"** "proibido ultrapassar".

overthrow [vb ,əʊvə'θrəʊ, n 'əʊvəθrəʊ] (pt -threw, pp -thrown) vt (of government) derrube m (Port), derrubada f (Br) ♦ vt (government, president) derrubar.

overtime ['əʊvətaɪm] n horas fpl extraordinárias.

overtones ['əʊvətəʊnz] npl (of anger, jealousy) ponta f; (political) implicações fpl.

overtook [,əʊvə'tʊk] pt → overtake.

overture ['əʊvə,tjʊər] n (MUS) abertura f.

overturn [,əʊvə'tɜːn] vi (boat) virar; (car) capotar.

overweight [,əʊvə'weɪt] adj gordo (-da).

overwhelm [,əʊvə'welm] vt: **I was ~ed with joy** fiquei feliz da vida.

overwhelming [,əʊvə'welmɪŋ] adj (feeling, quality) tremendo(-da); (victory, defeat, majority) esmagador(-ra).

overwork [,əʊvə'wɜːk] vt (staff, per-

son) sobrecarregar (com trabalho).

owe [əʊ] *vt* dever; **to ~ sb sthg** dever algo a alguém; **owing to** devido a.

owl [aʊl] *n* mocho *m*, coruja *f*.

own [əʊn] *adj* próprio(-pria) ◆ *vt* possuir, ter ◆ *pron*: **my ~** o meu (a minha); **a house of my ~** uma casa só minha; **on my ~** sozinho(-nha); **to get one's ~ back** vingar-se.

❑ **own up** *vi*: **to ~ up (to sthg)** confessar (algo), admitir (algo).

owner ['əʊnəʳ] *n* proprietário *m* (-ria *f*), dono *m* (-na *f*).

ownership ['əʊnəʃɪp] *n* posse *f*.

ox [ɒks] (*pl* **oxen**) *n* boi *m*.

Oxbridge ['ɒksbrɪdʒ] *n as Universidades de Oxford e Cambridge.*

oxen ['ɒksn] *pl* → **ox**.

oxtail soup ['ɒksteɪl-] *n* sopa *f* de rabo de boi.

oxygen ['ɒksɪdʒən] *n* oxigênio *m*.

oyster ['ɔɪstəʳ] *n* ostra *f*.

oz *abbr* = **ounce**.

ozone ['əʊzəʊn] *n* ozônio *m*.

ozone-friendly *adj* que não danifica a camada de ozônio.

ozone layer *n* camada *f* de ozônio.

P

p *abbr* = penny, pence; *(abbr of page)* pág.

pa [pɑː] *n (inf)* pai *m*.

PA *abbr (Brit)* = **personal assistant**, **public address system**.

pace [peɪs] *n (speed)* ritmo *m*; *(step)* passo *m*.

pacemaker ['peɪsˌmeɪkəʳ] *n (for heart)* marcapasso *m (Br)*, pacemaker *m (Port)*.

Pacific [pə'sɪfɪk] *n*: **the ~ (Ocean)** o (Oceano) Pacífico.

pacifier ['pæsɪfaɪəʳ] *n (Am: for baby)* chupeta *f*, chucha *f (Port)*.

pacifist ['pæsɪfɪst] *n* pacifista *mf*.

pack [pæk] *n (packet)* pacote *m*; *(of cigarettes)* maço *m*; *(Brit: of cards)* baralho *m*; *(rucksack)* mochila *f* ◆ *vt (suitcase, bag)* fazer; *(clothes, camera etc)* colocar na mala; *(to package)* empacotar ◆ *vi (for journey)* fazer as malas; **a ~ of lies** um monte de mentiras; **to ~ sthg into sthg** colocar algo em algo; **to ~ one's bags** fazer as malas.
❑ **pack up** *vi (pack suitcase)* fazer as malas; *(tidy up)* arrumar; *(Brit: inf: machine, car)* parar.

package ['pækɪdʒ] *n* pacote *m* ◆ *vt* empacotar.

package deal *n* acordo *m* global, acordo ou oferta cujas condições têm de ser todas respeitadas e aceitas.

package holiday *n* férias *fpl* com tudo incluído.

package tour *n* excursão *f* organizada.

packaging ['pækɪdʒɪŋ] *n (material)* embalagem *f*.

packed [pækt] *adj (crowded)* cheio (cheia).

packed lunch *n* almoço *m (que se leva de casa para a escola ou para o trabalho)*.

packet ['pækɪt] *n* pacote *m*; **it cost a**

~ *(Brit: inf)* custou um dinheirão.

packing ['pækɪŋ] *n (material)* embalagem *f*; **to do one's ~** fazer as malas.

pact [pækt] *n* pacto *m*.

pad [pæd] *n (of paper)* bloco *m*; *(of cotton wool)* disco *m*; *(of cloth)* almofada *f*; **elbow ~** cotoveleira *f*; **knee ~** joelheira *f*; **shin ~** caneleira *f*.

padded ['pædɪd] *adj (jacket)* acolchoado(-da); *(seat)* almofadado(-da).

padded envelope *n* envelope *m* almofadado.

padding ['pædɪŋ] *n (material)* forro *m*.

paddle ['pædl] *n (pole)* remo *m (pequeno)* ◆ *vi (wade)* chapinhar, patinhar; *(in canoe)* remar.

paddle boat *n* barco *m* a vapor *(com rodas propulsoras)*.

paddle steamer *n* barco *m* a vapor *(com rodas propulsoras)*.

paddling pool ['pædlɪŋ-] *n* piscina *f* para crianças.

paddock ['pædək] *n (at racecourse)* paddock *m*, recinto nos hipódromos para onde são levados os cavalos antes das corridas.

paddy field ['pædɪ-] *n* arrozal *m*.

padlock ['pædlɒk] *n* cadeado *m*.

pagan ['peɪgən] *adj* pagão(-gã) ◆ *n* pagão *m* (-gã *f*).

page [peɪdʒ] *n* página *f* ◆ *vt* chamar; **"paging Mr Hill"** "chamando o Sr. Hill".

paid [peɪd] *pt & pp* → **pay** ◆ *adj* pago(-ga).

pain [peɪn] *n* dor *f*; **to be in ~** estar com dores; **he's such a ~!** *(inf)* ele é um saco!
❑ **pains** *npl (trouble)* esforço *m*, trabalho *m*.

pained [peɪnd] *adj* angustiado(-da).

painful ['peɪnfʊl] *adj* doloroso(-osa).

painfully ['peɪnfʊlɪ] *adv (distressingly)*

penosamente; *(for emphasis)* extremamente.

painkiller ['peɪn,kɪləʳ] *n* analgésico *m*.

painless ['peɪnlɪs] *adj (operation, death)* indolor; *(unproblematic)* fácil.

painstaking ['peɪnz,teɪkɪŋ] *adj (worker)* meticuloso(-osa); *(attention, detail, care)* extremo(-ma).

paint [peɪnt] *n* tinta *f* ◆ *vt & vi* pintar; **to ~ one's nails** pintar as unhas.
⏤ **paints** *npl (tubes, pots etc)* tintas *fpl*.

paintbrush ['peɪntbrʌʃ] *n (of decorator)* broxa *f; (of artist)* pincel.

painter ['peɪntəʳ] *n* pintor *m* (-ra *f*).

painting ['peɪntɪŋ] *n (activity)* pintura *f; (picture)* quadro *m*.

paint stripper [-'strɪpəʳ] *n* removedor *m* de tinta.

paintwork ['peɪntwɜːk] *n* pintura *f*.

pair [peəʳ] *n (of two things)* par *m;* **in ~s** aos pares; **a ~ of pliers** um alicate; **a ~ of scissors** uma tesoura; **a ~ of shorts** um calção *(Br)*, uns calções *(Port);* **a ~ of tights** uma meia-calça *(Br)*, uns collants *(Port);* **a ~ of trousers** uma calça *(Br)*, um par de calças *(Port)*.

pajamas [pəˈdʒɑːməz] *(Am)* = **pyjamas**.

Pakistan [Brit ˌpɑːkɪˈstɑːn, Am ˌpækɪˈstæn] *n* Paquistão *m*.

Pakistani [Brit ˌpɑːkɪˈstɑːnɪ, Am ˌpækɪˈstænɪ] *adj* paquistanês(-esa) ◆ *n (person)* paquistanês *m* (-esa *f*).

pakora [pəˈkɔːrə] *npl* especialidade indiana feita com legumes fritos numa massa mole picante, servido como entrada com molhos picantes.

pal [pæl] *n (inf)* amigo *m* (-ga *f*).

palace ['pælɪs] *n* palácio *m*.

palatable ['pælətəbl] *adj* saboroso(-osa).

palate ['pælət] *n* paladar *m*.

pale [peɪl] *adj* pálido(-da).

pale ale *n* cerveja *f (clara e fraca)*.

Palestine ['pæləstaɪn] *n* Palestina *f*.

Palestinian [ˌpæləˈstɪnɪən] *adj* palestiniano(-na), palestino(-na) ◆ *n (person)* palestiniano *m* (-na *f*), palestino *m* (-na *f*).

palette ['pælət] *n* paleta *f*.

palm [pɑːm] *n (of hand)* palma *f;* **~ (tree)** palmeira *f*.

Palm Sunday *n* Domingo *m* de Ramos.

palpitations [ˌpælpɪˈteɪʃnz] *npl* palpitações *fpl*.

paltry ['pɔːltrɪ] *adj* mísero(-ra).

pamper ['pæmpəʳ] *vt* mimar.

pamphlet ['pæmflɪt] *n* folheto *m*.

pan [pæn] *n* panela *f*, tacho *m (Port)*.

pancake ['pænkeɪk] *n* panqueca *f*.

Pancake Day *n (Brit)* = terça-feira *f* de Carnaval, Dia *m* de Entrudo *(Port)*.

pancake roll *n* crepe *m* chinês.

panda ['pændə] *n* panda *m*.

panda car *n (Brit)* carro *m* da polícia.

pandemonium [ˌpændɪˈməʊnjəm] *n* pandemônio *m*.

pander ['pændəʳ] *vi:* **to ~ to sb's every whim** fazer todas as vontades a alguém; **the tabloid press ~s to popular prejudice** a imprensa sensacionalista gosta de alimentar os preconceitos dos seus leitores.

pane [peɪn] *n* vidro *m*, vidraça *f*.

panel ['pænl] *n (of wood)* painel *m; (group of experts)* equipe *f; (on TV, radio)* grupo *m* de convidados.

paneling ['pænəlɪŋ] *(Am)* = **panelling**.

panelling ['pænəlɪŋ] *n (Brit)* painéis *mpl*.

pang [pæŋ] *n* pontada *f;* **to feel ~s of guilt** ter a consciência pesada.

panic ['pænɪk] *(pt & pp* **-ked**, *cont* **-king)** *n* pânico *m* ◆ *vi* entrar em pânico.

panic-stricken [-'strɪkn] *adj* apavorado(-da), tomado(-da) pelo pânico.

panniers ['pænɪəz] *npl (for bicycle)* bolsas *fpl* para bicicleta.

panorama [ˌpænəˈrɑːmə] *n* panorama *m*.

panoramic [ˌpænəˈræmɪk] *adj* panorâmico(-ca).

pansy ['pænzɪ] *n (flower)* amor-perfeito *m*.

pant [pænt] *vi* arfar, ofegar.

panther ['pænθəʳ] *(pl inv OR* **-s)** *n* pantera *f*.

panties ['pæntɪz] *npl (inf)* calcinha *f (Br)*, cuecas *fpl (Port)*.

pantomime ['pæntəmaɪm] *n (Brit)* pantomima *f*.

pantry ['pæntrɪ] *n* despensa *f*.

pants [pænts] *npl (Brit: underwear)* cueca *f (Br)*, cuecas *fpl (Port); (Am: trousers)* calça *f (Br)*, calças *fpl (Port)*.

panty hose ['pæntɪ-] *npl (Am)* meia-calça *f (Br)*, collants *mpl (Port)*.

papa [pəˈpɑː] *n* papá *m*.

papadum ['pæpədəm] *n* tipo de bola-

cha, tipicamente indiana, frita, fina e estaladiça.

paper ['peɪpəʳ] *n (material)* papel *m;*
(newspaper) jornal *m; (exam)* prova *f;*
(at university) exame *m,* frequência *f*
♦ *adj* de papel ♦ *vt* decorar (com papel
de parede); **a piece of ~** *(sheet)* uma
folha de papel; *(scrap)* um pedaço de
papel.
❑ **papers** *npl (documents)* papéis *mpl,*
documentos *mpl.*

paperback ['peɪpəbæk] *n* livro *m* bro-
chado.

paper bag *n* saco *m* de papel.

paperboy ['peɪpəbɔɪ] *n* rapaz que dis-
tribui jornais de casa em casa.

paper clip *n* clipe *m.*

papergirl ['peɪpəgɜːl] *n* moça que dis-
tribui jornais de casa em casa.

paper handkerchief *n* lenço *m* de
papel.

paper knife *n* corta-papéis *m inv.*

paper shop *n* ~ tabacaria *f,* =
quiosque *m* de jornais.

paperweight ['peɪpəweɪt] *n* pesa-
papéis *m inv.*

paperwork ['peɪpəwɜːk] *n* papelada
f, burocracia *f*

paprika ['pæprɪkə] *n* colorau *m,*
pimentão-doce *m.*

par [pɑːʳ] *n (in golf)* par *m.*

paracetamol [,pærə'siːtəmɒl] *n* paracetamol *m.*

parachute ['pærəʃuːt] *n* pára-quedas
m.

parade [pə'reɪd] *n (procession)* desfile
m; (of shops) série *f* de pequenas lojas
(na mesma rua).

paradise ['pærədaɪs] *n (fig)* paraíso *m.*

paradox ['pærədɒks] *n* paradoxo *m.*

paradoxically [,pærə'dɒksɪklɪ] *adv*
paradoxalmente.

paraffin ['pærəfɪn] *n* parafina *f.*

paragraph ['pærəgrɑːf] *n* parágrafo *m.*

parallel ['pærəlel] *adj:* ~ **(to)** *(lines)*
paralelo(-la) (a).

paralysed ['pærəlaɪzd] *adj (Brit)* para-
lisado(-da), paralítico(-ca).

paralysis [pə'rælɪsɪs] *(pl* **-lyses** [-lɪsiːz])
n paralisia *f.*

paralyzed ['pærəlaɪzd] *(Am)* =
paralysed.

paramedic [,pærə'medɪk] *n* paramédi-
co *m (-ca f).*

paramount ['pærəmaʊnt] *adj* fundamental, vital; **of ~ importance** extre-

mamente importante, vital.

paranoid ['pærənɔɪd] *adj* paranói-
co(-ca).

parasite ['pærəsaɪt] *n* parasita *m.*

parasol ['pærəsɒl] *n (above table)*
guarda-sol *m (Br),* chapéu-de-sol *m*
(Port); (on beach) barraca *f* de praia *(Br),*
chapéu *m* de praia *(Port); (hand-held)*
sombrinha *f.*

parcel ['pɑːsl] *n* embrulho *m.*

parcel post *n* serviço *m* de enco-
mendas postais.

parched [pɑːtʃt] *adj (very dry)* resse-
cado(-da); **I'm ~** *(inf: very thirsty)* tenho
a garganta ressecada, estou morto de
sede.

parchment ['pɑːtʃmənt] *n* pergaminho *m.*

pardon ['pɑːdn] *excl:* ~? desculpe?,
como?; ~ **(me)!** perdão!; **I beg your ~!**
(apologizing) peço desculpa!; **I beg your**
~? *(asking for repetition)* desculpe?,
como?

parent ['peərənt] *n (father)* pai *m;*
(mother) mãe *f;* **my ~s** os meus pais.

Paris ['pærɪs] *n* Paris *s.*

parish ['pærɪʃ] *n (of church)* paróquia *f;*
(village area) = freguesia *f.*

park [pɑːk] *n* parque *m* ♦ *vt & vi (vehi-*
cle) estacionar.

park and ride *n* sistema que consiste
em estacionar o carro nos arredores da
cidade e apanhar o ônibus para o centro.

parking ['pɑːkɪŋ] *n* estacionamento
m.

parking brake *n (Am)* freio *m* de
mão *(Br),* travão *m* de mão *(Port).*

parking lot *n (Am)* (parque *m* de)
estacionamento *m.*

parking meter *n* parquímetro *m.*

parking space *n* espaço *m* OR lugar
m para estacionar.

parking ticket *n* multa *f* (por estacionar em lugar proibido).

parliament ['pɑːləmənt] *n* parlamento *m.*

parliamentary [,pɑːlə'mentərɪ] *adj*
parlamentar.

Parmesan (cheese) [pɑːmɪ'zæn-] *n*
(queijo) parmesão *m.*

parody ['pærədɪ] *n* paródia *f* ♦ *vt*
parodiar.

parole [pə'rəʊl] *n* liberdade *f* condicional; **on ~** em liberdade condicional.

parrot ['pærət] *n* papagaio *m.*

parry ['pærɪ] *vt (blow)* esquivar-se de.

parsley ['pɑːslɪ] n salsa f.

parsnip ['pɑːsnɪp] n cherivia f, cenoura f branca.

parson ['pɑːsn] n vigário m, pároco m.

part [pɑːt] n (portion) parte f; (of machine, car) peça f; (in play, film) papel m, parte; (of serial) episódio m; (Am: in hair) risco m ◆ adv em parte, parcialmente ◆ vi (couple) separar-se; **in this ~ of Portugal** nesta parte de Portugal; **to form ~ of** fazer parte de; **to play a ~ in** desempenhar um papel em; **to take ~ in** tomar parte em; **for my ~** quanto a mim; **for the most ~** geralmente, em geral; **in these ~s** por aqui, por estas partes.

part exchange n troca f, sistema que consiste em comprar algo novo dando como parte do pagamento algo usado; **in ~** em troca.

partial ['pɑːʃl] adj (not whole) parcial; **to be ~ to sthg** ter uma certa predileção por algo.

participant [pɑːˈtɪsɪpənt] n participante mf.

participate [pɑːˈtɪsɪpeɪt] vi: **to ~ (in)** participar (em).

participation [pɑːˌtɪsɪˈpeɪʃn] n participação f.

participle ['pɑːtɪsɪpl] n particípio m.

particle ['pɑːtɪkl] n partícula f.

particular [pɑːˈtɪkjʊlər] adj especial; (fussy) esquisito(-ta); **in ~** em particular; **nothing in ~** nada de especial.

❏ **particulars** npl (details) pormenores mpl, detalhes mpl.

particularly [pɑːˈtɪkjʊlələ] adv especialmente.

parting ['pɑːtɪŋ] n (Brit: in hair) repartido m (Br), risco m (Port).

partition [pɑːˈtɪʃn] n (wall) tabique m.

partly ['pɑːtlɪ] adv em parte.

partner ['pɑːtnər] n (husband, wife) cônjuge mf; (lover) companheiro m (-ra f); (in game, dance) parceiro m (-ra f); (COMM) sócio m (-cia f).

partnership ['pɑːtnəʃɪp] n sociedade f.

partridge ['pɑːtrɪdʒ] n perdiz f.

part-time adj & adv part-time, em meio expediente.

party ['pɑːtɪ] n (for fun) festa f; (POL) partido m; (group of people) grupo m; **to have a ~** dar uma festa.

pass [pɑːs] vt passar; (move past) passar por; (law) aprovar ◆ vi passar ◆ n (SPORT, document) passe m; (in mountain) desfiladeiro m, garganta f; (in exam) suficiente m, médio m; **to ~ sb sthg** passar algo a alguém.

❏ **pass by** vt fus (building, window etc) passar por ◆ vi passar.

❏ **pass on** vt sep (message) transmitir.

❏ **pass out** vi (faint) desmaiar.

❏ **pass up** vt sep (opportunity) deixar passar.

passable ['pɑːsəbl] adj (road) transitável; (satisfactory) aceitável, satisfatório(-ria).

passage ['pæsɪdʒ] n (corridor) passagem f, corredor m; (in book) passagem f, trecho m; (sea journey) travessia f.

passageway ['pæsɪdʒweɪ] n passagem f, corredor m.

passbook ['pɑːsbʊk] n caderneta f.

passenger ['pæsɪndʒər] n passageiro m (-ra f).

passerby [ˌpɑːsəˈbaɪ] n transeunte mf, passante mf.

passing ['pɑːsɪŋ] adj (trend) passageiro(-ra); (remark) de passagem.

❏ **in passing** adv por alto, de passagem.

passing place ['pɑːsɪŋ-] n (for cars) zona f para ultrapassagem.

passion ['pæʃn] n paixão f.

passionate ['pæʃənət] adj (showing strong feeling) apaixonado(-da); (sexually) ardente.

passive ['pæsɪv] n passiva f.

Passover ['pɑːsˌəʊvər] n: **(the) ~** a Páscoa dos judeus.

passport ['pɑːspɔːt] n passaporte m.

passport control n controle m de passaportes.

passport photo n fotografia f para passaporte.

password ['pɑːswɜːd] n senha f.

past [pɑːst] adj passado(-da); (former) antigo(-ga) ◆ prep (further than) depois de; (in front of) em frente de ◆ n (former time) passado m ◆ adv: **to go ~** passar; **the ~ month** o mês passado; **twenty ~ four** quatro e vinte; **the ~ (tense)** (GRAMM) o passado; **in the ~** no passado.

pasta ['pæstə] n massa f.

paste [peɪst] n (spread) pasta f; (glue) cola f.

pastel ['pæstl] n (for drawing) pastel m; (colour) tom m pastel.

pasteurized ['pɑːstʃəraɪzd] adj pasteurizado(-da).

pastille ['pæstɪl] *n* pastilha *f*.

pastime ['pɑːstaɪm] *n* passatempo *m*.

past participle *n* particípio *m* passado.

pastrami [pəs'trɑːmɪ] *n* carne de vaca defumada e picante.

pastry ['peɪstrɪ] *n* (for pie) massa *f*; (cake) pastel *m*.

pasture ['pɑːstʃəʳ] *n* pasto *m*, pastagem *f*.

pasty ['pæstɪ] *n* (Brit) empada *f*.

pat [pæt] *vt* (dog, friend) dar um tapinha (afetuosa) em.

patch [pætʃ] *n* (for clothes) remendo *m*; (of colour, damp) mancha *f*; (for skin) esparadrapo *m* (Br), penso *m* (Port); (for eye) pala *f*, penso; **a bad ~** (fig) um mau bocado.

patchwork ['pætʃwɜːk] *n* (of fields) colcha *f* de retalhos.

patchy ['pætʃɪ] *adj* (uneven) irregular; (incomplete) incompleto(-ta); (performance, game) com altos e baixos.

pâté ['pæteɪ] *n* pasta *f*, paté *m*.

patent [Brit 'peɪtənt, Am 'pætənt] *n* patente *f*.

patent leather *n* verniz *m* (cabedal).

paternal [pə'tɜːnl] *adj* paternal.

path [pɑːθ] *n* caminho *m*.

pathetic [pə'θetɪk] *adj* (pej: useless) inútil.

pathological [,pæθə'lɒdʒɪkl] *adj* patológico(-ca).

pathway ['pɑːθweɪ] *n* caminho *m*.

patience ['peɪʃns] *n* paciência *f*.

patient ['peɪʃnt] *adj* paciente ◆ *n* doente *mf*, paciente *mf*.

patio ['pætɪəʊ] (*pl* -s) *n* pátio *m*.

patriotic [Brit ,pætrɪ'ɒtɪk, Am ,peɪtrɪ'ɒtɪk] *adj* patriótico(-ca).

patrol [pə'trəʊl] *vt* patrulhar ◆ *n* (group) patrulha *f*.

patrol car *n* carro *m* de patrulha.

patron ['peɪtrən] *n* (fml: customer) cliente *mf*; **"~s only"** "só para clientes".

patronizing ['pætrənaɪzɪŋ] *adj* condescendente.

patter ['pætəʳ] *n* (of raindrops) tamborilar *m*.

pattern ['pætn] *n* (of shapes, colours) desenho *m*, padrão *m*; (for sewing) molde *m*.

patterned ['pætənd] *adj* estampado(-da).

paunch [pɔːntʃ] *n* pança *f*.

pause [pɔːz] *n* pausa *f* ◆ *vi* fazer uma pausa.

pave [peɪv] *vt* (with concrete, tarmac) pavimentar; (with stones) calçar; **to ~ the way for** preparar o caminho para.

pavement ['peɪvmənt] *n* (Brit: beside road) calçada *f* (Br), passeio *m* (Port); (Am: roadway) pavimento *m*, asfalto *m*.

pavilion [pə'vɪljən] *n* pavilhão *m*.

paving ['peɪvɪŋ] *n* calçamento *m*, pavimentação *f*.

paving stone *n* laje *f*.

pavlova [pæv'ləʊvə] *n* bolo feito de camadas de suspiro, creme batido e fruta.

paw [pɔː] *n* pata *f*.

pawn [pɔːn] *vt* empenhar ◆ *n* (in chess) peão *m*.

pawnbroker ['pɔːn,brəʊkəʳ] *n* penhorista *mf*.

pawnshop ['pɔːnʃɒp] *n* casa *f* de penhor.

pay [peɪ] (*pt & pp* **paid**) *vt* pagar; (person) pagar a ◆ *vi* (give money) pagar; (be profitable) compensar, dar lucro ◆ *n* ordenado *m*, salário *m*; **to ~ sb for sth** pagar a alguém (por) algo; **to ~ money into an account** depositar dinheiro numa conta; **to ~ attention (to)** prestar atenção (a); **to ~ sb a visit** visitar alguém, fazer uma visita a alguém; **to ~ by credit card** pagar com cartão de crédito.

❑ **pay back** *vt sep* (money) pagar; (person) pagar, devolver o dinheiro a.

❑ **pay for** *vt fus* (purchase) pagar (por).

❑ **pay in** *vt sep* (cheque, money) depositar.

❑ **pay out** *vt sep* (money) pagar.

❑ **pay up** *vi* pagar.

payable ['peɪəbl] *adj* (bill) pagável; **~ to** (cheque) em nome de, a ordem de.

payday ['peɪdeɪ] *n* dia *f* de pagamento.

payment ['peɪmənt] *n* pagamento *m*.

pay packet *n* (Brit: wages) pagamento *m*.

payphone ['peɪfəʊn] *n* telefone *m* público.

payroll ['peɪrəʊl] *n* folha *f* de pagamentos.

payslip ['peɪslɪp] *n* (Brit) recibo *m* de pagamento, contracheque *m*.

paystub ['peɪstʌb] *(Am)* = **payslip**.

PC *n* (abbr of personal computer) PC *m*; (Brit: abbr of police constable) policial *mf*

(Br), = polícia *mf (Port)*.

PE *abbr* = physical education.

pea [pi:] *n* ervilha *f*.

peace [pi:s] *n* paz *f*; **to leave sb in ~** deixar alguém em paz; **~ and quiet** paz e sossego.

peaceful ['pi:sful] *adj (place, day, feeling)* calmo(-ma); *(demonstration)* pacífico(-ca).

peacetime ['pi:staim] *n* tempo *m* de paz.

peach [pi:tʃ] *n* pêssego *m*.

peach melba [-'melbə] *n* peach melba *m*, pedaços de pêssego, cobertos com sorvete de baunilha e regados com molho de framboesa.

peacock ['pi:kɒk] *n* pavão *m*.

peak [pi:k] *n (of mountain)* pico *m*; *(of hat)* pala *f*; *(fig: highest point)* auge *m*.

peaked [pi:kt] *adj* com pala.

peak hours *npl* rush *m (Br)*, horas *fpl* de ponta *(Port)*.

peak rate *n* tarifa *f* alta.

peal [pi:l] *n (of bells)* repicar *m*; *(of thunder)* ribombar *m* ◆ *vi (bells)* repicar; **~ of laughter** gargalhadas *fpl*.

peanut ['pi:nʌt] *n* amendoim *m*.

peanut butter *n* manteiga *f* de amendoim.

pear [peəʳ] *n* pêra *f*.

pearl [pɜ:l] *n* pérola *f*.

peasant ['peznt] *n* camponês *m* (-esa *f*).

peat [pi:t] *n* turfa *f*.

pebble ['pebl] *n* seixo *m*.

pecan pie ['pi:kæn-] *n* torta *f* de noz-americana.

peck [pek] *vi (bird)* bicar.

peckish ['pekiʃ] *adj (Brit: inf)*: **I'm feeling ~** bem que eu comeria alguma coisa.

peculiar [pɪ'kju:ljəʳ] *adj (strange)* esquisito(-ta); **to be ~ to** *(exclusive)* ser característico de.

peculiarity [pɪˌkju:lɪ'ærətɪ] *n (special feature)* característica *f*.

pedal ['pedl] *n* pedal *m* ◆ *vi* pedalar.

pedal bin *n* lata *f* de lixo (com pedal).

pedalo ['pedələʊ] *(pl -s OR -es)* *n* gaivota *f*.

pedantic [pɪ'dæntɪk] *adj* rigoroso(-osa), picuinhas *(inv)*.

peddle ['pedl] *vt (drugs)* traficar; *(wares)* vender de porta em porta; *(rumour, gossip)* espalhar.

peddler ['pedlər] *(Am)* = **pedlar**.

pedestal ['pedɪstl] *n* pedestal *m*.

pedestrian [pɪ'destrɪən] *n* pedestre *m (Br)*, peão *m (Port)*.

pedestrian crossing *n* passagem *f* para pedestres *(Br)*, passadeira *f* (para peões) *(Port)*.

pedestrianized [pɪ'destrɪənaɪzd] *adj* para pedestre *(Br)*, pedonal *(Port)*.

pedestrian precinct *n (Brit)* zona *f* para pedestre.

pedestrian zone *(Am)* = **pedestrian precinct**.

pedigree ['pedɪgri:] *adj* de raça ◆ *n (of animal)* raça *f*.

pedlar ['pedlər] *n (Brit)* vendedor *m* (-ra *f*) ambulante.

pee [pi:] *vi (inf)* mijar ◆ *n*: **to have a ~** *(inf)* fazer chichi.

peek [pi:k] *vi (inf)* espiar, espreitar ◆ *n (inf)*: **to take OR have a ~ at sthg** dar uma espiadela em algo.

peel [pi:l] *n* casca *f* ◆ *vt* descascar ◆ *vi* cair.

peelings ['pi:lɪŋz] *npl* cascas *fpl*.

peep [pi:p] *n*: **to have a ~** dar uma espiadela.

peer [pɪəʳ] *vi* olhar com atenção; **to ~ at** olhar atentamente para.

peeved [pi:vd] *adj (inf)* fulo(-la), zangado(-da).

peevish ['pi:vɪʃ] *adj* rabugento(-ta).

peg [peg] *n (for tent)* estaca *f*; *(hook)* gancho *m*; *(for washing)* pregador *m (Br)*, mola *f* da roupa *(Port)*.

pejorative [pɪ'dʒɒrətɪv] *adj* pejorativo(-va).

pelican ['pelɪkən] *n* pelicano *m*.

pelican crossing *n (Brit)* travessia com sinais acionados manualmente pelos pedestres.

pellet ['pelɪt] *n (of mud, paper)* bolinha *f*; *(for gun)* chumbo *m*.

pelt [pelt] *n (animal skin)* pele *f* ◆ *vi (rain)* chover a cântaros ◆ *vt*: **to ~ sb with sthg** *(eggs, tomatoes)* atirar algo para alguém.

pelvis ['pelvɪs] *n* bacia *f*.

pen [pen] *n (ballpoint pen)* esferográfica *f*; *(fountain pen)* caneta *f* (de tinta permanente); *(for animals)* cerca *f*.

penalty ['penltɪ] *n (fine)* multa *f*; *(in football)* pênalti *m*, grande penalidade *f*.

penance ['penəns] *n* penitência *f*.

pence [pɛns] *npl* pence *mpl (moeda britânica)*; **it costs 20 ~** custa 20 pence.

penchant [*Brit* pãʃã, *Am* 'pentʃənt] *n*: **to have a ~ for** ter um fraco por; **to have a ~ for doing sthg** gostar de fazer algo.

pencil ['pensl] *n* lápis *m inv*.

pencil case *n* lapiseira *f (Br)*, portalápis *m inv (Port)*.

pencil sharpener *n* apontador *m (Br)*, apara-lápis *m inv (Port)*.

pendant ['pendənt] *n (on necklace)* pingente *m*.

pending ['pendɪŋ] *prep (fml)* até.

pendulum ['pendjuləm] *n* pêndulo *m*.

penetrate ['penɪtreɪt] *vt* penetrar.

penfriend ['penfrend] *n* penfriend *mf*, correspondente *mf*.

penguin ['peŋgwɪn] *n* pinguim *m*.

penicillin [penɪ'sɪlɪn] *n* penicilina *f*.

peninsula [pə'nɪnsjulə] *n* península *f*.

penis ['piːnɪs] *n* pênis *m inv*.

penknife ['pennaɪf] *(pl* **-knives** [-naɪvz]*) n* canivete *m*, navalha *f*.

pennant ['penənt] *n* galhardete *m*.

penniless ['penɪlɪs] *adj* sem um tostão.

penny ['penɪ] *(pl* **pennies***) n (coin in UK)* péni *m (moeda britânica); (coin in US)* centavo *m (Br)*, cêntimo *m (Port)*.

pen pal *n (inf)* correspondente *mf*.

pension ['penʃn] *n (for retired people)* aposentadoria *f (Br)*, reforma *f (Port); (for disabled people)* pensão *f*.

pensioner ['penʃənər] *n* aposentado *m (-da f) (Br)*, reformado *m (-da f) (Port)*.

pensive ['pensɪv] *adj* pensativo(-va).

Pentecost ['pentɪkɒst] *n* Pentecostes *m*.

penthouse ['penthaus, *pl* -hauzɪz] *n* cobertura *f*, apartamento de luxo situado no último andar de um edifício.

penultimate [pe'nʌltɪmət] *adj* penúltimo(-ma).

people ['piːpl] *npl* pessoas *fpl* ◆ *n (nation)* povo *m*; **the ~** *(citizens)* o povo.

pepper ['pepər] *n (spice)* pimenta *f; (vegetable)* pimentão *m (Br)*, pimento *m (Port)*.

peppercorn ['pepəkɔːn] *n* grão *m* de pimenta.

peppermint ['pepəmɪnt] *adj* de hortelã-pimenta ◆ *n (sweet)* bala *m* de hortelã-pimenta.

pepper pot *n* pimenteiro *m*.

pepper steak *n* bife *m* au poivre.

Pepsi® ['pepsɪ] *n* Pepsi® *f*.

per [pɜːr] *prep* por; **~ person/week** por pessoa/semana; **£20 ~ night** 20 libras por noite.

per annum [pər'ænəm] *adv* por ano.

perceive [pə'siːv] *vt* notar.

per cent *adv* por cento.

percentage [pə'sentɪdʒ] *n* percentagem *f*.

perception [pə'sepʃn] *n (of colour, sound, time)* percepção *f; (insight, understanding)* perspicácia *f*.

perceptive [pə'septɪv] *adj* perspicaz.

perch [pɜːtʃ] *n (for bird)* poleiro *m*.

percolator ['pɜːkəleɪtər] *n* cafeteira *f* de filtro.

percussion [pə'kʌʃn] *n* percussão *f*.

perennial [pə'renjəl] *adj (problem, feature)* permanente.

perfect [*adj & n* 'pɜːfɪkt, *vb* pə'fekt] *adj* perfeito(-ta) ◆ *vt* aperfeiçoar ◆ *n*: **the ~** *(tense)* o perfeito; **the past ~** *(tense)* o pretérito mais-que-perfeito composto.

perfection [pə'fekʃn] *n*: **to do sthg to ~** fazer algo na perfeição.

perfectionist [pə'fekʃənɪst] *n* perfeccionista *mf*.

perfectly ['pɜːfɪktlɪ] *adv (very well)* perfeitamente.

perforate ['pɜːfəreɪt] *vt* perfurar.

perforations [pɜːfə'reɪʃnz] *npl* picotado *m*.

perform [pə'fɔːm] *vt (task, operation)* realizar; *(play)* representar; *(concert)* dar; *(dance, piece of music)* executar ◆ *vi (actor, singer)* atuar.

performance [pə'fɔːməns] *n (of play)* representação *f; (of concert)* interpretação *f; (of film)* exibição *f; (by actor, musician)* atuação *f; (of car)* performance *f*.

performer [pə'fɔːmər] *n* artista *mf*.

perfume ['pɜːfjuːm] *n* perfume *m*.

perhaps [pə'hæps] *adv* talvez.

peril ['perɪl] *n* perigo *m*.

perimeter [pə'rɪmɪtər] *n* perímetro *m*.

period ['pɪərɪəd] *n* período *m; (Am: full stop)* ponto *m (final)* ◆ *adj (costume, furniture)* da época.

periodic [pɪərɪ'ɒdɪk] *adj* periódico (-ca).

period pains *npl* dores *fpl* menstruais.

peripheral [pə'rıfərəl] adj (vision, region) periférico(-ca).

periphery [pə'rıfərı] n periferia f.

perish [perıʃ] vi (die) morrer; (decay) deteriorar-se, estragar-se.

perishable ['perıʃəbl] adj perecível.

perk [pɜːk] n benefícios extras oferecidos pelo emprego, regalia f (Port).

perm [pɜːm] n permanente f ♦ vt: to have one's hair ~ed fazer uma permanente.

permanent ['pɜːmənənt] adj permanente.

permanent address n endereço m fixo.

permanently ['pɜːmənəntlı] adv permanentemente.

permeate ['pɜːmıeıt] vt infiltrar-se em.

permissible [pə'mısəbl] adj (fml) permissível.

permission [pə'mıʃn] n permissão f.

permissive [pə'mısıv] adj permissivo(-va).

permit [vb pə'mıt, n 'pɜːmıt] vt permitir ♦ n autorização f; to ~ sb to do sthg permitir a alguém fazer algo; "~ holders only" aviso indicando que no local só pode estacionar quem tiver uma autorização especial.

pernickety [pə'nıkətı] adj (inf) cheio (cheia) de nove horas.

perpendicular [,pɜːpən'dıkjuləʳ] adj perpendicular.

perpetual [pə'petʃuəl] adj perpétuo (-tua).

perplexing [pə'pleksıŋ] adj desconcertante.

persecute ['pɜːsıkjuːt] vt (oppress) perseguir.

perseverance [,pɜːsı'vıərəns] n perseverança f.

persevere [,pɜːsı'vıəʳ] vi perseverar, insistir.

persist [pə'sıst] vi persistir; to ~ in doing sthg persistir em fazer algo.

persistence [pə'sıstəns] n persistência f.

persistent [pə'sıstənt] adj persistente.

person ['pɜːsn] (pl **people**) n pessoa f; in ~ em pessoa.

personal ['pɜːsənl] adj pessoal; a ~ friend um amigo íntimo.

personal assistant n assistente mf pessoal.

personal belongings npl objetos mpl pessoais.

personal computer n computador m pessoal.

personality [,pɜːsə'nælətı] n personalidade f.

personally ['pɜːsnəlı] adv pessoalmente.

personal organizer n agenda f.

personal property n bens mpl móveis.

personal stereo n Walkman® m.

personify [pə'sɒnıfaı] vt personificar.

personnel [,pɜːsə'nel] npl pessoal m.

perspective [pə'spektıv] n perspectiva f.

Perspex® ['pɜːspeks] n (Brit) Perspex® m.

perspiration [,pɜːspə'reıʃn] n transpiração f.

persuade [pə'sweıd] vt: to ~ sb (to do sthg) persuadir alguém (a fazer algo); to ~ sb that ... persuadir alguém de que ....

persuasion [pə'sweıʒn] n (act of persuading) persuasão f; (belief) afinidade f.

persuasive [pə'sweısıv] adj persuasivo(-va).

pert [pɜːt] adj (person, reply) atrevido(-da), descarado(-da).

pertinent ['pɜːtınənt] adj pertinente.

perturb [pə'tɜːb] vt perturbar.

peruse [pə'ruːz] vt (read thoroughly) examinar; (read quickly) passar uma vista de olhos por.

perverse [pə'vɜːs] adj (delight, enjoyment) perverso(-sa); (contrary) difícil.

pervert ['pɜːvɜːt] n tarado m (-da f).

pessimist ['pesımıst] n pessimista mf.

pessimistic [,pesı'mıstık] adj pessimista.

pest [pest] n (insect, animal) praga f, inseto m nocivo; (inf: person) peste f.

pester ['pestəʳ] vt importunar.

pesticide ['pestısaıd] n pesticida m.

pet [pet] n animal m doméstico; **the teacher's** ~ o queridinho do professor.

petal ['petl] n pétala f.

peter ['piːtəʳ] : **peter out** vi (supplies, interest) esgotar-se.

pet food n comida f para animais domésticos.

petition [pı'tıʃn] n (letter) petição f, abaixo-assinado m.

petits pois [ˌpətiˈpwa] npl ervilhas fpl (pequenas e tenras).

petrified [ˈpɛtrɪfaɪd] adj petrificado (-da).

petrol [ˈpɛtrəl] n (Brit) gasolina f.

petrol bomb n (Brit) cocktail m OR coquetel m Molotov.

petrol can n (Brit) lata f de gasolina.

petrol cap n (Brit) tampa f do tanque de gasolina.

petroleum [pɪˈtrəʊljəm] n petróleo m.

petrol gauge n (Brit) indicador m do nível de gasolina.

petrol pump n (Brit) bomba f de gasolina.

petrol station n (Brit) posto m (de gasolina) (Br), estação f de serviço (Port).

petrol tank n (Brit) depósito m da gasolina.

pet shop n loja f de animais.

petticoat [ˈpɛtɪkəʊt] n combinação f.

petty [ˈpɛtɪ] adj (pej) (person) mesquinho(-nha); (rule) insignificante.

petty cash n fundo m para pequenas despesas.

petulant [ˈpɛtjʊlənt] adj petulante.

pew [pjuː] n banco m (de igreja).

pewter [ˈpjuːtəʳ] adj de peltre.

PG (abbr of parental guidance) abreviatura que indica que o filme não é aconselhável para menores de doze anos.

phantom [ˈfæntəm] n fantasma m, espectro m.

pharmacist [ˈfɑːməsɪst] n farmacêutico m (-ca f).

pharmacy [ˈfɑːməsɪ] n (shop) farmácia f.

phase [feɪz] n fase f.

PhD n (degree) = doutoramento m.

pheasant [ˈfɛznt] n faisão m.

phenomena [fɪˈnɒmɪnə] pl → phenomenon.

phenomenal [fɪˈnɒmɪnl] adj fenomenal.

phenomenon [fɪˈnɒmɪnən] (pl -mena) n fenômeno m.

phial [ˈfaɪəl] n ampola f.

philanthropist [fɪˈlænθrəpɪst] n filantropo m (-pa f).

philately [fɪˈlætəlɪ] n filatelia f.

Philippines [ˈfɪlɪpiːnz] npl: **the ~** as Filipinas.

philosopher [fɪˈlɒsəfəʳ] n filósofo m (-fa f).

philosophical [ˌfɪləˈsɒfɪkl] adj filosófico(-ca).

philosophy [fɪˈlɒsəfɪ] n filosofia f.

phlegm [flɛm] n (in throat) fleuma f (Br), catarro m.

phlegmatic [flɛgˈmætɪk] adj fleumático(-ca).

phobia [ˈfəʊbjə] n fobia f.

phone [fəʊn] n telefone m ◆ vt (Brit) telefonar para, ligar para ◆ vi (Brit) telefonar; **on the ~** (talking) no telefone; **we're not on the ~** (connected) não temos telefone.

⅃ phone up vt sep (Brit) telefonar para, ligar para ◆ vi (Brit) telefonar.

phone book n lista f telefônica.

phone booth n cabine f telefônica.

phone box n (Brit) cabine f telefônica, orelhão m (Br).

phone call n chamada f telefônica, telefonema m.

phonecard [ˈfəʊnkɑːd] n cartão m telefônico, Credifone® m (Port).

phone number n número m de telefone.

phonetics [fəˈnɛtɪks] n fonética f.

photo [ˈfəʊtəʊ] (pl -s) n fotografia f; **to take a ~ of** tirar uma fotografia de.

photo album n álbum m de fotografias.

photocopier [ˈfəʊtəʊˌkɒpɪəʳ] n fotocopiadora f.

photocopy [ˈfəʊtəʊˌkɒpɪ] n Xerox® m inv (Br), fotocópia f ◆ vt xerocar (Br), fotocopiar.

photograph [ˈfəʊtəgrɑːf] n fotografia f ◆ vt fotografar.

photographer [fəˈtɒgrəfəʳ] n fotógrafo m (-fa f).

photography [fəˈtɒgrəfɪ] n fotografia f.

phrasal verb [ˈfreɪzl-] n verbo m seguido de preposição.

phrase [freɪz] n expressão f.

phrasebook [ˈfreɪzbʊk] n guia m de conversação.

physical [ˈfɪzɪkl] adj físico(-ca) ◆ n exame m médico de aptidão.

physical education n educação f física.

physically [ˈfɪzɪklɪ] adv fisicamente.

physically handicapped adj deficiente físico(-ca).

physician [fɪˈzɪʃn] n médico m (-ca f).

physicist [ˈfɪzɪsɪst] n físico m (-ca f).

physics ['fiziks] n física f.
physiotherapy [,fiziəʊ'θerəpi] n
fisioterapia f.
physique [fi'ziːk] n físico m.
pianist ['piənist] n pianista mf.
piano [pi'ænəʊ] (pl -s) n piano m.
pick [pik] vt (select) escolher; (fruit,
flowers) apanhar, colher ♦ n (pickaxe)
picareta f; **to ~ a fight** procurar briga;
to ~ one's nose tirar meleca do nariz
(Br), tirar macacos do nariz (Port); **to
take one's ~** escolher à vontade.
❑ **pick on** vt fus implicar com.
❑ **pick out** vt sep (select) escolher; (see)
distinguir.
❑ **pick up** vt sep (lift up) pegar em;
(collect) ir buscar; (language) aprender;
(habit) apanhar; (bargain) conseguir;
(hitchhiker) dar uma carona a (Br), dar
boleia a (Port); (inf: woman, man)
paquerar (Br), engatar (Port) ♦ vi
(improve) recuperar; **to ~ up the phone**
(answer) atender o telefone.
pickaxe ['pikæks] n picareta f.
pickle ['pikl] n (Brit: food) pickle m;
(Am: pickled cucumber) pepino m de
conserva.
pickled onion ['pikld-] n cebola f em
conserva.
pickpocket ['pik,pɒkit] n batedor m
(-ra f) de carteiras (Br), carteirista mf
(Port).
pick-up (truck) n camioneta f,
carrinha f (Port).
picnic ['piknik] n piquenique m.
picnic area n área f para piqueni-
ques.
picture ['piktʃər] n (painting, drawing)
quadro m; (photograph) retrato m; (on
TV) imagem f; (film) filme m.
❑ **pictures** npl: **the ~s** (Brit) o cinema.
picture book n livro m ilustrado OR
de figuras.
picture frame n moldura f.
picturesque [,piktʃə'resk] adj pito-
resco(-ca).
pie [pai] n (savoury) empada f; (sweet)
torta f (Br), tarte f (Port).
piece [piːs] n (part, bit) pedaço m,
bocado m; (component, of clothing, of
music) peça f; (in chess) pedra f; **a 20p ~**
uma moeda de 20 pence; **a ~ of advice**
um conselho; **a ~ of furniture** um
móvel; **to fall to ~s** cair aos pedaços;
in one ~ (intact) inteiro, intacto; (unharmed) são e salvo.

piecemeal ['piːsmiːl] adj (fragmentary)
feito(-ta) aos poucos ♦ adv (little by little) aos poucos, por etapas.
pie chart n gráfico m de setores.
pier [piər] n cais m.
pierce [piəs] vt furar; **to have one's
ears ~d** furar as orelhas.
piercing ['piəsiŋ] adj (sound) estridente.
pig [pig] n porco m; (inf: greedy person)
alarde mf.
pigeon ['pidʒin] n pombo m.
pigeonhole ['pidʒinhəʊl] n escaninho
m.
piggybank ['pigibæŋk] n cofre m (Br),
mealheiro m (Port).
pigpen ['pigpen] (Am) = **pigsty**.
pigskin ['pigskin] adj de pele de
porco.
pigsty ['pigstai] n chiqueiro m.
pigtails ['pigteilz] npl tranças fpl (Br),
puxos mpl (Port).
pike [paik] n (fish) lúcio m.
pilau rice ['pilau-] n arroz à indiana
com várias cores, condimentado com diferentes especiarias orientais.
pilchard ['piltʃəd] n sardinha f grande.
pile [pail] n pilha f ♦ vt empilhar; **~s of**
(inf: a lot) montes de.
❑ **pile up** vt sep empilhar ♦ vi (accumulate) acumular-se.
piles [pailz] npl (MED) hemorróidas
fpl.
pileup ['pailʌp] n choque m em
cadeia.
pilfer ['pilfər] vi roubar.
pilgrim ['pilgrim] n peregrino m (-na
f).
pilgrimage ['pilgrimidʒ] n peregrinação f.
pill [pil] n comprimido m; **to be on
the ~** (contraceptive) tomar a pílula.
pillar ['pilər] n pilar m.
pillar box n (Brit) caixa f do correio
(Br), marco m de correio (Port).
pillion ['piljən] n: **to ride ~** viajar no
banco traseiro (de uma motocicleta).
pillow ['piləʊ] n (for bed) travesseiro
m, almofada f; (Am: on chair, sofa)
almofada f.
pillowcase ['piləʊkeis] n fronha f,
almofada f.
pilot ['pailət] n piloto m.
pilot light n piloto m.

pimp [pɪmp] n (inf) cafetão m (Br), chulo m (Port).

pimple ['pɪmpl] n borbulha f.

pin [pɪn] n (for sewing) alfinete m; (drawing pin) tachinha f (Br), pionés m (Port); (safety pin) alfinete de segurança; (Am: brooch) broche m; (Am: badge) crachá m, pin m ◆ vt (fasten) prender; **a two-~ plug** uma tomada f elétrica (de dois pinos); **~s and needles** formigueiro m.

pinafore ['pɪnəfɔːʳ] n (apron) avental m (Br), bata f (Port); (Brit: dress) vestido m de alças.

pinball ['pɪnbɔːl] n flippers mpl.

pincers ['pɪnsəz] npl (tool) turquês f.

pinch [pɪntʃ] vt (squeeze) beliscar; (Brit: inf: steal) roubar ◆ n (of salt) pitada f.

pincushion ['pɪnˌkʊʃn] n almofada f para alfinetes.

pine [paɪn] n pinheiro m ◆ adj de pinho.

pineapple ['paɪnæpl] n abacaxi m (Br), ananás m (Port).

pinetree ['paɪntriː] n pinheiro m.

pink [pɪŋk] adj cor-de-rosa (inv) ◆ n (colour) cor-de-rosa m inv.

pinkie ['pɪŋkɪ] n (Am) (dedo) mindinho m.

pinnacle ['pɪnəkl] n pináculo m.

PIN number [pɪn-] n código m pessoal, PIN m.

pinpoint ['pɪnpɔɪnt] vt (difficulty, cause) determinar; (position, target, leak) localizar.

pin-striped [-ˌstraɪpt] adj de listras.

pint [paɪnt] n (in UK) = 0,568 l, ~ meio litro m; (in US) = 0,473 l, ≈ meio litro; **a ~ (of beer)** (Brit) = uma caneca de cerveja.

pioneer [ˌpaɪə'nɪəʳ] n pioneiro m (-ra f) ◆ vt (new activity) explorar; (new invention, scheme) desenvolver.

pip [pɪp] n (of fruit) caroço m, pevide f (Port).

pipe [paɪp] n (for smoking) cachimbo m; (for gas, water) cano m.

pipe cleaner n limpador m de cachimbo.

pipeline ['paɪplaɪn] n (for oil) oleoduto m; (for gas) gasoduto m.

piper ['paɪpəʳ] n (MUS) gaiteiro m (-ra f).

pipe tobacco n tabaco m para cachimbo.

pirate ['paɪrət] n pirata m.

pirate radio n (Brit) rádio f pirata.

Pisces ['paɪsiːz] n Peixes m inv.

piss [pɪs] vi (vulg) mijar ◆ n: **to have a ~** (vulg) mijar, dar uma mijada; **it's ~ing down** (vulg) está chovendo canivetes (Br), está chovendo a potes (Port).

pissed [pɪst] adj (Brit: vulg: drunk) bêbado(-da) que nem um gambá; (Am: vulg: angry) fulo(-la).

pissed off adj (vulg): **to be ~ with** estar de saco cheio de.

pistachio [pɪ'stɑːʃɪəʊ] (pl -s) n pistache m (Br), pistácio m (Port) ◆ adj de pistácio.

pistol ['pɪstl] n pistola f.

piston ['pɪstən] n piston m, pistão m.

pit [pɪt] n (hole, for orchestra) poço m; (coalmine) mina f; (Am: in fruit) caroço m.

pitch [pɪtʃ] n (Brit: SPORT) campo m ◆ vt (throw) atirar; **to ~ a tent** montar uma barraca (de campismo).

pitch-black adj escuro(-ra) como breu.

pitcher ['pɪtʃəʳ] n (large jug) jarro m; (Am: small jug) jarra f.

pitchfork ['pɪtʃfɔːk] n forquilha f.

pitfall ['pɪtfɔːl] n (difficulty) armadilha f; (danger) perigo m.

pith [pɪθ] n (of orange) pele f branca.

pitiful ['pɪtɪfʊl] adj (arousing pity) lastimoso(-osa); (arousing contempt) ridículo(-la).

pitiless ['pɪtɪlɪs] adj impiedoso(-osa).

pitta (bread) ['pɪtə-] n pão m árabe; pão chato e oco.

pittance ['pɪtəns] n miséria f.

pitted ['pɪtɪd] adj (olives) descaroçado(-da), sem caroço.

pity ['pɪtɪ] n (compassion) pena f; **to have ~ on sb** ter pena de alguém; **it's a ~ (that)** ... é uma pena que ...; **what a ~!** que pena!

pivot ['pɪvət] n eixo m, pivô m.

pizza ['piːtsə] n pizza f.

pizzeria [ˌpiːtsə'riːə] n pizzaria f.

Pl. (abbr of Place) abreviatura do nome de certas ruas na Grã-Bretanha.

placard ['plækɑːd] n placar m.

placate [plə'keɪt] vt aplacar.

place [pleɪs] n lugar m; (house, flat) casa f; (at table) lugar, talher m ◆ vt (put) colocar; (an order, bet) fazer; **in the first ~** em primeiro lugar; **to take ~** ter lugar; **to take sb's ~** substituir alguém; **all over the ~** por todo o lado; **in ~ of** em lugar de.

place mat n descanso m (Br), individual m (Port).

placement ['pleɪsmənt] n (work experience) colocação f temporária, estágio m.

place of birth n local m de nascimento, naturalidade f.

placid ['plæsɪd] adj plácido(-da).

plagiarize ['pleɪdʒəraɪz] vt plagiar.

plague [pleɪg] n peste f.

plaice [pleɪs] (pl inv) n solha f.

plaid [plæd] n tecido de lã escocês.

plain [pleɪn] adj simples (inv), (yoghurt) natural; (clear) claro(-ra); (paper) liso(-sa); (pej: not attractive) sem atrativos ♦ n planície f.

plain chocolate n chocolate m preto OR negro.

plain-clothes adj vestido(-da) à paisana.

plain flour n (Brit) farinha f (sem fermento).

plainly ['pleɪnlɪ] adv (clearly) claramente.

plaintiff ['pleɪntɪf] n queixoso m (-osa f), demandante mf.

plait [plæt] n trança f ♦ vt entrançar.

plan [plæn] n (scheme, project) plano m; (drawing) planta f ♦ vt (organize) planear; **have you any ~s for tonight?** você tem planos para hoje à noite?; **according to ~** como estava previsto; **to ~ to do sthg, to ~ on doing sthg** pensar em fazer algo.

plane [pleɪn] n (aeroplane) avião m; (tool) plaina f.

planet ['plænɪt] n planeta m.

plank [plæŋk] n tábua f.

planning ['plænɪŋ] n planejamento m, planificação f.

planning permission n licença f para construir OR fazer obras.

plant [plɑːnt] n (living thing) planta f; (factory) fábrica f; (power, nuclear) central f ♦ vt (seeds, tree) plantar; (land) cultivar; **"heavy ~ crossing"** aviso que indica que na área circulam freqüentemente veículos pesados.

plantation [plæn'teɪʃn] n plantação f.

plaque [plɑːk] n placa f.

plaster ['plɑːstər] n (Brit: for cut) esparadrapo m (Br), penso m (Port); (for walls) estuque m; **in ~** (arm, leg) engessado.

plaster cast n (for broken bones) gesso m.

plastered ['plɑːstəd] adj (inf: drunk) bêbado(-da); **to get ~** embebedar-se.

plastic ['plæstɪk] n plástico m ♦ adj de plástico.

plastic bag n saca f OR saco m de plástico.

Plasticine® ['plæstɪsiːn] n (Brit) plastilina f (Br), plasticina f (Port).

plastic surgery n cirurgia f plástica.

plate [pleɪt] n (for food) prato m; (of metal) placa f; **a ~ of glass** um vidro, uma vidraça.

plateau ['plætəʊ] n planalto m.

plate-glass adj de vidro grosso.

platform ['plætfɔːm] n plataforma f.

platinum ['plætɪnəm] n platina f.

platoon [plə'tuːn] n pelotão m.

platter ['plætər] n (of food) travessa f (de comida).

plausible ['plɔːzəbl] adj plausível.

play [pleɪ] vt (sport, game) jogar; (instrument, music) tocar; (opponent) jogar contra; (CD, tape, record) pôr; (role, character) desempenhar ♦ vi (child) brincar; (in sport, game) jogar; (musician) tocar ♦ n (in theatre, on TV) peça f; (button on CD, tape recorder) play m.

❏ **play back** vt sep repetir, colocar de novo

❏ **play up** vi (machine, car) enguiçar, estar com problemas.

playboy ['pleɪbɔɪ] n playboy m.

player ['pleɪər] n (of sport, game) jogador m (-ra f); (of musical instrument) músico m (-ca f), intérprete mf; **guitar ~** guitarrista mf; **piano ~** pianista mf.

playful ['pleɪfʊl] adj brincalhão (-lhona).

playground ['pleɪgraʊnd] n (in school) recreio m; (in park etc) parque m infantil.

playgroup ['pleɪgruːp] n tipo de jardim-de-infância.

playing card ['pleɪɪŋ-] n carta f de jogar.

playing field ['pleɪɪŋ-] n parque m OR campo m de jogos.

playmate ['pleɪmeɪt] n companheiro m (-ra f) de brincadeiras.

playpen ['pleɪpen] n cercado m para bebês.

playroom ['pleɪrʊm] n sala f para brincadeiras.

playschool ['pleɪskuːl] = **playgroup**.

plaything ['pleɪθɪŋ] n brinquedo m.

playtime ['pleɪtaɪm] n recreio m.

playwright ['pleɪraɪt] n dramaturgo m (-ga f).

plc [Brit: abbr of public limited company) ~ S.A. (cotada na Bolsa).

plea [pliː] n (appeal) pedido m; (JUR): **to enter a ~ of guilty** declarar-se culpado.

plead [pliːd] vt alegar ♦ vi (JUR) alegar; (beg) pedir, rogar; **to ~ for sthg** pedir algo; **to ~ with sb to do sthg** rogar a alguém que faça algo; **he ~ed not guilty** declarou-se inocente.

pleasant ['pleznt] adj agradável.

please [pliːz] adv por favor ♦ vt agradar a; **yes ~!** sim, se faz favor!; **whatever you ~** o que quiser.

pleased [pliːzd] adj satisfeito(-ta), contente; **to be ~ with** estar satisfeito com; **~ to meet you!** prazer em conhecê-lo(-la)!

pleasing ['pliːzɪŋ] adj agradável.

pleasure ['pleʒər] n prazer m; **with ~** com prazer; **it's a ~!** é um prazer!

pleat [pliːt] n prega f.

pleated ['pliːtɪd] adj com OR de pregas.

pledge [pledʒ] n promessa f ♦ vt (promise to provide) prometer.

plentiful ['plentɪful] adj abundante.

plenty ['plentɪ] pron bastante; **~ of** bastante.

pliers ['plaɪəz] npl alicate m.

plight [plaɪt] n situação f deplorável.

plimsoll ['plɪmsəl] n (Brit) sapatilha f.

plod [plɒd] vi (walk slowly) arrastar-se, caminhar lentamente e com dificuldade.

plonk [plɒŋk] n (Brit: inf: wine) zurrapa f (Br), carrascão m (Port).

plot [plɒt] n (scheme) complot m; (of story, film, play) enredo m; (of land) pedaço m.

plough [plaʊ] n (Brit) charrua f ♦ vt (Brit) lavrar.

ploughman's (lunch) ['plaʊmənz-] n (Brit) prato composto por vários queijos, pão, pickles e salada servido frequentemente nos pubs.

plow [plaʊ] (Am) = **plough**.

ploy [plɔɪ] n estratagema m.

pluck [plʌk] vt (eyebrows, hair) arrancar, depilar (com pinça); (chicken) depenar.

plug [plʌg] n (with pins) tomada f elétrica, ficha f eléctrica (Port); (socket) tomada f, ficha (Port); (for bath, sink) tampa f, válvula f.

☐ **plug in** vt sep ligar (a tomada).

plughole ['plʌghəʊl] n ralo m.

plum [plʌm] n ameixa f.

plumber ['plʌmər] n encanador m (-ra f) (Br), canalizador m (-ra f) (Port).

plumbing ['plʌmɪŋ] n (pipes) canalização f.

plume [pluːm] n pluma f, pena f.

plump [plʌmp] adj roliço(-ça).

plum pudding n pudim natalício com frutos secos e especiarias servido com conhaque que se incendeia antes de servir.

plunder ['plʌndər] n (booty) saque m ♦ vt saquear, pilhar.

plunge [plʌndʒ] vi (fall, dive) mergulhar; (decrease) descer (em flecha).

plunge pool n piscina f pequena.

plunger ['plʌndʒər] n (for unblocking pipe) desentupidor m (de ventosa).

pluperfect (tense) [,pluː'pɜːfɪkt-] n: **the ~** o mais-que-perfeito.

plural ['plʊərəl] n plural m; **in the ~** no plural.

plus [plʌs] prep mais ♦ adj: **30 ~** trinta ou mais.

plush [plʌʃ] adj de luxo.

Pluto ['pluːtəʊ] n Plutão m.

ply [plaɪ] vt (trade) exercer; **to ~ sb with sthg** (food, drinks) não parar de oferecer algo a alguém, encher alguém com algo; (questions) assediar alguém com algo.

plywood ['plaɪwʊd] n compensado m (Br), contraplacado m (Port).

p.m. (abbr of post meridiem): **at 3 ~** às três da tarde, às 15h; **at 10 ~** às dez da noite, às 22h.

PMT n (abbr of premenstrual tension) síndrome f pré-menstrual.

pneumatic drill [njuː'mætɪk-] n perfuratriz f (Br), broca f pneumática.

pneumonia [njuː'məʊnjə] n pneumonia f.

poach [pəʊtʃ] vt (game) caçar furtivamente; (fish) pescar furtivamente; (copy) roubar ♦ vi (hunt) caçar (furtivamente); (fish) pescar (furtivamente).

poached egg [pəʊtʃt-] n ovo m pochê (Br), ovo m escalfado (Port).

poached salmon [pəʊtʃt-] n salmão m cozido.

poacher ['pəʊtʃəʳ] n (hunting) caçador m furtivo (caçadora f furtiva); (fishing) pescador m furtivo (pescadora f furtiva).

poaching ['pəʊtʃɪŋ] n (for game) caça f furtiva; (for fish) pesca f furtiva.

PO Box n (abbr of Post Office Box) caixa f postal (Br), apartado m (Port).

pocket ['pɒkɪt] n bolso m ♦ adj de bolso.

pocketbook ['pɒkɪtbʊk] n (notebook) bloco m de notas (pequeno); (Am: handbag) carteira f.

pocketknife ['pɒkɪtnaɪf] (pl -knives [-naɪvz]) n navalha f, canivete m.

pocket money n (Brit) mesada f (Br), semanada f (Port).

podgy ['pɒdʒɪ] adj (inf) roliço(-ça), gorducho(-cha).

podiatrist [pə'daɪətrɪst] n (Am) pedicuro m (-ra f), calista mf.

podium ['pəʊdɪəm] n pódio m.

poem ['pəʊɪm] n poema m.

poet ['pəʊɪt] n poeta m (-tisa f).

poetic [pəʊ'etɪk] adj poético(-ca).

poetry ['pəʊɪtrɪ] n poesia f.

poignant ['pɔɪnjənt] adj (moment, story) comovente.

point [pɔɪnt] n ponto m; (tip) ponta f; (most important thing) razão f; (Brit: electric socket) tomada f, ficha f (Port) ♦ vi: to ~ to apontar para; **five ~ seven** cinco vírgula sete; **what's the ~?** para quê?; **there's no ~** não vale a pena; **to be on the ~ of doing sthg** estar prestes a OR a ponto de fazer algo.

⊐ **points** npl (Brit: on railway) agulhas fpl.

⊐ **point out** vt sep (object, person) indicar; (fact, mistake) apontar.

point-blank adj (question, range) à queima-roupa; (denial, refusal) categórico(-ca) ♦ adv (accuse, ask) sem rodeios; (shoot) à queima-roupa; (deny, refuse) categoricamente.

pointed ['pɔɪntɪd] adj (in shape) pontiagudo(-da).

pointless ['pɔɪntlɪs] adj inútil.

point of view n ponto m de vista.

poised [pɔɪzd] adj (ready) pronto(-ta), preparado(-da); **to be ~ for sthg** estar pronto OR preparado para algo; **to be ~ to do sthg** estar pronto OR preparado para fazer algo.

poison ['pɔɪzn] n veneno m ♦ vt envenenar.

poisoning ['pɔɪznɪŋ] n envenenamento m.

poisonous ['pɔɪznəs] adj venenoso(-osa).

poke [pəʊk] vt (with finger, stick) cutucar (Br), tocar (Port); (with elbow) cutucar (Br), dar cotoveladas em; (fire) cutucar (Br), atiçar.

poker ['pəʊkəʳ] n (card game) póquer m.

poky ['pəʊkɪ] adj minúsculo(-la), apertado(-da).

Poland ['pəʊlənd] n Polônia f.

polar ['pəʊləʳ] adj polar.

polar bear ['pəʊlə-] n urso m polar.

Polaroid® ['pəʊlərɔɪd] n (photograph) fotografia f instantânea; (camera) máquina f de tirar fotografias instantâneas.

pole [pəʊl] n (of wood) poste m.

Pole [pəʊl] n (person) polonês (-esa f) (Br), polaco m (-ca f) (Port).

pole vault n salto m com vara.

police [pə'liːs] npl: **the ~** a polícia.

police car n rádio-patrulha f (Br), carro m da polícia.

police constable n (Brit) policial mf (Br), polícia mf (Port).

police force n forças fpl policiais.

policeman [pə'liːsmən] (pl -men [-mən]) n policial m (Br), polícia m (Port).

police officer n policial mf (Br), polícia mf (Port).

police station n delegacia f (Br), esquadra f (Port).

policewoman [pə'liːswʊmən] (pl -women [-wɪmɪn]) n policial f (Br), polícia f (Port).

policy ['pɒləsɪ] n (approach, attitude) política f; (for insurance) apólice f.

policy-holder n segurado m (-da f).

polio ['pəʊlɪəʊ] n poliomielite f, paralisia f infantil.

polish ['pɒlɪʃ] n (for cleaning) cera f ♦ vt encerar.

Polish ['pəʊlɪʃ] adj polonês(-esa) (Br), polaco(-ca) (Port) ♦ n (language) polonês m (Br), polaco m (Port) ♦ npl: **the ~** os poloneses (Br), os polacos (Port).

polished ['pɒlɪʃt] adj (floor) encerado(-da); (metal) polido(-da); (speech, performance) refinado(-da); (performer) bom (boa), esmerado(-da).

polite [pə'laɪt] *adj* educado(-da).

political [pə'lɪtɪkl] *adj* político(-ca).

politically correct [pə'lɪtɪklɪ-] *adj* politicamente correto(-ta).

politician [,pɒlɪ'tɪʃn] *n* político *m* (-ca *f*).

politics ['pɒlətɪks] *n* política *f*.

polka ['pɒlkə] *n* polca *f*.

polka dot *n* bolinha *f* (em tecido).

poll [pəʊl] *n* (survey) sondagem *f*; the ~s (election) as eleições.

pollen ['pɒlən] *n* pólen *m*.

polling booth ['pəʊlɪŋ-] *n* cabine *f* eleitoral.

polling station ['pəʊlɪŋ-] *n* mesa *f* OR centro *m* eleitoral.

pollute [pə'luːt] *vt* poluir.

pollution [pə'luːʃn] *n* poluição *f*.

polo ['pəʊləʊ] (pl -s) *n* pólo *m*.

polo neck *n* (Brit: jumper) gola *f* rulê (Br), camisola *f* de gola alta (Port).

polyester [,pɒlɪ'estər] *n* poliéster *m*.

polystyrene [,pɒlɪ'staɪriːn] *n* isopor® *m* (Br), esferovite *m* (Port).

polytechnic [,pɒlɪ'teknɪk] *n* escola *f* politécnica.

polythene bag ['pɒlɪθiːn-] *n* (Brit) saco *m* OR saca *f* de plástico.

pomegranate ['pɒmɪˌgrænɪt] *n* romã *f*.

pompom ['pɒmpɒm] *n* pompom *m*.

pompous ['pɒmpəs] *adj* pomposo (-osa).

pond [pɒnd] *n* lago *m*.

ponder ['pɒndər] *vt* refletir sobre.

pong [pɒŋ] *n* (Brit: inf) fedor *m*.

pontoon [pɒn'tuːn] *n* (Brit: card game) vinte-e-um *m*.

pony ['pəʊnɪ] *n* pônei *m*.

ponytail ['pəʊnɪteɪl] *n* rabo *m* de cavalo.

pony-trekking [-ˌtrekɪŋ] *n* (Brit) excursão *f* em pônei.

poodle ['puːdl] *n* caniche *m*.

pool [puːl] *n* (for swimming) piscina *f*; (of water, blood, milk) poça *f*; (small pond) lago *f*; (game) bilhar *m*.
❑ **pools** *npl* (Brit): the ~s ~ a loteca (Br), a loteria esportiva (Br), o Totobola® (Port).

poor [pɔːr] *adj* (short of money) pobre; (bad) mau (má); (expressing sympathy) coitado(-da), pobre ◆ *npl*: the ~ os pobres.

poorly ['pɔːlɪ] *adj* (Brit: ill) adoenta-

do(-da) ◆ *adv* mal.

pop [pɒp] *n* (music) música *f* pop ◆ *vt* (inf: put) meter ◆ *vi* (balloon) rebentar; **my ears popped** os meus ouvidos deram um estalido.
❑ **pop in** *vi* (Brit): I'll ~ **in after work** dou um pulo aí depois do trabalho.

pop concert *n* concerto *m* de música pop.

popcorn ['pɒpkɔːn] *n* pipoca *f*.

Pope [pəʊp] *n*: the ~ o Papa.

pop group *n* grupo *m* de música pop.

poplar (tree) ['pɒplər-] *n* álamo *m*, choupo *m*.

pop music *n* música *f* pop.

popper ['pɒpər] *n* (Brit) botão *m* de pressão (Br), mola *f* (Port).

poppy ['pɒpɪ] *n* papoula *f*.

Popsicle® ['pɒpsɪkl] *n* (Am) picolé *m* (Br), gelado *m* (de fruta) (Port).

pop socks *npl* meias *fpl* até ao joelho, meia-meia *f*.

pop star *n* pop star *f*.

popular ['pɒpjʊlər] *adj* (person, place, activity) popular; (opinion, ideas) generalizado(-da).

popularity [,pɒpjʊ'lærətɪ] *n* popularidade *f*.

popularize ['pɒpjʊləraɪz] *vt* (make popular) popularizar; (simplify) vulgarizar.

populated ['pɒpjʊleɪtɪd] *adj* povoado(-da).

population [,pɒpjʊ'leɪʃn] *n* população *f*.

porcelain ['pɔːsəlɪn] *n* porcelana *f*.

porch [pɔːtʃ] *n* (entrance) átrio *m*; (Am: outside house) terraço *m* (coberto), alpendre *m*.

porcupine ['pɔːkjʊpaɪn] *n* porcoespinho *m*.

pore [pɔːr] *n* poro *m*.
❑ **pore over** *vt fus* debruçar-se sobre, estudar atentamente.

pork [pɔːk] *n* carne *f* de porco.

pork chop *n* costeleta *f* de porco.

pork pie *n* empada *f* de carne de porco.

pornographic [,pɔːnə'græfɪk] *adj* pornográfico(-ca).

pornography [pɔː'nɒgrəfɪ] *n* pornografia *f*.

porous ['pɔːrəs] *adj* poroso(-osa).

porridge ['pɒrɪdʒ] *n* flocos *mpl* de aveia.

port [pɔːt] *n* porto *m*.

portable ['pɔːtəbl] *adj* portátil.

porter ['pɔːtər] *n* (*at hotel, museum*) porteiro *m* (-ra *f*); (*at station, airport*) carregador *m* (-ra *f*).

portfolio [,pɔːt'fəuljəu] (*pl* -s) *n* (*case*) pasta *f*; (*sample of work*) portfolio *m*.

porthole ['pɔːthəul] *n* vigia *f*.

portion ['pɔːʃn] *n* (*part*) porção *f*; (*of food*) dose *f*.

portly ['pɔːtlɪ] *adj* corpulento(-ta).

portrait ['pɔːtreɪt] *n* retrato *m*.

portray [pɔː'treɪ] *vt* (*in a play, film*) representar; (*describe, represent*) retratar, descrever.

Portugal ['pɔːtʃugl] *n* Portugal *s*.

Portuguese [,pɔːtʃu'giːz] *adj* português(-esa) ◆ *n* (*person*) português *m* (-esa *f*); (*language*) português *m* ◆ *npl*: **the ~** os portugueses.

pose [pəuz] *vt* (*problem, threat*) constituir ◆ *vi* (*for photo*) posar.

posh [pɒʃ] *adj* (*inf*) fino(-na), chique.

position [pə'zɪʃn] *n* posição *f*; **"~ closed"** "encerrado".

positive ['pɒzətɪv] *adj* positivo(-va); (*certain, sure*) seguro(-ra); **I'm absolutely ~** tenho a certeza absoluta.

possess [pə'zes] *vt* possuir.

possession [pə'zeʃn] *n* (*thing owned*) bem *m*.

possessive [pə'zesɪv] *adj* possessivo(-va).

possibility [,pɒsə'bɪlətɪ] *n* possibilidade *f*.

possible ['pɒsəbl] *adj* possível; **it's ~ that we may be late** é possível que cheguemos atrasados; **would it be ~ ...?** seria possível ...?; **as much as ~** o máximo possível; **if ~** se for possível.

possibly ['pɒsəblɪ] *adv* (*perhaps*) provavelmente.

post [pəust] *n* correio *m*; (*pole*) poste *m*; (*fml: job*) lugar *m* ◆ *vt* (*letter*) pôr no correio; (*parcel*) enviar; **by ~** pelo correio.

postage ['pəustɪdʒ] *n* franquia *f*; **~ and packing** custos *mpl* de envio; **~ paid** porte *m* pago.

postage stamp *n* (*fml*) selo *m* (postal).

postal ['pəustl] *adj* postal.

postal order *n* vale *m* postal.

postbox ['pəustbɒks] *n* (*Brit*) caixa *f* de coleta (*Br*), caixa *f* do correio (*Port*).

postcard ['pəustkɑːd] *n* (*cartão*) postal *m*.

postcode ['pəustkəud] *n* (*Brit*) código *m* postal.

poster ['pəustər] *n* poster *m*.

poste restante [,pəustres'tɑːnt] *n* (*Brit*) posta-restante *f*.

posterior [pɒ'stɪərɪər] *n* (*inf*) traseiro *m*.

post-free *adv* com porte pago.

postgraduate [,pəust'grædʒuət] *n* pós-graduado *m* (-da *f*).

posthumous ['pɒstjuməs] *adj* póstumo(-ma).

postman ['pəustmən] (*pl* -men [-mən]) *n* carteiro *m*.

postmark ['pəustmɑːk] *n* carimbo *m* (postal).

postmaster ['pəust,mɑːstər] *n* chefe *m* dos correios.

postmortem [,pəust'mɔːtəm] *n* (*autopsy*) autópsia *f*.

post office *n* (*building*) estação *f* de correios; **the Post Office ~** a Empresa Nacional dos Correios e Telégrafos (*Br*), ~ os CTT (*Port*).

postpone [,pəust'pəun] *vt* adiar.

postscript ['pəusskrɪpt] *n* (*to letter*) pós-escrito *m*.

posture ['pɒstʃər] *n* postura *f*.

postwoman ['pəust,wumən] (*pl* -women [-,wɪmɪn]) *n* carteira *f* (*Br*), mulher-carteiro *f* (*Port*).

pot [pɒt] *n* (*for cooking*) panela *f*; (*for jam, paint*) frasco *m*; (*for coffee, tea*) bule *m*; (*inf: cannabis*) maconha *f* (*Br*), erva *f* (*Port*); **a ~ of tea** um bule de chá.

potato [pə'teɪtəu] (*pl* -es) *n* batata *f*.

potato salad *n* salada *f* de batata.

potent ['pəutənt] *adj* (*argument, drink*) forte.

potential [pə'tenʃl] *adj* potencial ◆ *n* potencial *m*.

potentially [pə'tenʃəlɪ] *adv* potencialmente.

pothole ['pɒthəul] *n* (*in road*) buraco *m*.

potholing ['pɒt,həulɪŋ] *n* (*Brit*) espeleologia *f*; **to go ~** praticar espeleologia.

potion ['pəuʃn] *n* poção *f*.

pot plant *n* planta *f* de interior.

pot scrubber [-'skrʌbər] *n* esfregão *m*.

potshot ['pɒtʃɒt] *n*: **to take a ~ (at sthg)** disparar (contra algo), atirar (contra algo).

potted ['pɒtɪd] *adj (meat, fish)* de conserva; *(plant)* de vaso, de interior.

potter ['pɒtəʳ] *n* oleiro *m* (-ra *f*).

❏ **potter around** *vi (Brit)* ocupar-se de *tarefas agradáveis mas sem nenhuma importância.*

pottery ['pɒtərɪ] *n (clay objects)* cerâmica *f; (craft)* cerâmica, olaria *f.*

potty ['pɒtɪ] *n* penico *m (para crianças).*

pouch [paʊtʃ] *n (for money, tobacco)* bolsa *f.*

poultry ['pəʊltrɪ] *n (meat)* carne *f* de aves (domésticas) ♦ *npl (animals)* aves *fpl* domésticas.

pound [paʊnd] *n (unit of money)* libra *f; (unit of weight)* = 453,6 gr, libra ♦ *vi (heart)* palpitar; *(head)* latejar.

pour [pɔːʳ] *vt (liquid etc)* jogar; *(drink)* servir ♦ *vi (flow)* correr; **it's ~ing (with rain)** está chovendo canivetes *(Br)*, está a chover a cântaros *(Port).*

❏ **pour out** *vt sep (drink)* servir.

pouring ['pɔːrɪŋ] *adj (rain)* torrencial.

pout [paʊt] *vi* fazer beicinho.

poverty ['pɒvətɪ] *n* pobreza *f.*

poverty-stricken *adj* empobrecido(-da).

powder ['paʊdəʳ] *n* pó *m.*

powdered ['paʊdəd] *adj (milk, sugar)* em pó.

powder room *n* banheiro *m* para senhoras *(Br)*, casa *f* de banho para senhoras *(Port).*

power ['paʊəʳ] *n (control, authority)* poder *m; (ability)* capacidade *f; (strength, force)* força *f; (energy)* energia *f; (electricity)* eletricidade *f* ♦ *vt* alimentar, accionar; **to be in ~** estar no poder.

powerboat ['paʊəbəʊt] *n* barco *m* a motor.

power cut *n* corte *m* de energia.

power failure *n* falha *f* de energia.

powerful ['paʊəfʊl] *adj* forte; *(having control)* poderoso(-osa); *(machine)* potente.

powerless ['paʊəlɪs] *adj* impotente; **to be ~ to do sthg** não ter poderes para fazer algo, não poder fazer algo.

power point *n (Brit)* tomada *f* elétrica.

power station *n* central *f* elétrica.

power steering *n* direção *f* assistida.

practical ['præktɪkl] *adj* prático(-ca).

practicality [,præktɪ'kælətɪ] *n* aspecto *m* prático.

practical joke *n* partida *f.*

practically ['præktɪklɪ] *adv (almost)* praticamente.

practice ['præktɪs] *n (training, regular activity, custom)* prática *f; (training session)* sessão *f* de treino; *(MUS)* ensaio *m; (of doctor)* consultório *m; (of lawyer)* escritório *m* ♦ *vt (Am)* = **practise; out of ~** destreinado(-da).

practise ['præktɪs] *vt (sport, music, technique)* praticar ♦ *vi (train)* praticar; *(doctor, lawyer)* exercer ♦ *n (Am)* = **practice.**

Prague [prɑːg] *n* Praga *s.*

prairie ['preərɪ] *n* pradaria *f.*

praise [preɪz] *n* elogio *m* ♦ *vt* elogiar.

praiseworthy ['preɪz,wɜːðɪ] *adj* digno(-gna) de louvor.

pram [præm] *n (Brit)* carrinho *m* de bebê.

prance [prɑːns] *vi (person)* pavonear-se; *(horse)* dar pinotes.

prank [præŋk] *n* peça *f (Br)*, partida *f (Port).*

prawn [prɔːn] *n* camarão *m.*

prawn cocktail *n* cocktail *m* de camarão, entrada à base de camarão e *maionese com ketchup dispostos sobre uma camada de folhas de alface.*

prawn cracker *n* bolacha *f* de camarão, *tira-gosto frito chinês de farinha de arroz e camarão, fino e crocante.*

pray [preɪ] *vi* rezar; **to ~ for** *(fig)* rezar por; **to ~ for rain** rezar para que chova.

prayer [preəʳ] *n* oração *f.*

precarious [prɪ'keərɪəs] *adj* precário (-ria).

precaution [prɪ'kɔːʃn] *n* precaução *f.*

precede [prɪ'siːd] *vt (fml)* preceder.

precedence ['presɪdəns] *n:* **to take ~ over sthg** ter prioridade em relação a OR sobre algo.

precedent ['presɪdənt] *n* precedente *m.*

preceding [prɪ'siːdɪŋ] *adj* precedente.

precinct ['priːsɪŋkt] *n (Brit: for shopping)* zona *f* comercial (pedestre); *(Am: area of town)* circunscrição *f.*

precious ['preʃəs] *adj* precioso(-osa); *(memories, possession)* querido(-da).

precious stone *n* pedra *f* preciosa.

precipice ['presɪpɪs] *n* precipício *m.*

precise [prɪ'saɪs] *adj* preciso(-sa).

precisely [prɪ'saɪslɪ] *adv* precisamente.

precision [prɪ'sɪʒn] *n* precisão *f.*

precocious [prɪ'kəʊʃəs] *adj* precoce.

predator ['predətə'] *n (animal)* predador *m; (bird)* ave *f* de rapina.

predecessor ['priːdɪsesə'] *n* antecessor *m* (-ra *f*).

predicament [prɪ'dɪkəmənt] *n* situação *f* difícil.

predict [prɪ'dɪkt] *vt* prever.

predictable [prɪ'dɪktəbl] *adj* previsível.

prediction [prɪ'dɪkʃn] *n* previsão *f.*

predominant [prɪ'dɒmɪnənt] *adj* predominante.

predominantly [prɪ'dɒmɪnəntlɪ] *adv* predominantemente.

preempt [,priː'empt] *vt* adiantar-se a, antecipar-se a.

prefab ['priːfæb] *n (inf)* pré-fabricado *m.*

preface ['prefɪs] *n* prefácio *m.*

prefect ['priːfekt] *n (Brit: at school)* prefeito *m* (monitora *f*).

prefer [prɪ'fɜː'] *vt:* **to ~ sthg (to)** preferir algo (a); **to ~ to do sthg** preferir fazer algo.

preferable ['prefrəbl] *adj* preferível.

preferably ['prefrəblɪ] *adv* preferivelmente, de preferência.

preference ['prefərəns] *n* preferência *f.*

prefix ['priːfɪks] *n* prefixo *m.*

pregnancy ['pregnənsɪ] *n* gravidez *f.*

pregnant ['pregnənt] *adj* grávida.

prehistoric [,priːhɪ'stɒrɪk] *adj* pré-histórico(-ca).

prejudice ['predʒʊdɪs] *n* preconceito *m.*

prejudiced ['predʒʊdɪst] *adj* preconceituoso(-osa).

preliminary [prɪ'lɪmɪnərɪ] *adj* preliminar.

prelude ['preljuːd] *n (event):* **~ (to sthg)** prelúdio *m* (de algo).

premarital [,priː'mærɪtl] *adj* pré-matrimonial.

premature ['premə,tjʊə'] *adj* prematuro(-ra).

premeditated [,priː'medɪteɪtɪd] *adj* premeditado(-da).

premenstrual syndrome [,priː'menstruːl-] *n* síndrome *f* prémenstrual.

premenstrual tension = premenstrual syndrome.

premier ['premjə'] *adj* melhor ◆ *n* primeiro-ministro *m* (primeira-ministra *f*).

premiere ['premɪeə'] *n* estréia *f.*

premises ['premɪsɪz] *npl* instalações *fpl,* local *m;* **on the ~** no estabelecimento.

premium ['priːmjəm] *n (for insurance)* prêmio *m.*

premium-quality *adj* de primeira (qualidade).

premonition [,premə'nɪʃn] *n* premunição *f.*

preoccupied [,priː'ɒkjʊpaɪd] *adj* preocupado(-da).

prepacked [,priː'pækt] *adj* préembalado(-da).

prepaid ['priːpeɪd] *adj (envelope)* com porte pago, que não necessita de selo.

preparation [,prepə'reɪʃn] *n (preparing)* preparação *f.*
❑ **preparations** *npl (arrangements)* preparações *fpl.*

preparatory [prɪ'pærətrɪ] *adj* preparatório(-ria).

preparatory school *n (in UK)* escola particular, de preparação para o ensino secundário, para alunos dos sete aos doze anos; *(in US)* escola secundária particular destinada à preparação para o ensino superior.

prepare [prɪ'peə'] *vt* preparar ◆ *vi* preparar-se.

prepared [prɪ'peəd] *adj (ready)* preparado(-da); **to be ~ to do sthg** estar preparado para fazer algo.

preposition [,prepə'zɪʃn] *n* preposição *f.*

preposterous [prɪ'pɒstərəs] *adj* absurdo(-da).

prep school [prep-] = preparatory school.

prerequisite [,priː'rekwɪzɪt] *n* pré-requisito *m;* **to be a ~ of** OR **for sthg** ser um pré-requisito para algo.

preschool [,priː'skuːl] *adj* pré-escolar ◆ *n (Am)* pré-primário *m.*

prescribe [prɪ'skraɪb] *vt* receitar.

prescription [prɪ'skrɪpʃn] *n* receita *f* (médica).

presence ['prezns] *n* presença *f;* **in sb's ~** na presença de alguém.

present [*adj & n* 'preznt. *vb* prɪ'zent] *adj (in attendance)* presente; *(current)* atual ◆ *n (gift)* presente *m* ◆ *vt (give)* presentear; *(problem, challenge)* representar; *(portray, play, on radio or TV)* apresentar; **the ~** o presente; **the ~ (tense)** *(GRAMM)* o presente; **at ~** de momento; **to ~ sb to sb** apresentar alguém a alguém.

presentable [prɪˈzentəbl] *adj* apresentável.

presentation [ˌpreznˈteɪʃn] *n* apresentação *f*.

presenter [prɪˈzentəʳ] *n (of TV, radio programme)* apresentador *m (-ra f)*.

presently [ˈprezntlɪ] *adv (soon)* daqui a pouco; *(soon after)* daí a pouco; *(now)* atualmente, neste momento.

preservation [ˌprezəˈveɪʃn] *n (of wildlife, building, food)* conservação *f*; *(of order, peace)* manutenção *f*.

preservative [prɪˈzɜːvətɪv] *n* conservante *m*.

preserve [prɪˈzɜːv] *n (jam)* compota *f* ◆ *vt* conservar; *(order, peace)* manter.

preset [ˌpriːˈset] *(pt & pp* preset*)* *vt* programar.

president [ˈprezɪdənt] *n* presidente *mf*.

presidential [ˌprezɪˈdenʃl] *adj* presidencial.

press [pres] *vt (push firmly)* pressionar; *(button, switch)* apertar; *(iron)* passar (a ferro) ◆ *n*: **the ~** a imprensa; **to ~ sb to do sthg** insistir com alguém para que faça algo.

press conference *n* entrevista *f* coletiva *(Br)*, conferência *f* de imprensa *(Port)*.

pressed [prest] *adj*: **to be ~ for time/money** estar com falta de tempo/dinheiro, não ter tempo/dinheiro.

pressing [ˈpresɪŋ] *adj (problem, business, need)* urgente, premente; *(appointment)* inadiável.

press-stud *n* botão *m* de pressão *(Br)*, mola *f (Port)*.

press-ups *npl* flexões *fpl*.

pressure [ˈpreʃəʳ] *n* pressão *f*.

pressure cooker *n* panela *f* de pressão.

pressure gauge *n* manômetro *m*.

pressure group *n* grupo *m* de pressão.

pressurize [ˈpreʃəraɪz] *vt (Brit: force)*: **to ~ sb to do** OR **into doing sthg** pressionar alguém a fazer algo.

prestige [preˈstiːʒ] *n* prestígio *m*.

prestigious [preˈstɪdʒəs] *adj* prestigioso(-osa).

presumably [prɪˈzjuːməblɪ] *adv* presumivelmente.

presume [prɪˈzjuːm] *vt* presumir.

presumptuous [prɪˈzʌmptʃʊəs] *adj* presunçoso(-osa).

pretence [prɪˈtens] *n* fingimento *m*; **to make a ~ of doing sthg** fingir fazer algo.

pretend [prɪˈtend] *vt*: **to ~ to do sthg** fingir fazer algo; **she ~ed she was crying** ela fez de conta que estava chorando.

pretense [prɪˈtens] *(Am)* = **pretence**.

pretension [prɪˈtenʃn] *n* pretensão *f*.

pretentious [prɪˈtenʃəs] *adj* pretencioso(-osa).

pretext [ˈpriːtekst] *n* pretexto *m*; **on** OR **under the ~ of doing sthg** sob o pretexto de fazer algo; **on** OR **under the ~ that** sob o pretexto de que.

pretty [ˈprɪtɪ] *adj* bonito(-ta) ◆ *adv (inf) (quite)* bastante; *(very)* muito.

prevailing [prɪˈveɪlɪŋ] *adj (belief, opinion, fashion)* dominante, corrente; *(wind)* constante.

prevalent [ˈprevələnt] *adj* dominante, corrente.

prevent [prɪˈvent] *vt* evitar; **to ~ sb/sthg from doing sthg** impedir alguém/algo de fazer algo.

prevention [prɪˈvenʃn] *n* prevenção *f*.

preventive [prɪˈventɪv] *adj* preventivo(-va).

preview [ˈpriːvjuː] *n (of film)* pré-estréia *f (Br)*, anteestreia *f (Port)*; *(short description)* resumo *m*.

previous [ˈpriːvjəs] *adj* anterior.

previously [ˈpriːvjəslɪ] *adv* anteriormente.

prey [preɪ] *n* presa *f*.

price [praɪs] *n* preço *m* ◆ *vt* fixar o preço de; **to be ~d at** custar.

priceless [ˈpraɪslɪs] *adj (expensive)* de valor incalculável; *(valuable)* valiosíssimo(-ma).

price list *n* lista *f* de preços.

price tag *n* etiqueta *f*, preço *m*.

pricey [ˈpraɪsɪ] *adj (inf)* caro(-ra).

prick [prɪk] *vt* picar.

prickly [ˈprɪklɪ] *adj (plant, bush)* espinhoso(-osa).

prickly heat *n* brotoeja *f (provocada pelo calor)*.

pride [praɪd] n orgulho m ♦ vt: **to ~ o.s. on sthg** orgulhar-se de algo.

priest [priːst] n padre m.

priestess ['priːstɪs] n sacerdotisa f.

priesthood ['priːsthʊd] n: **the ~** (position, office) o sacerdócio; (priests) o clero.

prim [prɪm] adj (proper) ceremonioso (-osa).

primarily ['praɪmərɪlɪ] adv principalmente.

primary ['praɪmərɪ] adj primário (-ria).

❑ **primaries** npl (Am: POL) (eleições) primárias fpl.

primary school n escola f primária.

prime [praɪm] adj (chief) principal; (quality, beef, cut) de primeira.

prime minister n primeiro-ministro m (primeira-ministra f). ·

primer ['praɪmər] n (paint) (tinta de) base f; (textbook) cartilha f.

primitive ['prɪmɪtɪv] adj primitivo (-va).

primrose ['prɪmrəʊz] n primavera f.

prince [prɪns] n príncipe m.

Prince of Wales n Príncipe m de Gales.

princess [prɪnˈses] n princesa f.

principal ['prɪnsəpl] adj principal ♦ n (of school) diretor m (-ra f); (of university) reitor m (-ra f).

principle ['prɪnsəpl] n princípio m; **in ~** em princípio.

print [prɪnt] n (words) letra f (impressa); (photo) fotografia f; (of painting) reprodução f; (mark) impressão f ♦ vt (book, newspaper) imprimir; (publish) publicar; (write) escrever em letra de imprensa; (photo) revelar; **out of ~** esgotado.

❑ **print out** vt sep imprimir.

printed matter ['prɪntɪd-] n impressos mpl.

printer ['prɪntər] n (machine) impressora f; (person) impressor m (-ra f).

printout ['prɪntaʊt] n cópia f impressa, impressão f.

prior ['praɪər] adj (previous) prévio (-via); **~ to** (fml) antes de.

priority [praɪˈɒrətɪ] n prioridade f; **to have ~ over** ter prioridade sobre.

prison [prɪzn] n prisão f.

prisoner ['prɪznər] n prisioneiro m (-ra f).

prisoner of war n prisioneiro m (-ra f) de guerra.

prison officer n guarda mf de prisão.

privacy ['prɪvəsɪ] n privacidade f.

private ['praɪvɪt] adj privado(-da); (class, lesson) particular; (quiet) retirado(-da) ♦ n (MIL) soldado m raso; **in ~** em particular.

private health care n assistência f médica privada.

privately ['praɪvɪtlɪ] adv (meet, speak) em particular; (think, believe) no íntimo; **~ owned** (company) pertencente ao setor privado.

private property n propriedade f privada.

private school n escola f particular.

privatize ['praɪvɪtaɪz] vt privatizar.

privet ['prɪvɪt] n alfena f, alfenheiro m, ligustro m.

privilege ['prɪvɪlɪdʒ] n privilégio m; **it's a ~!** é uma honra!

prize [praɪz] n prêmio m.

prize-giving [-ˌgɪvɪŋ] n entrega f de prêmios.

prizewinner ['praɪzwɪnər] n premiado m (-da f), vencedor m (-ra f) (do prêmio).

pro [prəʊ] (pl -s) n (inf: professional) profissional mf.

❑ **pros** npl: **~s and cons** os prós e os contras.

probability [ˌprɒbəˈbɪlətɪ] n probabilidade f.

probable ['prɒbəbl] adj provável.

probably ['prɒbəblɪ] adv provavelmente.

probation [prəˈbeɪʃn] n (of prisoner) liberdade f condicional; (trial period) período m em experiência; **to be on ~** (employee) estar em experiência.

probation officer n assistente mf social (responsável por um preso em liberdade condicional).

probe [prəʊb] n (MED: for exploration) sonda f ♦ vt sondar.

problem ['prɒbləm] n problema m; **no ~!** (inf) não há problema!

procedure [prəˈsiːdʒər] n procedimento m.

proceed [prəˈsiːd] vi (fml) (continue) prosseguir; (act) proceder; (advance) avançar; **"~ with caution"** "avançar com precaução".

proceeds ['prəusiːdz] *npl* receita *f*, dinheiro *m* apurado

process ['prəuses] *n* processo *m*; **to be in the ~ of doing sthg** estar fazendo algo.

processed cheese ['prəusest-] *n (for spreading)* queijo *m* fundido; *(in slices)* queijo fundido em fatias.

procession [prə'seʃn] *n* procissão *f*.

proclaim [prə'kleɪm] *vt* proclamar.

procrastinate [prə'kræstɪneɪt] *vi* procrastinar, adiar.

procure [prə'kjuəʳ] *vt* arranjar, conseguir.

prod [prɒd] *vt (poke)* empurrar.

prodigal ['prɒdɪgl] *adj* pródigo(-ga).

prodigy ['prɒdɪdʒɪ] *n* prodígio *m*.

produce [*vb* prə'djuːs, *n* 'prɒdjuːs] *vt* produzir; *(cause)* provocar; *(show)* mostrar ♦ *n* produtos *mpl* agrícolas.

producer [prə'djuːsəʳ] *n* produtor *m* (-ra *f*).

product ['prɒdʌkt] *n* produto *m*.

production [prə'dʌkʃn] *n* produção *f*.

production line *n* linha *f* de produção.

productive [prə'dʌktɪv] *adj* produtivo(-va).

productivity [‚prɒdʌk'tɪvətɪ] *n* produtividade *f*.

profession [prə'feʃn] *n* profissão *f*.

professional [prə'feʃənl] *adj* profissional ♦ *n* profissional *mf*.

professor [prə'fesəʳ] *n (in UK)* professor *m* catedrático (professora *f* catedrática); *(in US)* professor *m* universitário (professora *f* universitária).

profile ['prəufaɪl] *n* perfil *m*.

profit ['prɒfɪt] *n (financial)* lucro *m* ♦ *vi*: **to ~ (from)** tirar proveito (de), lucrar (com).

profitability [‚prɒfɪtə'bɪlɪtɪ] *n* rentabilidade *f*.

profitable ['prɒfɪtəbl] *adj (financially)* lucrativo(-va), rentável.

profiteroles [prə'fɪtərəulz] *npl* profiteroles *mpl*, bolinhos de massa leve recheados com creme e cobertos de chocolate.

profound [prə'faund] *adj* profundo (-da).

profusely [prə'fjuːslɪ] *adv (sweat, bleed)* imenso; **to apologize ~** desfazer-se em desculpas.

program ['prəugræm] *n (COMPUT)* pro-

grama *m*; *(Am)* = **programme** ♦ *vt (COMPUT)* programar.

programme ['prəugræm] *n (Brit)* programa *m*.

programming ['prəugræmɪŋ] *n (COMPUT)* programação *f*.

progress [*n* 'prəugres, *vb* prə'gres] *n* progresso *m* ♦ *vi (work, talks, student)* progredir; *(day, meeting)* avançar; **to make ~ (improve)** progredir, melhorar; *(in journey)* avançar; **in ~** em curso.

progressive [prə'gresɪv] *adj (forward-looking)* progressivo(-va).

prohibit [prə'hɪbɪt] *vt* proibir; **"smoking strictly ~ed"** "é proibido fumar".

project ['prɒdʒekt] *n (plan)* projeto *m*; *(at school)* trabalho *m*.

projectile [prə'dʒektaɪl] *n* projétil *m*.

projection [prə'dʒekʃn] *n (estimate)* previsão *f*, estimativa *f*; *(protrusion)* saliência *f*.

projector [prə'dʒektəʳ] *n* projetor *m*.

prolific [prə'lɪfɪk] *adj* prolífico(-ca).

prolog ['prəulɒg] *(Am)* = **prologue**.

prologue ['prəulɒg] *n* prólogo *m*.

prolong [prə'lɒŋ] *vt* prolongar.

prom [prɒm] *n (Am: dance)* ~ baile *m* de finalistas.

promenade [‚prɒmə'nɑːd] *n (Brit: by the sea)* passeio *m* (à beira da praia), calçadão *m (Br)*.

prominent ['prɒmɪnənt] *adj* proeminente.

promiscuous [prɒ'mɪskjuəs] *adj* promíscuo(-cua).

promise ['prɒmɪs] *n* promessa *f* ♦ *vt & vi* prometer; **to show ~** ser prometedor; **to ~ sb sthg** prometer algo a alguém; **to ~ to do sthg** prometer fazer algo; **I ~ (that) I'll come** prometo que vou, prometo ir.

promising ['prɒmɪsɪŋ] *adj* prometedor(-ra).

promote [prə'məut] *vt* promover.

promotion [prə'məuʃn] *n* promoção *f*.

prompt [prɒmpt] *adj (quick)* imediato(-ta) ♦ *adv*: **at six o'clock ~** às seis em ponto.

promptly ['prɒmptlɪ] *adv (reply, react, pay)* imediatamente; *(arrive, leave)* pontualmente.

prone [prəun] *adj*: **to be ~ to sthg** ser propenso(-sa) a algo; **to be ~ to do sthg** ter tendência para fazer algo.

prong [prɒŋ] *n (of fork)* dente *m*.

pronoun ['prəʊnaʊn] n pronome m.

pronounce [prə'naʊns] vt (word) pronunciar.

pronunciation [prə,nʌnsɪ'eɪʃn] n pronúncia f.

proof [pruːf] n (evidence) prova f; **it's 12% ~** (alcohol) tem 12 graus.

prop [prɒp] : **prop up** vt sep (support) suster.

propaganda [,prɒpə'gændə] n propaganda f.

propeller [prə'pelər] n hélice f.

propelling pencil [prə'pelɪŋ-] n (Brit) lapiseira f (Br), porta-minas m inv (Port).

proper ['prɒpər] adj (suitable) adequado(-da); (correct, socially acceptable) correto(-ta).

properly ['prɒpəlɪ] adv corretamente.

proper noun n substantivo m próprio.

property ['prɒpətɪ] n propriedade f; (fml: building) imóvel m, prédio m.

prophecy ['prɒfɪsɪ] n profecia f.

prophesy ['prɒfɪsaɪ] vt profetizar.

prophet ['prɒfɪt] n profeta m (-tisa f).

proportion [prə'pɔːʃn] n (part, amount) porção f, parte f; (ratio, in art) proporção f.

proportional [prə'pɔːʃnl] adj proporcional; **to be ~ to sthg** ser proporcional a algo.

proportional representation [-,reprɪzen'teɪʃn] n representação f proporcional.

proportionate [prə'pɔːʃnət] adj: **~ (to)** proporcional (a).

proposal [prə'pəʊzl] n (suggestion) proposta f.

propose [prə'pəʊz] vt (suggest) propor ♦ vi: **to ~ to sb** pedir alguém em casamento.

proposition [,prɒpə'zɪʃn] n (offer) proposta f.

proprietor [prə'praɪətər] n (fml) proprietário m (-ria f).

prose [prəʊz] n (not poetry) prosa f; (SCH) retroversão f.

prosecute ['prɒsɪkjuːt] vt (JUR) processar, mover uma ação judicial contra ♦ vi (bring a charge) instaurar um processo judicial; (represent in court) representar o demandante.

prosecutor ['prɒsɪkjuːtər] n Promotor m Público (Promotora f Pública) (Br), Delegado m (-da f) do Ministério Público (Port).

prospect ['prɒspekt] n (possibility) possibilidade f, perspectiva f; **I don't relish the ~** não me agrada a perspectiva.

❏ **prospects** npl (for the future) perspectivas fpl.

prospective [prə'spektɪv] adj potencial.

prospectus [prə'spektəs] (pl -es) n prospecto m.

prosper ['prɒspər] vi prosperar.

prosperity [prɒ'sperətɪ] n prosperidade f.

prosperous ['prɒspərəs] adj próspero(-ra).

prostitute ['prɒstɪtjuːt] n prostituta f.

protagonist [prə'tægənɪst] n protagonista mf.

protect [prə'tekt] vt proteger; **to ~ sb/sthg against** proteger alguém/algo contra; **to ~ sb/sthg from** proteger alguém/algo de.

protection [prə'tekʃn] n proteção f.

protection factor n factor m de proteção.

protective [prə'tektɪv] adj protetor (-ra).

protein ['prəʊtiːn] n proteína f.

protest [n 'prəʊtest, vb prə'test] n (complaint) protesto m; (demonstration) passeata f (Br), protesto, manifestação f (Port) ♦ vt (Am: protest against) protestar contra ♦ vi: **to ~ (against)** protestar (contra).

Protestant ['prɒtɪstənt] n protestante mf.

protester [prə'testər] n manifestante mf.

prototype ['prəʊtətaɪp] n protótipo m.

protractor [prə'træktər] n transferidor m.

protrude [prə'truːd] vi sair.

proud [praʊd] adj orgulhoso(-osa); **to be ~ of** ter orgulho em.

prove [pruːv] (pp -d OR proven ['pruːvn]) vt (show to be true) provar; (turn out to be) revelar-se.

proverb ['prɒvɜːb] n provérbio m.

provide [prə'vaɪd] vt (supply) fornecer; **to ~ sb with sthg** fornecer algo a alguém.

❏ **provide for** vt fus (person) manter.

provided (that) [prə'vaɪdɪd-] conj desde que.

providing (that) [prə'vaɪdɪŋ-] = provided (that).

province ['prɒvɪns] n província f.

provision [prə'vɪʒn] n (of food, resources) fornecimento m; (in agreement, law) disposição f, cláusula f; (arrangement) precauções fpl; **to make ~ for** (future, eventuality) tomar precauções para.

❑ **provisions** npl (supplies) provisões fpl, mantimentos mpl.

provisional [prə'vɪʒənl] adj provisório(-ria).

provocative [prə'vɒkətɪv] adj provocador(-ra).

provoke [prə'vəʊk] vt provocar.

prow [praʊ] n proa f.

prowess ['praʊɪs] n proeza f.

prowl [praʊl] vi rondar.

proxy ['prɒksɪ] n: **by ~** por OR com procuração.

prudent ['pruːdnt] adj prudente.

prudish ['pruːdɪʃ] adj pudico(-ca).

prune [pruːn] n ameixa f seca ♦ vt (tree, bush) podar.

pry [praɪ] vi: **to ~ (into sth)** intrometer-se (em algo).

PS (abbr of postscript) PS.

psalm [sɑːm] n salmo m.

pseudonym ['sjuːdənɪm] n pseudônimo m.

psychiatric [ˌsaɪkɪ'ætrɪk] adj psiquiátrico(-ca).

psychiatrist [saɪ'kaɪətrɪst] n psiquiatra mf.

psychiatry [saɪ'kaɪətrɪ] n psiquiatria f.

psychic ['saɪkɪk] adj (person) mediúnico(-ca), espírita.

psychoanalysis [ˌsaɪkəʊə'næləsɪs] n psicanálise f.

psychoanalyst [ˌsaɪkəʊ'ænəlɪst] n psicanalista mf.

psychological [ˌsaɪkə'lɒdʒɪkl] adj psicológico(-ca).

psychologist [saɪ'kɒlədʒɪst] n psicólogo m (-ga f).

psychology [saɪ'kɒlədʒɪ] n psicologia f.

psychopath ['saɪkəpæθ] n psicopata mf.

psychotherapist [ˌsaɪkəʊ'θerəpɪst] n psicoterapeuta mf.

psychotic [saɪ'kɒtɪk] adj psicopático(-ca).

pt abbr = pint.

PTO (abbr of please turn over) v.s.f.f.

pub [pʌb] n ~ bar m.

puberty ['pjuːbətɪ] n puberdade f.

public ['pʌblɪk] adj público(-ca) ♦ n: **the ~** o público; **in ~** em público.

public-address system n sistema m de difusão pública OR (de reforço) de som.

publican ['pʌblɪkən] n (Brit) pessoa que gere um "pub".

publication [ˌpʌblɪ'keɪʃn] n publicação f.

public bar n (Brit) parte mais simples e menos confortável de um "pub".

public convenience n (Brit) banheiro m público (Br), casa f de banho pública (Port).

public footpath n (Brit) caminho m público.

public holiday n feriado m (nacional).

public house n (Brit: fml) ~ bar m.

publicity [pʌb'lɪsɪtɪ] n publicidade f.

publicize [pʌblɪ'saɪz] vt divulgar, dar a conhecer ao público.

public opinion n opinião f pública.

public relations npl relações fpl públicas. **public school** n (in UK) escola f particular; (in US) escola pública.

public telephone n telefone m público.

public transport n transporte m público OR coletivo.

publish ['pʌblɪʃ] vt publicar.

publisher ['pʌblɪʃəʳ] n (person) editor m (-ra f); (company) editora f.

publishing ['pʌblɪʃɪŋ] n (industry) indústria f editorial.

pub lunch n almoço servido num "pub".

pudding ['pʊdɪŋ] n (sweet dish) pudim m; (Brit: course) sobremesa f.

puddle ['pʌdl] n poça f.

puff [pʌf] vi (breathe heavily) ofegar ♦ n (of air) lufada f, (smoke) baforada f; **to ~ at** tirar baforadas de.

puffin ['pʌfɪn] n papagaio-do-mar m.

puff pastry n massa f folhada.

pull [pʊl] vt & vi puxar ♦ n: **to give sth a ~** dar um puxão em algo, puxar algo; **to ~ a face** fazer uma careta; **to ~ a muscle** distender um músculo; **"pull"** (on door) "puxe".

❑ **pull apart** vt sep (machine) desmontar; *(book)* desfazer.

❑ **pull down** *vt sep (lower)* baixar; *(demolish)* jogar abaixo, demolir.

❑ **pull in** *vi (train)* dar entrada *(em estação)*; *(car)* estacionar.

❑ **pull out** *vt sep (cork, plug)* tirar; *(tooth)* arrancar ◆ *vi (train)* partir; *(car)* sair; *(withdraw)* retirar-se.

❑ **pull over** *vi (car)* encostar.

❑ **pull up** *vt sep (trousers, sleeve)* arregaçar; *(socks)* puxar ◆ *vi (stop)* parar.

pulley ['pulɪ] *(pl -s)* n roldana f.

pull-out n *(Am: beside road)* área f de descanso.

pullover ['pul,əuvəʳ] n pulôver m.

pulp [pʌlp] n polpa f; *(of wood)* pasta f de papel ◆ *adj*: ~ **fiction** literatura f de cordel.

pulpit ['pulpɪt] n púlpito m.

pulse [pʌls] n (MED) pulso m.

puma ['pjuːmə] *(pl inv OR -s)* n puma m.

pump [pʌmp] n bomba f.

❑ **pumps** *npl (sports shoes)* sapatilhas fpl, ténis mpl *(Port)*.

❑ **pump up** *vt sep* encher.

pumpkin ['pʌmpkɪn] n abóbora f.

pun [pʌn] n trocadilho m.

punch [pʌntʃ] n *(blow)* murro m, soco m; *(drink)* ponche m ◆ *vt (hit)* esmurrar, dar um murro OR soco em; *(ticket)* picar, obliterar.

Punch and Judy show [-'dʒuːdɪ-] n ≃ show m de marionetes OR fantoches.

punch line n final m *(de uma anedota ou piada)*.

punch-up n *(Brit: inf)* briga f, pancadaria f.

punctual ['pʌŋktʃuəl] *adj* pontual.

punctuation [,pʌŋktʃu'eɪʃn] n pontuação f.

punctuation mark n sinal m de pontuação.

puncture ['pʌŋktʃəʳ] n furo m ◆ *vt* furar.

pungent ['pʌndʒənt] *adj (smell)* intenso(-sa), penetrante.

punish ['pʌnɪʃ] *vt*: **to ~ sb (for sthg)** castigar alguém (por algo), pôr alguém de castigo (por algo).

punishing ['pʌnɪʃɪŋ] *adj* penoso (-osa).

punishment ['pʌnɪʃmənt] n castigo m.

punk [pʌŋk] n *(person)* punk mf;

(music) música f punk.

punnet ['pʌnɪt] n *(Brit)* cestinho m, caixa f.

puny ['pjuːnɪ] *adj (person, limbs)* magricela; *(effort, attempt)* patético (-ca).

pup [pʌp] n *(young dog)* cachorrinho m *(Br)*, cachorro m *(Port)*.

pupil ['pjuːpl] n *(student)* aluno m (-na f); *(of eye)* pupila f.

puppet ['pʌpɪt] n fantoche m, marionete f.

puppy ['pʌpɪ] n cachorrinho m *(Br)*, cachorro m *(Port)*.

purchase ['pɜːtʃəs] *vt (fml)* comprar ◆ n *(fml)* compra f.

purchaser ['pɜːtʃəsəʳ] n comprador m (-ra f).

pure [pjuəʳ] *adj* puro(-ra).

puree ['pjuəreɪ] n purê m.

purely ['pjuəlɪ] *adv (only)* meramente.

purify ['pjuərɪfaɪ] *vt* purificar.

purity ['pjuərɪtɪ] n pureza f.

purple ['pɜːpl] *adj* roxo(-xa).

purpose ['pɜːpəs] n *(reason)* motivo m; *(use)* uso m; **on ~** de propósito.

purr [pɜːʳ] *vi (cat)* ronronar.

purse [pɜːs] n carteira f.

purser ['pɜːsəʳ] n comissário m de bordo.

pursue [pə'sjuː] *vt (follow)* perseguir; *(study, inquiry, matter)* continuar com.

pursuer [pə'sjuːəʳ] n perseguidor m (-ra f).

pursuit [pə'sjuːt] n *(of animal, criminal)* perseguição f; *(of happiness, goals)* busca f; *(occupation, activity)* atividade f; **leisure ~s** passatempos mpl.

pus [pʌs] n pus m.

push [puʃ] *vt (shove)* empurrar; *(button, doorbell)* apertar; *(product)* promover ◆ *vi (shove)* empurrar ◆ n: **to give sb/sthg a ~** empurrar alguém/algo, dar um empurrão em alguém/algo; **to ~ sb into doing sthg** levar alguém a fazer algo; **"push"** *(on door)* "empurre".

❑ **push in** *vi (in queue)* meter-se na frente.

❑ **push off** *vi (inf: go away)* pirar-se.

push-button telephone n telefone m de teclas.

pushchair ['puʃtʃeəʳ] n *(Brit)* carrinho m *(de bebê)*.

pushed [puʃt] *adj (inf)*: **to be ~ (for time)** não ter tempo.

pusher ['puʃəʳ] n *(drugs seller)* traficante *mf* OR passador *m* (-ra *f*).

push-ups *npl* flexões *fpl*.

pushy ['puʃɪ] *adj* agressivo(-va), insistente.

puss [pus] = **pussy (cat)**.

pussy (cat) ['pusɪ-] *n (inf)* gatito *m*, bichaninho *m*.

put [put] (*pt & pp* **put**) *vt* pôr; *(express)* exprimir; *(write)* escrever; *(a question)* colocar, fazer; **to ~ sthg at** *(estimate)* avaliar algo em; **to ~ a child to bed** pôr uma criança na cama; **to ~ money into sthg** pôr dinheiro OR investir em algo.

❏ **put aside** *vt sep (money)* pôr de lado.

❏ **put away** *vt sep (tidy up)* arrumar.

❏ **put back** *vt sep (replace)* repor; *(postpone)* adiar; *(clock, watch)* atrasar.

❏ **put down** *vt sep (on floor, table)* colocar; *(passenger, deposit)* deixar; *(Brit: animal)* matar, abater.

❏ **put forward** *vt sep (clock, watch)* adiantar; *(suggest)* sugerir.

❏ **put in** *vt sep (insert)* pôr em; *(install)* instalar.

❏ **put off** *vt sep (postpone)* adiar; *(distract)* distrair; *(repel)* dar nojo em; *(passenger)* deixar.

❏ **put on** *vt sep (clothes, make-up, CD)* pôr; *(television, light, radio)* acender, ligar; *(play, show)* montar; **to ~ on weight** engordar.

❏ **put out** *vt sep (cigarette, fire, light)* apagar; *(publish)* publicar; *(hand, arm, leg)* estender; *(inconvenience)* incomodar; **to ~ one's back out** deslocar uma vértebra.

❏ **put together** *vt sep* juntar.

❏ **put up** *vt sep (tent)* montar; *(statue)* erigir, erguer; *(building)* construir; *(umbrella)* abrir; *(a notice, sign)* afixar; *(price, rate)* aumentar, subir; *(provide with accommodation)* alojar ◆ *vi (Brit: in hotel)* ficar, hospedar-se.

❏ **put up with** *vt fus* aguentar, suportar.

putt [pʌt] *n* putt *m*, pancada *f* leve ◆ *vi* fazer um putt.

putter ['pʌtəʳ] *n (club)* putter *m*.

putting green ['pʌtɪŋ-] *n* green *m*, pequeno campo de golfe.

putty ['pʌtɪ] *n* betume *m*, massa *f* para vidros.

puzzle ['pʌzl] *n (game)* quebra-cabeças *m inv*; *(jigsaw)* puzzle *m*; *(mystery)* mistério *m* ◆ *vt* confundir.

puzzling ['pʌzlɪŋ] *adj* intrigante.

pyjamas [pə'dʒɑːməz] *npl (Brit)* pijama *m*.

pylon ['paɪlən] *n* poste *m* de alta tensão.

pyramid ['pɪrəmɪd] *n* pirâmide *f*.

Pyrenees [,pɪrə'niːz] *npl*: **the ~** os Pirineus.

Pyrex® ['paɪreks] *n* Pirex® *m*.

python ['paɪθn] *n (cobra)* piton *f*.

Q

quack [kwæk] n (noise) quá-quá m; (inf: doctor) charlatão m (-tona f), veterinário m (-ria f).

quadruple [kwɒˈdruːpl] vi quadruplicar ◆ adj: **sales are ~ last year's figures** as vendas aumentaram o quádruplo em relação ao ano passado.

quail [kweɪl] n codorna f (Br), codorniz f (Port).

quail's eggs npl ovos mpl de codorna.

quaint [kweɪnt] adj pitoresco(-ca).

quake [kweɪk] n (inf) terremoto m ◆ vi tremer.

qualification [ˌkwɒlɪfɪˈkeɪʃn] n qualificação f.

qualified [ˈkwɒlɪfaɪd] adj (trained) qualificado(-da).

qualify [ˈkwɒlɪfaɪ] vi (for competition) qualificar-se; (pass exam) formar-se.

quality [ˈkwɒlɪtɪ] n qualidade f ◆ adj de qualidade.

quantity [ˈkwɒntɪtɪ] n quantidade f.

quarantine [ˈkwɒrəntiːn] n quarentena f.

quarrel [ˈkwɒrəl] n discussão f ◆ vi discutir.

quarrelsome [ˈkwɒrəlsəm] adj conflituoso(-osa); **he's in a ~ mood today** ele está muito irritadiço hoje.

quarry [ˈkwɒrɪ] n (for stone) pedreira f; (for sand) areiro m.

quart [kwɔːt] n (in UK) = 1,136 l, = litro m; (in US) = 0,946 l, = litro.

quarter [ˈkwɔːtəʳ] n (fraction) quarto m; (Am: coin) moeda f de 25 centavos; (4 ounces) = 0,1134 kg, = cem gramas; (three months) trimestre m; (part of town) bairro m; **(a) ~ to five** (Brit) quinze para as cinco; **(a) ~ of five** (Am) quinze para as cinco; **(a) ~ past five** (Brit) cinco e quinze; **(a) ~ after five** (Am) cinco e quinze; **(a) ~ of an hour** um quarto de hora.

quarterfinal [ˌkwɔːtəˈfaɪnl] n quarta f de final.

quarterly [ˈkwɔːtəlɪ] adj trimestral ◆ adv trimestralmente ◆ n publicação f trimestral.

quarterpounder [ˌkwɔːtəˈpaʊndəʳ] n hambúrger m grande.

quartet [kwɔːˈtet] n quarteto m.

quartz [kwɔːts] adj (watch) de quartzo.

quartz watch n relógio m de quartzo.

quay [kiː] n cais m inv.

quayside [ˈkiːsaɪd] n cais m inv.

queasy [ˈkwiːzɪ] adj (inf) enjoado(-da), indisposto(-osta).

queen [kwiːn] n rainha f; (in cards) dama f.

queen mother n: **the ~** a rainha-mãe.

queer [kwɪəʳ] adj (strange) esquisito(-ta); (inf: ill) indisposto(-osta) ◆ n (inf: homosexual) bicha f (Br), maricas m inv (Port).

quench [kwentʃ] vt: **to ~ one's thirst** matar a sede.

query [ˈkwɪərɪ] n pergunta f.

quest [kwest] n: **~ (for)** busca f (de).

question [ˈkwestʃn] n pergunta f; (issue) questão f ◆ vt (person) interrogar; **it's out of the ~** está fora de questão.

questionable [ˈkwestʃənəbl] adj questionável.

question mark n ponto m de interrogação.

questionnaire [ˌkwestʃəˈneəʳ] n questionário m.

queue [kjuː] n (Brit) fila f, bicha f (Port) ◆ vi (Brit) fazer fila.
❑ **queue up** vi (Brit) fazer fila.

quiche [kiːʃ] n quiche m.

quick [kwɪk] adj rápido(-da) ◆ adv rapidamente, depressa.

quicken ['kwɪkn] *vt* apressar, acelerar ♦ *vi* acelerar-se.

quickly ['kwɪklɪ] *adv* rapidamente, depressa.

quicksand ['kwɪksænd] *n* areia *f* movediça.

quick-witted [-'wɪtɪd] *adj* vivo(-va).

quid [kwɪd] *(pl inv) n (Brit: inf)* libra *f.*

quiet ['kwaɪət] *adj* silencioso(-osa); *(calm, peaceful)* calmo(-ma); *(voice)* baixo(-xa) ♦ *n* sossego *m*, calma *f*; **keep ~!** está calado!; **to keep ~** *(not make noise)* estar calado; **please keep ~ about this** por favor não digam nada.

quieten ['kwaɪətn] : **quieten down** *vi* acalmar-se.

quietly ['kwaɪətlɪ] *adv* silenciosamente; *(calmly)* tranqüilamente.

quilt [kwɪlt] *n* edredom *m.*

quince [kwɪns] *n* marmelo *m.*

quirk [kwɜːk] *n* mania *f.*

quit [kwɪt] *(pt & pp* quit) *vi (resign)* demitir-se; *(give up)* desistir ♦ *vt (Am: school, job)* deixar, abandonar; **to ~ doing sthg** deixar de fazer algo, desistir de fazer algo.

quite [kwaɪt] *adv* bastante; **it's not ~ big enough** não é suficientemente grande; **it's not ~ ready** ainda não está pronto; **you're ~ right** você tem toda a razão; **~ a lot (of children)** bastantes (crianças); **~ a lot of money** bastante dinheiro.

quits [kwɪts] *adj (inf)*: **we're ~!** estamos quites!; **give me £10 and we'll call it ~!** dê-me 10 libras e assunto resolvido!

quiver ['kwɪvəʳ] *n (for arrows)* aljava *f*, carcás *m* ♦ *vi* tremer.

quiz [kwɪz] *(pl* -zes) *n* competição *f (que consiste em responder a perguntas de natureza variada).*

quizzical ['kwɪzɪkl] *adj (look, glance)* inquiridor(-ra); *(smile)* brincalhão (-lhona), zombeteiro(-ra).

quota ['kwəʊtə] *n* cota *f*, quota *f.*

quotation [kwəʊ'teɪʃn] *n (phrase)* citação *f; (estimate)* orçamento *m.*

quotation marks *npl* aspas *fpl.*

quote [kwəʊt] *vt (phrase, writer)* citar; *(price)* indicar ♦ *n (phrase)* citação *f; (estimate)* orçamento *m.*

R

rabbi ['ræbaɪ] *n* rabi *m*, rabino *m*.

rabbit ['ræbɪt] *n* coelho *m*.

rabbit hutch *n* coelheira *f*.

rabies ['reɪbiːz] *n* raiva *f*.

RAC *n* = TCB *(Br)*, ≃ ACP *(Port)*.

race [reɪs] *n (competition)* corrida *f*; *(ethnic group)* raça *f* ◆ *vi (compete)* competir; *(go fast)* correr; *(engine)* acelerar ◆ *vt (compete against)* competir com.

race car *(Am)* = **racing car**.

racecourse ['reɪskɔːs] *n* hipódromo *m*.

racehorse ['reɪshɔːs] *n* cavalo *m* de corrida.

racetrack ['reɪstræk] *n (for horses)* hipódromo *m*.

racial ['reɪʃl] *adj* racial.

racial discrimination *n* discriminação *f* racial.

racing ['reɪsɪŋ] *n*: **(horse) ~** corridas *fpl* de cavalos.

racing car *n* carro *m* de corrida.

racism ['reɪsɪzm] *n* racismo *m*.

racist ['reɪsɪst] *n* racista *mf*.

rack [ræk] *n (for coats)* cabide *m*; *(for bottles)* garrafeira *f*; *(for plates)* escorredor *m* de louça; **(luggage) ~** porta-bagagens *m inv*; **~ of lamb** peito *m* de carneiro.

racket ['rækɪt] *n (for tennis, badminton, squash)* raquete *f*; *(noise)* barulheira *f*.

racquet ['rækɪt] *n* raquete *f*.

radar ['reɪdɑːr] *n* radar *m*.

radiant ['reɪdjənt] *adj* radiante.

radiate ['reɪdɪeɪt] *vt* irradiar ◆ *vi (be emitted)* irradiar; *(spread from centre)* ramificar-se.

radiation [,reɪdɪ'eɪʃn] *n* radiação *f*.

radiator ['reɪdɪeɪtər] *n* radiador *m*.

radical ['rædɪkl] *adj* radical.

radically ['rædɪklɪ] *adv* radicalmente.

radii ['reɪdɪaɪ] *pl* → **radius**.

radio ['reɪdɪəu] *(pl* **-s***) n (device)* rádio *m*; *(system)* rádio *f* ◆ *vt (person)* chamar por rádio; **on the ~** na rádio.

radioactive [,reɪdɪəu'æktɪv] *adj* radioativo(-va).

radio alarm *n* rádio-despertador *m*.

radiology [,reɪdɪ'ɒlədʒɪ] *n* radiologia *f*.

radish ['rædɪʃ] *n* rabanete *m*.

radius ['reɪdɪəs] *(pl* **radii***) n* raio *m*.

RAF *n (abbr of Royal Air Force)* RAF *f*, força aérea británica.

raffle ['ræfl] *n* rifa *f*.

raft [rɑːft] *n (of wood)* jangada *f*; *(inflatable)* barco *m* de borracha.

rafter ['rɑːftər] *n* trave *f*, barrote *m*.

rag [ræg] *n (old cloth)* trapo *m*.

rag-and-bone man *n* trapeiro *m*.

rag doll *n* boneca *f* de trapos.

rage [reɪdʒ] *n* raiva *f*, fúria *f*.

ragged ['rægɪd] *adj (person, clothes)* esfarrapado(-da).

raid [reɪd] *n (attack)* ataque *m*; *(by police)* batida *f (Br)*, rusga *f (Port)*; *(robbery)* assalto *m* ◆ *vt (subj: police)* dar uma batida em; *(subj: thieves)* assaltar.

rail [reɪl] *n (bar)* barra *f*; *(for curtain)* trilho *m (Br)*, varão *m (Port)*; *(on stairs)* corrimão *m*; *(for train, tram)* trilho *m (Br)*, carril *m (Port)* ◆ *adj* ferroviário(-ria); **by ~** de trem *(Br)*, de comboio *(Port)*.

railcard ['reɪlkɑːd] *n (Brit)* cartão que permite aos jovens e aposentados obter descontos nas viagens de comboio.

railings ['reɪlɪŋz] *npl* grades *fpl*.

railroad ['reɪlrəud] *(Am)* = **railway**.

railway ['reɪlweɪ] *n (system)* ferrovia *f (Br)*, caminhos-de-ferro *mpl (Port)*; *(track)* estrada *f* de ferro *(Br)*, via-férrea *f (Port)*.

railway line *n (route)* linha *f* de trem *(Br)*, linha *f* dos caminhos-de-ferro *(Port)*; *(track)* estrada *f* de ferro *(Br)*, via-férrea *f (Port)*.

railway station *n* estação *f* ferro-viária *(Br)*, estação *f* dos caminhos-de-ferro *(Port)*.

railway track *n* estrada *f* de ferro *(Br)*, via-férrea *f (Port)*.

rain [reɪn] *n* chuva *f* ◆ *v impers* chover; it's ~ing está chovendo.

rainbow ['reɪnbəʊ] *n* arco-íris *m inv*.

raincoat ['reɪnkəʊt] *n* capa *f* de chuva *(Br)*, gabardina *f (Port)*.

raindrop ['reɪndrɒp] *n* gota *f* OR pingo *m* de chuva.

rainfall ['reɪnfɔ:l] *n* precipitação *f*.

rain forest *n* floresta *f* tropical (úmida).

rainy ['reɪnɪ] *adj* chuvoso(-osa).

raise [reɪz] *vt* levantar; *(increase)* aumentar; *(money)* angariar; *(child, animals)* criar ◆ *n (Am: pay increase)* aumento *m*.

raisin ['reɪzn] *n* passa *f* (de uva).

rake [reɪk] *n (tool)* ancinho *m*.

rally ['rælɪ] *n (public meeting)* comício *m*; *(motor race)* rali *m*, rally *m*; *(in tennis, badminton, squash)* troca *f* de bolas, rally.

ram [ræm] *n* carneiro *m* ◆ *vt (bang into)* bater contra.

Ramadan [ˌræmə'dæn] *n* Ramadão *m*.

ramble ['ræmbl] *n* passeio *m*, caminhada *f*.

rambler ['ræmblər] *n* caminhante *mf*.

ramp [ræmp] *n (slope)* rampa *f*; *(Brit: in road)* lombada *f*; *(Am: to freeway)* acesso *m*; **"ramp"** *(Brit)* "lombada".

rampant ['ræmpənt] *adj (inflation)* galopante; *(growth)* desenfreado(-da); **corruption was ~** proliferava a corrupção.

ramparts ['ræmpɑ:ts] *npl* muralhas *fpl*.

ramshackle ['ræmˌʃækl] *adj* em más condições.

ran [ræn] *pt* → **run**.

ranch [rɑ:ntʃ] *n* rancho *m*.

ranch dressing *n (Am)* tempero cremoso e picante para saladas.

rancher ['rɑ:ntʃər] *n* rancheiro *m* (-ra *f*).

rancid ['rænsɪd] *adj* rançoso(-osa).

random ['rændəm] *adj* ao acaso ◆ *n*: **at ~** ao acaso.

randy ['rændɪ] *adj (inf)* excitado(-da).

rang [ræŋ] *pt* → **ring**.

range [reɪndʒ] *n (of radio, telescope)* alcance *m*; *(of aircraft)* autonomia *f*; *(of prices)* leque *m*; *(of goods, services)* gama *f*, variedade *f*; *(of hills, mountains)* cadeia *f*, cordilheira *f*; *(for shooting)* linha *f* de tiro; *(cooker)* fogão *m* ◆ *vi*: **to ~ from ... to** oscilar entre ... e; **age ~** faixa *f* etária.

ranger ['reɪndʒər] *n* guarda *mf* florestal.

rank [ræŋk] *n (in armed forces, police)* patente *f* ◆ *adj (smell)* fétido(-da); *(taste)* horroroso(-osa).

ransack ['rænsæk] *vt (plunder)* pilhar.

ransom ['rænsəm] *n* resgate *m*.

rant [rænt] *vi* arengar.

rap [ræp] *n (music)* rap *m*.

rape [reɪp] *n (crime)* estupro *m* ◆ *vt* estuprar.

rapeseed ['reɪpsi:d] *n* semente *f* de colza.

rapid ['ræpɪd] *adj* rápido(-da).

❑ **rapids** *npl* rápidos *mpl*.

rapidly ['ræpɪdlɪ] *adv* rapidamente.

rapist ['reɪpɪst] *n* estuprador *m*.

rapport [ræ'pɔ:r] *n* relação *f*; **a ~ with/between** uma relação com/entre.

rapture ['ræptʃər] *n* excitação *f*.

rare [reər] *adj* raro(-ra); *(meat)* malpassado(-da).

rarely ['reəlɪ] *adv* raramente.

rarity ['reərətɪ] *n* raridade *f*.

rascal ['rɑ:skl] *n (dishonest person)* patife *mf*.

rash [ræʃ] *n (on skin)* erupção *f* cutânea, brotoeja *f* ◆ *adj* precipitado(-da).

rasher ['ræʃər] *n* fatia *f* (fina de bacon).

raspberry ['rɑ:zbərɪ] *n* framboesa *f*.

rat [ræt] *n* rato *m*, ratazana *f*.

ratatouille [ˌrætə'tu:ɪ] *n* ensopado de cebola, alho, tomate, pimentão, abobrinha e beringela.

rate [reɪt] *n (level)* índice *m*, taxa *f*; *(charge)* tarifa *f*, preço *m*; *(speed)* velocidade *f* ◆ *vt (consider)* considerar; *(deserve)* merecer; **~ of exchange** taxa de câmbio; **at any ~** *(at least)* pelo menos; *(anyway)* de qualquer modo; **at this ~** desse jeito, nesse passo.

rather ['rɑ:ðər] *adv (quite)* bastante; **I'd ~ have a beer** prefiro uma cerveja; **I'd ~ not** é melhor não; **would you ~ ...?** você prefere ...?; **~ than** em vez de; **that's ~ a lot** é um pouco demais.

ratify ['rætɪfaɪ] *vt* ratificar.

ratio ['reɪʃɪəʊ] *(pl -s) n* proporção *f*.

ration ['ræʃn] *n* porção *f*.

❑ **rations** *npl (food)* rações *fpl*.

rational [ˈræʃnl] *adj* racional.

rattle [ˈrætl] *n (of baby)* chocalho *m* ◆ *vi* chocalhar.

rattlesnake [ˈrætlsneɪk] *n* (cobra) cascavel *f*.

rave [reɪv] *n (party)* rave *f*.

raven [ˈreɪvn] *n* corvo *m*.

ravenous [ˈrævɔnɔs] *adj (person, animal)* faminto(-ta); *(appetite)* voraz.

ravine [rɔˈviːn] *n* ravina *f*.

raving [ˈreɪvɪŋ] *adj (beauty, success)* tremendo(-da); **~ mad** doido varrido (doida varrida).

ravioli [ˌrævɪˈɔʊlɪ] *n* ravioli *m*.

ravishing [ˈrævɪʃɪŋ] *adj (person)* belo(-la).

raw [rɔː] *adj (uncooked)* cru (crua); *(unprocessed)* bruto(-ta).

raw material *n* matéria-prima *f*.

ray [reɪ] *n* raio *m*.

rayon [ˈreɪɒn] *n* rayon *m*, seda *f* artificial.

razor [ˈreɪzəʳ] *n* lâmina *f* de barbear.

razor blade *n* lâmina *f* de barbear.

Rd *abbr* = **Road**.

re [riː] *prep* referente a, com respeito a.

RE *n (abbr of religious education)* ≃ religião *f* e moral.

reach [riːtʃ] *vt* chegar a; *(arrive at)* atingir; *(contact)* contatar ◆ *n:* **out of ~** fora de alcance; **within ~ of the beach** próximo da praia.

❑ **reach out** *vi:* **to ~ out (for)** estender o braço (para).

react [rɪˈækt] *vi* reagir.

reaction [rɪˈækʃn] *n* reação *f*.

reactor [rɪˈæktəʳ] *n (for nuclear energy)* reator *m*.

read [riːd] *(pt & pp* **read** [rɛd]) *vt* ler; *(subj: sign, note)* dizer; *(subj: meter, gauge)* marcar ◆ *vi* ler; **I read about it in the paper** fiquei sabendo pelo jornal.

❑ **read out** *vt sep* ler em voz alta.

readable [ˈriːdəbl] *adj (book)* agradável de ler.

reader [ˈriːdəʳ] *n (of newspaper, book)* leitor *m* (-ra *f*).

readership [ˈriːdəʃɪp] *n* número *m* de leitores.

readily [ˈrɛdɪlɪ] *adv (willingly)* de boa vontade; *(easily)* facilmente.

reading [ˈriːdɪŋ] *n* leitura *f*.

reading matter *n* leitura *f*.

readjust [ˌriːəˈdʒʌst] *vt* reajustar ◆ *vi:* **to ~ (to sthg)** adaptar-se (a algo).

readout [ˈriːdaʊt] *n (COMPUT)* visualização *f*.

ready [ˈrɛdɪ] *adj (prepared)* pronto (-ta); **to be ~ for sthg** *(prepared)* estar preparado para algo; **to be ~ to do sthg** *(willing)* estar disposto a fazer algo; *(likely)* estar prestes a fazer algo; **to get ~** preparar-se; **to get sthg ~** preparar algo.

ready cash *n* dinheiro *m* vivo, numerário *m*.

ready-cooked [-kʊkt] *adj* pré-cozido(-da).

ready-made *adj (ready to use)* (já) feito(-ta).

ready-to-wear *adj* de pronto para vestir.

reafforestation [ˈriːəˌfɒrɪsteɪʃn] *n* reflorestação *f*.

real [rɪəl] *adj* verdadeiro(-ra); *(life, world)* real; *(leather)* genuíno(-na) ◆ *adv (Am)* mesmo.

real ale *n (Brit)* cerveja feita e armazenada de modo tradicional.

real estate *n* bens *mpl* imóveis.

realism [ˈrɪəlɪzm] *n* realismo *m*.

realistic [rɪɔˈlɪstɪk] *adj* realista.

reality [rɪˈælətɪ] *n* realidade *f*; **in ~** na realidade.

realization [ˌrɪəlaɪˈzeɪʃn] *n (awareness, recognition)* consciência *f*; *(of ambition, goal)* realização *f*.

realize [ˈrɪəlaɪz] *vt (become aware of)* aperceber-se de; *(know)* saber; *(ambition, goal)* realizar.

really [ˈrɪəlɪ] *adv (for emphasis)* mesmo, muito; *(in reality)* realmente; **was it good? – not ~** foi bom? – nem por isso; **~?** *(expressing surprise)* a sério?

realtor [ˈrɪəltər] *n (Am)* agente *m* imobiliário (agente *f* imobiliária).

reap [riːp] *vt* colher.

reappear [ˌriːəˈpɪəʳ] *vi* reaparecer.

rear [rɪəʳ] *adj* traseiro(-ra) ◆ *n (back)* parte *f* de trás, traseira *f*.

rearmost [ˈrɪəməʊst] *adj* último (-ma).

rearrange [ˌriːəˈreɪndʒ] *vt (room, furniture)* mudar; *(meeting)* alterar.

rearview mirror [ˈrɪəvjuː-] *n* (espelho) retrovisor *m*.

rear-wheel drive *n* veículo *m* com tração nas rodas traseiras OR de trás.

reason ['ri:zn] *n* razão *f*, motivo *m*;
for some ~ por alguma razão.
reasonable ['ri:znəbl] *adj* razoável.
reasonably ['ri:znəblɪ] *adv* (quite)
razoavelmente.
reasoning ['ri:znɪŋ] *n* raciocínio *m*.
reassess [,ri:ə'ses] *vt* reexaminar.
reassurance [,ri:ə'ʃɔːrəns] *n* (comfort)
palavras *fpl* tranqüilizadoras OR de
conforto; (promise) garantia *f*.
reassure [,ri:ə'ʃɔːʳ] *vt* tranqüilizar.
reassuring [,ri:ə'ʃɔːrɪŋ] *adj* tranqüi-
lizador(-ra).
rebate ['ri:beɪt] *n* devolução *f*, reembolso *m*.
rebel [*n* 'rebl, *vb* rɪ'bel] *n* rebelde *mf*
♦ *vi* revoltar-se.
rebellion [rɪ'beljən] *n* rebelião *f*.
rebellious [rɪ'beljəs] *adj* rebelde.
rebound [rɪ'baund] *vi* (ball) ressaltar
(Br), pinchar (Port).
rebuild [,ri:'bɪld] (pt & pp -built) *vt*
reconstruir.
rebuke [rɪ'bju:k] *vt* repreender.
recall [rɪ'kɔːl] *vt* (remember) recordar-
se de, lembrar-se de.
recap ['ri:kæp] *n* (inf) resumo *m*, reca-
pitulação *f* ♦ *vt* & *vi* (inf: summarize)
recapitular.
recede [rɪ'si:d] *vi* (person, car) recuar;
(hopes, danger) desvanecer-se.
receding [rɪ'si:dɪŋ] *adj*: **~ hairline**
entradas *fpl*.
receipt [rɪ'si:t] *n* (for goods, money)
recibo *m*; **on ~ of** ao receber, mediante a recepção de.
receive [rɪ'si:v] *vt* receber.
receiver [rɪ'si:vəʳ] *n* (of phone) fone *m*
(Br), auscultador *m* (Port).
recent ['ri:snt] *adj* recente.
recently ['ri:sntlɪ] *adv* recentemente.
receptacle [rɪ'septəkl] *n* (fml) recipiente *m*.
reception [rɪ'sepʃn] *n* recepção *f*.
reception desk *n* recepção *f*.
receptionist [rɪ'sepʃənɪst] *n* recepcionista *mf*.
recess ['ri:ses] *n* (in wall) nicho *m*, vão
m; (Am: SCH) recreio *m*, intervalo *m*.
recession [rɪ'seʃn] *n* recessão *f*.
recharge [,ri:'tʃɑːdʒ] *vt* recarregar.
recipe ['resɪpɪ] *n* receita *f*.
recipient [rɪ'sɪpɪənt] *n* (of letter,
cheque) destinatário *m* (-ria *f*).

reciprocal [rɪ'sɪprəkl] *adj* recípro-
co(-ca).
recite [rɪ'saɪt] *vt* (poem) recitar; (list)
enumerar.
reckless ['rekləs] *adj* irresponsável.
reckon ['rekn] *vt* (inf: think): **to ~**
(that) achar que.
❑ **reckon on** *vt fus* contar, esperar.
❑ **reckon with** *vt fus* (expect) contar
com.
reclaim [rɪ'kleɪm] *vt* (baggage) recuperar.
reclining seat [rɪ'klaɪnɪŋ-] *n* assento
m reclinável.
recluse [rɪ'kluːs] *n* solitário *m* (-ria *f*).
recognition [,rekəg'nɪʃn] *n* reconhecimento *m*.
recognizable ['rekəgnaɪzəbl] *adj*
reconhecível.
recognize ['rekəgnaɪz] *vt* reconhecer.
recollect [,rekə'lekt] *vt* recordar-se
de.
recollection [,rekə'lekʃn] *n* lembrança *f*, recordação *f*; **I have no ~ of
what happened** não me lembro de
nada do que aconteceu.
recommend [,rekə'mend] *vt* recomendar; **to ~ sb to do sthg** recomendar a alguém que faça algo.
recommendation [,rekəmen'deɪʃn]
n recomendação *f*.
reconcile ['rekənsaɪl] *vt* (beliefs, ideas)
conciliar; (people) reconciliar; (resign):
to ~ o.s. to sthg conformar-se com
algo; **to ~ sthg with sthg** conciliar
algo com algo.
reconnaissance [rɪ'kɒnɪsəns] *n* reconhecimento *m*.
reconsider [,ri:kən'sɪdəʳ] *vt* reconsi-
derar.
reconstruct [,ri:kən'strʌkt] *vt* reconstruir.
record [*n* 'rekɔːd, *vb* rɪ'kɔːd] *n* (MUS)
disco *m*; (best performance, highest level)
recorde *m*; (account) registro *m* ♦ *vt*
(keep account of) registrar; (on tape) gravar.
recorded delivery [rɪ'kɔːdɪd-] *n*
(Brit) correio *m* registrado.
recorder [rɪ'kɔːdəʳ] *n* (tape recorder)
gravador *m*; (instrument) flauta *f*, pífaro
m.
record holder *n* detentor *m* (-ra *f*)
do recorde, recordista *mf*.
recording [rɪ'kɔːdɪŋ] *n* gravação *f*.
record player *n* toca-discos *m* inv

(Br), gira-discos *m inv (Port)*.

record shop *n* loja *f* de discos.

recover [rɪˈkʌvəˀ] *vt & vi* recuperar.

recovery [rɪˈkʌvərɪ] *n* recuperação *f*.

recovery vehicle *n (Brit)* reboque *m*.

recreation [ˌrekrɪˈeɪʃn] *n* distração *f*, divertimento *m*.

recreation ground *n* parque *m* OR campo *m* de jogos.

recriminations [rɪˌkrɪmɪˈneɪʃnz] *npl* recriminações *fpl*.

recruit [rɪˈkruːt] *n* recruta *mf* ♦ *vt* recrutar.

recruitment [rɪˈkruːtmənt] *n* recrutamento *m*.

rectangle [ˈrektæŋgl] *n* retângulo *m*.

rectangular [rekˈtæŋgjʊləˀ] *adj* retangular.

rectify [ˈrektɪfaɪ] *vt* retificar, corrigir.

recuperate [rɪˈkuːpəreɪt] *vi*: **to ~ (from sthg)** recuperar-se (de algo).

recur [rɪˈkɜːˀ] *vi* repetir-se.

recurrence [rɪˈkʌrəns] *n* repetição *f*.

recurrent [rɪˈkʌrənt] *adj* que se repete.

recycle [ˌriːˈsaɪkl] *vt* reciclar.

red [red] *adj (in colour)* vermelho(-lha), encarnado(-da); *(hair)* ruivo(-va) ♦ *n (colour)* vermelho *m*, encarnado *m*; **in the ~** com saldo negativo.

red cabbage *n* couve *f* roxa.

Red Cross *n* Cruz *f* Vermelha.

redcurrant [ˈredkʌrənt] *n* groselha *f*.

redden [ˈredn] *vt* tingir de vermelho ♦ *vi* ficar vermelho(-lha).

redecorate [ˌriːˈdekəreɪt] *vt* redecorar.

red-faced [-ˈfeɪst] *adj* vermelho(-lha).

red-haired [-ˈheəd] *adj* ruivo(-va).

red-handed [-ˈhændɪd] *adj*: **to catch sb ~** apanhar alguém com a boca na botija.

redhead [ˈredhed] *n* ruivo *m* (-va *f*).

red-hot *adj (metal)* incandescente, rubro(-bra).

redial [ˌriːˈdaɪəl] *vi* tornar a discar (o número de telefone).

redid [ˌriːˈdɪd] *pt* → **redo**.

redirect [ˌriːdɪˈrekt] *vt (letter)* mandar para o novo endereço; *(traffic, plane)* desviar.

rediscover [ˌriːdɪˈskʌvəˀ] *vt (re-experience)* voltar a descobrir.

red light *n (traffic signal)* sinal *m* vermelho.

redo [ˌriːˈduː] *(pt* **-did**, *pp* **-done)** *vt (do again)* tornar a fazer.

red pepper *n* pimentão *m* vermelho.

red tape *n (fig)* burocracia *f*.

reduce [rɪˈdjuːs] *vt (make smaller)* reduzir, diminuir; *(make cheaper)* saldar, reduzir o preço de ♦ *vi (Am: slim)* emagrecer.

reduced price [rɪˈdjuːst-] *n* preço *m* reduzido OR de saldo.

reduction [rɪˈdʌkʃn] *n* redução *f*.

redundancy [rɪˈdʌndənsɪ] *n (Brit: job loss)* demissão *f (Br)*, despedimento *m (Port)*.

redundant [rɪˈdʌndənt] *adj (Brit)*: **to be made ~** ser despedido(-da), perder o emprego.

red wine *n* vinho *m* tinto.

reed [riːd] *n* junco *m*.

reef [riːf] *n* recife *m*.

reek [riːk] *vi*: **to ~ (of)** feder (a).

reel [riːl] *n (of thread)* carro *m*; *(on fishing rod)* molinete *m*, carreto *m*.

refectory [rɪˈfektərɪ] *n* refeitório *m*, cantina *f*.

refer [rɪˈfɜːˀ] : **refer to** *vt fus (speak about)* fazer referência a, referir-se a; *(consult)* consultar.

referee [ˌrefəˈriː] *n (SPORT)* árbitro *m*.

reference [ˈrefrəns] *n* referência *f* ♦ *adj (book)* de consulta; *(library)* para consultas; **with ~ to** com referência a.

reference book *n* livro *m* de consulta.

reference number *n* número *m* de referência.

referendum [ˌrefəˈrendəm] *n* plebiscito *m (Br)*, referendo *m (Port)*.

refill [*n* ˈriːfɪl, *vb* ˌriːˈfɪl] *n (for pen)* recarga *f* ♦ *vt (voltar a)* encher; **would you like a ~?** *(inf: drink)* mais um copo?

refine [rɪˈfaɪn] *vt (oil, sugar)* refinar; *(details, speech)* aperfeiçoar.

refined [rɪˈfaɪnd] *adj (oil, sugar)* refinado(-da); *(person, manners)* requintado(-da); *(process, equipment)* avançado(-da).

refinement [rɪˈfaɪnmənt] *n (improvement)*: **~ (on sthg)** aperfeiçoamento *m* (de algo).

refinery [rɪˈfaɪnərɪ] *n* refinaria *f*.

reflect [rɪˈflekt] *vt & vi* refletir.

reflection [rɪˈflekʃn] *n (image)* reflexo *m.*

reflector [rɪˈflektəʳ] *n* refletor *m.*

reflex [ˈriːfleks] *n* reflexo *m.*

reflexive [rɪˈfleksɪv] *adj* reflexo(-xa), reflexivo(-va).

reforestation [riːˌfɒrɪˈsteɪʃn] = **reafforestation**.

reform [rɪˈfɔːm] *n* reforma *f* ◆ *vt* reformar.

refrain [rɪˈfreɪn] *n* refrão *m* ◆ *vi*: **to ~ from doing sthg** abster-se de fazer algo.

refresh [rɪˈfreʃ] *vt* refrescar.

refreshed [rɪˈfreʃt] *adj* repousado(-da).

refresher course [rɪˈfreʃəʳ-] *n* curso *m* de reciclagem.

refreshing [rɪˈfreʃɪŋ] *adj* refrescante.

refreshments [rɪˈfreʃmənts] *npl* lanches *mpl*, comes e bebes.

refrigerator [rɪˈfrɪdʒəreɪtəʳ] *n* geladeira *f (Br)*, frigorífico *m (Port)*.

refuel [ˌriːˈfjuəl] *vt* reabastecer ◆ *vi* reabastecer-se.

refuge [ˈrefjuːdʒ] *n* refúgio *m*; **to seek** OR **take ~** *(hide)* refugiar-se.

refugee [ˌrefjuˈdʒiː] *n* refugiado *m* (-da *f*).

refund [*n* ˈriːfʌnd, *vb* rɪˈfʌnd] *n* reembolso *m* ◆ *vt* reembolsar.

refundable [rɪˈfʌndəbl] *adj* reembolsável.

refurbish [ˌriːˈfɜːbɪʃ] *vt (building)* restaurar; *(office, shop)* renovar.

refusal [rɪˈfjuːzl] *n* recusa *f.*

refuse¹ [rɪˈfjuːz] *vt & vi* recusar; **to ~ to do sthg** recusar-se a fazer algo.

refuse² [ˈrefjuːs] *n (fml)* lixo *m.*

refuse collection [ˈrefjuːs-] *n (fml)* coleta *f* do lixo *(Br)*, recolha *f* do lixo *(Port)*.

refute [rɪˈfjuːt] *vt (fml)* refutar.

regain [rɪˈgeɪn] *vt (recover)* recuperar.

regard [rɪˈgɑːd] *vt (consider)* considerar ◆ *n*: **with ~ to** a respeito de; **as ~s** no que diz respeito a, quanto a.

⊔ **regards** *npl (in greetings)* cumprimentos *mpl*; **give them my ~s** dê-lhes os meus cumprimentos.

regarding [rɪˈgɑːdɪŋ] *prep* a respeito de, no que diz respeito a.

regardless [rɪˈgɑːdlɪs] *adv* apesar de tudo; **~ of** independentemente de.

reggae [ˈregeɪ] *n* reggae *m.*

regime [reɪˈʒiːm] *n* regime *m.*

regiment [ˈredʒɪmənt] *n* regimento *m.*

region [ˈriːdʒən] *n* região *f*; **in the ~ of** de cerca de, na região de.

regional [ˈriːdʒənl] *adj* regional.

register [ˈredʒɪstəʳ] *n* registro *m* ◆ *vt* registrar ◆ *vi (put one's name down)* inscrever-se; *(at hotel)* preencher o registro.

registered [ˈredʒɪstəd] *adj (letter, parcel)* registrado(-da).

registration [ˌredʒɪˈstreɪʃn] *n (for course, at conference)* inscrição *f.*

registration (number) *n* placa *f (Br)*, matrícula *f (Port).*

registry office [ˈredʒɪstrɪ-] *n* registro *m* civil.

regret [rɪˈgret] *n* arrependimento *m* ◆ *vt* lamentar, arrepender-se de; **to ~ doing sthg** arrepender-se de ter feito algo; **we ~ any inconvenience caused** lamentamos qualquer inconveniência.

regretfully [rɪˈgretfʊlɪ] *adv* com pesar.

regrettable [rɪˈgretəbl] *adj* lamentável.

regular [ˈregjʊləʳ] *adj* regular; *(normal, in size)* normal ◆ *n (customer)* cliente *mf* habitual, habitué *mf.*

regularly [ˈregjʊləlɪ] *adv* regularmente.

regulate [ˈregjʊleɪt] *vt* regular.

regulation [ˌregjʊˈleɪʃn] *n (rule)* regra *f.*

rehabilitate [ˌriːəˈbɪlɪteɪt] *vt* reabilitar.

rehearsal [rɪˈhɜːsl] *n* ensaio *m.*

rehearse [rɪˈhɜːs] *vt* ensaiar.

reign [reɪn] *n* reino *m* ◆ *vi* reinar.

reimburse [ˌriːɪmˈbɜːs] *vt (fml)* reembolsar.

reindeer [ˈreɪndɪəʳ] *(pl inv)* *n* rena *f.*

reinforce [ˌriːɪnˈfɔːs] *vt* reforçar.

reinforcements [ˌriːɪnˈfɔːsmənts] *npl* reforços *mpl.*

reins [reɪnz] *npl (for horse)* rédeas *fpl*; *(for child)* andadeira *f.*

reinstate [ˌriːɪnˈsteɪt] *vt (employee)* readmitir.

reiterate [riːˈɪtəreɪt] *vt* reiterar.

reject [rɪˈdʒekt] *vt* rejeitar.

rejection [rɪˈdʒekʃn] *n* rejeição *f.*

rejoice [rɪˈdʒɔɪs] *vi*: **to ~ (at** OR **in sthg)** ficar extremamente contente (com algo).

rejoin [ˌriːˈdʒɔɪn] *vt (motorway)* retomar, voltar a entrar em.

rejuvenate [rɪ'dʒuːvəneɪt] vt rejuvenescer.

rekindle [ˌriː'kɪndl] vt avivar.

relapse [rɪ'læps] n recaída f.

relate [rɪ'leɪt] vt (connect) relacionar ◆ vi: **to ~ to** (be connected with) estar relacionado(-da) com; (concern) dizer respeito a.

related [rɪ'leɪtɪd] adj (of same family) da mesma família, aparentado(-da); (connected) relacionado(-da).

relation [rɪ'leɪʃn] n (member of family) parente mf; (connection) relação f, ligação f; **in ~ to** em relação a. ❑ **relations** npl relações fpl.

relationship [rɪ'leɪʃnʃɪp] n (between countries, people) relações fpl; (between lovers) relação f; (connection) ligação f, relação.

relative ['relətɪv] adj relativo(-va) ◆ n parente mf.

relatively ['relətɪvlɪ] adv relativamente.

relax [rɪ'læks] vi (person) descontrair-se, relaxar.

relaxation [ˌriːlæk'seɪʃn] n (of person) descontração f, relaxamento m.

relaxed [rɪ'lækst] adj descontraído (-da), relaxado(-da).

relaxing [rɪ'læksɪŋ] adj relaxante, calmante.

relay ['riːleɪ] n (race) corrida f de revezamento (Br), corrida f de estafetas (Port).

release [rɪ'liːs] vt (set free) libertar, soltar; (let go of) largar, soltar; (record, film) lançar; (brake, catch) soltar ◆ n (record, film) lançamento m.

relegate ['relɪgeɪt] vt: **to be ~d** (SPORT) descer de divisão.

relent [rɪ'lent] vi (person) ceder; (wind, storm) abrandar.

relentless [rɪ'lentlɪs] adj (person) inflexível; (criticism, rain) implacável.

relevant ['reləvənt] adj relevante.

reliable [rɪ'laɪəbl] adj (person, machine) de confiança, confiável.

reliably [rɪ'laɪəblɪ] adv (dependably) sem falhar; **to be ~ informed (that)** ... saber por fontes seguras que ....

reliant [rɪ'laɪənt] adj: **~ on** dependente de.

relic ['relɪk] n (object) relíquia f.

relief [rɪ'liːf] n (gladness) alívio m; (aid) ajuda f.

relief road n itinerário alternativo que os motoristas podem usar em caso de congestionamento das vias principais.

relieve [rɪ'liːv] vt (pain, headache) aliviar.

relieved [rɪ'liːvd] adj aliviado(-da).

religion [rɪ'lɪdʒn] n religião f.

religious [rɪ'lɪdʒəs] adj religioso (-osa).

relinquish [rɪ'lɪŋkwɪʃ] vt renunciar a.

relish ['relɪʃ] n (sauce) molho m.

reluctance [rɪ'lʌktəns] n relutância f.

reluctant [rɪ'lʌktənt] adj relutante.

reluctantly [rɪ'lʌktəntlɪ] adv relutantemente.

rely [rɪ'laɪ] : **rely on** vt fus (trust) confiar em; (depend on) depender de.

remain [rɪ'meɪn] vi (stay) permanecer; (continue to exist) sobrar, restar. ❑ **remains** npl (of meal, body) restos mpl; (of ancient buildings etc) ruínas fpl.

remainder [rɪ'meɪndər] n resto m, restante m.

remaining [rɪ'meɪnɪŋ] adj restante.

remark [rɪ'mɑːk] n comentário m ◆ vt comentar.

remarkable [rɪ'mɑːkəbl] adj extraordinário(-ria), incrível.

remarry [ˌriː'mærɪ] vi voltar a casar.

remedial [rɪ'miːdjəl] adj (class) de apoio (pedagógico); (pupil) que necessita de apoio (pedagógico); (exercise, therapy) de reabilitação; (action) corretivo(-va).

remedy ['remədɪ] n remédio m.

remember [rɪ'membər] vt lembrar-se de ◆ vi (recall) lembrar-se; **to ~ doing sthg** lembrar-se de ter feito algo; **to ~ to do sthg** lembrar-se de fazer algo.

Remembrance Day [rɪ'membrəns-] n Dia m do Armistício, dia em que na Grã-Bretanha se presta homenagem aos soldados mortos nas grandes guerras.

remind [rɪ'maɪnd] vt: **to ~ sb of** (fazer) lembrar a alguém; **to ~ sb to do sthg** lembrar alguém de que tem de fazer algo.

reminder [rɪ'maɪndər] n (for bill, library book) aviso m.

reminisce [ˌremɪ'nɪs] vi: **to ~ about sthg** relembrar algo.

reminiscent [ˌremɪ'nɪsnt] adj: **~ of** (similar to) evocador(-ra) de.

remittance [rɪ'mɪtns] n (money) = vale m postal.

remnant ['remnənt] n resto m.

remorse [rɪ'mɔːs] n remorsos mpl.

remorseful [rɪˈmɔːsfʊl] *adj* cheio (cheia) de remorsos.

remorseless [rɪˈmɔːslɪs] *adj (cruelty, ambition)* sem piedade; *(advance, progress)* implacável.

remote [rɪˈməʊt] *adj* remoto(-ta).

remote control *n (device)* controle *m* remoto OR à distância.

removable [rɪˈmuːvəbl] *adj* removível.

removal [rɪˈmuːvl] *n* remoção *f*; *(change of house)* mudança *f*.

removal van *n* caminhão *m* de mudanças.

remove [rɪˈmuːv] *vt* remover.

remuneration [rɪˌmjuːnəˈreɪʃn] *n (fml)* remuneração *f*.

rendezvous [ˈrɒndɪvuː] *(pl inv* [ˈrɒndɪvuːz]*)* *n (meeting)* encontro *m*; *(place)* ponto *m* de encontro.

renegade [ˈrenɪɡeɪd] *n* renegado *m* (-da *f*).

renew [rɪˈnjuː] *vt* renovar.

renewable [rɪˈnjuːəbl] *adj* renovável.

renewal [rɪˈnjuːəl] *n (of activity)* ressurgimento *m*; *(of contract, licence, membership)* renovação *f*.

renounce [rɪˈnaʊns] *vt* renunciar.

renovate [ˈrenəveɪt] *vt* renovar.

renowned [rɪˈnaʊnd] *adj* célebre.

rent [rent] *n* renda *f*, arrendamento *m* ◆ *vt* arrendar.

rental [ˈrentl] *n* aluguel *m*.

reorganize [ˌriːˈɔːɡənaɪz] *vt* reorganizar.

repaid [ˌriːˈpeɪd] *pt & pp* → **repay**.

repair [rɪˈpeəʳ] *vt* reparar ◆ *n*: **in good ~** em boas condições.

❏ **repairs** *npl* consertos *mpl*.

repair kit *n* estojo *m* de ferramentas.

repay [ˌriːˈpeɪ] *(pt & pp* **-paid***)* *vt (money)* reembolsar; *(favour, kindness)* retribuir.

repayment [riːˈpeɪmənt] *n (money)* reembolso *m*.

repeat [rɪˈpiːt] *vt* repetir ◆ *n (on TV, radio)* repetição *f*.

repeatedly [rɪˈpiːtɪdlɪ] *adv* repetidamente.

repel [rɪˈpel] *vt* repelir.

repellent [rɪˈpelənt] *adj* repelente.

repent [rɪˈpent] *vi*: **to ~** *(of sthg)* arrepender-se (de algo).

repercussions [ˌriːpəˈkʌʃnz] *npl* repercussões *fpl*.

repertoire [ˈrepətwɑːʳ] *n* repertório *m*.

repetition [ˌrepɪˈtɪʃn] *n* repetição *f*.

repetitious [ˌrepɪˈtɪʃəs] *adj* repetitivo(-va).

repetitive [rɪˈpetɪtɪv] *adj* repetitivo(-va).

replace [rɪˈpleɪs] *vt (substitute)* substituir; *(faulty goods)* trocar; *(put back)* voltar a pôr no lugar.

replacement [rɪˈpleɪsmənt] *n (substitute)* substituto *m* (-ta *f*).

replay [ˈriːpleɪ] *n (rematch)* jogo *m* de desempate; *(on TV)* repetição *f*, replay *m*.

replenish [rɪˈplenɪʃ] *vt*: **to ~ sthg (with sthg)** reabastecer algo (de algo).

replica [ˈreplɪkə] *n* réplica *f*.

reply [rɪˈplaɪ] *n* resposta *f* ◆ *vt & vi* responder.

report [rɪˈpɔːt] *n (account)* relatório *m*; *(in newspaper, on TV, radio)* reportagem *f*; *(Brit: SCH)* boletim *m (Br)*, caderneta *f (Port)* (escolar) ◆ *vt (announce)* anunciar; *(theft, disappearance)* participar; *(person)* denunciar ◆ *vi (give account)* informar; *(for newspaper, TV, radio)* fazer uma reportagem; **to ~ to sb** *(go to)* apresentar-se a alguém; **to ~ (to sb) on** informar (alguém) sobre.

report card *n* boletim *m (Br)*, caderneta *f (Port)* (escolar).

reportedly [rɪˈpɔːtɪdlɪ] *adv* segundo se diz, ao que consta.

reporter [rɪˈpɔːtəʳ] *n* repórter *mf*.

represent [ˌreprɪˈzent] *vt* representar.

representative [ˌreprɪˈzentətɪv] *n* representante *mf*.

repress [rɪˈpres] *vt* reprimir.

repression [rɪˈpreʃn] *n* repressão *f*.

reprieve [rɪˈpriːv] *n (delay)* adiamento *m*.

reprimand [ˈreprɪmɑːnd] *vt* repreender.

reprisal [rɪˈpraɪzl] *n* represália *f*.

reproach [rɪˈprəʊtʃ] *vt* repreender.

reproachful [rɪˈprəʊtʃfʊl] *adj* reprovador(-ra).

reproduce [ˌriːprəˈdjuːs] *vt* reproduzir ◆ *vi* reproduzir-se.

reproduction [ˌriːprəˈdʌkʃn] *n* reprodução *f*.

reptile [ˈreptaɪl] *n* réptil *m*.

republic [rɪˈpʌblɪk] *n* república *f*.

Republican [rɪˈpʌblɪkən] *n (in US)*

republicano *m* (-na *f*) ♦ *adj (in US)* republicano(-na).

repulsive [rɪ'pʌlsɪv] *adj* repulsivo (-va).

reputable ['repjutəbl] *adj* de boa reputação.

reputation [repju'teɪʃn] *n* reputação *f*.

repute [rɪ'pju:t] *n (reputation)*: of good/ill ~ de boa/má reputação.

reputed [rɪ'pju:tɪd] *adj* reputado (-da); to be ~ to be/do sthg ter fama de ser/fazer algo.

reputedly [rɪ'pju:tɪdlɪ] *adv* supostamente.

request [rɪ'kwest] *n* pedido *m* ♦ *vt* pedir; to ~ sb to do sthg pedir a alguém que faça algo; available on ~ disponível a pedido do interessado.

request stop *n (Brit)* parada em que o ônibus só pára a pedido dos passageiros.

require [rɪ'kwaɪə̃r] *vt (subj: person)* necessitar de; *(subj: situation)* requerer, exigir; passengers are ~d to show their tickets pede-se aos passageiros que mostrem as passagens.

requirement [rɪ'kwaɪəmənt] *n (condition)* requisito *m*; *(need)* necessidade *f*.

rerun [*n* 'ri:rʌn, *vb* ri:'rʌn] *(pt* -ran, *pp* -run) *n (film, programme)* reposição *f*; *(similar situation)* repetição *f* ♦ *vt (film, programme)* repor; *(tape)* voltar a passar.

resat [ri:'sæt] *pt & pp* → **resit**.

rescue ['reskju:] *vt* salvar.

rescuer ['reskjuə̃r] *n* salvador *m* (-ra *f*).

research [rɪ'sɜ:tʃ] *n* pesquisa *f*, investigação *f*.

researcher [rɪ'sɜ:tʃə̃r] *n* pesquisador *m* (-ra *f*) *(Br)*, investigador *m* (-ra *f*) *(Port)*.

resemblance [rɪ'zembləns] *n* parecença *f*.

resemble [rɪ'zembl] *vt* parecer-se com.

resent [rɪ'zent] *vt* ressentir-se com.

resentful [rɪ'zentful] *adj* ressentido(-da).

resentment [rɪ'zentmənt] *n* ressentimento *m*.

reservation [rezə'veɪʃn] *n* reserva *f*; to make a ~ fazer uma reserva.

reserve [rɪ'zɜ:v] *n (SPORT)* reserva *mf (Br)*, suplente *mf; (for wildlife)*

reserva *f* ♦ *vt* reservar.

reserved [rɪ'zɜ:vd] *adj* reservado (-da).

reservoir ['rezəvwɑ:r] *n* reservatório *m*, represa *f*.

reset [ri:'set] *(pt & pp* reset) *vt (watch)* acertar; *(meter, device)* reajustar.

reshuffle [ri:'ʃʌfl] *n (POL)* reorganização *f*, reforma *f*.

reside [rɪ'zaɪd] *vi (fml)* residir.

residence ['rezɪdəns] *n (fml)* residência *f*; place of ~ *(fml)* (local *m* de) residência.

residence permit *n* autorização *f* de residência.

resident ['rezɪdənt] *n (of country)* habitante *mf; (of hotel)* hóspede *mf; (of area, house)* morador *m* (-ra *f*); "~s only" *(for parking)* "reservado para os moradores".

residential [rezɪ'denʃl] *adj* residencial.

residue ['rezɪdju:] *n* resíduo *m*.

resign [rɪ'zaɪn] *vi* demitir-se ♦ *vt*: to ~ o.s. to sthg resignar-se com algo, conformar-se com algo.

resignation [rezɪg'neɪʃn] *n (from job)* demissão *f*.

resigned [rɪ'zaɪnd] *adj*: to be ~ (to sthg) estar conformado(-da) (com algo).

resilient [rɪ'zɪlɪənt] *adj* forte.

resin ['rezɪn] *n* resina *f*.

resist [rɪ'zɪst] *vt* resistir a; I can't ~ cream cakes não resisto a bolos com creme; to ~ doing sthg resistir a fazer algo.

resistance [rɪ'zɪstəns] *n* resistência *f*.

resit [ri:'sɪt] *(pt & pp* -sat) *vt* repetir.

resolute ['rezəlu:t] *adj* resoluto(-ta).

resolution [rezə'lu:ʃn] *n* resolução *f*.

resolve [rɪ'zɒlv] *vt (solve)* resolver.

resort [rɪ'zɔ:t] *n (for holidays)* estância *f* (de férias); as a last ~ como último recurso.

 resort to *vt fus* recorrer a; to ~ to doing sthg recorrer a fazer algo.

resounding [rɪ'zaundɪŋ] *adj (noise, crash)* sonoro(-ra); *(success, victory)* retumbante.

resource [rɪ'sɔ:s] *n* recurso *m*.

resourceful [rɪ'sɔ:sful] *adj* desembaraçado(-da), expedito(-ta).

respect [rɪ'spekt] *n* respeito *m*; *(aspect)* aspecto *m* ♦ *vt* respeitar; with

~ **to** no que respeita a; **in some** ~s em alguns aspectos.

respectable [rɪ'spektəbl] *adj (person, job etc)* respeitável; *(acceptable)* decente.

respectful [rɪ'spektful] *adj* respeitador(-ra).

respective [rɪ'spektɪv] *adj* respectivo(-va).

respectively [rɪ'spektɪvlɪ] *adv* respectivamente.

respite [respaɪt] *n (pause)* descanso *m; (delay)* prolongamento *m* (de prazo).

resplendent [rɪ'splendənt] *adj* resplandecente.

respond [rɪ'spɒnd] *vi* responder.

response [rɪ'spɒns] *n* resposta *f*.

responsibility [rɪ,spɒnsə'bɪlətɪ] *n* responsabilidade *f*.

responsible [rɪ'spɒnsəbl] *adj* responsável; **to be ~ (for)** *(to blame)* ser responsável (por).

responsive [rɪ'spɒnsɪv] *adj (person)* receptivo(-va); ~ **to sthg** receptivo a algo.

rest [rest] *n (relaxation)* descanso *m; (for foot, head, back)* apoio *m* ♦ *vi (relax)* descansar ♦ *vt:* **to ~ sthg against sthg** encostar algo em algo; **the ~** *(remainder)* o resto; **to have a ~** descansar; **the ladder was ~ing against the wall** a escada estava encostada na parede.

restaurant ['restərɒnt] *n* restaurante *m*.

restaurant car *n (Brit)* vagão-restaurante *m (Br)*, carruagem-restaurante *f (Port)*.

restful [restful] *adj* tranqüilo(-la).

rest home *n (for old people)* lar *m*, asilo *m; (for sick people)* casa *f* de repouso.

restless ['restlɪs] *adj (bored, impatient)* impaciente; *(fidgety)* inquieto(-ta).

restore [rɪ'stɔːʳ] *vt (reintroduce)* restabelecer; *(renovate)* restaurar.

restrain [rɪ'streɪn] *vt* conter.

restrained [rɪ'streɪnd] *adj (person)* comedido(-da); *(tone)* moderado(-da).

restraint [rɪ'streɪnt] *n (rule, check)* restrição *f; (control)* restrições *fpl; (moderation)* comedimento *m*.

restrict [rɪ'strɪkt] *vt* restringir.

restricted [rɪ'strɪktɪd] *adj* restrito(-ta).

restriction [rɪ'strɪkʃn] *n* restrição *f*.

restrictive [rɪ'strɪktɪv] *adj* severo(-ra).

rest room *n (Am)* banheiro *m (Br)*, casa *f* de banho *(Port)*.

result [rɪ'zʌlt] *n* resultado *m* ♦ *vi:* **to ~ in** resultar em; **as a ~ of** em consequência de.

⎿ **results** *npl (of test, exam)* resultados *mpl*.

resume [rɪ'zjuːm] *vt & vi* recomeçar, retomar.

résumé ['rezjuːmeɪ] *n (summary)* resumo *m; (Am: curriculum vitae)* currículo *m*.

resumption [rɪ'zʌmpʃn] *n* recomeço *m*.

resurgence [rɪ'sɜːdʒəns] *n* ressurgimento *m*.

resurrection [,rezə'rekʃn] *n (RELIG):* **the ~** a Ressurreição (de Cristo).

resuscitation [rɪ,sʌsɪ'teɪʃn] *n* reanimação *f*.

retail ['riːteɪl] *n* venda *f* a varejo *(Br)*, venda *f* a retalho *(Port)* ♦ *vt* vender (a varejo) ♦ *vi:* **to ~ at** vender a.

retailer ['riːteɪləʳ] *n* varejista *mf (Br)*, retalhista *mf (Port)*.

retail price *n* preço *m* de venda ao público.

retain [rɪ'teɪn] *vt (fml)* reter.

retaliate [rɪ'tælɪeɪt] *vi* retaliar.

retaliation [rɪ,tælɪ'eɪʃn] *n* retaliação *f*.

retch [retʃ] *vi* ter ânsia de vômito *(Br)*, sentir vômitos *(Port)*.

reticent ['retɪsənt] *adj* reticente.

retina ['retɪnə] *n (pl* **-nas** OR **-nae** [-niː]*)* *n* retina *f*.

retire [rɪ'taɪəʳ] *vi (stop working)* aposentar-se *(Br)*, reformar-se *(Port)*.

retired [rɪ'taɪəd] *adj* aposentado(-da) *(Br)*, reformado(-da) *(Port)*.

retirement [rɪ'taɪəmənt] *n* aposentadoria *f (Br)*, reforma *f (Port)*.

retrain [,riː'treɪn] *vt* reciclar.

retreat [rɪ'triːt] *vi* retirar-se ♦ *n (place)* retiro *m*.

retrieval [rɪ'triːvl] *n* recuperação *f*.

retrieve [rɪ'triːv] *vt* recuperar.

retrospect ['retrəspekt] *n:* **in ~** a posteriori.

return [rɪ'tɜːn] *n (arrival back)* regresso *m; (Brit: ticket)* bilhete *m* de ida e volta ♦ *vt* devolver ♦ *vi* voltar, regressar ♦ *adj (Brit: journey)* de volta, de regresso; **by ~ of post** *(Brit)* na volta do correio; **in ~ (for)** em troca (de); **many happy ~s!** que se repita por muitos anos!; **to ~ sthg (to sb)** *(give back)* devolver algo (a alguém).

return flight *n* vôo *m* de volta.

return ticket *n* (*Brit*) bilhete *m* de ida e volta.

reunite [ˌriːjuːˈnaɪt] *vt* reunir.

rev [rev] *n* (*inf*: *of engine*) rotação *f* ◆ *vt* (*inf*): **to ~ sthg (up)** acelerar algo.

reveal [rɪˈviːl] *vt* revelar.

revel [ˈrevl] *vi*: **to ~ in sthg** deliciar-se OR deleitar-se com algo.

revelation [ˌrevəˈleɪʃn] *n* revelação *f*.

revenge [rɪˈvendʒ] *n* vingança *f*.

revenue [ˈrevənjuː] *n* receita *f*.

Reverend [ˈrevərənd] *n* reverendo *m*.

reversal [rɪˈvɜːsl] *n* (*of trend, policy, decision*) mudança *f*; (*of roles, order, position*) inversão *f*.

reverse [rɪˈvɜːs] *adj* inverso(-sa) ◆ *n* (AUT) marcha *f* à ré (*Br*), marcha *f* atrás (*Port*); (*of coin*) reverso *m*; (*of document*) verso *m* ◆ *vt* (*car*) dar marcha à ré com (*Br*), fazer marcha atrás com (*Port*); (*decision*) revogar ◆ *vi* (*car, driver*) dar marcha à ré (*Br*), fazer marcha atrás (*Port*); **in ~ order** na ordem inversa, ao contrário; **the ~** (*opposite*) o contrário; **to ~ the charges** (*Brit*) fazer uma chamada a cobrar no destinatário.

reverse-charge call *n* (*Brit*) chamada *f* a cobrar.

revert [rɪˈvɜːt] *vi*: **to ~ to** voltar a.

review [rɪˈvjuː] *n* (*of book, record, film*) crítica *f*; (*examination*) revisão *f* ◆ *vt* (*Am*: *for exam*) rever.

reviewer [rɪˈvjuːəʳ] *n* crítico *m* (-ca *f*).

revise [rɪˈvaɪz] *vt* rever ◆ *vi* (*Brit*) rever a matéria.

revision [rɪˈvɪʒn] *n* (*Brit*) revisão *f*.

revitalize [ˌriːˈvaɪtəlaɪz] *vt* revitalizar.

revival [rɪˈvaɪvl] *n* (*of person*) reanimação *f*; (*of economy*) retomada *f*; (*of custom*) recuperação *f*; (*of interest*) renovação *f*.

revive [rɪˈvaɪv] *vt* (*person*) reanimar; (*economy, custom*) recuperar.

revolt [rɪˈvəʊlt] *n* revolta *f*.

revolting [rɪˈvəʊltɪŋ] *adj* repugnante.

revolution [ˌrevəˈluːʃn] *n* revolução *f*.

revolutionary [ˌrevəˈluːʃnərɪ] *adj* revolucionário(-ria).

revolve [rɪˈvɒlv] *vi* (*go round*) girar; **to ~ around** (*be based on*) girar à volta de.

revolver [rɪˈvɒlvəʳ] *n* revólver *m*.

revolving door [rɪˈvɒlvɪŋ-] *n* porta *f* giratória.

revue [rɪˈvjuː] *n* (*teatro m de*) revista *f*.

revulsion [rɪˈvʌlʃn] *n* repugnância *f*.

reward [rɪˈwɔːd] *n* recompensa *f* ◆ *vt* recompensar.

rewarding [rɪˈwɔːdɪŋ] *adj* compensador(-ra), gratificante.

rewind [ˌriːˈwaɪnd] (*pt & pp* **-wound**) *vt* rebobinar.

rewire [ˌriːˈwaɪəʳ] *vt* substituir a instalação elétrica de.

rewound [ˌriːˈwaʊnd] *pt & pp* → rewind.

rewrite [ˌriːˈraɪt] (*pt* **-wrote**, *pp* **-written**) *vt* reescrever.

Reykjavik [ˈreɪkjəvɪk] *n* Reikjavik *s*.

rheumatism [ˈruːmətɪzm] *n* reumatismo *m*.

Rhine [raɪn] *n*: **the ~** o Reno.

rhinoceros [raɪˈnɒsərəs] (*pl inv* OR **-es**) *n* rinoceronte *m*.

rhododendron [ˌrəʊdəˈdendrən] *n* rododendro *m*.

rhubarb [ˈruːbɑːb] *n* ruibarbo *m*.

rhyme [raɪm] *n* (*poem*) rima *f* ◆ *vi* rimar.

rhythm [ˈrɪðm] *n* ritmo *m*.

rib [rɪb] *n* costela *f*.

ribbed [rɪbd] *adj* canelado(-da).

ribbon [ˈrɪbən] *n* fita *f*.

rice [raɪs] *n* arroz *m*.

rice pudding *n* = arroz-doce *m*.

rich [rɪtʃ] *adj* rico(-ca) ◆ *npl*: **the ~** os ricos; **to be ~ in sthg** ser rico em algo.

richness [ˈrɪtʃnɪs] *n* riqueza *f*.

rickety [ˈrɪkətɪ] *adj* pouco firme.

ricotta cheese [rɪˈkɒtə-] *n* ricota *m*, queijo muito semelhante ao requeijão.

rid [rɪd] *vt*: **to get ~ of** ver-se livre de, livrar-se de.

ridden [ˈrɪdn] *pp* → ride.

riddle [ˈrɪdl] *n* (*puzzle*) adivinha *f*; (*mystery*) enigma *m*.

riddled [ˈrɪdld] *adj* (*full*): **to be ~ with sthg** estar cheio(-a) OR crivado(-da) de algo.

ride [raɪd] (*pt* **rode**, *pp* **ridden**) *n* (*on horse, bike*) passeio *m*; (*in vehicle*) volta *f* ◆ *vt* (*horse*) andar a; (*bike*) andar de ◆ *vi* (*on horse*) andar OR montar a cavalo; (*on bike*) andar de bicicleta; (*in vehicle*) viajar; **to go for a ~** (*in car*) ir dar uma volta (de carro).

rider ['raɪdər] n (on horse) cavaleiro m
(amazona f); (on bike) ciclista mf.

ridge [rɪdʒ] n (of mountain) crista f;
(raised surface) rugosidade f.

ridicule ['rɪdɪkjuːl] n ridículo m ◆ vt
ridicularizar.

ridiculous [rɪ'dɪkjuləs] adj ridí-
culo(-la).

riding ['raɪdɪŋ] n equitação f.

riding school n escola f de equitação.

rife [raɪf] adj (widespread) generaliza-
do(-da).

rifle ['raɪfl] n espingarda f.

rift [rɪft] n (quarrel) desentendimento
m; ~ **between/in** desentendimento
entre/em.

rig [rɪg] n (oilrig) plataforma f petrolífera ◆ vt falsificar o resultado de.

right [raɪt] adj 1. (correct) certo(-ta);
to be ~ (person) ter razão; **to be** ~ **to
do sthg** fazer bem em fazer algo; **have
you got the** ~ **time?** você tem a hora
certa?; **is this the** ~ **way?** é este o
caminho certo?; **that's** ~! é isso
mesmo!, exatamente!

2. (fair) certo(-ta); **that's not** ~! isso
não está certo!

3. (on the right) direito(-ta); **the** ~ **side
of the road** o lado direito da estrada.
◆ n 1. (side): **the** ~ a direita.

2. (entitlement) direito m; **to have the** ~
to do sthg ter o direito de fazer algo.
◆ adv 1. (towards the right) à direita;
turn ~ **at the post office** vire à direita
junto aos correios.

2. (correctly) bem; **am I pronouncing it**
~? estou pronunciando isso bem?

3. (for emphasis) mesmo; ~ **here** aqui
mesmo; **I'll be** ~ **back** volto já; ~ **away**
imediatamente.

right angle n ângulo m reto.

righteous ['raɪtʃəs] adj (person)
justo(-ta), honrado(-da); (anger, indignation) justificado(-da).

rightful ['raɪtful] adj (share, owner)
legítimo(-ma); (place) devido(-da).

right-hand adj direito(-ta).

right-hand drive n veículo m com
volante à direita.

right-handed [-'hændɪd] adj (person)
destro(-tra); (implement) para pessoas
destras.

rightly ['raɪtlɪ] adv (correctly) corretamente; (justly) devidamente.

right of way n (AUT) prioridade f;

(path) direito m de passagem.

right-wing adj de direita.

rigid ['rɪdʒɪd] adj rígido(-da).

rigorous ['rɪgərəs] adj rigoroso(-osa).

rim [rɪm] n (of cup) borda f; (of glasses)
armação f; (of bicycle wheel) aro m; (of
car wheel) aro m (Br), jante f (Port).

rind [raɪnd] n (of fruit, cheese) casca f;
(of bacon) couro m (Br), courato m
(Port).

ring [rɪŋ] (pt rang, pp rung) n (for finger) anel m; (circle) círculo m; (sound)
toque m (de campainha, telefone); (on
electric cooker) disco m; (on gas cooker)
boca f (Br), bico m (Port); (for boxing)
ringue m; (in circus) arena f ◆ vt (Brit)
telefonar para, ligar para; (bell) tocar a
◆ vi (Brit: make phone call) telefonar;
(doorbell, telephone) tocar; (ears) zumbir; **to give sb a** ~ (phone call) telefonar
para alguém; **to** ~ **the bell** (of house,
office) tocar a campainha.

❏ **ring back** vt sep (Brit: person) voltar a
telefonar a ◆ vi (Brit) voltar a telefonar.

❏ **ring off** vi (Brit) desligar.

❏ **ring up** vt sep (Brit) telefonar para
◆ vi (Brit) telefonar.

ring binder n capa f de argolas, dossier m.

ringing ['rɪŋɪŋ] n (of doorbell, telephone) toque m; (in ears) zumbido m.

ringing tone ['rɪŋɪŋ-] n sinal m de
chamada.

ringlet ['rɪŋlɪt] n anel m de cabelo,
cacho m.

ring road n (estrada) perimetral f
(Br), circunvalação f (Port).

rink [rɪŋk] n rink m, pista f (de patinagem).

rinse [rɪns] vt (clothes, hair) enxaguar,
passar uma água (Br); (hands) lavar.

❏ **rinse out** vt sep (clothes) enxaguar,
passar uma água (Br); (mouth) bochechar.

riot ['raɪət] n (violent disturbance) distúrbio m.

rioter ['raɪətər] n desordeiro m (-ra f),
manifestante mf.

riot police npl polícia f de choque,
forças fpl de intervenção.

rip [rɪp] n rasgão m ◆ vt rasgar ◆ vi
rasgar-se.

❏ **rip up** vt sep rasgar em bocadinhos.

ripe [raɪp] adj maduro(-ra).

ripen ['raɪpn] vi amadurecer.

rip-off *n (inf)* roubo *m*.

ripple ['rɪpl] *n* onda *f*.

rise [raɪz] *(pt* **rose**, *pp* **risen** ['rɪzn]) *vi (move upwards)* elevar-se; *(sun, moon)* nascer; *(increase)* subir; *(stand up)* levantar-se ♦ *n* subida *f*; *(Brit: pay increase)* aumento *m*.

risk [rɪsk] *n* risco *m* ♦ *vt* arriscar; **to take a ~** correr um risco; **at your own ~** por sua conta e risco; **to ~ doing** sthg arriscar-se a fazer algo; **to ~ it** arriscar-se.

risky ['rɪskɪ] *adj* arriscado(-da).

risotto [rɪ'zɒtəʊ] *(pl* **-s)** *n* risoto *m*, prato à base de arroz com carne, marisco ou legumes.

risqué ['riːskeɪ] *adj* picante.

rissole ['rɪsəʊl] *n (Brit)* = croquete *m*.

ritual ['rɪtʃʊəl] *n* ritual *m*.

rival ['raɪvl] *adj* rival ♦ *n* rival *mf*.

rivalry ['raɪvlrɪ] *n* rivalidade *f*.

river ['rɪvə^r] *n* rio *m*.

river bank *n* margem *f* do rio.

riverbed ['rɪvəbed] *n* leito *m* do rio.

riverside ['rɪvəsaɪd] *n* beira-rio *f*.

rivet ['rɪvɪt] *n* rebite *m*.

Riviera [ˌrɪvɪ'eərə] *n*: **the (French) ~** a Riviera (francesa).

roach [rəʊtʃ] *n (Am: cockroach)* barata *f*.

road [rəʊd] *n* estrada *f*; **by ~** por estrada.

roadblock ['rəʊdblɒk] *n* controle *m* rodoviário.

road book *n* guia *m* das estradas.

road map *n* mapa *m* das estradas.

road safety *n* segurança *f* rodoviária OR na estrada.

roadside ['rəʊdsaɪd] *n*: **the ~** a beira (da estrada).

road sign *n* sinal *m* de trânsito.

road tax *n* imposto *m* de circulação.

roadway ['rəʊdweɪ] *n* rodovia *f*.

road works *npl* obras *fpl* na estrada.

roadworthy ['rəʊdˌwɜːðɪ] *adj* em condições de circular.

roam [rəʊm] *vi* vaguear.

roar [rɔː^r] *n (of crowd)* gritos *mpl*, brados *mpl*; *(of aeroplane)* ronco *m*; *(of lion)* rugido *m* ♦ *vi (crowd)* berrar, bradar; *(lion)* rugir.

roast [rəʊst] *n* assado *m* ♦ *vt* assar ♦ *adj* assado(-da); **~ beef** rosbife *m*; **~ chicken** frango *m* assado; **~ lamb** car-neiro *m* assado; **~ pork** lombo *m* (de porco assado); **~ potatoes** batatas *fpl* assadas.

rob [rɒb] *vt* assaltar; **to ~ sb of sthg** roubar algo de alguém.

robber ['rɒbə^r] *n* assaltante *mf*.

robbery ['rɒbərɪ] *n* assalto *m*.

robe [rəʊb] *n (Am: bathrobe)* roupão *m*.

robin ['rɒbɪn] *n* pisco-de-peito-ruivo *m*, pintarroxo *m (Port)*.

robot ['rəʊbɒt] *n* robô *m*.

robust [rəʊ'bʌst] *adj (person, health)* robusto(-ta); *(economy, defence, criti-cism)* forte.

rock [rɒk] *n* rocha *f*; *(Am: stone)* pedra *f*; *(music)* rock *m*; *(Brit: sweet)* pirulito *m* ♦ *vt (baby)* embalar; *(boat)* balançar; **on the ~s** *(drink)* com gelo.

rock and roll *n* rock and roll *m*.

rock climbing *n* escala *f*; **to go ~** ir escalar.

rocket ['rɒkɪt] *n (missile, space rocket)* foguete *m (Br)*, foguetão *m (Port)*; *(fire-work)* foguete *m*; *(salad plant)* rúcola *f*.

rocking chair ['rɒkɪŋ-] *n* cadeira *f* de balanço.

rocking horse *n* cavalo *m* de balanço.

rock 'n' roll [ˌrɒkən'rəʊl] *n* rock 'n' roll *m*.

rocky ['rɒkɪ] *adj (place)* rochoso(-osa).

rod [rɒd] *n (wooden)* vara *f*; *(metal)* barra *f*; *(for fishing)* vara *f* de pescar *(Br)*, cana *f (Port)*.

rode [rəʊd] *pt* → **ride**.

rodent ['rəʊdənt] *n* roedor *m*.

roe [rəʊ] *n* ovas *fpl* de peixe.

rogue [rəʊg] *n (likable rascal)* maroto *m* (-ta *f*); *(dishonest person)* trapaceiro *m* (-ra *f*).

role [rəʊl] *n* papel *m*.

roll [rəʊl] *n (of bread)* carcaça *f*, pão-zinho *m*; *(of film, paper)* rolo *m* ♦ *vi (ball, rock)* rolar; *(vehicle)* circular; *(ship)* balançar ♦ *vt (ball, rock)* fazer rolar; *(cigarette)* enrolar; *(dice)* lançar.

❏ **roll over** *vi (person, animal)* virar-se; *(car)* capotar.

❏ **roll up** *vt sep (map, carpet)* enrolar; *(sleeves, trousers)* arregaçar.

roller ['rəʊlə^r] *n (curler)* rolo *m* (de cabelo).

rollerblades ['rəʊləbleɪdz] *npl* patins *mpl* em linha.

rollerblading ['rəʊləˌbleɪdɪŋ] *n*: **to go**

~ ir patinar *(com patins em linha)*.

roller coaster *n* montanha-russa *f*.

roller skates *npl* patins *mpl* de rodas.

roller-skating ['rəʊlə-] *n* patinagem *f* sobre rodas.

rolling pin ['rəʊlɪŋ] *n* rolo *m* de pastel *(Br)*, rolo *m* da massa *(Port)*.

roll-on *n (deodorant)* roll-on *m*, bastão *m (Br)*.

ROM [rɒm] *(abbr of read only memory)* *n* ROM *f*.

Roman ['rəʊmən] *adj* romano(-na) ◆ *n* romano *m* (-na *f*).

Roman Catholic *n* católico *m* romano (católica *f* romana).

romance [rəʊ'mæns] *n* romance *m*.

Romania [ru:'meɪnjə] *n* Romênia *f*.

Romanian [ru:'meɪnjən] *adj* romeno(-na) ◆ *n (person)* romeno *m* (-na *f*); *(language)* romeno *m*.

Roman numerals *npl* numeração *f* romana.

romantic [rəʊ'mæntɪk] *adj* romântico(-ca).

Rome [rəʊm] *n* Roma *s*.

romper suit ['rɒmpə-] *n* macacão *m* (de criança).

roof [ru:f] *n (of building, cave)* telhado *m*; *(of car, caravan, tent)* teto *m*.

roof rack *n* bagageiro *m (Br)*, tejadilho *m (Port)*.

rooftop ['ru:ftɒp] *n* telhado *m*.

rook [rʊk] *n (bird)* gralha-calva *f*; *(chess piece)* torre *f*.

rookie ['rʊkɪ] *n (Am: inf)* novato *m* (-ta *f*).

room [ru:m, rʊm] *n (bedroom, in hotel)* quarto *m*; *(in building)* divisão *f*, sala *f*; *(space)* espaço *m*.

roommate ['ru:mmeɪt] *n* colega *mf* de quarto.

room number *n* número *m* do quarto.

room service *n* serviço *m* de quartos.

room temperature *n* temperatura *f* ambiente.

roomy ['ru:mɪ] *adj* espaçoso(-osa).

rooster ['ru:stə°] *n* galo *m*.

root [ru:t] *n* raiz *f*.

rope [rəʊp] *n* corda *f* ◆ *vt* amarrar.

rosary ['rəʊzərɪ] *n* terço *m*, rosário *m*.

rose [rəʊz] *pt* → **rise** ◆ *n (flower)* rosa *f*.

rosé ['rəʊzeɪ] *n (vinho)* rosé *m*.

rose bush *n* roseira *f*.

rosemary ['rəʊzmərɪ] *n* alecrim *m*.

rosette [rəʊ'zet] *n (badge)* emblema *m*.

rostrum ['rɒstrəm] *(pl* **-trums** OR **-tra** [-trə]*)* *n* tribuna *f*.

rosy ['rəʊzɪ] *adj (pink)* rosado(-da); *(promising)* cor-de-rosa *(inv)*.

rot [rɒt] *vi* apodrecer.

rota ['rəʊtə] *n* lista *f* de turnos.

rotate [rəʊ'teɪt] *vi* girar.

rotation [rəʊ'teɪʃn] *n* rotação *f*; **in ~** rotativamente.

rotten ['rɒtn] *adj (food, wood)* podre; *(inf: not good)* péssimo(-ma); **I feel ~** *(ill)* sinto-me péssimo.

rouge [ru:ʒ] *n* blush *m*.

rough [rʌf] *adj (surface, skin, cloth)* áspero(-ra); *(sea, crossing)* agitado(-da); *(person)* bruto(-ta); *(approximate)* aproximado(-da); *(conditions, wine)* mau (má); *(area, town)* perigoso(-osa) ◆ *n (on golf course)* rough *m*; **a ~ guess** um cálculo aproximado; **to have a ~ time** passar por um período difícil.

roughen ['rʌfn] *vt* tornar áspero(-ra).

roughly ['rʌflɪ] *adv (approximately)* aproximadamente; *(push, handle)* bruscamente, grosseiramente.

roulade [ru:'lɑːd] *n* rocambole *m (Br)*, torta *f (Port)*.

roulette [ru:'let] *n* roleta *f*.

round [raʊnd] *adj* redondo(-da).
◆ *n* 1. *(of drinks)* rodada *f*; **it's my ~** é a minha rodada.

2. *(of sandwiches)* sanduíche *m (Br)*, sandes *f inv (Port)*; *(of toast)* torrada *f*.

3. *(of competition)* volta *f*.

4. *(in golf)* partida *f*; *(in boxing)* assalto *m*.

5. *(of policeman, postman, milkman)* ronda *f*.

◆ *adv* 1. *(in a circle)*: **to go ~** andar em volta; **to spin ~** girar.

2. *(surrounding)* à volta; **it had a fence all (the way) ~** tinha uma cerca em toda a volta.

3. *(near)*: **~ about** em volta.

4. *(to one's house)*: **to ask some friends ~** convidar uns amigos (para casa); **we went ~ to her house** fomos até à casa dela.

5. *(continuously)*: **all year ~** *(durante)* todo o ano.

◆ *prep* 1. *(surrounding, circling)* à volta de; **they put a blanket ~ him** puseram

um cobertor em volta dele; **we walked ~ the lake** caminhamos em volta do lago; **to go ~ the corner** virar a esquina. **2.** *(visiting)*: **to go ~ a museum** visitar um museu; **to show sb ~ sthg** mostrar algo a alguém. **3.** *(approximately)* cerca de; **~ (about) 100** cerca de 100; **~ ten o'clock** cerca das OR por volta das dez horas. **4.** *(near)*: **~ here** aqui perto. **5.** *(in phrases)*: **it's just ~ the corner** *(nearby)* é logo ao virar da esquina; **~ the clock** 24 horas por dia.
❑ **round off** *vt sep (meal, day, visit)* terminar.

roundabout ['raʊndəbaʊt] *n (Brit) (in road)* cruzamento circular, rotunda *f (Port)*; *(in playground)* roda *f* (de parque infantil); *(at fairground)* carrossel *m*.

rounders ['raʊndəz] *n (Brit)* jogo de bola parecido com o baseball.

roundly ['raʊndlɪ] *adv (defeat)* completamente; *(criticize)* sem rodeios; *(deny)* redondamente.

round trip *n* viagem *f* de ida e volta.

roundup ['raʊndʌp] *n (summary)* resumo *m*.

rouse [raʊz] *vt (wake up)* acordar, despertar; *(excite)* instigar; *(give rise to)* despertar.

rousing ['raʊzɪŋ] *adj* entusiasmante.

route [ruːt] *n (way)* caminho *m*; *(of train)* linha *f*; *(of bus)* trajeto *m*; *(of plane)* rota *f* ◆ *vt (change course of)* mudar a rota de.

route map *n* (mapa do) trajeto *m*.

routine [ruːˈtiːn] *n* rotina *f* ◆ *adj* rotineiro(-ra).

row¹ [rəʊ] *n (line)* fila *f* ◆ *vt (boat)* impelir remando ◆ *vi* remar; **three times in a ~** três vezes seguidas.

row² [raʊ] *n (argument)* briga *f*; *(inf: noise)* algazarra *f*; **to have a ~** brigar.

rowboat ['rəʊbəʊt] *(Am)* = **rowing boat**.

rowdy ['raʊdɪ] *adj* turbulento(-ta).

rowing ['rəʊɪŋ] *n* remo *m*.

rowing boat *n (Brit)* barco *m* a remos.

royal ['rɔɪəl] *adj* real.

Royal Air Force *n*: **the ~** a força aérea britânica.

royal family *n* família *f* real.

Royal Navy *n*: **the ~** a marinha britânica.

royalty ['rɔɪəltɪ] *n (royal family)* realeza *f*.

RRP *(abbr of recommended retail price)* P.V.P.

rub [rʌb] *vt (back, eyes)* esfregar; *(polish)* polir ◆ *vi (with hand, cloth)* esfregar; *(shoes)* friccionar *(Br)*, roçar *(Port)*.
❑ **rub in** *vt sep (lotion, oil)* esfregar.
❑ **rub out** *vt sep* apagar.

rubber ['rʌbəʳ] *adj* de borracha ◆ *n* borracha *f*; *(Am: inf: condom)* camisinha *f (Br)*, preservativo *m*.

rubber band *n* elástico *m*.

rubber gloves *npl* luvas *fpl* de borracha.

rubber plant *n* borracheira *f*.

rubber ring *n* bóia *f*.

rubber stamp *n* carimbo *m* (de borracha).

rubbish ['rʌbɪʃ] *n (refuse)* lixo *m*; *(inf: worthless thing)* porcaria *f*; *(inf: nonsense)* disparate *m*.

rubbish bin *n (Brit)* lata *f* de lixo *(Br)*, caixote *m* do lixo *(Port)*.

rubbish dump *n (Brit)* depósito *m* de lixo *(Br)*, lixeira *f (Port)*.

rubble ['rʌbl] *n* entulho *m*, escombros *mpl*.

ruby ['ruːbɪ] *n* rubi *m*.

rucksack ['rʌksæk] *n* mochila *f*.

rudder ['rʌdəʳ] *n* leme *m*.

ruddy ['rʌdɪ] *adj (face, complexion)* corado(-da).

rude [ruːd] *adj (person)* mal-educado(-da); *(behaviour, joke, picture)* grosseiro(-ra).

rudimentary [ruːdɪˈmentərɪ] *adj* rudimentar.

rueful ['ruːfʊl] *adj (person, look)* arrependido(-da); *(smile)* de arrependimento.

ruffian ['rʌfjən] *n* rufião *m* (-fiona *f*).

ruffle ['rʌfl] *vt (hair)* desgrenhar, despentear; *(feathers, fur)* eriçar.

rug [rʌg] *n (for floor)* tapete *m*; *(Brit: blanket)* manta *f* (de viagem).

rugby ['rʌgbɪ] *n* rugby *m*, râguebi *m*.

rugged ['rʌgɪd] *adj (rocky, uneven)* acidentado(-da); *(sturdy)* resistente.

ruin ['ruːɪn] *vt* estragar.
❑ **ruins** *npl* ruínas *fpl*.

ruined ['ruːɪnd] *adj (building)* em ruínas; *(clothes, meal, holiday)* estragado (-da).

rule [ruːl] *n (law)* regra *f* ◆ *vt (country)* governar; **to be the ~** *(normal)* ser a regra; **against the ~s** contra as regras; **as a ~** geralmente.

❏ **rule out** *vt sep* excluir.

ruler [ruːləʳ] *n (of country)* governante *mf*; *(for measuring)* régua *f*.

rum [rʌm] *n* rum *m*.

rumble [rʌmbl] *n (of thunder)* ruído *m*; *(of stomach)* ronco *m* ◆ *vi (thunder)* trovejar, ribombar; *(stomach)* roncar.

rummage [rʌmɪdʒ] *vi:* **to ~ through** sthg remexer algo.

rumor [ruːməʳ] *(Am)* = **rumour**.

rumour [ruːməʳ] *n (Brit)* boato *m*.

rump steak [rʌmp-] *n* alcatra *f*.

rumpus [rʌmpəs] *n (inf)* chinfrim *m*.

run [rʌn] *(pt* **ran**, *pp* **run**) *vi* **1.** *(on foot)* correr; **we had to ~ for the bus** tivemos de correr para apanhar o ônibus. **2.** *(train, bus)* circular; **the bus ~s every hour** há um ônibus de hora em hora; **the train is running an hour late** o trem vem com uma hora de atraso; **this service doesn't ~ on Sundays** este serviço não se efetua aos domingos. **3.** *(operate)* funcionar; **to ~ on sthg** funcionar a algo; **leave the engine running** deixa o motor a funcionar. **4.** *(tears, liquid, river)* correr; **to leave the tap running** deixar a torneira aberta; **to ~ through** *(river, road)* atravessar; **the path ~s along the coast** o caminho segue ao longo da costa. **5.** *(play)* estar em cartaz OR cena; *(event)* decorrer; **"now running at the Palladium"** "em cartaz OR cena no Palladium". **6.** *(eyes)* chorar; *(nose)* escorrer *(Br)*, pingar *(Port)*. **7.** *(colour, dye, clothes)* desbotar. **8.** *(remain valid)* ser válido; **the offer ~s until July** a oferta é válida até julho. ◆ *vt* **1.** *(on foot)* correr; **to ~ a race** participar de uma corrida. **2.** *(manage, organize)* gerir. **3.** *(car, machine)* manter; **it's cheap to ~** é muito econômico. **4.** *(bus, train)* ter em circulação; **we're running a special bus to the airport** temos em circulação um ônibus especial para o aeroporto. **5.** *(take in car)* levar (de carro); **I'll ~ you home** eu levo você em casa. **6.** *(fill):* **to ~ a bath** encher a banheira.

◆ *n* **1.** *(on foot)* corrida *f*; **to go for a ~** ir dar uma corrida. **2.** *(in car)* passeio *m* de carro; **to go for a ~** ir dar um passeio de carro. **3.** *(of play, show):* **it had a two-year ~** esteve dois anos em cartaz. **4.** *(for skiing)* pista *f*. **5.** *(Am: in tights)* fio *m* puxado *(Br)*, foguete *m (Port)*. **6.** *(in phrases):* **in the long ~** a longo prazo.

❏ **run away** *vi* fugir.

❏ **run down** *vt sep (run over)* atropelar; *(criticize)* criticar ◆ *vi (clock)* parar; *(battery)* descarregar-se, gastar-se.

❏ **run into** *vt fus (meet)* encontrar; *(hit)* chocar com, bater em; *(problem, difficulty)* deparar com.

❏ **run out** *vi (be used up)* esgotar-se.

❏ **run out of** *vt fus* ficar sem.

❏ **run over** *vt sep (hit)* atropelar.

runaway [rʌnəweɪ] *n* fugitivo *m* (-va *f*).

rundown [rʌndaʊn] *n (report)* breve resumo *m*.

❏ **run-down** *adj (dilapidated)* delapidado(-da), velho(-lha); *(tired)* cansado(-da).

rung [rʌŋ] *pp* → **ring** ◆ *n (of ladder)* degrau *m*.

runner [rʌnəʳ] *n (person)* corredor *m* (-ra *f*); *(for door, drawer)* calha *f*; *(for sledge)* patim *m*.

runner bean *n* vagem *f (Br)*, feijão *m* verde (longo) *(Port)*.

runner-up *(pl* **runners-up***) n* segundo *m* classificado (segunda *f* classificada).

running [rʌnɪŋ] *n (SPORT)* corrida *f*; *(management)* gestão *f* ◆ *adj:* **three days ~** três dias seguidos; **to go ~** ir correr.

running water *n* água *f* corrente.

runny [rʌnɪ] *adj (sauce)* líquido(-da); *(egg, omelette)* mal-passado(-da); *(nose)* escorrendo *(Br)*, a pingar *(Port)*; *(eye)* lacrimejante.

run-of-the-mill *adj* normal.

runway [rʌnweɪ] *n* pista *f* (de aterrissagem).

rural [rʊərəl] *adj* rural.

ruse [ruːz] *n* truque *m*, estratagema *m*.

rush [rʌʃ] *n (hurry)* pressa *f*; *(of crowd)* onda *f* (de gente), afluência *f* ◆ *vi (move quickly)* ir correndo; *(hurry)* apressar-se ◆ *vt (work)* fazer às pressas; *(food)* comer às pressas; *(transport quickly)* levar urgentemente; **to be in a** ~ estar com OR ter pressa; **there's no** ~! não há pressa!; **don't** ~ **me!** não me apresse!

rush hour *n* hora *f* do rush *(Br)*, hora *f* de ponta *(Port)*.

rusk [rʌsk] *n* rosca *f* para bebês.

Russia ['rʌʃə] *n* Rússia *f.*

Russian ['rʌʃn] *adj* russo(-a) ◆ *n (person)* russo *m* (-a *f*); *(language)* russo *m.*

rust [rʌst] *n (corrosion)* ferrugem *f* ◆ *vi* enferrujar.

rustic ['rʌstɪk] *adj* rústico(-ca).

rustle ['rʌsl] *vi* fazer ruído.

rustproof ['rʌstpruːf] *adj* inoxidável.

rusty ['rʌstɪ] *adj (metal)* ferrugento (-ta); *(fig: language, person)* enferrujado(-da).

rut [rʌt] *n (furrow)* rodada *f*, marca *f* do pneu; **to be in a** ~ estar preso a uma rotina.

ruthless ['ruːθlɪs] *adj* implacável, sem piedade.

RV *n (Am: abbr of recreational vehicle)* reboque *m (Br)*, roulotte *f (Port)*.

rye [raɪ] *n* centeio *m.*

rye bread *n* pão *m* de centeio.

S

S (abbr of south, small) S.

Sabbath ['sæbəθ] n: **the ~** (for Christians) o domingo; (for Jews) o sábado.

sabotage ['sæbətu:ʒ] n sabotagem f ♦ vt sabotar.

saccharin ['sækərɪn] n sacarina f.

sachet ['sæʃeɪ] n pacote m.

sack [sæk] n (bag) saco ♦ vt despedir; **to get the ~** ser despedido.

sacred ['seɪkrɪd] adj sagrado(-da).

sacrifice ['sækrɪfaɪs] n (fig) sacrifício m.

sad [sæd] adj triste; (unfortunate) lamentável.

sadden ['sædn] vt entristecer.

saddle ['sædl] n (on horse) sela f; (on bicycle, motorbike) selim m.

saddlebag ['sædlbæg] n (on bicycle, motorbike) bolsa f; (on horse) alforge m.

sadistic [sə'dɪstɪk] adj sádico(-ca).

sadly ['sædlɪ] adv infelizmente.

sadness ['sædnɪs] n tristeza f.

s.a.e. n (Brit: abbr of stamped addressed envelope) envelope selado e sobrescritado.

safari [sə'fɑ:rɪ] n safari m.

safari park n reserva f (para animais selvagens).

safe [seɪf] adj seguro(-ra); (out of harm) em segurança ♦ n cofre m; **a ~ place** um local seguro; **(have a) ~ journey!** (faça) boa viagem!; **~ and sound** são e salvo.

safe-deposit box n caixa-forte f, cofre m.

safeguard ['seɪfgɑːd] n salvaguarda f, proteção f ♦ vt: **to ~ sb/sthg (against sthg)** salvaguardar alguém/algo (contra algo), proteger alguém/algo (de algo).

safekeeping [,seɪf'kiːpɪŋ] n: **she gave it to me for ~** ela deu-me para eu guardar.

safely ['seɪflɪ] adv em segurança.

safe sex n sexo m sem riscos.

safety ['seɪftɪ] n segurança f.

safety belt n cinto m de segurança.

safety pin n alfinete m de segurança.

saffron ['sæfrən] n açafrão m.

sag [sæg] vi (hang down) pender; (sink) ir abaixo.

sage [seɪdʒ] n (herb) salva f.

Sagittarius [,sædʒɪ'teərɪəs] n Sagitário m.

Sahara [sə'hɑːrə] n: **the ~ (Desert)** o (deserto do) Saara.

said [sed] pt & pp → say.

sail [seɪl] n vela f (de barco) ♦ vi velejar, navegar; (depart) zarpar ♦ vt: **to ~ a boat** velejar um barco; **to set ~** zarpar.

sailboat ['seɪlbəʊt] (Am) = **sailing boat**.

sailing ['seɪlɪŋ] n (activity) vela f; (departure) partida f; **to go ~** ir praticar vela.

sailing boat n barco m à vela.

sailing ship n veleiro m.

sailor ['seɪləʳ] n marinheiro m (-ra f).

saint [seɪnt] n santo m (-ta f).

sake [seɪk] n: **for my/their ~** por mim/eles; **for God's ~!** por amor de Deus!

salad ['sæləd] n salada f.

salad bar n (Brit: area in restaurant) bufê m de saladas; (restaurant) restaurante especializado em saladas.

salad bowl n saladeira f.

salad cream n (Brit) molho parecido com maionese utilizado para temperar saladas.

salad dressing n tempero m (para saladas).

salami [sə'lɑːmɪ] n salame m.

salary ['sælərı] *n* salário *m*, ordenado *m*.

sale [seɪl] *n* (selling) venda *f*; (at reduced prices) liquidação *f* (Br), saldo *m* (Port); **"for ~"** "vende-se"; **on ~** à venda.

❑ **sales** *npl* (COMM) vendas *fpl*; **the ~s** (at reduced prices) as liquidações (Br), os saldos (Port).

sales assistant [seɪlz-] *n* vendedor *m* (-ra *f*).

salesclerk ['seɪlzklɜːrk] (Am) = **sales assistant**.

salesman ['seɪlzmən] (pl **-men** [-mən]) *n* (in shop) vendedor *m*; (rep) representante *m* de vendas.

sales rep(resentative) *n* representante *mf* de vendas.

saleswoman ['seɪlzˌwʊmən] (pl **-women** [-ˌwɪmɪn]) *n* vendedora *f*.

saliva [sə'laɪvə] *n* saliva *f*.

salmon ['sæmən] (pl inv) *n* salmão *m*.

salmonella [ˌsælmə'nelə] *n* salmonela *f*.

salon ['sælɒn] *n* (hairdresser's) salão *m* (de cabeleireiro).

saloon [sə'luːn] *n* (Brit: car) sedã *m* (Br), carrinha *f* (de caixa fechada) (Port); (Am: bar) bar *m*; **~ (bar)** = pub *m*, (Brit) bar de hotel ou "pub", decorado de forma mais luxuosa, onde se servem bebidas a preços mais altos que nos outros bares.

salopettes [ˌsælə'pets] *npl* macacão *m* para esquiar.

salt [sɔːlt, sɒlt] *n* sal *m*.

saltcellar ['sɔːltˌselər] *n* (Brit) saleiro *m*.

salted peanuts ['sɔːltɪd-] *npl* amendoins *mpl* salgados.

salt shaker [-ˌʃeɪkər] (Am) = **saltcellar**.

saltwater ['sɔːltˌwɔːtər] *adj* de água salgada.

salty ['sɔːltɪ] *adj* salgado(-da).

salute [sə'luːt] *n* continência *f* ♦ *vi* fazer continência.

salvage ['sælvɪdʒ] *n* (property rescued) bens *mpl* OR objetos *mpl* salvos ♦ *vt* (rescue): **to ~ sthg (from)** salvar algo (de).

same [seɪm] *adj* mesmo(-ma) ♦ *pron*: **the ~** o mesmo (a mesma); **you've got the ~ book as me** você tem o mesmo livro que eu; **they look the ~** parecem iguais; **I'll have the ~ as her** vou tomar o mesmo que ela; **it's all the ~ to me** para mim tanto faz.

samosa [sə'məʊsə] *n* empada picante, de forma triangular, com recheio de carne picada e/ou verduras (especialidade indiana).

sample ['sɑːmpl] *n* amostra *f* ♦ *vt* (food, drink) provar.

sanctions ['sæŋkʃnz] *npl* (POL) sanções *fpl*.

sanctuary ['sæŋktʃʊərɪ] *n* (for birds, animals) reserva *f* ecológica.

sand [sænd] *n* areia *f* ♦ *vt* (wood) lixar.

❑ **sands** *npl* (beach) areal *m*.

sandal ['sændl] *n* sandália *f*.

sandbox ['sændbɒks] (Am) = **sandpit**.

sandcastle ['sændˌkɑːsl] *n* castelo *m* de areia.

sand dune *n* duna *f*.

sandpaper ['sændˌpeɪpər] *n* lixa *f*.

sandpit ['sændpɪt] *n* (Brit) caixa de areia para as crianças brincarem.

sandwich ['sænwɪdʒ] *n* sanduíche *m* (Br), sandes *f* inv (Port).

sandwich bar *n* local onde se vendem sanduíches e refrescos.

sandy ['sændɪ] *adj* (beach) arenoso(-osa); (hair) ruivo(-va).

sane [seɪn] *adj* (not mad) são (sã) (de espírito); (sensible) razoável, sensato(-ta).

sang [sæŋ] *pt* → **sing**.

sanitary ['sænɪtrɪ] *adj* sanitário(-ria).

sanitary napkin (Am) = **sanitary towel**.

sanitary towel *n* (Brit) toalha *f* higiênica (Br), penso *m* higiénico (Port).

sanity ['sænɪtɪ] *n* (saneness) saúde *f* mental; (good sense) sensatez *f*.

sank [sæŋk] *pt* → **sink**.

Santa (Claus) ['sæntə(klɔːz)] *n* Papai *m* Noel (Br), Pai *m* Natal (Port).

sap [sæp] *n* (of plant) seiva *f* ♦ *vt* (weaken) absorver, esgotar.

sapling ['sæplɪŋ] *n* árvore *f* jovem.

sapphire ['sæfaɪər] *n* safira *f*.

sarcastic [sɑː'kæstɪk] *adj* sarcástico (-ca).

sardine [sɑː'diːn] *n* sardinha *f*.

sardonic [sɑː'dɒnɪk] *adj* sardônico (-ca).

SASE *n* (Am: abbr of self-addressed stamped envelope) envelope selado e sobrescritado.

sash [sæʃ] n faixa f.

sat [sæt] pt & pp → **sit**.

Sat. (abbr of Saturday) sáb.

Satan ['seɪtn] n Satanás m.

satchel ['sætʃəl] n pasta f (da escola).

satellite ['sætəlaɪt] n (in space) satélite m; (at airport) sala f de embarque auxiliar.

satellite dish n antena f parabólica.

satellite TV n televisão f via satélite.

satin ['sætɪn] n cetim m.

satire ['sætaɪər] n sátira f.

satisfaction [,sætɪs'fækʃn] n satisfação f.

satisfactory [,sætɪs'fæktərɪ] adj satisfatório(-ria).

satisfied ['sætɪsfaɪd] adj satisfeito(-ta).

satisfy ['sætɪsfaɪ] vt satisfazer.

satisfying ['sætɪsfaɪɪŋ] adj (experience, feeling) ótimo(-ma).

satsuma [,sæt'suːmə] n (Brit) satsuma f (Port), espécie de tangerina.

saturate ['sætʃəreɪt] vt saturar.

Saturday ['sætədɪ] n sábado m; **it's ~** é sábado; **~ morning** sábado de manhã; **on ~** no sábado; **on ~s** aos sábados; **last ~** sábado passado; **this ~** este sábado; **next ~** o próximo sábado; **~ week, a week on ~** de sábado a oito (dias).

sauce [sɔːs] n molho m.

saucepan ['sɔːspən] n panela f (Br), tacho m (Port).

saucer ['sɔːsər] n pires m inv.

saucy ['sɔːsɪ] adj (inf) atrevido(-da).

Saudi Arabia [,saʊdɪ'reɪbjə] n Arábia f Saudita.

sauna ['sɔːnə] n sauna f.

saunter ['sɔːntər] vi caminhar (despreocupadamente).

sausage ['sɒsɪdʒ] n salsicha f, lingüiça f.

sausage roll n = folheado m de salsicha (Br), = pastel m de carne (Port).

sauté [Brit 'sauteɪ, Am sauteɪ] adj sauté (Br), salteado(-da) (Port).

savage ['sævɪdʒ] adj selvagem.

save [seɪv] vt (rescue) salvar; (money, time, space) poupar; (reserve) guardar; (SPORT) defender; (COMPUT) guardar (Port), salvar (Br) ♦ n defesa f.

❏ **save up** vi poupar; **to ~ up (for sthg)** poupar (para comprar algo).

saver ['seɪvər] n (Brit: ticket) bilhete de trem que apenas permite ao passageiro viajar fora das horas de rush a preço reduzido.

savings ['seɪvɪŋz] npl poupanças fpl, economias fpl.

savings account n (Am) conta f poupança.

savings and loan association n (Am) caixa f de crédito imobiliário.

savings bank n caixa f econômica.

savior ['seɪvjər] (Am) = **saviour**.

saviour ['seɪvjər] n (Brit) salvador m (-ra f).

savory ['seɪvərɪ] (Am) = **savoury**.

savoury ['seɪvərɪ] adj (Brit) salgado(-da).

saw [sɔː] (Brit pt **-ed**, pp **sawn**, Am pt & pp **-ed**) pt → **see** ♦ n (tool) serra f ♦ vt serrar.

sawdust ['sɔːdʌst] n serragem f (Br), serradura f (Port).

sawed-off shotgun [sɔːd-] (Am) = **sawn-off shotgun**.

sawn [sɔːn] pp → **saw**.

sawn-off shotgun n (Brit) espingarda f de cano serrado.

saxophone ['sæksəfəʊn] n saxofone m.

say [seɪ] (pt & pp **said**) vt dizer; (subj: clock, meter) marcar ♦ n: **I don't have a ~ in the matter** não tenho voto na matéria; **could you ~ that again?** podia repetir o que disse?; **~ we met at nine?** que tal encontrarmo-nos às nove?; **what did you ~?** (o que é) que você disse?

saying ['seɪɪŋ] n ditado m.

scab [skæb] n crosta f.

scaffold ['skæfəʊld] n (frame) andaime m; (for executions) cadafalso m.

scaffolding ['skæfəldɪŋ] n andaimes mpl.

scald [skɔːld] vt escaldar, queimar.

scale [skeɪl] n escala f; (of fish, snake) escama f; (in kettle) placa f, calcário m. ❏ **scales** npl (for weighing) balança f.

scallion ['skæljən] n (Am) cebolinha f.

scallop ['skɒləp] n vieira f.

scalp [skælp] n couro m cabeludo.

scalpel ['skælpəl] n bisturi m.

scamper ['skæmpər] vi correr.

scampi ['skæmpɪ] n camarões mpl fritos.

scan [skæn] vt (consult quickly) per-

correr, dar uma vista de olhos em ◆ *n*
(MED) exame *m*.
scandal ['skændl] *n* escândalo *m*.
scandalize ['skændəlaɪz] *vt* escandalizar.
Scandinavia [,skændɪ'neɪvjə] *n*
Escandinávia *f*.
Scandinavian [,skændɪ'neɪvjən] *adj*
escandinavo(-va) ◆ *n (person)* escandi-
navo *m* (-va *f*).
scant [skænt] *adj (attention)* pouco
(-ca).
scanty ['skæntɪ] *adj (amount, resources)*
escasso(-a); *(information)* pouco(-ca);
(dress) minúsculo(-la).
scapegoat ['skeɪpgəut] *n* bode *m*
expiatório.
scar [skuːʳ] *n* cicatriz *f*.
scarce ['skeəs] *adj* escasso(-a).
scarcely ['skeəslɪ] *adv (hardly)* mal; ~
anyone quase ninguém; ~ **ever** quase
nunca.
scare [skeəʳ] *vt* assustar.
scarecrow ['skeəkrəu] *n* espantalho
m.
scared ['skeəd] *adj* assustado(-da).
scarf ['skuːf] *(pl* **scarves)** *n (woollen)*
cachecol *m; (for women)* écharpe *f*.
scarlet ['skuːlət] *adj* vermelho(-lha),
escarlate.
scarves [skuːvz] *pl* → **scarf**.
scary ['skeərɪ] *adj (inf)* assustador
(-ra).
scathing ['skeɪðɪŋ] *adj (glance, criticism)* severo(-ra); *(reply)* mordaz.
scatter ['skætəʳ] *vt (seeds, papers)*
espalhar; *(birds)* dispersar ◆ *vi*
dispersar-se.
scatterbrain ['skætəbreɪn] *n (inf)*
cabeça *f* de vento (Br), cabeça-no-ar
mf (Port).
scenario [sɪ'nuːrɪəu] *(pl* -s) *n (possible
situation)* cenário *m*, panorama *m; (of
film, play)* enredo *m*, roteiro *m (Br)*.
scene [siːn] *n (in play, film, book)* cena
f; (of crime, accident) local *m; (view)*
panorama *m;* **the music** ~ o mundo da
música; **to make a** ~ armar um escândalo.
scenery ['siːnərɪ] *n (countryside)* paisagem *f; (in theatre)* cenário *m*.
scenic ['siːnɪk] *adj* pitoresco(-ca).
scent [sent] *n (smell)* fragrância *f; (of
animal)* rasto *m; (perfume)* perfume *m*.
sceptic ['skeptɪk] *n (Brit)* cético *m* (-ca
f).

sceptical ['skeptɪkl] *adj* cético(-ca).
schedule [*Brit* 'ʃedjuːl, *Am* 'skedʒul] *n
(of work, things to do)* programa *m*,
calendarização *f; (timetable)* horário *m;
(list)* lista *f* ◆ *vt (plan)* programar;
according to ~ de acordo com o previsto; **behind** ~ atrasado; **on** ~ *(plane,
train)* na hora (prevista).
scheduled flight [*Brit* 'ʃedjuːld-, *Am*
'skedʒuld-] *n* vôo *m* regular, vôo *m* de
linha.
scheme [skiːm] *n (plan)* projeto *m;
(pej: dishonest plan)* esquema *m*.
scheming ['skiːmɪŋ] *adj* cheio (cheia)
de truques.
schizophrenic [,skɪtsə'frenɪk] *adj*
esquizofrênico(-ca) ◆ *n* esquizofrênico
m (-ca *f*).
scholar ['skɒləʳ] *n* erudito *m* (-ta *f*);
Greek ~ helenista *mf;* **Latin** ~ latinista
mf.
scholarship ['skɒləʃɪp] *n (award)*
bolsa *f* de estudo.
school [skuːl] *n* escola *f; (university
department)* faculdade *f; (Am: university)* universidade *f* ◆ *adj* escolar; **at** ~
na escola.
school age *n* idade *f* escolar.
schoolbag ['skuːlbæg] *n* pasta *f* (da
escola).
schoolbook ['skuːlbuk] *n* livro *m*
escolar, manual *m* escolar OR didático.
schoolboy ['skuːlbɔɪ] *n* aluno *m*.
school bus *n* ônibus *m* escolar (Br),
autocarro *m* OR carrinha *f* da escola
(Port).
schoolchild ['skuːltʃaɪld] *(pl
-children* [-,tʃɪldrən]) *n* aluno *m* (-na *f*).
schooldays ['skuːldeɪz] *npl* tempos
mpl de escola.
schoolgirl ['skuːlgɜːl] *n* aluna *f*.
schooling ['skuːlɪŋ] *n* instrução *f*.
school-leaver [-,liːvəʳ] *n (Brit)* jovem
*que abandona os estudos após a escolari-
dade obrigatória*.
schoolmaster ['skuːl,muːstəʳ] *n (Brit)*
professor *m*.
schoolmistress ['skuːl,mɪstrɪs] *n
(Brit)* professora *f*.
schoolteacher ['skuːl,tiːtʃəʳ] *n* professor *m* (-ra *f*).
school uniform *n* uniforme *m*
escolar.
school year *n* ano *m* letivo.
science ['saɪəns] *n* ciência *f; (SCH)*
ciências *fpl*.

science fiction n ficção f científica.

scientific [ˌsaɪənˈtɪfɪk] adj científico (-ca).

scientist [ˈsaɪəntɪst] n cientista mf.

scintillating [ˈsɪntɪleɪtɪŋ] adj brilhante.

scissors [ˈsɪzəz] npl tesoura f; **a pair of ~** uma tesoura.

scold [skəʊld] vt ralhar com, repreender.

scone [skɒn] n bolo redondo por vezes com passas e que normalmente se come na hora do chá com manteiga e compota.

scoop [skuːp] n (for ice cream, flour) colher f grande; (of ice cream) bola f; (in media) furo m jornalístico (Br), exclusivo m (Port).

scooter [ˈskuːtər] n (motor vehicle) scooter f, lambreta f.

scope [skəʊp] n (possibility) possibilidade f; (range) alcance m.

scorch [skɔːtʃ] vt chamuscar.

scorching [ˈskɔːtʃɪŋ] adj (inf) abrasador(-ra).

score [skɔːr] n (total, final result) resultado m; (in test) ponto m (Br), pontuação f (Port) ◆ vt (SPORT) marcar; (in test) obter ◆ vi (SPORT) marcar; **what's the ~?** como é que está (o jogo)?

scoreboard [ˈskɔːbɔːd] n marcador m.

scorer [ˈskɔːrər] n marcador m (-ra f).

scorn [skɔːn] n desprezo m.

scornful [ˈskɔːnfʊl] adj desdenhoso (-osa); **to be ~ of** sthg desdenhar de algo.

Scorpio [ˈskɔːpɪəʊ] n Escorpião m.

scorpion [ˈskɔːpjən] n escorpião m.

Scot [skɒt] n escocês m (-esa f).

scotch [skɒtʃ] n uísque m escocês.

Scotch broth n sopa espessa feita com caldo de carne, verduras e cevada.

Scotch tape® n (Am) fita f durex® (Br), fita-cola f (Port).

Scotland [ˈskɒtlənd] n Escócia f.

Scotsman [ˈskɒtsmən] (pl -men [-mən]) n escocês m.

Scotswoman [ˈskɒtsˌwʊmən] (pl -women [-ˌwɪmɪn]) n escocesa f.

Scottish [ˈskɒtɪʃ] adj escocês(-esa).

scoundrel [ˈskaʊndrəl] n patife m.

scour [ˈskaʊər] vt (clean) esfregar, arear; (search) percorrer.

scout [skaʊt] n (boy scout) escoteiro m.

scowl [skaʊl] vi franzir a testa.

scramble [ˈskræmbl] n (rush) luta f ◆ vi (climb): **~ up/down a hill** subir/descer um monte (com dificuldade).

scrambled eggs [skræmbld-] npl ovos mpl mexidos.

scrap [skræp] n (of paper, cloth) tira f; (old metal) ferro m velho, sucata f.

scrapbook [ˈskræpbʊk] n álbum m de recortes.

scrape [skreɪp] vt (rub) raspar; (scratch) arranhar, esfolar.

scraper [ˈskreɪpər] n raspadeira f.

scrap paper n (Brit) papel m de rascunho.

scrapyard [ˈskræpjɑːd] n (depósito de) ferro-velho m.

scratch [skrætʃ] n (cut) arranhão m; (mark) risco m ◆ vt (cut) arranhar; (mark) riscar; (rub) coçar, arranhar; **to be up to ~** ter um nível satisfatório; **to start from ~** começar do nada.

scratch paper (Am) = **scrap paper**.

scrawl [skrɔːl] n rabisco m ◆ vt rabiscar.

scream [skriːm] n grito m ◆ vi gritar.

scree [skriː] n depósito de pedras que se desprenderam de uma encosta.

screech [skriːtʃ] n (of person, bird) guincho m; (of tyres, brakes, car) chio m, chiadeira f ◆ vi (person, bird) guinchar; (tyres, brakes, car) chiar.

screen [skriːn] n tela f (Br), ecrã m (Port); (hall in cinema) sala f de cinema; (panel) biombo m ◆ vt (film) exibir; (programme) emitir.

screening [ˈskriːnɪŋ] n (of film) exibição f.

screen wash n líquido m para o pára-brisas.

screw [skruː] n parafuso m ◆ vt (fasten) aparafusar; (twist) enroscar.

screwdriver [ˈskruːˌdraɪvər] n chave f de parafusos OR fendas.

scribble [ˈskrɪbl] vi escrevinhar, rabiscar.

script [skrɪpt] n (of play, film) roteiro m (Br), guião m (Port).

scroll [skrəʊl] n rolo m de papel/pergaminho.

scrounge [skraʊndʒ] vt (inf): **to ~ sthg (off sb)** filar algo (de alguém), cravar algo (a alguém).

scrounger [ˈskraʊndʒər] n (inf) filão m (-ona f) (Br), crava mf (Port).

scrub [skrʌb] vt esfregar.

scruff [skrʌf] n: **by the ~ of the**

neck pelo cangote.

scruffy ['skrʌfɪ] *adj* desmazelado (-da).

scrum(mage) ['skrʌm(ɪdʒ)] *n* formação *f*.

scrumpy ['skrʌmpɪ] *n* sidra com alto teor alcoólico proveniente do sudoeste da Inglaterra.

scruples ['skru:plz] *npl* escrúpulos *mpl*.

scrutinize ['skru:tɪnaɪz] *vt* examinar (minuciosamente).

scuba diving ['sku:bə-] *n* mergulho *m*.

scuff [skʌf] *vt* (furniture, floor) riscar; (heels) gastar.

scuffle ['skʌfl] *n* briga *f*.

sculptor ['skʌlptər] *n* escultor *m* (-ra *f*).

sculpture ['skʌlptʃər] *n* escultura *f*.

scum [skʌm] *n* (froth) espuma *f*; (inf: pej: worthless people) escumalha *f*, ralé *f*.

scurry ['skʌrɪ] *vi*: **to ~ off/away** escapulir, dar no pé.

scuttle ['skʌtl] ♦ *vi* (rush): **to ~ off/away** sair correndo, dar no pé.

scythe [saɪð] *n* segadeira *f*, gadanha *f*.

sea [si:] *n* mar *m*; **by ~** por mar; **by the ~** à beira-mar.

seabed ['si:bed] *n*: **the ~** o fundo do mar.

seafood ['si:fu:d] *n* marisco *m*.

seafront ['si:frʌnt] *n* orla *f* marítima.

seagull ['si:gʌl] *n* gaivota *f*.

seal [si:l] *n* (animal) foca *f*; (on bottle, container, official mark) selo *m* ♦ *vt* (envelope, container) selar.

sea level *n* nível *m* do mar.

sea lion *n* leão-marinho *m*.

seam [si:m] *n* (in clothes) costura *f*.

search [sɜ:tʃ] *n* procura *f*, busca *f* ♦ *vt* revistar ♦ *vi*: **to ~ for** procurar.

searchlight ['sɜ:tʃlaɪt] *n* holofote *m*.

seashell ['si:ʃel] *n* concha *f*.

seashore ['si:ʃɔ:r] *n* costa *f* (marítima).

seasick ['si:sɪk] *adj* enjoado(-da).

seaside ['si:saɪd] *n*: **the ~** a praia.

seaside resort *n* estância *f* balneária.

season ['si:zn] *n* (division of year) estação *f*; (period) temporada *f* ♦ *vt* (food) temperar; **in ~** (fruit, vegetables) da época; (holiday) em época alta; **out**

of ~ (fruit, vegetables) fora de época; (holiday) em época baixa.

seasonal ['si:zənl] *adj* sazonal.

seasoning ['si:znɪŋ] *n* tempero *m*, condimento *m*.

season ticket *n* passe *m*.

seat [si:t] *n* assento *m*; (place) lugar *m* ♦ *vt* (subj: building) ter lugar para; (subj: vehicle) levar; **"please wait to be ~ed"** aviso pelo qual se pede aos fregueses que esperem até serem conduzidos a uma mesa vaga.

seat belt *n* cinto *m* de segurança.

seating ['si:tɪŋ] *n* (capacity) lugares *mpl* (sentados).

seaweed ['si:wi:d] *n* alga *f* marinha.

seaworthy ['si:wɜ:ðɪ] *adj* em condições de navegar.

secluded [sɪ'klu:dɪd] *adj* isolado(-da).

seclusion [sɪ'klu:ʒn] *n* isolamento *m*; **to keep sb in ~** manter alguém isolado.

second ['sekənd] *n* segundo *m* ♦ *num* segundo *m* (-da *f*); **~ gear** segunda *f* (mudança), → **sixth**.

⌐ seconds *npl* (goods) artigos *mpl* de qualidade inferior; (inf: of food): **who wants ~?** quem quer repetir?

secondary school ['sekəndrɪ-] *n* escola *f* secundária.

second-class *adj* de segunda classe; (stamp) de correio normal.

second-hand *adj* de segunda mão.

secondly ['sekəndlɪ] *adv* segundo, em segundo lugar.

second-rate *adj* de segunda (categoria), medíocre.

Second World War *n*: **the ~** a Segunda Guerra Mundial.

secrecy ['si:krəsɪ] *n* sigilo *m*.

secret ['si:krɪt] *adj* secreto(-ta) ♦ *n* segredo *m*.

secretary [Brit 'sekrətrɪ, Am 'sekrəterɪ] *n* secretário *m* (-ria *f*).

Secretary of State *n* (Am: foreign minister) Secretário *m* (-ria *f*) de Estado, = Ministro *m* (-tra *f*) dos Negócios Estrangeiros; (Brit: government minister) ministro *m* (-tra *f*).

secretive ['si:krətɪv] *adj* (person) reservado(-da); (organization) sigiloso (-osa).

secretly ['si:krɪtlɪ] *adv* (plan, meet) em segredo; (hope, think) no íntimo.

sect [sekt] *n* seita *f*.

section ['sekʃn] *n* seção *f*.

sector ['sektər] *n* setor *m*.

secure [sɪ'kjuər] *adj* seguro(-ra) ♦ *vt (fix)* fixar; *(fml: obtain)* obter.

security [sɪ'kjuərətɪ] *n* segurança *f*.

security guard *n* segurança *m*, guarda *m*.

sedate [sɪ'deɪt] *adj* tranqüilo(-la) ♦ *vt* sedar.

sedative ['sedǝtɪv] *n* sedativo *m*.

sediment ['sedɪmǝnt] *n* sedimento *m*.

seduce [sɪ'djuːs] *vt* seduzir.

see [siː] *(pt* saw, *pp* seen) *vt* ver; *(accompany)* acompanhar; *(consider)* considerar ♦ *vi* ver; **I ~** *(understand)* estou entendendo; **I'll ~ what I can do** vou ver o que eu posso fazer; **to ~ to** sthg *(deal with)* tratar de algo; *(repair)* consertar algo; **~ you!** até mais!; **~ you later!** até logo!; **~ you soon!** até breve!; **~ p 14** ver pág. 14.
❏ **see off** *vt sep (say goodbye to)* despedir-se de.

seed [siːd] *n* semente *f*.

seedling ['siːdlɪŋ] *n* planta *f* jovem *(de sementeira)*.

seedy ['siːdɪ] *adj* sórdido(-da).

seeing (as) ['siːɪŋ-] *conj* visto que.

seek [siːk] *(pt & pp* sought) *vt (fml)* procurar.

seem [siːm] *vi* parecer ♦ *v impers*: **it ~s (that)** ... parece que ....

seemingly ['siːmɪŋlɪ] *adv (apparently)* aparentemente.

seen [siːn] *pp* → **see**.

seep [siːp] *vi (water, gas)* infiltrar-se.

seesaw ['siːsɔː] *n* gangorra *f (Br)*, baloiço *m (Port)*.

see-through *adj* transparente.

segment ['segmǝnt] *n (of fruit)* gomo *m*.

seize [siːz] *vt (grab)* agarrar; *(drugs, arms)* confiscar.
❏ **seize up** *vi (engine)* gripar; **my back ~d up** senti um espasmo nas costas.

seldom ['seldǝm] *adv* raramente.

select [sɪ'lekt] *vt* selecionar ♦ *adj* seleto(-ta).

selection [sɪ'lekʃn] *n* seleção *f*.

selective [sɪ'lektɪv] *adj* seletivo(-va).

self-assured [,selfǝ'ʃuǝd] *adj* seguro(-ra) de si.

self-catering [,self'keɪtǝrɪŋ] *adj (flat)* com cozinha; *(holiday)* em casa alugada.

self-centred [,self'sentǝd] *adj (per-*

son) egocêntrico(-ca).

self-confident [,self-] *adj* seguro(-ra) de si.

self-conscious [,self-] *adj* inibido(-da).

self-contained [,selfkǝn'teɪnd] *adj (flat)* independente *(com cozinha e banheiro)*.

self-control [,self-] *n* autodomínio *m*.

self-defence [,self-] *n* autodefesa *f*.

self-discipline [,self-] *n* autodisciplina *f*.

self-employed [,selfɪm'plɔɪd] *adj* que trabalha por conta própria, autônomo(-ma).

self-esteem [,self-] *n* auto-estima *f*.

self-explanatory [,selfɪk'splænǝtrɪ] *adj* claro(-ra).

self-important [,self-] *adj* cheio (cheia) de si.

selfish ['selfɪʃ] *adj* egoísta.

selfishness ['selfɪʃnɪs] *n* egoísmo *m*.

selfless ['selflɪs] *adj* abnegado(-da), desinteressado(-da).

self-portrait [,self-] *n* auto-retrato *m*.

self-raising flour [,self'reɪzɪŋ-] *n (Brit)* farinha *f* com fermento.

self-respect [,self-] *n* dignidade *f*, amor-próprio *m*.

self-restraint [,self-] *n* autodomínio *m*.

self-rising flour [,self'raɪzɪŋ-] *(Am)* = **self-raising flour**.

self-sacrifice [,self-] *n* abnegação *f*.

self-satisfied [,self-] *adj (person)* satisfeito consigo próprio (satisfeita consigo própria), ufano(-na).

self-service [,self-] *adj* self-service *(inv)*, de auto-serviço.

self-sufficient [,self-] *adj*: **~ (in sthg)** auto-suficiente (no que diz respeito a algo).

self-taught [,self-] *adj* autodidata.

sell [sel] *(pt & pp* sold) *vt & vi* vender; **to ~ for** vender-se por, ser vendido por; **to ~ sb sthg** vender algo a alguém.

sell-by date *n* data *f* limite de venda.

seller ['selǝr] *n* vendedor *m* (-ra *f*).

Sellotape® ['selǝteɪp] *n (Brit)* fita *f* durex® *(Br)*, fita-cola *f (Port)*.

semen ['siːmen] *n* sêmen *m*.

semester [sɪ'mestǝr] *n* semestre *m*.

semicircle ['semɪsɜːkl] n semicírculo m.

semicolon [ˌsemɪ'kəʊlən] n ponto m e vírgula.

semidetached [ˌsemɪdɪ'tætʃt] adj geminado(-da).

semifinal [ˌsemɪ'faɪnl] n semifinal f.

seminar ['semɪnɑːr] n seminário m.

semolina [ˌsemə'liːnə] n semolina f.

senate ['senɪt] n (in US): **the ~** o Senado.

senator ['senətər] n senador m (-ra f).

send [send] (pt & pp **sent**) vt enviar; (person) mandar; **to ~ sthg to sb** enviar algo a alguém.

❏ **send back** vt sep devolver.

❏ **send off** vt sep (letter, parcel) enviar; (SPORT) expulsar ◆ vi: **to ~ off (for sthg)** mandar vir (algo) pelo correio.

sender ['sendər] n remetente mf.

senile ['siːnaɪl] adj senil.

senior ['siːnjər] adj (in rank) superior ◆ n (Brit: SCH) aluno m (-na f) (de escola secundária); (Am: SCH) finalista mf.

senior citizen n idoso m (-osa f), pessoa f de idade.

sensation [sen'seɪʃn] n sensação f.

sensational [sen'seɪʃənl] adj sensacional.

sensationalist [sen'seɪʃnəlɪst] adj sensacionalista.

sense [sens] n sentido m; (common sense) bom-senso m ◆ vt sentir; **there is no ~ in waiting** não vale a pena esperar; **to make ~** fazer sentido; **~ of direction** sentido de orientação; **~ of humour** senso de humor.

senseless ['senslɪs] adj (stupid) insensato(-ta), sem sentido; (unconscious) inconsciente, sem sentidos.

sensible ['sensəbl] adj (person) sensato(-ta); (clothes, shoes) prático(-ca).

sensitive ['sensɪtɪv] adj sensível; (easily offended) suscetível; (subject, issue) delicado(-da).

sensual ['sensjʊəl] adj sensual.

sensuous ['sensjʊəs] adj sensual.

sent [sent] pt & pp → **send**.

sentence ['sentəns] n (GRAMM) frase f; (for crime) sentença f ◆ vt condenar.

sentimental [ˌsentɪ'mentl] adj (pej) sentimental.

sentry ['sentrɪ] n sentinela f.

Sep. (abbr of September) set.

separate [adj & n 'seprət, vb 'sepəreɪt] adj (different, individual) diferente, dis-

tinto(-ta); (not together) separado(-da) ◆ vt separar ◆ vi separar-se.

❏ **separates** npl (Brit: clothes) roupa feminina que pode ser usada em conjunto.

separately ['seprətlɪ] adv separadamente.

separation [ˌsepə'reɪʃn] n separação f.

September [sep'tembər] n setembro m; **at the beginning of ~** no início de setembro; **at the end of ~** no fim de setembro; **during ~** em setembro; **every ~** todos os meses de setembro, todos os anos em setembro; **in ~** em setembro; **last ~** setembro último OR passado; **next ~** no próximo mês de setembro; **this ~** setembro que vem; **2 ~ 1997** (in letters etc) 2 de setembro de 1997.

septic ['septɪk] adj infectado(-da).

septic tank n fossa f sética.

sequel ['siːkwəl] n (to book, film) continuação f.

sequence ['siːkwəns] n (series) série f; (order) ordem f.

sequin ['siːkwɪn] n lantejoula f.

Serb [sɜːb] = **Serbian**.

Serbia ['sɜːbjə] n Sérvia f.

Serbian ['sɜːbjən] adj sérvio(-via) ◆ n (person) sérvio m (-via f).

serene [sɪ'riːn] adj (calm) sereno(-na).

sergeant ['sɑːdʒənt] n (in police force) sargento m (Br), polícia m graduado (polícia f graduada) (Port); (in army) sargento m.

sergeant major n sargento-ajudante m.

serial ['sɪərɪəl] n seriado m (Br), série f (Port).

serial number n número m de série.

series ['sɪəriːz] (pl inv) n série f.

serious ['sɪərɪəs] adj sério(-ria); (accident, illness) grave; **are you ~?** você está falando sério?

seriously ['sɪərɪəslɪ] adv (really) de verdade; (badly) gravemente.

seriousness ['sɪərɪəsnɪs] n (of person, expression, voice) seriedade f; (of illness, situation, loss) gravidade f.

sermon ['sɜːmən] n sermão m.

serrated [sɪ'reɪtɪd] adj dentado(-da); **~ knife** faca f de serrilha.

servant ['sɜːvənt] n criado m (-da f).

serve [sɜːv] vt servir ◆ vi (SPORT) servir; (work) prestar serviço ◆ n (SPORT) serviço *m*; **the town is ~d by two air-ports** a cidade tem dois aeroportos; **to ~ as** *(be used for)* servir de; **"~s two"** "para duas pessoas"; **it ~s you right!** bem feito!

service ['sɜ:vɪs] *n* serviço *m*; *(at church)* culto *m* (Br), ofício *m* (Port); *(of car)* revisão *f* ♦ *vt (car)* fazer a revisão de; **"out of ~"** "fora de serviço"; **"~ included"** "serviço incluído"; **"~ not included"** "não inclui o serviço"; **can I be of any ~ to you?** *(fml)* em que posso servi-lo?

❏ **services** *npl (on motorway)* posto de gasolina com bares, banheiros etc.; *(of person)* serviços *mpl*.

service area *n* posto de gasolina com bares, banheiros, etc., área *f* de serviço (Port).

service charge *n* serviço *m*.

service department *n* seção *f* de atendimento ao consumidor.

service station *n* posto *m* de gasolina (Br), estação *f* de serviço (Port).

serviette [,sɜ:vɪ'et] *n* guardanapo *m*.

serving ['sɜ:vɪŋ] *n* porção *f*.

serving spoon *n* colher *f* para servir.

sesame seeds ['sesəmɪ-] *npl* sementes *fpl* de sésamo.

session ['seʃn] *n* sessão *f*.

set [set] *(pt & pp set)* *adj* **1.** *(fixed)* fixo(-xa); **~ lunch** = almoço *m* a preço fixo (Br), ementa *f* turística (Port).

2. *(text, book)* escolhido(-da).

3. *(situated)* situado(-da).

♦ *n* **1.** *(of stamps, stickers)* coleção *f*; *(for playing chess)* jogo *m*; *(of crockery)* aparelho *m*; *(of tools)* conjunto *m*.

2. *(TV)* aparelho *m*; **a TV ~** uma televisão, um televisor.

3. *(in tennis)* set *m*, partida *f*.

4. *(SCH)* grupo *m*.

5. *(of play)* cenário *m*.

6. *(at hairdresser's)*: **I'd like a shampoo and ~** queria lavar e pentear.

♦ *vt* **1.** *(put)* pôr.

2. *(cause to be)* pôr; **to ~ a machine going** pôr uma máquina em funcionamento.

3. *(clock, alarm, controls)* pôr; **~ the alarm for 7 a.m.** põe o despertador para despertar às sete.

4. *(fix)* fixar.

5. *(the table)* pôr.

6. *(a record)* estabelecer.

7. *(broken bone)* endireitar.

8. *(homework, essay)* marcar.

9. *(play, film, story)*: **to be ~** passar-se.

♦ *vi* **1.** *(sun)* pôr-se.

2. *(glue)* secar; *(jelly)* solidificar.

❏ **set down** *vt sep (Brit: passengers)* deixar.

❏ **set off** *vt sep (alarm)* fazer soar ♦ *vi* partir.

❏ **set out** *vt sep (arrange)* estabelecer ♦ *vi (on journey)* partir.

❏ **set up** *vt sep (barrier, equipment)* montar; *(meeting, interview)* marcar; *(committee)* criar.

setback ['setbæk] *n* contratempo *m*, revés *m*.

set meal *n* menu *m*, ementa *f* (Port).

set menu *n* menu *m* fixo, ementa *f* fixa (Port).

settee [se'ti:] *n* sofá *m*.

setting ['setɪŋ] *n (on machine)* posição *f*; *(surroundings)* cenário *m*.

settle ['setl] *vt (argument)* resolver; *(bill)* pagar, saldar; *(stomach, nerves)* acalmar; *(arrange, decide on)* decidir ♦ *vi (start to live)* estabelecer-se; *(bird, insect)* pousar; *(sediment, dust)* depositar-se.

❏ **settle down** *vi (calm down)* acalmar-se; *(sit comfortably)* instalar-se.

❏ **settle up** *vi* saldar as contas.

settlement ['setlmənt] *n (agreement)* acordo *m*; *(place)* povoado *m*, colônia *f*.

settler ['setlər] *n* colono *m* (-na *f*).

seven ['sevn] *num* sete, → **six**.

seventeen [,sevn'ti:n] *num* dezessete (Br), dezassete (Port), → **six**.

seventeenth [,sevn'ti:nθ] *num* décimo sétimo (décima sétima), → **sixth**.

seventh ['sevnθ] *num* sétimo(-ma), → **sixth**.

seventieth ['sevntjəθ] *num* septuagésimo(-ma), → **sixth**.

seventy ['sevntɪ] *num* setenta, → **six**.

several ['sevrəl] *adj* vários(-rias) ♦ *pron* vários *mpl* (-rias *fpl*).

severe [sɪ'vɪər] *adj (damage, illness, problem)* grave; *(weather conditions)* rigoroso(-osa); *(criticism, person, punishment)* severo(-ra); *(pain)* intenso(-sa).

severity [sɪ'verətɪ] *n (of damage, illness, problem)* gravidade *f*; *(of weather conditions)* rigor *m*; *(of storm)* violência *f*; *(of criticism, person, punishment)* severidade *f*.

sew [səʊ] (*pp* **sewn**) *vt & vi* coser, costurar.

sewage ['suːɪdʒ] *n* esgotos *mpl*, águas *fpl* residuais.

sewer ['sʊəʳ] *n* (cano de) esgoto *m*.

sewing ['səʊɪŋ] *n* costura *f*.

sewing machine *n* máquina *f* de costura.

sewn [səʊn] *pp* → **sew**.

sex [seks] *n* sexo *m*; **to have ~ (with)** ter relações sexuais (com).

sexist ['seksɪst] *n* sexista *mf*.

sexual ['sekʃʊəl] *adj* sexual; **~ equality** igualdade *f* dos sexos.

sexual harassment *n* assédio *m* sexual.

sexual intercourse *n* relações *fpl* sexuais.

sexy ['seksɪ] *adj* sexy.

shabby ['ʃæbɪ] *adj* (*clothes, room*) em mau estado; (*person*) esfarrapado (-da).

shack [ʃæk] *n* barraco *m*.

shade [ʃeɪd] *n* (*shadow*) sombra *f*; (*lampshade*) abajur *m*; (*of colour*) tom *m* ◆ *vt* (*protect*) proteger.

◡ **shades** *npl* (*inf: sunglasses*) óculos *mpl* escuros.

shadow ['ʃædəʊ] *n* sombra *f*.

shady ['ʃeɪdɪ] *adj* (*place*) com sombra; (*inf: person, deal*) duvidoso(-osa).

shaft [ʃɑːft] *n* (*of machine*) eixo *m*; (*of lift*) poço *m*.

shaggy ['ʃægɪ] *adj* (*dog*) peludo(-da); (*rug, carpet*) felpudo(-da); (*hair, beard*) hirsuto(-ta).

shake [ʃeɪk] (*pt* **shook**, *pp* **shaken** ['ʃeɪkn]) *vt* (*bottle*) agitar; (*tree, person*) abanar; (*rug*) sacudir; (*shock*) abalar ◆ *vi* tremer; **to ~ hands (with sb)** apertar a mão (a alguém), dar um aperto de mão (em alguém); **to ~ one's head** (*saying no*) negar com a cabeça.

shaky ['ʃeɪkɪ] *adj* (*chair, table*) frágil, trôpego(-ga); (*hand, writing, voice*) trémulo(-la); (*start*) acidentado(-da); (*finances*) instável; (*evidence, argument*) pouco sólido(-da); **I'm still a bit ~** ainda não me recuperei.

shall [*weak form* ʃəl, *strong form* ʃæl] *aux vb* **1.** (*expressing future*): **I ~ be ready soon** estarei pronto num instante.

2. (*in questions*): **~ I buy some wine?** quer que eu compre um vinho?; **~ we listen to the radio?** que tal se ouvisse-mos rádio?; **where ~ we go?** onde é que vamos?

3. (*fml: expressing order*): **payment ~ be made within a week** o pagamento deverá ser feito no prazo de uma semana.

shallot [ʃəˈlɒt] *n* cebolinha *f*, chalota *f*.

shallow ['ʃæləʊ] *adj* (*pond, water, grave*) raso(-sa).

shallow end *n* (*of swimming pool*) parte *f* rasa.

sham [ʃæm] *n* (*piece of deceit*) farsa *f*.

shambles ['ʃæmblz] *n* confusão *f*.

shame [ʃeɪm] *n* vergonha *f*; **it's a ~** é uma pena; **what a ~!** que pena!

shamefaced [ʃeɪmˈfeɪst] *adj* envergonhado(-da).

shameful ['ʃeɪmfʊl] *adj* vergonhoso(-osa).

shameless ['ʃeɪmlɪs] *adj* sem vergonha.

shampoo [ʃæmˈpuː] *n* (*liquid*) xampu *m* (*Br*), champô *m* (*Port*); (*wash*) lavagem *f*.

shandy ['ʃændɪ] *n* cerveja *f* com soda, panaché *m*.

shan't [ʃɑːnt] = **shall not**.

shape [ʃeɪp] *n* forma *f*; **to be in good/bad ~** estar em boa/má forma.

shapeless ['ʃeɪplɪs] *adj* (*clothes*) sem forma.

shapely ['ʃeɪplɪ] *adj* bem feito(-ta).

share [ʃeəʳ] *n* (*part*) parte *f*; (*in company*) ação *f* ◆ *vt* partilhar.

◡ **share out** *vt sep* partilhar.

shareholder ['ʃeəˌhəʊldəʳ] *n* acionista *mf*.

shark [ʃɑːk] *n* tubarão *m*.

sharp [ʃɑːp] *adj* (*blade, needle, teeth*) afiado(-da); (*clear*) nítido(-da); (*quick, intelligent*) perspicaz; (*rise, change, bend*) brusco(-ca); (*painful*) agudo(-da); (*food, taste*) ácido(-da) ◆ *adv* (*exactly*) em ponto.

sharpen ['ʃɑːpn] *vt* (*knife*) afiar; (*pencil*) apontar (*Br*), afiar (*Port*).

sharpener ['ʃɑːpnəʳ] *n* (*for pencil*) apontador *m* (*Br*), apara-lápis *m inv* (*Port*); (*for knife*) amolador *m*.

sharp-eyed [-'aɪd] *adj* perspicaz.

sharply ['ʃɑːplɪ] *adv* (*stand out, differ*) claramente; (*change, stop, criticize*) bruscamente.

shatter ['ʃætəʳ] *vt* (*break*) estilhaçar ◆ *vi* estilhaçar-se.

shattered ['ʃætəd] adj (Brit: inf: tired)
estourado(-da).

shave [ʃeɪv] vt (beard, legs) raspar;
(face) barbear ◆ vi barbear-se ◆ n: to
have a ~ barbear-se, fazer a barba.

shaver ['ʃeɪvə'] n barbeador m,
máquina f de barbear.

shaver point n tomada f (para
máquina de barbear).

shaving brush ['ʃeɪvɪŋ-] n pincel m
para a barba.

shaving cream ['ʃeɪvɪŋ-] n creme m
para a barba.

shaving foam ['ʃeɪvɪŋ-] n espuma f
para a barba.

shavings ['ʃeɪvɪŋz] npl aparas fpl.

shawl [ʃɔːl] n xale m.

she [ʃiː] pron ela; ~'s tall ela é alta.

sheaf [ʃiːf] (pl sheaves) n (of paper,
notes) maço m.

shear [ʃɪə'] (pt -ed, pp -ed OR shorn)
vt (sheep) tosquiar.
❏ shears npl (for gardening) tesoura f
de podar OR de jardim.

sheath [ʃiːθ] n (for knife) bainha f.

sheaves [ʃiːvz] pl → sheaf.

shed [ʃed] (pt & pp shed) n galpão m,
casinha de madeira em fundo de quintal
para guardar ferramentas de jardinagem,
etc. ◆ vt (tears, blood) derramar.

she'd [weak form ʃɪd, strong form ʃiːd]
= she had, she would.

sheen [ʃiːn] n brilho m.

sheep [ʃiːp] (pl inv) n ovelha f, carneiro m.

sheepdog ['ʃiːpdɒg] n cão m pastor.

sheepish ['ʃiːpɪʃ] adj embaraçado
(-da), envergonhado(-da).

sheepskin ['ʃiːpskɪn] adj de pele de
carneiro OR ovelha.

sheer [ʃɪə'] adj (pure, utter) puro(-ra);
(cliff) escarpado(-da); (stockings) fino
(-na).

sheet [ʃiːt] n (for bed) lençol m; (of
paper, metal, wood) folha f; a ~ of glass
um vidro, uma vidraça.

sheik(h) [ʃeɪk] n xeque m.

shelf [ʃelf] (pl shelves) n prateleira
f.

shell [ʃel] n (of egg, nut) casca f; (of oyster, clam, snail) concha f; (of turtle, crab)
carapaça f; (bomb) projétil m.

she'll [ʃiːl] = she will, she shall.

shellfish ['ʃelfɪʃ] n (food) marisco m.

shell suit n (Brit) roupa f de jogging
(de nylon brilhante).

shelter ['ʃeltə'] n abrigo m ◆ vt (protect) abrigar ◆ vi abrigar-se; to take ~
abrigar-se.

sheltered ['ʃeltəd] adj (place) abriga-
do(-da).

shelve [ʃelv] vt (plan, project) arquivar.

shelves [ʃelvz] pl → shelf.

shepherd ['ʃepəd] n pastor m.

shepherd's pie ['ʃepədz-] n empadão
de carne de vaca picada, cebola e especiarias.

sheriff ['ʃerɪf] n (in US) xerife m.

sherry ['ʃerɪ] n xerez m.

she's [ʃiːz] = she is, she has.

Shetland Islands ['ʃetlənd-] npl: the
~ as Ilhas Shetland.

shield [ʃiːld] n (of soldier, policeman)
escudo m ◆ vt proteger.

shift [ʃɪft] n (change) mudança f;
(period of work) turno m ◆ vt (move)
mover ◆ vi (move) mover-se; (change)
mudar.

shilling ['ʃɪlɪŋ] n (Brit) xelim m.

shimmer ['ʃɪmə'] vi tremeluzir, brilhar com luz trêmula.

shin [ʃɪn] n canela f.

shinbone ['ʃɪnbəʊn] n tíbia f.

shine [ʃaɪn] (pt & pp shone) vi brilhar
◆ vt (shoes) lustrar (Br), puxar o lustro
a (Port); (torch) apontar.

shingle ['ʃɪŋgl] n (on beach) seixos
mpl, cascalho m.
❏ shingles n (MED) zona f.

shiny ['ʃaɪnɪ] adj brilhante.

ship [ʃɪp] n navio m; by ~ de navio.

shipbuilding ['ʃɪpbɪldɪŋ] n construção f naval.

shipment ['ʃɪpmənt] n carregamento
m.

shipping ['ʃɪpɪŋ] n (ships) navios mpl.

shipwreck ['ʃɪprek] n (accident) naufrágio m; (wrecked ship) navio m nau-
fragado.

shipyard ['ʃɪpjɑːd] n estaleiro m.

shirk [ʃɜːk] vt fugir de.

shirt [ʃɜːt] n camisa f.

shirtsleeves ['ʃɜːtsliːvz] npl: to be in
(one's) ~ estar em mangas de camisa.

shiver ['ʃɪvə'] vi tremer.

shoal [ʃəʊl] n cardume m.

shock [ʃɒk] n (surprise) choque m;
(force) impacto m ◆ vt chocar; to be in
~ (MED) estar em estado de choque.

shock absorber [-əb,zɔːbə'] n
amortecedor m.

shocking [´ʃɒkɪŋ] adj (very bad) chocante.

shoddy [´ʃɒdɪ] adj (work, goods) de segunda.

shoe [ʃuː] n sapato m.

shoebrush [´ʃuːbrʌʃ] n escova f para sapatos.

shoehorn [´ʃuːhɔːn] n calçadeira f.

shoelace [´ʃuːleɪs] n cardaço m (Br), atacador m (Port).

shoe polish n graxa f.

shoe repairer's [-rɪˌpeərəz] n sapateiro m.

shoe shop n sapataria f.

shone [ʃɒn] pt & pp → shine.

shook [ʃʊk] pt → shake.

shoot [ʃuːt] (pt & pp shot) vt (kill, injure) dar um tiro em; (gun) disparar; (arrow) atirar; (film) filmar ♦ vi (with gun) atirar; (move quickly) passar disparado(-da); (SPORT) rematar ♦ n (of plant) broto m (Br), rebento m (Port).

shooting [´ʃuːtɪŋ] n (killing) assassinato m, morte f (a tiro); (hunting) caça-da f.

shop [ʃɒp] n loja f ♦ vi fazer compras.

shop assistant n (Brit) empregado m (-da f) (de balcão), vendedor m (-ra f).

shopkeeper [´ʃɒpˌkiːpər] n comerciante mf.

shoplifter [´ʃɒpˌlɪftər] n ladrão m (ladra f) de lojas.

shoplifting [´ʃɒpˌlɪftɪŋ] n roubo m em loja.

shopper [´ʃɒpər] n comprador m (-ra f), freguês m (-esa f).

shopping [´ʃɒpɪŋ] n compras fpl; to do the ~ fazer as compras; to go ~ ir às compras.

shopping bag n saco m de compras.

shopping basket n cesto m de compras.

shopping centre n centro m comercial, shopping m.

shopping list n lista f de compras.

shopping mall n centro m comercial.

shopsoiled [´ʃɒpsɔɪld] adj (Brit) danificado(-da).

shop steward n delegado m (-da f) sindical.

shop window n vitrine f, montra f (Port).

shopworn [´ʃɒpwɔːn] (Am) = shopsoiled.

shore [ʃɔːr] n (of river, lake) margem f; (of sea) costa f; on ~ em terra.

shorn [ʃɔːn] pp → shear.

short [ʃɔːt] adj (not tall) baixo(-xa); (in length, time) curto(-ta) ♦ adv (cut hair) curto ♦ n (Brit: drink) bebida f forte; (film) curta-metragem f; to be ~ of sthg (time, money) ter falta de algo; I'm ~ of breath estou sem fôlego; to be ~ for sthg (be abbreviation of) ser o diminutivo de algo; in ~ em resumo.
⊔ **shorts** npl (short trousers) calções mpl; (Am: underpants) cuecas fpl.

shortage [´ʃɔːtɪdʒ] n falta f, escassez f.

shortbread [´ʃɔːtbred] n biscoito m de manteiga.

short-change vt (in shop, restaurant) dar troco a menos a, roubar no troco de; (fig: treat unfairly) enganar, roubar.

short-circuit vi ter um curto-circuito.

shortcomings [´ʃɔːtˌkʌmɪŋz] npl defeitos mpl.

shortcrust pastry [´ʃɔːtkrʌst-] n massa f areada OR brisée.

short cut n atalho m.

shorten [´ʃɔːtn] vt encurtar.

shortfall [´ʃɔːtfɔːl] n: a ~ in/of um déficit em/de.

shorthand [´ʃɔːthænd] n estenografia f.

shorthand typist n (Brit) estenodatilógrafo m (-fa f).

short list n (Brit: for job, prize) lista f de candidatos selecionados.

shortly [´ʃɔːtlɪ] adv (soon) daqui a pouco, em breve; he arrived ~ before me ele chegou (um) pouco antes de mim.

shortsighted [ˌʃɔːt´saɪtɪd] adj (with poor eyesight) míope, curto(-ta) da vista.

short-sleeved [-ˌsliːvd] adj de manga curta.

short-staffed [-´stɑːft] adj: to be ~ estar com falta de pessoal, ter pessoal a menos.

short-stay car park n parque m de estacionamento de curta duração.

short story n conto m.

short-tempered [-´tempəd] adj irritável, com mau gênio.

short-term adj a curto prazo.

short wave n onda f curta.

shot [ʃɒt] pt & pp → shoot ♦ n (of gun)

tiro *m*; *(in football)* remate *m*; *(in tennis, golf etc)* jogada *f*; *(photo)* foto *f*; *(in film)* plano *m*; *(inf: attempt)* tentativa *f*; *(drink)* trago *m*.

shotgun [ˈʃɒtɡʌn] *n* espingarda *f*, caçadeira *f*.

should [ʃʊd] *aux vb* 1. *(expressing desirability)* dever; **we ~ leave now** devíamos ir embora agora. 2. *(asking for advice):* **~ I go too?** você acha que também devo ir? 3. *(expressing probability)* dever; **she ~ be home soon** ela deve estar chegando a casa. 4. *(ought to)* dever; **they ~ have won the match** eles é que deviam ter ganho o jogo. 5. *(fml: in conditionals):* **~ you need anything, call reception** se precisar de algo, ligue para a recepção. 6. *(fml: expressing wish):* **I ~ like to come with you** gostaria de ir contigo.

shoulder [ˈʃəʊldəʳ] *n* *(of person)* ombro *m*; *(of meat)* pá *f*; *(Am: of road)* acostamento *m* *(Br)*, zona *f* de paragem de urgência *(Port)*.

shoulder blade *n* omoplata *f*.

shoulder pad *n* chumaço *m*.

shoulder strap *n* alça *f*.

shouldn't [ˈʃʊdnt] = **should not**.

should've [ˈʃʊdəv] = **should have**.

shout [ʃaʊt] *n* grito *m* ♦ *vt & vi* gritar. ❏ **shout out** *vt sep* gritar.

shouting [ˈʃaʊtɪŋ] *n* gritos *mpl*.

shove [ʃʌv] *vt* *(push)* empurrar; *(put carelessly)* atirar com.

shovel [ˈʃʌvl] *n* pá *f*.

show [ʃəʊ] *(pp* **-ed** OR **shown)** *n* *(at theatre, on TV, radio)* espetáculo *m*; *(exhibition)* exibição *f*; *(of dogs)* concurso *m* ♦ *vt* mostrar; *(prove, demonstrate)* revelar; *(accompany)* acompanhar; *(film, TV programme)* passar ♦ *vi* *(be visible)* ver-se; *(film)* passar; **to ~ sthg to sb** mostrar algo a alguém; **to ~ sb how to do sthg** mostrar a alguém como fazer algo. ❏ **show off** *vi* exibir-se. ❏ **show up** *vi* *(come along)* aparecer; *(be visible)* ver-se.

show business *n* mundo *m* do espetáculo, show business *m*.

showdown [ˈʃəʊdaʊn] *n*: **to have a ~ with sb** resolver cara a cara as diferenças com alguém.

shower [ˈʃaʊəʳ] *n* *(for washing)* chu-

veiro *m*; *(of rain)* aguaceiro *m* ♦ *vi* tomar banho (de chuveiro); **to have a ~** tomar banho (de chuveiro).

shower cap *n* touca *f* de banho.

shower gel *n* gel *m* de banho.

shower unit *n* chuveiro *m* *(compartimento)*.

showing [ˈʃəʊɪŋ] *n* *(of film)* sessão *f*.

show jumping *n* competição *f* hípica de salto.

shown [ʃəʊn] *pp* → **show**.

show-off *n* *(inf)* exibicionista *mf*.

showroom [ˈʃəʊrʊm] *n* salão *m* de exposições.

shrank [ʃræŋk] *pt* → **shrink**.

shrapnel [ˈʃræpnl] *n* estilhaços *mpl*, metralha *f*.

shred [ʃred] *n* *(small piece)* tira *f* ♦ *vt* *(CULIN)* cortar em tiras muito finas; *(paper)* cortar em tiras.

shrewd [ʃruːd] *adj* *(person)* astuto (-ta); *(action, judgment, move)* inteligente.

shriek [ʃriːk] *n* grito *m* ♦ *vi* gritar; **a ~ of laughter** uma gargalhada; **to ~ with laughter** rir às gargalhadas.

shrill [ʃrɪl] *adj* estridente.

shrimp [ʃrɪmp] *n* camarão *m*.

shrine [ʃraɪn] *n* santuário *m*.

shrink [ʃrɪŋk] *(pt* **shrank**, *pp* **shrunk)** *n* *(inf: psychoanalyst)* psicanalista *mf* ♦ *vi* *(become smaller)* encolher; *(diminish)* diminuir.

shrivel [ˈʃrɪvl] *vi*: **to ~ (up)** secar, enrugar.

Shrove Tuesday [ʃrəʊv-] *n* Terça-feira *f* de Carnaval, Dia *m* de Entrudo *(Port)*.

shrub [ʃrʌb] *n* arbusto *m*.

shrug [ʃrʌɡ] *vi* encolher os ombros ♦ *n*: **she gave a ~** ela encolheu os ombros.

shrunk [ʃrʌŋk] *pp* → **shrink**.

shudder [ˈʃʌdəʳ] *vi* *(person):* **to ~ (with)** estremecer (de).

shuffle [ˈʃʌfl] *vt* *(cards)* embaralhar ♦ *vi* *(walk)* andar arrastando os pés.

shut [ʃʌt] *(pt & pp* **shut)** *adj* fechado(-da) ♦ *vt & vi* fechar. ❏ **shut down** *vt sep* fechar. ❏ **shut up** *vi* *(inf: stop talking)* calar-se.

shutter [ˈʃʌtəʳ] *n* *(on window)* persiana *f*; *(on camera)* obturador *m*.

shuttle [ˈʃʌtl] *n* *(plane)* avião *m* *(que faz vôos curtos regulares)*; *(bus)* serviço *m* regular.

shuttlecock [ˈʃʌtlkɒk] *n* peteca *f* (*Br*), volante *m* (*Port*).

shy [ʃaɪ] *adj* tímido(-da).

sibling [ˈsɪblɪŋ] *n* irmão *m* (-mã *f*).

sick [sɪk] *adj* (*ill*) doente; (*nauseous*) mal disposto(-osta); **to be ~** (*vomit*) vomitar; **to feel ~** sentir-se mal disposto; **to be ~ of** (*fed up with*) estar farto de.

sick bag *n* saco posto à disposição dos passageiros em aviões, barcos e ônibus para casos de enjôo.

sickbay [ˈsɪkbeɪ] *n* (*on ship*) enfermaria *f*; (*in school*) gabinete *m* médico.

sickening [ˈsɪknɪŋ] *adj* (*disgusting*) nauseabundo(-da).

sick leave *n* licença *f* por doença (*Br*), baixa *f* (*médica*) (*Port*).

sickly [ˈsɪklɪ] *adj* (*unhealthy*) adoentado(-da); (*nauseating*) enjoativo(-va).

sickness [ˈsɪknɪs] *n* (*illness*) doença *f*.

sick pay *n* auxílio-doença *m* (*Br*), subsídio *m* de doença (*Port*).

side [saɪd] *n* lado *m*; (*of road, river, pitch*) beira *f*; (*of coin*) cara *f*; (*Brit:* TV *channel*) canal *m*; (*page of writing*) página *f* ♦ *adj* (*door, pocket*) lateral; **at the ~ of** ao lado de; **on the other ~** no outro lado; **on this ~** neste lado; **~ by ~** lado a lado.

sideboard [ˈsaɪdbɔːd] *n* aparador *m*.

sideboards [ˈsaɪdbɔːdz] *npl* (*Brit*) suíças *fpl*, patilhas *fpl* (*Port*).

sideburns [ˈsaɪdbɜːnz] *npl* suíças *fpl*, patilhas *fpl* (*Port*).

sidecar [ˈsaɪdkɑːr] *n* side-car *m*.

side dish *n* acompanhamento *m*, guarnição *f*.

side effect *n* efeito *m* secundário, efeito *m* colateral.

sidelight [ˈsaɪdlaɪt] *n* (*Brit*) luz *f* lateral, farolim *m* (*Port*).

sideline [ˈsaɪdlaɪn] *n* (SPORT) linha *f* lateral.

side order *n* acompanhamento *m*, guarnição *f*.

side salad *n* salada *f* (*de acompanhamento*).

sideshow [ˈsaɪdʃəʊ] *n* barraca *f* (*de feira popular ou circo*).

side street *n* travessa *f*.

sidewalk [ˈsaɪdwɔːk] *n* (*Am*) passeio *m*.

sideways [ˈsaɪdweɪz] *adv* de lado.

siege [siːdʒ] *n* cerco *m*.

sieve [sɪv] *n* coador *m*; (*for flour*)

peneira *f* ♦ *vt* coar; (*flour*) peneirar.

sift [sɪft] *vt* (*sieve*) peneirar; (*fig: examine carefully*) estudar ♦ *vi:* **to ~ through sthg** (*evidence, applications*) estudar algo.

sigh [saɪ] *n* suspiro *m* ♦ *vi* suspirar.

sight [saɪt] *n* vista *f*; **at first ~** à primeira vista; **to catch ~ of** ver, avistar; **in ~** à vista; **to lose ~ of** perder de vista; **to be out of ~** (*hidden*) não estar visível; (*far away*) estar longe da vista.

❑ **sights** *npl* (*of country*) vistas *fpl*; (*of city*) locais *mpl* de interesse.

sightseeing [ˈsaɪtˌsiːɪŋ] *n:* **to go ~** fazer turismo.

sightseer [ˈsaɪtˌsiːər] *n* excursionista *mf*, turista *mf*.

sign [saɪn] *n* sinal *m* ♦ *vt* & *vi* assinar; **there's no ~ of her** dela, nem sinal.

❑ **sign in** *vi* (*at hotel, club*) assinar o registro (*ao chegar*).

signal [ˈsɪgnl] *n* sinal *m* ♦ *vi* fazer sinal.

signature [ˈsɪgnətʃər] *n* assinatura *f*.

significance [sɪgˈnɪfɪkəns] *n* significado *m*.

significant [sɪgˈnɪfɪkənt] *adj* significante.

sign language *n* linguagem *f* gestual.

signpost [ˈsaɪnpəʊst] *n* tabuleta *f*, sinal *m*.

sikh [siːk] *n* sikh *mf*, sique *mf*.

silence [ˈsaɪləns] *n* silêncio *m*.

silencer [ˈsaɪlənsər] *n* (*Brit:* AUT) silencioso *m*.

silent [ˈsaɪlənt] *adj* silencioso(-osa).

silhouette [ˌsɪluːˈet] *n* silhueta *f*.

silicon chip *n* chip *m* de silício.

silk [sɪlk] *n* seda *f*.

silky [ˈsɪlkɪ] *adj* acetinado(-da).

sill [sɪl] *n* bordo *m*.

silly [ˈsɪlɪ] *adj* bobo(-ba), tonto(-ta) (*Port*).

silver [ˈsɪlvər] *n* prata *f*; (*coins*) moedas *fpl* ♦ *adj* de prata.

silver foil *n* folha *f* OR papel *m* de alumínio.

silver-plated [-ˈpleɪtɪd] *adj* banhado(-da) a prata.

silverware [ˈsɪlvəweər] *n* (*objects made of silver*) prata *f*; (*Am: cutlery*) talheres *mpl*, faqueiro *m*.

similar [ˈsɪmɪlər] *adj* semelhante; **to be ~ to** ser semelhante a.

similarity [ˌsɪmɪˈlærətɪ] *n* semelhança *f*.

similarly [ˈsɪmɪləlɪ] *adv* igualmente.

simmer [ˈsɪmərˈ] *vi* cozinhar em fogo brando.

simple [ˈsɪmpl] *adj* simples (*inv*).

simple-minded *adj* simplório(-ria).

simplify [ˈsɪmplɪfaɪ] *vt* simplificar.

simply [ˈsɪmplɪ] *adv* simplesmente; (*easily*) facilmente.

simulate [ˈsɪmjʊleɪt] *vt* simular.

simultaneous [*Brit* ˌsɪməlˈteɪnjəs, *Am* ˌsaɪməlˈteɪnjəs] *adj* simultâneo(-nea).

simultaneously [*Brit* ˌsɪməlˈteɪnjəslɪ, *Am* ˌsaɪməlˈteɪnjəslɪ] *adv* simultaneamente.

sin [sɪn] *n* pecado *m* ◆ *vi* pecar.

since [sɪns] *adv* desde então ◆ *prep* desde ◆ *conj* (*in time*) desde que; (*as*) visto que; **ever ~** *prep* desde ◆ *conj* desde que.

sincere [sɪnˈsɪərˈ] *adj* sincero(-ra).

sincerely [sɪnˈsɪəlɪ] *adv* sinceramente; **Yours ~** ≃ Com os melhores cumprimentos.

sincerity [sɪnˈserətɪ] *n* sinceridade *f*.

sing [sɪŋ] (*pt* sang, *pp* sung) *vt & vi* cantar.

singe [sɪndʒ] *vt* chamuscar.

singer [ˈsɪŋərˈ] *n* cantor *m* (-ra *f*).

singing [ˈsɪŋɪŋ] *n* canto *m*.

single [ˈsɪŋgl] *adj* (*just one*) único(-ca); (*not married*) solteiro(-ra) ◆ *n* (*Brit: ticket*) bilhete *m* de ida; (*record*) single *m*; **every ~** cada um (uma) de; **every ~ day** todos os dias.

❏ **singles** *n* (*in tennis, badminton, pool*) simples *f inv* (*Br*), individuais *mpl* (*Port*) ◆ *adj* (*bar, club*) para solteiros.

single bed *n* cama *f* de solteiro.

single cream *n* (*Brit*) creme *m* magro fresco (*Br*), natas *fpl* frescas líquidas (*Port*).

single file *n*: **in ~** em fila indiana.

single-handed [-ˈhændɪd] *adv* sozinho(-nha), sem ajuda.

single parent *n* (*mother*) mãe *f* solteira; (*father*) pai *m* solteiro.

single room *n* quarto *m* de solteiro.

single track road *n* estrada *f* de uma só faixa OR via.

singular [ˈsɪŋgjʊlərˈ] *n* singular; **in the ~** no singular.

sinister [ˈsɪnɪstərˈ] *adj* sinistro(-tra).

sink [sɪŋk] (*pt* sank, *pp* sunk) *n* (*in kitchen*) pia *f*, lava-louça *m* (*Port*);

(*washbasin*) pia *f* ◆ *vi* (*in water, value*) afundar-se; (*in mud*) enterrar-se.

sink unit *n* pia *f* (*Br*), lava-louça *m* (*Port*).

sinner [ˈsɪnərˈ] *n* pecador *m* (-ra *f*).

sinuses [ˈsaɪnəsɪz] *npl* seios *mpl* nasais.

sip [sɪp] *n* gole *m* ◆ *vt* sorver.

siphon [ˈsaɪfn] *n* sifão *m* ◆ *vt* tirar com sifão.

sir [sɜːrˈ] *n* Senhor; **Dear Sir** Caro Senhor, Exmo. Sr.; **Sir Richard Blair** Sir Richard Blair.

siren [ˈsaɪərən] *n* sirene *f*.

sirloin steak [ˌsɜːlɔɪn-] *n* bife *m* de lombo de vaca.

sister [ˈsɪstərˈ] *n* (*relative*) irmã *f*; (*Brit: nurse*) enfermeira *f* chefe.

sister-in-law *n* cunhada *f*.

sit [sɪt] (*pt & pp* sat) *vi* sentar-se; (*be situated*) ficar ◆ *vt* (*to place*) sentar, colocar; (*Brit: exam*) fazer; **to be sitting** estar sentado.

❏ **sit down** *vi* sentar-se; **to be sitting down** estar sentado.

❏ **sit up** *vi* (*after lying down*) sentar-se; (*stay up late*) ficar acordado.

sitcom [ˈsɪtkɒm] *n* (*inf*) comédia *f* de situação.

site [saɪt] *n* (*place*) local *m*; (*building site*) obra *f*.

sitting [ˈsɪtɪŋ] *n* (*serving of meal*) turno *m*; (*session*) sessão *f*.

sitting room [ˈsɪtɪŋ-] *n* sala *f* de estar.

situated [ˈsɪtjʊeɪtɪd] *adj*: **to be ~** estar OR ficar situado(-da).

situation [ˌsɪtjʊˈeɪʃn] *n* situação *f*; **"~s vacant"** "ofertas de emprego".

six [sɪks] *num adj* seis (*inv*) ◆ *num n* seis *m inv*; **to be ~ (years old)** ter seis anos (de idade); **it's ~ (o'clock)** são seis horas; **a hundred and ~** cento e seis; **~ Hill St** Hill St, n° 6; **it's minus ~ (degrees)** estão seis graus negativos OR abaixo de zero; **~ out of ten** seis em dez.

sixteen [sɪksˈtiːn] *num* dezesseis (*Br*), dezasseis (*Port*), → **six**.

sixteenth [sɪksˈtiːnθ] *num* décimo sexto (décima sexta), → **sixth**.

sixth [sɪksθ] *num adj* sexto(-ta) ◆ *num pron* sexto *m* (-ta *f*) ◆ *num n* (*fraction*) sexto *m* ◆ *num adv* (*in race, competition*) em sexto (lugar); **the ~ (of September)** o dia seis (de setembro).

sixth form n (Brit) curso secundário de preparação para os "A levels", exames de acesso ao ensino superior.

sixth-form college n (Brit) escola secundária normal ou técnica.

sixtieth ['sɪkstɪəθ] num sexagésimo (-ma), → sixth.

sixty ['sɪkstɪ] num sessenta, → six.

size [saɪz] n (of room, bed, building, country) tamanho m; (of clothes, shoes, hats) número m; **what ~ do you take?** (of clothes) que tamanho OR número você veste?; (of shoes) que número você calça?; **what ~ is this?** que tamanho OR número é?

sizeable ['saɪzəbl] adj considerável.

sizzle ['sɪzl] vi chiar.

skate [skeɪt] n (ice skate, roller skate) patim m; (fish: pl inv) raia f ◆ vi (ice-skate) patinar; (roller-skate) andar de patins.

skateboard ['skeɪtbɔːd] n skate m.

skater ['skeɪtər] n patinador m (-ra f).

skating ['skeɪtɪŋ] n: **to go ~** (ice-skating) ir patinar; (roller-skating) ir andar de patins.

skating rink n rink m OR rinque m de patinagem.

skeleton ['skelɪtn] n (of body) esque-leto m.

skeptic ['skeptɪk] (Am) = **sceptic**.

sketch [sketʃ] n (drawing) esboço m; (humorous) sketch m ◆ vt (draw) esboçar.

sketchbook ['sketʃbʊk] n caderno m de desenho.

sketchpad ['sketʃpæd] n bloco m de desenho.

skewer ['skjuər] n espeto m (para churrasco).

ski [skiː] (pt & pp **skied**, cont **skiing**) n esqui m, ski m (Port) ◆ vi esquiar.

ski boots npl botas fpl de esquiar.

skid [skɪd] n derrapagem f ◆ vi derra-par.

skier ['skiːər] n esquiador m (-ra f).

skiing ['skiːɪŋ] n esqui m, ski m (Port); **to go ~** ir fazer esqui, ir esquiar; **a ~ holiday** umas férias fazendo esqui.

ski jump n (slope) pista f para saltos de OR com esquis; (event) salto m de OR com esquis.

skilful ['skɪlfʊl] adj (Brit) experiente, hábil.

ski lift n teleférico m, telesqui m.

skill [skɪl] n (ability) habilidade f; (tech-

nique) técnica f.

skilled [skɪld] adj (worker, job) espe-cializado(-da); (driver, chef) experiente, bom (boa).

skillful ['skɪlfʊl] (Am) = **skilful**.

skimmed milk ['skɪmd-] n leite m desnatado (Br), leite m magro.

skimp [skɪmp] vi: **to ~ on sthg** (on food, material) economizar em algo.

skimpy ['skɪmpɪ] adj (meal) parco(-ca); (skirt, dress) minúsculo(-la); (facts) insuficiente.

skin [skɪn] n pele f; (on milk) nata f.

skin diving n mergulho m (sem macacão ou escafandro, apenas com tubo respiratório).

skin freshener [-freʃnər] n tônico m (para a pele).

skinny ['skɪnɪ] adj magricela.

skin-tight adj muito justo(-ta).

skip [skɪp] vi (with rope) pular corda (Br), saltar à corda (Port); (jump) salti-tar ◆ vt (omit) passar na frente ◆ n (con-tainer) container m (grande para desperdícios).

ski pants npl calça f de esquiar.

ski pass n passe m (para esquiar).

ski pole n vara f de esqui.

skipper ['skɪpər] n capitão m (-tã f).

skipping rope ['skɪpɪŋ-] n corda f de pular.

skirmish ['skɜːmɪʃ] n escaramuça f.

skirt [skɜːt] n saia f.

ski slope n pista f de esqui.

ski tow n teleski m.

skittles ['skɪtlz] n (game) boliche m (Br), bowling m (Port).

skive [skaɪv] vi (Brit: inf): **to ~ (off)** faltar.

skull [skʌl] n crânio m.

skunk [skʌŋk] n gambá m (Br), doni-nha f fedorenta (Port).

sky [skaɪ] n céu m.

skylight ['skaɪlaɪt] n clarabóia f.

skyscraper ['skaɪ,skreɪpər] n arranha-céu m.

slab [slæb] n (of stone, concrete) laje f.

slack [slæk] adj (rope) frouxo(-xa); (careless) negligente; (not busy) calmo (-ma), parado(-da).

slacken ['slækn] vt & vi afrouxar.

slacks [slæks] npl calça f (Br), calças fpl (Port).

slam [slæm] vt bater com ◆ vi bater.

slander ['slɑːndər] n calúnia f.

slang [slæŋ] *n* gíria *f*.

slant [slɑːnt] *n (slope)* inclinação *f* ♦ *vi* inclinar-se.

slanting ['slɑːntɪŋ] *adj* inclinado(-da).

slap [slæp] *n (on face)* bofetada *f*; *(on back)* palmada *f* ♦ *vt (person, face)* esbofetear, dar uma bofetada em; *(back)* dar uma palmada em.

slapstick ['slæpstɪk] *n* palhaçada *f*.

slap-up *adj (Brit: inf)*: **a ~ meal** um banquete.

slash [slæʃ] *vt (cut)* cortar; *(fig: prices)* cortar em ♦ *n (written symbol)* barra *f* (oblíqua).

slate [sleɪt] *n (rock)* ardósia *f*; *(on roof)* telha *f* (de ardósia).

slaughter ['slɔːtəʳ] *vt* chacinar, massacrar.

slaughterhouse ['slɔːtəhaʊs, *pl* -haʊzɪz] *n* matadouro *m*.

slave [sleɪv] *n* escravo *m* (-va *f*).

slavery ['sleɪvərɪ] *n* escravatura *f*.

sleazy ['sliːzɪ] *adj* de má reputação.

sled [sled] = **sledge**.

sledge [sledʒ] *n* trenó *m*.

sledgehammer ['sledʒˌhæməʳ] *n* marreta *f*.

sleep [sliːp] *(pt & pp* **slept)** *n (nap)* sono *m* ♦ *vi* dormir ♦ *vt*: **the house ~s six** a casa tem lugar para seis pessoas dormirem; **try to get some ~** vê se você dorme; **I couldn't get to ~** não conseguia adormecer; **to go to ~** adormecer; **did you ~ well?** você dormiu bem?; **to ~ with sb** dormir com alguém.

sleeper ['sliːpəʳ] *n (train)* trem *m* noturno *(com couchettes ou camas)*; *(sleeping car)* vagão-cama *m (Br)*, carruagem-cama *f (Port)*; *(Brit: on railway track)* dormente *m (Br)*, travessa *f (Port)*; *(Brit: earring)* argola *f*.

sleeping bag ['sliːpɪŋ-] *n* saco *m* de dormir *(Br)*, saco-cama *m (Port)*.

sleeping car ['sliːpɪŋ-] *n* vagão-cama *m (Br)*, carruagem-cama *f (Port)*.

sleeping pill ['sliːpɪŋ-] *n* comprimido *m* para dormir.

sleeping policeman ['sliːpɪŋ-] *n (Brit)* rampa *f*.

sleepless ['sliːplɪs] *adj* sem dormir.

sleepwalk ['sliːpwɔːk] *vi (be a sleepwalker)* ser sonâmbulo(-la); *(walk in one's sleep)* andar durante o sono.

sleepy ['sliːpɪ] *adj (person)* sonolento(-ta); **I'm ~** estou com sono.

sleet [sliːt] *n* chuva *f* com neve ♦ *v impers*: **it's ~ing** está chovendo neve.

sleeve [sliːv] *n (of garment)* manga *f*; *(of record)* capa *f*.

sleeveless ['sliːvlɪs] *adj* sem mangas.

sleigh [sleɪ] *n* trenó *m*.

slender ['slendəʳ] *adj (person, waist)* esbelto(-ta); *(fingers, neck)* fino(-na); *(resources, means)* escasso(-a); *(hope, chance)* pequeno(-na).

slept [slept] *pt & pp* → **sleep**.

slice [slaɪs] *n* fatia *f* ♦ *vt* cortar.

sliced bread [slaɪst-] *n* pão *m* em fatias.

slick [slɪk] *adj (performance, operation)* bem conseguido(-da); *(pej: salesman)* com muita lábia ♦ *n* mancha *f* negra *(Br)*, maré *f* negra *(Port)*.

slide [slaɪd] *(pt & pp* **slid** [slɪd]) *n (in playground)* escorrega *m*; *(of photograph)* slide *m*, diapositivo *m*; *(Brit: hair slide)* travessão *m*, grampo *m (Br)*, gancho *m (Port)* ♦ *vi (slip)* escorregar.

sliding door [ˌslaɪdɪŋ-] *n* porta *f* deslizante OR corrediça.

slight [slaɪt] *adj (minor)* pequeno(-na); **the ~est** o menor (a menor), o mínimo (a mínima); **not in the ~est** absolutamente nada.

slightly ['slaɪtlɪ] *adv* ligeiramente.

slim [slɪm] *adj (person, waist)* delgado(-da); *(book)* fino(-na) ♦ *vi* emagrecer.

slime [slaɪm] *n (in pond etc)* lodo *m*; *(of snail, slug)* baba *f*.

slimming ['slɪmɪŋ] *n* emagrecimento *m*.

sling [slɪŋ] *(pt & pp* **slung)** *vt (inf: throw)* atirar ♦ *n*: **to have one's arm in a ~** estar com o braço na tipóia *(Br)*, trazer o braço ao peito *(Port)*.

slip [slɪp] *vi (slide)* escorregar ♦ *n (mistake)* deslize *m*; *(of paper)* pedaço *m*; *(half-petticoat)* anágua *f (Br)*, saiote *m (Port)*; *(full-length petticoat)* combinação *f*.

❑ **slip up** *vi (make a mistake)* cometer um deslize.

slipped disc [slɪpt-] *n* hérnia *f* discal.

slipper ['slɪpəʳ] *n* chinelo *m* (de quarto); *(winterweight)* pantufa *f*.

slippery ['slɪpərɪ] *adj* escorregadio (-dia).

slip road *n (Brit) (for joining motorway)* acesso *m*; *(for leaving motorway)* saída *f*.

slip-up n (inf) deslize m.

slit [slɪt] n racha f.

slob [slɒb] n (inf) (dirty) porco m (porca f); (lazy) lambão m (-bona f).

slogan [ˈsləʊgən] n slogan m.

slope [sləʊp] n (incline) inclinação f; (hill) encosta f; (for skiing) pista f ♦ vi (path, hill) descer; (floor, roof, shelf) ser inclinado(-da).

sloping [ˈsləʊpɪŋ] adj inclinado(-da).

sloppy [ˈslɒpɪ] adj (careless) descuidado(-da).

slot [slɒt] n ranhura f.

slot machine n (vending machine) distribuidora f automática; (for gambling) slot machine f.

Slovakia [sləˈvækɪə] n Eslováquia f.

slow [sləʊ] adj lento(-ta); (clock, watch) atrasado(-da) ♦ adv lentamente; "slow" (sign on road) = "reduza a velocidade"; a ~ train ~ um trem regional. ❏ **slow down** vt sep & vi abrandar, afrouxar.

slowly [ˈsləʊlɪ] adv lentamente.

slug [slʌg] n (animal) lesma f.

sluggish [ˈslʌgɪʃ] adj (person) molengão(-gona); (reaction, business) lento(-ta).

sluice [sluːs] n comporta f.

slum [slʌm] n (building) barraco m, barracão m.
❏ **slums** npl (district) favela f (Br), bairro m de lata (Port).

slumber [ˈslʌmbəʳ] n sono m.

slung [slʌŋ] pt & pp → **sling**.

slush [slʌʃ] n neve f meio derretida.

sly [slaɪ] adj manhoso(-osa).

smack [smæk] n (slap) palmada f ♦ vt dar uma palmada em.

small [smɔːl] adj pequeno(-na).

small ads npl (Brit) classificados mpl.

small change n troco m, dinheiro m miúdo OR trocado.

small hours npl madrugada f; in the ~ de madrugada.

smallpox [ˈsmɔːlpɒks] n varíola f.

small talk n conversa f banal.

smarmy [ˈsmɑːmɪ] adj bajulador(-ra).

smart [smɑːt] adj (elegant, posh) elegante; (clever) esperto(-ta).

smart card n smart card m, cartão com memória electrônica.

smarten [ˈsmɑːtn] : **smarten up** vt sep (appearance) melhorar; (room) arrumar; to ~ o.s up vestir-se melhor.

smash [smæʃ] n (SPORT) smash m; (inf: car crash) desastre m, acidente m ♦ vt (plate, window) partir ♦ vi (plate, vase etc) partir-se.

smashing [ˈsmæʃɪŋ] adj (Brit: inf) chocante (Br), bestial (Port).

smattering [ˈsmætərɪŋ] n: I have a ~ of Portuguese só sei umas palavras em português.

smear [smɪəʳ] n (slander) calúnia f ♦ vt (smudge) borrar; (spread): to ~ sthg onto sthg espalhar algo em algo; he ~ed his chest with oil ele espalhou óleo no peito.

smear test n preventivo m (Br), esfregaço m (Port).

smell [smel] (pt & pp -ed OR smelt) n cheiro m ♦ vt cheirar ♦ vi (have odour) cheirar; (have bad odour) cheirar mal; to ~ of sthg cheirar a algo.

smelly [ˈsmelɪ] adj mal cheiroso(-osa).

smelt [smelt] pt & pp → **smell**.

smile [smaɪl] n sorriso m ♦ vi sorrir.

smirk [smɜːk] n sorriso m falso.

smock [smɒk] n bata f.

smog [smɒg] n smog m, poluição f.

smoke [sməʊk] n (from fire, cigarette) fumaça f (Br), fumo m (Port) ♦ vt & vi fumar; to have a ~ fumar um cigarro.

smoked [sməʊkt] adj (meat, fish) defumado(-da); (cheese) curado(-da).

smoked salmon n salmão m defumado.

smoker [ˈsməʊkəʳ] n (person) fumante mf (Br), fumador m (-ra f) (Port).

smoking [ˈsməʊkɪŋ] n: "no ~" "proibido fumar".

smoking area n área f para fumantes.

smoking compartment n compartimento m para fumantes.

smoky [ˈsməʊkɪ] adj (room) enfumaçado(-da).

smolder [ˈsməʊldəʳ] (Am) = **smoulder**.

smooth [smuːð] adj (surface, road) plano(-na); (skin) macio(-cia); (takeoff, landing, wine) suave; (journey, flight) sem incidentes; (life) tranqüilo(-la); (mixture, liquid) homogêneo(-nea), cremoso(-osa); (pej: suave) meloso(-osa).
❏ **smooth down** vt sep alisar.

smother [ˈsmʌðəʳ] vt (cover) cobrir.

smoulder [ˈsməʊldəʳ] vi (Brit) (fire) arder lentamente (sem chama).

smudge [smʌdʒ] *n* mancha *f*.

smug [smʌg] *adj* satisfeito consigo próprio (satisfeita consigo própria).

smuggle [ˈsmʌgl] *vt* contrabandear; **to ~ in** *(sneak in)* introduzir clandestinamente.

smuggler [ˈsmʌglər] *n* contrabandista *mf*.

snack [snæk] *n* lanche *m*.

snack bar *n* lanchonete *f (Br)*, snack-bar *m (Port)*.

snag [snæg] *n (small problem)* pequeno problema *m*, inconveniente *m* ◆ *vi*: **to ~ (on sthg)** prender-se (em algo).

snail [sneɪl] *n* caracol *m*.

snake [sneɪk] *n* cobra *f*.

snap [snæp] *vt & vi (break)* partir ◆ *n (inf: photo)* foto *f*; *(Brit: card game)* = guerra *f*.

snapshot [ˈsnæpʃɒt] *n* fotografia *f*, foto *f*.

snare [sneər] *n* armadilha *f*.

snarl [snɑːl] *n* rosnadela *f* ◆ *vi (animal)* rosnar.

snatch [snætʃ] *vt (grab)* arrancar à força; *(steal)* roubar.

sneak [sniːk] *(Brit pt & pp* -**ed**, *Am pt & pp* -**ed** OR **snuck**) *n (Brit: inf)* queixinhas *mf inv* ◆ *vi*: **to ~ in/out** entrar/sair às escondidas OR sorrateiramente; **to ~ up on sb** surpreender OR assustar alguém.

sneakers [ˈsniːkəz] *npl (Am)* tênis *mpl*, sapatilhas *fpl*.

sneer [snɪər] *n* riso *m* sarcástico OR de escarninho ◆ *vi (smile unpleasantly)* sorrir desdenhosamente.

sneeze [sniːz] *n* espirro *m* ◆ *vi* espirrar.

sniff [snɪf] *vi (from cold, crying)* fungar ◆ *vt* cheirar.

snigger [ˈsnɪgər] *n* risinho *m* (dissimulado) ◆ *vi* rir furtivamente.

snip [snɪp] *vt* cortar (com tesoura), dar tesouradas em.

sniper [ˈsnaɪpər] *n* franco-atirador *m* (-ra *f*).

snippet [ˈsnɪpɪt] *n*: **I only heard ~s of their conversation** só ouvi trechos da conversa deles.

snivel [ˈsnɪvl] *vi* choramingar.

snob [snɒb] *n* snobe *mf*.

snobbish [ˈsnɒbɪʃ] *adj* snobe, pretencioso(-osa).

snobby [ˈsnɒbɪ] = **snobbish**.

snog [snɒg] *vi (Brit: inf)* beijar-se.

snooker [ˈsnuːkər] *n* sinuca *f (Br)*, snooker *m (Port)*.

snooze [snuːz] *n* soneca *f*.

snore [snɔːr] *vi* roncar, ressonar.

snorkel [ˈsnɔːkl] *n* respirador *m*, tubo *m* respiratório.

snort [snɔːt] *vi* fungar.

snout [snaut] *n* focinho *m*.

snow [snəu] *n* neve *f* ◆ *v impers*: **it's ~ing** está nevando.

snowball [ˈsnəubɔːl] *n* bola *f* de neve.

snowboarding [ˈsnəuˌbɔːdɪŋ] *n*: **to go ~** fazer snowboarding.

snowbound [ˈsnəubaund] *adj* bloqueado(-da) pela neve.

snowdrift [ˈsnəudrɪft] *n* monte *m* de neve *(formado pelo vento)*.

snowdrop [ˈsnəudrɒp] *n* campainha-branca *f*.

snowfall [ˈsnəufɔːl] *n (fall of snow)* nevada *f (Br)*, nevão *m (Port)*; *(amount)* queda *f* de neve.

snowflake [ˈsnəufleɪk] *n* floco *m* de neve.

snowman [ˈsnəumæn] *(pl* -**men** [-men]) *n* boneco-de-neve *m*.

snowplough [ˈsnəuplau] *n* máquina *f* para remoção de neve.

snowshoe [ˈsnəuʃuː] *n* raquete *f* de neve.

snowstorm [ˈsnəustɔːm] *n* tempestade *f* de neve.

snub [snʌb] *n* desfeita *f* ◆ *vt* ignorar.

snuck [snʌk] *pp* → **sneak**.

snug [snʌg] *adj (person)* aconchegado(-da); *(place)* aconchegante.

so [səu] *adv* 1. *(emphasizing degree)* tão; **don't be ~ stupid!** não seja tão idiota!; **it's ~ difficult (that ...)** é tão difícil (que ...); **~ much** tanto(-ta); **~ many** tantos(-tas).
2. *(referring back)*: **I don't think ~** acho que não; **I'm afraid ~** receio que sim; **~ you knew already** então você já sabia; **if ~** nesse caso.
3. *(also)* também; **~ do I** eu também.
4. *(in this way)* deste modo, assim.
5. *(expressing agreement)*: **~ there is** pois há, é verdade.
6. *(in phrases)*: **or ~** mais ou menos; **~ as** para; **~ that** para.
◆ *conj* 1. *(therefore)* por isso; **I'm away next week – I won't be there** não vou estar aqui na semana que vem, por isso não estarei presente.
2. *(summarizing)* então; **~ what have**

you been up to? então, o que é que você tem feito?
3. (in phrases): **~ what?** (inf) e depois?; **~ there!** (inf) pronto!, nada a fazer!

soak [səʊk] vt (leave in water) pôr de molho; (make very wet) ensopar, empapar ◆ vi: **to ~ through sthg** ensopar algo.

❏ **soak up** vt sep absorver.

soaked [səʊkt] adj encharcado(-da), ensopado(-da).

soaking ['səʊkɪŋ] adj encharcado (-da), ensopado(-da).

soap [səʊp] n sabonete m; (for clothes) sabão m.

soap opera n novela f (Br), telenovela f.

soap powder n sabão m em pó (Br), detergente m para a roupa (Port).

soar [sɔːr] vi (bird) pairar, planar; (balloon, kite) elevar-se no ar; (price) aumentar (repentinamente); (temperature) elevar-se (repentinamente); (unemployment) crescer a um ritmo acelerado.

sob [sɒb] n soluço m ◆ vi soluçar.

sober ['səʊbər] adj sóbrio(-bria).

so-called [-kɔːld] adj (misleadingly named) pseudo (pseuda), suposto (-posta); (widely known as) assim chamado(-da).

soccer ['sɒkər] n futebol m.

sociable ['səʊʃəbl] adj sociável.

social ['səʊʃl] adj social.

social club n clube m.

socialism ['səʊʃəlɪzm] n socialismo m.

socialist ['səʊʃəlɪst] adj socialista ◆ n socialista mf.

socialize ['səʊʃəlaɪz] vi: **to ~ (with sb)** confraternizar (com alguém).

social life n vida f social.

social security n previdência f social (Br), segurança f social (Port).

social services npl previdência f social (Br), segurança f social (Port).

social worker n assistente mf social.

society [sə'saɪətɪ] n sociedade f.

sociology [ˌsəʊsɪ'ɒlədʒɪ] n sociologia f.

sock [sɒk] n meia f, peúga f (Port).

socket ['sɒkɪt] n (for plug) tomada f, ficha f (Port); (for light bulb) casquilho m.

soda ['səʊdə] n (soda water) água f gaseificada OR com gás; (Am: fizzy

drink) refrigerante m.

soda water n água f gaseificada OR com gás.

sofa ['səʊfə] n sofá m.

sofa bed n sofá-cama m.

Sofia ['səʊfjə] n Sófia s.

soft [sɒft] adj (bed, food) mole; (skin, fur, fabric) macio(-cia), suave; (breeze, sound, tap) ligeiro(-ra); (voice) doce; (footsteps) leve.

soft cheese n queijo m cremoso.

soft drink n refrigerante m.

soften ['sɒfn] vt (skin, fabric) amaciar; (butter) amolecer; (blow, impact, effect) amortecer ◆ vi (skin, fabric) ficar mais macio(-cia); (butter) amolecer; (attitude) tornar-se mais brando(-da).

softly ['sɒftlɪ] adv (touch) delicadamente; (move) sem fazer barulho; (speak, sing) em voz baixa.

soft-spoken adj: **she's very ~** ela tem uma voz muito doce.

software ['sɒftweər] n software m.

soggy ['sɒgɪ] adj mole, empapado (-da).

soil [sɔɪl] n terra f.

soiled [sɔɪld] adj sujo(-ja).

solarium [sə'leərɪəm] n solário m, solarium m.

solar panel ['səʊlə-] n painel m solar.

sold [səʊld] pt & pp → **sell**.

solder ['səʊldər] n solda f ◆ vt soldar.

soldier ['səʊldʒər] n soldado m.

sold out adj esgotado(-da).

sole [səʊl] adj (only) adj único(-ca) ◆ n (of shoe) sola f; (of foot) planta f; (fish: pl inv) linguado m.

solemn ['sɒləm] adj solene.

solicitor [sə'lɪsɪtər] n (Brit) solicitador m (-ra f), advogado que apenas pode atuar nos tribunais de primeira instância.

solid ['sɒlɪd] adj sólido(-da); (chair, wall) resistente; (rock, gold, oak) maciço(-ça).

solidarity [ˌsɒlɪ'dærətɪ] n solidariedade f.

solitary ['sɒlɪtrɪ] adj solitário(-ria).

solitude ['sɒlɪtjuːd] n solidão f.

solo ['səʊləʊ] (pl -s) n solo m; **"~ m/cs"** (traffic sign) sinal indicando que no local apenas podem estacionar veículos de duas rodas.

soloist ['səʊləʊɪst] n solista mf.

soluble ['sɒljʊbl] adj solúvel.

solution [sə'luːʃn] n solução f.

solve [sɒlv] *vt* resolver.

solvent ['sɒlvənt] *adj (FIN)* dissolvente ◆ *n (substance)* dissolvente *m*.

some [sʌm] *adj* **1.** *(certain, large amount of)* algum (alguma); ~ **meat** algum carne; ~ **money** algum dinheiro; **I had ~ difficulty getting here** tive algumas dificuldades para chegar aqui. **2.** *(certain, large number of)* alguns (algumas); ~ **sweets** alguns doces; ~ **people** algumas pessoas; **I've known him for ~ years** já o conheço há alguns anos. **3.** *(not all)* alguns (algumas); ~ **jobs are better paid than others** alguns empregos são mais bem pagos que outros. **4.** *(in imprecise statements)* um (uma) ... qualquer; ~ **woman phoned** telefonou uma mulher qualquer. ◆ *pron* **1.** *(certain amount)* algum *m* (alguma *f*), parte *f*; **can I have ~?** posso ficar com algum OR parte?; ~ **of the money** algum dinheiro, parte do dinheiro. **2.** *(certain number)* alguns *mpl* (algumas *fpl*); **can I have ~?** posso ficar com alguns?; ~ **(of them) left early** alguns (deles) foram-se embora cedo. ◆ *adv (approximately)* aproximadamente; **there were ~ 7,000 people there** havia umas 7000 pessoas.

somebody ['sʌmbədɪ] = **someone**.

someday ['sʌmdeɪ] *adv* algum dia.

somehow ['sʌmhaʊ] *adv (some way or other)* de uma maneira ou de outra; *(for some reason)* por alguma razão; ~ **I don't think he'll come** tenho a impressão de que ele não virá.

someone ['sʌmwʌn] *pron* alguém.

someplace ['sʌmpleɪs] *(Am)* = **somewhere**.

somersault ['sʌməsɔːlt] *n* cambalhota *f*.

something ['sʌmθɪŋ] *pron* algo, alguma coisa; **it's really ~** é demais; **or ~** *(inf)* ou (qualquer) coisa parecida; ~ **like** *(approximately)* uns (umas), qualquer coisa como.

sometime ['sʌmtaɪm] *adv:* ~ **in June** em junho.

sometimes ['sʌmtaɪmz] *adv* às OR por vezes.

someway ['sʌmweɪ] *(Am)* = **somehow**.

somewhat ['sʌmwɒt] *adv* um pouco.

somewhere ['sʌmweəʳ] *adv (in unspecified place)* em algum lugar, em alguma parte; *(to specified place)* a alguma parte; ~ **around** OR **between** *(approximately)* aproximadamente.

son [sʌn] *n* filho *m*.

song [sɒŋ] *n* canção *f*.

son-in-law *n* genro *m*.

sonnet ['sɒnɪt] *n* soneto *m*.

soon [suːn] *adv (in a short time)* em breve; *(early)* cedo; **how ~ can you do it?** para quando é que estará pronto?; **as ~ as** assim que; **as ~ as possible** o mais cedo possível, assim que for possível; ~ **after** pouco depois; ~**er or later** mais cedo ou mais tarde.

soot [sʊt] *n* fuligem *f*.

soothe [suːð] *vt* acalmar.

sophisticated [səˈfɪstɪkeɪtɪd] *adj* sofisticado(-da).

soporific [ˌsɒpəˈrɪfɪk] *adj* soporífero(-ra).

sopping ['sɒpɪŋ] *adj:* ~ **(wet)** encharcado(-da), ensopado(-da).

soppy ['sɒpɪ] *adj (inf) (book, film)* sentimental; *(person)* piegas *(inv)*.

soprano [səˈprɑːnəʊ] *(pl* **-nos** OR **-ni** [-niː]*) n* soprano *mf*.

sorbet ['sɔːbeɪ] *n* sorvete *m* de frutas.

sorcerer ['sɔːsərəʳ] *n* feiticeiro *m*.

sordid ['sɔːdɪd] *adj* sórdido(-da).

sore [sɔːʳ] *adj (painful)* dolorido(-da); *(Am: inf: angry)* zangado(-da) ◆ *n* ferida *f*; **to have a ~ throat** estar com dor de garganta.

sorrow ['sɒrəʊ] *n* tristeza *f*.

sorry ['sɒrɪ] *adj:* **he isn't even ~** ele nem sequer está arrependido; **I'm ~!** desculpe!; **I'm ~ I'm late** desculpem o atraso; **I'm ~ about the mess** desculpe a confusão; **I'm ~ you didn't get the job** sinto muito que você não tenha conseguido o emprego; ~? *(asking for repetition)* perdão?; **to feel ~ for sb** sentir pena de alguém.

sort [sɔːt] *n* tipo *m* ◆ *vt* organizar; ~ **of** *(more or less)* mais ou menos.

❑ **sort out** *vt sep (classify)* organizar; *(resolve)* resolver.

so-so *adj (inf)* mais ou menos ◆ *adv (inf)* assim assim.

soufflé ['suːfleɪ] *n* suflê *m (Br)*, soufflé *m (Port)*.

sought [sɔːt] *pt & pp* → **seek**.

soul [səʊl] *n (spirit)* alma *f*; *(soul music)* música *f* soul.

sound [saʊnd] *n* som *m* ◆ *vt (horn, bell)* (fazer) soar ◆ *vi (make a noise)* soar; *(seem to be)* parecer ◆ *adj (in good condition)* sólido(-da); *(health)* sadio(-a); *(heart, mind)* são (sã), bom (boa); **to ~ like** *(make a noise like)* soar como; *(seem to be)* parecer ser.

sound effects *npl* efeitos *mpl* sonoros.

soundly ['saʊndlɪ] *adv (beat)* completamente; *(sleep)* profundamente.

soundproof ['saʊndpruːf] *adj* à prova de som.

soundtrack ['saʊndtræk] *n* trilha *f* sonora (Br), banda *f* sonora (Port).

soup [suːp] *n* sopa *f*.

soup spoon *n* colher *f* de sopa.

sour ['saʊəʳ] *adj (taste)* ácido(-da); *(milk)* azedo(-da); **to go ~** azedar.

source [sɔːs] *n (supply, origin)* fonte *f; (cause)* origem *f; (of river)* nascente *f*.

sour cream *n* creme *m* azedo (Br), natas *fpl* azedas (Port).

south [saʊθ] *n* sul *m* ◆ *adj (wind)* sul ◆ *adv (be situated)* ao sul; *(fly, walk)* para o sul; **in the ~ of England** no sul da Inglaterra.

South Africa *n* África *f* do Sul.

South America *n* América *f* do Sul.

southbound ['saʊθbaʊnd] *adj* em direção ao sul.

southeast [ˌsaʊθˈiːst] *n* sudeste *m*.

southerly ['sʌðəlɪ] *adj (wind)* do sul; **in a ~ direction** em direção ao sul, para o sul; **the most ~ point** o ponto mais ao sul.

southern ['sʌðən] *adj* do sul.

South Korea *n* Coréia *f* do Sul.

South Pole *n*: **the ~** o Pólo Sul.

southward ['saʊθwəd] *adj* em direção ao sul, para o sul.

southwards ['saʊθwədz] *adv* em direção ao sul, para o sul.

southwest [ˌsaʊθˈwest] *n* sudoeste.

souvenir [ˌsuːvəˈnɪəʳ] *n* lembrança *f*, recordação *f*.

sovereign ['sɒvrɪn] *n (ruler)* soberano *m* (-na *f*).

Soviet Union [ˌsəʊvɪət-] *n*: **the ~** a União Soviética.

sow[1] [saʊ] *(pp* **sown**) *vt (seeds)* semear.

sow[2] [saʊ] *n (pig)* porca *f*.

sown [saʊn] *pp* → **sow**[1].

soya ['sɔɪə] *n* soja *f*.

soya bean *n* semente *f* de soja.

soy sauce [ˌsɔɪ-] *n* molho *m* de soja.

spa [spɑː] *n* estância *f* hidromineral (Br), termas *fpl* (Port).

space [speɪs] *n* espaço *m* ◆ *vt* espaçar.

spacecraft ['speɪskrɑːft] *n* nave *f* espacial.

spaceman ['speɪsmæn] *(pl* **-men** [-men]) *n (inf)* astronauta *mf*.

spaceship ['speɪsʃɪp] *n* nave *f* espacial.

space shuttle *n* ônibus *m* espacial (Br), vaivém *m* espacial (Port).

spacesuit ['speɪssuːt] *n* macacão *m* espacial (Br), fato *m* espacial (Port).

spacious ['speɪʃəs] *adj* espaçoso (-osa).

spade [speɪd] *n (tool)* pá *f*.

❏ **spades** *npl (in cards)* espadas *fpl*.

spaghetti [spəˈgetɪ] *n* espaguete *m*.

Spain [speɪn] *n* Espanha *f*.

span [spæn] *pt* → **spin** ◆ *n (length)* distância *f*, palmo *m; (of time)* espaço *m* de tempo.

Spaniard ['spænjəd] *n* espanhol *m* (-la *f*).

spaniel ['spænjəl] *n* spaniel *m*, cão *m* de água (Port).

Spanish ['spænɪʃ] *adj* espanhol(-la) ◆ *n (language)* espanhol *m*.

spank [spæŋk] *vt* dar uma palmada em.

spanner ['spænəʳ] *n* chave-inglesa *f*.

spare [speəʳ] *adj (kept in reserve)* a mais; *(not in use)* disponível ◆ *n (spare part)* peça *f* sobressalente; *(spare wheel)* pneu *m* sobressalente ◆ *vt*: **to ~ sb sthg** *(money)* dispensar algo a alguém; **I can't ~ the time** não tenho tempo; **with ten minutes to ~** com dez minutos de antecedência.

spare part *n* peça *f* sobressalente.

spare ribs *npl* costeleta *f* de porco (Br), entrecosto *m* (Port).

spare room *n* quarto *m* de hóspedes.

spare time *n* tempo *m* livre.

spare wheel *n* pneu *m* sobressalente.

sparing ['speərɪŋ] *adj*: **to be ~ with** OR **of sthg** gastar menos de algo.

sparingly ['speərɪŋlɪ] *adv* com moderação.

spark [spɑːk] *n (from fire)* fagulha *f; (electric)* faísca *f*.

sparkle ['spɑːkl] *vi (jewel, stars, eyes)* cintilar, brilhar.

sparkling ['spɑːklɪŋ] *adj (mineral water, soft drink)* gaseificado(-da), com gás.

sparkling wine *n* espumante *m*.

spark plug *n* vela *f*.

sparrow ['spærəʊ] *n* pardal *m*.

sparse [spɑːs] *adj* escasso(-a).

spasm ['spæzm] *n (of muscle)* espasmo *m; (of coughing, anger)* ataque *m*.

spastic ['spæstɪk] *n (MED)* deficiente *mf* motor.

spat [spæt] *pt & pp* → **spit**.

spawn [spɔːn] *n* ovas *fpl*.

speak [spiːk] *(pt* **spoke**, *pp* **spoken)** *vt (language)* falar; *(say)* dizer ♦ *vi* falar; **who's ~ing?** *(on phone)* quem fala?; **can I ~ to Charlotte? ~ ing!** posso falar com a Charlotte? - é a própria!; **to ~ to sb about sthg** falar com alguém sobre algo.

❏ **speak up** *vi (more loudly)* falar mais alto.

speaker ['spiːkər] *n (person)* orador *m* (-ra *f*); *(loudspeaker)* altofalante *m; (of stereo)* altofalante *m (Br)*, coluna *f (Port)*; **a Portuguese ~** um lusófono, uma pessoa que fala português.

spear [spɪər] *n* lança *f*.

spec [spek] *n (Brit: inf)*: **on ~** à sorte.

special ['speʃl] *adj* especial ♦ *n (dish)* prato *m* do dia; **"today's ~"** "prato do dia".

special effects *npl* efeitos *mpl* especiais.

specialist ['speʃəlɪst] *n* especialista *mf*.

speciality [ˌspeʃɪˈælətɪ] *n* especialidade *f*.

specialize ['speʃəlaɪz] *vi*: **to ~ (in)** especializar-se (em).

specially ['speʃəlɪ] *adv* especialmente.

special offer *n* promoção *f*.

special school *n (Brit)* escola *f* especial *(para alunos com deficiências físicas ou problemas de aprendizagem)*.

specialty ['speʃltɪ] *(Am)* = **speciality**.

species ['spiːʃiːz] *n* espécie *f*.

specific [spəˈsɪfɪk] *adj* específico(-ca).

specifically [spəˈsɪfɪklɪ] *adv* especificamente.

specifications [ˌspesɪfɪˈkeɪʃnz] *npl (of machine, car)* ficha *f* técnica.

specify ['spesɪfaɪ] *vt* especificar.

specimen ['spesɪmən] *n* espécime *m*, espécimen *m*.

speck [spek] *n (of dust, soot)* cisco *m; (of blood)* pinta *f*.

specs [speks] *npl (inf)* óculos *mpl*.

spectacle ['spektəkl] *n* espetáculo *m*.

spectacles ['spektəklz] *npl* óculos *mpl*.

spectacular [spekˈtækjʊlər] *adj* espetacular.

spectator [spekˈteɪtər] *n* espectador *m* (-ra *f*).

spectrum ['spektrəm] *n (in physics)* espectro *m; (range)* leque *m*.

speculation [ˌspekjʊˈleɪʃn] *n* especulação *f*.

sped [sped] *pt & pp* → **speed**.

speech [spiːtʃ] *n (ability to speak)* fala *f; (manner of speaking)* maneira *f* de falar; *(talk)* discurso *m*.

speech impediment [-ɪmˌpedɪmənt] *n* defeito *m* na fala.

speechless ['spiːtʃlɪs] *adj*: **to be ~ (with)** ficar mudo(-da) (de).

speed [spiːd] *(pt & pp* **-ed** OR **sped)** *n* velocidade *f; (bicycle gear)* mudança *f* ♦ *vi (move quickly)* ir a grande velocidade; *(drive too fast)* dirigir com excesso de velocidade; **"reduce ~ now"** "reduza a velocidade".

❏ **speed up** *vi* acelerar.

speedboat ['spiːdbəʊt] *n* lancha *f*.

speed camera *n* radar *m (para o controle do excesso de velocidade nas estradas)*.

speeding ['spiːdɪŋ] *n* excesso *m* de velocidade.

speed limit *n* limite *m* de velocidade.

speedometer [spɪˈdɒmɪtər] *n* velocímetro *m*, conta-quilômetros *m inv*.

speedway ['spiːdweɪ] *n (SPORT)* motociclismo *m*, corridas *fpl* de motos; *(Am: road)* auto-estrada *f*.

speedy ['spiːdɪ] *adj* rápido(-da).

spell [spel] *(Brit pt & pp* **-ed** OR **spelt**, *Am pt & pp* **-ed)** *vt (word, name)* soletrar; *(subj: letters)* dar, formar a palavra ♦ *n (period)* período *m; (magic)* feitiço *m*.

spelling ['spelɪŋ] *n* ortografia *f*.

spelt [spelt] *pt & pp (Brit)* → **spell**.

spend [spend] *(pt & pp* **spent)** *vt (money)* gastar; *(time)* passar.

spendthrift ['spendθrɪft] *n* esbanjador *m* (-ra *f*), gastador *m* (-ra *f*).

spent [spent] *pt & pp* → **spend** ♦ *adj (fuel, force, patience)* gasto(-ta).

sperm [spɜ:m] (*pl inv* OR **-s**) *n (cell)* espermatozóide *m*; *(semen)* esperma *m*.

spew [spju:] *vi (flow, spread)*: **to ~ (out) from sthg** sair de algo.

sphere [sfɪəʳ] *n* esfera *f*.

spice [spaɪs] *n* especiaria *f* ◆ *vt* condimentar.

spicy ['spaɪsɪ] *adj* picante.

spider ['spaɪdəʳ] *n* aranha *f*.

spider's web *n* teia *f* de aranha.

spike [spaɪk] *n* espigão *m*.

spill [spɪl] (*Brit pt & pp* **-ed** OR **spilt** [spɪlt], *Am pt & pp* **-ed**) *vt* entornar ◆ *vi* entornar-se.

spin [spɪn] (*pt* **span** OR **spun**, *pp* **spun**) *vt (wheel, coin, chair)* rodar; *(washing)* centrifugar ◆ *n (on ball)* efeito *m*; **to go for a ~** *(inf)* ir dar uma volta.

spinach ['spɪnɪtʃ] *n* espinafre *m*.

spinal column ['spaɪnl-] *n* coluna *f* vertebral.

spinal cord ['spaɪnl-] *n* medula *f* espin(h)al.

spin-dryer *n (Brit)* centrifugadora *f*.

spine [spaɪn] *n (of back)* espinha *f* (dorsal), coluna *f* (vertebral); *(of book)* lombada *f*.

spiral ['spaɪərəl] *n* espiral *f*.

spiral staircase *n* escada *f* em caracol.

spire ['spaɪəʳ] *n* pináculo *m*.

spirit ['spɪrɪt] *n (soul)* espírito *m*; *(energy)* vigor *m*, energia *f*; *(courage)* coragem *f*; *(mood)* humor *m*.

❏ **spirits** *npl (Brit: alcohol)* bebidas *fpl* com teor alcoólico bem alto *(Br)*, bebidas *fpl* espirituosas *(Port)*.

spirited ['spɪrɪtɪd] *adj (debate)* animado(-da); *(action, defence)* energético (-ca); *(performance)* com brio.

spirit level *n* nível *m* de bolha de ar.

spiritual ['spɪrɪtʃʊəl] *adj* espiritual.

spit [spɪt] (*Brit pt & pp* **spat**, *Am pt & pp* **spit**) *vi (person)* cuspir; *(fire)* crepitar; *(food)* espirrar ◆ *n (saliva)* cuspe *m*; *(for cooking)* espeto *m* ◆ *v impers*: **it's spitting** está chuviscando.

spite [spaɪt] : **in spite of** *prep* apesar de.

spiteful ['spaɪtfʊl] *adj* maldoso(-osa).

spittle ['spɪtl] *n* cuspo *m*, saliva *f*.

splash [splæʃ] *n (sound)* chape *m* ◆ *vt* salpicar.

splendid ['splendɪd] *adj* esplêndido(-da).

splint [splɪnt] *n* tala *f*.

splinter ['splɪntəʳ] *n* falha *f*, lasca *f*.

split [splɪt] (*pt & pp* **split**) *n (tear)* rasgão *m*; *(crack, in skirt)* racha *f* ◆ *vt (wood, stone)* rachar; *(tear)* rasgar; *(bill, profits, work)* dividir ◆ *vi (wood, stone)* partir-se; *(tear)* rasgar-se.

❏ **split up** *vi (group, couple)* separar-se.

splutter ['splʌtəʳ] *vi (person)* balbuciar, gaguejar; *(engine)* engasgar-se.

spoil [spɔɪl] (*pt & pp* **-ed** OR **spoilt**) *vt (ruin)* estragar; *(child)* mimar.

spoilsport ['spɔɪlspɔ:t] *n* desmancha-prazeres *mf inv*.

spoilt [spɔɪlt] *pt & pp* → **spoil** ◆ *adj (food, dinner)* estragado(-da); *(child)* mimado(-da).

spoke [spəʊk] *pt* → **speak** ◆ *n* raio *m*.

spoken ['spəʊkn] *pp* → **speak**.

spokesman ['spəʊksmən] (*pl* **-men** [-mən]) *n* porta-voz *m*.

spokeswoman ['spəʊks,wʊmən] (*pl* **-women** [-,wɪmɪn]) *n* porta-voz *f*.

sponge [spʌndʒ] *n (for cleaning, washing)* esponja *f*.

sponge bag *n (Brit)* estojo *m* de toalete.

sponge cake *n* = pão-de-ló *m*.

sponsor ['spɒnsəʳ] *n (of event, TV programme)* patrocinador *m* (-ra *f*).

sponsored walk [spɒnsəd-] *n* caminhada patrocinada com fins benificentes.

sponsorship ['spɒnsəʃɪp] *n* patrocínio *m*.

spontaneous [spɒn'teɪnjəs] *adj* espontâneo(-nea).

spooky ['spu:kɪ] *adj (inf)* assustador (-ra).

spool [spu:l] *n* rolo *m*.

spoon [spu:n] *n* colher *f*.

spoonful ['spu:nfʊl] *n* colherada *f*, colher *f*.

sporadic [spə'rædɪk] *adj* esporádico(-ca).

sport [spɔ:t] *n* esporte *m (Br)*, desporto *m (Port)*.

sporting ['spɔ:tɪŋ] *adj* esportivo(-va) *(Br)*, desportivo(-va) *(Port)*; **to have a ~ chance of doing sthg** ter uma boa chance de fazer algo.

sports car [spɔ:ts-] *n* carro *m* esporte *(Br)*, carro *m* desportivo *(Port)*.

sports centre [spɔ:ts-] *n* centro *m* esportivo (Br), pavilhão *m* de desportos *(Port)*.

sports jacket [spɔːts-] n jaqueta f de esporte (Br), casaco m de desporto OR desportivo (Port).

sportsman ['spɔːtsmən] (pl **-men** [-mən]) n esportista m (Br), desportista m (Port).

sportsmanship ['spɔːtsmənʃɪp] n espírito m esportivo (Br), desportivismo m (Port).

sports shop [spɔːts-] n loja f de artigos de esporte (Br), loja f de artigos de desporto (Port).

sportswear ['spɔːtsweəʳ] n roupa f de esporte (Br), roupa f desportiva (Port).

sportswoman ['spɔːts,wumən] (pl **-women** [-,wɪmɪn]) n esportista f (Br), desportista f (Port).

sporty ['spɔːtɪ] adj (inf: person) esportivo(-va) (Br), desportivo(-va) (Port).

spot [spɒt] n (of paint, rain, blood) gota f, pingo m; (on dog, leopard) mancha f; (on skin) borbulha f; (place) lugar m, sítio m (Port) ◆ vt notar, reparar em; **on the ~** (at once) imediatamente; (at the scene) no local.

spotless ['spɒtlɪs] adj impecável, imaculado(-da).

spotlight ['spɒtlaɪt] n projetor m.

spotted ['spɒtɪd] adj (material) de bolas.

spotty ['spɒtɪ] adj com borbulhas.

spouse [spaus] n (fml) esposo m (-sa f).

spout [spaut] n bico m.

sprain [spreɪn] vt torcer.

sprang [spræŋ] pt → spring.

spray [spreɪ] n (of aerosol, perfume) spray m; (droplets) gotas fpl; (of sea) espuma f ◆ vt (car) pintar com pistola; (crops) pulverizar; (paint, water etc) esguichar.

spread [spred] (pt & pp spread) vt (butter, jam) barrar; (glue, disease, news) espalhar; (map, tablecloth, blanket) estender; (legs, fingers, arms) abrir ◆ vi (disease, fire, news) espalhar-se; (stain) alastrar ◆ n (food): **chocolate ~** pasta f de chocolate, Tulicreme® m.

❏ **spread out** vi (disperse) espalhar-se.

spree [spriː] n: **to go on a spending/drinking ~** gastar/beber à valer.

spring [sprɪŋ] (pt sprang, pp sprung) n (season) primavera f; (coil) mola f; (in ground) nascente f ◆ vi (leap) saltar; **in (the) ~** na primavera.

springboard ['sprɪŋbɔːd] n prancha f (de saltos).

spring-cleaning [-'kliːnɪŋ] n limpezas fpl de primavera.

spring onion n cebolinha f.

spring roll n crepe m chinês.

springtime ['sprɪŋtaɪm] n: **in (the) ~** na primavera.

springy ['sprɪŋɪ] adj (carpet, ground) mole; (rubber) elástico(-ca); (mattress) de molas.

sprinkle ['sprɪŋkl] vt: **to ~ sthg with sugar/flour** polvilhar algo com açúcar/farinha; **to ~ water on sthg** salpicar algo com água.

sprinkler ['sprɪŋkləʳ] n (for fire) extintor m (automático de incêndios); (for grass) regador m (automático), aspersor m.

sprint [sprɪnt] n (race) corrida f de velocidade ◆ vi (run fast) dar uma corrida.

Sprinter® ['sprɪntəʳ] n (Brit: train) trem m interurbano, trem que serve pequenas distâncias.

sprout [spraut] n (vegetable) couve-de-Bruxelas f.

spruce [spruːs] n espruce m.

sprung [sprʌŋ] pp → spring ◆ adj (mattress) de molas.

spud [spʌd] n (inf) batata f.

spun [spʌn] pt & pp → spin.

spur [spɜːʳ] n (for horse rider) espora f; **on the ~ of the moment** sem pensar duas vezes.

spurt [spɜːt] vi jorrar.

spy [spaɪ] n espião m (-pia f).

spying ['spaɪɪŋ] n espionagem f.

squabble ['skwɒbl] n briga f ◆ vi: **to ~ (about OR over sthg)** brigar (por algo).

squad [skwɒd] n (of police) brigada f; (group of players) equipe f.

squadron ['skwɒdrən] n (of planes) esquadrilha f; (of warships) esquadra f; (of soldiers) esquadrão m.

squall [skwɔːl] n tempestade f, borrasca f.

squalor ['skwɒləʳ] n sordidez f.

squander ['skwɒndəʳ] vt desperdiçar.

square [skweəʳ] adj (in shape) quadrado(-da) ◆ n (shape) quadrado m; (in town) praça f; (of chocolate) pedaço m; (on chessboard) casa f; **2 ~ metres** 2 metros quadrados; **it's 2 metres ~** tem 2 metros de lado; **we're (all) ~ now**

(not owing money) agora estamos quites.

squarely ['skweəlı] *adv (directly)* exatamente; *(honestly)* francamente.

squash [skwɒʃ] *n (game)* squash *m*; *(Brit: drink)* bebida à base de suco de fruto concentrado e água; *(Am: vegetable)* abóbora *f* ♦ *vt* esmagar.

squat [skwɒt] *adj* atarracado(-da) ♦ *n (building)* edifício abandonado e ocupado clandestinamente ♦ *vi (crouch)* agachar-se.

squatter ['skwɒtə'] *n (Brit)* ocupante *mf* ilegal, squatter *mf*.

squawk [skwɔːk] *vi (bird)* gritar.

squeak [skwiːk] *vi* chiar.

squeal [skwiːl] *vi* chiar.

squeamish ['skwiːmɪʃ] *adj*: **I'm ~ about the sight of blood** não posso ver sangue.

squeeze [skwiːz] *vt* espremer.

❏ **squeeze in** *vi* arranjar lugar.

squid [skwɪd] *n* lula *f*.

squint [skwɪnt] *n* estrabismo *m* ♦ *vi* semicerrar os olhos; **to ~ at** olhar com os olhos semi-cerrados para.

squirrel [*Brit* 'skwɪrəl, *Am* 'skwɜːrəl] *n* esquilo *m*.

squirt [skwɜːt] *vi* esguichar.

Sri Lanka [ˌsriː'læŋkə] *n* Sri Lanca *m*.

St *(abbr of Street)* R.; *(abbr of Saint)* S. *mf*, Sta. *f*.

stab [stæb] *vt (with knife)* apunhalar, esfaquear.

stable ['steɪbl] *adj* estável ♦ *n* estábulo *m*.

stack [stæk] *n (pile)* pilha *f*; **~s of** *(inf: lots)* pilhas de.

stadium ['steɪdjəm] *n* estádio *m*.

staff [stɑːf] *n (workers)* pessoal *m*.

stag [stæg] *n (pl inv OR -s)* *n* veado *m* (macho).

stage [steɪdʒ] *n (phase)* fase *f*; *(in theatre)* palco *m*.

stagecoach ['steɪdʒkəutʃ] *n* diligência *f*.

stage fright *n* medo *m* do palco.

stagger ['stægə'] *vt (arrange in stages)* escalonar ♦ *vi* cambalear.

stagnant ['stægnənt] *adj* estagnado(-da).

stagnate [stæg'neɪt] *vi* estagnar.

staid [steɪd] *adj* conservador(-ra), antiquado(-da).

stain [steɪn] *n* nódoa *f*, mancha *f* ♦ *vt* manchar.

stained glass window [steɪnd-] *n* vitral *m*.

stainless steel ['steɪnlɪs-] *n* aço *m* inoxidável.

stair [steə'] *n* degrau *m*.

❏ **stairs** *npl* escadas *fpl*.

staircase ['steəkeɪs] *n* escadaria *f*.

stairway ['steəweɪ] *n* escadaria *f*.

stairwell ['steəwel] *n* vão *m* das escadas.

stake [steɪk] *n (share)* parte *f*; *(in gambling)* aposta *f*; *(post)* estaca *f*; **at ~** em jogo.

stale [steɪl] *adj (bread)* duro(-ra); *(crisps, biscuits)* mole.

stalemate ['steɪlmeɪt] *n (deadlock)* beco *m* sem saída, impasse *m*; *(in chess)* empate *m*.

stalk [stɔːk] *n (of flower, plant)* pé *m*, caule *m*; *(of fruit)* galho *m (Br)*, píncaro *m (Port)*; *(of leaf)* galho *(Br)*, pecíolo *m (Port)*.

stall [stɔːl] *n (at exhibition)* stand *m*; *(in market, at fair)* barraca *f* ♦ *vi (car, plane, engine)* morrer *(Br)*, ir abaixo *(Port)*.

❏ **stalls** *npl (Brit: in theatre)* platéia *f*.

stallion ['stæljən] *n* garanhão *m*.

stamina ['stæmɪnə] *n* resistência *f*.

stammer ['stæmə'] *vi* gaguejar.

stamp [stæmp] *n (for letter)* selo *m*; *(in passport, on document)* carimbo *m* ♦ *vt (passport, document)* carimbar ♦ *vi*: **to ~ on sthg** esmagar algo com o pé; **to ~ one's foot** bater com o pé no chão.

stamp album *n* álbum *m* de selos.

stamp-collecting [-kəˌlektɪŋ] *n* filatelia *f*.

stampede [stæm'piːd] *n* debandada *f*.

stamp machine *n* distribuidor *m* automático de selos.

stance [stæns] *n (posture)* postura *f*; **~ (on sthg)** *(attitude)* posição *f* (em relação a algo).

stand [stænd] *(pt & pp stood)* *vi (be on feet)* estar de OR em pé; *(be situated)* ficar; *(get to one's feet)* levantar-se ♦ *vt (place)* pôr, colocar; *(bear, withstand)* agüentar, suportar ♦ *n (in market, at fair)* barraca *f*; *(at exhibition)* stand *m*; *(for newspapers)* banca *f* de jornais *(Br)*, quiosque *m (Port)*; *(for umbrellas)* bengaleiro *m*; *(for coats)* cabide *m*; *(for bike, motorbike)* descanso *m*; *(at sports stadium)* arquibancada *f (Br)*, bancada *f (Port)*; **to ~ sb a drink** pagar uma bebida para alguém; **to be ~ing** estar de OR em pé; **"no ~ing"** *(Am: AUT)* "zona de estacionamento e parada proibida".

❏ **stand back** *vi* afastar-se.

❏ **stand for** *vt fus (mean)* representar; *(tolerate)* tolerar.

❏ **stand in** *vi:* **to ~ in for sb** substituir alguém.

❏ **stand out** *vi (be conspicuous)* dar nas vistas; *(be superior)* destacar-se.

❏ **stand up** *vi (be on feet)* estar de OR em pé; *(get to one's feet)* levantar-se ◆ *vt sep (inf: boyfriend, girlfriend)* deixar plantado(-da).

❏ **stand up for** *vt fus* defender.

standard ['stændəd] *adj (normal)* normal, padrão *(inv)* ◆ *n (level)* nível *m*; *(point of comparison)* média *f*; *(for product)* norma *f*; **to be up to ~** estar à altura.

❏ **standards** *npl (principles)* princípios *mpl*.

standard-class *adj (Brit: on train)* de segunda classe.

standard lamp *n (Brit)* abajur *m* de pé *(Br)*, candeeiro *m* de pé *(Port)*.

standard of living *n* padrão *m* de vida *(Br)*, nível *m* de vida.

standby ['stændbaɪ] *adj (ticket)* sem reserva, de última hora.

stand-in *n (replacement)* substituto *m* (-ta *f*); *(stunt person)* dublê *mf (Br)*, duplo *m* (-pla *f*) *(Port)*.

standing order ['stændɪŋ-] *n* transferência *f* bancária.

standing room ['stændɪŋ-] *n (at sports ground, theatre)* lugares *mpl* em pé.

standpoint ['stændpɔɪnt] *n* ponto *m* de vista.

standstill ['stændstɪl] *n:* **to be at a ~** *(traffic)* estar parado(-da), estar imobilizado(-da); **to come to a ~** *(car, train)* parar, imobilizar-se; *(negotiations, work)* cessar.

stank [stæŋk] *pt* → **stink**.

staple ['steɪpl] *n (for paper)* grampo *m (Br)*, agrafo *m (Port)*.

stapler ['steɪplə'] *n* grampeador *m (Br)*, agrafador *m (Port)*.

star [stɑː'] *n* estrela *f* ◆ *vt (subj: film, play etc):* **"starring ..."** "com ...".

❏ **stars** *npl (horoscope)* horóscopo *m*.

starboard ['stɑːbəd] *adj* de estibordo.

starch [stɑːtʃ] *n (for clothes)* goma *f*; *(in food)* amido *m*.

stare [steə'] *vi:* **to ~ at** fitar, olhar fixamente (para).

starfish ['stɑːfɪʃ] *(pl inv)* n estrela-do-mar *f*.

starling ['stɑːlɪŋ] *n* estorninho *m*.

starry ['stɑːrɪ] *adj* estrelado(-da).

Stars and Stripes *n:* **the ~** a bandeira dos Estados Unidos.

start [stɑːt] *n (beginning)* início *m*, começo *m*; *(starting place)* ponto *m* de partida ◆ *vt (begin)* começar; *(car, engine)* ligar; *(business, club)* montar ◆ *vi (begin)* começar; *(car, engine)* pegar; *(begin journey)* sair, partir; **prices ~ at** OR **from £5** preços a partir de 5 libras; **to ~ doing sthg** OR **to do sthg** começar a fazer algo; **to ~ with ...** para começar ....

❏ **start out** *vi (on journey)* partir; *(be originally)* começar.

❏ **start up** *vt sep (car, engine)* ligar; *(business, shop)* montar.

starter ['stɑːtə'] *n (Brit: of meal)* entrada *f*; *(of car)* motor *m* de arranque; **for ~s** *(in meal)* como entrada.

starter motor *n* motor *m* de arranque.

starting point ['stɑːtɪŋ-] *n* ponto *m* de partida.

startle ['stɑːtl] *vt* assustar.

startling ['stɑːtlɪŋ] *adj* surpreendente.

starvation [stɑː'veɪʃn] *n* fome *f*.

starve [stɑːv] *vi (have no food)* passar fome; **I'm starving!** estou esfomeado OR morto de fome!

state [steɪt] *n* estado *m* ◆ *vt (declare)* declarar; *(specify)* especificar, indicar; **the State** o Estado; **the States** os Estados Unidos.

statement ['steɪtmənt] *n (declaration)* declaração *f*; *(from bank)* extrato *m* de conta.

state school *n* escola *f* pública.

statesman ['steɪtsmən] *(pl* **-men** [-mən]*) n* homem *m* de estado, estadista *m*.

static ['stætɪk] *n (on radio, TV)* interferências *fpl*.

station ['steɪʃn] *n* estação *f*.

stationary ['steɪʃnərɪ] *adj* estacionário(-ria).

stationer's ['steɪʃnəz] *n (shop)* papelaria *f*.

stationery ['steɪʃnərɪ] *n* artigos *mpl* de papelaria.

stationmaster ['steɪʃn,mɑːstəʳ] *n* chefe *mf* de estação.

station wagon *n (Am)* perua *f (Br)*, carrinha *f (Port)*.

statistics [stə'tɪstɪks] *npl (figures)* estatísticas *fpl*.

statue ['stætʃuː] *n* estátua *f.*

Statue of Liberty *n*: the ~ a Estátua da Liberdade.

stature ['stætʃəʳ] *n* estatura *f.*

status ['steɪtəs] *n (legal position)* estado *m; (social position)* status *m (Br)*, estatuto *m (Port); (prestige)* prestígio *m*, status *m.*

statutory ['stætjʊtrɪ] *adj* legal.

staunch [stɔːntʃ] *adj* leal ◆ *vt* estancar.

stave [steɪv] (*pt & pp* -**d** OR **stove**) *n (MUS)* pauta *f.*

❑ **stave off** *vt sep (disaster, defeat)* adiar, protelar; *(hunger)* saciar, aplacar.

stay [steɪ] *n (time spent)* estadia *f* ◆ *vi (remain)* ficar; *(as guest)* ficar (hospedado); *(Scot: reside)* morar, viver; **where are you ~ing?** onde você está hospedado?; **to ~ the night** passar a noite.

❑ **stay away** *vi (not attend)* não ir; *(not go near)* ficar longe.

❑ **stay in** *vi* ficar em casa.

❑ **stay out** *vi (from home)* ficar fora.

❑ **stay up** *vi* ficar acordado.

STD code *n* indicativo *m.*

stead [sted] *n*: **to stand sb in good ~** ser muito útil para alguém.

steadfast ['stedfɑːst] *adj (supporter)* leal, fiel; *(resolve)* inabalável; *(gaze)* fixo(-xa).

steadily ['stedɪlɪ] *adv (gradually)* gradualmente; *(regularly)* regularmente; *(calmly)* calmamente.

steady ['stedɪ] *adj (not shaking, firm)* firme; *(gradual)* gradual; *(stable)* estável; *(job)* fixo(-xa) ◆ *vt (table, ladder)* firmar.

steak [steɪk] *n* bife *m.*

steak and kidney pie *n* empada de carne de vaca e rins.

steakhouse ['steɪkhaʊs, *pl* -haʊzɪz] *n* restaurante especializado em bifes.

steal [stiːl] *(pt* stole, *pp* stolen) *vt* roubar; **to ~ sthg from sb** roubar algo de alguém.

stealthy ['stelθɪ] *adj* furtivo(-va).

steam [stiːm] *n* vapor *m* ◆ *vt (food)* cozer no vapor.

steam boat ['stiːmbəʊt] *n* barco *m* a vapor.

steam engine *n* máquina *f* a vapor.

steamer ['stiːməʳ] *n (ship)* navio *m* a vapor.

steam iron *n* ferro *m* a vapor.

steamroller ['stiːm,rəʊləʳ] *n* cilindro *m.*

steel [stiːl] *n* aço *m* ◆ *adj* de aço.

steep [stiːp] *adj (hill, path)* íngreme; *(increase, drop)* considerável.

steeple ['stiːpl] *n* torre *f* da igreja, campanário *m.*

steeplechase ['stiːpltʃeɪs] *n* corrida *f* de obstáculos.

steer [stɪəʳ] *vt (car)* dirigir *(Br)*, conduzir *(Port); (boat, plane)* pilotar.

steering ['stɪərɪŋ] *n* direção *f.*

steering wheel *n* volante *m.*

stem [stem] *n (of plant)* talo *m*, caule *m; (of glass)* pé *m.*

stench [stentʃ] *n* fedor *m.*

stencil ['stensl] *n* stencil *m.*

step [step] *n (stair, rung)* degrau *m; (pace, measure, stage)* passo *m* ◆ *vi*: **to ~ on sthg** pisar em algo; **"mind the ~"** "cuidado com o degrau".

❑ **steps** *npl (stairs)* escadas *fpl.*

❑ **step aside** *vi (move aside)* desviar-se, afastar-se.

❑ **step back** *vi (move back)* recuar, afastar-se.

step aerobics *n* step *m.*

stepbrother ['step,brʌðəʳ] *n* meio-irmão *m.*

stepdaughter ['step,dɔːtəʳ] *n* enteada *f.*

stepfather ['step,fɑːðəʳ] *n* padrasto *m.*

stepladder ['step,lædəʳ] *n* escada *f* portátil, escadote *m (Port).*

stepmother ['step,mʌðəʳ] *n* madrasta *f.*

stepping-stone ['stepɪŋ-] *n (in river)* pedra *f; (fig: way to success)* trampolim *m.*

stepsister ['step,sɪstəʳ] *n* meia-irmã *f.*

stepson ['stepsʌn] *n* enteado *m.*

stereo ['sterɪəʊ] (*pl* -**s**) *adj* estereofônico(-ca) ◆ *n (hi-fi)* aparelhagem *f; (stereo sound)* estereofonia *f*, estéreo *m.*

stereotype ['sterɪətaɪp] *n* estereótipo *m.*

sterile ['steraɪl] *adj (germ-free)* esterilizado(-da).

sterilize ['stɛrəlaɪz] *vt* esterilizar.

sterling ['stɜ:lɪŋ] *adj (pound)* esterlino(-na) ◆ *n* libra *f* esterlina.

sterling silver *n* prata *f* de lei.

stern [stɜ:n] *adj* severo(-ra) ◆ *n* popa *f*.

steroid ['stɪərɔɪd] *n* esteróide *m*.

stethoscope ['steθəskəup] *n* estetoscópio *m*.

stew [stju:] *n* ensopado *m*, guisado *m*.

steward ['stjuəd] *n (on plane, ship)* comissário *m* de bordo; *(at public event)* organizador *m*.

stewardess ['stjuədɪs] *n* aeromoça *f (Br)*, hospedeira *f* de bordo *(Port)*.

stewed [stju:d] *adj (fruit)* cozido(-da).

stick [stɪk] *(pt & pp* **stuck)** *n (of wood)* pau *m*; *(for sport)* stick *m*; *(of celery)* tira *f (Br)*, troço *m (Port)*; *(walking stick)* bengala *f* ◆ *vt (glue)* colar; *(push, insert)* meter, pôr; *(inf: put)* meter, pôr ◆ *vi (become attached)* grudar-se *(Br)*, pegar-se *(Port)*; *(jam)* encravar.

❏ **stick out** *vi* sobressair.

❏ **stick to** *vt fus (decision, principles, promise)* manter-se fiel a.

❏ **stick up** *vt sep (poster, notice)* afixar ◆ *vi*: **your hair is ~ing up!** você está com o cabelo todo arrepiado!

❏ **stick up for** *vt fus* defender.

sticker ['stɪkər] *n* adesivo *m (Br)*, autocolante *m (Port)*.

sticking plaster ['stɪkɪŋ-] *n* esparadrapo *m (Br)*, penso *m* (rápido) *(Port)*.

stick shift *n (Am: car)* veículo *m* com mudanças manuais.

stick-up *n (inf)* assalto *m* à mão armada.

sticky ['stɪkɪ] *adj (substance, hands, sweets)* pegajoso(-osa); *(label, tape)* adesivo(-va), autocolante *(Port)*; *(weather)* úmido(-da).

stiff [stɪf] *adj (firm)* rijo(-ja); *(sheet)* teso(-sa); *(neck)* duro(-ra); *(back, person)* dolorido(-da); *(door, latch, mechanism)* emperrado(-da) ◆ *adv*: **to be bored ~** *(inf)* estar morrendo de tédio.

stiffen ['stɪfn] *vi (muscles, person)* ficar rígido(-da); *(hinge, handle)* emperrar; *(competition, resolve)* endurecer.

stifle ['staɪfl] *vt (suffocate)* sufocar; *(suppress)* abafar.

stifling ['staɪflɪŋ] *adj (heat)* sufocante.

stigma ['stɪgmə] *n (disgrace)* estigma *m*.

stile [staɪl] *n* conjunto de degraus que facilita a passagem das pessoas por cima de uma vedação ou vala no campo.

stiletto heels [stɪ'letəu-] *npl (shoes)* sapatos *mpl* com saltos finos.

still [stɪl] *adv* ainda ◆ *adj (motionless)* imóvel; *(quiet, calm)* calmo(-ma); *(not fizzy)* sem gás; **we've ~ got 10 minutes** ainda temos 10 minutos; **~ more** ainda mais; **to stand ~** estar quieto.

stillborn ['stɪlbɔ:n] *adj* nati-morto (nati-morta).

still life *(pl* **-s)** *n* natureza-morta *f*.

stilted ['stɪltɪd] *adj* forçado(-da).

Stilton ['stɪltn] *n* queijo *m* Stilton, *queijo azul inglês com sabor forte e amargo, comido tradicionalmente acompanhado de vinho do Porto*.

stilts [stɪlts] *npl* pernas *fpl* de pau *(Br)*, andas *fpl (Port)*.

stimulate ['stɪmjuleɪt] *vt* estimular.

stimulating ['stɪmjuleɪtɪŋ] *adj (physically)* revigorante; *(mentally)* estimulante.

stimulus ['stɪmjuləs] *(pl* **-li** [-laɪ]) *n* estímulo *m*.

sting [stɪŋ] *(pt & pp* **stung)** *vt* picar ◆ *vi (skin, eyes)* arder.

stingy ['stɪndʒɪ] *adj (inf)* pão-duro(-ra) *(Br)*, forreta *(Port)*.

stink [stɪŋk] *(pt* **stank** OR **stunk**, *pp* **stunk)** *vi* cheirar mal.

stinking ['stɪŋkɪŋ] *adj (inf: headache, cold)* horroroso(-osa).

stint [stɪnt] *n (period of time)* período *m* ◆ *vi*: **to ~ on sthg** poupar em algo.

stipulate ['stɪpjuleɪt] *vt* estipular.

stir [stɜ:r] *vt (move around, mix)* mexer.

stir-fry *n* prato chinês em que pedaços de legumes e carnes são fritos rapidamente em óleo bem quente ◆ *vt* fritar rapidamente.

stirrup ['stɪrəp] *n* estribo *m*.

stitch [stɪtʃ] *n (in sewing, knitting)* ponto *m*; **to have a ~** sentir uma pontada do lado.

❏ **stitches** *npl (for wound)* pontos *mpl*.

stoat [stəut] *n* arminho *m*.

stock [stɒk] *n (of shop)* estoque *m*; *(FIN)* títulos *mpl*, acções *fpl*; *(CULIN)* caldo *m* ◆ *vt (have in stock)* ter em estoque; **in ~** em estoque, armazenado; **out of ~** esgotado.

stockbroker ['stɒk,brəukər] *n* corretor *m* (-ra *f*) da bolsa.

stock cube *n* cubo *m* de caldo.

Stock Exchange *n* bolsa *f* de valo-res.

stockholder ['stɒk,həʊldəʳ] *n (Am)* acionista *mf*.

Stockholm ['stɒkhəʊm] *n* Estocolmo *s*.

stocking ['stɒkɪŋ] *n* meia *f*.

stock market *n* bolsa *f*, mercado *m* de valores.

stocktaking ['stɒk,teɪkɪŋ] *n* inventá-rio *m*.

stocky ['stɒkɪ] *adj* atarracado(-da).

stodgy ['stɒdʒɪ] *adj (food)* pesado(-da).

stole [stəʊl] *pt* → **steal**.

stolen ['stəʊln] *pp* → **steal**.

stomach ['stʌmək] *n (organ)* estôma-go *m*; *(belly)* barriga *f*.

stomachache ['stʌməkeɪk] *n* dor *f* de estômago.

stomach upset [-'ʌpset] *n* indispo-sição *f* estomacal.

stone [stəʊn] *n (substance)* n pedra *f*; *(in fruit)* caroço *m*; *(measurement: pl inv)* = 6,35 kg; *(gem)* pedra preciosa ◆ *adj* de pedra.

stonewashed ['stəʊnwɒʃt] *adj* pré-lavado(-da) com pedras.

stood [stʊd] *pt & pp* → **stand**.

stool [stuːl] *n (for sitting on)* banco *m*, mocho *m (Port)*.

stoop [stuːp] *vi (bend over)* abaixar-se; *(hunch shoulders)* corcovar-se.

stop [stɒp] *n* parada *f (Br)*, paragem *f (Port)* ◆ *vt* parar ◆ *vi* parar; *(stay)* ficar; **to ~ sb/sthg from doing sthg** impedir alguém/algo de fazer algo; **to ~ doing sthg** parar de fazer algo; **to put a ~ to sthg** pôr termo OR fim a algo; **"stop"** *(road sign)* "stop"; **"stopping at ..."** *(train, bus)* "com paradas em ...". ❏ **stop off** *vi* parar.

stopover ['stɒp,əʊvəʳ] *n* parada *f (Br)*, paragem *f (Port)*; *(on plane journey)* escala *f*.

stoppage ['stɒpɪdʒ] *n (strike)* greve *f*, paralisação *f*; *(in sports match)* inter-rupção *f*.

stopper ['stɒpəʳ] *n* tampa *f*.

stopwatch ['stɒpwɒtʃ] *n* cronômetro *m*.

storage ['stɔːrɪdʒ] *n* armazenamento *m*, armazenagem *f*.

storage heater *n (Brit)* termo-acumulador *m*, aquecedor que acumula calor durante a noite para o emitir duran-te o dia.

store [stɔːʳ] *n (shop)* loja *f*; *(supply)* estoque *m* ◆ *vt* armazenar.

storehouse ['stɔːhaʊs, pl -haʊzɪz] *n* armazém *m*.

storekeeper ['stɔː,kiːpəʳ] *n (Am)* comerciante *mf*, dono *m* (-na *f*) de loja.

storeroom ['stɔːrʊm] *n (in shop)* armazém *m*; *(in house)* dispensa *f*.

storey ['stɔːrɪ] *(pl -s) n (Brit)* andar *m*.

stork [stɔːk] *n* cegonha *f*.

storm [stɔːm] *n (bad weather)* tempes-tade *f*.

stormy ['stɔːmɪ] *adj (weather)* tem-pestuoso(-osa).

story ['stɔːrɪ] *n (account, tale)* história *f*; *(news item)* artigo *m*; *(Am)* = **storey**.

stout [staʊt] *adj (fat)* corpulento(-ta), forte ◆ *n (drink)* cerveja *f* preta.

stove [stəʊv] *pt & pp* → **stave** ◆ *n (for cooking)* fogão *m*; *(for heating)* estufa *f*.

stow [stəʊ] *vt*: **to ~ sthg (away)** *(luggage)* arrumar algo; *(files)* arquivar algo; *(treasure)* esconder algo.

stowaway ['stəʊəweɪ] *n* passageiro *m* clandestino (passageira *f* clandestina).

straddle ['strædl] *vt (subj: person)* escarranchar-se em.

straggler ['strægləʳ] *n* atrasado *m* (-da *f*).

straight [streɪt] *adj (not curved)* direi-to(-ta); *(road, line)* reto(-ta); *(hair)* liso(-sa); *(consecutive)* consecutivo(-va); *(drink)* puro(-ra) ◆ *adv (in a straight line)* reto(-ta); *(upright)* direito; *(directly)* diretamente; *(without delay)* imediata-mente; **~ ahead** sempre em frente; **~ away** imediatamente, já; **~ in front** mesmo em frente.

straighten ['streɪtn] *vt* endireitar; *(room, desk)* arrumar. ❏ **straighten out** *vt sep (mis-understanding)* esclarecer.

straight face *n*: **to keep a ~** manter-se sério(-ria), conter o riso.

straightforward [,streɪt'fɔːwəd] *adj (easy)* simples *(inv)*.

strain [streɪn] *n (force)* força *f*; *(nervous stress)* stress *m*; *(tension)* tensão *f*; *(injury)* distenção *f* ◆ *vt (muscle, eyes)* forçar; *(food, tea)* coar.

strained [streɪnd] *adj (forced)* força-do(-da); *(tense)* tenso(-sa); *(ankle, shoulder)* deslocado(-da); *(muscle)* dis-tendido(-da).

strainer ['streɪnəʳ] *n* passador *m*, coa-dor *m*.

strait [streɪt] n estreito m.

straitjacket [ˈstreɪtˌdʒækɪt] n camisa-de-força f.

straitlaced [ˌstreɪtˈleɪst] adj puritano(-na).

strand [strænd] n (of cotton, wool) linha f, fio m; a ~ of hair um cabelo.

stranded [ˈstrændɪd] adj (person, car) preso(-sa); (boat) encalhado(-da).

strange [streɪndʒ] adj estranho(-nha).

stranger [ˈstreɪndʒər] n (unfamiliar person) estranho m (-nha f), desconhecido m (-da f); (person from different place) forasteiro m (-ra f).

strangle [ˈstræŋgl] vt estrangular.

strap [stræp] n (of bag) alça f; (of camera, shoe) correia f; (of watch) pulseira f.

strapless [ˈstræplɪs] adj sem alças.

strapping [ˈstræpɪŋ] adj bem constituído(-da).

Strasbourg [ˈstræzbɜːg] n Estrasburgo s.

strategic [strəˈtiːdʒɪk] adj estratégico(-ca).

strategy [ˈstrætɪdʒɪ] n estratégia f.

Stratford-upon-Avon [ˌstrætfədəpɒnˈeɪvn] n Stratford-Upon-Avon s.

straw [strɔː] n palha f; (for drinking) canudo m (Br), palhinha f (Port).

strawberry [ˈstrɔːbərɪ] n morango m.

stray [streɪ] adj (animal) abandonado(-da) ♦ vi vaguear.

streak [striːk] n (stripe, mark) listra f, risca f; (period) período m.

stream [striːm] n (river) riacho m; (of traffic, people) torrente f; (of water, air) corrente f.

streamlined [ˈstriːmlaɪnd] adj (aerodynamic) com um perfil aerodinâmico; (efficient) eficiente.

street [striːt] n rua f.

streetcar [ˈstriːtkɑːr] n (Am) bonde m (Br), eléctrico m (Port).

street light n poste m de iluminação, candeeiro m de rua (Port).

street plan n mapa m (das ruas).

streetwise [ˈstriːtwaɪz] adj esperto (-ta).

strength [streŋθ] n força f; (of structure) solidez f; (strong point) ponto m forte; (of feeling, wind, smell) intensidade f; (of drink) teor m alcoólico; (of drug) dosagem f.

strengthen [ˈstreŋθn] vt reforçar.

strenuous [ˈstrenjuəs] adj (exercise, activity) esgotante; (effort) vigoroso

(-osa), tremendo(-da).

stress [stres] n (tension) stress m; (on word, syllable) acento m tônico ♦ vt (emphasize) pôr a tônica em; (word, syllable) acentuar.

stressful [ˈstresfʊl] adj desgastante.

stretch [stretʃ] n (of land, water) extensão f; (of time) período m ♦ vt esticar ♦ vi (land, sea) estender-se; (person, animal) estirar-se, espreguiçar-se; to ~ one's legs (fig) esticar as pernas.

❏ **stretch out** vt sep (hand) estender ♦ vi (lie down) estender-se ao comprido, deitar-se.

stretcher [ˈstretʃər] n maca f.

strict [strɪkt] adj rigoroso(-osa).

strictly [ˈstrɪktlɪ] adv (absolutely) estritamente; (exclusively) exclusivamente; ~ speaking a bem dizer.

stride [straɪd] n passada f.

strident [ˈstraɪdnt] adj (voice, sound) estridente.

strife [straɪf] n rixas fpl, conflitos mpl.

strike [straɪk] (pt & pp struck) n (of employees) greve f ♦ vt (fml: hit) agredir; (fml: collide with) colidir OR chocar com; (a match) acender ♦ vi (refuse to work) fazer greve; (happen suddenly) ocorrer; the clock struck eight o relógio bateu oito horas.

striker [ˈstraɪkər] n (person on strike) grevista mf; (in football) ponta-de-lança mf.

striking [ˈstraɪkɪŋ] adj (noticeable) impressionante; (attractive) atraente.

string [strɪŋ] n cordel m, fio m; (of pearls, beads) colar m; (of musical instrument, tennis racket) corda f; (series) série f; a piece of ~ um cordel, um fio.

string bean n feijão m verde, vagem f.

stringed instrument [strɪŋd-] n instrumento m de cordas.

stringent [ˈstrɪndʒənt] adj severo(-ra), austero(-ra).

strip [strɪp] n (of paper, cloth etc) tira f; (of land, water) faixa f ♦ vt (paint) raspar; (wallpaper) arrancar ♦ vi (undress) despir-se.

stripe [straɪp] n risca f, listra f.

striped [straɪpt] adj de listras.

strip-search vt revistar (mandando tirar a roupa a alguém).

strip show n espetáculo m de striptease.

striptease [ˈstriptiːz] n striptease m.

strive [straɪv] (*pt* **strove,** *pp* **striven** ['strɪvn]) *vi:* **to ~ for** sthg lutar por algo; **to ~ to do** sthg esforçar-se por fazer algo.

stroke [strəuk] *n* (MED) trombose *f*; *(in tennis)* batida *f*; *(in golf)* tacada *f*; *(swimming style)* estilo *m* ◆ *vt* fazer festas em; **a ~ of luck** um golpe de sorte.

stroll [strəul] *n* passeio *m*.

stroller ['strəulər] *n* (Am: pushchair) carrinho *m* de bebê.

strong [strɒŋ] *adj* forte; *(structure, bridge, chair)* sólido(-da); *(accent)* forte, acentuado(-da).

strongbox ['strɒŋbɒks] *n* caixa-forte *f*.

stronghold ['strɒŋhəuld] *n (fig: bastion)* bastião *m*.

strongly ['strɒŋlɪ] *adv (built)* solidamente; *(advise)* vivamente; *(taste, smell)* intensamente; *(support)* plenamente; **to ~ oppose** sthg opor-se completamente a algo.

strove [strəuv] *pt* → **strive.**

struck [strʌk] *pt & pp* → **strike.**

structure ['strʌktʃər] *n (arrangement, organization)* estrutura *f*; *(building)* construção *f*.

struggle ['strʌgl] *n (great effort)* luta *f* ◆ *vi (fight)* lutar; *(in order to get free)* debater-se; **to ~ to do** sthg esforçar-se por fazer algo.

stub [stʌb] *n (of cigarette)* ponta *f*; *(of cheque, ticket)* talão *m*.

stubble ['stʌbl] *n (on face)* barba *f* por fazer.

stubborn ['stʌbən] *adj (person)* teimoso(-osa).

stuck [stʌk] *pt & pp* → **stick** ◆ *adj* preso(-sa).

stuck-up *adj (inf)* presunçoso(-osa), pedante.

stud [stʌd] *n (on boots)* pitão *m*, piton *m*; *(fastener)* botão *m* de pressão (Br), mola *f* (Port); *(earring)* brinco *m*.

student ['stju:dnt] *n* estudante *mf*.

student card *n* carteira *f* de estudante.

students' union ['stju:dnts-] *n (place)* associação *f* de estudantes.

studio ['stju:dɪəu] (*pl* **-s**) *n (for filming, broadcasting)* estúdio *m*; *(of artist)* atelier *m*.

studio apartment (Am) = **studio flat.**

studio flat *n* (Brit) conjugado *m* (Br), estúdio *m* (Port).

studious ['stju:djəs] *adj* estudioso (-osa), aplicado(-da).

studiously ['stju:djəslɪ] *adv* cuidadosamente.

study ['stʌdɪ] *n* estudo *m*; *(room)* escritório *m* ◆ *vt (learn about)* estudar; *(examine)* examinar ◆ *vi* estudar.

stuff [stʌf] *n (inf) (substance)* coisa *f*; *(things, possessions)* coisas *fpl*, tralha *f* ◆ *vt (put roughly)* enfiar; *(fill)* rechear.

stuffed [stʌft] *adj (food)* recheado(-da); *(inf: full up)* cheio (cheia); *(dead animal)* embalsamado(-da).

stuffing ['stʌfɪŋ] *n* recheio *m*.

stuffy ['stʌfɪ] *adj (room, atmosphere)* abafado(-da).

stumble ['stʌmbl] *vi (when walking)* tropeçar.

stumbling block ['stʌmblɪŋ-] *n* entrave *m*, obstáculo *m*.

stump [stʌmp] *n (of tree)* toco *m*.

stun [stʌn] *vt (shock)* chocar.

stung [stʌŋ] *pt & pp* → **sting.**

stunk [stʌŋk] *pt & pp* → **stink.**

stunning ['stʌnɪŋ] *adj* espantoso(-osa).

stunt [stʌnt] *n (for publicity)* golpe *m* OR truque *m* publicitário; *(in film)* cena *f* arriscada.

stunt man *n* dublê *mf* (Br), duplo *m* (Port).

stupendous [stju:'pendəs] *adj (inf: wonderful)* estupendo(-da).

stupid ['stju:pɪd] *adj* estúpido(-da).

stupidity [stju:'pɪdətɪ] *n* estupidez *f*.

sturdy ['stɜ:dɪ] *adj* robusto(-ta).

stutter ['stʌtər] *vi* gaguejar.

stye [staɪ] *n* terçol *m*, terçolho *m* (Port).

style [staɪl] *n* estilo *m*; *(design)* modelo *m* ◆ *vt (hair)* pentear.

stylish ['staɪlɪʃ] *adj* elegante.

stylist ['staɪlɪst] *n (hairdresser)* cabeleireiro *m* (-ra *f*).

stylus ['staɪləs] (*pl* **-es**) *n (on record player)* agulha *f*.

suave [swɑ:v] *adj* polido(-da).

sub [sʌb] *n (inf) (substitute)* substituto *m* (-ta *f*); *(Brit: subscription)* assinatura *f*; *(Am: filled baguette)* sanduíche *m*.

subconscious [sʌb'kɒnʃəs] *adj* subconsciente ◆ *n:* **the ~** o subconsciente.

subdued [səb'dju:d] *adj (person)* abatido(-da); *(lighting, colour)* tênue.

subject [*n* 'sʌbdʒekt, *vb* səb'dʒekt] *n (topic)* tema *m*; *(at school)* disciplina *f*; *(at university)* cadeira *f*; (GRAMM) sujeito *m*; *(fml: of country)* cidadão *m* (-dã *f*)

◆ *vt*: **to ~ sb to sthg** submeter alguém a algo; **~ to availability** dentro do limite do estoque disponível; **they are ~ to an additional charge** estão sujeitos a um suplemento.

subjective [səb'dʒektɪv] *adj* subjetivo(-va).

subjunctive [səb'dʒʌŋktɪv] *n* subjuntivo *m* (*Br*), conjuntivo *m* (*Port*).

sublet [sʌb'let] (*pt & pp* **sublet**) *vt* subalugar, subarrendar.

sublime [sə'blaɪm] *adj* sublime.

submarine [ˌsʌbmə'riːn] *n* submarino *m*.

submerge [səb'mɜːdʒ] *vt* submergir.

submit [səb'mɪt] *vt* apresentar ◆ *vi* submeter-se.

subordinate [sə'bɔːdɪnət] *adj* (*GRAMM*) subordinado(-da).

subscribe [səb'skraɪb] *vi* (*to magazine, newspaper*) assinar.

subscriber [səb'skraɪbəʳ] *n* assinante *mf*.

subscription [səb'skrɪpʃn] *n* assinatura *f*.

subsequent [ˈsʌbsɪkwənt] *adj* subseqüente.

subsequently [ˈsʌbsɪkwəntlɪ] *adv* subseqüentemente, posteriormente.

subside [səb'saɪd] *vi* (*ground*) abater, aluir; (*feeling*) desaparecer, dissipar-se; (*noise*) diminuir.

subsidence [səb'saɪdns] *n* (*of building*) desmoronamento *m*; (*of ground*) abaixamento *m*.

subsidiary [səb'sɪdjərɪ] *adj* secundário(-ria) ◆ *n*: **~ (company)** subsidiária *f*, filial *f*.

subsidize [ˈsʌbsɪdaɪz] *vt* subsidiar.

subsidy [ˈsʌbsɪdɪ] *n* subsídio *m*.

substance [ˈsʌbstəns] *n* substância *f*.

substantial [səb'stænʃl] *adj* substancial.

substantially [səb'stænʃəlɪ] *adv* substancialmente, consideravelmente; (*true*) em grande parte; (*complete*) praticamente.

substitute [ˈsʌbstɪtjuːt] *n* (*replacement*) substituto *m* (-ta *f*); (*SPORT*) suplente *mf*.

subtitles [ˈsʌbˌtaɪtlz] *npl* legendas *fpl*.

subtle [ˈsʌtl] *adj* subtil.

subtlety [ˈsʌtltɪ] *n* subtileza *f*.

subtract [səb'trækt] *vt* subtrair.

subtraction [səb'trækʃn] *n* subtração *f*.

suburb [ˈsʌbɜːb] *n* subúrbio *m*; **the ~s** os subúrbios.

subway [ˈsʌbweɪ] *n* (*Brit: for pedestrians*) passagem *f* subterrânea; (*Am: underground railway*) metrô *m*.

succeed [sək'siːd] *vi* (*be successful*) ter êxito OR sucesso ◆ *vt* (*fml: follow*) seguir; **to ~ in doing sthg** conseguir fazer algo.

success [sək'ses] *n* êxito *m*, sucesso *m*.

successful [sək'sesful] *adj* (*plan, person*) bem sucedido(-da); (*film, book, TV programme*) de sucesso.

successive [sək'sesɪv] *adj* sucessivo (-va); **four ~ days** quatro dias seguidos OR consecutivos.

succinct [sək'sɪŋkt] *adj* sucinto(-ta).

succulent [ˈsʌkjʊlənt] *adj* suculento(-ta).

succumb [sə'kʌm] *vi*: **to ~ (to sthg)** sucumbir (a algo).

such [sʌtʃ] *adj* (*of stated kind*) tal, semelhante; (*so great*) tamanho(-nha), tal ◆ *adv*: **~ a lot** tanto; **~ a lot of books** tantos livros; **it's ~ a lovely day** está um dia tão bonito; **she has ~ good luck** ela tem tanta sorte; **~ a thing should never have happened** uma coisa assim nunca deveria ter acontecido; **~ as** tal como.

suck [sʌk] *vt* (*sweet*) chupar; (*thumb*) chupar; (*nipple*) mamar em.

sudden [ˈsʌdn] *adj* repentino(-na); **all of a ~** de repente.

suddenly [ˈsʌdnlɪ] *adv* de repente.

suds [sʌdz] *npl* espuma *f* (de sabão).

sue [suː] *vt* processar.

suede [sweɪd] *n* camurça *f*.

suet [ˈsuɪt] *n* sebo *m*.

suffer [ˈsʌfəʳ] *vt & vi* sofrer; **to ~ from** (*illness*) sofrer de.

sufferer [ˈsʌfrəʳ] *n* doente *mf*.

suffering [ˈsʌfrɪŋ] *n* sofrimento *m*.

sufficient [sə'fɪʃnt] *adj* (*fml*) suficiente.

sufficiently [sə'fɪʃntlɪ] *adv* (*fml*) bastante, suficientemente.

suffix [ˈsʌfɪks] *n* sufixo *m*.

suffocate [ˈsʌfəkeɪt] *vi* sufocar.

sugar [ˈʃʊgəʳ] *n* açúcar *m*.

sugar beet *n* beterraba *f*.

sugarcane [ˈʃʊgəkeɪn] *n* cana-de-açúcar *f*.

sugary [ˈʃʊgərɪ] *adj* (*food, drink*) açucarado(-da).

suggest [sə'dʒest] *vt* sugerir; **to ~**

doing sthg sugerir fazer algo.

suggestion [sə'dʒestʃn] *n* sugestão *f*.

suggestive [sə'dʒestɪv] *adj (remark, behaviour)* sugestivo(-va); ~ **of** sthg *(reminiscent)* que sugere algo.

suicide ['sʊɪsaɪd] *n* suicídio *m*; **to commit** ~ suicidar-se.

suit [suːt] *n (man's clothes)* terno *m (Br)*, fato *m (Port)*; *(woman's clothes)* conjunto *m*; *(in cards)* naipe *m*; *(JUR)* processo *m* ◆ *vt (subj: clothes, colour, shoes)* ficar bem em; *(be convenient for)* convir a; *(be appropriate for)* ser apropriado(-da) para.

suitable ['suːtəbl] *adj* apropriado (-da), conveniente; **to be** ~ **for** ser apropriado OR conveniente para.

suitcase ['suːtkeɪs] *n* mala *f*.

suite [swiːt] *n (set of rooms)* suíte *f*; *(furniture)* conjunto *m* de mobília.

suited ['suːtɪd] *adj*: **to be** ~ **to** sthg *(suitable)* servir para algo; **I'm not** ~ **to this humid weather** não me dou bem com este tempo úmido; **they are very well** ~ estão bem um para o outro.

sulk [sʌlk] *vi* amuar.

sulky ['sʌlkɪ] *adj* amuado(-da).

sullen ['sʌlən] *adj* taciturno(-na), carrancudo(-da).

sultana [səl'tɑːnə] *n (Brit)* sultana *f*.

sultry ['sʌltrɪ] *adj (weather, climate)* abafado(-da).

sum [sʌm] *n* soma *f*.

❏ **sum up** *vt sep (summarize)* resumir, sumariar.

summarize ['sʌməraɪz] *vt* resumir.

summary ['sʌmərɪ] *n* resumo *m*, sumário *m*.

summer ['sʌməʳ] *n* verão *m*; **in (the)** ~ no verão; ~ **holidays** férias *fpl* de verão.

summer school *n* cursos *mpl* de verão.

summertime ['sʌmətaɪm] *n* verão *m*.

summit ['sʌmɪt] *n (of mountain)* topo *m*, cume *m*; *(meeting)* conferência *f* de cúpula *(Br)*, cimeira *f (Port)*.

summon ['sʌmən] *vt (send for)* convocar; *(JUR)* intimar.

sumptuous ['sʌmptʃʊəs] *adj* suntuoso(-osa).

sun [sʌn] *n* sol *m* ◆ *vt*: **to** ~ **o.s.** apanhar sol; **to catch the** ~ bronzear-se; **to sit in the** ~ sentar-se no sol; **out of the** ~ na sombra.

Sun. *(abbr of Sunday)* dom.

sunbathe ['sʌnbeɪð] *vi* apanhar OR tomar banho de sol.

sunbed ['sʌnbed] *n* aparelho *m* de raios ultravioletas.

sun block *n* protetor *m* solar *(com fator de proteção total)*.

sunburn ['sʌnbɜːn] *n* queimadura *f* solar.

sunburnt ['sʌnbɜːnt] *adj* queimado(-da) (de sol).

sundae ['sʌndeɪ] *n* sundae *m*, sorvete regado com molho de fruta ou chocolate, polvilhado com frutos secos (nozes, avelãs, etc) e servido com creme batido.

Sunday ['sʌndɪ] *n* domingo *m*, → Saturday.

Sunday school *n* catequese *f*.

sundial ['sʌndaɪəl] *n* relógio *m* de sol.

sundown ['sʌndaʊn] *n* pôr *m* do sol.

sundress ['sʌndres] *n* vestido *m* de alças.

sundries ['sʌndrɪz] *npl (on bill)* artigos *mpl* diversos.

sunflower ['sʌn,flaʊəʳ] *n* girassol *m*.

sunflower oil *n* óleo *m* de girassol.

sung [sʌŋ] *pt* → **sing**.

sunglasses ['sʌn,glɑːsɪz] *npl* óculos *mpl* de sol, óculos escuros.

sunhat ['sʌnhæt] *n* chapéu-de-sol *m*.

sunk [sʌŋk] *pp* → **sink**.

sunlight ['sʌnlaɪt] *n* luz *f* do sol.

sun lounger [-,laʊndʒəʳ] *n* espreguiçadeira *f*.

sunny ['sʌnɪ] *adj (day, weather)* de sol, ensolarado(-da); *(room, place)* ensolarado(-da).

sunrise ['sʌnraɪz] *n* nascer *m* do sol.

sunroof ['sʌnruːf] *n* teto *m* solar.

sunset ['sʌnset] *n* pôr-do-sol *m*.

sunshade ['sʌnʃeɪd] *n* sombrinha *f*.

sunshine ['sʌnʃaɪn] *n* luz *f* do sol; **in the** ~ ao sol.

sunstroke ['sʌnstrəʊk] *n* insolação *f*.

suntan ['sʌntæn] *n* bronzeado *m*.

suntan cream *n* creme *m* bronzeador, bronzeador *m*.

suntan lotion *n* loção *f* bronzeadora, bronzeador *m*.

super ['suːpəʳ] *adj (wonderful)* chocante *(Br)*, formidável ◆ *n (petrol)* gasolina *f* super.

superb [suː'pɜːb] *adj* magnífico(-ca), soberbo(-ba).

superficial [,suːpə'fɪʃl] *adj* superficial.

superfluous [suːˈpɔːfluəs] *adj* supér-fluo(-flua).

Superglue® [ˈsuːpəgluː] *n* cola *f* ultra-rápida.

superhuman [ˌsuːpəˈhjuːmən] *adj* sobre-humano(-na).

superimpose [ˌsuːpərɪmˈpəʊz] *vt*: **to ~ sthg on sthg** sobrepor algo a algo.

superintendent [ˌsuːpərɪnˈtendənt] *n* (*Brit: of police*) = subchefe *m* (-fa *f*).

superior [suːˈpɪərɪər] *adj* superior ◆ *n* superior *mf*.

superlative [suːˈpɜːlətɪv] *adj* superlativo(-va) ◆ *n* superlativo *m*.

supermarket [ˈsuːpəˌmɑːkɪt] *n* supermercado *m*.

supernatural [ˌsuːpəˈnætʃrəl] *adj* sobrenatural.

superpower [ˈsuːpəˌpaʊər] *n* super-potência *f*.

Super Saver® *n* (*Brit*) *bilhete de trem com preço reduzido, sob certas condições*.

supersede [ˌsuːpəˈsiːd] *vt* suplantar.

supersonic [ˌsuːpəˈsɒnɪk] *adj* supersônico(-ca).

superstitious [ˌsuːpəˈstɪʃəs] *adj* supersticioso(-osa).

superstore [ˈsuːpəstɔːr] *n* hiper-mercado *m*.

supervise [ˈsuːpəvaɪz] *vt* supervisionar.

supervisor [ˈsuːpəvaɪzər] *n* (*of workers*) supervisor *m* (-ra *f*), encarregado *m* (-da *f*).

supper [ˈsʌpər] *n* (*main meal*) jantar *m*, ceia *f*; **to have ~** jantar, cear.

supple [ˈsʌpl] *adj* flexível.

supplement [*n* ˈsʌplɪmənt, *vb* ˈsʌplɪment] *n* suplemento *m* ◆ *vt* completar, complementar.

supplementary [ˌsʌplɪˈmentərɪ] *adj* suplementar.

supplier [səˈplaɪər] *n* fornecedor *m* (-ra *f*), abastecedor *m* (-ra *f*).

supply [səˈplaɪ] *n* (*store*) reserva *f*; (*providing*) fornecimento *m* ◆ *vt* fornecer; **to ~ sb with sthg** fornecer algo a alguém.

❑ **supplies** *npl* provisões *fpl*.

support [səˈpɔːt] *n* (*backing, encouragement*) apoio *m*; (*supporting object*) suporte *m* ◆ *vt* (*cause, campaign, person*) apoiar; (*SPORT*) torcer por (*Br*), ser adepto de (*Port*); (*hold up*) suportar; (*a family*) sustentar.

supporter [səˈpɔːtər] *n* (*SPORT*) torce-dor *m* (-ra *f*) (*Br*), adepto *m* (-ta *f*) (*Port*); (*of cause, political party*) partidário *m* (-ria *f*).

suppose [səˈpəʊz] *vt*: **to ~ (that)** supor que ◆ *conj* = **supposing**; **I ~ so** suponho que sim.

supposed [səˈpəʊzd] *adj* (*alleged*) suposto(-osta); **it's ~ to be quite good** é supostamente bastante bom; **you were ~ to be here at nine** você era para estar aqui às nove.

supposedly [səˈpəʊzɪdlɪ] *adv* supostamente.

supposing [səˈpəʊzɪŋ] *conj* supondo que.

suppress [səˈpres] *vt* (*uprising, revolt, emotions*) reprimir; (*information, report*) ocultar.

supreme [soˈpriːm] *adj* supremo(-ma).

surcharge [ˈsɜːtʃɑːdʒ] *n* sobretaxa *f*.

sure [ʃʊər] *adj* (*certain to happen*) certo(-ta); (*with no doubts*) seguro(-ra) ◆ *adv* (*inf: yes*) claro; **are you ~?** você tem certeza?; **to be ~ of o.s.** ser seguro de si; **to make ~ (that)** ... assegurar-se de que ...; **for ~** com certeza.

surely [ˈʃʊəlɪ] *adv* com OR de certeza.

surf [sɜːf] *n* surf *m* ◆ *vi* fazer surfe.

surface [ˈsɜːfɪs] *n* superfície *f*; **"temporary road ~"** "asfaltamento temporário" (*Br*), "traçado temporário" (*Port*).

surface area *n* área *f* de superfície.

surface mail *n* correio *m* por via terreste.

surfboard [ˈsɜːfbɔːd] *n* prancha *f* de surfe.

surfing [ˈsɜːfɪŋ] *n* surf *m*; **to go ~** ir fazer surfe.

surge [sɜːdʒ] *n* (*of electricity*) sobre-tensão *f*; (*of interest, support*) onda *f*; (*of sales, applications*) aumento *m* (repentino) ◆ *vi* (*people, vehicles*): **~ forward** avançar em massa.

surgeon [ˈsɜːdʒən] *n* cirurgião *m* (-giã *f*).

surgery [ˈsɜːdʒərɪ] *n* (*treatment*) cirurgia *f*; (*Brit: building*) consultório *m*; (*Brit: period*) horário *m* de atendimento, horas *fpl* de consulta.

surgical [ˈsɜːdʒɪkl] *adj* (*instrument, gown*) cirúrgico(-ca).

surgical spirit *n* (*Brit*) álcool *m* etílico.

surly [ˈsɜːlɪ] *adj* mal-humorado(-da).

surmount [sɜːˈmaʊnt] *vt* vencer, superar.

surname ['sɜːneɪm] *n* sobrenome *m* (*Br*), apelido *m* (*Port*).

surpass [sə'pɑːs] *vt* ultrapassar, exceder.

surplus ['sɜːpləs] *n* excedente *m*.

surprise [sə'praɪz] *n* surpresa *f* ◆ *vt* (*astonish*) surpreender.

surprised [sə'praɪzd] *adj* surpreso(-sa).

surprising [sə'praɪzɪŋ] *adj* surpreendente.

surprisingly [sə'praɪzɪŋlɪ] *adv*: **it was ~ good** foi melhor do que esperávamos; **not ~** como seria de esperar.

surrender [sə'rendəʳ] *vi* render-se ◆ *vt* (*fml: hand over*) entregar.

surreptitious [ˌsʌrəp'tɪʃəs] *adj* subreptício(-cia).

surround [sə'raund] *vt* rodear.

surrounding [sə'raundɪŋ] *adj* circundante, à volta.

surroundings *npl* arredores *mpl*.

surveillance [sɜː'veɪləns] *n* vigilância *f*.

survey ['sɜːveɪ] (*pl* **-s**) *n* (*investigation*) inquérito *m*; (*poll*) sondagem *f*; (*of land*) levantamento *m* topográfico; (*Brit: of house*) inspeção *f*, vistoria *f*.

surveyor [sə'veɪəʳ] *n* (*Brit: of houses*) inspetor *m* (-ra *f*), perito *m* (-ta *f*); (*of land*) agrimensor *m* (-ra *f*).

survival [sə'vaɪvl] *n* sobrevivência *f*.

survive [sə'vaɪv] *vi* sobreviver ◆ *vt* sobreviver a.

survivor [sə'vaɪvəʳ] *n* sobrevivente *mf*.

susceptible [sə'septəbl] *adj* suscetível; **to be ~ to sthg** ser suscetível a algo.

suspect [*vb* sə'spekt, *n & adj* 'sʌspekt] *vt* (*mistrust*) suspeitar de ◆ *n* suspeito *m* (-ta *f*) ◆ *adj* suspeito(-ta); **to ~ sb of sthg** suspeitar que alguém tenha feito algo; **to ~ (that)** suspeitar que.

suspend [sə'spend] *vt* suspender.

suspender belt [sə'spendə-] *n* cinta-liga *f* (*Br*), cinto *m* de ligas (*Port*).

suspenders [sə'spendəz] *npl* (*Brit: for stockings*) cinto *m* de ligas; (*Am: for trousers*) suspensórios *mpl*.

suspense [sə'spens] *n* suspense *m*.

suspension [sə'spenʃn] *n* suspensão *f*.

suspension bridge *n* ponte *m* pênsil.

suspicion [sə'spɪʃn] *n* (*mistrust, idea*) suspeita *f*; (*trace*) vestígio *m*.

suspicious [sə'spɪʃəs] *adj* (*behaviour,*

situation) suspeito(-ta); **to be ~ of** (*distrustful*) desconfiar OR suspeitar de.

sustain [sə'steɪn] *vt* (*maintain, prolong*) manter; (*feed*) sustentar; (*suffer*) sofrer; (*withstand*) agüentar, suportar.

SW *abbr* = **short wave**.

swallow ['swɒləʊ] *n* (*bird*) andorinha *f* ◆ *vt & vi* engolir.

swam [swæm] *pt* → **swim**.

swamp [swɒmp] *n* pântano *m*.

swan [swɒn] *n* cisne *m*.

swap [swɒp] *vt* (*possessions, places*) trocar de; (*ideas, stories*) trocar; **to ~ sthg for sthg** trocar algo por algo.

swarm [swɔːm] *n* (*of bees*) enxame *m*.

swarthy ['swɔːðɪ] *adj* moreno(-na).

swastika ['swɒstɪkə] *n* suástica *f*, cruz *f* gamada.

swat [swɒt] *vt* esmagar, matar.

sway [sweɪ] *vt* (*influence*) influenciar ◆ *vi* (*swing*) balançar, oscilar.

swear [sweəʳ] (*pt* **swore**, *pp* **sworn**) *vi* (*use rude language*) praguejar; (*promise*) jurar ◆ *vt*: **to ~ to do sthg** jurar fazer algo.

swearword ['sweəwɜːd] *n* palavrão *m*, asneira *f*.

sweat [swet] *n* suor *m* ◆ *vi* suar.

sweater ['swetəʳ] *n* suéter *m* (*Br*), camisola *f* (*Port*).

sweatshirt ['swetʃɜːt] *n* sweatshirt *f*, suéter *m* de algodão (*Br*), camisola *f* de algodão (*Port*).

sweaty ['swetɪ] *adj* (*skin, clothes*) suado(-da).

swede [swiːd] *n* (*Brit*) nabo *m*.

Swede [swiːd] *n* sueco *m* (-ca *f*).

Sweden ['swiːdn] *n* Suécia *f*.

Swedish ['swiːdɪʃ] *adj* sueco(-ca) ◆ *n* (*language*) sueco *m* ◆ *npl*: **the ~** os suecos.

sweep [swiːp] (*pt & pp* **swept**) *vt* (*with brush, broom*) varrer.

sweet [swiːt] *adj* doce; (*smell*) agradável ◆ *n* (*Brit*) (*candy*) bala *f* (*Br*), rebuçado *m* (*Port*); (*dessert*) doce *m*; **how ~ of you!** que gentileza a sua!

sweet-and-sour *adj* agridoce.

sweet corn *n* milho *m*.

sweeten ['swiːtn] *vt* adoçar.

sweetener ['swiːtnəʳ] *n* (*for drink*) adoçante *m*.

sweetheart ['swiːthɑːt] *n* (*term of endearment*) querido *m* (-da *f*); (*boyfriend or girlfriend*) namorado *m* (-da *f*).

sweetness ['swiːtnɪs] *n* doçura *f*; (*of*

smell) fragrância *f.*

sweet pea *n* ervilha-de-cheiro *f.*

sweet potato *n* batata-doce *f.*

sweet shop *n (Brit)* confeitaria *f.*

swell [swɛl] *(pp* **swollen)** *vi (ankle, arm etc)* inchar.

swelling ['swɛlɪŋ] *n* inchaço *m.*

sweltering ['swɛltərɪŋ] *adj (weather)* abrasador(-ra); *(person)* encalorado(-da).

swept [swɛpt] *pt & pp* → **sweep.**

swerve [swɜːv] *vi (vehicle)* dar uma guinada.

swift [swɪft] *adj* rápido(-da) ◆ *n (bird)* andorinhão *m.*

swig [swɪg] *n (inf)* gole *m,* trago *m.*

swim [swɪm] *(pt* **swam,** *pp* **swum)** *vi (in water)* nadar ◆ *n:* **to go for a ~** ir dar um mergulho.

swimmer ['swɪməʳ] *n* nadador *m* (-ra *f).*

swimming ['swɪmɪŋ] *n* natação *f;* **to go ~** ir nadar.

swimming baths *npl (Brit)* piscina *f* municipal.

swimming cap *n* touca *f* de banho.

swimming costume *n (Brit)* traje *m* de banho *(Br),* fato *m* de banho *(Port).*

swimming pool *n* piscina *f.*

swimming trunks *npl* calções *mpl* de banho.

swimsuit ['swɪmsuːt] *n* traje *m* de banho *(Br),* fato *m* de banho *(Port).*

swindle ['swɪndl] *n* fraude *f.*

swine [swaɪn] *(pl inv OR* **-s)** *n (inf: person)* canalha *mf.*

swing [swɪŋ] *(pt & pp* **swung)** *n (for children)* balanço *m* ◆ *vt (move from side to side)* balançar ◆ *vi (move from side to side)* balançar-se.

swipe [swaɪp] *vt (credit card etc)* passar pela ranhura.

Swiss [swɪs] *adj* suíço(-ça) ◆ *n (person)* suíço *m* (-ça *f)* ◆ *npl:* **the ~** os suíços.

Swiss cheese *n* queijo *m* suíço.

swiss roll *n* rocambole *m* (doce) *(Br),* torta *f* (doce) *(Port).*

switch [swɪtʃ] *n (for light, power)* interruptor *m; (for TV, radio)* botão *m* ◆ *vt (change)* mudar de; *(exchange)* trocar ◆ *vi* mudar.

❏ **switch off** *vt sep (light, radio)* apagar, desligar; *(engine)* desligar.

❏ **switch on** *vt sep (light, radio)* acender, ligar; *(engine)* ligar.

switchboard ['swɪtʃbɔːd] *n* PBX *m.*

Switzerland ['swɪtsələnd] *n* Suíça *f.*

swivel ['swɪvl] *vi* girar.

swollen ['swəʊln] *pp* → **swell** ◆ *adj (ankle, arm etc)* inchado(-da).

swoop [swuːp] *vi (fly downwards)* descer em vôo picado; *(pounce)* atacar de surpresa.

swop [swɒp] = **swap.**

sword [sɔːd] *n* espada *f.*

swordfish ['sɔːdfɪʃ] *(pl inv)* *n* peixe-espada *m (Br),* agulhão *m (Port).*

swore [swɔːʳ] *pt* → **swear.**

sworn [swɔːn] *pp* → **swear.**

swot [swɒt] *n (Brit: inf: person)* caxias *mf (Br),* marrão *m* (-ona *f) (Port)* ◆ *vi (Brit: inf):* **to ~ for** *(sthg)* queimar as pestanas (em algo), marrar (para algo) *(Port).*

swum [swʌm] *pp* → **swim.**

swung [swʌŋ] *pt & pp* → **swing.**

sycamore ['sɪkəmɔːʳ] *n* bordo *m,* plátano-bastardo *m.*

syllable ['sɪləbl] *n* sílaba *f.*

syllabus ['sɪləbəs] *n* programa *m* (de estudos).

symbol ['sɪmbl] *n* símbolo *m.*

symbolize ['sɪmbəlaɪz] *vt* simbolizar.

symmetry ['sɪmɪtrɪ] *n* simetria *f.*

sympathetic [ˌsɪmpə'θetɪk] *adj (understanding)* compreensivo(-va).

sympathize ['sɪmpəθaɪz] *vi:* **to ~ (with)** *(feel sorry)* compadecer-se (de); *(understand)* compreender.

sympathizer ['sɪmpəθaɪzəʳ] *n* simpatizante *mf.*

sympathy ['sɪmpəθɪ] *n (understanding)* compreensão *f.*

symphony ['sɪmfənɪ] *n* sinfonia *f.*

symptom ['sɪmptəm] *n* sintoma *m.*

synagogue ['sɪnəgɒg] *n* sinagoga *f.*

syndrome ['sɪndrəʊm] *n* síndrome *f.*

synonym ['sɪnənɪm] *n* sinônimo *m;* **to be a ~ for** OR **of sthg** ser sinônimo de algo.

syntax ['sɪntæks] *n* sintaxe *f.*

synthesizer ['sɪnθəsaɪzəʳ] *n* sintetizador *m.*

synthetic [sɪn'θetɪk] *adj* sintético (-ca).

syphon ['saɪfn] = **siphon.**

syringe [sɪ'rɪndʒ] *n* seringa *f.*

syrup ['sɪrəp] *n (for fruit etc)* calda *f.*

system ['sɪstəm] *n* sistema *m; (for gas, heating etc)* instalação *f.*

systematic [ˌsɪstə'mætɪk] *adj* sistemático(-ca).

T

ta [tɑː] *excl (Brit: inf)* obrigado!

tab [tæb] *n (of cloth, paper etc)* etiqueta *f*; *(bill)* conta *f*; **put it on my ~** ponha na minha conta.

table ['teɪbl] *n (piece of furniture)* mesa *f*; *(of figures etc)* quadro *m*.

tablecloth ['teɪblklɒθ] *n* toalha *f* de mesa.

table lamp *n* abajur *m* (de mesa) (Br), candeeiro *m* (de mesa) (Port).

tablemat ['teɪblmæt] *n* descanso *m* para pratos *(Br)*, individual *m* (Port).

tablespoon ['teɪblspuːn] *n* colher *f* de sopa.

tablet ['tæblɪt] *n (pill)* comprimido *m*; *(of soap)* barra *f*; *(of chocolate)* tablete *f*.

table tennis *n* pingue-pongue *m*, tênis *m* de mesa.

table wine *n* vinho *m* de mesa.

tabloid ['tæblɔɪd] *n* jornal *m* sensacionalista, tablóide *m*.

tacit ['tæsɪt] *adj* tácito(-ta).

taciturn ['tæsɪtɜːn] *adj* taciturno (-na).

tack [tæk] *n (nail)* tacha *f*.

tackle ['tækl] *n (in football, hockey)* ataque *m*; *(in rugby, American football)* placagem *f*; *(for fishing)* apetrechos *mpl* ♦ *vt (in football, hockey)* carregar; *(in rugby, American football)* placar; *(deal with)* enfrentar.

tacky ['tækɪ] *adj (inf: jewellery, design etc)* cafona (Br), piroso(-sa) (Port).

taco ['tækəʊ] *(pl -s) n* taco *m*, espécie de crepe de farinha de milho frito recheado normalmente com carne picada e feijão *(especialidade mexicana)*.

tact [tækt] *n* tato *m*.

tactful ['tæktfʊl] *adj* com muito tato, diplomático(-ca).

tactical ['tæktɪkl] *adj* tático(-ca).

tactics ['tæktɪks] *npl* tática *f*, estratégia *f*.

tactless ['tæktlɪs] *adj* pouco diplomático(-ca).

tadpole ['tædpəʊl] *n* girino *m*.

tag [tæg] *n (label)* etiqueta *f*.

tagliatelle [ˌtæglɪə'telɪ] *n* talharins *mpl*.

tail [teɪl] *n* cauda *f*.
◻ **tails** *n (of coin)* coroas *fpl* ♦ *npl (formal dress)* fraque *m*.

tailback ['teɪlbæk] *n (Brit)* fila *f* de carros.

tailcoat ['teɪlkəʊt] *n* fraque *m*.

tailgate ['teɪlgeɪt] *n (of car)* porta *f* do porta-malas.

tailor ['teɪlə'] *n* alfaiate *m*.

tailor-made *adj* feito(-ta) sob medida.

tailwind ['teɪlwɪnd] *n* vento *m* de popa.

tainted ['teɪntɪd] *adj (reputation)* manchado(-da); *(profits, money)* sujo(-ja); *(Am: food)* estragado(-da).

Taiwan [ˌtaɪ'wɑːn] *n* Taiwan *s*, Formosa *f*.

take [teɪk] *(pt took, pp taken) vt* 1. *(carry, drive, contain)* levar.
2. *(hold, grasp)* segurar.
3. *(do, make)*: **to ~ a bath/shower** tomar um banho/uma ducha; **to ~ an exam** fazer um exame; **to ~ a photo** tirar uma foto.
4. *(require)* requerer; **how long will it ~?** quanto tempo é que vai demorar?
5. *(steal)* tirar.
6. *(train, taxi, plane, bus)* apanhar.
7. *(route, path, road)* seguir por.
8. *(medicine)* tomar.
9. *(size in clothes)* vestir; *(size in shoes)* calçar; **what size do you ~?** *(in clothes)* que tamanho você veste?; *(in shoes)* que número você calça?
10. *(subtract)* tirar, subtrair.
11. *(accept)* aceitar; **do you ~ travel-**

ler's cheques? vocês aceitam cheques de viagem?; **to ~ sb's advice** seguir os conselhos de alguém.

12. *(react to)* reagir a; **to ~ sthg the wrong way** levar algo a mal.

13. *(control, power, attitude)* assumir; **to ~ charge of** assumir a responsabilidade de; **to ~ an interest in sthg** interessar-se por algo.

14. *(tolerate)* agüentar.

15. *(assume)*: **I ~ it that ...** presumo que ....

16. *(pulse)* medir; *(temperature)* tirar.

17. *(rent)* alugar.

❑ **take apart** *vt sep* desmontar.

❑ **take away** *vt sep (remove)* levar; *(subtract)* tirar, subtrair.

❑ **take back** *vt sep (thing borrowed)* devolver; *(person)* levar (de volta); *(accept)* aceitar de volta; *(statement)* retirar.

❑ **take down** *vt sep (picture, decorations, curtains)* remover.

❑ **take in** *vt sep (include)* incluir; *(understand)* perceber; *(deceive)* enganar; *(clothes)* apertar.

❑ **take off** *vi (plane)* levantar vôo, decolar ♦ *vt sep (remove)* tirar; **to ~ a day/week off** *(as holiday)* tirar um dia/uma semana de folga.

❑ **take out** *vt sep (from container, pocket)* tirar; *(library book)* pegar *(Br)*, requisitar *(Port)*; *(insurance policy)* fazer; *(loan)* pedir; **to ~ sb out for dinner** convidar alguém para jantar fora.

❑ **take over** *vi* assumir o controle.

❑ **take up** *vt sep (begin)* dedicar-se a; *(use up)* ocupar; *(trousers, skirt, dress)* subir a bainha de.

takeaway ['teɪkə,weɪ] *n (Brit) (shop)* loja *que vende comida para viagem*; *(food)* comida *f* para viagem.

taken ['teɪkn] *pp* → **take**.

takeoff ['teɪkɒf] *n (of plane)* decolagem *f*.

takeout ['teɪkaʊt] *(Am)* = **takeaway**.

takeover ['teɪk,əʊvər] *n (of company)* aquisição *f*.

takings ['teɪkɪŋz] *npl* receita *f*.

talc [tælk] = **talcum powder**.

talcum powder ['tælkəm-] *n* (pó de) talco *m*.

tale [teɪl] *n (story)* conto *m*; *(account)* história *f*.

talent ['tælənt] *n* talento *m*.

talented ['tæləntɪd] *adj* talentoso

(-osa); **she's very ~** ela tem muito talento.

talk [tɔːk] *n (conversation)* conversa *f*; *(speech)* conferência *f* ♦ *vi* falar; **to ~ to sb (about sthg)** falar com alguém (sobre algo); **to ~ with sb** falar com alguém.

❑ **talks** *npl* negociações *fpl*.

talkative ['tɔːkətɪv] *adj* tagarela.

talk show *n* talk-show *m*, programa *m* de entrevistas.

tall [tɔːl] *adj* alto(-ta); **how ~ are you?** qual é a sua altura?; **I'm six feet ~** meço 1.80 m.

tally ['tælɪ] *n* registro *m* ♦ *vi* bater certo.

talon ['tælən] *n* garra *f*.

tambourine [,tæmbə'riːn] *n* pandeireta *f*.

tame [teɪm] *adj (animal)* domesticado(-da).

tamper ['tæmpər] : **tamper with** *vt fus (machine)* mexer em; *(records, file)* alterar, falsificar; *(lock)* tentar forçar.

tampon ['tæmpɒn] *n* tampão *m*.

tan [tæn] *n (suntan)* bronzeado *m* ♦ *vi* bronzear ♦ *adj (colour)* cor-de-mel (inv).

tangent ['tændʒənt] *n (in geometry)* tangente *f*; **to go off at a ~** divagar.

tangerine [,tændʒə'riːn] *n* tangerina *f*.

tangible ['tændʒəbl] *adj* tangível.

tangle ['tæŋgl] *n (mass)* emaranhado *m*.

tank [tæŋk] *n* tanque *m*.

tanker ['tæŋkər] *n (truck)* caminhão-cisterna *m*.

tanned [tænd] *adj (suntanned)* bronzeado(-da).

Tannoy® ['tænɔɪ] *n* (sistema *m* de) altofalantes *mpl*.

tantalizing ['tæntəlaɪzɪŋ] *adj* tentador(-ra).

tantrum ['tæntrəm] *n*: **to have OR throw a ~** fazer birra.

tap [tæp] *n (for water)* torneira *f* ♦ *vt (hit)* bater (ligeiramente) com.

tap dance *n* sapateado *m*.

tape [teɪp] *n (cassette, video)* fita *f (Br)*, cassete *f*; *(in cassette, strip of material)* fita *f*; *(adhesive material)* fita-cola *f* ♦ *vt (record)* gravar; *(stick)* colar com fita-cola.

tape measure *n* fita *f* métrica.

taper ['teɪpər] *vi (corridor)* tornar-se mais estreito(-ta); *(trousers)* afunilar.

tape recorder *n* gravador *m*.
tapestry ['tæpɪstrɪ] *n* tapeçaria *f*.
tap water *n* água *f* da torneira.
tar [tɑːʳ] *n* alcatrão *m*.
target ['tɑːgɪt] *n* alvo *m*.
tariff ['tærɪf] *n* (price list) lista *f* de preços; (Brit: menu) menu *m*; (at customs) tarifa *f*.
tarmac ['tɑːmæk] *n* (at airport) pista *f*. ❏ **Tarmac®** *n* (on road) asfalto *m*, macadame *m* betuminoso.
tarnish ['tɑːnɪʃ] *vt* (make dull) embaciar; (fig: damage) manchar.
tarpaulin [tɑːˈpɔːlɪn] *n* lona *f* alcatroada, oleado *m*.
tart [tɑːt] *n* (sweet) tarte *f*.
tartan ['tɑːtn] *n* tartã *m*, tecido de lã com os xadrezes tipicamente escoseses.
tartare sauce [tɑːtə-] *n* molho *m* tártaro, molho usado para acompanhar peixe, feito com maionese, ervas aromáticas, alcaparras e pepino de conserva picado.
task [tɑːsk] *n* tarefa *f*.
tassel ['tæsl] *n* borla *f*.
taste [teɪst] *n* (flavour) sabor *m*, gosto *m*; (discernment, sense) gosto ◆ *vt* (sample) provar; (detect) detectar o sabor de ◆ *vi*: **to ~ of sthg** ter gosto de algo; **it ~s bad/good** tem um gosto ruim/bom; **to have a ~ of sthg** (food, drink) provar algo; (fig: experience) experimentar algo; **bad/good ~** mau/bom gosto.
tasteful ['teɪstfʊl] *adj* com bom gosto.
tasteless ['teɪstlɪs] *adj* (food) insípido(-da); (comment, decoration) de mau gosto.
tasty ['teɪstɪ] *adj* saboroso(-osa).
tatters ['tætəz] *npl*: **in ~** (clothes) em farrapos; (confidence, reputation) destruído(-da).
tattoo [təˈtuː] (pl -s) *n* (on skin) tatuagem *f*; (military display) desfile *m* militar.
tatty ['tætɪ] *adj* (Brit) (inf) (flat) caindo aos pedaços; (clothes) surrado(-da); (area) degradado(-da).
taught [tɔːt] *pt & pp* → teach.
taunt [tɔːnt] *vt* gozar de, troçar de ◆ *n* piada *f*, boca *f* (Port).
Taurus ['tɔːrəs] *n* Touro *m*.
taut [tɔːt] *adj* (rope, string) esticado(-da); (muscles) tenso(-sa).
tax [tæks] *n* imposto *m*, taxa *f* ◆ *vt* (goods) lançar imposto sobre; (person)

cobrar impostos a.
taxable ['tæksəbl] *adj* tributável, sujeito(-ta) a impostos.
tax allowance *n* rendimento *m* mínimo não tributável.
taxation [tækˈseɪʃn] *n* impostos *mpl*.
tax collector *n* cobrador *m* (-ra *f*) de impostos.
tax disc *n* (Brit) plaqueta *f* (Br), selo *m* automóvel (Port).
tax-free *adj* isento(-ta) de imposto, tax-free (inv).
taxi ['tæksɪ] *n* táxi *m* ◆ *vi* (plane) andar (pela pista).
taxi driver *n* taxista *mf*, motorista *mf* de táxi.
tax inspector *n* fiscal *mf*.
taxi rank *n* (Brit) ponto *m* de táxi (Br), praça *f* de táxis (Port).
taxi stand (Am) = taxi rank.
taxpayer ['tæks,peɪəʳ] *n* contribuinte *mf*.
tax relief *n* benefício *m* fiscal.
TB *abbr* = tuberculosis.
T-bone steak *n* bife *m* com osso (em forma de T).
tea [tiː] *n* chá *m*; (afternoon meal) lanche *m*; (evening meal) jantar *m*.
tea bag *n* saquinho *m* de chá.
tea break *n* (Brit) pausa *f* para o chá (durante as horas de trabalho).
teacake ['tiːkeɪk] *n* pãozinho doce com passas.
teach [tiːtʃ] (pt & pp taught) *vt & vi* ensinar; **to ~ sb sthg, to ~ sthg to sb** ensinar algo a alguém; **to ~ sb (how) to do sthg** ensinar alguém a OR como fazer algo.
teacher ['tiːtʃəʳ] *n* professor *m* (-ra *f*).
teaching ['tiːtʃɪŋ] *n* ensino *m*.
tea cloth *n* pano *m* de prato.
tea cosy *n* (Brit) abafador *m* (para o bule do chá).
tea cozy (Am) = tea cosy.
teacup ['tiːkʌp] *n* xícara *f* de chá.
team [tiːm] *n* (SPORT) time *m* (Br), equipa *f* (Port); (group) equipe *f*.
teammate ['tiːmmeɪt] *n* colega *mf* de equipe.
teamwork ['tiːmwɜːk] *n* trabalho *m* de equipe.
teapot ['tiːpɒt] *n* bule *m*.
tear[1] [teəʳ] (pt tore, pp torn) *vt* (rip) rasgar ◆ *vi* (rip) rasgar-se; (move quickly) precipitar-se ◆ *n* (rip) rasgão *m*.

❏ **tear up** vt sep rasgar.

tear² [tɪər] n lágrima f.

teardrop ['tɪədrɒp] n lágrima f.

tearful ['tɪəfʊl] adj (person) em lágrimas, choroso(-osa).

tearoom ['tiːrʊm] n salão m de chá.

tease [tiːz] vt (make fun of) gozar de.

tea set n serviço m de chá.

teaspoon ['tiːspuːn] n colher f de chá.

teaspoonful ['tiːspuːnˌfʊl] n colher f de chá.

teat [tiːt] n (of animal) teta f; (Brit: of bottle) bico m (Br), tetina f (Port).

teatime ['tiːtaɪm] n hora f do lanche.

tea towel n pano m de prato.

technical ['teknɪkl] adj técnico(-ca).

technical drawing n desenho m técnico.

technicality [ˌteknɪˈkælətɪ] n (detail) pormenor m técnico.

technically ['teknɪklɪ] adv tecnicamente.

technician [tekˈnɪʃn] n técnico m (-ca f).

technique [tekˈniːk] n técnica f.

technological [ˌteknəˈlɒdʒɪkl] adj tecnológico(-ca).

technology [tekˈnɒlədʒɪ] n tecnologia f.

teddy (bear) ['tedɪ-] n ursinho m (de pelúcia).

tedious ['tiːdjəs] adj tedioso(-osa).

tee [tiː] n tee m.

teenager ['tiːnˌeɪdʒər] n adolescente mf.

teens [tiːnz] npl adolescência f.

teeth [tiːθ] pl → tooth.

teethe [tiːð] vi: he's teething os dentes dele estão começando a nascer.

teetotal [tiːˈtəʊtl] adj abstêmio (-mia).

teetotaler [tiːˈtəʊtlər] (Am) = teetotaller.

teetotaller [tiːˈtəʊtlər] n (Brit) abstêmio m (-mia f).

TEFL ['tefl] (abbr of Teaching (of) English as a Foreign Language) n ensino do inglês como língua estrangeira.

telecommunications [ˌtelɪkəmjuːnɪˈkeɪʃnz] npl telecomunicações fpl.

telegram ['telɪgræm] n telegrama m.

telegraph ['telɪgrɑːf] n telégrafo m ◆ vt telegrafar.

telegraph pole n poste m telegráfico.

telephone ['telɪfəʊn] n telefone m ◆ vt telefonar para ◆ vi telefonar; **to be on the ~** (talking) estar no telefone; (connected) ter telefone.

telephone book n catálogo m (Br), lista f telefônica.

telephone booth n cabine f telefônica.

telephone box n cabine f telefônica.

telephone call n chamada f telefônica, telefonema m.

telephone directory n catálogo m (Br), lista f telefônica.

telephone number n número m de telefone.

telephonist [tɪˈlefənɪst] n (Brit) telefonista mf.

telephoto lens [ˌtelɪˈfəʊtəʊ-] n teleobjetiva f.

telescope ['telɪskəʊp] n telescópio m.

teletext ['telɪtekst] n teletexto m.

televise ['telɪvaɪz] vt transmitir pela televisão.

television ['telɪˌvɪʒn] n televisão f; **what's on (the) ~ tonight?** o que é que tem na televisão hoje à noite?

television set n aparelho m de televisão, televisor m.

telex ['teleks] n telex m.

tell [tel] (pt & pp told) vt (inform) dizer; (story, joke) contar; (truth, lie) dizer, contar; (distinguish) distinguir ◆ vi: **can you ~?** dá para notar?; **can you ~ me the time?** podia dizer-me as horas?; **to ~ sb sthg** dizer algo a alguém; **to ~ sb about sthg** contar algo a alguém; **to ~ sb how to do sthg** dizer a alguém como fazer algo; **to ~ sb to do sthg** dizer a alguém para fazer algo; **to ~ the difference** ver a diferença.

❏ **tell off** vt sep ralhar com, repreender.

teller ['telər] n (in bank) caixa mf.

telltale ['telteɪl] n fofoqueiro m (-ra f) (Br), queixinhas mf inv (Port).

telly ['telɪ] n (Brit: inf) televisão f.

temp [temp] n empregado m temporário (empregada f temporária); ◆ vi trabalhar como empregado temporário.

temper ['tempər] n: **to be in a ~** estar de mau humor, estar irritado(-da); **to**

lose one's ~ perder a paciência, irritar-se.

temperament ['tɛmprəmənt] n temperamento m.

temperamental [ˌtɛmprə'mɛntl] adj temperamental.

temperate ['tɛmprət] adj temperado(-da).

temperature ['tɛmprətʃər] n temperatura f; **to have a ~** ter febre.

tempestuous [tɛm'pɛstjuəs] adj tempestuoso(-osa).

temple ['tɛmpl] n (building) templo m; (of forehead) têmpora f.

temporarily [Brit 'tɛmprərəlɪ, Am ˌtɛmpə'rɛrɪlɪ] adv temporariamente.

temporary ['tɛmprərɪ] adj temporário(-ria).

tempt [tɛmpt] vt tentar; **to be ~ed to do sthg** estar OR sentir-se tentado a fazer algo.

temptation [tɛmp'teɪʃn] n tentação f.

tempting ['tɛmptɪŋ] adj tentador (-ra).

ten [tɛn] num dez, → **six**.

tenacious [tɪ'neɪʃəs] adj tenaz.

tenant ['tɛnənt] n inquilino m (-na f).

tend [tɛnd] vi: **to ~ to do sthg** ter tendência para fazer algo.

tendency ['tɛndənsɪ] n tendência f.

tender ['tɛndər] adj (affectionate) meigo(-ga); (sore) dolorido(-da); (meat) tenro(-ra) ♦ vt (fml: pay) pagar.

tendon ['tɛndən] n tendão m.

tenement ['tɛnəmənt] n cortiço m (Br), prédio m OR bloco m de apartamentos (Port) (normalmente em zonas degradadas e pobres de uma cidade).

tennis ['tɛnɪs] n tênis m.

tennis ball n bola f de tênis.

tennis court n quadra f de tênis (Br), campo m de tênis (Port).

tennis racket n raquete f de tênis.

tenor ['tɛnər] n (singer) tenor m.

tenpin bowling ['tɛnpɪn-] n (Brit) boliche m (Br), bowling m.

tenpins ['tɛnpɪnz] (Am) = **tenpin bowling**.

tense [tɛns] adj tenso(-sa) ♦ n tempo m; **the present ~** o presente.

tension ['tɛnʃn] n tensão f.

tent [tɛnt] n barraca f, tenda f.

tentacle ['tɛntəkl] n tentáculo m.

tentative ['tɛntətɪv] adj (unconfident, hesitant) hesitante; (temporary, not final) provisório(-ria).

tenth [tɛnθ] num décimo(-ma), → **sixth**.

tent peg n estaca f.

tent pole n poste m de barraca.

tenuous ['tɛnjuəs] adj tênue.

tepid ['tɛpɪd] adj tépido(-da), morno (morna).

tequila [tɪ'kiːlə] n tequilha f.

term [tɜːm] n (word, expression) termo m; (at school) período m; (at university) = semestre m; **in the long ~** a longo prazo; **in the short ~** a curto prazo; **in ~s of** no que diz respeito a; **in business ~s** do ponto de vista comercial.

❏ **terms** npl (of contract) termos mpl; (price) preço m.

terminal ['tɜːmɪnl] adj (illness) incurável ♦ n terminal m.

terminate ['tɜːmɪneɪt] vi (train, bus) terminar a viagem OR o trajeto.

terminus ['tɜːmɪnəs] n estação f terminal, terminal m.

terrace ['tɛrəs] n (patio) terraço m; **the ~s** (at football ground) a arquibancada (Br), a geral (Port).

terraced house ['tɛrəst-] n (Brit) casa que faz parte de uma fileira de casas do mesmo estilo e pegadas.

terrain [tɛ'reɪn] n terreno m.

terrible ['tɛrəbl] adj terrível; **to feel ~** sentir-se péssimo(-ma) OR muito mal.

terribly ['tɛrəblɪ] adv (extremely) extremamente, terrivelmente; (very badly) imensamente, terrivelmente; **I'm ~ sorry!** sinto muito!

terrier ['tɛrɪər] n terrier m.

terrific [tə'rɪfɪk] adj (inf) incrível.

terrified ['tɛrɪfaɪd] adj aterrorizado(-da).

terrifying ['tɛrɪfaɪɪŋ] adj aterrorizador(-ra).

territory ['tɛrɪtrɪ] n território m.

terror ['tɛrər] n terror m.

terrorism ['tɛrərɪzm] n terrorismo m.

terrorist ['tɛrərɪst] n terrorista mf.

terrorize ['tɛrəraɪz] vt aterrorizar.

terse [tɜːs] adj seco(-ca).

test [tɛst] n teste m; (of blood) análise f ♦ vt (check) testar; (give exam to) avaliar; (dish, drink) provar; **driving ~** exame m de motorista (Br), exame m de condução (Port).

testicles ['tɛstɪklz] npl testículos mpl.

testify ['tɛstɪfaɪ] vi (JUR) testemunhar,

depor; **to ~ to sthg** *(be proof)* teste-munhar algo.

testimony [*Brit* 'testimani, *Am* 'testə‚məuni] *n (JUR)* testemunho *m*.

testing ['testɪŋ] *adj* difícil.

test match *n (Brit)* partida *f* interna-cional.

test tube *n* tubo *m* de ensaio.

test-tube baby *n* bebê *m* de pro-veta.

tetanus ['tetənəs] *n* tétano *m*.

text [tekst] *n (written material)* texto *m; (textbook)* manual *m*.

textbook ['tekstbuk] *n* manual *m*.

textile ['tekstaɪl] *n* têxtil *m*.

texture ['tekstʃəʳ] *n* textura *f*.

Thai [taɪ] *adj* tailandês(-esa).

Thailand ['taɪlænd] *n* Tailândia *f*.

Thames [temz] *n*: **the ~** o Tâmisa.

than [*weak form* ðən, *strong form* ðæn] *conj* que ♦ *prep*: **you're better ~ me** você é melhor (do) que eu; **I'd rather stay in ~ go out** prefiro ficar em casa do que sair; **more ~ ten** mais de dez.

thank [θæŋk] *vt*: **to ~ sb (for sthg)** agradecer a alguém (por) algo.

❑ **thanks** *npl* agradecimentos *mpl* ♦ *excl* obrigado!, obrigada!; **~s to** graças a; **many ~s** muito obrigado OR obrigada.

thankful ['θæŋkful] *adj* agradecido (-da); **to be ~ for sthg** estar agradeci-do por algo.

thankless ['θæŋklɪs] *adj* ingrato(-ta).

Thanksgiving ['θæŋks‚gɪvɪŋ] *n* Dia *m* de Ação de Graças.

thank you *excl* obrigado!, obriga-da!; **~ very much!** muito obrigado!; **no ~!** não, obrigado!

that [ðæt, *weak form of pron and conj* ðət] *(pl* those) *adj* **1.** *(referring to thing, person mentioned)* esse (essa); **I prefer ~ book** prefiro esse livro.

2. *(referring to thing, person further away)* aquele (aquela); **~ book at the back** aquele livro lá atrás; **I'll have ~ one** quero aquele (ali) OR esse.

♦ *pron* **1.** *(referring to thing, person men-tioned)* esse *m (essa f); (indefinite)* isso; **what's ~?** o que é isso?; **who's ~?** *(on the phone)* quem fala?; *(pointing)* e esse, quem é?; **~'s interesting** que interes-sante.

2. *(referring to thing, person further away)* aquele *m (aquela f); (indefinite)* aquilo; **is ~ Lucy?** *(pointing)* aquela é a

Lucy?; **I want those at the back** quero aqueles lá atrás; **what's ~ on the roof?** o que é aquilo no telhado?

3. *(introducing relative clause)* que; **a shop ~ sells antiques** uma loja que vende antiguidades; **the film ~ I saw** o filme que eu vi; **the room ~ I slept in** o quarto onde OR em que dormi.

♦ *adv* assim tão; **it wasn't ~ bad/good** não foi assim tão mau/bom; **it didn't cost ~ much** não custou tanto assim.

♦ *conj* que; **tell him ~ I'm going to be late** diga-lhe que vou chegar atrasado.

thatched [θætʃt] *adj (building)* com telhado de colmo.

that's [ðæts] = that is.

thaw [θɔː] *vi (snow, ice)* derreter ♦ *vt (frozen food)* descongelar.

the [*weak form* ðə, *before vowel* ðɪ, *strong form* ðiː] *definite article* **1.** *(gen)* o (a), os (as) *(pl)*; **~ book** o livro; **~ apple** a maçã; **~ girls as meninas**; **~ Wilsons** os Wilson; **to play ~ piano** tocar piano.

2. *(with an adjective to form a noun)* o (a), os (as) *(pl)*; **~ British** os britânicos; **~ young** os jovens; **~ impossible** o impossível.

3. *(in dates)*: **~ twelfth** o dia doze; **~ forties** os anos quarenta.

4. *(in titles)*: **Elizabeth ~ Second** Elizabeth Segunda.

theater ['θɪətəʳ] *n (Am) (for plays, drama)* = theatre; *(for films)* cinema *m*.

theatre ['θɪətəʳ] *n (Brit)* teatro *m*.

theatregoer ['θɪətə‚gəuəʳ] *n* freqüen-tador *m* (-ra *f)* de teatro.

theatrical [θɪætrɪkl] *adj* teatral.

theft [θeft] *n* roubo *m*.

their [ðeəʳ] *adj* seu (sua), deles (delas); **~ house** a casa deles, a sua casa.

theirs [ðeəz] *pron* o seu (a sua), o/a deles (o/a delas); **a friend of ~** um amigo deles OR seu; **these books are ~** estes livros são (os) deles OR seus; **these are ours – where are ~?** estes são os nossos – onde estão os deles?

them [*weak form* ðəm, *strong form* ðem] *pron (direct object)* os *mpl* (as *fpl); (indirect object)* lhes; *(after prep)* eles *mpl* (elas *fpl)*; **I know ~** eu os conheço; **it's ~** são eles; **send this to ~** manda-lhes isto; **tell ~** diga-lhes; **he's worse than ~** ele é pior do que eles; **Charlotte and Ricky brought it with ~** a Charlotte e o Ricky trouxeram-no com eles.

theme [θiːm] n tema m.

theme park n parque de diversões baseado num tema específico.

theme tune n tema m musical.

themselves [ðəmˈselvz] pron (reflexive) se; (after prep) eles mpl próprios (elas fpl próprias), si mpl próprios (si fpl próprias); **they did it ~** fizeram-no eles mesmos OR próprios; **they blame ~** eles culpam-se a si próprios; **they hurt ~** eles machucaram-se.

then [ðen] adv (at time in past) então, naquela altura; (at time in future) nessa altura; (next, afterwards) depois; (in that case) então; **from ~ on** daí em diante; **until ~** até aí.

theoretical [θɪəˈretɪkl] adj teórico(-ca), teorético(-ca).

theorize [ˈθɪəraɪz] vi (develop theory): **to ~ (about sthg)** teorizar (sobre algo).

theory [ˈθɪərɪ] n teoria f; **in ~** em teoria.

therapist [ˈθerəpɪst] n terapeuta mf.

therapy [ˈθerəpɪ] n terapia f.

there [ðeəʳ] adv (available, existing, present) lá, ali; (at, in, to that place) lá ◆ pron: **~ is/are** há; **is Bob ~, please?** (on phone) o Bob está?; **I'm going ~ next week** vou lá para a semana; **it's right ~ by the phone** está aí mesmo ao lado do telefone; **over ~** ali; **~'s someone at the door** tem alguém na porta; **~ are several people waiting** várias pessoas estão à espera; **~ you are** (when giving) aqui tem.

thereabouts [ˌðeərəˈbaʊts] adv: **or ~** aproximadamente.

thereafter [ˌðeərˈuːftəʳ] adv (fml) daí em diante, conseqüentemente.

thereby [ˌðeəˈbaɪ] adv (fml) assim, conseqüentemente.

therefore [ˈðeəfɔːʳ] adv portanto, por isso.

there's [ðeəz] = there is.

thermal underwear [ˌθɜːml-] n roupa f de baixo térmica.

thermometer [θəˈmɒmɪtəʳ] n termômetro m.

Thermos (flask)® [ˈθɜːməs-] n garrafa f térmica.

thermostat [ˈθɜːməstæt] n termostato m.

thesaurus [θɪˈsɔːrəs] (pl -es) n dicionário m de sinônimos.

these [ðiːz] pl → this.

thesis [ˈθiːsɪs] (pl theses [ˈθiːsiːz]) n tese f.

they [ðeɪ] pron eles mpl (elas fpl).

they'd [ðeɪd] = they had, they would.

they'll [ðeɪl] = they shall, they will.

they're [ðeəʳ] = they are.

they've [ðeɪv] = they have.

thick [θɪk] adj (in size) grosso (grossa); (fog) cerrado(-da); (forest, vegetation) denso(-sa); (hair) abundante; (liquid, sauce, smoke) espesso(-a); (inf: stupid) estúpido(-da); **it's 1 metre ~** tem 1 metro de espessura.

thicken [ˈθɪkn] vt (sauce, soup) engrossar ◆ vi (mist, fog) tornar-se mais cerrado, aumentar.

thicket [ˈθɪkɪt] n matagal m.

thickness [ˈθɪknɪs] n (of wood, wall, line) espessura f; (of forest, vegetation) densidade f; (of hair) grossura f.

thickset [ˌθɪkˈset] adj atarracado(-da).

thick-skinned [-ˈskɪnd] adj insensível.

thief [θiːf] (pl thieves) n ladrão m (ladra f).

thieve [θiːv] vt & vi furtar.

thieves [θiːvz] pl → thief.

thigh [θaɪ] n coxa f.

thimble [ˈθɪmbl] n dedal m.

thin [θɪn] adj (in size) fino(-na); (not fat) magro(-gra); (soup, sauce) pouco espesso(-a), líquido(-da).

thing [θɪŋ] n coisa f; **the ~ is** o que se passa é que, acontece que.

❏ **things** npl (clothes, possessions) coisas fpl; **how are ~s?** (inf) como (é que) vão as coisas?

thingummyjig [ˈθɪŋəmɪdʒɪg] n (inf) coisa f.

think [θɪŋk] (pt & pp thought) vt (believe) achar, pensar; (have in mind, expect) pensar ◆ vi pensar; **to ~ (that)** achar OR pensar que; **to ~ about** pensar em; **to ~ of** pensar em; (remember) lembrar-se de; **to ~ of doing sthg** pensar fazer algo; **I ~ so** acho que sim; **I don't ~ so** acho que não; **do you ~ you could ...?** você acha que podia ...?; **to ~ highly of sb** ter muito boa opinião de alguém.

❏ **think over** vt sep refletir sobre.

❏ **think up** vt sep imaginar.

third [θɜːd] num terceiro(-ra), → sixth.

thirdly [ˈθɜːdlɪ] adv terceiro, em terceiro lugar.

third party insurance n seguro m contra terceiros.

third-rate adj de terceira.

Third World n: the ~ o Terceiro Mundo.

thirst [θɜːst] n sede f.

thirsty [ˈθɜːstɪ] adj: to be ~ ter sede.

thirteen [ˌθɜːˈtiːn] num treze, → six.

thirteenth [ˌθɜːˈtiːnθ] num décimo m terceiro (décima f terceira), → sixth.

thirtieth [ˈθɜːtɪəθ] num trigésimo (-ma), → sixth.

thirty [ˈθɜːtɪ] num trinta, → six.

this [ðɪs] (pl these) adj 1. (referring to thing, person) este (esta); **these chocolates are delicious** estes chocolates são deliciosos; ~ **morning/week** esta manhã/semana; **I prefer ~ book** prefiro este livro; **I'll have ~ one** quero este.
2. (inf: used when telling a story): **there was ~ man ...** havia um homem ....
♦ pron (referring to thing, person) este m (esta f); (indefinite) isto; ~ **is for you** isto é para ti; **what are these?** o que é isto?, o que é que são estas coisas?; ~ **is David Gregory** (introducing someone) este é o David Gregory; (on telephone) aqui fala David Gregory.
♦ adv: **it was ~ big** era deste tamanho; **I don't remember it being ~ tiring** não me lembro de ser tão cansativo assim.

thistle [ˈθɪsl] n cardo m.

thorn [θɔːn] n espinho m.

thorny [ˈθɔːnɪ] adj espinhoso(-osa).

thorough [ˈθʌrə] adj minucioso (-osa).

thoroughbred [ˈθʌrəbred] n puro-sangue m inv.

thoroughfare [ˈθʌrəfeəʳ] n (fml) rua f principal.

thoroughly [ˈθʌrəlɪ] adv (completely) completamente.

those [ðəʊz] pl → that.

though [ðəʊ] conj se bem que ♦ adv no entanto; **even ~ it was raining** apesar de estar chovendo.

thought [θɔːt] pt & pp → think ♦ n (idea) ideia f; (thinking) pensamento m; (careful consideration) reflexão f.
⊐ **thoughts** npl (opinion) opinião f.

thoughtful [ˈθɔːtfʊl] adj (quiet and serious) pensativo(-va); (considerate) atencioso(-osa).

thoughtless [ˈθɔːtlɪs] adj indelicado(-da).

thousand [ˈθaʊznd] num mil; **a** OR **one ~ mil; ~s of milhares de,** → six.

thousandth [ˈθaʊzntθ] num milésimo(-ma), → sixth.

thrash [θræʃ] vt (inf: defeat heavily) derrotar.

thread [θred] n (of cotton etc) linha f ♦ vt (needle) enfiar (uma linha em).

threadbare [ˈθredbeəʳ] adj surrado (-da), puído(-da).

threat [θret] n ameaça f.

threaten [ˈθretn] vt ameaçar; **to ~ to do sthg** ameaçar fazer algo.

threatening [ˈθretnɪŋ] adj ameaçador(-ra).

three [θriː] num três, → six.

three-D n: **in ~** em três dimensões.

three-dimensional [-dɪˈmenʃənl] adj (picture, film, image) em três dimensões; (object) tridimensional.

threefold [ˈθriːfəʊld] adj triplo(-pla) ♦ adv: **to increase ~** triplicar.

three-piece suite n conjunto m de um sofá e duas poltronas.

three-ply adj (wool, rope) com três fios; (wood) com três espessuras.

three-quarters [-ˈkwɔːtəz] n três quartos mpl; ~ **of an hour** três quartos de hora.

threshold [ˈθreʃhəʊld] n (fml: of door) limiar m, soleira f.

threw [θruː] pt → throw.

thrifty [ˈθrɪftɪ] adj poupado(-da).

thrill [θrɪl] n (sudden feeling) sensação f, arrepio m; (exciting experience) experiência f incrível ♦ vt emocionar, fazer vibrar de excitação.

thrilled [θrɪld] adj encantado(-da).

thriller [ˈθrɪləʳ] n filme m de suspense.

thrilling [ˈθrɪlɪŋ] adj emocionante, excitante.

thrive [θraɪv] vi (plant, animal, person) desenvolver-se; (business, tourism, place) prosperar.

thriving [ˈθraɪvɪŋ] adj (person, community, business) próspero(-ra); (plant) com um bom crescimento.

throat [θrəʊt] n garganta f.

throb [θrɒb] vi (head) latejar; (noise, engine) vibrar.

throne [θrəʊn] n trono m.

throng [θrɒŋ] n multidão f.

throttle [ˈθrɒtl] n (of motorbike) válvula f reguladora.

through [θruː] prep (to other side of, by

means of) através de; *(because of)* graças a; *(from beginning to end of)* durante; *(throughout)* por todo(-da) ♦ *adv (from beginning to end)* até o fim ♦ *adj:* **I'm ~ (with it)** *(finished)* já acabei; **you're ~** *(on phone)* já tem ligação; **~ traffic** trânsito de passagem; **a ~ train** um trem direto; **"no ~ road"** *(Brit)* "rua sem saída"; **Monday ~ Thursday** *(Am)* de segunda a quinta-feira; **to let sb ~** deixar alguém passar; **to go ~ sthg** atravessar algo.

throughout [θruːˈaʊt] *prep (day, morning, year)* ao longo de todo(-da); *(place, country, building)* por todo(-da) ♦ *adv (all the time)* sempre, o tempo todo; *(everywhere)* por todo o lado.

throw [θrəʊ] *(pt* **threw** [θruː], *pp* **thrown** [θrəʊn]) *vt* atirar; *(javelin, dice)* lançar; *(a switch)* ligar; **to ~ sthg in the bin** jogar algo no lixo *(Br)*, deitar algo para o lixo *(Port)*.

❏ **throw away** *vt sep (get rid of)* jogar fora.

❏ **throw out** *vt sep (get rid of)* jogar fora; *(person)* pôr na rua.

❏ **throw up** *vi (inf: vomit)* vomitar.

throwaway [ˈθrəʊəˌweɪ] *adj (product)* descartável; *(bottle)* sem depósito.

throw-in *n (Brit: in football)* lançamento *m* da linha lateral.

thrown [θrəʊn] *pp* → **throw**.

thru [θruː] *(Am)* = **through**.

thrush [θrʌʃ] *n (bird)* tordo *m*.

thrust [θrʌst] *(pt & pp* **thrust**) *n (of sword)* estocada *f*; *(of knife)* facada *f*; *(of troops)* investida *f* ♦ *vt:* **to ~ sthg into sthg** enfiar algo em algo.

thud [θʌd] *n* barulho *m* seco.

thug [θʌg] *n* marginal *mf*.

thumb [θʌm] *n* polegar *m* ♦ *vt:* **to ~ a lift** pedir carona *(Br)*, pedir boleia *(Port)*.

thumbtack [ˈθʌmtæk] *n (Am)* percevejo *m (Br)*, pionés *m (Port)*.

thump [θʌmp] *n (punch)* soco *m*; *(sound)* barulho *m* seco ♦ *vt* dar um soco em; **he ~ed him** ele deu-lhe um soco.

thunder [ˈθʌndəʳ] *n* trovões *mpl*, trovoada *f*.

thunderbolt [ˈθʌndəbəʊlt] *n* raio *m*.

thunderclap [ˈθʌndəklæp] *n* trovão *m*.

thunderstorm [ˈθʌndəstɔːm] *n* tem-

pestade *f* (acompanhada de trovoada), temporal *m*.

thundery [ˈθʌndərɪ] *adj* de trovoada.

Thurs. *(abbr of Thursday)* 5ª, quin.

Thursday [ˈθɜːzdɪ] *n* quinta-feira *f*, → **Saturday**.

thus [ðʌs] *adv (fml) (as a consequence)* conseqüentemente, por conseguinte; *(in this way)* assim.

thwart [θwɔːt] *vt* gorar.

thyme [taɪm] *n* tomilho *m*.

thyroid [ˈθaɪrɔɪd] *n* tiróide *f*.

tiara [tɪˈɑːrə] *n* diadema *m*.

Tibet [tɪˈbet] *n* Tibete *m*.

tic [tɪk] *n* tique *m*.

tick [tɪk] *n (written mark)* sinal *m* de visto; *(insect)* carrapato *m (Br)*, carraça *f (Port)* ♦ *vt* marcar OR assinalar (com sinal de visto) ♦ *vi (clock, watch)* fazer tiquetaque.

❏ **tick off** *vt sep (mark off)* marcar OR assinalar (com sinal de visto).

ticket [ˈtɪkɪt] *n (for travel, cinema, match)* bilhete *m*; *(label)* etiqueta *f*; *(for traffic offence)* multa *f*.

ticket collector *n* revisor *m* (-ra *f*).

ticket inspector *n* revisor *m* (-ra *f*).

ticket machine *n* distribuidor *m* automático de bilhetes.

ticket office *n* bilheteira *f*.

tickle [ˈtɪkl] *vt* fazer cócegas a ♦ *vi* fazer cócegas.

ticklish [ˈtɪklɪʃ] *adj:* **to be ~** ter cócegas.

tick-tack-toe *n (Am)* jogo-da-velha *m (Br)*, jogo *m* de galo *(Port)*.

tidal [ˈtaɪdl] *adj (river)* com marés; *(barrier)* contra a maré.

tidbit [ˈtɪdbɪt] *(Am)* = **titbit**.

tiddlywinks [ˈtɪdlɪwɪŋks] *n (game)* jogo *m* de fichas *(Br)*, jogo *m* da pulga *(Port)*.

tide [taɪd] *n (of sea)* maré *f*.

tidy [ˈtaɪdɪ] *adj (room, desk, person)* arrumado(-da); *(hair, clothes)* cuidado(-da).

❏ **tidy up** *vt sep* arrumar.

tie [taɪ] *(pt & pp* **tied**, *cont* **tying**) *n (around neck)* gravata *f*; *(draw)* empate *m*; *(Am: on railway track)* dormente *m (Br)*, chulipa *f (Port)* ♦ *vt* atar; *(knot)* fazer, dar ♦ *vi (draw)* empatar.

❏ **tie up** *vt sep* atar; *(delay)* atrasar.

tiebreak(er) [ˈtaɪbreɪk(əʳ)] *n (in tennis)* tie-break *m*; *(extra question)* pergunta f de desempate.

tiepin ['taɪpɪn] n alfinete m de gravata.

tier [tɪəʳ] n (of seats) fila f, fileira f.

tiff [tɪf] n desentendimento m.

tiger ['taɪgəʳ] n tigre m.

tight [taɪt] adj apertado(-da); (drawer,
tap) preso(-sa); (rope, material) estica-
do(-da); (inf: drunk) bêbado(-da) ♦ adv
(hold) com força, bem; **my chest feels
~** estou um pouco congestionado (dos
brônquios).

tighten ['taɪtn] vt apertar.

tightfisted [ˌtaɪt'fɪstɪd] adj (inf) sovina.

tightly ['taɪtlɪ] adj (hold, fasten) com
força.

tightrope ['taɪtrəʊp] n corda f
bamba.

tights [taɪts] npl meia-calça f (Br),
collants mpl (Port); **a pair of ~** um par
de meias-calças, umas meias-calças.

tile ['taɪl] n (for roof) telha f; (for floor)
ladrilho m; (for wall) azulejo m.

tiled [taɪld] adj (roof) de telha; (floor)
de ladrilhos; (wall) de azulejos.

till [tɪl] n caixa f registradora ♦ prep &
conj até; **I'll wait ~ he arrives** esperarei
até ele chegar OR até que ele chegue.

tiller ['tɪləʳ] n barra f do leme.

tilt [tɪlt] vt inclinar ♦ vi inclinar-se.

timber ['tɪmbəʳ] n (wood) madeira f;
(of roof) trave f.

time [taɪm] n tempo m; (measured by
clock) horas fpl; (moment) altura f; (occasion) vez f ♦ vt (measure) cronometrar;
(arrange) prever; **I haven't got (the) ~**
não tenho tempo; **it's ~ to go** está na
hora de irmos embora; **what's the ~?**
que horas são?; **do you have the ~,
please?** você tem horas, por favor?;
two ~s two dois vezes dois; **five ~s as
much** cinco vezes mais; **in a month's ~**
daqui a um mês; **to have a good ~**
divertir-se; **all the ~** sempre, o tempo
todo; **every ~** sempre; **from ~ to ~** de
vez em quando, de tempos em tem-
pos; **for the ~ being** por enquanto; **in
~ (arrive)** a tempo; **in good ~** com
tempo; **last ~** a última vez; **most of
the ~** a maior parte do tempo; **on ~** na
hora; **some of the ~** parte do tempo;
this ~ desta vez; **two at a ~** dois de
cada vez.

time difference n diferença f horá-
ria.

time lag n intervalo m.

timeless ['taɪmlɪs] adj eterno(-na).

time limit n prazo m, limite m de
tempo.

timely ['taɪmlɪ] adj oportuno(-na).

time off n tempo m livre; **to take ~**
tirar férias.

time-out n (SPORT) tempo m morto.

timer ['taɪməʳ] n cronômetro m, relógio m.

time scale n período m.

time share n propriedade adquirida
por várias pessoas com o direito de
utilizá-la por um determinado período a
cada ano durante as suas férias.

timetable ['taɪmˌteɪbl] n horário m;
(of events) programa m.

time zone n fuso m horário.

timid ['tɪmɪd] adj tímido(-da).

timing ['taɪmɪŋ] n: **the ~ of the
remark was unfortunate** o comentário
foi feito num momento extremamente inoportuno; **the ~ of the election is
crucial** a data das eleições é fundamental.

tin [tɪn] n (metal) estanho m; (container) lata f ♦ adj de estanho, de lata.

tin can n lata f.

tinfoil ['tɪnfɔɪl] n papel m OR folha f
de alumínio.

tinge [tɪndʒ] n ponta f.

tingle ['tɪŋgl] vi: **my feet are tingling**
meus pés estão formigando.

tinker ['tɪŋkəʳ] vi: **to ~ with sthg**
mexer em algo.

tinkle ['tɪŋkl] n (Brit: inf: phone call):
to give sb a ~ dar uma ligada para
alguém.

tinned food [tɪnd-] n (Brit) comida f
enlatada, conservas fpl.

tin opener [-ˌəʊpnəʳ] n (Brit) abridor
m de latas (Br), abre-latas m inv (Port).

tinsel ['tɪnsl] n fios mpl de ouropel
(usados para decorar a árvore de Natal).

tint [tɪnt] n (for hair) tinta f (para o
cabelo).

tinted glass [ˌtɪntɪd-] n vidro m colorido OR fumê.

tiny ['taɪnɪ] adj pequenininho(-nha),
minúsculo(-la).

tip [tɪp] n (point, end) ponta f; (to waiter, taxi driver etc) gorjeta f; (piece of
advice) dica f; (rubbish dump) depósito
m de lixo (Br), lixeira f (Port) ♦ vt (waiter, taxi driver etc) dar uma gorjeta a;
(tilt) inclinar; (pour) despejar.

❑ **tip over** vt sep entornar ◆ vi entornar-se.

tipped [tɪpt] adj (cigarette) com filtro.

tipsy ['tɪpsɪ] adj (inf) alegre.

tiptoe ['tɪptəʊ] vi andar na ponta dos pés ◆ n: **on ~** na ponta dos pés.

tire [taɪəʳ] vi cansar-se ◆ n (Am) = **tyre**.

tired ['taɪəd] adj cansado(-da); **to be ~ of** (fed up with) estar farto(-ta) de.

tired out adj exausto(-ta), esgotado(-da).

tireless ['taɪəlɪs] adj incansável.

tiresome ['taɪəsəm] adj cansativo(-va), entediante.

tiring ['taɪərɪŋ] adj cansativo(-va).

tissue ['tɪʃuː] n (handkerchief) lenço m de papel.

tissue paper n papel m de seda.

tit [tɪt] n (vulg: breast) mama f.

titbit ['tɪtbɪt] n (Brit: of food) guloseima f.

titillate ['tɪtɪleɪt] vt excitar, titilar.

title ['taɪtl] n título m.

titter ['tɪtəʳ] vi rir-se baixinho.

T-junction n cruzamento m (em forma de T).

to [unstressed before consonant tə, unstressed before vowel tu, stressed tuː] prep
1. (indicating direction) para; **to go ~ Brazil** ir ao Brasil; **to go ~ school** ir para a escola.
2. (indicating position) a; **~ the left/right** à esquerda/direita.
3. (expressing indirect object) a; **to give sthg ~ sb** dar algo a alguém; **give it ~ me** dê-me isso; **to listen ~ the radio** ouvir rádio.
4. (indicating reaction, effect): **~ my surprise** para surpresa minha; **it's ~ your advantage** é em seu benefício.
5. (until) até; **to count ~ ten** contar até dez; **we work from nine ~ five** trabalhamos das nove (até) às cinco.
6. (in stating opinion) para; **~ me, he's lying** para mim, ele está mentindo.
7. (indicating change of state): **to turn ~ sthg** transformar-se em algo; **it could lead ~ trouble** pode vir a dar problemas.
8. (Brit: in expressions of time) para; **it's ten ~ three** são dez para as três; **at quarter ~ seven** às quinze para as sete.
9. (in ratios, rates): **40 miles ~ the gallon** ~ 7 litros por cada 100 quilômetros.

10. (of, for): **the answer ~ the question** a resposta à pergunta; **the key ~ the car** a chave do carro; **a letter ~ my daughter** uma carta para a minha filha.
11. (indicating attitude) (para) com; **to be rude ~ sb** ser grosseiro (para) com alguém.
◆ with infinitive **1.** (forming simple infinitive): **~ walk** andar; **~ laugh** rir.
2. (following another verb): **to begin ~ do sthg** começar a fazer algo; **to try ~ do sthg** tentar fazer algo.
3. (following an adjective): **difficult ~ do** difícil de fazer; **pleased ~ meet you** prazer em conhecê-lo; **ready ~ go** pronto para partir.
4. (indicating purpose) para; **we came here ~ look at the castle** viemos para ver o castelo.

toad [təʊd] n sapo m.

toadstool ['təʊdstuːl] n cogumelo m venenoso.

toast [təʊst] n (bread) torradas fpl; (when drinking) brinde m ◆ vt (bread) torrar; **a piece** OR **slice of ~** uma torrada.

toasted sandwich ['təʊstɪd-] n sanduíche m quente (Br), tosta f (Port).

toaster ['təʊstəʳ] n torradeira f.

toastie ['təʊstɪ] n = **toasted sandwich**.

tobacco [tə'bækəʊ] n tabaco m.

tobacconist's [tə'bækənɪsts] n tabacaria f.

toboggan [tə'bɒgən] n tobogã m.

today [tə'deɪ] n hoje m ◆ adv (on current day) hoje; (these days) hoje em dia.

toddler ['tɒdləʳ] n criança f (que começa a dar os primeiros passos).

toddy ['tɒdɪ] n = **ponche** m quente.

to-do (pl -s) n (inf) confusão f, rebuliço m.

toe [təʊ] n (of person) dedo m do pé.

toe clip n estribo m do pedal.

toenail ['təʊneɪl] n unha f do pé.

toffee ['tɒfɪ] n puxa-puxa m (Br), caramelo m (Port).

toga ['təʊgə] n toga f.

together [tə'geðəʳ] adv juntos(-tas); **~ with** juntamente OR junto com.

toil [tɔɪl] n (fml) labuta f ◆ vi (fml) trabalhar sem descanso, labutar.

toilet ['tɔɪlɪt] n (room) banheiro m (Br), casa f de banho (Port); (bowl) vaso *m* sanitário *(Br)*, sanita *f (Port)*; **to go to the ~** ir ao banheiro; **where's the ~?** onde é o banheiro?

toilet bag *n* estojo *m* de toilette.

toilet paper *n* papel *m* higiênico.

toiletries ['tɔilitriz] *npl* artigos *mpl* de toalete.

toilet roll *n* rolo *m* de papel higiênico.

toilet water *n* água-de-colônia *f*.

token ['təʊkn] *n (metal disc)* ficha *f*.

told [təʊld] *pt & pp* → **tell**.

tolerable ['tɒlərəbl] *adj* tolerável.

tolerance ['tɒlərəns] *n* tolerância *f*.

tolerant ['tɒlərənt] *adj* tolerante.

tolerate ['tɒləreit] *vt* tolerar.

toll [təʊl] *n (for road, bridge)* pedágio *m (Br)*, portagem *f (Port)*.

tollbooth ['təʊlbuːθ] *n* pedágio *m (Br)*, portagem *f (Port)*.

toll-free *adj (Am)* gratuito(-ta).

tomato *[Brit* təˈmɑːtəʊ, *Am* təˈmeitəʊ*]* *(pl* **-es***) n* tomate *m*.

tomato juice *n* suco *m* de tomate.

tomato ketchup *n* ketchup *m*.

tomato puree *n* concentrado *m* de tomate.

tomato sauce *n* molho *m* de tomate.

tomb [tuːm] *n* túmulo *m*.

tomboy ['tɒmbɔi] *n* menina *f* moleque *(Br)*, maria-rapaz *f (Port)*.

tombstone ['tuːmstəʊn] *n* lápide *f*, pedra *f* tumular.

tomcat ['tɒmkæt] *n* gato *m (*macho*)*.

tomorrow [təˈmɒrəʊ] *n* amanhã *m* ◆ *adv* amanhã; **the day after ~** depois de amanhã; **~ afternoon** amanhã à tarde; **~ morning** amanhã de manhã; **~ night** amanhã à noite.

ton [tʌn] *n (in Britain)* = 1016 kg; *(in U.S.)* = 907 kg; *(metric tonne)* tonelada *f*; **~s of** *(inf)* toneladas de.

tone [təʊn] *n (of voice, colour)* tom *m*; *(on phone)* sinal *m*.

tongs [tɒŋz] *npl (for hair)* ferro *m* (para enrolar o cabelo); *(for sugar)* pinça *f*.

tongue [tʌŋ] *n* língua *f*.

tongue-in-cheek *adj* irônico(-ca).

tongue-tied *adj* incapaz de falar *(por timidez ou nervos)*.

tongue-twister *n* trava-língua *m*, expressão *f* difícil de dizer.

tonic ['tɒnik] *n (tonic water)* água *f*

tônica; *(medicine)* tônico *m*.

tonic water *n* água *f* tônica.

tonight [təˈnait] *n* esta noite *f* ◆ *adv* hoje à noite.

tonne [tʌn] *n* tonelada *f*.

tonsil ['tɒnsl] *n* amígdala *f*.

tonsillitis [ˌtɒnsɪˈlaitis] *n* amigdalite *f*.

too [tuː] *adv (excessively)* demais, demasiado; *(also)* também; **it's not ~ good** não é lá muito bom; **it's ~ late to go out** é tarde demais OR é demasiado tarde para sair; **~ many** demasiados(-das); **~ much** demasiado(-da).

took [tʊk] *pt* → **take**.

tool [tuːl] *n* ferramenta *f*.

tool box *n* caixa *f* da ferramenta.

tool kit *n* jogo *m* de ferramentas.

tooth [tuːθ] *(pl* **teeth***) n* dente *m*.

toothache ['tuːθeik] *n* dor *f* de dentes.

toothbrush ['tuːθbrʌʃ] *n* escova *f* de dentes.

toothpaste ['tuːθpeist] *n* pasta *f* de dentes.

toothpick ['tuːθpik] *n* palito *m* (para os dentes).

top [tɒp] *adj (highest)* de cima; *(best, most important)* melhor ◆ *n (highest part)* topo *m*, alto *m*; *(of table, bed)* cabeçeira *f*; *(best point)* primeiro *m* (-ra *f*); *(lid, cap)* tampa *f*; *(garment)* blusa *f (Br)*, camisola *f (Port)*; *(of street, road)* final *m (Br)*, cimo *m (Port)*; **at the ~ (of)** *(in highest part)* no topo (de); **on ~ of** *(on highest part of)* em cima de; *(of mountain)* no topo de; *(in addition to)* além de; **at ~ speed** a toda velocidade; **~ gear** = quinta *f*.

❑ **top up** *vt sep (glass, drink)* voltar a encher ◆ *vi (with petrol)* completar *(Br)*, atestar *(Port)*.

top floor *n* último andar *m*.

top hat *n* cartola *f*.

topic ['tɒpik] *n* tópico *m*.

topical ['tɒpikl] *adj* atual.

topless ['tɒplis] *adj*: **to go ~** fazer topless.

topmost ['tɒpməʊst] *adj* mais alto(-ta).

topped [tɒpt] *adj*: **~ with sthg** *(food)* com algo (por cima).

topping ['tɒpiŋ] *n*: **with a chocolate ~** coberto(-ta) com chocolate; **the ~ of your choice** *(on pizza)* com os ingredientes que desejar.

topple ['tɒpl] *vt* derrubar ◆ *vi* cair.

top-secret adj altamente secreto (-ta).

topspin ['tɒpspɪn] n topspin m, efeito m por cima.

topsy-turvy [ˌtɒpsɪ'tɜːvɪ] adj de pernas para o ar.

torch [tɔːtʃ] n (Brit: electric light) lanterna f.

tore [tɔːʳ] pt → **tear**[1].

torment [tɔː'ment] vt (annoy) atormentar.

torn [tɔːn] pp → **tear**[1] ◆ adj (ripped) rasgado(-da).

tornado [tɔː'neɪdəʊ] (pl -es OR -s) n tornado m.

torpedo [tɔː'piːdəʊ] (pl -es) n torpedo m.

torrent ['tɒrənt] n torrente f.

torrential [tɒ'renʃəl] adj torrencial.

torrid ['tɒrɪd] adj (hot) tórrido(-da); (passionate) abrasador(-ra).

tortoise ['tɔːtəs] n tartaruga f.

tortoiseshell ['tɔːtəʃel] n tartaruga f (material).

torture ['tɔːtʃəʳ] n tortura f ◆ vt torturar.

Tory ['tɔːrɪ] n conservador m (-ra f), membro do partido conservador britânico.

toss [tɒs] vt (throw) atirar; (coin) atirar ao ar; (salad, vegetables) misturar, mexer.

tot [tɒt] n (inf: small child) pequeno m (-na f), pequerrucho m (-cha f) (Port); (of drink) trago m.

total ['təʊtl] adj total ◆ n total m; **in** ~ no total.

totalitarian [ˌtəʊtælɪ'teərɪən] adj totalitário(-ria).

totally ['təʊtəlɪ] adv (entirely) totalmente, completamente; **I** ~ **agree** concordo plenamente.

totter ['tɒtəʳ] vi cambalear.

touch [tʌtʃ] n (sense) tato m; (small amount) pitada f; (detail) toque m, retoque m ◆ vt tocar em; (move emotionally) tocar ◆ vi tocar-se; **to get in** ~ **(with sb)** entrar em contato (com alguém); **to keep in** ~ **(with sb)** manter o contato (com alguém).

□ **touch down** vi (plane) aterrissar (Br), aterrar (Port).

touchdown ['tʌtʃdaʊn] n (of plane) aterrissagem f (Br), aterragem f (Port); (in American football) ensaio m.

touched [tʌtʃt] adj (grateful) comovido(-da).

touching ['tʌtʃɪŋ] adj (moving) comovente.

touchline ['tʌtʃlaɪn] n linha f de fundo.

touchy ['tʌtʃɪ] adj (person) suscetível; (subject, question) melindroso(-osa).

tough [tʌf] adj (resilient) forte; (hard, strong) resistente; (meat, terms, policies) duro(-ra); (difficult) difícil.

toughen ['tʌfn] vt endurecer.

toupee ['tuːpeɪ] n chinó m.

tour [tʊəʳ] n (journey) volta f; (of city, castle etc) visita f; (of pop group, theatre company) turnê f, digressão f ◆ vt visitar, viajar por; **on** ~ em turnê OR digressão.

tourism ['tʊərɪzm] n turismo m.

tourist ['tʊərɪst] n turista mf.

tourist class n classe f turística.

tourist information office n centro m de turismo.

tournament ['tɔːnəmənt] n torneio m.

tour operator n agência f OR operador m de viagens.

tout [taʊt] n cambista mf (Br), revendedor m (-ra f) de bilhetes (a um preço mais alto) (Port).

tow [təʊ] vt rebocar.

toward [tə'wɔːd] (Am) = **towards**.

towards [tə'wɔːdz] prep (Brit) (in the direction of) em direção a; (facing, to help pay for) para; (with regard to) para com; (near, around) perto de.

towaway zone ['təʊəweɪ-] n (Am) zona de estacionamento proibido sob pena de reboque.

towel ['taʊəl] n toalha f.

toweling ['taʊəlɪŋ] (Am) = **towelling**.

towelling ['taʊəlɪŋ] n (Brit) tecido m para toalhas, (pano) turco m (Port).

towel rail n toalheiro m.

tower ['taʊəʳ] n torre f.

tower block n (Brit) arranha-céu m, espigão m.

Tower Bridge n Tower Bridge f, famosa ponte levadiça londrina.

towering ['taʊərɪŋ] adj muito alto(-ta).

Tower of London n: **the** ~ a torre de Londres.

town [taʊn] n (small) vila f; (larger) cidade f; (town centre) centro m (da cidade).

town centre n centro m da cidade.

town council n ~ câmara f municipal.

town hall *n* prefeitura *f (Br)*, câmara *f* municipal *(Port)*.

town planning *n (study)* urbanismo *m*.

towpath ['təupɑ:θ] *n* caminho *m* de sirga.

towrope ['təurəup] *n* cabo *m* de reboque.

tow truck *n (Am)* reboque *m*.

toxic ['tɒksɪk] *adj* tóxico(-ca).

toy [tɔɪ] *n* brinquedo *m*.

toy shop *n* loja *f* de brinquedos.

trace [treɪs] *n* indício *m*, vestígio *m* ♦ *vt (find)* localizar.

tracing paper ['treɪsɪŋ-] *n* papel *m* vegetal OR de decalque.

track [træk] *n (path)* caminho *m; (of railway)* via *f; (SPORT)* pista *f; (song)* música *f*.

❑ **track down** *vt sep* localizar.

tracksuit ['træksu:t] *n* roupa *f* de treino OR jogging *(Br)*, fato *m* de treino *(Port)*.

traction ['trækʃn] *n (MED):* **in ~** sob tração.

tractor ['træktər] *n* trator *m*.

trade [treɪd] *n (COMM)* comércio *m; (job)* ofício *m* ♦ *vt* trocar ♦ *vi* comercializar, negociar.

trade fair *n* feira *f* industrial.

trade-in *n* troca *f, sistema que consiste em dar um artigo velho como entrada para comprar um novo.*

trademark ['treɪdmɑ:k] *n* marca *f* (registada).

trader ['treɪdər] *n* comerciante *mf*.

tradesman ['treɪdzmən] *(pl* **-men** [-mən]) *n (deliveryman)* entregador *m; (shopkeeper)* comerciante *m*.

trade union *n* sindicato *m*.

trading ['treɪdɪŋ] *n* comércio *m*.

tradition [trə'dɪʃn] *n* tradição *f*.

traditional [trə'dɪʃənl] *adj* tradicional.

traffic ['træfɪk] *(pt & pp* **-ked,** *cont* **-king)** *n (cars etc)* trânsito *m* ♦ *vi:* **to ~ in** traficar.

traffic circle *n (Am)* rotunda *f*.

traffic island *n* placa *f* (de refúgio para pedestres).

traffic jam *n* engarrafamento *m*.

trafficker ['træfɪkər] *n* traficante *mf*.

traffic lights *npl* sinais *mpl* de trânsito, semáforos *mpl*.

traffic warden *n (Brit)* guarda *mf*

de trânsito *(Br)*, polícia *mf* de trânsito *(Port)*.

tragedy ['trædʒədɪ] *n* tragédia *f*.

tragic ['trædʒɪk] *adj* trágico(-ca).

trail [treɪl] *n (path)* caminho *m; (marks)* rasto *m* ♦ *vi (be losing)* estar perdendo.

trailer ['treɪlər] *n (for boat, luggage)* atrelado *m,* reboque *m; (Am: caravan)* trailer *m (Br)*, caravana *f (Port); (for film, programme)* trailer *m*, excertos *mpl*.

train [treɪn] *n (on railway)* trem *m (Br)*, comboio *m (Port)* ♦ *vt & vi* treinar; **by ~** de trem.

train driver *n* maquinista *mf*.

trained [treɪnd] *adj* qualificado(-da).

trainee [treɪ'ni:] *n* estagiário *m* (-ria *f*).

trainer ['treɪnər] *n (of athlete etc)* treinador *m* (-ra *f*).

❑ **trainers** *npl (Brit: shoes)* tênis *m inv (Br)*, sapatilhas *fpl (Port)*.

training ['treɪnɪŋ] *n (instruction)* estágio *m; (exercises)* treino *m*.

training shoes *npl (Brit)* tênis *m inv (Br)*, sapatilhas *fpl (Port)*.

trait [treɪt] *n* traço *m*.

traitor ['treɪtər] *n* traidor *m* (-ra *f*).

trajectory [trə'dʒektərɪ] *n* trajetória *f*.

tram [træm] *n (Brit)* bonde *m (Br)*, eléctrico *m (Port)*.

tramp [træmp] *n* vagabundo *m* (-da *f*), mendigo *m* (-ga *f*).

trample ['træmpl] *vt* espezinhar.

trampoline ['træmpəli:n] *n* trampolim *m*.

trance [trɑ:ns] *n* transe *m*.

tranquil ['træŋkwɪl] *adj* tranqüilo (-la), sereno(-na).

tranquilizer ['træŋkwɪlaɪzər] *(Am)* = **tranquillizer.**

tranquillizer ['træŋkwɪlaɪzər] *n (Brit)* calmante *m*.

transaction [træn'zækʃn] *n* transação *f*.

transatlantic [,trænzət'læntɪk] *adj* transatlântico(-ca).

transcend [træn'send] *vt* transcender.

transcript ['trænskrɪpt] *n* transcrição *f*.

transfer [*n* 'trænsfɜ:r, *vb* træns'fɜ:r] *n* transferência *f; (picture)* decalcomania *f; (Am: ticket)* bilhete que permite fazer transferências durante a viagem ♦ *vt* transferir ◆ vi (change bus, plane etc) efetuar transferências; "~s" (in airport) "transferências" (Br), "transbordos" (Port).

transfer desk n balcão m de informação para passageiros em trânsito.

transform [træns'fɔːm] vt transformar.

transfusion [træns'fjuːʒn] n transfusão f.

transient ['trænzɪənt] adj passageiro (-ra).

transistor radio [træn'zɪstəʳ-] n transistor m.

transit ['trænsɪt] : **in transit** adv durante a viagem.

transitive ['trænzɪtɪv] adj transitivo (-va).

transit lounge n sala f de espera (para onde vão os passageiros em trânsito).

transitory ['trænzɪtrɪ] adj transitório(-ria).

translate [træns'leɪt] vt traduzir.

translation [træns'leɪʃn] n tradução f.

translator [træns'leɪtəʳ] n tradutor m (-ra f).

transmission [trænz'mɪʃn] n transmissão f.

transmit [trænz'mɪt] vt transmitir.

transmitter [trænz'mɪtəʳ] n transmissor m.

transparency [træns'pærənsɪ] n (for overhead projector) transparência f, diapositivo m (Br), acetato m (Port).

transparent [træns'pærənt] adj transparente.

transplant ['trænsplɑːnt] n transplante m.

transport [n 'trænspɔːt, vb træn'spɔːt] n transporte m ◆ vt transportar.

transportation [trænspɔː'teɪʃn] n (Am) transporte m.

transpose [træns'pəʊz] vt inverter a ordem de.

trap [træp] n armadilha f ◆ vt: **to be trapped** (stuck) estar preso(-sa).

trapdoor [træp'dɔːʳ] n alçapão m.

trapeze [trə'piːz] n trapézio m.

trash [træʃ] n (Am) lixo m.

trashcan ['træʃkæn] n (Am) lata f de lixo (Br), contentor m de lixo (Port).

trauma ['trɔːmə] n trauma m.

traumatic [trɔː'mætɪk] adj traumático(-ca).

travel ['trævl] n viagem f ◆ vt (distance) percorrer ◆ vi viajar.

travel agency n agência f de viagens.

travel agent n agente mf de viagens; ~'s (shop) agência f de viagens.

Travelcard ['trævlkɑːd] n bilhete normalmente válido por um dia para viajar nos transportes públicos de Londres.

travel centre n (in railway, bus station) balcão m de informações e venda de bilhetes.

traveler ['trævlər] (Am) = **traveller**.

travel insurance n seguro m de viagem.

traveller ['trævləʳ] n (Brit) viajante mf.

traveller's cheque n traveller's cheque m, cheque m de viagem.

travelsick ['trævəlsɪk] adj enjoado(-da) (durante uma viagem).

travesty ['trævəstɪ] n paródia f.

trawler ['trɔːləʳ] n traineira f.

tray [treɪ] n bandeja f, tabuleiro m.

treacherous ['tretʃərəs] adj (person) traiçoeiro(-ra); (roads, conditions) perigoso(-osa).

treachery ['tretʃərɪ] n traição f.

treacle ['triːkl] n (Brit) melaço m.

tread [tred] (pt trod, pp trodden) n (of tyre) piso m, zona f de rolagem ◆ vi: **to ~ on sthg** pisar em algo.

treason ['triːzn] n traição f.

treasure ['treʒəʳ] n tesouro m.

treasurer ['treʒərəʳ] n tesoureiro m (-ra f).

treat [triːt] vt tratar ◆ n (special thing) presente m; **to ~ sb to sthg** oferecer algo a alguém.

treatise ['triːtɪs] n: **~ (on sthg)** tratado m (sobre algo).

treatment ['triːtmənt] n tratamento m.

treaty ['triːtɪ] n tratado m.

treble ['trebl] adj triplo(-pla).

tree [triː] n árvore f.

treetop ['triːtɒp] n copa f (de árvore).

tree-trunk n tronco m de árvore.

trek [trek] n caminhada f.

trellis ['trelɪs] n grade f de ripas cruzadas.

tremble ['trembl] vi tremer.

tremendous [trɪ'mendəs] adj (very large) tremendo(-da); (inf: very good) espetacular.

tremor ['trɛmər] *n (small earthquake)* sismo *m*, tremor *m* de terra.

trench [trɛntʃ] *n (ditch)* vala *f*; *(MIL.)* trincheira *f*.

trend [trɛnd] *n* tendência *f*.

trendy ['trɛndɪ] *adj (inf) (person)* que segue a moda; *(place)* muito na moda.

trespass ['trɛspəs] *vi* trespassar; **"no ~ing"** "entrada proibida".

trespasser ['trɛspəsər] *n* intruso *m* (-sa *f*); **"~s will be prosecuted"** "é proibido passar, sob pena de multa".

trestle table *n* mesa *f* de cavalete.

trial ['traɪəl] *n (JUR)* julgamento *m*; *(test)* prova *f*; **a ~ period** um período de experiência.

triangle ['traɪæŋgl] *n* triângulo *m*.

triangular [traɪˈæŋgjʊlər] *adj* triangular.

tribe [traɪb] *n* tribo *f*.

tribunal [traɪˈbjuːnl] *n* tribunal *m*.

tributary ['trɪbjʊtrɪ] *n* afluente *m*.

tribute ['trɪbjuːt] *n*: **to be a ~ to** *(be due to)* dever-se a; **to pay ~ to** render homenagem a.

trick [trɪk] *n* truque *m* ♦ *vt* enganar; **to play a ~ on sb** pregar uma peça em alguém.

trickery ['trɪkərɪ] *n* artifícios *mpl*.

trickle ['trɪkl] *vi (liquid)* pingar.

tricky ['trɪkɪ] *adj* difícil.

tricycle ['traɪsɪkl] *n* triciclo *m*.

trifle ['traɪfl] *n (dessert)* sobremesa que consiste em bolo ensopado em xerez coberto com fruta, creme de leite, amêndoas e creme batido.

trigger ['trɪgər] *n* gatilho *m*.

trim [trɪm] *n (haircut)* corte *m* (de cabelo) ♦ *vt (hair)* cortar (as pontas de); *(beard, hedge)* aparar.

trimmings ['trɪmɪŋz] *npl (on clothing)* enfeites *mpl*; *(CULIN)* acompanhamentos *mpl*.

trinket ['trɪŋkɪt] *n* bugiganga *f*.

trio ['triːəʊ] *(pl -s)* *n* trio *m*.

trip [trɪp] *n (journey)* viagem *f*; *(outing)* excursão *f* ♦ *vi* tropeçar.
❑ **trip up** *vi* tropeçar.

tripe [traɪp] *n (CULIN)* dobrada *f*, tripas *fpl*.

triple ['trɪpl] *adj* triplo(-pla).

triple jump *n*: **the ~** o triplo salto.

triplets ['trɪplɪts] *npl* trigêmeos *mpl* (-meas *fpl*).

tripod ['traɪpɒd] *n* tripé *m*.

trite [traɪt] *adj* batido(-da).

triumph ['traɪəmf] *n* triunfo *m*.

trivia ['trɪvɪə] *n* trivialidades *fpl*.

trivial ['trɪvɪəl] *adj (pej)* trivial.

trod [trɒd] *pt* → **tread**.

trodden ['trɒdn] *pp* → **tread**.

trolley ['trɒlɪ] *(pl -s)* *(Brit: in supermarket, at airport, for food)* carrinho *m*; *(Am: tram)* bonde *m* *(Br)*, trólei *m* *(Port)*.

trombone [trɒmˈbəʊn] *n* trombone *m*.

troops [truːps] *npl* tropas *fpl*.

trophy ['trəʊfɪ] *n* troféu *m*.

tropical ['trɒpɪkl] *adj* tropical.

tropics ['trɒpɪks] *npl*: **the ~** os trópicos.

trot [trɒt] *vi (horse)* andar a trote, trotar ♦ *n*: **on the ~** *(inf)* de seguida; **three on the ~** três seguidos.

trouble ['trʌbl] *n* problemas *mpl* ♦ *vt (worry)* preocupar; *(bother)* incomodar; **to be in ~** ter problemas; **to get into ~** meter-se em problemas; **to take the ~ to do sthg** dar-se ao trabalho de fazer algo; **it's no ~** não custa nada, não é problema nenhum.

troubled ['trʌbld] *adj (worried, upset)* preocupado(-da); *(life, time)* difícil; *(place)* agitado(-da).

troublemaker ['trʌblmeɪkər] *n* desordeiro *m* (-ra *f*).

troublesome ['trʌblsəm] *adj (knee, cold)* problemático(-ca); *(person, car, job)* que só causa problemas.

trough [trɒf] *n (for animals)* cocho *m*.

troupe [truːp] *n* companhia *f*.

trouser press ['traʊzər-] *n* dispositivo para engomar calças.

trousers ['traʊzəz] *npl* calças *fpl*; **a pair of ~** uma calça *(Br)*, um par de calças *(Port)*.

trout [traʊt] *(pl inv)* *n* truta *f*.

trowel ['traʊəl] *n (for gardening)* colher *f* de jardineiro.

truant ['truːənt] *n*: **to play ~** matar aula *(Br)*, fazer gazeta *(Port)*.

truce [truːs] *n* trégua *f*.

truck [trʌk] *n* caminhão *m* *(Br)*, camião *m* *(Port)*.

truck driver *n* camionheiro *m* (-ra *f*) *(Br)*, camionista *mf* *(Port)*.

trucker ['trʌkər] *n (Am)* camionheiro *m* (-ra *f*) *(Br)*, camionista *mf* *(Port)*.

truck farm *n (Am)* viveiro *m* agrícola.

trudge [trʌdʒ] *vi* arrastar-se, caminhar com dificuldade.

true [truː] *adj* verdadeiro(-ra); **it's ~ é** verdade.

truffle ['trʌfl] *n (sweet)* brigadeiro *m*, trufa *f*; *(fungus)* trufa *f*.

truly ['truːlɪ] *adv*: **yours ~** ≃ com os melhores cumprimentos, cordialmente.

trumpet ['trʌmpɪt] *n* trompete *m*.

trumps [trʌmps] *npl* trunfo *m*.

truncheon ['trʌntʃən] *n* cassetete *m*, cacete *m*.

trunk [trʌŋk] *n (of tree)* tronco *m*; *(Am: of car)* mala *f* (do carro), portabagagens *m (Port)*; *(case, box)* baú *m*; *(of elephant)* tromba *f*.

trunk call *n (Brit)* chamada *f* (telefônica) interurbana.

trunk road *n (Brit)* ≃ estrada *f* nacional.

trunks [trʌŋks] *npl (for swimming)* sunga *f (Br)*, calções *fpl* (de banho) *(Port)*.

trust [trʌst] *n (confidence)* confiança *f* ◆ *vt (believe, have confidence in)* confiar em; *(fml: hope)*: **to ~ (that)** esperar que.

trusted ['trʌstɪd] *adj* de confiança.

trusting ['trʌstɪŋ] *adj* confiante.

trustworthy ['trʌst,wɜːðɪ] *adj* de confiança.

truth [truːθ] *n (true facts)* verdade *f*; *(quality of being true)* veracidade *f*.

truthful ['truːθful] *adj (statement, account)* verídico(-ca); *(person)* honesto(-ta).

try [traɪ] *n (attempt)* tentativa *f* ◆ *vt (attempt)* tentar; *(experiment with, test, seek help from)* experimentar; *(food)* provar; *(JUR)* processar ◆ *vi* tentar; **to ~ to do sthg** tentar fazer algo.

❑ **try on** *vt sep (clothes)* experimentar.

❑ **try out** *vt sep (plan, idea)* pôr à prova; *(car, machine)* testar.

trying ['traɪɪŋ] *adj* difícil.

T-shirt *n* camiseta *f (Br)*, T-shirt *f (Port)*.

tub [tʌb] *n (of margarine etc)* pacote *m*, caixa *f*; *(inf: bath)* banheira *f*.

tubby ['tʌbɪ] *adj (inf)* gorducho(-cha).

tube [tjuːb] *n* tubo *m*; *(Brit: inf: underground)* metrô *m*; **by ~** em metrô.

tuberculosis [tjuːˌbɜːkjuˈləʊsɪs] *n* tuberculose *f*.

tube station *n (Brit: inf)* estação *f* do metrô.

tubing ['tjuːbɪŋ] *n* tubo *m*.

tubular ['tjuːbjʊləʳ] *adj* tubular.

tuck [tʌk] : **tuck in** *vt sep (shirt)* enfiar (dentro das calças); *(child, person)* aconchegar ◆ *vi (inf)*: **~ in!** pode comer!

tuck shop *n (Brit)* lojinha *f* de balas (da escola) *(Br)*, bar *m* (da escola) *(Port)*.

Tudor ['tjuːdəʳ] *adj* Tudor *(inv) (século XVI)*.

Tues. *(abbr of Tuesday)* 3ª, ter.

Tuesday ['tjuːzdɪ] *n* terça-feira *f*, → Saturday.

tuft [tʌft] *n* tufo *m*.

tug [tʌg] *vt* puxar (com força).

tug-of-war *n* cabo-de-guerra *m (Br)*, jogo *m* da corda *(Port)*, jogo em que cada uma das equipes puxa o seu lado da corda para ver quem tem mais força.

tuition [tjuːˈɪʃn] *n* aulas *mpl*; **private ~** aulas *fpl* particulares.

tulip ['tjuːlɪp] *n* tulipa *f*.

tumble ['tʌmbl] *vi* cair.

tumbledown ['tʌmbldaʊn] *adj* caindo aos pedaços.

tumble-dryer ['tʌmbldraɪəʳ] *n* máquina *f* de secar roupa.

tumbler ['tʌmbləʳ] *n (glass)* copo *m* de uísque.

tummy ['tʌmɪ] *n (inf)* barriga *f*.

tummy upset *n (inf)* dor *f* de barriga.

tumor ['tuːməʳ] *(Am)* = **tumour**.

tumour ['tjuːməʳ] *n (Brit)* tumor *m*.

tuna (fish) [*Brit* 'tjuːnə, *Am* 'tuːnə] *n* atum *m*.

tuna melt *n (Am)* torrada com atum e queijo suíço fundido.

tune [tjuːn] *n* melodia *f* ◆ *vt (radio, TV)* sintonizar; *(engine, instrument)* afinar; **in ~** afinado; **out of ~** desafinado.

tuneful ['tjuːnful] *adj* melodioso (-osa).

tuner ['tjuːnəʳ] *n (for radio, TV)* sintonizador *m*.

tunic ['tjuːnɪk] *n* túnica *f*.

Tunisia [tjuːˈnɪzɪə] *n* Tunísia *f*.

tunnel ['tʌnl] *n* túnel *m*.

turban ['tɜːbən] *n* turbante *m*.

turbine ['tɜːbaɪn] *n* turbina *f*.

turbo ['tɜːbəʊ] *(pl* **-s)** *n (car)* turbo *m*.

turbulence ['tɜːbjʊləns] *n* turbulência *f*.

turbulent ['tɜ:bjulənt] *adj* agitado (-da).

tureen [təˈriːn] *n* terrina *f*.

turf [tɜ:f] *n* (*grass*) gramado *m* (*Br*), relva *f* (*Port*).

Turk [tɜ:k] *n* turco *m* (-ca *f*).

turkey ['tɜ:kɪ] (*pl* -s) *n* peru *m*.

Turkey *n* Turquia *f*.

Turkish ['tɜ:kɪʃ] *adj* turco(-ca) ♦ *n* (*language*) turco *m* ♦ *npl*: **the ~** os turcos.

Turkish delight *n* doce gelatinoso coberto de açúcar em pó.

turmoil ['tɜ:mɔɪl] *n* turbilhão *m*.

turn [tɜ:n] *n* (*in road*) cortada *f*; (*of knob, key, switch*) volta *f*; (*go, chance*) vez *f* ♦ *vt* virar; (*become*) tornar-se, ficar; (*cause to become*) pôr, deixar ♦ *vi* (*person*) virar-se; (*car*) virar; (*rotate*) girar; (*milk*) azedar; **it's your ~** é a sua vez; **at the ~ of the century** na virada do século; **to take it in ~s** to do sthg fazer algo revezando; **to ~ into** sthg (*become*) transformar-se em algo; **to ~ left/right** virar à esquerda/direita; **to ~ sthg into sthg** transformar algo em algo; **to ~ sthg inside out** virar algo pelo avesso.

❏ **turn back** *vt sep* (*person*) mandar voltar ♦ *vi* voltar.

❏ **turn down** *vt sep* (*radio, volume, heating*) baixar; (*offer, request*) recusar.

❏ **turn off** *vt sep* (*light, TV, engine*) desligar; (*water, gas, tap*) fechar ♦ *vi* (*leave road*) virar.

❏ **turn on** *vt sep* (*light, TV, engine*) ligar; (*water, gas, tap*) abrir.

❏ **turn out** *vt sep* (*light, fire*) apagar ♦ *vi* (*be in the end*) acabar; (*come, attend*) aparecer; **to ~ out to be sthg** acabar por ser algo.

❏ **turn over** *vi* (*in bed*) virar-se; (*Brit: change channels*) mudar de canal ♦ *vt sep* (*page, card, omelette*) virar.

❏ **turn round** *vt sep* (*car, table etc*) virar ♦ *vi* (*person*) virar-se.

❏ **turn up** *vt sep* (*radio, volume, heating*) aumentar ♦ *vi* (*come, attend*) aparecer.

turning ['tɜ:nɪŋ] *n* cortada *f*.

turnip ['tɜ:nɪp] *n* nabo *m*.

turnpike ['tɜ:npaɪk] *n* (*Am*) rodovia *f* com pedágio (*Br*), auto-estrada *f* com portagem (*Port*).

turnstile ['tɜ:nstaɪl] *n* borboleta *f* (*Br*), torniquete *m* (*Port*).

turntable ['tɜ:n,teɪbl] *n* (*on record player*) prato *m*.

turn-up *n* (*Brit: on trousers*) dobra *f*.

turpentine ['tɜ:pəntaɪn] *n* terebintina *f*, aguarrás *f*.

turps [tɜ:ps] *n* (*Brit: inf*) terebintina *f*, aguarrás *f*.

turquoise ['tɜ:kwɔɪz] *adj* turquesa (*inv*).

turret ['tʌrɪt] *n* (*on castle*) torinha *f* (*Br*), torreão *m* (*Port*).

turtle ['tɜ:tl] *n* tartaruga *f*.

turtleneck ['tɜ:tlnek] *n* camisola *f* de meia gola.

tusk [tʌsk] *n* defesa *f*.

tussle ['tʌsl] *n* luta *f*.

tutor ['tjuːtər] *n* (*private teacher*) professor *m* (-ra *f*) particular, explicador *m* (-ra *f*).

tutorial [tjuːˈtɔːrɪəl] *n* ≈ seminário *m*.

tuxedo [tʌkˈsiːdəʊ] (*pl* -s) *n* (*Am*) smoking *m*.

TV *n* televisão *f*; **on ~** na televisão.

tweed [twiːd] *n* tweed *m*.

tweezers ['twiːzəz] *npl* pinça *f*.

twelfth [twelfθ] *num* décimo segundo (décima segunda), → **sixth**.

twelve [twelv] *num* doze, → **six**.

twentieth ['twentɪəθ] *num* vigésimo (-ma); **the ~ century** o século vinte, → **sixth**.

twenty ['twentɪ] *num* vinte, → **six**.

twice [twaɪs] *adv* duas vezes; **it's ~ as good** é duas vezes melhor; **~ as much** o dobro.

twiddle ['twɪdl] *vt* dar voltas em, brincar com ♦ *vi*: **to ~ with sthg** brincar com algo.

twig [twɪg] *n* galho *m*.

twilight ['twaɪlaɪt] *n* crepúsculo *m*, lusco-fusco *m*.

twin [twɪn] *n* gêmeo *m* (-mea *f*).

twin beds *npl* camas *fpl* separadas.

twine [twaɪn] *n* barbante *m* (*Br*), cordel *m* (*Port*).

twinge [twɪndʒ] *n* pontinha *f*.

twinkle ['twɪŋkl] *vi* (*star, light*) cintilar; (*eyes*) brilhar.

twin room *n* quarto *m* duplo.

twin town *n* cidade *f* irmanada.

twirl [twɜ:l] *vt & vi* girar, rodar.

twist [twɪst] *vt* torcer; (*bottle top, lid, knob*) girar.

twisting ['twɪstɪŋ] *adj* cheio (cheia) de curvas.

twit [twɪt] *n* (*Brit: inf*) idiota *mf*.

twitch [twɪtʃ] *n* tique *m* ◆ *vi (muscle)* contrair-se; *(eye)* palpitar.

two [tu:] *num* dois (duas), → **six**.

two-door *adj* de duas portas.

twofaced [,tu:'feɪst] *adj* falso(-sa), hipócrita.

twofold ['tu:fəʊld] *adj* duplo(-pla) ◆ *adv*: **to increase ~** duplicar.

two-piece *adj* de duas peças.

twosome ['tu:səm] *n (inf)* dupla *f*.

tycoon [taɪ'ku:n] *n* magnata *m*.

tying ['taɪɪŋ] *cont* → **tie**.

type [taɪp] *n (kind)* tipo *m* ◆ *vt & vi*

bater à máquina *(Br)*, escrever à máquina *(Port)*.

typewriter ['taɪp,raɪtəʳ] *n* máquina *f* de escrever.

typhoid ['taɪfɔɪd] *n* febre *f* tifóide.

typhoon [taɪ'fu:n] *n* tufão *m*.

typical ['tɪpɪkl] *adj* típico(-ca).

typing ['taɪpɪŋ] *n* datilografia *f*.

typist ['taɪpɪst] *n* datilógrafo *m* (-fa *f*).

tyranny ['tɪrənɪ] *n* tirania *f*.

tyrant ['taɪrənt] *n* tirano *m* (-na *f*).

tyre ['taɪəʳ] *n (Brit)* pneu *m*.

U

U *adj (Brit: film)* para todos.

U-bend *n* sifão *m*.

udder ['ʌdər] *n* tetas *fpl*, úbere *m*.

UFO *n (abbr of unidentified flying object)* OVNI *m*.

ugly ['ʌglɪ] *adj* feio (feia).

UHF *n (abbr of ultra-high frequency)* UHF *f*.

UHT *adj (abbr of ultra heat treated)* UHT.

UK *n*: the ~ o Reino Unido.

Ukraine [juːˈkreɪn] *n*: the ~ a Ucrânia.

ulcer ['ʌlsər] *n* úlcera *f*.

Ulster ['ʌlstər] *n* Úlster *m*.

ulterior [ʌlˈtɪərɪər] *adj*: ~ motives segundas intenções *fpl*.

ultimate ['ʌltɪmət] *adj (final)* final; *(best, greatest)* máximo(-ma).

ultimately ['ʌltɪmətlɪ] *adv* no final das contas.

ultimatum [ˌʌltɪˈmeɪtəm] *(pl -tums OR -ta* [-tə]) *n* ultimato *m*.

ultrasound ['ʌltrəsaʊnd] *n* ultra-sons *mpl; (scan)* ecografia *f*.

ultraviolet [ˌʌltrəˈvaɪələt] *adj* ultravioleta.

umbilical cord [ʌmˈbɪlɪkl-] *n* cordão *m* umbilical.

umbrella [ʌmˈbrelə] *n* guarda-chuva *m*, chapéu-de-chuva *m (Port)*.

umpire ['ʌmpaɪər] *n* árbitro *m*.

umpteen [ˌʌmpˈtiːn] *num adj (inf)*: ~ times não sei quantas vezes, "n" vezes.

umpteenth [ˌʌmpˈtiːnθ] *num adj (inf)*: for the ~ time pela enésima OR milésima vez.

UN *n (abbr of United Nations)*: the ~ a ONU.

unable [ʌnˈeɪbl] *adj*: to be ~ to do sthg não ser capaz de fazer algo; I'm afraid I'm ~ to attend sinto muito

mas não poderei estar presente.

unacceptable [ˌʌnəkˈseptəbl] *adj* inaceitável.

unaccompanied [ˌʌnəˈkʌmpənɪd] *adj (child, luggage)* desacompanhado(-da), sozinho(-nha).

unaccustomed [ˌʌnəˈkʌstəmd] *adj*: to be ~ to sthg não estar acostumado(-da) a algo.

unadulterated [ˌʌnəˈdʌltəreɪtɪd] *adj (unspoiled)* não adulterado(-da).

unanimous [juːˈnænɪməs] *adj* unânime.

unanimously [juːˈnænɪməslɪ] *adv* unanimemente.

unappetizing [ˌʌnˈæpɪtaɪzɪŋ] *adj* pouco apetitoso(-osa).

unassuming [ˌʌnəˈsjuːmɪŋ] *adj* despretensioso(-osa).

unattended [ˌʌnəˈtendɪd] *adj* sem vigilância, abandonado(-da).

unattractive [ˌʌnəˈtræktɪv] *adj* pouco atraente.

unauthorized [ʌnˈɔːθəraɪzd] *adj* não autorizado(-da).

unavailable [ˌʌnəˈveɪləbl] *adj* não disponível.

unavoidable [ˌʌnəˈvɔɪdəbl] *adj* inevitável.

unaware [ˌʌnəˈweər] *adj*: to be ~ (that) ignorar que; to be ~ of sthg não ter conhecimento de algo.

unbearable [ʌnˈbeərəbl] *adj* insuportável.

unbeatable [ʌnˈbiːtəbl] *adj* imbatível.

unbelievable [ˌʌnbɪˈliːvəbl] *adj* inacreditável.

unbias(s)ed [ʌnˈbaɪəst] *adj* imparcial.

unbutton [ʌnˈbʌtn] *vt* desabotoar.

uncalled-for [ʌnˈkɔːld-] *adj (remark)* injusto(-ta); *(criticism)* injustificado(-da).

uncanny [ʌn'kænɪ] adj estranho(-nha), inquietante.

uncertain [ʌn'sɜːtn] adj (not definite) incerto(-ta); (not sure) indeciso(-sa).

uncertainty [ʌn'sɜːtntɪ] n incerteza f.

unchanged [ʌn'tʃeɪndʒd] adj na mesma.

unchecked [ʌn'tʃekt] adj (growth, expansion) livre, desenfreado(-da) ♦ adv (grow, spread) livremente, desenfreadamente.

uncivilized [ʌn'sɪvɪlaɪzd] adj não civilizado(-da), primitivo(-va).

uncle ['ʌŋkl] n tio m.

unclean [ʌn'kliːn] adj sujo(-ja).

unclear [ʌn'klɪəʳ] adj pouco claro (-ra); (not sure) pouco seguro(-ra).

uncomfortable [ʌn'kʌmftəbl] adj incômodo(-da); **to feel ~** (awkward) sentir-se pouco à vontade.

uncommon [ʌn'kɒmən] adj (rare) invulgar.

unconcerned [ʌnkən'sɜːnd] adj ~ (about) (not anxious) pouco ansioso(-sa).

unconscious [ʌn'kɒnʃəs] adj (after accident) inconsciente; **to be ~ of** não ter consciência de.

unconventional [ʌnkən'venʃənl] adj pouco convencional.

unconvinced [ʌnkən'vɪnst] adj cético(-ca); **to remain ~** continuar a não acreditar.

unconvincing [ʌnkən'vɪnsɪŋ] adj pouco convincente.

uncooperative [ʌnkəʊ'ɒpərətɪv] adj pouco cooperativo(-va).

uncork [ʌn'kɔːk] vt tirar a rolha de.

uncouth [ʌn'kuːθ] adj rude.

uncover [ʌn'kʌvəʳ] vt descobrir.

undecided [ʌndɪ'saɪdɪd] adj (person) indeciso(-sa); (issue) por resolver.

undeniable [ʌndɪ'naɪəbl] adj inegável.

under ['ʌndəʳ] prep (beneath) embaixo de (Br), debaixo de (Port); (less than) menos de; (according to) segundo; (in classification) em; **children ~ ten** crianças com menos de dez anos; **~ the circumstances** nas OR dadas as circunstâncias; **to be ~ pressure** estar sob pressão.

underage [ʌndər'eɪdʒ] adj menor de idade.

undercarriage ['ʌndə,kærɪdʒ] n trem m de aterrissagem.

undercharge [ʌndə'tʃɑːdʒ] vt: **they ~d me by about £2** me cobraram umas duas libras a menos.

underdeveloped [ʌndədɪ'veləpt] adj subdesenvolvido(-da).

underdog ['ʌndədɒg] n: **the ~** o mais fraco.

underdone [ʌndə'dʌn] adj mal cozido(-da), cru (crua).

underestimate [ʌndər'estɪmeɪt] vt subestimar.

underexposed [ʌndərɪk'spəʊzd] adj (photograph) com exposição insuficiente.

underfoot [ʌndə'fʊt] adv debaixo dos pés.

undergo [ʌndə'gəʊ] (pt -went, pp -gone) vt (change, difficulties) sofrer; (operation) submeter-se a.

undergraduate [ʌndə'grædjʊət] n estudante m universitário (não licenciado) (estudante f universitária (não licenciada)).

underground ['ʌndəgraʊnd] adj (below earth's surface) subterrâneo (-nea); (secret) clandestino(-na) ♦ n (Brit: railway) metrô m (Br), metropolitano m (Port).

undergrowth ['ʌndəgrəʊθ] n vegetação f rasteira, mato m.

underhand [ʌndə'hænd] adj escuso (-sa), dúbio(-bia).

underline [ʌndə'laɪn] vt sublinhar.

undermine [ʌndə'maɪn] vt (weaken) enfraquecer.

underneath [ʌndə'niːθ] prep embaixo de (Br), debaixo de (Port) ♦ adv debaixo, embaixo, por baixo ♦ n parte f inferior OR de baixo.

underpaid ['ʌndəpeɪd] adj mal pago(-ga).

underpants ['ʌndəpænts] npl cueca f (de homem).

underpass ['ʌndəpɑːs] n passagem f subterrânea.

underrated [ʌndə'reɪtɪd] adj (person) subestimado(-da); **I think it's a much ~ film/book** não acho que tenha sido dado o devido valor ao filme/livro.

undershirt ['ʌndəʃɜːt] n (Am) camiseta f (Br), camisola f interior (Port).

underskirt ['ʌndəskɜːt] n anágua f (Br), saiote m (Port).

understand [ʌndə'stænd] (pt & pp -stood) vt entender; (believe) crer ♦ vi entender; **I don't ~** não entendo; **to**

make o.s. understood fazer-se entender.

understandable [ˌʌndəˈstændəbl] *adj*
compreensível.

understanding [ˌʌndəˈstændɪŋ] *adj*
compreensivo(-va) ◆ *n* (*agreement*)
acordo *m*; (*knowledge*) conhecimento
m; (*interpretation*) interpretação *f*; (*sympathy*) compreensão *f*.

understatement [ˌʌndəˈsteɪtmənt]
n: that's an ~ isso é um eufemismo.

understood [ˌʌndəˈstʊd] *pt & pp* →
understand.

understudy [ˈʌndəˌstʌdɪ] *n* (ator)
substituto *m* ((atriz) substituta *f*).

undertake [ˌʌndəˈteɪk] (*pt* -took, *pp*
-taken) *vt* empreender; to ~ to do
sthg comprometer-se a fazer algo.

undertaker [ˈʌndəˌteɪkər] *n* agente *m*
funerário (agente *f* funerária).

undertaking [ˌʌndəˈteɪkɪŋ] *n* (*promise*) promessa *f*; (*task*) tarefa *f*.

undertook [ˌʌndəˈtʊk] *pt* → undertake.

underwater [ˌʌndəˈwɔːtər] *adj* suba-
quático(-ca) ◆ *adv* debaixo da água.

underwear [ˈʌndəweər] *n* roupa *f* de
baixo (*Br*), roupa *f* interior (*Port*).

underwent [ˌʌndəˈwent] *pt* → undergo.

undesirable [ˌʌndɪˈzaɪərəbl] *adj* indesejável.

undid [ˌʌnˈdɪd] *pt* → undo.

undies [ˈʌndɪz] *npl* (*inf*) roupa *f* de
baixo (*Br*), roupa *f* interior (*Port*).

undisputed [ˌʌndɪˈspjuːtɪd] *adj* indiscutível.

undo [ˌʌnˈduː] (*pt* -did, *pp* -done) *vt*
(*coat, shirt*) desabotoar; (*shoelaces, tie*)
desamarrar, desapertar; (*parcel*) abrir.

undone [ˌʌnˈdʌn] *adj* (*coat, shirt*) desa-
botoado(-da); (*shoelaces, tie*) desamar-
rado(-da), desapertado(-da).

undoubtedly [ʌnˈdaʊtɪdlɪ] *adv* sem
dúvida (alguma).

undress [ʌnˈdres] *vi* despir-se ◆ *vt*
despir.

undressed [ʌnˈdrest] *adj* despi-
do(-da); to get ~ despir-se.

undue [ˌʌnˈdjuː] *adj* excessivo(-va).

unearth [ʌnˈɜːθ] *vt* desenterrar.

unease [ʌnˈiːz] *n* mal-estar *m*.

uneasy [ʌnˈiːzɪ] *adj* inquieto(-ta).

uneducated [ʌnˈedjʊkeɪtɪd] *adj*
inculto(-ta).

unemployed [ˌʌnɪmˈplɔɪd] *adj* desem-

pregado(-da) ◆ *npl*: the ~ os desempregados.

unemployment [ˌʌnɪmˈplɔɪmənt] *n*
desemprego *m*.

unemployment benefit *n*
auxílio-desemprego *m* (*Br*), subsídio *m*
de desemprego (*Port*).

unequal [ˌʌnˈiːkwəl] *adj* desigual.

unerring [ˌʌnˈɜːrɪŋ] *adj* infalível.

uneven [ˌʌnˈiːvn] *adj* (*surface, speed,
beat*) irregular; (*share, distribution, competition*) desigual.

uneventful [ˌʌnɪˈventfʊl] *adj* sem
incidentes, tranqüilo(-la).

unexpected [ˌʌnɪkˈspektɪd] *adj* ines-
perado(-da).

unexpectedly [ˌʌnɪkˈspektɪdlɪ] *adv*
inesperadamente.

unfailing [ʌnˈfeɪlɪŋ] *adj* constante,
inabalável.

unfair [ˌʌnˈfeər] *adj* injusto(-ta).

unfairly [ˌʌnˈfeəlɪ] *adv* injustamente.

unfaithful [ˌʌnˈfeɪθfʊl] *adj* infiel.

unfamiliar [ˌʌnfəˈmɪljər] *adj* desco-
nhecido(-da); to be ~ with não estar
familiarizado(-da) com.

unfashionable [ˌʌnˈfæʃnəbl] *adj* fora
de moda.

unfasten [ˌʌnˈfɑːsn] *vt* (*button*) desabotoar; (*belt, strap*) desapertar; (*knot*)
desfazer.

unfavourable [ˌʌnˈfeɪvrəbl] *adj* desfavorável.

unfinished [ˌʌnˈfɪnɪʃt] *adj* inacaba-
do(-da).

unfit [ˌʌnˈfɪt] *adj*: to be ~ (*not healthy*)
não estar em forma; to be ~ for sthg
(*not suitable*) não ser adequado(-da)
para algo.

unfold [ʌnˈfəʊld] *vt* (*map, sheet*) desdobrar.

unforeseen [ˌʌnfɔːˈsiːn] *adj* imprevis-
to(-ta).

unforgettable [ˌʌnfəˈgetəbl] *adj*
inesquecível.

unforgivable [ˌʌnfəˈgɪvəbl] *adj* imperdoável.

unfortunate [ʌnˈfɔːtʃnət] *adj*
(*unlucky*) infeliz; (*regrettable*) lamentável.

unfortunately [ʌnˈfɔːtʃnətlɪ] *adv*
infelizmente.

unfounded [ˌʌnˈfaʊndɪd] *adj* infunda-
do(-da).

unfriendly [ˌʌnˈfrendlɪ] *adj* hostil.

unfurnished [ˌʌnˈfɜːnɪʃt] adj sem mobília.

ungainly [ʌnˈɡeɪnlɪ] adj desajeitado(-da).

ungrateful [ʌnˈɡreɪtfʊl] adj ingrato(-ta).

unhappy [ʌnˈhæpɪ] adj (sad) infeliz; (not pleased) descontente; **to be ~ about sthg** não estar feliz OR contente com algo.

unharmed [ʌnˈhɑːmd] adj ileso(-sa).

unhealthy [ʌnˈhelθɪ] adj (person) doente, pouco saudável; (food, smoking) prejudicial para a saúde; (place) pouco saudável.

unheard-of [ʌnˈhɜːd-] adj (unknown, completely absent) inexistente; (unprecedented) sem precedente, inaudito(-ta).

unhelpful [ˌʌnˈhelpfʊl] adj (person) imprestável; (advice, information) inútil.

unhurt [ʌnˈhɜːt] adj ileso(-sa).

unhygienic [ˌʌnhaɪˈdʒiːnɪk] adj pouco higiênico(-ca).

unification [ˌjuːnɪfɪˈkeɪʃn] n unificação f.

uniform [ˈjuːnɪfɔːm] n uniforme m.

unify [ˈjuːnɪfaɪ] vt unificar.

unilateral [ˌjuːnɪˈlætərəl] adj unilateral.

unimportant [ˌʌnɪmˈpɔːtənt] adj sem importância, pouco importante.

uninhabited [ˌʌnɪnˈhæbɪtɪd] adj desabitado(-da).

uninjured [ˌʌnˈɪndʒəd] adj ileso(-sa).

unintelligent [ˌʌnɪnˈtelɪdʒənt] adj pouco inteligente.

unintentional [ˌʌnɪnˈtenʃənl] adj involuntário(-ria).

uninterested [ˌʌnˈɪntrəstɪd] adj desinteressado(-da), pouco interessado(-da).

uninteresting [ˌʌnˈɪntrestɪŋ] adj sem interesse, pouco interessante.

union [ˈjuːnjən] n (of workers) sindicato m.

Union Jack n: **the ~** a bandeira do Reino Unido.

unique [juːˈniːk] adj único(-ca); **to be ~ to sthg** típico(-ca) de.

unisex [ˈjuːnɪseks] adj unisex inv (Br), unissexo (inv) (Port).

unison [ˈjuːnɪzn] n uníssono m; **in ~** em uníssono.

unit [ˈjuːnɪt] n unidade f; (group) equipe f.

unite [juːˈnaɪt] vt (people) unir; (country, party) unificar ◆ vi unir-se.

united [juːˈnaɪtɪd] adj unido(-da).

United Kingdom n: **the ~** o Reino Unido.

United Nations npl: **the ~** as Nações Unidas.

United States (of America) npl: **the ~** os Estados Unidos (da América).

unity [ˈjuːnətɪ] n unidade f.

universal [ˌjuːnɪˈvɜːsl] adj universal.

universe [ˈjuːnɪvɜːs] n universo m.

university [ˌjuːnɪˈvɜːsətɪ] n universidade f.

unjust [ʌnˈdʒʌst] adj injusto(-ta).

unkempt [ʌnˈkempt] adj (person) desalinhado(-da); (hair) despenteado(-da).

unkind [ʌnˈkaɪnd] adj cruel.

unknown [ʌnˈnəʊn] adj desconhecido(-da).

unlawful [ʌnˈlɔːfʊl] adj (activity) ilegal; (behaviour) que atenta contra a lei; (killing) não justificado(-da).

unleaded (petrol) [ʌnˈledɪd-] n gasolina f sem chumbo.

unleash [ʌnˈliːʃ] vt (fury, violence) desencadear.

unless [ənˈles] conj a não ser que.

unlike [ʌnˈlaɪk] prep (different to) diferente de; (in contrast to) ao contrário de; **it's ~ her to be late** ela não é de chegar atrasada.

unlikely [ʌnˈlaɪklɪ] adj (not probable) pouco provável; **she's ~ to agree** é pouco provável que ela concorde.

unlimited [ʌnˈlɪmɪtɪd] adj ilimitado(-da); **~ mileage** = quilometragem ilimitada.

unlisted [ʌnˈlɪstɪd] adj (Am: phone number) que não consta da lista telefônica.

unload [ʌnˈləʊd] vt descarregar.

unlock [ʌnˈlɒk] vt abrir (com chave), destrancar.

unlucky [ʌnˈlʌkɪ] adj (unfortunate) infeliz; (bringing bad luck) que traz má sorte.

unmarried [ʌnˈmærɪd] adj solteiro(-ra).

unmistakable [ˌʌnmɪˈsteɪkəbl] adj inconfundível.

unnatural [ʌnˈnætʃrəl] adj (unusual) invulgar; (behaviour, person) pouco natural.

unnecessary [ʌnˈnesəsərɪ] adj desnecessário(-ria).

unnerving [ʌnˈnɜːvɪŋ] adj desconcertante.

unnoticed [ʌnˈnəʊtɪst] adj despercebido(-da).

unobtainable [ʌnəbˈteɪnəbl] adj inacessível.

unobtrusive [ʌnəbˈtruːsɪv] adj discreto(-ta).

unoccupied [ʌnˈɒkjʊpaɪd] adj (place, seat) desocupado(-da).

unofficial [ʌnəˈfɪʃl] adj não oficial.

unorthodox [ʌnˈɔːθədɒks] adj pouco ortodoxo(-xa).

unpack [ʌnˈpæk] vt desfazer ♦ vi desfazer as malas.

unpleasant [ʌnˈplɛznt] adj desagradável.

unplug [ʌnˈplʌg] vt desligar (na tomada).

unpopular [ʌnˈpɒpjʊləʳ] adj impopular, pouco popular.

unprecedented [ʌnˈprɛsɪdəntɪd] adj sem precedente.

unpredictable [ʌnprɪˈdɪktəbl] adj imprevisível.

unprepared [ʌnprɪˈpeəd] adj mal preparado(-da).

unprotected [ʌnprəˈtɛktɪd] adj desprotegido(-da).

unqualified [ʌnˈkwɒlɪfaɪd] adj (person) sem qualificação.

unravel [ʌnˈrævl] vt (knitting, threads) desmanchar; (mystery, puzzle) resolver.

unreal [ʌnˈrɪəl] adj irreal.

unrealistic [ʌnrɪəˈlɪstɪk] adj pouco realista, irrealista.

unreasonable [ʌnˈriːznəbl] adj absurdo(-da), irracional.

unrecognizable [ʌnrɛkəɡˈnaɪzəbl] adj irreconhecível.

unrelated [ʌnrɪˈleɪtɪd] adj: to be ~ (to sthg) não estar relacionado(-da) (com algo).

unrelenting [ʌnrɪˈlɛntɪŋ] adj inexorável, constante.

unreliable [ʌnrɪˈlaɪəbl] adj pouco confiável, de pouca confiança.

unrequited [ʌnrɪˈkwaɪtɪd] adj não correspondido(-da).

unresolved [ʌnrɪˈzɒlvd] adj por resolver.

unrest [ʌnˈrɛst] n agitação f.

unroll [ʌnˈrəʊl] vt desenrolar.

unruly [ʌnˈruːlɪ] adj rebelde.

unsafe [ʌnˈseɪf] adj (dangerous) perigoso(-osa); (in danger) inseguro(-ra).

unsatisfactory [ʌnsætɪsˈfæktərɪ] adj insatisfatório(-ria).

unscathed [ʌnˈskeɪðd] adj ileso(-sa).

unscrew [ʌnˈskruː] vt (lid, top) desenroscar.

unseemly [ʌnˈsiːmlɪ] adj impróprio(-pria).

unselfish [ʌnˈsɛlfɪʃ] adj altruísta, desinteressado(-da).

unsettled [ʌnˈsɛtld] adj (person) perturbado(-da); (weather, region) instável; (argument) por resolver; (account, bill) por pagar.

unshaven [ʌnˈʃeɪvn] adj (face, chin) por barbear; (person) com a barba por fazer.

unsightly [ʌnˈsaɪtlɪ] adj feio (feia).

unskilled [ʌnˈskɪld] adj (worker) sem qualificação.

unsociable [ʌnˈsəʊʃəbl] adj insociável.

unsound [ʌnˈsaʊnd] adj (building, structure) inseguro(-ra); (argument, method) errôneo(-nea).

unspoiled [ʌnˈspɔɪlt] adj intacto(-ta), não destruído(-da).

unstable [ʌnˈsteɪbl] adj instável.

unsteady [ʌnˈstɛdɪ] adj instável; (hand) trêmulo(-la).

unstuck [ʌnˈstʌk] adj: to come ~ (label, poster etc) descolar-se.

unsuccessful [ʌnsəkˈsɛsfʊl] adj mal sucedido(-da).

unsuitable [ʌnˈsuːtəbl] adj inadequado(-da).

unsure [ʌnˈʃɔːʳ] adj: to be ~ (about) não ter certeza (de).

unsuspecting [ʌnsəˈspɛktɪŋ] adj desprevenido(-da).

unsweetened [ʌnˈswiːtnd] adj sem açúcar.

untangle [ʌnˈtæŋgl] vt desemaranhar.

untidy [ʌnˈtaɪdɪ] adj desarrumado(-da).

untie [ʌnˈtaɪ] (cont untying) vt (knot) desatar; (person) desprender.

until [ənˈtɪl] prep & conj até; wait ~ he arrives espera até ele chegar OR até que ele chegue.

untimely [ʌnˈtaɪmlɪ] adj (premature) prematuro(-ra); (inopportune) inoportuno(-na).

untold [ʌnˈtəʊld] adj (incalculable,

vast) incalculável.

untoward [ʌntɔ'wɔːd] *adj (event)* fora do normal; *(behaviour)* impróprio (-pria).

untrue [ʌn'truː] *adj* falso(-sa).

untrustworthy [ʌn'trʌstwɜːðɪ] *adj* indigno(-gna) de confiança.

untying [ʌn'taɪɪŋ] *cont* → **untie**.

unusual [ʌn'juːʒl] *adj (not common)* invulgar; *(distinctive)* fora do vulgar.

unusually [ʌn'juːʒəlɪ] *adv (more than usual)* excepcionalmente.

unwelcome [ʌn'welkəm] *adj* indesejado(-da).

unwell [ʌn'wel] *adj* mal disposto (-osta); **to feel ~** sentir-se mal.

unwieldy [ʌn'wiːldɪ] *adj (object, tool)* difícil de manejar; *(system, method)* pouco eficiente; *(bureaucracy)* pesado(-da).

unwilling [ʌn'wɪlɪŋ] *adj:* **to be ~ to do sthg** não estar disposto(-osta) a fazer algo.

unwind [ʌn'waɪnd] *(pt & pp* **unwound)** *vt* desenrolar ♦ *vi (relax)* relaxar.

unwise [ʌn'waɪz] *adj* imprudente.

unworthy [ʌn'wɜːðɪ] *adj (undeserving):* **to be ~ of** não merecer.

unwound [ʌn'waʊnd] *pt & pp* → unwind.

unwrap [ʌn'ræp] *vt* desembrulhar.

unzip [ʌn'zɪp] *vt* abrir o fecho ecler de.

up [ʌp] *adv* **1.** *(towards higher position, level)* para cima; **to go ~** subir; **prices are going ~** os preços estão subindo; **we walked ~ to the top** subimos até o cume; **to pick sthg ~** apanhar algo.

2. *(in higher position):* **she's ~ in her bedroom** está lá em cima no seu quarto; **~ there** ali OR lá em cima; **put your hands ~, please!** levantem as mãos, por favor!

3. *(into upright position):* **to stand ~** pôr-se em OR de pé; **to sit ~** *(from lying position)* sentar-se; *(sit straight)* sentar-se direito.

4. *(northwards):* **~ in Scotland** na Escócia.

5. *(in phrases):* **to walk ~ and down** andar de um lado para o outro; **to jump ~ and down** dar pulos; **~ to six weeks** até seis semanas; **~ to ten people** até dez pessoas; **are you ~ to**

travelling? você está em condições de viajar?; **what are you ~ to?** o que você está tramando?; **it's ~ to you** depende de você; **~ until ten o'clock** até às dez horas.

♦ *prep* **1.** *(towards higher position):* **to walk ~ a hill** subir um monte; **I went ~ the stairs** subi as escadas.

2. *(in higher position)* no topo de; **~ a hill** no topo de um monte; **~ a ladder** no topo de uma escada.

3. *(at end of):* **they live ~ the road from us** eles vivem no final da nossa rua.

♦ *adj* **1.** *(out of bed)* levantado(-da); **I was ~ at six today** levantei-me às seis hoje.

2. *(at an end):* **time's ~** acabou-se o tempo.

3. *(rising):* **the ~ escalator** a escada rolante ascendente.

♦ *n:* **~s and downs** altos e baixos *mpl.*

upbringing [ʌp'brɪŋɪŋ] *n* educação *f.*

update [ʌp'deɪt] *vt* atualizar.

upheaval [ʌp'hiːvl] *n* reviravolta *f.*

upheld [ʌp'held] *pt & pp* → **uphold.**

uphill [ʌp'hɪl] *adv:* **to go ~** subir.

uphold [ʌp'həʊld] *(pt & pp* **-held)** *vt* defender.

upholstery [ʌp'həʊlstərɪ] *n (material)* estofo *m.*

upkeep [ʌpkiːp] *n* manutenção *f.*

uplifting [ʌp'lɪftɪŋ] *adj* animador(-ra), entusiasmante.

up-market *adj* de alta categoria.

upon [ə'pɒn] *prep (fml: on)* em, sobre; **~ hearing the news ...** ao ouvir a notícia ....

upper [ʌpər] *adj* superior ♦ *n (of shoe)* gáspeas *fpl.*

upper class *n:* **the ~** a alta sociedade.

uppermost [ʌpəməʊst] *adj (highest)* mais alto(-ta).

upper sixth *n (Brit: SCH)* segundo e último ano do curso opcional que prepara os alunos de 18 anos para os exames "A level".

upright [ʌpraɪt] *adj* direito(-ta) ♦ *adv* direito.

uprising [ʌp,raɪzɪŋ] *n* revolta *f,* insurreição *f.*

uproar [ʌprɔːr] *n (commotion)* tumulto *m; (protest)* indignação *f.*

uproot [ʌp'ruːt] *vt* desenraizar.

upset [ʌpˈset] (*pt & pp* **upset**) *adj (distressed)* transtornado(-da) ◆ *vt* transtornar; *(knock over)* derrubar; **to have an ~ stomach** estar indisposto (-osta).

upshot [ˈʌpʃɒt] *n* resultado *m*.

upside down [ˌʌpsaɪd-] *adj* invertido(-da), ao contrário ◆ *adv* de pernas para o ar.

upstairs [ʌpˈsteəz] *adj* de cima ◆ *adv (on a higher floor)* lá em cima; **to go ~** ir lá para cima.

upstart [ˈʌpstɑːt] *n* pessoa que consegue um cargo de alto nível nem sempre por mérito e que se mostra extremamente arrogante.

upstream [ˌʌpˈstriːm] *adv (sail)* rio acima; *(swim)* contra a corrente ◆ *adj:* **to be ~ (from sthg)** ficar a montante (de algo).

upsurge [ˈʌpsɜːdʒ] *n:* **~ of/in sthg** aumento *m* de/em algo.

uptight [ʌpˈtaɪt] *adj (inf: person)* nervoso(-osa); **to get ~ about sthg** enervar-se com algo.

up-to-date *adj (modern)* moderno (-na); *(well-informed)* atualizado(-da).

upturn [ˈʌptɜːn] *n:* **~ (in sthg)** melhoria *f* (em algo).

upward [ˈʌpwəd] *adj (movement)* para cima; *(trend)* ascendente.

upwards [ˈʌpwədz] *adv* para cima; **~ of 100 people** mais de 100 pessoas.

urban [ˈɜːbən] *adj* urbano(-na).

urban clearway [-ˈklɪəweɪ] *n (Brit)* rua onde não é permitido parar nem estacionar.

Urdu [ˈʊəduː] *n* urdu *m*.

urge [ɜːdʒ] *vt:* **to ~ sb to do sthg** incitar alguém a fazer algo.

urgency [ˈɜːdʒənsɪ] *n* urgência *f*.

urgent [ˈɜːdʒənt] *adj* urgente.

urgently [ˈɜːdʒəntlɪ] *adv (immediately)* urgentemente.

urinal [jʊəˈraɪnl] *n (fml)* urinol *m*.

urinate [ˈjʊərɪneɪt] *vi (fml)* urinar.

urine [ˈjʊərɪn] *n* urina *f*.

urn [ɜːn] *n (for ashes)* urna *f*; *(for tea, coffee)* lata *f*.

us [ʌs] *pron (direct)* nos; *(indirect, after prep)* nós; **they know ~** conhecem-nos; **it's ~** somos nós; **send it to ~** envia-nos isso; **tell ~** diga-nos; **they're worse than ~** são piores que nós; **we brought it with ~** trouxemo-lo connosco.

US *n (abbr of United States):* **the ~** os E.U.A.

USA *n (abbr of United States of America):* **the ~** os E.U.A.

usable [ˈjuːzəbl] *adj* utilizável.

use [*n* juːs, *vb* juːz] *n* uso *m* ◆ *vt* usar; *(run on)* levar; **to be of ~** ser útil; **to have the ~ of sthg** poder utilizar algo; **to make ~ of sthg** aproveitar algo; **"out of ~"** "fora de serviço"; **to be in ~** estar em funcionamento; **it's no ~** não vale a pena; **what's the ~?** de que vale?; **to ~ sthg as sthg** usar algo como algo; **"~ before ..."** "consumir de preferência antes de ...".

❑ **use up** *vt sep* gastar.

used [*adj* juːzd, *aux vb* juːst] *adj* usado(-da) ◆ *aux vb:* **I ~ to live near here** costumava viver perto daqui; **I ~ to go there every day** costumava ir lá todos os dias; **to be ~ to sthg** estar acostumado a algo; **to get ~ to sthg** acostumar-se a algo.

useful [ˈjuːsfʊl] *adj* útil.

useless [ˈjuːslɪs] *adj* inútil; *(inf: very bad)* péssimo(-ma).

user [ˈjuːzər] *n (of product, machine)* utilizador *m* (-ra *f*), usuário *m* (-ria *f*) *(Br)*; *(of public service)* usuário *m* (-ria *f*) *(Br)*, utente *mf (Port)*.

user-friendly *adj* fácil de usar.

usher [ˈʌʃər] *n (at cinema, theatre)* lanterninha *m (Br)*, arrumador *m (Port)*.

usherette [ˌʌʃəˈret] *n* lanterninha *f (Br)*, arrumadora *f (Port)*.

USSR *n:* **the (former) ~** a (antiga) U.R.S.S.

usual [ˈjuːʒəl] *adj* habitual; **as ~** *(in the normal way)* como de costume; *(as often happens)* como sempre.

usually [ˈjuːʒəlɪ] *adv* normalmente.

usurp [juːˈzɜːp] *vt* usurpar.

utensil [juːˈtensl] *n* utensílio *m*.

uterus [ˈjuːtərəs] *(pl -ri [-raɪ], -ruses)* *n* útero *m*.

utilize [ˈjuːtɪlaɪz] *vt (fml)* utilizar.

utmost [ˈʌtməʊst] *adj* extremo(-ma) ◆ *n:* **to do one's ~** fazer o possível e o impossível.

utter [ˈʌtər] *adj* total ◆ *vt* proferir.

utterly [ˈʌtəlɪ] *adv* totalmente.

U-turn *n (in vehicle)* meia-volta *f*, reviravolta *f*.

V

vacancy ['veɪkənsɪ] *n* vaga *f;* **"vacancies" "vagas"; "no vacancies"** "completo".

vacant ['veɪkənt] *adj (room, seat)* vago(-ga); **"vacant" "livre".**

vacate [və'keɪt] *vt (fml: room, house)* vagar, desocupar.

vacation [və'keɪʃn] *n (Am)* férias *fpl* ◆ *vi (Am)* passar férias; **to go on ~** ir de férias.

vacationer [və'keɪʃənər] *n (Am) (throughout the year)* pessoa *f* de férias; *(in summer)* veranista *mf (Br)*, veraneante *mf (Port).*

vaccinate ['væksɪneɪt] *vt* vacinar.

vaccination [,væksɪ'neɪʃn] *n* vacinação *f.*

vaccine [*Brit* 'væksiːn, *Am* væk'siːn] *n* vacina *f.*

vacuum ['vækjuəm] *vt* aspirar.

vacuum cleaner *n* aspirador *m* de pó.

vagina [və'dʒaɪnə] *(pl* **-nas** OR **-nae** [-niː]) *n* vagina *f.*

vagrant ['veɪgrənt] *n* vagabundo *m* (-da *f).*

vague [veɪg] *adj* vago(-ga).

vaguely ['veɪglɪ] *adv* vagamente.

vain [veɪn] *adj (pej: conceited)* vaidoso (-osa); **in ~** em vão.

Valentine card ['væləntaɪn-] *n* cartão *m* do Dia de São Valentim.

Valentine's Day ['væləntaɪnz-] *n* Dia *m* dos Namorados OR de São Valentim.

valet ['væleɪ, 'vælɪt] *n (in hotel)* empregado *m* de hotel *(encarregado do serviço de lavandaria).*

valet service *n (in hotel)* serviço *m* de lavandaria; *(for car)* serviço de lavagem de automóveis.

valiant ['væljənt] *adj* valente.

valid ['vælɪd] *adj (ticket, passport)* válido(-da).

validate ['vælɪdeɪt] *vt (ticket)* validar.

Valium® ['vælɪəm] *n* Valium® *m.*

valley ['vælɪ] *(pl* **-s)** *n* vale *m.*

valuable ['væljuəbl] *adj* valioso(-osa). ❏ **valuables** *npl* objetos *mpl* de valor.

valuation [,vælju'eɪʃn] *n* avaliação *f.*

value ['væljuː] *n (financial)* valor *m; (usefulness)* sentido *m;* **a ~ pack** um pacote de tamanho econômico; **to be good ~ (for money)** ter um preço módico, estar em conta. ❏ **values** *npl (principles)* valores *mpl.*

valued ['væljuːd] *adj* precioso(-osa).

valve [vælv] *n* válvula *f.*

van [væn] *n* caminhonete *f (Br)*, carrinha *f (Port).*

vandal ['vændl] *n* vândalo *m* (-la *f).*

vandalism ['vændəlɪzm] *n* vandalismo *m.*

vandalize ['vændəlaɪz] *vt* destruir, destroçar.

vanilla [və'nɪlə] *n* baunilha *f.*

vanish ['vænɪʃ] *vi* desaparecer.

vanity ['vænətɪ] *n* vaidade *f.*

vantagepoint ['vɑːntɪdʒ,pɔɪnt] *n (for view)* posição *f* estratégica.

vapor ['veɪpər] *(Am)* = **vapour.**

vapour ['veɪpər] *n (Brit)* vapor *m.*

variable ['veərɪəbl] *adj* variável.

variation [,veərɪ'eɪʃn] *n* variação *f.*

varicose veins ['værɪkəʊs-] *npl* varizes *fpl.*

varied ['veərɪd] *adj* variado(-da).

variety [və'raɪətɪ] *n* variedade *f.*

variety show *n* espetáculo *m* de variedades.

various ['veərɪəs] *adj* vários(-rias).

varnish ['vɑːnɪʃ] *n (for wood)* verniz *m* ◆ *vt (wood)* envernizar.

vary ['veərɪ] *vt & vi* variar; **to ~ from sthg to sthg** variar entre algo e algo; **"prices ~"** "os preços variam".

vase [Brit vɑːz, Am veɪz] n jarra f.
Vaseline® ['væsəliːn] n vaselina f.
vast [vɑːst] adj vasto(-ta).
vat [væt] n tina f (Br), bidon m (Port).
VAT [væt, viːeiˈtiː] n (abbr of value added tax) ICM/S (Br), I.V.A m (Port).
vault [vɔːlt] n (in bank) caixa-forte f; (ceiling) abóbada f; (in church) cripta f.
VCR n (abbr of video cassette recorder) vídeo m.
VDU n (abbr of visual display unit) monitor m.
veal [viːl] n vitela f.
veer [vɪər] vi (vehicle, road) virar.
veg [vedʒ] abbr = **vegetable**.
vegan ['viːgən] adj vegetalista♦ n vegetalista mf, pessoa vegetariana que não consome carne, peixe ou derivados animais, tais como ovos ou leite.
vegetable ['vedʒtəbl] n vegetal m, legume m.
vegetable oil n óleo m vegetal.
vegetarian [ˌvedʒɪˈteərɪən] adj vegetariano(-na) ♦ n vegetariano m (-na f).
vegetation [ˌvedʒɪˈteɪʃn] n vegetação f.
vehement ['viːɪmənt] adj veemente.
vehicle ['viːəkl] n veículo m.
veil [veɪl] n véu m.
vein [veɪn] n veia f.
Velcro® ['velkrəu] n Velcro® m.
velocity [vɪˈlɒsətɪ] n velocidade f.
velvet ['velvɪt] n veludo m.
vendetta [venˈdetə] n vendeta f.
vending machine ['vendɪŋ-] n máquina f de venda automática.
vendor ['vendɔːr] n vendedor m (-ra f).
veneer [vəˈnɪər] n (of wood) folheado m.
venetian blind [vɪˌniːʃn-] n persiana f (Br), estore m laminado (Port).
vengeance ['vendʒəns] n vingança f; with a ~ para valer.
venison ['venɪzn] n carne f de veado.
venom ['venəm] n veneno m.
vent [vent] n (for air, smoke etc) saída f de ar, ventilador m.
ventilation [ˌventɪˈleɪʃn] n ventilação f.
ventilator ['ventɪleɪtər] n ventilador m.
venture ['ventʃər] n aventura f ♦ vi (go) aventurar-se.
venue ['venjuː] n local m (de determi-

nado acontecimento esportivo ou cultural).
veranda [vəˈrændə] n terraço m coberto, alpendre m.
verb [vɜːb] n verbo m.
verbal ['vɜːbl] adj verbal.
verdict ['vɜːdɪkt] n (JUR) veredicto m; (opinion) parecer m.
verge [vɜːdʒ] n (of road) acostamento m (Br), berma f (Port); (of lawn, path) beira f; **"soft ~s"** "acostamento mole" (Br), "bermas baixas" (Port).
verify ['verɪfaɪ] vt verificar.
vermin ['vɜːmɪn] n bichos mpl (nocivos ou parasitários).
vermouth ['vɜːməθ] n vermute m.
versa → **vice versa**.
versatile ['vɜːsətaɪl] adj versátil.
verse [vɜːs] n (of song, poem) verso m; (poetry) versos mpl.
versed [vɜːst] adj: **to be well ~ in** sthg ser versado(-da) em algo.
version ['vɜːʃn] n versão f.
versus ['vɜːsəs] prep versus, contra.
vertebra ['vɜːtɪbrə] (pl -bras OR -brae [-briː]) n vértebra f.
vertical ['vɜːtɪkl] adj vertical.
vertigo ['vɜːtɪgəu] n vertigens fpl.
very ['verɪ] adv muito ♦ adj: that's the ~ thing I need é disso mesmo que eu preciso; you're the ~ person I wanted to see era mesmo com você que eu queria falar; ~ much muito; not ~ não muito; my ~ own room o meu próprio quarto.
vessel ['vesl] n (fml: ship) embarcação f.
vest [vest] n (Brit: underwear) camiseta f (Br), camisola f interior (Port); (Am: waistcoat) colete m.
vet [vet] n (Brit) veterinário m (-ria f).
veteran ['vetrən] n veterano m (-na f).
veterinarian [ˌvetərɪˈneərɪən] (Am) = **vet**.
veterinary surgeon ['vetərɪnrɪ-] (Brit: fml) = **vet**.
veto ['viːtəu] (pl -es) n veto m ♦ vt vetar.
VHF n (abbr of very high frequency) VHF f.
VHS n (abbr of video home system) VHS m.
via ['vaɪə] prep via.
viable ['vaɪəbl] adj viável.
viaduct ['vaɪədʌkt] n viaduto m.

vibrate [vaɪˈbreɪt] vi vibrar.

vibration [vaɪˈbreɪʃn] n vibração f.

vicar [ˈvɪkəʳ] n vigário m, pároco m.

vicarage [ˈvɪkərɪdʒ] n casa f paroquial.

vice [vaɪs] n (moral fault) vício m; (crime) crime m; (Brit: tool) torno m.

vice-president n vice-presidente m (-ta f).

vice versa [ˌvaɪsɪˈvɜːsə] adv vice-versa.

vicinity [vɪˈsɪnətɪ] n: **in the ~** nas proximidades.

vicious [ˈvɪʃəs] adj (attack, animal) violento(-ta); (comment) cruel.

vicious circle n círculo m vicioso.

victim [ˈvɪktɪm] n vítima f.

victimize [ˈvɪktɪmaɪz] vt tratar injustamente.

Victorian [vɪkˈtɔːrɪən] adj vitoriano(-na) (segunda metade do séc. XIX).

victorious [vɪkˈtɔːrɪəs] adj vitorioso(-osa).

victory [ˈvɪktərɪ] n vitória f.

video [ˈvɪdɪəʊ] (pl **-s**) n vídeo m; (videotape) cassete f vídeo, videocassete f ♦ vt (using video recorder) gravar; (using camera) filmar; **on ~** em vídeo.

video camera n câmara f de vídeo.

video cassette n videocassete f, cassete f de vídeo.

video game n jogo m de vídeo.

video recorder n videogravador m.

video shop n locadora f de vídeo (Br), clube m de vídeo (Port).

videotape [ˈvɪdɪəʊteɪp] n cassete f vídeo, videocassete f.

vie [vaɪ] (pt & pp **vied**, cont **vying**) vi: **to ~ with sb (for sthg)** competir com alguém (por algo).

Vienna [vɪˈenə] n Viena s.

Vietnam [Brit ˌvjetˈnæm, Am ˌvjetˈnɑːm] n Vietnam m.

view [vjuː] n (scene, field of vision) vista f; (opinion) opinião f; (attitude) visão f ♦ vt (look at) ver; **in my ~** na minha opinião; **in ~ of** (considering) tendo em consideração; **to come into ~** aparecer.

viewer [ˈvjuːəʳ] n (of TV) telespectador m (-ra f).

viewfinder [ˈvjuːˌfaɪndəʳ] n visor m.

viewpoint [ˈvjuːpɔɪnt] n (opinion) ponto m de vista; (place) miradouro m.

vigilant [ˈvɪdʒɪlənt] adj (fml) atento(-ta).

vigorous [ˈvɪɡərəs] adj vigoroso(-osa).

vile [vaɪl] adj horrível, horroroso (-osa).

villa [ˈvɪlə] n casa f, vivenda f (Port).

village [ˈvɪlɪdʒ] n lugarejo m, aldeia f.

villager [ˈvɪlɪdʒəʳ] n habitante mf da aldeia.

villain [ˈvɪlən] n (of book, film) vilão m (-lã f) da fita; (criminal) criminoso m (-osa f).

vinaigrette [ˌvɪnɪˈɡret] n vinagrete m, molho para saladas feito com azeite, vinagre, sal, pimenta e ervas aromáticas.

vindicate [ˈvɪndɪkeɪt] vt justificar.

vindictive [vɪnˈdɪktɪv] adj vingativo(-va).

vine [vaɪn] n (grapevine) videira f; (climbing plant) trepadeira f.

vinegar [ˈvɪnɪɡəʳ] n vinagre m.

vineyard [ˈvɪnjəd] n vinha f, vinhedo m.

vintage [ˈvɪntɪdʒ] adj (wine) vintage (inv) ♦ n (year) colheita f, ano m.

vinyl [ˈvaɪnɪl] n vinil m.

viola [vɪˈəʊlə] n (MUS) rabeca f.

violate [ˈvaɪəleɪt] vt (law, human rights) violar.

violence [ˈvaɪələns] n violência f.

violent [ˈvaɪələnt] adj violento(-ta).

violet [ˈvaɪələt] adj roxo(-xa), violeta (inv) ♦ n (flower) violeta f.

violin [ˌvaɪəˈlɪn] n violino m.

violinist [ˌvaɪəˈlɪnɪst] n violinista mf.

VIP n (abbr of very important person) VIP mf.

viper [ˈvaɪpəʳ] n víbora f.

virgin [ˈvɜːdʒɪn] n virgem mf.

Virgo [ˈvɜːɡəʊ] (pl **-s**) n Virgem f.

virile [ˈvɪraɪl] adj viril.

virtually [ˈvɜːtʃʊəlɪ] adv praticamente.

virtual reality [ˈvɜːtʃʊəl-] n realidade f virtual.

virtue [ˈvɜːtjuː] n virtude f; **by ~ of** em virtude de, pelo fato de.

virtuous [ˈvɜːtʃʊəs] adj virtuoso(-osa).

virus [ˈvaɪrəs] n vírus m inv.

visa [ˈviːzə] n visto m.

viscose [ˈvɪskəʊs] n viscose f.

visibility [ˌvɪzɪˈbɪlətɪ] n visibilidade f.

visible ['vɪzəbl] *adj* visível.

visit ['vɪzɪt] *vt* visitar ♦ *n* visita *f*.

visiting hours ['vɪzɪtɪŋ-] *npl* horas *fpl* de visita.

visitor ['vɪzɪtə'] *n* (to person) visita *f*; (to place) visitante *mf*.

visitor centre *n* (Brit) estabelecimento que inclui um centro de informação, lojas, cafeteria, etc e que se encontra em locais de interesse turístico.

visitors' book *n* livro *m* de visitantes.

visitor's passport *n* (Brit) passaporte *m* provisório.

visor ['vaɪzə'] *n* (helmet) viseira *f*; (of hat) pala *f*.

visual ['vɪʒuəl] *adj* visual.

vital ['vaɪtl] *adj* vital.

vitamin [Brit 'vɪtəmɪn, Am 'vaɪtəmɪn] *n* vitamina *f*.

vivacious [vɪ'veɪʃəs] *adj* vivaz, animado(-da).

vivid ['vɪvɪd] *adj* vivo(-va).

VLF (abbr of very low frequency) freqüência extremamente baixa.

V-neck *n* (design) decote *m* em bico OR em V.

vocabulary [və'kæbjulərɪ] *n* vocabulário *m*.

vocal cords *npl* cordas *fpl* vocais.

vocation [vəʊ'keɪʃn] *n* vocação *f*.

vocational [vəʊ'keɪʃənl] *adj* profissional.

vociferous [və'sɪfərəs] *adj* vociferante.

vodka ['vɒdkə] *n* vodca *f*.

voice [vɔɪs] *n* voz *f*.

voice mail *n* correio *m* de voz.

void [vɔɪd] *adj* (invalid) nulo(-la).

volcano [vɒl'keɪnəʊ] (*pl* -es OR-s) *n* vulcão *m*.

volley ['vɒlɪ] (*pl* -s) *n* (in tennis) vôlei *m* ♦ *vt* bater em (antes que haja ressalto).

volleyball ['vɒlɪbɔːl] *n* voleibol *m*.

volt [vəʊlt] *n* volt *m*.

voltage ['vəʊltɪdʒ] *n* voltagem *f*.

volume ['vɒljuːm] *n* volume *m*.

voluntarily [Brit 'vɒləntrɪlɪ, Am ,vɒlən'terəlɪ] *adv* voluntariamente.

voluntary ['vɒləntrɪ] *adj* voluntário (-ria).

volunteer [,vɒlən'tɪə'] *n* voluntário *m* (-ria *f*) ♦ *vt*: to ~ to do sthg oferecer-se para fazer algo.

vomit ['vɒmɪt] *n* vômito *m* ♦ *vi* vomitar.

vote [vəʊt] *n* (choice) voto *m*; (process, number of votes) votação *f* ♦ *vi*: to ~ (for) votar (em).

voter ['vəʊtə'] *n* eleitor *m* (-ra *f*).

voting ['vəʊtɪŋ] *n* votação *f*.

vouch [vaʊtʃ] : **vouch for** *vt fus* (person, child) responder por; **I can ~ for its accuracy** posso lhe garantir que está correto.

voucher ['vaʊtʃə'] *n* vale *m*.

vow [vaʊ] *n* voto *m*, juramento *m* ♦ *vt*: to ~ (that) jurar que; to ~ to do sthg jurar fazer algo.

vowel ['vaʊəl] *n* vogal *f*.

voyage ['vɔɪɪdʒ] *n* viagem *f*.

vulgar ['vʌlgə'] *adj* ordinário(-ria), vulgar.

vulnerable ['vʌlnərəbl] *adj* vulnerável; ~ to sthg (to being hurt) vulnerável a algo; (to criticism, influence) sujeito(-ta) a algo.

vulture ['vʌltʃə'] *n* abutre *m*.

vying ['vaɪɪŋ] *cont* → **vie**.

W

W *(abbr.of west)* O.

wad [wɒd] *n (of paper, banknotes)* maço *m; (of cotton)* bola *f,* novelo *m.*

waddle ['wɒdl] *vi* bambolear-se.

wade [weɪd] *vi* caminhar *(com dificuldade pela água).*

wading pool ['weɪdɪŋ-] *n (Am)* piscina *f* infantil.

wafer ['weɪfəʳ] *n* bolacha *f (muito fina e leve).*

waffle ['wɒfl] *n (pancake)* = waffle *m (Br),* talassa *f (Port)* ◆ *vi (inf)* dizer palha.

wag [wæg] *vt* abanar.

wage [weɪdʒ] *n* ordenado *m.*

❏ **wages** *npl* ordenado *m.*

wage packet *n (pay)* ordenado *m.*

wager ['weɪdʒəʳ] *n* aposta *f.*

wagon ['wægən] *n (vehicle)* carroça *f; (Brit: of train)* vagão *m.*

wail [weɪl] *n* lamento *m,* gemido *m* ◆ *vi (person, baby)* chorar.

waist [weɪst] *n* cintura *f.*

waistcoat ['weɪskəʊt] *n* colete *m.*

waistline ['weɪstlaɪn] *n* cintura *f,* cinta *f.*

wait [weɪt] *n* espera *f* ◆ *vi* esperar; **to ~ for sb to do sthg** esperar que alguém faça algo; **I can't ~!** mal posso esperar!

❏ **wait for** *vt fus* esperar por; **I'm ~ing for someone** estou à espera de alguém.

waiter ['weɪtəʳ] *n* garçon *m,* empregado *m (de mesa) (Port).*

waiting list ['weɪtɪŋ-] *n* lista *f* de espera.

waiting room ['weɪtɪŋ-] *n* sala *f* de espera.

waitress ['weɪtrɪs] *n* garçonete *f (Br),* empregada *f (de mesa) (Port).*

waive [weɪv] *vt (rule)* não aplicar; *(right)* prescindir de.

wake [weɪk] *(pt* woke, *pp* woken) *vt & vi* acordar.

❏ **wake up** *vt sep & vi* acordar.

Waldorf salad ['wɔːldɔːf-] *n* salada *f* Waldorf, *salada de maçã, nozes e aipo com maionese.*

Wales [weɪlz] *n* País *m* de Gales.

walk [wɔːk] *n (hike)* caminhada *f; (stroll)* passeio *m; (path)* trilho *m,* caminho *m* ◆ *vi* andar; *(as hobby)* caminhar ◆ *vt (distance)* andar; *(dog)* passear; **to go for a ~** dar um passeio; **it's a short ~** não é muito longe (a pé), fica a dois passos; **to take the dog for a ~** levar o cachorro a passear, passear o cachorro; **"walk"** *(Am)* sinal luminoso *que indica aos pedestres que podem atravessar;* **"don't ~"** *(Am)* sinal luminoso *que indica aos pedestres que não podem atravessar.*

❏ **walk away** *vi* ir-se embora.

❏ **walk in** *vi* entrar.

❏ **walk out** *vi (leave angrily)* ir-se embora.

walker ['wɔːkəʳ] *n* caminhante *mf.*

walkie-talkie [ˌwɔːkɪ'tɔːkɪ] *n* walkie-talkie *m.*

walking ['wɔːkɪŋ] *n:* **to go ~** fazer caminhadas.

walking boots ['wɔːkɪŋ-] *npl* botas *fpl* de montanha.

walking stick ['wɔːkɪŋ-] *n* bengala *f.*

Walkman® ['wɔːkmən] *n* walkman® *m.*

wall [wɔːl] *n (of building, room)* parede *f; (in garden, countryside, street)* muro *m.*

wallchart ['wɔːltʃɑːt] *n* mapa *m.*

wallet ['wɒlɪt] *n* carteira *f (de documentos).*

wallpaper ['wɔːlˌpeɪpəʳ] *n* papel *m* de parede.

wally ['wɒlɪ] *n (Brit: inf)* palerma *mf.*

walnut ['wɔːlnʌt] *n (nut)* noz *f.*

walrus ['wɔːlrəs] (pl inv OR **-es**) n morsa f.

waltz [wɔːls] n valsa f.

wand [wɒnd] n varinha f de condão.

wander ['wɒndə'] vi vagar, perambular.

want [wɒnt] vt (desire) querer; (need) precisar de; **to ~ to do sthg** querer fazer algo; **to ~ sb to do sthg** querer que alguém faça algo.

wanted ['wɒntɪd] adj: **to be ~ (by the police)** ser procurado(-da) (pela polícia).

war [wɔː'] n guerra f.

ward [wɔːd] n (in hospital) enfermaria f.

warden ['wɔːdn] n (of park) guarda mf; (of youth hostel) encarregado m (-da f).

warder ['wɔːdə'] n guarda mf (prisional).

wardrobe ['wɔːdrəʊb] n guarda-roupa m, armário m.

warehouse ['weəhaʊs, pl -haʊzɪz] n armazém m.

warfare ['wɔːfeə'] n guerra f.

warhead ['wɔːhed] n ogiva f.

warm [wɔːm] adj quente; (friendly) caloroso(-osa) ♦ vt aquecer.
❑ **warm up** vt sep aquecer ♦ vi aquecer; (do exercises) fazer exercícios de aquecimento.

war memorial n monumento m aos mortos na guerra.

warm-hearted [-'hɑːtɪd] adj bondoso(-osa).

warmly ['wɔːmlɪ] adv (in a friendly way) calorosamente; **to dress ~** agasalhar-se.

warmth [wɔːmθ] n calor m.

warn [wɔːn] vt avisar; **to ~ sb about** sthg avisar alguém de algo; **to ~ sb not to do sthg** avisar alguém para não fazer algo.

warning ['wɔːnɪŋ] n aviso m.

warp [wɔːp] vt & vi (wood) empenar.

warrant ['wɒrənt] n (JUR) mandato m ♦ vt (fml: justify) justificar.

warranty ['wɒrəntɪ] n (fml) garantia f.

warrior ['wɒrɪə'] n guerreiro m (-ra f).

Warsaw ['wɔːsɔː] n Varsóvia s.

warship ['wɔːʃɪp] n navio m de guerra.

wart [wɔːt] n verruga f (Br), cravo m (Port).

wartime ['wɔːtaɪm] n tempo m de guerra.

wary ['weərɪ] adj receoso(-osa); **to be ~ of sthg/of doing sthg** recear algo/fazer algo.

was [wɒz] pt → **be**.

wash [wɒʃ] vt lavar ♦ vi lavar-se ♦ n: **to give sthg a ~** dar uma lavada em algo; **to have a ~** lavar-se; **to ~ one's hands** lavar as mãos.
❑ **wash up** vi (Brit: do washing-up) lavar a louça; (Am: clean o.s.) lavar-se.

washable ['wɒʃəbl] adj lavável.

washbasin ['wɒʃˌbeɪsn] n pia f, lavatório m (Port).

washbowl ['wɒʃbəʊl] n (Am) pia f, lavatório m (Port).

washer ['wɒʃə'] n (ring) bucha f, anilha f.

washing ['wɒʃɪŋ] n (activity) lavagem f; (clothes) roupa f suja.

washing line n corda f de estender a roupa, varal m (Br), estendal m (Port).

washing machine n máquina f de lavar roupa.

washing powder n sabão m em pó (Br), detergente m para a roupa (Port).

washing-up n (Brit): **to do the ~** lavar a louça.

washing-up bowl n (Brit) bacia f de lavar louça, lava-louças m inv (Port).

washing-up liquid n (Brit) detergente m para a louça.

washroom ['wɒʃrʊm] n (Am) banheiro m (Br), casa f de banho (Port).

wasn't [wɒznt] = **was not**.

wasp [wɒsp] n vespa f.

waste [weɪst] n (rubbish) lixo m ♦ vt (money, energy, opportunity) desperdiçar; (time) perder; **a ~ of money** um desperdício de dinheiro; **a ~ of time** um desperdício OR uma perda de tempo.

wastebin ['weɪstbɪn] n lata f de lixo (Br), caixote m do lixo (Port).

wasteful ['weɪstfʊl] adj (person) esbanjador(-ra); (activity) pouco econômico(-ca).

waste ground n terreno m abandonado, descampado m.

wastepaper basket [ˌweɪst'peɪpə'-] n cesta f de lixo (Br), cesto m dos papéis (Port).

watch [wɒtʃ] n (wristwatch) relógio m (de pulso) ♦ vt (observe) ver; (spy on) espiar, vigiar; (be careful with) ter cuidado com.
❑ **watch out** vi (be careful) ter cuidado;

weather

to ~ out for *(look for)* estar atento a.
watchdog ['wɒtʃdɒg] *n (dog)* cão *m* de
guarda; **a consumer ~** *uma organização
de defesa do consumidor.*
watchmaker ['wɒtʃ,meikə'] *n* relo-
joeiro *m* (-ra *f*).
watchman ['wɒtʃmən] *(pl* **-men**
[-mən]) *n* vigia *m*.
watchstrap ['wɒtʃstræp] *n* pulseira *f*
de relógio.
water ['wɔːtə'] *n* água *f* ♦ *vt (plants,
garden)* regar ♦ *vi (eyes)* lacrimejar; **to
make one's mouth ~** dar água na
boca.
water bottle *n* cantil *m*.
watercolour ['wɔːtə,kʌlə'] *n* aquarela *f*.
watercress ['wɔːtəkres] *n* agrião *m*.
waterfall ['wɔːtəfɔːl] *n* queda *f*
d'água, catarata *f*.
water heater *n* aquecedor *m* (de
água) *(Br)*, esquentador *m (Port)*.
watering can ['wɔːtərɪŋ-] *n* regador
m.
water level *n* nível *m* de água.
water lily *n* nenúfar *m*.
waterlogged ['wɔːtəlɒgd] *adj (land)*
alagado(-da), alagadiço(-ça).
water main *n* conduta *f* (principal)
da água.
watermark ['wɔːtəmɑːk] *n (in paper)*
marca *f* de água; *(showing water level)*
marca do nível de água.
watermelon ['wɔːtə,melən] *n* melancia *f*.
waterproof ['wɔːtəpruːf] *adj* à prova
de água.
water purification tablets
[-pjʊərɪfɪ'keiʃn-] *npl* comprimidos *mpl*
para purificar a água.
water skiing *n* esqui *m* aquático.
watersports ['wɔːtəspɔːts] *npl*
esportes *mpl* aquáticos.
water tank *n* tanque *m* de água.
watertight ['wɔːtətait] *adj* à prova
d'água.
watery ['wɔːtəri] *adj (food, drink)*
aguado(-da).
watt [wɒt] *n* watt *m*, vátio *m*; **a 60-~
bulb** uma lâmpada de 60 watts.
wave [weiv] *n* onda *f* ♦ *vt (hand)* acenar com; *(flag)* agitar ♦ *vi (move hand)*
acenar, dizer adeus.
wavelength ['weivleŋθ] *n* comprimento *m* de onda.
waver ['weivə'] *vi (person, resolve, con-*

fidence) vacilar; *(voice)* hesitar; *(flame,
light)* oscilar.
wavy ['weivi] *adj* ondulado(-da).
wax [wæks] *n* cera *f*.
waxworks ['wækswɔːks] *(pl inv)* *n*
museu *m* de cera.
way [wei] *n (manner, means)* maneira *f*,
forma *f*; *(route, distance travelled)*
caminho *m*; *(direction)* direção *f*; **which
~ is the station?** para que lado é a
estação?; **the town is out of our ~** a
cidade não fica no nosso caminho; **to
be in the ~** estar à frente; **to be on the**
OR **one's ~** *(coming)* estar a caminho;
to get out of the ~ sair da frente; **to
get under ~** começar; **it's a long ~ to
the station** a estação fica muito longe;
to be a long ~ away ficar muito longe;
to lose one's ~ perder-se, perder o
caminho; **on the ~ back** na volta; **on
the ~ there** no caminho; **that ~** *(like
that)* daquela maneira, assim; *(in that
direction)* por ali; **this ~** *(like this)* assim;
(in this direction) por aqui; **"give ~"** "dê
preferência"; **"~ in"** "entrada"; **"~
out"** "saída"; **no ~!** *(inf)* nem pensar!
waylay [,wei'lei] *(pt & pp* **-laid)** *vt*
abordar.
wayward ['weiwəd] *adj* rebelde.
WC *n (abbr of water closet)* WC *m*.
we [wiː] *pron* nós; **~'re young** (nós)
somos jovens.
weak [wiːk] *adj* fraco(-ca); *(not solid)*
frágil.
weaken ['wiːkn] *vt* enfraquecer.
weakling ['wiːklɪŋ] *n* fracote *m* (-ta *f*).
weakness ['wiːknɪs] *n (weak point)*
fraqueza *f*; *(fondness)* fraco *m*.
wealth [welθ] *n* riqueza *f*.
wealthy ['welθi] *adj* rico(-ca).
wean [wiːn] *vt (baby, kitten)* desmamar.
weapon ['wepən] *n* arma *f*.
weaponry ['wepənri] *n* armamento
m.
wear [weə'] *(pt* **wore**, *pp* **worn)** *vt
(clothes, shoes, jewellery)* usar ♦ *n
(clothes)* roupa *f*; **~ and tear** uso *m*.
❑ **wear off** *vi* desaparecer.
❑ **wear out** *vi* gastar-se.
weary ['wiəri] *adj* cansado(-da).
weasel ['wiːzl] *n* doninha *f*.
weather ['weðə'] *n* tempo *m*; **what's
the ~ like?** como está o tempo?; **to be
under the ~** *(inf)* estar um pouco
adoentado.

weathercock ['weðəkɒk] n cata-vento m.

weather forecast n previsão f do tempo.

weather forecaster [-,fɔːkɑːstəʳ] n meteorologista mf.

weather report n boletim m meteorológico.

weather vane [-veɪn] n cata-vento m.

weave [wiːv] (pt wove, pp woven) vt tecer.

weaver ['wiːvəʳ] n tecelão m (tecedeira f).

web [web] n (of spider) teia f.

Web site n (COMPUT) site m.

Wed. (abbr of Wednesday) 4ª, quar.

we'd [wiːd] = we had, we would.

wedding ['wedɪŋ] n casamento m.

wedding anniversary n aniversário m de casamento.

wedding cake n bolo m de noiva.

wedding dress n vestido m de noiva.

wedding ring n aliança f.

wedge [wedʒ] n (of cake) fatia f; (of wood etc) cunha f, calço m.

Wednesday ['wenzdɪ] n quarta-feira f, → Saturday.

wee [wiː] adj (Scot) pequeno(-na) ◆ n (inf) chichi m.

weed [wiːd] n erva f daninha.

weedkiller ['wiːd,kɪləʳ] n herbicida m.

weedy ['wiːdɪ] adj (Brit: inf: feeble) fracote(-ta).

week [wiːk] n semana f; a ~ today daqui a uma semana OR oito dias; in a ~'s time daqui a uma semana OR oito dias.

weekday ['wiːkdeɪ] n dia m útil.

weekend [,wiːk'end] n fim-de-semana m.

weekly ['wiːklɪ] adj semanal ◆ adv semanalmente ◆ n semanário m.

weep [wiːp] (pt & pp wept) vi chorar.

weigh [weɪ] vt pesar; how much does it ~? quanto é que (isso) pesa?

weight [weɪt] n peso m; to lose ~ emagrecer; to put on ~ engordar.

❏ **weights** npl (for weight training) pesos mpl.

weightlifting ['weɪt,lɪftɪŋ] n halterofilia f.

weight training n musculação f.

weighty ['weɪtɪ] adj de peso.

weir [wɪəʳ] n represa f.

weird [wɪəd] adj esquisito(-ta), estranho(-nha).

welcome ['welkəm] adj bem-vindo(-da) ◆ n boas-vindas fpl ◆ vt (greet) dar as boas-vindas a; (be grateful for) agradecer ◆ excl bem-vindo!; you're ~ to use our car você pode usar o nosso carro à vontade; to make sb feel ~ fazer alguém sentir-se bem-vindo; you're ~! de nada!

weld [weld] vt soldar.

welfare ['welfeəʳ] n (happiness, comfort) bem-estar m; (Am: money) subsídio m da segurança social.

welfare state n: the ~ o estado-previdência.

well [wel] (compar better, superl best) adj bom (boa) ◆ adv bem ◆ n poço m; to get ~ melhorar; to go ~ correr bem; ~ done! muito bem!; it may ~ happen pode muito bem acontecer; it's ~ worth it vale bem a pena; as ~ (in addition) também; as ~ as (in addition to) assim como.

we'll [wiːl] = we shall, we will.

well-advised adj: you would be ~ to ask her first seria prudente perguntar-lhe primeiro.

well-behaved [-bɪ'heɪvd] adj bem comportado(-da).

wellbeing [,wel'biːɪŋ] n bem-estar m.

well-built adj bem constituído(-da), robusto(-ta).

well-done adj (meat) bem passado(-da).

well-dressed [-'drest] adj bem vestido(-da).

wellington (boot) ['welɪŋtən-] n bota f de borracha, galocha f.

well-kept adj (garden) bem cuidado(-da); (secret) bem guardado(-da).

well-known adj conhecido(-da).

well-meaning adj bem-intencionado (-da).

well-nigh adv praticamente.

well-off adj (rich) rico(-ca).

well-paid adj bem pago(-ga), bem remunerado(-da).

well-read [-red] adj culto(-ta).

well-timed [-'taɪmd] adj oportuno (-na).

well-to-do adj rico(-ca), abastado (-da).

well-wisher [-,wɪʃəʳ] n simpatizante mf.

welly ['welɪ] n (Brit: inf) bota f de

borracha, galocha *f*.
Welsh [welʃ] *adj* galês(-esa) ◆ *n (language)* galês *m* ◆ *npl*: **the ~** os galeses.
Welshman ['welʃmən] (*pl* **-men** [-mən]) *n* galês *m*.
Welsh rarebit [-'reəbɪt] *n* torrada com queijo derretido.
Welshwoman ['welʃ,wumən] (*pl* **-women** [-,wɪmɪn]) *n* galesa *f*.
went [went] *pt* → **go**.
wept [wept] *pt & pp* → **weep**.
were [wɜːr] *pt* → **be**.
we're [wɪər] = **we are**.
weren't [wɜːnt] = **were not**.
west [west] *n* oeste *m* ◆ *adj* ocidental, oeste ◆ *adv (be situated)* a oeste; *(fly, walk)* em direção ao oeste, para o oeste; **in the ~ of England** no oeste da Inglaterra.
westbound ['westbaund] *adj* em direção ao oeste.
West Country *n*: **the ~** o sudoeste da Inglaterra, especialmente os condados de Somerset, Devon e a Cornualha.
West End *n*: **the ~** *(of London)* o West End, famosa área londrina onde se encontram as grandes lojas, cinemas e teatros.
westerly ['westəlɪ] *adj (wind)* de oeste; **in a ~ direction** em direção ao oeste; **the most ~ point** o ponto mais a oeste.
western ['westən] *adj* ocidental ◆ *n* western *m*, filme *m* de cow-boys.
West Indian *adj* antilhano(-na) ◆ *n (person)* antilhano *m* (-na *f*).
West Indies [-'ɪndiːz] *npl* Antilhas *fpl*.
Westminster ['westmɪnstər] *n* Westminster, bairro do centro de Londres.
Westminster Abbey *n* abadia *f* de Westminster.
westward ['westwəd] *adj*: **in a ~ direction** em direção ao oeste.
westwards ['westwədz] *adv* em direção ao oeste, para o oeste.
wet [wet] (*pt & pp* **wet** OR **-ted**) *adj (soaked, damp)* molhado(-da); *(rainy)* chuvoso(-osa) ◆ *vt* molhar; **to get ~** molhar-se; **"~ paint"** "tinta fresca".
wet suit *n* traje *m* de mergulho *(Br)*, fato *m* de mergulho *(Port)*.
we've [wiːv] = **we have**.
whack [wæk] *n (inf)* pancada *f* ◆ *vt (inf)* dar uma pancada em.
whale [weɪl] *n* baleia *f*.

wharf [wɔːf] (*pl* **-s** OR **wharves** [wɔːvz]) *n* cais *m* inv.
what [wɒt] *adj* **1.** *(in questions)* que; **~ colour is it?** de que cor é?; **he asked me ~ colour it was** ele perguntou-me de que cor era.
2. *(in exclamations)* que; **~ a surprise!** mas que surpresa!; **~ a beautiful day!** mas que dia lindo!
◆ *pron* **1.** *(in questions)* o que; **~ is going on?** o que é que está acontecendo?; **~ is that?** o que é isso?; **~ is that thing called?** como é que se chama aquilo?; **~ is the problem?** qual é o problema?; **she asked me ~ had happened** ela perguntou-me o que é que tinha acontecido; **she asked me ~ I had seen** ela perguntou-me o que é que eu tinha visto.
2. *(in questions: after prep)* que; **~ are they talking about?** de que é que eles estão falando?; **~ is it for?** para que é isso?; **she asked me ~ I was thinking about** ela perguntou-me em que é que eu estava pensando.
3. *(introducing relative clause)* o que; **I didn't see ~ happened** não vi o que aconteceu; **you can't have ~ you want** você não pode ter o que quer.
4. *(in phrases)*: **~ for?** para quê?; **~ about going out for a meal?** que tal irmos comer fora?
◆ *excl* o quê!
whatever [wɒt'evər] *pron*: **take ~ you want** leve o que quiser; **~ I do, I'll lose** faça o que fizer, perco sempre; **~ that may be** seja lá o que for.
whatsoever [,wɒtsəu'evər] *adj*: **nothing ~** nada; **none ~** nenhum(-ma); **to have no interest ~ in sthg** não ter interesse nenhum em algo.
wheat [wiːt] *n* trigo *m*.
wheel [wiːl] *n (of car, bicycle etc)* roda *f*; *(steering wheel)* volante *m*.
wheelbarrow ['wiːl,bærəu] *n* carrinho *m* de mão.
wheelchair ['wiːl,tʃeər] *n* cadeira *f* de rodas.
wheelclamp ['wiːl,klæmp] *n* garra *f*, imobilizador *m*.
wheezy ['wiːzɪ] *adj*: **to be ~** respirar com dificuldade.
whelk [welk] *n* búzio *m*.
when [wen] *adv & conj* quando.
whenever [wen'evər] *conj* sempre que; **~ you like** quando você quiser.

where [weəʳ] *adv & conj* onde; **that's ~ you're wrong** aí é que você se engana.

whereabouts [ˈweərəbauts] *adv* onde ◆ *npl* paradeiro *m*.

whereas [weərˈæz] *conj* enquanto que.

whereby [weəˈbaɪ] *conj (fml)* pelo (pela) qual.

wherever [weərˈevəʳ] *conj* onde quer que; **~ that may be** onde quer que isso seja; **~ you like** onde você quiser.

whet [wet] *vt*: **to ~ sb's appetite (for sthg)** abrir o apetite de alguém (para algo).

whether [ˈweðəʳ] *conj (indicating choice, doubt)* se; **~ you like it or not** queira ou não queira.

which [wɪtʃ] *adj (in questions)* qual, que; **~ room do you want?** qual é o quarto que você quer?, que quarto você quer?; **~ one?** qual (deles)?; **she asked me ~ room I wanted** ela perguntou-me qual OR que quarto eu queria.

◆ *pron* 1. *(in questions)* qual; **~ is the cheapest?** qual é o mais barato?; **~ do you prefer?** qual (é o que) você prefere?; **he asked me ~ was the best** ele perguntou-me qual era o melhor; **he asked me ~ I preferred** ele perguntou-me qual é que eu preferia; **he asked me ~ I was talking about** ele perguntou-me de qual (é que) eu estava falando.

2. *(introducing relative clause: subject)*: **take the one ~ is nearer to you** leva o que está mais perto de você; **I can't remember ~ was better** não me lembro de qual era o melhor; **the house ~ is on the corner** a casa da esquina.

3. *(introducing relative clause: object, after prep)* que; **the television ~ I bought** a televisão que eu comprei; **the settee on ~ I'm sitting** o sofá em que estou sentado.

4. *(referring back)* o que; **he's late, ~ annoys me** ele está atrasado, o que me aborrece; **he's always late, ~ I don't like** ele está sempre atrasado, o que eu odeio.

whichever [wɪtʃˈevəʳ] *pron* o que (a que) ◆ *adj*: **~ place you like** o lugar que você preferir; **~ way you do it** faça como fizer.

whiff [wɪf] *n (smell)* cheirinho *m*.

while [waɪl] *conj (during the time that)* enquanto; *(although)* se bem que; *(whereas)* enquanto que ◆ *n*: **a ~** um pouco; **a ~ ago** há algum tempo; **it's been quite a ~ since I last saw him** há muito que não o vejo; **for a ~** durante algum tempo; **in a ~** daqui a pouco.

whilst [waɪlst] *conj* = while.

whim [wɪm] *n* capricho *m*.

whimper [ˈwɪmpəʳ] *vi (dog)* gamir; *(child)* choramingar.

whine [waɪn] *vi (make noise)* gemer; *(complain)* queixar-se; *(dog)* ganir.

whinge [wɪndʒ] *vi (Brit)*: **to ~ (about)** queixar-se (de).

whip [wɪp] *n* chicote *m* ◆ *vt* chicotear.

whipped cream [wɪpt-] *n* creme *m* batido *(Br)*, natas *fpl* batidas *(Port)*, chantilly *m*.

whip-round *n (Brit: inf)*: **to have a ~** fazer uma coleta.

whirlpool [ˈwɜːlpuːl] *n (Jacuzzi)* Jacuzzi® *m*.

whirlwind [ˈwɜːlwɪnd] *n* remoinho *m* (de vento), furacão *m*.

whirr [wɜːʳ] *vi* zumbir.

whisk [wɪsk] *n (utensil)* vara *f* de arames, batedor *m* de ovos manual ◆ *vt (eggs, cream)* bater.

whiskers [ˈwɪskəz] *npl (of person)* suiças *fpl*, patilhas *fpl* (Port); *(of animal)* bigodes *mpl*.

whiskey [ˈwɪskɪ] *(pl -s)* *n* uísque *m (irlandês ou americano)*.

whisky [ˈwɪskɪ] *n* uísque *m (escocês)*.

whisper [ˈwɪspəʳ] *vt & vi* murmurar.

whistle [ˈwɪsl] *n (instrument)* apito *m*; *(sound)* assobio *m* ◆ *vi* assobiar.

white [waɪt] *adj* branco(-ca); *(coffee, tea)* com leite ◆ *n (colour)* branco *m*; *(of egg)* clara *f*; *(person)* branco *m* (-ca *f*).

white bread *n* pão *m* (branco).

white-hot *adj* incandescente.

White House *n*: **the ~** a Casa Branca.

white lie *n* mentirinha *f*.

whiteness [ˈwaɪtnɪs] *n* brancura *f*.

white sauce *n* molho *m* branco.

white spirit *n* aguarrás *f*, essência *f* de petróleo.

whitewash [ˈwaɪtwɒʃ] *vt* caiar.

white wine *n* vinho *m* branco.

whiting [ˈwaɪtɪŋ] *(pl inv)* *n* faneca *f*.

Whitsun [ˈwɪtsn] *n* Pentecostes *m*.

whizz [wɪz] *n (inf)*: **to be a ~ at sthg**

ser um gênio em algo ♦ *vi* passar a grande velocidade.

whizz kid *n* (*inf*) menino-prodígio *m* (menina-prodígio *f*).

who [hu:] *pron* (*in questions*) quem; (*in relative clauses*) que.

who'd [hu:d] = **who had, who would**.

whoever ['hu:'evər] *pron* quem; **~ it is** quem quer que seja, seja quem for.

whole [həʊl] *adj* inteiro(-ra) ♦ *n*: **the ~ of the journey** a viagem inteira, toda a viagem; **on the ~** em geral.

wholefoods ['həʊlfu:dz] *npl* produtos *mpl* dietéticos.

whole-hearted *adj* total.

wholemeal bread ['həʊlmi:l-] *n* (*Brit*) pão *m* integral.

wholesale ['həʊlseɪl] *adv* (*COMM*) por atacado.

wholesome ['həʊlsəm] *adj* saudável.

wholewheat bread ['həʊl,wi:t-] (*Am*) = **wholemeal bread**.

who'll [hu:l] = **who will**.

wholly ['həʊlɪ] *adv* totalmente.

whom [hu:m] *pron* (*fml: in questions*) quem; (*in relative clauses: after prep*) que; **to ~** a quem.

whooping cough ['hu:pɪŋ-] *n* coqueluche *f* (*Br*), tosse *f* convulsa (*Port*).

whopping ['wɒpɪŋ] *adj* (*inf*) tremendo(-da).

whore [hɔ:ʳ] *n* puta *f*.

who're ['hu:əʳ] = **who are**.

whose [hu:z] *adj* (*in questions*) de quem; (*in relative clauses*) cujo(-ja) ♦ *pron* de quem; **~ book is this?** de quem é este livro?

why [waɪ] *adv* & *conj* porque; **~ not?** porque não?; **tell me ~** (diz-me) porquê; **I know ~** James isn't here eu sei porque é que o James não está.

wick [wɪk] *n* (*of candle, lighter*) mecha *f*, pavio *m*.

wicked ['wɪkɪd] *adj* (*evil*) mau (má); (*mischievous*) travesso(-a).

wicker ['wɪkəʳ] *adj* de vime.

wickerwork ['wɪkəwɜ:k] *n* trabalho *m* em verga OR vime.

wide [waɪd] *adj* largo(-ga); (*range, variety, gap*) grande ♦ *adv*: **to open sthg ~** abrir bem algo; **how ~ is the road?** qual é a largura da estrada?; **it's 12 metres ~** tem 12 metros de largura; **~ open** escancarado, aberto de par em par.

wide-angle lens *n* (objectiva) grande angular *f*.

wide-awake *adj* completamente acordado(-da).

widely ['waɪdlɪ] *adv* muito.

widen ['waɪdn] *vt* (*make broader*) alargar ♦ *vi* (*gap, difference*) aumentar.

wide-ranging [-'reɪndʒɪŋ] *adj* vasto (-ta).

widespread ['waɪdspred] *adj* generalizado(-da).

widow ['wɪdəʊ] *n* viúva *f*.

widower ['wɪdəʊəʳ] *n* viúvo *m*.

width [wɪdθ] *n* largura *f*.

wield [wi:ld] *vt* (*weapon*) brandir; (*power*) exercer.

wife [waɪf] (*pl* **wives**) *n* esposa *f*, mulher *f*.

wig [wɪg] *n* peruca *f*.

wiggle ['wɪgl] *vt* (*inf*) mexer; (*tooth*) balançar.

wild [waɪld] *adj* (*animal, land, area*) selvagem; (*plant*) silvestre; (*uncontrolled*) descontrolado(-da); (*crazy*) louco(-ca); **to be ~ about** (*inf*) ser louco por.

wilderness ['wɪldənɪs] *n* (*barren land*) deserto *m*; (*overgrown land*) selva *f*.

wild flower *n* flor *f* silvestre.

wildlife ['waɪldlaɪf] *n* a fauna e a flora.

wildly ['waɪldlɪ] *adv* (*applaud, shout*) como um louco (uma louca); (*guess, suggest*) ao acaso; (*shoot*) indiscriminadamente, em todos os sentidos; (*funny, different*) extremamente.

will[1] [wɪl] *aux vb* **1.** (*expressing future tense*): **it ~ be difficult to repair** vai ser difícil de arranjar; **~ you be here next Friday?** você vai estar aqui na próxima sexta?; **I ~ see you next week** vejo-lhe para a semana; **yes I ~** sim; **no I won't** não.

2. (*expressing willingness*): **I won't do it** recuso-me a fazê-lo.

3. (*expressing polite question*): **~ you have some more tea?** você quer mais um chá?

4. (*in commands, requests*): **~ you please be quiet!** pode ficar calado, por favor!; **close that window, ~ you?** feche a janela, faz favor.

will[2] [wɪl] *n* (*document*) testamento *m*; **against my ~** contra a minha vontade.

willing ['wɪlɪŋ] *adj*: **to be ~ to do sthg** estar disposto(-osta) a fazer algo.

willingly ['wılıŋlı] *adv* de boa vontade.

willow ['wıləu] *n* salgueiro *m*.

willpower ['wıl,pauə^r] *n* força *f* de vontade.

wilt [wılt] *vi (plant)* murchar.

wily ['waılı] *adj* astuto(-ta), matreiro (-ra).

wimp [wımp] *n (inf)* banana *f (Br)*, medricas *mf inv (Port)*.

win [wın] *(pt & pp* **won**) *n* vitória *f* ◆ *vt* ganhar; *(support, approval)* obter ◆ *vi* ganhar.

wince [wıns] *vi (pull face)* fazer uma careta; **to ~ at sthg** *(memory, thought)* estremecer com algo; **to ~ with sthg** *(pain, embarrassment)* encolher-se com algo.

winch [wıntʃ] *n* guincho *m*.

wind[1] [wınd] *n (air current)* vento *m*; *(in stomach)* gases *mpl*.

wind[2] [waınd] *(pt & pp* **wound**) *vi (road, river)* serpentear ◆ *vt*: **to ~ sthg round sthg** enrolar algo à volta de algo.

❏ **wind up** *vt sep (Brit: inf: annoy)* gozar; *(car window)* subir; *(clock, watch)* dar corda em.

windbreak ['wındbreık] *n* guarda-vento *m*.

windfall ['wındfɔːl] *n (unexpected gift)* presente *m* caído do céu.

winding ['waındıŋ] *adj* sinuoso(-osa).

wind instrument [wınd-] *n* instrumento *m* de sopro.

windmill ['wındmıl] *n* moinho *m* de vento.

window ['wındəu] *n* janela *f*; *(of shop)* vitrine *f*.

window box *n* floreira *f* de janela.

window cleaner *n* limpador *m* (-ra *f*) de janelas.

window ledge *n* peitoril *m* da janela.

windowpane ['wındəu,peın] *n* vidro *m*, vidraça *f*.

window seat *n (on plane)* lugar *m* ao lado da janela.

window-shopping *n*: **to go ~** ir ver vitrines.

windowsill ['wındəusıl] *n* peitoril *m* da janela.

windpipe ['wındpaıp] *n* traquéia *f*.

windscreen ['wındskriːn] *n (Brit)* pára-brisas *m inv*.

windscreen wipers *npl (Brit)* lava-

dor *m* de pára-brisas *(Br)*, limpa-pára-brisas *m inv (Port)*.

windshield ['wındʃiːld] *n (Am)* pára-brisas *m inv*.

Windsor Castle ['wınzə-] *n* o Castelo de Windsor.

windsurfing ['wınd,sɜːfıŋ] *n* windsurfe *m*; **to go ~** fazer windsurfe.

windy ['wındı] *adj* ventoso(-osa), com muito vento; **it's ~** está ventando muito.

wine [waın] *n* vinho *m*.

wine bar *n (Brit) bar de certa categoria especializado em vinhos, que serve também refeições ligeiras.*

wine cellar *n* adega *f*.

wineglass ['waınglɑːs] *n* copo *m* de vinho.

wine list *n* lista *f* dos vinhos.

wine tasting [-,teıstıŋ] *n* prova *f* de vinhos.

wine waiter *n* garçon *m* que serve o vinho.

wing [wıŋ] *n* asa *f*; *(Brit: of car)* pára-lamas *m inv*, guarda-lamas *m inv (Port)*; *(of building)* ala *f*.

❏ **wings** *npl*: **the ~s** *(in theatre)* os bastidores.

winger ['wıŋə^r] *n (SPORT)* ponta *m*, extremo *m*.

wink [wıŋk] *vi* piscar o olho.

winner ['wınə^r] *n* vencedor *m* (-ra *f*).

winning ['wınıŋ] *adj (person, team)* vencedor(-ra); *(ticket, number)* premiado(-da).

winter ['wıntə^r] *n* inverno *m*; **in (the) ~** no inverno.

winter sports *npl* esportes *mpl* de inverno.

wintertime ['wıntətaım] *n* inverno *m*.

wint(e)ry ['wıntrı] *adj* de inverno, invernal.

wipe [waıp] *vt* limpar; **to ~ one's hands/feet** limpar as mãos/os pés.

❏ **wipe up** *vt sep & vi* limpar.

wiper ['waıpə^r] *n (windscreen wiper)* lavador *m* de pára-brisas *(Br)*, limpa-pára-brisas *m inv (Port)*.

wire ['waıə^r] *n* arame *m*; *(electrical wire)* fio *m* (elétrico) ◆ *vt (plug)* montar.

wireless ['waıəlıs] *n* rádio *m*.

wiring ['waıərıŋ] *n* instalação *f* elétrica.

wisdom ['wızdəm] *n (of person)* sabedoria *f*.

wisdom tooth n dente m do siso.

wise [waɪz] adj (person) sábio(-bia); (decision, idea) sensato(-ta).

wisecrack ['waɪzkræk] n piada f.

wish [wɪʃ] n (desire) desejo m ◆ vt: I ~ I was younger quem me dera ser mais novo; I ~ you'd told me earlier que pena você não me disse isso antes; to ~ for sthg desejar algo; to ~ to do sthg (fml) desejar fazer algo; to ~ sb happy birthday dar os parabéns a alguém; to ~ sb luck desejar boa sorte a alguém; if you ~ (fml) se assim o desejar; best ~es cumprimentos.

wit [wɪt] n (humour) espírito m; (intelligence): to have the ~ to do sthg ter a inteligência suficiente para fazer algo. ❑ **wits** npl (intelligence, mind): to have OR keep one's ~s about one estar alerta OR atento(-ta).

witch [wɪtʃ] n bruxa f.

with [wɪð] prep 1. (in company of) com; ~ come ~ me/us vem comigo/conosco; can I go ~ you? posso ir com você?; we stayed ~ friends ficamos em casa de amigos. 2. (in descriptions) com; a man ~ a beard um homem de barba; a room ~ a bathroom um quarto com banheiro. 3. (indicating means, manner) com; I washed it ~ detergent lavei-o com detergente; they won ~ ease ganharam com facilidade. 4. (indicating emotion) de; to tremble ~ fear tremer de medo. 5. (regarding) com; be careful ~ that! tenha cuidado com isso! 6. (indicating opposition) com; to argue ~ sb discutir com alguém. 7. (indicating covering, contents): to fill sthg ~ sthg encher algo com OR de algo; packed ~ people cheio de gente; topped ~ cream coberto com creme.

withdraw [wɪð'drɔ:] (pt -drew, pp -drawn) vt (take out) retirar; (money) levantar ◆ vi (from race, contest) desistir.

withdrawal [wɪð'drɔ:əl] n (from bank account) levantamento m.

withdrawal symptoms npl síndrome f da abstinência.

withdrawn [wɪð'drɔ:n] pp → withdraw.

withdrew [wɪð'dru:] pt → withdraw.

wither ['wɪðəʳ] vi murchar.

withhold [wɪð'həʊld] (pt & pp -held)

vt (salary) reter; (information) ocultar.

within [wɪð'ɪn] prep (inside) dentro de; (certain distance) a; (certain time) em ◆ adv dentro; ~ 10 miles of ... a 10 milhas de ...; it arrived ~ a week chegou em menos de uma semana; ~ the next week durante a próxima semana.

without [wɪð'aʊt] prep sem; ~ doing sthg sem fazer algo.

withstand [wɪð'stænd] (pt & pp -stood) vt resistir a, agüentar.

witness ['wɪtnɪs] n testemunha f ◆ vt (see) testemunhar.

witticism ['wɪtɪsɪzm] n dito m espirituoso.

witty ['wɪtɪ] adj espirituoso(-osa).

wives [waɪvz] pl → wife.

wizard ['wɪzəd] n feiticeiro m, mago m.

wobble ['wɒbl] vi (chair, table) balançar; (legs, hands) tremer.

wobbly ['wɒblɪ] adj (table, chair) pouco firme.

woe [wəʊ] n mágoa f.

wok [wɒk] n wok f, frigideira chinesa grande e com fundo redondo, usada especialmente para cozinhar em fogo alto.

woke [wəʊk] pt → wake.

woken ['wəʊkn] pp → wake.

wolf [wʊlf] (pl wolves ['wʊlvz]) n lobo m.

woman ['wʊmən] (pl women) n mulher f.

womanly ['wʊmənlɪ] adj feminino (-na).

womb [wu:m] n útero m.

women ['wɪmɪn] pl → woman.

won [wʌn] pt & pp → win.

wonder ['wʌndəʳ] vi (ask o.s.) perguntar a si mesmo(-ma) ◆ n (amazement) maravilha f; to ~ if perguntar a si mesmo se; I ~ if I could ask you a favour? podia fazer-me um favor?; I ~ if they'll come será que eles vêm?

wonderful ['wʌndəfʊl] adj maravilhoso(-osa).

wonderfully ['wʌndəfʊlɪ] adv (very well) maravilhosamente; (for emphasis) extremamente.

won't [wəʊnt] = will not.

woo [wu:] vt cortejar.

wood [wʊd] n (substance) madeira f; (small forest) bosque m; (golf club) taco m de madeira.

wooden ['wʊdn] adj de madeira.

woodland ['wʊdlənd] n floresta f.

woodpecker ['wʊd,pekəʳ] *n* pica-pau *m*.

woodwind ['wʊdwɪnd] *n*: **the ~** os instrumentos de sopro de madeira.

woodwork ['wʊdwɜːk] *n (SCH)* carpintaria *f*.

woodworm ['wʊdwɜːm] *n* carcoma *m*, caruncho *m*.

wool [wʊl] *n* lã *f*.

woolen ['wʊlən] *(Am)* = **woollen**.

woollen ['wʊlən] *adj (Brit)* de lã.

woolly ['wʊlɪ] *adj (Brit)* de lã.

wooly ['wʊlɪ] *(Am)* = **woolly**.

Worcester sauce ['wʊstəʳ-] *n* molho *m* inglês.

word [wɜːd] *n* palavra *f*; **in other ~s** em outras palavras; **to have a ~ with sb** falar com alguém.

wording ['wɜːdɪŋ] *n* texto *m*.

word processing [-'prəʊsesɪŋ] *n* processamento *m* de texto.

word processor [-'prəʊsesəʳ] *n* processador *m* de texto.

wore [wɔːʳ] *pt* → **wear**.

work [wɜːk] *n* trabalho *m*; *(painting, novel etc)* obra *f* ♦ *vi* trabalhar; *(operate, have desired effect)* funcionar; *(take effect)* ter efeito ♦ *vt (machine, controls)* operar; **out of ~** desempregado, sem trabalho; **to be at ~** estar trabalhando; **to be off ~** *(on holiday)* estar de folga; **the ~s** *(inf: everything)* tudo; **how does it ~?** como é que funciona?; **it's not ~ing** não está funcionando.

❑ **work out** *vt sep (price, total)* calcular; *(solution, reason, plan)* descobrir; *(understand)* perceber ♦ *vi (result, be successful)* resultar; *(do exercise)* fazer exercício; **it ~s out at £20 each** *(bill, total)* sai a 20 libras cada.

workable ['wɜːkəbl] *adj (plan, idea)* viável; *(system)* passível de funcionar.

workaholic [,wɜːkə'hɒlɪk] *n* viciado *m* (-da *f*) no trabalho.

workday ['wɜːkdeɪ] *n (not weekend)* dia *m* de semana, dia útil.

worked up [,wɜːkt-] *adj* exaltado (-da).

worker ['wɜːkəʳ] *n* trabalhador *m* (-ra *f*).

workforce ['wɜːkfɔːs] *n* mão-de-obra *f*.

working ['wɜːkɪŋ] *adj (in operation)* em funcionamento; *(having employment)* que trabalha; *(day, conditions)* de trabalho.

❑ **workings** *npl (of system, machine)* mecanismo *m*.

working class *n*: **the ~** a classe trabalhadora.

working hours *npl* horário *m* de trabalho.

working order *n*: **to be in good ~** estar funcionando bem.

workload ['wɜːkləʊd] *n* carga *f* OR quantidade *f* de trabalho.

workman ['wɜːkmən] *(pl* **-men** [-mən]) *n* trabalhador *m* (manual), operário *m*.

workmanship ['wɜːkmənʃɪp] *n (of person)* arte *f*; *(of object)* trabalho *m*.

workmate ['wɜːkmeɪt] *n* colega *mf* de trabalho.

work of art *n* obra *f* de arte.

workout ['wɜːkaʊt] *n* sessão *f* de exercícios.

work permit *n* autorização *f* de trabalho.

workplace ['wɜːkpleɪs] *n* local *m* de trabalho.

workshop ['wɜːkʃɒp] *n (for repairs)* oficina *f*.

work surface *n* bancada *f*.

worktop ['wɜːktɒp] *n (Brit)* bancada *f*, aparador *m*.

world [wɜːld] *n* mundo *m* ♦ *adj* mundial; **the best in the ~** o melhor do mundo.

world-class *adj* de primeira categoria.

world-famous *adj* mundialmente famoso(-osa).

worldwide [,wɜːld'waɪd] *adv* no mundo inteiro.

worm [wɜːm] *n* minhoca *f*.

worn [wɔːn] *pp* → **wear** ♦ *adj (clothes, carpet)* gasto(-ta).

worn-out *adj (clothes, shoes etc)* gasto(-ta); *(tired)* exausto(-ta).

worried ['wʌrɪd] *adj* preocupado (-da).

worry ['wʌrɪ] *n* preocupação *f* ♦ *vt* preocupar ♦ *vi*: **to ~ (about)** preocupar-se (com).

worrying ['wʌrɪɪŋ] *adj* preocupante.

worse [wɜːs] *adj & adv* pior; **to get ~** piorar; **~ off** em pior situação.

worsen ['wɜːsn] *vi* piorar.

worship ['wɜːʃɪp] *n (church service)* culto *m* ♦ *vt* adorar.

worst [wɜːst] *adj & adv* pior ♦ *n*: **the ~** o pior (a pior).

writhe

worth [wɜ:θ] *prep*: **how much is it ~?** quanto é que vale?; **it's ~ £50** vale 50 libras; **it's ~ seeing** vale a pena ver; **it's not ~ it** não vale a pena; **fifty pounds' ~ of traveller's cheques** cheques de viagem no valor de 50 libras.

worthless [wɜ:θlis] *adj (jewellery, possessions)* sem valor; *(person, undertaking)* inútil.

worthwhile [,wɜ:θ'waɪl] *adj* que vale a pena.

worthy [wɜ:ðɪ] *adj* merecedor(-ra); **to be ~ of sthg** merecer algo.

would [wʊd] *aux vb* 1. *(in reported speech)*: **she said she ~ come** ela disse que vinha.
2. *(indicating condition)*: **what ~ you do?** o que é que você faria?; **what ~ you have done?** o que é que você teria feito?; **I ~ be most grateful** ficaria muito agradecido.
3. *(indicating willingness)*: **she ~n't go** ela não queria ir embora; **he ~ do anything for her** ele faria qualquer coisa por ela.
4. *(in polite questions)*: **~ you like a drink?** você quer beber alguma coisa?; **~ you mind closing the window?** importa-se de fechar a janela?
5. *(indicating inevitability)*: **he ~ say that** não me surpreende que ele tenha dito isso.
6. *(giving advice)*: **I ~ report him if I were you** eu, no seu lugar, denunciava-o.
7. *(expressing opinions)*: **I ~ prefer** eu preferia; **I ~ have thought (that)** ... eu pensava que ....

wouldn't [wʊdnt] = **would not**.

would've [wʊdəv] = **would have**.

wound[1] [wu:nd] *n* ferida *f* ◆ *vt* ferir.

wound[2] [waʊnd] *pt & pp* → **wind**[2].

wove [wəʊv] *pt* → **weave**.

woven [wəʊvn] *pp* → **weave**.

wrangle [ræŋgl] *n* disputa *f* ◆ *vi* discutir; **to ~ with sb (over sthg)** discutir com alguém (sobre algo).

wrap [ræp] *vt (package)* embrulhar; **to ~ sthg round sthg** enrolar algo em volta de algo.

❏ **wrap up** *vt sep (package)* embrulhar ◆ *vi (dress warmly)* agasalhar-se.

wrapper [ræpər] *n (for sweet)* papel *m*.

wrapping [ræpɪŋ] *n* invólucro *m*, embrulho *m*.

wrapping paper *n* papel *m* de embrulho.

wrath [rɒθ] *n* ira *f*.

wreak [ri:k] *vt*: **to ~ havoc** causar estragos.

wreath [ri:θ] *n* coroa *f* de flores, grinalda *f*.

wreck [rek] *n (of plane, car)* destroços *mpl*; *(of ship)* restos *mpl* ◆ *vt (destroy)* destruir; *(spoil)* estragar; **to be ~ed** *(ship)* naufragar.

wreckage [rekɪdʒ] *n (of plane, car)* destroços *mpl*; *(of building)* escombros *mpl*.

wren [ren] *n* carriça *f*.

wrench [rentʃ] *n (tool)* chave *f* inglesa.

wrestle [resl] *vi* lutar; **to ~ with sb** lutar com alguém.

wrestler [reslər] *n* lutador *m* (-ra *f*) de luta livre.

wrestling [reslɪŋ] *n* luta *f* livre.

wretch [retʃ] *n* desgraçado *m* (-da *f*).

wretched [retʃɪd] *adj (miserable)* desgraçado(-da); *(very bad)* péssimo (-ma).

wriggle [rɪgl] *vi* mexer-se, contorcer-se; **I ~d free** consegui escapar contorcendo-me.

wring [rɪŋ] *(pt & pp wrung)* *vt* torcer.

wringing [rɪŋɪŋ] *adj*: **to be ~ wet** estar encharcado(-da) OR ensopado (-da).

wrinkle [rɪŋkl] *n* ruga *f*.

wrist [rɪst] *n* pulso *m*.

wristwatch [rɪstwɒtʃ] *n* relógio *m* de pulso.

writ [rɪt] *n* mandato *m* judicial.

write [raɪt] *(pt wrote, pp written)* *vt* escrever; *(cheque, prescription)* passar; *(Am: send letter to)* escrever a ◆ *vi* escrever; **to ~ (to sb)** *(Brit)* escrever (para alguém).

❏ **write back** *vi* responder.

❏ **write down** *vt sep* anotar.

❏ **write off** *vt sep (Brit: inf: car)* destruir ◆ *vi*: **to ~ off for sthg** escrever pedindo algo.

❏ **write out** *vt sep (essay)* escrever; *(list)* fazer; *(cheque, receipt)* passar.

write-off *n*: **the car was a ~** o carro ficou completamente destruído.

writer [raɪtər] *n (author)* escritor *m* (-ra *f*).

writhe [raɪð] *vi* contorcer-se, torcer-se.

writing [ˈraɪtɪŋ] *n (handwriting)* letra *f;* *(written words)* texto *m; (activity)* escrita *f;* in ~ por escrito.
writing desk *n* escrivaninha *f.*
writing pad *n* bloco *m* de notas.
writing paper *n* papel *m* de carta.
written [ˈrɪtn] *pp* → **write** ♦ *adj* escrito(-ta).
wrong [rɒŋ] *adj* errado(-da) ♦ *adv* mal; **what's** ~? o que é que está acontecendo?; **something's** ~ **with the car** o carro está com algum problema; **to be in the** ~ estar errado; **to get sthg** ~ enganar-se em algo; **to go** ~ *(machine)* avariar; "~ **way**" *(Am)* sinal de sentido proibido.
wrongful [ˈrɒŋful] *adj* injusto(-ta), injustificado(-da).
wrongly [ˈrɒŋlɪ] *adv* mal.
wrong number *n* número *m* errado; **sorry, you've got the** ~ desculpe, é engano.
wrote [rəʊt] *pt* → **write.**
wrought iron [rɔːt] *n* ferro *m* forjado.
wrung [rʌŋ] *pt & pp* → **wring.**
wry [raɪ] *adj (amused)* irônico(-ca); *(displeased)* descontente.

xenophobia [ˌzenəˈfəʊbjə] *n* xenofobia *f*.
xing (*Am: abbr of crossing*): **"ped ~"** "travessia para pedestres" *(Br)*, "passagem de peões" *(Port)*.
XL (*abbr of extra-large*) XL.

Xmas [ˈeksməs] *n (inf)* Natal *m*.
X-ray *n (picture)* raio-X *m* ◆ *vt* fazer uma radiografia a; **to have an ~** fazer uma radiografia.
xylophone [ˈzaɪləfəʊn] *n* xilofone *m*.

yacht [jɒt] *n* iate *m*.
yachting [ˈjɒtɪŋ] *n* navegação *f* com iate; **to go ~** ir andar de iate.
yachtsman [ˈjɒtsmən] (*pl* -men [-mən]) *n* dono ou piloto de um iate.
Yank [jæŋk] *n (Brit: inf)* ianque *mf*.
Yankee [ˈjæŋkɪ] *n (Brit: inf)* ianque *mf*.
yap [jæp] *vi (dog)* ladrar, latir.
yard [jɑːd] *n (unit of measurement)* = 91,44 cm, jarda *f*; *(enclosed area)* pátio *m*; *(Am: behind house)* jardim *m*.
yard sale *n (Am)* venda de objectos usados organizada pelo dono no jardim da casa.
yardstick [ˈjɑːdstɪk] *n* critério *m*.
yarn [jɑːn] *n (thread)* linha *f*.
yawn [jɔːn] *vi* bocejar.
yd *abbr* = **yard**.
yeah [jeə] *adv (inf)* sim.
year [jɪər] *n* ano *m*; **next ~** o ano que vem; **this ~** este ano; **I'm 15 ~s old**

tenho 15 anos; **I haven't seen her for ~s** *(inf)* há anos que não a vejo.
yearly [ˈjɪəlɪ] *adj* anualmente.
yearn [jɜːn] *vi*: **to ~ for sthg/to do sthg** ansiar por algo/por fazer algo.
yeast [jiːst] *n* fermento *m*.
yell [jel] *vi* gritar.
yellow [ˈjeləʊ] *adj* amarelo(-la) ◆ *n* amarelo *m*.
yellow lines *npl* linhas *fpl* amarelas.
Yellow Pages® *n*: **the ~** as Páginas Amarelas.
yelp [jelp] *n (dog)* latir; *(person)* gritar.
yeoman of the guard [ˈjəʊmən-] (*pl* **yeomen of the guard** [ˈjəʊmən-]) *n* alabardeiro *m* da guarda real (britânica).
yes [jes] *adv* sim; **to say ~** dizer que sim.
yesterday [ˈjestədɪ] *n* ontem *m* ◆ *adv* ontem; **the day before ~** anteontem; **~ afternoon** ontem à tarde; **~ mor-**

ning ontem de manhã.

yet [jɛt] *adv* ainda ♦ *conj* contudo; **have they arrived ~?** já chegaram?; **the best one ~** o melhor até agora; **not ~** ainda não; **I've ~ to do it** ainda não o fiz; **~ again** mais uma vez; **~ another delay** mais um atraso.

yew [juː] *n* teixo *m*.

yield [jiːld] *vt (profit)* render; *(interest)* ganhar ♦ *vi (break, give way)* ceder; **"yield"** *(Am:* AUT) sinal de perda de prioridade.

YMCA *n* = ACM, associação internacional de jovens cristãos que oferece alojamento a um preço acessível.

yob [jɒb] *n (Brit: inf)* arruaceiro *m*.

yoga ['jəʊɡə] *n* ioga *m ou f*.

yoghurt ['jɒɡət] *n* iogurte *m*.

yolk [jəʊk] *n* gema *f*.

York Minster [jɔːkˈmɪnstəʳ] *n* a catedral de York.

Yorkshire pudding ['jɔːkʃə-] *n* pudim *m* de York, espécie de pudim feito com uma massa semelhante à dos crepes cozido no forno e servido tradicionalmente com rosbife.

you [juː] *pron* **1.** *(subject: singular)* você, tu; *(subject: singular polite form)* o senhor (a senhora), você (Port); *(subject: plural)* vocês; *(subject: plural polite form)* os senhores (as senhoras); **do ~ speak Portuguese?** *(singular)* você fala português?; *(polite form)* (o senhor) fala português?; **~ Brazilians** vocês brasileiros.

2. *(direct object: singular)* o (a), te; *(direct object: singular polite form)* o senhor (a senhora); *(direct object: plural)* os (as), vos; *(direct object: plural polite form)* os (as), os senhores (as senhoras); **I saw ~** *(singular)* eu o vi; **can I help ~?** *(polite form: singular)* em que posso ajudá-lo?; *(polite form: plural)* em que posso ajudá-los?; **I'll see ~ later** *(plural)* vejo-os mais tarde.

3. *(indirect object: singular)* lhe, te; *(indirect object: singular polite form)* lhe; *(indirect object: plural)* lhes, vos; **I would like to ask ~ something** *(polite form: singular)* gostaria de perguntar algo a você; **didn't I tell ~ what happened?** *(polite form: plural)* não lhes contei o que aconteceu?

4. *(after prep: singular)* você, ti; *(after prep: singular polite form)* o senhor (a senhora), si; *(after prep: plural)* vocês;

(after prep: plural polite form) os senhores (as senhoras); vós; **this is for ~** isto é para você/o senhor, etc; **with ~** *(singular)* com você, contigo; *(singular: polite form)* com o senhor (a senhora); *(plural)* com vocês, convosco; *(plural: polite form)* com os senhores (as senhoras).

5. *(indefinite use: subject):* **the coffee ~ get in Brazil is very strong** o café que se bebe no Brasil é muito forte; **~ never know** nunca se sabe.

6. *(indefinite use: object):* **exercise is good for ~** exercício faz bem (para a saúde).

you'd [juːd] = **you had, you would**.

you'll [juːl] = **you will**.

young [jʌŋ] *adj* novo (nova) ♦ *npl*: **the ~** os jovens.

younger ['jʌŋɡəʳ] *adj (brother, sister)* mais novo (nova).

youngest ['jʌŋɡəst] *adj (brother, sister)* mais novo (nova).

youngster ['jʌŋstəʳ] *n* jovem *mf*.

your [jɔːʳ] *adj* **1.** *(singular subject)* o seu (a sua), o teu (a tua); *(singular subject: polite form)* o/a do senhor (da senhora); *(plural subject)* o vosso (a vossa); *(plural subject: polite form)* o/a dos senhores (das senhoras); **~ dog** o seu/teu/vosso cão, o cão do senhor (da senhora), o cão dos senhores (das senhoras); **~ house** a sua/tua/vossa casa, etc; **~ children** os seus/teus/vossos filhos, etc.

2. *(indefinite subject):* **it's good for ~ health** é bom para a saúde.

you're [jɔːʳ] = **you are**.

yours [jɔːz] *pron (singular subject)* o seu (a sua), o teu (a tua); *(singular subject: polite form)* o/a do senhor (da senhora); *(plural subject)* o vosso (a vossa); *(plural subject: polite form)* o/a dos senhores (das senhoras), **a friend of ~** un amigo seu/teu/vosso/do senhor/da senhora/dos senhores/das senhoras; **these shoes are ~** estes sapatos são (os) seus/teus/vossos, etc; **these are mine – where are yours?** estes são os meus – onde estão os seus/teus/vossos, etc?

yourself [jɔːˈself] *pron* **1.** *(reflexive: singular)* se, te; *(reflexive: plural)* se; **did you hurt ~?** *(singular)* você se machucou?

2. *(after prep: singular)* você mesmo

(-ma), tu mesmo(-ma); *(after prep: plural)* vocês mesmos(-mas); *(after prep: singular polite form)* vós mesmo(-ma); *(after prep: plural polite form)* os senhores mesmos (as senhoras mesmas), vós mesmos(-mas), ; **did you do it ~?** *(singular)* você fez isso sozinho?; *(polite form)* foi o senhor mesmo que o fez?; **did you do it yourselves?** vocês fizeram isso sozinhos?; *(polite form)* foram os senhores mesmos que o fizeram?

youth [juːθ] *n* juventude *f*; *(young man)* jovem *m*.

youth club *n* clube *m* de jovens.

youthful [ˈjuːθfʊl] *adj* juvenil.

youth hostel *n* albergue *m* da juventude *(Br)*, pousada *f* da juventude *(Port)*.

you've [juːv] = **you have**.

Yugoslav [ˈjuːgəʊˌslɑːv] = **Yugoslavian**.

Yugoslavia [ˌjuːgəˈslɑːvɪə] *n* Iugoslávia *f (Br)*, Jugoslávia *f (Port)*.

Yugoslavian [ˌjuːgəʊˈslɑːvɪən] *adj* iugoslavo(-va) *(Br)*, jugoslavo(-va) *(Port)* ◆ *n* iugoslavo *m* (-va *f*) *(Br)*, jugoslavo *m* (-va *f*) *(Port)*.

yuppie [ˈjʌpɪ] *n* yuppie *mf*.

yuppy = **yuppie**.

YWCA *n* = ACM *f*, associação internacional de jovens cristãs que oferece alojamento a um preço acessível.

Z

zany ['zeɪnɪ] *adj (inf)* disparatado (-da).

zap [zæp] *vi (rush)*: **she's always zapping off to new places** ela passa a vida viajando para lugares diferentes.

zeal [zi:l] *n* zelo *m*, fervor *m*.

zealous ['zeləs] *adj* zeloso(-osa), fervoroso(-osa).

zebra [*Brit* 'zebrə, *Am* 'zi:brə] *n* zebra *f*.

zebra crossing *n (Brit)* faixa *f* (para pedestres) *(Br)*, passadeira *f* (para peões) *(Port)*.

zenith [*Brit* 'zenɪθ, *Am* 'zi:nəθ] *n (fig: highest point)* zênite *m*, auge *m*.

zero ['zɪərəʊ] *n* zero *m*; **five degrees below ~** cinco graus abaixo de zero.

zest [zest] *n (of lemon, orange)* raspa *f*, zesto *m*.

zigzag ['zɪgzæg] *vi* ziguezaguear.

zinc [zɪŋk] *n* zinco *m*.

zip [zɪp] *n (Brit)* fecho ecler *m* ◆ *vt* fechar o fecho ecler de.

❏ **zip up** *vt sep* fechar o fecho ecler de.

zip code *n (Am)* código *m* postal.

zip fastener *n (Brit)* = **zip**.

zipper ['zɪpəʳ] *n (Am)* fecho ecler *m*.

zit [zɪt] *n (inf)* borbulha *f*.

zodiac ['zəʊdɪæk] *n* zodíaco *m*.

zone [zəʊn] *n* zona *f*.

zoo [zu:] *(pl -s) n* zôo *m*.

zoology [zəʊ'ɒlədʒɪ] *n* zoologia *f*.

zoom [zu:m] *vi (inf: move quickly)*: **to ~ past** passar voando; **to ~ off** sair voando.

zoom lens *n* zoom *m*.

zucchini [zu'ki:nɪ] *(pl inv) n (Am)* abobrinha *f (Br)*, courgette *f (Port)*.